San Jose, CA, USA

CHI

May 7 - 12

2016 #chi4good

Association for Computing Machinery

SIGCHI

Proceedings

The 34th Annual CHI Conference on Human Factors in Computing Systems

San Jose Convention Center

https://chi2016.acm.org

Association for
Computing Machinery

Advancing Computing as a Science & Profession

The Association for Computing Machinery
2 Penn Plaza, Suite 701
New York, New York 10121-0701

ISBN: 978-1-4503-3362-7 (Digital)

ISBN: 978-1-4503-4633-7 (Print)

Additional copies may be ordered prepaid from:

ACM Order Department
PO Box 30777
New York, NY 10087-0777, USA

Phone: 1-800-342-6626 (USA and Canada)
+1-212-626-0500 (Global)
Fax: +1-212-944-1318
E-mail: acmhelp@acm.org
Hours of Operation: 8:30 am – 4:30 pm ET

Printed in the USA

CHI 2016 is the premier world-wide conference for Human-Computer Interaction (HCI) and this year took place in the heart of Silicon Valley, San Jose, California. The Proceedings and Extended Abstracts represent today's most innovative, novel and creative work in HCI. These Proceedings and Abstracts have added over one-thousand documents in the ACM Digital Library. Across all tracks, CHI received nearly 5000 submissions and accepted over 1000 that can be seen today. These include almost 600 rigorously reviewed papers and notes selected from over 2200 submissions. These Proceedings and Abstracts also document two days of workshops, symposia and meetings involving over 800 participants, a record number for CHI conferences.

The CHI 2016 conference includes two days of focused workshops and four days of technical content, including CHI's prestigious technical program, with 16 parallel sessions of rigorously reviewed research Papers, engaging Panels, Case Studies and Special Interest Groups (SIGs), Conference highlights also include student research, design, and game competitions, and last-minute SIGs for discussing current topics. The popular alt.chi forum enters its eleventh year of provocation within the HCI community. The conference also showcases Interactivity and Interactivity Research Demos, which are hands-on demonstrations of the best in technology and innovation. And we're particularly proud this year to include documents from our new Art Exhibition, held at the *Works/San Jose Gallery* in conjunction with the CHI conference.

We began our conference planning process with three core ideas: "**CHI in Silicon Valley**": emphasizing local engagement in this vibrant community, "**#chiforgood**": HCI in the community, both during the workshop time and at appropriate points during the conference, and a "**More Humane Conference and Planning Process**": lots of transparency, early planning, no surprises, data-driven decisions and taking into account the importance of families, work/life balance, and the like.

From this, the overall theme of the conference emerged, **#chi4good**: addressing issues of social good through the innovation and creativity of the CHI community. To this end we held a Day of Service on the Saturday before the conference with hundreds of CHI attendees working on projects for non-profit and area arts organizations, and we have continued that theme throughout the conference by hosting the Diversity and Inclusion Lunch, brought childcare back to the conference for the first time in many years, and introduced the lunch@chi program to facilitate small group lunches on the first day of the conference. We've introduced CHI's first Diversity & Inclusion Statement, and our keynote speakers, represent the vibrancy, diversity and excitement of the wide field of HCI with particular emphasis on #chi4good. This year's speakers were chosen from among crowd-sourced suggestions from the CHI community and they are: Dayo Olopade, (Journalist and author of *The Bright Continent*); Kimberly Bryant (Founder, Black Girls Code), in conversation with Sarah Guthals, (Co-Founder of ThoughtSTEM); Marissa Meyer (President & CEO of Yahoo), in conversation with Terry Winograd (Professor Emeritus, Stanford University); Vishal Sikka (CEO of Infosys), in conversation with computing pioneer Alan Kay (Viewpoints Research Institute); and Salman Khan (founder, Khan Academy).

With careful consultation from the community, we have enhanced the CHI conference experience from submission and review processes, to more participation possibilities at the conference. Peer-reviewed papers have more space for references and will receive a wider range of better-matched reviews. There are more curated venues and more input into the selection of keynote speakers.

We are deeply indebted to an enormous number of volunteers, without whom CHI 2016 would not be possible, including over 4000 reviewers, 222 senior members of the program committee, nearly 100 members of the CHI 2016 conference organization committee and, of course, the more than 180 student volunteers.

The CHI conference is supported by the efforts of SIGCHI, (the Special Interest Group on Computer-Human Interaction) of the Association for Computing Machinery (ACM) and the ACM, and we are indebted for their ongoing support, organization, and leadership into the future.

Jofish Kaye, Yahoo, CHI 2016 General Conference Co-Chair

Allison Druin, University of Maryland / National Park Service, CHI 2016 General Conference Co-Chair

Cliff Lampe, University of Michigan, CHI 2016 Technical Program Chair

Dan Morris, Microsoft, CHI 2016 Papers Co-Chair

Juan Pablo Hourcade, University of Iowa, CHI 2016 Papers Co-Chair

Loren Terveen, University of Minnesota, President, ACM SIGCHI Executive Committee

Scooter Morris, University of San Francisco, ACM SIGCHI Vice President for Conferences

Table of Contents

VOLUME 1

Table of Contents

Table of Contents

Table of Contents

Table of Contents

Table of Contents

Table of Contents

Table of Contents

Table of Contents

Table of Contents

Table of Contents

Table of Contents

Table of Contents

Table of Contents

Table of Contents

Table of Contents

Table of Contents

Table of Contents

Table of Contents

Table of Contents

Table of Contents

Table of Contents

Table of Contents

Table of Contents

Table of Contents

Table of Contents

Table of Contents

Table of Contents

Table of Contents

Table of Contents

Table of Contents

Table of Contents

Designing Engaging Games Using Bayesian Optimization

Mohammad M. Khajah
University of Colorado
Boulder, CO
mohammad.khajah@colorado.edu

Brett D. Roads
University of Colorado
Boulder, CO
brett.roads@colorado.edu

Robert V. Lindsey
University of Colorado
Boulder, CO
robert@boulderanalytics.com

Yun-En Liu
University of Washington
Seattle, WA
yunliu@cs.washington.edu

Michael C. Mozer
University of Colorado
Boulder, CO
mozer@colorado.edu

ABSTRACT

We use Bayesian optimization methods to design games that maximize user engagement. Participants are paid to try a game for several minutes, at which point they can quit or continue to play voluntarily with no further compensation. Engagement is measured by player persistence, projections of how long others will play, and a post-game survey. Using Gaussian process surrogate-based optimization, we conduct efficient experiments to identify game design characteristics—specifically those influencing difficulty—that lead to maximal engagement. We study two games requiring trajectory planning, the difficulty of each is determined by a three-dimensional continuous design space. Two of the design dimensions manipulate the game in user-transparent manner (e.g., the spacing of obstacles), the third in a subtle and possibly covert manner (incremental trajectory corrections). Converging results indicate that overt difficulty manipulations are effective in modulating engagement only when combined with the covert manipulation, suggesting the critical role of a user's self-perception of competence.

Author Keywords

engagement; persistence; motivation; games; difficulty manipulation; optimization; Gaussian processes

ACM Classification Keywords

I.2.1 Artificial Intelligence: Learning; H.1.2 Information Systems: User/Machine Systems; G.3 Probability and Statistics: Experimental Design

ACM 978-1-4503-3362-7/16/05$15.00
DOI: http://dx.doi.org/10.1145/2858036.2858253

INTRODUCTION

Interest has recently surged in applying game-like mechanics to enhance engagement in a variety of domains, such as personal health [9, 14], scientific discovery [16, 6], and education [7, 25, 24, 23]. This research is based on the hypothesis that increased engagement will improve user experiences, data collection, and outcomes. Although engagement is a broad construct [10], it has been operationalized via subjective-self reports, physiological measures, player preferences, and observations of in-game player behavior [27]. In the present work we measure engagement using player persistence, which has been explored previously in game engagement research [25, 36] and in the gambling psychology literature [15], as well as using projections of other players' persistence and post-experiment subjective surveys engagement.

In gaming, as in related domains, a key design decision that affects engagement is how difficult to make challenges presented to users. If challenges are trivial, users become bored and lose interest; if challenges are overwhelming and utterly impossible, users quit from frustration. Successful design identifies the not-too-easy, not-too hard challenge level that seduces users. We focus on manipulations of difficulty to modulate engagement in this work, although the methods we present are suitable for exploring any aspect of game design to achieve any measurable outcome.

Difficulty manipulations can be static or dynamic. *Static manipulations* modulate initial game configuration and design before game play begins based on population-level play-testing data or simulations of player behavior. Static manipulations have been used to match a particular game statistic [37, 13], reduce uncertainty about an underlying cognitive model [30], and maximize success or persistence rates in an educational game [23]. In contrast, *dynamic manipulations* modulate game design parameters on the fly in reaction to player behavior or performance; examples include matching simulated players' skill [2], selecting exercises that maximize information per mistake [18], adapting AI to move into game states that maximize persistence [11], and adjusting the user interface to maximize performance [26]. Static and dynamic difficulty manipulations can be combined to discover a dynamic difficulty adjustment (DDA) scheme that works across individuals [21]. The dynamic difficulty manipulation is parameterized and the parameters are determined to be appropriate for a population of users. In this work we focus exclusively on static difficulty manipulations but our method applies to any parametrized measure of difficulty, including DDA.

Game difficulty parameters are typically based on the player's physical or mental capabilities (e.g., the player's reflexes and perceptual ability determine how small or fast enemies can be before the player is overwhelmed), but the player's *perception* of difficulty is also important. For instance, players are more engaged playing a game in which suspenseful audio messages warn of potential enemies than an identical game without the messages [17]. players are also more engaged when they told that the game has adaptive AI, when it actually does not [8]. In these two examples, the player's perception of difficulty was manipulated, through suspense and pre-game instructions, whilst the actual game difficulty was held constant. In this work we introduce a novel twist in which we manipulate the actual difficulty whilst holding the perception of difficulty constant.

The goal of our work is to design games that maximize engagement for a population of users via manipulation of static difficulty. Ordinarily, design decisions are made with A/B testing or with a designer's intuitions. A literature has begun to emerge that leverages the vast quantities of user data that can be collected with online software to *optimize* the design through more systematic and comprehensive experimentation. We will discuss past approaches that have been used to optimize over design spaces, and we will present a novel approach using a technique referred to as *Bayesian optimization.* The method we present could theoretically be applied to any game after it is released in the wild, leading to automated improvement of the software with minimal intervention by designers. In the optimization framework, the role of designers is to specify a space of designs over which exploration will take place.

Recent Research on Game Optimization

Recent research has used an on-line educational gaming platform to search a design space to maximize player retention. The platform, called BrainPop, is a popular site used primarily in grade 4-8 classrooms. It offers multiple games, and students can switch among the games. Usage is divided into sessions, and engagement is measured by the length of a session and the number of rounds played within a session. Lomas et al. [25] conducted randomized controlled trials on four dimensions affecting game difficulty, the Cartesian product of which had $2 \times 8 \times 9 \times 4 = 576$ designs. Each of 69,642 anonymous user sessions were randomly assigned to a design, statistical hypothesis testing showed that less challenging designs were more engaging.

As an alternative to exhaustive search through design space, Liu et al. [23] devised a heuristic, greedy search strategy that involved selecting one dimension at a time, marginalizing over the as-yet-unselected dimensions. This strategy was used to identify the design maximizing user persistence in a five-dimensional space with 64 designs; we will return to this experiment shortly. Lomas [24] used multi-armed bandits to efficiently search a design space and minimize regret—defined as games that users chose *not* to play. In experiments with relatively few distinct designs (5 or 6), more games are played overall with bandit assignment of designs than with random assignment.

The three search strategies just described—exhaustive, greedy, and bandit-based—deal adequately with nominal (categorical) dimensions but are not designed to exploit ordinal (ranked) or cardinal (numerical) dimensions. Further, the exhaustive and bandit strategies cannot leverage structure in the design space unless they make the strong and unreasonable assumption that choices on the dimensions are independent.

BAYESIAN OPTIMIZATION

We propose an alternative methodology to search for engagement-maximizing designs: Bayesian optimization (BO). To motivate this methodology, suppose one wishes choose a font size for a web site to maximize the duration that visitors stay on the site. We might posit a quadratic model to formalize the relationship between font size, denoted x, and stay duration, denoted y: $y(x) = \beta_0 + \beta_1 x + \beta_2 x^2$, where the coefficients $\boldsymbol{\beta} \equiv \{\beta_0, \beta_1, \beta_2\}$ are unknown. If we randomly assign visitors to conditions, as in A-B testing, we will collect many noisy (x, y) observations. We can the fit the $\boldsymbol{\beta}$ parameters to the observations and use the resulting parameterized function, $y(x)$ to identify the font size x that maximizes stay duration y. The function serves as a surrogate for the true implicit function that describes reality. With sufficient data, the surrogate will be a good approximation to the true implicit function. In this approach, although each data point is noisy, each data point constrains the overall shape of the function; in concert, a relatively small amount of noisy data can serve to identify the function optimum. This benefit arises because the values of x define a continuum.

BO extends this simple method in three respects. First, instead of using a parametric model—a model of fixed, prespecified form—that makes strong assumptions about the relationship between dependent and independent variables, BO uses a more powerful class of nonparametric surrogate models whose only constraint is that the function $y(x)$ must be locally smooth. Consequently, BO can infer arbitrary sorts of structure in the design space. Second, BO is a Bayesian methodology: instead of searching for the best fitting parameter values, referred to as a maximum likelihood estimate, BO computes the posterior distribution over parameter values. The posterior effectively allows BO to assess the *uncer-*

tainty in its predictions. Third, instead of choosing random x for testing, BO uses *active-selection heuristics* to select x in order to be data efficient. These heuristics trade off exploration and exploitation, that is, trade off testing regions of the design space where parameter values are uncertain versus those where optima are likely to be given the data previously collected. These heuristics leverage the Bayesian representation of uncertainty.

BO typically assumes a prior probability distribution over all possible smooth functions, $f(x)$. (This is a generalization of the notion of assuming a prior distribution over the parameters $\boldsymbol{\beta}$.) This prior is known as a *Gaussian process (GP)* prior. The term Gaussian comes from the assumption that sets of points on the function are jointly Gaussian. Rather than assuming a certain degree of smoothness of the function, GPs are nonparametric: the data specify the degree of smoothness. GPs can model ordinal and cardinal dimensions to discover functional relationships between designs and outcomes. GPs are also efficient in their use of data [35], leading to strong predictions with orders of magnitude less data than utilized by previously tested methods. This efficiency arises from the underlying assumption of smoothness, i.e., nearby points in the design space yield similar degrees of engagement. By contrast, the common multi-armed bandits approach assumes that each arm, or design, is independent which prevents the method from exploiting observations from similar designs.

BO can be used with models other than GPs. For example, BO was recently used to adaptively select control dynamics that maximize a user's in-game performance [26]. Here the user is assumed to behave according to a Markov decision process (MDP). This approach outperformed the traditional multi-armed bandits approach. In our case however, we want to adjust game designs statically over a population of users, which makes GPs a natural choice. As we noted earlier, it is trivial to combine static and dynamic manipulations, e.g., BO could optimize the discount parameter of the MDP.

In our context, Bayesian optimization with GPs infers a surrogate function that characterizes the relationship between designs and a latent valuation. Each design is a parameterization of a game, and the valuation is our measure of engagement. Starting with a Gaussian process (GP) prior and observations of human behavior, the optimization procedure computes a posterior over functions and uses this posterior to guide subsequent experimentation. With a suitable exploration strategy, globally optimal solutions can be obtained.

Bayesian optimization with GPs has recently been applied to the design of a shoot-'em-up game. Zook et al. [37] searched over several design parameters to achieve a gameplay objective: having the enemy hit the player exactly six times during an attack. Optimizing gameplay is different than optimizing engagment in one critical regard: the *observation model* required. The observation model is a probabilistic mapping from the latent valuation represented by the GP to observed behavior (called a likelihood in the general GP literature). Because engagement is a characteristic of the player's cognitive state, the observation model is a cognitive theory of how the state of engagement induced by a given game design influences behavior. Similar probabilistic models have been developed for a variety of human responses, e.g., preference [5], two-alternative forced choice with guessing [21], and similarity judgment [31]. Here, we develop and justify a probabilistic model to predict behavioral measures of engagement from the latent index of engagement.

An Illustration of the Bayesian Approach

In this section, we re-analyze an existing data set and show the value of Bayesian methods. The data set is from Liu et al. [23], who constructed a game called *Treefrog Treasure* to teach fractions. In this game, the player guides a frog to jump to a series of targets which are specified as fractions on a number line. The game can be configured in one of 64 designs, specified in a discrete $2 \times 2 \times 2 \times 4$ space. The dimensions determine the representation of the target and the number line (pie chart or symbolic), presence/absence of tick marks and animations, and the number of hints provided (1-4). Over 360,000 trials were collected from 34,000 players with design changing randomly every other trial. Players could quit the game on any trial at their discretion. Engagement is quantified by the probability that, for a trial of design $\mathcal{A}$, a player will complete the next trial (and not quit). We call this the *persistence* induced by $\mathcal{A}$.

We use the data resampling and aggregation procedure of Liu et al. to marginalize over two irrelevant aspects of the data—the design of the next trial and the specific fractions tested. Figure 1a shows the empirical persistence across designs, and Figure 1b shows the same result but smoothed via a GP classifier. The model provides a clear interpretation of which design dimensions matter, in contrast to the raw data. In support of the robustness of the model, it produces the same interpretation across regroupings of the data. Further, the model produces a prediction of engagment over the design space that is consistent with that obtained by the approach of Liu et al. [23], which they validated on a test set. For example, persistence is higher without animations (the bottom row of cubes). Animations provide a visual tutorial in dividing up number lines into fractions, and might make problems easier; however, they also take control away from the player for several seconds and could therefore be distracting. These results suggest that the distraction effect overpowers any possible learning gains, underscoring the importance of engagement in any optimization process for online games.

This simulation used a logistic observation model—yielding observations in [0,1]—and a squared exponential kernel with ARD distance measure, for a total of 6 hyperparameters which were drawn via elliptical slice

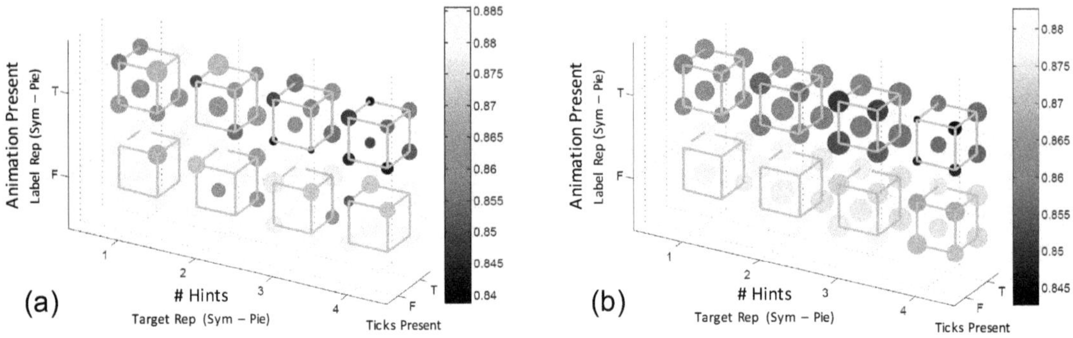

Figure 1. Persistence probability of Treefrog Treasure players over the design space: (a) empirical mean; (b) GP-posterior mean. Each disk represents a design. Color denotes persistence and diameter is inversely proportional to variance of (a) aggregated observations and (b) the GP posterior.

sampling. This kernel effectively computes a weighted Hamming distance on the binary dimensions.

From Persistence to Total Play Duration

The logistic observation model is a natural choice to characterize persistence on a single trial. However, this model assumes that after each trial, the player flips a biased coin to decide whether to continue. Because the coin flips after each trial are independent of one another, the model predicts an exponential distribution for total play duration.

The exponential distribution is not a particularly realistic characterization of human activity times. The best studied measure of time in human behavior is the response latency, which has been characterized by positively skewed distributions in which the variance grows with the mean, e.g., an ex-Gaussian [12] or Weibull density [32]. Evidence about usage-duration distributions is harder to find. Miyamoto et al. [28] performed an analysis of 20 MOOCs and found a positively skewed distribution for both the number of sessions and hours a student would engage with a course. Andersen et al. [1] also observed what appears to be a mixture of positively skewed distribution and an impulse near 0 representing individuals who lost interest immediately.

In order for Bayesian optimization to produce sensible results, we require an observation model that represents the mapping from latent states of engagement to a play duration. In the next section, we propose four alternative observation models that seem well matched to empirical distributions. We evaluate these models via simulation experiments.

Selecting an Observation Model

Our goal is to identify a model that is robust to misspecification: we would like the model to work well even if real-world data—engagement as measured by the duration of play—are not distributed according to the model's assumptions. The observation models must have three properties to be suitable for representing play-duration distributions: (1) nonnegative support, (2) variance that increases with the mean, and (3) probability mass at zero to represent individuals who express no interest in voluntary play. To satisfy these three properties, our generative process assumes that play duration, denoted V, is given by $V = CT$, where

$$C|\pi \sim \text{Bernoulli}(\pi)$$

is an individual's binary choice to continue playing or not and T is the duration of play if they continue. Criterion 1 rules out the popular ex-Gaussian density because it has nonzero probability for negative values. We tested four alternative distributional assumptions for T:

$$T \sim \text{Gamma}\left(\alpha, \frac{\alpha}{e^{f(\boldsymbol{x})}}\right)$$
$$T \sim \text{Weibull}\left(k, \frac{e^{f(\boldsymbol{x})}}{\Gamma\left(1+\frac{1}{k}\right)}\right)$$
$$T \sim \ln \mathcal{N}\left(f(\boldsymbol{x}) - \frac{\sigma^2}{2}, \sigma^2\right)$$
$$T \sim \text{Wald}\left(\lambda, e^{f(\boldsymbol{x})}\right)$$

where $\boldsymbol{x}$ is a game design and $f(\boldsymbol{x})$ is the latent valuation and has a GP prior. The first parameter of the Gamma, Weibull, and Wald distributions specify the *shape*, and the second parameter specifies the *rate*, *scale*, and *mean*, respectively. The two parameters of the log-Normal distribution specify the mean and variance, respectively. These four distributions all share the same mean, $e^{f(\boldsymbol{x})}$, but have different higher-order moments. Note that the Gamma distribution includes the exponential as a special case. To allow a design's valuation $f(\boldsymbol{x})$ to influence the choice C as well as the play duration T, we define $\text{logit}(\pi) \equiv \beta_0 + \beta_1 f(\boldsymbol{x})$. This general form includes design invariance as a special case ($\beta_1 = 0$).

We performed synthetic experiments with each of these four observation models. To evaluate robustness to misspecification, we evaluated each model using the same four models to simulate the underlying generative process (i.e., to generate synthetic data meant to represent human play durations). Synthetic data for these experiments were obtained by probing a valuation function, $f(\boldsymbol{x})$, that represents the engagement associated with a design $\boldsymbol{x}$. For $f(\boldsymbol{x})$, we used a mixture of two to four

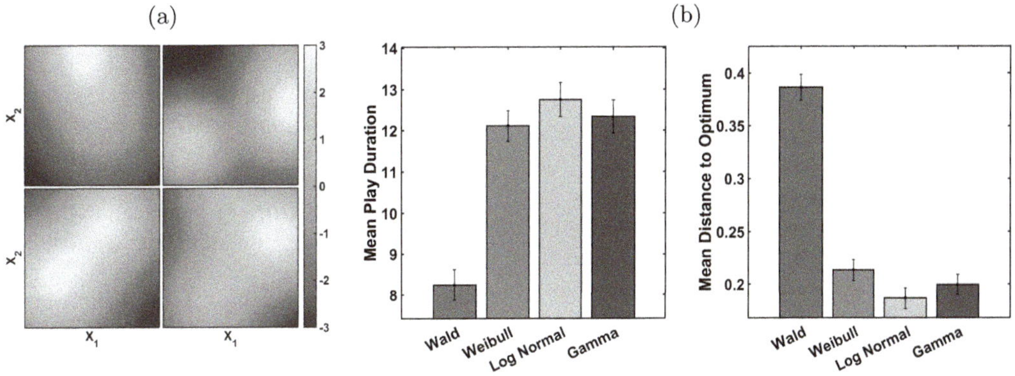

Figure 2. Simulation experiment. (a) Examples of the 2D functions used for generating synthetic data. (b) Results of synthetic experiment. The left and right plots depict the mean function value (higher is better) and the mean distance to the true optimum (lower is better) for various observation models. Results are averaged over four different generative-process models, 100 replications of each simulation, the last 10 trials per replication. Error bars indicate ±1 standard error.

Gaussians with randomly drawn centers, spreads, and mixture coefficients, defined over a 2D design space. For examples, see Figure 2a. We generate synthetic observations by mapping the function value through the assumed generative process. The goal of Bayesian optimization is to recover the function optimum from synthetic data. We performed 100 replications of the simulated experiment, each with a different randomly drawn mixture of Gaussians and with $\beta_0 = 0$ and $\beta_1 = 1$. For the generative models, we need to assume values for the free parameters, and we used $\alpha = 2$, $k = 2$, $\sigma^2 = 1$ and $\lambda = 4$. (These parameters settings are used to generate the synthetic data and are not shared with the Bayesian optimization method; rather, the method must recover these parameters from the synthetic data.)

To perform Bayesian optimization, we require an *active-selection policy* that determines where in design space to probe next. The *probability of improvement* and *expected improvement* policies are popular heuristics in the Bayesian optimization literature. Both policies balance exploration and exploitation without additional tuning parameters. However, since the variance increases with the mean in our observation models, both policies tend to degenerate to pure exploitation. Instead, we chose Thompson sampling [4], which is not susceptible to this degeneracy. For each replication of the simulated experiment, we ran 40 active selection rounds with 5 observations (simulated subjects) per round. The GP used the squared exponential Automatic-Relevance-Determination (ARD) kernel whose hyperparameters were inferred by slice sampling.

For each combination of the four distributions as observation model and for each combination of the four distributions as generative model, we ran the battery of 100 experiment replications each with 200 simulated subjects. The simulation results are summarized in Figure 2b. We collected two different measures of performance. The bar graph on the left shows, for each distribution as the observation model, the mean play duration over the 200 simulated subjects and the 400 replications of each experiment (100 replications with each of four generative models). The bar graph on the right shows the mean distance of the inferred optimum to the true optimum. Superior performance is indicated by a higher play duration and a lower distance to the true optimum. The log-Normal distribution as observation model shows a slight advantage over the Weibull and Gamma distributions, and a large advantage over the Wald. By both measures of performance, the log-Normal distribution is most robust to incorrect assumptions about the underlying generative process. We use this observation model in the human studies that follow. This decision may seem strange in light of recent work that shows that Weibull is appropriate to model play times [34]. But that work measured *total play time* across multiple sessions as opposed to our present setup where we measure play time in a single session.

EXPERIMENTS

Let us take a step back and remind the reader of our overall agenda. We wish to maximize retention (play duration) over a game design space. The dimensions of this space affect difficulty. We described a powerful methodology, Bayesian optimization, that can be used to efficiently search a continuous, multi-dimensional design space to identify an optimum design. Through a re-analysis of existing data and through simulation studies, we demonstrated that this methodology is promising and effective, and we developed a model that is appropriate for the dependent variable of play duration.

Finally, we can now turn to describing experiments. Our experiments were conducted using Amazon's Mechanical Turk platform. The inspiration for using this platform came from earlier studies we conducted on Turk. In one study requiring participants to induce concepts from exemplars, we received post-experiment messages from participants asking if we could provide additional exemplars for them to use to improve their skills. In another study involving foreign language learning, participants who completed the study asked for the vocabulary list. In all cases, the participants' motivation was to learn, not to receive additional compensation.

Given that Turk participants are willing to voluntarily commit time to activities that they find engaging, we devised a method for measuring *voluntary time on activity* or *VTA*. In each of our experiments, participants are required to play a game for sixty seconds. During the mandatory play period, a clock displaying remaining time is displayed. When the mandatory play period ends, the clock is replaced by a button that allows the participant to terminate the game and and receive full compensation. Participants are informed that they can continue playing with no further compensation. VTA is measured as the lag between the button appearance and the button press.

The traditional method of assessing engagement is a post-experiment survey (e.g., [29, 27]). Recently, however, VTA-like measures have been explored. Sharek and Wiebe [33] tested several versions of a game on Turk and quantified engagement by the frequency of clicking on a game clock to reveal whether the minimum required play time had passed. Also, in work we described earlier [25, 24, 23], engagement was measured by how likely a player is to switch to a different game. In gambling psychology, VTA has been extensively used to study the effect of near-misses on time spent playing slot machines [15].

Overt Versus Covert Difficulty Manipulations

In our experiments, we distinguish between *overt* and *covert* manipulations of game difficulty. Overt manipulations are those to which players readily attribute causal effects on difficulty, such as the speed of an enemy or the height of a wall. Overt manipulations tend to be visually salient and directly perceived from the game lay out. In contrast, covert manipulations are more subtle and involve aspects of the game to which players may not be attending or may not have an explicit theory relating these manipulations to game difficulty. An example of a covert manipulation might be the proximity that a bullet's trajectory needs to come to an enemy in order to hit the enemy.

Although we know of no prior work in which difficulty is covertly manipulated, there is a related literature in which the appearance of difficulty is manipulated without affecting the actual difficulty. Some of this work falls under the banner of the *illusion of control* [19]. In a classic study, subjects drew a card against an awkward or confident-looking confederate, winning the round if they had the highest card. Before each round, subjects placed a bet that they'd win. Subjects who played against the awkward confederate bet, on average, 47% more than those who played against a confident confederate, despite the objective probability of winning—the difficulty—being the same in both cases. In the context of video games, two examples we cited earlier [17, 8] show that players are more engaged when the perception of challenge was manipulated, rather than the actual challenge. We hypothesize that the effectiveness of these manipulations is due to the fact that individuals readily overestimate their sense of agency—the amount of control they have over an outcome [22]. Unlike these previous efforts that manipulate the perception of difficulty whilst keeping the actual difficulty constant, a covert manipulation does the opposite. We may assist the player in navigating a game, thereby changing the actual difficulty, whilst giving the play an illusion that success is attributed to their own competence and skill.

In our experiments, we evaluate the effectiveness of overt versus covert difficulty manipulations on engagement.

Two Games and Three Difficulty Manipulations

The two games we studied are simple, popular trajectory-planning games: Flappy Bird and Spring Ninja. In Flappy Bird, the objective is to keep a bird in the air by flapping its wings to resist gravity and avoid hitting the ground, the top of the screen, or vertical pipes (Figure 3a). In Spring Ninja, the objective is to wind a spring to the proper tension so that the player jumps from one pillar to the next and avoids falling to the ground (Figure 3b). The player holds and releases a mouse button to jump. The longer the player holds, the further the ninja jumps. Both Flappy Bird and Spring Ninja involve trajectory planning, but the former requires real-time decision making whilst the latter allows players to take their time in planning the next jump.

We manipulated two overt factors affecting the difficulty of Flappy Bird—the horizontal spacing between pipes and the vertical gap between pipes—as well as one covert factor, which we refer to as the *assistance.* Assistance acts as a force that, when the wings are flapped, steers the bird toward the gap between the next pair of pipes. In Spring Ninja, we manipulated two overt factors—the horizontal spacing between the pillars and the visible extent of a projected trajectory (the blue curve in Figure 3b)—as well as the amount of covert assistance. The assistance in Spring Ninja corrects the trajectory of the player if the trajectory falls within a certain distance of the ideal trajectory. In both games, the assistance level can be adjusted to range from no assistance whatsoever to essentially a guarantee that nearly any action taken by the player will result in success. For moderate levels of assistance, the manipulation can be quite subtle. We have no experimental evidence that players were unaware of our 'covert' support, but anecdotally, players who tested our games with low-to-moderate levels of assistance were surprised when they were informed that game dynamics were modulating to guide them along. Indeed, it was shocking to realize that one could perform relatively well with eyes closed.

Flappy Bird: Experimental Methodology and Results

We conducted two studies with Flappy Bird. In the first study, we tested 958 participants. Each participant was

Figure 3. (a) Flappy Bird: The player flaps bird's wings to keep it aloft and to avoid hitting pipes. (b) Spring Ninja: The player jumps from one pillar to another by compressing springs in the ninja's shoes. The blue trajectory is the projected jump path for the given spring compression level.

assigned to a random point in the three dimensional, continuous design space. The large number of participants in this *random-assignment* experiment enabled us to fit an accurate model that characterizes the relationship between the game design and latent engagement, much as we fit data from the Treefrog Treasure game which was collected by random assignment (Figure 1). In the second study, we ran the experiment again from scratch and tested 201 participants. Participants were assigned to designs chosen by an *active-selection* policy, Thompson sampling as described earlier. Active selection chooses a design for each participant based on the model estimated based on all previous participants.

Our pilot experiments suggested that randomly seeding Bayesian active selection is necessary, as is often done with BO. Consequently, we assigned the first 55 participants in the active-selection study to a Sobol-generated set of random points in design space. Sobol sequences [20] are attractive because they evenly cover design space, as opposed to a sequence generated from a pseudo-random number generator. After the seeding phase, we performed rounds of Bayesian optimization using Thompson sampling with five subjects tested at each selected design.

The design space consisted of three dimensions: pipe spacing, pipe gap, and covert assistance. Each dimension was quantized to 10 levels.[1] Participants were given game instructions and were told that to receive compensation (20 cents) they must play for 60 seconds, but they could continue playing without further compensation for as long as they wished. During the mandatory-play period, a countdown timer in the corner of screen indicated the time remaining. During the mandatory-play period, multiple rounds of the game were played. Each round was initiated with a mouse click and ended when the bird crashed. When the mandatory time was reached, the time-remaining display was replaced by a 'finish' button. Because individuals might not notice the button mid-round, we excluded the round in play, and defined VTA to be the time (in seconds) beginning with a mouse click to initiate the first round once the finish button had appeared.

At any time, clicking finish took participants to a final screen that indicated how much time they had spent beyond the mandatory time; this number could be zero if no new rounds were played following the mandatory time. Participants were asked to enter how long they expected *other* mechanical turk players to voluntarily play. The two dependent measures available then were the *experiential* and *projected* VTA. In pilot experiments we treated both measures as independent so there were two observations per participant. However, this led to non-smooth model fits to the data so we decided to use the projected VTA exclusively as our measure of engagement. Projected VTA is less contaminated by confounds, e.g., the player would have liked to continue but had another obligation, or the player continued for several rounds only because they had not noticed the finish button. Although it may seem that we are ignoring the important behavioral signal in the experiential VTA, we are still making use of that signal because the experiential VTA is provided as a reference when participants are asked to specify the projected VTA. In the random-assignment study, we displayed the experiential VTA on the screen and asked participants to enter the projected VTA. In the active-selection study, to emphasize the experiential VTA, we incorporated a slider control that is initially anchored on their experiential VTA (see top of Figure 4). The slider had a range of at least 0-100, and if the experiential VTA was greater than 100, the top end was set to twice the experiential VTA, rounded up to the nearest multiple of 100.

In the active-selection study, we included a short questionnaire about the participant's experience in the game. The questionnaire consisted of 6 true/false items with each item phrased such that "true" corresponds to an engaging game. The first four phrases in the questionnaire (Figure 4) were taken from the Game Engagement Questionnaire [3].

[1]This quantization may seem strange given that BO can handle continuous dimensions. However, 10 levels allows for fine distinctions, and allows us to avoid local-optimization techniques such as hill climbing needed for continuous spaces.

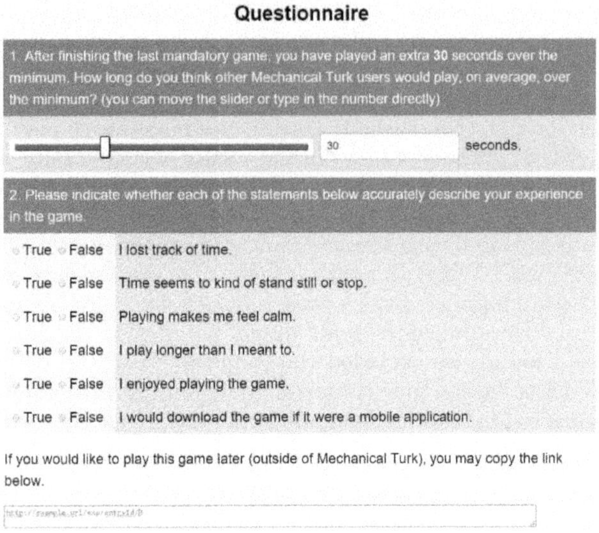

Figure 4. The post-experiment questionnaire.

Figure 5a and 5b show the model posterior mean VTA over the three dimensional design space in the random-assignment and active-selection studies, respectively. The remarkable finding is that the two independent studies yield very similar outcomes: the optimal design identified by the two studies is in almost exactly the same point in design space (the red squres in the Figures). The random-assignment study should yield reliable results due to the relatively large number of participants tested.

An important question here is whether the predictions of the model are related to the observations. Because repeated observations within the same game design are highly variable, we averaged observations for each design tested and determined the correlation with the expected VTA predicted by the model. We included in this analysis only designs for which we had four or more observations in our random-assignment experiment. We obtain a Spearman correlation of 0.65. This coefficient is close to the value obtained by fitting the model to synthetic data generated by the model itself (0.50 ± 0.1, 10 replications). The fact that the model predicts the actual data as well as if not better than the synthetic data suggests that the model is appropriate for the task. (We used the random-assignment experiment for this analysis; a similar analysis for the active-selection experiment is not sensible given the dependence among samples.)

To compare the efficiency of random-assignment vs. active selection, we randomly sampled 200 observations from the random-assignment study and fitted our model using only those observations. We then calculated the distance between the optimum found using 200 observations and the optimum found using the full set of 958 observations. We replicated this procedure 50 times, each time sampling a different subset of observations. The mean distance over these 50 replications was 0.70 (std. error ± 0.03). In contrast, the distance was 0.28 in the active selection study, using the same number of observations. This result indicates that with matched budgets for data collection, the active-selection study is more efficient than random selection in converging on the optimum.

The Figures indicate that engagement is sensitive to each dimension in the design space. There is not much hint of an interaction across the dimensions. Notably, with minimal covert assistance (the upper-left array in each Figure), the other two overt difficulty dimensions have little or no impact on engagement, and are not sufficient to motivate participants to continue playing voluntarily. Thus, we conclude that covert assistance is key to engaging our participants. Consistent with the hypothesis that participants need to be unaware of the assistance, the experiments show that engagement is poor with maximum assistance (the lower-right array in each Figure). With maximum assistance, the manipulation causes the bird to appear to be pulled into the gap, and this is therefore no longer covert in nature.

To obtain further converging evidence in support of the optimum identified in Figures 5a and 5b, we fitted a Gaussian process model to questionnaire scores. We defined the score as the number of 'true' responses made by the participant. The higher the score, the higher the engagement because we phrased questionnaire items such that an affirmative response indicated engagement. We used Gaussian process regression with a Gaussian observation model to fit the scores. (Our VTA model is appropriate for fitting play-time observations, whereas the scores lie in a fixed range of 0-6.) Figure 5c shows the model posterior mean score over the three dimensional design space. The notable result here is that the posterior mean score looks similar to the posteriors from the random-assignment and active-selection studies. More importantly, the predicted optima—marked by red squares—lie in almost exactly the same place in 5a, 5b and 5c. Whereas the posterior inferred from the questionnaire scores looks different, e.g., for assistance=1, we remind the reader that the objective of BO is to find the maximum of a function, rather than map out the full design space. The consistency across studies and across response measures provides converging evidence that increase our confidence in the experiment outcomes, and also provide support for the appropriateness of using VTA as measure of engagement in place of a more traditional questionnaire.

Spring Ninja: Experimental Methodology and Results

We conducted a single study with Spring Ninja with 325 participants. As in the active-selection Flappy Bird study, we seeded the optimization procedure with participants evaluated with designs generated from a Sobol sequence, 54 in total. The remaining participants were tested in groups of five with a game design chosen from an active-selection policy, Thompson sampling. We did not conduct a random-assignment study with Spring Ninja due to time constraints and because, in addition

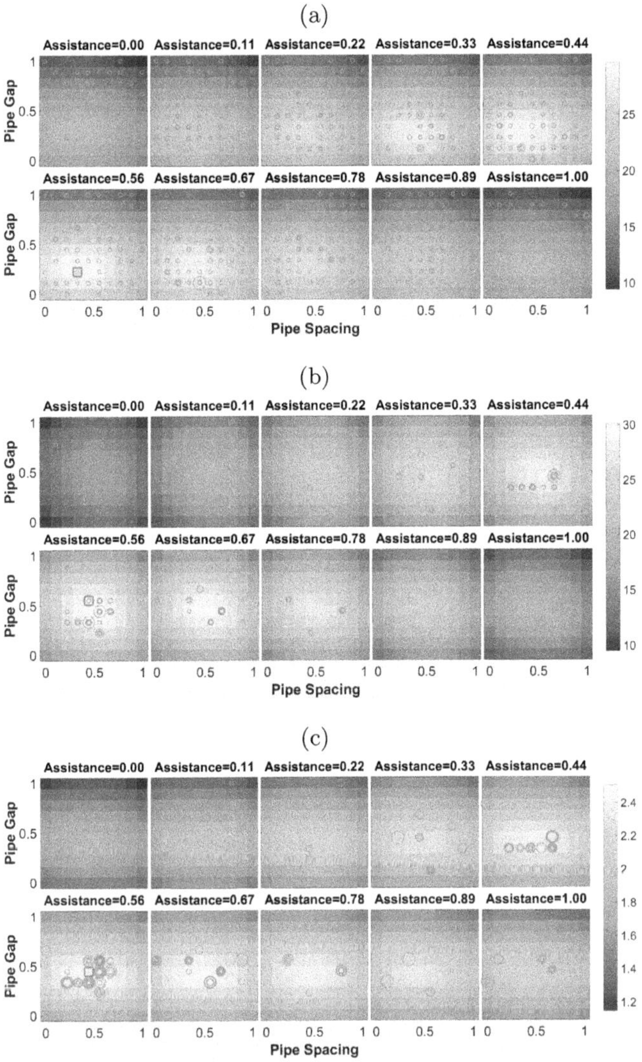

Figure 5. Bayesian model fits of VTA (in seconds) over the Flappy Bird design space for (a) the random-assignment and (b) active selection studies. Each array corresponds to a fixed level of assistance, with the upper left array being no assistance (level 0) and the lower right array being maximal assistance (level 1). For each fixed level of assistance, the corresponding array depicts model-fit VTA across the range of horizontal spacings between pipes (x axis) and vertical gaps (y axis). The pipe gap and pipe spacing is calibrated such that a level of 0 is a challenging game, unlikely to be played well by a novice, and 1 is readily handled by a novice. The circles correspond to observations with the radii indicating the magnitudes of the observations. At locations with multiple observations, there are co-centric circles. Red squares indicate the locations of the predicted global maximum. (c) An analogous Bayesian model fit to the questionnaire score, which indicates the number of items with an affirmative response. Higher scores indicate greater engagement.

to cited literature on the efficiency of Bayesian optimization, we have already established the effectiveness of our active selection method in Flappy Bird, which is a similar three-parameter game.

The design space of Spring Ninja consisted of three dimensions: the spacing between pillars, the visible extent of the projected trajectory and the covert assistance. Each dimension was quantized into 10 levels in the range 0–1 with 0 and 1 corresponding to difficult and easy game settings, respectively. The optimization procedure sought to maximize the VTA, defined for this game as the number of jumps a player would make after the appearance of the finish button.

As in the Flappy Bird studies, Spring Ninja participants were required to play for a minimum of 60 seconds in order to receive compensation (20 cents). A countdown timer was shown in the corner of the screen and replaced with a finish button when the timer reached zero. The timer counted down only from the time at which the participant began compressing the spring and stopped after the ninja landed on a pillar or fell off the screen. When the player falls off the screen, a game-over screen is shown offering the player to start a new game or—if the mandatory play time had elapsed—finish the experiment. When the finish button is clicked, participants are redirected to a post-experiment screen in which they specify their projection of others' VTA and respond to the same questionnaire as in the Flappy Bird studies (Figure 4).

We measure the VTA in Spring Ninja differently than in Flappy Bird because the former is turn-based whereas the latter is continuous. Specifically, Spring Ninja players are likely to notice between jumps when the countdown timer hits zero and the finish button appears because they are not under time pressure. We could define VTA as the time after the finish button appears but this poses a problem when we ask participants for the projected VTA since there is a mismatch between the game's sense of time—time advances only when the Ninja is flying or about to fly—and real world time. So a participant would be perplexed if they found out that they have played for only 20 seconds extra when they have actually played for one more minute. Indeed, we received several emails from pilot participants complaining about this issue. To avoid this problem, we instead measure the number of jumps after the finish button appears. The number of jumps is agnostic to the way the game measures time and is a non-negative quantity that is directly proportional to VTA so we can still use our VTA model. We shall continue to refer to the number of voluntary jumps as the VTA.

Figures 6a and 6b show model posteriors over VTA (in number of jumps) and questionnaire scores, respectively, fit in the same way as we did in the Flappy Bird study. High engagement is obtained for the mid-range of design parameter settings. The predicted optima by the two measures are very close, as indicated by the red squares. Consistent with the Flappy Bird study, the Spring Ninja results indicate that the two overt difficulty manipulations have little impact on engagement when no covert assistance is provided (the upper left array), yet with

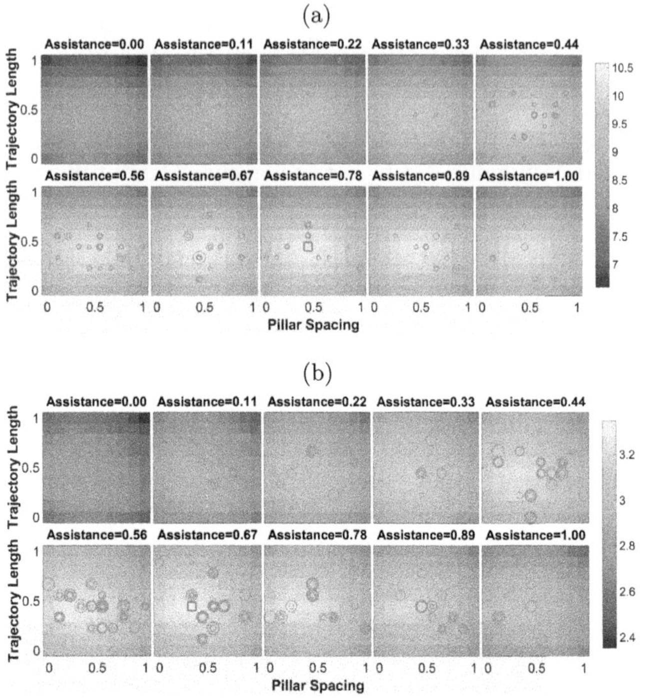

Figure 6. (a) Model predicted VTA (in ninja jumps) over the Spring Ninja design space. Each array shows VTA for a range of trajectory lengths and horizontal spacings between the pillars. The trajectory length and pillar spacing is scaled such that 0 is a challenging game, unlikely to be played well by a novice, and 1 is readily handled by a novice. Each of the 10 arrays represents a fixed level of assistance, with 0 being none and 1 being maximal. Each cell in an array corresponds to a setting of the trajectory length and the horizontal spacing between pillars. The circles correspond to observations with the radii indicating the magnitudes of the observations. At locations with multiple observations, there are co-centric circles. Red squares indicate the locations of the predicted global maximum. (b) An analogous Bayesian model fit to the questionnaire score, which indicates the number of items with an affirmative response. Higher scores indicate greater engagement.

moderate covert assistance, engagement significantly increases.

DISCUSSION

In this article, we've applied an increasingly popular tool from the machine learning literature, Bayesian optimization, to a problem of intense interest in the fields of gaming and gamification: How do you design software to engage users? In contrast to traditional A/B testing, Bayesian optimization allows us to search a continuous multi-dimensional design space for a maximally engaging game design. Bayesian optimization is data efficient in that it draws strong inferences from noisy observations. Consequently, experimentation with users on suboptimal designs can be minimized. When placed in a live context, Bayesian optimization can be used to continually improve the choice of designs for new users.

Bayesian optimization is a collection of three components: (1) Gaussian process regression to model design spaces, (2) a probabilistic, generative theory of how observations (voluntary usage times) are produced, and (3) an active-selection policy that specifies what design to explore next. A key component of the research described in this article is our exploration of candidate generative theories, and a contribution of our work is the specification of a theory that is robust to misspecification, i.e., robust to the possibility that humans behave differently than the theory suggests.

We collected multiple measures of engagement, including experiential and predicted voluntary time on activity and a post-usage survey with questions indicative of engagement. We argue that predicted voluntary time may be a better measure than experiential, if the experiential time is used as an anchor to predict the usage time of other individuals. We also showed that usage time and the survey yield highly consistent predictions of maximally engaging designs. The converging evidence from these two very different measures gives us confidence in our interpretations of the data.

Beyond our methodological contributions, we explored a fundamental question regarding engagement and game difficulty. Moving beyond the well-trodden notion that game difficulty can affect engagement, we compared covert versus overt manipulations of difficulty. We found that overt manipulations on their own were relatively ineffective in modulating engagement (at least over the range of designs we tested), yet they became quite effective when coupled with a covert manipulation in which we provided assistance in a subtle manner, possibly skirting the player's awareness. We believe that players attributed the improved performance resulting from our covert manipulation of game dynamics to their own competence. Their boost in perceived competence led to increased engagement. We envision that this covert-assistance trick could be used to draw players into a game and then be gradually removed as the player's true skill increases.

In future research, we plan to address three limitations of the present work. First, we would like to conduct longer-term usage studies to show that the effects we observe on engagement scale up with longer use of software. Second, we would like to explicity evaluate the player's perception of task difficulty under different levels of covert assistance, rather than relying on anecdotal evidence. Third, rather than optimize design parameters for a user population as a whole, the same methodology could be applied to optimize for a specific user, conditioned on their play history. For such a task, the data efficiency of Bayesian optimization is critical.

ACKNOWLEDGMENTS

This research was supported by NSF grants SES-1461535, SBE-0542013, and SMA-1041755.

REFERENCES

1. E Andersen, Y Liu, R Snider, R Szeto, and Z Popovic. 2011. Placing a value on aesthetics in online casual games. In *Proceedings of the SIGCHI Conference on Human Factors in Computing Systems*. ACM, New York, 1275–1278.
2. G. Andrade, G. Ramalho, H. Santana, and V. Corruble. 2005. Challenge-sensitive action selection: an application to game balancing. In *Intelligent Agent Technology, IEEE/WIC/ACM International Conference on*. 194–200. DOI: http://dx.doi.org/10.1109/IAT.2005.52
3. Jeanne H Brockmyer, Christine M Fox, Kathleen A Curtiss, Evan McBroom, Kimberly M Burkhart, and Jacquelyn N Pidruzny. 2009. The development of the Game Engagement Questionnaire: A measure of engagement in video game-playing. *Journal of Experimental Social Psychology* 45, 4 (2009), 624–634.
4. Olivier Chapelle and Lihong Li. 2011. An empirical evaluation of thompson sampling. In *Advances in neural information processing systems*. 2249–2257.
5. Wei Chu and Zoubin Ghahramani. 2005. Preference learning with Gaussian processes. In *In Proceedings of the 22nd International Conference on Machine Learning*. ACM, New York, 137–144.
6. Seth Cooper, Firas Khatib, Adrien Treuille, Janos Barbero, Jeehyung Lee, Michael Beenen, Andrew Leaver-Fay, David Baker, Zoran Popović, and others. 2010. Predicting protein structures with a multiplayer online game. *Nature* 466, 7307 (2010), 756–760.
7. Simone de Sousa Borges, V. H. S. Durelli, H. M. Reis, and S. Isotani. 2014. A systematic mapping on gamification applied to education. In *Proceedings of the 29th Annual ACM Symposium on Applied Computing*. ACM, New York, 216–222.
8. Alena Denisova and Paul Cairns. 2015. The Placebo Effect in Digital Games: Phantom Perception of Adaptive Artificial Intelligence. In *Proceedings of the 2015 Annual Symposium on Computer-Human Interaction in Play*. ACM, 23–33.
9. Fitocracy. 2015. Fitocracy. (2015). https://www.fitocracy.com/
10. J A Fredricks, P C Blumenfeld, and A H Paris. 2004. School engagement: Potential of the concept, state of the evidence. *Review of Educational Research* 74 (2004), 59–109.
11. B. Harrison and D.L. Roberts. 2013. Analytics-driven dynamic game adaption for player retention in Scrabble. In *Computational Intelligence in Games (CIG), 2013 IEEE Conference on*. 1–8. DOI: http://dx.doi.org/10.1109/CIG.2013.6633632
12. R H Hohle. 1965. Inferred components of reaction times as functions of foreperiod duration. *Journal of Experimental Psychology* 69 (1965), 382–386.
13. Aaron Isaksen, Dan Gopstein, and Andy Nealen. 2015. Exploring game space using survival analysis. In *Foundations of Digital Games*.
14. David Jurgens, James McCorriston, and Derek Ruths. 2015. An Analysis of Exercising Behavior in Online Populations. In *Ninth International AAAI Conference on Web and Social Media*.
15. Jeffrey I Kassinove and Mitchell L Schare. 2001. Effects of the" near miss" and the" big win" on persistence at slot machine gambling. *Psychology of Addictive Behaviors* 15, 2 (2001), 155.
16. Firas Khatib, Frank DiMaio, Seth Cooper, Maciej Kazmierczyk, Miroslaw Gilski, Szymon Krzywda, Helena Zabranska, Iva Pichova, James Thompson, Zoran Popović, and others. 2011. Crystal structure of a monomeric retroviral protease solved by protein folding game players. *Nature structural & molecular biology* 18, 10 (2011), 1175–1177.
17. Christoph Klimmt, Albert Rizzo, Peter Vorderer, Jan Koch, and Till Fischer. 2009. Experimental evidence for suspense as determinant of video game enjoyment. *CyberPsychology & Behavior* 12, 1 (2009), 29–31.
18. Janne V. Kujala, Ulla Richardson, and Heikki Lyytinen. 2010. A Bayesian-optimal principle for learner-friendly adaptation in learning games. *Journal of Mathematical Psychology* 54, 2 (2010), 247 – 255. DOI: http://dx.doi.org/10.1016/j.jmp.2009.10.001
19. Ellen J Langer. 1975. The illusion of control. *Journal of personality and social psychology* 32, 2 (1975), 311.
20. G Levy. 2002. An introduction to quasi-random numbers. (2002). http://www.nag.co.uk/IndustryArticles/introduction_to_quasi_random_numbers.pdf
21. Robert V Lindsey, Michael C Mozer, William J Huggins, and Harold Pashler. 2013. Optimizing Instructional Policies. In *Advances in Neural Information Processing Systems 26*, C.J.C. Burges, L. Bottou, M. Welling, Z. Ghahramani, and K.Q. Weinberger (Eds.). Curran Associates, 2778–2786.
22. K Linser and T Goschke. 2007. Unconscious modulation of the conscious experience of voluntary control. *Cognition* 104 (2007), 459–475.
23. Y.-E. Liu, T. Mandel, E. Brunskill, and Z. Popovic. 2014. Towards automatic experimentation of educational knowledge. In *Proceedings of the SIGCHI Conference on Human Factors in Computing Systems*. ACM, New York, 3349–3358.

24. Derek Lomas, Jodi Forlizzi, Nikhil Poonwala, Nirmal Patel, Sharan Shodhan, Kishan Patel, Ken Koedinger, and Emma Brunskill. 2015. Interface Design Optimization as a Multi-Armed Bandit Problem. In *Proceedings of the SIGCHI Conference on Human Factors in Computing Systems*. ACM, New York.

25. J. D. Lomas, K. Patel, J. L. Forlizzi, and K. R. Koedinger. 2013. Optimizing challenge in an educational game using large-scale design experiments. In *Proceedings of the SIGCHI Conference on Human Factors in Computing Systems*. ACM, New York, 89–98.

26. MM Hassan Mahmud, Benjamin Rosman, Subramanian Ramamoorthy, and Pushmeet Kohli. 2014. Adapting interaction environments to diverse users through online action set selection. In *Proceedings of the AAAI 2014 Workshop on Machine Learning for Interactive Systems*. Citeseer.

27. Elisa D. Mekler, Julia Ayumi Bopp, Alexandre N. Tuch, and Klaus Opwis. 2014. A Systematic Review of Quantitative Studies on the Enjoyment of Digital Entertainment Games. In *Proceedings of the 32Nd Annual ACM Conference on Human Factors in Computing Systems (CHI '14)*. ACM, New York, NY, USA, 927–936. DOI: http://dx.doi.org/10.1145/2556288.2557078

28. Y R Miyamoto, C A Coleman, J J Williams, J Whitehill, S O Nesterko, and J Reich. 2015. Beyond Time-on-Task: The Relationship between Spaced Study and Certification in MOOCs. http://dx.doi.org/10.2139/ssrn.2547799, *Journal of Learning Analytics* (2015). Accessed: 2015-01-09.

29. H L O'Brien and E. G. Toms. 2010. The development and evaluation of a survey to measure user engagement. *J. of the Am. Soc. for Information Science and Technlogy* 61 (2010), 50–69.

30. Anna N Rafferty, Matei Zaharia, Thomas L Griffiths, and others. 2012. Optimally designing games for cognitive science research. In *Proceedings of the 34th Annual Conference of the Cognitive Science Society*.

31. B. Roads and M. C. Mozer. 2015. Improving Human-Computer Cooperative Classification Via Cognitive Theories of Similarity. (2015).

32. Jeffrey N Rouder, Jun Lu, Paul Speckman, DongChu Sun, and Yi Jiang. 2005. A hierarchical model for estimating response time distributions. *Psychonomic Bulletin & Review* 12, 2 (2005), 195–223.

33. D Sharek and E Wiebe. 2015. Measuring Video Game Engagement Through the Cognitive and Affective Dimensions. *Simulation & Gaming* 45, 4-5 (Jan. 2015), 569–592.

34. R. Sifa, C. Bauckhage, and A. Drachen. 2014. The Playtime Principle: Large-scale cross-games interest modeling. In *Computational Intelligence and Games (CIG), 2014 IEEE Conference on*. 1–8. DOI: http://dx.doi.org/10.1109/CIG.2014.6932906

35. Jasper Snoek, Hugo Larochelle, and Ryan P Adams. 2012. Practical Bayesian optimization of machine learning algorithms. In *Advances in neural information processing systems*. 2951–2959.

36. Ben G. Weber, Michael John, Michael Mateas, and Arnav Jhala. 2011. Modeling Player Retention in Madden NFL 11. In *Innovative Applications of Artificial Intelligence (IAAI)*. AAAI Press, AAAI Press, San Francisco, CA.

37. A Zook, E Fruchter, and M O Riedl. 2014. Automatic playtesting for game parameter tuning via active learning. In *Proc. of the 9th Intl. Conf. on the Foundations of Digital Games*, T Barnes and I Bogost (Eds.). Soc. for the Adv. of the Science of Digital Games, Ft. Lauderdale, FL.

Operationalising and Evaluating Sub-Optimal and Optimal Play Experiences through Challenge-Skill Manipulation

Madison Klarkowski, Daniel Johnson, Peta Wyeth,
Mitchell McEwan, Cody Phillips, Simon Smith
Queensland University of Technology (QUT), Brisbane, Australia
{m15.clark, dm.johnson, peta.wyeth, m1.mcewan, c1.phillips, simon.smith}@qut.edu.au

ABSTRACT
The study examines the relationship of challenge-skill balance and the player experience through evaluation of competence, autonomy, presence, interest/enjoyment, and positive and negative affect states. To manipulate challenge-skill balance, three video game modes – boredom (low challenge), balance (medium challenge), and overload (high challenge) – were developed and experimentally tested (n = 45). The study showed that self-reported positive affect, autonomy, presence, and interest/enjoyment differed between the levels. The balance condition generally performed well in terms of positive player experiences, confirming the key role challenge-skill balance plays in designing for optimal play experiences. Interestingly, the study found significantly lower negative affect scores when playing the boredom condition. Greater feelings of competence were also reported for the boredom condition than the balance and overload conditions. Finally, some measures point to overload as a more enjoyable experience than boredom, suggesting possible player preference for challenge > skill imbalance over skill > challenge imbalance. Implications for design and future research are presented.

Author Keywords
Video games; player experience; self-determination; presence; challenge.

ACM Classification Keywords
K.8.0 Personal Computing: General- games.

INTRODUCTION
One of the most prominent challenges in player experience research is finding or designing video games that allow for useful player experience comparisons to be made. Comparing the player experience across two different video games is sometimes valuable, but it is usually difficult to find games that only differ on the variable of interest. This creates a challenge for researchers seeking to better understand the player experience in terms of isolating which features of games and contexts of play influence the player experience in particular ways.

CHI'16, May 07-12, 2016, San Jose, CA, USA
© 2016 ACM. ISBN 978-1-4503-3362-7/16/05$15.00
DOI: http://dx.doi.org/10.1145/2858036.2858563

The current study forms part of a larger program of research seeking to understand the psychophysiological states associated with different aspects of the player experience. The first step in this research was to create video game play experiences that provide useful points of comparison. One accessible aspect of games that is commonly manipulated is challenge-skill balance, a core contributor to the player experience in that it is considered a robust predictor of game enjoyment that emerges through flow [33]. While the impact of challenge-skill balance on flow has been investigated in previous work, the understanding of the influence of challenge-skill on other constructs of the play experiences is still being developed.

As such, the aim of the current study is to explore the role of challenge-skill balance on the player experience. To do this, three video game conditions were manipulated to be representative of challenge-skill balance and imbalance, so that the impact of boredom (low challenge), balance (medium challenge) and overload (high challenge) could be examined. Various subjective measures associated with the player experience were used, including need satisfaction, presence, interest and enjoyment, and positive and negative affect states. While there is an assumed understanding of the role that challenge-skill has in the player experience, understanding of how challenge-skill balance influences different aspects of the player experience is still being developed. By employing various player experience measures to investigate experiential phenomena associated with the play experience, a novel understanding of challenge-skill balance can be gained. This will allow greater insight into how challenge-skill balance should be designed to facilitate positive player experiences

Our results show greater positive affect, autonomy, presence, and interest/enjoyment when playing the balance condition as opposed to the boredom and overload conditions. Interestingly, results also showed less negative affect in the boredom condition than in the balance and overload conditions, possibly speaking to impact on emotional engagement or mental stimulation in low-challenge game experiences. Similar rated levels of competence between the balance and boredom conditions indicates that competence may be limited as a predictor of a positive play experience.

Finally, participants reported greater enjoyment and positive affect for the overload condition than the boredom condition, suggesting that some challenge-skill imbalances are preferable to others.

This study represents an effort to examine the impact of challenge-skill balance and imbalance on wider subjective experiential phenomena. Our findings allow for a better understanding of the player experience associated with differing levels of challenge-skill balance. Our findings also present implications for game designers seeking to build optimal game experiences, strengthening the role of challenge-skill balance as a core element of a positive play-experience and as a precursor to many positive experiential phenomena, such as presence and autonomy. This research is also useful for researchers aiming to build or evaluate games or game levels for use in experimental studies, revealing that greater negative affect does not necessarily indicate a negative play experience and reported competence does not necessarily indicate a positive play experience. The reported process for altering the challenge-skill variable in a complex game environment may also be beneficial to experimental designs. Finally, challenge-skill balance is potentially relevant to a breadth of activities; as such the broader research community may benefit from these results by considering our findings in serious games or work-based software (for example, vocational training games), gamification, or in non-gaming contexts such as pedagogical and learning research, particularly when considering optimal challenge.

BACKGROUND

Self-Determination Theory and Needs Satisfaction

The player experience poses a notable challenge for evaluation [19]. As the concept of 'fun' is difficult to define and partial to personal preference, research instead examines the experience through the lens of experiential phenomena associated with video game play [5]. Amongst the phenomena commonly evaluated include presence, motivation, engagement, and affect.

Motivation and needs satisfaction in video games has been evaluated through the application of Self-Determination Theory (SDT), an established psychological theory of motivation concerned with the fulfillment of universal needs of competence, relatedness, and autonomy. SDT primarily addresses factors that enable intrinsic motivation, a core motivation for play and sport [27]. The development of the Player Experience of Needs Satisfaction (PENS) scale has allowed researchers to examine SDT through a measure uniquely developed for player experience evaluation [27]. Through SDT, PENS evaluates autonomy, competence, and relatedness.

Autonomy speaks to the sense of volition or willingness when doing a task [9], and is positively associated with increased intrinsic motivation. Enabling a sense of freedom and choice for players, the provision of opportunities that interest them, and the avoidance of factors that diminish volition (such as controlling or limited tasks) promotes autonomy, in turn promoting willingness to engage in the activity [27].

Competence addresses feelings of effectiveness and a need for challenge within the game [27]. To achieve satisfied competence, players should be optimally challenged, receive positive feedback to enhance perceived competence, and be presented with the opportunity to improve on his/her abilities and skills. The need for optimal challenge is perhaps best satisfied by careful consideration for challenge-skill balance, in which the skill of the player does not either exceed or fail to meet the challenges presented by the game (see Challenge-Skill Balance).

Finally, *relatedness* investigates feelings of connection to others [27]. Within games, this primarily pertains to experiences of relatedness to human others in multiplayer games; however, this also addresses the sense of connection to computer-controlled non-player characters (NPCs) [27].

PENS also evaluates presence and intuitive controls, core influences on the player experience [27]. Presence is described as the feeling of being 'within' the game world, facilitated by engaging narrative and visually pleasing aesthetics; it is described by the International Society of Presence Research as *"[occurring] when part or all of a person's perception fails to accurately acknowledge the role of technology that makes it appear that s/he is in a physical location and environment different from her/his actual location and environment in the physical world."* [12] Presence is theorised to be positively associated with increased intrinsic motivation. Intuitive controls assists in enabling feelings of competence, autonomy (by not stymieing the player with awkward or difficult controls), and presence (by facilitating feelings of 'being there' through to provision of an intuitive control scheme that does not require active consideration) [27].

PENS has revealed less competence and autonomy when engaged in co-located play with others than solo play or play online [32]. Studies have also revealed autonomy, competence, and relatedness as positive predictors of game enjoyment and future play, and positive association between autonomy and competence and post-play mood [27].

The concept of presence in games has been explored beyond PENS literature. Presence is positively related to space exploration and the need for discovery within game worlds [31], and has been identified as a key contributor to greater enjoyment of games [18]. Games played on higher difficulties (that is, games that have not been identified as 'easy'), in first-person view, or with realistic environments have also been identified as more likely to provoke feelings of presence [22].

Affect

Another experiential phenomena of the play experience is impact on affect; or, the state feelings or emotions of the player throughout the experience. There is some ambiguity within literature concerning 'mood' and 'affect'. While the terms are often used interchangeably, such as in Ravaja et al.'s study of phasic emotional responses [23], there is an important distinction between the two. While affective states are emotions experienced during an event (or, in the context of this research topic, within player experience), mood is a lasting disposition that may impact on a person's overall perception of an event [30]. The glossary of the American Psychiatric Association states, "*affect is momentary (like weather), while, mood is a prolonged emotion (like climate)*". Within the context of player experience evaluation, it is necessary to measure affective states, as these are the emotions experienced during play [19].

Positive affect has been linked with positive player experiences, such as competence satisfaction [27], convergence between the player's experiences of self and the player's ideal self during play [21], and prosocial play [28]. Conversely, a study by Jennett et al. [13] examined the relationship between fast-paced games, negative affect, and state anxiety; while they found negative affect and state anxiety was higher for faster-paced games than slow games, the results were not significant. As such, Jennett et al. recommends negative affect and emotions for further study [28] [5].

Enjoyment

Research has consistently identified enjoyment as a central reason for, and a core aspect of, playing video games [10]. While it is pervasively understood that video games provide an enjoyable experience, the dimensions of this experience and how to design for this experience are still not fully understood [33]. Enjoyment has been identified as a multifaceted construct that relates to physiological, affective, cognitive, and behavioural dimensions [10] [33]. Research has also coupled enjoyment with intrinsic motivation [26].

Challenge and Challenge-Skill Balance

Much of game design is rooted in the concept that players seek, and are driven by, challenge [17]. Successfully completing challenging tasks in game environments generates a sense of greater self-efficacy and accomplishment for players [17]. Research also suggests that simply undertaking optimally challenging activities – not just the experience of succeeding at the task – is an enjoyable experience in itself [1], establishing challenge-based game play as an intrinsically motivating activity.

Abuhamdeh and Csikszentmihalyi found that optimal enjoyment of an activity occurs during moderately challenging experiences, in which the activity is perceived as neither too easy nor too difficult [1]. Likewise, challenge-skill balance is achieved when the skills or abilities of the player are evenly met by the challenges represented by the game or task. Should a game be too difficult or too easy for the player, the player experience is assumed to be negatively impacted [2].

Despite this, the notion of challenge is not yet well-defined within games literature, and consequently has been the nexus of much research investigating the play experience [7]. Experience of challenge has been found to be dependent on both game genre (as well as the advent of emotional challenge in narrative-driven titles) [6], and the relationship of the player with the game or gaming in general [2] [17]. Research investigating engagement in an educational game found that players were more engaged, and played longer, when the game presented an easy challenge as opposed to a moderate challenge [17], which contradicts the aforementioned notion of optimal challenge. The researchers suggested that a possible explanation for the outcome was the lack of prior experience amongst their players, and that it is possible that challenge-seeking behaviours may only occur after some level of expertise is acquired. This is supported by other research that discovered that 'casual' players of a game gained more enjoyment out of easier difficulties, regardless of their aptitude in the game, whereas 'experienced' players' enjoyment of the game was predicated upon challenge [2].

Flow

Flow describes a mental state characterised by total absorption in and enjoyment of an activity [8]. Flow is often achieved in instances of challenge-skill balance [15], in which the challenge or demands of the task are adequately met by the skill or ability of the person completing the task. Should the participant find the task overwhelming or too simple, the potential for flow is lessened. While some literature suggests that challenge-skill balance is a necessary antecedent to the experience of flow [8], other research suggests it is simply a robust predictor of flow [24] [11]. A revisited model of flow suggests that the original model conflagrates antecedents, states, and consequences, and that antecedents (such as challenge-skill balance) should instead be construed as predictors of, and not a part of, the flow state [4]. Video games have been identified as possessing ideal characteristics to invoke and maintain the flow experience, with the caveat that only games that provide a match between difficulty and player skill are likely achieve a flow state [29].

PREVIOUS RESEARCH

This study builds upon our previous research [16], in which the challenges of operationalising and measuring flow in video games are discussed. While the overload condition prompted significantly less flow than the balance and boredom conditions, no significant differences were found between balance and boredom. Some proposed explanations for this include improper condition design (the boredom condition may still have allowed for a positive play experience), the potential for high ratings of flow to not actually be occurring in the scale used due to the wording of some items, or that, as suggested in some literature, challenge-skill balance plays a more diminished role in flow than assumed. The boredom condition has since been altered towards greater skill > challenge imbalance through the removal of enemy agents entirely. Multiple measures of the player experience were evaluated against the redesigned conditions. A gap was identified in the literature on evaluation of challenge-skill balance and imbalance impact on play constructs other than flow, immersion, and performance; as such, the experience of presence, competence, autonomy, interest/enjoyment and affect are reported for this paper.

STUDY DESCRIPTION

A within-subjects experiment was designed to measure the effects of challenge-skill balance and imbalance on the play experience. The study made use of three game conditions modified to be representative of dimensions of challenge-skill balance and challenge-skill imbalance. The impact of challenge-skill balance and imbalance on the player experienced was measured across multiple subjective self-report surveys that evaluate the experience of experiential phenomena commonly associated with play.

Measures

PANAS

The Positive and Negative Affect Schedule (PANAS) is a subjective measure of affect, which uses two subscales: positive affect and negative affect. Each of the subscales contains 10 adjective items, which are rated on a 1-5 Likert scale, with 5 being "Extremely". The positive affect subscale includes adjective items such as "Interested", "Enthusiastic" and "Alert", while the negative affect subscale includes adjective items such as "Irritable", "Ashamed" and "Afraid". Scores for each subscale can range from 10-50, with higher scores being indicative of higher positive affect or higher negative affect. It is important to note that positive affect and negative affect exist in parallel rather than on a continuum of affect.

PENS

Three of the needs-satisfaction subscales were included in the study design: competence, autonomy, and presence, which are thought to be core components of the player experience [27]. The Player Experience of Needs Satisfaction scale has been shown to be a statistically reliable measure [14]. While the Player Experience of Needs Satisfaction contains a subscale for relatedness, this subscale was excluded from the study on the grounds that the game is a single player experience and no non-player characters were present in the game. Similarly, the intuitive controls subscale was excluded from the study as the control setup was not being manipulated in any way.

Items are rated on a Likert scale of 1 – 7 ('7' representing 'Strongly Agree'), and are as are as follows:

- Competence: *"I felt very capable and effective when playing."*
- Autonomy: *"I did things in the game because they interested me."*
- Presence: *"I experienced feelings as deeply in the game as I have in real life."*

IMI

Rooted in self-determination theory, the Intrinsic Motivation Inventory (IMI) is a scale for measuring subjective experiences in relation to an activity [26]. It is considered to be a reliable measure of its subscales, interest/enjoyment, competence, effort, value, pressure and perceived choice (autonomy). An additional subscale has since been added, though has not yet been validated (relatedness). As the Intrinsic Motivation Inventory and Player Experience of Needs Satisfaction are similarly rooted in Self-Determination Theory, it was determined that inclusion of the needs-satisfaction subscales from the Intrinsic Motivation Inventory would be largely repetitious, and that those subscales (competence, autonomy, relatedness) should not be included in the study design. However the interest/enjoyment subscale of the Intrinsic Motivation Inventory does not have an analogue in the Player Experience of Needs Satisfaction, and will be used to gauge the interest and enjoyment of participants across the experimental conditions. Items are rated on a Likert scale of 1 – 7 ('7' representing 'very true'), and are as follows:

- *"I would describe this activity as very interesting."*
- *"I enjoyed doing this activity very much."*

Game

The game chosen for this study was Valve Corporation's *Left 4 Dead 2,* a post-apocalyptic zombie first-person shooter. This was due to its high production levels, popularity within the gaming community, and intuitive gameplay. The game was also chosen due to its native inclusion of Dynamic Difficulty Adjustment (DDA) in the form of an entity known as the 'AI Director'. DDA provides real-time adjustment of the game's difficulty in response to player performance, ensuring a similar play experience regardless of individual ability or expertise.

The three modified game conditions all took place within a map named 'The Port'. In this level, participants explored an industrial complex to retrieve sixteen gas canisters with the help of three companion AI. Once all sixteen gas canisters were emptied into a fuel tank, a bridge would lower, granting access to a car and finishing the level. As this mission generally took longer than the ten-minute gameplay sessions, no participants completed this mission; this was intended to prevent a victory condition from occurring for the more skilled players, and to ensure all participant had identical play durations. An exception to this is five participants who completed the objectives in the boredom condition before the allotted time passed, requiring early termination of the play session before reaching the car ('beating' the level).

Manipulations

Game conditions that only differed on the challenge-skill variable were required for the study. To achieve this, three conditions were designed towards manipulating challenge-skill balance and imbalance: 'balance' (medium challenge), 'boredom' (low challenge), and 'overload' (high challenge). The challenge of each game condition was directly altered to accomplish this. The game level chosen featured two key challenges: successfully collecting and delivering sixteen gas canisters, and surviving combat with enemy agents (zombies). The challenge of gas canister collection was dependent on the challenge of enemy agents: canisters were clearly marked and highlighted in the map, and canister collection was only inhibited through the presence of enemy AI. To this end, combat was the only feature of the game directly altered.

	Balance	Boredom	Overload
Common enemy agents	Standard	None	Extreme
Special enemy agents	Standard	None	Extreme
Collecting canisters	Standard	Standard	Standard
DDA	Enabled	Disabled	Disabled

Table 1. Challenge manipulation in the game conditions.

Left 4 Dead 2 features two types of enemy agents: common and special. Common enemy zombies are slow-moving, attack through melee hits only, often move in 'herds', and natively have low health. Special enemy zombies have unique abilities (such as spitting pools of acid, or pouncing on the player), move alone, require special tactics to eliminate, and have lower spawn rates than common enemy zombies. Both these enemy types were modified for each game condition: in boredom, they were removed entirely; in balance, they appeared as they would in standard *Left 4 Dead 2* and were influenced by DDA; finally, in overload, spawn rates, health, responsiveness, herd size, and damage dealt were radically increased. For challenge manipulated across all conditions, please refer to Table 1.

The conditions were developed so as to be extreme enough in difference that players of any skill level would experience challenge > skill in the Overload condition, skill > challenge in the Boredom condition, and a match of skill and challenge in the Balance condition. As such, the paper operates under the assumption that the conditions were successful in achieving this.

Some features of *Left 4 Dead 2* were altered for all conditions for the preservation of experimental integrity and inhibition of potential confounds. These alterations include:

- The achievement system was disabled to ensure no players experienced a reward for achieving something that other players did not (for example, killing five 'Hunter' type special enemies).
- Sprays, player-chosen images that can be 'pasted' into the game world by pressing a button, were also disabled.
- Players were restricted to only one of four playable characters ('Nick').
- Weapon choice was eliminated from the game. In the default game, players may choose to play with a sniper rifle, machete, assault rifle, chainsaw, and so on. To ensure a similar experience across all conditions and experiments, only the assault rifle as the primary weapon and pistol as the secondary weapon were enabled.
- In all conditions, the 'Witch'- a rare special enemy type with the ability to instantly kill a novice player and their AI teammates –was removed.

Balance Condition

Figure 1. Screenshot of the 'balance' condition.

The balance condition was designed for challenge-skill balance. This condition remained almost identical to the standard version of *Left 4 Dead 2*, with the exception of the alterations made for all conditions as detailed previously, as the native presence of DDA (in the form of the 'AI director') allowed for challenge-skill match for each participant. DDA is often used in video games as a solution to challenge-skill imbalance in both single player [2] and multiplayer [3] contexts, ensuring that the play experience is neither too easy nor too difficult. As such, this condition design assumes that the AI Director is successful in promoting a challenge-skill match experience.

To this end, game difficulty was set to 'normal' in the map editor. Common enemy zombies had 50 health, and would spawn in herd sizes respective to the player performance as judged by the AI director. The player and their AI-controlled teammates had 100 points of health each, and would take 2 damage per hit to their front and 1 damage per hit to their back. The AI Director (DDA) was enabled. Refer to Figure 1 for a screenshot of the typical play experience for the balance condition.

Boredom Condition

Figure 2. Screenshot of the 'boredom' condition.

The boredom was designed for challenge-skill imbalance, where the skill of the player far exceeded the challenge of the game. In this condition, enemies were removed entirely from the game. The gameplay in this condition consisted entirely of retrieving the gas canisters scattered throughout the map. As the gas canisters are highlighted in the map in all conditions, finding the canisters did not represent much challenge; additionally, the large size of the map and the distribution of the canisters ensured a repetitive experience. Despite the removal of combat altogether, the inclusion of canister collection and travel in the virtual world ensures the game remains sufficiently game-like. Refer to Figure 2 for a screenshot of the typical play experience for the boredom condition.

Overload Condition

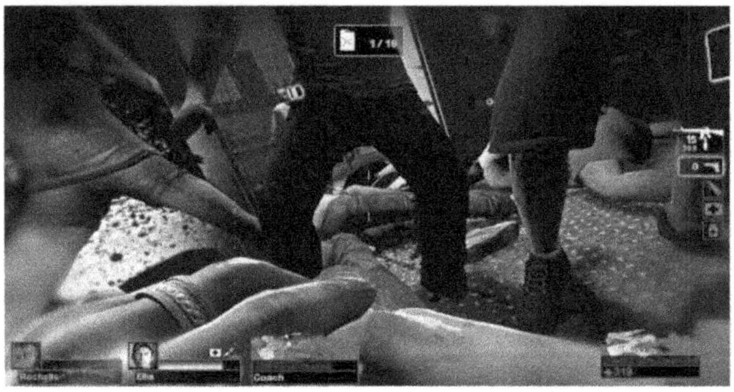

Figure 3. Screenshot of the 'Overload' condition.

Similar to the boredom condition, the overload condition was also designed for challenge-skill imbalance. In this condition, the challenge-skill imbalance was accomplished through challenge outstripping player skill. This was achieved through extra enemy health, drastically increased enemy count, extra damage taken from enemy hits and friendly fire, and reduced friendly AI line-of-sight range. The high spawn rate of enemy AI also reduced the potential for 'cooldown spots' [20] that allow players time to heal, regroup, and restock on ammunition.

To this end, game difficulty was set to 'expert' in the map editor. Common enemy health was raised from 50 (in the balance condition) to 1000. The player and their AI-controlled teammates had 100 points of health each, and would take 20 damage per hit to their front and 10 damage per hit to their back. All special enemies, including the 'tank', had their health multiplied by 4; this gave tanks 16,000 health points. In addition to this, zombies were more likely to spawn behind the player, there was no game-enforced limit on how many zombies could be present in the map at a time, and special infected spawn rate was increased. Refer to Figure 3 for a screenshot of the typical play experience for the overload condition.

Participants

Forty-five participants (thirty-three male), aged 17 – 29 (mean age of 22.1, $SD = 3.75$), volunteered for the study. A demographics survey distributed at the start of the experiment asked for their estimation of their experience with video games; on a Likert scale of 1 – 7, with '7' representing 'extremely experienced' and '1' 'not at all experienced'. Participants self-rated as an average of 6.1 ($SD = 1.08$) for 'general experience with video games' and 5.2 ($SD = 1.85$) for 'experience with first-person shooters'. Participants were recruited through word-of-mouth, undergraduate lectures, and online flyers, and were compensated for their time with video game keys.

Experimental Environment

The experiments took place in a laboratory environment on gaming PCs. The experimenter sat behind a partition in the corner of the laboratory, facilitating participant comfort through lack of direct observation. Experiments were conducted on one participant at a time, ensuring that only the participant and one researcher were present in the room during data collection.

Process

Upon entering the laboratory, participants were briefed on the experiment procedure and the tasks they were to undertake. Participants were then set-up with instruments used to record their physiological signals, of which the results are not reported for this paper. Participants would then answer a short demographics survey and spend approximately five minutes playing a custom tutorial for the game. The tutorial took place in the same map as the game conditions, and introduced the player to game mechanic basics such as shooting, using medkits, interacting with doors, and picking up gas canisters.

The study employed a repeated measures experiment design to offset learning effect; as such, 23 participants played the balance condition first, and 22 participants played the boredom condition first. The overload condition was always played last to prevent residual frustration influencing the experience of the boredom and flow conditions. Each condition self-terminated after ten minutes of playtime.

After each of the three game conditions, participants would spend five to ten minutes completing a questionnaire on their player experience. The results from the competence, autonomy, and presence subscales of PENS, the interest/enjoyment subscale of the IMI, and the results from PANAS are reported in this paper.

RESULTS

No issues were found with singularity or multicollinearity, and so a repeated measures multivariate analysis of variance was conducted on all the subjective self-response measures using the experimental condition as the within-subjects factor. Outliers were assessed by inspection of a box plot. One extreme outlier was identified for negative affect that was causing violations to the assumption of normality for that measure, but analysis with and without the participant revealed no changes in the pattern of results so the full sample was included in all analyses. Mauchly's Test indicated that the assumption of sphericity had been violated for PENS Autonomy ($W = .865$, $\chi2(2) = 6.071$, $p = .048$), IMI Interest/Enjoyment ($W = .767$, $\chi2(2) = 11.115$, $p = .004$), and PANAS Positive Affect ($W = .637$, $\chi2(2) = 18.973$, $p < .001$), so Greenhouse-Geisser adjustments ($\varepsilon = .881$, $\varepsilon = .881$, $\varepsilon = .733$) were used for their within-subjects univariate analyses. Wilk's Lambda and an alpha level of $p < .05$ was used as the significance test for the RM MANOVA results, while a Bonferroni adjustment was applied to pairwise comparisons to control the experiment-wise error rate. The repeated-measures MANOVA revealed a significant multivariate within-subjects effect of condition on the subjective response measures ($F(12, 32) = 12.572$, $p < .001$, $\eta p2 = .825$).

PANAS: Positive & Negative Affect

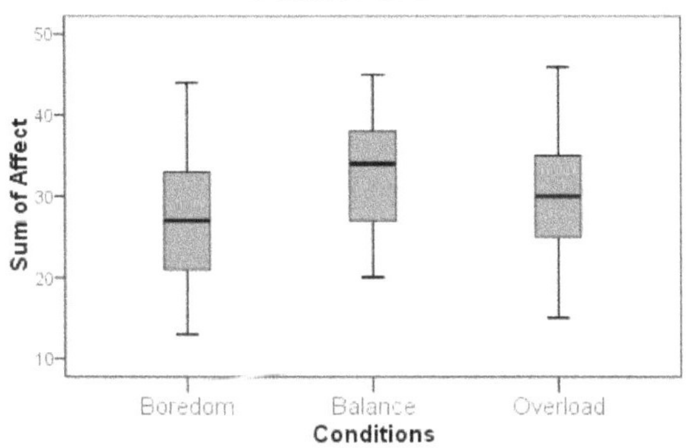

Figure 4. Sum of positive affect across each play condition

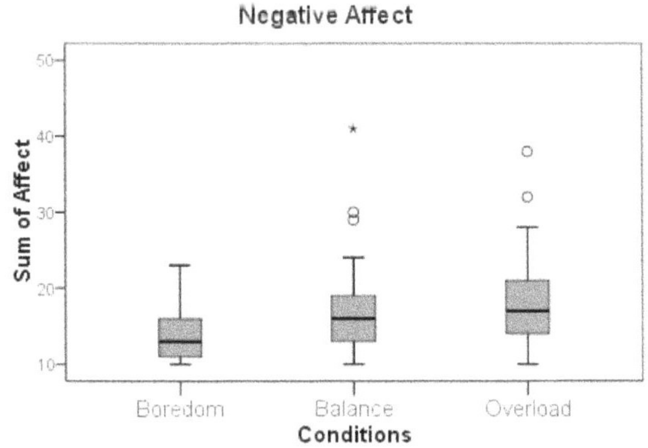

Figure 5. Sum of negative affect across each play condition

Significant univariate main effects were observed for both PANAS positive affect ($F(1.450, 63.799) = 15.884$, $p < .001$, $\eta p2 = .265$) and negative Affect ($F(2, 88) = 10.616$, $p < .001$, $\eta p2 = .194$). Post-hoc analysis revealed that participants reported significantly greater positive affect in the balance ($M = 33.49$, $SD = 6.97$) condition than in both the boredom ($M = 26.25$, $SD = 7.91$, $p < .001$) and overload ($M = 30.27$, $SD = 7.91$, $p = .002$) conditions. Additionally, participants reported significantly greater positive affect in the overload condition than in the boredom condition ($p = <.05$). In terms of negative affect, participants reported significantly less negative affect in the boredom ($M = 14.09$, $SD = 3.76$) condition than in both the balance ($M = 17.11$, $SD = 5.84$, $p = .005$) and overload ($M = 17.60$, $SD = 6.10$, $p < .001$) conditions. No significant difference in negative affect was found between the overload and balance conditions. Please refer to Figures 4 and 5 for graphs presenting affect findings.

IMI: Interest/Enjoyment

Post-hoc analysis revealed that for the main effect on IMI Interest/Enjoyment participants reported significant differences between all three conditions, such that the balanced condition ($M = 5.5$, $SD = .955$) showed significantly higher interest/enjoyment levels than both the boredom ($M = 3.49$, $SD = 1.56$, $p < .001$) and overload ($M = 4.99$, $SD = 1.36$, $p = .015$) conditions, and the overload condition also showed higher interest/enjoyment than the boredom condition ($p < .001$). Please refer to Figure 6 for a graph representing the results for interest/enjoyment.

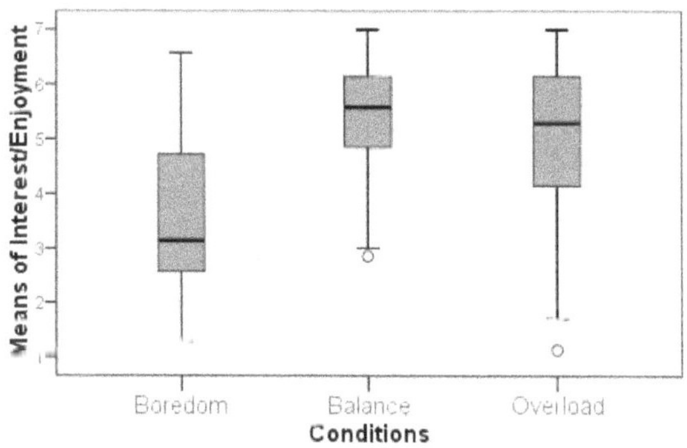

Figure 6. Means of interest/enjoyment across each play condition

PENS: Competence, Autonomy, & Presence

Significant univariate main effects were observed for competence ($F(2, 88) = 37.842$, $p < .001$, $\eta p2 = .462$), autonomy ($F(1.727, 75.978) = 15.441$, $p < .001$, $\eta p2 = .26$), and presence ($F(2, 88) = 17.019$, $p < .001$, $\eta p2 = .279$). Post-hoc analysis revealed that for the main effect on competence, participants reported significantly less competence in the overload condition ($M = 2.98$, $SD = 1.46$) than in the balance ($M = 4.90$, $SD = 1.58$, $p < .001$) and boredom ($M = 5.13$, $SD = 1.39$, $p < .001$) conditions. No significant difference found between balance and boredom. For main effect on autonomy, the balance condition (M = 4.30, SD = 1.31) showed significantly higher autonomy than both the boredom (M = 3.38, SD = 1.49, p = .001) and overload conditions (M = 3.19, SD = 1.22, p < .001), with no significant difference reported between the boredom and overload conditions. Finally, the main effect on presence revealed that the balance condition (M = 3.93, SD = 1.28) showed significantly higher presence than both the boredom (M = 3.06, SD = 1.14, p < .001) and overload (M = 3.24, SD = 1.24, p < .001) conditions, with no significant difference revealed between the boredom and overload conditions. Refer to Figures 7 - 9 for the graph presenting competence, autonomy, and presence findings.

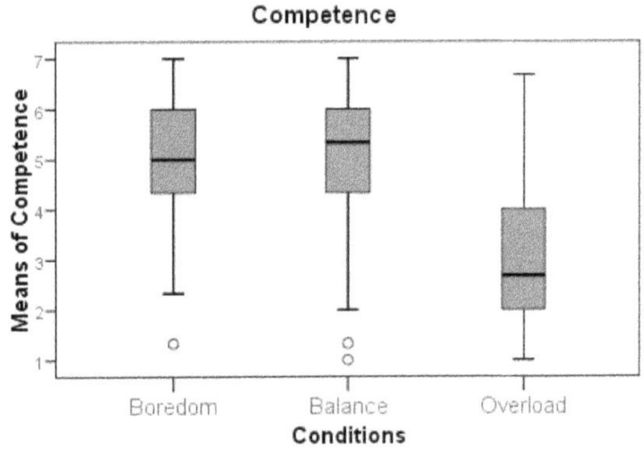

Figure 7. Means of competence across each play condition

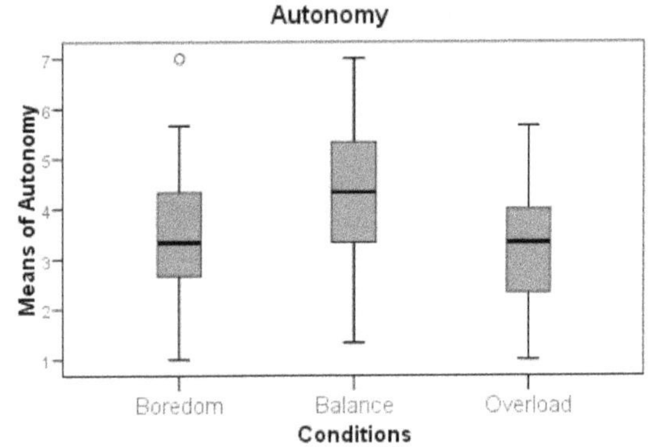

Figure 8. Means of autonomy across each play condition

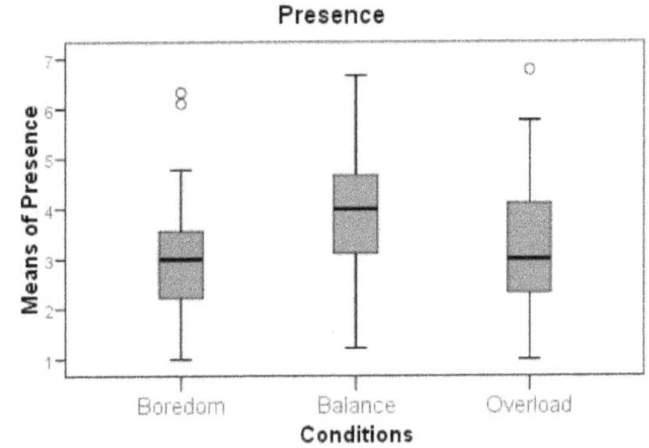

Figure 9. Means of presence across each play condition

DISCUSSION

Generally, the self-report measures supported the balance condition as the optimal play experience amongst the three conditions. The balance condition rated higher for measures indicative of a positive play experience for almost all measures, with surprising exceptions for negative affect and competence. The impact of overload and boredom on the experience of play was also interesting, and points to disparities in sub-optimal play experiences in that different sub-optimal experiences may not be reported the same way.

Affect

While participants reported greater positive affect in the balance and overload condition than the boredom condition, and greater positive affect in the balance condition than the overload condition, greater negative affect was also found in the balance and overload conditions than in the boredom condition. This could be attributed to less emotional engagement for both positive and negative affect: the boredom condition, through absence of any challenge, did not implicitly evoke feelings of pride (through achievement, or overcoming a difficult obstacle), enthusiasm, or excitement; likewise, the banal nature of the task potentially did not allow for feelings of shame, nervousness, or distress due to absence of threat or failure. The boring nature of the boredom condition was corroborated anecdotally through comments made by participants in a 'General Comments' field in the respective condition surveys, including:

"No zombies or challenges makes it boring"

"Only boring due to the easiness and repetitiveness of the task at hand."

"No enemys (sic) *not as much fun"*

Increased negative affect in the balance and overload conditions support Jennett et al.'s hypothesis that faster-paced games lead to greater negative affect [13]. In terms of games design and research, it may be pertinent to be aware that less negative affect does not necessarily translate to a more optimal play experience, and, in fact, could be indicative of a sub-optimal experience through lessened mental stimulation or emotional engagement.

Positive affect appears to remain a reliable predictor of optimal play experiences, with a caveat in that those who experienced challenge > skill imbalance still reported greater positive affect than those who experienced skill > challenge imbalance. Again, anecdotal participant feedback in the surveys indicated that the condition performed as expected in terms of providing an overwhelming play experience:

"Wasn't expecting it to be that hard."

"I died 3 times, I really suck :("

"... the amount of zombies seemed overwhelming for the task requested by the game."

"Overall this session was frustrating and I definitely felt a sense of 'lack of control', such that I didn't see a point in

trying to complete the level, knowing that it wasn't going to happen."

Despite this, it is possible that the experience remained 'fun' despite the excessive challenge of the condition. Some feedback indicated that participants may have had fun despite the challenge-skill imbalance:

"I had more determination to complete the objective even though I kept dying. Just getting one or two cans was enough"

"It had its moments, such as when everyone was away from me and I was healing up myself, only at the VERY LAST MOMENT a zombie hitting me in the back - that was kind of cool."

Interestingly, this may tentatively point to challenge > skill imbalance as a more enjoyable experience than the reverse; that is, overwhelming the player may lead to more positive experiences or affect than underwhelming or boring the player. Another explanation may be that the presence of combat in a combat-based game, regardless of challenge-skill balance or imbalance, is inherently more fun than or preferable to the complete absence of combat. However, when considering previous research that suggests a preference amongst casual or inexperienced players for low challenge [17] [2], it is important to consider that the findings in the present study may reflect the relatively high levels of self-reported experience among participants.

Interest/Enjoyment

Participants reported significantly greater interest/enjoyment for the balance condition than for both the boredom and overload conditions, and was rated highly overall, supporting the balance condition as the optimal play experience in terms of interest/enjoyment. On the surface, this result contradicts the findings of greater negative affect in the balance condition than the boredom condition; however, as previously discussed, this can likely be attributed to generally heightened mental or emotional stimulation in the balance condition. This finding also represents further evidence that challenge-skill balance plays an important role in the player experience, as other research supports [15] [20].

As with positive affect, participants also reported greater interest/enjoyment in the overload condition than for the boredom condition, again possibly pointing to a more positive play experience with challenge > skill imbalance than skill > challenge imbalance. It is also possible that the inclusion of combat mechanics was sufficient to elicit this improvement.

Competence, Autonomy, and Presence

No significant differences were found for competence between the boredom and balance conditions. This may be because some PENS competence items are able to be rated highly for both experiences of challenge-skill balance and skill > challenge imbalance. For example:

- *I felt very capable and effective when playing.*

The absence of sufficient challenge in the boredom condition removes opportunity for failure or error. As such, it may be that feelings of competence are not inhibited, allowing players to experience mastery over the condition's simple fetch task.

Another item more directly addresses challenge-skill balance, however, academic use of the commercial PENS scale does not extend to publishing this item. The item enquires about the player's experience of challenge-skill balance, but does not specify if the absence of balance is the result of challenge exceeding skill or skill exceeding challenge. It is possible that participants responded to this item using either interpretation. That is, disagreement with the item could be indicative of both ability exceeding the challenge, or challenge exceeding ability. It is possible that participants interpreted disagreement with this item as representative of an inability to meet the condition's challenges, potentially affecting rating for this subscale. Another possibility is that participants may have sought out their own challenge for this condition – for example, attempting to collect all the fuel canisters before the condition self-terminated. This is supported by anecdotal comments provided to the experimenter through the survey comments, as follows:

"... given the trivial difficulty, I set a challenge to myself to speedrun the game as quickly as possible (given my limited skills) ..."

"I kinda made my own game out of juggling the canisters."

Finally, experience of competence in instances of sub-optimal or low challenge has been identified in previous PENS literature. Described as 'mastery in action', this experience occurs when players are granted the opportunity to "*deliver a superlative performance without having to work too hard*" [25]. Importantly, these authors note this is not intended to represent the whole of the gameplay experience – rather, developers should provide opportunities for mastery in action as well as optimally challenging play. Thus, it is possible that the findings in the current study reflect participants' experience of 'mastery in action' during the boredom condition and this resulted in high ratings of competence. However, this is arguably less likely given that the whole gameplay experience (in the boredom condition) was low challenge and 'mastery in action' is more likely to occur in situations where it is a 'break' from more optimally challenging play.

All potential explanations point to implications for designers and player experience researchers. Firstly, a high competence rating may not be indicative of challenge-skill balance; researchers should take care to ensure the game artefact does not feature skill > challenge imbalance even in the event of a positive competence rating (unless the intention is to provide a 'mastery in action' experience). Secondly, should the players be setting their own challenge within an intentional skill > challenge imbalance condition, this highlights challenges associated with designing for a boring play experience while keeping the game artefact 'game-like' (that is, not negating potential for invented challenge through the removal of interactive elements). Researchers and designers may wish to evaluate if players are creating their own challenges within a post-game interview.

Participants reported significantly greater autonomy in the balance condition than in the boredom and overload condition, potentially positioning challenge-skill balance as a precursor of autonomy (or challenge-skill imbalance as inhibitors of autonomy). In the boredom condition, the linear task and absence of combat may have contributed to this: instead of being able to defeat enemy agents in interesting or entertaining ways, participants were relegated to the repetitive task of canister collection. Likewise, in the overload condition, participants were almost immediately overwhelmed by a large number of enemy agents, and thus constrained to the starting area of the map. Often, participant movement was restricted either through incapacitation or enemy AI body blocking. As the enemy presence was continuous and overwhelming, it is also possible that the condition left no room for strategy or target prioritization, forcing the player to simply 'spray and pray' (shoot randomly at enemies).

It is notable that the boredom condition did not elicit greater autonomy than the overload condition, as the boredom condition provided participants with the ability to freely explore the game world, choose their own routes, and not remain near their AI teammates for safety. It is possible that the presence of a clear challenge, even one that is overwhelming for the participant, was able to balance this. Alternatively, the absence of an achievable goal in both the boredom and overload conditions may have prompted participants to feel as though there are no meaningful choices to be made.

Finally, participants reported significantly greater presence in the balance condition than the boredom and overload conditions. This again supports challenge-skill balance as a possible antecedent to the experience of presence, or challenge-skill imbalance as inhibitors of presence, as supported by other research [22]. It is likely that the overload condition interrupted or obstructed the experience of presence due to unrealistic or notably skewed gameplay, thus taking players 'out of' the game. Similarly, the complete absence of zombies in boredom condition is at odds with the story of the game world (as told by NPC commentary, world assets, and prior knowledge of the game), again potentially breaking the illusion of being transported to within the game. It is also possible that a lack of mental stimulation in the boredom condition prompted participants' minds to wander, impeding focus on the game itself. When designing for presence in the game world, this points to the importance of obtaining challenge-skill balance.

IMPLICATIONS FOR FUTURE RESEARCH

While this study attempted to gain insight on the general play experience through evaluation of multiple common experiential phenomena associated with play, experimental limits and time constraints prevented measurement of some constructs. These include immersion, engagement, and relatedness. Study of the impact of challenge-skill balance on these constructs is a recommended path of inquiry for future research. Additionally, the discovery of relatively increased negative affect in 'fast-paced' games (as present in the overload and balance conditions) supports the hypothesis of previous research [13]. Further investigation is needed before any firm conclusions can be made about the presence and implications of negative-affect in either optimal or fast-paced play experiences. The potential challenges of measuring competence in games, especially as the experience of competence may not be indicative of an optimal game experience, also warrant further exploration. Additionally, future research may benefit from a direct measure of individual player skill or performance. This would allow for a robust examination of the skill-challenge relationship. Manipulation of challenge beyond game combat mechanics would also allow for greater insight to the effect of challenge-skill balance and imbalance in video game play. The preservation of consistent play styles (i.e. not removing difficult mechanics) may also prove beneficial for future research.

CONCLUSION

The comparison and evaluation of challenge-skill balance and imbalance on competence, autonomy, presence, affect, and interest/enjoyment has revealed implications of the effect of challenge-skill balance on the play experience. The current study highlights the important role challenge-skill balance plays in achieving the optimal play experience through presence, autonomy, interest/enjoyment, and positive affect. The challenges of designing game conditions that only differ on the variable of interest are discussed, pointing to unexpected player experiences such as competence through easy tasks, invented challenge, and preference for challenge > skill imbalance over skill > challenge imbalance. Greater reported competence for the boredom condition also points to challenges in measuring and interpreting competence in situations in which challenge-skill balance may be compromised. Greater negative affect is also identified as not contradictory to positive affect and play experiences. Finally, further research is recommended in regards to the impact of challenge-skill on other play experience constructs (such as immersion or engagement), the measurement of challenge-skill balance and imbalance, and the measurement of competence in challenge-skill balance.

ACKNOWLEDGMENTS

We thank Valve Corporation for supporting this research by kindly providing game keys for participant compensation.

REFERENCES

1. Sami Abuhamdeh and Mihaly Csikszentmihalyi. 2012. The Importance of Challenge for the Enjoyment of Intrinsically Motivated, Goal-Directed Activities. *Personality and Social Psychology Bulletin* 38, 3: 317-330.
2. Justin T. Alexander, John Sear, and Andreas Oikonomou. 2013. An investigation of the effects of game difficulty on player enjoyment. *Entertainment Computing* 4, 1: 53-62.
3. Alexander Baldwin, Daniel Johnson, Peta Wyeth, and Penelope Sweetser. 2013. A framework of Dynamic Difficulty Adjustment in competitive multiplayer video games. In *2013 IEEE International Games Innovation Conference* (IGIC), 16-19.
4. Nicholas D. Bowman. 2008. A PAT on the Back: Media Flow Theory Revis(it)ed. *Rocky Mountain Communication Review* 4, 1: 27-39.
5. Elizabeth A. Boyle, Thomas M. Connolly, Thomas Hainey and James M. Boyle. 2012. Engagement in digital entertainment games: A systematic review. *Computers in Human Behavior* 28, 3: 771-780.
6. Tom Cole, Paul Cairns, and Marco Gillies. 2015. Emotional and Functional Challenge in Core and Avant-grade Games. In *Proceedings of the 2015 Annual Symposium on Computer-Human Interaction in Play* (CHI PLAY '15), 121-126. http://dl.acm.org/citation.cfm?doid=2793107.2793147
7. Anna L. Cox, Paul Cairns, Pari Shah, and Michael Carroll. 2012. Not Doing But Thinking: The Role of Challenge in the Gaming Experience. In *Proceedings of the SIGCHI Conference on Humans Factors in Computing Systems* (CHI '12), 79-88. http://dl.acm.org/citation.cfm?doid=2207676.2207689
8. Mihaly Csikszentmihalyi. 1990. *Flow: The Psychology of Optimal Experience.* Harper Perennial.
9. Edward L. Deci and Richard M. Ryan. 2000. The "what" and "why" of goal pursuits: Humans needs and the self-determination of behavior. *Psychological Inquiry* 11, 4: 227-268.
10. Xiaowen Fang, Susy Chan, Jacek Brzezinski and Chitra Nair. 2010. Development of an Instrument to Measure Enjoyment of Computer Game Play. *International Journal of Human-Computer Interaction* 26, 9: 868-886.
11. Carlton Fong, Diana Zaleski, and Jennifer Leach. 2014. The challenge-skill balance and antecedents of flow: a meta-analytic investigation. *Journal of Positive Psychology* 10, 5: 425-446.
12. International Society for Presence Research. 2000. The Concept of Presence: Explication Statement. Retrieved September 18, 2015 from http://ispr.info/
13. Charlene Jennett, Anna L. Cox, Paul Cairns, Samira Dhoparee, Andrew Epps, Tim Tijs and Alison Walton. 2008. Measuring and Defining the Experience of Immersion in Games. *Internation Journal of Human-Computer Studies* 66, 9: 641-661.
14. Daniel M. Johnson and John Gardner. 2010. Personality, Motivation and Video Games. In *22nd Conference of the Computer-Human Interaction Special Interest Group of Australia on Computer-Human Interaction* (OZCHI '10), 276-279. http://dl.acm.org/citation.cfm?doid=1952222.1952281
15. Johannes Keller and Herbert Bless. 2008. Flow and regulatory compatibility: An experimental approach to the flow model of intrinsic motivation. *Journal of Personality and Social Psychology Bulletin* 34, 2: 196-209.
16. Madison Klarkowski, Daniel Johnson, Peta Wyeth, Simon Smith, and Cody Phillips. 2015. Operationalising and Measuring Flow in Video Games. In *Proceedings of the Annual Meeting of the Australian Special Interest Group for Computer Human Interaction* (OzCHI '15), 114-118. http://dl.acm.org/citation.cfm?doid=2838739.2838826
17. Derek Lomas, Kishan Patel, Jodi L. Forlizzi, and Kenneth R. Koedinger. 2013. Optimizing Challenge in an Educational Game Using Large-Scale Design Experiments. In *Proceedings of the SIGCHI Conference on Human Factors in Computing Systems* (CHI '13), 89-98. http://dl.acm.org/citation.cfm?doid=2470654.2470668
18. Matthew Lombard and Theresa Ditton. At the Heart of It All: The Concept of Presence. 1997. *Journal of Computer-Mediated Communication* 3, 2: 0.
19. Regan L. Mandryk and M. Stella Atkins. 2007. A fuzzy physiological approach for continuously modelling emotion during interaction with play technologies. *International Journal of Human-Computer Studies* 65, 4: 329-347.
20. Lennart Nacke and Craig A. Lindley. 2008. Flow and immersion in first-person shooters: measuring the player's gameplay experience. In *Proceedings of the 2008 Conference on Future Play: Research, Play, Share* (Future Play '08), 81-88. http://dl.acm.org/citation.cfm?doid=1496984.1496998
21. Andrew K. Przybylski, Netta Weinstein, Kou Murayama, Martin F. Lynch and Richard M. Ryan. 2012. The Ideal Self at Play: The Appeal of Video Games That Let You Be All You Can Be. *Psychological Science* 23, 1: 69-76.
22. Niklas Ravaja, Mikko Salminen, Jussi Holopainen, Timo Saari, Jari Laarni, and Aki Järvinen. 2004. Emotional Response Patterns and Sense of Presence during Video Games: Potential Criterion Variables for Game Design. In *Proceedings of the Third Nordic*

Conference on Human-Computer Interaction (NordiCHI '04), 339-347. http://dl.acm.org/citation.cfm?doid=1028014.1028068

23. Niklas Ravaja, Timo Saari, Mikko Salminen, Jari Laarni and Kari Kallinen. 2006. Phasic emotional reactions to video game events: a psychophysiological investigation. *Media Psychology* 8, 4: 343-367.
24. Falko Rheinberg, Regina Vollmeyer and Stefan Engeser. 2003. Die Erfassung des Flow-Erlebens [The assessment of flow experience]. In *Diagnostik von Selbstkonzept, Lernmotivation und Selbstregulation [Diagnosis of Motivation and Self-Concept]*, 261-279.
25. Scott Rigby and Richard Ryan. 2007. The Player Experience of Needs Satisfaction (PENS): An applied model and methodology for understanding key components of the player experience. Retrieved from immersyve.com/PENS_Sept07.pdf
26. Richard M. Ryan. 1982. Control and Information in the Intrapersonal Sphere: An Extension of Cognitive Evaluation Theory. *Journal of Personality and Social Psychology* 43, 3: 450-461.
27. Richard Ryan., Rigby, C. Scott Rigby, and Andrew Przybylski. 2006. The Motivational Pull of Video Games: A Self-Determination Theory Approach. *Motivation and Emotion* 30, 4: 347-363.
28. Muniba Saleem, Craig A. Anderson, and Douglas A. Gentile. 2012. Effects of Prosocial, Neutral, and Violent Video Games on College Students' Affect. *Aggressive Behavior* 38, 4: 263-271.
29. John L. Sherry. 2004. Flow and Media Enjoyment. *Communication Theory* 14, 4: 328-347.
30. Andrew Sims. 1988. *Symptoms in the Mind: An Introduction to Descriptive Psychopathology.* Saunders Ltd.
31. Paul Skalski, Francis Dalisay, Matthew Kushin and Yung-I Liu. 2012. Need for Presence and Other Motivations for Video Game Play across Genres. In *Proceedings of the Presence Live! International Society for Presence Research Annual Conference* (ISPR '12).
32. Kellie Vella, Daniel M. Johnson, and Leanne Hides. 2013. Positively playful: When videogames lead to player wellbeing. In *Proceedings of the First International Conference on Gameful Design, Research and Applications* (Gamification '13), 99-102. http://dl.acm.org/citation.cfm?doid=2583008.2583024
33. Peta Wyeth, Daniel M. Johnson, and Penelope Sweetser. 2012. Conceptualising, operationalising and measuring the player experience in videogames. In *Extended Proceedings of the Fun and Games Conference 2012* (Fun and Games '12), 90-93.

How to Present Game Difficulty Choices? Exploring the Impact on Player Experience

Jan D. Smeddinck[1], Regan L. Mandryk[2], Max V. Birk[2], Kathrin M. Gerling[3], Dietrich Barsilowski[1], Rainer Malaka[1]
[1]Digital Media Lab, TZI, University of Bremen, Germany, lastname@tzi.de
[2]University of Saskatchewan, Saskatoon, SK, CA, firstname.lastname@usask.ca
[3]University of Lincoln, Lincoln, UK, kgerling@lincoln.ac.uk

ABSTRACT

Matching game difficulty to player ability is a crucial step toward a rewarding player experience, yet making difficulty adjustments that are effective yet unobtrusive can be challenging. This paper examines the impact of automatic and player-initiated difficulty adjustment on player experience through two studies. In the first study, 40 participants played the casual game THYFTHYF either in motion-based or sedentary mode, using menu-based, embedded, or automatic difficulty adjustment. In the second study, we created an adapted version of the commercially available game *fl0w* to allow us to carry out a more focused study of sedentary casual play. Results from both studies demonstrate that the type of difficulty adjustment has an impact on perceived autonomy, but other player experience measures were not affected as expected. Our findings suggest that most players express a preference for manual difficulty choices, but that overall game experience was not notably impacted by automated difficulty adjustments.

Author Keywords

Game difficulty; player experience; game-user research; flow; dynamic difficulty adjustments; feedback.

INTRODUCTION

Research has demonstrated a breadth of benefits of games, for example, on player cognition [22], physical health [33], and general well-being [44]. Therefore, games are now targeting broad audiences with heterogeneous expectations and abilities. Particularly in the area of serious games, researchers and designers are often addressing audiences with special needs, for example, young children [21], people with disabilities [25,28], or older adults [23]. A crucial step in this process is ensuring that games meet the needs of players to provide a positive, empowering experience. To this end, it is important to provide balanced gameplay that does not overwhelm individual players by being too challenging and that enables players of different abilities to play together [26]. Balancing game settings to achieve captivating experiences that can harness the full motivational potential of games is challenging, and previous work has only begun to explore this area. Manual difficulty choices, typically presented as menu settings, have long been an important element of games [11]. In addition to predefined difficulty level choices that change the base level for usually ongoing difficulty increases as a game progresses, dynamic difficulty adjustments (DDA) in games can improve gameplay [30]. A growing body of work is concerned with automated difficulty adjustments, which not only promise to reduce the burden placed on players and avoid breaking the magic circle – the special place in time and space created by a game [29,43] – but also bear the potential to influence a large amount of fine-grained variables. However, selecting matching settings for individual players is a complex problem, involving the unpredictability of human agents and the variety and interplay of game settings.

CHI'16, May 07 - 12, 2016, San Jose, CA, USA

ACM 978-1-4503-3362-7/16/05…$15.00
DOI: http://dx.doi.org/10.1145/2858036.2858574.

Thus, recent work suggests improvements in manual difficulty choices that can also interact with dynamic difficulty adjustment [11,12]. Based on flow theory [16], the work highlights the challenge of difficulty balancing and adjustments in games with an emphasis on the importance of enabling *personal control* whilst retaining *autonomy* and *avoiding interrupting the flow* of an activity, leading to the concept of *player-oriented difficulty choices* that are embedded within the game world [11]. While related work presents a theoretical basis for the interaction with game difficulty choices, we found no reported empirical evaluations on this topic.

Stemming from our research in the area of full-body motion-based games for health, we were interested in the question: *"Do different modes of presenting difficulty choices impact the player experience?"* The concept of player-oriented difficulty choices suggests the method of embedding the choices in a way that blends with the game world, while the most common solution employed in games on the market are difficulty settings in classic menus that may adhere roughly with the visual style of the game, but do not blend with the regular game interaction or mechanics. Games with DDA frequently offer no additional difficulty choices.

We test the hypothesis that *embedded* difficulty choices lead to a better overall player experience by retaining autonomy and control, and by avoiding interruptions of the gaming that endanger immersion or might force players out of the magic circle when compared to traditional *menu* difficulty choices or *auto*matic difficulty adjustments without interaction options. Our work contributes empirical insights relating to the impact of different modalities for interacting with game difficulty choices on player experience and preferences.

BACKGROUND

Getting the level of challenge to match the capabilities and needs of a player is a core element of good player experience. This has long been discussed in game user research [14], and the most cited psychological foundation on the balance of challenges and skills is flow theory [16].

Flow in Games

Csikszentmihalyi [17] describes flow as state of being fully "in the zone" when engaging with an activity. This can have positive effects, such as increased motivation to perform an activity again, which may be explained through a feeling of enjoyment related to evolutionary benefits of performing certain activities [17]. The most prominent precondition that is required if flow is to be achieved is an optimal balance of risk of failure (in games e.g., losing a move, a life, a level, or the entire game) and the chance to attain the goals (in games e.g., winning some points, a bonus, a level, or the entire game) when performing an activity [41]. The entire set of conditions that are prerequisites for flow experiences are in short: clear goals, immediate feedback, match of challenges and skills, action and awareness merge, concentration on the task at hand, sense of potential and control, loss of self-consciousness, sense of time altered; resulting in an experience becoming autotelic [17]. Seeing these conditions, it is not surprising that Csikszentmihalyi frequently uses games as examples of activities that can induce flow. Related work lists explicit examples of how the facilitating factors for flow are present in games [13,31,48]. Because the balance of challenge and skills is an important precondition, and skills differ between people, it becomes clear why balancing challenges is such an important aspect of game design [41]. It also becomes clear why most games still offer manual difficulty choices in setting menus: even after iterative testing and balancing, average solutions are likely suboptimal.

Difficulty Choices in Games

Game difficulty choices that are presented in menus with typical labels such as "easy, medium, hard" can be found even in very early and simple games. The "classic way to present difficulty choices" has arguably evolved largely as a matter of technical circumstance and the prominent use of difficulty selection menus today is arguably the result of established customs. Although manual – i.e., explicit – feedback has been used for difficulty adjustments with unusual input modalities (such as biofeedback), and has shown increased immersion and affect [34], menus with multiple levels of one monolithic and unspecific parameter remain the most common form of difficulty choice UI.

Dynamic Difficulty Adjustments and User-guidance

Because the difficulty of a game is often the product of many different game variables, and because it can change from one moment to the next, manual difficulty choices are not always compatible with seeking the optimal game experience. *Dynamic difficulty adjustments* (DDA) that automatically adjust difficulty based on threshold heuristics [30], or on machine learning models [18], have been explored as a reasonable alternative. Such systems have even been used in regular consumer games, such as *Half-Life 2* and *Max Payne* [1,3] and in serious games [2,47].

There are great potential benefits to DDA, such as high frequency and detailed adjustments [3,30], and in theory they merely require an adequate *performance evaluation* and an *adjustment mechanism* [1]. However, DDA adoption faces challenges, because decisions that contradict the will of the players are potentially harmful to player experience, and in the details of the implementation, assessing affective states is hard [32], especially when the tools should be unintrusive. Balancing adjustment mechanisms is extremely challenging due to the very personalized nature of the outcomes. Especially when first confronted with a new player, be it for balancing between players, or for adjusting the difficulty for an individual player, such DDA or adaptive systems suffer from cold-start problems. Even if the cold-start problems can be overcome and players are provided with a well-matched player experience that results in continued play, adaptive systems suffer the risk of getting stuck in local extrema, or alternatively of enacting strongly fluctuating difficulty settings (rubber banding), which may result in unacceptably balanced play sessions.

Asking players to provide explicit feedback can provide a direction and extent of settings that supports a DDA system to function well. Existing work on user-guided adaptive systems focuses on which information the guidance provides and how it can improve the system [9,50]. User modeling and adaptive systems work also looks at explicit feedback for user-guidance under the term (advisory) dialogue / communication [37] and some approaches are explicitly built around flow theory, with boredom [8] and frustration [27] as critical measures. However, while in traditional software having an explicit dialogue about the adaptive system may often be acceptable, in games, this might endanger immersion [11]. It is therefore important to consider the effects that the presence and presentation of manual difficulty choices have on game user experience.

Difficulty Choices and Flow in Games

Flow in games has been discussed by a number of researchers in the field [11,13,48]. In this work, we focus on the work by Chen, as the concept of player-oriented (embedded) difficulty choices was introduced in this work [11,12]. He builds on arguments for DDA, suggesting that frequent difficulty adjustments can support flow in games, and that allowing players to exert user-guidance by providing explicit feedback can provide a feeling of "being in control" and can also inform more adequate adaptations. Chen is cautious that frequent interactions with difficulty setting menus might be disruptive to being immersed in a game, which would in-turn be detrimental to experiencing flow, and so he develops the concept of embedded difficulty choices, which are implemented in such a manner that they blend with the actual game, so that the feeling of being in control as an autonomous actor is provided, while players remain in the magic circle [29] of the game world.

In his line of arguments, Chen relies heavily on flow theory and the theoretical advantages of the embedded difficulty choice approach intuitively appear coherent in this light. He also presents an informal study with two games (called *Traffic Light* and *fl0w*) to underline the arguments, with the latter one being specifically designed to implement embedded difficulty choices. However, despite the large number of references to the work in related literature (> 500 references), we could not find an empirical investigation of the effects of embedding player difficulty choices into the core of the interactive experience (or *player-oriented DDA*).

Self-Determination Theory and Flow

Considering the prerequisites for flow, embedded difficulty choices appear prone to be supportive of flow experiences. However, the benefits can also be reasoned based on other motivational theories, such as self-determination theory, which may be beneficial due to the following reasons:

Flow as an indicator for player experiences is highly debated and *"it simplifies the dynamics of intrinsic motivation"* [17] (p. 83), whereas the self-determination theory (SDT) approach has seen growing adoption in player experience research [6,7,46]. SDT in games is assessed using the *Player Experience of Needs Satisfaction* (PENS) questionnaire [42], and results in subscales that can directly inform game design decisions as opposed to the common flow scales [36,49]; flow is a multi-dimensional construct and a matter of present experience – a process variable – that is difficult to measure [5]. For example, the levels of satisfaction of autonomy or competence have been shown to be good indicators of the motivational power of games [40], and they are linked to "feeling in control". Links between flow and SDT and its measures for intrinsic motivation have been discussed in related work [42] making connections via the aspect of presence / immersion. Csikszentmihalyi also acknowledges similarities between flow and SDT, highlighting the aspect of autonomy. In his view, flow theory arose from an interest in what propels people to initiate or continue actions because they enjoy the performance in the present [17], while other theories (such as needs satisfaction) are more outcome oriented. If SDT and flow theory set a different emphasis (in which SDT is concerned with the preconditions and building factors for intrinsic motivation, and flow theory is concerned with the current and sustained experience of intrinsically motivated activities), then arguably the major SDT dimensions of competence and autonomy needs satisfaction can be interpreted as provisions for flow experiences, mapping in particular to balance of challenge and skills and the sense of potential and control.

EXPECTED IMPACT OF DIFFICULTY CHOICE MODES

Based on this theoretical background, we explore approaches to game difficulty adjustment in a comparative study with three conditions and the following expectations:

Menu – Players select one option from multiple levels of a single difficulty parameter that is presented with through a classic WIMP (windows, icons, menus, pointer) interface.
H_{mA1}: Players will experience higher levels of *autonomy* relative to conditions without explicit choices (here: *auto*).
H_{mB1}: Players will experience reduced *presence / immersion* relative to conditions where the gaming experience is not interrupted by elements that do not blend seamlessly with the game world (here: *embedded* and *auto*).

Auto – An implementation of dynamic difficulty adjustments that are performed automatically and where the players are not able to make explicit difficulty choices.
H_{aA1}: Players will experience reduced levels of *autonomy* relative to conditions with explicit difficulty choices.
H_{aB1}: Players will experience increased *presence / immersion* relative to conditions where the gaming experience is interrupted by elements that do not blend seamlessly with the game world (here: *menu*).

Embedded – Building on the approach of player-oriented difficulty choices [11], players make explicit difficulty choices by interacting with the game world, integrating closely with the visual design and game mechanics.
H_{eA1}: Players will experience increased levels of *autonomy* relative to conditions where explicit difficulty choices are not possible (here: *auto*).
H_{aB1}: Players will experience increased *presence / immersion* relative to conditions where the gaming experience is interrupted by elements that do not blend seamlessly with the game world.

These assumptions were considered most reasonable based on related work, while other effects were also deemed possible. In the *auto* condition, for example, with a DDA system in place, control over difficulty is executed by the system. This may be appreciated by the players, if they are not interested in executing control over this aspect of their interactive experience and the system does not make obvious mistakes. Yet, players might also (to an extent) appreciate full control over those aspects of the system [45]. Conditions with manual (explicit) control might also have an impact on perceived competence need satisfaction; although, in this case, the direction does not appear clear. The impact might be positive (due to perceived control of the system), or negative (e.g. due to becoming aware of requiring "easier" settings). We therefore opted to include competence in our measures but did not attach a directed hypothesis during our investigation.

We were motivated to this research by our ongoing efforts in the area of motion-based games for health. With applications in the context of therapy (where extrinsic motivation and heteronomy play an important role) re-gaining competence and autonomy (thus boosting intrinsic motivation) can be valuable. On the other hand, matching the individual capabilities and needs of different members of very heterogeneous target groups is especially important in such use cases and could benefit from the timely adjustment of multiple parameters, calling for automated support with difficulty choices. In this light, the concept of embedded feedback bears the promise that expression takes place in an unobtrusive manner, as a meaningful part of the interactions with the game world.

STUDY 1: THE IMPACT OF DIFFERENT INTERACTION STYLES FOR GAME DIFFICULTY CHOICES

In order to explore the impact of different modalities for game difficulty choices on the player experience, we conducted a study based on a casual skill game called *The Higher You Fly, The Harder You Fall* (THYFTHYF). In order to attain connectivity of the findings to our ongoing research on full-body motion-based games, the study was implemented as a mixed design with a two level between-groups independent variable of *controller type* being either *motion-based input*, or *gamepad input* and a three level within-subjects independent variable *game difficulty choice interaction modality*. For the purpose of this paper we focus on the within-subjects analysis of the *gamepad* group and only remark on selected between group comparisons.

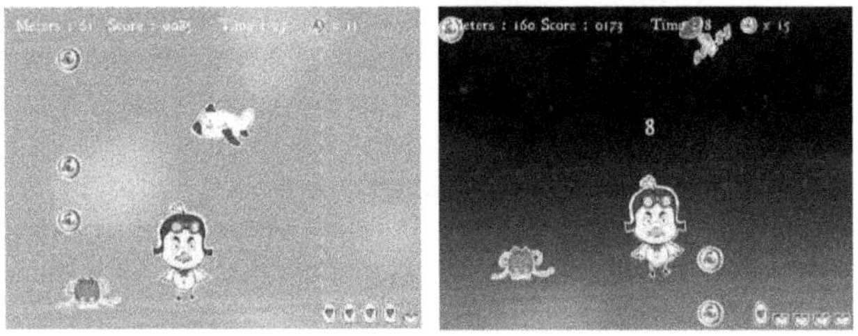

Figure 1. Two screenshots of the game THYFTHYF taken at different height (progress) levels show common game objects.

Design & Implementation

The game was selected to fulfill a number of requirements: It should transparently and immediately reflect changes in player performance, in order to assure that players would experience effects of their difficulty choices. This includes offering dense in-game and post-game audio-visual feedback. The game was also balanced following pilot study runs to include the possibilities of feeling overstrained, or of losing, even within a short time.

In the game THYFTHYF, the player controls a bird player character (PC) with the goal to fly as high as possible whilst collecting points on the way (cf. Figure 1). It can be played with two types of controls: *motion-based control*, where the player is tracked with a Kinect (v1) and has to move her/his arms, mimicking the motion with which a bird flaps its wings and *gamepad control* (here: XBOX360 controller), where the player repeatedly pushes and releases the continuous trigger buttons, also mimicking the motion with which a bird flaps its wings. The game world is composed of tiles. Each tile belongs to one of three classes: ground, sky and space. At runtime, the tiles are procedurally placed and populated with "good items", which increase the player's score if they are collected by hitting them with the player character and "enemies", which hurt the player character when contacted and give a sideways impact to the player character that reduces the current balance. The PC can be moved upward by "flapping" both wings at equal speed, where the frequency controls the speed. The direction of flight can be controlled by executing wing-flapping movements with a relatively faster speed on one side (causing the bird to "lean" to the opposite side). If the PC leans too far to either side or stops flapping the wings for too long, it falls down a bit and the player loses a life (starting with a supply of five per round). If all lives are lost, the bird falls all the way to the ground and the player has to start flying up again from ground level with newly refreshed lives. These design decisions were made to assure comparable stimuli; the duration was set to 60 seconds per round. The difficulty, realized by changing speed, balance support and of bad/good objects, increases with increasing height in the level as offsets of base parameters that were influenced by the manual or automatic difficulty choices. After each round, a summary screen showed the final score.

Difficulty Choice Interaction Modalities

A player-oriented embedded difficulty choice mode was implemented in the form of five different start boosts that reflected the five levels present in the alternative difficulty selection menu (cf. Figure 2). Selections in the difficulty menu would be reflected in a different duration of a jetpack starting boost. Higher boosts would result in increased difficulty settings, whereas lower boosts result in lower difficulty settings. Both modalities were invoked at the beginning of each round in order to assure comparable exposure. The player would also receive a boost start in the DDA only condition without any explicit difficulty choices.

Dynamic Difficulty Adjustments

Performance based DDA was implemented to allow for a condition without difficulty choices. The mechanism was designed to be limited to a controllable number of effectors, while allowing for distinctly notable adjustments. In the context of the three challenge mechanics that were present in the game (height, collection/avoidance, and balance), the *performance metrics* were defined as follows:

Over the last 5 rounds – weighted by recentness –, the height reached, the ratio of bad objects hit, the ratio of good objects collected and the times out of balance were each evaluated by threshold-based heuristics. The balance was set in a way that required the players to perform at a challenging level in order to reach the space level, which always started at a fixed height relative to the final starting position (after a starting boost), and to assure that players don't struggle with "out-of-balance" events too much, enabling them to collect coins, while avoiding enemies. Before each session, the according *difficulty parameters* of max speed / fall speed, number of bad / good objects, and balance support (via damping) were adjusted.

Figure 2: Left/right: Embedded difficulty choice / menu difficulty choice in THYFTHYF.

THYFTHYF was implemented in C# based on .NET 3.5, the XNA 4.0 framework and the Kinect 1.8 SDK.

Setup & Procedure

Trials of the laboratory study lasted about 60 minutes. We recruited from the local student body, and each participant received $10 CAD compensation for their time. Figure 3 illustrates the technical setup. The study language was English. The procedure was performed with 40 participants (19f, 21m, age: M = 26.88, SD = 5.79, min/max = 18/45), who were randomly assigned to the sedentary (gamepad) or the motion-based (Kinect) group. Four participants said they never play video games in a typical week, 16 said they play up to three hours per week and two participants said they play more than 35 hours/week, with the rest spending between 3 hours and 35 hours a week gaming. They have been gaming since 10.76 years on average (SD = 6.7).

Following the greeting and gathering of informed consent, participants were asked to complete a pre-study questionnaire before engaging in a warmup round with a short introduction by demonstration and explanation of the core game mechanics. Each subject then participated in four trials of gameplay consisting of three one-minute rounds interspersed with a difficulty choice in the conditions *embedded* and *menu*, followed by a fixed set of post-trial questionnaires. The fourth (and last) trial always featured a zero effect menu choice placebo condition that was omitted from analysis and report for brevity. The difficulty choice modality conditions *embedded*, *menu,* and *none* were presented in Latin square randomized order to counter-balance potential learning-, customization- and fatigue-effects. Lastly, the participants completed a short personality trait index and responded to a semi-structured interview about experiences and preferences.

The independent variable of *controller type* (motion-based vs. sedentary) was added to the design in order to facilitate carrying over results, because potential interaction effects (e.g. of feeling more / less in control or autonomous when exposed in regard to one's physical appearance and skills while playing motion-based games) might exist. We found no evidence for meaningful interaction effects and for reasons of brevity, the analysis of that group was largely omitted from this report. Notable fixed variables include design choices around interacting with explicit user feedback, which was always collected between one round of gameplay and the next (fixed intervals) and not based on the players' volition to assure comparable outcomes. Players were informed that they could influence the difficulty of the game and would be asked to do so between rounds. It was explained to them, what each difficulty choice in both the *menu* and the *embedded* condition would mean before the respective conditions.

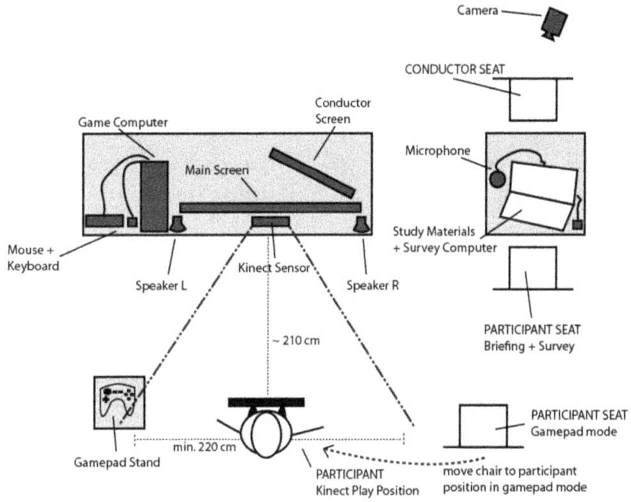

Figure 3: The technical setup of the study.

Measures

In addition to demographic background information, gaming preferences, and a brief personality questionnaire (TIPI), we measured *affect* with the *Positive and Negative Affect Schedule* (PANAS) [15], *player experience* with the *Player Experience of Needs Satisfaction* (PENS) [39] questionnaire (the dimensions *interest-enjoyment* and *effort-importance* of the *Intrinsic Motivation Inventory* (IMI) [35] were added as additional dimensions rooted in SDT to augment the PENS results), and a *Task Load Index* (TLX) was collected as a measure of *frustration* rooted in usability research, as the interaction with difficulty choices was realized either "inside" a game, or with regular GUI components. The questionnaires were presented in the order of introduction in this text and with randomized item order. Each questionnaire was completed multiple times by each participant (once after each trial) and the PANAS was also completed once before the first trial in order to facilitate relative offset calculations that compensate for individual differences in initial affect. The participants were instructed to consider their entire interaction sessions with the game (including interface components). Before the final interview, players also reported a ranking of their preference for the difficulty choice modalities together with responses to a number of question items regarding their usual perception of – and interaction with – difficulty choices in games. Video recordings and observational protocols completed the data collection.

Results & Analysis

The quantitative experiential measures were analyzed with a general linear model facilitating a mixed design repeated-measures analysis of variance (ANOVA) at a significance level of $\alpha = .05$ and Mauchly's sphericity tests, as well as Bonferroni adjustments prior to post-hoc pairwise t-tests for multiple comparisons. The analysis was performed in R with the *ezStats* package for the ANOVA operations, and variances were winsorized [19] (leveling outliers in the top/bottom .2 quantiles to the trim edge values). The results were confirmed using SPSS (version 20) and are summarized in Table 1 and Table 2.

STUDY 1 (PANAS, PENS, IMI)	embedded [M (SD)]:	menu [M (SD)]:	auto [M (SD)]:
positive affect	2.95 (.77)	2.96 (.68)	2.94 (.82)
positive affect (MB)	3.37 (.74)	3.44 (.75)	3.29 (.74)
negative affect	1.59 (.53)	1.58 (.64)	1.54 (.46)
competence	2.72 (.9)	2.8 (.7)	2.83 (.81)
presence / immersion	2.83 (.74)	2.84 (.73)	2.73 (.71)
autonomy	3.07 (.75)**	2.9 (.74)	2.68 (.9)**
relatedness	2.73 (.68)	2.77 (.75)	2.65 (.97)
intuitive control*	2.93 (.72)	3.03 (.74)	3.11 (.88)
intuitive cont. (MB)*	3.52 (.76)	3.57 (.55)	3.57 (.77)
interest enjoyment	3.34 (.53)	3.38 (.47)	3.3 (.61)
effort-importance	3.71 (.61)	3.71 (.44)	3.7 (.62)

Table 1: Mean (M) and standard deviation (SD) results of study 1. All items were recorded on 5 pt. Likert scales. Group effects comparing between sedentary and motion-based (MB) are indicated with (*). Within-subjects effects between the embedded, menu, and auto conditions are indicated with (**).

There were no significant effects on the *positive affect* or on the *negative affect* scale. Notably higher *positive affect* than *negative affect* and also higher *positive affect* in the *motion-based* (MB) game group are in line with the following measures and suggest that the scale is sensitive to changes in affect caused by the experience of playing different versions of the game. While the lack of significances does not prove the absence of effects, we assume that there are no large effects on *affect* between the three conditions, because the means between all conditions are very close.

The PENS results on the *competence* and *presence / immersion* dimensions show a similar picture. While the result on *competence* appeared difficult to predict due to the complex interaction of self-perceived, practical skill and interacting with difficulty choices, *presence / immersion* could be expected to be lowered in the *menu* condition, which was not the case in our sample and the similarity in means suggests an absence of strong effects. There was a significant difference on the PENS *autonomy* dimension ($F(2,76) = 5.01$, $p = .009$, gen. $\eta^2 = .02$ [4], Mauchly not sig.) with post-hoc pairwise comparisons confirming a sig. diff. between *embedded* and *auto* ($p = .02$). This finding can be seen as evidence to support an increased sense of autonomy needs satisfaction in the *embedded* condition that was predicted based on Chen's arguments. However, there is no discernable difference between the *embedded* and the *menu* condition. The PENS dimensions *relatedness* and *intuitive control* showed no significant differences on the indep. variable *difficulty selection*, as expected, while *intuitive control* was sig. increased under the *motion-based* control condition ($F(1,38) = 6.33$, $p = .016$, gen. $\eta^2 = .12$ [4], Mauchly not sig.), which could also be expected, as the game was originally designed to be motion-based.

The IMI dimensions *interest-enjoyment* and *effort-importance* showed remarkable similarity in means and no significant differences, suggesting that both player enjoyment and motivation were not notably different under the different difficulty choice modalities.

STUDY 1 (TLX)	embedded [M (SD)]:	menu [M (SD)]:	auto [M (SD)]:
physical demand*	.8 (10.33)	.65 (10.93)	1.15 (10.68)
phys. dem. (MB)*	11.05 (4.76)	8.35 (6.18)	9.5 (6.41)
mental demand	2.9 (7.02)	3.15 (7.34)	3.1 (8.5)
temporal demand*	7.35 (5.37)	7.1 (3.87)	6.75 (3.35)
temp. dem. (MB)*	2.3 (8.02)	2.35 (8.7)	2.05 (10.45)
performance*	-1.9 (7.72)	-.3 (8.3)	-1 (9.46)
perf. (MB)*	3.65 (8.42)	4.15 (7.21)	3.45 (7.07)
effort	8.15 (3.82)	8.25 (3.6)	7.4 (5.06)
frustration	-.75 (8.4)	-1.65 (8.93)	-1.95 (9.78)

Table 2: The mean (M) and standard deviation (SD) results of the TLX in study 1. All items were recorded on 40 pt. Likert scales (range -20 to 20). Group effects comparing between sedentary and motion-based (MB) are indicated with (*).

The TLX dimension *physical demand* showed no differences between the within-subject conditions, although the *motion-based* game group recorded significantly higher *physical demand* ($F(1,38) = 11.6$, $p = .002$, gen. $\eta^2 = .22$ [4], Mauchly not sig.), providing further evidence for the sensibility of the chosen measures. The TLX *mental demand* and *temporal demand* dimensions showed no significant differences, although the mean of the *temp. dem. auto* condition appears lowered, which seems reasonable given the lack of a manual selection process. *Temporal demand* appears sig. decreased in the *motion-based* game group ($F(1,38) = 5.66$, $p = .023$, gen. $\eta^2 = .11$ [4], Mauchly not sig.), which cannot be explained by observable differences in actual time spent and seems contradictory to the physical effort measure, hinting at a potential interaction with overall motivational effects. There were no sig. diffs. on *difficulty choice* in the TLX *performance* dimension, although there was a sig. diff. between *sedentary* and *motion-based* ($F(1,38) = 4.43$, $p = .042$, gen. $\eta^2 = .09$ [4], Mauchly not sig.), which may be a secondary effect to the observed difference in *physical demand.* While THYFTHYF appears to be a rather high-*effort* game, the final TLX dimensions of *effort* and *frustration* showed no further sig. diffs., hinting at a further lack of notable negative or positive effects of the *difficulty choice modality*.

Interviews

In the interviews, three out of four participants said that they *like being able to change settings*, as opposed to being *more happy just playing the game*. Regarding the difficulty selection in THYFTHYF, one participant expressed it this way *"I did like being able to choose the difficulty settings because it felt like I could cater the game to how well I played, but I also liked playing the game itself"*, while some others expressed notions such as: *"I'm just more happy playing the game"*. Some participants added that they *appreciate a broad range of (difficulty) settings*.

When asked *how they decided which difficulty to select*, participants mentioned various strategies they followed to make difficulty choices ranging from *depending on last time*, over *first easier then harder* and *just stay in the middle*, to *just hard* and *first easiest, then hardest*, and in three cases even just *random* (which was only mentioned with embedded difficulty selection but not regarding the menu). A common notion was *"I just did it based on how it felt the previous time I played it"*.

Players expressed a broad range of opinions regarding how difficult they found it to play the game, ranging from *too easy* (2) over *okay / all right* to *too hard* (4 mentions, 3 of those relating to difficult controls; occurring in both controller type groups). 20 participants added that they generally *prefer games to be challenging (or hard)*.

Regarding whether they felt that their difficulty selections made a difference, 22 participants explicitly said they *noted that their difficulty selections made a difference*. Three did not clearly reply to this question, while 15 did *not clearly say that they noted differences*. However, some added positive unasked remarks on the DDA, such as *"I liked the idea that the game difficulty was automatically adjusted to my performance"*. In those parts of the open-ended discussion elements that led to players making a statement whether they like the idea of DDA in general, 9 were positive about DDA, while 6 expressed rather negative connotations. During the post-study interviews, the participants were eventually informed about the difficulty selection interaction modality manipulation and later question items named the conditions, which may explain why some participants expressed preferences for automatic adjustments or manual adjustments.

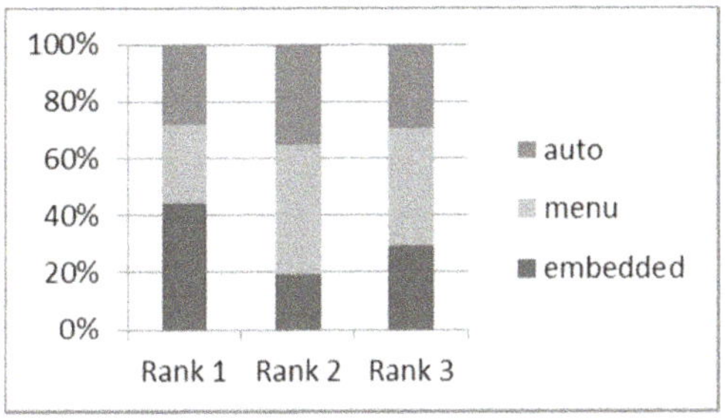

Figure 4: Ranking by participants regarding preference in study 1 (with the game THYFTHYF).

The ranking of all conditions (cf. Figure 4) in comparison after completion of the trials does not show significant results on the Friedman rank sum test. While *embedded* received slightly more first rank preferences, Exact Wilcoxon-Pratt Signed-Rank Tests also did not show any notable contrasts in pairwise comparisons.

While the findings seem to support Chen's cautioning of an impact on the player *autonomy*, *presence/immersion* does not appear to be impacted and the difficulty choice modality similarly has *no notable impacts* on a large variety of enjoyment related measures. We were intrigued by the lack of significant effects on presence / immersion and any secondary or related experiential measures (especially interest-enjoyment, effort-importance, and affect).

STUDY 2: THE IMPACT OF DIFFERENT LEVELS OF FEEDBACK EXPLICITNESS IN CHEN'S GAME FLOW

Results from study 1 showed a surprising homogeneity, especially of the resulting directly enjoyment-related measures, which were thought to react to the different game difficulty choice modes. This partially contradicted predictions that we drew from Chen's considerations. However, Chen's arguments relate directly to his own game implementations. Our game THYFTHYF – while also being a casual game – bears quite a number of differences, especially with regard to how difficulty choices were triggered and how the embedded difficulty choice mode integrated into the game world and the game mechanics. We thus repeated the study in a comparable setup with Chen's well-known game *fl0w* in order to further investigate the unexpected absence of effects and to seek confirmation for the effect on autonomy.

Design & Implementation

In the game *fl0w*, which can be described as a casual atmospheric game, the player controls a microorganism that can chase and "eat" (collide with the mouth section) available food items that float around in multiple fluid-like layers of a game world that may have been imagined as a petri dish. The player organism moves towards the position of the mouse cursor on screen, when the left button is clicked. With increasing "depth", other microorganisms are present in the layers and some will attack the player's organism by attempting to "eat" some of its components. The player organism can similarly "fight" other organisms by "eating them" piece-by-piece. The embedded difficulty choice mode originally implemented in the game allows players to move up and down through different difficulty layers of their own volition by eating either a special red piece (one layer down; harder) or a special blue piece (one layer up; easier) as shown in the instructions screenshot in Figure 5. The game *fl0w* was converted to *Haxe* based on the *AS2* source code made available by J. Chen [10].

Difficulty Choice Interaction Modalities

In addition to the original embedded difficulty choices method, we implemented a traditional menu, which could be opened at any time during play by clicking the right mouse button (see Figure 6), as well as a fully automatic DDA method, relating to the methods *embedded*, *menu*, and *auto* from study 1. The most notable difference in difficulty selection, aside from the selection upon the players' volition at arbitrary times during game play in *fl0w* was that THYFTHYF uses a five point difficulty choice scale, whereas the difficulty choice in *fl0w* is binary.

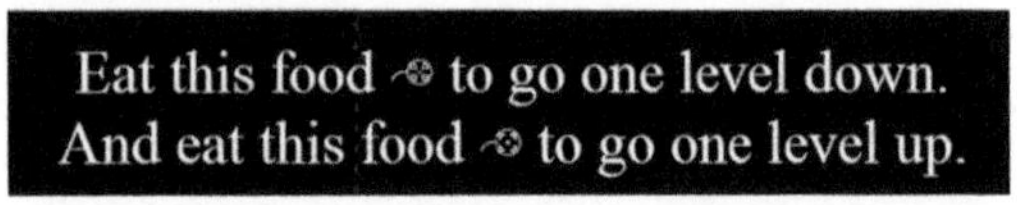

Figure 5: Instructions for the condition *embedded*.

Instructions provided for the condition *menu* were: *"Click the right mouse button at any time to change the level."*

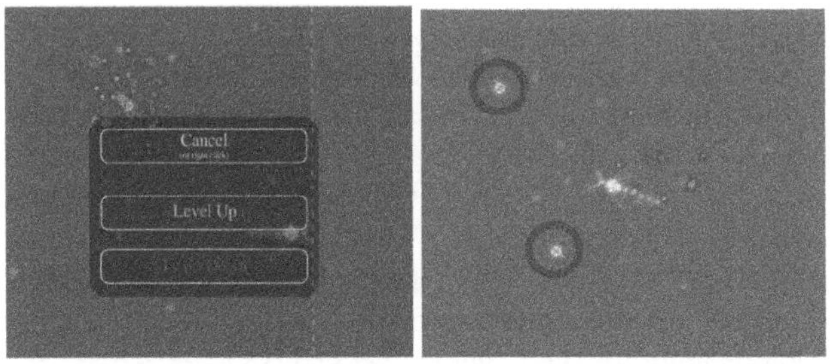

Figure 6: Difficulty choice interaction styles for the condition *menu* (left) and *embedded* (right; red circles are clarification markers not present in the game). Left background elements and right game assets: © Jenova Chen / thatgamecompany.

Dynamic Difficulty Adjustments

In order to automatically increase difficulty, a timer-based heuristic check was performed regularly to determine whether any other organisms or food items were still visible to the player. If there were no further other organisms alive in the layer, as well as no more than two food items available, the difficulty level was increased by moving one layer down. The mechanism for automatically decreasing difficulty was kept as originally implemented in *fl0w*, meaning that the player's creature would automatically be moved up one layer if its health status (as expressed by intact body segments) fell one level due to an attack by another creature.

Setup & Procedure

The study setup duplicated the setup from study 1 with the following adjustments for brevity: The BPNS and TIPI personality trait questionnaires were skipped, as they were not of interest to this comparison study. Study 2 also did not feature interviews or a motion-based game condition (safe to omit due to the between groups mixed design of study 1). Latin square randomization was maintained for the order of within-subjects conditions.

The study was completed by 18 participants (7f, 11m, age: M = 26.78, SD = 5.71, min/max = 20/45) to test whether effects with notable effect sizes would occur. Four participants said they never play video games in a typical week, seven said they play up to 3 hours per week and none said that they played more than 21 hours per week. They have been gaming since 13.28 years on average (SD = 6.64). Participants did not receive monetary compensation and were conveniently sampled mostly from a student population in Germany. The study language was English.

Results & Analysis

There were no significant effects on the *positive affect* or on the *negative affect* scale (cf. Table 3), mirroring results of study 1 and suggesting again the absence of large effects between the three conditions, because the means are very similar. Also in agreement with study 1, the PENS results on the *competence* and *presence / immersion* dimensions show a similar picture with the lack of an effect on *presence / immersion* in contrast to the menu condition, contradicting the expectations. The significant difference on the PENS *autonomy* dimension from study 1 was confirmed (F(2,34) = 4.17, p = .024, gen. η^2 = .05 [4], Mauchly not sig.) with post-hoc pairwise comparisons confirming a sig. diff. between *menu* and *auto* (p = .047). This finding can be seen as evidence to support an increased sense of *autonomy* needs satisfaction in the *menu* condition that was predicted based on the Chen's arguments, providing a helpful complement to the significant difference found in post-hoc pairwise comparison between the *embedded* and *auto* condition in study 1, while again finding very similar means in the *embedded* and the *menu* conditions. The PENS dimensions *relatedness* and *intuitive control* showed no significant differences, as expected, and in agreement with study 1. Findings were also repeated for the IMI dimensions *interest-enjoyment* and *effort-importance*, which show remarkable similarity in means, including the *embedded* condition, and no significant differences.

STUDY 2 (PANAS, PENS, IMI)	**embedded** [M (SD)]:	**menu** [M (SD)]:	**auto** [M (SD)]:
positive affect	26.79 (3.57)	26.97 (5.65)	26.02 (5.72)
negative affect	12.57 (2.65)	12.13 (1.83)	12.94 (1.99)
competence	3.37 (.6)	3.47 (.49)	3.61 (.47)
presence / immersion	2.67 (.62)	2.6 (.77)	2.63 (.7)
autonomy	3.06 (.7)	3.17 (.67)*	2.84 (.47)*
relatedness	1.69 (.66)	1.72 (.6)	1.65 (.6)
intuitive control	4.42 (.51)	4.35 (.39)	4.56 (.45)
interest enjoyment	3.67 (.5)	3.82 (.36)	3.64 (.39)
effort-importance	2.89 (.67)	2.69 (.58)	2.71 (.39)

Table 3: Mean (M) and standard deviation (SD) results of study 2. All items were recorded on 5 pt. Likert scales (pos. and neg. affect use mean sums of item scores; range 10 - 50). Within-subjects effects are indicated with (*).

The TLX dimensions *physical demand* and *performance* (cf. Table 4) showed no significant differences, also repeating the findings from study 1. The TLX *effort* (F(2,34) = 6.47, p = .004, gen. η^2 = .11, Mauchly not sig.) and *frustration* (F(2,34) = 3.6, p = .038, gen. η^2 = .07, Mauchly not sig.) dimensions did, however, show sig. diffs., with post-hoc pairwise comparisons showing a sig. diff. between *embedded* and *manual* on the *effort* dimension (p = .011) and between *embedded* and *auto* on the *frustration* dimension (p = .047). This finding is not in line with the results from study 1, yet it appears reasonable considering the game design of *fl0w*, as players are required to make an effort to chase the special food item of their liking in order to move one layer up or down (which affects the difficulty level accordingly). That argument can be supported with the results from the *mental demand*, and the *temporal demand* dimensions, which show higher mean scores for the *embedded* condition and for which the ANOVA returns a trend ($F(2,34) = 3.24$, $p = .051$, gen. $\eta^2 = .04$, Mauchly not sig.) in the case of *temporal demand*. Pairwise comparison hints at the contrast between *embedded* and *auto* ($p = .069$) as the main cause.

STUDY 2 (TLX)	embedded [M (SD)]:	menu [M (SD)]:	auto [M (SD)]:
physical demand	2.36 (1.03)	2.7 (1.07)	2.72 (.89)
performance	13.87 (3.45)	13.81 (3.15)	14.03 (2.77)
effort	8.28 (3.23)*	5.97 (2.36)*	6.76 (2.69)
frustration	4.52 (2.25)*	3.8 (1.86)	3.18 (1.94)*
mental demand	8.52 (3.82)	7.91 (4.55)	7.56 (4.72)
temporal demand	8.67 (3.36)	7.37 (3.58)	7.17 (3.34)

Table 4: The mean (M) and standard deviation (SD) results of the TLX in study 2. All items were recorded on 20 pt. Likert scales (range 1 to 20). Sig. effects are indicated with (*).

The ranking of all conditions (cf. Figure 7) in comparison after completion of the trials does not show significant results on the Friedman Rank Sum Test ($\chi^2(2) = 3.44$, $p = .18$), although *embedded* received the highest total score and an Exact Wilcoxon-Pratt Signed-Rank Test comparing *embedded* with *auto* shows a trend ($Z = 1.82$, $p = .08$, $r = .3$; suggesting a medium effect size).

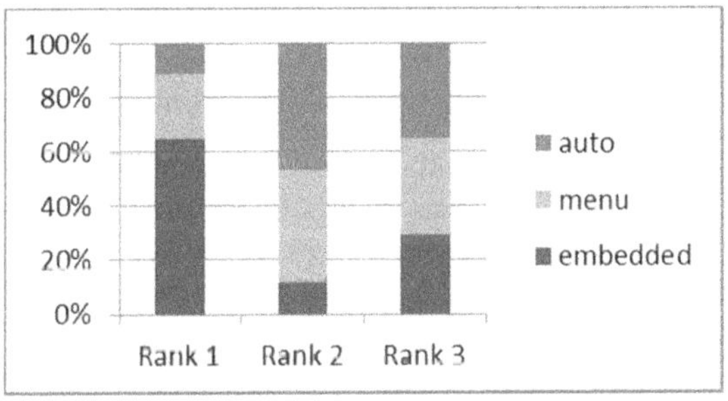

Figure 7: Ranking by participants regarding preference in study 2 (with the game *fl0w*).

Study 2 repeated the specific player experience items from study 1 almost exactly. We confirmed an effect on *autonomy*. There are significant differences between study 1 and 2 in the TLX dimensions *effort* and *frustration*, which are supported by differences in means on the *mental demand* and *temporal demand* dimensions. If interpreted as a classical "task load index", these measures put *embedded* in a worst position regarding usability. For game design choices, high task loads arguably need not necessarily be seen as adverse, because – given the right circumstances – overcoming challenges in a game generates positive player experiences (the similarity in most PENS and IMI player experience scales may be interpreted to support this argument). At the same time, frustrating controls can hinder game experiences. Either way, game designers can benefit from an awareness of possible frustrations triggered by their game difficulty choice implementations.

DISCUSSION

In this paper, we presented two studies on the impact of game difficulty choice interaction modes on player experience, focusing on potential effects on autonomy and presence/immersion for which outcome expectations were discussed based on related work.

We found evidence for a reduced autonomy needs satisfaction if no explicit difficulty choice is present, which appears in line with the expectations given the presence of manual difficulty choices in the other conditions. However, we could neither find a significant impact on presence / immersion in the case of non-embedded difficulty choices nor on any other player experience measure (with the reasonable exception of TLX measures in study 2), indicating that the differences in perceived autonomy did not have any strong impact on the overall enjoyment, motivation and affect; or in short on most of the game experience. The significant differences and trends measured on the TLX dimensions mentioned in the analysis of study 2 point towards the embedded difficulty choice being a potential source of frustration, due to the considerable effort that it required when seeking out the special food items that are not always in the same position and not always in close reach, thereby breaking interaction best practices when considered from a usability point of view. While further investigations about how players perceive difficulty choices in the forms of game mechanical elements and settings interfaces could help clarify such assumptions, the notable closeness of all modalities on most player experience measures indicates that the impact of the game difficulty selection modality on the overall game experience is likely to be small enough to allow for other considerations to guide game designers' choices of modality. With complex motion-based games for health, for example, where large numbers of sensible difficulty-related variables can be influenced by difficulty adjustments, this suggests that a strong role of DDA / adaptivity could lead to player experiences that are at least comparable to those that can be achieved when notable manual difficulty choices are present, even if they were well embedded.

While elements of choice have been linked to increased cognitive and affective engagement in learning scenarios [20], the suggested link to game enjoyment may not have results that are as large as an intuitive theoretical understanding suggests. The strong homogeneity in results between studies 1 and 2 suggests that these negative results were not accidental for the genre of casual games, and the similarities in means across conditions in the measures without significant findings indicate that strong effects on the overall player experience are unlikely to exist. The comparison with the motion-based group in study 1 serves as an indicator that the employed measures did pick up on relevant player experience factors, adding to our confidence in interpreting the large number of homogenous results.

The TLX as a classic demand measure was included because it has been used in the context of games by other researchers [24,38]. Our study provides further evidence for the sensitivity of the separate dimensions in game user research. While it requires careful interpretation in games, as desirable challenges may be part of the game design, it can be seen as an asset in the young area of game user research, where reliable psychometrics are still rare.

Limitations & Future Work

A number of limitations should be noted. Explicit feedback to an adaptive system is an unusual game design element. A further study that investigates the framing of "pre-play settings" (e.g. settings menu) vs. "post-play feedback" might thus deliver interesting additional insights. However, from our observation and the user responses during the interviews, we gather that the menu-feedback condition was seen as being similar to typical difficulty settings that are usually accessible through a main menu. It is also not clear in how far experiences related to flow are triggered in short episodes of casual game-play, although other researchers suggest that flow can emerge from a broad range of durations of captivating activities [11,17]. More highly immersive, longer-term gaming sessions might lead to different reactions to the offered difficulty choice modes.

A number of specific game design choices that were made when preparing the games and setup offer opportunities for further investigations in alternative design choices. The point of intervention for the DDA, for example, was set to be between rounds for study 1, whereas continuous or sparser adjustments are also feasible. Likewise, if an adaptive mechanism is present, feedback can strongly influence the DDA settings, adjusting not only the specific game mechanical variables, but also the estimated optimal performance thresholds for an individual player (moving from fixed threshold DDA to an individual solution). Other feedback mechanisms, such as (implicit) general affective feedback, more specific technical feedback, or feedback on multiple dimensions, may be taken into account, and other intervals for providing feedback (or other modalities to express volition) could be evaluated. Because both games were "casual", many other game types offer opportunities for further investigations on game difficulty choices. Due to the differences between the embedded difficulty choice modalities in study 1 and 2 (i.e., it was always available yet required effort to attain in study 2, whereas it was only available once per game round in study 1), further studies might expand on our results by focusing on frequency and ease of access as independent variables.

CONCLUSION

We presented an investigation of the impact of difficulty adjustments that were performed either through manual control via a classic selection menu, through an embedded difficulty choice, or with an automatic heuristics-based DDA system, on game user experience. With prior considerations regarding the impact based largely on flow theory, we presented a transfer of the expectations to the dimensions measured by validated game user research tools rooted in self-determination theory. The expected effect on autonomy was observed in the data based on a study with a game of our own design, however, no impact on presence / immersion could be found, which contradicted our outcome expectations. In the interviews, many players expressed that they prefer the presence of manual difficulty choices in games, yet our participants were more likely to be positive about DDA than to be negative about it and did not remark negatively on the presence of DDA. This ambiguity, together with a lack of notable differences on any resulting game experience measure besides the PENS dimension of autonomy, prompted us to repeat the study design with the game *fl0w*. Because Chen employed the latter to argue for the benefits of his concept of embedded (player-oriented) difficulty choices, we aimed to double-check for potential biases introduced with specific game design decisions of our game. The findings were largely repeated, including the surprisingly similar means across conditions on almost all game experience dimensions. Due to the repeated absence of effects in both studies, we find the evidence to be worth reporting. Significant differences in the TLX dimensions of effort and frustration in study 2 were found; these can be explained by game design aspects of the *embedded* mode in *fl0w*, which requires players to manually seek out special game objects in order to influence the game difficulty. Since no game motivation related measure besides autonomy showed an impact between conditions in either study, we conclude that in practical (casual) game design, all versions could lead to a very similar game experience.

Our findings suggest that the game difficulty choice interaction mode in casual games might play a minor role compared to other game design choices. These could therefore be prioritized by game designers. Letting other considerations influence the choice of game difficulty interaction modality, or opting for common and simple difficulty selection menus, appear to be reasonable choices. In terms of game user research and arguments on game design based in motivation theory, we could only partially confirm our expectations, which appeared firmly rooted in theory and intuitively logical. Hence, we can only support the call for empirical investigations of game design theory so that designers are enabled to make more certain, well-informed, and detailed decisions.

ACKNOWLEDGMENTS

We thank the *GRAND NCE*, the *Klaus Tschira Stiftung*, as well as the *Federal Ministry of Education and Research, Germany* (BMBF) for funding, and members of the *Interaction Lab* at the University of Saskatchewan, the *Digital Media Lab* at the University of Bremen, the original THYFTHYF developer team, as well as all study participants, Rodrigo Vicencio-Moreira, Jenny Cramer, Jenova Chen, and *thatgamecompany* for their kind support.

REFERENCES

1. Ernest Adams. 2010. *Fundamentals of Game Design*. New Riders.
2. Gazihan Alankus, Amanda Lazar, Matt May, and Caitlin Kelleher. 2010. Towards customizable games

for stroke rehabilitation. *Proceedings of the 28th international conference on Human factors in computing systems*, ACM, 2113–2122. http://doi.org/10.1145/1753326.1753649

3. Christine Bailey and Michael Katchabaw. 2005. An experimental testbed to enable auto-dynamic difficulty in modern video games. *Proceedings of the 2005 GameOn North America Conference*, 18–22. Retrieved September 21, 2015 from http://mmm.csd.uwo.ca/faculty/katchab/pubs/gameonna2005_add.pdf
4. Roger Bakeman. 2005. Recommended effect size statistics for repeated measures designs. *Behavior Research Methods* 37, 3: 379–384. http://doi.org/10.3758/BF03192707
5. Gary Bente. 2009. Making the implicit explicit. Embedded measurement in serious games.
6. Max Birk and Regan L. Mandryk. 2013. Control your game-self: effects of controller type on enjoyment, motivation, and personality in game. *Proceedings of the SIGCHI Conference on Human Factors in Computing Systems*, ACM, 685–694. http://doi.org/10.1145/2470654.2470752
7. Max V. Birk, Regan L. Mandryk, Matthew K. Miller, and Kathrin M. Gerling. 2015. How Self-Esteem Shapes Our Interactions with Play Technologies. *Proceedings of the 2015 Annual Symposium on Computer-Human Interaction in Play*, ACM, 35–45. http://doi.org/10.1145/2793107.2793111
8. Guillaume Chanel, Cyril Rebetez, Mireille Bétrancourt, and Thierry Pun. 2008. Boredom, engagement and anxiety as indicators for adaptation to difficulty in games. *Proceedings of the 12th international conference on Entertainment and media in the ubiquitous era*, ACM, 13–17. http://doi.org/10.1145/1457199.1457203
9. Darryl Charles and Michaela Black. 2004. Dynamic player modeling: A framework for player-centered digital games. *Proc. of the International Conference on Computer Games: Artificial Intelligence, Design and Education*, 29–35. Retrieved November 26, 2012 from http://research.rmutp.ac.th/paper/cu/DynamicPlayerModelling.pdf
10. Jenova Chen. 2006. *fl0w - source code*. Retrieved September 25, 2015 from http://www.thatgamecompany.com/forum/viewtopic.php?p=4255&sid=5af8dfad64831dfb41b7bc4e66c1a165#p4255
11. Jenova Chen. 2007. Flow in games (and everything else). *Commun. ACM* 50, 4: 31–34. http://doi.org/10.1145/1232743.1232769
12. Jenova Chen. Flow in Games. Retrieved September 19, 2011 from http://jenovachen.com/flowingames/Flow_in_games_final.pdf
13. Ben Cowley, Darryl Charles, Michaela Black, and Ray Hickey. 2008. Toward an Understanding of Flow in Video Games. *Comput. Entertain.* 6, 2: 20:1–20:27. http://doi.org/10.1145/1371216.1371223
14. Chris Crawford. 1984. *The Art of Computer Game Design*. Osborne/McGraw-Hill.
15. John R. Crawford and Julie D. Henry. 2004. The Positive and Negative Affect Schedule (PANAS): Construct validity, measurement properties and normative data in a large non-clinical sample. *British Journal of Clinical Psychology* 43, 3: 245–265.
16. Mihaly Csikszentmihalyi. 1990. *Flow: The Psychology of Optimal Experience*. Harper & Row, New York.
17. Mihaly Csikszentmihalyi and K. Rathunde. 1992. The measurement of flow in everyday life: toward a theory of emergent motivation. Nebraska Symposium on Motivation. Nebraska Symposium on Motivation 40: 57–97.
18. Anders Drachen, Alessandro Canossa, and Georgios N. Yannakakis. 2009. Player modeling using self-organization in tomb raider: underworld. *Computational Intelligence and Games*, 2009. CIG 2009. IEEE Symposium on, 1–8.
19. David M. Erceg-Hurn and Vikki M. Mirosevich. 2008. Modern robust statistical methods: An easy way to maximize the accuracy and power of your research. *American Psychologist* 63, 7: 591–601. http://doi.org/10.1037/0003-066X.63.7.591
20. Terri Flowerday and Gregory Schraw. 2003. Effect of Choice on Cognitive and Affective Engagement. *The Journal of Educational Research* 96, 4: 207–215. http://doi.org/10.1080/00220670309598810
21. Sandro Franceschini, Simone Gori, Milena Ruffino, Simona Viola, Massimo Molteni, and Andrea Facoetti. 2013. Action Video Games Make Dyslexic Children Read Better. *Current Biology*. http://doi.org/10.1016/j.cub.2013.01.044
22. Yue Gao and Regan L. Mandryk. 2012. The Acute Cognitive Benefits of Casual Exergame Play. *Proceedings of the 2012 ACM annual conference on Human Factors in Computing Systems*, 1863–1872.
23. Kathrin Maria Gerling, Frank Paul Schulte, Jan Smeddinck, and Maic Masuch. 2012. Game Design for Older Adults: Effects of Age-Related Changes on Structural Elements of Digital Games. In *Entertainment Computing - ICEC 2012*, Marc Herrlich, Rainer Malaka and Maic Masuch (eds.).

Springer Berlin Heidelberg, 235–242. Retrieved January 18, 2013 from http://link.springer.com/chapter/10.1007/978-3-642-33542-6_20

24. Kathrin M. Gerling, Kristen K. Dergousoff, and Regan L. Mandryk. 2013. Is Movement Better?: Comparing Sedentary and Motion-based Game Controls for Older Adults. *Proceedings of Graphics Interface 2013*, Canadian Information Processing Society, 133–140. Retrieved September 21, 2015 from http://dl.acm.org/citation.cfm?id=2532129.2532153

25. Kathrin M. Gerling, Regan L. Mandryk, Matthew Miller, Michael R. Kalyn, Max Birk, and Jan D. Smeddinck. 2015. Designing Wheelchair-Based Movement Games. *ACM Trans. Access.* Comput. 6, 2: 6:1–6:23. http://doi.org/10.1145/2724729

26. Kathrin M. Gerling, Matthew Miller, Regan L. Mandryk, Max Birk, and Jan Smeddinck. 2014. Effects of Balancing for Physical Abilities on Player Performance, Experience and Self-Esteem in Exergames. *CHI'14: Proceedings of the 2014 CHI Conference on Human Factors in Computing Systems.* Retrieved February 11, 2014 from https://hci.usask.ca/uploads/331-paper122.pdf

27. Kiel M. Gilleade and Alan Dix. 2004. Using frustration in the design of adaptive videogames. *Proceedings of the 2004 ACM SIGCHI International Conference on Advances in computer entertainment technology, ACM*, 228–232. http://doi.org/10.1145/1067343.1067372

28. Hamilton A. Hernandez, T. C. Graham, Darcy Fehlings, et al. 2012. Design of an exergaming station for children with cerebral palsy. *Proceedings of the 2012 ACM annual conference on Human Factors in Computing Systems*, 2619–2628. Retrieved May 24, 2013 from http://dl.acm.org/citation.cfm?id=2208652

29. Johan Huizinga. 2008. *Homo ludens: proeve eener bepaling van het spel-element der cultuur*. Amsterdam University Press.

30. Robin Hunicke. 2005. The case for dynamic difficulty adjustment in games. *Proceedings of the 2005 ACM SIGCHI International Conference on Advances in computer entertainment technology*, 429–433.

31. Marshall G. Jones. 1998. Creating Electronic Learning Environments: Games, Flow, and the User Interface. Retrieved September 17, 2015 from http://eric.ed.gov/?id=ED423842

32. Arvid Kappas. 2010. Smile when you read this, whether you like it or not: Conceptual challenges to affect detection. *IEEE Transactions on Affective Computing*, 1, 1: 38–41.

33. Pamela M. Kato. 2012. Evaluating Efficacy and Validating Games for Health. *Games for Health Journal* 1, 1: 74–76. http://doi.org/10.1089/g4h.2012.1017

34. K. Kuikkaniemi, T. Laitinen, M. Turpeinen, T. Saari, I. Kosunen, and N. Ravaja. 2010. The influence of implicit and explicit biofeedback in first-person shooter games. *Proceedings of the 28th international conference on Human factors in computing systems*, 859–868. Retrieved August 17, 2012 from http://dl.acm.org/citation.cfm?id=1753453

35. E McAuley, T Duncan, and V V Tammen. 1989. Psychometric properties of the Intrinsic Motivation Inventory in a competitive sport setting: a confirmatory factor analysis. *Research quarterly for exercise and sport* 60, 1: 48–58.

36. Giovanni B. Moneta. 2012. On the Measurement and Conceptualization of Flow. In *Advances in Flow Research*, Stefan Engeser (ed.). Springer New York, 23–50. Retrieved September 17, 2015 from http://link.springer.com/chapter/10.1007/978-1-4614-2359-1_2

37. A. Quilici. 1994. Forming user models by understanding user feedback. *User Modeling and User-Adapted Interaction* 3, 4: 321–358.

38. Leonard Reinecke, Ron Tamborini, Matthew Grizzard, Robert Lewis, Allison Eden, and Nicholas David Bowman. 2012. Characterizing Mood Management as Need Satisfaction: The Effects of Intrinsic Needs on Selective Exposure and Mood Repair. *Journal of Communication* 62, 3: 437–453. http://doi.org/10.1111/j.1460-2466.2012.01649.x

39. Scott Rigby and Richard Ryan. 2007. *The Player Experience of Need Satisfaction(PENS): an applied model and methodology for understanding key components of the player experience.*

40. Scott Rigby and Richard Ryan. 2011. *Glued to Games: How Video Games Draw Us In and Hold Us Spellbound.* Praeger.

41. Ute Ritterfeld, Michael Cody, and Peter Vorderer. 2009. *Serious Games: Mechanisms and Effects.* Routledge.

42. Richard M. Ryan, C. Scott Rigby, and Andrew Przybylski. 2006. The Motivational Pull of Video Games: A Self-Determination Theory Approach. *Motivation and Emotion* 30, 4: 344–360. http://doi.org/10.1007/s11031-006-9051-8

43. Katie Salen and Eric Zimmerman. 2003. *Rules of play: game design fundamentals.* MIT Press, Cambridge, Mass.

44. Rosa García Sánchez, Alasdair G. Thin, Jannicke Baalsrud Hauge, et al. 2012. Value Propositions for Serious Games in Health and Well-Being. In *Serious*

Games Development and Applications, Minhua Ma, Manuel Fradinho Oliveira, Jannicke Baalsrud Hauge, Heiko Duin and Klaus-Dieter Thoben (eds.). Springer Berlin Heidelberg, 150–157. Retrieved July 5, 2013 from http://link.springer.com/chapter/10.1007/978-3-642-33687-4_12

45. Thomas B. Sheridan. 2001. Rumination on automation, 1998. *Annual Reviews in Control* 25: 89–97. http://doi.org/10.1016/S1367-5788(01)00009-8

46. Jan David Smeddinck, Marc Herrlich, and Rainer Malaka. 2015. Exergames for Physiotherapy and Rehabilitation: A Medium-term Situated Study of Motivational Aspects and Impact on Functional Reach. *Proceedings of the 33rd Annual ACM Conference on Human Factors in Computing Systems*, ACM, 4143–4146. http://doi.org/10.1145/2702123.2702598

47. Jan Smeddinck, Sandra Siegel, and Marc Herrlich. 2013. Adaptive Difficulty in Exergames for Parkinson's disease Patients. *Proceedings of Graphics Interface 2013*.

48. Penelope Sweetser and Peta Wyeth. 2005. GameFlow: A Model for Evaluating Player Enjoyment in Games. *Comput. Entertain.* 3, 3: 3–3. http://doi.org/10.1145/1077246.1077253

49. Jane Webster and And Others. 1993. The Dimensionality and Correlates of Flow in Human-Computer Interactions. *Computers in Human Behavior* 9, 4: 411–26.

50. Philip Zigoris and Yi Zhang. 2006. Bayesian adaptive user profiling with explicit & implicit feedback. *Proceedings of the 15th ACM international conference on Information and knowledge management*, ACM, 397–404. http://doi.org/10.1145/1183614.1183672

Peak-End Effects on Player Experience in Casual Games

Carl Gutwin[1], Christianne Rooke[1], Andy Cockburn[2], Regan L. Mandryk[1], Benjamin Lafreniere[3]
[1]University of Saskatchewan, Saskatoon, Canada
[2]University of Canterbury, Christchurch, New Zealand
[3]Autodesk Research, Toronto, Canada
gutwin@cs.usask.ca, christianne.r@usask.ca, andy@cosc.canterbury.ac.nz, regan@cs.usask.ca, ben.lafreniere@gmail.com

ABSTRACT
The peak-end rule is a psychological heuristic observing that people's retrospective assessment of an experience is strongly influenced by the intensity of the peak and final moments of that experience. We examine how aspects of game player experience are influenced by peak-end manipulations to the sequence of events in games that are otherwise objectively identical. A first experiment examines players' retrospective assessments of two games (a pattern matching game based on Bejeweled and a point-and-click reaction game) when the sequence of difficulty is manipulated to induce positive, negative and neutral peak-end effects. A second experiment examines assessments of a shootout game in which the balance between challenge and skill is similarly manipulated. Results across the games show that recollection of *challenge* was strongly influenced by peak-end effects; however, results for *fun, enjoyment,* and *preference to repeat* were varied – sometimes significantly in favour of the hypothesized effects, sometimes insignificant, but never against the hypothesis.

Author Keywords
Peak-end theory; player experience; game design.

ACM Classification Keywords
H.5.m. Information interfaces and presentation (e.g., HCI).

INTRODUCTION
Peak-end theory suggests that people's retrospective evaluation of an experience is strongly influenced by the *peak* and *end* moments of that experience. That is, rather than objectively considering the experience as a whole, people tend to base their assessments on the most intense and final moments of the experience. For example, Kahneman and colleagues have shown that when people undergo a painful experience (such as colonoscopy), their memory of the overall experience is substantially coloured by the final moments of the procedure [21, 28, 29]. This overweighting of the final moments of experience can lead to surprising outcomes, such as reliable preferences for longer experiences that contain more total pain (but finish with lower pain levels) over shorter experiences with less total pain that finish abruptly.

HCI researchers have recently shown that peak-end theory also affects people's evaluations of their experiences with interactive systems. Cockburn and colleagues [6] manipulated *effort* in an interactive task by changing the number of sliders that had to be set on each of a sequence of pages. Their study showed that people significantly preferred sequences that had a less effortful peak (only a few sliders on a middle page) and a less effortful end (few sliders on the last page) compared to other sequences with an identical number of sliders but in a different arrangement. In other work, Hassenzahl and Sandweg [18] showed that the terminating level of mental effort during an interaction negatively correlated with perceived usability, and Harrison et al. [16, 17] showed that variations in the pace for visual feedback influenced people's preferences for progress bars.

Peak-end theory suggests that there are other kinds of experiences in human-computer systems that could be affected by the ordering and sequencing of events. In particular, computer games are an area where different qualities of the experience – such as difficulty or balance, and their variation over time – could have strong effects on the player's subjective assessments of the game's challenge, their own performance, or their preferences. Games provide an interesting platform for examining peak-end effects because the activities involved are designed to be highly engaging and immersive (e.g., fighting a series of enemies); games may also generate stronger momentary experiences than other forms of daily interactive tasks, allowing more sensitive experimental examination of peak-end effects. In addition, game designers are already interested in understanding how game event sequencing affects experiences – they consider order when positioning cut-scenes and pacing when designing levels [27], and they explicitly evaluate play experience [3, 30, 34]. Finally, replay and retention rate is a major concern for game designers, and a player's willingness to replay a game is strongly connected to their memory of the experience.

There is little information, however, about whether or how peak-end theory affects game experience, or what variables in games lead to effects. Early peak-end studies manipulated pain [2, 21, 28, 29]; others have examined pleasurable experiences [9, 11]; and HCI studies have shown effects

CHI'16, May 07 - 12, 2016, San Jose, CA, USA

ACM 978-1-4503-3362-7/16/05…$15.00
DOI: http://dx.doi.org/10.1145/2858036.2858419

when manipulating effort that is predominantly mental [18] and physical [6]. In games, there are several variables that could be manipulated. First, *difficulty* is a fundamental part of the game experience [27], and games are often set up to have increasing difficulty (e.g., the "boss fight" at the end of a sequence). Second, the *balance* between difficulty and skill has been discussed as an important element of game design [1]; optimal balance occurs when difficulty and ability are well matched (which can lead to the user experiencing "flow" [8, 34]).

To provide game designers with information about the effects of peak-end theory in games, we carried out two studies. Because peak-end experiences could have effects on more than just overall preference, we tested several aspects of play experience including perception of performance, challenge, tension, effort, and enjoyment. The first study manipulated difficulty level in two different games ("Match-3", based on Bejeweled, and "Whac-A-Germ", which is a point-and-click reaction game). Players rated their experiences following paired game sequences that altered the timing of periods of difficult and easy play (to create hypothetical peak-end effects), while equalizing the overall difficulty of each sequence.

The second study manipulated the balance between difficulty and skill using a shootout game and a computer-controlled opponent. Participants played a series of calibration rounds to determine their skill level, and then compared pairs of games that presented a sequence of enemies. The sequences were configured to induce positive and negative peak-end effects by distributing periods of difficulty/skill balance and imbalance through the sequence.

In both studies, we asked participants to rate various aspects of their experience after each sequence, and we also asked them to make forced-choice comparisons between them (e.g., which was more fun, which was more difficult, and which would you choose to repeat)

Results of the studies show that peak-end effects can strongly influence several aspects of player experience. First, in two of the three games (Match-3 and Shootout), we found significant effects on people's perceptions of the game and of their own performance – finishing with more difficult play made participants think that the sequence overall was more difficult, and led to changes in their perceptions of performance and enjoyment. Second, in the Match-3 game, we also found that the sequences had a significant effect on which of the two versions people saw as more fun and which they would prefer to repeat. The Whac-A-Germ game, in contrast, showed only an effect of perceived challenge.

These are important results for game designers, demonstrating that the sequence of game difficulty and challenge can have strong effects on several aspects of people's retrospective assessment of play experience, as predicted by the peak-end rule. While game designers already have some intuitions about sequencing difficulty (e.g., matching skill and challenge, or providing increasing difficulty in successive levels), our work provides a theoretical framework for explaining current practice, and opens opportunities for well-founded further research.

RELATED WORK

Peak-End Effects

Kahneman et al.'s [21] 'cold-pressor' experiment had subjects immerse their arm in painfully cold water in two conditions: 'short' and 'long'. Both conditions started identically with the arm submerged in 14° C water for one minute. In the 'short' condition the participants then removed their arm from the water, but in the 'long' condition their arm remained submerged for an additional 30 seconds during which the water gradually warmed to a still painful 15° C. When asked which condition the subjects would prefer to repeat, a significant majority (69%) chose to repeat the 'long' condition – preferring more total pain with a less painful ending, to less pain overall.

Fredrickson and Kahneman [13] similarly observed that the duration of negative experiences had little impact on retrospective evaluation. Subjects viewed unpleasant and pleasant film clips that varied in intensity and duration, giving continuous ratings of their momentary experiences. They were then asked to rank the clips in order of overall pleasantness. Findings showed *duration neglect* – rankings were unaffected by the duration of experience, as indicated by a correlation between rankings and a weighted average of momentary experience (which is independent of duration), and an absence of correlation between rankings and the total pleasantness/unpleasantness (which depends on duration).

In subsequent work, Kahneman et al. [19, 20, 22] presented three different types of 'utility' that might be used to characterize an experience: *instant utility*, which is the experience of a particular moment; *total utility*, which is the sum total of momentary experiences, and *remembered utility*, which is the user's memory of the experience. Importantly, Kahneman's studies demonstrate that *remembered utility* and *total utility* are very different measures of experience. As we substantially live in our memories, and make judgments and choices based upon them, *remembered utility* is particularly important.

The overweighted influence of the peak and ending moments of experience has been confirmed in many studies beyond painful and unpleasant stimuli. This includes the pleasure of receiving gifts [11], assessment of life quality (James Dean and Alexander Solzhenitzyn effects [9]), article pricing [23, 26], effortful study [12], enjoyment of gambling [7], and customer service experiences [10].

Relatively few studies in HCI have examined peak-end effects. Hassenzahl and Sandweg [18] examined correlations between perceived usability and various manipulations of mental effort during an interactive task, including conditions that manipulated peak and terminating mental effort. Results showed that the terminating level of mental effort correlated negatively with usability assessment, which they attributed to a recency effect. In their studies of progress bars, Harrison et al. [16, 17] referred to peak-end effects when explaining user preferences for progress bars that showed accelerating rates of progress. Finally, Cockburn et al. [6] recently directly examined peak-end effects as a method for manipulating users' retrospective assessment of interactive experiences. Their experiment examined user preferences for interfaces that altered the distribution of a constant total workload across a series of interactive pages. Results showed a significant preference for a series that combined a positive peak and end over a series that combined a negative peak and end. However, results were not significant for either series where only peak or end was manipulated.

Observing and experimenting with peak-end effects requires two components: first, experimenters must manipulate the sequence of subjects' momentary experiences, while keeping the objective total content of those experiences equitable; second, experimenters require a way to measure subjects' retrospective assessment of experience. When experiments involve direct pain, straightforward manipulations are possible (although with ethical challenges), including cold water immersion [21] and pressure induced by a vice-clamp [2]. Furthermore, the effectiveness of these measures can be easily validated through real-time subject reporting on the pain received [21]. Retrospective assessments are typically assessed through rating scales and through the use of forced preference choices, which ask participants which of two experiences they would choose to repeat.

Controlling and validating the momentary affective experience during human-computer interaction is challenging because users can respond differently to controlled elements. For example, when manipulating page workload in a study of peak-end effects in HCI [6], some participants reported a positive sense of accomplishment when a page contained high workload, while others reported a negative sense of burden. Neurological measures (e.g., EEG and fMRI) and autonomic activity measures (e.g., heart rate, pupil dilation, and skin conductivity) are promising technologies for understanding subjective experiences, but they remain largely under development for these applications (see [5] for a review).

Our studies, described below, use various measures of subjective experience (including self-report measures on various dimensions of experience and overall preference) to examine retrospective assessment of play experience in games where we manipulate objective game difficulty and difficulty-skill balance.

Sequencing, Challenge, and Player Experience in Games

Games are intended to provide a very different experience compared to other types of interactive systems – they are designed to entertain rather than to support stand-alone productivity or communication tasks [27]. As a result, there is considerable research into ways of evaluating player experience in games, much of which has focused on aspects of experience related to enjoyment, immersion, self-determination, fun, motivation, and suspense [3, 27, 30].

Although sequencing is an important part of game design (e.g., in following a narrative path, or in designing the ultimate goal of winning the game), the effects of different sequencing approaches on measures of experience has not been studied as widely. Work in other domains, however (notably in research into gambling) has looked at the idea of sequencing. Researchers have found that gamblers' memories are biased towards extreme events in a sequence, such as wins or jackpots [14] and have found strong peak-end effects on people's retrospective assessment of a sequence of events at a slot machine [35]. The reward structures of these games (e.g., the payout interval) has strong effects on people's willingness to keep playing, and the idea of reward structures has also been explored in the context of video games [3, 27]. However, "Creating a game that establishes immediate and continued motivation to continue playing over long periods of time is a very complex issue" ([27], p.6). Finally some researchers have looked at the ways that points of repeated failure in games (such as repeatedly dying at a particular spot) can negatively affect perception of an otherwise fun game [4].

Several games researchers have examined how a game's *challenge* should be designed in order to provide a good experience [1, 34]. Some games have progressively-harder levels, often culminating in a "boss fight" against a very difficult computer opponent (e.g., the Bowser level in Super Mario 64, see Figure 3). However, simply increasing difficulty level is not the only way to design challenge – researchers have noted that challenge should be matched to the player's level of skill (i.e., game balancing). As Pagulayan and colleagues state, "Too easy is boring and too hard is unfair. Either perception can make a person cease playing" ([27] p.6). When challenge and skill are appropriately matched, players can enter a "flow" state of intense focus and control, and a loss of awareness of self and time [1]. Similarly, researchers have shown that game suspense is greatest when players are slightly behind in a competitive match, and that enjoyment is highest when the outcome is uncertain [1]. The concept of balance does not state how different difficulty levels will affect retrospective experience, other than to suggest that balanced challenge and skill leads to positive experiences.

In contrast to the idea of skill/difficulty balance, there are several examples of games that are successful even though they are extremely easy or difficult. First, some games provide almost no challenge to the user, and instead focus on regular rewards, allowing the user to enter a state of "blissful productivity" with little effort [25]. For example, "Zen Mode" in *Bejeweled* (bejeweled.popcap.com, see Figure 1) allows players to continue indefinitely, with no time limit and with the game always providing at least one move on the board. Similarly, a genre of "clicker" games (such as *Cookie Clicker*) has very low difficulty – all the player needs to do

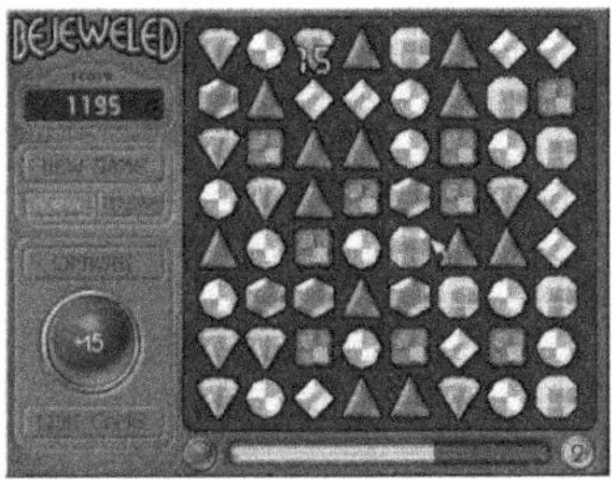

Figure 1. Bejeweled

Figure 2. Clicker Heroes

Figure 3. Super Mario 64

Figure 4. QWOP

to progress is to click the mouse button. These games are surprisingly popular – there are dozens of titles tagged as "Clicker" on the Steam platform, and one game, *Clicker Heroes*, has tens of thousands of players and a "very positive" rating (Figure 2).

At the other end of the challenge spectrum, some games are designed to be extremely difficult yet are also popular. For example, there are numerous lists of "hardest video games of all time" that celebrate extreme difficulty, and some games such as QWOP (foddy.net, Figure 4) appear to have been designed to prevent players from succeeding, while drawing on physical comedy [33]. These games can still provide a satisfying player experience, however, because games create a high degree of failure tolerance in players, and in some cases failure can be enjoyable (e.g., an accomplishment may be more rewarding after repeated failure). For example, researchers found that a particularly difficult game level, in which players repeatedly died, was rated as the most enjoyable [4].

STUDY 1: MANIPULATING DIFFICULTY

Our first study examines peak-end effects caused by different sequences of game difficulty. We chose game difficulty as our manipulation of momentary experience for two reasons. First, difficulty is a parameter that game designers can typically easily control by manipulating factors such as the number, speed, and firing rate of enemies, the rate of play (e.g., scroll speed or time per move), or the number of solutions available at any point. Second, previous interaction studies have demonstrated that different forms of 'difficulty' (mental effort [18] and physical workload [6]) have successfully induced peak-end effects. Together, these suggested that game difficulty could be a widely applicable and sensitive means for examining peak-end effects.

Methods

Games: Match-3 and Whac-A-Germ

We developed two custom games for this study, called Match-3 and Whac-A-Germ. Match-3 (Figure 5) is based on Bejeweled – the player clicks on sets of at least three contiguous tiles that are the same color. Unlike Bejeweled, tiles do not slide down once cleared – instead, each correctly selected set is grayed out. The objective of the game is to click as many sets as possible within five seconds. A falling white ball shows the remaining time for each game screen (Figure 5, right).

We created sequences of varying difficulty by algorithmically altering the number and size of the sets of contiguous tiles available within each game screen. The availability of many large sets makes the game easier, whereas fewer, smaller sets make the game harder. Figure 5 shows a medium difficulty game screen containing 9 sets and 34 tiles within them; Figure 6 (left) shows an easy screen containing 12 sets and 60 tiles; and Figure 6 (right) shows a hard screen containing 4 sets and 13 tiles.

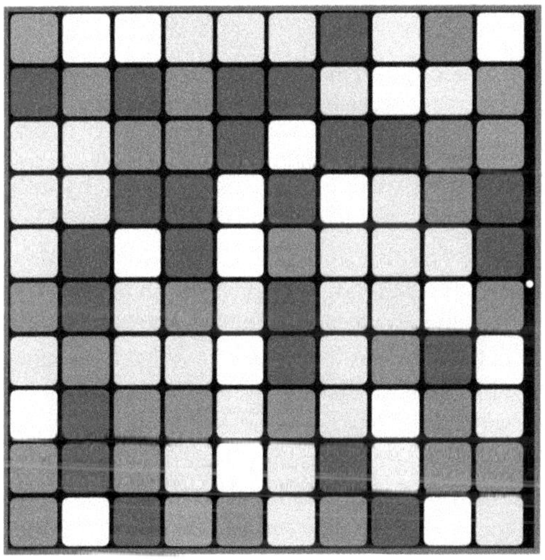

Figure 5. Match-3, medium difficulty. Goal of the game is to click on as many contiguous regions of three same-color tiles as possible before the timer (falling ball at right) finishes.

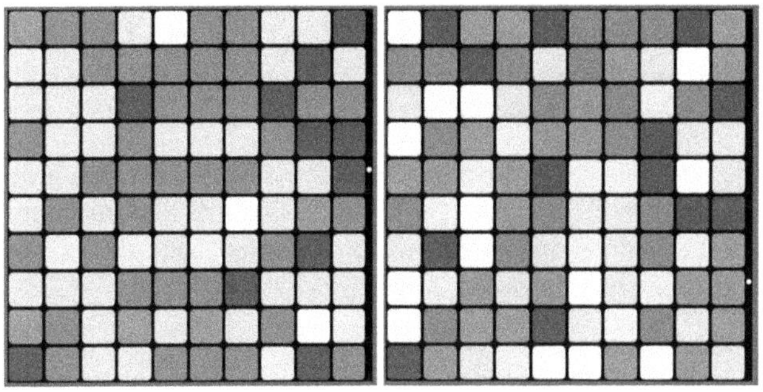

Figure 6. Match-3, easy (left) and hard (right) difficulty.

Match-3 games contained 15 screens, with the difficulty sequences described below. In all games, the total number of tiles in the sets was identical.

The second game was a targeting task motivated by the fairground game Whac-A-Mole. In our version, called Whac-A-Germ (Figure 7), players clicked as quickly as possible on a series of "germs" appearing on the screen. There were 15 germs in each round of the game. Difficulty was manipulating using the Fitts' Law index of difficulty (ID) – in easy tasks the germ was large and close to the player's cursor; and in hard tasks the germ was small and far away. The sequences of difficulties followed the patterns described below. The sum of the difficulties for each complete sequence was identical.

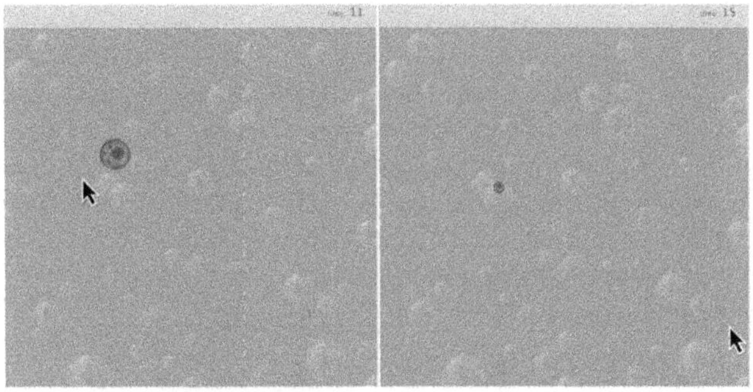

Figure 7. Whac-A-Germ, easy (left) and hard (right). Other screens were between these difficulties.

Difficulty Sequences (Experimental Conditions)

We designed three difficulty sequences to test hypothetically positive, negative, and neutral peak-end effects. The Match-3 sequences are shown in Figure 8 (the y-axis shows the total number of tiles available to be cleared in each screen). The *Positive* sequence contains easy screens (many tiles available) at its middle and end. The *Negative* sequence has screens with high difficulty at the middle and end. The *Neutral* sequence has screens with identical difficulty throughout. Note that the total objective difficulty of all sequences is identical. Whac-A-Germ sequences were the same shape as those shown in Figure 8 (achieved by manipulating Fitts' Law index of difficulty).

Participants and Apparatus

Twelve participants were recruited from a local university (7 female; mean age 27.7 years). Seven participants stated that they did not play computer games, and five stated that they played less than three hours per week. All were familiar with mouse input (>8 hrs/week).

The two games were written in Processing and were run on a Windows 7 computer, with a 21-inch 1080p monitor. Questionnaire responses were recorded on the same computer using an online form.

Procedure

Participants completed a demographics questionnaire and were introduced to the games. Participants then played twelve games in each system (Match-3 and Whac-A-Germ, order counterbalanced), divided into six pairs. The six pairs comprised three comparisons in two possible orders for the conditions shown in Figure 8: Negative vs. Positive, Neutral vs. Positive, Neutral vs. Negative.

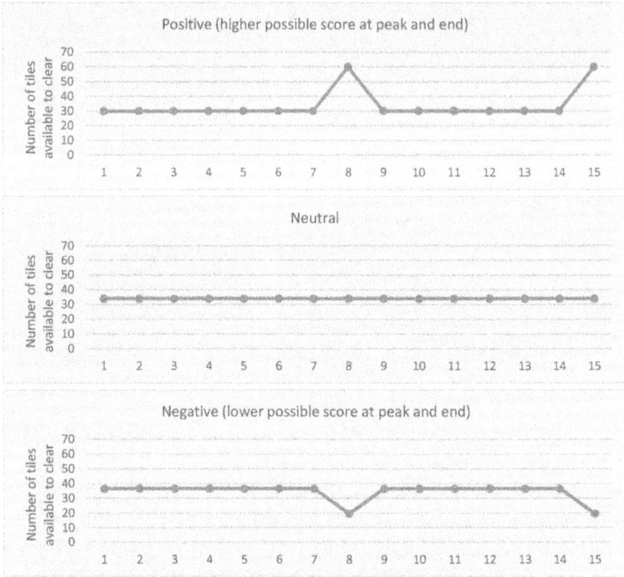

Figure 8. Difficulty sequences for Match-3 game showing number of tiles available per screen (more tiles mean lower difficulty). All three sequences have the same total difficulty.

After each game, participants completed a questionnaire asking about their experience in that game. For Match-3, we asked about perceived performance, ability to see matches on the board, player speed, and game difficulty; for Whac-A-Germ, we asked about perceived performance, perceived accuracy, player speed, and game difficulty. All questions used a 1-9 scale (low to high).

After each pair, participants answered four forced-choice questions, selecting between the two games of the pair – which game was more fun, which was more interesting, which was more challenging, and which the player would prefer to repeat. Once all pairs and questionnaires for one system (Match-3 or Whac-A-Germ) were finished, the player repeated the process for the other game.

Design and Research Questions

Questionnaire responses on the 1-9 scale were analysed using Friedman tests. Forced-choice responses were analysed using a binomial test. Our hypotheses for the study were predominantly exploratory, but we anticipated that participants' rankings and preferences would be positively influenced by our Positive conditions, and negatively influenced by the Negative conditions.

Results

Match-3: Post-Game Responses

We asked four questions (1-9 scale) at the end of each Match-3 game, regarding players' perception of their performance, their speed, their ability to see matches on the board, and the difficulty of the game. Results are shown in Figure 9.

Friedman tests showed significant differences for Player speed (χ^2=4.83, p<.05) and Difficulty (χ^2=10.29, p<.01), but not for Performance (χ^2=5.29, p=.071) or Ability to see matches (χ^2=2.38, p=.30).

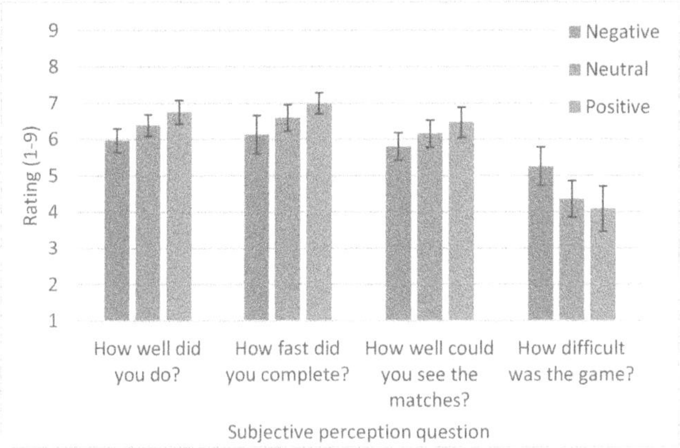

Figure 9. Match-3: mean post-game participant ratings ±s.e.

Match-3: Comparison of Sequences

After each pair of sequences, we asked participants four forced-choice questions about the pair (see Table 1). Binomial tests on the counts found several significant differences (p<.05). For the pair with the largest expected difference (Positive to Negative), there were significantly more responses choosing the Positive sequences as more fun, more interesting, and easier. In addition, there were significantly more responses choosing the Positive sequence to repeat. For the other pairs with smaller expected differences (Positive-Neutral and Neutral-Negative), players stated that Positive was more interesting than Neutral, that Neutral was more challenging than Positive, and Negative more challenging than Neutral.

	Of the two games you just played, which: was more fun?	was more interesting?	was more challenging?	would you repeat?
Positive peak and end	**10**	**18**	**5**	**18**
Negative peak and end	**5**	**6**	**19**	**6**
Binomial p-value	**.0033**	**.011**	**.011**	**.011**
Positive peak and end	16	**18**	**6**	14
Neutral (no peak or end)	8	**6**	**18**	10
Binomial p-value	.076	**.011**	**.011**	.27
Neutral (no peak or end)	15	9	**5**	13
Negative peak and end	9	15	**19**	11
Binomial p-value	.15	.15	**.0033**	.42

Table 1. Participant counts for comparison questions (significant differences in bold).

Whac-A-Germ: Post-Game Responses

We asked four questions (1-9 scale) at the end of each game (perceived performance, accuracy in clicking, player speed, and the difficulty of the game). Results are shown in Figure 10. Friedman tests did not show any significant effects of Sequence on any of these questions (Performance: χ^2=0.5, p=.78; Accuracy: χ^2=3.29, p=.19; Speed: χ^2=4.67, p=.097; Difficulty: χ^2=0.54, p=.76).

Whac-A-Germ: Comparison of Sequences

After each pair of sequences, we asked participants four choice questions about the pair (see Table 2). Binomial tests on the counts found only one difference – significantly more participants chose the Negative sequence as more challenging than the Positive sequence (p<.05).

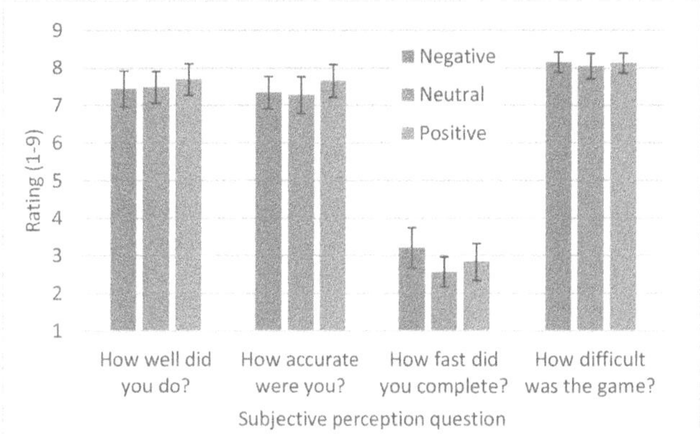

Figure 10. Whac-A-Germ: mean post-game participant ratings

	Of the two games you just played, which: was more fun?	was more interesting?	was more challenging?	would you repeat?
Positive peak and end	12	12	**6**	15
Negative peak and end	12	12	**18**	9
Binomial p-value			**.011**	.14
Positive peak and end	13	12	8	13
Neutral (no peak or end)	11	12	16	11
Binomial p-value	.42		.076	.42
Neutral (no peak or end)	11	11	8	10
Negative peak and end	13	13	16	14
Binomial p-value	.42	.42	.076	.27

Table 2. Participant counts for comparison questions (significant differences in bold).

STUDY 2: MANIPULATING BALANCE

The results of Study 1 consistently showed that participants' perception of *challenge* was influenced by manipulation of peak-end experience. The relationship between the challenge of an experience and a person's skill levels are well known to strongly influence engagement in that experience [8, 34] – high levels of challenge with insufficient skills will lead to frustration; insufficient challenge with high skills leads to boredom; and a *balance* between challenge and skill can optimize user engagement.

As the balance between challenge and skill is a key consideration for game designers, Study 2 specifically uses *skill-challenge balance* as the experiential factor that is manipulated through peak-end event sequencing. An initial calibration session is used to determine the participants' skill levels, and peak-end experiences are constructed by creating game sequences that vary the timing of moments that have *appropriate balance*, are *too easy*, and are *too hard*, relative to the users' skill.

Methods

Game: Space Shootout

We built a simple one-on-one shooting game with spaceships at the top and bottom of the screen (bottom controlled by the player, top controlled by the computer). The player moved their ship left and right with the 'h' and 'l' keys, fired the gun with the 'k' key, and invoked a temporary shield (one second duration) with the 'z' key. The object of the game was to shoot the opponent's ship, and when this occurred, the round finished; the game was designed to have several rounds (so that we could create different difficulty sequences).

The computer enemy was designed to have a variable level of difficulty (from 0 to 20) through programmatic control of four elements: the enemy's speed, the enemy's fire rate, the likelihood that the enemy would use its shield when needed, and the likelihood that the enemy would change direction in the face of incoming fire. The algorithm was hand-tuned in pilot testing until it provided a very low starting difficulty at level 0 (trivial for any player to beat), a gradual increase from level 0 to 20, and an extremely high difficulty at level 20 (essentially impossible to beat).

Figure 11. Shootout game: player at bottom, enemy at top.

Balance Sequences (Experimental Conditions)

To test for peak-end effects when manipulating skill-challenge balance (as opposed to simple difficulty in Study 1), we created sequences that used an appropriate balance as the positive momentary experience (corresponding to Study 1's easy peak-and-end sequence), and an inappropriate balance as the negative momentary experience (corresponding to Study 1's difficult peak-and-end condition). Importantly, there are two forms of inappropriate balance: too easy and too hard.

The sequences are illustrated in Figures 12 and 13. The overall hypothesis for these sequences is that people may remember sequences that end with an appropriate balance differently than sequences that are unbalanced at the end. Furthermore, there may be differences between different forms of imbalance (too easy or too hard).

Participants and Apparatus

Twelve participants were recruited from a local university (5 female; mean age 27.5 years). Gaming experience varied: four people stated that they did not usually play computer games, four stated that they played less than three hours per week, and four played between 3 and 10 hours/week.

As in the first study, the game system was written in Processing and ran on a mid-range Windows 7 computer, with a 21-inch 1080p monitor. Questionnaire responses were recorded on the same computer using an online form.

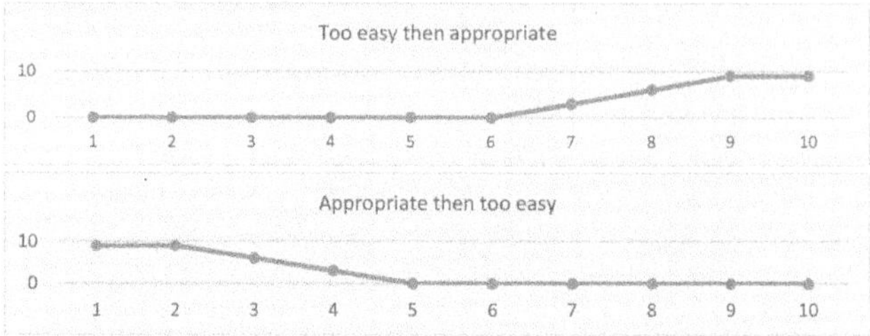

Figure 12. Example difficulty levels for sequences in shootout game (easy version): sequences are exactly inverted, with appropriate difficulty at either start or end. Note: overall line was adjusted up or down based on player calibration.

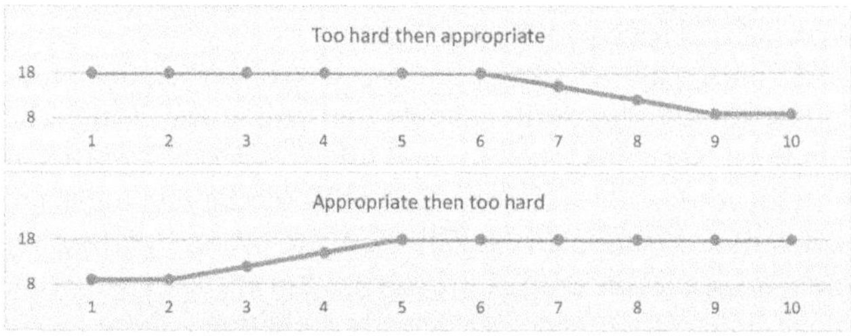

Figure 13. Example difficulty for sequences in shootout game (hard version).

Procedure

Participants completed a demographics questionnaire and were introduced to the shootout game. Participants then completed a calibration session in which they played 20 rounds against enemies of increasing difficulty – the object of the calibration was to determine three difficulty levels: one that was too easy, one that was too hard, and one where the player was evenly matched to the computer opponent. The experimenter determined the balanced level by choosing a round that was one of the longest (neither player was able to win easily) and where the participant either won the round or had won in the previous round. This level was used to set the difficulty levels of the sequences as described above.

In the second phase of the study, participants played pairs of games with matched but inverted difficulty sequences. Instead of simply changing difficulty as in the first study, we manipulated whether the challenge was too easy, too hard, or evenly matched. The *Too-Easy* pair (see Figure 12) had one sequence that had enemies that were too easy then finished with enemies that were evenly matched to the player, and one sequence that began evenly matched and then became too easy. The *Too-Hard* pair (Figure 13) had one sequence that was too hard then evenly matched, and one that was even and then too hard.

After each game, participants completed a validated scale asking about their experience in that game. We used the Intrinsic Motivation Inventory (IMI) questionnaire, which measures four dimensions of experience: enjoyment, perceived competence, effort, and tension [24] using 18 items rated on a 1-5 scale: 1=Strongly Disagree; 5=Strongly Agree. After each pair, participants also answered the forced-choice questions used in Study 1: these asked which game was more fun, more interesting, more challenging, and which the player would prefer to repeat.

Design and Hypotheses

For the post-game questions, we combined the questions from the IMI into the four constructs; the IMI is a validated instrument that allows the use of ANOVA on the combined scores for enjoyment, competence, effort, and tension [24]. For the forced-choice questions, we counted the number of participants choosing each response and compared counts using a Binomial test. Our hypotheses in Study 2 were again exploratory: we expected sequences ending with appropriate balance to be seen as preferable, but the effects on play experience are hard to predict, given the many ways that players view success and difficulty in games.

Results

Shootout: Post-Game Responses

Mean results for the IMI are shown in Figures 14 and 15 (Too-Easy and Too-Hard versions of the game respectively). RM-ANOVA showed that in the Too-Easy version, there were significant main effects of Perceived Competence ($F_{1,11}$=9.68, p=.01, η^2=.47) and Tension ($F_{1,11}$=5.47, p=.039, η^2=.33). For the Too-Hard version, there were effects of Perceived Competence ($F_{1,11}$=13.3, p=.004, η^2=.55) and Effort ($F_{1,11}$=7.8, p=.018, η^2=.41).

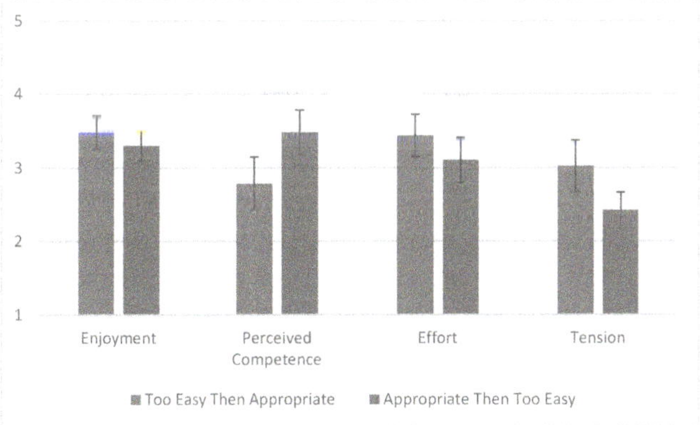

Figure 14. Shootout (too-easy version): mean post-game participant ratings (±s.e.)

These results show that players saw themselves as more competent when the sequence ended with a set of too-easy enemies, and also when the sequence ended with a set of too-hard enemies (see below for discussion of this result). In the too-easy games, players rated tension higher when the game ended with appropriate balance; and in the too-hard games, players stated that that they put in more effort when the game ended with balanced difficulty.

Shootout: Comparison of Sequences

After each pair, we asked participants four choice questions about the pair (see Table 3). Binomial tests on the counts found only one difference, in the Too-Easy version – significantly more participants felt that the sequence that ended with appropriate balance was more challenging than the appropriate-then-too-easy sequence.

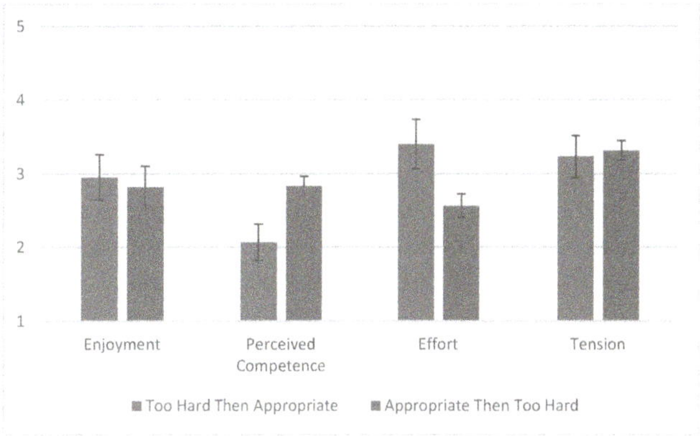

Figure 15. Shootout (too-hard version): mean post-game participant ratings

	Of the two games you just played, which: was more fun?	was more interesting?	was more challenging?	would you repeat?
Too Easy → Appropriate	5	8	**10**	6
Appropriate → Too Easy	7	4	**2**	6
Binomial p-value	.77	.19	**.019**	
Too Hard → Appropriate	6	6	5	5
Appropriate → Too Hard	6	6	7	7
Binomial p-value			.77	.77

Table 3. Participant counts for comparison questions (significant differences in bold).

DISCUSSION

The two studies provide several main findings:

- In Match-3, sequences with positive peaks and ends were judged as significantly more fun, more interesting, and less challenging than sequences with negative peaks and ends (despite identical total objective difficulty). Players also rated their own speed significantly higher with positive sequences, and were significantly more likely to choose the positive sequence to play again.
- In Whac-A-Germ, the only significant difference found was that players saw negative sequences as significantly more challenging than positive sequences.
- In the too-easy version of Shootout, players rated their own competence significantly higher when the sequence ended with too-easy enemies (compared to appropriately balanced), and also rated these sequences as less tense.
- In the too-hard version of Shootout, players rated their competence significantly higher when the sequence ended with too-hard enemies, but also rated their own effort as significantly lower in these sequences.
- The only difference in the forced choice selections between Shootout sequences was that the sequence ending with appropriate skill/difficulty balance was chosen as

being more challenging significantly more frequently than the sequence ending with easy enemies.

- There were no significant differences in enjoyment for the different sequences of Shootout, nor did players choose any one sequence as more fun or more replayable.

The following sections discuss possible reasons underlying the results, consider some of the surprising outcomes from the study, connect our findings back to larger issues of game design and peak-end theory, and identify experimental limitations and opportunities for further work.

Strong peak-end effects of difficulty in Match-3

Adjusting the difficulty of the screens in the Match-3 game led to strong differences in people's perceptions of the sequences – they thought the positive sequence was more fun, more interesting, and more worthy of replay.

Possible explanations concern the style of game, the way in which people think about difficulty in this game, and the possibility that we hit a sweet spot within the range of difficulties chosen. The gameplay mechanics are extremely simple – similar to the "clicker" games described earlier, which have very low challenge but are still seen as rewarding by players. In these games, obtaining easy rewards is a key component of gameplay, unlike other genres (such as completing a quest or achieving a goal). In Match-3, therefore, players may have felt that "easier is better," and thus may have had stronger memories of the sequence that allowed them to do particularly well (i.e., Positive peak and end). It is also possible that the difficulty of "easy" configurations was well matched to our participants' skill, giving an engaging final experience.

Few peak-end effects of difficulty in Whac-A-Germ

In contrast to Match-3, the only effect of difficulty sequence in Whac-A-Germ was that people felt that the negative sequence was more challenging than the positive sequence (despite its objectively neutral total content). It is possible that the absence of other effects arises from the way in which difficulty and reward influenced its gameplay. Even though people did feel that the negative sequences were more challenging, the manipulation of difficulty in Whac-A-Germ appears to have had a weaker effect on momentary experiences than in Match-3. In Match-3, being successful on a screen was rewarding (e.g., it was satisfying to clear a large amount of the screen), and success was directly correlated to the difficulty of the screen. In Whac-A-Germ, there was no difference in reward based on difficulty, and the game behaved the same regardless of whether the player had clicked on a small far target or a large close one.

In addition, every screen in Whac-A-Germ had the same level of success – that is, clicking on the germ advanced to the next target. There was no time limit, and little to motivate or engage the player. Therefore, every screen had the same success experience regardless of difficulty. Although people's perception of overall difficulty was affected by the sequencing (small, distant targets are objectively harder than big, near ones), this may have had less effect on play experience (small, distant targets are no more 'fun' or engaging than big, near ones). Consequently, participants' preferences and ratings were largely unaffected by our manipulations.

Consistent peak-end effects on perception of challenge

People's responses in both studies showed that their perception of game challenge was consistently altered by the sequencing of difficulty in the game – by the peak and end experiences in Study 1, and by the end experience in Study 2. These results were consistent in three different kinds of games involving three different mechanics (matching, targeting, and fighting an opponent).

There are two issues to consider when interpreting this finding: what it says about the existence of peak-end effects in games, and what its implications are for game design. The consistency of the result provides strong evidence for a difficulty-based peak-end effect in games. In both studies, sequences that finished with a higher difficulty level were reliably seen as more difficult overall, even though the objective total difficulty was identical.

Although game designers may already know that the final experience of a game is important (e.g., a poor ending could "leave a bad taste in the player's mouth"), there is still little understanding of the specific effects of sequencing, and our results suggest that evaluations of play experience could be influenced in ways that designers are not considering.

For example, when running evaluation tests for a game, designers may receive feedback that a game is too hard if the evaluation session ends with a difficult set of events. This could lead designers to rebalance the overall game, which might result in a game that is too easy in sections of the sequence. Multi-player settings are another evaluation scenario that could be complicated by peak-end effects. In multi-user online play, the game has little control over the difficulty faced by the player – and our results show that differences in the sequences of enemies could lead to large differences in a player's perception of overall difficulty.

Perception of competence, effort, & tension in Shootout

There were also interesting effects on player perceptions in the Shootout game. First, it is puzzling that perceived competence went up significantly both when the sequence ended with too-easy enemies, and also with too-hard enemies. The too-easy case seems logical and conforms to peak-end theory – it is likely that participants viewed themselves as more competent during easy play, and their retrospective assessment of competence was substantially influenced by their terminating experience. However, the too-hard case seems out of place. A speculative explanation is that players may have been reacting to the near-impossibility of the game – that is, when the game is impossible to win, players may have started to attribute the reason for their performance to external sources (i.e., that the game was far too difficult) rather than to themselves. This explanation is reflected in prior psychology findings that people have a tendency to accept the credit for their successes, while attributing failure to external sources [32].

Another finding that might initially appear surprising is that participants' retrospective assessment of effort was lower following the too-hard ending. However, we suspect this is due to the players giving up when they became unable to compete due to excessive challenge – their effort was therefore very low (or nil) in the final moments. Similarly, the participants' recollections of tension were significantly lower following a too-easy ending, which reflects a lack of challenge during the final moments.

It is important to reiterate that although we cannot definitively state why people had these perceptions of their experience, their perceptions were definitely altered by the change in sequence. This implies again that game evaluators should be aware of potential peak-end effects.

Preferences for easier and harder games in Shootout

The Shootout study did not show any effects on enjoyment, fun, interest, or willingness to repeat one sequence over another. This suggests that in a game like Shootout, there is not the same connection between difficulty and enjoyment as observed for Match-3. In Shootout, there seems to be a much more complex relationship between people's preferences and the level of skill/challenge balance.

It seems surprising, for example, that in Study 2, players did not prefer sequences that ended with an appropriate difficulty level – even though it appeared that their memories of the sequences were in fact influenced by the ending balance (too-hard and too-easy). As expected, players indicated that the sequence ending with too-hard enemies was more difficult than the sequence ending with appropriate balance, however, their preference choices were split between too-hard and appropriate endings. Similarly mixed choice results were found for the too-easy sequences (except for challenge, as discussed earlier).

These conflicting results suggest that in some games, easier may be preferred to balanced; and in others, harder may be preferred. We had assumed that an appropriate balance between skill and difficulty would be seen as the preferable option (as suggested by previous literature [1,26]), but this was not the case in our study.

Despite the seemingly obvious logic behind balancing skill and difficulty, there are a few reasons why players might choose a sequence that they recall as being too-difficult or too-easy. In some settings, people actually want things to be highly challenging. As described above, some games are extraordinarily difficult, but have attracted a large following. Given that the Shootout game was very simple in terms of gameplay, it may have been that some players saw increased difficulty as the only thing that would make the game interesting over a longer term. Similarly, some of our participants may have seen the too-easy condition as a satisfying success experience, leading them to state a preference for the sequence that ended with easy enemies.

These equivocal results show that even though peak-end effects are occurring in our games, the connection between difficulty and repetition choice in our experiments is not as clear as the connection between pain and choice that Kahneman originally studied.

Experimental limitations and further work

Although several of our findings conform to the peak-end rule, others failed to show predicted effects. Reliable generalisation of the peak-end rule to game settings therefore requires further study. This includes analysis of different distributions of game content (e.g., experience curves other than those shown in Figure 8), manipulation of experiential factors such as fun or comedy [33], and studying different types of gamers (e.g., different expertise, and those with different preferences [15]). There are also opportunities to examine the effect of peak experiences in isolation, as our studies only examined combined peak and end experiences (Study 1) and end effects (Study 2).

CONCLUSIONS

The peak-end rule is a psychological heuristic stating that people's retrospective assessment of an experience is substantially influenced by the intensity of the peak and terminating moments of that experience. It has been validated in many areas involving human quality judgments, but it has received relatively little attention in HCI and less still in gaming, where the remembered quality of experience is likely to be a fundamental factor influencing potential future play.

Results from the three different games examined in this paper show that peak-end effects occurred when the sequence of difficulty and challenge-skill balance was manipulated. Users' recollection of challenge was uniformly affected by peak-end sequence manipulations, despite the tested conditions being objectively identical in total content. Peak-end manipulations also led to significant differences in recalled fun, interest and willingness to repeat in one of the three games.

This work provides initial insights into how a widely known but under used (in HCI) psychological phenomenon influences game experiences. There are abundant opportunities for further work in examining how different parameters of momentary experience induce peak-end effects – our experiments used only relatively crude manipulations of difficulty and challenge-skill balance. There are also extensive opportunities for examining and understanding the conditions under which peak-end retrospective assessments translate into desired positive outcomes, such as recalled enjoyment and fun.

ACKNOWLEDGMENTS

This work was supported by NSERC, the GRAND NCE, and the SurfNet research network.

REFERENCES

1. Abuhamdeh, S. and Csikszentmihalyi, M. The importance of challenge for the enjoyment of intrinsically motivating, goal-directed activities. *Personality and Social Psychology Bulletin 38*, 3 (2012), 317-330.
2. Ariely, D. Combining Experiences Over Time: The Effects of Duration, Intensity Changes and On-Line Measurements on Retrospective Pain Evaluations. *Journal of Behavioral Decision Making 11* (1998), 19-45.
3. Bernhaupt, R. (ed.), *Game User Experience Evaluation.* Springer, 2015.
4. Birk, M., Luerig, C. and Mandryk, R.L. A Metric for Automatically Flagging Problem Levels in Games from Prototype Walkthrough Data *Academic MindTrek '15*, Tampere, Finland, 2015, To appear. .
5. Brave, S. and Nass, C. Emotion in human-computer interaction. in Julie, A.J. and Andrew, S. eds. *The human-computer interaction handbook*, L. Erlbaum Associates Inc., 2003, 81-96.
6. Cockburn, A., Quinn, P. and Gutwin, C. Examining the peak-end effects of subjective experience. in *Proceedings of CHI'15: ACM Conference on Human Factors in Computing Systems*, ACM Press, (2015), 357-366.
7. Cowley, E. and Farrell, C. Retrospective evaluations: Will chance versus luck oriented individuals select different moments of an experience? *Advances in Consumer Research*, San Antonio, United States, 2006, http://www.acrwebsite.org/volumes/v33/naacr_v33_32.pdf.
8. Csikszentmihalyi, M. *Flow: The Psychology of Optimal Experience*. Harper and Row, New York, 1991.
9. Diener, E., Wirtz, D. and Oishi, S. End effects of rated life quality: the James Dean Effect. *Psychol Sci. 12*, 2 (2001), 124-128.
10. Dixon, M. and Verma, R. Sequence effects in service bundles: Implications for service design and scheduling. *Journal of Operations Management 31*, 3 (2013), 138--152.
11. Do, A., Rupert, A. and Wolford, G. Evaluations of pleasurable experiences: The peak-end rule. *Psychonomic Bulletin & Review 15*, 1 (2008), 96-98.
12. Finn, B. Ending on a High Note: Adding a Better End to Effortful Study. *Journal of Experimental Psychology: Learning, Memory, and Cognition 36*, 6 (2010), 1548-1553.
13. Fredrickson, B. and Kahneman, D. Duration neglect in retrospective evaluations of affective episodes. *Journal of Personality and Social Psychology 65*, 1 (1993), 45-55.
14. Griffiths, M. Fruit machine gambling: The importance of structural characteristics. *Journal of Gambling Studies 9*, 2 (1993), 101-120.
15. Hamari, J. and Tuunanen, J. Player types: A meta-synthsis. *Transactions of the Digital Games Research Association 1*, 2 (2014), 29-53.
16. Harrison, C., Amento, B., Kuznetsov, S. and Bell, R. Rethinking the progress bar. in *Proceedings of the 20th annual ACM symposium on User interface software and technology*, ACM, (2007), 115-118.
17. Harrison, C., Yeo, Z. and Hudson, S.E. Faster progress bars: manipulating perceived duration with visual augmentations. in *Proceedings of the SIGCHI Conference on Human Factors in Computing Systems*, ACM, (2010), 1545-1548.
18. Hassenzahl, M. and Sandweg, N. From mental effort to perceived usability: transforming experiences into summary assessments *CHI '04 Extended Abstracts on Human Factors in Computing Systems*, ACM, Vienna, Austria, 2004, 1283-1286
19. Kahneman, D. Evaluation by Moments: Past and Future. in Kahneman, D. and Tversky, A. eds. *Choices, Values and Frames*, Cambridge University Press New York, 2000.
20. Kahneman, D. Experience Utility and Objective Happiness: A Moment-Based Approach. in Kahneman, D. and Tversky, A. eds. *Choices, Values and Frames*, Cambridge University Press New York, 2000.
21. Kahneman, D., Fredrickson, B., Schreiber, C. and Redelmeier, D. When More Pain Is Preferred to Less: Adding a Better End. *Journal of Personality and Social Psychology 65*, 1 (1993), 401-405.
22. Kahneman, D., Wakker, P. and Sarin, R. Back to Bentham? Explorations of Experienced Utility. *The Quarterly Journal of Economics 112*, 2 (1997), 375-405.
23. Langer, T., Sarin, R. and Weber, M. The retrospective evaluation of payment sequences: duration neglect and peak-and-end effects. *Journal of Economic Behavior & Organization 58*, 1 (2005), 157-175.
24. McAuley, E., Duncan, T. and Tammen, V.V. Psychometric properties of the Intrinsic Motivation Inventory in a competitive sport setting: a confirmatory factor analysis. *Res Q Exerc Sport 60*, 1 (1989), 48-58.
25. McGonigal, J. 2014. Games Can Make a Better World. from http://janemcgonigal.com/2014/01/06/transcript-games-can-make-a-better-world/.
26. Nasiry, J. and Popescu, I. Dynamic Pricing with Loss-Averse Consumers and Peak-End Anchoring. *Operations Research 59*, 6 (2011), 1361--1368.
27. Pagulayan, R.J., Keeker, K., Wixon, D., Romero, R.L. and Fuller, T. User-centered design in games. in Jacko, J., A and Sears, A. eds. *The human-computer interaction handbook*, L. Erlbaum Associates Inc., 2003, 883-906.
28. Redelmeier, D.A. and Kahneman, D. Patients' memories of painful medical treatments: real-time and retrospective evaluations of two minimally invasive procedures. *Pain 66*, 1 (1996), 3--8.

29. Redelmeier, D.A., Katz, J. and Kahneman, D. Memories of colonoscopy: a randomized trial. *Pain 104*, 1 (2003), 187--194.
30. Ryan, R., Rigby, C.S. and Przybylski, A. The Motivational Pull of Video Games: A Self-Determination Theory Approach. *Motivation and Emotion 30*, 4 (2006), 344-360.
31. Siang, A.C. and Radha Krishna, R. Theories of learning: a computer game perspective. in *Multimedia Software Engineering, 2003. Proceedings. Fifth International Symposium on*, (2003), 239-245.
32. Streufert, S. and Streufert, S.C. Effects of conceptual structure, failure, and success on attribution of causality and interpersonal attitudes. *Journal of Personality and Social Psychology 11*, 2 (1969), 138-147.
33. Švelch, J. Comedy of Contingency: Making Physical Humor in Video Game Spaces. *International Journal of Communication 8* (2014), 2530-2552.
34. Sweetser, P. and Wyeth, P. GameFlow: a model for evaluating player enjoyment in games. *Comput. Entertain. 3*, 3 (2005), 3-3.
35. Yu, E., C., Lagnado, D., A. and Chater, N. Retrospective evaluations of gambling wins: Evidence for a 'peak-end' rule *Proceedings of the 30th Annual Conference of the Cognitive Science Society*, 2008, 77-82.

"My Doctor is Keeping an Eye on Me!": Exploring the Clinical Applicability of a Mobile Food Logger

Yoojung Kim[1], Sookyoung Ji[1], Hyunjeong Lee[1],
Jeong-Whun Kim[2], Sooyoung Yoo[3], Joongseek Lee[1]
User Experience Lab, Seoul National University, Seoul, South Korea[1]
Department of Otorhinolaryngology, Seoul National University Bundang Hospital, Seongnam, South Korea[2]
Center for Medical Informatics, Seoul National University Bundang Hospital, Seongnam, South Korea[3]
{tendtoyj, purpler7, hyunjeong.lee, kimemail, yoosoo0, joonlee8}@snu.ac.kr

ABSTRACT
By enabling people to track their lifestyles, including activity level, sleeping, and diet, technology helps clinicians to treat patients suffering from "lifestyle diseases." However, despite its importance compared to other lifestyle factors, it is not easy to record food intake consistently. Although researchers have attempted to solve this problem, most have not considered its applicability in the clinical context. In this paper, we aim to (1) understand food-journaling practices and (2) explore the applicability of lifestyle data in the clinical context. By observing 20 patients who recorded data including food logs, steps, and sleeping time, we found that patients recorded their food logs diligently, as they were conscious of clinicians. Clinicians were surprised by the high adherence rate of journaling and tried to overlap food data with other data, such as steps, sleeping time, etc. This paper contributes by providing qualitative insights for designing applicable strategies utilizing lifestyle data in the clinical context.

Author Keywords
Food journaling; Lifestyle Disease; Personal Informatics; Self-tracking; Clinical Context.

INTRODUCTION
The rapid spread of smartphones and wearable devices has enabled people to quantify every aspect of their daily lives, including their walking, sleeping, eating, and smoking. These kinds of lifestyle factors, are crucial to preventing and managing diseases [23, 25, 34]. However, the medical world has not made good use of personal lifestyle data, even though, anyone who has visited their doctor's clinic has heard the following advice: "Exercise more, watch what you eat, and do not smoke or drink." Moreover, lifestyle diseases are increasing globally [25], and lifestyle management and modification are becoming as important as medication treatment and surgery. Thus, collecting data on activity level, sleeping, and diet, etc. is also extremely important.

CHI'16, May 07-12, 2016, San Jose, CA, USA
© 2016 ACM. ISBN 978-1-4503-3362-7/16/05…$15.00
DOI: http://dx.doi.org/10.1145/2858036.2858145

Despite its importance [23, 25], it is far more difficult to record food intake compared to other lifestyle factors. Thus, the development of food-intake recording techniques has long been an interest. The HCI field and industry have both made many attempts to overcome the challenges of food journaling. Popular applications such as Noom Coach, MyFitnessPal, etc. somewhat overcame the limitations of the traditional method of food-intake recording through the semi-automation of journaling and database updating. Attempts to reduce users' recording effort and minimize content loss have led to fully automated food-journaling solutions [2, 26]. On the other hand, Cordeiro et al. argued that full automation might undermine the mindfulness benefit of food journaling and proposed a photo-based lightweight food-journaling application for the self-reporting of food intake [11].

Although previous works have made many contributions, there are still several problems related to food journaling. First, until the recent studies such as Bentley et al.'s work [5], most of the preceding works have dealt with food journaling only and have not thought of food data as a part of lifestyle data. This could be considered a limited approach, because eating is not an isolated habit but is interrelated with other habits, and considering other habits offers a more valuable and extended point of view. For example, people often eat too much given their amount of daily activity or eat high-calorie food at night, and it is hard to understand these aspects if only food journaling is considered. Second, the applicability of food intake data collected by food loggers as a lifestyle factor is rarely considered in the clinical context. Despite technological advances and a plethora of studies on food journaling in the HCI field, in the actual medical field, the paper based diary is still a popular method, as it is not only cost-efficient but also accessible. However, there has been relatively less interest in exploring the clinical applicability of mobile food loggers.

A new strategy must be developed that utilizes food logs interrelated with other data, such as steps and sleeping time, in the clinical context. Thus, in this paper, we aim to (1) understand the clinical applicability of food-journaling practices and (2) explore clinicians' requirements when utilizing lifestyle data. To do so, we conducted interviews with clinicians and field deployment study to examine this topic.

RELATED WORK

We reviewed previous works related to food logging for behavior modification and the burden of using such data in the clinical context for patients and healthcare providers.

Food Journaling for Behavior Modification

Food journaling is considered the most traditional method of tracking food intake. There are two indications for using journaling: (1) to record in detail for expert analysis or assessment and (2) to self-monitor one's behavior [11]. The former is focused on the healthcare providers' side, while the latter is focused on building patients' awareness during the process of recording.

Food journaling is one of the representative examples of journaling to improve health behaviors [20]. Self-monitoring food intake is considered the cornerstone of behavioral treatment of obesity and other chronic disorders that can be managed by dietary modification, such as end-stage renal disease (ESRD), diabetes, and dyslipidemia [34]. Previous studies have shown that people who are aware of their current behavior are more likely to lose weight [3, 31]. In this sense, the automation of food journaling may not be the answer, since it may eliminate the positive effects of self-monitoring [11].

Despite these positive effects, adherence remains a recognized challenge. Food journaling, especially by paper, is an arduous task that leads to fatigue [4, 13], and therefore, continuous recording is highly unlikely. Research has shown that adherence to self-monitoring is less than ideal [3], and others have reported that adherence deteriorates over time [7]. Therefore, self-logging studies try to minimize the burden of users to encourage long-term usage. Technological support, from electronic diaries [8] to smartphone applications, has somewhat lowered the burden of the traditional paper-based method. Carter et al. [8] found that the recording rate via smartphones is significantly higher than that via websites or paper. The general input methods of various smartphone health applications (e.g., MyFitnessPal, Noom Coach, Lose It) aims to lower users' burden, by modularizing menus and portions.

Patient Logging Burden vs. Clinical Use

In terms of lowering the capture burden, studies have suggested alternative input methods, such as employing photo-based food journaling [11, 22], using chewing sounds [2, 26], or scanning receipts [24]. Although focused on sleeping behavior, Choe et al. [9] provided meaningful findings: suggesting that widgets reduced the number of steps and gave users high access to the capture tool.

Simple information can be easier to record, but be of little use. The negative effects of data oversimplification should also be considered, especially when the self-logging data is intended not only for self-monitoring but also for medical usage. As discussed in [9], professional engagement is necessary regarding data interpretation. When considering the involvement of experts, the dimension of clinical usage should also be considered alongside increasing the usability of the capture tool. For instance, photo-based food journaling increases adherence; however, in the clinical setting, it is difficult for clinicians to go over every food photo. Lack of time is recognized as one of the biggest barriers to clinicians' engagement with patient-collected life-log data in medical checkups [10].

Recent studies [10] represent the growing interest in integrating life-log data into the clinical context. Health applications (e.g., Calorie Counter & Activity Tracker, Food & Fitness Planner) in the market also support multiple logging of diverse data, yet remain unexplored in the clinical context. Chung et al. [10] presented valuable findings related to the employment of life-log data within the clinical setting. However, the findings were drawn from interviews, some of which included hypothesized situations. Thus, in this study, we aim to provide further empirical findings through a field study.

CLINICIAN INTERVIEWS

The preliminary interviews were conducted to understand the way in which food intake data is currently used during medical examinations. We recruited five medical specialists (otorhinolaryngology, family medicine, obstetrics & gynecology, rehabilitation medicine, and urology) from Seoul National University Bundang Hospital who showed interest in the topic. Researchers met doctors one on one for 40 to 60 minutes on average, and each doctor was rewarded with $100. We asked them how they would use/are using food-intake records, and what types of data they would consider useful for actual diagnosis and prescription.

Current Usage of and Need for Food Records

Data usage, type, and importance differ depending upon the characteristics of the disease being treated. For departments that treat lifestyle diseases, such as obesity, food diaries are important references. In departments that treat diseases for which lifestyle is considered a risk factor, dietary information can also be required. However, due to constraints, medical staff members approximate patients' eating habits by asking them in person during examinations, which only represents partial or perceived information. *"Weight control is a crucial part of treating obstructive sleep apnea syndrome. If patients do not lose weight, they rarely improve. On the contrary, by just losing weight, many patients actually show improvement. However, for now, the majority of doctors do not conduct interventions for patients' weight loss because of their difficulty."* (Otolaryngologist, M, 46)

When treating lifestyle diseases, medical specialists need to derive patterns in (1) nutritional content, (2) total calorie intake, and (3) daily distributions (time and frequency) from food-intake records collected. On the other hand, when weight and food management are additionally recommended for disease improvement, rather than such detailed information, medical specialists want to identify whether patients maintain regular diets. They expect to provide more helpful weight-control advice based on this data. However, for the additional analysis and research of clinical results, most specialists report that they also need the raw data on patients' food-intake recordings so that they can access it as necessary.

Potential Benefits and Challenges

Medical practitioners claimed that patients' diet records are being used for self-monitoring and as a communication tool between the medical staff and patient. That is, clinicians believe that food records will contribute to patients' awareness of their eating habits and increase the effects of doctors' medical advice.

While such benefits were identified, the following issues were reported as barriers: (1) Patients often fail to continue recording (continuity) and (2) the records might not accurately represent their diets (reliability). Even if the patients diligently record every detail, medical practitioners encounter practical barriers during the process of analyzing and reviewing the data. First, clinicians are not able to examine every record due to a lack of time (in the case of university hospitals in Korea, examination time is extremely restricted due to the high numbers of outpatient clinics). Therefore, the raw data collected from patients should be summarized/patternized prior to medical checkups. Second, at present, the analysis process is not automated and it significantly depends on the effort of nutritionists, and consequently a high amount of time and money is consumed. Third, the collected food intake data is not integrated in the hospital information system. Such restricted accessibility discourages clinicians from cross-referencing the food intake data with other patient data. Even though food intake data is recognized as meaningful, clinicians often encounter such practical difficulties. These issues were considered during our field study.

FIELD STUDY

Through the interviews with medical specialists, we analyzed the challenges of food-intake recording and explored the potential uses of the data obtained by journaling. We developed an app to focus on the consistent collection of data used by clinicians during medical checkups, and collected requirements from medical experts through interviews. This study was approved by the Institutional Review Board of Seoul National University Bundang Hospital (IRB #B-1504-296-302).

mFood Logger

The food-logging app was made as simple as possible to focus on the difficulties regarding data acquisition. Popular food-tracking applications, such as Noom Coach and MyFitnessPal, are weight-loss goal driven. Therefore, we did not use these applications, since we were concerned about negative reactions from patients because of diet-biased feedback. Medical staff members doubted the possibility of consistent data acquisition based on their prior experience with paper food diaries. Therefore, accessibility was the top priority of the application design [9]. We developed an app with three buttons for indicating users' feelings of fullness after a meal along with a free text box for selective input about the context of the food intake (Figure 1). We could obtain the timestamp and subjective fullness when the user pressed a button. Meal context, such as menus or nutritional information, was inserted as free text. Referring to previous studies [6, 9] on the importance of reminders, we attached a small (1x1cm) physical sticker as an ambient reminder on the patients' smartphones.

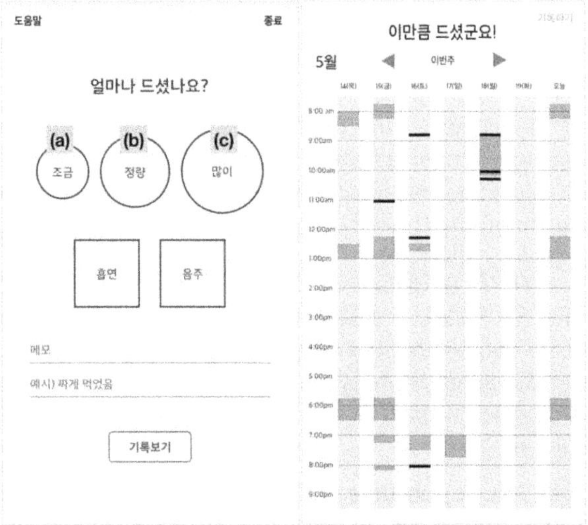

Figure 1. The interface of mFood Logger. <Left> The logging page. Button (a), (b), (c) refers to portion size: "little", "just right", and "too much". Rectangular buttons below refer to "smoking" and "drinking" (Right) The weekly summary view.

Maximize Accessibility

Consistency was our top priority. During the interviews, doctors doubted that the patients would consistently record food intake based of prior experience. Clinicians emphasized that data should be collected for at least a certain period to identify patterns and trends. Therefore, we minimized the page depth of our application and the amount of information collected to lower the burden of users and support consistency. We divided the features into two simple parts, (1) record and (2) view, maintaining single depth for each part. We also developed a widget so patients could record right from their home screen.

Enrich the Context

To enrich the context, we provided free text input for patients who desired to log additional information. We did not predetermine the structure of the input so that patients could freely log whatever they thought was important (e.g., what they ate, how they felt about the food, where they ate, or with whom they ate). We did not suggest items beforehand, because patients might have felt pressured. Timestamps from the button input were also automatically recorded; however, a previous study [9] showed that timestamp data is inaccurate due to frequent backfilling. Therefore, the free text input could help compensate for inaccurate data from missed logging. Moreover, free-text entries could also help identify what patients considered important regarding their nutritional intake.

Simplify Feedback
Another aim was to simplify feedback. We were originally interested in how the doctors used the collected data and how the patients reacted to the intervention. However, feedback from applications has been found to be an important factor to affect users' motivation [12]. Therefore, we kept feedback neutral and eliminated judgments or evaluations. We visualized the weekly input (Figure 1). Each bar represents a day, and the vertical axis represents time. Green represents food, orange alcohol, and black smoking. Through this visualization, patients obtained basic information about their eating habits, such as regularity and frequency.

Participants
First, we recruited six medical experts from Seoul National University Bundang Hospital. We assumed that interest in food intake data would differ according to specialty. Therefore, doctors from diverse specialties were recruited: internal medicine (C01, C04), otorhinolaryngology (C02), family medicine (C03), obstetrics & gynecology (C05), and rehabilitation medicine (C06). Every clinician except for C01 and C04 are those who have also participated in the preliminary interview. The doctors recruited patients who were suffering from lifestyle diseases (Table 1). The patients were screened based on two criteria: whether they possessed a smartphone and whether they were capable of using their smartphone at a basic level. The patients' employment statuses were as follows: employed (9), self-employed (6), full-time homemaker (3), etc. (4). The patients were highly educated overall: Most were high school graduates (8) or university graduates or above (14).

We asked patients to log their food intake on our mobile app. Patients were also provided with wearable devices (Misfit/Fitbit), which we asked them to use to log activity and sleep data. They had control over the data via the web (individual ID/PW) so that they could delete data they did not desire to share. The field study lasted for eight weeks, and excluding the two dropouts, we obtained data from a total of 20 patients (Table 1). The two patients could not visit the hospital for the required checkups due to the sudden Middle East Respiratory Syndrome (MERS) situation in South Korea and an unexpected business trip.

Patient Interviews
We first conducted 30–60-minute semi-structured interviews to determine the original nutritional behaviors of the patients. We asked the patients about their perceptions of health and health management strategies. After the interviews, we explained the procedure and installed the mFood Logger on their smartphones. During the field study, patients had to complete two phone interviews. We asked patients if they had noticed anything new about their eating patterns, if anything about the process was inconvenient, and how they felt about the medical intervention. Lastly, we inquired about the changes in their health behavior, experience of app use and data-integrated checkups. The checkup sessions and interviews were recorded under permission. Rewards of $300 were given to the patients who went through two checkups and four interviews. Patients who dropped out were rewarded $50 per checkup or interview. No reward was promised based on the activity, sleep, and food-intake data.

PID	Sex	Age	Disease	CID
P01	M	60	Hypertension, heart disease	
P02	M	55	Heart disease	
P03	F	65	Hypertension, Hyperlipidemia	C01
P04	F	64	Diabetes mellitus,heart disease	
P05	F	51	Hypertension, Hyperlipidemia, Diabetes mellitus	
P06	M	42	Hyperlipidemia, Obesity, Sleep Apnea	
P07	M	47	Diabetes mellitus, Sleep Apnea	
P08	F	25	Sleep Apnea, Chronic rhinosinusitis	C02
P09	M	50	Hypertension, Sleep Apnea	
P10	F	53	Sleep Apnea, Chronic rhinosinusitis	
P11	M	54	Hypertension	C03
P12	M	58	Obesity	
P13	M	47	Hypertension, Hyperlipidemia, Diabetes mellitus	
P14	M	67	Hypertension, Obesity, Sleep Apnea, heart disease	C04
P15	M	45	Hyperlipidemia	
P16	F	48	Diabetes mellitus, Myoma uteri	C05
P17	F	59	Hypertension, Breast cancer	
P18	F	53	Diabetes mellitus, Breast cancer	
P19	F	43	Breast cancer	C06
P20	F	71	Hypertension, Diabetes mellitus, Breast cancer	

Table 1. Demographic information of the patients.

Medical Checkups Using Food Logs
To explore the difficulties and possibilities of using food-intake data in the medical context, we arranged two checkups during the eight-week field study. Researchers attended the checkups and observed how doctors used the data (Figure 4). After each checkup, we opened workshops which all the participating clinicians were asked to attend. The clinicians exchanged their experience about the checkup and opinion about the clinician view.

The two checkup sessions at a three-week interval were designed to promote data sharing in the natural workflow. To do so, as mentioned in the preliminary clinician interviews, data summarization, automated analysis, and system integration were considered. We (1) analyzed and summarized the data before the scheduled checkups, (2) visualized diverse charts for the clinician web interface separate from mFood Logger, and (3) provided this data on

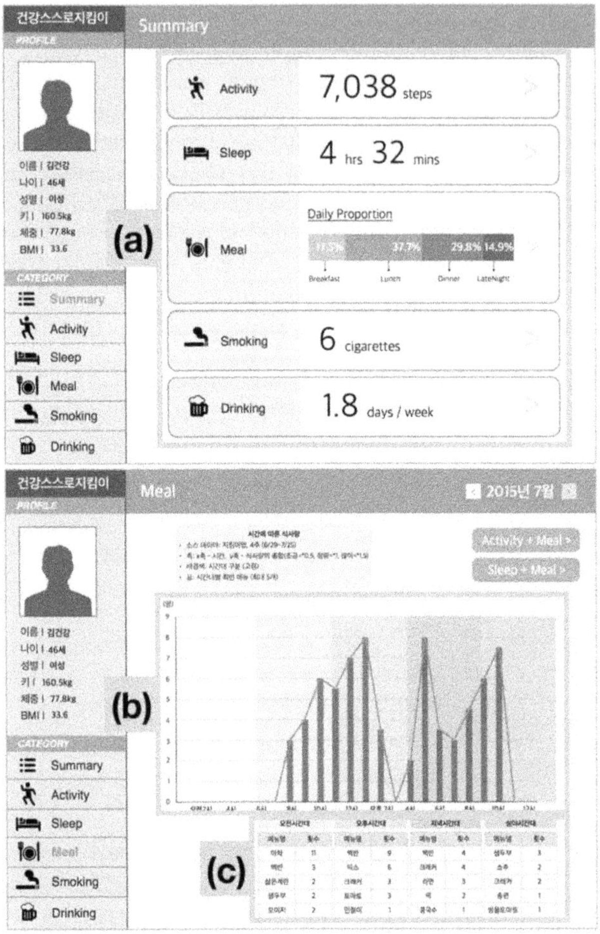

Figure 2. Examples of the clinician web interface. (a) The summary view that shows the average of the patient-logged data. More detailed information of each data was provided as individual views. (b) Portion size (calculated by button input) per time (c) Top ranked menus per time.

the EMR. Direct integration to the hospital system was attempted but was unattainable due to hospital network security. Instead, the visualized data was made accessible through a link on the EMR screen (Figure 2). In consideration of the clinicians' lack of experience in impromptu life-log data interpretation, data was sent to the clinicians at least 12 hours prior to the checkup so they could review it in advance.

The clinician web interface was iteratively designed while reflecting the requirements identified during the clinician interviews. A summary view and individual views for each type of data were given (Figure 2). The summary view was designed considering the fact that clinicians cannot examine every record. During the first checkup, summaries of the frequency, time, and menu of meals were provided. We modified the data presented in the second checkup after conducting a workshop with the doctors. During the second checkup, we provided data about mealtime, subjective fullness, and menu.

After the second checkup, we conducted another workshop with medical experts to obtain further requirements.

Data Analysis

Three types of data—(1) logs, (2) patient interview transcripts, and (3) checkup observations—were analyzed.

First, we collected activity and sleep logs automatically by the Fitbit and Misfit APIs and manual food intake logs from the food journaling app (mFood Logger). We analyzed the adherence rate of each lifestyle log. In the case of automatically collected logs, we calculated their "collection rate" by counting the days that had data input during the experiment. In the case of manual logs by mFood Logger, we calculated the "food journaling rate" by counting the days patients logged at least three or more times. The results will be mainly discussed in the Patient Side section of our findings.

Secondly, in order to analyze the patient interview transcripts, we went through three ideation sessions in which we analyzed the transcripts. We theorized the main issues using grounded theory [28], which consists of the stages of coding, noting, and integrating. In the first stage, researchers open coded the transcripts independently. After reading each line of the interviews, researchers wrote down the key phrases or sentences on post-it notes to break down the transcripts and identify key points. In the second stage, researchers added notes on each code by checking similar concepts, considering what they had discussed in the previous session. During the last stage, by using an affinity diagram repetitively, we grouped the notes by their main topics and finally established seven issues. Each stage was followed by active discussion. The results will be mainly discussed in the Patient Side section of our findings.

Thirdly, we observed how the collected food intake data was used during actual medical examinations. A total of 40 examinations were observed (2 examinations x 20 patients) and recorded. Researchers transcribed the 40 recordings and used utterance-by-utterance analysis. The results will be mainly discussed in the Clinician Side section.

FINDINGS

The findings of the field study were derived by analyzing both the patient side and the clinician side.

Patient Side

The first notable characteristic was that the presence of the doctor significantly affected food journaling behavior, as it contributed in forming a sense of duty toward food journaling among patients. That is, it ensured patients did not forget to journal and led to more precise descriptions of what they had eaten. The second notable point was that the patients improved their perceptions of the data and their health behavior. Lastly, patients had difficulty in consistently recording their food intake, because they often forgot. Our findings support previous studies that have revealed the difficulties of food journaling [11].

Clinicians' Encouragement of Journaling

Many patients performed their food journaling diligently, which might have been caused by the influence of the doctors. The average food journaling, sleep data-collection, and activity data-collection rates were 81%, 88.2%, and 94.9%, respectively. The food journaling rate was lower than the activity and sleep data-collection rates. However, considering that food journaling data was collected manually and that an average of three meals per day was assumed, 81% is a relatively high rate.

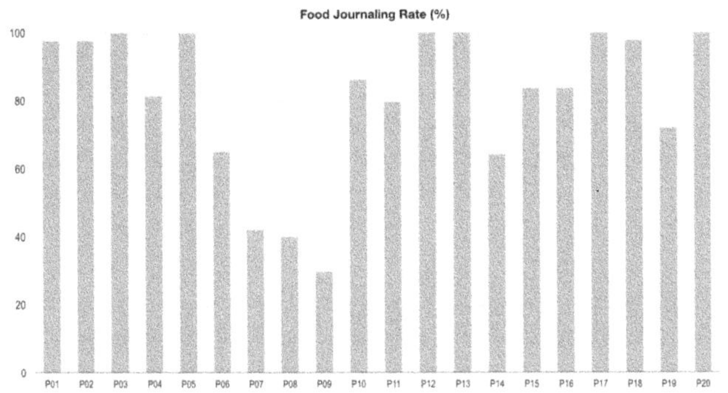

Figure 3. Food journaling rate of each patient. A relatively high journaling rates was identified (Avg.=81.0, SD=22.3).

When the food journaling rate of each patient was examined individually, a majority of the patients scored relatively high journaling rates (Figure 3). There were six patients who had journaling rates of 100%, which means they logged three times or more every day. On the other hand, the first quartile consisting of five patients (P06, P07, P08, P09, P14) had journaling rates under 76%. However, through the interviews, we identified that most of these patients stated that they originally ate less than three times a day. P06 said he ate once a day and had been trying intermittent fasting. Similarly, P08 reported that he regularly skipped breakfast, and P07 was under a strict meal plan after surgery.

The number of data entries from patients was also high. A total of 5,500 records were submitted, containing 2,877 memos and 2,326 button-clicking entries. The memos required more effort from users, but the higher number of memos versus button-clicking entries may have been due to the characteristics of the free-text-type memo. The patients freely wrote diverse memos, and some patients even separated their memos into multiple entries.

Importantly, patients regarded the doctors as supervisors, and their presence naturally led to a sense of obligation among patients. *"Since I knew that the doctors were going to view my records, I put more effort into it."* (P17) Some patients were influenced even more strongly, reporting that they felt pressure or that they considered food journaling their obligation. Interestingly, although patients did not consider themselves self-motivated and showed relatively passive attitudes, their journaling rates remained high. *"It was because the doctor told me to do it. If not, why would I? There's no inner motivation..."* (P01).

However, the passive and negative attitudes patients showed in the early stages slowly changed. In the early stages, they considered food journaling a chore to get finished, whereas as time passed, they started to interpret the entries by themselves and discover patterns from the data they had collected. Patients started to see food journaling more positively after they saw that the collected data could help them to better understand their eating habits. *"I found out that my eating habits were not as good as I thought they would be. I started to think that I should be more careful about what I eat"* (P17).

Some patients went beyond examining their habits and showed a desire to change their diets or reduce portion sizes. Signs of improvement showed the mindfulness effect of food journaling. *"There are times when I eat meat several times a day, like chicken at lunch and pork for dinner. Before, I would just vaguely think that I ate too much meat. But now, if I see that kind of record, I start reflecting upon my diet and try to improve my next meal."* (P16) In some cases, patients not only avoided high-calorie foods and reduced portion sizes but also searched for additional information and managed their nutritional intake. *"I was aware that I had to write down everything I ate. So sometimes, I would be like 'Is it okay to eat this much?' I also tried to eat carbohydrates, fat... and especially protein. Even when I went to buffets, I tried to eat more protein."* (P14) This implies that clinicians' encouragement of journaling could lead patients to modify their behavior.

Detailed Journaling and Caregiving Feedback

Another interesting aspect was that patients started to record in enhanced detail. Patients expected that medical staff would check and evaluate their record data, and, therefore, started to write what they ate in detail, once they got used to recording. P05 started out with brief menu names. However, after experiencing the first data checkup session with the doctor, she started recording in detail, such as moving information from the nutrition label, or describing her portion size in diverse measures. As for the patients who put in additional effort into journaling, they started expecting detailed feedback from their doctors. They considered a detailed checkup the reward of their extra effort and desired the other to acknowledge their effort. *"I thought that doctors couldn't thoroughly know what I ate from the original amount of information I was journaling. So if I were eating a snack, I would input the calories on the label, and so. Doctors may understand my eating behavior better."* (P05)

Some patients claimed that they would not mind if they had to invest more time and effort, if guaranteed for a detailed feedback from the doctor. This implies that a presence of a doctor or medical staff and their feedback can positively affect the quality of data collected. *"It doesn't take like 10-20 minutes. If I have to do it anyway, taking 1-2 more minutes is not a problem if I could get a better checkup."* (P19) Patients who were suffering from diseases that were relatively more closely affected by dietary intake said that they expected disease-aware feedback, such as a customized menu or dietary guideline. *"I have diabetes, so while I'm journaling, I wonder if I'm keeping my diet on the right track. It would be nice if I could receive feedback of what sort of side menus I should eat etc.... "* (P18)

Patients showed positive reactions toward friendly feedback from doctors, rather than requesting concrete and objective information such as calories. Simple words of encouragement or affirmation affected patients. *"The doctor said it's okay to eat pizza, once in a while. After looking at my intake records, he assumed that I was undergoing too much stress. After the checkup, I went home and ordered some Chinese food. It tasted so good. I loosened up a bit and felt okay to eat like that once in a while."* (P17) This implies that mechanic feedback may not be the answer to satisfactory feedback. Chronic disease is a state patients have to live with, and this may lead to an elongated sense of stress [15]. This point may be easily overlooked, when entirely relying on systematic feedback, both content-wise and communication-wise. Patients traditionally experience moderation and regulation. As inferred in P17's quote, emotional interaction may also be an important factor of feedback.

Enhancing Perceptions of Data via Communication

Patients enhanced their perception of the data through the data integration checkups. The communication with doctors enriched how patients interpret data, and this led to an increased sense of awareness. Each patient (total of 20) went through two checkups. During the 40 checkups, the doctors utilized the food-intake data by showing it to patients, explaining notable points, and planning possible future modifications. Patients identified their eating habits and tried to improve their behaviors in line with the doctors' recommendations. *"After the checkup, I realized that my lifestyle patterns were likely to make me gain weight."* (P14)

Patients were strongly motivated to modify their behaviors based upon what the doctors said rather than the effect of the self-awareness formed through the act of recording their eating behavior. A majority of the patients showed excessive trust and dependence on medical experts. *"If my husband told me, I probably wouldn't really listen. But if it's from a doctor, then I really think that I should pay attention."* (P04) Patients showed that they immediately trusted and accommodated the doctors' suggestions. *"I'm trying to follow what the doctor said. I'm not the type who really listens to others. But now I eat salads more than three days a week."* (P11)

Discussion about patients' willingness to accommodate doctors' suggestions is necessary. It is critically important that patients follow the directions of medical experts. Through that process, patients' self-awareness is enhanced, and this encourages healthy behaviors and the modification of original eating behaviors. However, this may lead to a passive attitude and cause patients to wait for instructions from an external presence. During the user study, we observed patients who showed heteronomous attitudes. *"[I do this] because the doctor told me to. How could I keep doing this on my own?"* (P01) Doctor–patient communication consisted of orders that were obeyed, and patients stayed passive and heteronomous. However, such communication traits did not affect the journaling rate, and surprisingly, those who showed passive attitudes tended to have even higher journaling rates.

Ambient Reminder for Self-Logging

Previous studies have identified that the most cited reason for not journaling is forgetting. This was also found in the field study. Even though the overall level of adherence was high, patients still cited that they often forgot to journal. Patients reported that there were situations in which they were more prone to forgetting and that they still forgot from time to time even after they got used to journaling. *"I would often forget to log my dinner meal if I was at an outing or meeting likely to involve drinking."* (P11) If journaling did not happen during or right after consumption, the sticker triggered the behavior. The sticker helped patients think back and identify when their last meal was and whether they had recorded it. *"When I saw the sticker, I remembered and looked at the recordings on my app to see if I'd left anything out."* (P12) The usefulness of the sticker was also cited by a majority of patients. Some said that they recorded less and left things out when there was no sticker (during the eight-week experiment, the sticker had worn off toward the end, and some patients had to remove it from their smartphones). *"When I'm busy, everything is hurried. I still remembered when I had the sticker on, but now I forget more often."* (P13) This result shows how ambient reminders can also support consistent journaling [6, 14, 21].

Another interesting point was that some patients considered the wearable device itself an ambient reminder. *"After I stopped wearing the wearable device, I also started to skip journaling what I had eaten."* (P19) Another notable finding was that the device was used to track activity and sleep, but it also served as an ambient reminder of food journaling. Patients perceived activity, sleep, and food intake together as a whole symbol, representing lifestyle improvement. Many patients, therefore, perceived the wearable device and mFood Logger as a reminder of "health." *"After wearing the device (Fitbit), when I was eating something, let's say an apple, I would think of whether it was okay to eat it or not. It made me think about stuff. I just kind of fiddled with it when I was bored, sometimes unintentionally. But in some way, it was... like a symbol of health."* (P09) This implies that consistent food journaling may increase when understood within a more comprehensive context, such as a healthy lifestyle.

Clinician Side

We conducted our field study while considering the difficulties pointed out from previous studies, such as workflow integration [10], and by doing so, we derived rich findings, including specific challenges and benefits. Lack of time [10] was not reported as a challenge, while clinicians said that they were able to promote communication. Clinicians also reported their lack of confidence in lifestyle data interpretation, and their level of interest varied. However, the detailed requests from clinicians who have actually used such data during medical checkups suggest the potential of overcoming such challenges.

Lack of Confidence in Planning

The level of usage of lifestyle data, including food data during medical checkups, differed with specialty. The general case was *showing*, when the clinicians read the collected lifestyle data along with the patient, and *explaining*, when the clinicians descriptively explained the data to their patients. Only a few cases of *planning*, when clinicians suggested a specific plan based on the lifestyle data, were witnessed. During the 40 examinations, clinicians (1) showed the food data 21 times, (2) explained the food data 17 times, such as identifying eating behavior patterns, and (3) only provided specific plans 13 times.

C01, C04, and C06 focused on *showing* data and by doing so triggered communication with the patients. They commented that "explaining the lifestyle data" increased "communication with patients" (C01) and enabled a more thorough "history taking" (C06). In other words, the data summary provided on the EMR helped clinicians understand the patients' lifestyle in a relatively shorter amount of time. C01 reported as follows: *"If I ask the patient how he has been and what he has eaten, this already amounts to a few sentences. It was more effective to read right from the data summary and quickly grasp the big picture rather than asking."* (C01) This shows that data summarization and workflow integration (in our case, being able to view lifestyle data on the EMR) help overcome time limitation and support time-efficient communication.

However, it was difficult to overcome clinicians' lack of confidence with just the data summary. C01 and C04 rarely suggested plans for their patients. On the other hand, C02, C03, and C05, who were relatively more interested and confident in interpreting lifestyle data, actively explained the data to their patients and used it to suggest plans. They also made the most use of the food-intake data. *"[Explain] Your mealtimes are quite delayed, and since you rarely exercise, too many calories are stored during the nighttime. This may be the reason you find it hard to lose weight. (...) [Plan] I recommend you eat your meals and your nighttime snacks a bit earlier."* (C02, Medical Examination of P08). As observed in the utterance, clinicians had to identify the relationship between food intake data and other lifestyle data in order to give specific plans. To support this process, there is a need to thoroughly examine how clinicians practically use lifestyle data.

Learning from Experience

We were able to identify the relative importance within the food data components and the specific needs regarding data visualization during the field study. Interestingly, although we collected and visualized lifestyle data based upon clinicians' needs by referring to the initial interviews, their comments and requirements changed or became more detailed after their first actual practice.

First, we identified the relative importance of the food data components. Before the field study, clinicians said that the time, frequency, and portion size were equally important data. However, during the field study, clinicians claimed that the most important food data was "portion size." During the first examination, we provided doctors with summaries of objective data, such as mealtime and frequency. However, all six doctors who participated in the experiment claimed that despite being relatively subjective, "portion size is must-have information" (C01, C02, C03). Doctors said that without knowing how much the patient ate, it is difficult to interpret a meaningful pattern, even though the information about what they ate (menus) is provided. In other words, portion size is necessary data to determine whether the patient needs behavior modification. Reflecting such feedback, during the second examination, we provided data summaries focused on portion size.

Secondly, clinicians started to give specific requirements regarding data visualization and raised the necessity of additional data mapping. Doctors required data that represented the regularity of patients' mealtimes, such as "at what time of the day they eat" so that they could interpret the average "daily pattern at a glance" (C03). The third distinctive point was "unusual moments" (C01), such as eating out, skipping meals, or eating late at night. This is because the irregular context of meals described above is correlated to overeating, gorging, and unbalanced nutritional intake. In addition, since doctors considered skipping meals important information, they brought up the necessity of distinguishing if a user forgot to record or if they actually skipped a meal by adding a "skip" button. Likewise, distinguishing a late meal and a midnight snack was also an issue.

Understanding Patients Further by Overlapping Data

As mentioned above, it is important to understand the food intake data within the context of other lifestyle data in order to provide specific plans. Clinicians saw potential in cross-referencing food intake data with other lifestyle data. However, since doctors cannot concretely relate a certain outcome to a certain lifestyle factor, they lacked enough evidence to determine cause and effect.

Even so, clinicians still said it was meaningful to understand the tendencies within an individual patient. During the workshop, C02 and C03 suggested overlapping "activity" (C02, C03) data with food intake so that "the input–output of energy balance" can be considered. Energy balance has been implemented in some healthcare applications, and medical experts confirm its medical value. Moreover, C03 proposed overlapping food intake with sleep data based on the evidence that irregular sleeping may evoke irregular eating. This request was reflected, and during the second checkup, we added the (1) "food+activity data" and (2) "food+sleep data" views. As for the (1) "food+activity data" view, the area graph of the meal portions (food) and the line graph of the steps (activity), were overlapped by synchronizing the time axes (2) and as for the "food+sleep data" view, the last meal hour of the day was overlapped with the sleeping hours.

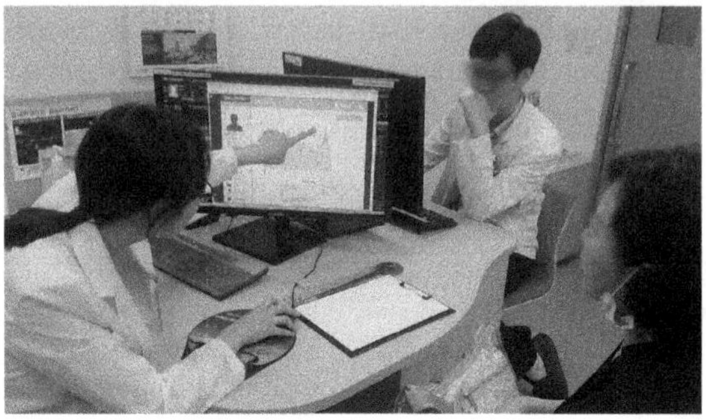

Figure 4. A medical checkup using food logs (food+activity data view).

There remain requirements that were notable but not reflected due to practical issues. "Alcohol" (C02) was also mentioned as a possible correlative variable with food intake, since drinking mostly accompanies high-calorie side dishes and late-night eating. Moreover, all of the doctors requested the food intake data be overlapped with clinical outcome data, such as weight or blood pressure.

DISCUSSION

We now summarize and discuss the lessons based on the findings.

Usable vs. Useful Data

Whereas usability is critical for the consistency of recording, the collected data should also be medically valuable. This predicament derives from the contradictory relationship between the two criteria: usability and usefulness. The validity of the collected data—which, in the case of food journaling, depends on how well the reports replicate actual intake—is the most important requirement of doctors. However, users find detailed reporting more arduous, since describing everything is labor intensive. Therefore, doctors' attempts to obtain more accurate data may prevent them from obtaining any data at all. The opposite is also problematic, since oversimplified or invalid data is of no value, even if it is collected consistently. Thus, data collection by self-reported food journaling needs to balance user-friendliness and medical usefulness. "What kind of information?" and "How many times?" may be possible questions to ask to get closer to finding such a balance.

This research focused on obtaining the simplest, yet meaningful, data to begin with so that we could collect a significant amount of data to explore its potential in a clinical context. That is why we focused on simplifying input and thereby lowering the burden of capture. In a wider sense, however, the possibility of enhancing usability not just by lowering the burden but also by helping users gain motivation is worthy of discussion. Increasing the perception of value and motivating users may be especially critical when they first start collecting data and therefore find it hard to generate any meaning from it. For instance, as more and more data was accumulated and especially after such data was used during medical checkups, patients showed higher tolerance to recording. Some patients even increased their burden of capture, because they were motivated by clinicians' comments. This shows that although usability and data usefulness may start off contradictory, the two can end up supporting one another after a certain balance is found.

Meanwhile, we should not overlook the fact that the usefulness of data in the clinical context also includes practical workflow issues. Even if the data is sufficient in size and high in credibility, such data cannot be used without considering the integration within the current workflow, system standardization, and visualization. A few additional issues were considered due to the site of the study (university hospital in South Korea): average medical checkup time being under five minutes, remote medical examinations being illegal, and EMR security issues. Similar issues, such as the medical laws of the applicable country and the degree of cooperation of field experts, should be checked beforehand, since these issues may also affect data accumulation and analysis. It is therefore important to conduct iterative field tests to collect and reflect requirements.

Healthy Food vs. Healthy Lifestyle

Food-intake data was more valuable when overlapped with other lifestyle data rather than being solely presented. This is because eating is related to other life activities, such as sleeping and exercising. The causes of lifestyle diseases are correlated, and the clinicians attempted to interpret the food data in relation with other lifestyle data. However, up to now, food-journaling studies have focused solely on dietary management. The two main goals of previous studies have been (1) lowering the burden of input [2, 11, 26] and (2) increasing validity by detailed input [33]. Recent wearable healthcare mobile applications such as Fitbit enable manual food-logging features, which allow users to view their personal health data as a whole. Such approaches should also be explored in a clinical context.

Ambient vs. Obtrusive Reminders

One of the most important aspects of food journaling is reminding users to log. Previous studies have shown that forgetting often hinders consistent food journaling [11]. Therefore, many studies use notification reminders to support in-the-moment logging [5, 6]. This not only minimizes the possibility of forgetting but also builds self-awareness and supports behavior modification. The mFood Logger also used a reminder but selected an ambient reminder rather than a direct notification, as we were concerned that direct notification would increase stress or intensify passive attitudes. Therefore, by placing a small sticker on smartphones, we induced self-awareness.

Still, patients reported that they often forgot to record what they had eaten, which supported the findings of previous studies [11]. However, interestingly, patients often recalled their meals or snacks and recorded them later on when they saw the sticker. The log data shows that many entries were late. However, as mentioned, the journaling rate remained high, meaning that at some point, patients acknowledged that they had missed an entry and recorded their food intake retroactively. *"If I missed a day, I recalled what I ate that day. I think this helped me look back at my day and evaluate what I did wrong... what I needed to work on the next day."* (P05)

Moreover, although not directly related to food journaling, some patients mentioned that the wearable devices acted as reminders to record. This is an interesting point that requires further investigation.

Self-Directed vs. Other-Directed Attitude

The trusting attitudes that patients showed toward doctors' orders is another point worthy of discussion. The authority of the doctors positively influenced data collection. *"You know, it's just a kind of admiration."* (P17) Patients' expectations that the doctors would review the reports turned food journaling into a sort of obligation. The average journaling rate of the 20 patients (81.04%) highly exceeded researchers' original estimates. Free text entries were also frequent, and some patients even made their input more detailed. This shows that the doctors served as both observers and motivators.

However, this alone cannot be considered an effective way of increasing data collection. The intervention of a clinician increased food-logging rates, but it simultaneously contributed to the formation of passive attitudes among patients. As for the doctors, correcting the behaviors of patients is their duty, and therefore, from that perspective, patients are expected to wait for their decisions to be made and recommendations to be given. This tendency may have appeared more strongly, since this study was conducted in an Asian culture country. According to Tanan et al., there exists a difference in the physician patient relationship between America and Asia [27]. In Asian culture, the physician–patient relationship is more hierarchal and reciprocal rather than egalitarian and contractual. Moreover, patients within the Asian culture tend to show more respect and deference for physicians' authority and suggestions [27]. The doctor–patient relationship in Korea also shows similar aspects, and this may be an additional reason for the conforming attitudes witnessed during the field study. However, the authoritarianism of medical experts is not restricted to Asian cultures. Therefore, even if cultural issues are considered, the intervention of clinicians may still have affected the other-directed attitudes observed in our field study.

However, since building self-awareness is equally important in food journaling, absentminded, mechanical journaling should be avoided. Therefore, in the clinical context, challenges remain in terms of making patients more self-directed and self-aware. During the field study, patients initially showed other-directed attitudes, but after the first medical examination, the communication with doctors helped trigger self-directed attempts at sense making. *"I eat too much bread, too many carbs. The doctor said that wasn't an appropriate diet for me. Now I eat a lot of vegetables the next day if I happen to eat too many carbs."* (P15) Communication with doctors helped P15 become aware of his eating habits and improve them through self-regulation. Designers of healthcare technologies, including food journaling technologies, should consider the attitudes patients form in the clinical context.

CONCLUSION

In this paper, we tried to understand food journaling practices in the clinical context and investigate how clinicians could use lifestyle data, including food logs, in situ. Through a field study with 20 patients and 6 clinicians, we gained insights into designing future healthcare technologies using lifestyle data. We also discovered that food journaling is more valuable when it is combined with other lifestyle data.

The key findings from the field study are as follows. First, the patients were significantly conscious of the clinicians, even during the period when they did not come for a checkup. The patients considered the doctors as supervisors, which led them to record their food logs diligently. Most patients desired detailed feedback about their logs and personalized diagnoses based on their lifestyle data. Second, the clinicians wanted to cross-reference the food intake data with other lifestyle data. However, clinicians lack concrete medical evidence about the relationship between lifestyle data and outcomes; therefore, further studies need to focus on investigating the medical value of lifestyle data.

The limitation of this study was that we did not fully control all the conditions. We also could not investigate the interrelationship between lifestyle data quantitatively. Despite these limitations, this paper provides qualitative insights for designing applicable strategies utilizing lifestyle data in the clinical context.

ACKNOWLEDGEMENT

This research was supported by a grant of the Korea Health Technology R&D Project through the Korea Health Industry Development Institute (KHIDI), funded by the Ministry of Health & Welfare, Republic of Korea (grant number: HI14C3213).

REFERENCES

1. Adrienne H. Andrew, Gaetano Borriello, James Fogarty. 2013. Simplifying mobile phone food diaries: design and evaluation of a food index-based nutrition diary. *In Proceedings of the 7th International Conference on Pervasive Computing Technologies for Healthcare*, 260-263.
2. Oliver Amft, Mathias Stäger, Paul Lukowicz, and Gerhard Tröster. 2005. Analysis of Chewing Sounds for Dietary Monitoring, *UbiComp 2005: Ubiquitous Computing*, 3660:56-72.Raymond C Baker, Daniel S. Kirschenbaum. 1993. Self-monitoring may be

necessary for successful weight control. *Behavior Therapy* 24, 3: 377-394.

3. Raymond C. Baker, and Daniel S. Kirschenbaum. 1998. Weight control during the holidays: highly consistent self-monitoring as a potentially useful coping mechanism. *Health Psychology* 17.4: 367.

4. Elizabeth Barrett-Connor. 1991. Nutrition epidemiology: how do we know what they ate?. *The American journal of clinical nutrition* 54, 1:182S-187S.

5. Frank Bentley, Konrad Tollmar, Peter Stephenson, Laura Levy, Brian Jones, Scott Robertson, Ed Price, Richard Catrambone, and Jeff Wilson. 2013. Health Mashups: Presenting statistical patterns between wellbeing data and context in natural language to promote behavior change. *ACM Transactions on Computer-Human Interaction (TOCHI)* 20.5 (2013): 30. DOI: http://dx.doi.org/10.1145/2503823

6. Frank Bentely, and Konrad Tollmar. 2013. The Power of Mobile Notifications to Increase Wellbeing Logging Behavior. In *Proceedings of the SIGCHI Conference on Human Factors in Computing Systems* (CHI'12), 1095-1098. DOI: 10.1145/2470654.2466140

7. Lora E. Burke, Melanie Warziski, Terry Starrett, Jina Choo, Edvin Music, Susan Sereika, Susan Stark, and Mary Ann Sevick, 2005. Self-Monitoring Dietary Intake: Current and Future Practices. *Journal of Renal Nutrition* 15, 3: 281-290.

8. Michelle Clare Carter, Victoria Jane Burley, Camilla Nykjaer, Janet Elizabeth Cade. 2013. Adherence to a smartphone application for weight loss compared to website and paper diary: pilot randomized controlled trial. *Journal of medical Internet research*, 15(4): e32. DOI: 10.2196/jmir.2283

9. Eun Kyoung Choe, Bongshin Lee, Matthew Kay, Wanda Pratt, and Julie A. Kientz. 2015. SleepTight: low-burden, self-monitoring technology for capturing and reflecting on sleep behaviors. *In Proceedings of the 2015 ACM International Joint Conference on Pervasive and Ubiquitous Computing* (UbiComp' 15). ACM, New York, NY, USA, 121-132. DOI: http://dx.doi.org/10.1145/2750858.2804266

10. Chia-Fang Chung, Jonathan Cook, Elizabeth Bales, Jasmine Zia, Sean A. Munson. 2015. More Than Telemonitoring: Health Provider Use and Nonuse of Life-Log Data in Irritable Bowel Syndrome and Weight Management. *Journal of medical Internet research* 17(8): e203. DOI:10.2196/jmir.4364

11. Felicia Cordeiro, Elizabeth Bales, Erin Cherry, and James Fogarty. 2015. Rethinking the Mobile Food Journal: Exploring Opportunities for Lightweight Photo-Based Capture. *In Proceedings of the 33rd Annual ACM Conference on Human Factors in Computing Systems* (CHI '15), 3207-3216. http://doi.acm.org/10.1145/2702123.2702154

12. Felicia Cordeiro, Daniel A. Epstein, Edison Thomaz, Elizabeth Bales, Arvind K. Jagannathan, Gregory D. Abowd, and James Fogart. 2015. Barriers and Negative Nudges: Exploring Challenges in Food Journaling. *In Proceedings of the 33rd Annual ACM Conference on Human Factors in Computing Systems*, 1159-1162.

13. Mary Ruth Craig, Alan R. Kristal, Carrie L. Cheney, and Ann L. Shattuck. 2000. The prevalence and impact of 'atypical'days in 4-day food records. *Journal of the American Dietetic Association* 100, 4: 421-427.

14. Sunny Consolvo, Predrag Klasnja, David W. McDonald, Daniel Avrahami, Jon Froehlich, Louis LeGrand, Ryan Libby, Keith Mosher, James A. Landay. 2008. Flowers or a robot army?: encouraging awareness & activity with personal, mobile displays. *UbiComp '08 Proceedings of the 10th international conference on Ubiquitous computing*. 54-63.

15. Carolyn Ehrlich, Elizabeth Kendall, Nicolette Frey, Michelle Denton, and Steve Kisely. 2015. Consensus building to improve the physical health of people with severe mental illness: a qualitative outcome mapping study. *BMC Health Services Research* 15:83.

16. Block Gladys. 1982. A review of validations of dietary assessment methods. *American journal of epidemiology* 115, 4: 492-505.

17. John C. Guare, Rena R.Wing, Marsha D. Marcus, Leonard H. Epstein, List R. Burton, and William E. Gooding. 1989. Analysis of changes in eating behavior and weight loss in type II diabetic patients: which behaviors to change. *Diabetes Care* 12, 7: 500-503.

18. Michael R. Hufford, Saul Shiffman. 2003. Assessment methods for patient-reported outcomes. *Disease Management & Health Outcomes* 11, 2:77-86.

19. G Biro, KFAM Hulshof, L Ovesen, JA Amorim Cruz for the EFCOSUM Group. 2002. Selection of methodology to assess food intake. *European journal of clinical nutrition*, 56: S25-32.

20. Frederick H. Kanfer. 1970. Self-monitoring: Methodological limitations and clinical applications. *Journal of consulting and clinical psychology* 35, 2:148-152.

21. Matthew L. Lee, Anind K. Dey. 2014. Real-time feedback for improving medication taking. *CHI '14 Proceedings of the SIGCHI Conference on Human Factors in Computing Systems*. 2259-2268 DOI: http://dx.doi.org/10.1145/2556288.2557210

22. Arab Lenore, D Estrin, D H Kim, J Burke, and J Goldman. 2011. Feasibility testing of an automated image-capture method to aid dietary recall. *European journal of clinical nutrition* 65.10 : 1156-1162.

23. Using Therapeutic Lifestyle. Can Lifestyle Modifications Using Therapeutic Lifestyle Changes (TLC) Reduce Weight and the Risk for Chronic Disease?. *Research to Practice Series*, No. 7.

24. Jennifer Mankoff, Gray Hsieh, Ho Chak Hung, Sharon Lee, and Elizabeth Nitao. 2002. Using low-cost sensing to support nutritional awareness. *UbiComp 2002: Ubiquitous Computing*. 2498: 371-378.

25. Elina Mattila, Ilkka Korhonen, Jukka H. Salminen, Aino Ahtinen, Esa Koskinen, Antti Sa¨rela, Juha Pa¨rkka¨, and Raimo Lappalainen. 2010. Empowering Citizens for Well-being and Chronic Disease Management With Wellness Diary. *Information Technology in Biomedicine, IEEE Transactions on* 14, 2: 456-463.

26. Tauhidur Rahman, Alexander T. Adams, Mi Zhang, Erin Cherry, Bobby Zhou, Huaishu Peng, Tanzeem Choudhury 2014. BodyBeat: a mobile system for sensing non-speech body sounds. In Proceedings of the 12th annual international conference on Mobile systems, applications, and services, 2-13. DOI: http://dx.doi.org/10.1145/2594368.2594386

27. Tana Nilchaikovit, James M. Hill, Jimmie C. Holland. 1993. The effects of culture on illness behavior and medical care: Asian and American differences. *General hospital psychiatry*, 15(1), 41-50. doi:10.1016/0163-8343(93)90090-B

28. Bernard H. Russell, Gery W. Ryan. 2009. *Analyzing qualitative data: Systematic approaches*. SAGE publications.

29. Dale A. Schoeller. 1990. How accurate is self-reported dietary energy intake?. *Nutrition reviews* 48, 10: 373-379.

30. Katie A. Siek, Kay H. Connelly, Yvonne Rogers, Paul Rohwer, Desiree Lambert, and Janet L. Welch. 2006. When do we eat? An evaluation of food items input into an electronic monitoring application. *In Proceedings of the First International Conference on Pervasive Computing Technologies for Healthcare* (Pervasive Health) (IEEE), 1-10.

31. William A. Sperduto, Harley S. Thompson, and Richard M. O'Brien. 1986. The effect of target behavior monitoring on weight loss and completion rate in a behavior modification program for weight reduction. *Addictive behaviors* 11, 3: 337-340.

32. Arthur A. Stone, Joseph E.Schwartz, John M. Neale, Saul Shiffman, Christine A. Marco, Mary Hickcox, Jean Paty, Laura S. Porter, and Laura J. Cruise. 1998. comparison of coping assessed by ecological momentary assessment and retrospective recall (personality processes and individual differences). *JPers Soc Psychol*, 74:1670-1680.

33. Walter C. Willett, Laura Sampson, Meir J. Stampfer, Bernard Rosner, Christopher Bain, Jelia Witschi, Charles H. Hennekens, and Frank E. Speizer. 1985. Reproducibility and validity of a semiquantitative food frequency questionnaire. *American journal of epidemiology* 122, 1: 51-65.

34. World Health Organization. 2003. Diet, nutrition and the prevention of chronic diseases. *WHO Technical Report Series* 916.

Crumbs: Lightweight Daily Food Challenges to Promote Engagement and Mindfulness

Daniel A. Epstein[1], Felicia Cordeiro[1], James Fogarty[1], Gary Hsieh[2], Sean A. Munson[2]
[1]Computer Science & Engineering, [2]Human Centered Design & Engineering
DUB Group, University of Washington
{depstein, felicia0, jfogarty}@cs.washington.edu, {garyhs, smunson}@uw.edu

ABSTRACT

Many people struggle with efforts to make healthy behavior changes, such as healthy eating. Several existing approaches promote healthy eating, but present high barriers and yield limited engagement. As a lightweight alternative approach to promoting mindful eating, we introduce and examine *crumbs*: daily food challenges completed by consuming one food that meets the challenge. We examine crumbs through developing and deploying the iPhone application *Food4Thought*. In a 3-week field study with 61 participants, crumbs supported engagement and mindfulness while offering opportunities to learn about food. Our 2x2 study compared *nutrition* versus *non-nutrition* crumbs coupled with *social* versus *non-social* features. *Nutrition* crumbs often felt more purposeful to participants, but *non-nutrition* crumbs increased mindfulness more than *nutrition* crumbs. *Social* features helped sustain engagement and were important for engagement with *non-nutrition* crumbs. *Social* features also enabled learning about the variety of foods other people use to meet a challenge.

Author Keywords

Food; daily challenges; mindfulness; personal informatics.

ACM Classification Keywords

H.5.m. Information interfaces and presentation (e.g., HCI).

INTRODUCTION

Daily interventions such as reminders, tips, or challenges, are a popular and effective method for promoting a variety of aspects of well-being [11,35]. Challenges provide small, achievable goals that give a clear indication of whether they have been completed, and can support competition or fun. Daily challenges have been shown to promote behavior change [11] and provide feedback on efforts toward larger goals [12].

Mindfulness focuses attention on the present activities [23] and can lead to healthier behaviors. In our focus on food, we build upon a definition of mindfulness as "*non-judgmental awareness of physical and emotional sensations associated with eating*" [19]. Mindfulness is therefore explicitly not corrective, does not make behavior change recommendations, and does not judge food "good" or "bad." Food mindfulness can help people understand why they eat [19,42], cope with cravings [1], avoid eating disorders [5,24], and manage obesity [24,34]. Successful methods for promoting food mindfulness have included hosting information sessions and discussions [5,24] and providing people with manuals [1]. Other common food tracking techniques, such as journaling, can also promote mindfulness of food choices [6,10,14,27,41]. However, people find food journals difficult and burdensome, often feel judged by tracking tools, and report abandoning their efforts due to these feelings of judgment [14,15].

CHI'16, May 07-12, 2016, San Jose, CA, USA
© 2016 ACM. ISBN 978-1-4503-3362-7/16/05···$15.00
http://dx.doi.org/10.1145/2858036.2858044

We draw on research on daily challenges [35,41] and photo-based food journaling [6,14] to develop the concept of *crumbs:* lightweight food-based daily challenges. A crumb is a daily challenge that a person completes by taking a picture of and consuming one food or meal that meets the challenge requirement. We design and evaluate four variants of an experience using crumbs: examining the role of a *social* experience in daily food challenges and the *nutritional* nature of those challenges.

We also incorporate successful social features found in other self-tracking domains, such as leaderboards and competition [12,40] or forums [37] in physical activity. We assess the value of social features in our current approach by comparing a personal version of the crumbs intervention with a version in which people post pictures of completed crumbs to a shared Facebook group. Although prior work suggests social experiences can help *or* hurt participation [15,17,30,31], we hypothesize that providing a social experience among people completing the same crumb can help people stay engaged with the intervention.

Noting arguments in research for both prescriptive and open-ended wellness applications, we develop and evaluate two types of crumbs. A *nutrition* crumb is nutritionally prescriptive (e.g., "Eat something high in fiber"). In contrast, *non-nutrition* crumbs are prescriptive, but not about the nutritional content (e.g., "Eat something that reminds you of your childhood"). We hypothesize non-nutrition crumbs can provide mindfulness benefits while potentially embracing the celebratory nature of food [22] and not making people feel as judged about nutritional choices and intake [14,15].

These features are combined into an iPhone application, *Food4Thought*. We evaluate our designs in a three-week field experiment with 61 participants, divided into a 2x2 design comparing *social* vs. *non-social* interventions and *nutrition* vs. *non-nutrition* crumbs. We evaluate participant engagement, mindfulness, and changes in foods consumed.

We found that crumbs generally supported mindfulness and offered opportunities to learn about food. Participants who received nutrition crumbs reported they more often learned about the nutritional makeup of their food, but participants who received non-nutritional crumbs reported larger gains in eating mindfulness. *Social* features helped sustain engagement, were particularly important to engagement with non-nutrition crumbs, and created an opportunity to learn about the variety of foods people use to complete a challenge.

The primary contributions of this work include:

- We introduce and evaluate the concept of a crumb: a lightweight food-related daily challenge.
- Our results offer important insights into creating effective daily food challenges. A more nutritionally prescriptive challenge may result in people learning more about their nutrition, while a more creative and fun challenge may be more effective in improving mindfulness.
- We build upon existing research on the benefits of social features in self-tracking apps. We demonstrate the benefit of social features in supporting engagement, highlighting how these features increase the sense of motivation and accountability while also providing opportunities to learn from other participants.

BACKGROUND AND MOTIVATION

Many people seek to improve their diet in some way, and many approaches have been developed to help people in this general goal. These include more prescriptive techniques (e.g., following a specific diet or reaching certain goals for nutritional content) as well more open-ended techniques (e.g., mindfulness exercises or journaling food eaten without other specific requirements about what is eaten). Regardless of technique, awareness of food and the act of eating is typically a key component of the intervention.

In developing and evaluating crumbs and Food4Thought, we were motivated by research on the benefits and challenges of food journaling, the benefits of increased food mindfulness, and the potential of daily goals and social features to promote engagement. We now review this literature.

Food Journaling

Food journaling is one of the most commonly recommended techniques for gaining awareness of food eaten and for self-regulation of diet. Early food journaling methods used lengthy interviews and questionnaires to collect an understanding of patient eating habits [28]. Paper diaries were later introduced, assisting recall by allowing people to record food nearer to the time of eating. Mobile food tracking applications have more recently become available, and many people prefer them to paper diaries [8].

Despite the prevalence of journaling, food journalers often find it tedious to keep an accurate record of all food consumed, and often fall out of the habit [15]. To reduce the burden, research has examined tracking only meal components (e.g., vegetables, grains) [3], taking meal photos [6,10,14], or marking a meal as "healthy" or not [29]. Byrne et al. demonstrated the potential for an intervention to change eating habits based on one photo of food per day. Adolescents used their app to take a photo of their breakfast, and then used these photos to take care of a virtual pet [10].

People can also give up journaling food or become frustrated with it because it makes them feel judged. In particular, the emphasis on quantification and calorie budgets in many journals can also create feelings of judgment that lead people to abandon journaling [14,15].

Eating Mindfulness

Mindful eating interventions are another technique that also focuses on attention and awareness [23]. Mindfulness focuses attention on present experiences without judgment and without saying what the experience should be [19,23]. Mindfulness interventions are not based in "good" or "bad", nor in prescriptive behavior change. Framson et al. define eating mindfulness as "*non-judgmental awareness of physical and emotional sensations associated with eating*" [19]. Eating mindfulness practices have been found to decrease cravings [1] and reduce BMI for those overweight [24,34].

Many mindful eating programs have taken a Cognitive Behavioral Therapy approach to helping people identify and adopt healthier habits. These often involve in-person sessions [24] or daily home mindfulness exercises [2], spanning multiple months. These mindfulness interventions are designed to mitigate serious eating disorders, and are fairly time-consuming and demanding of participants.

Supporting Engagement & Reducing Barriers in Tracking

In this research, we strive to address two barriers people encounter when engaging with common food interventions. To do so, we design an intervention that imposes lower burdens and that people perceive as less judgmental.

To address our first goal, we draw upon research in small, daily challenges and upon research in social engagement.

Engaging with Small, Daily Challenges

Setting small, achievable goals is a key strategy for behavior change (i.e., take small steps [18]). Goal-setting theory further suggests people exert the most effort when given specific goals [26]. Concrete challenges remove ambiguity about whether and when goals are attained. Publicizing completion of challenges enables public celebration of achievement, which further increases its salience [13].

The use of daily goals has been explored in various research projects and commercial products. Many physical activity applications suggest daily goals (e.g., Houston [12], FitBit). These daily goals tend to be basic and repetitive (e.g., number of steps or active minutes per day). Such goals are effective when tracking requires little effort and feedback is persistent [12], but more varied and interesting goals may support greater engagement and learning opportunities over time.

The Daily Challenge program [11] is one example of a wellness program based on varied, small goals. This program presented participants with a challenge each day, such as reading about where they should store fruit, taking the stairs at work, learning about the salt content of their lunch, or learning about a local issue. In a 30-day trial, participants in this program had greater improvements in well-being scores than participants who received an e-health newsletter [11].

Importantly, we did not design crumbs to replace journaling of all foods for people working to achieve a specific nutrition budget. Crumbs require people engage in only one daily challenge, which consists of photographing just one food selection that meets the challenge's requirements. Informed by results on daily challenges [11] and Byrne et al.'s success with using daily food photos to motivate behavior change in youth, we anticipated that this design of crumbs could present lower barriers but still be sufficient to result in benefits for people generally seeking to improve their eating.

Social Features and Engagement

Prior research also examines social features for increasing engagement in technology-mediated health and wellness interventions. Social features have been used to increase emotional support, informational support, accountability, and motivation [17]. These include sharing goals and progress with one's social network [16,30,31] or on peer support communities (e.g., [6,12], FitBit) and providing opportunities to discuss barriers and ask questions in support forums [37]. Results have been mixed: social features sometimes lead to greater engagement or participation (e.g., [37]), but sometimes have no effect because participants are reluctant to use social features (e.g., [32]), or sometimes the effects cancel each other out (e.g., [31]).

Grouping people who have a common goal has been shown to motivate participation in mobile-social health applications [7]. Other studies have placed people in groups with shared goals as a way to create a shared experience, sense of togetherness, and sometimes competition (e.g., [25]). The Daily Challenge website allows participants to form social ties with other participants, and then to see who among their connections has completed each challenge. Researchers found participants who were socially connected completed 1.85 times as many challenges as those without social ties [35]. However, participants were not randomized into social or non-social conditions, so it was impossible to determine if the social connections increased engagement or if the increased engagement and social connections were instead both a consequence of higher interest in the activity. In this study, we test that casual connection.

Prescriptive vs. Non-Prescriptive

To address the second barrier (i.e., that interventions can be perceived as judgmental, contributing to abandonment), we build upon prior research suggesting activities may not need to be prescriptive to promote mindfulness. The designers of VERA argue that open-ended systems which encourage reflection can offer flexibility that may appeal to people [6]. Grimes and Harper argue the design space for health and wellness systems should include celebratory technology, incorporating positive interactions people have with food to allow room for creativity and pleasure [22]. O'Hara et al. describe using photo mementos of meals as one such technology [33]. Instead of limiting daily goals to nutrition-based or health-oriented challenges (e.g., "eat 100 grams of fiber"), it may be just as beneficial to offer more fun, open-ended challenges (e.g., "eat something purple"). As a result, we designed and evaluated both nutritionally prescriptive and non-nutritionally prescriptive crumbs.

Research Questions

We designed a study to explore and evaluate different points in the design space for lightweight daily food challenges. We sought to design engaging food tracking experiences that would improve eating mindfulness and provide opportunities to learn about food. We selected eating mindfulness as an outcome because it can support many healthy eating goals and is not tied to any single food outcome (e.g., achieving a calorie budget). It can therefore benefit a broad range of people.

We specifically investigated the following research questions:

RQ1. Do crumbs (i.e., lightweight daily food challenges), offer an engaging food tracking experience that results in food mindfulness and learning?

We hypothesized that crumbs can support an engaging experience and would benefit mindfulness and learning.

RQ2. Does (a) engagement or (b) mindfulness differ whether participants receive nutritionally prescriptive challenges or challenges that are not nutritionally prescriptive?

We had competing hypotheses. Non-nutrition crumbs might be more fun and engaging, as they are less prescriptive and allow participants to reflect on or celebrate their behaviors, leading to greater mindfulness. On the other hand, nutrition crumbs may promote greater consideration of the health consequences of food choices and thus greater mindfulness. We also believed nutrition crumbs might provoke additional opportunities to learn about the nutritional makeup of foods, often considered a benefit of traditional food journal methods.

RQ3. Does a discussion board supporting conversation about challenges and sharing challenge achievement with other participants (a) change engagement in the challenges or (b) result in different mindfulness outcomes?

We hypothesized social features would lead to greater engagement and thus greater mindfulness. We further believed social features would provide opportunities for participants to learn from each other.

SYSTEM DESIGN

To evaluate crumbs as tools for engagement, mindfulness, and learning, we developed the mobile food journaling app Food4Thought. Rather than requiring tedious tracking of all foods, it encourages journaling one food or meal a day that meets a daily challenge. The system has two components: (1) a mobile photo-based food journaling app, and (2) a private Facebook group to which photos meeting the day's challenge are posted. We selected Facebook as the social platform because it incorporates the app into many people's routines. It offers methods for encouragement (e.g., likes, comments) and communication (e.g., comments). People also see Food4Thought posts when accessing Facebook for other reasons. Because the Facebook group was private, posts were only visible to others in the study, creating a cohort effect similar to other systems (e.g., [6,7,12,25,35], FitBit).

The mobile app displays a notification of the day's crumb at a configurable time (default 9am), a lesson learned from other journaling systems [9]. A person completes a challenge by taking a picture of a food they ate (Figure 1a, 1b), indicating whether it meets the day's challenge, and adding an optional message. A person can look back at the previous day's challenges (Figure 1e) and at all pictures they have taken with the app (Figure 1f). If an entry meets the challenge, the picture and message are sent to the Facebook group (Figure 1d). Photos are posted to a separate album for each day's challenge, and each photo appears in the group's feed. At midnight each day, Food4Thought automatically posts the number of people who completed the previous day's challenge and a link to the corresponding album. This allows seeing an overview of food others ate to complete the challenges, which later sections will discuss as an important element of the design.

CRUMB DEVELOPMENT AND SELECTION

We define a crumb as a food-related challenge completed by consuming *one* food or meal that meets the challenge. Crumbs begin with a statement of "Eat something …" and end with an attribute of food (e.g., "Eat something crunchy"). To accomplish a crumb, a person must eat a food with that characteristic by the end of the day. This small, actionable challenge requires additional thought about food consumed to complete it, and could therefore increase mindfulness. Crumbs also provide opportunities for food journaling to be fun, social, or competitive while supporting learning.

Nutritionally and Non-Nutritionally Prescriptive Crumbs

We designed and studied two types of crumbs: nutritionally prescriptive and non-nutritionally prescriptive. A nutrition crumb is a challenge that requires thinking about the nutritional makeup of food (e.g., the amount of protein, low sugar, high fiber). A specific example is "Eat something high in vitamin B-12." We chose this type of crumb to be consistent with nutritional information tracked in current food journaling applications.

Inspired by prior work [6,22], we designed non-nutritionally prescriptive crumbs to promote a less corrective and more creative approach to healthy eating. A non-nutrition crumb emphasizes general food attributes (e.g., color or shape, the letter a food begins with, a food's preparation). A specific example is "Eat something that is triangular." Non-nutrition crumbs may imply nutritional values (e.g., "Eat something

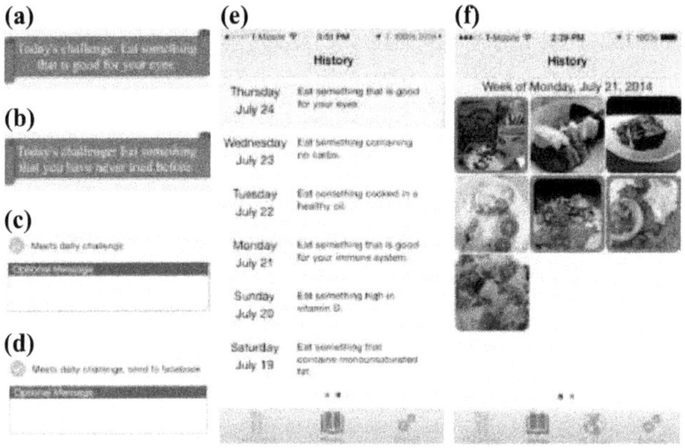

Figure 1. Food4Thought is a mobile food journaling app providing daily challenges and a historical log of food photos. We developed four versions based on a 2x2 design comparing (a) nutrition and (b) non-nutrition crumbs, and (c) non-social and (d) social interventions. Food4Thought included looking back at (e) completed challenges and (f) all pictures taken.

cooked in a microwave", "Eat something that is a dessert"), but are not nutritionally prescriptive. A person completing these crumbs may still make nutritionally beneficial choices (e.g., reheated roasted vegetables, nonfat yogurt), although it is not required (e.g., a pizza roll, an ice cream sundae).

Two members of the research team generated 202 total crumbs. We found it easier to ideate for non-nutritionally prescriptive crumbs, and so we unintentionally generated unequal numbers of the two categories: 42 nutrition and 160 non-nutrition. The supplementary materials contain a full list of crumbs generated.

Verification of Crumb Categories

People have varying beliefs about nutrition, and validity of our experiment required the crumbs in each category reliably be considered as nutritionally prescriptive or non-nutritionally prescriptive. To verify and categorize our crumbs, we obtained opinions from people on Amazon Mechanical Turk. We required Turkers have a 90%+ HIT acceptance rate and at least 100 HITs approved. Given food's cultural nature, we required all Turkers be from the United States to ensure some similarity in food background. Each HIT required rating five different crumbs presented on a single page. We paid Turkers $0.15 per HIT. Turkers rated each crumb according to their agreement with several statements on 5-item Likert scales. Statements included: (1) "I could easily complete this challenge", (2) "This challenge would be difficult to complete", and (3) "This challenge requires me to think about the nutritional makeup of food."

To identify spam responses, we asked both (1) "easily complete" and (2) "difficult to complete" as questions about opposites, to filter responses from Turkers who responded similarly to both questions. We removed all responses where Turkers agreed or disagreed with both questions (i.e., on the same side of a 3 rating on our 5-item Likert scale, labeled as "neutral"). We also removed all responses from a Turker if they gave the same Likert value across all statements for

	Nutrition		Non-Nutrition	
Social	S^+N^+	N=18: 5M, 13F Age: avg 30.17, min 22, max 59	S^+N^-	N=22: 4M, 18F Age: avg 27.64, min 18, max 65
Non-Social	S^-N^+	N=10: 2M, 8F Age: avg 26.78, min 19, max 36	S^-N^-	N=11: 2M, 9F Age: avg 27.20, min 18, max 40

Table 1. Our field study had four conditions, with participants randomly assigned, weighted toward the social conditions.

five or more crumbs. In total, we removed 7.84% of responses as spam. After spam removal, an average of 14.3 Turkers (min: 9, max: 19) evaluated each crumb.

Filtering and Categorizing Crumbs

Before categorizing crumbs as nutrition or non-nutrition, we filtered out potentially controversial crumbs to ensure a clear distinction. For a crumb to be controversial: (1) the median "nutritional makeup" rating from all Turkers must be a neutral 3, or (2) the interquartile range must be greater than two, indicating high variance in Turker responses. We categorized 42 crumbs as controversial (8 by first criterion, 34 by the second, totaling 20.8%). We did not use these crumbs in our field study of Food4Thought.

Remaining crumbs were grouped by median rating of their "nutritional makeup." Crumbs with a median greater than 3 were grouped as "nutrition" (53 crumbs) and the remaining as "non-nutrition" (107 crumbs). For 149 (93%) crumbs, Turkers agreed with the research team's initial assessment. The remaining 11 (7%) were categorized differently ("vegan", "vegetarian", "organic", "fresh and in-season", "grain," "starchy," "colorless," "salty," "citrus," "you would eat before running," "cooked in a healthy oil"). Turkers believed these challenges required considering the nutritional makeup of food, while the research team had not.

We believe the majority of the controversial and differently categorized crumbs arose from Turkers thinking through, and subsequently rating, which food they might eat to complete the crumb, rather than rating the crumb itself. For example, the challenge "Eat something yellow" might lead a person to think of a banana. If they consider this a nutritional fruit, they may deem the challenge to be nutritional. However, the challenge does not prescribe something healthy and could also be met with a lemon tart.

FIELD STUDY OF LIGHTWEIGHT DAILY FOOD CHALLENGES

We conducted a 3-week field deployment of Food4Thought with 61 participants, split in four groups in a 2x2 design: receiving *nutrition* (N^+) or *non-nutrition* crumbs (N^-), and being in a Facebook group *social* (S^+) or a *non-social* (S^-) condition. Participant demographics appear in Table 1.

Participants and Crumb Selection

We recruited from Facebook, Twitter, and university and local mailing lists, describing our study as "using a food application with a random daily challenge." Participants needed to have a Facebook account, own and use an iPhone, and remain in North America during the study (to keep similar time zones within the Facebook group and to ensure similar food opportunities).

Day	Nutrition Crumbs (Eat something…)	Non-nutrition Crumbs (Eat something…)
1	high in fiber.	that is homemade.
2	low in sugar.	that starts with the letter 'A'.
3	high in vitamin C.	cooked on a skillet.
4	under 4 grams of saturated fat.	that is spicy.
5	low in sodium.	that is yellow.
6	with at least 20 grams of protein.	that reminds you of your teenage years.
7	that is organic.	that you would eat in the spring.
8	low in carbs.	that starts with the letter 'S'.
9	that is salty.	that is a dessert.
10	that is good for your eyes.	that is squishy.
11	that you would eat before running.	that is room-temperature.
12	that is whole-grain.	that you would eat on a picnic.
13	high in potassium.	that starts with the letter 'Q'.
14	high in Omega-3.	from a package.
15	that is dairy-free.	that is sour.
16	that is colorless.	traditionally French.
17	that is good for your liver.	that is blue.
18	low on the glycemic index.	that you would eat on Halloween.
19	that is vegan.	that starts with the letter 'W'.
20	high in vitamin A.	cooked in an oven.
21	that is good for your hair.	that you have never tried before.

Table 2. Participants received daily crumbs for 3 weeks, and were assigned to nutrition or non-nutrition conditions.

We stratified participants by Facebook use, ensuring each social condition had equal proportions of people who regularly posted to and read their Facebook timelines. Three people had limited Internet access, so we placed them in the non-social groups such that unreliable Facebook access would not weaken the social intervention. Beyond this, condition assignment was made randomly. Groups contained unequal numbers of participants to ensure social groups had critical mass. Groups were assigned during recruitment, and some participants did not complete recruitment. Six did not start the study after recruitment (4 S^+N^+, 1 S^+N^-, 1 S^-N^+): three did not install Food4Thought, two did not log in, and one dropped out after learning she was pregnant. This participant reported that food photos in her Facebook feed were incompatible with her pregnancy-related nausea.

Using the results from the Mechanical Turk evaluation, we selected challenges to integrate into Food4Thought based on our split of nutrition and non-nutrition crumbs. Within the split, challenges were randomly selected (Table 2).

Procedure

The study consisted of a pre-study survey, a three-week field deployment, a post-study survey, and an optional post-study interview. Participants installed Food4Thought on their own phones. They were compensated $30 and required only to complete the surveys and leave Food4Thought installed for the duration of the study, so challenges would appear daily. Crumb completion was not financially incentivized, and most participants did not complete all crumbs received.

The initial survey contained installation instructions, demographic questions, and questions regarding prior food journaling experience. The final survey contained multiple choice and Likert-type questions about experiences using Food4Thought. Both are available in supplementary materials.

To better understand experiences with Food4Thought and crumbs, we also interviewed 19 participants about their experiences (6 S^+N^+, 6 S^+N^-, 4 S^-N^+, 3 S^-N^-). We selected interview participants based on their responses to open-ended questions in the post-survey (we sought participants who enjoyed or disliked aspects of the study), activity in the social groups, and varied uses of the application (such as journaling all food consumed). An external service transcribed interview recordings, and the research team identified themes and representative quotes.

Measures and Evaluation Metrics

Engagement

We recorded the number of food photos taken with the app (including those marked as completing daily challenges and those not). Social engagement in the social conditions was observed by reading Facebook comments and likes. Usage data was supplemented with survey and interview findings.

Eating Mindfulness

To evaluate the impact of Food4Thought as a mindfulness intervention, we compared scores pre- and post-intervention on the Fred Hutchinson Mindful Eating Scale, a validated scale for mindful eating behaviors [19]. The authors of the scale describe it as "*non-judgmental awareness of physical and emotional sensations associated with eating.*" This scale asks people about their observations and actions around eating, two key principles in mindfulness. In contrast to other eating scales (e.g., the emotional eating scale [4], the three-factor eating questionnaire [39], the binge-eating questionnaire [20]), it is general purpose and does not measure a particular nutritional goal or problem. It is therefore well-suited to participant goals of generally healthy eating.

Questions ask about the frequency of certain food behaviors on a 4-point scale (from Never/Rarely to Usually/Always), of how aware a person is of their food when they are eating (e.g., "*I notice when there are subtle flavors in the food I eat*"), what distracts them from eating (e.g., "*My thoughts tend to wander while I am eating*"), and external factors that contribute to them eating (e.g., "*I recognize when I'm eating and not hungry*"). We used this scale to answer RQ2b and RQ3b. We used three questions from each of the awareness, distraction, and external scales to reduce time burden of the survey. We did not include questions for scales less relevant to our research questions, specifically disinhibition (i.e., "*the inability to stop eating even when full*") and emotional (i.e., "*eating in response to negative emotional states*") scales.

To assist interpretation of these scales, we note that people currently completing at least two hours of yoga per week score 0.30 better on the summary score of the Mindful Eating Scale (i.e., an average of the subscores), while people who have practiced yoga for at least five years score 0.26 better than people who have never practiced yoga [19].

Participants completed this questionnaire in both pre-study and post-study surveys, and we compared change in scores. Four participants did not complete this questionnaire (one in each condition). We report on the remaining 57 participants.

Across all participants, awareness and external scores were highly correlated (r=0.49, p<0.001). We combine them into a single score, and report the change in combined score and change in distraction score from before and after the study.

FIELD STUDY RESULTS

We present our field deployment results in terms of overall Food4Thought usage and our three research questions.

Overall Application Usage

Over the three-week study, participants took 951 pictures of food, 551 of which they identified as completing the daily crumb (some completed the crumb multiple times per day). Participants recorded an average of 15.6 meals (min 1, max 92, average 0.7 per day), 9 of which completed crumbs. Each crumb was completed by at least four participants. Additionally, a server issue for three days potentially resulted in a small loss of data (we estimate approximately 20 entries lost in total, based on participant self-reported estimates).

72% of participants reported they enjoyed receiving crumbs and 46% wanted to continue. S^-N^-9 checked each day's challenge before she went to bed: "*often times I would be pretty excited about the next day's challenge and so I would look at midnight to see tomorrow's challenge.*" S^+N^-5 even described "*gaming the app*" by changing her phone time and date to look ahead at the next few challenges.

Engagement and Mindfulness with Crumbs

Figure 2 shows usage across study conditions over time. Negative binomial regression analysis with participants as a random effect (Table 3) showed a decrease in the number of challenges completed over time (Table 3 Days in Study, 95% CI: 0.8-0.9 fewer people complete a challenge per day across the study). Use of a system often decreases as its novelty wears off, and the effects of reminders also wear off over time [9,21,38]. Participants also described being more engaged at different times in the study: "*I think towards the end I got a little bit lazier*" (S^-N^-9), "*Towards the middle, I would get a little bit forgetful*" (S^+N^-13), "*at the end I got more into the rhythm of it*" (S^+N^+11). Reasons for less engagement included: "*a little bit forgetful*" (S^+N^-13), "*other things going on that just had my attention*" (S^+N^+11), "*vacation*" (S^+N^-5), and "*a new job*" (S^-N^-9).

During post-study interviews, participants also remarked that Food4Thought increased mindfulness. S^+N^+17 said "*As it is, I've been trying to eat healthier, but it's definitely made me more aware*" and that the crumb was on her mind throughout the day "*I always had it on my mind throughout the day, so I definitely think it helped.*" 37 (61%) participants agreed or strongly agreed challenges made them think about food choices for the day. Overall, nutrition and non-nutrition crumbs both prompted participants to think about their food choices for the day, supporting our hypotheses for RQ1.

Changing Food Choices

In both the pre-study and post-study surveys, we asked participants to estimate how many servings of fruits and vegetables and how many servings of high-fat foods

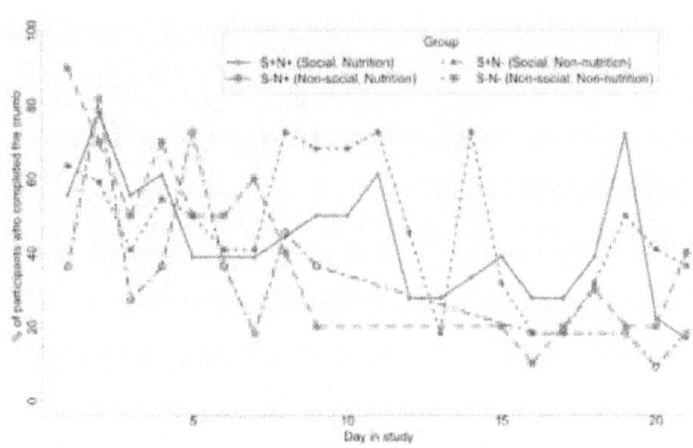

Figure 2. Certain challenges, particularly in the social conditions, resulted in greater completion.

Count Model Coefficients

Variable	Estimate	Std. Error	p
(Intercept)	0.472	0.397	0.584
Social	0.028	0.468	0.371
Nutrition	0.122	0.517	0.204
Social*Nutrition	-0.837	0.586	0.153
Weekend	-0.321	0.152	0.035*
Days in Study	-0.161	0.026	<0.001***
Social*Days in Study	0.102	0.026	<0.001***
Nutrition*Days in Study	-0.005	0.023	0.821

*** p<0.001 ** p<0.01 * p< 0.05 . p< 0.1

Table 3. Challenge completion rate decreased over the study. The effect was mitigated in the social conditions.

(e.g., red meat) they consumed over the past seven days. Participants across all conditions reported increasing their fruit and vegetable consumption since using the application (t_{55}=1.74, p<0.05) but leaving their high-fat consumption unchanged (t_{55}=-0.68, p≈0.75). While we cannot distinguish whether participants changed eating behaviors as a result of the application or overall study participation, this is a promising indicator that crumbs may lead to behavior change.

In the surveys and interviews, many participants said they changed what they ate to complete a challenge: "*There was one day, eat something that has an A and I ate applesauce for breakfast instead of some other fruit. The same thing with 'eat something sour'. I ate yogurt for breakfast, for that reason*" (S^+N^-9) and "*one of the ones that was high in Omega 3, so I decided to have fish for dinner instead of whatever I was going to ordinarily have*" (S^-N^+9).

In some cases, participants changed what they ate for the better: "*I know oranges are very hard to peel, they're kind of annoying, they make your hands dirty, but I know I probably should be eating them, so that one I ate*" (S^-N^+5). However, some changes were for the worse: "*there were days like, 'Eat something from a package.' That was actually the first day of my vacation... we had just filled our kitchen with amazing beautiful fruits and vegetables, and I would not have eaten anything from a package that day, at all, if I hadn't had that challenge*" (S^+N^-5).

Additional Journaling

Although we designed Food4Thought for daily completion of crumbs, people could also use it to keep a photo-based journal of other food. We define 'journaling behavior' as logging food that does not complete a crumb. Although participants in social conditions completed more crumbs than participants in non-social conditions, participants in non-social conditions created slightly more journal entries (Table 4b Social, 95% CI 0.05 to 0.11 more foods during the study). We believe participants in social conditions viewed participation in social challenges as the primary purpose of the app, while some participants in the non-social conditions saw Food4Thought as a food journaling application with the challenges as supplemental feature (e.g., S^-N^+8 described them as "*a nice added bonus*").

Differences between Nutrition and Non-Nutrition Crumbs

We used negative binomial regression analysis to characterize correlations between application usage and study condition. Results are summarized in Table 4, with interaction effects summarized in Figure 3. Table 5 summarizes the difference between food mindfulness scores pre-study and post-study.

Engagement (RQ2a)

Participants who received nutrition crumbs completed more challenges than those who received non-nutrition crumbs (Table 4a Nutrition, 95% CI 1.2-2.3 more crumbs out of 21 during the study). Participants in nutrition crumb conditions said challenges often encouraged improvements they already wanted to make, so they were more motivated to complete them: "*'something low in sugar'. That, in particular, just aligns with my personal dietary beliefs*" (S^-N^+3). People in non-nutrition conditions often felt crumbs were arbitrary or did not have a benefit, which made them less inclined to complete them: "*the arbitrariness of the challenges, like eating a food that begins with the letter 'S' ... It didn't seem like they had a point*" (S^+N^-5); "*I didn't understand what I was getting out of doing the challenge*" (S^-N^-1). This is counter to our expectation non-nutrition crumbs would lead to higher engagement, though the next section notes social features interacted with crumb type: participants were more engaged with non-nutrition crumbs in the social condition.

Mindfulness (RQ2b)

We observed a negative effect of nutrition-focused crumbs on the combined awareness and external scores (Table 5a Nutrition, 95% CI: 0.26-1.85 decrease). Given the overall increase in mindfulness reported in the previous section (Table 5a Intercept, 95% CI: 0.25-1.35 increase), this means that although participation in the study contributed to awareness, it had less of an effect in the nutrition conditions. This is consistent with our hypothesis that the corrective nature of nutritionally prescriptive challenges can interfere with the non-judgmental nature of mindfulness.

Opportunities for Learning

Participants in nutrition and non-nutrition conditions said they looked up foods: "*For almost all of the letter ones, I Googled lists of foods that start with 'A', lists of foods that start with 'Q'*" (S^+N^-5), "*I Googled, saw what was high in Vitamin C*" (S^-N^+9). Crumbs that involved looking up foods were the favorite for participants in the nutrition condition,

(a) Challenges Completed

	Count Model Coefficients		
Variable	Estimate	Std. Error	p
(Intercept)	1.645	0.133	<0.001***
Social	0.662	0.149	<0.001***
Nutrition	0.495	0.171	0.004**
Social*Nutrition	-0.539	0.199	0.007**

(b) Journal Pictures

(Intercept)	3.005	0.067	<0.001***
Social	-2.599	0.187	<0.001***
Nutrition	-0.528	0.113	<0.001***
Social*Nutrition	0.005	0.314	0.735

*** p<0.001 ** p<0.01 * p< 0.05 . p< 0.1

Table 4. Regression results for (a) Number of challenges completed and (b) Number of pictures taken in support of a food journal, varied by level of social and nutrition variables. The intercept indicates a baseline level, while other variables denote the influence of the study conditions. Social*Nutrition denotes the influence of both conditions (S^+N^+) compared to when one condition was absent (S^+N^-), (S^-N^+).

(a) **(b)**

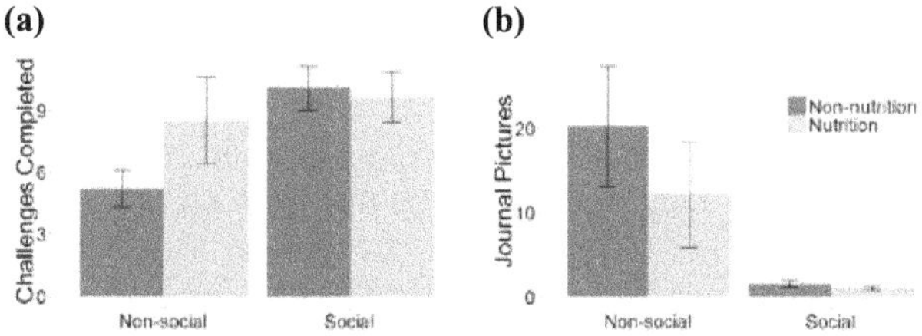

Figure 3. Observed interaction effects between conditions for (a) challenges completed and (b) journaling behavior. Error bars represent 95% confidence intervals.

as they found them more fun: "*the ones that required me to look something up were more fun*" (S^+N^+13). A few participants also said they enjoyed when crumbs made them learn about nutritional factors they did not otherwise consider: "*My favorite ones were... the Vitamin D ones and the 'eat something low on the glycemic index,' I guess those are two things I didn't know much about*" (S^+N^+17).

Participants also liked learning about new foods and their health benefits: "*I liked the 'eat something good for your liver' challenge because I had to look up things that were good for my liver, so I learned something new*" (S^+N^+3). Even when not looking up food, participants reported looking more closely at their food and its health benefits, such as S^+N^+8: "*it made me more conscious of what I was eating ... make me more aware of, 'Hey, what's the health benefit of my Greek yogurt.'*"

Role and Effects of Social Features

The social intervention amplified engagement, especially for non-nutrition crumbs. Participants in the social condition also described learning from other participants.

Engagement (RQ3a)

Participants in the social conditions completed more crumbs than those in non-social conditions (Table 4a Social, 95% CI 1.5 to 2.6 more out of 21 during the study). Participants in the social condition maintained their interest in the study longer (there is an interaction effect between days and being in the social condition; Table 3 Social*Days in Study, 95% CI 1.05-1.17 more people complete a challenge per day in the social condition), supporting our hypothesis in RQ3a that social features promote engagement. In interviews and surveys, participants in the social condition described how the social experience increased their motivation and accountability: "*You just don't want to be the person that doesn't complete any challenges*" (S^+N^-13). S^+N^-3 found posts by others to be motivational, "*It was really interesting to be able to see what everyone else was doing and everyone was kind of really motivated about it... motivating me to [complete challenges].*" Some other participants in the social group became competitive with one another, wanting to complete the crumb in a better or more creative way than others: "*I wanted to do something that was a better fit for the challenge than other people did*" (S^+N^-9).

(a) Awareness & External

	Linear Model Coefficients		
Variable	Estimate	Std. Error	p
(Intercept)	0.796	0.274	0.005**-
Social	-0.662	0.336	0.054.
Nutrition	-1.055	0.398	0.011*
Social*Nutrition	0.920	0.490	0.066.

(b) Distraction

(Intercept)	-0.334	0.184	0.076.
Social	0.451	0.226	0.051.
Nutrition	0.481	0.268	0.078.
Social*Nutrition	-0.753	0.330	0.026*

*** p<0.001 ** p<0.01 * p< 0.05 . p< 0.1

Table 5. Across Food4Thought, we find (a) improvements in food awareness, particularly in non-nutrition conditions, and (b) declines in identification of food distractions.

Social features are most important for engagement with non-nutrition crumbs. We observed an interaction between social features and whether crumbs were nutrition-focused (Figure 3, Table 4a Social*Nutrition, 95% CI 0.4 to 0.9 more non-nutrition crumbs in the social condition, in addition to the strong effect of the social condition itself). Participants in the social condition were more likely to complete non-nutrition crumbs than participants in the non-social condition. Social interaction may have given these otherwise "arbitrary" non-nutrition crumbs a purpose or meaning.

Participants in the social conditions also commented that notifications about posts by others reminded them to engage with the application. S^+N^-4 said "*Sometimes throughout the day I would forget and then I would see some people post stuff on Facebook I would say, 'Oh yeah. I need to go do that'.*" These reminders, as well as the accountability and competitive aspects of the social group, likely supported the higher completion rate and lower drop-out over time.

Experiences with sharing. Participants generally desired more social interaction. S^+N^-9 jokingly recommended we "*make people post more*" when asked for potential study changes. S^+N^+11 tried to engage socially, but was unhappy with her responses: "*I put a little comment on [a post], the guy replied and we moved on, but I was hoping for*

(a) (b)

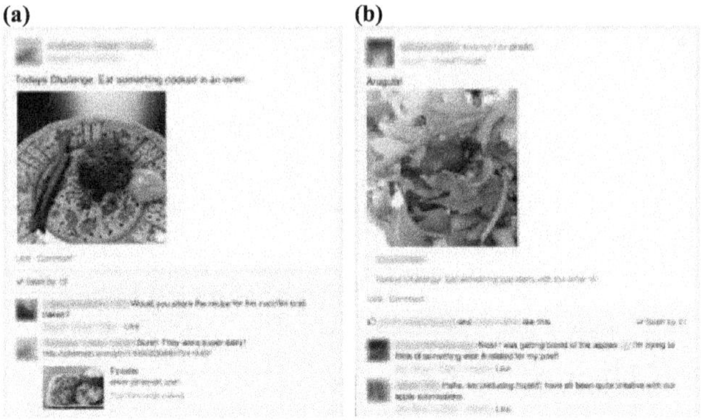

Figure 4. People in social conditions used Food4Thought to (a) learn from others such as by asking for a recipe, or (b) demonstrate creativity in their food choices.

conversation." But most felt social interaction was supportive: "*We're very supportive of others, people were asking for recipes for things that they made and stuff. It was just nice. It's a group of strangers who were all doing the same thing*" (S^+N^-6). Participants regularly liked posts, and occasionally asked for recipes (Figure 4a). Some felt uncomfortable sharing pictures of their food with people who were not friends: "*I felt a bit awkward initially sharing what I'm eating*" (S^+N^-3). However, when asked if they would have completed as many challenges without the group, most agreed with S^+N^-13: "*I would have completed less.*"

Figure 4b shows a discussion between participants about the creativity of their responses to a challenge. Participants worried about being creative, and many often thought of the same foods to complete a challenge. For "Eat something that starts with an 'A'", there were several apple posts, followed by a discussion of how nice it was to for someone to complete the challenge with arugula. Seeing that others shared a picture of the same food they had planned discouraged some participants from completing a challenge: "*if someone else thought of something before me then I felt like I couldn't use that as my challenge because someone else had taken it*" (S^+N^-4), "*if a bunch of people had put 'carrots', I'm not going to put 'carrots'*" (S^-N^+9).

Results support our hypothesis for RQ3a: a social experience made crumbs more engaging than individually completing them by offering motivation, accountability, and competition.

Mindfulness (RQ3b)

Participants in the nutrition-social condition experienced a decrease in identification of food distractions (Table 5b Social*Nutrition, 95% CI 0.09-1.41 decrease). It is possible that the additional social reminders were sometimes a distraction or that social engagement with crumbs took their attention away from the eating experience.

Opportunities for Learning

As in the non-social condition, participants in the social condition looked up foods that completed a crumb. Participants in the social condition further learned through discussion on their posts and by seeing others post in the Facebook group about what foods completed a crumb: "*My favorite ones were... the Vitamin D ones and the 'eat something low on the glycemic index,' I guess those are two things I didn't know much about*" (S^+N^+7). Many commented their diet was boring: "*I'm pretty boring, I tend to eat the same thing for breakfast and lunch every day*" (S^+N^+10). They used the Facebook group to learn about other foods: "*it was nice to see the variety of how some people completed the challenges*" (S^+N^+8), "*I was looking at what others are doing and that gave me some ideas*" (S^+N^-3). Others asked for recipes of dishes that looked good: "*I got a couple recipes which I'm really excited about*" (S^+N^-4). Participants in the social conditions preferred crumbs for which they wanted to see the responses of others, such as creative or tricky challenges: "*The homemade challenge was memorable because I enjoyed seeing what everyone else posted.*" (S^+N^-20), "*the squishy one, I couldn't think of anything and enjoyed seeing what others came up with*" (S^+N^-2).

DISCUSSION

Table 6 summarizes our findings. Our overall results show the potential for low-burden and non-corrective eating interventions. People can obtain benefits in their eating, as demonstrated by the increase in reported food mindfulness, learning about food, and changes in diet, with challenges that require eating and recording only one food per day. Not only are non-nutritionally prescriptive challenges effective, they actually lead to *greater* gains in mindfulness than nutritionally prescriptive crumbs. The remainder of this section discusses challenges around engagement and re-engagement with these activities as well as future opportunities for crumbs.

Designing for Engagement: Difficulty

We sought to design crumbs to be specific and achievable, but open-ended enough that they did not push a particular health goal and could be achieved in a variety of ways. Although participants engaged with crumbs, they still had trouble completing crumbs that were too difficult or required planning. When asked why they did not complete a crumb, 57% of participants indicated they had already decided what they would eat that day, and the challenge did not fit into their plan. Participants also sometimes had trouble identifying foods to complete a challenge (51%) or found a challenge too difficult to complete (31%). S^+N^-5 said "*there's like four foods that begin with the letter 'Q.'*"

In designing the difficulty of a set of crumbs, it is important to consider that crumbs may be situationally difficult. S^+N^+4 said: "*I was really bad on weekends. I left my phone places and didn't have it for long periods of time.*" Participants completed fewer challenges on weekends (Table 3 Weekend, 95% CI 0.57-0.98 fewer people), but it may be possible to design challenges more suited to weekend lifestyles. Varying difficulty to match events in a person's life might help keep a person engaged, and could support playful approaches to promoting mindfulness [21]. S^+N^-5 did not think the crumb itself determined the difficulty, but rather context in her life: "*the hardness felt less to do with the challenge and more to do with my life in that day.*" Designs could consider such

Questio	Measure	Findings
RQ1 (crumbs)	Engagement	Participants completed an average of 9 crumbs. 72% enjoyed receiving crumbs, 46% wanted to continue receiving them. Challenge completion decreased over time (95% CI: 0.8 to 0.9 fewer people per day).
	Mindfulness	Increase in combined awareness and external scores (95% CI: 0.5 to 1.7), decrease in food distraction score (95% CI: 0.0 to 0.8).
RQ2 (nutrition features)	Engagement	Participants completed more crumbs in nutrition conditions than non-nutrition (95% CI: 1.2 to 2.3). Nutrition crumbs better reflected people's food beliefs and felt less arbitrary.
	Mindfulness	Decrease in combined awareness and external score for participants in nutrition conditions (95% CI: 0.1 to 1.7). Non-nutritionally prescriptive crumbs promoted more mindfulness.
RQ3 (social features)	Engagement	Participants completed more crumbs in social conditions than non-social (95% CI: 1.5 to 2.6). Social condition participants did not want to let others in their group down, and found social interaction supportive.
	Mindfulness	No significant effects on the Mindful Eating Scale. Participants in social conditions reported Facebook notifications served as an extra reminder to participate.

Table 6. Crumbs increased mindfulness and created opportunities for learning in an engaging and low-burden manner.

factors as when a person plans meals, as advance notice of crumbs could inform grocery shopping. As another possible direction, a longer period could be provided for complete crumbs (e.g., "Eat something spicy this week"). S^+N^+10 supported this, stating: *"If I knew it sooner... I could plan to incorporate this into whatever I'm eating."*

Designing for Engagement: Social

Although non-nutrition crumbs promoted greater mindfulness, people were less engaged with them on their own. Based on reactions from study participants, we believe it took the social feature to give meaning to these otherwise arbitrary challenges. Future designers and researchers of mindfulness systems and other non-judgmental or non-prescriptive wellness activities might also use social features to give them meaning, or they might work to identify other techniques to create engagement around these activities.

Participants also noted opportunities for social features to be developed further. S^+N^+11 recommended the researchers *"cast some questions out to the group to try and stimulate some interaction between the group members"*, consistent with recommendations from prior work [36]. Another approach is to group people with similar food goals, values, or expertise to promote a shared experience, or simply to evaluate Food4Thought with a group of pre-existing friends.

Social information can also support re-engagement. Although engagement decreased as the study went on, we observed significant spikes in engagement in the social conditions (e.g., at day 13 in the non-nutrition condition: "Eat something that starts with the letter 'Q'", at day 19 of the nutrition condition: "Eat something that is vegan"), but no corresponding spikes in the non-social conditions. When social participants saw an influx of posts completing a challenge, they felt motivated to complete the challenge as well: *"A lot of people were posting in [the Facebook group], so I wanted to post also"* (S^+N^-9). Although this temporary engagement did not sustain to other days, it suggests social features paired with lightweight challenges have a potential to help re-engage people in self-tracking after a lapse.

Future Opportunities for Crumbs

To explore the design space, we designed and selected a broad range of crumbs for inclusion in our study. Future research on crumbs might focus on understanding what aspects of those crumbs contribute to engagement and mindfulness, in both individual and social use. For example, from our study it remains unclear how specific nutrition crumbs should be. "At least 20 grams of protein" is more prescriptive than "high in protein", and may therefore feel more judgmental.

Future crumbs, or sequences of crumbs, could be personalized to individual goals, dietary excesses, or deficiencies (e.g., a vegetarian might request crumbs that exclude meats and promote a need for other proteins). A preliminary questionnaire could identify a person's food-related goals and use them to customize a sequence of crumbs, or the survey could assess a person's food knowledge and provide challenges intended to teach them something new about food. S^-N^+8 recommended that challenges *"be tailored more to where I know I'm weak."*

We also believe there is opportunity to design and evaluate sequences of crumbs for people diagnosed with a health condition with associated food requirements. For example, someone recently diagnosed with irritable bowel syndrome might participate in crumbs that help them discover substitutes for foods that commonly trigger symptoms. We imagine collaboration with nutrition experts and clinicians when designing crumbs to support these targeted goals.

CONCLUSION

We developed Food4Thought to evaluate the notion of a crumb, a lightweight food-related daily challenge that people complete by taking a picture of and consuming one food or meal that meets the challenge's requirement. We also examined how nutritionally prescriptive versus non-nutritionally prescriptive crumbs and the presence of social features affect engagement and mindful eating. We did not design crumbs to replace journaling of all foods for people working to achieve a specific nutrition budget, but did show that they can provide important benefits. Nutrition and non-nutrition crumbs, whether completed individually or socially, increased mindfulness and created opportunities for learning. Although nutrition crumbs had higher participation levels and prompted people to learn more about the nutritional content of food, non-nutrition crumbs resulted in a greater increase in mindfulness. Social participation sustained engagement better than private participation, and social features supported engagement with non-nutrition crumbs. Our findings show the potential of these lightweight, even non-nutritionally prescriptive interventions, and we urge further design and study of such approaches.

ACKNOWLEDGMENTS

We thank Elena Agapie, Elizabeth Bales, Morgan Dixon, and Ravi Karkar. This work was funded in part by the Intel Science and Technology Center for Pervasive Computing, the Agency for Healthcare Research and Quality (1R21HS023654), and the National Science Foundation (OAI-1028195 & SCH-1344613).

REFERENCES

1. Hugo J. E. M. Alberts, Sandra Mulkens, Maud Smeets, and Roy Thewissen. (2010). Coping with food cravings. Investigating the potential of a mindfulness-based intervention. *Appetite*, *55*(1), 160–163. http://doi.org/cfj8dz
2. Hugo J. E. M. Alberts, Roy Thewissen, and Loes Raes. (2012). Dealing with problematic eating behaviour. The effects of a mindfulness-based intervention on eating behaviour, food cravings, dichotomous thinking and body image concern. *Appetite*, *58*(3), 847–851. http://doi.org/fxjm5k
3. Adrienne Andrew, Gaetano Borriello, and James Fogarty. (2013). Simplifying Mobile Phone Food Diaries: Design and Evaluation of a Food Index-Based Nutrition Diary. *Proceedings of the International Conference on Pervasive Computing Technologies for Healthcare (PervasiveHealth '13)*, 260–263. http://doi.org/bbkk
4. Bruce Arnow, Justin Kenardy, and W. Stewart Agras. (1995). The Emotional Eating Scale: The Development of a Measure to Assess Coping with Negative Affect by Eating. *The International Journal of Eating disorders*, *18*(1), 79–90. http://doi.org/fs28bx
5. Ruth A. Baer, Sarah Fischer, and Debra B. Huss. (2005). Mindfulness and Acceptance in the Treatment of Disordered Eating. *Journal of Rational-Emotive & Cognitive-Behavior Therapy*, *23*(4), 281–300. http://doi.org/dkc49g
6. Eric P. S. Baumer, Sherri Jean Katz, Jill E. Freeman, Phil Adams, Amy L. Gonzales, JP Pollak, Daniela Retelny, Jeff Niederdeppe, Christine M. Olson, and Geri K. Gay. (2012). Prescriptive Persuasion and Open-Ended Social Awareness: Expanding the Design Space of Mobile Health. *Proceedings of the ACM Conference on Computer Supported Cooperative Work (CSCW '12)*, 475–484. http://doi.org/bbkm
7. Eric P. S. Baumer, Vera Khovanskaya, Phil Adams, John P. Pollak, Stephen Voida, and Geri Gay. (2013). Designing for Engaging Experiences in Mobile Social-Health Support Systems. *IEEE Pervasive Computing*, *12*(3), 32–39. http://doi.org/bbkn
8. Jeannette M. Beasley, William T. Riley, Amanda Davis, and Jatinder Singh. (2008). Evaluation of a PDA-based dietary assessment and intervention program: a randomized controlled trial. *Journal of the American College of Nutrition*, *27*(2), 280–286. http://doi.org/bbkp
9. Frank Bentley and Konrad Tollmar. (2013). The Power of Mobile Notifications to Increase Wellbeing Logging Behavior. *Proceedings of the SIGCHI Conference on Human Factors in Computing Systems (CHI '13)*, 1095–1098. http://doi.org/f2zs59
10. Sahara Byrne, Geri Gay, J. P. Pollack, Amy Gonzales, Daniela Retelny, Theodore Lee, and Brian Wansink. (2012). Caring for Mobile Phone-Based Virtual Pets can Influence Youth Eating Behaviors. *Journal of Children and Media*, *6*(1), 83–99. http://doi.org/dskw69
11. Nathan K. Cobb and Josée Poirier. (2014). Effectiveness of a Multimodal Online Well-Being Intervention: A Randomized Controlled Trial. *American Journal of Preventive Medicine*, *46*(1), 41–48. http://doi.org/bbkq
12. Sunny Consolvo, Katherine Everitt, Ian Smith, and James A. Landay. (2006). Design Requirements for Technologies that Encourage Physical Activity. *Proceedings of the SIGCHI Conference on Human Factors in Computing Systems (CHI '06)*, 457–466. http://doi.org/b2wmz3
13. Sunny Consolvo, Predrag Klasnja, David W. McDonald, and James A. Landay. (2009). Goal-setting Considerations for Persuasive Technologies that Encourage Physical Activity. *Proceedings of the International Conference on Persuasive Technology (Persuasive '09)*. http://doi.org/cddnsz
14. Felicia Cordeiro, Elizabeth Bales, Erin Cherry, and James Fogarty. (2015). Rethinking the Mobile Food Journal: Exploring Opportunities for Lightweight Photo-Based Capture. *Proceedings of the SIGCHI Conference on Human Factors in Computing Systems (CHI '15)*, 3207–3216. http://doi.org/bbkc
15. Felicia Cordeiro, Daniel A. Epstein, Edison Thomaz, Elizabeth Bales, Arvind K. Jagannathan, Gregory D. Abowd, and James Fogarty. (2015). Barriers and Negative Nudges: Exploring Challenges in Food Journaling. *Proceedings of the SIGCHI Conference on Human Factors in Computing Systems (CHI '15)*, 1159–1162. http://doi.org/bbdt
16. Franco Curmi, Maria Angela Ferrario, Jen Southern, and Jon Whittle. (2013). HeartLink : Open Broadcast of Live Biometric Data to Social Networks. *Proceedings of the SIGCHI Conference on Human Factors in Computing Systems (CHI '13)*, 1749–1758. http://doi.org/bbkr

17. Daniel A. Epstein, Bradley H. Jacobson, Elizabeth Bales, David W. McDonald, and Sean A. Munson. (2015). From "nobody cares" to "way to go!": A Design Framework for Social Sharing in Personal Informatics. *Proceedings of the ACM Conference on Computer Supported Cooperative Work (CSCW '15)*. http://doi.org/bbks
18. BJ Fogg. (2009). Creating Persuasive Technologies: An Eight-Step Design Process. *Proceedings of the International Conference on Persuasive Technology (Persuasive '09)*. http://doi.org/b4vd4k
19. Celia Framson, Alan R. Kristal, Jeanette M. Schenk, Alyson J. Littman, Steve Zeliadt, and Denise Benitez. (2009). Development and validation of the Mindful Eating Questionnaire. *Journal of the American Dietetic Association*, *109*, 1439–1444. http://doi.org/fjzb7h
20. Jim Gormally, Sionag Black, Sandy Daston, and David Rardin. (1982). The Assessment of Binge Eating Severity among Obese Persons. *Addictive Behaviors*, *7*(1), 47–55. http://doi.org/b29mxz
21. Rúben Gouveia, Evangelos Karapanos, and Marc Hassenzahl. (2015). How Do We Engage With Activity Trackers ? A Longitudinal Study of Habito. *Proceedings of the ACM International Joint Conference on Pervasive and Ubiquitous Computing (UbiComp '15)*, 1305–1316. http://doi.org/10.1145/2750858.2804290
22. Andrea Grimes and Richard Harper. (2008). Celebratory Technology : New Directions for Food Research in HCI. *Proceedings of the SIGCHI Conference on Human Factors in Computing Systems (CHI '08)*, 467–476. http://doi.org/cvc429
23. Jon Kabat-Zinn. (1990). *Full Catastrophe Living: Using the Wisdom of Your Body and Mind to Face Stress, Pain, and Illness*. Dell Publishing, New York. http://doi.org/fb57wh
24. Jean Kristeller, Ruth Q. Wolever, and Virgil Sheets. (2014). Mindfulness-Based Eating Awareness Training (MB-EAT) for Binge Eating: A Randomized Clinical Trial. *Mindfulness*, *5*, 282–297. http://doi.org/bbkt
25. James J. Lin, Lena Mamykina, Silvia Lindtner, Gregory Delajoux, and Henry B. Strub. (2006). Fish'n'Steps: Encouraging Physical Activity with an Interactive Computer Game. *Proceedings of the International Conference on Ubiquitous Computing (UbiComp 2006)*, 261–278. http://doi.org/crcvd9
26. Edwin A. Locke and Gary P. Latham. (2002). Building a practically userful theory of goal setting and task motivation: a 35-year odyssey. *American Pyschologist*, *57*(9), 705–717. http://doi.org/d4d932
27. Jennifer Mankoff, Gary Hsieh, Ho Chak Hung, Sharon Lee, and Elizabeth Nitao. (2002). Using Low-Cost Sensing to Support Nutritional Awareness. *Proceedings of the International Conference on Ubiquitous Computing (UbiComp '02)*, 1–8. http://doi.org/cf5gf2
28. Jean W. Marr. (1971). Individual dietary surveys: purposes and methods. *World Review of Nutrition and Dietetics*, *13*, 105 – 64. http://doi.org/bbkv
29. Elina Mattila, Juha Pärkkä, Marion Hermersdorf, Jussi Kaasinen, Janne Vainio, Kai Samposalo, Juho Merilahti, Juha Kolari, Minna Kulju, Raimo Lappalainen, and Ilkka Korhonen. (2008). Mobile diary for wellness management-results on usage and usability in two user studies. *IEEE Transactions on Information Technology in Biomedicine*, *12*(4), 501–512. http://doi.org/fpfv5s
30. Sean A. Munson and Sunny Consolvo. (2012). Exploring Goal-Setting, Rewards, Self-Monitoring, and Sharing to Motivate Physical Activity. *Proceedings of the International Conference on Pervasive Computing Technologies for Healthcare (PervasiveHealth '12)*, 25–32. http://doi.org/bbn8
31. Sean A. Munson, Erin Krupka, Caroline Richardson, and Paul Resnick. (2015). Effects of Public Commitments and Accountability in a Technology-Supported Physical Activity Intervention. *Proceedings of the SIGCHI Conference on Human Factors in Computing Systems (CHI '15)*, 1135–1144. http://doi.org/bbkw
32. Sean A. Munson, Debra Lauterbach, Mark W. Newman, and Paul Resnick. (2010). Happier Together: Integrating a Wellness Application into a Social Network Site. *Persuasive Technology*, 27–39. http://doi.org/fsm763
33. Kenton O'Hara, John Helmes, Abigail Sellen, Richard Harper, Martijn Bhömer, and Elise van den Hoven. (2012). Food for Talk: Phototalk in the Context of Sharing a Meal. *Human-Computer Interaction*, *27*, 124–150. http://doi.org/10.1080/07370024.2012.656069

34. G. A. O'Reilly, L. Cook, D. Spruijt-Metz, and D. S. Black. (2014). Mindfulness-based interventions for obesity-related eating behaviours: A literature review. *Obesity Reviews*, *15*, 453–461. http://doi.org/bbkx

35. Josée Poirier and Nathan K. Cobb. (2012). Social influence as a driver of engagement in a web-based health intervention. *Journal of Medical Internet research*, *14*(1), e36. http://doi.org/bbkz

36. Paul J. Resnick, Adrienne W. Janney, Lorraine R. Buis, and Caroline R. Richardson. (2010). Adding an Online Community to an Internet-Mediated Walking Program. Part 2: Strategies for Encouraging Community Participation. *Journal of Medical Internet research*, *12*(4), e72. http://doi.org/fxc3pg

37. Caroline R. Richardson, Lorraine R. Buis, Adrienne W. Janney, David E. Goodrich, Ananda Sen, Michael L. Hesse, Kathleen S. Mehari, Laurie A. Fortlage, Paul J. Resnick, Brian J. Zikmund-Fisher, Victor J. Stretcher, and John D. Piette. (2010). An Online Community Improves Adherence in an Internet-Mediated Walking Program. Part 1: Results of a Randomized Controlled Trial. *Journal of Medical Internet research*, *12*(4). http://doi.org/bh5ngp

38. Jason J. Saleem, Emily S. Patterson, Laura Militello, Marta L. Render, Greg Orshansky, and Steven M. Asch. (2005). Exploring Barriers and Facilitators to the Use of Computerized Clinical Reminders. *Journal of the American Medical Informatics Association*, *12*(4), 438–447. http://doi.org/cr6q5g

39. Albert J. Stunkard and Samuel Messick. (1985). The Three-Factor Eating Questionnaire to Measure Dietary Restraint, Disinhibition and Hunger. *Journal of Psychosomatic Research*, *29*(1), 71–83. http://doi.org/bkthvb

40. Tammy Toscos, Anne Faber, Kay Connelly, and Adity Mutsuddi Upoma. (2008). Encouraging Physical Activity in Teens: Can Technology Help Reduce Barriers to Physical Activity in Adolescent Girls? *Proceedings of the International Conference on Pervasive Computing Technologies for Healthcare (PervasiveHealth '08)*, 218–221. http://doi.org/cvmffx

41. Christopher C. Tsai, Gunny Lee, Fred Raab, Gregory J. Norman, Timothy Sohn, William G. Griswold, and Kevin Patrick. (2007). Usability and Feasibility of PmEB: A Mobile Phone Application for Monitoring Real Time Caloric Balance. *Mobile Networks and Applications*, *12*, 173–184. http://doi.org/bg67bf

42. Brian Wansink. (2004). Environmental Factors That Increase the Food Intake and Consumption Volume of Unknowing Consumers. *Annual Review of Nutrition*, *24*, 455–79. http://doi.org/fp2pgr

Evaluation of a Food Portion Size Estimation Interface for a Varying Literacy Population

Beenish M. Chaudhry[1], Christopher Schaefbauer[2], Ben Jelen[3], Katie A. Siek[3], Kay Connelly[3]

[1]University of Notre Dame
384 A Nieuwland Science Center, Notre Dame, IN 46556
bchaudhr@nd.edu

[2]University of Colorado
111 Engineering Drive, Boulder CO 80309
schaefba@colorado.edu

[3]Indiana University
919 E 10th St, Bloomington, IN 47408
{bcjelen, ksiek, connelly}@indiana.edu

ABSTRACT
Portion size estimation is important for managing dietary intake in many chronic conditions. We conducted a 6-week field study with nine varying literacy dialysis patients to explore the usability and feasibility of a dietary intake mobile application that emphasizes portion size estimation. Seven participants demonstrated sustained use of the application and improved their self-efficacy, knowledge, and ability to estimate portion sizes in pre- and post-study assessments. Participants reported moments when portion size information in the application differed from their prior understanding, challenging them to reconcile dissonant information. Although participants acquired new knowledge about portion sizes, they struggled to accurately estimate portion sizes in situ for most foods. Despite using the application consistently, rating it highly, and exhibiting learning, we found that self-efficacy and knowledge are not sufficient to support improved behaviors in everyday life.

Author Keywords
Portion estimate; User Interface Design; Mobile Devices; Low Literacy; Self-Efficacy; Health; Behavior Change

ACM Classification Keywords
H.5.2 Information interfaces and presentation (User interfaces): Graphical User Interfaces (GUI), Screen Design, User-centered Design.

INTRODUCTION
People with chronic illness, such as obesity, chronic kidney disease, and cardiovascular disease, must continuously manage their nutrition for maintenance and intervention to avoid the risk of severe health consequences. Since food portion sizes influence nutrient consumption, estimating and tracking portion sizes is a necessary enabler for nutritional assessment. Therefore, people with chronic illnesses critically need a system with accurate portion size estimation to collect this data.

CHI'16, May 07 - 12, 2016, San Jose, CA, USA

ACM 978-1-4503-3362-7/16/05…$15.00
DOI: http://dx.doi.org/10.1145/2858036.2858554

Typically, people can estimate food portion sizes by using nutritional labels or by making volume comparisons with various objects known as estimation aids or reference objects. Despite the popularity of these methods, they can be problematic because people misunderstand labels [23], cannot always have estimation aids with them, and can forget comparison amounts. In addition, these techniques require people to track and calculate total daily intake – tasks that demand reading, writing, and numeracy skills often lacking in low literacy people. As a result, low literacy populations often find it difficult to manage their portion sizes, and are at risk of poor health outcomes.

Technology can help people manage particular aspects of their illnesses and enable them to practice preventative behaviors [24, 28]. Until recently, most technical solutions did not address specific needs of low socioeconomic (low SES) groups – constituting almost 1.4 billion people in the world [35]. Researchers have started to design sociotechnical solutions that can empower low SES groups who often have low literacy skills to handle various life challenges [2, 16] but more research is still needed– especially in health critical applications.

We explored the feasibility of a mobile dietary intake monitoring tracking application, DIMA, for a low SES and low literacy population [13], however DIMA included portion size estimation for fluids only. For this study, we extended DIMA with a picture-based portion size estimation module for all types of foods, DIMA-P. We deployed DIMA-P in a six-week study with nine participants who had chronic kidney disease stage V (CKD V). Our aim was to explore how participants used DIMA-P in situ. In describing our study, we make following contributions:

1. An interactive portion size estimation aid design that met the needs and the abilities of low literacy users;

2. Qualitative analysis of participants' comments about the application that sheds light on how the tool was used;

3. A quantitative analysis showing improved self-efficacy of portion size estimation.

These contributions will help the design community increase their knowledge and understanding about designing effective health behavior change technologies for low literacy populations.

MOTIVATION

We work with CKD V patients who often find it very difficult to comply with their strict dietary regimen [6]. Typically, CKD patients must limit their daily diet to no more than 1 liter of fluid, 2 grams of sodium, 2 grams of potassium, and 1 gram of phosphorus [18]. Transgressions in nutrient consumption can result in serious health consequences and sometimes death [26]. The only treatment is extra dialysis, which causes physical discomfort to patients and increases healthcare costs. We focused on low literacy adults because they often lack skills needed to determine their food portion sizes [23]. Indeed, their limited literacy is a potential contributor to poor CKD outcomes [5]. Moreover, current methods of nutritional assessment for CKD patients are invasive – health providers assess how CKD patients adhere to their diet via blood work, and weighing patients between dialysis sessions to assess fluid consumption.

RELATED WORK

Mobile and ubiquitous computing fields are exploring novel methods for managing and tracking dietary intake. Recent examples include sensors for emotional eating support [8], food photography based healthy food rating systems [19], and electronic food diaries to create food entries [1]. But relatively limited work has been done to design health applications for people with low literacy skills. Moreover, food portion size estimation in diet tracking applications has not been sufficiently explored for people who want to increase their ability to estimate.

Diet Management Applications

Recent research in designing food recording technologies for low literacy users tackle design issues with respect to the effort involved in tracking. Photograph-based food diaries can minimize the effort involved in tracking; however, such journals often do not provide any nutritional information. Cordeiro and colleagues developed a photograph-based mobile food journal that people could use to document their socio-emotional and other contextual information based on their dietary goals [15]. Other designs enable users to understand nutrition with respect to their health goals [19, 29]. Other researchers explored simplified food diaries that focus on recording food groups as opposed to specific nutrients or food items [1, 3], but found that users prefer more detailed food diaries [1].

Technologies that specifically target dietary intake in low SES populations include interactive nutritional educational programs that are either game-based [21] or use multimedia to promote learning [20, 33]. Other researchers have developed mobile application-based interventions for low socioeconomic individuals to provide support for healthy eating. SnackBuddy explores how family members use a sociotechnical system to support each other's healthy behavior [39]; whereas, DIMA engages an individual in reflection of their own health data [13]. Another notable technology solution for low SES individuals is Grimes and colleagues' voice forum that allows low SES users to exchange their food memories using voice recordings [20].

Portion Estimation Technologies

Three main classes of technologies in this domain are: food photograph based applications; human computing based commercial nutritional assessment services; and experimental, automatic portion estimation prototypes. We discuss representative projects in each class.

Portion Size Photographs based Applications

Dietitians typically use native and web-based desktop applications during nutritional assessment recall interviews [44, 46]. These applications consist of photographs of one meal in multiple portion sizes making them resource intensive and unsuitable for mobile devices. Applications such as MAPMAAL are less resource intensive as they allow dietitians to manipulate meal photographs by rubbing away its parts via a touch screen [12]. These interface designs support reporting (not necessarily in situ) and recalling rather than learning and understanding portion sizes. They may also require regular updates with new meal photographs and nutritional values prior to use. We evaluated interface designs based on portion size estimation strategies people regularly use [10], thus DIMA-P's interface has fewer and static images that assisted in designing a low resource intensive mobile applications with minimal updates.

Human Computing Based Portion Estimation

Some web and mobile nutritional assessment applications (e.g., MycaNutrition, http://www.mycanutrition.com) accept dietary intake through alternative input mechanisms such as camera and voice [31]. A human facilitator then performs portion size estimation and sends nutritional feedback to the user. These systems have the capability to simplify portion size estimation tasks, but may be unsuitable for low literacy, chronically ill populations because they: (a) do not always provide real-time feedback; (b) could be inaccurate either because the user is unable to accurately describe their food selection to the system or the human (e.g., mechanical Turk) is not appropriately trained to provide accurate feedback; (c) are mainly for tracking purposes and not designed to help people learn portion estimation skills. We wanted people to improve not only their ability to track their diets, but also create opportunities for them to practice and develop skills that can lead to long-term behavior changes.

Automated Portion Size Estimation

Automated portion size estimation systems offload the task of portion size estimation from the user. This class includes systems augmented with external hardware such as cameras [48, 49] and ambient-embedded sensor devices, such as a dining table that determines consumed food amounts via container's weight change [9]. Another example is a sensor-

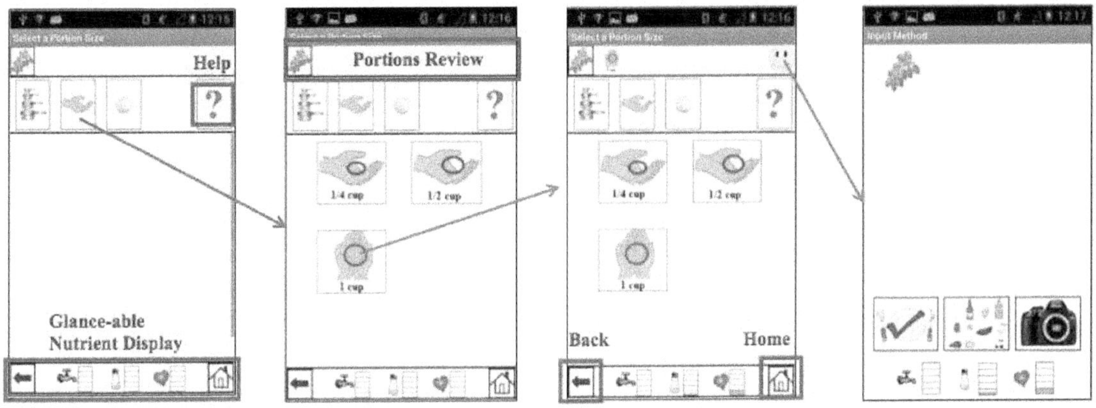

(a) Estimation Aids (b) Hand Gestures (c) Two Handfuls (d) Current Meal (Home)

Figure 1 © Beenish Chaudhry. Recording two handfuls of grapes on DIMA-P: (a) Portion Estimation Interface for Fruits with no Estimation Aid selected; (b) Hand Gestures Estimation Strategy selected, three possible portion estimates; (c) Two Handfuls selected and Smiley face is evident because user has not exceeded nutrient limits; (d) Home Page after entering grapes

rich cup that identifies the type and amount of liquid consumed [27]. On-body sensor devices can estimate food portion size based on timing and count variables of the chewing cycle structure [32]. Experimental studies suggest these automated systems can be highly accurate and robust in estimating food portion sizes. This is promising in terms of providing accurate feedback to users, however such systems are still experimental and do not allow users to interact with the data such that they can understand or improve their portion estimation skills.

In summary, current systems are not focusing on empowering or improving the portion size estimation abilities of individuals. Most do not specifically target low literacy people who have special needs and limitations with respect to using and interacting with informational technologies. Our research tries to fill in these gaps while increasing our understanding around designing behavior change technologies.

APPLICATION OVERVIEW

For this study, we extended the original DIMA application with a portion size estimation module informed by prior work [10]. DIMA is a diet tracking mobile application that we designed and developed through an iterative user-centered design process. DIMA provides users with the ability to record their meals via a picture-based interface. To locate a food item, the user must traverse a set of food category screens via a simple linear navigation. The food categories were a combination of USDA-recommended categories and target-user defined categories based on a prior study [42]. By grouping food items under categories, we limited the number of pictures to show on the small screen of a smartphone and not overwhelm the user. In the extended version of DIMA, referred to as DIMA-P, after selecting a food item, the user views the portion size estimation module. The module consisted of twenty-four distinct interfaces - a subset of the interfaces is shown in Figure 2. Each interface consisted of 2-4 reference objects or household containers specific to the chosen food's shape, size, and physical state (i.e., solid – definite geometric shape, amorphous – no defined shape, or liquids – container's shape). From that interface, the user can select an appropriate portion size and immediately see a visualization of its effect on their cumulative nutrient intake. Users view the real-time feedback and can adjust their current or future meals.

In designing this picture-based module, we aimed to enhance low literacy, chronically ill people's: (a) ability to estimate food portion sizes; and (b) self-efficacy in using estimation aids and household containers. We incorporated constructs specified in the Integrated Theory of Health Behavior Change (ITHBC) in the portion estimation module's design. ITHBC suggests that health behavior change can be enhanced by fostering knowledge and beliefs, increasing self regulation skills and abilities, and enhancing social facilitation [34]. (Since we wanted to focus on understanding participants' own ability to use and learn from the estimation module, we did not incorporate social facilitation in this version), In addition, we incorporated goal-setting, where the application sets the (nutrient consumption) goals for the user based on health professional's recommendations.

The topmost section of any interface from the estimation module is called Portions Review section (Figure 1.b). This is where the currently selected portion sizes can be seen. The bottommost section is the glance-able nutrient display (Figure 1.a) where current intake amounts of three critical nutrients – fluid, sodium, and potassium are displayed. Clicking the glance-able display opens the feedback page where additional nutrient values are visible. The HOME and BACK icons (Figure 1.c) are on either end of the nutrient display allowing the user to exit if they decide not want to save the current recording.

Let's assume Sally wants to decide how many grapes to eat. She first selects grapes by navigating through the food category screens, as described in our prior publication [13] on the DIMA application. After Sally selects grapes, the screen in Figure 1.a opens where she can select an estimation aid from: measuring cups, hand gestures, and spherical objects. If she wants to use hand gestures to estimate the amount of grapes to eat, she clicks the hand gestures. The screen then changes to Figure 1.b where she can select the appropriate portion estimates obtainable from various hand gestures.

Each of these portion estimates is linked to a nutritional entry in the underlying database. When a portion estimate is selected, the associated nutritional values are displayed in the glance-able nutrient display (Figure 1.a) in real time. Changes to the nutrient display provide Sally with the opportunity to learn about the effect of a portion size on her daily cumulative intake and the nutritional content of the targeted food item. This awareness can help shape her beliefs and knowledge about her intake. Sally can also open the help page by clicking the Help icon (Figure 1.a) to learn more about estimation aids.

If Sally's selection puts any of the nutrients above 80% of her restricted limits or nutrient intake goals, the associated nutrient chart in the glance-able display becomes red. By monitoring changes to the glance-able display, Sally can learn to self-regulate either by decreasing her portion size or changing what she is eating. Otherwise, she can continue to record up to six portions at one time – for instance if she desires to eat more grapes, she can select another handful. The selected portion images are stored in the Portions Review bar (Figure 1.b). Sally can edit Portions Review bar by clicking it. The nutrient values in the glance-able display change in real-time as Sally adds or deletes portions from Portions Review. Through these intentional interactions and enacted feedback, Sally can plan her meals easily. The ability to modify portion sizes provides Sally with the flexibility needed to keep within her strict dietary limits – the closer to these limits she gets, the more creative she needs to be to figure out what she can eat.

If Sally's selection of portions keeps her below her recommended amounts, a smiley face appears in the right corner of Portions Review bar to let her know that she is staying within her nutritional limits. If her choices redden any nutrient chart in the glance-able display, a check mark appears in place of the smiley face. Ultimately, Sally has to click either the smiley face or the check icon to save portion sizes (Figure 1.c) and exit the estimation module.

METHODS

In this paper, we analyze the portion size estimation module's usage; participants' reactions to the module; challenges and successes of the module; and changes in participants' self-efficacy and estimation abilities.

Study Design

After receiving ethics board approval, we conducted a 6-week field study with low-SES CKD V patients. The recruitment and interviews were conducted in a dialysis unit during the first two hours of dialysis to accommodate participants' comfort and schedules. Participants were paid $25 after the baseline interview, $25 after self-monitoring for 6-weeks, and $25 after the post self-monitoring interview. Compensation was not tied to application usage.

Baseline Assessment

At the first meeting, individuals completed a background questionnaire and Newest Vital Sign (NVS) [47]. NVS is an assessment that measures ability to read, understand, calculate, and apply health information.

During the second meeting, participants were trained to use the mobile phone and DIMA-P. To ensure that participants could use the application on their own, they had to pass a competency assessment test consisting of thirteen tasks. The tasks included things like making a food entry, interpreting the feedback page, and opening the help page of estimation module. Until participants could successfully complete all thirteen tasks on their own, they could not enter the next phase. Each participant passed the test after 3-5 training sessions, each lasting for 40-60 minutes. Number of training sessions did not correlate with literacy and no one could pass the test in the first try.

Once a participant passed his competency test, we conducted three Portion Size Estimation Tests. The first test, *Pictures,* assessed participants' ability to select an image from the estimation module that accurately represented portion size of a pre-weighed food sample. Twelve food samples were used in this test. Participants received 1 for correct answer and 0 otherwise. The second test, *Apportion*, evaluated participants' ability to portion out ten food samples in specified amounts (the researcher was trained to identify correct amount based on known facts, for example, half an apple is half a cup, and 4 ounces of rice is ¾ of the provided 6-ounce container). Correct responses received a 1, and 0 otherwise. In the third test, *Containers*, participants provided their estimates of the volumes of 12 real household utensils and containers. Similarly, participants were given 1 for a correct response, and 0 otherwise. Finally, participants took the Portion Size Estimation Self-Efficacy Scale (PSESES), a validated instrument developed by Ayala [4] to measure two aspects of self-efficacy specific to portion size estimation: judging portion sizes in various situations, and using estimation aids and household containers. The questions were read aloud to participants who answered on a 5-point Likert Scale.

Self-Monitoring

After the completion of the Portion Estimation tests, participants entered 6-weeks of self-monitoring. They

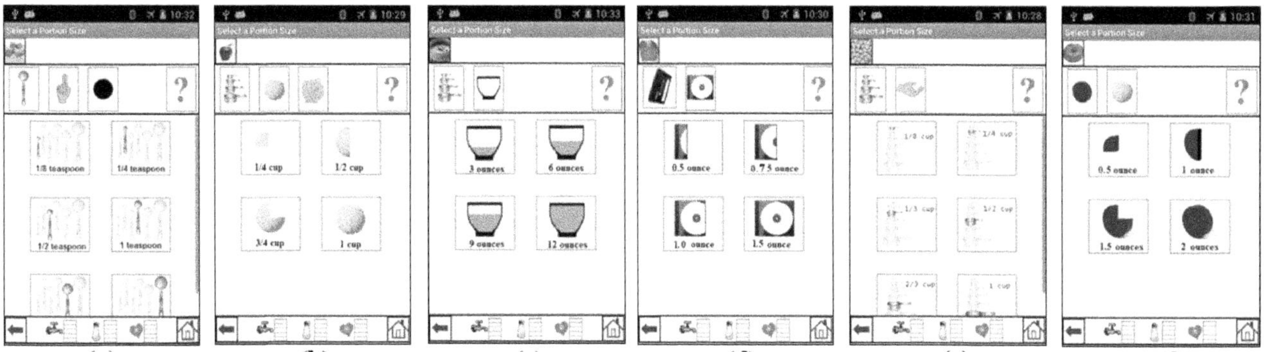

(a) (b) (c) (d) (e) (f)

Figure 2 © Beenish Chaudhry. Example Interfaces from Portion Size Estimation Module (a) Measuring Spoons for Condiments (b) Tennis Ball for Fruits (c) 12 ounce Bowl for Soup (d) CD Case for Breads (e) Measuring Cups for Legumes (f) Hockey Puck for Bakery Items

received a 25-page picture-based user manual showing how to use DIMA-P, including taking pictures, entering food items, and estimating portions. During this phase, participants recorded their dietary intake and portion sizes. They also photographed their meals both before and after eating. They placed a reference object, e.g., card deck, in these photographs to help us estimate food amounts against a standard sized object. We had face-to-face encounters with the participants three times a week during the first two weeks of self-monitoring for a total of 6 times. During each meeting, we resolved issues related to application usage, and answered questions related to the study. For the remaining four weeks, we were accessible via phone.

End of Self-Monitoring Assessment

At the end of six weeks, we met with participants to collect their phones, and conduct an end of study assessments. We conducted the same Portion Size Estimation Tests and the PSESES instrument we had used at the baseline. Participants verbally responded to the modified Rawl usability questionnaire [36], which consists of 25 closed and 3 open-ended questions, asking participants to evaluate attractiveness, comprehensibility, user-friendliness, and usefulness of the application. Participants also explained their responses to closed questions that were written and used in the qualitative analysis. In addition, they also responded to a context of use questionnaire consisting of 25 closed and 3 open-ended questions. Finally, participants responded to eight open-ended questions that assessed their self-efficacy of self-regulating their portion intake.

Participants

We approached 15 patients in an urban dialysis facility and eleven agreed to participate. Two patients dropped out within the first week (due to difficulty seeing the screen due to cataracts, and feeling too sick to participate). In this paper, we report on the nine patients who completed the study. The study sample included two women and seven men – everyone was Black/African American with an average age of 49.4 years (SD = 8.0 years). All participants were on Medicaid and lived in a low-income neighborhood. Participants had on average 12.6 years of education and demonstrated varying reading and functional literacy levels based on NVS scores. Two participants scored 0-1, suggesting a high likelihood of limited literacy; three scored 2-3 indicating the possibility of limited literacy, and four scored 4-5 signifying adequate literacy. We classify those who demonstrated high likelihood and possibility of limited literacy as low literacy – marked with † in Table 1.

Participants' technology familiarity ratings can be described as: (a) low – did not use computers more than once a month and never used a mobile phone before the study; (b) medium – used computers a few times a month and may have used a mobile phone before; (c) high – used a computer every day, and had also used a mobile phone including a few mobile application games before. None of the participants used computers for anything other than chatting, surfing and social networking.

Six participants reported watched their portion sizes while eating either by not cooking too much or by eyeballing the amount they put on their plates. Only two participants were familiar with the term 'estimation aid.' None of the participants reported tracking or calculating their daily nutritional intake despite a strict and prescribed nutritional regimen. Six participants regularly had problems maintaining their blood phosphorous within a normal range.

Analysis

The data collected during the study included: (i) application usage logs; (ii) inter-dialytic weight gain and blood nutrient levels; (iii) participants' food and fluid entries and portion sizes recorded during the self-monitoring phase (meal logs); (iv) meal photographs captured by participants both before and after they ate; (v) participants' responses to the pre- and post-study portion size estimation tests; (vii) pre- and post-study responses to PSESES instrument; (viii) post-study knowledge of reference objects; (ix) post-study responses to modified 28-item Rawl usability questionnaire; (x) responses to context of use questionnaire; and (xi) participants' post-study comments and impressions about using a portion size estimation module.

	Tech Fam.	Years of Ed.	NVS	Use Days	Average Daily Portion Sizes
P1*†	Medium	14	3	42	8.76
P2	Low	13	4	17	5.86
P3†	Low	14	2	27	3.52
P4*†	Low	12	3	41	8.14
P5†	Medium	12	0	-	-
P6*	Medium	12	5	42	9.19
P7†	Medium	13.5	1	34	3.08
P8*	High	12	5	40	8.97
P9	Medium	11	5	28	3.39

Table 1. Participants' Tech Familiarity, Literacy Levels, and Application Use (Key: Ed. = Education; Fam. = Familiarity)

In this paper, we focus on how participants used the portion estimation interface, how they felt about using it, and how their self-efficacy and portion estimation abilities changed. We used logs of all participants except P5 because their logs were accidently erased during extraction from the device. We used the Data Package in Microsoft Excel for quantitative analysis of application usage logs. To determine accuracy of portion sizes recorded in meal logs, the primary author determined the ground truth of estimates using a combination of methods such as fiduciary marker, container sizes, and packaging information in corresponding meal photographs. The estimate was determined to be accurate if participants selected the portion size that was closest for the particular estimation aid they chose to use. For example, if they were recording 1.5 ounces and chose the hand estimation aid, a full-cupped hand was the closest (representing 2 ounces); whereas if they used the deck of cards estimation aid, half a deck was the closest (representing 1.5 ounces).

The qualitative data included participants' unstructured, written responses to the usability and self-efficacy instruments, and their reflections on their experience with the portion size estimation interface recorded during the interviews. Two researchers independently coded the data at the sentence level using Dedoose. Codes emerged through open and inductive processes, which the research team then iteratively refined to develop consensus. A total of 23 codes were initially generated, then grouped into the main themes described in this paper.

RESULTS

A majority of the participants demonstrated sustained use of the application. Participants' literacy skills tested in NVS did not have any relationship with the usage of estimation module. Overall, participants found the estimation module easy to use and apply. Time and effort involved in using the module did not cause any concern. The major successes of the estimation module included its effectiveness in helping participants develop and practice portion estimation skills and learn knowledge. This led to improved self-efficacy and increased awareness of one's eating habits. Some of the challenges included lack of specific reference objects for some food items, and inapplicability of a certain class of reference objects to some participants.

Application Usage

We classified participants into two groups according to their frequency of recordings with the portion estimation interface. The first group recorded an average of 8-9 portion sizes per day, and the second recorded an average of 3-4 portion sizes per day. This helped us define an active participant (marked with * in Table 1) as one who recorded at least six portion sizes on at least half of the study days.

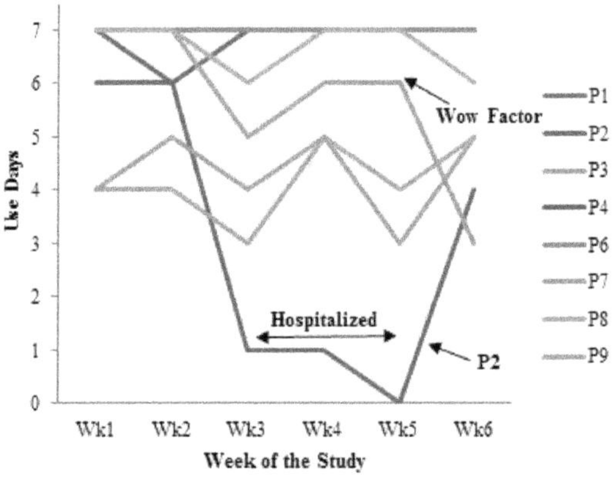

Figure 3 © Beenish Chaudhry. Use Days by Week

We also studied DIMA-P usage in terms of the number of days they used the application (use days) in each week of the study (Figure 3). Five participants showed a drop in use days in the third week. This corresponds to the time when the researcher stopped face-to-face meetings with the participants. Five participants increased usage in the last week, including P2 who did not use DIMA-P from week 3 to week 5 due to a hospital admission. One participant (P7) showed a significant decrease in the application use over the course of the study – a phenomenon known as the "wow factor" (Figure 3) [13]. Overall, even the most infrequent users used the application somewhat regularly during the study. Moreover, there was an increase in use days in the last week among most participants, suggesting incentives could have been a motive.

To understand how participants' daily interactions with the application changed over the course of the study, we used a quality of use metric also used in the original DIMA study [13]. A day was rated High (2) if more than one recording was made in a day, Medium (1) for only one recording, and Low (0) for no recording during the day. Based on weekly averages of the daily ratings, we found that four participants maintained high and two maintained low quality of use. The remaining two (one of them was P2) decreased their quality of use from high, in the first two weeks, to medium, in the final two weeks. The majority of participants had multiple interactions with DIMA-P every day during the study. This result is similar to the first pilot study, where there was no portion size estimation module.

User Experience

From the usage logs, we learn that the recording time with DIMA-P was longer than with DIMA, 35.4 seconds versus 13.5 seconds. However, use days and quality of use metrics show that introducing portion estimation, which increased task completion time, did not significantly change the usage. From the usability questionnaire, we learn that, overall, participants found the application easy to use (Median=4; SD=0.97). They also found it easy to do portion size estimation with DIMA-P (Median=5; SD=0.73). They thought the information on the portion estimation interface easy to understand (Median=5; SD=0.53). Watching their dietary intake with DIMA-P was a satisfactory experience for most participants (Median= 4; SD=0.44). Finally, most participants were willing to use the application again (Median=4; SD=0.93), and also wanted to recommend it to others having trouble managing their diet (Median=4; SD=1.32).

Portion Size Estimation Module's Usage

To understand how participants used the portion estimation interface, what they felt about using it, and how well it fulfilled their portion estimation needs, we describe the six key themes that emerged from participants' post-study comments about their experiences. We discuss each theme with supporting quotes from participants.

Strategies in Selecting Aid Portions

Participant developed metrics to ensure they were accurately interpreting the information on the estimation interfaces. Individual seemed to gravitate towards a small set of aids they wanted to apply based on three criteria:

Flexibility: an aid's ability to define a portion size even when it did not fit a food's shape or composition – "*Deck of cards was my gauge*" (P7†).

Physical Availability: an aid's availability in the physical world even when it was not difficult to imagine other presented aids. "*It was not difficult to imagine the size of baseball; but I did not want to do it. I just relied on my hands*" (P6*). "*If I am not sure how much I am eating, I would drop it in a measuring cup to check*" (P4*†).

Relevance: the number of times an aid was used or interacted with by the participant in the real world. The lesser an object's relevance to participants, the harder it was for them to create its mental image and find it useful. "*I have not looked at the hockey puck for a long time so I forget, and it becomes difficult to imagine*" (P2). "*For people who are not into sports, find something else to measure"* (P8*).

Conflict between internal beliefs and external information

Participants consistently reported a feeling of surprise or disbelief around what the application told them was a certain portion size. When first beginning to use the application, users identified a misalignment between their own beliefs around what a portion size of a food looked like and what the application told them. Many users aligned their beliefs with the application information and then reported integrating that knowledge into their practice – "*I was shocked to find out, it was different. My perception about values of different containers was not correct. Before you just drown it in gravy because it tastes good, but now you know how it is, you are taking in too much*" (P8*).

Participants described two processes that helped them reconcile the information provided in the application with their beliefs – performing confirmatory testing to check the accuracy of the application and continued application use. P2 used a physical version of the aid to confirm information in the application – "*it is not believable that the object is that much weight but when you look at the actual size of the object it becomes believable. I [had] not looked at the deck of cards for a long time so I forgot.*" P5† used a scale to confirm the application's information – "*I had to weight it out ... to match the pictures on the screen.*" Instead of conducting confirmatory testing, P1*† continued practicing with the application to develop confidence in the application's estimators – "*I had knowledge of certain sizes but I was not right; it helped me [to] practice.*"

For a few participants, some images remained unbelievable after continuing to use the application. P2 had difficulty because the images of the objects were too unfamiliar to be deciphered properly. P2 pointed out that they could not believe "*an image [pointing to ¼ of cassette] is 0.25 ounce bread.*" They admitted they were not able to identify the object in the image. P8* also reported having difficulty believing the application, even after continued use: "*Some of the portion sizes are not believable like I cannot believe that cheese about the size of 2 playing cards side by side is 1 ounce.*" P8* cited their disbelief of some of the estimators as their primary frustration with the application.

Learning through application use

Participants described three different ways that they gained knowledge and skills through using the application: 1) *specific, factual information*; 2) *practical skill-based knowledge*; and 3) *personal information about an individual's own behavior.*

During the post-study interview, some participants reported being able to learn specific factual information around what size different portion aids represented – "*5 crackers = ½ ounce; mini muffin = 3 ounces; fist = 1 cup*" (P8*) and "*I had knowledge of certain sizes but I was not right; it helped me practice what my dietitian always tells me to do; I remember 1 Golf ball = 1 ounce; Fist = 1 cup; Handful = ½ cup; deck of cards = 3 ounces of meat*" (P1*†) – and conversions between measurement units – "*show more comparisons like 4 tablespoons = 1/4 cup*" (P7†).

One thing that users appreciated greatly was the opportunity afforded by the application to practice their portion size estimation skills. Some participants wished they had more time to use the application, as they had just started learning to manage their health outcomes. "*The study should have been for at least 90 days. I think you see more changes* [in health outcomes i.e. inter-dialytic weight gain and portion estimation skills] *in this time period*" (P8*). Many suggested that they gained some level of skills that they would be able to take forward in their life, even without having the application or reference objects in their lives.

Main Uses: Reference and Feedback

Participants admitted that the applications helped them make choices when they were approaching limits. "*I slowed down when it was red and I tried to watch what I eating" (*P4*). However, participants noted that the application could have suggested specific foods or portion sizes based on their current intake: "*It needs to be dynamic and tell people how much to eat* [when they are close to their recommended limits]" (P3†).

Participants also admitted that the application helped them eat less and work towards their own specific goals. "*It taught me how to eat less*" (P1*†). "*Documenting helps you make better choices and how much to eat*" (P3†). Participants were also interested in seeing how consuming a certain portion size would affect their weight gain between two dialysis sessions: "*It should show how it* [a portion] *is going to change my weight*" (P7†).

Limitations of the Estimation interface

Participants thought the estimation interface needed to be more specific in identifying different scenarios - such as when different preparations of the same food could vary greatly. One individual reported, "*It just had too little options for cooking, like potato you can eat it mashed or cubed or fries. Some of the places, it was not enough options like candies come in so many different shapes and sizes. There is a very long candy and some potatoes are grown as finger potatoes*" (P8*). This was also an issue in home-prepared food versus restaurant food – "*I think choices need to be more definitive. For example, there are so many different sizes of hotdogs. I know at home they are small size but when you go to convenience store they are bigger*" (P3†). A better clarification of portion images was also desired. "*Some of the portion pictures need more explanation, for example the meat about the size of card deck is 3 ounces with bones or without bones"* (P2).

Another emergent concept was the time and effort to enter all the ingredients of a prepared meal to get more accurate feedback. "*Sometimes you eat so many things and then you have to think about portion size for each one of them and it becomes time consuming but I want to lose weight and want to track everything that I am eating"* (P1*†).

In our face-to-face contact during self-monitoring phase, several participants pointed out that they were having trouble maintaining their blood phosphorous levels. We note that these participants would have benefited from having phosphorous in the glance-able nutrient display – currently it is only shows fluid, sodium and potassium.

Successes	Concerns/ Challenges
Flexibility of reference objects	Irrelevance/ unavailability of certain reference objects
Promotion of knowledge and learning with respect to portion size estimation	Mismatch between internal belief and external representation
An opportunity to practice skills and apply knowledge	Lack of specific reference objects for portion estimation with respect to prepared meals
Improvement in decision making and self-efficacy	Time and effort involved in estimating portion sizes
Awareness of one's own behaviors was promoted by real-time feedback	Limitations with respect to understanding/ managing overall personal health

Table 2. Estimation Module's Successes and Challenges

Portion Size Estimation Self-Efficacy

During the post-study interviews, participants made comments that suggested an increase in their self-efficacy around measuring portion sizes and integrating portion size measurement into their eating practices. "*I knew about estimation aids from my dietitian but I never used them. This tool helped me practice what my dietitian always tells me to do*" (P1*†). Another concept emerged around participant's confidence in their knowledge of their own practices. "*I was already measuring my fluid but it helped me realize how quickly I ate 4 ounces of peanut butter"* (P3†), and "*It added a lot of knowledge. It showed me what the heck I was doing and how to do it better*" (P7†).

Self-Efficacy in	Pre-Study	Post-Study
Estimating portion sizes in various situations	4.13 (SD=1.17)	4.60 (SD=0.92)
Using estimation aids and household containers	3.33 (SD=1.25)	4.56 (SD=0.90)

Table 3. Descriptive Statistics for Subscales of PSESES

In their post-study reflections, participants pointed out that before the study, they thought they knew portion sizes. But during the study they learned that their perceptions were not necessarily accurate. "*Before I thought I could* [estimate portion sizes] *but I found out I could not. Like my idea of ½ cup was more than a fist. But now I know better*" (P8*). "*It helped me learn to do the right thing. I thought I could do it before but it makes more sense now*" (P9).

The mean score on both subscales of PSESES improved post-study. A paired t-test comparing pre and post-test responses to the PSESES questionnaire revealed a significant difference in participants' confidence in estimating portion sizes, $t(8) = 3.32$, $p=.011$, and their confidence in using estimation aids and household containers, $t(8) = 3.62$, $p =$

.004. These results, although with a small sample, support the finding that participants felt a greater sense of self-efficacy in estimating portion sizes and using estimation aids and household containers to support their assessment of portion size.

Pre and Post Portion Size Estimation Tests

	Pictures (Max=12)		Measure (Max=10)		Containers (Max=12)	
	Pre	Post	Pre	Post	Pre	Post
P1*†	3	6	5	6	4	6
P2	2	4	6	9	2	2
P3†	2	4	3	5	5	8
P4*†	3	6	6	4	3	6
P5†	5	6	3	1	3	4
P6*	6	6	5	6	5	5
P7†	4	5	4	4	4	4
P8*	2	6	6	5	2	4
P9	2	5	6	5	1	3
Mean	3.22	5.22	4.89	5	3.22	4.67

Table 4. Portion Estimation Test Scores

Not only did participants increase confidence in estimating portion sizes, they also demonstrated increased accuracy in the portion size estimation tests. From the test scores (Table 4), we learn that eight participants improved their scores on *Pictures*, four improved on *Apportion* and six improved on *Containers*. Paired t-tests comparing participants' pre and post scores on the *Pictures* and *Containers* test revealed significant improvement in their ability to estimate portion sizes: $t(8) = 4.99$, $p < .001$, and $t(8) = 3.51$, $p < .001$, respectively. We found no significant change in participants' scores for the *Apportion* test, $t(8) = .48$, $p=.32$. The positive effect on the *Pictures* test, but not the *Apportion* test suggests participants became more skilled at estimating portion sizes of food once it was portioned out, however they still had difficulty in creating an amount of food matching a specified quantity.

In Situ Estimation Accuracy

In comparing participants' portion size estimates for 600 food and 144 drink items, as recorded in the application, to the actual portion sizes based on the pictures they took, we found that participants accurately measured more than half of their portions, 58.2%. The inter-dialytic weight gain data helped us bolster the accuracy of these estimations. The in situ estimation accuracy of most food categories did not seem to change over the course of the study, except liquids and eggs that showed improvement over time. Participants had more difficulty measuring portion sizes of solid (69% correct) and amorphous foods (62%) compared to liquids (95%). Snacks (32%) and crackers (14%) had lowest percentage accuracies but they were also recorded infrequently (44 and 28 total recordings respectively). Moreover, also like earlier work [12], protein portions, such as meat pieces or slices represented the greatest challenge to participants, (36% accurate estimates) suggesting a need to focus on education and reference objects that effectively support the estimation of these items.

DISCUSSION

In this section, we highlight novel conceptual understandings about health behavior change technologies and issues surrounding their in situ use based on our findings. We discuss how cognitive dissonance and manual logging can be leveraged in design for changing users' beliefs about health behaviors and empowering them to take greater control of their health. Finally, we discuss the importance of data triangulation in the evaluation of behavior change applications.

Leveraging Cognitive Dissonance

At times, participants demonstrated disbelief when information on the estimation interface conflicted with their current knowledge. Festinger's Theory of Cognitive Dissonance [17] suggests that this mental inconsistency would put individuals in a state of psychological discomfort. The psychological discomfort would, in turn, prompt individuals to act in order to reconcile their contradictory beliefs. As Consolvo and colleagues summarized, users have four options for recourse when faced with this discomfort – changing their behavior, changing their knowledge, rationalizing the dissonance, or avoiding the information and situations that reinforce the dissonance [14].

In our study, participants primarily engaged in changing their knowledge in response to dissonance between information in the application and their current knowledge. This differs from much of the prior HCI research, where interventions have directly targeted behavior change by creating dissonance between users' behaviors and their beliefs [22, 7, 40]. When participants in our study were confronted with information inconsistent with their current knowledge or beliefs, many stopped to consider the information and actively engaged in reconciling their prior knowledge with the new information. For several, this took the form of testing, where participants used scales or physical objects to confirm what the application was telling them.

Although we found that the cognitive dissonance created through DIMA-P primarily had a positive effect, it is well documented that cognitive dissonance can also cause users to avoid situations that reinforce the psychological discomfort [7, 41]. Systems that create dissonance could alienate users and lead them to stop using the application or reduce their engagement with it [11]. P8 highlighted her disbelief of some portion size estimators as the one negative aspect of the application. Although this supports the idea that creating dissonance has the risk of engendering negative attitudes in users, ultimately P8 continued using the application throughout the study period and highlighted the way the new knowledge helped her in practice. In our case, users could reconcile this new knowledge by engaging physical versions of the estimators and scales to test the accuracy of the application. This helped them remain engaged with the application instead of abandoning it. Applications that aim to use cognitive dissonance as a method to support knowledge development or behavior change must provide users with the ability to reconcile dissonant information by integrating and supporting methods to verify application claims.

In addition to providing opportunities for users to confirm information in the application, prior research also suggests that facilitating expert or peer communication for users could help them resolve disbelief [28, 30]. Gaming could also be used as a strategy to educate users and present potentially dissonant information. The gaming element can increase engagement and comfort with new concepts - helping reduce the negative side effects of cognitive dissonance. Grimes-Parker's work on educating low SES populations about food is an example of this approach [21].

Involving Users in Input

There has been an effort to develop systems that automate the process of collecting dietary information from users [9, 27, 48, 49] or estimating portion size through semi-automated methods [31]. Although this relieves the burden of entry and portion size estimation from users, which addresses a major barrier in long-term engagement with behavior change applications [45, 43], our research suggests that this may miss out on some of the most valuable learning opportunities for users. In our study, participants developed knowledge, skills, and self-efficacy around estimating portion sizes that transcended the application itself. Almost all of this development came from the process of entering food into the application and using the aid to estimate portion sizes. Automated portion size systems would take these learning opportunities away from users, disempowering them from developing their own skills in portion size estimation. For low literacy users, this is especially problematic, as these kinds of foundational skills are valuable for use in everyday life.

Other researchers have identified the process of logging health behaviors in self-monitoring applications as a key moment for learning, reflection, and awareness raising [8, 15, 37]. When users are removed from the logging process, feedback can be out of context and there are missed opportunities for just-in-time feedback. Similar to this prior research, our work challenges the idea that we should automate the logging of behaviors and instead suggests that we should develop systems to make entry more engaging and valuable for users. By actively engaging users in the process of entering their food and estimating their portion sizes, we enhanced their self-efficacy and provided them with knowledge and skills that could be applied outside the application. Previous research has used just-in-time feedback when behaviors are logged and game progression as ways to promote self-logging and make it a valuable experience for users [39]. More work should be done to explore ways to make the self-logging process more valuable and engaging for users.

Data Triangulation

We aimed to target self-efficacy and portion size estimation skills by designing features that supported two out of three behavioral health constructs of ITHBC (a) foster knowledge and beliefs, and (b) enhance self-regulation skills and abilities. Our analysis of pre and post-study tests shows that participants' self-efficacy of portion size estimation, and their knowledge and skills around portion size estimation have improved. However, on analyzing in-situ meal recordings we found that participants were inconsistent in their ability to translate their knowledge and skills into accurate portion size estimations for different types of food in everyday life. The theory postulates that improving these two constructs should impact health behaviors. Our results highlight a gap between theory and practice, uncovered only through data triangulation.

One possible problem with DIMA-P was the lack of support for the social facilitation construct of ITHBC. If participants had obtained feedback on their in-situ portion size estimates over the course of the study, it is possible that they could have self-identified shortcomings in their techniques and consequently rectified them. Prior work has found that peer or expert feedback on one's diet can help improve people awareness of their dietary intake [30, 52].

Other research has used data triangulation to find gaps between theory and practice [30] and inconsistencies in people's perceptions and behaviors [38]. Indeed, Klasnja and colleagues suggest that early stage HCI research in behavior change technologies should focus on efficacy evaluations and studies that help gain deeper understanding of people's technology use [25]. We join them in their suggestion by adding that data triangulation (especially with in-situ data) is critical for understanding the nuances in people's use of technology, and for uncovering future research directions.

LIMITATIONS

While we acknowledge that a sample size of 7-9 people is small, Klasnja and colleagues argue that piloting an early research interface in a long study with fewer participants makes better sense in uncovering errors [25]. The smaller sample size helped us looked at specific design issues and needs of the participants in more detail. Moreover, we only had one view of meal photographs that might have affected our assessment of participants' accuracy of estimation.

ACKNOWLEDGMENTS

We gratefully acknowledge Earlham College Faculty Research Grant for supporting this research work. We are also thankful to the Indiana University Hospital, Indianapolis for giving us the permission to conduct this study with the CKD V patients in their dialysis unit. Finally, we thank reviewers for providing us valuable comments that helped us improve the quality of this publication.

REFERENCES

1. Adrienne H. Andrew, Gaetano Borriello and James Fogarty. 2013. Simplifying Mobile Phone Food Diaries: Design and Evaluation of a Food Index-Based Nutrition Diary. In *Proceedings of in Pervasive Computing Technologies for Healthcare (PervasiveHealth '13),* 260-263. http://dx.doi.org/10.4108/icst.pervasivehealth.2013.252101
2. Ingrid Arreola, Zan Morris, Matthew Francisco, Kay Connelly, Kelly Caine, and Ginger White. 2014. From checking on to checking in: designing for low socio-economic status older adults. In *Proceedings of the SIGCHI Conference on Human Factors in Computing Systems (CHI '14),* 1933-1936. http://dx.doi.org/10.1145/2556288.2557084
3. Erik Arsand, Ragnhild Varmedal, and Gunnar Hartvigsen. 2007. Usability of a Mobile Self-help Tool for People with Diabetes: The Easy Health Diary. In *Proceedings of IEEE International Conference on Science and Automation (CASE '07)*, 863-868. http://dx.doi.org/ 10.1109/COASE.2007.4341807.
4. Guadalupe Xochitl Ayala. 2006. An Experimental Evaluation of Group- versus Computer-based Intervention to Improve Food Portion Size Estimation Skills. *Health Education Research 21*, 1 (2006), 133-145.
5. Nancy D. Berkman, Stacey L. Sheridan, Katrina E. Donahue, David J. Halpern, and Karen Crotty. 2011. Low Health Literacy and Health Outcomes: An Updated Systematic Review. *Ann Intern Med. 155*, 2 (2011), 97-107.
6. Jeremy Brown and Ray Fitzpatrick. 1988. Factors influencing compliance with dietary restrictions in dialysis patients. *J Psychosom Res 32*, 2 (1988), 191–196.
7. Sahara Byrne, et al. 2012. Caring for Mobile Phone-Based Virtual Pets can Influence Youth Eating Behaviors. *J. Child. Media 6*; 1 (2012), 83–99.
8. Erin A. Carroll, Mary Czerwinski, Asta Roseway, Ashish Kapoor, Paul Johns, Kael Rowan, and M. C. Schraefel. Food and Mood: Just-in-Time Support for Emotional Eating. In *Proceedings of IEEE Affective Computing and Intelligent Interaction (ACII '13)*, 252-257. http://dx.doi.org/10.1109/ACII.2013.48.
9. Keng-Hao Chang, Shih-Yen Liu, Jr-ben Tian, Hao-Hua Chu, and Cheryl Chen. 2005. Dietary-Aware Dining Table - Tracking What and How Much You Eat. In *Proceedings of Workshop on Smart Object Systems*, 61-68. http://tair.lib.ntu.edu.tw:8000/20060927122839835408.
10. Beenish Chaudry, Kay Connelly, Katie A. Siek, and Janet L. Welch. 2011. The design of mobile portion size estimation interface for low literacy populations. In *Proceedings of the 5th International Conference on Pervasive Computing Technologies for Healthcare (PervasiveHealth '11)*, 160–167. http://dx.doi.org/10.4108/icst.pervasivehealth.2011.246.
11. Eun Kyoung Choe. 2011. Design of persuasive technologies for healthy sleep behavior. In *Proc. 13th Int. Conf. Ubiquitous Comput (UbiComp '11)*, 507-510.
12. Rob Comber, Jack Weeden, Jennifer Hoare, Stephen Lindsay, Gemma Teal, Alastair Macdonald, Lisa Methven, Paula Moynihan, and Patrick Olivier. 2012. Supporting visual assessment of food and nutrient intake in a clinical care setting. In *Proceedings of the SIGCHI Conference on Human Factors in Computing Systems (CHI '12)*, 919-922. http://dx.doi.org/10.1145/2207676.2208534
13. Kay Connelly, Katie A Siek, Beenish Chaudry, Josette Jones, Kim Astroth, and Janet L Welch. 2012. An Offline Mobile Nutrition Monitoring Intervention for Varying-Literacy Patients receiving Hemodialysis: A Pilot Study Examining the Usage and Usability. *J Am Med Inform Assoc 19*, 5 (2012), 705-712.
14. Sunny Consolvo, David McDonald, and James Landay. 2009. Theory-driven design strategies for technologies that support behavior change in everyday life. In *Proceedings of the 27th international conference on Human factors in computing systems (CHI '09)*, 405–414.
15. Felicia Cordeiro, Elizabeth Bales, Erin Cherry, and James Fogarty. 2015. Rethinking the Mobile Food Journal: Exploring Opportunities for Lightweight Photo-Based Capture. In *Proceedings of the 33rd Annual ACM Conference on Human Factors in Computing Systems (CHI '15)*, 3207-3216. http://dx.doi.org/10.1145/2702123.2702154.
16. Sebastien Cuendet, Indrani Medhi, Kalika Bali, and Edward Cutrell. 2013. VideoKheti: making video content accessible to low-literate and novice users. In *Proceedings of the SIGCHI Conference on Human Factors in Computing Systems (CHI '13)*, 2833-2842. http://dx.doi.org/10.1145/2470654.2481392
17. Leon Festinger. A theory of cognitive dissonance. Stanford University Press, 1957.
18. Denis Fouque, Marianne Vennegoor, Piet Ter Wee, Christoph Wanner, Ali Basci, Bernard Canaud, Patrick Haage, Klaus Konner, Jeroen Kooman, Alejandro Martin-Malo, Lucianu Pedrini, Francesco Pizzarelli, James Tattersall, Jan Tordoir, and Raymond Vanholder. 2007. EBPG Guideline on Nutrition. *Nephrology Dialysis Transplantation 22,* (2007), 45-87.
19. Feng Gao, Enrico Costanza, and M. C. Schraefel. 2012. "Honey=sugar" means unhealthy: investigating how people apply knowledge to rate food's healthiness. In *Proceedings of the 2012 ACM Conference on*

Ubiquitous Computing (UbiComp '12), 71-80. http://dx.doi.org/10.1145/2370216.2370228

20. Andrea Grimes, Martin Bednar, Jay David Bolter, and Rebecca E. Grinter. 2008. EatWell: sharing nutrition-related memories in a low-income community. In *Proceedings of the 2008 ACM conference on Computer supported cooperative work (CSCW '08)*, 87-96. http://dx.doi.org/10.1145/1460563.1460579.
21. Andrea Grimes, Vasudhara Kantroo, and Rebecca E. Grinter. 2010. Let's play!: mobile health games for adults. In *Proceedings of the 12th ACM international conference on Ubiquitous computing (UbiComp '10)*, 241-250. http://dx.doi.org/10.1145/1864349.1864370.
22. Ha He, Saul Greenberg, and Elaine Huang. 2010. One size does not fit all: applying the transtheoretical model to energy feedback technology design. In *Proceedings of the Conference on Human in computing systems (CHI '10)*, 927–936.
23. Mary Margaret Huizinga, Adam J. Carlisle, Kerri L. Cavanaugh, Dianne L. Davis, Rebecca P. Gregory, David G. Schlundt, and Russel L. Rothman. 2009. Literacy, Numeracy and Portion-Size Estimation Skills. *Am J Prev Med 36*, 4 (2009), 324–328
24. Maia L. Jacobs, James Clawson, and Elizabeth D. Mynatt. 2014. My journey compass: a preliminary investigation of a mobile tool for cancer patients. In *Proceedings of the SIGCHI Conference on Human Factors in Computing Systems (CHI '14)*, 663-672. http://dx.doi.org/10.1145/2556288.2557194
25. Predrag Klasnja, Sunny Consolvo, and Wanda Pratt. 2011. How to evaluate technologies for health behavior change in HCI research. In *Proceedings of the SIGCHI Conference on Human Factors in Computing Systems (CHI '11)*, 3063-3072. http://dx.doi.org/10.1145/1978942.1979396.
26. John E. Leggat Jr, Sean M. Orzol, Tempie E. Hulbert-Shearon, Thomas A. Golper, Camille A. Jones, Philip J. Held, and Friedrich K. Port. 1998. Noncompliance in Hemodialysis: Predictors and Survival Analysis. *Am J Kidney Dis 32*, 1 (1998), 139–145
27. Jonathan Lester, Desney Tan, Shwetak Patel, and A.J. Bernheim Brush. 2010. Automatic Classification of Daily Fluid Intake. In *Proceedings of Pervasive Computing Technologies for Healthcare (PervasiveHealth '10)*, 1-8. http://dx.doi.org/10.4108/ICST.PERVASIVEHEALTH2010.8906.
28. Julie Maitland and Matthew Chalmers. 2011. Designing for peer involvement in weight management. In *Proceedings of the SIGCHI Conference on Human Factors in Computing Systems (CHI '11)*, 315-324. http://dx.doi.org/10.1145/1978942.1978988
29. Lena Mamykina, Andrew D. Miller, Catherine Grevet, Yevgeniy Medynskiy, Michael A. Terry, Elizabeth D. Mynatt, and Patricia R. Davidson. 2011. Examining the impact of collaborative tagging on sensemaking in nutrition management. In *Proceedings of the SIGCHI Conference on Human Factors in Computing Systems (CHI '11)*, 657-666. http://dx.doi.org/10.1145/1978942.1979037
30. Lena Mamykina, Elizabeth Mynatt, Patricia Davidson, and Daniel Greenblatt. 2008. MAHI: investigation of social scaffolding for reflective thinking in diabetes management. In *Proceeding of the twenty-sixth annual SIGCHI conference on Human factors in computing systems (CHI '08)*, 477–486.
31. Jon Noronha, Eric Hysen, Haoqi Zhang, and Krzysztof Z. Gajos. 2011. Platemate: crowdsourcing nutritional analysis from food photographs. In *Proceedings of the 24th annual ACM symposium on User interface software and technology (UIST '11)*.
32. Sebastian Päßler, Wolf-Joachim Fischer. 2011. Food Intake Activity Detection Using a Wearable Microphone System. In *Proceedings of the Seventh International Conference on Intelligent Environments*, 298-301. http://dx.doi.org/10.1109/IE.2011.
33. Andrea Parker, Vasudhara Kantroo, Hee Lee, Miguel Osornio, Mansi Sharma, and Rebecca Grinter. 2012. Health promotion as activism: building community capacity to effect social change. In *Proceedings of the SIGCHI Conference on Human Factors in Computing Systems (CHI '12)*, 99–108.
34. Polly Ryan. 2009. Integrated theory of health behavior change. *Clin. Nurse Specialty 23*, 3: 161-172.
35. Martin Ravallion and Shaohua Chen. 2009. Weakly Relative Poverty. *World Bank Policy Research Working Paper Series*, 4844.
36. Charles L. Rawls. 2000. *Performance Support and Usability: An Experimental Study of Electronic Performance Support Interfaces*. PhD Dissertation. University of Central Florida, Orlando, FL.
37. Eric Robinson, et al. 2013. Development and feasibility testing of a smart phone based attentive eating intervention. *BMC Public Health 13*, 1 (2013), 639-646.
38. Yvonne Rogers, William R. Hazlewood, Paul Marshall, Nick Dalton, and Susanna Hertrich. 2010. Ambient influence: can twinkly lights lure and abstract representations trigger behavioral change?. In *Proceedings of the 12th ACM international conference on Ubiquitous computing (UbiComp '10)*. 261-270.
39. Chris Schaefbauer, Danish Khan, Amy Le, Garrett Sczechowski, and Katie Siek. 2015. Snack Buddy: Supporting Healthy Snacking in Low Socioeconomic Status Families. In *Proceedings of the 2015 ACM*

conference on Computer supported cooperative work (CSCW 2015), 1045–1057.

40. Victoria Schwanda, Steven Ibara, Lindsay Reynolds, and Dan Cosley. 2011. Side effects and gateway tools: advocating a broader look at evaluating persuasive systems. In *Proceedings of the Conference on Human in computing systems (CHI '11)*, 345–348

41. Christina Schwind, Jürgen Buder, and Friedrich Hesse. 2011. I Will Do It, But I Don't Like It: User Reactions to Preference-Inconsistent Recommendations. In *Proceedings of the SIGCHI Conference on Human Factors in Computing Systems (CHI '11)*, 349–352.

42. Katie Siek, Kay Connelly, and Yvonne Rogers. 2006. Pride and prejudice: learning how chronically ill people think about food. In *Proceedings of the SIGCHI conference on Human Factors in computing systems (CHI '06)*. 947–950.

43. Katie Siek, Kay Connelly, Yvonne Rogers, Paul Rohwer, Desiree Lambert, and Janet Welch. 2006. When do we eat? An evaluation of food items input into an electronic food monitoring application. *In Pervasive Health '06.*

44. Amy F. Subar, Jennifer Crafts, Thea Palmer Zimmerman, Michael Wilson, Beth Mittl, Noemi G. Islam, Suzanne McNutt, Nancy Potischman, Richard Buday, Stephen G. Hull, Tom Baranowski, Patricia M. Guenther, Gordon Willis, Ramsey Tapia, Frances E. Thompson. 2010. Assessment of the Accuracy of Portion Size Reports Using Computer-based Food Photograph Aids in the Development of an Automated Self-Administered 24-hour Recall. *J Am Diet Assoc 110*, 1 (2010), 55-64.

45. Christopher C. Tsai, Gunny Lee, Fred Raab, Gregory J. Norman, Timothy Sohn, William G. Griswold, Kevin Patrick. 2007. Usability and Feasibility of PmEB: A Mobile Phone Application for Monitoring Real Time Caloric Balance. *Mob. Networks Appl. 12*, 2–3 (2007), 173–184.

46. Carine Vereeckena, Sophie Dohogne, Marc Covents and Lea Maes. 2010. How Accurate are Adolescents in Portion-Size Estimation using the Computer Tool Young Adolescents' Nutrition Assessment on Computer (YANA-C)? *British J Nutr. 103*, 12 (2010), 1844-1850.

47. Barry D. Weiss, Mary Z. Mays, William Martz, Kelley Merriam Castro, Darren A. DeWalt, Michael P. Pignone, Joy Mockbee, and Frank A. Hale. 2005. Quick Assessment of Literacy in Primary Care: The Newest Vital Sign. *Annals of Family Medicine 3*, 6 (2005), 514-522.

48. Insoo Woo, Karl Otsmo, SungYe Kim, David S. Ebert, Edward J. Delp, and Carol J. Boushey. 2010. Automatic portion estimation and visual refinement in mobile dietary assessment. In *Proceedings of Society of Photographic Instrumentation Engineers (SPIE* '10), 7533.

http://dx.doi.org/10.1117/12.849051.

49. Fengqing Zhu, Marc Bosch, Insoo Woo, SungYe Kim, Carol J. Boushey, David S. Ebert, Edward J. Delp. 2010. The use of mobile devices in aiding dietary assessment and evaluation. *IEEE J Sel Top Signal Process 4*, 4 (2010), 756 – 766.

Examining Unlock Journaling with Diaries and Reminders for In Situ Self-Report in Health and Wellness

Xiaoyi Zhang[1], Laura R. Pina[1,2], James Fogarty[1]
[1]Computer Science & Engineering, [2]Human Centered Design & Engineering
DUB Group, University of Washington
{ xiaoyiz, lpina, jfogarty }@cs.washington.edu

ABSTRACT

In situ self-report is widely used in human-computer interaction, ubiquitous computing, and for assessment and intervention in health and wellness. Unfortunately, it remains limited by high burdens. We examine *unlock journaling* as an alternative. Specifically, we build upon recent work to introduce single-slide unlock journaling gestures appropriate for health and wellness measures. We then present the first field study comparing unlock journaling with traditional diaries and notification-based reminders in self-report of health and wellness measures. We find unlock journaling is less *intrusive* than reminders, dramatically improves *frequency* of journaling, and can provide equal or better *timeliness*. Where appropriate to broader design needs, unlock journaling is thus an overall promising method for in situ self-report.

Author Keywords

Personal informatics; self-tracking; experience sampling.

ACM Classification Keywords

H.5.2. Information interfaces and presentation (e.g., HCI).

INTRODUCTION AND MOTIVATION

The use of mobile devices for prompted in situ self-report has become common across a variety of disciplines, sometimes called experience sampling [3,15,23], diaries [8,34,36,41], or ecological momentary assessment [21,40,44]. Applications of these methods are too broad to enumerate, but research in the CHI community has included studies of mobile device adoption [34], of time management and interruptions [17,24,26,35,38], of relating sensed behavior traces to explicit reports [20,27], of location privacy preferences [13], and informing and evaluating mobile and ubiquitous computing applications [7,11,12,14,41]. The CHI community is also actively exploring self-tracking through the lenses of personal informatics [32], the Quantified Self [10], and lived informatics [16,18,37]. We are particularly interested in the increasing applications of these techniques to self-monitoring in health and wellness (e.g., [6,28]).

CHI'16, May 07-12, 2016, San Jose, CA, USA

ACM 978-1-4503-3362-7/16/05...$15.00
DOI: http://dx.doi.org/10.1145/2858036.2858360

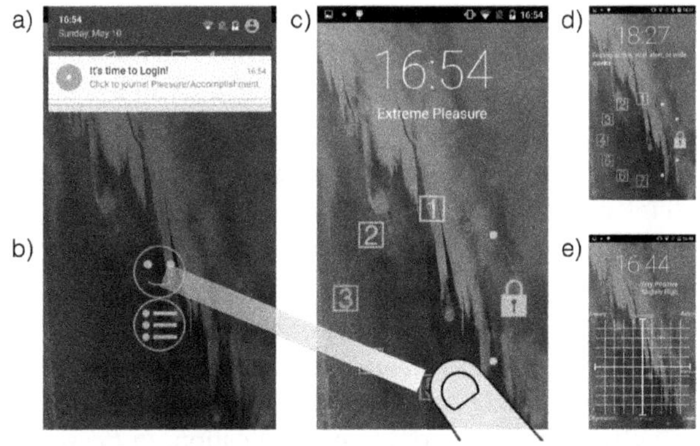

Figure 1. We examine unlock journaling, in which unlocking a phone also journals an in situ self-report. We present the first study comparing to diaries and notification-reminders.

Unfortunately, potential benefits of these techniques remain limited by their high burdens. Quantified Selfers report the burdens of self-tracking often create a fatigue that leads them to abandon self-tracking [10]. Experience sampling research has found the frequency of prompts must be limited to mitigate annoyance they create [19,27]. Intrusiveness of prompts can also be reduced using context awareness and decision theory methods to focus prompts at appropriate times and reduce the total number of prompts [25,26,38]. Health and wellness applications face the additional challenge that the act of journaling is often itself intended to promote mindfulness and self-monitoring (i.e., self-report serves both assessment and treatment [29]). Too much of a focus on sensing, automating data collection, or minimizing journaling may therefore undermine the entire purpose [42].

Initial methods used beepers (i.e., pagers) to prompt people to complete paper diaries [15]. This same basic approach continues in mobile interfaces that present a survey with multiple questions requiring minutes to complete. In contrast, recent work explores more lightweight journaling interfaces. Choe et al.'s SleepTight uses a phone lockscreen widget for journaling of potential sleep disruptors with as little as a single tap [9]. We build upon work by Truong et al., repurposing the otherwise wasted action of unlocking a phone (i.e., the slide to unlock gesture) to allow a small optional action [46]. Figure 1 illustrates our LogIn system, which modifies the unlock gesture to enable single-slide unlock journaling of health and wellness self-reports for sleepiness [22], pleasure and accomplishment [31], or mood [39].

Although repurposing the unlock gesture is appealing in its potential to reduce burdens of journaling, no prior work has compared this with traditional approaches. Researchers and designers thus lack information regarding how unlock journaling for health and wellness might be expected to perform in practice. We therefore present a field study in which 24 people each journal a health and wellness measure for 18 days. We compare unlock journaling with diaries and notification-based reminders, finding that unlock journaling is less *intrusive* than reminders, dramatically improves *frequency* of journaling, and can provide equal or better *timeliness*. Where appropriate to broader design needs, unlock journaling is thus a promising method for in situ self-report.

The specific contributions of this work therefore include:

- We expand the design of single-slide unlock journaling gestures to support (1) selection among multiple measures to journal, and (2) journaling a two-dimensional measure.
- We present the first field study comparing unlock journaling with traditional diaries and notification-based reminders for self-report of health and wellness measures.

RELATED WORK

The CHI community adopted diary studies as an alternative to field observation, which requires a researcher be present [36]. People often forget to journal, so methods evolved to provide reminders via beepers (i.e., pagers) [15], mobile devices [3], and text messages [1]. As devices became more common and capable, techniques have been updated to leverage advances in mobile media capture [8,34], automatic sensing [19,25], mobile notifications [5], and context awareness [25,26,38]. Enabled by these advances, an important thread of research has examined how those advances impact in-situ self-report [3,5,8,43].We similarly contribute by examining the potential of unlock journaling as a new low-burden approach to in situ self-report, focusing on health and wellness applications.

We build directly on Truong et al.'s Slide to X technique [46]. This technique assigns a dual purpose to the unlock gesture, aiming to preserve its extreme simplicity while having that same gesture perform a simple, optional task. They propose Slide to QuantifySelf, but do not field such an application, nor do they compare to data collection with traditional diaries or notification-based reminders. We extend the single-slide gestures illustrated by Truong et al. to support common health and wellness measures. We also present the first field study comparing single-slide unlock journaling to traditional approaches. Additional examples of lightweight lockscreen interaction include small crowdsourcing tasks in Twitch [47], a crossing-based interface for email review in ProactiveTasks [2], and single-tap journaling via a lockscreen widget in SleepTight [9]. None of these provide the guidance we contribute on how single-slide unlock journaling might perform for a variety of health and wellness measures.

DESIGN OF LOGIN

LogIn is our implementation of unlock journaling, focused on validated health and wellness measures selected to be representative of needs in this space [22,31,39]. This section details our design of singe-slide unlock journaling in LogIn.

Our first measure is the Stanford Sleepiness Scale, a 7-point one-dimensional scale administered multiple times per day to identify sleep debt and patterns of alertness [22]. Such a scale is supported by the original Likert-type design in Slide to X [46], though we modify the design to preserve Android conventions and avoid thumb occlusion. Drop targets appear when a person touches the unlock handle, a text explanation of a target is provided by sliding the handle to it, and releasing the handle then simultaneously journals the selection and unlocks the phone (Figure 1d, 2a).

Our second measure is for pleasure and accomplishment, implemented as a pair of 5-point one-dimensional scales. A person working with a therapist to assess and treat depressive symptoms may journal whether activities create a sense of pleasure or accomplishment, as such activities are important to behavioral activation in managing symptoms [4,31,33]. The original Slide to X interactions do not support single-slide selection of what to journal, so we introduce choosing from *multiple handles* to slide. A person chooses which scale to journal by touching the appropriate handle, then the interaction proceeds as before (Figure 1b, 1c, 2b).

Our third measure is Russell's Affect Grid, a two-dimensional measure of mood (i.e., pleasure and arousal) appropriate for journaling throughout the day [39]. The original Slide to X interactions do not support single-slide gesturing to journal in a two-dimensional scale. This is challenging in part because of the need to allow selection from the grid while preserving the default slide to unlock interaction (i.e., Figure 2d). We resolve this by introducing *layers* in the slide interaction. A person slides the handle to a grid icon, which activates the grid layer, then slides to the desired value and releases (Figure 1e, 2c), simultaneously journaling and unlocking.

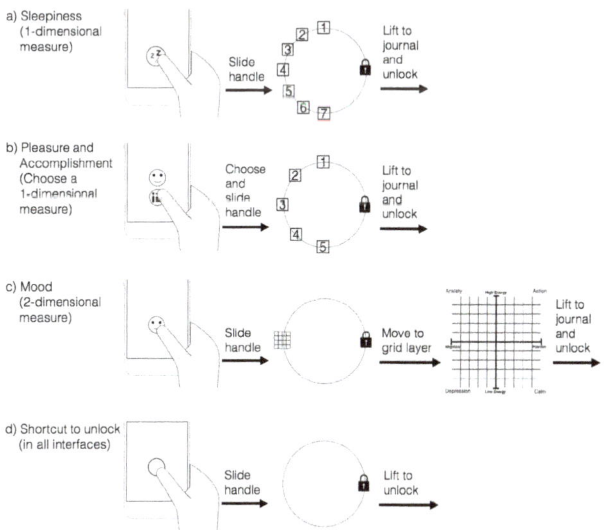

Figure 2. We design single-slide unlock gestures to support journaling of sleepiness (i.e., a rating scale), pleasure and accomplishment (i.e., choosing the scale to journal), and mood (i.e., a two-dimensional scale). All designs make journaling optional, preserving the simplicity of the default unlock.

Journaling is always optional, and all designs preserve the default unlock gesture (Figure 2d). Journaling is therefore visible and easy but not required, as required journaling could result in people recording less reliable data while attempting to quickly access their phone. Although it is important our field evaluation is based in commonly-used measures, we also again note these measures were selected to be representative of needs in this space. Other health and wellness measures could likely be supported through these interactions or through designs based on their insights (e.g., choosing among layers via multiple slide targets).

Implementation. LogIn is implemented for Android, which provides a public API for customizing the lockscreen. Unlock journaling thus replaces the default unlock gesture (i.e., is not an additional step in the interaction). Any system password is preserved and entered after the unlock gesture (i.e., at the same point in the overall interaction sequence).

FIELD EVALUATION

Our evaluation examines unlock journaling in a field study focused on health and wellness self-report, comparing to traditional diaries and notification-based reminders.

Design and Procedure

We use a 2x3 within-subjects design, examining the impact of interfaces with *unlock journaling* (with, without) and *notifications* (none, traditional, aggressive) on *intrusiveness*, *frequency*, and *timeliness* of journaling in health and wellness.

Traditional notifications conditions generated a platform notification reminding the participant to journal (Figure 1a). *Aggressive notifications* added sound/vibration. Notifications were generated every 30 minutes in a configurable 12-hour window, applying a small random jitter to avoid grouping with any notifications from other applications at the same approximate time. The participant configured this window at the beginning of the study. For comparison, unlock journaling was only presented during this same window.

Base Functionality. All conditions provided an app which allowed journaling at will (i.e., participants could journal at any time, without needing to wait for a notification or first lock their phone). A simple app also visualized a participant's data, allowing them to view their journal at will. Note that the condition *without unlock journaling* and *none notifications* is a traditional *diary* (i.e., can enter and view data, but does not otherwise surface itself or remind participants to journal).

Journaling Domain. To maximize participant interest in the task, we screened participants for interest and allowed them to choose their journaling domain from sleepiness, pleasure and accomplishment, or mood. Each participant used different interfaces for journaling in their chosen domain over the course of their participation.

Procedure. Participants used their own Android phones to journal with LogIn over the course of 18 days. Each of the 6 conditions was used for 2 consecutive days, with a rest day between conditions. The LogIn app automatically switched interface conditions at midnight. To account for possible carryover effects (e.g., fatigue, learning, varying interest), we counterbalanced conditions using a balanced Latin Square.

Participation began with a brief interview, during which we installed LogIn on the participant's phone. We explained the study, then they chose their domain and configured their 12-hour journaling window. We emphasized compensation was not dependent on frequency of interaction, only a need to leave LogIn installed and return for a brief exit interview. Participants were compensated with a $20 gift card.

Participants

We recruited through local email lists, linking to a questionnaire screening for use of a phone running Android 4.2 or above and for interest in three domains. From the eligible pool, we randomly selected 24 participants, reporting an average age of 26.1 years (min 19, max 47, med 24), 14 male, 10 female. 11 chose to journal sleepiness, 6 pleasure and accomplishment, and 7 mood. Reporting motivation to journal in their chosen domain on a 7-point Likert scale, 15 reported motivation 7, 7 motivation 6, and 2 motivation 5.

Results

Participants journaled an average of 147 entries in 12 days (min 36, max 255, med 149), or 12.2 per day. When unlock journaling was active in the interface condition, they unlocked without journaling an average of 228 times, or 38 per day. We analyze their reported *intrusiveness* of conditions and their *frequency* and *timeliness* of journaling by condition.

We use mixed-model analyses of variance, with *participant* as a random effect (i.e., accounting for individual differences). We model *domain* and *study day*, but find no significant results (i.e., no differences by journaling domain and no carryover effects). We model *unlock journaling*, *notifications*, and their interaction. Figure 3 presents our primary results. To control for other independent variables, means reported in Figure 3 and this section are all least squares means.

Intrusiveness. At the end of each 12-hour study window, an alert asked participants to rate *intrusiveness* of that day's condition on a 5-point Likert scale. We find the addition of *unlock journaling* is reported as more *intrusive* (2.12 vs. 2.38, $F_{1,258} = 11.7, p \approx .001$). We find a main effect for *notifications* ($F_{2,258} = 12.7, p < .001$), and Tukey's HSD finds *aggressive* (2.94) is reported as more *intrusive* than *traditional* (2.27, $F_{1,258} = 51.3, p < .001$), with both more *intrusive* than *none* (1.55, $F_{1,258} = 218, p < .001$, $F_{1,258} = 57.9, p < .001$).

Of particular interest is a contrast between *unlock journaling* and *notifications* (e.g., a designer choosing one or the other to enhance a *diary* that has neither). Tukey's HSD finds addition of *notifications* is more intrusive than *unlock journaling* (2.22 vs. 1.77, $F_{2,258} = 11.8, p \approx .001$). Part of this may be that unlock journaling is surfaced during normal interaction, which P18 explained as: "*I have so many different reminder and buzzing things and don't know which one is the journal reminder. But if I see this lockscreen, I know I am supposed to do it ... it is very easy.*"

Frequency. We define *frequency* as the number of entries a person journals in a day. We find the addition of *unlock journaling* doubles *frequency* (16.1 vs. 7.9 entries per day, $F_{1,258} = 188, p < .001$). We find a main effect for *notifications* ($F_{2,258} = 31.4$, $p < .001$). Tukey's HSD finds *aggressive* (14.3) and *traditional* (13.0) yield greater *frequency* than *none* (8.8, $F_{1,258} = 57.5$, $p < .001$, $F_{1,258} = 33.6$, $p < .001$), but not significantly different from each other ($F_{1,258} = 3.19$, $p \approx .075$). Part of *unlock journaling*'s higher *frequency* and a lack of improvement with *aggressive notifications* may be that notifications become less effective if delivered too often or too aggressively, contributing to *intrusiveness* instead of increasing *frequency*, as P7 explained: "*for the days there were many notifications, I feel like 'Ugh, leave me alone'*".

We find a significant interaction between *unlock journaling* and *notifications* ($F_{2,258} = 13.1$, $p < .001$). Tukey's HSD finds the *diary* condition (i.e., *none without unlock*) yields significantly less *frequency* than other conditions (2.5, all pairs $p < .001$). The *diary* condition provided no reminder to journal, and some reported forgetting entirely (e.g., P9 said "*I rarely remember if I don't have any notifications and (the lockscreen) is shown nothing. You can see from what I did ... I probably hardly journal anything.*" Of 13 days that participants had a *frequency* of 0, 10 are in the *diary* condition (including 1 from p1, who did not journal on 3 days and made only 36 entries over the entire study).

The contrast between *unlock journaling* and *notifications* is again of particular interest, and we find that *unlock journaling* improves *frequency* significantly more than *traditional notifications* (15.0 vs. 9.8, $F_{1,258} = 25.6$, $p < .001$) or *aggressive notifications* (15.0 vs. 11.5, $F_{1,258} = 11.5, p \approx .001$).

Timeliness. Our final analysis examines *timeliness* separately from *frequency*, as some domains may require journaling near a particular time. Considering only cases where a self-report was provided, we examine average proximity to the nearest 30-minute interval (i.e., when notification was or would have been made). We define proximity as two-sided, ranging from 0 to 15. We exclude 13 days with *frequency* 0.

We find the addition of *unlock journaling* improves *timeliness* (7.8 vs. 9.3, $F_{1,245} = 49.5$, $p < .001$). We find a main effect for *notifications* ($F_{2,245} = 42.9$, $p < .001$), and Tukey's HSD finds *aggressive* (7.3) improves *timeliness* over *traditional* (8.8, $F_{1,245} = 33.8$, $p < .001$), and both improve over *none* (9.6, $F_{1,245} = 83.1, p < .001, F_{1,245} = 11.9, p < .001$).

We are again particularly interested in a contrast between *unlock journaling* and *notifications* (e.g., a designer choosing one or the other to enhance a *diary* that has neither). Tukey's HSD finds addition of *unlock journaling* or *notifications* to a *diary* to be indistinguishable in their impact on *timeliness* (8.6 vs. 9.3, $F_{2,245} = 4.28$, $p \approx .040$, but failing the test's adjustment for multiple comparisons).

Notifications (columns) × **Unlock Journaling** (rows)

Intrusiveness (1 to 5)	None	Traditional	Aggressive
With Unlock	1.77	2.31	3.08
Without Unlock	1.33	2.22	2.81

without unlock 2.12 < with unlock 2.38
none 1.55 < traditional 2.27 < aggressive 2.94
none with unlock 1.77 < traditional without unlock 2.22

Frequency (entries per day)	None	Traditional	Aggressive
With Unlock	15.0	16.2	17.1
Without Unlock	2.5	9.8	11.5

with unlock 16.1 > without unlock 7.9
aggressive 14.3 ≈ traditional 13.0 > none 8.8
significant interaction (i.e., low value for none without unlock)
none with unlock 15.0 > traditional without unlock 9.8
none with unlock 15.0 > aggressive without unlock 11.5

Timeliness (minutes)	None	Traditional	Aggressive
With Unlock	8.6	8.2	6.7
Without Unlock	10.7	9.3	7.9

with unlock 7.8 < without unlock 9.3
aggressive 7.3 < traditional 8.8 < none 9.6
none with unlock 8.6 ≈ traditional without unlock 9.3

Figure 3. Summary of analyses, all as least squares means. Compared to notifications, unlock journaling is less *intrusive*, dramatically improves *frequency*, with equal or better *timeliness*.

DISCUSSION

If choosing between unlock journaling or notifications, our results suggest unlock journaling will be perceived as less *intrusive* (1.77 vs. 2.22), yield greater *frequency* of journaling (15.0 vs. 9.8), with comparable *timeliness* (8.6 vs. 9.3). Unlock journaling can also be combined with notifications, improving *frequency* and *timeliness* with a small increase in *intrusiveness*. These results motivate additional longer-term comparisons and studies of other characteristics of unlock journaling (e.g., different reporting windows, long-term fatigue, reliability of self-report collected in this manner).

Unlock journaling is limited to self-report that can be reduced to single-swipe gestures. We have extended the space of such gestures, but interesting opportunities for future work include pairing unlock journaling with other methods (e.g., with wearable eating detection [45] for lightweight verification of sensed data). LogIn also adds some complexity to a phone's unlocking mechanism. Although not a concern for our participants, this complexity could be a challenge for some.

Finally, Lathia et al. note the design of experience sampling implies bias in the resulting data [30]. This is unavoidable, as every method has a bias, but should be considered in applying a method. Experience sampling is already biased toward times a person can respond, and unlock journaling may magnify this to times when they are already accessing their phone. Depending on the application, this is potentially offset by the greater frequency of journaling.

There remain significant opportunities to extend this first field study comparing unlock journaling with traditional diaries and notification-based reminders in self-report of health and wellness measures. But our overall results suggest that, where appropriate to broader design needs, unlock journaling is a promising method for in situ self-report.

ACKNOWLEDGMENTS

This work is sponsored in part by the Intel Science and Technology Center for Pervasive Computing, Nokia Research, the AHRQ under award 1R21HS023654, and the NSF under awards OAI-1028195 and SCH-1344613.

REFERENCES

1. Jacob Anhøj and Claus Møldrup. (2004). Feasibility of Collecting Diary Data from Asthma Patients through Mobile Phones and SMS (Short Message Service): Response Rate Analysis and Focus Group Evaluation from a Pilot Study. *Journal of Medical Internet Research*, *6*(4), e42. http://doi.org/dfvrrg
2. Nikola Banovic, Christina Brant, Jennifer Mankoff, and Anind K. Dey. (2014). ProactiveTasks: The Short of Mobile Device Use Sessions. *Proceedings of the International Conference on Human-Computer Interaction with Mobile Devices & Services (MobileHCI 2014)*, 243–252. http://doi.org/bbn9
3. Lisa Feldman Barrett and Daniel J. Barrett. (2001). An Introduction to Computerized Experience Sampling in Psychology. *Social Science Computer Review*, *19*(2), 175–185. http://doi.org/d4tqhc
4. J.S. Beck and A.T. Beck. (2011). *Cognitive Behavior Therapy: Basics and Beyond.* Guilford Press.
5. Frank Bentley and Konrad Tollmar. (2013). The Power of Mobile Notifications to Increase Wellbeing Logging Behavior. *Proceedings of the SIGCHI Conference on Human Factors in Computing Systems (CHI 2013)*, 1095–1098. http://doi.org/f2zs59
6. Lora E. Burke, Jing Wang, and Mary Ann Sevick. (2011). Self-Monitoring in Weight Loss: A Systematic Review of the Literature. *Journal of the American Dietetic Association*, *111*(1), 92–102. http://doi.org/ct2ph2
7. Scott Carter, Jennifer Mankoff, and Jeffrey Heer. (2007). Momento: Support for Situated Ubicomp Experimentation. *Proceedings of the SIGCHI Conference on Human Factors in Computing Systems (CHI 2007)*, 125–134. http://doi.org/d69b3v
8. Scott Carter and Jennifer Mankoff. (2005). When Participants do the Capturing: The Role of Media in Diary Studies. *Proceedings of the SIGCHI Conference on Human Factors in Computing Systems CHI (2005)*, 899–908. http://doi.org/dqfsph
9. Eun Kyoung Choe, Bongshin Lee, Matthew Kay, Wanda Pratt, and Julie A. Kientz. (2015). SleepTight: Low-Burden, Self-Monitoring Technology for Capturing and Reflecting on Sleep Behaviors. *Proceedings of the ACM International Joint Conference on Pervasive and Ubiquitous Computing (UbiComp 2015)*, 121–132. http://doi.org/bbpb
10. Eun Kyoung Choe, Nicole B. Lee, Bongshin Lee, Wanda Pratt, and Julie A. Kientz. (2014). Understanding Quantified-Selfers' Practices in Collecting and Exploring Personal Data. *Proceedings of the ACM Conference on Human Factors in Computing Systems (CHI 2014)*, 1143–1152. http://doi.org/bbpd
11. Karen Church, Mauro Cherubini, and Nuria Oliver. (2014). A Large-Scale Study of Daily Information Needs Captured In Situ. *ACM Transactions on Computer-Human Interaction*, *21*(2). http://doi.org/bbpf
12. Sunny Consolvo, Predrag Klasnja, David W. McDonald, Daniel Avrahami, Jon E. Froehlich, Louis LeGrand, Ryan Libby, Keith Mosher, and James A. Landay. (2008). Flowers or a Robot Army?: Encouraging Awareness & Activity with Personal, Mobile Displays. *Proceedings of the International Conference on Ubiquitous Computing (UbiComp 2008)*, 54–63. http://doi.org/dk9hqb
13. Sunny Consolvo, Ian E. Smith, Tara Matthews, Anthony LaMarca, Jason Tabert, and Pauline Powledge. (2005). Location Disclosure to Social Relations: Why, When, & What People Want to Share. *Proceedings of the SIGCHI Conference on Human Factors in Computing Systems (CHI 2005)*, 81–90. http://doi.org/dk5d5v
14. Sunny Consolvo and Miriam Walker. (2003). Using the Experience Sampling Method to Evaluate Ubicomp Applications. *IEEE Pervasive Computing*, *2*(2), 24–31. http://doi.org/cmbg6h
15. Mihaly Csikszentmihalyi and Reed Larson. (1987). Validity and Reliability of the Experience-Sampling Method. *The Journal of Nervous and Mental Disease*, *175*(9), 526–536. http://doi.org/bwb7km
16. Daniel A. Epstein, An Ping, James Fogarty, and Sean A. Munson. (2015). A Lived Informatics Model of Personal Informatics. *Proceedings of the ACM International Joint Conference on Pervasive and Ubiquitous Computing (UbiComp 2015)*, 731–742. http://doi.acm.org/10.1145/2750858.2804250
17. James Fogarty, Scott E. Hudson, Christopher G. Atkeson, Daniel Avrahami, Jodi Forlizzi, Sara Kiesler, Johnny C. Lee, and Jie Yang. (2005). Predicting Human Interruptibility with Sensors. *ACM Transactions on Computer-Human Interaction*, *12*(1), 119–146. http://doi.org/fpqwt3

18. Thomas Fritz, Elaine M. Huang, Gail C. Murphy, and Thomas Zimmermann. (2014). Persuasive Technology in the Real World: A Study of Long-Term Use of Activity Sensing Devices for Fitness. *Proceedings of the ACM Conference on Human Factors in Computing Systems (CHI 2014)*, 487–496. http://doi.org/bbdv

19. Jon E. Froehlich, Mike Y. Chen, Sunny Consolvo, Beverly L. Harrison, and James A. Landay. (2007). MyExperience: A System for In Situ Tracing and Capturing of User Feedback on Mobile Phones. *Proceedings of the International Conference on Mobile Systems, Applications and Services (Mobisys 2007)*, 57–70. http://doi.org/c8smx6

20. Jon E. Froehlich, Mike Y. Chen, Ian E. Smith, and Fred Potter. (2006). Voting with your Feet: An Investigative Study of the Relationship Between Place Visit Behavior and Preference. *Proceedings of the International Conference on Ubiquitous Computing (UbiComp 2006)*, 333–350. http://doi.org/dw2bxj

21. Eric Granholm, Catherine Loh, and Joel Swendsen. (2008). Feasibility and Validity of Computerized Ecological Momentary Assessment in Schizophrenia. *Schizophrenia Bulletin*, *34*(3), 507–14. http://doi.org/bb5ch2

22. Eric Hoddes, Vincent Zarcone, and William Dement. (1972). Development and Use of Stanford Sleepiness Scale. *Psychophysiology*, *9*(1), 150.

23. Stefan E Hormuth. (1986). The Sampling of Experiences In Situ. *Journal of Personality*, *54*(1), 262–293. http://doi.org/fr7bs4

24. James M. Hudson, Jim Christensen, Wendy A. Kellogg, and Thomas Erickson. (2002). "I'd be overwhelmed, but it's just one more thing to do": Availability and Interruption in Research Management. *Proceedings of the SIGCHI Conference on Human Factors in Computing Systems (CHI 2002)*, 97–104. http://doi.org/dq59k7

25. Stephen S. Intille, Emmanuel Munguia Tapia, John Rondoni, Jennifer Beaudin, Chuck Kukla, Sitij Agarwal, Ling Bao, and Kent Larson. (2003). Tools for Studying Behavior and Technology in Natural Settings. *Proceedings of the International Conference on Ubiquitous Computing (UbiComp 2003)*, 157–174. http://doi.org/dghjhz

26. Ashish Kapoor and Eric Horvitz. (2008). Experience Sampling for Building Predictive User Models: A Comparative Study. *Proceeding of the SIGCHI Conference on Human Factors in Computing Systems (CHI 2008)*, 657–666. http://doi.org/d6sr59

27. Predrag Klasnja, Beverly L. Harrison, Louis LeGrand, Anthony LaMarca, Jon E. Froehlich, and Scott E. Hudson. (2008). Using Wearable Sensors and Real Time Inference to Understand Human Recall of Routine Activities. *Proceedings of the International Conference on Ubiquitous Computing (UbiComp 2008)*, 154–163. http://doi.org/fwkjv6

28. Predrag Klasnja and Wanda Pratt. (2012). Healthcare in the Pocket: Mapping the Space of Mobile-Phone Health Interventions. *Journal of Biomedical Informatics*, *45*(1), 184–198. http://doi.org/c8t7t9

29. William J. Korotitsch and Rosemery O. Nelson-Gray. (1999). An Overview of Self-Monitoring Research in Assessment and Treatment. *Psychological Assessment*, *11*(4), 415–425. http://doi.org/fs8szw

30. Neal Lathia, Kiran K. Rachuri, Cecilia Mascolo, and Peter J. Rentfrow. (2013). Contextual Dissonance: Design Bias in Sensor-Based Experience Sampling Methods. *Proceedings of the ACM International Joint Conference on Pervasive and Ubiquitous Computing (UbiComp 2013)*, ACM Press, 183–192. http://doi.org/bbpg

31. C.W. Lejuez, Derek R. Hopko, Ron Acierno, Stacey B. Daughters, and Sherry L. Pagoto. (2011). Ten Year Revision of the Brief Behavioral Activation Treatment for Depression: Revised Treatment Manual. *Behavior Modification*, *35*(2), 111–161. http://doi.org/d2cgds

32. Ian Li, Anind K. Dey, and Jodi Forlizzi. (2010). A Stage-Based Model of Personal Informatics Systems. *Proceedings of the ACM Conference on Human Factors in Computing Systems (CHI 2010).*, 557–566. http://doi.org/bh8zsb

33. C.R. Martell, S. Dimidijian, and R. Herman-Dunn. (2013). *Behavioral Activation for Depression: A Clinician's Guide*. Guilford Press.

34. Leysia Palen and Marilyn Salzman. (2002). Voice-Mail Diary Studies for Naturalistic Data Capture Under Mobile Conditions. *Proceedings of the ACM Conference on Computer Supported Cooperative Work (CSCW 2002)*, 87–95. http://doi.org/drg82q

35. Martin Pielot, Tilman Dingler, Jose San Pedro, and Nuria Oliver. (2015). When Attention is Not Scarce - Detecting Boredom from Mobile Phone Usage. *Proceedings of the ACM International Joint Conference on Pervasive and Ubiquitous Computing (UbiComp 2015)*, 825–836. http://doi.acm.org/10.1145/2750858.2804252

36. John Rieman. (1993). The Diary Study: A Workplace-Oriented Research Tool to Guide Laboratory Efforts. *Proceedings of the SIGCHI Conference on Human Factors in Computing Systems (CHI 1993)*, 321–326. http://doi.org/cxn7sw

37. John Rooksby, Mattias Rost, Alistair Morrison, and Matthew Chalmers Chalmers. (2014). Personal Tracking as Lived Informatics. *Proceedings of the ACM Conference on Human Factors in Computing Systems (CHI 2014)*, 1163–1172. http://doi.org/bbdz

38. Stephanie Rosenthal, Anind K. Dey, and Manuela Veloso. (2011). Using Decision-Theoretic Experience Sampling to Build Personalized Mobile Phone Interruption Models. *Proceedings of the International Conference on Pervasive Computing (Pervasive 2011)*, 170–187. http://doi.org/d2fcbj

39. James A. Russell, Anna Weiss, and Gerald A. Mendelsohn. (1989). Affect Grid: A Single-Item Scale of Pleasure and Arousal. *Journal of Personality and Social Psychology*, *57*(3), 493–502.

40. Saul Shiffman. (2009). Ecological Momentary Assessment (EMA) in Studies of Substance Use. *Psychological Assessment*, *21*(4), 486–497. http://doi.org/csttmw

41. Timothy Sohn, Kevin A. Li, William G. Griswold, and James D. Hollan. (2008). A Diary Study of Mobile Information Needs. *Proceeding of the CHI Conference on Human Factors in Computing Systems (CHI 2008)*, 433–442. http://doi.org/fjrb85

42. Arthur A. Stone, Christine A. Bachrach, Jared B. Jobe, Howard S. Kurtzman, and Virginia S. Cain (eds.). (1999). *The Science of Self-Report: Implications for Research and Practice*. Psychology Press.

43. Arthur A. Stone, Saul Shiffman, Joseph E Schwartz, Joan E Broderick, and Michael R Hufford. (2003). Patient Compliance with Paper and Electronic Diaries. *Controlled Clinical Trials*, *24*(2), 182–199. http://doi.org/bnwr3b

44. Arthur A. Stone and Saul Shiffman. (2003). Ecological Momentary Assessment (EMA) in Behavorial Medicine. *Journal of Happiness Studies*, *4*(1), 35–52. http://doi.org/bdjp7x

45. Edison Thomaz, Irfan Essa, and Gregory D. Abowd. (2015). A Practical Approach for Recognizing Eating Moments with Wrist-Mounted Inertial Sensing. *Proceedings of the 2015 ACM International Joint Conference on Pervasive and Ubiquitous Computing (UbiComp 2015)*, 1029–1040. http://dx.doi.org/10.1145/2750858.2807545

46. Khai N. Truong, Thariq Shihipar, and Daniel J. Wigdor. (2014). Slide to X: Unlocking the Potential of Smartphone Unlocking. *Proceedings of the ACM Conference on Human Factors in Computing Systems (CHI 2014)*, 3635–3644. http://doi.org/bbph

47. Rajan Vaish, Keith Wyngarden, Jingshu Chen, Brandon Cheung, and Michael S. Bernstein. (2014). Twitch Crowdsourcing: Crowd Contributions in Short Bursts of Time. *Proceedings of the ACM Conference on Human Factors in Computing Systems (CHI 2014)*, 3645–3654. http://doi.org/bbpj

Delineating the Operational Envelope of Mobile and Conventional EDA Sensing on Key Body Locations

Panagiotis Tsiamyrtzis
Dept. of Statistics
Athens Univ. of Econ. & Bus.
pt@aueb.gr

Malcolm Dcosta
Computational Physiology Lab
Univ. Of Houston
mtdcosta2@uh.edu

Dvijesh Shastri
Computer Science
Univ. of Houston-Downtown
shastrid@uhd.edu

Eswar Prasad
Computational Physiology Lab
Univ. of Houston
emanapuram@uh.edu

Ioannis Pavlidis
Computational Physiology Lab
Univ. of Houston
ipavlidis@uh.edu

ABSTRACT

Electrodermal activity (EDA) is an important affective indicator, measured conventionally on the fingers with desktop sensing instruments. Recently, a new generation of wearable, battery-powered EDA devices came into being, encouraging the migration of EDA sensing to other body locations. To investigate the implications of such sensor/location shifts in psychophysiological studies we performed a validation experiment. In this experiment we used startle stimuli to instantaneously arouse the sympathetic system of $n = 23$ subjects while sitting. Startle stimuli are standard but minimal stressors, and thus ideal for determining the sensor and location resolution limit. The experiment revealed that precise measurement of small EDA responses on the fingers and palm is feasible either with conventional or mobile EDA sensors. By contrast, precise measurement of small EDA responses on the sole is challenging, while on the wrist even detection of such responses is problematic for both EDA modalities. Given that affective wristbands have emerged as the dominant form of EDA sensing, researchers should beware of these limitations.

Author Keywords

Electrodermal Activity (EDA); skin conductance; affective sensors; wearable sensors; startle

ACM Classification Keywords

H.5.2 Information Interfaces and Presentation (e.g. HCI): User Interfaces; Input devices and strategies

INTRODUCTION

Sympathetic signals are fundamental indicators of emotional state in affective human studies [1]. Peripheral sensing of sympathetic signals primarily targets transient perspiratory responses, also known as electrodermal activity (EDA) [2]. Conventionally, EDA is measured with clinical instruments that are grid-powered, have limited Internet connectivity, and feature tethered probes. These probes are attached to the subject's fingers. Such conventional sensing schemes restrict mobility, and in some cases interfere with the subject's task (e.g., dexterous action studies [10]). The availability of more autonomous and unobtrusive forms of EDA sensing has increased with the proliferation of mobile computing [11].

There are several mobile EDA sensors in wristband or other wearable forms. These include the Q Sensor (Affectiva, Waltham, Massachusetts), the Shimmer3 GSR + Optical Pulse Development Kit (Shimmer, Dublin, Ireland), and the E4 Wristband (Empatica, Milan, Italy). There are also several conventional EDA instruments built around desktop data acquisition modules. These include the Powerlab (ADInstruments, Bella Vista, New South Wales), the MP 150 (Biopac, Goleta, California), and others.

The technology within each family of EDA instruments (conventional vs. mobile) is largely the same, but there are differences across families. Specifically, both instrument families use Ag/AgCl disc electrodes with contact areas of 1.0 cm^2 for their recordings, as recommended in the literature [4]; they differ, however, in terms of power mode (AC vs. DC), packaging (large vs. small form factor), standard communication capabilities (wired vs. wireless), and wearable options. The power mode has some implications in measurement accuracy (AC is better [2]), while the wearable options in the mobile family of sensors offer flexibility but also present a challenge. The challenge stems from the fact that sympathetically induced EDA responses differ in their strength among various body locations [2, 18]. Unfortunately, the strongest responses do not necessarily correlate with the most 'wearable' body locations. The combination of lesser accuracy with lesser responses may bias results in mobile studies of subject affect. Such biases have not been sufficiently appreciated or studied in the literature.

M. van Dooren et al. investigated the relative strength of EDA responses on 16 body locations [18]. They aroused subjects via emotional film segments, measuring responses with a conventional EDA device. The study concluded that EDA measurements at the foot were most similar with those of the finger. In contrast, arm, back, and armpit traces differed most

CHI 2016, May 7–12, 2016, San Jose, California, USA.
Copyright © 2016 ACM ISBN 978-1-4503-3362-7/16/05 ...$15.00.
http://dx.doi.org/10.1145/2858036.2858536

from the finger trace. Ranogajec and Geršak also found that EDA finger responses are comparable to EDA foot responses [14].

Poh et al. [13] compared the measurements of mobile EDA sensors on subjects' wrists against measurements taken with conventional EDA sensors on subjects' fingers; the stimuli included physical activity, mental arithmetic, Stroop, and horror movies. Then, Poh and other researchers used mobile EDA sensors to collect affective signals from daily activities including reading, walking, and sleeping [13, 16]. They also used mobile EDA sensors in an epilepsy study [12]. The range of applications kept expanding. Chaspari et al. [3] used mobile EDA sensing to model verbal response latencies in autistic children. McDuff et al. [8] used mobile EDA sensing to quantify user emotions in a reflection study of past events. Overwhelmingly, in all these studies researchers used the wristband form of mobile EDA sensing and reported interesting findings.

To summarize, some researchers investigated the strength of EDA responses at several body locations using a conventional EDA device for the measurements; thus, they studied the location effect but not the sensor effect [18]. Other researchers attempted to investigate the sensor effect by using conventional EDA sensors on the subjects' fingers and mobile EDA sensors on the subjects' wrists; in doing so, they confounded sensor effect with location effect [13]. Importantly, the stimuli used in all these studies were emotionally complex and thus, non-ideal for inter-subject comparison. This leaves the investigation of mobile EDA sensing incomplete. We aim to fill this gap by answering two questions: (a) What is the EDA sensor effect at body locations with wearability potential? (b) What are the body's EDA responses in these locations when sympathetic arousal takes place in its most primal form? Stimuli used in prior studies were capable of generating complex emotions, which might depend on the subject's genotype and phenotype. In contrast, we use auditory startle stimuli in our study. Auditory startle is known to invoke a threshold response on the fingers of healthy subjects [6]. This is the least common denominator when it comes to subject arousal, allowing us to establish a firm basis for comparisons.

An EDA device that successfully captures startle responses on the fingers, meets the 'gold standard', as it has the capability of measuring a ubiquitous sympathetic arousal of low intensity and minimal duration at a prime neurophysiological site. Conventional EDA devices belong to this category. Even a gold standard device, however, may not capture startle responses on a different body location (e.g., wrist), where there may be lower concentration of perspiration glands and sparser innervation. Hence, an EDA device should be validated for every intended body location.

Using EDA sensors on body locations that have not been validated against the gold standard may introduce bias into sympathetic measurements in the form of underestimation. With the proliferation of mobile affective studies, this is becoming a pressing question.

METHODS

Ethics Statement. The experimental procedures were approved by the University of Houston's Institutional Review Board (IRB), and were performed in accordance with the approved guidelines. Informed consent was obtained from each subject before conducting the experiments.

Subjects. We recruited subjects through email solicitations and flyer posting in the university campus community (population about $35,000$). We excluded children (< 18), subjects with hearing impairments, and subjects on medications. Age brings psychological and physiological changes that are especially prominent during developmental and late years [2]; for this reason, we did not include children and older adults (> 59) in the subject pool. The use of auditory startle stimuli in the experiment necessitated the exclusion of subjects with hearing problems. Certain medications affect sympathetic responses [5]; to simplify screening and minimize confounding factors, we excluded all medication cases.

Experimental Design. After each subject consented, s/he filled out a biographic questionnaire, the Trait Anxiety Inventory (TAI), and the State Anxiety Inventory (SAI) [17]. The last two meant to check if any pathological or extraordinary conditions were biasing responses. Next, we asked each subject to wash her/his hands and feet prior to sensor attachment. We waited 10 min for normal moisture levels to reestablish on their skin, before attaching the sensors. This preparation ensured optimal and uniform skin conditions in the attachment areas for all subjects. We used Galvanic Skin Response probes connected to an ADInstruments PowerLab data acquisition unit (ADInstruments, Bella Vista, Australia) as conventional EDA sensors (C EDA); we used Q Sensor sets (Affectiva,Waltham, Massachusetts) [15] as mobile EDA sensors ($\mathcal{M}$ EDA).

This was a validation experiment that aimed to isolate the sensor effect from the location effect in EDA measurements. Ideally, for the sensor validation part we needed to test if the C EDA sensor and the $\mathcal{M}$ EDA sensor give the same measurement on the same body location at the same time. The recommended test locations are the fingers and palm, where the sympathetic responses are known to be strong. Because it is impossible to attach the C and $\mathcal{M}$ sensors on the same location, however, we used the bilateral symmetry of the human body as a workaround. The results show that the C sensor measurements on the fingers and palm of the right hand were in agreement with the $\mathcal{M}$ sensor measurements on the fingers and palm of the left hand, respectively (see RESULTS section). For this to happen both of the following conditions had to be true: (a) The C and $\mathcal{M}$ sensors had to have similar capability and (b) the subject pool had to have bilateral symmetry. Hence, our subject pool had bilateral symmetry and this is not surprising, because the great majority of the human population has bilateral symmetry in its functional responses under non-extreme conditions [7].

A total of $n = 25$ subjects fulfilling the inclusion/exclusion criteria volunteered for the experiment. We attached seven

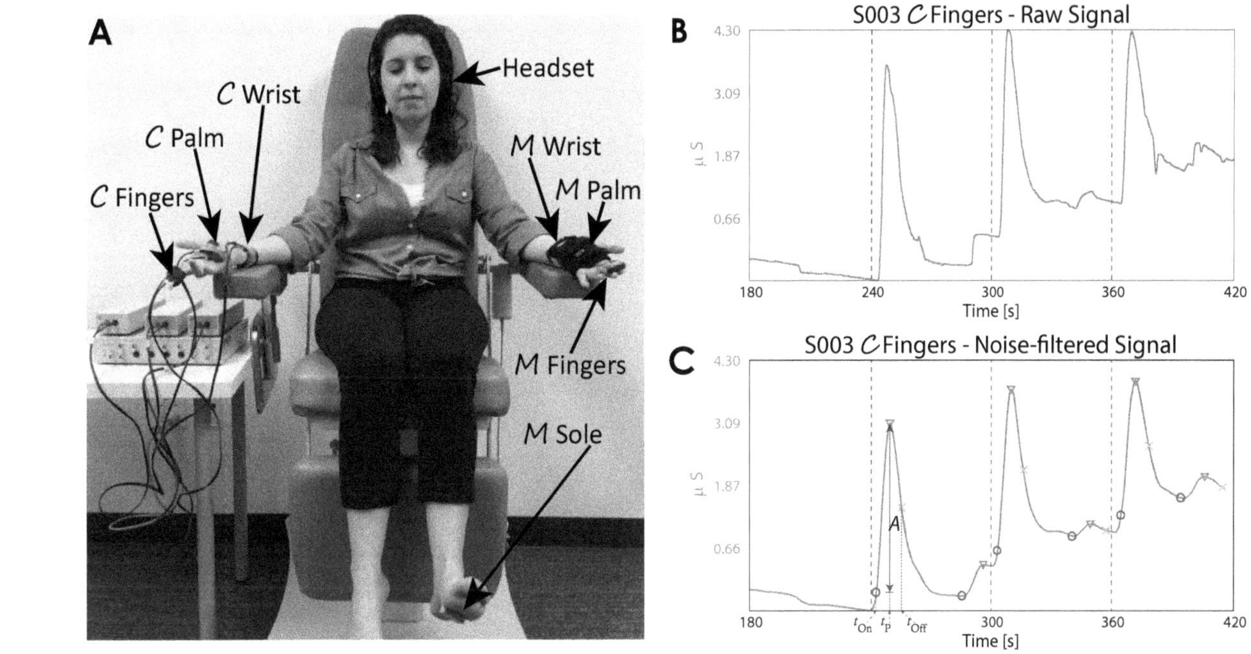

Figure 1. Experiment and sample outcome. A, Experimental setup, demonstrating all seven nodes. B, Raw EDA signal on the fingers of subject S003, captured via the conventional sensing device. The dotted lines mark the occurrence of the three stimuli. Only the last minute of the baseline period is depicted to economize space. C, The signal after noise filtering. There are multiple arousals after each stimulus; circles mark onsets, triangles mark peaks, and crosses mark offsets; t_{on}, denotes the time of Onset occurrence, t_p the time of Peak occurrence, and t_{off} the time of Offset occurrence; A stands for the arousal's amplitude.

EDA sensors to each subject: three sets of a conventional EDA sensor (C EDA) on the subject's right half and four sets of a mobile EDA sensor ($\mathcal{M}$ EDA) on the subject's left half. Specifically, we had the following sensor-location pairs (aka nodes - Fig. 1A):

- Conventional EDA on the right hand fingers (C Fingers)
- Conventional EDA on the right palm (C Palm)
- Conventional EDA on the right wrist (C Wrist)
- Mobile EDA on the left hand fingers ($\mathcal{M}$ Fingers)
- Mobile EDA on the left palm ($\mathcal{M}$ Palm)
- Mobile EDA on the left wrist ($\mathcal{M}$ Wrist)
- Mobile EDA on the left sole ($\mathcal{M}$ Sole)

One of the 25 subjects had missing conventional signals due to a technical problem. For another subject the recorded EDA responses across body locations had a low signal to noise ratio, rendering analysis impossible. Hence, we excluded these two subjects from any further consideration. The usable data set included $n = 23$ subjects (11 males / 12 females; age: 23.91 ± 8.12). Figure 2, Fig. 3, and Fig. 4 depict the analyzed data set for the finger, wrist, and sole locations, respectively, facilitating cross-sensor and cross-location comparisons.

The main experiment lasted seven minutes for each subject. During these seven minutes, the subject listened to soothing music via a headset in a near dark room. This soothing music was interrupted three times with a glass breaking sound, which served as the auditory startle stimulus. The first stimulus was delivered in the fourth minute. After that, two more stimuli were delivered at one-minute interval each. All sensor measurements were synchronized and recorded throughout the experiment. Hence, our usable data bank accrued 161 EDA signals (23 subjects $\times$ 7 EDA signals per subject - one for each node).

Signal Processing. The C sensor samples at the rate of 25 points per second, while the $\mathcal{M}$ sensor samples at the rate of 32 points per second. For this reason, we resampled the $\mathcal{M}$ signals down to 25 points per second to establish uniformity across the signal bank. Then, we applied a moving window filter twice to reduce noise. We set the window size at $W = 125$ points. We arrived at this selection by performing sensitivity analysis with window sizes $W = 25 \times k,\ k = 1, 2, 3, \ldots$ We chose the size of the increment to be 25 points because it matches the minimum resolution (i.e., rate of sampling). At $k = 5$ we attained optimal performance by substantially reducing noise without destructing signal information; at $k > 5$ the signals exhibited over-smoothing, which affected the performance of the Peak and Onset detection algorithms.

Even under the best circumstances, EDA signals are not only noisy (Fig. 1B) but also variable. An electrodermal response may feature more than one Peak. Such peaks correspond to multiple neurophysiological firings provoked by a single stimulus [2]. Hence, for each stimulus a subject can experience none, one, or several peaks (Fig. 1C). For this reason, signal abstraction is quintessential to fair comparisons; noise filtering

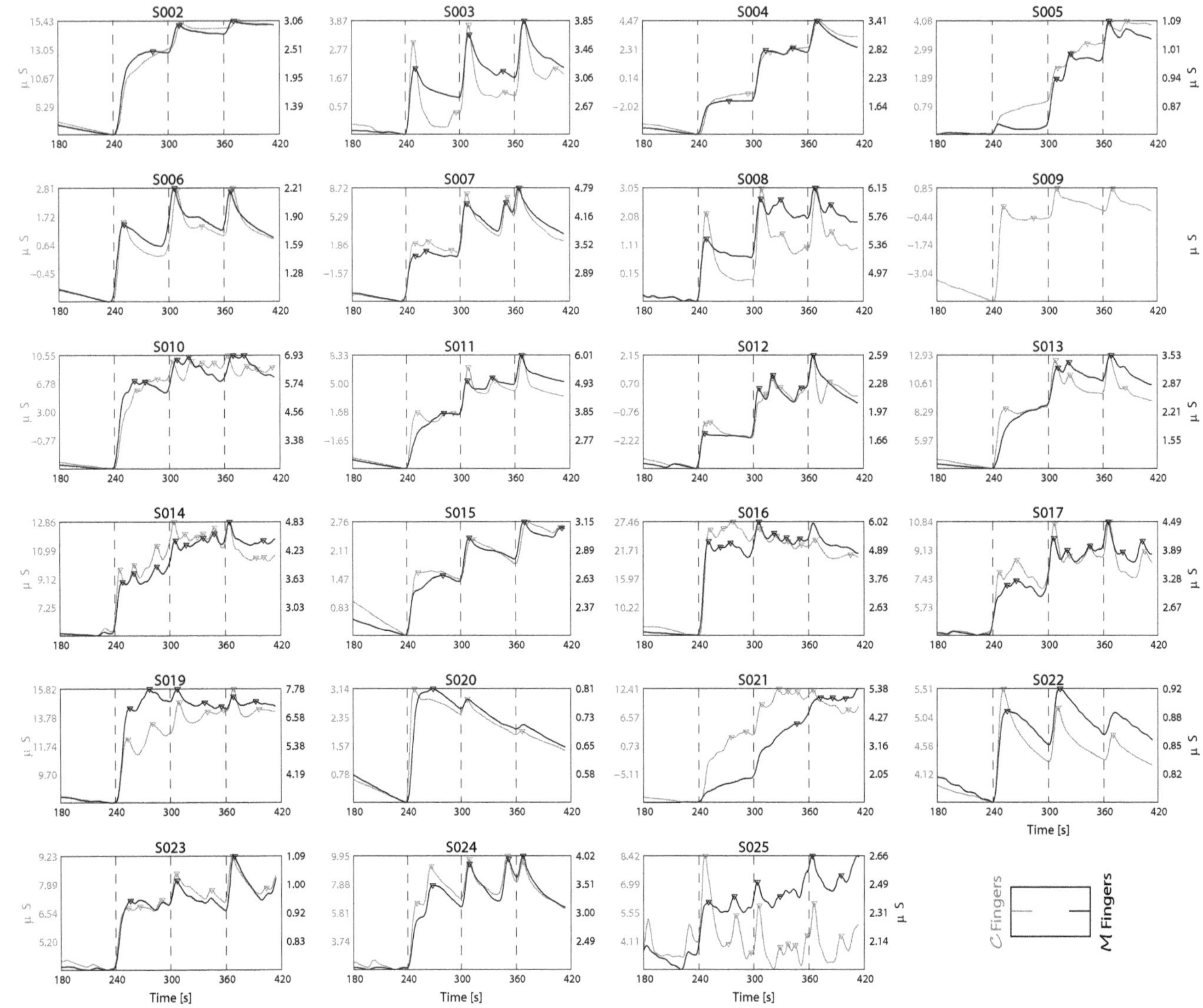

Figure 2. C and $\mathcal{M}$ EDA responses on the fingers per subject. From the four minutes of baseline only the last minute is depicted in the graphs to economize space. Vertical dotted lines identify stimuli times and inverted triangles denote peaks, facilitating arousal comparison. The $\mathcal{M}$ EDA signal for subject S009 was not collected due to technical reasons. The graphs confirm qualitatively the high responsiveness of the fingers location and the agreement between the two sensor modalities.

alone is not sufficient. What is of interest here is the ability of the sensor to measure the essence of the stimulus' response at the specific site. A normal neurophysiological response (arousal) can be reconstructed to a good approximation from three key points in the corresponding EDA signal [2]: Onset, Peak, and Offset. The Onset point represents the start of the EDA activation; the Peak point represents the culmination of the activation; and, the Offset point represents the ebbing of the activation.

On the noise-filtered signals, we focused on the non-baseline period from $t = 4$ to 7 min. We divided this period into three segments: $S_1 = [4, 5)$ min, $S_2 = [5, 6)$ min, and $S_3 = [6, 7]$ min; each segment included the respective stimulus S_1 , S_2 , S_3 and the period up to the delivery of the next stimulus or the end of the experiment. Within each segment we sought arousals (firings), each characterized by a Peak and an Onset. An Offset might or might not have existed, depending on the recovery rate and the timing of the next arousal. To facilitate curve analysis we performed averaging on the noise-filtered signals reducing the resolution down to two points per second. Then, we executed the following algorithmic steps:

1. **Peak Detection:** We applied a Peak detection algorithm on the non-baseline portion of each signal - $S_1 \cup S_2 \cup S_3$. The template we used for Peak detection was a 5-tuple structure fulfilling the following condition: $P(t-2) < P(t-1) < P(t) > P(t+1) > P(t+2)$, where $P(t)$ is the signal intensity P recorded at time t. In essence, this template is the discrete definition of the derivative test for locating curve maxima. Figure 2, Fig. 3A, and Fig. 4 depict the peaks located by the template matching algorithm for all legitimate signals in

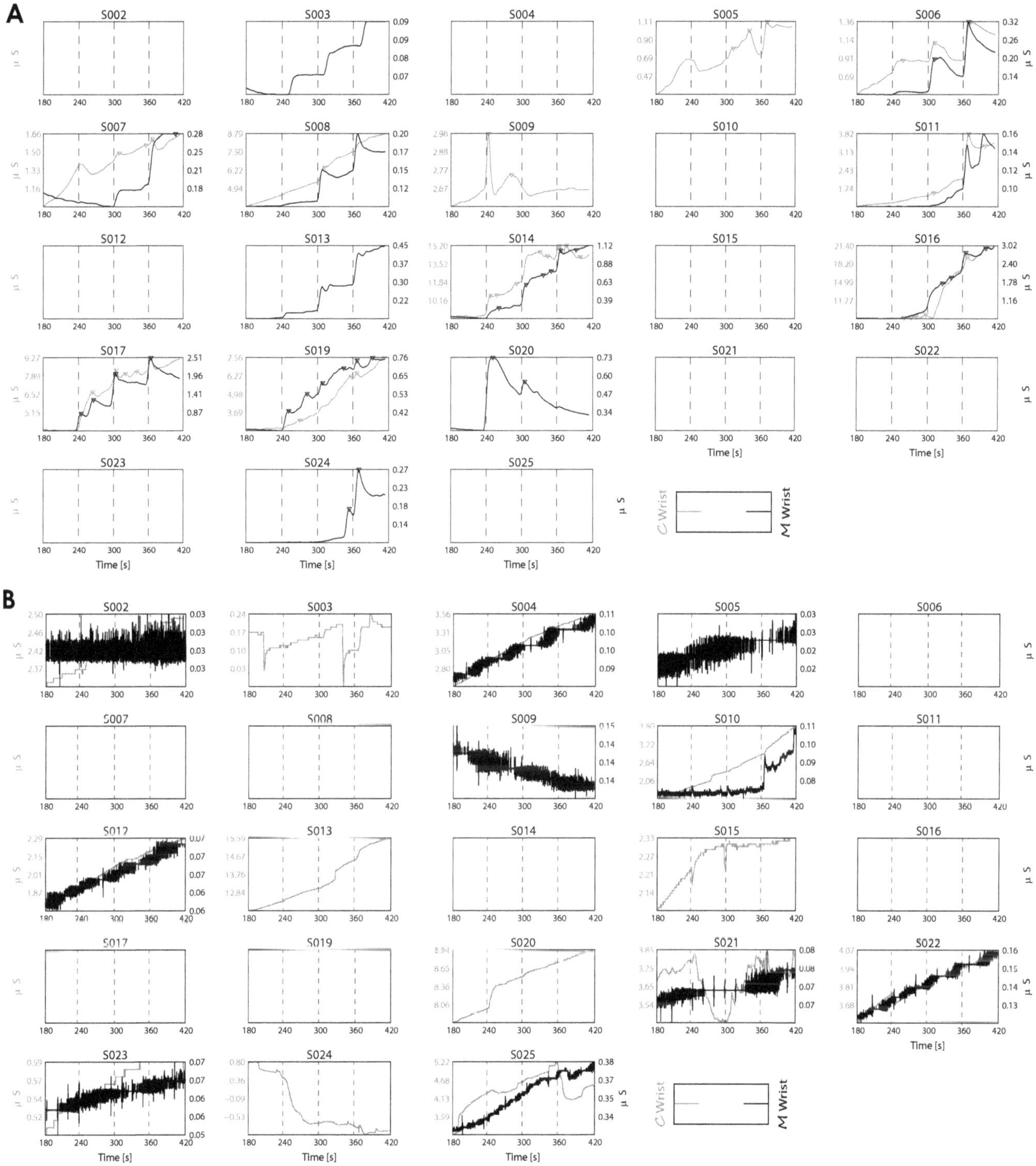

Figure 3. $\mathcal{C}$ **and** $\mathcal{M}$ **EDA responses on the wrist per subject. From the four minutes of baseline only the last minute is depicted in the graphs to economize space. Vertical dotted lines identify stimuli times and inverted triangles denote peaks, facilitating arousal comparison. A, Signals manifesting sympathetic responses on the wrist. B, Signals manifesting the absence of sympathetic responses on the wrist (complement to panel A), which were excluded from further processing and analysis. The graphs confirm qualitatively the low responsiveness of the wrist location, a result that was documented quantitatively in the text.**

the finger, wrist, and sole nodes. For the palm node, signals and results were quite similar to the finger node. The Peak detection algorithm accurately located almost all legitimate peaks in our signal bank. It failed to locate peaks only in a couple of very weak wrist signals, where there is inherently ambiguity as to what constitutes a Peak - see S003 and S013 in Figure 3A.

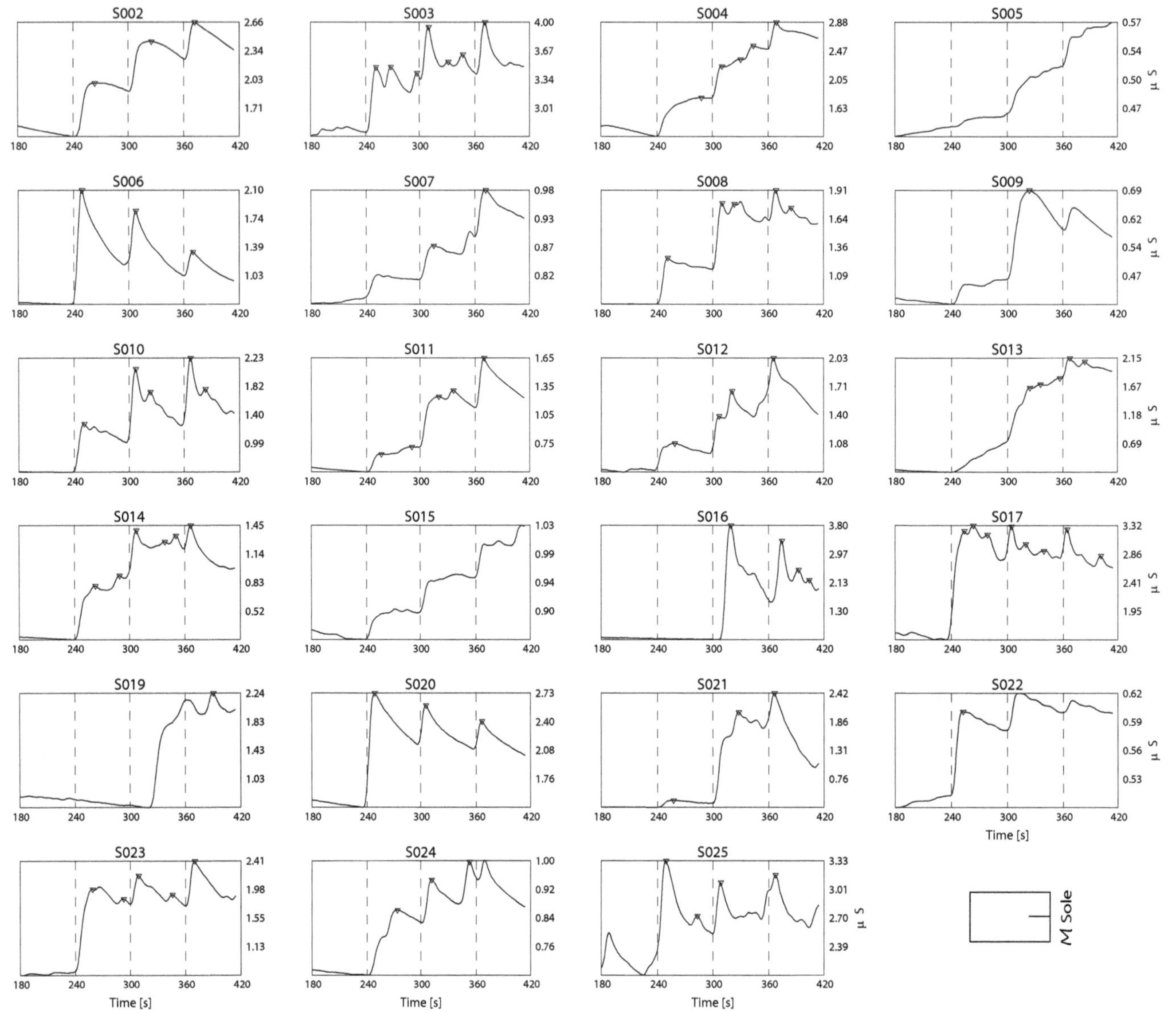

Figure 4. $\mathcal{M}$ EDA responses on the sole per subject. From the four minutes of baseline only the last minute is depicted in the graphs to economize space. Vertical dotted lines identify stimuli times and inverted triangles denote peaks, facilitating arousal comparison. The graphs confirm qualitatively the responsiveness of the sole location, a result that was documented quantitatively in the text. However, amplitude correlations with the finger and palm locations are not strong, suggesting that precise EDA measurements on the sole may be challenging.

2. **Detection of First Onset:** Between each stimulus and the first Peak that followed it within the respective segment, we determined the corresponding Onset; this was the Onset of the first arousal in response to the specific stimulus. We computed the intensity of this first Onset as $P_S + 10\%(\text{Peak}_1 - P_S)$, where P_S denotes the signal intensity at the time of the stimulus and Peak_1 denotes the first Peak.

3. **Detection of Additional Onsets:** When multiple firings took place in response to a stimulus, then more than one Peak points existed within the respective segment S_i, $i = 1, 2, 3$. We located the Onset point corresponding to such an additional Peak in the valley between this additional Peak and the preceding Peak. The template we used for this was a 3-tuple structure fulfilling the following condition: $P(t-1) > P(t) < P(t+1)$, where $P(t)$ is the signal intensity P recorded at time t.

4. **Offset Detection:** For each Peak we determined the matching Offset as the 50% × (Peak - Onset) drop-off point. If this point occurred after the next Onset or stimulus, then it was rejected and the Offset was treated as a missing value; this is an indication that the subject had not recovered at the time a new arousal set in.

RESULTS

Peaks are the most characteristic points of an electrodermal response. Hence, our analysis proceeds at two levels:

Detection level We pay attention to the occurrence of peaks, as proxies of neurophysiological responses; the absence of peaks signifies the absence of a response at a node.

Measurement level We pay attention to the parameters of the neurophysiological responses recorded at the various nodes. These parameters include the times of occurrence for Onset (t_{on}), Peak (t_p), and Offset (t_{off}) as well as the amplitude of the recorded response (A = Peak - Onset). The times t_{on}, t_p, and t_{off} quantify the arousal's evolution, while the amplitude quantifies the arousal's intensity (Fig. 1C).

To ensure that the subjects' trait and state anxiety levels did not affect manifestation of sympathetic activation [9], we obtained their trait (TAI) and state (SAI) anxiety psychometrics [17]. Then, we examined in each node the correlations between the number of peaks detected per subject versus the corresponding TAI and SAI scores. None of these correlations was statistically significant ($p > 0.05$).

Detection Level Analysis

The number of peaks denote responsiveness to stimuli, with zero peaks signifying a non-responsive subject in the specific node. Different subjects exhibited different levels of responsiveness at different nodes. As we observe in Fig. 5, the wrist locations had the highest number of non-responsive subjects irrespective of the sensor type. This indicates that wrists responded poorly to stimuli. The rest of the locations had minimal numbers of non-responsive subjects, indicating the regular presence of arousals in response to stimuli.

We are interested to examine if indeed the proportion of non-responsive subjects differed significantly among the nodes. To do so we use the Binomial distribution. In each node we sampled 23 subjects, where each subject presented a binary outcome: failure, if s/he was non-responsive or success, if s/he had at least one arousal. Hence, for each node if we call Y_i the random variable that denotes the outcome of subject i and θ the unknown probability of success, we have $Y_i|\theta \sim Bernoulli(\theta)$, giving:

$$Y_i = \begin{cases} 0 & \text{if no peaks in the entire experiment} \\ 1 & \text{if at least one peak in the entire experiment} \end{cases} \quad (1)$$

We count the total number of successes in the 23 subjects, forming the random variable $X|\theta \sim Binomial(n, \theta)$, $n = 23$:

$$X = \sum_{i=1}^{n} Y_i \quad (2)$$

As we observe in Fig. 5, the maximum likelihood estimates (MLE) at the wrists are quite smaller compared to the other locations. In fact, running a seven-sample test for equality of proportions shows that there are significant differences among the seven nodes ($p < 0.01$). Next, we exclude the two wrist nodes that appear to be the culprit and we compare the proportions in the remaining five nodes. This time the test returns a non-significant number ($p > 0.05$), which indicates that with the exception of the wrist nodes, all the other nodes are statistically equivalent in terms of peak presence.

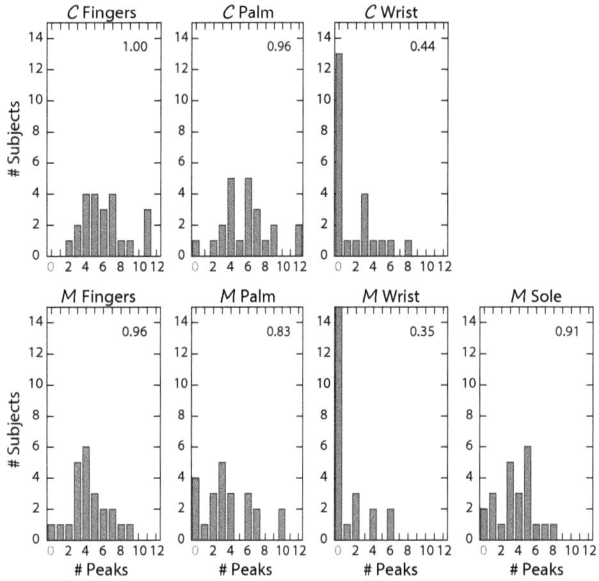

Figure 5. Responsiveness of subjects per node. Each bar chart depicts the distribution of the number of subjects over different levels of response (i.e., number of recorded peaks in the node). Red bars indicate the number of completely non responsive subjects for the specific node. The maximum likelihood estimates (MLE, $\hat{\theta} = X/n$) for getting at least one peak appear on the upper right corner of the node's panel.

Measurement Level Analysis

We start the measurement level analysis by studying the relationship of arousal timing between each pair of nodes, taking into account all three stimuli. Figure 6 shows a matrix that is split along its diagonal. The matrix portion below the diagonal shows the scatterplots of Onset (t_{on}), Peak (t_p), and Offset (t_{off}) times for all node pairs. The matrix portion above the diagonal shows the correlation coefficients for the corresponding scatterplots. As indicated both visually and numerically, the timing agreement between nodes is exceptionally high. Hence, the arousal's evolution is captured accurately at the locations of interest (fingers, palm, wrist, sole), irrespective of the type of sensor used. One has to note, however, that in the case of wrist nodes, the number of points is small. This is consistent with the finding in Fig. 5. Arousal detection at the wrist is rare, but when it occurs, both the C and $\mathcal{M}$ sensors track equally well its evolution.

Next, we study the relationship of arousal intensity between each pair of nodes, taking into account all three stimuli. Figure 7 also shows a matrix that is split along its diagonal. The matrix portion below the diagonal shows the amplitude (A) scatterplots for all node pairs. The matrix portion above the diagonal shows the correlation coefficients for the corresponding scatterplots. As indicated both visually and numerically, the agreement is poor for pairs involving one wrist node, irrespective of the sensor type attached to this wrist node. Agreement is also poor for pairs involving the mobile sole node. Agreement gets at least moderately strong for pairs involving fingers, palms, or finger-palm, irrespective of the sensing modality.

This brings to the fore a problem with EDA sensing: while the timing of the phenomenon is accurately captured across

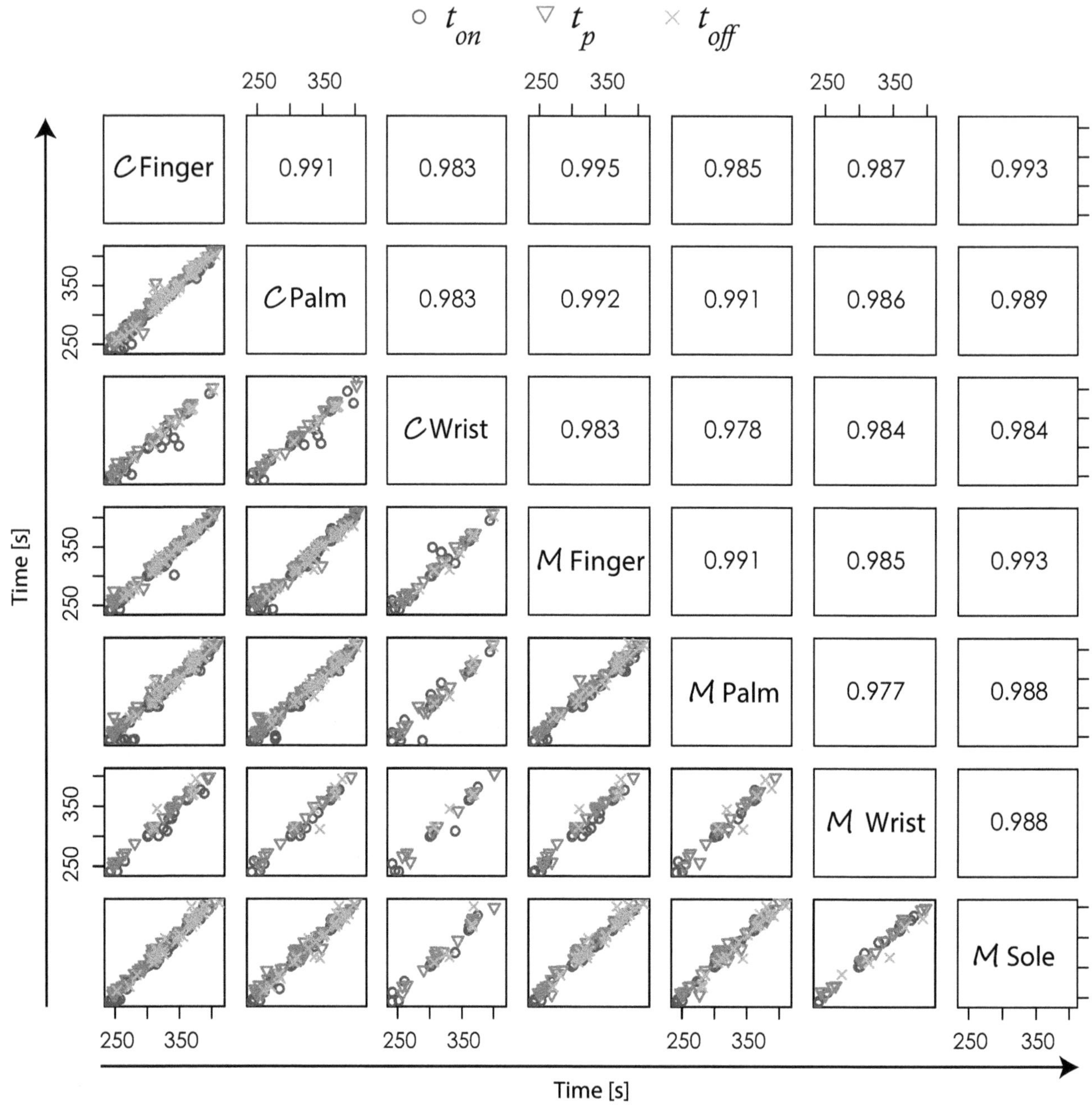

Figure 6. Arousal timing relationships between nodes. BELOW THE DIAGONAL: Scatter-plots of Onset (t_{on}), Peak, (t_p), and Offset (t_{off}) times for the various node pairs. ABOVE THE DIAGONAL: The Pearson correlation coefficients that correspond to the strength of the linear relationships depicted in the scatter-plots below the diagonal (all are significant, $p < 0.01$).

locations and sensor types, the magnitude of the phenomenon poses a challenge. This challenge is bigger for the sole and insurmountable for the wrist location, irrespective of the sensor type.

DISCUSSION

We recognize the importance of quantifiable and objective information the EDA responses can provide to studies of subject affect. Traditionally, EDA sensing is performed on the fingers with conventional EDA devices. Although, this has serious usability problems, it captures well minimal bursts of sympathetic activation. The new mobile EDA sensors, attached on various body locations, have obvious usability advantages. However, one has to be careful not to compromise measurement accuracy or if s/he does, s/he should at least be aware of it.

In this study we found that in response to minimal standardized sympathetic stimuli, conventional EDA devices are in moderate agreement with mobile EDA devices on the fingers and palm. At the same time, we found that both conventional and

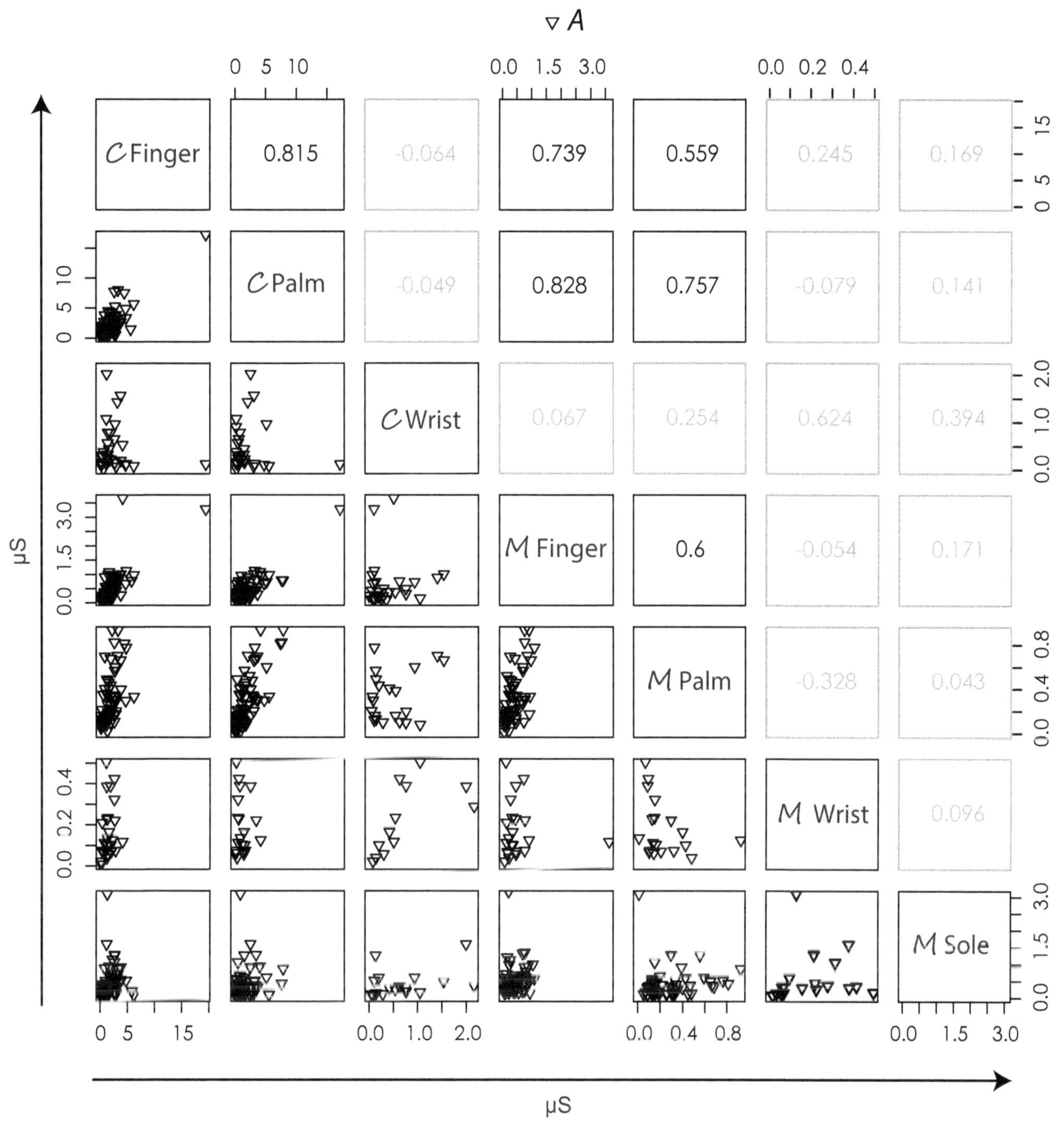

Figure 7. Arousal intensity relationships between nodes. BELOW THE DIAGONAL: Scatter-plots of amplitude (*A*) for the various node pairs. ABOVE THE DIAGONAL: The Pearson correlation coefficients that correspond to the strength of the linear relationships depicted in the scatter-plots below the diagonal (coefficients in bold are significant, $p < 0.01$).

mobile EDA devices give significantly inferior measurements when attached to the wrist. Actually, not only measurement but also mere detection of sympathetic responses on the wrist is quite challenging. Given the proliferation of mobile EDA devices, often in the form of affective wristbands, and the accompanying marketing hype, these results are a waking call for a more careful examination of operational limitations; otherwise, the introduction of measurement bias in affective studies appears likely. A simple way for researchers to guard against this, is to screen their subjects through a startle experiment, ensuring that they produce sympathetic responses on the wrist before embarking on their study.

Another body location - the sole - that is a candidate site for wearable EDA sensing provides strong detection capability, but relatively poor measurement capability.

This study tested sensors and locations in a stationary context. While this was necessary to minimize confounding factors and establish a clear first-level comparison, it certainly does not account for additional effects that are present in practice. The main such effect is ambulatory motion that needs to be studied in the future.

ACKNOWLEDGMENTS

This material is based upon work supported by the National Science Foundation via grant # IIS-1249208, entitled 'EAGER: The Effect of Stress and the Role of Computer Mediation on Exam Performance'. Any opinions, findings, and conclusions or recommendations expressed in this paper are those of the authors and do not necessarily reflect the views of the funding agency.

REFERENCES

1. John L Andreassi. 2000. *Psychophysiology: Human behavior & physiological response*. Psychology Press, New York, New York.
2. Wolfram Boucsein. 2012. *Electrodermal activity*. Springer Science & Business Media, New York, New York.
3. Theodora Chaspari, Daniel Bone, James Gibson, Chi-Chun Lee, and Shrikanth Narayanan. May 26-31, 2013. Using physiology and language cues for modeling verbal response latencies of children with ASD. In *Proceedings of the 2013 IEEE International Conference on Acoustics, Speech and Signal Processing (ICASSP)*. IEEE, Vancouver, BC, Canada, 3702–3706.
4. Don C Fowles, Margaret J Christie, Robert Edelberg, William W Grings, David T Lykken, and Peter H Venables. 1981. Publication recommendations for electrodermal measurements. *Psychophysiology* 18, 3 (1981), 232–239.
5. Alan S Horn, Joseph T Coyle, and Solomon H Snyder. 1971. Catecholamine uptake by synaptosomes from rat brain structure-activity relationships of drugs with differential effects on dopamine and norepinephrine neurons. *Mol. Pharmacol.* 7, 1 (1971), 66–80.
6. Peter J Lang, Margaret M Bradley, and Bruce N Cuthbert. 1990. Emotion, attention, and the startle reflex. *Psychol. Rev.* 97, 3 (1990), 377–395.
7. AL MacMillan and JM Spalding. 1969. Human sweating response to electrophoresed acetylcholine: A test of postganglionic sympathetic function. *J Neurol Neurosurg Psychiatry* 32, 2 (1969), 155–160.
8. Daniel McDuff, Amy Karlson, Ashish Kapoor, Asta Roseway, and Mary Czerwinski. May 5-10, 2012. AffectAura: An intelligent system for emotional memory. In *Proceedings of the SIGCHI Conference on Human Factors in Computing Systems (CHI '10)*. ACM, Austin, TX, 849–858.
9. Richard S Neary and Marvin Zuckerman. 1976. Sensation seeking, trait and state anxiety, and the electrodermal orienting response. *Psychophysiology* 13, 3 (1976), 205–211.
10. I Pavlidis, P Tsiamyrtzis, D Shastri, A Wesley, Y Zhou, P Lindner, P Buddharaju, R Joseph, A Mandapati, B Dunkin, and others. 2012. Fast by nature-how stress patterns define human experience and performance in dexterous tasks. *Sci. Rep.* 2 (2012), 305; doi: 10.1038/srep00305.
11. Rosalind W Picard. 2010. Emotion research by the people, for the people. *Emot Rev* 2, 3 (2010), 250–254.
12. Ming-Zher Poh, Tobias Loddenkemper, Nicholas C Swenson, Shubhi Goyal, Joseph R Madsen, and Rosalind W Picard. September 1-4, 2010a. Continuous monitoring of electrodermal activity during epileptic seizures using a wearable sensor. In *Proceedings of the 32nd Annual International Conference of the IEEE Engineering in Medicine and Biology Society (EMBC 2010)*. IEEE, Buenos Aires, Argentina, 4415–4418.
13. Ming-Zher Poh, Nicholas C Swenson, and Rosalind W Picard. 2010b. A wearable sensor for unobtrusive, long-term assessment of electrodermal activity. *IEEE Trans. Biomed. Eng.* 57, 5 (2010), 1243–1252.
14. Slaven Ranogajec and Gregor Geršak. September 22-24, 2014. Measuring site dependency when measuring skin conductance. In *Proceedings of the Twenty-Third International Electrotechnical and Computer Science Conference ERK 2014*, Vol. 23. IEEE Region 8, Portorož, Slovenia, 155–158.
15. Rozalind W Picard *et al.*, inventors; Massachusetts Institute of Technology, assignee. 2012 Mar 20. Washable wearable biosensor. (March 20 2012 Mar 20). United States patent US 8,140,143.
16. Akane Sano and Rosalind W Picard. August 30-September 3, 2011. Toward a taxonomy of autonomic sleep patterns with electrodermal activity. In *Proceedings of the 33rd Annual International Conference of the IEEE Engineering in Medicine and Biology Society (EMBC 2011)*. IEEE, Boston, MA, 777–780.
17. Charles D Spielberger. 2010. State-Trait Anxiety Inventory. In *The Corsini Encyclopedia of Psychology*, Irving B Weiner and Edward W Craighead (Eds.). John Wiley & Sons, Inc., Hoboken, New Jersey.
18. Marieke van Dooren, Joris H Janssen, and others. 2012. Emotional sweating across the body: Comparing 16 different skin conductance measurement locations. *Physiol Behav* 106, 2 (2012), 298–304.

SpiroCall: Measuring Lung Function over a Phone Call

Mayank Goel[1], Elliot Saba[1], Maia Stiber[2], Eric Whitmire[1], Josh Fromm[1], Eric C. Larson[3], Gaetano Borriello[1], Shwetak N. Patel[1]

[1]Computer Science and Engineering, Electrical Engineering
DUB Group
University of Washington
Seattle, WA 98195
{mayankg, sabae, emwhit, jwfromm, gaetano, shwetak}@uw.edu

[2]Inglemoor High School
Kenmore, WA 98028
mwstiber@gmail.com

[3]Computer Science and Engineering
Southern Methodist University
Dallas, TX 75205
eclarson@lyle.smu.edu

ABSTRACT
Cost and accessibility have impeded the adoption of spirometers (devices that measure lung function) outside clinical settings, especially in low-resource environments. Prior work, called SpiroSmart, used a smartphone's built-in microphone as a spirometer. However, individuals in low- or middle-income countries do not typically have access to the latest smartphones. In this paper, we investigate how spirometry can be performed from *any* phone—using the standard telephony voice channel to transmit the sound of the spirometry effort. We also investigate how using a 3D printed vortex whistle can affect the accuracy of common spirometry measures and mitigate usability challenges. Our system, coined SpiroCall, was evaluated with 50 participants against two gold standard medical spirometers. We conclude that SpiroCall has an acceptable mean error with or without a whistle for performing spirometry, and advantages of each are discussed.

Author Keywords
Health sensing; spirometry; mobile phone sensing; signal processing; machine learning.

ACM Classification Keywords
H.5.m. Information interfaces and presentation (*e.g.,* HCI): Miscellaneous.

INTRODUCTION
Portability, low-cost, and sensing capabilities provide mobile phones a distinct advantage in health sensing. Phone-based health applications often save patients from using and carrying dedicated medical devices. This advantage is particularly apparent in the management of chronic diseases, where patients frequently use health tests to monitor disease progression and manage treatment.

CHI'16, May 07-12, 2016, San Jose, CA, USA
 ISBN 978-1-4503-3362-7/16/05...$15.00.
http://dx.doi.org/10.1145/2858036.2858401

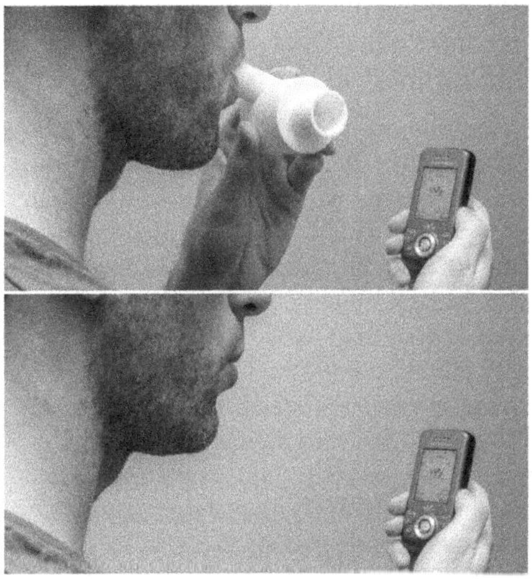

Figure 1. A user using SpiroCall on a feature phone (Sony w580i) with, and without a SpiroCall whistle.

Recently, a number of health applications have been developed to estimate physiological measures such as heart rate [13], respiratory rate [8,12], pupillary dilation [14], and newborn jaundice [5]. Larson *et al.* [9] introduced SpiroSmart, a smartphone-based spirometer that measures a user's lung function using the phone's built-in microphone. Spirometry is the mainstay for measuring lung function and standard of care for diagnosing chronic lung impairments, such as asthma, chronic obstructive pulmonary disease (COPD), and cystic fibrosis. During spirometry tests, participants forcefully exhale as much air as they can from their lungs. The spirometer measures the instantaneous flow and cumulative volume of exhaled air. It then calculates multiple lung function measures to help diagnose and manage various pulmonary conditions.

Introduced in 2012, SpiroSmart [9] is a smartphone application that records the user's exhalation and sends the audio data generated to a central server. The server then calculates the expiratory flow rate using a physiological model of the vocal tract and a model of the reverberation of sound around the user's head. SpiroSmart was an important step in making spirometry more accessible, and since its introduction, it has been involved in numerous clinical studies. SpiroSmart is currently deployed in multiple locations around the world, including Seattle and Tacoma in USA, Khulna in Bangladesh, and Pune in India. Thus far, we have collected data for around two thousand patients using SpiroSmart with encouraging results. While an analysis of the collected data is not the focus of this paper, we highlight four challenges that have surfaced from the SpiroSmart deployments: (1) SpiroSmart requires a smartphone; (2) usability and training challenges exist; (3) a patient with severely low lung function might not generate any sound; and (4) algorithms created from audio collected on a specific smartphone model may not generalize to other models or brands. In this paper, we critically examine ways to address these challenges and evaluate our proposed solutions with a set of 50 new patients.

Smartphones are becoming prevalent at a breathtaking rate, yet more than half of the mobile phone users in sub-Saharan Africa and South Asia will still be using a non-smartphone (or feature phone) in 2020 [4]. A major portion of the population suffering from lung impairments lives in these low resource environments. In fact, according to a recent WHO report, more than 90% COPD deaths occur in low- and middle-income countries [19]. Thus, we believe that phone-based spirometers need to work on all mobile phones, and not just programmable smartphones. Even smartphones, the diversity of phone manufacturers and models makes it challenging to manage custom applications for every type of mobile phone.

To this end, we present *SpiroCall* (Figure 1), a call-in service that measures lung function on *any* mobile phone without the need for a locally running application. Unlike SpiroSmart, it transmits the collected audio using the standard voice telephony channel. A server receives the data of degraded audio quality and calculates clinically relevant lung function measures and reports to the participants using audio or text message. The ability to use a server to analyze audio data transmitted from any mobile phone, be it a feature phone or smartphone, eliminates the need to develop a specialized application for every phone platform. SpiroCall combines multiple regression algorithms to provide reliable lung function estimates despite the degraded audio quality over a voice communication channel.

Although the call-in service removes the need for a smartphone, there are other significant usability challenges that are more difficult to mitigate: how a user holds the phone (angle, microphone occlusion, *etc.*), the distance from the user's mouth to the phone, and how wide a user opens their mouth. Recognizing that some people may not be able to master the technique needed to perform this maneuver, we also designed a simple and low-cost 3D-printed whistle accessory. The whistle (Figure 1, *Top*) generates vortices as the user exhales through it [17,18], changing its resonating pitch in proportion to the flow rate. The whistle does not have any moving parts and is as simple as any spirometer mouthpiece. Despite the additional hardware, the whistle offers several important advantages: (1) the acoustic properties of the whistle are more consistent than a user's vocal tract and generate audible sounds even at lower flow rates, (2) the whistle removes the effect of distance from the user's mouth, and (3) precisely controlling mouth shape and phone orientation are less important. In this paper, we investigate viability of the call-in service approach with and without the whistle.

We evaluated SpiroCall in a controlled study with 50 patients. We compare SpiroCall to two FDA approved spirometers and evaluate the effect of using the voice communication channel on the performance of SpiroCall. Each patient performed spirometry efforts with and without the whistle on two different phones recording the audio through the cell phone network and two smartphones recording the audio locally through an app. Participants used two different sizes of vortex whistles to determine whether different sizes work better for different individuals. Our results show that without a whistle, SpiroCall has a mean error of 7.2% for the four major clinically relevant lung function measures. For FEV1% (the most commonly used diagnostic measure [2]), the mean error is 6.2%. With a whistle, SpiroCall has a mean error of 8.3% for the four measures, and 7.3% for FEV1%. Although, using the whistle leads to higher average error in lung function estimation, it performs more consistently for people with lower lung function and produces fewer over-estimations of lung function (*i.e.*, false negatives), as compared to when not using a whistle.

The main contribution of this paper is a demonstration that *every* mobile phone in the world can be used as a spirometer. This contribution comes in four parts: (1) an algorithm to estimate lung function from a standard telephony voice channel's degraded audio signal; (2) a custom-designed whistle that reduces usability and performance challenges; (3) a comparison of the call-in service and the whistle against two clinical spirometers (using different phones); and (4) a demonstration of how poor quality audio, transmitted across the standard telephony voice channel, can be utilized for modeling and inference.

BACKGROUND OF SPIROMETRY

Spirometry is the most widely employed pulmonary function test. Many different types of spirometers are available, ranging from big, clinical spirometers to portable, home spirometers. Their cost also varies from $1,000 USD to $5,000 USD. During a spirometry test, the patient takes the deepest breath possible and then exhales with maximum force for as long as possible. The spirometer measures the amount and speed of airflow and calculates various lung function measures based on the test. Four of the most important lung function measures are:

(1) **Forced Vital Capacity (FVC):** Total volume of air expelled during the expiration,

(2) **Forced Expiratory Volume in one second (FEV_1):** Volume of air expelled in the first second of expiration,

(3) **FEV_1/FVC (FEV1%):** Ratio of FEV_1 and FVC, and

(4) **Peak Expiratory Flow (PEF):** Maximum expiratory flow rate reached during the test.

A healthy individual's lung function measures are generally at least 80% of the values predicted based on their age, height, and gender [7]. Abnormal values of FEV1% are (expressed as a percent of predicted value) [10]:

- Mild to Medium Lung Dysfunction: 60-79%,
- Moderate Lung Dysfunction: 40-59%, and
- Severe Lung Dysfunction: below 40%.

Apart from the numerical measures, spirometers also generate flow *vs.* time, flow *vs.* volume, and volume *vs.* time plots. Figure 2 shows examples of FV plots. In a healthy individual, the descending limb of the FV plot is almost a straight line (black, solid line in Figure 2). As obstruction to the airflow increases, the flow rate decreases faster than exponentially after reaching its maximum value (PEF). Therefore, it attains a curved or "scooped" slope (blue, dashed line in Figure 2). For an individual suffering from a restrictive lung disease, such as cystic fibrosis, the respiratory muscles weaken and the patient's lung capacity (FVC) decreases (red, dashed line in Figure 2).

DESIGN OF SPIROCALL

The previous work of SpiroSmart offloaded a significant chunk of computation to a server, with the audio transferred via an Internet connection. Thus, the received audio was lossless and free of artifacts. In SpiroCall, we leverage the voice communication channel to transmit the audio data to a server. The server then uses machine learning to compute lung function measures. The features used by our machine learning model fall into three categories: temporal envelope detection, spectrogram processing, and linear predictive coding (LPC). The cellphone channel (GSM) uses LPC to encode voice. This means that even though the GSM channel compresses the audio signal, the values of LPC coefficients remain largely preserved. Landlines, or POTS (Plain Old Telephone Service) is also an attractive option as a communication channel. However, we do not focus on POTS in this paper because GSM networks are far more prevalent than landlines in the developing world.

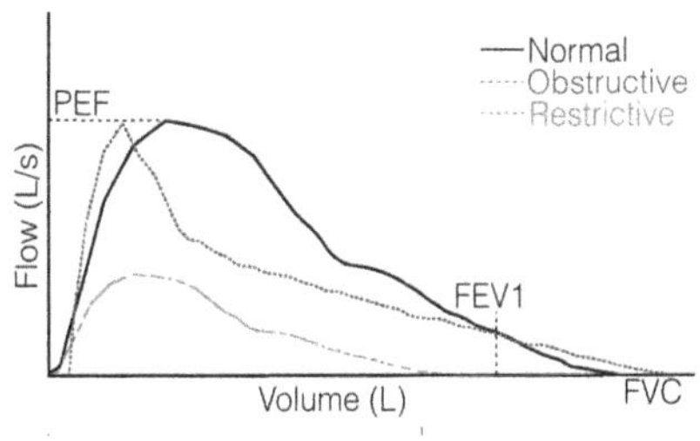

Figure 2. Example of different Flow *vs.* Volume curves and major lung function measures.

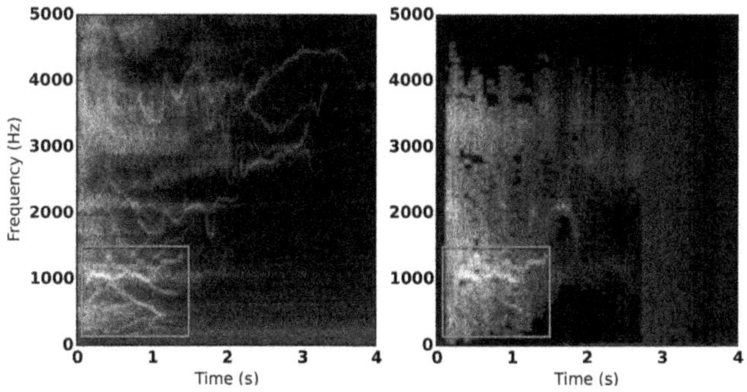

Figure 3. *(Left)* Spectrogram of a spirometry effort recorded locally, and *(Right)* recorded through the voice channel. The GSM network downsamples the audio, and the data over 4 kHz is lost. However, the data in our main region of interest (red square) is largely reconstructable.

Lung Function Estimate without Whistle

Figure 3 shows spectrograms of a spirometry effort recorded locally on a smartphone *(Left)* and the same effort after the data is sent through a GSM cell phone network *(Right)*. The device type is an iPhone 4S in both cases. There are significant differences between the two spectrograms as the voice undergoes many changes as it goes through a communication channel. Although different communication networks use different speech coding techniques, all GSM/UMTS speech-coding algorithms share similarities in their treatment of speech and are based upon the same underlying linear prediction approach.

First, all GSM voice coding technologies use a source-filter model for speech. That is, the "source" estimates the lung or glottis excitation, and the "filter" estimates how the vocal tract blurs this excitation into continuous sound. Parameters of the source and filter are then transmitted through the channel, instead of the raw audio. The most common method for separating out the source excitation from the vocal tract filter is to use LPC. An artifact of the LPC calculation is that the strong frequency resonances are preserved (and are calculable directly from the LPC coefficients). These resonances are also the primary features in our algorithms. As such, we expect the LPC encoding to preserve much of the important information in the signal. An example of this is shown in Figure 3 – the fundamental resonance is easily seen in both recordings (inside the red box), despite many smaller details, such as higher harmonics of the fundamental resonance and all spectral energy above 4 kHz, being lost.

Additionally, the transmission process suppresses low-energy components in the signal, as can be seen in Figure 3 *(Right)* where the energy of the signal abruptly cuts off in patches. In contrast, the signal maintains high fidelity and stays above the noise floor for the initial (and relatively louder) segment of the effort (inside the red box in Figure 3, *Right*).

Algorithm for Lung Function Estimation over a Voice Channel without a Vortex Whistle

In order to deal with the drastic variation in sound quality as the data goes through a GSM channel, we sought to evaluate what modifications are necessary to the algorithm proposed in the original SpiroSmart paper [9].

We use the microphone as an uncalibrated pressure sensor and the received pressure values are transformed using three approaches (Figure 4): (1) envelope detection, (2) resonance tracking in the frequency domain, and (3) linear predictive coding (LPC). The envelope of the signal can be assumed to be a reasonable approximation of the flow rate because it is a measure of the overall signal power (or amplitude) at low frequencies. In the frequency domain, resonances can be assumed to be amplitudes excited by reflections in the vocal tract and mouth opening—and therefore should be proportional to the flow rate that causes them. Finally, we can use linear prediction as a flow approximation. Linear prediction assumes that a signal can be divided into a source and a shaping filter and it estimates the source power and shaping filter coefficients. The "filter" in our case approximates the vocal tract. The "source variance" is an estimate of the white noise process exciting the vocal tract filter—in our case, this approximates the power of the flow rate from the lungs. Each approach generates multiple time-domain flow-rate estimations.

We extract separate feature sets for FEV1, FVC, and PEF from these time-domain flow-rate estimations. For example, PEF is defined as the maximum flow reached in an effort. Thus, for a given flow-rate estimation, we take the max value and use it as a feature for PEF regression. In contrast, FVC is defined as the total volume of air exhaled. Thus, integrating the flow-rate estimation with respect to time gives us a feature for FVC regression. Using this approach, we generate 3 sets of of 38 features for FEV1, FVC, and PEF, each. We do not use any regression algorithm to estimate FEV1%. This value is simply a ratio of the estimated FEV1 and FVC.

Considering that the GSM channel uses LPC to encode sound, the LPC-based features used in our algorithms remain largely preserved. The envelope detection-based features are based on the coarse amplitude of sound with respect to time; in most cases these features remain preserved as well. The spectral features are most affected by the GSM channel because the high frequency details are completely lost. However, upon analysis we realized that the resonances within the first harmonics were strong enough that most spectral features contain some relevant information.

In the original algorithm, the calculated features were sent to a random forest regression that, because it has no underlying linear model, had trouble exploiting some of the linearity in the feature data. The algorithm performed poorly on the data collected through the GSM channel and it over-estimated the lung function for participants with obstructed lungs (FEV1% < 0.8). Therefore, we have updated the algorithm to employ an ensemble of four different regression algorithms (Figure 4), with the aim that each regression would provide a different perspective. We run the regressions using the *scikit-learn* toolkit in Python and use leave-one-patient-out cross-validation to avoid overfitting. Furthermore, we keep all the parameters for all the algorithms at their default values and do not tune them for the collected data.

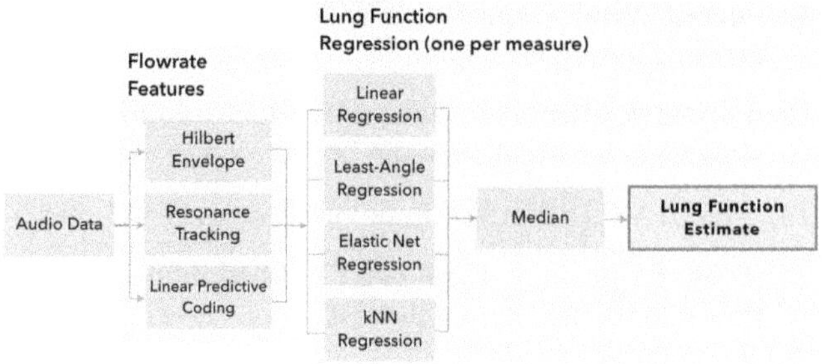

Figure 4. Flowchart for lung function estimation without whistle.

The first regression is a linear regression that tries to find a linear relationship between the features and the ground truth lung function value. The second regression uses least angle regression (LARS) [3]. LARS selects the most useful features using a variant of forward feature selection, but the underlying model is assumed to be linear. The third regression uses the elastic net algorithm [20], which eliminates features in a slightly different way than LARS. This regression uses a combination of LASSO regression and ridge regression for regularization that is often more stable. Finally we use enclosing k-Nearest Neighbor regression (k = 2) [6], which finds the convex hull of the data in the feature space and fits a locally linear regression. Though the underlying model is assumed linear, the local fitting often can fit many different types of nonlinearity. We find the final regression estimate by taking the median of these four regressions. We use this same process for FEV1, FVC, and PEF measures. As mentioned, FEV1% is calculated as a ratio of the estimated FEV1 and FVC values.

Additionally, there are situations when the test is performed in a noisy environment or the channel itself might be noisy. To deal with such situations, the system automatically detects the level of background noise by looking at the mean absolute amplitude of the recorded sound for a 250 ms window immediately before the user exhales. This is the period when the user is most silent and we use it as an opportunity to measure the ambient noise level. If the amplitude of sound within this window is estimated to be above an empirically determined threshold, the environment is considered unsuitable for data collection. The threshold used here is same as the one used in the SpiroSmart clinical trials.

Lung Function Estimate with Whistle

SpiroCall faces three audio sensing challenges, (1) variability of different phones, (2) low sound amplitude for severely impaired patients, and (3) inconsistency of the distance between a user's mouth and the microphone. Bernard Vonnegut, in 1954, designed a whistle that changed its pitch in proportion to flow rate and called it a vortex whistle [17]. Later, Watanabe and Sato suggested modifications to vortex whistle construction for use in spirometry efforts [16,18,21]. In their study, they used pitch tracking to convert the vortex whistle sound to an estimate of flow rate. Considering pitch tracking is resilient to variations across devices, such as gain and frequency response, the whistle could make SpiroCall independent of distance, channel, and device. The whistle has no moving parts and thus, is as simple as any spirometer mouthpiece—mass-producible for less than 10 cents (US). We decided to test the design proposed in [16] to see if it could be used as a flow-sound transducer instead of the user's vocal tract. However, we found the proposed design unsuitable for spirometry and modified it based on a pilot study with 15 participants.

The vortex whistle consists of three sections: the inlet, the cylindrical cavity, and the downstream tube. The *inlet* is a cylindrical pipe that is tangentially connected to the cylindrical cavity on its curved surface. The user blows through this tube. The *cylindrical cavity* allows the air inside to swirl around the chamber. The *downstream tube* is attached perpendicular to the cylindrical cavity. When the air enters the cylindrical cavity, it starts rotating along the circumference of the cavity, thereby forming a vortex, and moves toward the downstream tube. The arrows in Figure 5 *(Left)* show the result of a simulation of airflow within the whistle. The color of the arrow denotes the simulated velocity of the air. When the air leaves the cylindrical cavity, the vortex becomes unstable and whips around at an angular velocity that is proportional to the rotational velocity of the vortex. This unstable vortex generates sound as it leaves the downstream tube.

The frequency produced by the whistle is affected by several factors, including the dimensions of the whistle [17]:

$$F = \frac{U}{2\pi R_{CC} A} \sin\theta \sqrt{\frac{1}{R_f(L_{DST}+\Delta L_{DST})}} \quad (1)$$

where F is frequency, U is input flow rate, R_{CC} is the radius of the vortex in the cylindrical cavity, A is the cross-sectional area of the inlet, R_f is radius of the air in the downstream tube, L_{DST} is the length of the downstream tube, and ΔL_{DST} is the length of the vortex formed at the outlet of the whistle. The *sin* term refers to the angle between the formed vortex and cylindrical plane. This term is difficult to calculate mathematically, necessitating that the quantity be determined through calibration [16]. Typical values range between 0.35 up to 0.95 [16].

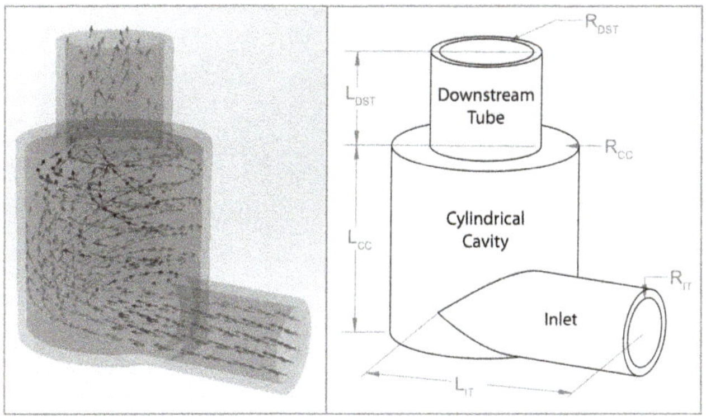

Figure 5. *(Left)* 3D rendering of the whistle. The arrows show the airflow and the colors denote the velocity. Red is faster and blue is slower. *(Right)* Dimensions (in mm) of the two whistles: Small: R_{CC} = 20, R_{DST} = 11, R_{IT} = 8, L_{IT} = 50, L_{DST} = 24, L_{CC} = 40. Big: R_{CC} = 37.5, R_{DST} = 12.5, R_{IT} = 8, L_{IT} = 74, L_{DST} = 27, L_{CC} = 35.

We modified the design suggested in [16] to ensure that the whistle's response remains linear even at flow rates around 15 L/s (verified via SolidWorks™ simulations). This flow rate is well above the peak flow rate attainable by individuals with height up to 210 cm. We designed two sizes of the whistle (dimensions shown in Figure 5, *Right*), as different sizes will have different pitch gradients.

We 3D-printed the whistles on a Stratasys BST768 printer using ABS plastic material. Our evaluation of both the whistle sizes with 50 participants demonstrated that the bigger whistle performed better because it had a steeper pitch gradient. From a usability standpoint, 34 out of 50 participants also preferred using the bigger whistle, because it was easier to handle.

Algorithm for Lung Function Estimation with Whistle

When a vortex whistle is used, we can simplify the audio processing considerably because the whistle pitch changes linearly in response to flow rate. Simple pitch tracking can estimate the flow rate over time. We can calibrate the parameters of this linear relationship (bias and slope) using a few example spirometry efforts. For a particular vortex whistle with set dimensions, these parameters only need to be calibrated once.

Whistle Pitch Extraction: All audio data is resampled to 44.1 kHz to ensure uniformity in the processing across devices with different sampling rates. We first process the spectrogram of the effort to track the pitch. We segment the data into frame durations of 46 ms with a step size of 3 ms between frames. Next, we find the peak magnitude in the spectrogram (Figure 6) and search for the peak frequency within 0.25 seconds. The peak frequency (Figure 6, top of the white curve) corresponds to the PEF of the spirometry effort. We track pitch backward and forward in time from that point, stopping when the spectral energy ceases to trend towards lower frequencies. This helps us ignore wheezing at the end of a spirometry effort that may overwhelm the

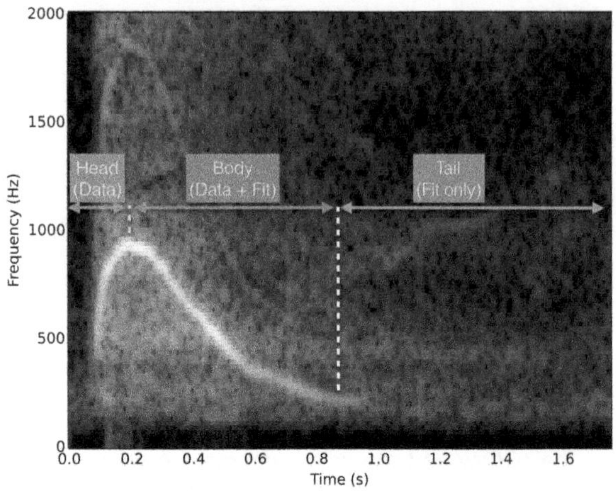

Figure 6. The blue and orange regions are associated with the pitch tracked by the algorithm. The green region is extrapolated based on information in the blue region.

main whistle audio amplitude. For each frame, we fit a quadratic polynomial to the frequency bin of interest and its two neighbors to attain sub-bin accuracy in our peak frequency estimates [11]. We stop pitch tracking once the resonance passes below a certain empirically determined pitch threshold, as the whistle mouthpiece does not resonate well at lower flow rates and therefore lower frequencies.

For example, in Figure 6, the pitch can be tracked up to 1 s. This means that while we can infer the FEV_1 value from the pitch data, the FVC value needs an extrapolated curve.

Tail Extrapolation: After the flow achieves its peak value (PEF), the flow rate decays exponentially for a healthy individual and decays faster than exponentially for an individual with obstructive lung impairments. Therefore, when we extrapolate the pitch curve, we cannot just use an exponential fit function. We apply a combination of exponential and exponential of exponential fits, so that the system automatically adapts to different types of flow-time curves, including the ones where the flow rate decay faster

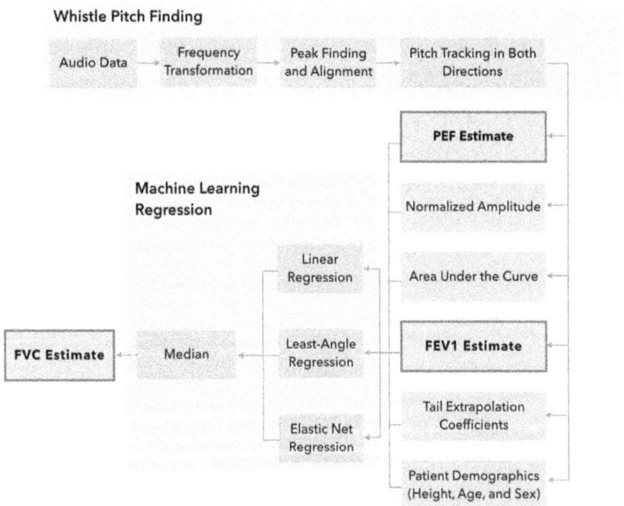

Figure 7. Flowchart for lung function estimation with whistle.

than exponentially . We fit the following function to the tail end of the flow-time curve:

$$x(t) = \left(a_0 e^{-b_0 t} + a_1 e^{-b_1 t^2}\right) \cdot a_2 e^{e^{-b_3 t}} \qquad (2)$$

We use the entire descending limb of the tracked pitch to fit our extrapolation function. The green area (Tail Fit only) in Figure 6 shows the time over which the curve is extrapolated. The blue area (Body, Data+Fit) represents the phase in time during which reliable resonance tracking data is available. However in order to transition smoothly from resonance-tracking to extrapolation, we cross-fade from resonance-tracked data to extrapolated data within the blue region. We evaluated our extrapolation function by applying it to the set of groundtruth flow-time curves to ensure it was able to model the tail end of a user's exhalation. Although the extrapolation function worked exceptionally on groundtruth data (mean error = 3.2%), when we evaluated the extrapolation on the audio data received from SpiroCall devices, our FVC estimates had an average error of 15%. We therefore decided to estimate the FVC through a regression model, using the extrapolated curve as a feature in the regression.

FVC Regression Model: Although our tail extrapolation method did not provide an adequate volume (FVC) measure, it still provided a good, albeit noisy, estimate in most cases. We, therefore, encode the pitch tracking output as a set of regression features. Figure 7 shows all the features used in the regressions. The features can be broken down into the three phases of the pitch tracking in Figure 6: *Head, Body,* and *Tail.* We use the estimated PEF, *i.e.,* the peak frequency of the tracked pitch, as the representative feature from the *Head* section of the curve. We also use the peak amplitude (normalized) of the overall audio. From the *Body* section of the curve, we use the area under the pitch-tracking curve until the end of the body section, and the area under the curve until the end of 1 sec, *i.e.,* FEV_1 estimate. The next set of features comes from the *Tail* extrapolation. We use the coefficients generated by the tail extrapolation as an encoding of the curve in the *Tail* region of the curve. Specifically, we use a_0, a_1, and $a_2$from Equation (2) as features in the regression. Apart from these features, we also use height, age, and sex as our demographic features. It is common practice in spirometers to record a patient's physical details as this information helps the device in calculating predicted normal lung function for the patient.

Similar to the no-whistle condition, the regression algorithm employs an ensemble of three regressions: linear, LARS, and elastic net regressions. We combine the outputs of all regressions and select a median of their estimates as the final FVC estimate. We use leave-one-patient-out cross validation in all levels of learning to avoid overfitting.

EVALUATION

To evaluate SpiroCall, we created an extensive dataset of audio samples and ground truth spirometry data. We recruited 50 participants (30 males, 20 females), ranging in age from 21 to 67 years (M = 30) through flyers and email messages in the university. The study sessions were conducted in a non-clinical lab setting and lasted for approximately 30 minutes. 20% of participants had mild to moderate lung obstruction, *i.e.,* FEV1% < 0.80 (Table 1).

The SpiroCall study used a within-subjects 2 × 2 × 3 factorial design. The factors and levels were:

- ***Phone Type:*** *iPhone* and *non-iPhone.* We used two non-iPhone devices: Samsung Note 3 and Sony Ericsson W580i. We used the W580i (feature phone) to evaluate the performance of SpiroCall on an approximately 10-year-old device.
- ***Channel Type:*** *Local recording* or *voice channel recording.* We kept the iPhone consistent in both channels to analyze the performance of SpiroCall if only the channel is changed.
- ***Whistle:*** *No whistle, small whistle,* and *big whistle.* We recorded audio data for two whistles to understand if different participants preferred different sizes or if one size gave results that were more reliable that the other.

All the conditions were counterbalanced and we randomized the order of the whistles.

Experimental Setup

We collected the audio data on four phones, two iPhone 4S smartphones, a Samsung Galaxy Note 3, and a Sony Ericsson W580i feature phone. All four phones were in front of the user at roughly an arm's length away (Figure 8). The distance was not formally controlled or varied. One of the iPhones and the Samsung Note recorded the audio data locally at 32 kHz and 44.1 kHz, respectively. The other two devices sent the data over the GSM voice channel. These phones placed phone calls to different Google Voice accounts that recorded the data in the form of voicemail messages. Google Voice saved the audio data as 44.1 kHz

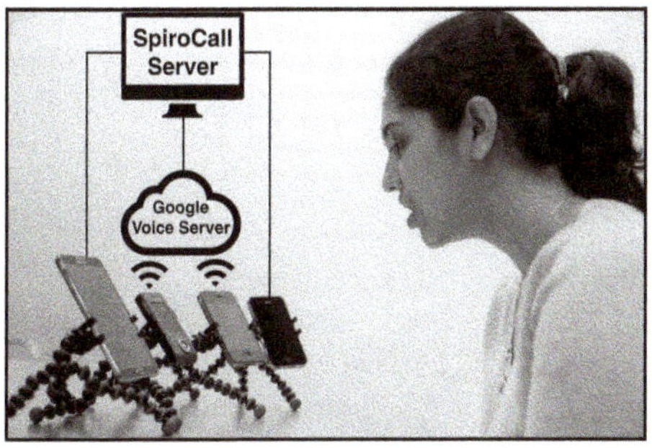

Figure 8. SpiroCall experimental setup. We recorded the data on four phones at the same time. Two phones recorded the audio locally. The other two phones called Google Voice numbers and sent the audio data over the GSM channel to the Google Voice server.

Table 1. Demographic information of the participants.

Participant Demographics (N = 50)	
Males (n, %)	30 (60%)
Age (yrs) (mean, range)	30 (21 – 67)
Height (cm) (mean, range)	172 (155 – 188)
Reported Lung Ailments Asthma: 10 (20%), Bronchitis: 2 (4%), COPD: 2 (4%), Cystic Fibrosis: 1 (2%), Sarcoidisis: 1 (2%)	
Low Lung Function (n, %)	16 (32%)
Never Performed Spirometry (n, %)	30 (60%)

MP3 files, but the GSM channel band-limited the data to less than 8 kHz. The difference between the local recordings and those done over the GSM channel is shown in Figure 3.

We transferred the data from the local phones (iPhone 4S and Samsung Note) to the computer over a USB connection at the end of the study. We downloaded the data from the Google Voice accounts as MP3 files to a computer.

Procedure

We collected the ground truth for the participants on two FDA-approved clinical spirometers: the nSpire Koko Legend and the NDD EasyWare spirometer. We used the two spirometers to answer two questions: (1) whether the participants got fatigued as the session progressed, and (2) how much variability exists between the outputs of the two devices. We recorded the variability between the clinical devices to use it as a benchmark for SpiroCall's performance. The participants performed at least 15 spirometry efforts (three each for: two clinical spirometers, two whistles, and one without whistle). Spirometry measurements are completely effort-dependent and some fatigue can build up when performing this many efforts. Therefore, we recorded efforts on one clinical spirometer at the beginning of the session and on another spirometer at the end of the session. We randomized the order for each participant.

At the start of each session, we explained the forced expiratory maneuver to the participants and we asked them to practice using the spirometer. Once the participants were able to perform an acceptable maneuver according to the ATS criteria for reproducibility [10], three efforts were recorded using the spirometer. Next, we introduced the participants to SpiroCall.

The four phones (Phone Type × Channel Type) recorded the audio simultaneously, thus saving the participants from performing tests with each device type separately. One of the authors, who was trained to administer spirometry efforts, gave feedback to the participants regarding the acceptability and quality of the efforts. In the future, it will be straightforward to have a system that automatically determines if an effort was too low in volume.

Note that collecting the SpiroCall data and the clinical spirometer data at the same time is impossible, so explicit ground truth was unknown. Instead, each effort from SpiroCall was associated with the best effort selected by the clinical spirometer. As per the ATS criteria, the spirometer selects the effort with the highest FVC as the best one [2,10].

RESULTS

In this section, we discuss the performance of SpiroCall when compared to the two clinical spirometers in terms of accuracy of estimated lung function measures and false positives *vs.* false negatives. We consider an estimate to be a false negative if the groundtruth FEV1% is below 0.8 and SpiroCall predicts the value to be above 0.8 [2]. We break down these results by *Phone Type* and *Channel Type.* We also compare the performance of SpiroCall with and without a vortex whistle. Finally, we discuss the accuracy and usefulness of the flow-volume curves generated by SpiroCall. Based on our evaluation we conclude that SpiroCall can help in screening and monitoring patients with lung impairments in low resource regions.

Two Ground Truth Devices

As mentioned, we used two clinical spirometers to collect groundtruth. We compared their respective lung function measure and found that PEF had the maximum difference of 9.2% between the two devices, and FEV1, FVC, and FEV1% had a difference of 5.1%, 5.2%, and 3.2%, respectively. However, none of these differences are statistically significant (based on an F-test, $p>0.05$). We also studied the effect of order to understand if fatigue played any role in exaggerating the difference between the two devices. In a 2-way ANOVA test with *presentation order* of the two spirometers as a between-subjects factor, we found that the difference in estimates of PEF and FEV1 were statistically significant ($p<0.05$). This finding suggests that the participants got fatigued by the time the session ended. Therefore, we use the results from the *first* spirometer that the participants used as their groundtruth or reference device. While this means that the reference device was not consistent across participants, the difference in device performance was not found to be significant and should not strongly affect the final analysis. In addition, we corrected for fatigue by counter-balancing between all *Phone, Channel*, and *Whistle Type* conditions for all participants.

Lung Function Estimate without Whistle

We break down the comparison of measurements from SpiroCall and the clinical spirometers by evaluating how well it performs for different lung function measures and the number of outliers and false negatives.

Accuracy of Lung Function Measures

The graphs in Figure 9 *(Left)* present the percentage error of each measure without a whistle. For all lung function measures, the algorithm returns an average error of less than 10%. There is no significant difference between the performance of smartphones recording the data locally in an app (Samsung Note and Apple iPhone) and phones running over the voice communication channel (Sony W580i and Apple iPhone 4S). The performance is best for FEV1%, which is the most common measure of lung function used in diagnosis because it is typically most consistent [10,15]. The mean error rate for FEV1% is below 6% for all the four conditions. The ATS acceptability criteria require lung function measures to be within 7% to 10% of one another [15]. For most patients, SpiroCall performs well within the expected level of variation, even if the patient did not have a smartphone and performed the test on a phone call. However, it is important to evaluate the outliers (with error higher than twice the standard deviation) and see whether the lung function measures are under-estimated or over-estimated. We use twice the standard deviation because the first standard deviation is within the ATS acceptability criteria [15] and the result cannot be considered an outlier.

Outliers and Patients with Low Lung Function

In order to understand the direction of the bias, we use the modified Bland-Altman plots [1] in Figure 10. The figure shows the percentage difference between SpiroCall and the output of a spirometer *versus* the spirometer measurement of FEV1%. Lines indicating $\pm 2\sigma$ (red dashes). We focus solely on FEV1% because it is the most common lung function measure for diagnosis. If the percentage difference is positive, then the lung function was over-estimated (false negative). It can be seen in Figure 10, *Top-Left* and *Top-Right,* that SpiroCall (both without whistle) tend to over-

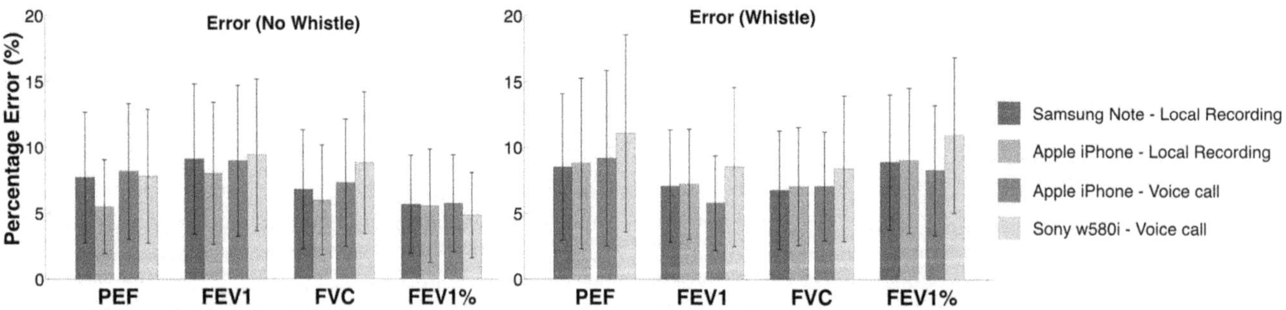

Figure 9. Percent error for different lung function measures on different devices without whistle (Left), and with whistle (Right). The first two devices recorded the data locally in an app; the next two devices recorded the data over a phone call. The error bars show standard deviation.

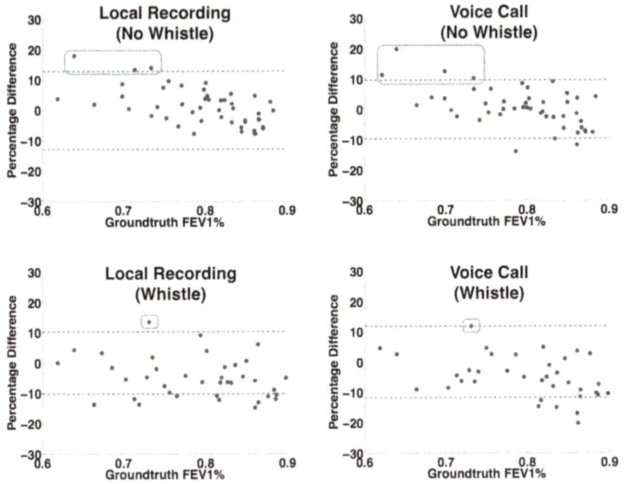

Figure 10. Bland-Altman plots of percent error of FEV1% (without and with whistle) for local and voice call recordings versus the value obtained from the clinical spirometer. The false negatives are highlighted inside grey boxes. ±2σ (red dashes) are also shown.

estimate the actual value for some patients with low lung function (FEV1% < 0.8), *i.e.,* a false negative. We highlight the false negatives inside the gray boxes. In any medical device, it is more acceptable to have a false positive than a false negative. The main reason the system currently has more false negatives for low lung function is because the algorithm is data driven and the population with higher lung function is better represented. Therefore, the model tends to bias towards the median value. Considering the signal-to-noise ratio is lower for the devices connected over the GSM channel, the false negatives are slightly more pronounced in case of voice call (Figure 10, *Top Right*).

One way to quantify the model's bias towards higher lung function is to calculate the statistical effect of lung function measure (FEV1% in this case) on the error of the model. We tested for effects of groundtruth FEV1% on the percent error through a chi-square test. We found that there was a significant effect of the groundtruth FEV1% on the accuracy of SpiroCall ($p<0.05$). As such, the performance of SpiroCall might degrade further if tested on more highly obstructed patients. Although the bias is only slight and there are relatively few false negatives, from a diagnostic perspective, it could mean that patients are screened improperly.

Lung Function Estimate with Whistle

The bias in the performance of the system due to groundtruth lung function of the user prompted us to explore the possibility of using a whistle for the users of SpiroCall.

Comparison of Two Whistle Sizes

We used two sizes of the vortex whistle in our study. Both whistles had slightly different gradient of pitch with respect to the input flow. We performed a two-sample F-test for equal variances on the percentage error for the four lung function measures for both whistle sizes. We observed a significant effect (*$p<0.01$*) of size on FVC and FEV1%, in favor of the bigger whistle. The percentage difference between the two whistles was 0.24%, 4.22%, 2%, and 2.13% for PEF, FEV1, FVC, and FEV1%, respectively. Considering the bigger whistle worked significantly better, our analysis of SpiroCall only includes the larger whistle.

Accuracy of Lung Function Measures

Bar graphs shown in Figure 9 *(Right)* display the percentage error of each lung function measure for each device and connection type with a whistle. The Sony Ericsson W580i performed the worst among all the phones. However, the difference was not statistically significant (F-test, $p>0.05$). Among the lung functions, the error was highest for PEF, but it is worthwhile to note that the variance in PEF was also the highest for the groundtruth spirometers. The most widely used lung function measure, FEV1%, has less than 8% mean error for three of the four device types.

Outliers and Patients with Low Lung Function

In order to understand the direction of the bias present in whistle results, Figure 10 *(Bottom)* shows modified Bland-Altman plots of FEV1%, displaying percentage difference between SpiroCall (with whistle) and the spirometer *versus* the spirometer measure. From these plots, we show that the whistle mitigates false negatives. We highlight the false negatives inside gray boxes. Most of the error for the whistle comes from false positives. When comparing local recordings and voice calls, there is no significant performance difference (F-test, $p>0.05$). However, using the whistle, we eliminate the bias in the estimate that we saw in case of no whistle. This means the whistle may be a superior screening tool, especially for patients with very low lung function. We quantify this effect of bias as before by considering the effects of groundtruth FEV1% on the percent error through a chi-square test. We found that there was *no significant effect* of the groundtruth FEV1% on the accuracy of SpiroCall across devices ($p>0.05$)

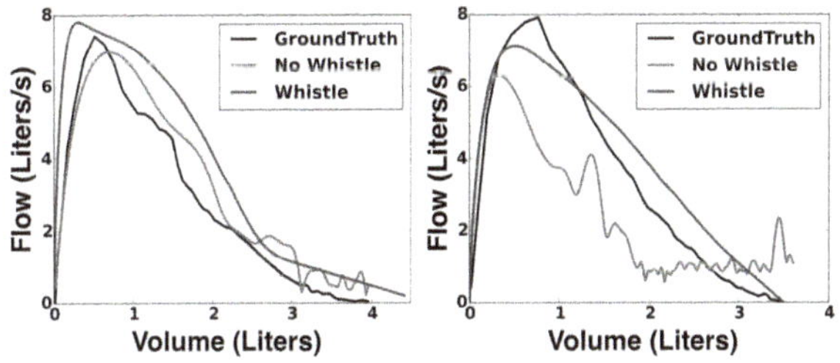

Figure 11. Two Flow *vs.* Volume curves generated by SpiroCall with a whistle and without a whistle.

Curves Generated by SpiroCall

We now shift our discussion from lung function measures to the shape of the flow-volume curves. The spirometry curves serve two purposes: (1) to evaluate if the patients performed the effort sufficiently, and (2) to help in diagnosis by showing the descending limb of the FV curve. A technician looks at the slope of the FV curve from the start of the test to PEF. This slope should be as steep as possible, indicating that the initial blast of air was truly maximal. The investigator also looks to see if the user coughs during the spirometry maneuver. Coughing makes the descending edge of the FV curve non-monotonic as the user ends up inhaling during a cough. Therefore, it is important to evaluate how SpiroCall performs in generating these curves.

Figure 11 shows example flow-volume curves generated by SpiroCall without the whistle and with the whistle; we find that the curves generated without a whistle can be unreliable. The no-whistle (green) curve in the Figure 12 *(Right)* has an inaccurate shape because the latter half of the effort by the patient was very quiet. When the GSM channel compressed the audio, this segment was heavily compressed and not reconstructed accurately. However, these curves can still be used for validity assessment of the efforts. The initial part of the effort is always very loud and reconstructed accurately. Therefore, the investigator can still look at the ascending slope at the start of the test. For cough information, we envision that the Hilbert envelopes of the temporal audio data can be attached along with the spirometry curves, which would make any coughs clearly visible. However, in cases where the spirometry curves are of importance, we suggest the use of a whistle. The whistle generates a direct mapping to the Flow *vs.* Time curve and the final Flow *vs.* Volume curves are usually very accurate. We recognize that a more rigorous evaluation of the spirometry curves is important. This is part of our on-going work, where we are sending all the curves generated by SpiroCall to medical practitioners for quality assessment at Spirometry 360[1].

DISCUSSION

SpiroCall offers two approaches to performing spirometry through a call-in service: with a vortex whistle and without. The performance of both approaches is very promising and the mean error of the four major lung function measures is 6.2%, which is well within the ATS criteria for a clinical spirometer. However, the system sometimes over-estimates lung function when used without a whistle. We believe that this limitation stems from the fact that without a whistle, the algorithm depends on the spread and variation in its training data to remove the bias in its estimation. We plan to combine the SpiroCall clinical evaluation with ongoing SpiroSmart clinical trials.

The linear relationship between flow-rate and pitch makes the vortex whistle reliable for estimating lung function measures and spirometry curves with significantly fewer false negatives and almost no bias toward high lung function. Another major advantage with the whistle is that its estimation model is generalizable across devices and channels. In fact, it calculates PEF and FEV_1 directly, without any statistical modeling. For the patients with obstructive lung impairments such as asthma and COPD, the lung function measure that changes most drastically is FEV_1. If the patient only needs to track their FEV_1 with fine granularity (a common practice for many patients), SpiroCall can use a much simpler computation with a whistle, without any machine learning. Moreover, it will be easier to judge a valid effort because the shape of the curve is more faithfully represented.

SpiroCall's performance is promising as the mean performance loss due to use of the call-in service is only around 1%. The flexibility between channels and the possibility of using a whistle allows SpiroCall to make spirometry accessible. However, this only demonstrates the feasibility of sensing. It remains unclear how the user, in general, could use spirometers without any guidance from trained personnel. Although SpiroSmart tries to bridge this gap with a rich visual interface, it will be more difficult for SpiroCall to train the user. It is possible that in future work we could implement audio feedback between spirometry efforts, or have a health worker train the user before they are able to use SpiroCall independently.

[1] www.spirometry360.org

CONCLUSION

In order to make spirometry more accessible, it is important to remove its dependence on smartphones. We introduced SpiroCall, a combination of call-in service and a simple whistle that turns *every* mobile phone in the world into a spirometer. The phone sends the audio data generated during a spirometry effort over the GSM voice channel and calculates the results on a central server. Our evaluation shows that we can use SpiroCall to reliably measure lung function in low resource regions. SpiroCall's call-in service's mean error is comparable to a clinical spirometer and does not degrade substantially when compared to local recordings made on a smartphone. The whistle helps in improving the performance with patients with degraded lung function. SpiroCall also serves as a demonstration that researchers can perform sensing on all mobile phones, not just smartphones, by leveraging the voice channel for data transfer.

REFERENCES

1. J M Bland and D G Altman. 1986. Statistical methods for assessing agreement between two methods of clinical measurement. *Lancet* 1, 8476: 307–10. Retrieved July 9, 2014 from http://www.ncbi.nlm.nih.gov/pubmed/2868172
2. Robert O Crapo, John L Hankinson, Charles Irvin, and Neil R. MacIntyre. 1994. Standardization of Spirometry. *American Journal of Respiratory and Critical Care Medicine*, 7.
3. Bradley Efron, Trevor Hastie, Iain Johnstone, and Robert Tibshirani. 2014. Least angle regression. *The Annals of Statistics* 32, 2: 407–499. Retrieved December 4, 2014 from http://projecteuclid.org/euclid.aos/1083178935

4. Ericsson. 2015. *Ericsson Mobility Report: On the Pulse of the Networked Society.*

5. Lilian de Greef, Mayank Goel, Min Joon Seo, et al. 2014. BiliCam: Using Mobile Phones to Monitor Newborn Jaundice. *Proceedings of the 2014 ACM International Joint Conference on Pervasive and Ubiquitous Computing 2014*, ACM Press. http://doi.org/10.1145/2638728.2638803

6. Maya R Gupta, Eric K Garcia, and Erika Chin. 2008. Adaptive local linear regression with application to printer color management. *IEEE transactions on image processing : a publication of the IEEE Signal Processing Society* 17, 6: 936–945. http://doi.org/10.1109/TIP.2008.922429

7. R J Knudson, R C Slatin, M D Lebowitz, and B Burrows. 1976. The maximal expiratory flow-volume curve. Normal standards, variability, and effects of age. *The American review of respiratory disease* 113, 5: 587–600. Retrieved December 4, 2014 from http://www.ncbi.nlm.nih.gov/pubmed/1267262

8. Jiri Kroutil, Alexandr Laposa, and Miroslav Husak. 2011. Respiration monitoring during sleeping. *Proceedings of the 4th International Symposium on Applied Sciences in Biomedical and Communication Technologies - ISABEL '11*, ACM Press, 1–5. http://doi.org/10.1145/2093698.2093731

9. Eric C Larson, Mayank Goel, Gaetano Boriello, Sonya Heltshe, Margaret Rosenfeld, and Shwetak N Patel. 2012. SpiroSmart : Using a Microphone to Measure Lung Function on a Mobile Phone. *UbiComp'12.*

10. M R Miller, J Hankinson, V Brusasco, et al. 2005. Standardisation of spirometry. *The European respiratory journal* 26, 2: 319–38. http://doi.org/10.1183/09031936.05.00034805

11. Dennis R. Morgan and Michael G. Zierdt. 2009. Novel signal processing techniques for Doppler radar cardiopulmonary sensing. *Signal Processing* 89, 1: 45–66. http://doi.org/10.1016/j.sigpro.2008.07.008

12. Rajalakshmi Nandakumar, Shyamnath Gollakota, and Nathaniel Watson. 2015. Contactless Sleep Apnea Detection on Smartphones. *Proceedings of the 13th Annual International Conference on Mobile Systems, Applications, and Services - MobiSys '15*: 45–57. http://doi.org/10.1145/2742647.2742674

13. Michael R Neuman. Vital signs: heart rate. *IEEE pulse* 1, 3: 51–5. http://doi.org/10.1109/MPUL.2010.939179

14. Sohail Rafiqi, Chatchai Wangwiwattana, Jasmine Kim, Ephrem Fernandez, Suku Nair, and Eric C Larson. 2015. Pupil Ware : Towards Pervasive C ognitive Load Measurement using Commodity Devices. *Proc. 8th Int. Conf. PErvasive Technol. Relat. to Assist. Environ.*

15. Alessandro Rubini, Andrea Parmagnani, and Michela Bondì. 2011. Daily variations in lung volume measurements in young healthy adults. *Biological Rhythm Research* 42, 3: 261–265. http://doi.org/10.1080/09291016.2010.505456

16. Hiroshi Sato and Kajiro Watanabe. 2000. Experimental study on the use of a vortex whistle as a flowmeter. *IEEE Transactions on Instrumentation and Measurement* 49, 1: 200–205. http://doi.org/10.1109/19.836334

17. Bernard Vonnegut. 1954. A Vortex Whistle. *The Journal of the Acoustical Society of America* 26, 1: 18–20.

18. Kajiro Watanabe and Hiroshi Sato. 1994. Vortex Whistle as a Flow Meter. *Proc. Advanced Technologies in Instrumentation and Measurement*, 1225–1228.

19. World Health Organization. 2015. Chronic obstructed pulmonary diseases (COPD). Retrieved September 9, 2015 from http://www.who.int/mediacentre/factsheets/fs315/en/

20. Hui Zou and Trevor Hastie. 2005. Regularization and variable selection via the elastic net. *Journal of the Royal Statistical Society: Series B (Statistical Methodology)* 67, 2: 301–320. http://doi.org/10.1111/j.1467-9868.2005.00503.x

21. 佐藤浩志, 大原昌幸, 渡辺嘉二郎, and 佐藤秀昭. 1999. Application of the Vortex Whistle to the Spirometer. 計測自動制御学会論文集 35, 7: 840–845.

Interacting with Predictions: Visual Inspection of Black-box Machine Learning Models

Josua Krause
New York University
New York, NY, USA
josua.krause@nyu.edu

Adam Perer
IBM T.J. Watson Research Center
Yorktown Heights, NY, USA
adam.perer@us.ibm.com

Kenney Ng
IBM T.J. Watson Research Center
Yorktown Heights, NY, USA
kenney.ng@us.ibm.com

ABSTRACT
Understanding predictive models, in terms of interpreting and identifying actionable insights, is a challenging task. Often the importance of a feature in a model is only a rough estimate condensed into one number. However, our research goes beyond these naïve estimates through the design and implementation of an interactive visual analytics system, *Prospector*. By providing interactive partial dependence diagnostics, data scientists can understand how features affect the prediction overall. In addition, our support for localized inspection allows data scientists to understand how and why specific datapoints are predicted as they are, as well as support for tweaking feature values and seeing how the prediction responds. Our system is then evaluated using a case study involving a team of data scientists improving predictive models for detecting the onset of diabetes from electronic medical records.

Author Keywords
interactive machine learning; predictive modeling; partial dependence; visual analytics; model visualization

ACM Classification Keywords
H.5.m. Information Interfaces and Presentation (e.g. HCI): Miscellaneous

INTRODUCTION
In the era of data-driven analytics, there is growing demand to generate and deploy predictive models in a variety of domains so that the patterns unearthed from massive amounts of data can be leveraged and converted into actionable insights. Predictive modeling is defined as the process of developing a mathematical tool or model that generates an accurate prediction [24]. As an example, in healthcare, if one can model the data characteristics of patients who will likely develop diabetes, healthcare institutions could deploy such a model on their patient databases, and automatically flag high risk patients to clinicians to make sure they are being treated appropriately. However, building such models on noisy, real-world data is quite challenging.

Data scientists often turn to machine learning, where the goal is to create predictive models based on information automatically learned from data with ground truth. However, these machine learning techniques are often black-boxes and may be selected based only on performance metrics such as high accuracy scores, and not necessarily based on the interpretability and actionable insights of the model. There has recently been a variety of techniques to inject humans-in-the-loop when building predictive models based on machine learning, from interactive training [1] to interactive feature selection [23]. However, interactive systems to effectively assess and evaluate the interpretability and actionable insights of a predictive model that go beyond simple accuracy metrics is still lacking. We believe bringing humans into the loop at this stage can possibly lead to better models and consequently improved outcomes when the models are deployed.

Our research aims to support data scientists to go beyond judging predictive models solely based on their accuracy scores by also including model interpretability and actionable insights. Towards this goal, we developed *Prospector*, a novel visual analytics system designed to help analysts better understand predictive models. *Prospector* leverages the concept of partial dependence, a diagnostic technique that was designed to communicate how features affect the prediction, and makes this technique fully interactive. *Prospector* also supports localized inspection, so users can understand why certain data results in a specific prediction, and even lets users hypothesize new data by tweaking values and seeing how the predictive model responds. We also demonstrate, through a case study, how the system can lead to important insights for clinical researchers building models that try to predict patient outcomes based on electronic medical records.

Concretely, our contributions include:

- A design and implementation of an interactive visual analytics system, *Prospector*, for assessing the interpretability and actionable insights of trained predictive models by supporting:
  - Interactive partial dependence diagnostics to understand how features affect the prediction overall. There

CHI'16, May 07 - 12, 2016, San Jose, CA, USA

ACM 978-1-4503-3362-7/16/05...$15.00
DOI: http://dx.doi.org/10.1145/2858036.2858529

are novel visual representations, sampling strategies, and support for comparing multiple models.

– Localized inspection to understand how and why specific data points are predicted as they are. Users can interactively tweak feature values and see how the prediction responds, as well as find the most impactful features using a novel local feature importance metric.

• A case study of data scientists using *Prospector* to improve predictive models for detecting the onset of diabetes trained from electronic medical record data.

MOTIVATION

Machine Learning for Predictive Modeling

Data scientists often use machine learning to create predictive models based on known properties of training data, which acts as the ground truth. Machine learning algorithms typically work in two phases: the training phase and the prediction phase. In the training phase, parameters of the model are learned using training data. The prediction phase then computes predictions using the trained model. Below, we describe several machine learning algorithms that are commonly used and also utilized in the case study.

A decision tree is one such algorithm, which is a tree whose nodes are rules that decide how to proceed down the branches of the tree, according to the range of values for a specific feature. The decision making starts at the root of the tree and leaves carry the prediction results. Decision trees are popular in machine learning as they allow data scientists to model arbitrary functions. However, the more nodes a tree has, the harder it is to understand the reasoning behind outcomes. Logistic regression is another popular algorithm that is easier to understand, as features can only positively or negative influence the prediction, and the rate of influence is fixed. This is achieved by defining a hyper-plane in the feature vector space, where the outcome of the prediction depends on how close to and on which side of the hyper-plane a point is.

Another popular algorithm is random forests, which combine the output of multiple decision trees. A random forest is an example of an ensemble model, which combines the output of several weak machine learning models to yield an overall better result with less bias and variance than a single strong model. However, this makes ensemble models less interpretable since each weak model has only a small influence on the outcome.

Predictive Modeling in Healthcare

In order to make our contributions concrete, we utilize a motivating scenario that emerged from our case study. The case study involves a team of five data scientists interested in using predictive modeling on a longitudinal database of electronic medical records. The research team has a background in healthcare analytics and their database contains 4,000 patients from a major hospital in the United States. The team is interested in building a predictive model to predict if a patient is at risk of developing diabetes, a chronic disease of high blood sugar levels that may cause serious health complications.

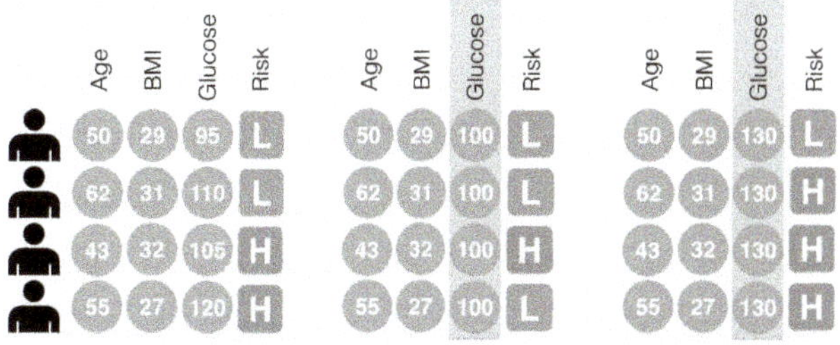

Figure 1. An illustration of how partial dependence is computed for the feature "Glucose". On the left are four patients' original feature values. In the middle, the "Glucose" values are all changed to 100, and the corresponding predictions change. Similarly, on the right, the "Glucose" values are all changed to 130, and again the risks are different. This demonstrates the impact of the "Glucose" feature on risk prediction.

The team of data scientists manages to develop a highly accurate predictive model for detecting patients at high risk of developing diabetes. They determine its effectiveness by measuring the common metrics used by predictive models (e.g., accuracy and AUC scores [24]). They also followed the best practices of building predictive models. They worked with clinical researchers to properly define cohorts of patients with diabetes (cases) and matched patients without diabetes (controls) by thoroughly searching through the electronic medical records. They constructed features based on lab tests, diagnosis codes, procedures, demographics, and patient conditions from the records. They used cross-validation to ensure their models were robust. They used a variety of state-of-the-art feature selection methods to utilize the most informative features in the model while keeping it as generalizable as possible. And they used a variety of effective classifiers to do the training and evaluation. After trying various combinations of these techniques, the model with the highest accuracy metrics was selected and presented to the appropriate stakeholders at the healthcare institution.

Their stakeholders were impressed by the high accuracy scores of the model. But when they asked the data scientists for more information about what was inside of the model, the reports only described the top features of the model and their associated "importance" weights. The stakeholders recognized many of the feature names, and it appeared to make clinical sense. However, there were also some surprising ones that led to intellectual discussions. But the stakeholders demanded to know more. They wanted a clearer sense of how certain features impacted the prediction. Furthermore, they wanted to understand how the values associated with the features (e.g., the results associated with lab tests) impacted the prediction. They also were curious to interact with the model to test hypotheses about how the model would react to hypothetical patients of interest. When confronted with these questions, the data scientists shrugged. In the data scientist's defense, it is difficult to summarize and interpret complex models and there are few tools and techniques available to address the stakeholders' requests. So now the stakeholders are faced with a hard decision: do they deploy a predictive model in their institution that appears to have high accuracy but is also somewhat of a black-box?

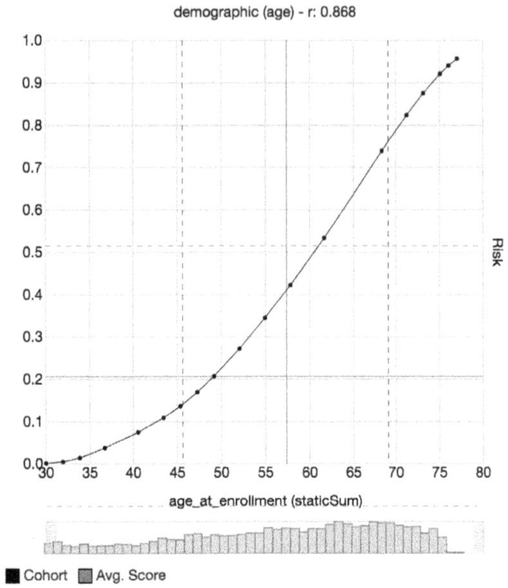

Figure 2. Partial dependence plots. The black curve shows the average predicted risk (probability of a certain outcome) if for all rows in the data the value of this feature was the given value of the horizontal axis. The red line shows the average predicted risk for the original data. The vertical line shows the mean of the observed values and the histogram below the plot shows the distribution of observed values. Dotted lines show the range of one standard deviation around the mean values.

Although this scenario is motivated by our case study, our other projects and interviews suggest these are not atypical requirements. Our work is motivated to support the development of more comprehensible predictive models.

Partial Dependence

The most widely used technique to understand the relationship between a feature and a prediction is by computing partial dependence [14, 16]. The idea of partial dependence plots is to treat predictive models as a black-box and observe how changes in the input affect prediction outcomes. When inspecting only the partial dependence of one input feature at a time, Formula (1) can be used to compute a partial dependence plot.

$$pdp_f(v) = \frac{1}{N}\sum_{i}^{N} pred(x_i) \text{ with } x_{if} = v \qquad (1)$$

N is the number of rows in the input matrix x, *pred* is the prediction function that takes one input row, a feature vector, and returns an outcome probability, and f is the feature used to compute the partial dependence plot. The formula computes the average outcome over all input rows while changing the value of feature f to the input value v for each row x_i. The original input data is kept fixed. This allows for observing the influence of f on the predicted probabilities.

In order to make this function more concrete, consider the illustrative example in Figure 1, where each input row is a patient, and each column is a feature. The last column represents the output of the predictive model that predicts if a patient is at low-risk or high-risk for developing diabetes. In Figure 1a, the patients' original feature values (age, BMI (Body Mass Index, a standard way to quantify obesity), and glucose level (a standard way to determine diabetes)) are shown. If one wants to examine the impact of the glucose feature on the prediction, partial dependence can be applied by keeping all of the other features (age, bmi) as they were, but fixing glucose to a set of fixed values to see how that feature impacts the prediction. For example, in Figure 1b, the glucose values (highlighted in yellow) are fixed to 100, which yields predictions of only 1 patient being high risk, instead of the original 2. Conversely, in Figure 1c, glucose is fixed to 180, and 3 patients are predicted to have high risk. Thus, there appears to be partial dependence of glucose on the prediction.

Partial dependence is typically visualized as a partial dependence plot, as shown in Figure 2,which is a line graph that plots the fixed values for the target feature on the x-axis, and the corresponding predicted risk (probability of a certain outcome) on the y-axis.

RELATED WORK

Motivation for Interpretability

Modern machine learning algorithms are able to create more reliable and precise models but they are increasingly complex and come with the price of being harder and harder to interpret (Breiman [7]). This inverse relation of understandability versus expressiveness of a model introduces the need to find ways to improve the interpretability of complex models to overcome this disadvantage. Lim [28] asks questions such as "*Why* did X happen?", "*Why* not Y?", "*What* happens *if* I do Z?", and "*How* do I make X happen?" to explain complex mechanisms like machine learning models. Our system allows users to interactively ask and answer such questions. Kulesza *et al.* [25] use explanatory debugging by conveying how a model came to its prediction in order to be able to correct mistakes. On the other hand, Patel *et al.* [33] use multiple classifiers to better understand input data. Steeg and Galstyan [45, 41] use total correlation to build a hierarchy of features explaining their role in the data.

Algorithm Specific Model Visualization

In the past, research has primarily focused on understanding and interacting with specific machine learning algorithms. Often the focus is on the internal weights of the trained models. For Bayesian networks, showing probabilities of the nodes (Becker *et al.* [5]) and how the input is propagated (Correa *et al.* [18]) has been used. For Support Vector Machines, projection techniques (Caragea *et al.* [8]) and Nomograms (Jakulin *et al.* [17]) to see the "cut" in the data points were utilized. Visualizing and interpreting the graph of a neural network has also been used by Tzeng and Ma [43]. Kim *et al.* [22, 20] introduce graphical models that allow for interpretability of its features. [20] use a colored matrix of features by category to show distinguishable features computed by their model. Caruana *et al.* [9] use high-performance generalized additive models (GA^2Ms) that allows visual inspection of the influence of its input features on the outcome much like partial dependence.

Model Result Visualization

However, showing only internal, algorithm specific weights is often not enough. Plate *et al.* [36] and Olden [31] show how input features influence the outcome of neural network classifications. Xu *et al.* [46] interprets the graph of a neural network used for image classification to retrieve which part of an image was responsible for a specific classification result. These techniques aim in the same direction as partial dependence but are limited to only neural networks. They cannot be used to support the ability to compare different machine learning models across algorithms.

Having access to the internals of a machine learning algorithm also allows direct interaction with the models and to improve them on the fly. BaobabView (van den Elzen and van Wijk [44]) offers interactive decision tree construction. Steed *et al.* [40, 39] guides regression model creation by enhancing interaction with the input data. EnsembleMatrix (Talbot *et al.* [42]) allows users to combine already computed classification models to build ensemble models. Some recent interactive machine learning tools [1, 2, 3, 4, 19, 21, 26, 29, 32]) are more algorithm agnostic, but depend on general performance measures like confusion matrices, area under ROC curve (AUC) measures, result distribution of data points, and feature weights according to model independent statistics.

Frank and Hall [13] use 2D projections of the data to show results for multiple classification algorithms, as well as Rheingans and desJardins [37] with self-organizing maps.

Probing Models

Partial dependence was proposed by Friedman [14] for analyzing gradient boosting models and has since been used for other models as well (*e.g.* Ehrlinger [12] uses partial dependence to analyze the behavior of random forests in the *R* package *ggRandomForests*).

Cortez and Embrechts [10, 11] and Kim *et al.* [22] use sensitivity analysis to analyze and compare machine learning models of different algorithms. Sensitivity analysis is similar to partial dependence except that it uses a few base vectors (usually the mean, median, or quartiles of all observed values) instead of computing the probabilities over all input points. This method is faster than partial dependence but may miss critical details about the prediction function especially if the function is strongly non-linear.

Goldstein *et al.* [15] extends the idea of partial dependence by using Individual Conditional Expectation (ICE) plots which show one line for each row of the input data. We found, however, that this often clutters the plots too much and makes them harder to interpret. We experimented further with showing standard deviations and quartiles of the partial dependence line but discarded this approach since the spread of the partial dependence results is always expected to be large unless one feature dominates the classification significantly and is able to solely change the classification even for the furthest data points.

By not restricting ourselves to sampling only the observed input space, our approach on partial dependence enables a deeper analysis of the machine learning model. Furthermore, accepting the costs of computing partial dependence over all input points yields proper results even for highly non-linear models, while also not overwhelming users with too much detail. This is strengthened even further by our novel approach of using implementation details of the inspected models to improve the sampling and the representation of the results.

SYSTEM

In order to integrate partial dependence and localized inspection into our pipeline we propose *Prospector*, a web-based interface. The server side of *Prospector* can load any machine learning model accessible via python, or integrate with existing predictive modeling pipelines such as PARAMO [30]. Although this paper demonstrates the system on clinical data, the tool is able to handle predictive models for other domains. For example, the tool has also been used with exploring models that predict real estate prices, as well as classic data sets from the UCI Machine Learning Repository [27].

In this section, we first describe *Prospector*'s novel enhancements of partial dependence plots. Then, we describe how *Prospector* leverages partial dependence to support localized inspection. Finally, we describe the workflow of how these techniques are integrated into *Prospector*'s UI.

Partial Dependence Plots

Partial dependence is typically visualized as a partial dependence plot, which is a line graph that plots the fixed values for the target feature on the horizontal axis, and the corresponding predicted risk (probability of a certain outcome) on the vertical axis. In *Prospector*, we enhance the plot by adding a red reference line with the average predicted risk of the model on the original data, as shown in Figure 2. In addition, a black vertical line indicates the average observed value of the input data for the current feature. Both reference lines are accompanied with dotted lines showing one standard deviation in both directions from the mean value. To help with validating insights and assigning importance, a histogram of the observed values in the original data is also shown below the plot.

Sampling Partial Dependence

One of our core contributions is the ability to effectively treat partial dependence as a black-box for inspection. However, naïvely treating the predictive model as black-box may lead to inaccuracies in the generated plot. Often only observed input values are used for sampling which leaves the prediction function for other values undefined, even though those values might be of particular interest for understanding the internals of the model. Furthermore, the interpolation between those sample points may ignore inherent features of the prediction function. For example, Ehrlinger [12] shows the usage of partial dependence plots via random forest models. The prediction function for those models can only change between thresholds appearing in the nodes of the trees. For all other values the prediction remains constant. However, the interpolation between sample points used in the examples is polynomial. This leads to the following misrepresentations of the prediction function: (i) some sampled prediction values are not included in the interpolation; (ii) the interpolation is a curve where it should be a constant which alludes to values

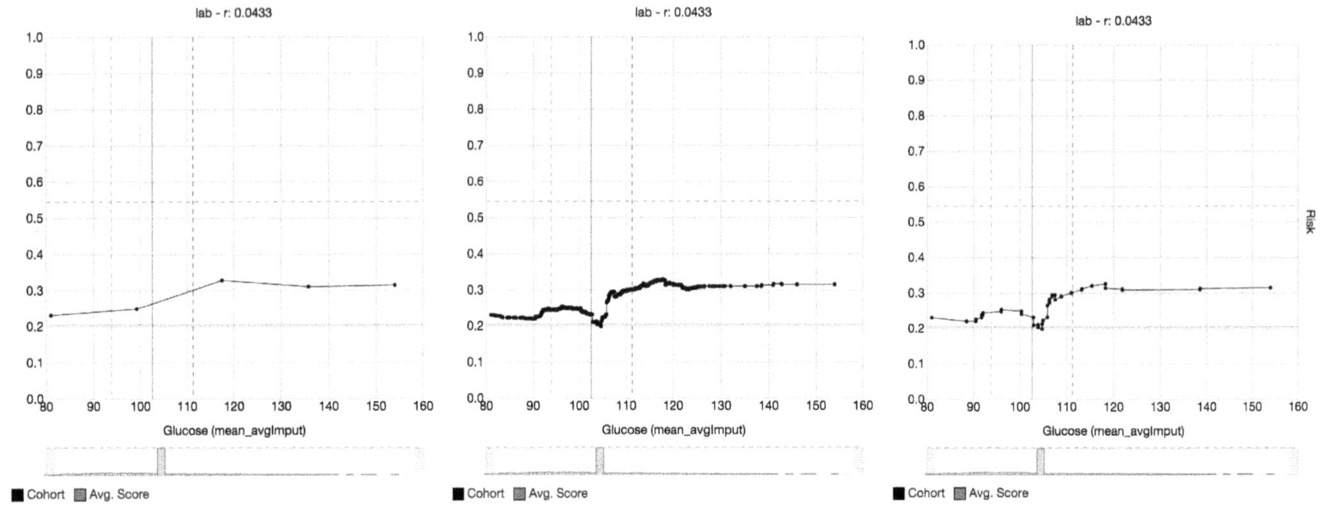

Figure 3. Different sampling strategies for partial dependence plots. The leftmost plot uses a naïve sampling which misses the dip in the predicted risk for a Glucose value around 105. Using the thresholds of the trees in the random forest the middle plot shows all details of the displayed model. The rightmost plot simplifies this by detecting co-linear points and summarizing them into lines improving readability. The dip in the predicted risk is due to imputation of missing values to the mean of the observed values. This increase in local noise shifts the prediction towards the overall average predicted risk (the horizontal red line). Most patients have never had their Glucose value measured.

that are impossible to achieve with the prediction function; (iii) steps are interpolated as curves which gives the impression of a smooth ascent of values when it should be a series of sudden jumps.

We overcome those inaccuracies by acknowledging inherent properties of the prediction functions of our models. This is only possible by leveraging the internal design of model algorithms and therefore, *Prospector* must more effectively sample the range of the input features. For example, in decision tree or forest models, where the predicted risk will not change between thresholds of the nodes of those models' trees *Prospector* utilizes the knowledge that the plot will be a step function by only sampling values at the thresholds of the given feature to accurately compute the complete plot (see Figure 3). It does this by inspecting the decision rules in the nodes of the model to retrieve those thresholds.

However some models, such as random forest models, produce a large number of points where the outcome might change which leads to a cluttered plot that impairs readability. One solution to this is to simplify the generated plot by finding almost co-linear points and reducing them to the endpoints. Such visual optimizations support more comprehensible plots that are easier to read while still being accurate representations. Other machine learning algorithms may not require such optimizations.

Prospector also enhances partial dependence plots by taking into account the context of the original data values. For example, certain features only make sense as integer values (*e.g.* the number of times a laboratory test was performed) and it does not make sense to show non-integer values in the plots. Such features can be heuristically detected by inspecting the set of values in the original data set and *Prospector* restricts those features to only have integer values as input. Similarly, in the partial dependence plot, only integer values are computed. Furthermore, for predictive models using step functions the plot is horizontally shifted by 0.5 so that jumps happen between values. This eases reading the actual value at the integer points. Even though this improvement leads to a slight misrepresentation of the prediction function for non-observable values the readability of the plot is significantly improved to support user tasks. For non-integer data types, these optimizations are not necessary.

Local Inspection

Our second core contribution is leveraging our implementation of partial dependence to support the user task of local inspection. Users can use *Prospector* to inspect specific data points of interest and see how the models predict how they behave. In addition, if the users are curious about how a particular data point's risk might change if it had different values, a user can explore this as well. The idea of localized inspection is illustrated in Figure 4 using our running example of diabetes prediction. At the top, the original patient's feature values are shown, along with the patient's original predicted low risk of having diabetes. Suppose the analyst was curious to see how the patient's risk would change if his BMI was

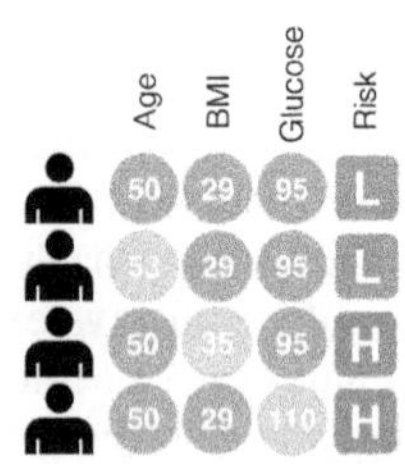

Figure 4. This illustration provides an explanation of how local inspection works. On the top row are the patient's original feature values and the corresponding prediction. On the bottom three rows, users changed certain values of the patient, highlighted in yellow, and such values impacted the prediction.

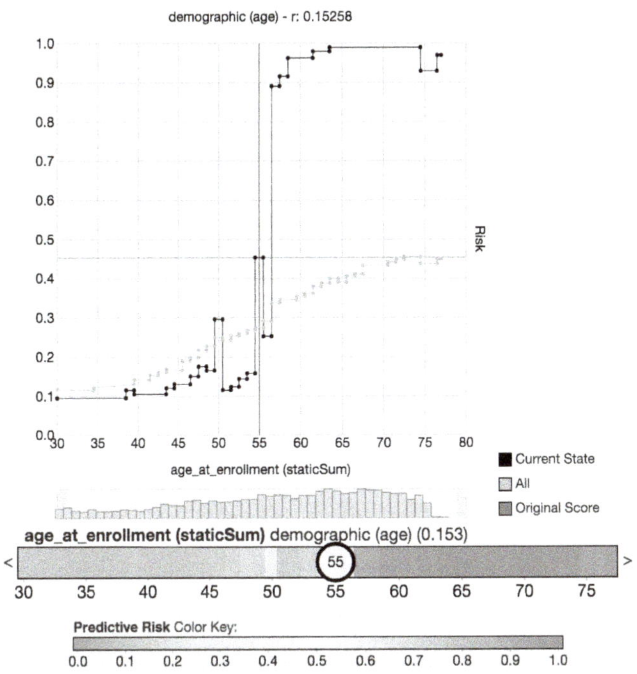

Figure 5. The same feature shown as line plot (top) and partial dependence bar (middle). Color indicates the predicted risk for the outcome. The color mapping is shown at the bottom.

increased to 35. Localized inspection allows users to interactively change this value, and see the corresponding prediction. In order to streamline this kind of exploration we fully compute the predicted risk for all values of BMI similar to partial dependence. As seen in Figure 4 we do this for all features independently yielding local partial dependence plots for each feature using a single input row.

Partial Dependence Bars

In order to increase interactivity, encourage exploration, and display a larger number of features at once, we use a novel visual encoding, *partial dependence bars*, a color bar representation of a partial dependence plot, shown in Figure 5. The horizontal axis of a partial dependence bar represents the range of values of a feature, and the color at a given position represents the predicted risk for that value. Color is mapped to a three-point color scale, where blue represents low risk, yellow represents medium risk, and red represents high risk. As these bars are meant to aid local inspection, the current feature value of the datapoint being inspected is positioned along the horizontal axis and annotated as a circular label. Users can drag this circular label left or right to inspect how changes in the feature value affect the predicted risk as well as the local partial dependence of other features.

Local feature importance

The fourth novel contribution of our research is a technique to simplify the exploration of the predicted risk space by automatically finding features where a small change in value yields a significantly large change on the predicted risk.

While manipulating values of specific features allows users to test hypotheses on how features of interest may impact the prediction, if users wish to simply understand how to most impact the prediction, manipulating features one-by-one to test impact is an inefficient process. Instead, *Prospector* can employ local feature importance, a novel technique that computes the impact of a given feature on the model according to the current values. This localized feature importance comes in two different flavors: as a feature importance number and as actual suggestions for value changes.

A straight-forward way to define a localized importance of features is to look at the range of possible predicted risks the feature can create starting from the given data point. Formula (2) computes the local importance I of a given feature f for the given feature vector p. It sums up the entirety of changes in outcomes for all values v for feature f. The outcome changes are weighted by ω the likelihood of changing the value from p_f to v. p^* is the modified feature vector where its value for f is set to v and $pred$ is the prediction function.

$$I_f(p) = \int_{-\infty}^{\infty} [pred(p^*) - pred(p)]\ \omega(v, p_f)\, dv \qquad (2)$$

$$\text{with } p^*_f = v \text{ and } p^*_g = p_g \text{ for } g \neq f$$

$$\omega(v, p_f) = \frac{1}{\sigma_f \sqrt{2\pi}} \exp\left(-\frac{(v - p_f)^2}{2\sigma_f^2}\right)$$

In order for different features to be comparable, ω takes the distribution of values in the input data into account. In features with a high spread, a larger change is more likely than in a feature with a narrow value range. We model the likelihood of the change using a normal distribution with the reference value p_f as mean and the standard deviation σ_f of the observed values of f as standard deviation. Ordering the features according to this local importance yields features that are likely to decrease the predicted risk first, then features that have a low impact on the predicted risk, and finally features that are likely to increase the predicted risk.

Instead of computing local feature importance for all possible changes, it is more practically useful to compute the importance according to the most *impactful* change for a feature. An impactful change is the smallest change needed to have the largest change in the predicted outcome. Note that this is different from the slope of the function since an impactful change might be after a valley or ridge. Again, in order to have comparable results, the distribution of values in the input data is taken into account.

$$\arg\max_{v} \left[s\ [pred(p^*) - pred(p)]\ \omega(v, p_f)\right] \qquad (3)$$

Formula (3) finds the most impactful change of a feature. s is either 1 or -1 depending on whether to search for the largest increase or decrease. All other variables are the same as in Formula (2). The changes yielding the highest impact can be interpreted as suggestions for changing a data point.

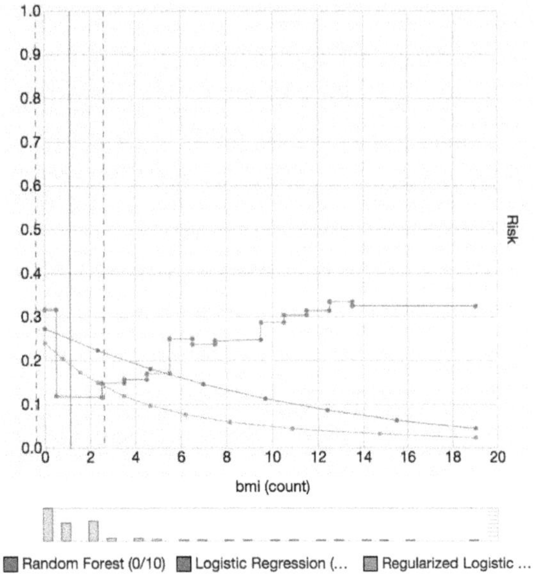

Figure 6. Comparison of three machine learning models on the number of measured BMI values. The two regression models (logistic regression in blue and regularized logistic regression in green) can express only a single slope (downwards or upwards) whereas the random forest in red can model the strong decrease in predicted risk going from no BMI measures to one measure as well as the later increase again if a patient has several BMI measures. The random forest is more expressive, but the distribution of input values in the histogram below the plot hint the model might be overfitting as most of the observed values are 2 or less.

Comparing Multiple Models

Prospector also supports plotting multiple models in the same plot. As the input domain and the output range are the same across different machine learning models on the same data, partial dependence plots can also be used to compare multiple models as shown in Figure 6. This is useful for comparing the expressiveness of models and seeing which models are possibly under- or over-fitting the input data.

Workflow

In order to support the workflow of clinical researchers, as described above in the Motivation, *Prospector*'s UI is organized into three main tabs: patient selection, patient inspection, and partial dependence plots.

Patient Selection

The patient selection tab allows users to find patients they may want to inspect, based on their ground truth (*e.g.* whether they actually had diabetes) and their predicted risk (*e.g.* assessed likelihood by the predictive model of having the disease). *Prospector* provides a visual summary of the patient population by providing a patient selection visualization. The visualization, as seen in Figure 7, consists of two columns dividing the population according to their ground truth (case patients being those actually diagnosed with diabetes and control patients being not). Each column is then separated into bins of predicted probabilities in steps of 0.1 which can be clicked to select the group of patients fitting those criteria. For instance, if a case patient was predicted with a low risk score, that patient would appear in the top of the right column. If a bin is too small to provide a clickable area, a box at the side of the column is displayed to allow choosing even small populations. The selected population is then shown next to the visualization with the individual prediction results shown for each entry.

In order to get more details about patients before selecting, users can hover over a patient in the list and see a summary for the patient, as shown in Figure 8. In addition to the predicted risk and the ground truth, the interface shows the top 5 most impactful features, for both increasing and decreasing predicted risk, according to the local feature importance described above. For each impactful feature, the original data value is shown as well as the suggested change and what the resulting predicted risk would be if such a change was made. This summary provides a preview of how amenable a particular patient's predicted risk is to changing and which features are mostly responsible for their current predicted risk.

Patient Inspection

After users select a patient of interest, the UI switches to the patient inspection tab with the selected patient's data loaded, as shown in Figure 9. All of the features' partial dependence bars are shown in a scrollable list, with the patient's feature values selected with circular labels. Users can drag the circular label to change the value of any feature and see the predicted risk change in real-time. Users can also select a feature and see the corresponding typical partial dependence plot of the feature. In this plot the local partial dependence of the current patient is shown as black curve and the global partial dependence of the whole population is shown in gray. The partial dependence plot is also clickable and users can change the feature value here as well, changing the black vertical line that, in this plot, shows the current value.

Users can change the sort order of the partial dependence bars by using the buttons at the top. In addition to sorting by the feature weight and relevance as determined by the predictive model, users can also sort according to our local feature importance and impactful changes as described above. If impactful changes are chosen as the sort order, the suggested changes to each feature are indicated with a white circular label in the partial dependence bar, as shown in the bottom left of Figure 9.

Often after analysts have inspected a particular patient, they may wish to find other patients similar to them to see how they react to the predictive model. If users wish to find patients similar to the one they are inspecting, they can click on the "Neighborhood" button and *Prospector* will automatically find the closest patients to the current set of values using feature-wise Euclidean distance. This similar set of patients are then used as the population in the patient selection tab that users can navigate.

Partial Dependence Plots

If users wish to browse the global partial dependence plots of a feature of interest, they can navigate to the third tab. Users can view multiple models at once by using a combo-box at the top of the user interface to select the models they wish to view in the plot. Each selected model is assigned a unique color using a quantitative color scale, and a color-coded key

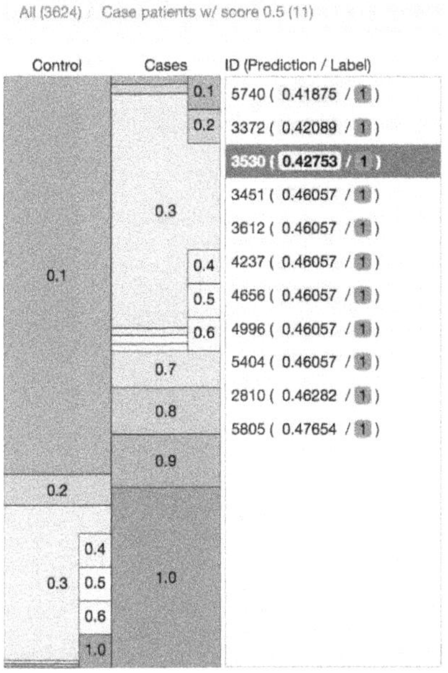

Figure 7. The interface for selecting a patient. The left side shows the distribution of patients within different ranges of predicted risk. The columns indicate the ground truth. On the right side a list shows the patients of the currently selected range.

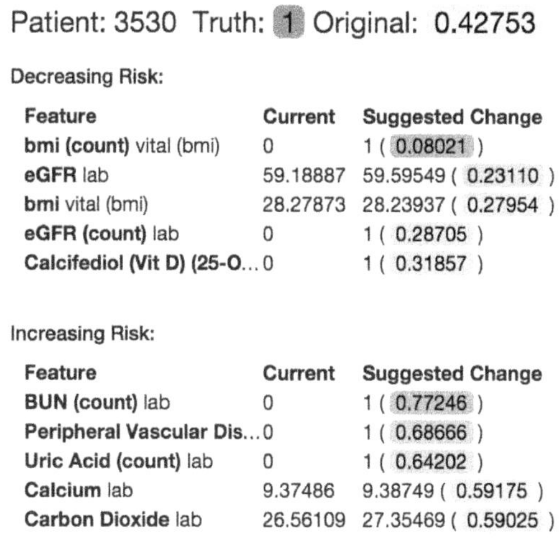

Figure 8. The summary of one patient. The header line indicates the patient id, the ground truth, and the predicted risk. For both decreasing and increasing the predicted risk the top 5 most impactful features are shown. Each feature shows its current value and the suggested change with the highest impact along with how the predicted risk would change.

is displayed beneath the plot. If more than one model is selected, the red "Avg. Score" helper line is not shown. Users can also filter the global population to a subset population of interest by using a predicted probability bin or the "Neighborhood" of a patient in the patient selection tab. This alters the plot accordingly allowing for a more focused analysis for *e.g.* mispredicted patients, outliers, or patient neighborhoods.

CASE STUDY: PREDICTING DIABETES

In order to evaluate the utility of *Prospector*, we chose to conduct a case study utilizing a team of real data scientists building their own predictive models on their own real-world datasets to demonstrate its effectiveness at reaching insights in practice. There is a growing belief in the visualization community that traditional evaluation metrics (e.g. measuring task time completion or number of errors) are often insufficient to evaluate visualization systems [6, 35, 38]. Using the evaluation methodology developed by Perer and Shneiderman [34], we conducted a 4-month long-term case study with a team of five data scientists interested in using predictive modeling on a longitudinal database of electronic medical records. The research team is interested in building a predictive model to predict if a patient is at risk of developing diabetes using a database of 4,000 patients from a major hospital in the United States. Due to sensitive data agreements, this team wished to remain anonymous.

The initial phase of the case study involved understanding the data scientists' current tools and needs. They presented their typical results after building predictive models, sharing stories of success when their stakeholders were pleased, as well as examples of less successful results when their stakeholders demanded answers they couldn't provide with existing tools. Their use cases and experiences shaped the design and requirements of the tool.

After the tool was developed, there were bi-weekly meetings with the data science team in which we discussed the current interface and identified shortcomings of the interface, necessary UI enhancements, and components that were not worth developing further. Some of the elements originally proposed turned out not to be useful, such as overlaying distributions of risk in the partial dependence plots or using ICE plots [15]. However, focusing the meetings on examining the team's predictive models together using *Prospector* allowed us to determine which elements helped improve both the models and their comprehension of the models.

Understanding Model Classes

Initially, the data scientists were unsure which type of predictive models to build. Although they had used simpler models in the past, such as decision trees and logistic regression, they were eager to use random forest models due the promise of higher accuracy but were worried about how interpretable the results would be. After building models using both logistic regression and random forests, they were curious to use partial dependence plots to understand the trade-offs of both approaches. An example of such trade-offs can be seen in Figure 6, which is a partial dependence plot of two logistic regression models and one random forest. Interestingly, for this feature (which refers to the number of times patients got their BMI recorded), the model types disagree substantially for higher values in the plot. This is surprising since the inspected feature is most important for all models and all models perform equally well using standard statistics like accuracy or AUC.

While all three models have a decrease in average predicted risk when the count goes from 0 to 2, the logistic regression models continue to trend downward. However, the random forest model (in red), illustrates the predictive risk increases

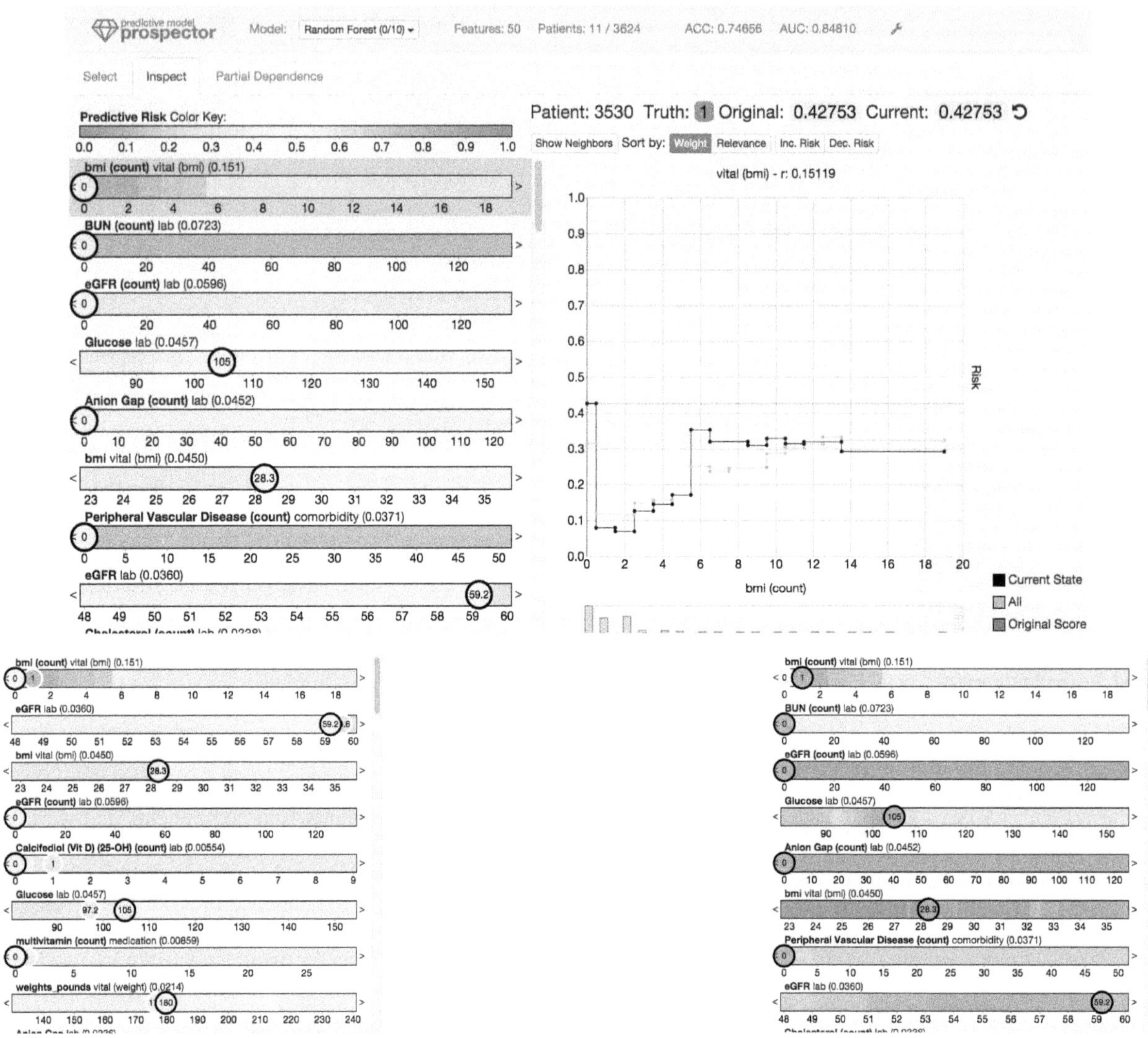

Figure 9. The user interface of *Prospector* is shown at the top. The bottom left shows suggestions on what changes (white circles) would decrease the predicted risk the most. The bottom right shows how the color plots change due to changing a value (namely changing the bmi value from 0 to 1). Fully white circles show the original value of the given patient.

as the count gets higher than two. The data scientists were surprised to learn how differently the model classes treated this feature, but using the tool, they were able to devise a two-fold explanation. On one hand, logistic regression models are not expressive enough to model the late increase after the initial drop, as logistic regression models are bound by a single curve. On the other hand, most of the observed data points of the feature are zero, one, and two while the higher values occur extremely rare, as the histogram below the plot clearly illustrates. This led the data scientist team to question whether to model everything as precisely as possible or using a simpler model for the sake of generality.

Unexpected Effects of Data Imputation

Due to limitations of their database, many of the patients were missing Glucose lab test results. During the feature construction phase, the team made a decision that in order to work around the missing values, each patient who did not have a value would be given the average observed value of all other patients. This imputation technique is popular among predictive modelers, as simply removing all patients without such data would make the data quite small. However, once the data science team began to explore the Glucose feature in the tool, as shown in Figure 3, they began to realize the dramatic effects their imputation strategy can have. Due to the imputation, patients that are either cases or controls often have the same lab test values which increases the noise of the predicted risk. The partial dependence plot illustrates that, as noise increases, the predicted probability gets closer to the population average leading to a valley in the machine learning model. Exploring this feature in *Prospector* suggested that a better strategy for handling missing values would be needed to overcome this problem.

The Need for Localized Inspection

Discussions in bi-weekly interviews also led to the development of the localized inspection of patients which aims to answer the following questions:

1. What impact does a feature have on an actual patient?
2. Does the model behave correctly on a case-to-case basis?
3. What are the most important features for a given patient?
4. Why are certain patients not being accurately predicted?
5. Can we identify high impact actionable features?

The last question about identifying actionable features was of particular importance to the data science team. They were interested to know if the model could be used to learn features that could be acted upon by the patients or their doctors to reduce the risk of diabetes. However, the data science team were disappointed to learn, via *Prospector*, that many of the highest ranking features were not actionable. For instance, some of the most predictive features for a high risk of diabetes involved having a high count of the number of lab tests. Informing patients to get fewer lab tests would likely not correlate to lower risk of diabetes. Instead, these lab test counts were likely a proxy for other features that correlated to more complicated or more sickly patients seeing their doctors more regularly and thus getting more lab tests. Other demographic features that were highly predictive, like age, simply have no intervention as well. The data science team then reconsidered which features should be a part of the predictive model, by creating features that are actionable and omitting others. Of course, the model cannot know this by itself – no matter what sophisticated feature selection algorithms are used – so the access *Prospector* provides is critical for this process.

Impact into Data Scientists' Workflow

In addition to learning new insights about their predictive models, the tool also impacted the team's workflow. Prior to *Prospector*, after each new predictive model was built, a data scientist would manually generate a set of reports describing the model. Typically, this would involve exporting a list of the model's top features and their weights, and generating a bar chart for the other team members to review. They would present these bar chart summaries during review meetings and discuss if the model seemed sensible enough. If they believe the list of features made sense, they would then present this chart to their stakeholders. If it didn't, they would brainstorm how to improve the predictive model (such as changing the classification or feature selection algorithms) and then repeat this process. While this manual approach led to the deployment of predictive models in the past, many iterations were required and understanding impactful values of features were rarely considered.

Once *Prospector* was integrated into their workflow, many of these shortcomings were overcome. No longer did a data scientist need to generate a set of manual reports. Instead, the predictive model can be loaded into the tool directly. Since the tool is interactive, it also allows the team to ask questions that may have not been considered when static charts were created. The tool also allowed them to ask questions beyond the top features that contributed to the models. They could ask more patient-centric questions such as "Why is this patient not being classified correctly?" by drilling down to incorrectly predicted patients and exploring the most impactful features for them. Beyond exploration, *Prospector* was also used to communicate models to the stakeholders, which allowed stakeholders to ask questions and see the results in real-time. This rapid feedback helped gain support for deploying predictive models in future projects. As a result of these successes, *Prospector* is now a part of their predictive modeling workflow and is used for other work than predicting the onset of diabetes.

CONCLUSION AND DISCUSSION

In this paper, we demonstrated how the design and implementation of an interactive visual analytics system, *Prospector*, can help data scientists assess the interpretability and actionable insights of trained predictive models. *Prospector* accomplishes this by supporting interactive partial dependence diagnostics for understanding how features affect the prediction overall by featuring novel visual representations, sampling strategies, and support for comparing multiple models. Furthermore, *Prospector* supports localized inspection so data scientists can understand how and why specific datapoints are predicted as they are. With support to interactively tweak feature values and see how the prediction responds, as well as finding the most impactful features using a novel local feature importance metric, data scientists can interact with models on a deeper level than possible with common tools. Finally, we presented a case study, in the spirit of #chi4good, which involved a team of data scientists using *Prospector* to improve predictive models for detecting the onset of diabetes. Their extended use of the tool led to better predictive models, as well as better communication of their models to their stakeholders.

Despite the novel features of *Prospector* and its successful case study, there is still much future work to continue to give users full comprehension of predictive models. *Prospector* relies on partial dependence for one input feature at a time, but this approach relies on the orthogonality of input features. However, in real-world data, this is not often the case, as features may be correlated. *Prospector* can only model changes along one axis at a time as it cannot take correlations or influences between features into account. We plan to address this limitation in future work by modeling valid sets of input points and visualizing how they react to changes in one or more features. Another limitation is that *Prospector* was built to view predictive models after they had been built using users' own predictive modeling pipeline of choice. However, this flexibility limits the ability for users to directly impact their predictive models based on insights reached during exploration. Also, *Prospector* can only handle single-class predictions, but we plan to extend this functionality to multi-class predictions in the future. Our future work also intends to integrate *Prospector* more directly into the predictive modeling pipeline so users can directly modify features for feature construction and feature selection and see how their models improve in a single user interface. Despite these limitations, providing users with advanced visual tools to inspect black-boxes of machine learning shows great promise and helps users comprehend and retain control of their predictive models without sacrificing accuracy.

REFERENCES

1. Saleema Amershi, Max Chickering, Steven M. Drucker, Bongshin Lee, Patrice Simard, and Jina Suh. 2015. ModelTracker: Redesigning Performance Analysis Tools for Machine Learning. (April 2015), 337–346.
2. Saleema Amershi, James Fogarty, Ashish Kapoor, and Tan Desney. 2011a. Designing for Effective End-user Interaction with Machine Learning. In *Proceedings of the 24th Annual ACM Symposium Adjunct on User Interface Software and Technology (UIST '11 Adjunct)*. ACM, New York, NY, USA, 47–50.
3. Saleema Amershi, James Fogarty, and Daniel Weld. 2012. Regroup: Interactive Machine Learning for On-demand Group Creation in Social Networks. In *Proceedings of the SIGCHI Conference on Human Factors in Computing Systems (CHI '12)*. ACM, New York, NY, USA, 21–30.
4. Saleema Amershi, Bongshin Lee, Ashish Kapoor, Ratul Mahajan, and Blaine Christian. 2011b. CueT: Human-guided Fast and Accurate Network Alarm Triage. In *Proceedings of the SIGCHI Conference on Human Factors in Computing Systems (CHI '11)*. ACM, New York, NY, USA, 157–166.
5. Barry Becker, Ron Kohavi, and Dan Sommerfield. 2002. Information Visualization in Data Mining and Knowledge Discovery. Morgan Kaufmann Publishers Inc., San Francisco, CA, USA, Chapter Visualizing the Simple Baysian Classifier, 237–249.
6. Enrico Bertini, Heidi Lam, and Adam Perer. 2011. Summaries: a special issue on evaluation for information visualization. *Information Visualization* 10, 3 (2011).
7. Leo Breiman. 2001. Statistical Modeling: The Two Cultures. *Statist. Sci.* 16, 3 (08 2001), 199–231.
8. Doina Caragea, Dianne Cook, and Vasant Honavar. 2001. Gaining Insights into Support Vector Machine Pattern Classifiers Using Projection-Based Tour Methods. In *Proceedings of the KDD Conference*. 251–256.
9. Rich Caruana, Yin Lou, Johannes Gehrke, Paul Koch, Marc Sturm, and Noemie Elhadad. 2015. Intelligible Models for HealthCare: Predicting Pneumonia Risk and Hospital 30-day Readmission. In *Proceedings of the 21th ACM SIGKDD International Conference on Knowledge Discovery and Data Mining (KDD '15)*. ACM, New York, NY, USA, 1721–1730.
10. Paulo Cortez and Mark J. Embrechts. 2011. Opening black box Data Mining models using Sensitivity Analysis. In *Computational Intelligence and Data Mining (CIDM), IEEE Symposium on*. 341–348.
11. Paulo Cortez and Mark J. Embrechts. 2013. Using sensitivity analysis and visualization techniques to open black box data mining models. *Information Sciences* 225 (2013), 1–17.
12. John Ehrlinger. 2015. ggRandomForests: Random Forests for Regression. (2015). R package version 1.1.4.
13. Eibe Frank and Mark Hall. 2003. Visualizing Class Probability Estimators. In *Knowledge Discovery in Databases (PKDD)*, Nada Lavra, Dragan Gamberger, Ljupo Todorovski, and Hendrik Blockeel (Eds.). Lecture Notes in Computer Science, Vol. 2838. Springer Berlin Heidelberg, 168–179.
14. Jerome H. Friedman. 2001. Greedy function approximation: A gradient boosting machine. *Annals of Statistics* 29, 5 (10 2001), 1189–1232.
15. Alex Goldstein, Adam Kapelner, Justin Bleich, and Emil Pitkin. 2014. Peeking Inside the Black Box: Visualizing Statistical Learning With Plots of Individual Conditional Expectation. *Journal of Computational and Graphical Statistics* (March 2014).
16. Trevor Hastie, Robert Tibshirani, and Jerome Friedman. 2001. *The elements of statistical learning: data mining, inference, and prediction*. Springer Verlag.
17. Aleks Jakulin, Martin Možina, Janez Demšar, Ivan Bratko, and Blaž Zupan. 2005. Nomograms for Visualizing Support Vector Machines. In *Proceedings of the Eleventh ACM SIGKDD International Conference on Knowledge Discovery in Data Mining (KDD '05)*. ACM, New York, NY, USA, 108–117.
18. David Correa Martins Jr., Evaldo A. de Oliveira, Ulisses de Mendonça Braga Neto, Ronaldo Fumio Hashimoto, and Roberto Marcondes Cesar Jr. 2013. Signal propagation in Bayesian networks and its relationship with intrinsically multivariate predictive variables. *Information Sciences* 225 (March 2013), 18–34.
19. Ashish Kapoor, Bongshin Lee, Desney Tan, and Eric Horvitz. 2010. Interactive Optimization for Steering Machine Classification. In *Proceedings of the SIGCHI Conference on Human Factors in Computing Systems (CHI '10)*. ACM, New York, NY, USA, 1343–1352.
20. Been Kim, Finale Doshi-Velez, and Julie A Shah. 2015a. Mind the Gap: A Generative Approach to Interpretable Feature Selection and Extraction. In *Advances in Neural Information Processing Systems*.
21. Been Kim, Kayur Patel, Afshin Rostamizadeh, and Julie Shah. 2015b. Scalable and interpretable data representation for high-dimensional complex data. In *Association for the Advancement of Artificial Intelligence (AAAI)*.
22. Been Kim, Cynthia Rudin, and Julie A Shah. 2014. The Bayesian Case Model: A Generative Approach for Case-Based Reasoning and Prototype Classification. In *Advances in Neural Information Processing Systems*. 1952–1960.
23. Josua Krause, Adam Perer, and Enrico Bertini. 2014. INFUSE: Interactive Feature Selection for Predictive Modeling of High Dimensional Data. *Visualization and Computer Graphics, IEEE Transactions on* 20, 12 (Dec 2014), 1614–1623.
24. Max Kuhn and Kjell Johnson. 2013. *Applied Predictive Modeling*. Springer London, Limited.

25. Todd Kulesza, Margaret Burnett, Weng-Keen Wong, and Simone Stumpf. 2015. Principles of Explanatory Debugging to Personalize Interactive Machine Learning. In *Proceedings of the 20th International Conference on Intelligent User Interfaces (IUI '15)*. ACM, New York, NY, USA, 126–137.

26. Carson K. Leung and Kyle W. Joseph. 2014. Sports Data Mining: Predicting Results for the College Football Games. *Procedia Computer Science* 35 (September 2014), 710–719. Knowledge-Based and Intelligent Information & Engineering Systems 18th Annual Conference (KES), Proceedings of.

27. Moshe Lichman and Kevin Bache. 2013. UCI Machine Learning Repository. (2013). `http://archive.ics.uci.edu/ml`

28. Brian Y. Lim. 2012. *Improving Understanding and Trust with Intelligibility in Context-aware Applications*. Ph.D. Dissertation. Pittsburgh, PA, USA. Advisor(s) Dey, Anind K. AAI3524680.

29. Shubhanshu Mishra, Jana Diesner, Jason Byrne, and Elizabeth Surbeck. 2015. Sentiment Analysis with Incremental Human-in-the-Loop Learning and Lexical Resource Customization. In *Proceedings of the 26th ACM Conference on Hypertext & Social Media (HT '15)*. ACM, New York, NY, USA, 323–325.

30. Kenney Ng, Amol Ghoting, Steven R. Steinhubl, Walter F. Stewart, Bradley Malin, and Jimeng Sun. 2013. PARAMO: A PARAllel predictive MOdeling platform for healthcare analytic research using electronic health records. *Journal of Biomedical Informatics* (2013).

31. Julian D. Olden and Donald A. Jackson. 2002. Illuminating the "black box": a randomization approach for understanding variable contributions in artificial neural networks. *Ecological Modelling* 154, 12 (2002), 135–150.

32. Kayur Patel, Naomi Bancroft, Steven Drucker, James Fogarty, and James Landay. 2010. Gestalt: Integrated Support for Implementation and Analysis in Machine Learning. In *Proceedings of the 23rd annual ACM symposium on User interface software and technology (UIST)*. ACM, New York, NY, 37–46.

33. Kayur Patel, Steven M. Drucker, James Fogarty, Ashish Kapoor, and Desney S. Tan. 2011. Using Multiple Models to Understand Data. In *Proceedings of the 22nd International Joint Conference on Artificial Intelligence (IJCAI)*, Toby Walsh (Ed.). IJCAI/AAAI, 1723–1728.

34. Adam Perer and Ben Shneiderman. 2008. Integrating statistics and visualization: case studies of gaining clarity during exploratory data analysis. In *Proceedings of the twenty-sixth annual SIGCHI conference on Human factors in computing systems*. 265–274.

35. Catherine Plaisant. 2004. The challenge of information visualization evaluation. In *Proceedings of the working conference on Advanced visual interfaces*. ACM, 109–116.

36. Tony Plate, Joel Bert, John Grace, and Pierre Band. 1997. Visualizing the Function Computed by a Feedforward Neural Network. *Progress in Connectionist-Based Information Systems: Proceedings of The Fourth International Conference on Neural Information Processing (ICONIP'97)* 1 (1997), 306–309.

37. Penny Rheingans and Marie desJardins. 2000. Visualizing high-dimensional predictive model quality. In *Visualization*. 493–496.

38. Ben Shneiderman and Catherine Plaisant. 2006. Strategies for evaluating information visualization tools: multi-dimensional in-depth long-term case studies. In *Proceedings of the 2006 BELIV Workshop*. 1–7.

39. Chad A. Steed, Patrick J. Fitzpatrick, J. Edward Swan II, and T.J. Jankun-Kelly. 2009a. Tropical Cyclone Trend Analysis Using Enhanced Parallel Coordinates and Statistical Analytics. *Cartography and Geographic Information Science* 36, 3 (2009), 251–265.

40. Chad A. Steed, J. Edward Swan II, T.J. Jankun-Kelly, and Patrick J. Fitzpatrick. 2009b. Guided analysis of hurricane trends using statistical processes integrated with interactive parallel coordinates. In *Visual Analytics Science and Technology (VAST), IEEE Symposium on*. 19–26.

41. Greg Ver Steeg and Aram Galstyan. 2015. Maximally Informative Hierarchical Representations of High-Dimensional Data. In *AISTATS'15*.

42. Justin Talbot, Bongshin Lee, Ashish Kapoor, and Desney S. Tan. 2009. EnsembleMatrix: Interactive Visualization to Support Machine Learning with Multiple Classifiers. In *Proceedings of the SIGCHI Conference on Human Factors in Computing Systems (CHI '09)*. ACM, New York, NY, USA, 1283–1292.

43. Fan-Yin Tzeng and Kwan-Liu Ma. 2005. Opening the Black Box - Data Driven Visualization of Neural Networks. In *Proceedings of IEEE Visualization '05 Conference*. IEEE, 383–390.

44. Stef van den Elzen and Jarke J. van Wijk. 2011. BaobabView: Interactive construction and analysis of decision trees. In *Visual Analytics Science and Technology (VAST), IEEE Conference on*. 151–160.

45. Greg Ver Steeg and Aram Galstyan. 2014. Discovering Structure in High-Dimensional Data Through Correlation Explanation. In *Advances in Neural Information Processing Systems 27*, Z. Ghahramani, M. Welling, C. Cortes, N.D. Lawrence, and K.Q. Weinberger (Eds.). Curran Associates, Inc., 577–585.

46. Kelvin Xu, Jimmy Ba, Ryan Kiros, Kyunghyun Cho, Aaron Courville, Ruslan Salakhudinov, Rich Zemel, and Yoshua Bengio. 2015. Show, Attend and Tell: Neural Image Caption Generation with Visual Attention. In *Proceedings of the 32nd International Conference on Machine Learning (ICML-15)*. 2048–2057.

Musically Informed Sonification for Chronic Pain Rehabilitation: Facilitating Progress & Avoiding Over-doing

Joseph W. Newbold[1], Nadia Bianchi-Berthouze[1], Nicolas E. Gold[3], Ana Tajadura-Jiménez[1,2], Amanda CdC Williams[4]

[1]UCL Interaction Centre London, UK

[2]Universidad Loyola Andalucía Seville, Spain

[3]Dept. of Computer Science UCL, London, UK

[4]Dept. of Clinical, Educational & Health Psychology UCL, London, UK

{joseph.newbold.14, n.berthouze, n.gold, a.tajadura, amanda.williams }@ucl.ac.uk

ABSTRACT

In self-directed chronic pain physical rehabilitation it is important that the individual can progress as physical capabilities and confidence grow. However, people with chronic pain often struggle to pass what they have identified as safe boundaries. At the same time, over-activity due to the desire to progress fast or function more normally, may lead to setbacks. We investigate how musically-informed movement sonification can be used as an implicit mechanism to both avoid overdoing and facilitate progress during stretching exercises. We sonify an end target-point in a stretch exercise, using a stable sound (i.e., where the sonification is musically resolved) to encourage movements ending and an unstable sound (i.e., musically unresolved) to encourage continuation. Results on healthy participants show that instability leads to progression further beyond the target-point while stability leads to a smoother stop beyond this point. We conclude discussing how these findings should generalize to the CP population.

Author Keywords

Musically informed sonification; physical rehabilitation; auditory feedback

ACM Classification Keywords

H.5.2 User Interfaces: Auditory (non-speech) feedback

INTRODUCTION

Self-directed chronic pain (CP) rehabilitation is challenging and emotionally distressing [4]. In CP, that is pain that persists past the expected time of healing and it is not justified by physical damage [22], it can create anxiety towards movements that are perceived as threatening (e.g., stretching). It can be difficult to achieve progress due to fear of increase pain. At the same time, there is the danger of over-activity induced by the desire and personal expectations of progressing quickly which can cause set-backs and becoming bed-bound for weeks [15]. In this paper we explored how musically informed movement sonification can be used to invite progress during exercise, or discourage overdoing.

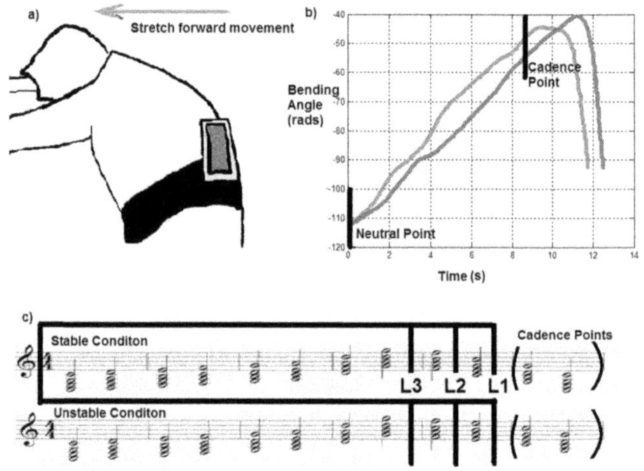

Figure 1. a) shows the stretch forward movement (trunk bend angle) tracked by a smartphone-based system. b) An example of the output recorded: the movement towards and past the cadence point for stable (blue) and unstable (red) conditions. This example illustrates the difference in amount of stretching beyond the cadence point. c) An overview of the sonification stimuli used, all ending on either a stable or unstable cadence point, with three lengths L1, L2 and L3 (derived by removing one or two chords from before the cadence point, followed by either the stable or unstable cadence).

Sound and visual feedback for rehabilitation has been used to provide rewards as it enhances the perception of moving (self-efficacy) [16, 24], enables a better control of the body with respect to trajectories/targets [25] and shifts the attention away from pain [9, 16]. Typically, the achievement of targets is rewarded through changes in the sonification, e.g., the ending of sound beyond the target, dynamically changing sound (increasing tone scales) to indicate progression [25, 16]. Deviations from the set targets (e.g., going beyond it) are signalled by an alteration of the sound, by stopping or by an auditory alert to signal wrong-doing [16, 24].

In this paper, we contribute a new method of sonifying target points based on the idea of harmonic stability. Musical harmony can be thought of as a series of tensions and relaxations: points of tension where the music feels as though it

CHI'16, May 07 - 12, 2016, San Jose, CA, USA

ISBN 978-1-4503-3362-7/16/05. . . $15.00
DOI: http://dx.doi.org/10.1145/2858036.2858302

should continue (unstable) and points of resolution where the music feels concluded (stable) [1]. For example, in a pop song there may be a build in tension before the chorus, partly achieved through aspects of musical instability and which will often become resolved at the end of the chorus. This aspect of music has been shown to be understood implicitly by people without musical training, through day-to-day exposure [1, 23, 21, 14]. By exploiting the sense of agency over the heard sounds derived from the sonification of one's body movement (i.e., the feeling that the sounds heard are being produced by one's own body movement [18]) and the musical resolution obtained using harmonic stability levels, we aim to provide the perception that the level of resolution of the sonification is created by the person's internal decision to either conclude a movement or not. We investigate whether the target point of a movement (e.g., stretching forward), being stable or unstable, can affect the behaviour at that point. In particular, we explore the possibility of stable contexts to conveying the feeling that a movement is reaching an end, thus encouraging stopping, and unstable contexts for target points to producing the desire to continue. The novel contribution of this work is in the demonstration of the effect of harmonic structure when used in a sonification of movement. We aim to use this musical structure as part of an embodied interaction and whether the musical structure of harmonic stability is perceived as the conclusion of the movement.

BACKGROUND

Sound feedback for physical Rehabilitation

Sonification of movement has been used in many contexts: for optimisation, e.g., sports [13, 2], dance [3] or motor-learning [7, 17]. Several works have also investigated the use of sound feedback to aid rehabilitation. Wallis et al. developed a system for the rehabilitation of arm mobility in stroke patients that used musical sound feedback driven by movement within a given space [25]. The progression of the feedback was driven by the individual's movement. The ending of movement was incentivised by using harmonic resolution and an auditory alert to indicate completion. Undesired movement was indicated using other auditory alerts. This work shows the use of harmonic structure within a defined space to provide a rewarding end. However, it does not explore the uses of harmony to encourage continuation or how the harmonic resolution affects the movement.

Vogt et al. focus on helping people undergoing physiotherapy to better understand their body and movement [24]. The system used two scenarios, a woodland scene where layers of sound were added with movement, and one where movement drove the playback of a musical sample/text, with inhibitory sounds used to avoid deviation from the movement. Again this work used a definite end point, not allowing progression past a predefined point.

Singh et al. used sonification specifically to aid CP rehabilitation [16]. Each individual defined their own exercise space consisting of a neutral start point, a comfortable amount of stretching and a final target amount of stretch. The sonification used these points to space a melodic progression within the exercise space: an ascending melody marked the progression from the start to the comfortable point and from this point a descending melody marked the progression to the target point. Participants reported higher performance and self-efficacy with this feedback.

The work described above defined an end to the movement to inform an individual that they are moving outside of the given space through a change in the sonification. Sound feedback has also been shown to affect the perception of body appearance and/or the body physical capabilities (e.g., body strength) and these may have an effect on movement behaviour [18, 19]. These mechanisms exploit the concept of agency, that is the perception of the sound as direct sensory feedback of one's own action. Hence careful manipulations of sonification are perceived as consequences of one's own motor behaviour rather than externally imposed [6, 20]

Implicit music understanding

Musical stability can be thought of as how much a piece of music has concluded. Bigand demonstrated that this aspect of music is understood by people without explicit musical training, and that tonal factors are important for both musicians and non-musicians for determining the stability [1]. Sears' recent work on perception of cadence also demonstrates the ability of non-musically trained people to identify differing stabilities of cadences [14]. Cadences represent a specific way in which musical stability can be manipulated. A cadence consists of two chords used most commonly at the end of a musical phrase that define whether it either continued or concluded. The ratings for different cadences taken from Mozart's Piano Sonata No. 3, K. 281 were given by musicians and non-musicians. Sears' work showed that similar completion ratings were given by both musicians and non-musicians for a series of different cadences.

These works show that the understanding of musical stability and cadential closure are acquired to some degree implicitly without musical training. Using this understanding, we aim to create a musically-informed sonification which would allow better progression and discourage over-activity. Our approach is grounded in neuroscience theories of motor-to-sensory transformations showing implicit associations between sounds and movement (e.g., sound pitch and direction of movement) [8] and that sensory feedback is used to update motor predictions and implicitly biases the subsequent movements [27].

HARMONIC STABILITIES EFFECT ON MOVEMENT

Motivation and Hypothesis

This experiment investigates the use of stable and unstable cadences for defining the target point of a movement; for example, a set amount of trunk bending, as shown in Figure 1.a. Participants were given sound feedback driven by their movement and asked to use the sound to inform them that they have reached the target point. A stretch forward movement, often used in the rehabilitation of chronic lower back pain, was chosen for its past use as an example of an anxiety-inducing movement for people with CP [16].

We hypothesised that a target point sonified by stable cadences would lead to a more natural stop, whereas with unstable cadences a more prolonged movement past the target point would be observed (**Hypothesis 1**). We also hypothesised stable cadences would provide a stronger sense of reward and motivation than unstable ones (**Hypothesis 2**).

Materials

Our sonification is based on that used by Singh *et al.* consisting of a set of ascending tones followed by a set of descending tones ending at the final-target point [16]. The use of a simply shaped sound was considered important as it was easier to interpret while executing a feared movement, as such we used the same shape but added harmonic structuring. The target point sonification was based on the conceptual sonification design framework proposed in [12]. A set of six conditions was created: three stable (ST) and three unstable (UN). For the descending part, three different lengths were used: 3 chords (L1), 2 chords (L2) and 1 chord long (L3) for both ST and the UN of the sound, as shown in Figure 1.b. The reasoning behind the different length stimuli was to avoid learning bias, where participants would learn after how many chords the feedback stopped. The cadences were chosen following a validation study with 38 participants who rated the stability of six different cadences and different length stimuli. The unstable condition was left unresolved and participants returned to the initial position once they realised no more chords would be triggered.

Participants

A total of 21 healthy paid participants were recruited for the study (age=21-75, 14 female and 7 male). Four participants from the study were discounted from the analyses, three as they failed to consistently reach the final cadence point and one due to exceeding the range of the sensor. For this study we recruited from the general population, instead of any specific rehabilitation population, this was done for two reasons: 1) to ensure it would be safe to use within a rehabilitation context and 2) as there should be no difference in the perception of the sonification or its effect on movement between rehabilitation and non-rehabilitation populations. 13 out of the 17 participants were found to be below the mean score for General Musical Sophistication subscale of the Goldsmith musical sophistication index in the general population (81.58) [10], therefore we assume the effects seen are not due to musical training.

Experimental Design & procedure

To achieve the sonification, a smart-phone application was used: the phone was placed on the participant's lower back, via a support band, and used its integrated gyroscope to measure the bending of the trunk during the stretching forward which drives the sonification, it operated at ~50 FPS with minimal frame loss. First, measures of each participant's neutral position (i.e., standing up right) and a maximum stretch position were taken. The stretch space between neutral position and target point was then divided into 11 equal segments so that as the participant stretches the next chord in the sequence played. The final two chords of this sequence gave either a ST or UN target point within the stretch space (dependent on the length). Behavioural and self-reported measures were taken:

Stretch distance: The amount of stretch beyond the cadence point, as measured by the phone gyroscope, was used as a measure of how far participants continued to stretch before stopping to return to the neutral position.

Time of return: The time taken between the cadence point and the maximum amount of stretch before returning (the stretch distance) was used as a measure of the participants response time to the final cadence (i.e., how long it took them to realise they had reached the target point).

Self-reported measures: Measures of perceived stability, perceived motivation to continue, perceived amount of stretch and perceived reward at the target point were taken with 7-point Likert-type response items.

A randomised within-subjects design was used and consisted of 12 trials, including two repetitions of the six conditions. The participants were first introduced to the experiment and given a demonstration of the smart-phone application. They were instructed to stretch forward at a steady pace allowing each chord to sound and to use the music produced to inform them when they had reached the target point (i.e., the end of the feedback). After each stretch a questionnaire was used to collect the self-report measures. The study was approved by the ethics committee of UCL.

RESULTS

Behavioural data was normalised using individual z-scores. The trials were submitted to repeated measures analyses of variance (ANOVA) with stability, length and repetition as within-subjects factors, and musical expertise as between-subjects factor, followed by Bonferroni-corrected pairwise comparisons. Self-reported data were analysed with Friedman tests, followed by Bonferroni-corrected Wilcoxon signed rank tests. Results are summarized in Figure 2.

Stretch distance: Significant effects were found both for stability ($F(1,14) = 25.744$, $p < .001$, $\eta^2 = .632$) and length ($F(2,60) = 15.201$, $p < .001$, $\eta^2 = .503$), with no significant interaction. Bonferroni-corrected pairwise comparisons showed that people stretched more in L3 than in L1 ($p < .001$), and in L2 than in L1 ($p = .037$). No significant effect was seen due to repetition. *Participants stretched on average more in the UN and less in the longest condition L1.*

Time of return: Significant effects were found for stability ($F(1,14) = 13.917$, $p = .002$, $\eta^2 = .481$) and length ($F(2,60) = 8.000$, $p = .002$, $\eta^2 = .348$), with no significant interaction. A significant difference was found between L1 and L3 (p =

.006). Again no effect of repetition was found. *Participants responded quicker to ST, and to the longest L1 vs L3.*

Self-reported measures: Wilcoxon signed rank tests showed no significant differences between the two repetitions for each item. Thus, the repetitions were averaged resulting in six conditions. A series of Friedman tests found significant differences for: perceived stability ($\eta^2(5) = 47.357$, $p < .001$), perceived stretch ($\eta^2(5) = 12.139$, $p = .033$) and perceived reward ($\eta^2(5) = 38.180$, $p < .001$), but not for perceived motivation. Subsequent Wilcoxon tests (the adjusted significance level was at $p = 0.055$) showed that STL3 was significantly less stable than STL1 ($Z = -2.866$, $p = .004$) and STL2 ($Z = -3.005$, $p = .003$). ST conditions were significantly more stable than their UN counterparts for L1 ($Z = -3.209$, $p = .001$), L2 ($Z = -3.625$, $p = .001$) and L3 ($Z = -3.423$, $p = .001$). For perceived reward, significant differences were found between STL1 and STL3 ($Z = - 2.806$, $p = .005$). ST conditions were found more rewarding than their UN counterparts for L1 ($Z = -3.054$, $p = .002$), L2 ($Z = -3.160$, $p = .002$) but not L3.Significant effects were not found for perceived stretch.

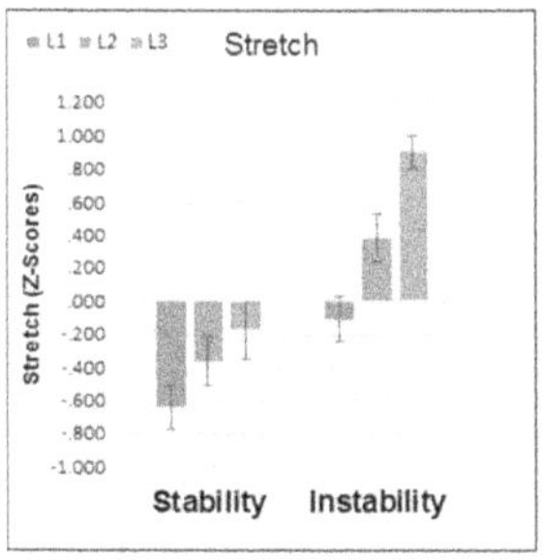

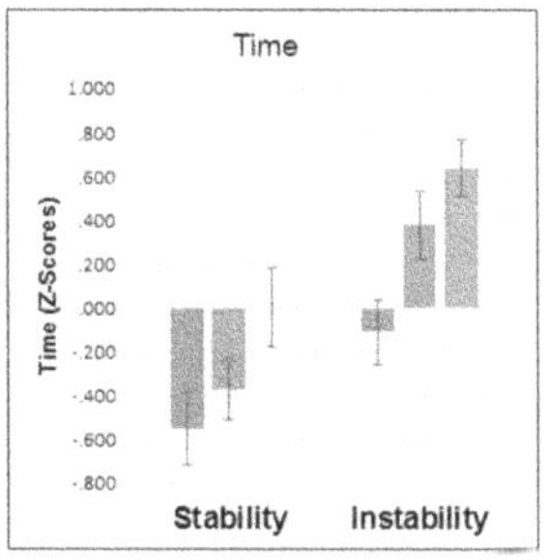

	STL1	STL2	STL3	UNL1	UNL2	UNL3
Stability	1(1-6)	1.5(1-5.5)	3(1-6.5)	5(1-7)	6(1-7)	5.5(3-7)
Motivation	4(1-7)	5(1-7)	4.5(1-7)	2.5(1-6.5)	3.5(1-7)	4(1-7)
Stretch	6(4-7)	5.5(2-7)	5(1.5-7)	5.5(2-7)	5.5(2.5-7)	5.5(1-7)
Reward	5.5(4.5-6.5)	5.5(3.5-6.5)	5(2.5-6)	4(1-6.5)	3.5(1.5-6)	4(1-6)

Figure 2. Experimental results: (top) mean (SE) stretch & time; (bottom) median (range) values for self-reported data for stable (ST) and unstable (UN) cadences of lengths L1-3.

DISCUSSION

The results show that, in music-based sonifications of movement, ST can be used to promote ending and conversely UN can be used to encourage continuation of movement after the target point. As hypothesized, we found that for UN there was additional movement after the cadence point and that for ST the time of return was quicker. Results also show that the length of the sonification prior to the cadence had significant effects on both stretch distance and time of return. Furthermore, ST endings were as expected more rewarding than UN. These results are in keeping with Bigand's suggestion that musical stability is implicitly understood [1]. They are also in line with previous neuroscience works on motor-to-sensory transformations showing that sensory feedback received on one's actions can implicitly bias subsequent motor behaviour [27] and constitute a novel contribution to this area of research in which there are only few studies looking at sound feedback [19]. These previous studies mostly used distorted versions of sounds that naturally accompany body movement. However we show that implicit associations between body movement and musical sound can also have an effect on motor behaviour. Results also suggest that the length of the sonification prior to the cadence point can modify movement behaviour, as significant effects of sonification length were found on stretch distance and time of return. This should be taken with caution. We hypothesize that it could be due to the knowledge of the maximum stretch so that as they stretched further they were more expectant of the ending.

Though our study was carried out with healthy participants, we feel these preliminary results can be generalised for a musically-informed sonification for CP rehabilitation. The key differences between this population and that with CP are pain on movement, and anxiety. Previous work has shown that self-calibrated sonification of movement can refocus attention from pain and anxiety to movement by providing an external focus [16] and sound/music can be used to manage anxiety and even reduce pain [11, 5]. Moreover, our approach directly mimics the verbal instructions of physiotherapists [15]: the UN cadence mimics their use of continuous tense during movement to focus on moving and encourage progress; the ST cadence mimics direct verbal instructions to specify targets and avoid overdoing.

The present results also show that ST endings were significantly more rewarding than those that do not reach musical conclusion, this is beneficial in terms of reducing overdoing. Self-efficacy is especially important in CP as it links to fear and anxiety of movement [26]. The importance of marking the end of a movement was also seen in Wallis et al. [25] for other kinds of rehabilitation.

At the same time, the UN cadence was perceived as less rewarding. However, in the context of rehabilitation, an UN cadence would be used to encourage movement past a point, then followed by a ST cadence at a final target to both resolve musically and reward movement. Naturally the next step will be to verify its use in this context.

CONCLUSION & FUTURE WORK

These results demonstrate how harmonic stability can be used to promote movement for a rehabilitation context. We demonstrate the application of implicit musical understood theory [1, 14] to create a musically-informed movement sonification. We show that endings of different stabilities can be used to either encourage movement or provide a definite end point and how these definite ends are seen as more rewarding. This work primarily focuses on the rehabilitation applications of this sonification; however, this could be used elsewhere, for example: motor learning/optimisation for sport/training, where sound feedback has already been shown to be effective in the past [7, 13, 2, 17].

ACKNOWLEDGMENTS

Supported by EPSRC EP/H017178/1 'Emo&Pain' and ESRC ES/K001477/1 'The Hearing Body' grants.

REFERENCES

1. Emmanuel Bigand. 1997. Perceiving musical stability: The effect of tonal structure, rhythm, and musical expertise. *Journal of Experimental Psychology: Human Perception and Performance.* (1997). http://psycnet.apa.org/journals/xhp/23/3/808/
2. Daniel Cesarini, Thomas Hermann, and Bodo E Ungerechts. 2014. An Interactive Sonification System for Swimming Evaluated by Users. In *SoniHED- Conference on Sonification of Health and Enviromental Data.*
3. Tobias Großhauser, Bettina Blasing, Corinna Spieth, and Thomas Hermann. 2012. Wearable Sensor-Based Real-Time Sonification of Motion and Foot Pressure in Dance Teaching and Training. *Journal of the Audio Engineering Society* 60, 7/8 (2012), 589. http://pub.uni-bielefeld.de/publication/2528002
4. IASP. 2014. Unrelieved pain is a major global healthcare problem. (2014). http://www.efic.org/userfiles/PainGlobalHealthcareProblem.pdf
5. Katherine Finlay, 2014. Music-induced analgesia in chronic pain: Efficacy and assessment through a primary-task paradigm. *Psychology of Music,*
6. Gunther Knoblich and Bruno H. Repp. 2009. Inferring agency from sound. *Cognition* 111, 2 (May 2009), 248–262. DOI http://dx.doi.org/10.1016/j.cognition.2009.02.007
7. Amir Lahav, Elliot Saltzman and Gottfried Schlaug. 2007. Action representation of sound: audiomotor recognition network while listening to newly acquired actions. *The Journal of Neuroscience: The Official Journal of the Society for Neuroscience*, 27(2), 308–14.
8. Fumiko Maeda, Ryota Kanai, and Shinsuke Shimojo. 2004. Changing pitch induced visual motion illusion. *Current biology* 14, 23 (Dec. 2004), R990–1. DOI: http://dx.doi.org/10.1016/j.cub.2004.11.018
9. Yoky Matsuoka, Sonya Allin, & Roberta Klatzky. 2002. "The tolerance for visual feedback distortions in a virtual environment". *Physiology & Behavior.*
10. Daniel Mullensiefen, Bruno Gingras, Jason Musil,¨ and Lauren Stewart. 2014. The musicality of non-musicians: an index for assessing musical sophistication in the general population. *PloS one* 9, 2 (Jan. 2014), e89642. DOI: http://dx.doi.org/10.1371/journal.pone.0089642
11. Mark Nazemi, Maryam Mobini, Tyler Kinnear, Diane Gromala, 2013, "Soundscapes: A prescription for managing anxiety in a clinical setting," In *Proceedings of the SIGCHI Conference on Human Factors in Computing Systems (CHI '13).* ACM, Paris, France
12. Joseph W. Newbold, Nadia Bianchi-Berthouze, Nicolas E. Gold, and Amanda Williams. 2015. Musically Informed Sonification for Self-Directed Chronic Pain Physical Rehabilitation. In *Sound and Music Computing.*
13. Nina Schaffert, Klaus Mattes, and Alfred Oliver Effenberg. 2011. The sound of rowing stroke cycles as acoustic feedback. In *Proceedings of the 17th International Conference on Auditory Display (ICAD 2011).*
14. David Sears, William E Caplin, and Stephen McAdams. 2014. Perceiving the Classical Cadence. *Music Perception: An Interdisciplinary Journal* 31, 5 (2014), 397–417.
15. Aneesha Singh, Annina Klapper, Jinni Jia, Antonio Fidalgo, Ana Tajadura-Jimenez, Natalie Kanakam,´ Nadia Bianchi-Berthouze, and Amanda Williams. 2014. Motivating People with Chronic Pain to Do Physical Activity: Opportunities for Technology Design. In *Proceedings of the SIGCHI Conference on Human Factors in Computing Systems (CHI '14).* ACM, New York, NY, USA, 2803–2812. DOI: http://dx.doi.org/10.1145/2556288.2557268
16. Aneesha Singh, Davide Pollarolo, Stefano Piana, Gualtiero Volpe, Ana Tajadura-Jiménez, Giovanna Varni, Hane Aung, Isaac Pouw, Amanda Williams, Antonio Camurri, and Nadia Berthouze. 2015. Go with the flow: Tracking, Analysis and Sonification of Movement and Breathing to Build Confidence in Activity Despite Chronic Pain. *HCI* 30 (2015).
17. Kevin M Smith and David Claveau. 2014. The Sonification and Learning of Human Motion. *20th International Conference on Auditory Display (ICAD 2014)* (2014). http://smartech.gatech.edu/handle/1853/52049
18. Ana Tajadura-Jiménez, Maria Basia, Ophelia Deroy, Merle Fairhurst, Nicolai Marquardt, and Nadia Bianchi-Berthouze. 2015. As light as your footsteps: altering walking sounds to change perceived body weight, emotional state and gait. (2015), 2943–2952.
19. Ana Tajadura-Jiménez, Nadia Berthouze, Enrico Furfaro, and Frederic Bevilacqua. 2015. Sonification of virtual and real surface tapping: evaluation of behavior changes, surface perception and emotional indices. *IEEE MultiMedia* (2015), 1–1. DOI:http://dx.doi.org/10.1109/MMUL.2015.30
20. Ana Tajadura-Jiménez, Manos Tsakiris, Torsten Marquardt, and Nadia Bianchi-Berthouze. 2015. Action sounds update the mental representation of arm dimension: contributions of kinaesthesia and agency. *Frontiers in psychology* 6 (Jan. 2015), 689. DOI:http://dx.doi.org/10.3389/fpsyg.2015.00689
21. Barbara Tillmann, Emmanuel Bigand, and Francois Madurell. 1998. Local versus global processing of harmonic cadences in the solution of musical puzzles. (1998). DOI: http://dx.doi.org/10.1007/s004260050022
22. Dennis C. Turk and Thomas E. Rudy. 1987. IASP taxonomy of chronic pain syndromes: preliminary assess-

ment of reliability. *Pain* 30, 2 (Aug. 1987), 177–189. DOI: http://dx.doi.org/10.1016/0304-3959(87)91073-6

23. Michel Vallieres, Daphne Tan, William E Caplin, and Stephen McAdams. 2009. Perception of intrinsic formal functionality: An empirical investigation of Mozarts materials. *Journal of Interdisciplinary Music Studies* 3, 1-2 (2009), 17–43.

24. Katharina Vogt, D Pirro, and Ingo Kobenz. 2009. Physiosonic-movement sonification as auditory feedback. In *Proceedings of the 15th International Conference on Auditory Display, Copenhagen, Denmark*. 1–7. http://iem.kug.ac.at/fileadmin/ media/iem/projects/2009/physio.pdf

25. Richard Isaac Wallis, Todd Ingalls, Thanassis Rikakis, Loren Olsen, Yinpeng Chen, Weiwei Xu, and Hari Sundaram. 2007. Real-time sonification movement for an immersive stroke rehabilitation environment. In *Pro-Proceedings of the 13th International Conference on Auditory Display (ICAD 2007)*. 497–503. http://www.icad.org/node/2460

26. Steve R Woby, Martin Urmston, and Paul J Watson. 2007. Self-efficacy mediates the relation between pain-related fear and outcome in chronic low back pain patients. *European journal of pain (London, England)* 11, 7 (Oct. 2007), 711–8. DOI: http://dx.doi.org/10.1016/j.ejpain.2006.10.009

27. Daniel M. Wolpert and Zoubin Ghahramani. 2000. Computational principles of movement neuroscience. *Nature neuroscience* 3 Suppl (Nov. 2000), 1212–7. DOI: http://dx.doi.org/10.1038/81497

KeDiary: Using Mobile Phones to Assist Patients in Recovering from Drug Addiction

Chuang-Wen You†, Ya-Fang Lin◇, Cheng-Yuan Li†‡, Yu-Lun Tsai*, Ming-Chyi Huang⊔, Chao-Hui Lee⊔, Hao-Chuan Wang◇, Hao-Hua Chu‡
†Intel-NTU CCC Center, ‡Dept. of Computer Science and Information Engineering, and *Dept. of Electrical Engineering, National Taiwan University, Taipei, Taiwan
◇Institute of Information Systems and Applications, National Tsing Hua University, Hsinchu, Taiwan
⊔Taipei City Psychiatric Center, Taipei City Hospital Songde Branch, Taipei, Taiwan
cwyou@ntu.edu.tw, s103065533@m103.nthu.edu.tw, d99922035@csie.ntu.edu.tw, b00901158@ntu.edu.tw, {mch, a1046}@tpech.gov.tw, haochuan@cs.nthu.edu.tw, hchu@csie.ntu.edu.tw

ABSTRACT
Ketamine is an addictive drug that has been shown to inflict considerable physical and mental damage on users. Due in part to its low cost, ketamine has become one of the most popular club drugs among young adults and teenagers in Southeast Asia. This paper proposes a phone-based support system (KeDiary) with Bluetooth-enabled device for the screening of saliva, as a means of assisting ketamine-dependent patients to self-monitor their ketamine use following acute withdrawal treatment. We also conducted a practical experiment to evaluate the feasibility of the proposed system, wherein three ketamine-dependent patients self-administered tests at least once per day over a period of three weeks. Follow-up interviews with the same users helped in the further refinement of the proposed self-monitoring system.

ACM Classification Keywords
D.4.m. Information Systems Applications: Miscellaneous.

Author Keywords
Drug addiction; addiction recovery; mobile system; chi4good.

INTRODUCTION
The recreational use of ketamine has gained considerable popularity in Southeast Asia and many other parts of the world [13], due to its low cost and the lack of international control on the ingredients used in ketamine production. One previous study conducted in Taiwan reported that 47% of the urine samples in a dance club tested positive for ketamine [21]. Ketamine abuse can lead to severe physical and mental harm, including kidney dysfunction, depression, and impaired memory [27, 29]. Among those treated, 40~60% of patients experience relapses after leaving rehabilitation centers [6].

Current treatment techniques for drug withdrawal can be broken down into two stages: (1) acute withdrawal and (2) follow-up maintenance. Patients with serious drug dependency are commonly required to enter a rehab center to stop using drugs. During the follow-up maintenance program, patients intermittently revisit the rehab center to receive follow-up outpatient abstinence treatment to maintain abstinence in daily life.

After leaving rehab centers, psychiatrists will ask patients to maintain abstinence during outpatient abstinence treatment. Patients can self-manage their drug use behavior by participating in self-help support groups [15, 18], such as Narcotics Anonymous (NA) [7], or through contact with experts and individuals with similar experience, such as the online forums on Reddit [9]. However, many patients might still suffer from mild withdrawal symptoms in the early phase of this treatment stage and probably experience periods of relapse. Therefore, patients are encouraged keep a drug diary [30]; however, they often fail to record their drug use. Without complete and accurate data on the behavior of patients, psychiatrists are limited in the assistance they can provide. Previous researchers have explored alternative methods for the detection of a drug use through the analysis of electrocardiogram signals in a controlled environment [28] or while undergoing physical activities, such as walking [20]. However, none of these screening techniques have taken advantage of modern smartphone technology to facilitate the implementation of support systems to assist patients in recovering from ketamine addiction. We believe that a phone-based system could provide recovery support whenever and wherever needed, while facilitating the provision of after-care treatment, reducing costs, and improving the effectiveness of existing drug withdrawal treatment.

From a chronic care perspective, the treatment regimens used for addictive disorders and those of diabetes are quite similar [25], due in a large part to the way that the stages of treatment are arranged, i.e., initial acute inpatient treatment followed by a maintenance program. Several phone-based support systems have been developed to assist patients in controlling diabetes [22], dealing with alcohol dependence [33], and quitting smoking [17]. These studies have been highly instructional with regard to the aspect of "cheating", in which patients lie about their level of compliance with the treatment requirements. However, prolonged participation in continuing care [23, 24, 26] has seldom been addressed in the field of ketamine addiction. In this study, we developed a phone-based support system to facilitate the monitoring of ketamine use with a

CHI'16, May 07 - 12, 2016, San Jose, CA, USA

ACM 978-1-4503-3362-7/16/05$15.00
DOI: http://dx.doi.org/10.1145/2858036.2858185

customized saliva-screening device wirelessly connected to the patient's smartphone. The primary target in this study was treatment-seeking patients with a severe addiction to ketamine.

The contributions of this paper include a comprehensive outline of the design, implementation, and qualitative evaluation of KeDiary self support system for ketamine addiction. Follow-up interviews with the same users provide valuable data with which to further refine the proposed self-monitoring system.

MAINTAIN ABSTINENCE IN DAILY LIFE

As with alcohol-dependent patients [33], those addicted to ketamine are expected to revisit the hospital regularly for follow-up maintenance programs following the completion of acute withdrawal treatment. Tracking ketamine use when patients revisit the rehab center requires that patients provide either blood or urine samples. When taking urine tests at the rehab center, patients are escorted into a lavatory and observed by a police officer to ensure the integrity of the collected urine samples. In contrast, urine tests conducted at home are prone to falsification. Thus, we initially evaluated the screening procedures by conducting half-hour surveys with seven patients undergoing withdrawal treatment in a rehab center. The sample included five males and two females with an average age of 33.9 years (30~37 years with a standard deviation of 2.5 years). During half-hour semi-structured interviews, several of the patients described how easy it was to cheat when taking urine tests at home. One patient even reported collecting urine samples from his five-year-old son. Participants also described the process of taking urine tests everyday as burdensome and tedious.

These observations suggest the need for a home-based self-administered ketamine screening test that is difficult to falsify but easy to use.

KEDIARY DESIGN & IMPLEMENTATION

The KeDiary system comprises a portable Bluetooth-enabled saliva-screening device, a smartphone app, and a backend server. These components are described in the following.

Saliva-Screening Device

Fig. 1(a) presents the proposed saliva-screening device and a replaceable single-use test cassette. Compared to urine and blood screening, saliva testing is fast and can be conducted almost anywhere [16]. Patients simply spit saliva into a straw on the saliva-screening device (Fig. 1(a)), which is a 3D printed plastic box (5.1 cm × 10.3 cm × 5.7 cm). The saliva-screening device contains a customized main board equipped with a TI CC2541 microcontroller [12] and an off-the-shelf serial camera module [4]. The microcontroller triggers the camera module to capture images of the reaction zone of the test strip. When the CC2541 microcontroller receives an image from the camera, a Bluetooth Low Energy (BLE) radio is used to transmit images to the patient's smartphone. Three white LEDs located between the camera and reaction zone are used for illumination [10]. Before taking a test, patients simply clip a single-use test cassette into the opening of a device. The device is powered by a lithium-ion battery, which is recharged approximately once a month using a TI BQ24040 charger [11]

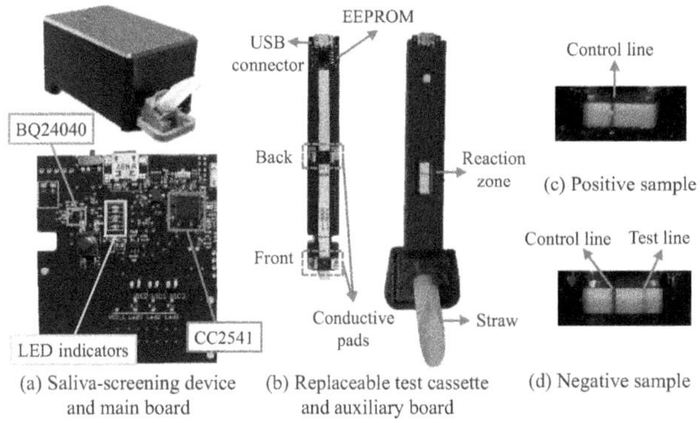

Figure 1: (a) Saliva-screening device and main board. (b) Replaceable test cassette and auxiliary board showing (c) positive and (d) negative line patterns, which appear in the reaction zone of the cassette.

via USB interface. Three single-color LEDs are mounted on the main board to inform patients of the device status: green (device is running), red (ready for screening), red blinking (screening on-going), and yellow (charging).

Fig. 1(b) presents a single-use test cassette, which was fabricated using a 3D printer. The test cassette includes a saliva test strip (with a cutoff sensitivity of 50 ng/ml) [8] and an auxiliary circuit board containing an Atmel AT24C01D EEPROM [1], a micro USB connector, and two pairs of conductive pads. The conductive pads on the ends of the strip detect the absorption of saliva. After the saliva enters the straw, it flows into the front end cotton wick of the strip through a small drain, which causes a reduction in resistance between the front pair of conductive pads, thereby indicating that the user has indeed provided a sample. The eventual absorption of saliva by the back-end cotton wick causes a drop in resistance between the pair of rear pads, indicating that the saliva has propagated through the reaction zone. After the saliva reacts with the chemicals used to coat the strip for a given period of time, the camera is triggered to take several images of the reaction zone. Photos and saliva absorption readings are then sent back to the smartphone for processing. To ensure the integrity of testing, each cassette is assigned a unique ID stored in the EEPROM.

KeDiary Phone Application

The KeDiary system provides support functions to enable the self-monitoring of ketamine use via saliva tests and then provide a summary of the patient's progress in maintaining abstinence. By leveraging experience gained using a mobile support system for alcoholics [33], KeDiary exploits the same set of behavioral theories that help patients to develop skills required to maintain abstinence. The KeDiary system is based on self-efficacy theory [14], cognitive behavioral therapy [32], and self-determination theory [19]. By performing self-monitoring, patients show their determination to exert control over their behavior and increase their self-efficacy [14, 19]. A review of the drug-use log enables users to recognize which situations trigger their drug cravings to develop coping strategies [32]. The app provides two functional modules: (1) drug use detection and (2) progress visualization.

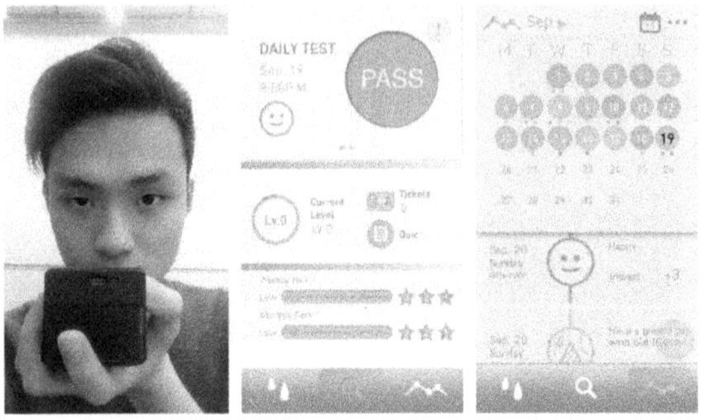

(a) Picture taken by the phone camera (b) Screening result page (c) Monthly visualization page

Figure 2: Exemplar picture (a) taken by the phone application while the user performs a saliva test and screenshots of the (b) screening result page and (c) monthly visualization page.

Drug use detection: This module is used to screen for ketamine excreted into saliva, which can typically be detected in a saliva sample even one to two days after ingestion [8]. The app reminds patients to perform at least one mandatory saliva test each day to ensure that the ketamine is detected before being metabolized in the liver.

The KeDiary system includes several mechanisms to prevent cheating. Patients begin the screening test by inserting a new cassette into the saliva-screening device. When the patient presses the start button on the app, the phone automatically connects to the screening device via Bluetooth and validates the authenticity of the cassette. In cases of validation failure, such as when a used cassette is inserted, the patient is requested to insert a new/unused cassette. To reinforce the validity of testing, patients must present their faces as well as the screening device to the camera on the phone (Fig. 2(a)), so that the video recorded by the phone captures the whole saliva-spitting action. This makes it possible to verify the identity of the user through manually reviewing videos uploaded to the server from the phone. After the saliva sample is provided, the app waits ten minutes for the test strip to absorb the saliva, during which time the patient can browse the coping skills provided by an appointed psychiatrist.

Photos of the test strip are then sent to the app for conversion into gray-scaled images. Dark lines in the reaction zone are screened by the app to determine whether the test outcome is negative (two lines as shown in Fig. 1(d)), positive (one control line as shown in Fig. 1(c)), or invalid (no control line). Fig. 2(b) shows the phone app notifying patients of the results, which are also uploaded to a backend server. The accuracy of the saliva screening device was tested in an experiment involving the collection of 246 saliva samples (50 positives and 196 negatives) from patients in a rehab center. Screening accuracy was 93%, which is considered sufficient for the daily screening of ketamine.

Progress visualization: Fig. 2(b) presents a visualization of patient progress with regard to ketamine abstinence. Following the completion of each saliva test, the phone app summarizes the time and outcome of the test in a dashboard located at the top of the screening result page. Patient abstinence can also be presented in calendar view, as shown in Fig. 2(c).

Backend Server

The server also generates a summary of the patient's abstinence performance and sends it to psychiatrists to enable continual monitoring. The server checks for milestone achievements and when detected, sends encouraging messages to the patient's phone.

PRELIMINARY FEASIBILITY STUDY

To collect patient feedback concerning KeDiary use, we conducted a three-week study involving three ketamine-dependent patients who had been interviewed in the earlier pilot study. This study was approved by the Institutional Review Board of Taipei City Hospital (IRB No.: TCHIRB-1040411).

Participants

The three participants were screened by psychiatrists using explicit inclusion and exclusion criteria. All participants had to meet the following: (1) met DSM-IV criteria of substance use disorder [3], (2) completed abstinence, (3) used ketamine as the main drug of abuse, and (4) were able to read and provide informed consent. The sample included one male and two females aged between 31 and 37 years, with an average age of 34 years and a standard deviation of 3 years. After explaining the goal of the study, the participants were asked to provide informed consent. Each participant was reimbursed approximately US$10 for each visit to compensate for travel costs to and from the hospital for follow-up assessments. All participants collected ground-truth ketamine use data using the timeline follow-back (TLFB) method [5].

Each patient was provided a portable saliva-screening device, which was paired to his/her smartphone. We also installed the KeDiary phone app on their smartphones and asked participants to use them as their primary phones during the study.

Procedure

The experiment was conducted in three stages: (1) pre-study medical assessment, (2) three-week real-world study with KeDiary, and (3) post-study interviews. In the pre-study medical assessment, we collected data related to baseline ketamine consumption and compliance, which were measured using the TLFB method based on follow-up medical reviews, obtained from participants' self-reports. Patients attended a 30-minute training session to learn how to use the app and screening device.

Patients were expected to attend weekly medical reviews at the rehab center to enable the collection of ground-truth data and answer any questions related to the use of KeDiary. In cases where patients failed to attend the scheduled medical reviews, follow-up phone calls were used to arrange further appointments. A maximum of three contact attempts were made to ensure the retention of each patient. All three participants attended the post-study interviews. Audio recorders were set up to record one-hour semi-structured interviews addressing the daily use of the application, their opinions of the support functions, and notable behavioral changes following their experience with KeDiary.

Self-monitoring Adherence

To evaluate the monitoring adherence, we defined the completion rate as the percentage of days during the study period in which participants completed at least one saliva screening test. The average completion rate was 81%, with only minor fluctuations over the three-week period. Patient P1 exhibited the poorest adherence and missed sampling sessions one day during the study. That patient attributed this lapse to a mix up between two smartphones, which resulted in the patient's missing several reminders. Patients P2 and P3 did not miss any screening tests and achieved 100% completion rates.

Findings

The data used in qualitative analysis were retrieved from audio recordings obtained during interviews after being transcribed manually. Each transcript underwent iterative coding independently by three experienced researchers. We focused on codes with a reasonable degree of agreement among different coders to identify major themes based on thematic analysis [31]. The three salient themes identified in this open coding process are described as follows.

Exploring the screening device's sensing capability & limit

Patients sought to identify the factors that could affect the testing of saliva samples. For example, P3 was afraid that what she ate or drank prior to the test could affect the results.

"Yesterday, I performed two tests: one before and one after dinner. [...] I wanted to make sure the food intake wouldn't change my saliva and make me fail the test. After this experiment, I figured it's fine to eat before testing." — (P3)

P1 explored the sensing limit of the device by reducing her ketamine dose in order to pass the test.

"I was surprised ... that the saliva-screening device actually detected my ketamine use. I thought the system wouldn't be able to detect it since I reduced the dose, and smoked (not snorted) only a little. But it did detect it!" — (P1)

Strong reaction to positive screening results and demand a channel to explain

All three patients had been in and out of rehab centers. Each withdrawal session involved considerable time and effort; therefore, they reacted strongly when the screening results were positive, claiming that the device was reporting "false positives". Positive results were interpreted as a personal insults and the patients sought to rectify them immediately.

"I could not accept positive results when I was not using ketamine. [...] Or, I'll take a photo of the strip and send you the photo to show you that there were obviously two lines on the strip (i.e., negative line pattern)." — (P3)

Occasionally, the patients sought to defend themselves by reporting stories of circumstances beyond their control. The patients commented that the phone app ought to include a channel by which to provide a legitimate explanation in order to reverse positive screening test results.

"I think the saliva-screening device was confused by the anesthetic applied by my dentist, when I had a tooth extracted earlier in the afternoon. The dentist applied a lot of anesthetic. I swear that I did not use ketamine." — (P2)

This channel could help the patients to save face in this embarrassing situation. Without a channel to explain their side, patients may consider quitting the program altogether.

Protection of patient privacy

In many Asian countries, ketamine (the drug) use is socially unacceptable and illegal; therefore, patients expressed a strong need to protect their privacy. This is particularly true when patients have yet to tell their family members or friends of their addiction to ketamine. They want to make sure that the use of KeDiary on their phone will not reveal their history of drug use.

"Is the uploaded data secure? I cannot allow any of my friends or family members to open the app and see my phone records. [...] I don't want them to know I am participating in this study." — (P1)

Patients who already told friends and/or family members about their ketamine addiction were willing to share negative screening results; however, they remained adamant about concealing positive results, which they claim should be shared only with trusted professionals, e.g., psychiatrists and researchers.

"I am less concerned that my friends might use my phone and stumble on the app. The one exception is my boyfriend's family members. All they know is that I have been diagnosed with a depressive disorder. [...] I cannot allow anyone (not even my mom) to know about my positive results. I might be willing to tell you (i.e., a researcher) or my psychiatrist, as long as you don't tell my mom." — (P3)

The name of the app and the icon used to open it should not reveal any connection to drug addiction. The app should also include a password to restrict unauthorized access.

CONCLUSION

This study presents a phone-based support system to enable the self-monitoring of ketamine use by recovering patients after returning to everyday life. A three-week study including three ketamine-dependent patients revealed three main findings: (1) Patients explored the sensing capability and limits of the screening device; (2) Patients reacted strongly to positive screening results and demanded a channel by which to present explanations; and (3) patients expressed a strong need to protect their privacy with regard to their addiction and app use. These findings are valuable in guiding the future design of support systems for this user population.

The KeDiary system has a number of limitations in its current form. First, to gain experience in the development of a support system for drug-addicted patients, we targeted a schedule III drug (ketamine) [2] with a moderate to low potential for physical and psychological dependence as our initial target drug. Nonetheless, we believe that this system could easily be extended to the screening of other drugs simply by changing the saliva test strips in the cassette. Second, we recruited only three patients for our evaluation. Future studies should test KeDiary using a larger sample size.

REFERENCES

1. Atmel AT24C01D. http://www.atmel.com/devices/AT24C01D.aspx.
2. Commonly Abused Drugs Charts | National Institute on Drug Abuse (NIDA). http://www.drugabuse.gov/drugs-abuse/commonly-abused-drugs-charts.
3. DSM-IV Criteria Substance Related Disorders. https://datashare.nida.nih.gov/assessment/d/dsm-iv-criteria-substance-related-disorders.
4. Grove - Serial Camera Kit. http://www.seeedstudio.com/wiki/Grove_-_Serial_Camera_Kit.
5. Instrument: Timeline Followback Method Assessment. http://cde.drugabuse.gov/instrument/d89c8e23-16e5-625a-e040-bb89ad43465d.
6. "Mindfulness" Meditation Can Help Reduce Addiction Relapse Rates. http://www.drugfree.org/join-together/mindfulness-meditation-can-help-reduce-addiction-relapse-rates-study/.
7. Narcotics Anonymous. https://www.na.org.
8. Rapid Response Signal Drug Saliva Test Cassette. http://www.btnx.com/Product.aspx?id=1997.
9. Reddit: The Front Page of the Internet. https://www.reddit.com.
10. SML-E1 Series : LEDs - Rohm. http://rohmfs.rohm.com/en/products/databook/datasheet/opto/led/chip_mono/sml-e1.pdf.
11. Texas Instruments BQ24040. http://www.ti.com/product/bq24040.
12. Texas Instruments CC2541. http://www.ti.com/product/cc2541.
13. United Nations Office on Drug and Crime (UNODC). World Drug Report 2010. https://www.unodc.org/documents/wdr/WDR_2010/World_Drug_Report_2010_lo-res.pdf.
14. Albert Bandura. 1994. Self-efficacy. In V. S. Ramachaudran (Ed.), *Encyclopedia of Human Behavior* 4 (1994). Academic Press, New York, NY, USA, 71–81.
15. Stephanie H. Cook, José A. Bauermeister, Deborah Gordon-Messer, and Marc A. Zimmerman. 2013. Online Network Influences on Emerging Adults' Alcohol and Drug Use. *Journal of Youth and Adolescence* 42, 11 (2013), 1674–1686. DOI: http://dx.doi.org/10.1007/s10964-012-9869-1 .
16. Alim Fatah and Jeffrey P. Cohn. Developments in Drug Testing: Saliva as an Alternate to Urine and Blood. https://www.ncjrs.gov/App/publications/abstract.aspx?ID=232891.
17. Caroline Free, Rosemary Knight, Steven Robertson, Robyn Whittaker, Phil Edwards, Weiwei Zhou, Anthony Rodgers, John Cairns, Michael G Kenward, and Ian Roberts. 2011. Smoking Cessation Support Delivered via Mobile Phone Text Messaging (txt2stop): A Single-blind, Randomised Trial. *The Lancet* 378, 9785 (2011), 49–55. DOI: http://dx.doi.org/10.1016/S0140-6736(11)60701-0 .
18. Marc Galanter, Helen Dermatis, Stephen Post, and Courtney Santucci. 2013. Abstinence from Drugs of Abuse in Community-based Members of Narcotics Anonymous. *Journal of Studies on Alcohol and Drugs* 74, 2 (2013), 349–352. DOI: http://dx.doi.org/10.15288/jsad.2013.74.349 .
19. David H. Gustafson, Bret R. Shaw, Andrew Isham, Timothy Baker, Michael G. Boyle, and Michael Levy. 2011. Explicating an Evidence-Based, Theoretically Informed, Mobile Technology-Based System to Improve Outcomes for People in Recovery for Alcohol Dependence. *Substance Use & Misuse* 46, 1 (2011), 96–111. DOI: http://dx.doi.org/10.3109/10826084.2011.521413 .
20. Syed Monowar Hossain, Amin Ahsan Ali, Md. Mahbubur Rahman, Emre Ertin, David Epstein, Ashley Kennedy, Kenzie Preston, Annie Umbricht, Yixin Chen, and Santosh Kumar. 2014. Identifying Drug (Cocaine) Intake Events from Acute Physiological Response in the Presence of Free-living Physical Activity. In *Proceedings of the 13th International Symposium on Information Processing in Sensor Networks (IPSN '14)*. IEEE Press, Piscataway, NJ, USA, 71–82. DOI: http://dl.acm.org/citation.cfm?id=2602339.2602348 .
21. Ahai Chang Lua, Huei Ru Lin, Yong Te Tseng, An Ren Hu, and Pei Chi Yeh. 2003. Profiles of Urine Samples from Participants at Rave Party in Taiwan: Prevalence of Ketamine and MDMA Abuse. *Forensic Science International* 136, 1-3 (2003), 47–51. DOI: http://dx.doi.org/10.1016/S0379-0738(03)00261-5 .
22. Lena Mamykina, Andrew D. Miller, Elizabeth D. Mynatt, and Daniel Greenblatt. 2010. Constructing Identities Through Storytelling in Diabetes Management. In *Proceedings of the SIGCHI Conference on Human Factors in Computing Systems (CHI '10)*. ACM, New York, NY, USA, 1203–1212. DOI: http://dx.doi.org/10.1145/1753326.1753507 .
23. James R. McKay. 2005. Is There a Case for Extended Interventions for Alcohol and Drug Use Disorders? *Addiction* 100, 11 (2005), 1594–1610. DOI: http://dx.doi.org/10.1111/j.1360-0443.2005.01208.x .
24. James R. McKay. 2009. Continuing Care Research: What We've Learned and Where We're Going. *Journal of Substance Abuse Treatment* 36, 2 (2009), 131–145. DOI: http://dx.doi.org/10.1016/j.jsat.2008.10.004 .
25. A. Thomas McLellan. 2002. Have We Evaluated Addiction Treatment Correctly? Implications from a Chronic Care Perspective. *Addiction* 97, 3 (2002), 249–252. DOI: http://dx.doi.org/10.1046/j.1360-0443.2002.00127.x .

26. A. Thomas McLellan, James R. McKay, Robert Forman, John Cacciola, and Jack Kemp. 2005. Reconsidering the Evaluation of Addiction Treatment: From Retrospective Follow-up to Concurrent Recovery Monitoring. *Addiction* 100, 4 (2005), 447–458. DOI:http://dx.doi.org/10.1111/j.1360-0443.2005.01012.x .

27. Celia J. Morgan and H. Valerie Curran. 2012. Ketamine Use: A Review. *Addiction* 107, 1 (2012), 27–38. DOI: http://dx.doi.org/10.1111/j.1360-0443.2011.03576.x .

28. Annamalai Natarajan, Abhinav Parate, Edward Gaiser, Gustavo Angarita, Robert Malison, Benjamin Marlin, and Deepak Ganesan. 2013. Detecting Cocaine Use with Wearable Electrocardiogram Sensors. In *Proceedings of the 2013 ACM International Joint Conference on Pervasive and Ubiquitous Computing (UbiComp '13)*. ACM, New York, NY, USA, 123–132. DOI: http://dx.doi.org/10.1145/2493432.2493496 .

29. S.H. Ng, M.L. Tse, H.W. Ng, and F.L. Lau. 2010. Emergency Department Presentation of Ketamine Abusers in Hong Kong: A Review of 233 Cases. *Hong Kong Med. J.* 16, 1 (2010), 6–11.

30. Shulamith L. A. Straussner. 2013. *Clinical Work with Substance-Abusing Clients (3rd Ed.)*. Guilford Publications.

31. Braun Virginia and Clarke Victoria. 2006. Using Thematic Analysis in Psychology. *Qualitative Research in Psychology* 3, 2 (2006), 77–101. DOI: http://dx.doi.org/10.1191/1478088706qp063oa .

32. Nora D. Volkow. 2011. *Principles of Drug Addiction Treatment: A Research-Based Guide (2nd Ed.)*. DIANE Publishing Company.

33. Chuang-Wen You, Kuo-Cheng Wang, Ming-Chyi Huang, Yen-Chang Chen, Cheng-Lin Lin, Po-Shiun Ho, Hao-Chuan Wang, Polly Huang, and Hao-Hua Chu. 2015. SoberDiary: A Phone-based Support System for Assisting Recovery from Alcohol Dependence. In *Proceedings of the 33rd Annual ACM Conference on Human Factors in Computing Systems (CHI '15)*. ACM, New York, NY, USA, 3839–3848. DOI: http://dx.doi.org/10.1145/2702123.2702289 .

The 32 Days Of Christmas: Understanding Temporal Intent in Image Search Queries

Frank R. Bentley, Joseph 'Jofish' Kaye, David A. Shamma, John Alexis Guerra-Gomez
Yahoo
San Francisco, CA USA
[fbentley, jofish, jguerra]@yahoo-inc.com, aymans@acm.org

ABSTRACT
Temporal terms, such as 'winter', 'Christmas', or 'January' are often used in search queries for personal images. But how do people's memories and perceptions of time match with the actual dates when their images were captured? We compared the temporal terms that 74 Flickr users used to search their own photo collections, and compared them to the date captured data in the target image. We also conducted a larger study across several billion images, comparing user-applied tags for holidays and seasons to the dates the images were captured. We demonstrate that various query terms and tags can be in conflict with the actual dates photos were taken for specific types of temporal terms up to 40% of the time. We will conclude by highlighting implications for search systems where users are querying for personal content by date.

ACM Classification Keywords
H.5.m. Information Interfaces and Presentation (e.g. HCI): Miscellaneous

Author Keywords
Photos; Search; Date; Temporal; Queries, Memory

INTRODUCTION
Along with the growth of the smartphone, personal photo collections have grown in size as it has become easier to capture large numbers of photos. These photos are now increasingly being stored in collections on computers or in the cloud, with 1.8 billion photos being uploaded per day [6]. But how can people find the one photo they are looking for out of a collection of many thousands of personal photographs?

It seems obvious, but the difficulty in photo search is inherently one of description. That is to say, photos are images, but we are using words to find them. If you have a document, the words which you use to search are usually in the document that you are trying to find. But there is another layer of disconnect in image search. Recent advances in machine vision begin to describe the objects in the photograph: 'cat', 'tree'. However some of the most salient facts that people remember about photographs include the context around them. Specifically the time, date, location, and sharing history of a photo have been shown to be salient aspects that people remember [2, 7, 8, 10].

But how accurately do people remember these details? When trying to query photos from their collection, how accurately would people remember aspects of the date (year, month, season, etc.) or location of the event? This is compounded by the problem that everyday perceptions of holidays and seasons are much broader than strict definitions of those events. For example, a company Christmas party may happen any time between late November and early January. Likewise, if it is cold and snowing on the 3rd of December, it feels like winter, even though "real" winter is still almost a month away, beginning on the 21st of December.

In this note, we will explore user generated queries on 1,492 personal images from 74 diverse participants on a large photo sharing site (Flickr) to better understand how people think about dates in their own photo collections, as well as the details that people remember or misremember about their past events when searching for photographs in their collections. We will also explore a large-scale dataset of tags from Flickr images and relate temporally-based tags to the dates when these photos were captured. Tying both datasets together, we will conclude with implications from this work on the creation of tools for photo organization and search.

RELATED WORK
The CHI community has been studying photo organization for some time, including ways to query personal photo collections based on metadata in the photos. In the mid-2000s, as camera phones were beginning to enter the mainstream, many researchers explored how we could automatically tag photos with relevant mobile-sensed contextual information, such as temporal, spatial, and social metadata [4]. In particular, time and location could be used to infer data such as daylight or weather conditions. Other work [7] showed that participants were fairly bad at remembering the exact date of a photo. However, specifics as to which aspects of the date participants got wrong, as well as how far off they were in their errors was not explored in this work, making it difficult to design the details of temporal search systems from the data presented. Others

CHI'16, May 07–12, 2016, San Jose, CA, USA.
© 2016 ACM ISBN 978-1-4503-3362-7/16/05...$15.00.
DOI http://dx.doi.org/10.1145/2858036.2858255.

examined how people remember a photo using a rigid interface to direct participants down traceable paths (e.g. Year→Season or Year→Month) to find photos in their collections [2]. While time, location, and people in the photo were the most salient aspects of a photo, dates themselves were often misremembered and often off by one major unit such as a month or a season in this small-scale lab study. In this work, we wanted to scale up this task, with 74 participants and years worth of photos.

Searching for photos is important, as many researchers have shown people rarely manually tagging their photos so that they could be found again. In their Requirements for Photoware work, Frohlich et al. [5] explored audio annotations and other mechanisms for adding additional narrative information to photos. Ames et al. explored Requirements for Mobile Photoware [1] where annotating images is a large part of the focus. Overall, this work highlights the need for tools to better help people find photos in their growing collections. As mobile camera phones continue to be a part of our daily lives, our collections will continue to grow, and recalling older images becomes more difficult. We set out to explore what people remember about the temporal aspects of their images, some many years old, in our study.

METHODS

We studied this question through a mixed-methods approach incorporating both user-generated queries for specific photos by 74 diverse participants, and a second study of the metadata of large numbers of photographs on Flickr. Together, these studies explored people's temporal views of particular photos and events, and led us to specific ways to modify search algorithms to move beyond rigid definitions of temporal terms to meet the likely intent of the searcher.

Interactive Survey

In early 2015, we conducted an online study with 74 active Flickr users (with at least 500 photos) from the United States. 53% of participants were female; 60% were aged 26–35 and 36% were aged 36–45.

The study gathered queries that participants entered to find their own images. We first required participants to log into their personal Flickr accounts and then selected 20 photos from their collection using the Flickr API. To achieve diversity in the images, and automatically select images that a person might actually want to search for, five of the photos were from the set of 100 most recently taken photos, five had people in them (as identified by the Flickr recognition engine), five were taken outdoors, and five came from a set of high Flickr "interesting" scores (often with many favorites and comments). If participants did not have five images in a category, the remaining images were chosen randomly from the remainder of their collection. From the initial set of 20, participants were able to choose images that they did not want to share with the research team, and these images were replaced with additional images from their collection before proceeding.

For each image, participants were asked to provide a query that they would use to find this image in their Flickr collection. They were given a free text field, similar to the existing Flickr

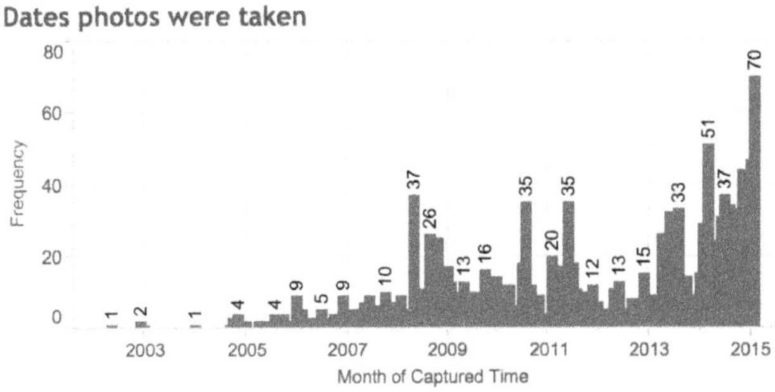

Figure 1. The dates that the photos in our survey were taken. Note that the median date is from 2011, and there are many older images, making the task of searching by date more difficult, yet realistic as photo collections grow.

search bar, and nothing in the survey through this point mentioned any particular interest in times, location, or other ways to find photos. After providing a query for all 20 images, additional questions were asked on another page of the survey to probe on specific aspects of the images. The survey concluded with basic demographic information. On average, the survey took 15 minutes to complete, and participants were paid $4.

Data Footprints

To explore the patterns we saw in our $n = 74$ sample at larger scale, we queried the full Flickr database to extract the image-taken date field from each photo that the owner had tagged with a temporal term. We began looking for images tagged with 'christmas', and then five terms for seasons (spring, summer, fall, autumn and winter). We repeated this for a total of 56 temporally- or holiday-related search terms, including halloween, christmas, passover, eid, bastille, guy fawkes, pride, ski week, and so on. Each pattern was then visualized in Tableau in several different ways—by day of the year, by day of the week, and so on—to help identify different patterns. We treat as ground truth the date the photograph was taken as recorded in the image's EXIF metadata. This makes the assumption, of course, that this date is accurate. As shown in [9], 93% of geotagged images on Flickr had accurate timestamps within 48 hours. This tends to be less of a problem for mobile photos, as phones generally set their time from the network.

FINDINGS

In this section we will explore findings from both studies, which we will tie together when forming implications for design. Through analyzing data from search queries as well as from tags, we are able to develop a broader understanding of people's perceptions of temporal terms for personal images.

Interactive Survey

From the online survey, we gathered users' intended search queries for 1,492 images. For each image, we also asked if the participant had taken the photo themselves, and 1135 (76%) had been captured by the person taking the survey. The majority of photos were taken between 2004 and 2015 according to the EXIF metadata, with the median age photo taken in 2011. A histogram of dates captured can be seen in Figure 1. Most participants therefore had a large range of

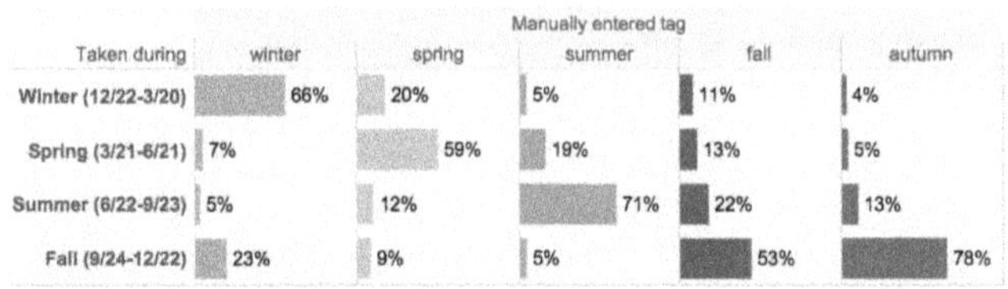

Figure 2. Photos tagged with particular season names do not necessarily occur in the canonical season. Note, especially, that 22% of Winter images actually were taken in the Fall, and 21% of images tagged Spring were taken in the Winter.

images from several years represented in the images selected for the survey.

Looking at the queries that participants provided, only 162 of the 1492 queries (10.8%), succeeded in finding the target image via the Flickr search API. We were particularly interested in examining queries with temporal terms in them, to see how participants remembered and expressed the dates of the various events. Twelve percent of all queries contained a temporal term: e.g. a year (69% of these queries), season (36%), holiday (18%), or month (11%). Note that some queries had combinations of these, such as 'December 2011'.

However, frequently these temporal terms did not match the EXIF date on the photo, and thus resulted in the search failing to find the target image. In looking at all queries with year-based terms, 27% of the time the year did not match the captured date on the target image. Month-based queries fared worse, with 33% of the months mentioned in the queries not matching the image data. Finally, season-based queries had the largest rate of error, with 40% of queries with season-based terms not matching the calendar definitions of the seasons.

Examining season-based queries illustrates how search systems can better adapt to people's memories of time. For example, all queries with the term 'winter' had EXIF dates between December 1 and March 31. However, using the calendar definition of winter (December 21st–March 20) as most systems do today, 20% of these images did not match the queries.

Data Footprints

Working with large-scale data confirmed our impressions from the small-scale study. For example, Figure 2 shows an analysis of when photos tagged with different seasons were actually taken. We are comparing manually tagged images (including the synonyms 'autumn' and 'fall' for completeness) with the four seasons as defined by the solstices and equinoxes for the Northern Hemisphere. Antipodean seasons may legitimately explain the 5% of images tagged 'winter' which were taken during the summer, or, similarly, the 5% of images tagged 'summer' taken during the winter. But we believe that the off-by-one cases, like fall photographs labeled winter, suggest the photo represents the *experience* of winter, regardless of the arbitrary and objective reality of the calendar.

One issue in using large datasets as guidance to inform translation of temporal terms to specific dates is the long tail of responses. For example, Figure 3, represents every photograph tagged with the word 'thanksgiving' on Flickr. The six days between November 22 and 27th inclusive, the darkest blue area,

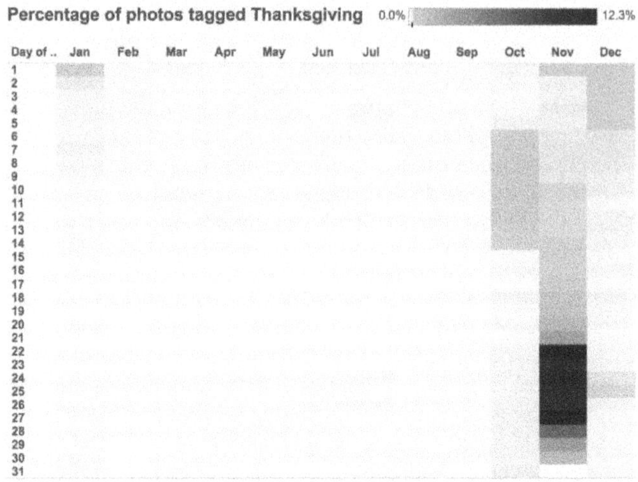

Figure 3. The relative frequencies by day of the year of photographs on Flickr tagged 'thanksgiving'. Note the dark blue area showing American Thanksgiving, and the much lighter gray area in early October representing Canadian Thanksgiving.

covers 65% of the photos. Expanding that range to November 15–30 covers 83%. Expanding to all of November covers 85%, and including October (and thus Canadian Thanksgiving, in dark grey in early October) brings the total to 90%. But that means that 10% of all photos tagged thanksgiving are outside of this range. Every grey square in Figure 3 represents a total of a minimum of 40 photographs taken on that day between 2003 and 2014 inclusive, uploaded to Flickr and tagged 'thanksgiving' with the only white spaces being days that don't exist, like February 30th or April 31st. Repeated manual verification of public photos tagged thanksgiving on arbitrarily chosen dates confirms is not an error: it merely reflects the very long tail of such datasets. Such photographs tagged thanksgiving may include pumpkins or turkeys, autumnal leaves or cornucopias, all images culturally associated with the holiday. This underlines the need for careful search algorithm design to support such diverse practices.

The tagged data reveals that not all temporal search terms are quite so complicated. Some holidays are celebrated and captu photographically on a single day throughout the year, such as Canada Day, on July 1st, or Boxing Day, on December 26th. Treating searches for those terms as searches for photographs on the day itself, or one day on either side to allow for complications of time zones and inaccuracies, will generally return the majority of desired images. Others have more complicated temporal patterns. The lunar festivals of Easter, Passover, Chinese New Year, Eid Al-Adha, Eid Al-Fitr and so on move in a regular (if complicated) way when expressed on the solar calendar, as shown in Figure 5.

Even a term that one would expect to have minimal temporal change can turn out to have temporal patterns: photographs tagged 'birthday' are primarily taken on Saturdays (38%), then Sundays (24%), and then Fridays (12%). The remaining 26% is evenly distributed among the other days of the week as seen in Figure 5. This suggests, for example, that if a system was

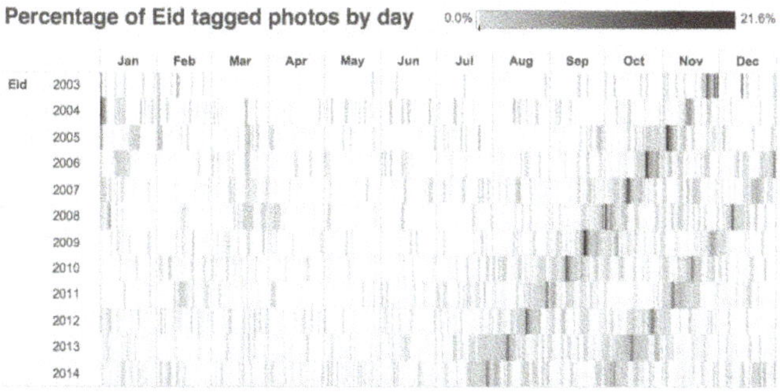

Figure 4. The Hijri (Muslim) Calendar is based off a lunar cycle with no leap correction. Here we see two "Eids" (holidays), Eid Al-Fitr and Eid Al-Adha, shifting dates as it moves across the Gregorian, solar calendar.

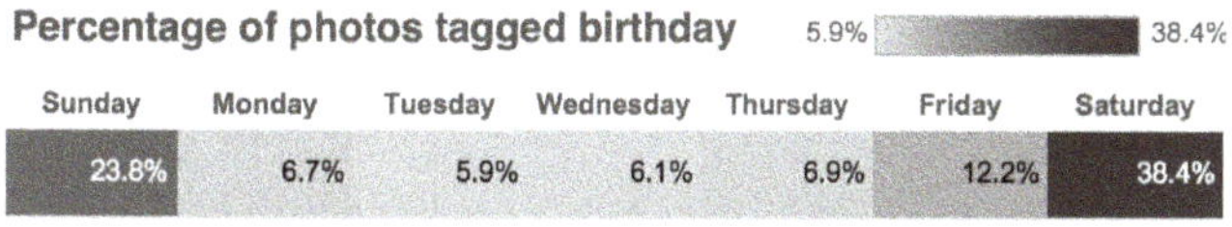

Figure 5. The relative frequencies by day of the week of photographs tagged 'birthday'. Birthday photos tend to be taken during weekends.

searching for a birthday photograph then there would be value in expanding the search term to nearby weekends.

Similarly, Halloween falls on October 31st. But Figure 6 shows photographs of the event are clustered on the Friday, Saturday and Sunday *before* Halloween. While 28% of the images tagged Halloween are taken on October 31st, the five days after Halloween contain only 10% of the images compared to 30% in the five days before Halloween.

Finally, to address the question posed in the title of the paper, when is Christmas? More photos tagged 'christmas' are taken on December 25th than any other day: 19%. Christmas Eve is a close second, at 12%. In other languages, this difference practically goes away: 9.2% of photos tagged 'noel' are taken on Christmas Eve, and 9.6% are on Christmas; 'navidad' photos are 11.3% on Christmas Eve and 12.0% on Christmas. But Christmas photos are taken throughout December. Looking at dates with at least 1% of the photos tagged 'Christmas' we find that every day from December 1st to January 1st hits that definition, with December 2nd barely scraping in; that makes 32 days of Christmas.

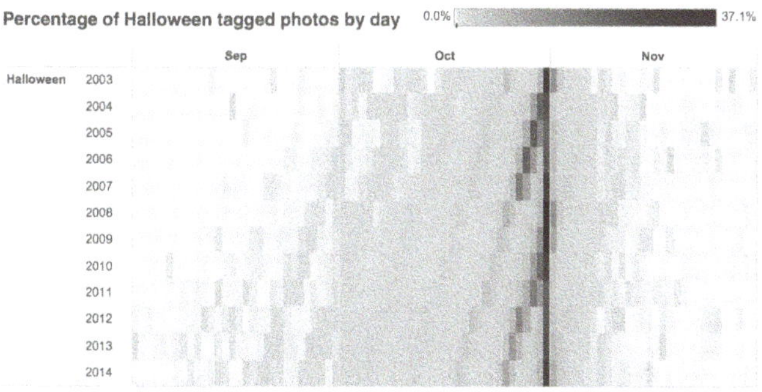

Figure 6. Photos tagged with Halloween are more likely to occur in the week before the holiday, with higher density on the weekend before.

IMPLICATIONS FOR DESIGN

This work highlights the importance of understanding people's perceptions of temporal aspects of their own events when designing organization and search systems. We have seen, through analyzing people's own search queries on their personal photos, and by examining the tags that people apply to their photos, that temporal terms often extend far beyond the calendar definitions in a type of vocabulary mismatch [3].

Beyond photos, other systems where people refer to dates in finding content (web search, calendar search, social network search, etc.) should consider people's understanding of time phrases and not stick to canonical dates. Specifically, search systems should extend ranges for season-based terms to extend more broadly beyond the strict calendar range. Especially in places with strong seasons, a snowy December 3rd definitely feels like winter, and our data shows that people do remember these events in this way. Currently, Flickr defines Christmas to be Dec 24–25, while Google+ defines it as Dec 23–25, and Facebook rewrites the query term 'Christmas' to 'December' and does not seem to rank based on proximity to the 25th.

Search systems should also show results for adjacent temporal ranges. For example, searches for 'July' should have easy ways to see the June or August results. Year-based searches such as '2011' should likely also include results from 2010 and 2009 for cases where people mis-remembered and need to easily expand their query to find the target result.

Finally, returning the title of this paper, holidays should not be seen as only specific dates. Some holidays, especially ones that take place over longer time periods or involve travel such as Christmas, can often include events over an entire month, and our search systems should support this broader context of the term beyond just December 24th and 25th. Likewise, one might approximate Thanksgiving as the entire 4-day weekend or even the entire week around the event, using weighted algorithms to represent differing probabilities.

CONCLUSION

We have analyzed the ways that participants naturally thought of temporal terms when searching for or tagging photos in their own collections. Through showing that memory of years, months, and seasons can be off of standard definitions up to 40% of the time, we have demonstrated the need for alternative solutions to help people find content when using temporal information. We have provided several clear implications for design for those who are building content organization and search applications.

Future work can explore these same types of errors and misremembrances on other types of metadata including locations, people in the photos, or social history of the photo (e.g. who it was sent to). Additional work can explore these same temporal memory issues for other types of content including searching for email, files, or news. As search becomes more important across content types in our lives, and as the amount of content that we have to search increases, understanding human perception and memory of temporal terms will only become more important.

REFERENCES

1. Morgan Ames, Dean Eckles, Mor Naaman, Mirjana Spasojevic, and Nancy Van House. 2010. Requirements for mobile photoware. *Personal and Ubiquitous Computing* 14, 2 (2010), 95–109.
2. Frank Bentley and Crysta Metcalf. 2006. Flexible Views: Annotating and finding context-tagged mobile content. In *Ubicomp 2006 workshop on Pervasive Image Capture and Sharing*. Citeseer.
3. W Bruce Croft, Donald Metzler, and Trevor Strohman. 2010. *Search engines: Information retrieval in practice*. Addison-Wesley Reading.
4. Marc Davis, Simon King, Nathan Good, and Risto Sarvas. 2004. From context to content: leveraging context to infer media metadata. In *Proceedings of the 12th annual ACM international conference on Multimedia*. ACM, 188–195.
5. David Frohlich, Allan Kuchinsky, Celine Pering, Abbe Don, and Steven Ariss. 2002. Requirements for photoware. In *Proceedings of the 2002 ACM conference on Computer supported cooperative work*. ACM, 166–175.
6. Mary Meeker. 2014. 2014 Internet Trends. (2014). http://www.kpcb.com/internet-trends
7. Mor Naaman, Susumu Harada, QianYing Wang, Hector Garcia-Molina, and Andreas Paepcke. 2004. Context data in geo-referenced digital photo collections. In *Proceedings of the 12th annual ACM international conference on Multimedia*. ACM, 196–203.
8. Meredith Ringel, Edward Cutrell, Susan Dumais, and Eric Horvitz. 2003. Milestones in time: The value of landmarks in retrieving information from personal stores. In *Proc. Interact*, Vol. 2003. 184–191.
9. Bart Thomee, Jose G Moreno, and David A Shamma. 2014. Who's Time Is It Anyway?: Investigating the Accuracy of Camera Timestamps. In *Proceedings of the ACM International Conference on Multimedia*. ACM, 909–912.
10. Steve Whittaker, Ofer Bergman, and Paul Clough. 2010. Easy on that trigger dad: a study of long term family photo retrieval. *Personal and Ubiquitous Computing* 14, 1 (2010), 31–43.

Influence of Content Layout and Motivation on Users' Herd Behavior in Social Discovery

Yanzhen Yue
Agency for Science, Technology and Research, Singapore
yanzhengyue@gmail.com

Xiaojuan Ma
Hong Kong University of Science and Technology, Hong Kong
mxj@cse.ust.hk

Zhenhui Jiang
National University of Singapore, Singapore
jiang@comp.nus.edu.sg

ABSTRACT
Social product discovery is an emerging paradigm that enables users to seek information and inspiration from peer-contributed contents. Researchers have observed herd behaviors in social discovery, i.e., basing beliefs and decisions on what similarly situated others have done. In this paper, we explore the effects of content layout and motivation on users' herd behaviors in social discovery. We conduct an eye-tracking study with 120 participants to compare goal- and action-oriented users' behaviors on a grid versus waterfall style social discovery site. The results show that users have a higher tendency to herd on a grid-style website, more so for goal-oriented users.

Author Keywords
Social discovery; herd; layout; grid; waterfall; motivation.

ACM Classification Keywords
H.5.m. Information interfaces and presentation (e.g., HCI): Miscellaneous.

INTRODUCTION
Social discovery is a rising paradigm that empowers exploration of desirable digital contents in user-generated online catalogues [11]. Social product discovery services such as Pinterest (pinterest.com) and Fancy (fancy.com) aim to "connect everyone through the 'things' that people find interesting" [7]. Thriving business in this area has attracted academia and industry to investigate factors that may affect how users behave during social discovery [??].

Social product discovery allows a user to seek information, recommendation, and inspiration from a peer-shared, peer-reviewed product inventory. Prior work has found that the number of "likes" is the strongest predictor of users' re-pin actions in Pinterest [7]. This indicates the existence of herd phenomenon in social discovery, i.e., basing beliefs and decisions on others' choices and actions [15, 18, 2, 3]. The question then arises as to whether and how interface design

CHI'16, May 07-12, 2016, San Jose, CA, USA

DOI: http://dx.doi.org/10.1145/2858036.2858497

Figure 1. Grid (left) and waterfall (right) content layout on social discovery sites.

of social discovery sites can influence users' tendency to herd, i.e., to what extent users are inclined to rely on informational social cues in their judgment process, whether or not they reach a final conclusion.

Although many social product discovery sites employ a tile-based interface to display user-contributed contents, the spatial arrangement of the tiles can vary. Some sites, such as fancy.com, wanelo.com, and shopcade.com, place contents in structured grids, i.e., fixed-size rectangle cells aligned both vertically and horizontally (Figure 1 left). Other sites, such as pinterest.com, mogujie.com, and meilishuo.com, have adopted a trendy waterfall layout, which consists of rectangle blocks that are only aligned in columns (Figure 1 right). Online retail research has shown that grid layout is favored for its ability to facilitate planned, goal oriented users, whereas irregular item placement can engage action-oriented users in longer exploration [19, 9]. However, whether content layout can affect the herding tendency of users with different motives is still under-investigated.

In this paper, we explore the interplay between content layout and user motivation on potential herd behaviors in social discovery. We exploit eye tracking to capture goal- and action-oriented users' herding tendency through their attention allocation on various cues when visiting a grid- versus waterfall-style social discovery site. Different from prior work (e.g., [6, 18]) that merely used questionnaires to detect existence of herd behaviors in decisions, we are able to gain deeper insights into users' mental process from gaze behaviors. We find that goal-oriented users' attention to products with considerably more likings drops significantly when browsing a waterfall-style webpage than a grid-style one, which suggests a reduction in their tendency to herd.

LITERATURE REVIEW AND HYPOTHESES

We first review herd behavior in online contexts, and then present related work on how environmental and personal factors may affect users' behaviors.

Online Users' Herd Behavior

Herd behavior reflects informational social influences on decision making [15]. Prior research has identified two primary triggers of the tendency to herd: "uncertainty about the decision" and "observation of others' actions" [18]. Herding tendency can be particularly prominent in social discovery because: (1) social discovery sites offer a wide range of contents that reflect contributors' diverse tastes and interests, which adds more uncertainty to users' choices; and (2) social discovery sites make information about predecessors' actions more easily accessible to their users, such as the number of "Like" or "Favorite". Researchers have discovered herding behaviors in social discovery of different contents, such as ebooks [2] and software [20], especially if financial concerns are involved in the final decision [3].

In this paper, we aim to explore how environmental and personal factors impact users' reliance on informational social cues in social discovery. Since action-oriented users may not necessary make a decision, we employ three measures as indicators of herding tendency in the viewing process: (1) the proportion of the number of popular items clicked to view details over the total number of items clicked based on system logs, (2) the proportion of time spent on viewing popular items over the total time on-site captured by eye tracking, and (3) the average amount of time spent on viewing a popular item. Based on the review of literature, we proposed a set of hypotheses.

Content Layout and Processing Fluency

Online retailing studies have examined the influence of content layout on users' purchase intent [19, 12, 4]. However, little work has looked into how interface design may affect users' selective attention to assorted information cues, which consequently causes or inhibits herd behaviors.

Inspired by environmental psychology, we conceptualize different content layouts by their physical characteristics of an environment, in particular visual access [13]. For example, tiles in a grid layout are identical in size, making the same type of information across different tiles in a row aligned horizontally. This improves the efficiency of visual scanning. On the contrary, the waterfall design is more visually complex and thus yields higher perceptual load.

Overall, the waterfall layout is more perceptually harder-to-process than the grid layout. The processing fluency of the informational social cue – the number of likes – is more severely impaired in a waterfall design than the more salient product images. Since people tend to weight fluent information more heavily in judgment making [1, 15]; hence, we hypothesize that: *H1. Users have a higher tendency to herd on a grid-style social discovery site than on a waterfall-style site, i.e., (H1a) higher ratio of popular contents clicked, (H1b) higher ratio of time on popular contents, and (H1c) longer popular product viewing time.*

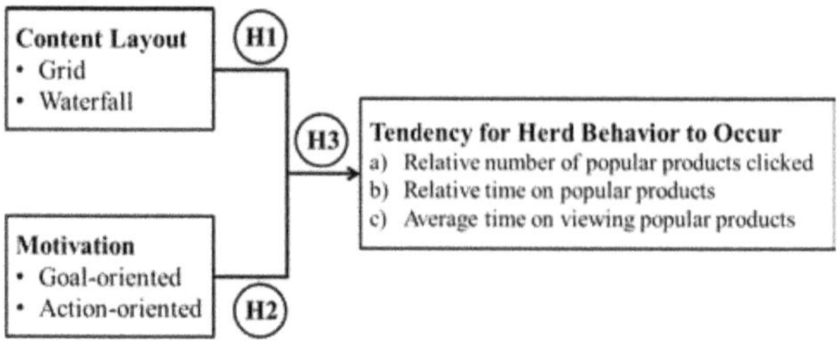

Figure 2. Research model and hypotheses (H1~H3).

Motivation and Cue Selection

Research on persuasion indicates that motivation also affects people's cue selection in information processing [14]. Goal-oriented users visit social discovery sites with plans in mind and thus primarily seek cues that can help compare and eliminate candidates [14], and thus they are more likely to use quantitative informational social cues that are intuitive indicators of product popularity such as the number of "Like". In contrast, action-oriented users do not have a specific target; instead, they explore matches to the desired end state based on more descriptive information [8]. These users tend to rely more on their own subjective responses to affective cues such as attractiveness of product images rather than other people's opinions [14]. Hence, we hypothesize that: *H2. Goal-oriented users have a higher tendency to herd than action-oriented users, i.e., (H2a) higher ratio of popular products clicked, (H2b) higher ratio of time on popular products, and (H2c) longer popular product viewing time.*

Interaction between Content Layout and Motivation

As discussed earlier, action-oriented users are more inclined to explore [19], and a less structured, perceptually disfluent interface design may further encourage them to look into affective, descriptive cues [8]. On the contrary, an orderly arrangement provides goal-oriented users easier visual access to diagnostic social cues which can facilitate quick judgment [19, 14]. Therefore, we hypothesize that: *H3. Interface layout and motivation have an interaction on users' tendency to herd, i.e., waterfall layout induces a more significant decrease in (H3a) the ratio of popular products clicked, (H3b) the ratio of time on popular products, and (H3c) length of time viewing each popular product for goal-oriented than action-oriented users compared to grid layout.*

RESEARCH METHOD

To test the proposed hypotheses, we conducted a controlled laboratory experiment with a 2×2 between-factorial design (Figure 2), i.e., two types of interface layout (grid versus waterfall) × two types of motivations (goal- versus action-oriented). We recruited 30 participants for each condition (a total of 120 people) to ensure sufficient statistical power of 0.8 for medium effect size (f=.25) [5].

		df	F	Sig.	η^2
Layout (L)	% Click on pop. item (1a)	1	3.98	0.04	0.04
	% Time on pop. item (1b)	1	5.45	0.02	0.05
	% Time on social cue	1	20.42	0.00	0.16
	Time on social cue	1	14.06	0.00	0.11
Motive (M)	% Time on pop. item (2b)	1	6.78	0.01	0.06
	Time on pop. item (2c)	1	4.90	0.03	0.04
	Time on social cue	1	4.87	0.03	0.04
	Reliance on social cue	1	8.01	0.01	0.06
L × M	% Click on pop. item (3a)	1	4.27	0.04	0.04
	% Time on pop. item (3b)	1	4.38	0.04	0.04
	Time on pop. item (3c)	1	24.06	0.00	0.18
	Time on social cue	1	11.90	0.00	0.10

Table 1. MANOVA results on the ratio of popular products clicked, ratio of time on popular products, ratio of time on social cues, average time on popular products and social cues, and perceived reliance on social cues.

Experimental Website Design

We developed two experimental websites for the two layout designs respectively (Figure 1). Regardless of the style, each content tile contained the same amount of information, including a product image, a short product description, the number of "Likes", and snippets of two user reviews. In the waterfall layout, we randomly adjusted the height of product images within a threshold adopted from Pinterest. Viewers can scroll up and down in the product catalogs, and click on a product tile to open a separate product page with detailed information. Both experimental websites applied the same design to the product pages.

We presented the same set of 147 products coming from the gift category of Pinterest on both sites. To alleviate the potential gender bias, we included equal samples of gender-specific and gender-neutral products. Among all the products displayed on the interfaces, we picked 10% as popular products with over 100 likings, which cover a wide range of merchandise types, e.g., clothes, shoes, digital products, accessories, books, etc. The number of likes for the rest of products followed a normal distribution (Max. = 64), based on our investigation of the popularity ratings on Pinterest and several rounds of pilot studies. Pilot participants suggested that it felt unnatural when the liking difference between popular and ordinary products was too big and hard-to-distinguish when it was too small.

Participants, Procedure, and Data Collection

We recruited 120 participants with diverse academic backgrounds from a public university. Among these participants, 65.8% were female, 93% were between 19 to 23 years old (M=21.30, SD=2.76). All the participants had over seven years of Internet experience, and 92% had online shopping experiences.

We randomly assigned the participants to one of the four experiment conditions, i.e., goal-oriented versus action-oriented × grid versus waterfall layout. The order of the products and the location of the popular items were randomized for each participant. We gave different instructions to manipulate the shopping orientation, similar to [6]. More specifically, we asked goal-oriented users to purchase a birthday gift for their friend and write down the selected product in the post-study questionnaire. Different from the conventional visual search task of locating a predetermined target among distractors e.g., [8, 16], we only provided a scenario and there was no right or wrong regarding participants' final decision [21]. On the contrary, we told action-oriented users to visit the social commerce website for personal enjoyment.

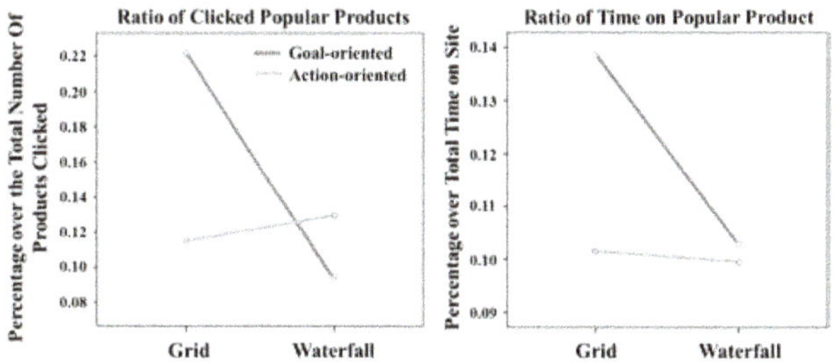

Figure 3. Comparison of the ratio of clicks (left) and time (right) on a popular product between goal- and action-oriented users given grid versus waterfall design.

After reading the instruction, participants are free to browse the given experimental website on a Dell Precision T1700 desktop computer (Win 7 OS, 19-inch screen size). When participants feel that they have sufficiently fulfilled the task, they can stop viewing. After rating perceived herding tendency and perceived reliance on social cues on a 7-point Likert Scale, the participants receive a compensation of $ 6.

A backend script logs every user interaction with the experimental websites. Furthermore, participants' gaze movement was recorded by a Tobii Eyetracker TX60. Hence, we can identify products attended by viewers and specify the particular regions within each tile that have been scanned, and compute the duration of each fixated attention.

RESULTS AND ANALYSIS

In general, there is no significant difference in gender, age and other demographic distributions across the four experimental conditions. We used ratios in our analysis to eliminate individual differences.

Hypotheses Testing on Tendency to Herd

We conducted MANOVA analysis on the three measures of herding tendency with Bonferroni correction, i.e., the ratio of popular products clicked, the ratio of time on popular products, and average time on popular product (Table 1).

Waterfall Layout Suppresses Herding Tendency

There is no significant difference between grid and waterfall layout in terms of the average time that users spent on a popular product (H1c rejected). However, MANOVA results indicate significant main effects of content layout (Table 1) on the percentage of popular items among all the products clicked (Figure 3 left, M = 18% for grid and 12% for waterfall, H1a accepted) and the ratio of time spent on popular products (Figure 3 right, M = 12% for grid and 10% for waterfall design, H1b accepted). We conducted a Chi-square Goodness-of-Fit test comparing the

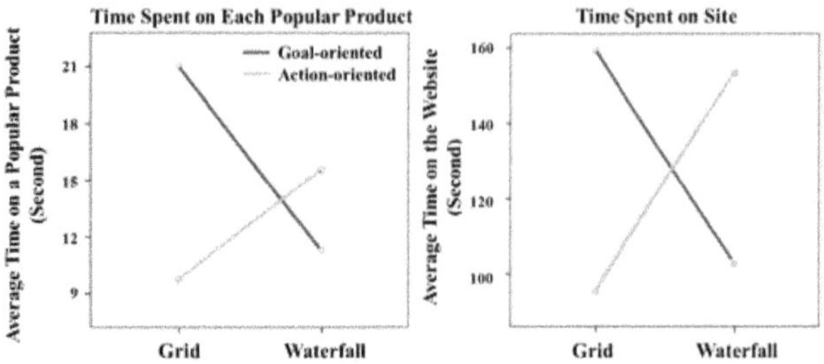

Figure 4. Comparison of the average time (left) on a popular product and on the social discovery site (right) between goal- and action-oriented users given grid versus waterfall design.

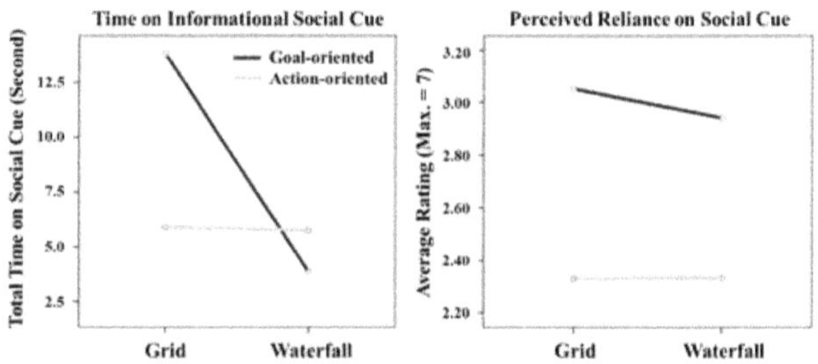

Figure 5. Comparison of the time (left) and perceived reliance (right) on informational social cues between goal- and action-oriented users given grid versus waterfall design.

occurrence of popular products among all the ones clicked with the hypothesized 10% under equal chance. Significant deviation from the hypothesized value is found in grid condition ($\chi^2(1)=7.11$, $p<0.05$) but not in the waterfall condition, suggesting that waterfall design in general effectively encourages users to allocate their attention more evenly across all products.

We further analyzed the impact of layout on cue selection. Overall, participants spent 9.88 seconds in total (8.1% of total time on site) on informational social cues on the grid-style social discovery site; in comparison, they spent significantly less time 4.52 seconds in total (3.8%) on social cues on a waterfall design (Table 1, Figure 4 left). This confirms that processing disfluency caused by a visual design can reduce social cue weighting in judgment.

Goal-oriented Users are more Inclined to Herd

Although motivation does not seem to affect the proportion of popular items among all the products clicked (H2a rejected), Chi-square Goodness-of-Fit Test suggests a significant deviation between the actual ratio of popular products clicked and the hypothesized 10% in goal-oriented condition (M=17%; $\chi^2(1)=5.44$, $p<0.05$) but not for action-oriented users (M=13%). In addition, MANOVA results show that motivation has a significant effect (Table 1) on the percentage of time looking at popular items (Figure 3 right, H2b accepted) and the amount of time people spent on each popular product (Figure 4 left, H2c accepted). More specifically, goal-oriented users on average spent 12% (M=16 seconds) of their time (10%, M=13 seconds for action-oriented users) on products with over 100 Likes.

Both subjective ratings and eye-tracking data suggest that goal-oriented users pay more attention to the social cues than action-oriented ones (Table 1, Figure 5). The formal group also rate their herding inclination marginally higher than the latter group (MANOVA $p = 0.07$), indicating that motivation can influence users' reliance on social cues, which ultimately affect their likelihood to herd.

Significant Interaction Effect between Layout and Motivation

We find significant interaction effects in all three measures (Table 1, H3 accepted). In particular, the decrease of the ratio of time on popular products from grid to waterfall design is more dramatic for goal-oriented than for action-oriented users (Figure 3 right). It is because unplanned users generally rely less on the social cues (Figure 5 right), and thus their judgment process is rarely affected when such information becomes hard to locate in the waterfall design (Figure 5 left).

We notice that in the waterfall condition, the average time that an action-oriented user spent on looking at a popular product increases compared to the grid condition, while that of a goal-oriented user drops considerably. This may be introduced by the significant interaction effect on the total time on site (Figure 4 right, MANOVA: $F(1,55)=21.17$, $p<0.05$, $\eta^2=0.16$). Consistent with existing online retailing literature e.g., [19], irregular layout can retain shoppers for a longer period, and thus the absolute time on checking each item, whether popular or not, is likely to be increased. The relative popular product viewing time however remains rather constant as H1a is rejected (Figure 3 right). Overall, grid layout can better facilitate systematic search, whereas waterfall design is good for unplanned exploration.

CONCLUSION AND FUTURE WORK

In this paper, we present an eye-tracking study with 120 participants to explore the influence of interface design (grid versus waterfall) and motivation (goal-oriented versus action-oriented) on users' potential herd behavior in social product discovery. The results show that users have a higher tendency to herd on a grid-style website, and the effect is stronger for goal-oriented users.

Our study had some limitations. We did not collect the participants' personal interests among the product categories beforehand. It would be nice to compare such information to their viewing behaviors to rule out the potential confounding factor of interest. Also, paying attention to social cues does not necessarily mean that users would ultimately base their belief on them. In the future, we will further analyze the scanpath and combine eye-tracking with other measures to detect actual herd behaviors. We also plan to investigate how other product, user, interface, and contextual factors may influence users' perceptions and actions in social discovery.

ACKNOWLEDGMENTS

We thank all the participants, and thank the Ministry of Education (MOE) of Singapore [Grant Number: T1 251RES1401] for its financial support.

REFERENCES

1. Adam L. Alter and Daniel M. Oppenheimer. 2008. Effects of fluency on psychological distance and mental construal (or why New York is a large city, but New York is a civilized jungle). *Psychological Science.* 19, 2: 161-167.
2. Yi-Fen Chen. 2008. Herd behavior in purchasing books online. *Computers in Human Behavior.* 24, 5: 1977-1992.
3. Yi-Fen Chen and Ya-Ju Wang. 2010. Effect of herd cues and product involvement on bidder online choices. *Cyberpsychology, Behavior, and Social Networking.* 13(4): 423-428.
4. Terry L. Childers, Christopher L. Carr, Joann Peck, and Stephen Carson. 2002. Hedonic and utilitarian motivations for online retail shopping behavior. *Journal of retailing.* 77, 4: 511-535.
5. Jacob Cohen. 1977. *Statistical power analysis for the behavioral sciences.* Lawrence Erlbaum Associates, Inc.
6. Liqiong Deng and Poole, M. S. 2010. Affect in Web Interfaces: A Study of the Impacts of Webpage Visual Complexity and Order. *MIS Quarterly.* 34(4): 711-730
7. Eric Gilbert, Saeideh Bakhshi, Shuo Chang, and Loren Terveen. 2013. "I need to try this"?: a statistical overview of pinterest. In *Proceedings of the SIGCHI Conference on Human Factors in Computing Systems* (CHI '13). ACM, New York, NY, USA, 2427-2436.
8. Joseph H. Goldberg, Mark J. Stimson, Marion Lewenstein, Neil Scott, and Anna M. Wichansky. 2002. Eye tracking in web search tasks: design implications. In *Proceedings of the 2002 symposium on Eye tracking research & applications*. 51-58. ACM.
9. Marc Hassenzahl and Daniel Ullrich. 2007. To do or not to do: Differences in user experience and retrospective judgments depending on the presence or absence of instrumental goals. *Interacting with Computers.* 19, 4: 429-437.
10. E. Tory Higgins. 1998. Promotion and prevention: Regulatory focus as a motivational principle. *Advances in experimental social psychology.* 30: 1-46.
11. Xin Li, Lei Guo, and Yihong Eric Zhao. 2008. Tag-based social interest discovery. In *Proceedings of the 17th international conference on World Wide Web.* 675-684. ACM.
12. Emmanouela E. Manganari, George J. Siomkos, Irini D. Rigopoulou, and Adam P. Vrechopoulos. 2011. Virtual store layout effects on consumer behaviour: applying an environmental psychology approach in the online travel industry. *Internet Research.* 21, 3: 3-346.
13. Daniel R. Montello. The contribution of space syntax to a comprehensive theory of environmental psychology. 2007. In *Proceedings of the 6th International Space Syntax Symposium.* 1–12.
14. Michel Tuan Pham and Tamar Avnet. 2004. Ideals and oughts and the reliance on affect versus substance in persuasion. *Journal of Consumer Research.* 30, 4: 503-518.
15. Anuj K.Shah and Daniel M. Oppenheimer. 2007. Easy does it: The role of fluency in cue weighting. *Judgment and Decision Making.* 2, 6: 371-379.
16. Sav Shrestha and Kelsi Lenz. 2007. Eye gaze patterns while searching vs. browsing a website. *Usability News* 9, 1: 17.
17. Uri Simonsohn and Dan Ariely. 2008. When rational sellers face nonrational buyers: evidence from herding on eBay. *Management science.* 54(9): 1624-1637.
18. Heshan Sun. 2013. A longitudinal study of herd behavior in the adoption and continued use of technology. *Mis Quarterly.* 37(4): 1013-1041.
19. Adam P.Vrechopoulos, Robert M. O'Keefe, Georgios I. Doukidis, and George J. Siomkos. 2004. Virtual store layout: an experimental comparison in the context of grocery retail. *Journal of Retailing.* 80, 1: 13-22.
20. Eric A. Walden and Glenn J. Browne. 2009. Sequential adoption theory: a theory for understanding herding behavior in early adoption of novel technologies. *Journal of the Association for Information Systems.* 10(1): 1.
21. Yanzhen Yue, Xiaojuan Ma, and Zhenhui Jiang. 2014. Share your view: impact of co-navigation support and status composition in collaborative online shopping. In *Proceedings of the SIGCHI Conference on Human Factors in Computing Systems* (CHI '14). ACM, New York, NY, USA, 3299-3308.
22. Ping Zhang, Lina Zhou, and Hans-Dieter Zimmermann. 2013. Advances in Social Commerce Research: Guest Editors' Introduction. *Electronic Commerce Research and Applications.* 12: 221-223.

Age-related Differences in the Content of Search Queries when Reformulating

Saraschandra Karanam
Utrecht University
Utrecht, The Netherlands
s.karanam@uu.nl

Herre van Oostendorp
Utrecht University
Utrecht, The Netherlands
h.vanoostendorp@uu.nl

ABSTRACT

This study investigated the change in the content of the queries when performing reformulations in relation to age and task difficulty. Results showed that both generalization and specialization strategies were applied significantly more often for difficult tasks compared to simple tasks. Young participants were found to use specialization strategy significantly more often than old participants. Generalization strategy was also used significantly more often by young participants, especially for difficult tasks. Young participants were found to reformulate much longer than old participants. The semantic relevance of queries with the target information was found to be significantly higher for difficult tasks compared to simple tasks. It showed a decreasing trend across reformulations for old participants and remained constant for young participants, indicating that as old participants reformulated, they produced queries that were further away from the target information. Implications of these findings for design of information search systems are discussed.

Author Keywords

Information Search; Aging; Reformulation Strategies; Task Difficulty.

ACM Classification Keywords

H.5.4 Information Interfaces and Presentation: Hypertext / Hypermedia—*Navigation*; H.3.3 Information Storage and Retrieval: Information Search and Retrieval—*Search Process*; J.4 Computer Applications: Social and Behavioral Sciences—*Psychology*

INTRODUCTION

The Internet was once thought to be of not much use to older adults. Complexity and difficulty to learn its usage added to this perception [12, 26]. However, this is no longer the case, as is evident from the fact that they are now one of the fastest growing users of the Internet [1, 9]. Recent studies show that older adults are now as enthusiastic as younger adults in using the web [38]. The Internet is known to decrease isolation by enabling alternate means of communication with near and dear, foster independence, enhance attention and memory [33] and keep the mind active, thereby increasing overall health and well-being of the elderly [25].

However, a number of barriers still exist preventing large scale adoption and usage of the Internet by the elderly. Due to the natural decline in their motor skills and fluid intelligence involving processing speed, cognitive flexibility or ability to switch processing strategies, attentional control and visuospatial span [14, 15, 36], they are known to be slow and less efficient when using the Internet. Crystallized intelligence, on the other hand, increases and/or becomes more stable with aging. Crystallized intelligence involves prior knowledge, experience and vocabulary skills. Therefore it is higher for older adults compared to younger adults [14, 15, 36].

Searching for information on the Internet can often be challenging and involves several cognitive processes such as memory (formulating relevant queries), attention (understanding the visual layout of the website or search engine result pages (SERPs, henceforth)), problem solving (information can be found in multiple locations and there could be multiple paths leading to them), comprehension (understanding the search results provided by a search engine) and decision making (choosing a relevant search result, reformulating unfruitful queries). These cognitive processes are known to be affected by the above aging-related declines in cognitive abilities. Much research has already been conducted on how aging-related decline in cognitive abilities influence either positively or negatively the performance on an information search task [5, 31]. Older adults were in general found to spend longer on search result pages, open fewer search results and reformulate queries less often than younger adults, especially for difficult tasks. Also, they were found to generate fewer queries than younger adults [21]. In another study, it was found that the performance of younger adults was better than that of older adults, especially on difficult and impossible tasks. Younger adults not only used more queries but also more keywords per query compared to older adults when solving difficult and impossible tasks. More precisely, it was difficult for older adults to reformulate unsuccessful queries [10]. Overall, older adults generate less queries, use less keywords per query, reformulate less, spend longer time evaluating the search results, spend more time evaluating the content of websites opened from SERPs, switch less number of times between SERPs and websites and find it difficult to reformulate unsuccessful queries [5, 29]. However, older adults are known to adapt their search

CHI 2016, May 7–12, 2016, San Jose, California, USA.

ACM ISBN 978-1-4503-3362-7/16/05 ...$15.00.
http://dx.doi.org/10.1145/2858036.2858444

and navigation strategies exploiting their higher crystallized knowledge to compensate for their decreased fluid capabilities when performing information search tasks using the Internet [7, 8, 10, 29]. Information search tasks on the Internet are usually carried out in two phases: first, using a search engine and formulating queries relevant to one's goal (search by query) and second, navigating on websites opened by clicking on one or more of the search results (search by navigation) [28]. We focus on the first phase, i.e., interaction with a search engine in this paper.

AGING AND SEARCH STRATEGIES

A number of researchers have looked into the search strategies employed by younger and older adults when solving information search tasks using a search engine. Youmans et al. [37] conducted a study in which older adults were found to follow a more structured and methodical approach to information search such as careful selection of query terms and spending longer time evaluating the search results whereas younger adults were found to follow a more impulsive strategy that involved more switches between search results and more clicks on irrelevant search results.

A more recent study by [4] looked at the three important phases in an information search process: planning (dividing a problem into sub-problems, formulating the first query), evaluating (assessing the relevance of search results) and controlling (modifying the query and strategy if required). In line with one of their earlier studies [3], they found significant differences in the amount of time allocated to the three phases of information search in relation to age and task difficulty. Younger adults were found to control their strategy more than older adults enabling them to perform better especially at difficult and impossible tasks.

In another study [6], it was found that there are significant age differences in the amount of resources allocated to exploration (number of search results opened for any given query) phase and exploitation (number of websites and hyperlinks within those websites visited for any given query) phase of an information search process. Older adults were found to do more exploitation in terms of spending longer time and viewing more information compared to younger adults. They even found that the older adults were adaptive in adjusting the two processes depending on the difficulty of the task.

Research on search strategies has so far overlooked the age related differences in reformulation strategies and the actual content of the queries during reformulations. By actual content, we mean here the semantic aspects of the query terms. These, precisely, form the main focus of this paper. Of all the different kinds of query reformulation strategies that the information retrieval domain has extensively looked at [17, 18, 32, 35], we focus on the two most common types: *generalization* and *specialization* in our study. These are concerned with modifying the content of the queries and are interesting from a cognitive perspective. Some recent studies have shown that people highly familiar with the topic of search prefer generalization whereas people less familiar with the topic of search prefer specialization as a reformulation strategy [16]. People more familiar with the topic of search were also found to use less queries, more relevant keywords per query, select more relevant results and were more successful in solving tasks, especially the difficult ones [27, 30]. Choice of reformulation strategy employed was also shown to be influenced by the type of search task [24], however, this and the earlier studies did not incorporate any age-related differences. The two main issues that this paper addresses are:

(a) Age-related differences in reformulation strategies in relation to difficulty of task.

(b) Variation in the content of the queries during reformulations in relation to age, difficulty of the task and the target information sought.

Semantic relevance was used in the past as a metric to evaluate the content of hyperlink texts (to predict navigation behavior on websites) [13, 19] or the content of the search results on the SERPs (to predict interaction behavior with search engines) [21]. In both cases, semantic relevance was computed in relation to the user goal and not with the target information. As far as we know, this is the first study that investigates the content of the queries in relation to the target information sought.

Outcomes of this study would be valuable for designing and embedding support mechanisms for various reformulation strategies into search and information retrieval systems.

RESEARCH QUESTIONS

Based on the findings from previous studies, we formulated the following research questions and hypotheses for the current study:

(a) How often do younger and older adults make use of generalization and specialization strategies when reformulating search queries? (**RQ1**). Because, reformulating a query is a cognitively effortful process, we hypothesize that younger adults would use both generalization and specialization more often than older adults (**Hyp1**).

(b) How does the frequency of usage of generalization and specialization strategies when reformulating queries vary in relation to difficulty of a task? (**RQ2**). We hypothesize that difficult tasks would require more reformulations and therefore more generalizations and specializations than simple tasks (**Hyp2**).

(c) How does the semantic relevance of a query with the target information sought vary in relation to age and difficulty of a task? (**RQ3**). The Construction-Integration model of text comprehension [22] states that comprehension of text happens cyclically in two phases: *construction phase* during which a representation of a new piece of text and all possible meanings of the text are generated and *integration phase* during which using reader's prior knowledge and context, a single coherent meaning is selected by filtering all those representations that do not fit to the context. We assume that this model also applies to information search and hypothesize that solving difficult search tasks successfully urges users to activate a greater number of related concepts from Long Term Memory into Working Memory

[22]. Assuming that these activated concepts are included as terms in the search queries formulated by users, we hypothesize that the semantic relevance of a query with the target information would be higher for difficult tasks compared to simple tasks (**Hyp3a**). Also, based on the outcomes of the study by [4], in which younger adults were found to be better at controlling phase of information search (modifying the query and strategy if required, which resulted in their higher performance) compared to older adults, we hypothesize that the semantic relevance of queries generated by younger adults would be higher than that of older adults (**Hyp3b**).

EXPERIMENT

We briefly report here the results of an experiment conducted to collect behavioral data from participants and check if the results are in line with prior outcomes from aging-related literature. Next to that we report the main issue of this study: the analysis of the type of reformulation strategy and the content of the queries during reformulations in relation to age and task difficulty.

Method

Participants

24 young participants (16 males and 8 females) ranging from 18 to 31 years (M = 22.7, SD = 3.31), and 24 old participants (14 males and 10 females) ranging from 65 to 88 years (M = 73.58, SD = 6.74) participated in the study.

Design

We followed a 2 (Age: Young vs. Old) X 2 (Task Difficulty: Simple vs. Difficult) mixed design with age as between-subjects variable and task difficulty as within-subjects variable.

Material

The experiment was conducted with twelve simulated information search tasks [2]: six simple and six difficult, all from the domain of health. For simple tasks, participants in most cases could find the answer easily either in the snippets of the search engine results or in one of the websites referred to by the search engine results. For instance, for a task like *"Wat is de belangrijkste functie van zweetklieren? (What is the main function of sweat glands?)"*, user could use the words like *"functie van zweetklieren (function of sweat glands)"* from the task description itself as queries. One can easily find the answer *"regelen de lichaamstemperatuur (regulation of body temperature)"* within the snippets of the corresponding search results without having to click on any of them. For difficult tasks, users had to frame queries using their knowledge and understanding of the task, the answer was not easily found in the snippets of search engine results and often they had to evaluate information from multiple websites. As an example, for the task *"Elbert, 76 jaar oud, heeft al een paar jaar last van een brandend gevoel bij het plassen. Hij plast's nachts meer dan normaal en hij klaagt over het gevoel dat zijn blaas dan niet helemaal leeggemaakt wordt. Sinds kort heeft hij ook een scherpe pijn in de heup, onderrug en zijn bekken. In de laatste 6 maanden is hij 12 kilo afgevallen. Wat zou de oorzaak van zijn klachten kunnen zijn? (Elbert, 76 years old has been suffering for few years from burning sensation while passing urine. He passes urine more often than normal at night and complains of a feeling that the bladder is not empty completely. Lately, he also developed acute pain in the hip, lower back and pelvis region. He also lost 12 kilos in the last 6 months. What problem could he be suffering from?)"*, users had to formulate multiple queries such as *"niersteen pijn in rug (kidney stones pain in the back)"*, *"branderig gevoel bij plassen (burning sensation when urinating)"*, *"blaasontsteking (urinary infection)"* to find the answer. The answer to this task *"prostaatkanker (prostate cancer)"* is also not found easily in the snippets of the search results of the queries, unless the query is very specific. The tasks were all presented in Dutch.

Procedure

Participants first did a demographic questionnaire in which they were asked details about their age, gender, familiarity with search engines (on a Likert scale of 1(A bit) to 4 (Very Much)) and computer experience (number of years). Based on these self-reported ratings, old participants (M=2.63, SD=1.01) were found to be significantly less experienced with search engines than young participants (M=3.75, SD=0.68) $t(46)$ = 4.52, p<.001. Old participants were significantly longer experienced with computers (M=22.7 years, SD=9.43) than young participants (M=15.33 years, SD=4.09) $t(46)$ = 3.1, p<.005. They were next presented with a fluid intelligence test: a computerized version of the Trail Making Test (TMT Part B) [34]. Participants were shown 25 circles containing both numbers (1 to 13) and alphabets (A to L) on the computer screen. The participants had to click on the circles in ascending pattern alternating between numbers and alphabets (1-A-2-B-3-C and so on) starting from the number 1. If the circle clicked by a participant is right, it turned green, otherwise it turned red. We measured the time taken to finish the test correctly. In line with the traditional cognitive aging literature, significant differences were found in fluid abilities of young and old participants. Old participants took significantly longer to finish this test ($t(46)$=5.13, p<.001) than young participants indicating that they had significantly lower fluid abilities compared to young participants.

After the TMT test, participants were allowed a break of five minutes. They were then presented with twelve information search tasks (six simple and six difficult) in a counter balanced order. Participants were first shown the task and then directed to the home page of Google's search engine. Participants were not allowed to use any other search engine. We show in Figure 1 the main screen of our interface that participants used while solving the information search tasks. Participants could enter queries as they normally would on any browser and the corresponding search results appeared. The task description was made available to the participant at all times in the top left corner. An empty text box was provided in the top right corner for the participant to enter his/her answer. All the queries generated by the users, the corresponding search engine result pages and the URLs opened by them were logged in the back-end using Visual Basic. We first analyze the performance in terms of time, clicks, accuracy and reformulations and later analyze the type of reformulation strategy and the semantic content of the queries during reformulations more deeply.

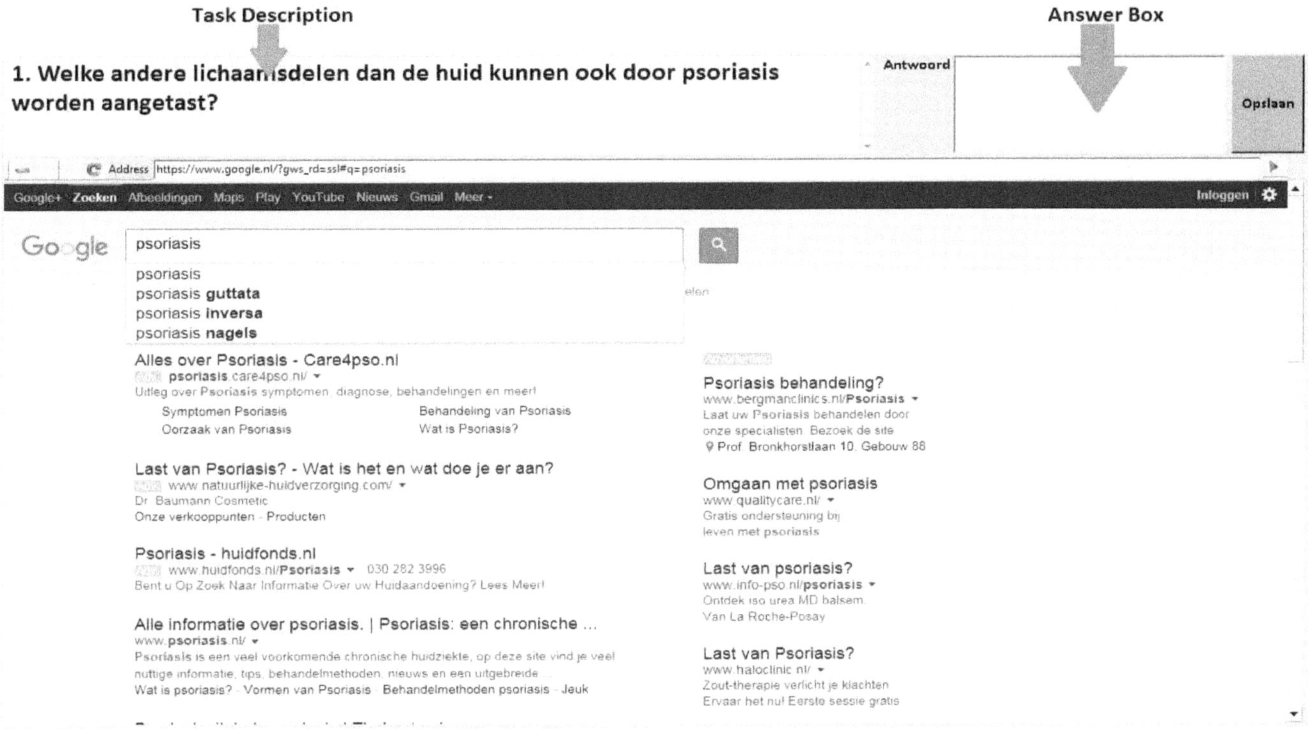

Figure 1. Interface showing the main screen in which the information search tasks are solved.

Analysis of Search Outcomes

Measures

Task-completion time is computed from the moment of opening a browser and typing in the first query to the moment of answering the question. This includes the time it takes in typing queries, evaluating search results, clicking on one of the search results, evaluating the content of websites opened from the search results and finally typing the answers.

Number of clicks is the total number of clicks made by a participant for each task. This includes the clicks made on the search results as well as the clicks made on websites opened from the search results.

Accuracy is measured as 1, 0.5 or 0 depending on whether the participant's answer was correct (in which case the score is 1) or partially correct (in which case the score is 0.5) or wrong (in which case the score is 0).

Number of reformulations is the total number of unique queries that a user could come up with for each task in the process of answering it (e.g., if participant added, deleted keywords or created new ones, we counted them as reformulations of query).

Data of only those tasks was included in the analysis for which the participants successfully completed the tasks. 37 data points out of a total number of (12 tasks X 48 participants) = 576 data points (6.4%) were therefore dropped. For all the four dependent variables, a 2 (Age: Young vs. Old) X 2 (Task Difficulty: Simple vs. Difficult) mixed ANOVA was conducted with age as between-subjects variable and task difficulty as within-subjects variable.

Results

Task-completion time Figure 2a shows the mean task-completion time in relation to age and task difficulty. The main effect of age was significant $F(1,46) = 579.37$, $p<.001$. The main effect of task difficulty was significant $F(1,46) = 90.07$, $p<.001$. The interaction of age and task difficulty was also significant $F(1,46) = 11.63$, $p<.001$.

Number of clicks Figure 2b shows the relationship between age and task difficulty for mean number of clicks. The main effect of age was significant $F(1,46) = 15.54$, $p<.001$. The main effect of task difficulty was significant $F(1,46) = 21.89$, $p<.001$. The interaction of age and task difficulty was significant $F(1,46) = 8.46$, $p<.01$.

Accuracy As can be seen from Figure 2c, the main effect of age was significant $F(1,46) = 17.18$, $p<.001$. The main effect of task difficulty was significant $F(1,46) = 196.4$, $p<.001$. Interaction of age and task difficulty was not significant ($p>.05$).

Number of reformulations Figure 2d shows the mean number of reformulations in relation to age and task difficulty. The main effect of age was significant $F(1,46) = 26.92$, $p<.001$. The main effect of task difficulty was significant $F(1,46) = 31.35$, $p<.001$. The interaction of age and task difficulty was significant $F(1,46) = 12.21$, $p<.001$.

Summarizing the main behavioral outcomes, we found that difficult tasks took significantly longer to complete, significantly more clicks were made, were answered significantly less accu-

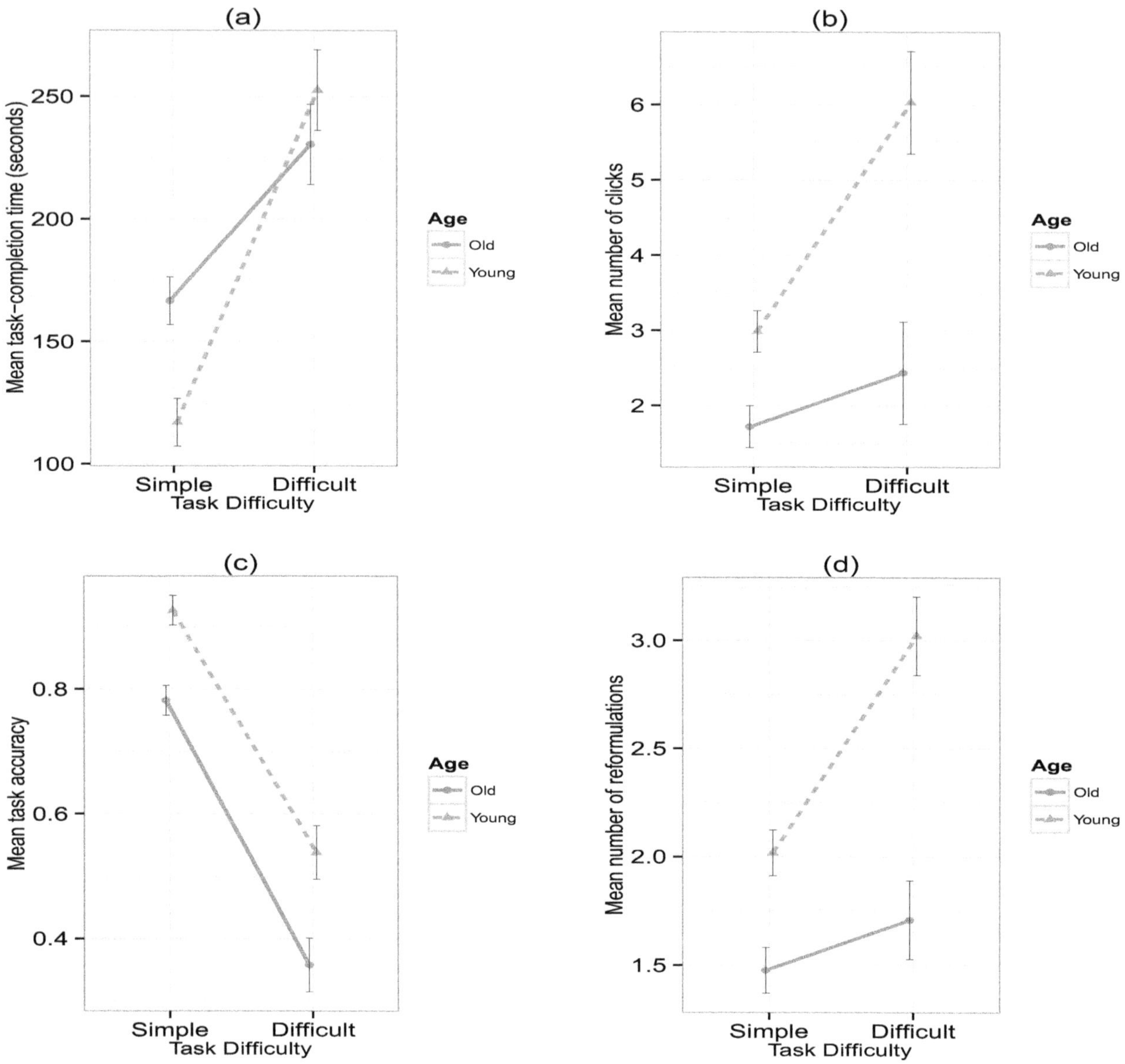

Figure 2. Analysis of search performance in terms of (a) task-completion time, (b) clicks, (c) accuracy and (d) number of reformulations in relation to age and task difficulty.

rately than simple tasks and significantly more reformulations were made than simple tasks. Young participants were found to be significantly faster in completing the tasks, especially the simple ones. Accuracy of young participants was significantly higher than that of old participants. Old participants were found to click significantly less and reformulate queries significantly less often than young participants. We next analyze the type of reformulation strategy and the semantic content of the queries during reformulations in more detail.

Analysis of Reformulation Strategies

Of all the different types of query reformulations, we focus on *generalization* and *specialization* in our study as these are concerned with modifying the content of the queries and are interesting from a cognitive perspective. We also had other types of reformulations in our data such as spelling corrections (58), repeating same query again (7), converting a query string into its plural form (3), use of special operators such as AND or double quotes (2), reordering words in a query (2) which were dropped from the analysis as these were not many compared to the total number of reformulations we had (together 10.18%). We used a slightly modified version of generalization and specialization as defined in [24].

Measures

Generalization of Query If the user finds that the search results are too narrow, he/she normally generalizes the query by using superordinate terms or by removing some terms. Therefore, if Q_i and Q_{i+1} are two consecutive queries, Q_{i+1} is a generalization of Q_i if Q_i and Q_{i+1} have at least one query term

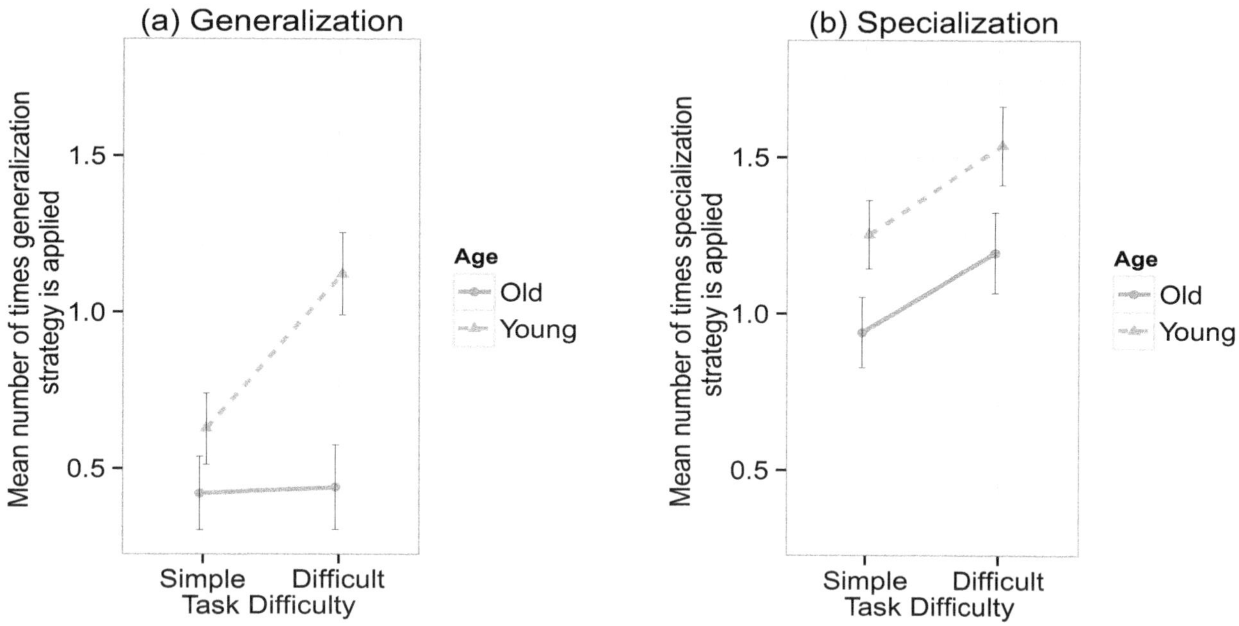

Figure 3. Mean number of times (a) generalization and (b) specialization strategies are applied by young and old participants in relation to task difficulty.

in common, Q_{i+1} contains fewer or equal number of terms than Q_i and/or Q_{i+1} contains some new terms not present in Q_i [24]. For the example task in the difficult category discussed above, if the queries are *"niersteen pijn in rug (kidney stones pain in the back)"*, *"branderig gevoel bij plassen (burning sensation when urinating)"*, *"blaasontsteking (urinary infection)"* then the number of times generalization strategy is applied is 3. However, if the queries are *"niersteen pijn in rug (kidney stones pain in the back)"*, *"pijn bij plassen (pain when urinating)"*, *"pijn bij plassen en gewichtsverlies (pain when urinating and weight loss)"*, then the number of times generalization strategy is applied is only 1.

Specialization of Query If the user is not satisfied with the search results, and finds them to be too generic, he/she normally makes the query more specific by adding new terms. Therefore, if Q_i and Q_{i+1} are two consecutive queries, Q_{i+1} is a specialization of Q_i if Q_i and Q_{i+1} have at least one query term in common, Q_{i+1} contains more terms than Q_i and/or Q_{i+1} contains some new terms not present in Q_i [24].Taking the same example task as above, for the queries in the first case, the number of times specialization strategy was applied is 0 as all three queries were generated by using completely new terms. However, for the queries in the second case, the number of times specialization strategy is applied is 1 as the third query is generated by adding additional terms (weight loss) to the second query.

Semantic Relevance of Query (SRQ) For each task and each query corresponding to that task, semantic relevance was computed between the query and the target information sought using a technique called Latent Semantic Analysis (LSA, henceforth) [23]. LSA is a machine-learning technique that builds a semantic space representing a given user population's understanding of words, short or whole texts by applying statistical computations, singular value decomposition and represents them as a vector in a multidimensional space of about 300 dimensions. The cosine value (+1 if identical and 0 if unrelated) between two vectors in this representation gives the measure of the semantic relatedness. It has been shown that higher semantic relevance between two texts relates to higher overlap in the meanings associated with those two texts. LSA has been successfully put to use in applications such as information retrieval, essay grading, synonymy tests, automatic tutors, etc [11].

We used 70,000 Dutch documents (consisting of 60% newspaper articles and 40% medical and health related articles) as a corpus to create first a semantic space in Dutch. The LSA values were then computed between a query and each of the headings and search snippets of search results from the corresponding SERP using this space. For a detailed procedure to compute semantic similarities, refer [20]. This is repeated for all queries of the task and a mean LSA value is computed. This is repeated again for all the tasks of a participant and finally for all the participants. This metric gives us an estimate of how close in semantic similarity the queries generated by the participants are to the target information.

Results

For all three dependent variables, a 2 (Age: Young vs. Old) X 2 (Task Difficulty: Simple vs. Difficult) mixed ANOVA was conducted with age as between-subjects variable and task difficulty as within-subjects variable.

Generalization of Query As shown in Figure 3a, the main effect of age was significant $F(1,41) = 9.08$, $p<.005$. Generalization strategy was applied significantly more often by young

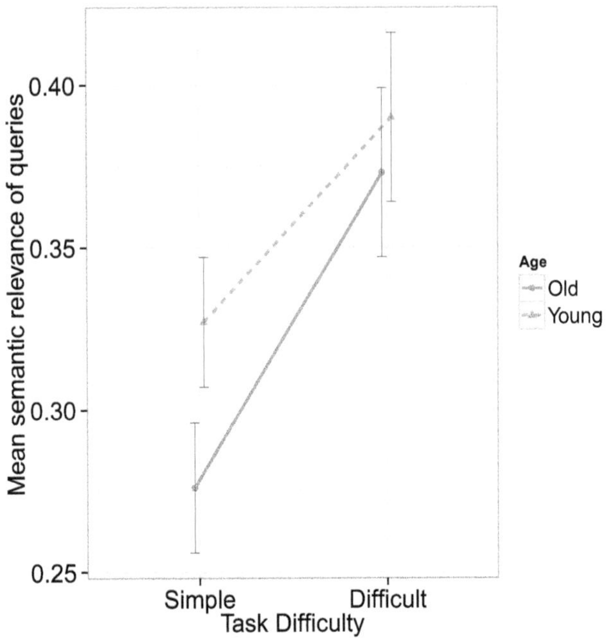

Figure 4. Mean semantic relevance of queries with target in relation to age and task difficulty.

participants compared to old participants. The main effect of task difficulty was significant $F(1,41) = 6.98, p<.05$. Difficult tasks demanded more generalizations than simple tasks. The interaction of age and task difficulty was significant $F(1,41) = 5.98, p<.005$. Post-hoc tests showed that the number of times the generalization strategy was applied by young participants was significantly more than that of old participants, especially for difficult tasks.

Specialization of Query As shown in Figure 3b, the main effect of age was significant $F(1,41) = 8.04, p<.01$. The specialization strategy was applied significantly more often by young participants compared to old participants. The main effect of task difficulty was significant $F(1,41) = 4.76, p<.05$. The number of times specialization strategy was applied for difficult tasks was significantly higher than that for simple tasks. The interaction of age and task difficulty was not significant ($p>.05$).

Semantic Relevance of Query It is evident from Figure 4 that the main effect of task difficulty was significant $F(1,46) = 9.47$, $p<.005$. The mean semantic relevance of queries for difficult tasks was significantly higher than that for simple tasks. The main effect of age and the interaction of age and task difficulty were not significant ($p>.05$).

We next analyzed the mean semantic relevance of the queries with the target information at a more granular level by looking at each reformulation cycle separately. First cycle corresponds to first query, second cycle corresponds to the second query, third cycle corresponds to the third query and so on. Mean semantic relevance was computed for all the queries of all the tasks of a particular type (simple and difficult separately), generated by young and old participants in each reformulation cycle. It would have been interesting to perform this analysis separately also for generalization and specialization strategies, but we restrict ourselves to simple and difficult tasks for now because of lack of sufficient data. To achieve higher reliability, only those cycles were considered for which there were at least 5 queries (per reformulation cycle). By doing so, only 2.8% of data was excluded from the analysis. The resulting graphs are shown in Figure 5. We can observe from Figure 5 that young participants reformulated much longer than old participants.

We conducted 4 different one-way ANOVAs (for simple old, difficult old, simple young and difficult young) with cycle (reformulation cycle 1 vs 2 vs 3 and so on as repeated measures) as independent variable and mean LSA value of the SERP generated by queries in a reformulation cycle as dependent variable. The main effect of cycle on mean LSA value was weakly significant $F(2,56) = 2.55, p<.09$, for simple old and not ($p>.05$) for others. For simple old, post-hoc tests showed that the mean LSA value of the SERPs in reformulation cycle 3 was significantly less ($p<.05$) than that in the first cycle. There was also a significant linear trend $F(2,56) = 5.03, p<.05$, for simple old and a weaker trend for difficult old $F(1, 66) = 3.52, p<.07$, indicating that as old participants reformulated, they produced queries which were further away from the target information.

We next checked the difference in mean LSA value of the SERPs between the starting (first query) and ending points (last query) of a search session. We found no significant difference in the starting points of young and old participants, for both simple and difficult tasks. However, at the ending points, young participants (M=.45, SD=.45, for simple tasks and M=.48, SD=.40 for difficult tasks) end up significantly higher than old participants (M=.14, SD=.17 for simple tasks and M=.12, SD=.14 for difficult tasks), $t(20) = 2.3, p<.05$ (for simple tasks), $t(8) = 2.28, p=.06$ (for difficult tasks), indicating that the semantic relevance of queries with target information decreases with further reformulations for old participants whereas it remains constant for young participants.

Summarizing the analyses on reformulation strategies, we found that both generalization and specialization strategies were applied significantly more often for difficult tasks compared to simple tasks. Young participants were found to use the specialization strategy significantly more often than old participants. The generalization strategy was also used significantly more often by young participants, especially for difficult tasks. The semantic relevance of queries with the target information was found to be significantly higher for difficult tasks compared to simple tasks. Although the mean semantic relevance of queries with target information was overall similar for young and old participants, it remained constant for young participants and decreased for old participants with further reformulations. Also, young participants were found to reformulate much longer than old participants.

CONCLUSIONS AND DISCUSSION

This study was designed mainly to investigate deeper the query reformulation strategies and the content of the queries during

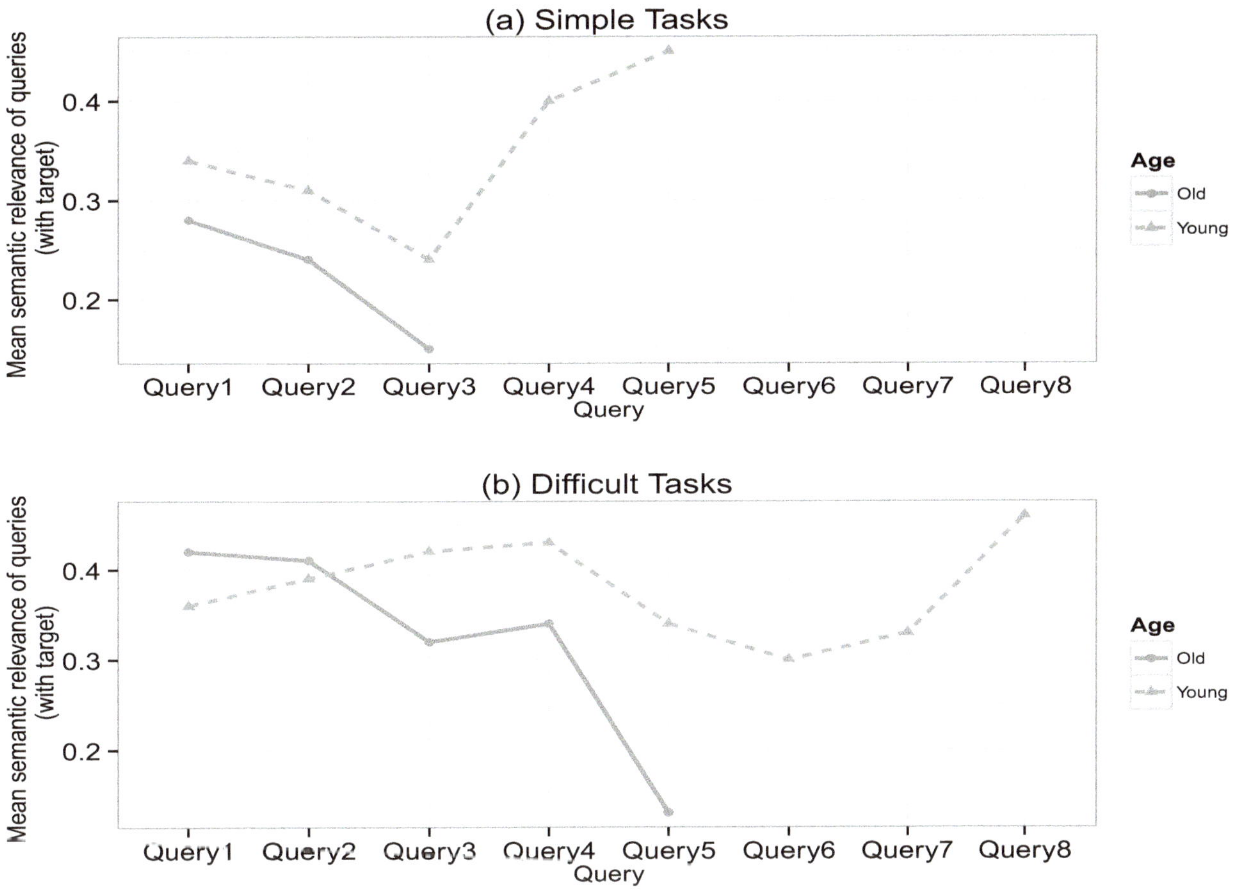

Figure 5. Mean semantic relevance of queries with target at each reformulation cycle for (a) simple and (b) difficult tasks.

reformulations in relation to age and task difficulty. A behavioral study in which 24 young and 24 old participants solved six simple and six difficult information search tasks was conducted. Analysis of behavioral outcomes showed that difficult tasks took significantly longer to complete, significantly more clicks were made, were answered significantly less accurately than simple tasks and significantly more reformulations were made than simple tasks. Younger adults were found to be significantly faster in completing tasks, especially the simple ones. Accuracy of younger adults was significantly higher than that of older adults. Older adults were found to click significantly less and reformulate queries significantly less often than younger adults. These results were in line with the outcomes of previous studies [4, 10, 21] and therefore provide stronger foundation to the main contributions of this study.

We formulated three main research questions regarding reformulation strategies and the content of queries. First, how often do younger and older adults make use of generalization and specialization strategies when reformulating search queries? Because, reformulating a query is a cognitively effortful process, we hypothesized that younger adults would use both generalization and specialization more often than older adults. Second, how does the frequency of usage of generalization and specialization strategies when reformulating queries vary in relation to difficulty of a task? We hypothesized that difficult tasks would require more reformulations and therefore more generalizations and specializations than simple tasks. Third, how does the semantic relevance of a query with the target information sought vary in relation to age and difficulty of a task? Based on the Construction-Integration model of text comprehension [22], difficult tasks would require activation of higher number of concepts (related to the task) in the Working Memory compared to simple tasks. Assuming that these activated concepts are included as terms in the search queries formulated by participants, we hypothesized that the semantic relevance of a query with the target information would be higher for difficult tasks compared to simple tasks. Also, because we think that younger adults would do much more activity in terms of number of search queries used, number of search results clicked and the number of pages of the websites opened from the search results explored, compared to older adults, we hypothesized that the semantic relevance of queries generated by younger adults would be higher than that of older adults.

Analysis of reformulation strategies showed that both generalization and specialization strategies were applied significantly more often for difficult tasks compared to simple tasks (**Hyp1**). Younger adults were found to use specialization strategy significantly more often than older adults. Generalization strategy was also used significantly more often by younger adults, especially for difficult tasks (**Hyp2**). The semantic relevance of queries with the target information was found to be significantly higher for difficult tasks compared to simple tasks (**Hyp3a**). We could not find evidence in our data that could show that the semantic relevance of queries used by younger adults would be higher than that of the queries used by older adults (**Hyp3b**). However, we found that the semantic relevance of the queries generated by younger adults remained constant and that of the queries generated by older adults showed a decreasing trend as they reformulated further.

A deeper analysis with type of reformulation (not reported above) as a factor revealed a significant main effect of type of reformulation $F(1, 174) = 45.63$, $p<.001$. Specialization strategy was used significantly more often than generalization strategy. The interaction of type of reformulation with age or task difficulty was not significant ($p>.05$).

The age related differences in the number of reformulations (generalizations and specializations) may be due to the lower fluid abilities of older adults compared to younger adults based on the performance on Trail Making Test. This needs to be verified by incorporating TMT scores into the analysis. Also, these results seem to be confirming the outcomes of [4] in which they found that the younger adults were more efficient in the controlling phase (reformulation of queries, coming out of unsuccessful searches etc.) of an information search task. The age related differences in the semantic relevance of queries in terms of the increasing trend for younger adults and decreasing trend for older adults as they reformulate further, may be due to the fact that younger adults were found to use specialization and generalization strategies more often than older adults. Queries in later cycles do not bring older adults closer to the target information but take them even farther away (lower SRQ). They seem to use keywords which have, over cycles, decreasing semantic relevance to the target information, in contrast to younger adults. This applies not only to simple but also to difficult tasks. We also saw that the performance in terms of accuracy was lower for older adults. An explanation of lower accuracy of older adults could be that older adults do not succeed in generating queries relevant to the target information which in turn could be because they are not able to apply proper reformulation strategies like specialization and generalization. We did indeed find significant age related differences for both.

IMPLICATIONS FOR SYSTEM DESIGN

The results from this study have implications to the design of systems that support performing information search tasks using the Internet. It is important to take into account the difficulties faced by older adults when designing such systems. First, if the search systems could detect that search results are too narrow or too broad and accordingly give suggestions to generalize or to specialize, this would be very helpful, especially for old people. Second, one can imagine a search engine monitoring semantic relevance of SERPs with respect to the queries in a search session. Whenever it shows a decreasing trend or falls below a threshold value, the system can automatically warn users to consider reformulating that query. A third possibility would be to provide support along the lines of [19] in which the semantic similarity between the user goal and the hyperlink text has been successfully used to generate navigation support. Highly similar links based on their LSA value between the goals and the link were emphasized to the participant. It would be interesting to complete this approach with similar support on the search result pages (by emphasizing results with high LSA value to the goal) in order to enhance search performance. These three types of interventions could enhance particularly for older adults their search performance.

ACKNOWLEDGMENTS

We would like to thank Guillermo de Jorge Botana from Department of Evolutionary and Educational Psychology, National Distance Education University, Madrid, Spain and Ricardo Olmos Albacete from Department of Social and Methodological Psychology, Autonoma University of Madrid, Madrid, Spain, for help with creating a semantic space. We thank Floortje van Oosten for assistance in testing participants and for her expertise in judging the adequacy of materials. This research was supported by Netherlands Organization for Scientific Research (NWO), ORA Plus project MISSION (464-13-043), and carried out in collaboration with University of Toulouse and University of Illinois.

REFERENCES

1. Anne Aula. 2005. User study on older adults use of the Web and search engines. *Universal Access in the Information Society* 4, 1 (2005), 67–81.
2. Pia Borlund and Peter Ingwersen. 1997. The development of a method for the evaluation of interactive information retrieval systems. *Journal of documentation* 53, 3 (1997), 225–250.
3. Aline Chevalier, Aurélie Dommes, and Jean-Claude Marquié. 2011. Information searching on the web: the cognitive difficulties experienced by older users in modifying unsuccessful information searches. In *Engineering Psychology and Cognitive Ergonomics*. Springer, 225–232.
4. Aline Chevalier, Aurélie Dommes, and Jean-Claude Marquié. 2015. Strategy and accuracy during information search on the Web: Effects of age and complexity of the search questions. *Computers in Human Behavior* 53 (2015), 305–315.
5. Aline Chevalier, Aurélie Dommes, and Daniel Martins. 2013. The effects of ageing and website ergonomic quality on internet information searching. *Ageing and Society* 33, 06 (2013), 1009–1035.
6. Jessie Chin, Evan Anderson, Chieh-Li Chin, and Wai-Tat Fu. 2015. Age differences in information search: An exploration-exploitation tradeoff model. In *Proceedings of the Human Factors and Ergonomic Society (HFES 2015)*. 85–89.
7. Jessie Chin and Wai-Tat Fu. 2010. Interactive effects of age and interface differences on search strategies and

performance. In *Proceedings of the SIGCHI Conference on Human Factors in Computing Systems*. ACM, 403–412.

8. Jessie Chin, Wai-Tat Fu, and Thomas Kannampallil. 2009. Adaptive information search: age-dependent interactions between cognitive profiles and strategies. In *Proceedings of the SIGCHI Conference on Human Factors in Computing Systems*. ACM, 1683–1692.
9. Jérôme Dinet, Eric Brangier, Gabriel Michel, Robin Vivian, Sophie Battisti, and Rémi Doller. 2007. Older people as information seekers: Exploratory studies about their needs and strategies. In *Universal Acess in Human Computer Interaction. Coping with Diversity*. Springer, 877–886.
10. Aurelie Dommes, Aline Chevalier, and Sarah Lia. 2011. The role of cognitive flexibility and vocabulary abilities of younger and older users in searching for information on the web. *Applied Cognitive Psychology* 25, 5 (2011), 717–726.
11. Susan T Dumais. 2004. Latent semantic analysis. *Annual review of information science and technology* 38, 1 (2004), 188–230.
12. Jacqueline K Eastman and Rajesh Iyer. 2004. The elderly's uses and attitudes towards the Internet. *Journal of Consumer Marketing* 21, 3 (2004), 208–220.
13. Wai-Tat Fu and Peter Pirolli. 2007. SNIF-ACT: A cognitive model of user navigation on the World Wide Web. *Human–Computer Interaction* 22, 4 (2007), 355–412.
14. John L Horn. 2012. The Theory of Fluid and Crystallized Intelligence in Relation to Concepts of Cognitive Psychology and Aging in. In *Aging and cognitive processes*. Vol. 8. Springer Science & Business Media, 237–278.
15. John L Horn and Raymond B Cattell. 1967. Age differences in fluid and crystallized intelligence. *Acta psychologica* 26 (1967), 107–129.
16. Rong Hu, Kun Lu, and Soohyung Joo. 2013. Effects of topic familiarity and search skills on query reformulation behavior. *Proceedings of the American Society for Information Science and Technology* 50, 1 (2013), 1–9.
17. Jeff Huang and Efthimis N Efthimiadis. 2009. Analyzing and evaluating query reformulation strategies in web search logs. In *Proceedings of the 18th ACM conference on Information and knowledge management*. ACM, 77–86.
18. Bernard J Jansen, Amanda Spink, and Bhuva Narayan. 2007. Query modifications patterns during web searching. In *Information Technology, 2007. ITNG'07. Fourth International Conference on*. IEEE, 439–444.
19. Ion Juvina and Herre van Oostendorp. 2008. Modeling semantic and structural knowledge in Web navigation. *Discourse Processes* 45, 4-5 (2008), 346–364.
20. Saraschandra Karanam, Herre van Oostendorp, and Bipin Indurkhya. 2012. Evaluating CoLiDeS+ Pic: the role of relevance of pictures in user navigation behaviour. *Behaviour & Information Technology* 31, 1 (2012), 31–40.
21. Saraschandra Karanam, Herre van Oostendorp, Mylène Sanchiz, Aline Chevalier, Jessie Chin, and Wai Tat Fu. 2015. Modeling and predicting information search behavior. In *Proceedings of the 5th International Conference on Web Intelligence, Mining and Semantics*. ACM, 7.
22. Walter Kintsch. 1998. *Comprehension: A paradigm for cognition*. Cambridge university press.
23. Thomas K Landauer, Peter W Foltz, and Darrell Laham. 1998. An introduction to latent semantic analysis. *Discourse processes* 25, 2-3 (1998), 259–284.
24. Chang Liu, Jacek Gwizdka, Jingjing Liu, Tao Xu, and Nicholas J Belkin. 2010. Analysis and evaluation of query reformulations in different task types. *Proceedings of the American Society for Information Science and Technology* 47, 1 (2010), 1–9.
25. David Mellor, Lucy Firth, and Kathleen Moore. 2008. Can the Internet Improve the Well-being of the Elderly? *Ageing international* 32, 1 (2008), 25–42.
26. Tracy L Mitzner, Julie B Boron, Cara Bailey Fausset, Anne E Adams, Neil Charness, Sara J Czaja, Katinka Dijkstra, Arthur D Fisk, Wendy A Rogers, and Joseph Sharit. 2010. Older adults talk technology: Technology usage and attitudes. *Computers in human behavior* 26, 6 (2010), 1710–1721.
27. Sophie Monchaux, Franck Amadieu, Aline Chevalier, and Claudette Mariné. 2015. Query strategies during information searching: Effects of prior domain knowledge and complexity of the information problems to be solved. *Information Processing & Management* 51, 5 (2015), 557–569.
28. Christopher Olston and Ed H Chi. 2003. ScentTrails: Integrating browsing and searching on the Web. *ACM Transactions on Computer-Human Interaction (TOCHI)* 10, 3 (2003), 177–197.
29. Richard Pak and Margaux M Price. 2008. Designing an information search interface for younger and older adults. *Human Factors: The Journal of the Human Factors and Ergonomics Society* 50, 4 (2008), 614–628.
30. Ira Puspitasari, Koichi Moriyama, Ken-ichi Fukui, and Masayuki Numao. 2015. Effects of Individual Health Topic Familiarity on Activity Patterns During Health Information Searches. *JMIR medical informatics* 3, 1 (2015).
31. Tara L Queen, Thomas M Hess, Gilda E Ennis, Keith Dowd, and Daniel Grühn. 2012. Information search and decision making: Effects of age and complexity on strategy use. *Psychology and aging* 27, 4 (2012), 817.

32. Soo Young Rieh and others. 2006. Analysis of multiple query reformulations on the web: The interactive information retrieval context. *Information Processing & Management* 42, 3 (2006), 751–768.

33. Karin Slegers, Martin PJ Van Boxtel, and Jelle Jolles. 2012. Computer use in older adults: determinants and the relationship with cognitive change over a 6year episode. *Computers in Human Behavior* 28, 1 (2012), 1–10.

34. Esther Strauss, Elisabeth MS Sherman, and Otfried Spreen. 2006. *A compendium of neuropsychological tests: Administration, norms, and commentary*. Oxford University Press, USA.

35. Jaime Teevan, Eytan Adar, Rosie Jones, and Michael AS Potts. 2007. Information re-retrieval: repeat queries in Yahoo's logs. In *Proceedings of the 30th annual international ACM SIGIR conference on Research and development in information retrieval*. ACM, 151–158.

36. Jing-Jen Wang and Alan S Kaufman. 1993. Changes in fluid and crystallized intelligence across the 20-to 90-year age range on the K-BIT. *Journal of Psychoeducational Assessment* 11, 1 (1993), 29–37.

37. Robert J Youmans, Brooke Bellows, Christian A Gonzalez, Brittany Sarbone, and Ivonne J Figueroa. 2013. Designing for the wisdom of elders: age related differences in online search strategies. In *Universal Access in Human-Computer Interaction. User and Context Diversity*. Springer, 240–249.

38. Panayiotis Zaphiris, Sri Kurniawan, and Mariya Ghiawadwala. 2007. A systematic approach to the development of research-based web design guidelines for older people. *Universal Access in the Information Society* 6, 1 (2007), 59–75.

Steel-Sense: Integrating Machine Elements with Sensors by Additive Manufacturing

Tatyana Vasilevitsky
The Hebrew University of Jerusalem
Jerusalem, Israel
tatyana.vasilevitsk@mail.huji.ac.il

Amit Zoran
The Hebrew University of Jerusalem
Jerusalem, Israel
zoran@cs.huji.ac.il

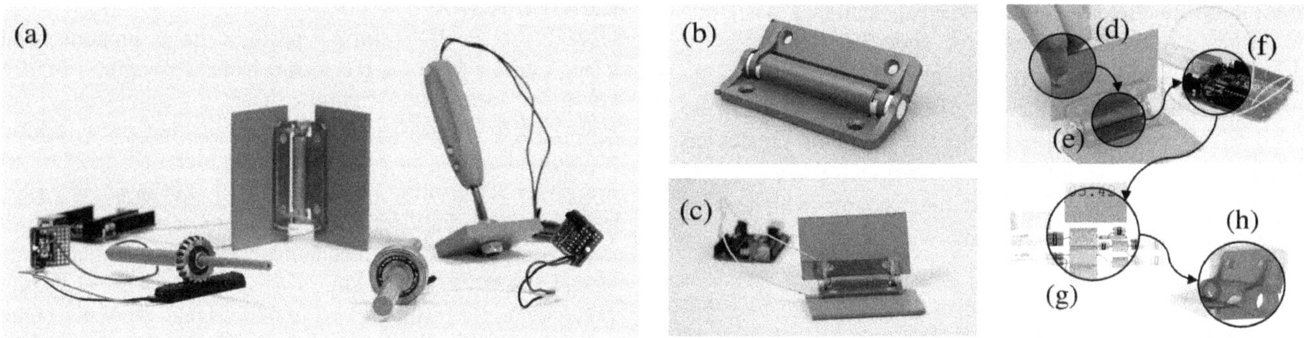

Figure 1. (a) Steel-Sense: four 3D-printed metal machine elements augmented with sensing abilities. From left to right: a voltage divider integrated inside a gear; a variable capacitor embedded in a hinge; an electronic switch within a ball bearing; and a pressure sensor within a screw (and its dedicated screwdriver). For example: (b) the virtual model of the hinge (rendered with VRay), and (c) the 3D-printed hinge system. An operation scenario: (d) a change in the hinge's opening angle (e) changes its capacitance. (f) An Arduino microcontroller measures the resulting capacitance. (g) A Grasshopper script uses the output data (h) to control the virtual model, mirroring the physical hinge.

ABSTRACT
Many interactive devices use both machine elements and sensors, simultaneously but redundantly enabling and measuring the same physical function. We present Steel-Sense, an approach to joining these two families of elements to create a new type of HCI design primitive. We leverage recent developments in 3D printing to embed sensing in metal structures that are otherwise difficult to equip with sensors, and present four design principles, implementing (1) an electronic switch integrated within a ball bearing; (2) a voltage divider within a gear; (3) a variable capacitor embedded in a hinge; and (4) a pressure sensor within a screw. Each design demonstrates a different sensing principle, and signals its performance through (1) movement; (2) position; (3) angle (4) or stress. We mirror our elements physical performance in a virtual environment, evaluate our designs electronically and structurally, and discuss future work and implications for HCI research.

CHI'16, May 07-12, 2016, San Jose, CA, USA

DOI: http://dx.doi.org/10.1145/2858036.2858309

Author Keywords
3D Printing; Sensors; Digital Fabrication; Hybrid Design; Machine Elements; Additive Manufacturing; Metal Printing.

ACM Classification Keywords
H.5.2 Information interfaces and presentation: User Interfaces - Input devices and strategies.

INTRODUCTION
Sensors and machine elements are key components in the construction of many interactive devices. Machine elements determine the potential of a device's physical freedom, while sensors measure the actual use of this potential. Although sensor design is a common research field within HCI (see the Related Work section), the study of machine elements seems foreign to traditional HCI, where many researchers use off-the-shelf components in developing their projects. Furthermore, in many designs these two families of elements are used together, but the integration between them has not been explored, as designers still rely on traditional separation between machine elements and sensors. We wish to study the possibility of merging these two families of components, seeking to use both efficiently (saving space and material), and forming a new interactive space in HCI.

Like sensors, machine elements come in a variety of types and meet a wide range of needs, satisfying structural requirements, and controlling motion and/or user mechanical input [21]. Bearings, axles, seals, gears, screws and other elements are produced in mass quantities, reducing their cost to bare minimum. While offering an extensive portfolio of designs, the industrial standards that dictate the forms and dimensions of such elements limit design freedom, introducing rigid constraints on the making process. In the realm of customization enabled by digital fabrication, the *need* to constrain the design process with rigid standards and catalogues seems out-of-date.

Additive Manufacturing (AM) calls for a revision of traditional disciplinary boundaries [3], enabling designers to produce specific solutions for specific needs. AM of metal parts makes conductive objects that can be used to 3D print sensors, and complicated 3D structures that can be used to 3D print machine elements [15]. This creates an opportunity to bridge mechanical design with sensors, and link the research in 3D-printed mechanisms with that of digitally fabricated sensors. Thus, with Steel-Sense we are motivated to free the design of sensor and machine elements from industrial standards, integrating sensors into structures with complex physical constraints using existing AM material and processes. Additionally, Steel-Sense contributes a new family of *double agent* elements—*facilitating mechanical performance while evaluating the same performance*.

With Steel-Sense, mechanical actions (such as angular and linear movement, motion transmitting, and structural alignments) and sensorial (electromagnetic) measurements are considered as a single performing unit, rather than simply combining sensors with machine elements as current solutions offer [7,18]. We envision these hybrid elements impacting the traditional design of interactive systems, as they offer a new interactive vocabulary of *performing* and *measuring* in a single unit.

In this paper, we span our new design space using four fundamental Steel-Sense principals, illustrated by the combination of fundamentally different machine elements and sensing capabilities. As the components described below are likely the most common machine elements, they are the best suited to establishing the Steel-Sense concept, rather than suggesting specific products. In the present work, we emphasize the technology (see Fig. 1) of a Steel-Sense (1) ball bearing; (2) gear; (3) hinge; and (4) screw. We 3D printed (1) a differential *rotary motion* detector for a ball bearing using an embedded switch; (2) a differential *linear motion* detector with a voltage divider embedded in a linear gear; (3) an *angle detector* using a variable capacitor in the shape of a hinge axle, and (4) an embedded sensing mechanism to measure *force* applied to a screw. We evaluated the structural performance of the new designs with the Finite Element Method (FEM), and also ran electronic performance measurements and analysis. A future work will broaden the discussion on HCI implications; here, we discuss the potential of several HCI applications based on our current design-cases.

This paper is structured around a presentation of the new designs, followed by structural and signal evaluation for each of the four machine elements. In the next section, we review related work, before presenting the technology itself in the Steel-Sense section. We discuss implications to HCI before concluding the work in the last section.

RELATED WORK

Several recent 3D printing projects have demonstrated designs with a high degree of mechanical freedom [28,29]. Along the same lines, Schmitt offers a parametric design procedure to customize 3D-printed machine parts, taking into consideration the specifications (tolerance, resolution) of a given 3D printing technology [10]. Yet in many cases, designers and engineers are bound to traditional design paradigms, paralleling mechanical and sensorial systems instead of merging them. For example, in [12] the researchers 3D printed two parallel gear systems. One converted a servomotor's rotary motion to linear motion, while a second measured movement on the same axis. While these parallel systems are common within traditional practices, 3D printing metal structures allows us to hybridize such systems, developing specific solutions while reducing cost and space.

In HCI, researchers have already started to explore the intersection of 3D printing and interactive components, as in the 3D-printed optics by Willis et al. [27]. In the last several years a vast body of work has been published on 2D-printed (customizable) electronics and sensors [4,7,9,14], and we can expect the development of fully functional 3D-printed electronics, likely beginning with conductive traces layered on a 3D model, etc., as suggested by Voxel8 [16]. In our work, we propose several interactive design primitives. This approach, of suggesting a new interaction potential using a finite set of interactive grammars, is common within HCI research, as seen in projects such as Sticky Actuator [21] and PneUI [26].

STEEL-SENSE

Steel-Sense presents four different 3D-printed machine elements integrated with four different sensing capabilities. These elements produce electronic signals echoing their mechanical performance. A ball bearing, a gear, a hinge, and a screw (plus a screwdriver) were designed to perform as similarly as possible to traditional machine elements, yet with small structural changes that enable them to function as motion, angle, and pressure sensors.

Design and Fabrication

Currently there are several AM technologies available from online services that enable digital fabrication of metal parts. The high-end process offered by *Stratasys* provides full sintering of metal powder using Direct Metal Laser

Sintering (DMLS) for stainless steel, titanium, aluminum and other alloys [13]. While this is a costly process (see below), cheaper options are available from *Shapeways* [11] and *i.materialize*. A hybrid printing/casting option is offered for metals with lower melting points, such as brass, bronze, silver, and gold. These materials can be easily cast from 3D-printed wax models. An even cheaper hybrid option (with probably the lowest resolution) digitally layers steel powder (60%) and deposits it with melted bronze (40%).

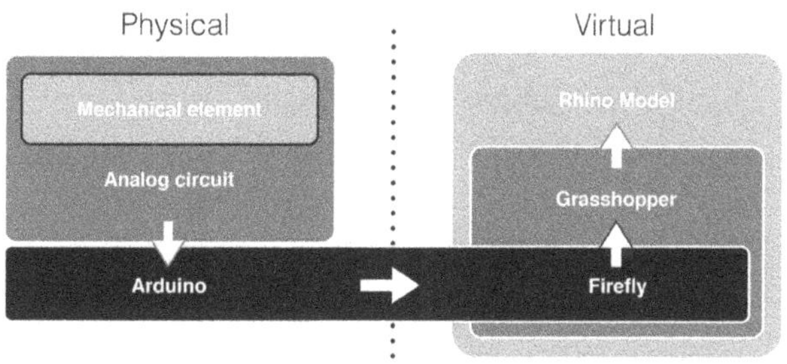

Figure 2. The data from the physical element and its circuit affect the virtual model in Rhino, flowing through Arduino and Firefly to Grasshopper.

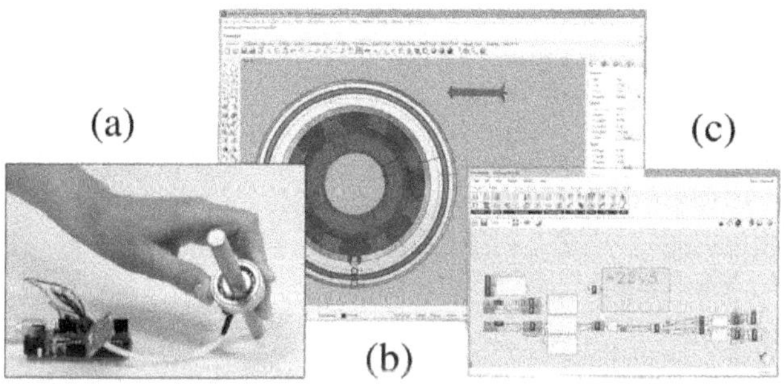

Figure 3. Dataflow from the physical machine element (ball bearing) (a) to the virtual model (b) using Grasshopper (c), Firefly and Arduino.

We compare the costs, as of August 25, 2015, of the same part (one of the hinge pieces) with the three technologies. Stratasysdirect DMLS Stainless Steel varies from $419 (Stainless Steel 17-4PH) to $457 (Stainless Steel 316L) for a single print. Raw bronze costs $63.63 (Shapeways) or $75.55 (i.materialise), while a steel/brass hybrid costs $22.76 (Shapeways) or $25.85 (i.materialise). The detailed specifications and accuracy of these processes can be found in the references. Generally speaking, the DMLS process is lower in resolution than wax printing, but post-print surface treatment can achieve a very smooth result.

All of our metal parts were designed in Rhino and 3D printed in wax, then made in bronze. While DMLS Stainless Steel is a superior AM process for our application, due to its significantly higher production cost we demonstrate our designs using a less expensive, less durable metal. Plastic parts (insulators) were printed by Shapeways using Selective Laser Sintering (SLS) of nylon 12 (the cost of SLS nylon is negligible compared to metal prints). To integrate capacitance and resistance into our designs, we use special SLS materials offered by Stratasysdirect: NyTek™ 1200 GF (nylon 12 plus glass for a higher dielectric constant) and NyTek™ 1200 CF (nylon 12 plus carbon for a weak conductivity). A detailed design for each element is presented below in the corresponding sections.

In addition to the mechanical designs, we implement analog circuits to read data from the sensors using an Arduino board. The data is transferred from the Arduino to a PC via USB (using the Arduino's serial port). Virtual models (in Rhino) mirror the physical performance of the machine element through Grasshopper (a parametric plug-in to Rhino) and Firefly (a Grasshopper plugin for Arduino integration, see Fig. 2 and Fig. 3).

Principals of Elements Evaluation

As we revise well-known elements with stable performance, it is necessary to visualize how our design affects them structurally. To evaluate the mechanical performance of our design (as presented in each section), we ran FEM simulations for each part using Scan&Solve (an FEM plugin for Rhino). We discuss the structural implication of our new designs below. For the simulations, we assumed these elements were printed in DMLS Stainless Steel 17-7 (which is superior to bronze for most real applications), and compare our hybrid designs to traditional ones made from the same material. We intentionally pushed the simulation to extreme (failure) conditions, comparing our designs to traditional components under the same conditions to easily visualize differences in failure performance. More advanced structural evaluation is needed in the future, as we present only our initial results here.

Machine Element (1): A Switch Ball Bearing

Our first hybrid element is a ball bearing (Fig. 3-4): a bearing mechanism between a fixed axle and a rotating part, separated by a ring of small balls that reduce rotational friction and support loads. Ball bearings come in a diverse range of shapes and sizes, and can be made from a variety of metals, plastics, and even ceramics. Bearings are fundamental in any mechanical design with degrees of freedom, as they allow movement. While we relied on a common ball bearing design, our solution will also fit alternative ball bearings.

Our ball bearing (printed from bronze and nylon 12, 17.1 mm radius, 10.3 mm wide) implements a differential angular motion detector in the form of a two-way single pole switch (Fig. 4e), counting quarter circles (90 degrees rotations). The outer ring supports the whole inner structure, and encloses two isolated side rings (see Fig. 4a-b). Each of these side rings has four pins (90 degree from each other, Fig. 4c) inside, but isolated from, the outer ring. A nylon case sets the angle between the inner ring and the balls.

The outer ring of the ball bearing is grounded at all times. Both side rings are supplied with a voltage of 5V, and each is

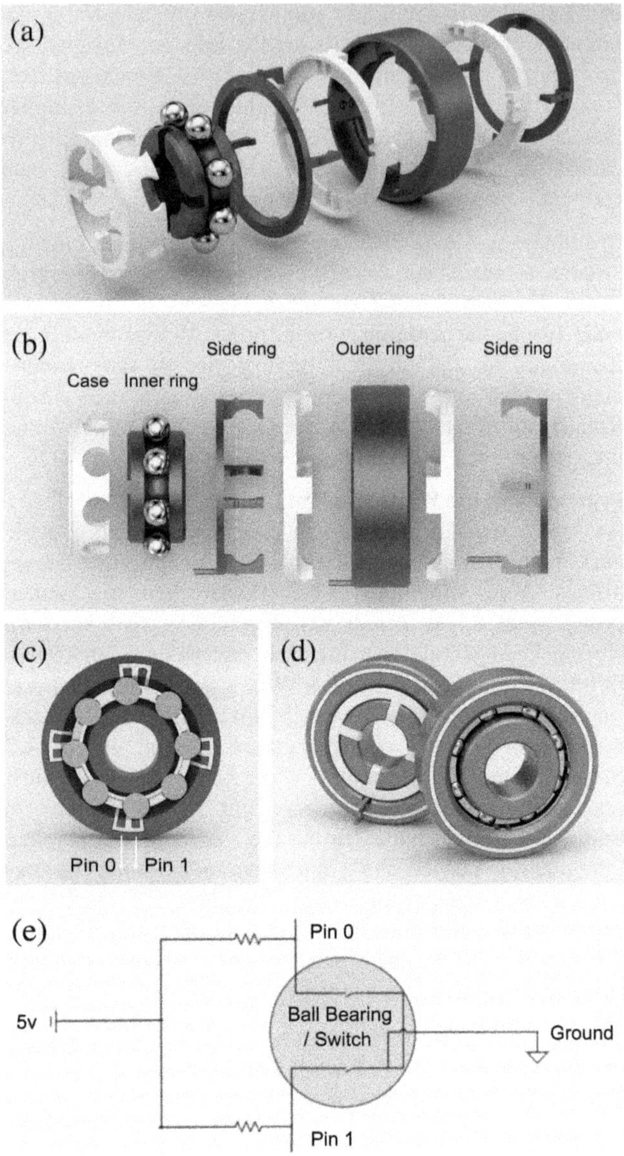

Figure 4. (a-d) The design of the 3D printed switch ball bearing using bronze, nylon, and steel balls. (e) The analog circuit design. Rendered in VRay.

connected to an analog pin on the microcontroller. During the rotation of the ball bearing, contact with the outer ring may be made by either pin (or both simultaneously). When the outer ring makes contact, the current flows to ground through a resistor, bringing the analog pin from 5V to ground. To best evaluate the performance of our ball bearing, we use analog data polling to monitor the voltage on the pins. However, digital polling may be preferred for some practical applications.

In the firmware, the angle counter is set to 0 on the ball upon initiation. The firmware samples the analog pins periodically and detects the contact between the side and the outer ring. We use a sequence of input samples to determine the rotation angle and angular speed. We use

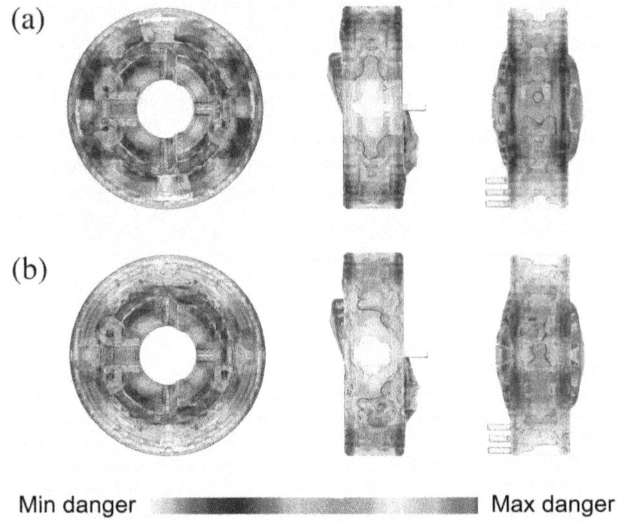

Figure 5. FEM simulation of torque (500KNm) applied to the inner ring, aligned with the ball bearing rotation plane, tested on our ball bearing switch design (a) and compared to a standard design (b). Colors represent risk (danger) to structural integrity.

$(P_i^{\{H,L\}},T)$ to describe the state of pin $i \in [0,1]$ at time T, when $\{H,L\}$ represent High/Low. For example, (P_0^H,T) means Pin 0 is High at time T, and the notation $<(P_0^{\{H,L\}},T),(P_1^{\{H,L\}},T)>$ describes the state of both pins at a given time T, thus describing the whole system. Using this notation, we can describe clockwise rotation with the following series (by switching the states of the two pins, we describe counterclockwise rotation):

contact with pin 0	**contact with both pins**	**contact with pin 1**
$<(P_0^L,t),(P_1^H,t)>$	$<(P_0^L,t+1),(P_1^L,t+1)>$	$<(P_0^H,t+2),(P_1^L,t+2)>$

The firmware running on the Arduino polls the state of the pins and attempts to find a series as described above. Arduino's analog resolution is 1024, with the values [0:1024] representing voltage values of 0-5V. For our purposes, anything in the lower half of the resolution ([0:512] will be taken as low, and the rest of the values will be high. The program samples the inputs once every 5ms and averages the reading from the last 10 samples, in order to reduce noise. Each instance of the described series indicates 1/4 turn. We set the orientation such that clockwise rotation is counted as (+1), and counterclockwise as (-1). The resulting sum is the number of 1/4 turns made by the ball bearing, which is the data output to the serial port. Grasshopper uses this output to rotate the ball bearing model and display the angle of rotation.

Ball Bearing Performance

FEM simulation is used to evaluate the new design. We simulate a torque on the inner ring, aligned with the ball bearing rotation plane. In Fig. 5 we present the results of two designs: the first is our ball bearing switch, and the second is a similar, more traditional, design with a unified outer ring, rather than separate side and outer rings.

The two simulations have similar results: i.e., the new design does not introduce a significant risk caused by static torque. Nevertheless, manual operation of the ball suggests a friction problem, as the rotation of the inner part is not smooth. This is a direct result of the lower accuracy of the 3D printed process compared to the professional standards of ball bearings, and can be improved by accurate post-machining.

For the electrical output, we note a tradeoff of reliability versus stability. As the angular speed increases, a higher sampling frequency is required to catch the voltage transitions. However, the greater sampling rate introduces an increasing amount of noise, which can be reduced with better surface contact, as noted in *Design Process and Constraints*. Fig. 6 shows the voltage output for both pins for different speeds of rotation over a few seconds and a complete turn, with a sampling rate of 13.333 Hz.

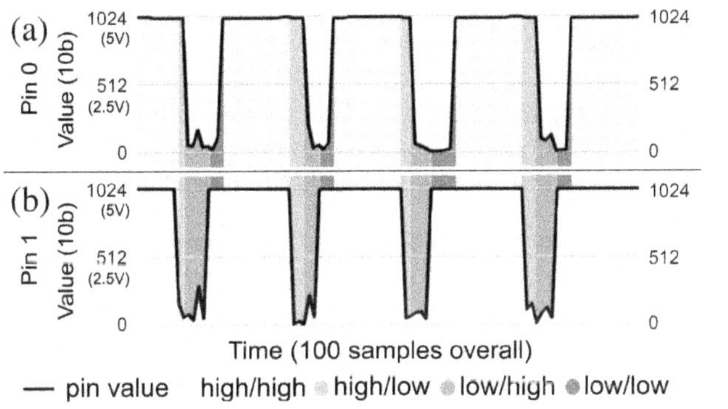

Figure 6. Voltage outputs measured by two Arduino pins (a-b), over 100 samples taken with a 75ms sampling interval. The gray key represents logic state.

Machine Element (2): A Voltage Divider Gear

A gear is a set of toothed elements, either wheels or linear bars that work together to transfer one type of driving force to another. While the applications for gears are innumerable, here we present a simple system with a wheel and a linear gear that transfers rotation to linear motion. We revise a traditional linear gear (the *track*, 67 x 8.5 x 11.9 mm) by separating it into four alternating-tooth systems, connected together to a single housing using NyTek™ 1200 CF (nylon 12 with carbon) SLS. The main industrial use of NyTek™ 1200 CF is to improve the thermal performance of nylon 12 as a common SLS material. However, the conductivity of the carbon also makes it a good resistor [1], allowing us to implement a voltage divider between the four alternating-tooth systems.

In essence, the gear moving on the track functions as a potentiometer—by changing the resistance of the circuit as it moves on the track, it also changes the voltage on the wheel. The track consists of repeated sequences of three resistors connected in series. This design creates voltage dividers on the track, with a different voltage value for every position (see Fig 7). Since the shape of our resistor is complex and the current flows along many paths, it is hard to calculate the resistance numerically. Therefore, the resistance and voltage were determined empirically from measurements. Because the resistance values vary between sequences, the expected voltage levels vary as well. As the variance is bounded by 0.25V, we associate ranges of that size to each position.

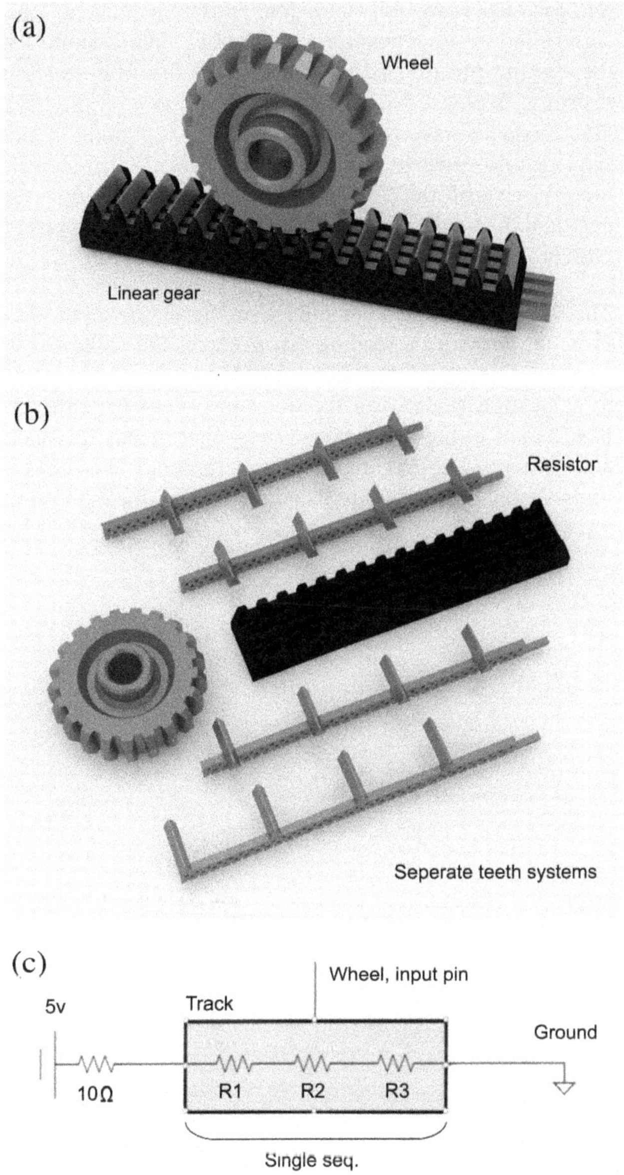

Figure 7. (a-b) The design of the 3D printed voltage divider gear (c), using the conductivity/resistance of the nylon-carbon SLS enclosure. Rendered in VRay.

The wheel itself is connected to an analog pin on the Arduino board, which reads the outgoing voltage from the circuit. The firmware routinely samples the voltage at the input pin to determine the position of the wheel on the track as it rests between two of the teeth. Since the track provides different resistance values, the level of voltage on the input pin readings can fall into four different ranges, each corresponding to a position on the track. We assume that the starting position of the wheel is at the first series of resistors. Between every fourth and fifth tooth on the track, the resistance reverts from 5V to 0V, beginning a new sequence. In order to prevent the gear wheel from shorting the 5V pin of the Arduino when moving through this position, a small resistor (10Ohm) buffers between the Arduino's ground pin and its 5V pin.

The firmware samples the voltage on the analog input every 2ms, and provides a reading that averages the values of the previous five samples. The value of the reading is translated to a location (index) on the track by a lookup table, and then output to the serial port. Grasshopper reads this value and converts it to angle and distance in order to rotate and translate the gear model to its corresponding location on the track model.

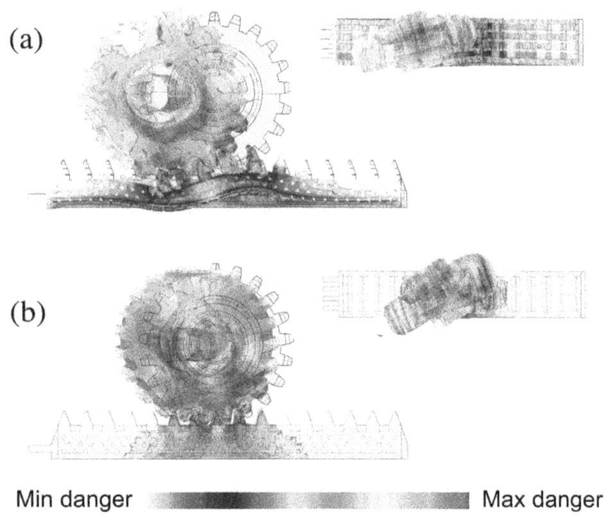

Figure 8. FEM simulation of torque (100KNm) applied to the gear wheel, aligned with the rotation plane, tested on our design (a) and compared to a standard design (b). Colors represent risk (danger) to structural integrity.

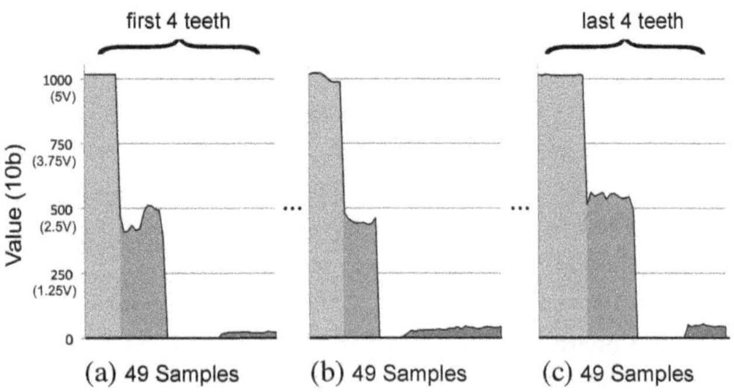

Figure 9. Voltage measurements of the gear wheel transitioning between the teeth on the track, taken from three different sets of teeth.

Gear Performance

As with the ball bearing, an FEM simulation (Fig. 8) supplies initial structural analysis of the gear performance, simulating torque applied to the wheel. Here, the new design fails significantly more often than the traditional design, which has a unified linear gear instead of split teeth. In extreme conditions, the wheel of the traditional design bends a little, while our modified linear gear deforms significantly due to the weak connection of each tooth to its base. This effect can be reduced by using wider teeth that are more strongly connected to their bases and/or by using a side support.

When the wheel is held steady between two teeth on the track, the sampled voltage varies by approximately 0.025V, (at 50HZ). Therefore, a narrow average (only a few samples before and after) is enough for a reliable estimation of the gear's position, unlike the results from the ball bearing. This has a direct effect on the sensors' response time. The smaller the sampling intervals and number of samples for which it averages the values, the more sensitive it is to rapid changes.

As the resistance values are not identical between the resistor sequences, the voltage readings obtained are not identical either. Since the firmware is unaware of the existence of sequences, this necessitates a wider window of accepted values that can be mapped to each position. The size of the windows is different for each position. Fig. 9 shows the voltage values distribution for the different positions.

Machine Element (3): A Variable Capacitor Hinge

A hinge allows an angle of rotation between two elements, and usually consists of a circular bearing mechanism between two joints. It can connect many different elements and come in a wide variety of shapes and sizes. We present a variable capacitor hinge that relies on the device's circular bearing (using 45.6mm from the hinge's total length of 65mm), where one rounded conductive surface (4.2mm radius) moves around a second conductive rounded surface (4.95mm radius). As these surfaces move, their overlapping areas (the capacitor's terminals) change, thus changing the potential capacitance between them (see Fig. 10). By measuring the device's capacitance, we can determine the angle of the hinge.

Capacitance normally depends on the dimensions and design of the device's terminals, the distance between them, and the dielectric constant of an insulator. Like the rest of the printed devices in this paper, we used bronze printing for the conductive parts of the hinge. For the insulator, we chose NyTek™ 1200 GF SLS (nylon 12 and glass). This material has a dielectric constant of 6.3 (where nylon 12 has only around 3 [23]), due to the glass particles. This significantly improved the capacitance of our hinge, and thus its angular resolution.

The capacitance of our hinge ranges from 5pF to 22pF. To get a reliable measurement for these values, we took advantage of the Arduino's inner capacitance. The Arduino's analog pin acts as a second capacitor with a known value. For the Arduino UNO boards we use, this value is approximately 30pF [20]. Another capacitor is connected in series to the capacitor under test. The inner capacitor may be charged or discharged by changing the output to high or low, respectively. As both capacitors are connected in series, raising the pin to 5V causes current to flow through both. Once the voltage between them settles close to its final value (approximately 30ns), it can be sampled and used to determine the capacitance of the unknown capacitor. In stable state $C_1 = V_{out}C_2/(V_{in}-V_{out})$ where C_2=23pF, V_{in}=5V and C_1 is our unknown capacitor.

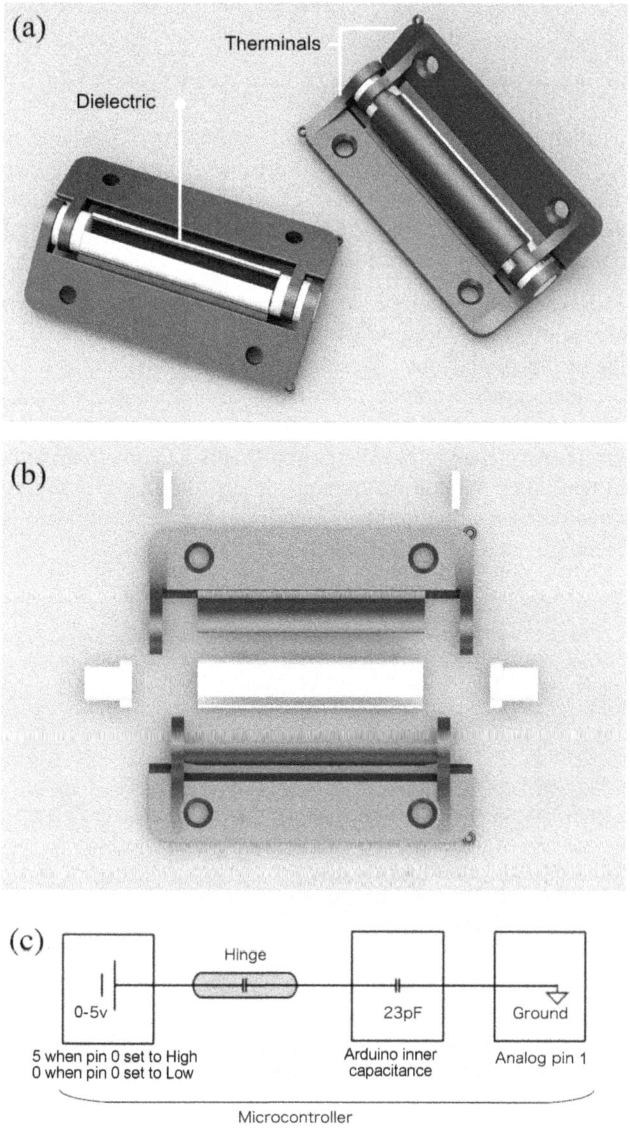

Figure 10. (a-b) The design of the 3D-printed varying capacitance hinge and its analog circuit (c), using the improved dialectic constant of a nylon-glass SLS insulator cylinder. Rendered in VRay.

The firmware charges the capacitors by setting the output pin to high. It sets the input pin to input mode and samples the voltage between the two capacitors. The capacitance is deduced from the sample using the equation described above. The angle of the hinge is then derived from the capacitance with a third-degree polynomial, obtained using Matlab's *polyfit* on 20 capacitance samples from one cycle of opening the hinge from 0 to 180 degrees.

For angle A and capacitance c the relation is given by $A(c) = -0.0189c^3+0.7265c^2-14.5779c+160.3188$. After calculating the angle, the firmware sets the output pin to low, and the input pin to output mode in order to discharge the capacitors before the next measurement cycle, and waits 300ms for the system to stabilize. The wait time, greater than needed to discharge, is a safety measure to avoid starting the cycle with a charged capacitor, which could damage the microcontroller.

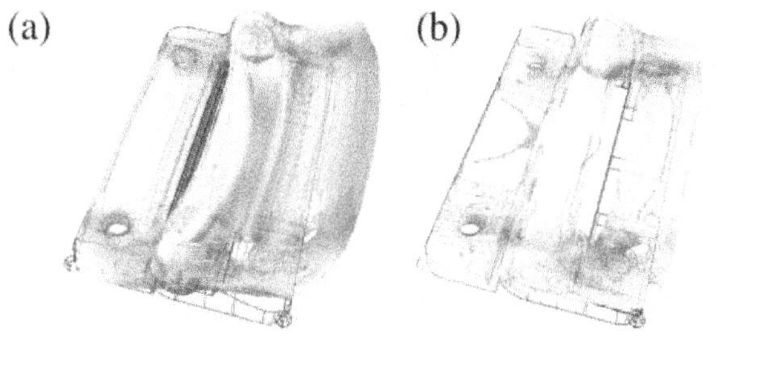

Figure 11. FEM simulation of force applied to the hinge (10KN, pushing apart its two terminals), tested on our design (a) and compared to a standard design (b). Colors represent risk (danger) to structural integrity.

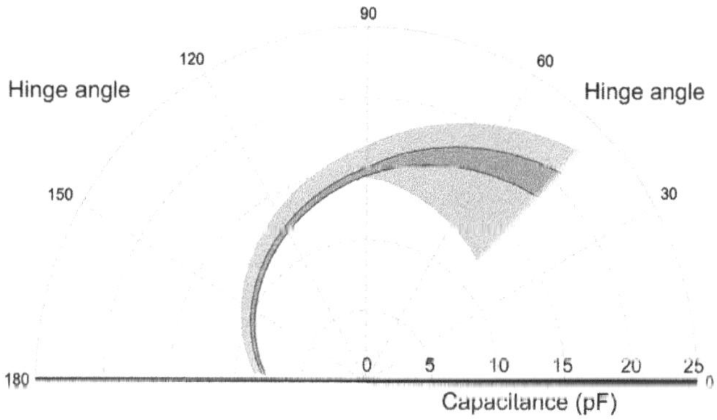

Figure 12. Capacitance values of the hinge measured by the Arduino as a function of the hinge's opening angle. The continuous values were (linearly) interpolated from three data points (45, 90 and 180 degrees). The dark color represents the mean and standard deviation around them, where most of the data found.

Hinge Performance

Because a significant percentage of the hinge's bearing is used for the variable capacitor (instead of operating as a close reinforced rotating axis), it weakens the structural performance of the device, as seen in the FEM simulation (Fig. 11). The tradeoff between the strength and capacitance of the device is obvious. Future development of AM materials with a higher dielectric constant will enable major improvements, allowing a reduction in the terminals' length.

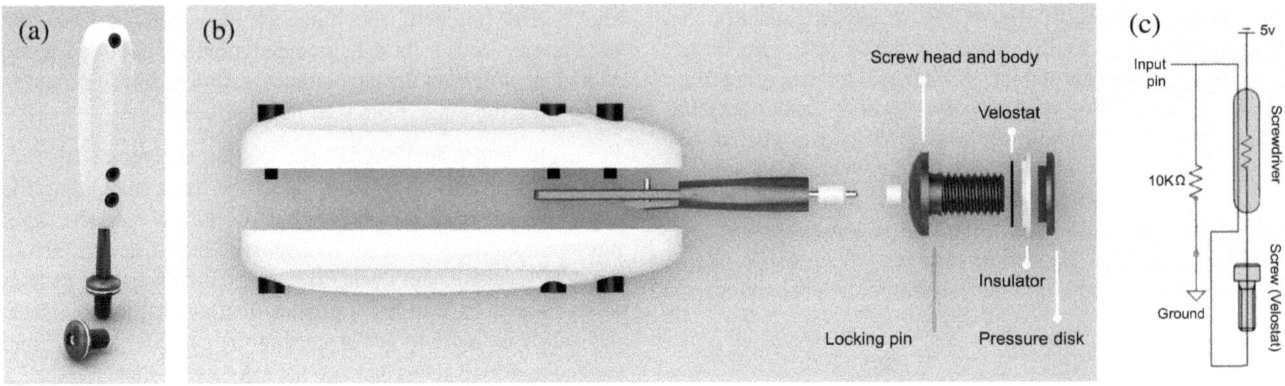

Figure 13. (a-b) The design of the 3D-printed Velostat pressure-sensing screw and its screwdriver and analog circuit (c). Rendered in VRay.

The capacitance measurement obtained from the hinge while it holds at a steady angle fluctuates by approximately 1pF. The relation of capacitance to angle is not linear. Rather, as the angle decreases, the change in capacitance becomes less significant. Fig.12 contains shows the samples taken over 15 seconds at 45, 90, and 180 degrees.

Machine Element (4): A Velostat Screw

Many applications require the stress applied by or on a screw to be precisely tuned. However, the relevant information necessary to make these adjustments is not always available. Unlike our earlier devices, here we chose to rely on an existing sensing material and embed it in our design. Velostat is a thin (0.1mm) pressure-sensitive conductive material: squeezing it will reduce the resistance [25]. We designed a 3D-printed screw (see Fig. 13) with a special disk isolated from the main body of the screw, located between the screwhead and the base surface (the radius of the screwhead being 7.9mm). Three layers of Velostat sheets were placed between this ring and the screwhead. When the screw is driven into a surface, it changes its resistance due to pressure applied to the ring. A special 3D-printed screwdriver can read this pressure while driving the screw (see. Fig 14).

Since the screw changes its resistance as pressure is applied, the best way to deduce its resistance at a given time is by using a simple voltage divider circuit. To measure its value, we connect the screw in series to a 5KOhm resistor (using the special screwdriver) and supply it with an incoming voltage of 5V. For the unknown resistor R_1, a resistor with a known value R_2=5K, input voltage V_{in}=5V, and the sampled voltage V_{out}, we can easily find $R_1 = R_2(V_{in}/V_{out}-1)^{-1}$. In a similar vein with the previous components, the firmware samples the V_{out} every 100ms and averages the result with the adjacent samples, after which it calculates the resistance with the given formula. A simple Grasshopper program displays a visualization of the change in the screw's location, based on the assumption that a rise in pressure indicates change in position.

Screw Performance

Compared to traditional screw design, the additional ring we place underneath the screwhead does not significantly weaken the screw's structure. Only when the screwhead is subjected to an extreme (and unrealistic) pressure can we detect some differences in the FEM simulation between our design and a traditional (unified) one (see Fig. 15). We do not consider this a significant concern.

The resulting sensor is very sensitive. A slight change in pressure on the screw is enough to change its resistance in the realm of KOhms. Therefore, the electrical output must be toned down to achieve a workable data set. Fig. 16 shows the voltage obtained for various levels of pressure on the screw. Any change in voltage represents KOhms of change in resistance. As the evaluation reveals, the screw is highly sensitive to a value range of 125-750g. Further evaluation is recommended for higher values.

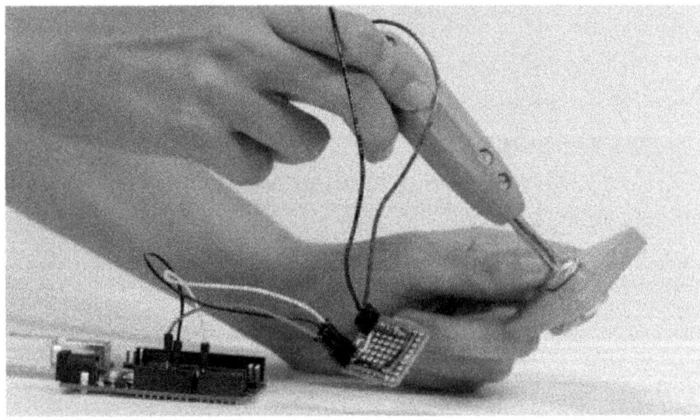

Figure 14. Operation scenario of the Velostat screw and the dedicated screwdriver, which is designed to read the information from the screw while driving it.

Design Process and Constraints

Steel-Sense is a hybrid design paradigm relying on traditional design and fabrication tools. We envision an integration of our technical paradigm within an existing design-flow, rather than suggesting a new process. Thus, the design process, limitations and constraints of Steel-Sense are equal to those of the selected 3D printing technology. The scale and resolution of the hybrid elements are bounded only by the fabrication process. For example, as the resolution of the ball bearing is determined by the number of pins embedded in the outer ring, the designer can decide to add more pins if space allows.

Alternatively, a shorter distance between the hinge terminals can improve its capacitance. However, this distance is a factor of the 3D-printed dielectric, and with current SLS technologies, wall thickness cannot be thinner than 0.8mm.

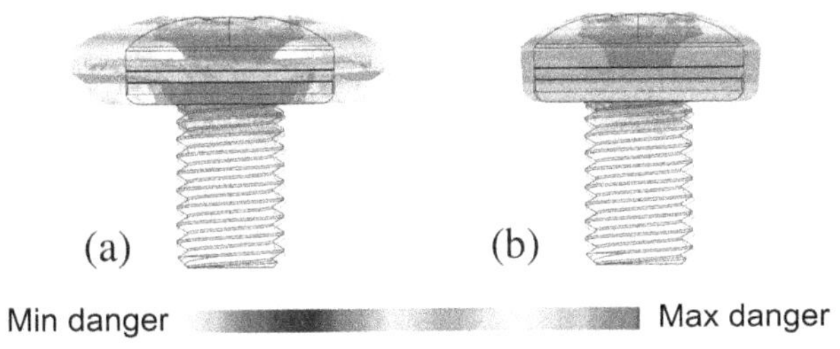

Figure 15. FEM simulation of torque applied to the screw (500KNm), in the direction of the screwing axis, tested on our design (a) and compared to a standard design (b). Colors represent risk (danger) to structural integrity.

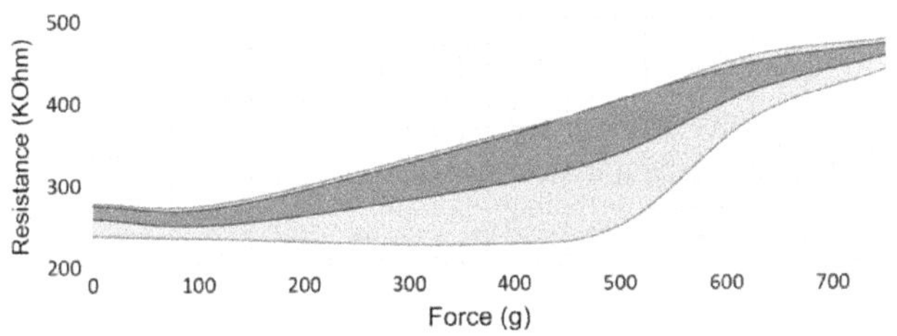

Figure 16. Voltage values of the screw measured by the Arduino as a function of applied force (measured at 0, 125, 375, 500, 625 & 750 g). The plot is a spline interpolation. The dark color represents the mean with the standard deviation around it, where most of the data found.

Generally speaking, the 3D printing process falls short compared to the accuracy of traditional machining, and our AM elements lack the operational smoothness of common machine elements. Until the accuracy of AM improves, this can be solved by post-machining the elements via milling, lathing, drilling, etc., as is already done for high-end DMLS parts. Additionally, while using our bare hands to work with the printed elements, we noted unstable electronic behavior caused by the conductivity of our skin affecting the sensors. For future real-world applications, we recommend that such hybrid elements be insulated.

IMPLICATIONS FOR THE DESIGN OF INPUT DEVICES

Today, digital fabrication technologies contribute to a growing portfolio of new designs, interactions and technical solutions. Many new interactive scenarios require compact sensing solutions to control and improved performance. Additionally, many applications need small mechanical and sensorial solutions to improve their designs and lower their cost while merging the physical with the virtual. Here, we review potential applications for Steel-Sense, considering the different principles we presented and different production costs.

Professional, high-end hybrid solutions Considering the high production costs of DMLS, we believe the main professional application for Steel-Sense is in custom, one-off solutions that require unique designs. As the main applications of DMLS technologies are already in producing unique one-offs for special needs [15], we hope our work will inspire designers and engineers to reconsider the designs of these and other hybrid-printed parts, introducing entirely new possibilities for designing interactive machines.

For example, the ball bearing demonstrates a seamless integration principle: without affecting the mechanical properties of the bearing structure, we augment the element with new sensorial capabilities. Such a design could be ideal for high-end, professional mountain or road bicycles. As these bicycles use expensive fabrication technologies and composite materials to gain improved performance, the high cost of DMLS may not be a significant barrier for this application. A titanium DMLS ball bearing could sense wheel movement very accurately, without the need to attach external sensing devices that can add weight, impact the aerodynamic design of the bicycles, and be easily damaged if not fully enclosed. Moreover, such a ball bearing could be custom designed to fit unique requests, integrating it as part of a wider in-wheel system. By tracking both wheels in this way, riders, coaches, and designers could collect valuable information and analyze it to improve performance.

3D-printed custom mechatronics Steel-Sense contributes a new design principle, showing how standard 3D printing materials can be used to implement capacitors and resistors: a 3D-printed nylon-carbon composite can function as a resistor, and a nylon-glass composite as a dialectic. Together with 3D-printed conductors and insulators, these enable the design of complicated forms and structures that can implement capacitive sensors, voltage dividers, varying resistors and capacitors, and more. While we presented a simple gear-voltage divider that can ease the integration of sensing within space-tight 3D-printed gears, we believe the potential here is much wider. Thus, we will explore it farther in our future work. One example is in developing fully interactive, 3D-printed mechatronics, or 3D-printed custom transmitter-receiver devices. Using one of the less expensive options for 3D printing metals would keep costs low, making these applications relevant to many DIY projects.

The shift from virtual to physical in HCI encouraged researchers to investigate different designs and scenarios for physical interactive prototypes [8], many of them made using AM [19]. Haptic input devices [5] harness physical degrees of freedom for sensing, with a virtual model that reacts to physical action. As these haptic devices contain bearings and hinges, this is a good use case for considering various capacitor solutions. Moreover, while we have presented a varying capacitor hinge, a similar concept can be applied to a telescopic arm, using one of the cheaper metal 3D printing options. Together, they would enable easy DIY design and rapid prototyping of custom haptic

Figure 17. A futuristic concept design for a two-worlds ((a) physical, (b) virtual) model of a 3D-printed tractor toy which has all of our machine element designs embedded as integral parts: ball-bearings in the front wheels to measure distance; a voltage divider gear to detect the angle of the steering wheel; a variable capacitor hinge to report whether the engine doors are open, and by how much; and a screw that can apply pressure to the back wheels (and report on it) to add friction and slow them down. Both figures were rendered in VRay.

scanners, relying on angular and linear degrees of freedom, as an example of 3D printed mechatronics.

Mass-production of machine elements While this paper focuses on the affordances of 3D printing, the implications of Steel-Sense go beyond the AM realm. A direct example relies on our pressure sensor screw. While a screw is a simple element, many people do not use it properly. We envision our 3D-printed design evolving into a mass-produced smart screw product, rather than a solely custom design solution. For example, if a user drives a screw too hard, it may crack wooden surfaces; in a cement plaster wall, over-screwing can destroy the threads of the screw holes. While a simple application inside a smart screwdriver can solve these problems, we believe such a solution may also lead to broader applications. A screw element that can report on its own pressure through a screwdriver agent invites us to conceptualize new opportunities. Just as recent developments in computer graphics seek ways to assist in design, construction and assembly of furniture [2, 16], intelligent construction elements such as screws can virtually mirror the building process and supply real-time instructions and alarms in potentially dangerous situations.

Integrated System As an example of future integrated implications for Steel-Sense, Fig. 17 shows a concept design for a 3D-printed tractor toy that has all of our machine elements designs embedded as integral parts of the tractor. A virtual model mirrors the physical one, relying on the data received from the sensors. As interactive compact physical/virtual toys are already common [24], we believe applications like this one may receive great benefits from the Steel-Sense hybrid design paradigm. Using one of the cheaper metal 3D printed options mentioned earlier, DIY toys can easily be tracked and control virtual scripts, sharing their physical performance and recording it for future use, learning, and interactive scenarios.

CONCLUSIONS

This paper presents Steel-Sense, a new approach to augmenting machine elements with sensing capabilities using AM. While machine elements act in the physical domain, and sensors are used to report on the virtual one, our hybrid elements suggest a new integrated territory. We contribute a hybrid design paradigm, illustrated by 3D-printed metal parts to facilitate both sensors and machine elements in a single component. We present four design primitives, implementing (1) an electronic switch, (2) a voltage divider, (3) a variable capacitor, and (4) an existing sensing material (Velostat) embedded inside 3D-printed machine elements. In addition, we build simple analog/digital systems, mirroring the physical devices and their performance in the virtual (PC) environment. Our evaluations show that while there are a few technical limitations that can be improved, the designs are reliable and stable, and fulfill our initial motivation.

We see the potential of Steel-Sense to contribute wise, compact, customable and interactive mechatronics to HCI. We envision this new family of hybrid elements impacting the traditional design of interactive system, as they offer a new interactive vocabulary. Moreover, Steel-Sense presents a new paradigm of interactive units equipped to *perform* while *measuring*. To articulate the potential of these hybrid units for HCI and design, we hope to farther develop a theoretical framework for this new design space and describe how it interacts with traditional design paradigms.

ACKNOWLEDGMENTS

We deeply appreciate all the friends and colleagues who supported and assisted us in completing this work: N.W. Gong, P. Schmitt, R. Fattal, G. Ron, J. A. Paradiso, M. Feldmeier, M. Mizrahi, S, Olberding and C. L. Evers.

REFERENCES

1. Athreya, S. R., Kalaitzidou, K., Das, S. 2010. Processing and characterization of a carbon black-filled electrically conductive Nylon-12 nanocomposite produced by selective laser sintering. Materials Science and Engineering: A, 527, Issues 10–11, 25 April 2010. doi:10.1016/j.msea.2009.12.028

2. Fu, C.W., Song, P., Yan, X., Yang, L.W., Jayaraman, P.K., and Cohen-Or, D. 2015. Computational interlocking furniture assembly. ACM Trans. Graph. 34, 4, Article 91 (July 2015), 11 pages. DOI=http://dx.doi.org/10.1145/2766892

3. Gershenfeld, N. 2007. Fab: The Coming Revolution on Your Desktop--from Personal Computers to Personal Fabrication. Basic Books (February 6, 2007).

4. Gong, N.-W., Steimle, J., Olberding, S., Hodges, S., Gillian, N., Kawahara, Y., and Paradiso, J. A. 2014. PrintSense: a versatile sensing technique to support multimodal flexible surface interaction. In Proceedings of the SIGCHI Conference on Human Factors in Computing Systems (CHI '14). ACM, New York, NY, USA, 1407-1410. DOI=http://dx.doi.org/10.1145/2556288.2557173

5. Geomagic® Haptic Devices website. 2015. Retrieved at September 25, 2015 from http://www.geomagic.com/en/products-landing-pages/haptic

6. Gong, N.-W., Zoran, A. and Paradiso, J. A. 2013. Inkjet-printed conductive patterns for physical manipulation of audio signals. In Proceedings of the adjunct publication of the 26th annual ACM symposium on User interface software and technology (UIST '13 Adjunct). ACM, New York, NY, USA, 13-14. DOI=http://dx.doi.org/10.1145/2508468.2514932.

7. Innovative Products - SENSOR BEARINGS FOR INDUSTRIAL MACHINERY. NSK Europe website. Retrieved December 26, 2015, from http://www.nskeurope.com/cps/rde/xchg/eu_en/hs.xsl/innovative-sensor-bearings-for-industrial-machinery.html

8. Ishii, H., Leithinger, D., Follmer, S., Zoran, A., Schoessler, P., and Counts, J. 2015. TRANSFORM: Embodiment of "Radical Atoms" at Milano Design Week. In Proceedings of the 33rd Annual ACM Conference Extended Abstracts on Human Factors in Computing Systems (CHI EA '15). ACM, New York, NY, USA, 687-694. DOI=http://dx.doi.org/10.1145/2702613.2702969

9. Kawahara, Y., Hodges, S., Gong, N.-W., Olberding, S. and Steimle, J. 2014. Building Functional Pervasive Computing Prototypes using Conductive Inkjet Printing. In IEEE Pervasive Computing, (Volume:13 , Issue: 3), July-Sept. 2014. DOI=http://doi.ieeecomputersociety.org/10.1109/MPRV.2014.41

10. Schmitt, P. 2011. Original Machines: Developing Tools and Methods for Object-Oriented Mechatronics. PhD dissertation, Massachusetts Institute of Technology. Dept. of Architecture. Program in Media Arts and Sciences.

11. Shapeways website - 3D Printing Service and Marketplace. (n.d.). Retrieved August 23, 2015, from http://www.shapeways.com/materials/wax

12. Shilkrot, R., Maes, P., Paradiso, J. A., and Zoran, A. 2015. Augmented Airbrush for Computer Aided Painting (CAP). ACM Trans. Graph. 34, 2, Article 19 (March 2015). DOI=http://dx.doi.org/10.1145/2699649

13. Stratasys Direct Manufacturing website - 3D PRINTING & MANUFACTURING. (n.d.). Retrieved August 23, 2015, from https://www.stratasysdirect.com/materials/direct-metal-laser-sintering/

14. Steimle, J. 2015. Printed electronics for human-computer interaction. In ACM Interactions 22, 3 (April 2015), 72-75. DOI=http://dx.doi.org/10.1145/2754304

15. Systems and Solutions for Metal Manufacturing. EOS website. Retrieved August 23, 2015, from http://www.eos.info/systems_solutions/metal

16. The World's First 3D Electronics Printer. Voxel8 website. Retrieved August 23, 2015, from http://www.voxel8.co/

17. Li, H., Hu, R., Alhashim, I., and Zhang, H. 2015. Foldabilizing furniture. ACM Trans. Graph. 34, 4, Article 90 (July 2015), 12 pages. DOI=http://dx.doi.org/10.1145/2766912

18. Motor encoder units. SKF website. Retrieved December 26, 2015, from http://www.skf.com/us/products/bearings-units-housings/engineered-products/sensor-bearing-units/motor-encoder-units/index.html?switch=y

19. Nakagaki, K., Inamura, C., Totaro, P., Shihipar, T., Akikyama, C., Shuang, Y., and Ishii. H. 2015. Linked-Stick: Conveying a Physical Experience using a Shape-Shifting Stick. In Proceedings of the 33rd Annual ACM Conference Extended Abstracts on Human Factors in Computing Systems (CHI EA '15). ACM, New York, NY, USA,1609-1614. DOI=http://dx.doi.org/10.1145/2702613.2732712

20. Capacitance measurement with the Arduino Uno. Nethercott website . Retrieved August 24, 2015, from http://wordpress.codewrite.co.uk/pic/2014/01/21/cap-meter-with-arduino-uno/

21. Niiyama, R., Sun, X., Yao, L., Ishii, H., Rus, D., and Kim, S. 2015. Sticky Actuator: Free-Form Planar Actuators for Animated Objects. International Conference on Tangible, Embedded, and Embodied Interaction (TEI'15), ACM, New York, NY, USA, 77-84. DOI=http://dx.doi.org/10.1145/2677199.2680600
22. Norton, R. L. 2010. Machine Design, (4th Edition), Prentice-Hall.
23. Material Properties of SLS Thermoplastics. JR Prototypes website. Retrieved August 23, 2015, from http://www.jrprototypes.com/sls-prototypes/sls-material-properties.htm
24. Patkar, M. (2013, September 10). 8 Cool Smartphone-Controlled Toys You Secretly Desire! Retrieved August 23, 2015, from http://www.makeuseof.com/tag/8-cool-smartphone-controlled-toys-you-secretly-desire
25. PRESSURE-SENSITIVE CONDUCTIVE SHEET (VELOSTAT/LINQSTAT). (n.d.). Retrieved August 23, 2015, from https://www.adafruit.com/products/1361
26. Yao, L., Niiyama, R., Ou, J., Follmer, S., Silva, C. D., and Ishii, .. 2013. PneUI: pneumatically actuated soft composite materials for shape changing interfaces. In Proceedings of the 26th annual ACM symposium on User interface software and technology (UIST '13). ACM, New York, NY, USA, 13-22. DOI=http://dx.doi.org/10.1145/2501988.2502037
27. Willis, K., Brockmeyer, E., Hudson, S. and Poupyrev, I. 2012. Printed optics: 3D printing of embedded optical elements for interactive devices. In Proceedings of the 25th annual ACM symposium on User interface software and technology (UIST '12). ACM, New York, NY, USA, 589-598. DOI=http://dx.doi.org/10.1145/2380116.2380190
28. Zoran, A. 2011. "The 3D Printed Flute: Digital Fabrication and Design of Musical Instruments," Journal of New Music Research (JNMR), volume 40, issue 4, December 2011.
29. Zoran, A, Shilkrot, R, and Paradiso, J.A. 2013. Human-computer interaction for hybrid carving. In Proceedings of the 26th annual ACM symposium on User interface software and technology (UIST '13). ACM, New York, NY, USA, 433-440. DOI=http://dx.doi.org/10.1145/2501988.2502023

xPrint: A Modularized Liquid Printer for Smart Materials Deposition

Guanyun Wang[1], Lining Yao[2], Wen Wang[3], Jifei Ou[2], Chin-Yi Cheng[4], Hiroshi Ishii[2]

[1]Zhejiang University
Hangzhou, China
guanyun@zju.edu.cn

[2]MIT Media Lab
Cambridge, USA
{liningy, jifei, ishii}
@media.mit.edu

[3]Chemical Engineering MIT
Cambridge, USA
wwen@mit.edu

[4]Design Computation MIT
Cambridge, USA
chinyich@mit.edu

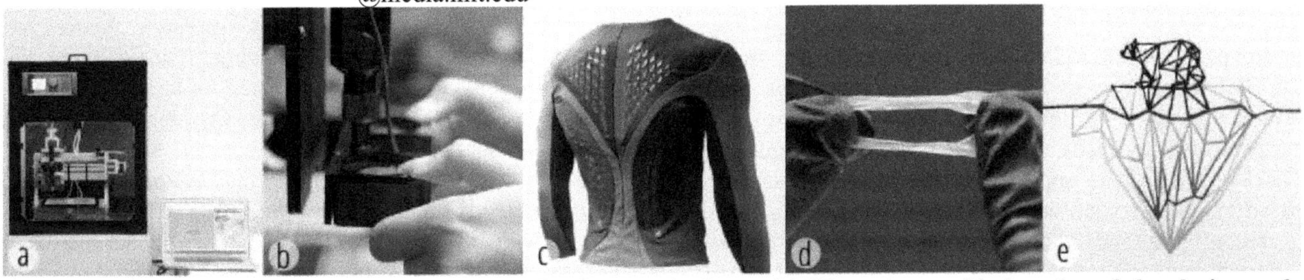

Figure 1: xPrint system. (a) Open hardware and software platform; (b) Magnet assembly based modular design and alignment; (c) Outcome of one user test: a sweat activated transformable garment; (d) Printed pH responsive calcium alginate gel sample; (e) Outcome of one user test: an animated painting on paper.

ABSTRACT

To meet the increasing requirements of HCI researchers who are looking into using liquid-based materials (e.g., hydrogels) to create novel interfaces, we present a design strategy for HCI researchers to build and customize a liquid-based smart material printing platform with off-the-shelf or easy-to-machine parts. For the hardware, we suggest a magnetic assembly–based modular design. These modularized parts can be easily and precisely reconfigured with off-the-shelf or easy-to-machine parts that can meet different processing requirements such as mechanical mixing, chemical reaction, light activation, and solution vaporization. In addition, xPrint supports an open-source, highly customizable software design and simulation platform, which is applicable for simulating and facilitating smart material constructions. Furthermore, compared to inkjet or pneumatic syringe–based printing systems, xPrint has a large range of printable materials from synthesized polymers to natural micro-organism-living cells with a printing resolution from 10μm up to 5mm (droplet size). In this paper, we will introduce the system design in detail and three use cases to demonstrate the material variability and the customizability for users with different demands (e.g., designers, scientific researchers, or artists).

CHI'16, May 07 - 12, 2016, San Jose, CA, USA

ACM 978-1-4503-3362-7/16/05…$15.00
DOI: http://dx.doi.org/10.1145/2858036.2858281

Author Keywords

Liquid deposition modeling printer; 3D printing; Smart material printing; Functional material printing; Responsive material printing; Smart material interface; Physical interface; Shape changing interface.

ACM Classification Keywords

H.5.m. Information interfaces and presentation (e.g., HCI): Miscellaneous

INTRODUCTION

Smart functional materials such as transformable living materials and shape memory polymers are gaining increasing attention from researchers in the fields of science, engineering, and design [4, 27]. In particular, in the human–computer interaction (HCI) community, active materials that could response to external controllable stimuli to create functional and interactive interfaces are emerging as research directions [22]. Meanwhile, there are an increasing number of new responsive liquid-state materials that are used for creating novel input and output devices [13, 30]. However, the toolsets that HCI community could choose from to process liquid-state raw materials are limited. Therefore, it is necessary to design a customized high-precision printing platform that can be used for depositing a variety of liquid materials at a wide range of viscosities that could effectively facilitate the design of interactive objects and promote the use of novel materials in HCI research.

The ideal platform should be able to shorten the time required to create smart material based interfaces, and to fabricate more precise prototypes. However, the ability to integrate multiple materials into one digital fabrication process remains a challenge with commercially available printing platforms. The major problems are unavoidable hardware configuration constraints and non-open sourced firmware [7, 26]. To solve these, the maker community has been exploring pneumatic syringe–based extrusion printing, especially for food printing [23]. In some engineering labs, they have built their own research tools (e.g. 3D bioprinting [17] and 3D-printing for chemical synthesis [28]). However, these sophisticated equipment or open-platform and high-precision liquid solution modeling (LSM) printing systems are not readily available for outsiders. Through this work, we hope to address those challenges and bring LSM-based 2D and 3D printing to the fab table.

In this paper, we present the xPrint system, a clear strategy for HCI researchers to build their own deposition digital printer to process liquid materials with off-the-shelf components and easily machinable parts in a short time. The key part of the approach is the magnetic assembly–based modular design, which makes it extendable and easy to reconfigure and align with high precision to meet different material requirements (e.g., mechanical mixing, chemical reaction, light activation, and solution vaporization). Furthermore, xPrint can process a wide range of printable materials with various viscosities from synthesized polymers to natural micro-organisms with its printing resolution from 10μm to 5mm (droplet size). In addition, we have developed an open-source, highly customizable software and simulation platform to help synchronize the changing of hardware components and the generation of G-codes for different 1D, 2D, and 3D printing path settings. To demonstrate the material variability and customizability for different users, we invited three users (a designer, a scientific researcher, and an artist) to test our system.

RELATED WORK

Bio-printing

Recently, bio-printing has become an emerging technology for constructing and fabricating biomaterials in the field of bioengineering. Most state-of-the-art bio-printing technologies are inkjet- or extrusion-based. Inkjet printers enable precise control over the locations of droplets and thus give users great flexibility. There are numerous research papers detailing the hardware technology [29, 30], demonstrating a step-by-step approach to integrating the inkjet head to a CNC router. Despite great progress in inkjet-based bio-printing, this technique still faces some limitations. One of the main restrictions is the low upper limit for the viscosity of bio-ink. Cell aggregation and sedimentation in the cartridge and clogging of the nozzles are limitations associated with this technique [6].

The method using a pressure- or extrusion-based printing system has been used for quite a long time. Extrusion-based bio-printing is a combination of a fluid-dispensing system that includes a pneumatic or mechanical system with an automated robotic system for extrusion and writing [12, 15]. For example, BioBot [3] is specifically designed for printing biological materials, which overcomes the viscosity limitation and clogging problem in an inkjet system. However, the trade-off is the printing precision and material portfolio, which can only be applied on a limited printing scale with specific materials.

Functional Material Printing Systems

Researchers in the field of additive manufacturing have been developing new instruments and platforms for printing materials beyond static plastic. Jennifer Lewis' group created a deposition method based on a 3D printing system that allows one to create 3D structures with conductive materials [9, 18]. However, their research focuses on material invention and characterization. The software and hardware setup of the printing system is less documented, making it difficult to rebuild such a system for printing other functional materials. More recently, a team at MIT presented a multi-materials printing system that prints liquid conductive and magnetic materials [25]. The system is built with off-the-shelf components and costs relatively little ($7000) compared to high-end multi-material printers. However, the system uses inkjet print heads for deposition, which only allow nanoparticles to pass through. This becomes a major constraint if one needs to print larger size particles such as cells or spores.

Digital Fabrication Tools for Unconventional Materials

Previous research has led to a variety of fabrication processes and tools for smart or unconventional materials. PrintScreen [19] is a versatile platform to fabricate customized flexible interactive screens with thin-film electroluminescence characteristics. ShrinkyCircuits [11] uses an inexpensive pre-stressed polymer film to present a novel compositing prototyping technique that produces circuits in minutes. Protopiper [1] is introduced as a digital bending approach that allows users to sketch room-sized objects at actual scale with plastic tubes. Hudson creates a felting machine [10] with a solid additive manufacturing method to open new possibilities in the creation of interactive objects that are soft and flexible. To compensate existing toolsets and materials portfolios for creating interactive interfaces, we propose the development of a platform that can handle a large pool of novel smart materials in a liquid state.

Open Source Fabrication and Modular Printer

Modularization and open source systems are gaining increased attention in the field of digital fabrication and the maker movement. Peek introduces a method of making a desktop CNC machine with cardboard folding and HDPE snap fit as its supporting structure [21]. All designs being open source allows users to customize the gantry according to their individual needs. Fab@Home [5] is an open-source mass-collaboration developing personal fabrication technology aimed at bringing personal fabrication into homes. Moyer also introduced methods of customizing a digitally controlled dispenser [16]. For scientific research, modular science creates a modular hackable software and hardware system for lab automation to improve reproducibility and the exchange of scientific information

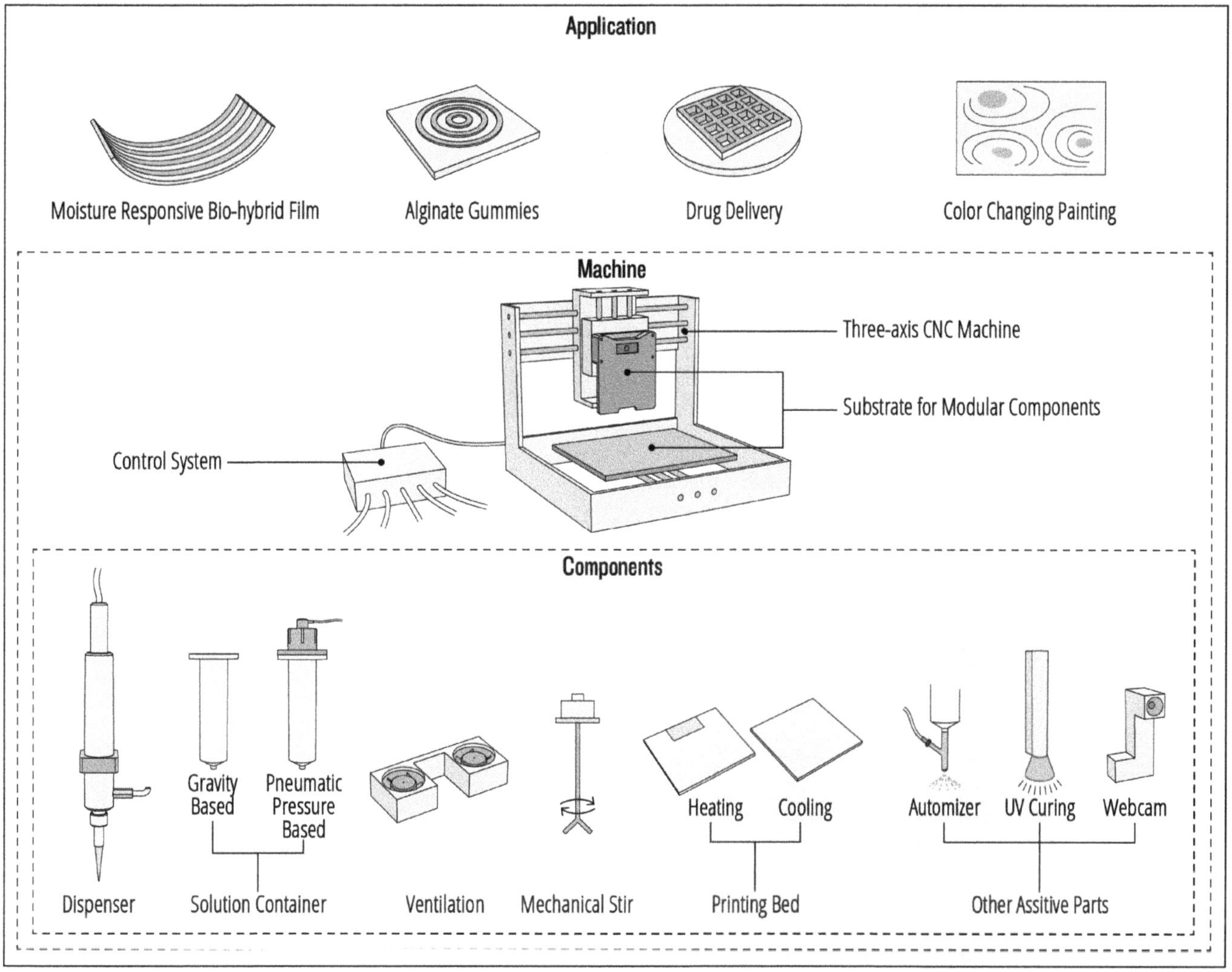

Figure 2: Hardware platform of xPrint: machine based and modular components.

[14]. Inspired by those works, our goal is to create an open source hardware and software platform for depositing liquid-based smart materials.

XPRINT SYSTEM

xPrint contains off-the-shelf hardware components, and a software platform developed on top of open source plugins (Figure 3). xPrint is designed with a few goals in mind: A highly customizable modular design to accommodate different material printing requirements; an easy work flow from geometry design through G-code generation and machine control to material fabrication; a high-precision system that covers printing droplet width from 10μm up to 5mm; good usability for a large user group including designers, artists, and scientific researchers; and safety and hygiene.

Hardware Platform

The hardware system includes a machine base and modular components (Figure 2). It is built with off-the-shelf components and easily machinable parts.

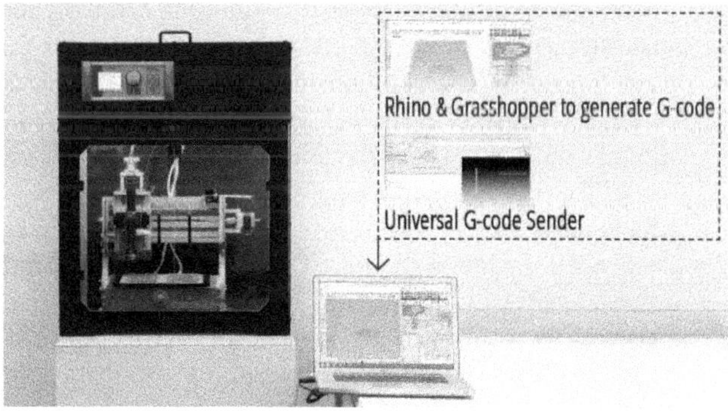

Figure 3: xPrint system: An integrated, customizable hardware and software platform

Machine Base

The machine includes a standard three-axis CNC platform, two mounting substrates for attaching modular components, and a central control system. In our demo system, we use a CNC kit (F8 version) from Zen Toolworks [31]. A higher end CNC platform will help increase the printing resolution. The mounting substrates are used to mount the central dispenser and other configurable modular components. They have embedded magnets at particular locations to hold all the modular components at the same places each time. The Breakout control board supports up to five one-axis stepper motors, five input ports, and five extra output ports to accept signals and send commands to the modular components.

Modular Components

We chose the essential modules based on the tasks required of our printer: Printing liquid solution–based smart material and forming 2D or 3D composite structures. The modularized parts can be reconfigured to meet different material requirements for solidification, such as mechanical mixing, chemical reaction, light activation, and solution vaporization.

All modular components are designed with specific mechanical structures and magnet assemblies for easy plugging/unplugging and configuration. To save space and keep them clean, all components can rest on top of the ceiling of the printer case (Figure 4-1). Figure 4-2 describes the locations of each component, and the corresponding magnet placements. All modules are designed in such a way that the magnets ensure the same exact placement location each time.

- The dispenser is the central component. It is a progressive cavity pump–based dispensing head (EcoPen 300 from ViscoTec-America Inc.) that covers droplet widths from 10μm up to 5mm. The dispenser is controlled by the central control system; customized G-code can turn the dispenser on and off on demand.
- Solution container: There are two types of solution container. Liquid that flows quickly with its own gravity can be loaded into the gravity-based container without a cap; a closed container with controllable pneumatic pressure is used for solutions with higher viscosity.
- Ventilation: Certain solutions only solidify when water or other chemicals evaporate. In this case, a ventilation module with two speed-tunable fans can be placed on top of the printing platform.
- Mechanical stir: Some materials are particles suspended inside a liquid. Those materials are not soluble and may form into sediment. This problem becomes very obvious when it comes to living cells printing [20]. Mechanical stirring is a useful approach to prevent sedimentation.
- Camera: We currently use a webcam to remotely track printing progress; however, more interesting work can be done with a live video stream if computer vision is combined. For example, an object can be detected and set to be the initial location of the printing path.
- UV Curing lamp: A large group of materials can be made UV-curable, the most common of which are resins. Under the scope of smart materials, we explore

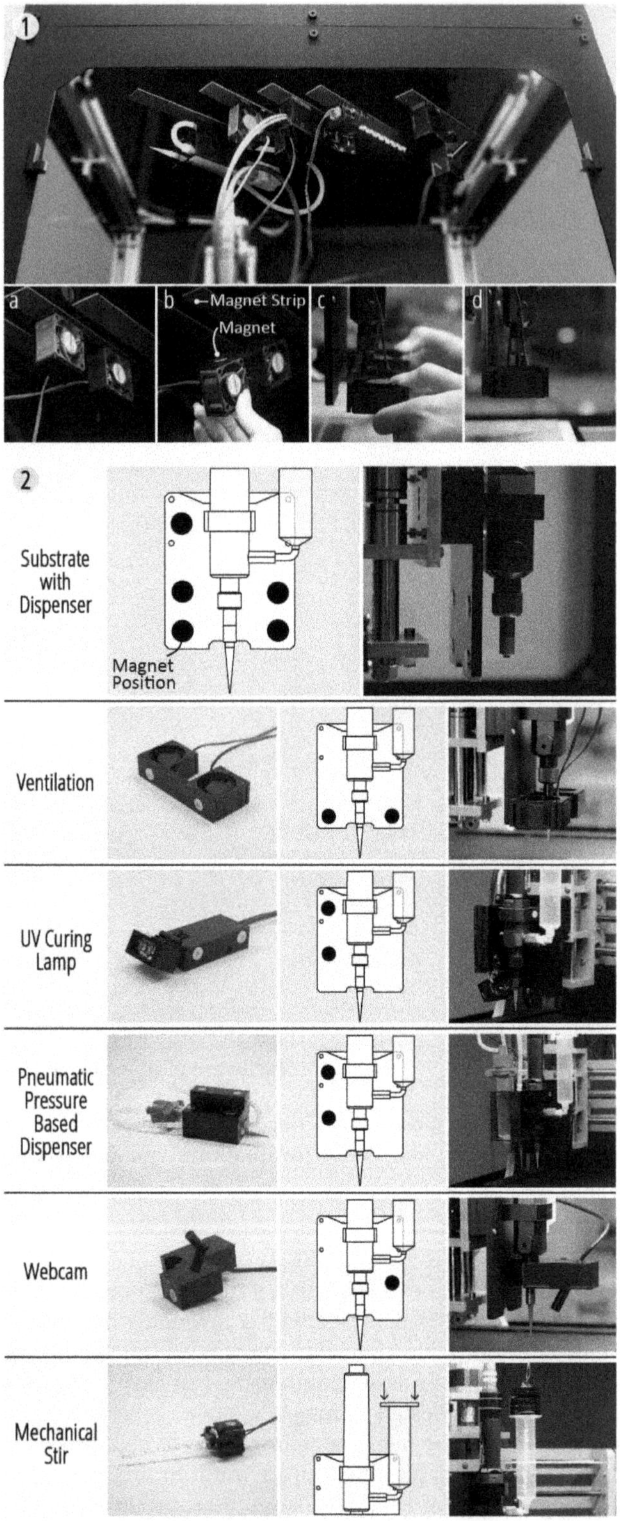

Figure 4: Modular components with magnetic assembly

color-changing resin, and moisture-responsive hydrogel.

- Pneumatic atomizer: Coating is a universal process for both material and chemical research, and industrial layered composite materials. For liquid solutions, we use atomization to coat the surface evenly, or coat the surface with pre-mounted masks.

Software

In a software system, the workflow includes design, simulation, and communication (Figure 5). Since our targeted use cases involve people with different levels of digital design and modeling skills, and different software feature requirements to design different printing paths, we decided our software design strategy as follows: A set of parametric tools based on the most commonly used printing path; customizable with parameter sliders.

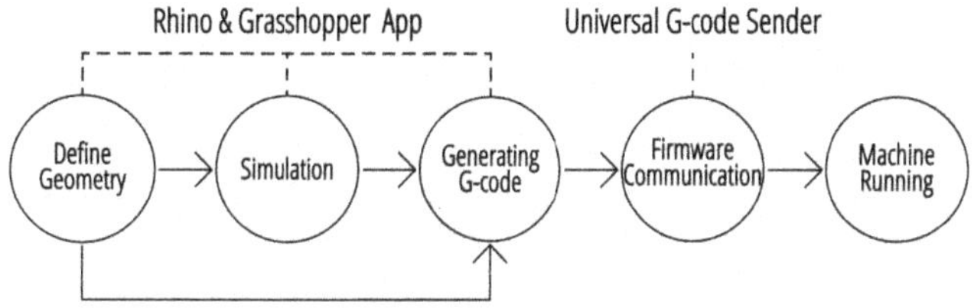

Figure 5: Workflow of the xPrint software platform.

The software platform is built on top of an open source algorithmic modeling platform, Grasshopper [8], which enables both graphic programming and a visual user interface. Thus far, we have the basic toolsets to handle 1D, 2D and 3D structures; more customized variations can be easily developed on top of the current platform.

Since different materials require specific hardware configurations and control settings, we suggest a customized software platform to facilitate the G-code generation process. The customized G-code controls the CNC platforms and some modular components that need synchronization, such as the dispenser and the UV curable light.

- 1D Tool – Offsetting a line path

If the goal is to print one open or closed line, once or multiple times, with a certain width, this is the correct tool to use. Since the print head has maximum line width (~5mm), if the targeted width is larger than 5mm, a more offset line path can be generated with a slider (Figure 6).

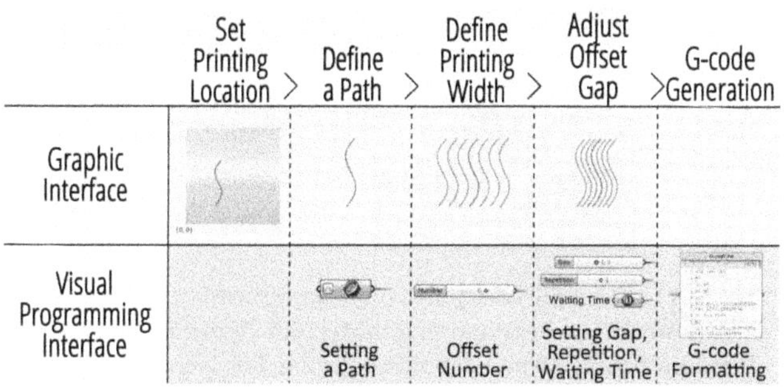

Figure 6: Graphic user interface for offsetting a 1D line.

- 2D Tool – Filling a geometry

The user draws a closed curve to indicate the region for printing, and then the tool will generate a printing path to fill the region; the distance, or line gap is adjustable through a slider. If the printing needs to be looped a few times, the time of looping and waiting time in between can be adjusted (Figure 7).

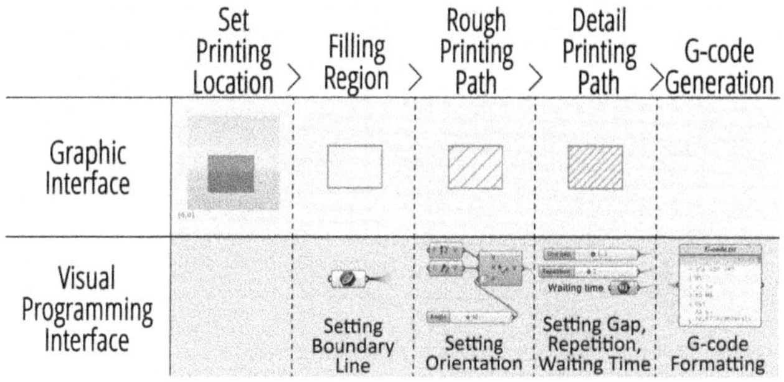

Figure 7: Graphic user interface for filling a 2D geometry.

- 3D Tool – Slicing and filling each layer

This tool slices the model vertically, and then fills each slice with a line path. It enables a user to define the height gap between each slide, and the gap between each line (Figure 8).

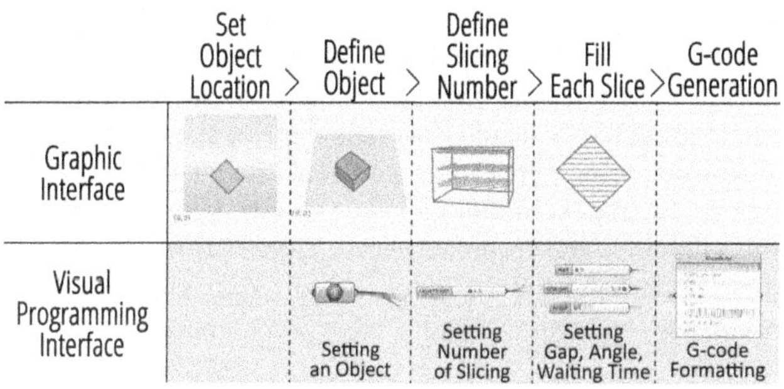

Figure 8: Graphic user interface for slicing a 3D model

- Customized G-code

We assigned some G-code with new functions, to gain extra controllability over the extra modular components (Table 1).

Table 1: G-code customization

G-code	Old function	New Function	Control Circuit
M3	Turn the spindle clockwise	Turn on the trigger for the Dispenser Module	Output a high signal to the dispenser control board
M5	Stop the spindle	Turn off the trigger for the Dispenser Module	Output a low signal to the dispenser control board
UV0	NA	Turn on the UV light	Output a high signal to the UV light control board
UV1	NA	Turn off the UV light	Output a low signal to the UV light control board

- Simulation

Simulation is tightly related to the specific material's responsiveness, and the printing structure. We implemented one tool, which simulates a hinge folding–based transformation if an actuator material is printed on a bi-layer structure. Measurements of the bending curvature from the material sample sets are fed into the Stoney formula, which serves as the modeling basis for simulating the material's behavior; the evolutionary computing method is used to speed up the real-time simulation. Further simulation can be developed, and this is to demonstrate the feasibility of an integrated system with the same software platform (Figure 9).

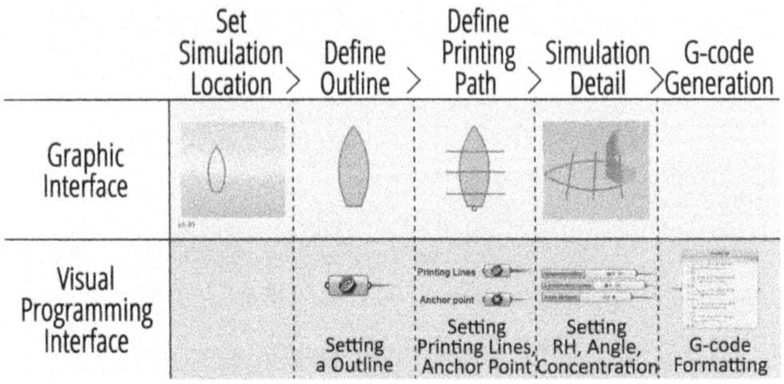

Figure 9: Simulating a bi-layer hinge folding structure

PRINTING MATERIAL OPTIONS

xPrint focuses on printing smart, particularly active materials, which come in a liquid solution and solidify under particular chemical reactions or physical transformations. Although mainstream 3D printers do not support many smart materials, there is a big pool of commercial and research materials that we can choose from to test our printer. The relevant properties of the candidate smart material solution include particle sizes, means of solidification, and responsiveness. Figure 10 highlights the smart materials that we have tested using xPrint; it also maps its potential to handle other smart materials in the future.

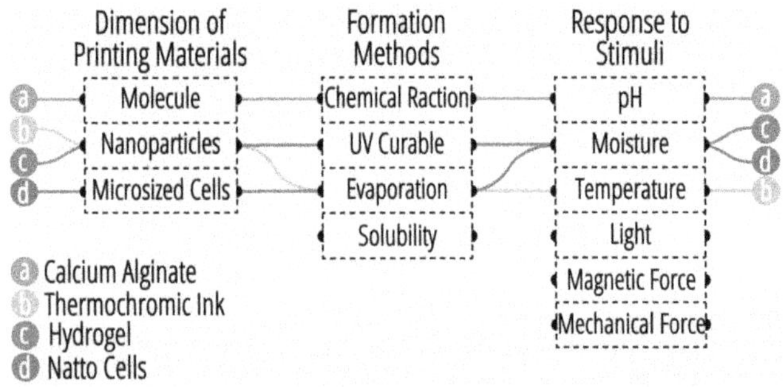

Figure 10: The space of solution based smart materials

In Figure 10, we presented three different levels. 1) The dimension information of the liquid starting materials (material science level); 2) solidification or formation methods for materials processing (fabrication level); and 3) the responsiveness of the fabricated objects (application level). In our paper, we have explored the intersection between the three rows and mapped the current printing examples with the different colors emphasized in the use case.

To demonstrate the system's flexibility to accommodate different types of smart material, we chose four materials from either commercial sources or research publications, or designed four different system configurations to print them (Figure 11).

- Natto cells as RH responsive actuators (Figure 11-1): Natto cells are reported as nanoactuators [30]; the cells can be suspended in water and deposited onto latex to form bi-layer thin films upon water evaporation. In the xPrint system, a Natto cell and water solution requires the central dispenser module, the gravity-based container module, the ventilation module, and the heating plate module to speed up the evaporation process. The outcome is a bi-layer origami structure that reversibly folds and unfolds based on changes in the surrounding relative humidity.
- Calcium alginate as a pH responsive material (Figure 11-2): Alginate is a well-known low-cost pH responsive polymer [24]. The liquid sodium alginate solution can form a gel when it meets a calcium solution. The gel forms due to the replacement of alginate ions with calcium ions when the two liquid solutions meet. In the xPrint system, we use the central dispenser module to first deposit a thin line of liquid alginate, then use the pneumatically controlled container module with a luer fitting brush tip to deposit calcium solution following the same printing path. The gel forms immediately as the brush passes by the liquid alginate lines. 3D structures can thus be formed layer by layer.

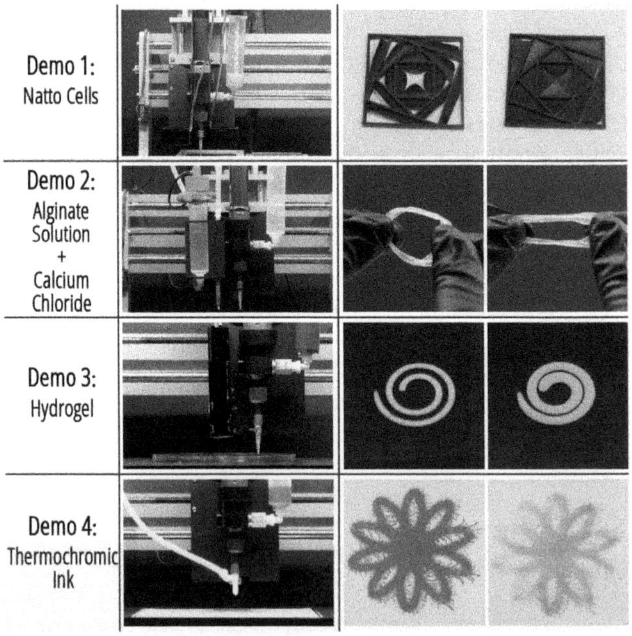

Figure 11: Four different modular configurations are used to print four different functional materials. Demo 1: Natto cells form humidity responsive films; Demo 2: Calcium alginate gels are stretchy and responsive to PH; Demo 3: UV-curable hydrogels swell in water; Demo 4: Thermochromic ink printed on paper.

- Hydrogel swells in water (Figure 11-3): The solution we used is poly(ethylene glycol) di(meth)acrylate

(PEGDA), a UV curable hydrogel [2]. In its gel phase, it can swell up to 42% when submerged in water. PEGDA has been used for several bio-applications, particularly in the field of tissue engineering and drug delivery, due to the advantages of its 3D structure, biocompatibility, and biodegradability. The hydrogel formation is trigged by UV radiation, where free radicals are released from the initiator resulting in the gels crosslinking. The pre-polymer solidifies within 10 seconds when high intensity and focused UV light is applied. In xPrint, we use the central dispenser module and the UV curing lamp module to print the hydrogel.

- Thermochromic film that changes color with temperature (Figure 11-4): We suspended commercial thermochromic powder into a water solution, and coated it on top of paper or other films. With xPrint, we use the atomizer dispensing module to spray the coating. The atomizer is controlled by positive air pressure.

USE CASES

We invited three users with different backgrounds (one fashion designer, one scientist, and one artist) to design and fabricate, with our tested material options to test the usability of the xPrint system and the quality of work that can be produced by our targeted users. No participant had prior experience of using this platform, and each had little experience using 3D modeling or parametric design software. We gave them 1.5 hours training on the hardware and software platforms, covering workflow and safety measures. Following half an hour of practice, all three users were able to use the platform by themselves. We then allowed each participant a maximum of two weeks to design and fabricate their objects.

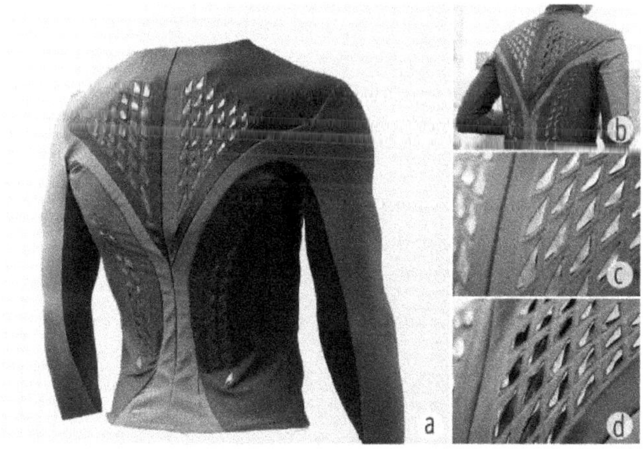

Figure 12: The sweat-actuated flaps on the back of a garment.

Fashion Designer: Transformable Garment with Natto Cells Printing

Oksana is a fashion designer from the Royal College of Art. She has over five years of female garment design experience, and her design interest is adaptive and responsive clothing. She was inspired by the Natto cell–actuated film, and decided to design her own transformable garment. The garment reacts to body sweat and the flaps on the back open up to accelerate the sweat vaporization process (Figure 12).

Tools

She used the central dispenser, the ventilation module, the mechanical stirrer, and the heating plate. For software, she used the 2D line filling tool.

Workflow

She combined the traditional garment manufacturing process with the new material fabrication. She started from hand sketches and thermal fusing tests to combine the responsive film with fabric, then printed film sheets, laser cut the films into units, assembled the back panel, and sewed the garment.

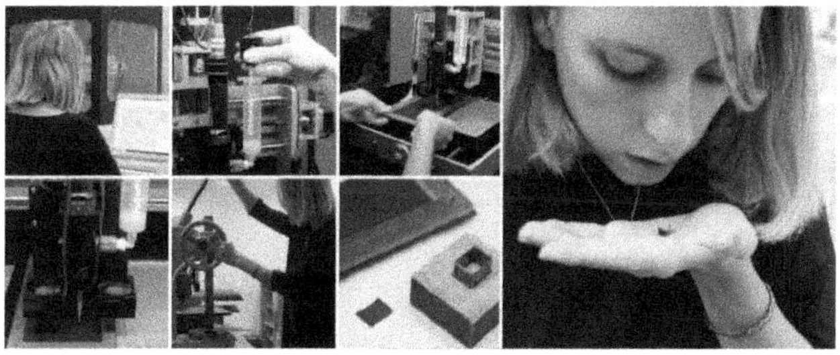

Figure 13: Workflow of a fashion designer, printing her sweat-responsive garment with Natto cells

User Experience

In the process, Oksana tried to print the Natto cell solution in multiple layers to enhance the biofilm responsive effect. When the machine printed the second time before the original printing had evaporated completely in previous trials, the newly printed solution was dragged by the tip of the dispenser, which resulted in uneven evaporation and defects in the biofilm. We reminded her to adjust the speed of the fan and the temperature of the heating plate to make sure that the first-layer solution evaporated more rapidly, and she followed our suggestions; however, the new biofilm cracked due to the over-dehydration caused by the strong wind and high temperature. After 1.5 hours of experimenting, she finally got an appropriate setting to ensure that the solution evaporated just enough before the next layer was printed.

User Feedback

She commented that the integration of a printer required higher precision in terms of fabrication and composite fabric assembly, while traditional garments are usually done in a more casual way; she found the printer very easy to use, although the speed was still too slow for daily design use. After two weeks of intensively working on the garment, she mentioned that she now felt her colleagues back at her home school "are doing things that are so boring." She suggested that integrating responsiveness into fashion is very powerful, and the xPrint enables precise control of the film making process.

Scientist: Drug delivery with Hydrogel Printing

Eve is a postdoc working in the field of biological engineering. Her research focus is the use of multi-functional materials to study the response of living systems; she hopes to apply her ideas in biomedical applications. In this study, her research interest is to print hydrogel capsules and study drug delivery effects. The biocompatible hydrogel has a dual function; first, it is a carrier of a sample drug that needs to be tested for toxicity in living cells. Second, the swelling response of the hydrogel towards water is an interesting effect to study, and is related to the drug release rate. She hopes to use a simple instrument to demonstrate the drug delivery concept and measure the speed for different volumes of gel to optimize the dosing rate.

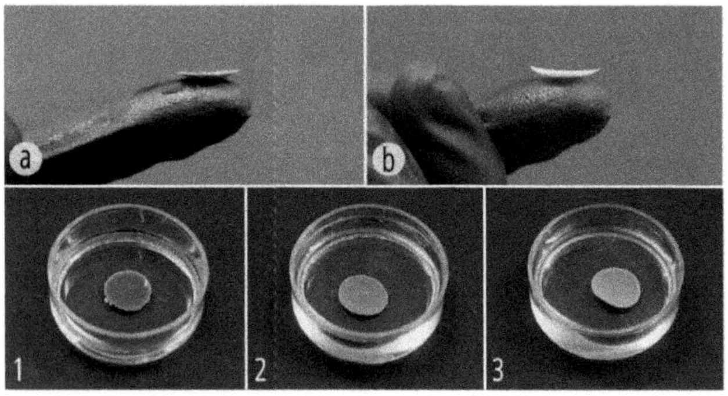

Figure 14: Printed water-responsive hydrogel structures for drug delivery. a) Drug capsule in its unswollen state; b) Drug capsule in its swollen state

Tools

For materials, she chose to use a conventional UV curing biocompatible hydrogel.

For hardware configuration, she chose the central dispenser and the UV curing lamp module. The printing bed is a petri-dish for hygiene purposes; she used the 3D slicing tool to generate the G-code for printing.

Workflow

She started by brainstorming ideas of how such a hydrogel material can be printed in terms of the processing time and feasible pattern. It took her a slightly longer time to finish a relatively simple geometry. She seemed very used to the machine operation processes, including loading material, cleaning the printing bed, and adjusting flow rate. After printing, she tested the hydrogel transformation and drug release in a solvent in terms of both the shape and color of the drug. She used the data to estimate a rough range for the drug release rate, and she mentioned that she is very used to procedural operation in her lab (Figure 15).

User Experience

Eve wanted to print a 3D structure like a piece of a pill. In the beginning, she was unfamiliar with the quantity of printing and the power of UV curing. For instance, the hydrogel would be stiffer with a thinner layer and the UV curing time was extended between each run. However, the hydrogel would become softer as the quantity of deposited materials increased or the UV curing time shortened. In addition, since Eve utilized multiple-layer printing, the UV curing time would affect the original layers' stiffness indirectly. Then, to achieve suitable stiffness in the drug carrier structure, she spent more time precisely adjusting the curing time setting and the quantity of printing. After testing for 3 hours, she printed satisfactory samples with various sizes and thicknesses.

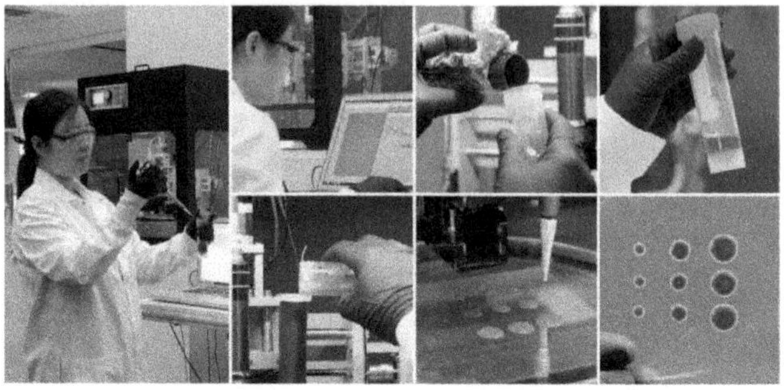

Figure 15: Workflow of the scientific user, printing her water-responsive drug capsules.

User Feedback

Eve mentioned that it is a "very useful" platform, and she asked how much such a platform would cost, and was very surprised by how little people might need to spend to have such a platform. She noted that she had heard of hydrogel printing systems in her field, but noted that it is still just emerging as a technology. It is either built by another engineering lab that has collaborations going on, or it will "cost a ton." "Any scientific research equipment costs a lot!" She was also surprised by the simplicity of the software platform. In addition, the printing platform normally occupies a large lab space and is not portable. It is difficult to move the whole instrument into a small biological safety cabinet for *in situ* printing and testing. "Our instruments usually have very complicated control software, which takes days of training and learning". Finally, she suggested that although the resolution is yet to be improved for printing high resolution structures and scaffolds, which bioprinters often claim as a capability, it can be a "very useful" low end printing system for chemistry or biology research labs to test their ideas. It can also be adjusted to print different materials for other purposes.

Artist: Animated painting with Thermochromic Ink Printing

Samuel is a freelance artist, good at graphic design and creative painting. He likes to explore new ways of drawing in his work, and has used thermochromic ink in his painting previously. In this user study, he created a "digital style" color changing painting (Figure 16).

Tools

The hardware modules he used were a dispenser and the ventilation module. In addition, he used the 1D tool to generate his line drawing.

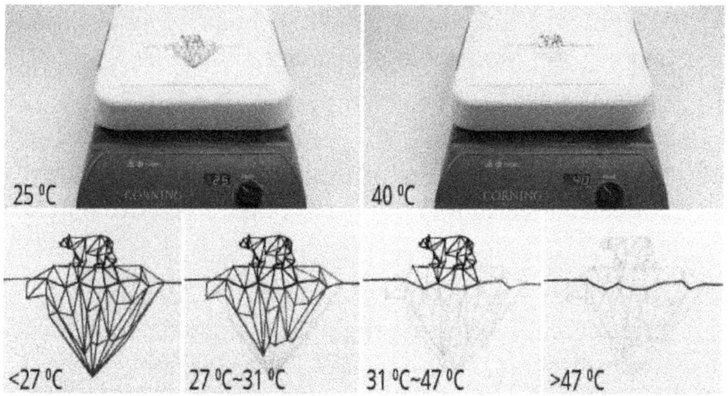

Figure 16: Melting Iceberg, the visual elements of the digital painting disappears sequentially.

Workflow

It took him two days to finish the design and fabrication of the painting. He spent one day getting familiar with the effects of thermochromic ink deposition, and he explored the effects when a few parameters were changed during the printing process such as the distance between the dispenser and the paper and the flow rate of the dispenser. On the second day he focused on the creation of the line drawing in the software and the actual printing of the drawing.

Figure 17: Workflow of an artist, printing his animated painting with thermochromic ink

User Experience

Samuel had a higher requirement for the effect of curves. He spent two hours printing the same single line square by changing to different types of nozzle (e.g., normal nozzle, brush, and atomizer) and different nozzle sizes to achieve satisfactory results. Evenly, he tried to control the air pressure in different powers for the atomizer and different distances between the brush dispenser and the paper in the process of printing.

Feedback

He mentioned he felt a sense of "co-creation" with the machine. He could never create a "digital but tangible" drawing without the assistance of the machine. It was "like a copy you print out of your inkjet printer after you draw it in Illustrator," but it had a level of interactivity. When he commented on that, he placed his painting on top of a hot plate and demonstrated how the different components disappeared as he turned up the temperature. Finally, he suggested that the software should add one more function that can preview the final line effects with different printing settings, such as the dispenser flow rate, the distance between the dispenser and the paper, and the different nozzle dimensions.

CHALLENGES AND FUTURE WORK

Fine-tune the material properties and control the machine modules for printing.

The viscosity and curing time of the material is critical. For example, the hydrogel material we used had a very low viscosity; it flowed a bit around the edges before solidifying on the printing bed, which affects its final printing resolution and quality. Fine tuning the viscosity and the UV light intensity are key in this case. In theory, the current xPrint should work for almost all liquid smart material solution, as long as they solidify under certain environmental conditions once printed. However, in reality, the machine and material parameters have to be finely tuned and adjusted, sometimes with the help of experts from chemistry or material science fields.

Control axis and CNC moving speed.

During our use study, we learned about how printing on both sides of a thin film to create composite structures is desirable. For improvement, we would like to build a rotatory printing platform that can flip the printing bed upside down; we would also like to increase the printing speed by replacing the current servo motors with faster steadier ones.

Multi-material printing with customized central dispenser.

We currently use an off-the-shelf central dispenser; it is very precise, but costly and limited to one print head. For the next step, we would like to develop our own open source progressive cavity pump–based dispensing system. We would like to have multiple containers that can print more than one material simultaneously. This will open doors for 3D printing with supporting structures and composite material printing with embedded functions.

Open source hardware and software.

Although this paper details all of our design principles, we would like to construct a wiki page to share our source code for the software design and simulation platform, and document our machine design process. Community has a strong power to improve such systems through practice and comments.

CONCLUSION

In this paper, we presented a liquid depositing modeling printing system. We emphasized its wide coverage of printing resolutions and its modular design to accommodate liquid material solutions that solidify under different environment stimuli such as mechanical mixing, chemical reaction, and ambient vaporization. We hope such a platform can be a helpful toolkit for those who are interested in conducting design and research in the area of fabricating smart materials and transformable, especially for shape changing interfaces.

REFERENCES

1. Agrawal, H., Umapathi, U., Kovacs, R., Frohnhofen, J., Chen, H.-T., Mueller, S., Baudisch, P. 2015. Protopiper: Physically Sketching Room-Sized Objects at Actual Scale. *Proc. of UIST 2015*, 427-436.
2. Beamish, J.A., Zhu, J., Kottke-Marchant, K., Marchant, R.E. 2010. The effects of monoacrylated poly (ethylene glycol) on the properties of poly (ethylene glycol) diacrylate hydrogels used for tissue engineering. *Journal of Biomedical Materials Research Part A 92*, 441-450.
3. BioBot. Available from: http://www.biobots.io/.
4. Chen, X., Mahadevan, L., Driks, A., Sahin, O. 2014. Bacillus spores as building blocks for stimuli-responsive materials and nanogenerators. *Nature nanotechnology 9*, 137-141.
5. Fab@home. Available from: http://www.fabathome.org/.
6. Ferris, C.J., Gilmore, K.G., Wallace, G.G. 2013. Biofabrication: an overview of the approaches used for printing of living cells. *Applied microbiology and biotechnology 97*, 4243-4258.
7. FormLabs. Available from: http://formlabs.com/.
8. Grasshopper. Available from: http://www.grasshopper3d.com/.
9. Hardin, J.O., Ober, T.J., Valentine, A.D., Lewis, J.A. 2015. Microfluidic Printheads for Multimaterial 3D Printing of Viscoelastic Inks. *Advanced Materials*.
10. Hudson, S.E. 2014. Printing teddy bears: a technique for 3D printing of soft interactive objects. *Proc. of CHI 2014*, 459-468.
11. Lo, J., Paulos, E. 2014. ShrinkyCircuits: sketching, shrinking, and formgiving for electronic circuits. *Proc. of UIST 2014*, 291-299.
12. Mironov, V. 2003. Printing technology to produce living tissue. *Expert opinion on biological therapy 3*, 701.
13. Miruchna, V., Walter, R., Lindlbauer, D., Lehmann, M., von Klitzing, R., Müller, J. 2015. GelTouch: Localized Tactile Feedback Through Thin, Programmable Gel. *Proc. of UIST 2015*, 3-10.
14. ModularScience. Available from: https://www.modularscience.com/.
15. Mogas-Soldevila, L., Duro-Royo, J., Oxman, N. 2014. Water-Based Robotic Fabrication: Large-Scale Additive Manufacturing of Functionally Graded Hydrogel Composites via Multichamber Extrusion. *3D Printing and Additive Manufacturing 1*, 141-151.
16. Moyer, I.E. 2014. A gestalt framework for virtual machine control of automated tools. *Massachusetts Institute of Technology*.
17. Murphy, S.V., Atala, A. 2014. 3D bioprinting of tissues and organs. *Nature biotechnology 32*, 773-785.
18. Muth, J.T., Vogt, D.M., Truby, R.L., Mengüç, Y., Kolesky, D.B., Wood, R.J., Lewis, J.A. 2014. Embedded 3D printing of strain sensors within highly stretchable elastomers. *Advanced Materials 26*, 6307-6312.
19. Olberding, S., Wessely, M., Steimle, J. 2014. Printscreen: fabricating highly customizable thin-film touch-displays. *Proc. of UIST 2014*, 281-290.
20. Parsa, S., Gupta, M., Loizeau, F., Cheung, K.C. 2010. Effects of surfactant and gentle agitation on inkjet dispensing of living cells. *Biofabrication 2*, 025003.
21. Peek, N. 2010. Rapid prototyping of green composites.
22. Rasmussen, M.K., Pedersen, E.W., Petersen, M.G., Hornbæk, K. 2012. Shape-changing interfaces: a review of the design space and open research questions. *Proc. of CHI 2012*, 735-744.
23. Rutzerveld, C. *Edible Growth*. 2015; Available from: http://www.chloerutzerveld.com/edible-growth-2014.
24. Shi, J., Alves, N.M., Mano, J.F. 2006. Drug Release of pH/Temperature-Responsive Calcium Alginate/Poly (*N*-isopropylacrylamide) Semi-IPN Beads. *Macromolecular bioscience 6*, 358-363.
25. Sitthi-Amorn, P., Ramos, J.E., Wangy, Y., Kwan, J., Lan, J., Wang, W., Matusik, W. 2015. MultiFab: a machine vision assisted platform for multi-material 3D printing. *ACM Transactions on Graphics (TOG) 34*, 129.
26. Stratasys. Available from: http://www.stratasys.com/3d-printers/design-series.
27. Sun, L., Huang, W.M., Ding, Z., Zhao, Y., Wang, C.C., Purnawali, H., Tang, C. 2012. Stimulus-responsive shape memory materials: a review. *Materials & Design 33*, 577-640.
28. Symes, M.D., Kitson, P.J., Yan, J., Richmond, C.J., Cooper, G.J., Bowman, R.W., Vilbrandt, T., Cronin, L. 2012. Integrated 3D-printed reactionware for chemical synthesis and analysis. *Nature Chemistry 4*, 349-354.
29. Wilson, W.C., Boland, T. 2003. Cell and organ printing 1: protein and cell printers. *The Anatomical Record Part A: Discoveries in Molecular, Cellular, and Evolutionary Biology 272*, 491-496.
30. Yao, L., Ou, J., Cheng, C.-Y., Steiner, H., Wang, W., Wang, G., Ishii, H. 2015. bioLogic: Natto Cells as Nanoactuators for Shape Changing Interfaces. *Proc. of CHI 2015*, 1-10.
31. Zentoolworks. Available from: http://www.zentoolworks.com/.

Cilllia - 3D Printed Micro-Pillar Structures for Surface Texture, Actuation and Sensing

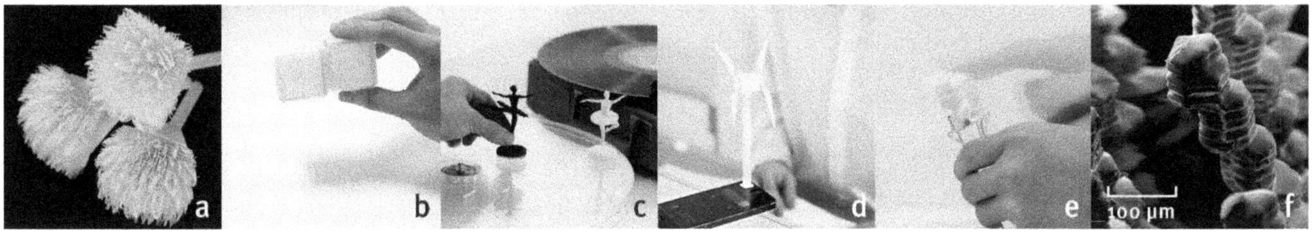

Figure 1. Printed Objects with Cilllia. (a) Printed Flowers with fine surface details; (b) Mechanical adhesion surface; (c) Passively actuated dancing figures; (d) Ambient actuated object for notification; (d) Acoustic sensing of swiping gesture; (e) Scanning electron microscope (SEM) image of the printed hair structure.

Jifei Ou[1], Gershon Dublon[1], Chin-Yi Cheng[2], Felix Heibeck[1], Karl Willis[3], Hiroshi Ishii[1]

[1]MIT Media Lab,
Cambridge, USA
{jifei, gershon, heibeck, ishii}
@media.mit.edu

[2]MIT Architecture,
Cambridge, USA
chinyich@media.mit.edu

[3]Addimation, Inc
San Francisco, USA
karl@karlddwillis.com

ABSTRACT
This work presents a method for 3D printing hair-like structures on both flat and curved surfaces. It allows a user to design and fabricate hair geometries that are smaller than 100 micron. We built a software platform to let users quickly define the hair angle, thickness, density, and height. The ability to fabricate customized hair-like structures not only expands the library of 3D-printable shapes, but also enables us to design passive actuators and swipe sensors. We also present several applications that show how the 3D-printed hair can be used for designing everyday interactive objects.

Author Keywords
3D Printing; Surface Texture; Actuated Interfaces; Acoustic Sensing; Digital Fabrication; Hair.

ACM Classification Keywords
H.5.2. Information interfaces and presentation: User Interfaces.

INTRODUCTION
Throughout nature, hair-like structures can be found on animals and plants at many different scales. Beyond ornamentation, hair provides warmth and aids in the sense of touch. Hair is also a natural responsive material that interfaces between the living organism and its environment by creating functionalities like adhesion, locomotion, and sensing. Inspired by how hair achieves those properties with its unique high aspect ratio structure, we are exploring ways of digitally designing and fabricating hair structures on man-made objects that not only have fine texture on the surface, but also can sense touch and be actuated. Material science and mechanical engineers have long been investigating various methods of fabricating hair-like structure [17][21]. In this paper, we present *Cilllia,* our exploration of hair fabrication using Stereolithography (SLA) 3D printing, as well as acoustic methods for hair-based actuation and sensing. This research is driven by the vision of Radical Atoms[12] , which proposes a group of physical materials as a dynamic manifestation of digital information.

3D printing is rapidly expanding the possibilities for how physical objects are fabricated [16]. Its layer-by-layer fabrication process has tremendous potential to enable the fabrication of physical objects not previously possible. High-resolution 3D printers have become increasingly affordable and widely available, enabling the fabrication of micron-scale structures. In this paper we present *Cilllia*, a bottom-up printing pipeline to fully utilize the capability of current high-resolution photopolymer 3D printers to generate large amounts of fine hair on the surfaces of 3D objects. We introduce methods, algorithms, and design tools for the fabrication of *Cilllia*, and explore its capability of actuating and sensing touch. Using these techniques, we demonstrate the use of *Cilllia* for toy and interactive object design.

CHI'16, May 07-12, 2016, San Jose, CA, USA
© 2016 ACM. ISBN 978-1-4503-3362-7/16/05...$15.00 DOI: http://dx.doi.org/10.1145/2858036.2858257

The ability to 3D print hair-like structures opens up new possibilities for personal fabrication and interaction. We can quickly prototype objects with highly customized fine surface textures that have mechanical adhesion properties, or brushes with controllable stiffness and texture. A 3D printed figure can translate vibration into a controlled motion based on the hair geometry, and printed objects can now sense human touch direction and velocity.

In this paper, we present the following contributions:

1. A bottom-up approach for generating 3D printable micro-pillar structures.
2. A graphical user interface that allows users to easily design hair structure.
3. Examples of encoding physical movement into hair structures
4. An acoustic method for sensing finger swipe direction and velocity on hairy surfaces.
5. Example applications that demonstrate how 3D printed hair can be implemented and used in everyday objects and actuated tangible interfaces.

As high-resolution 3D printers become increasingly available and affordable, we envision a future where physical materials' properties, whether optical or mechanical, electrical or biological, can be encoded and decoded directly by users. This allows us to customize and fabricate interactive objects as needed.

HAIR IN DIGITAL FABRICATION AND HCI

Natural hair and fur provides a rich visual and tactile texture palette. In the field of computer graphics, numerous works have been done to simulate the natural movement of hair [3]. Traditionally, synthetic hair/fur on a surface is produced with specific machining and chemical processes that have been widely used in fashion and product design. Recently, as materiality has become increasingly important in tangible interfaces design, researchers in HCI have presented works on rapid prototyping object with soft/furry surface textures [23][6][8], These efforts have focused on using soft/furry materials to construct physical objects. *Cilllia* explores how to digitally control hair/fur geometry and directly print it with commercially available stereolithography printers. This enables designers to freely customize the surface detail of their design.

Inspired by the versatile capabilities of hair structures in the biological world (self-cleaning, sensing, protection, warmth, actuation, adhesion, camouflage, etc.), we aim to explore a large design space with 3D printable hair. In the context of design and HCI, we are interested in how to use hair to not only create fine surface texture, but also to utilize its structure to create active surfaces that can output physical motion and receive human gesture input. Prior work shows a variety of approaches to actuate tabletop objects [7][9][19] and touch sensing on surfaces [10][13][22]. We demonstrate that by arranging the hair geometry and directionality on the surface with our tools, we can print surfaces that are capable of serving as both an actuating and sensing mechanism with help of a single transducer. This could be useful for designing future I/O coincident devices/materials.

CILLLIA FOR SURFACE TEXTURE FABRICATION

In this section, we introduce a novel approach to 3D print hair-like structure on both flat and curved surfaces. Our approach allows user to individually control the geometry of individual hair, such as height, thickness and angle, as well as properties of the hair array, such as density and location. We then present three example applications to demonstrate the capabilities of our hair printing approach.

All the test and examples shown in this paper, unless stated differently, are printed on a commercially available Digital Light Processing (DLP) 3D printer (Autodesk Ember Printer). The DLP printer takes stacks of bitmap images from the CAD models and directly projects the image onto the liquid resin layer by layer. The printer can support overhang structure within 60 degrees during printing (based on our empirical tests). The printer has a feature resolution of 50 μm on the X and Y-axis, and 25 μm on Z-axis. The build volume is 64 by 40 by 150 mm. The print material is near UV light photopolymer (available on //spark.autodesk.com/ember/shop).

Challenges on Digital Representation of Hair Structures

Although the resolution of recent 3d printers has been improving, it is still considered impractical to directly print fine hair arrays on object's surfaces. This is due to the lack of an efficient digital representation of CAD models with fine surface texture [20]. Most of the current commercially available 3D printers use a layer-by-layer method to deposit/solidify materials into shapes that are designed in the CAD. The process follows a top-down pipeline, in which users create digital 3D models, and then a program slices the models into layers for the printer to print. In the field of computer graphics, the standard way to represent surface texture is through lofting bitmaps on the CAD model to create an optical illusion. These representations do not actually capture the 3-dimensional structure. It is difficult and impractical to create many thousands of small hairs with real geometry using conventional CAD systems. The data for describing the total geometry becomes extremely large and rendering such complex structures can also be computationally expensive.

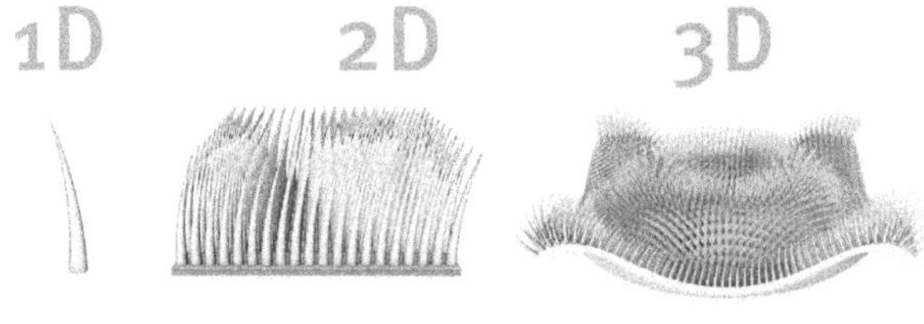

Figure 2. The three-folds design of 3D printing hair-like structure.

Printing Hair-like Structure

We propose a bottom-up 3D printing approach to design and fabricate hair-like structures without first making 3D CAD model, where user directly generate printing layers that contains hair structure information for the 3D printer. The method can be viewed from 3 layers:

1. Single hair's geometry (1D): height, thickness, angle and profile.
2. Hair array on flat surfaces (2D): varying single hair geometry across the array on a 2D surface.
3. Hair array on curved surfaces (3D): generating hair array on arbitrary curved surfaces. (Figure 2)

Single Hair Geometry

Compared to other surfaces textures, such as wrinkle, hair is simpler to describe mathematically. It is usually a high aspect ratio cone that is vertical/angled to the surface. The height, thickness and profile might vary from one to another. As we know, the diameter of a cone continuously decreases from the base to the tip. However, the smallest unit in DLP printer is a pixel. Therefore we need to find a way to construct a model that could approximate the geometry of a cone. As shown in Figure 3(a), we set the base of a pillar to be a matrix of array (e.g. 3 by 3 pixels). As the layer increases, the pixels linearly reduce in a spiral stairs manner, leaving the top layer with just 1 pixel. This method gives us the highest resolution control of the printed cone shape. We can also add acceleration to the base pixel reducing velocity to create hair with a different profile.

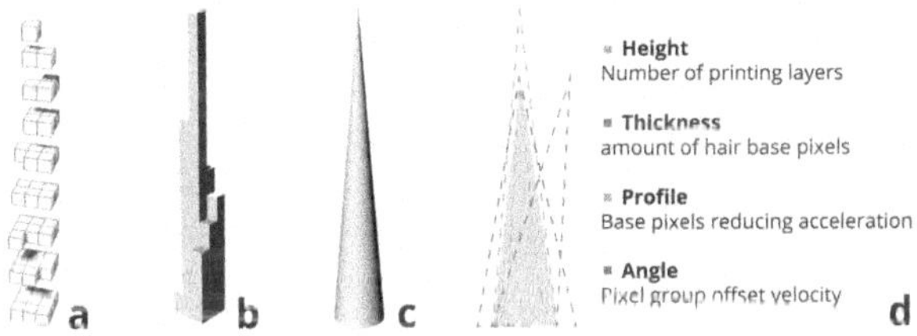

Figure 3. (a) A pixel by pixel, layer by layer approach to generate hair; (b) visualization of (a) after printing; (c) ideal shape of printed hair. (d) Parameters of single hair geometry.

For tilting the hair to a certain angle, we can offset the pixel group in X or Y direction every few layers. As the printer has the double resolution on the Z compared to the X and Y axis (25μm vs. 50μm), The relationship of tilted angle and layer is:

$$\tan\theta = (L / 2) \times P$$

where L is the number of layers, and P is the numbers of offsetting pixels. Figure 3(d) summarizes the relationship between basic physical hair geometry and pixel information.

We successfully printed a series of sample surfaces with oriented hair. Figure 4 shows that our printed geometry matches the computer visualization.

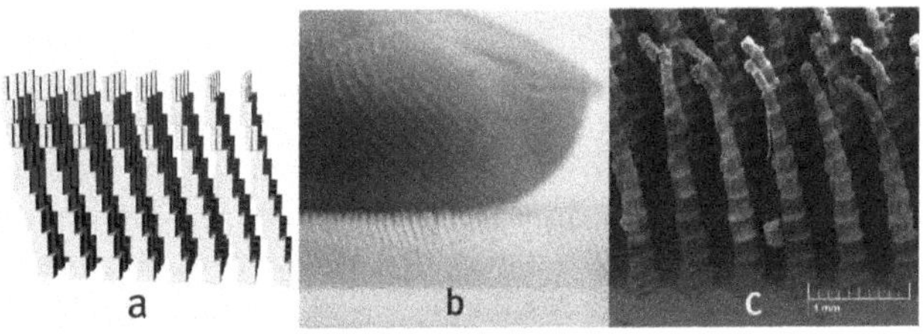

Figure 4. (a) Computer visualization of printed hair; (b) close view of actual printed hair; (c) SEM photo of the (b).

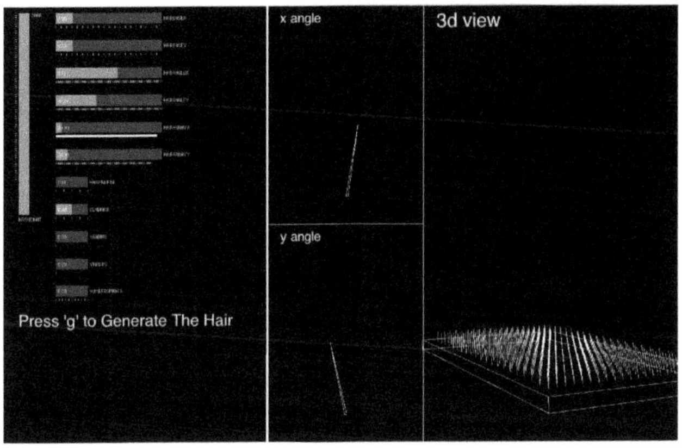

Figure 5. A graphical user interface to quickly change the parameters of the hair structure.

Through a graphical user interface we designed, users can easily change the parameters of the hair geometry. It visualizes the hair structures as well as generating bitmaps for printing. (Figure 5)

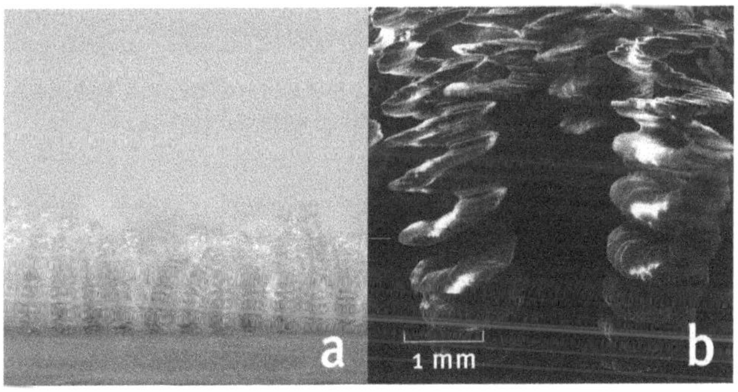

Figure 6. (a) Printed spring shape hair; (b) SEM photo of (a).

We can also generate curved hair by offsetting the pixel group in a spiral layer by layer. Figure 6 shows a spring shape hair.

Hair Array on Flat Surfaces

The ability to individually control hair geometry can be applied to thousands across a flat surface. In order to quickly do that, we use a color mapping method that allows one to make a RGB bitmap in Photoshop, then turn it into a hair array. The values of the R, G and B of each pixel are correspondent to one parameter of hair geometry. The algorithm checks the bitmap every few pixels to create a new hair based on the pixel's color. One can therefore easily vary the density of the hair by changing how frequently the bitmap is checked.

Based on our experience, height and angle are the most common parameters that need to be varied frequently. We therefore map the R-value to the angle of X-axis, G-value to the angle of Y-axis and B-value to the height of the hair. Figure 7 shows the bitmaps, hair rendering and printed models. We use this method to create the conveyor panels in the later section. In the future, we plan to develop a more general approach to encode hair geometry information into one bitmap image, where other parameters such as profile and thickness can be included as well.

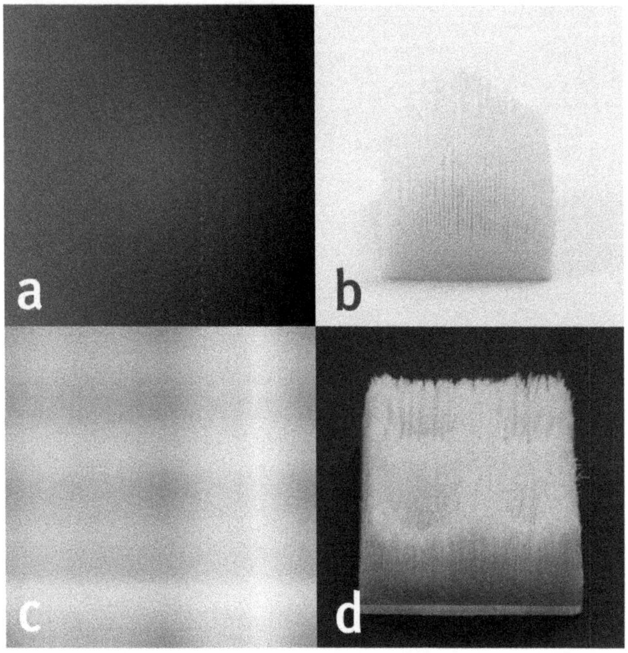

Figure 7. (a)(c) The color bitmap for generating hair printing; (b)(d) actual printed hair generated by (a)(c).

Hair Array on Curved Surfaces

In order to apply the presented techniques to a variety of models, it is desirable to print hair on an arbitrary curved surface. To do that, we developed a hybrid method; where user only create the curved surface in a CAD software, then generate bitmaps that contains pixels of hair array.

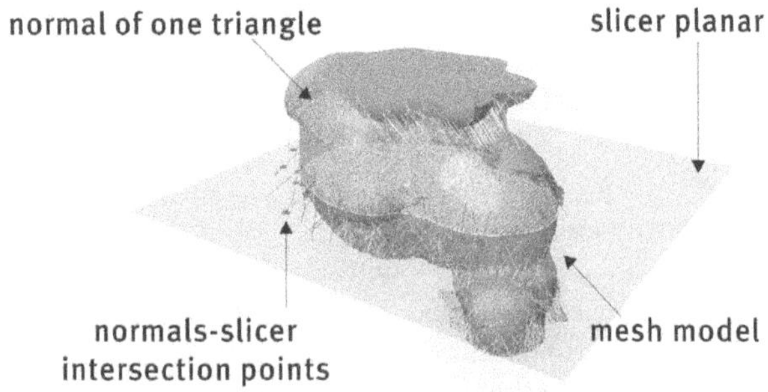

Figure 8. Hair generating while slicing a mesh model.

To do that, we first import the STL file and position it in the correct printing position. Then we find the centroid location of each triangle on the mesh and shoot a ray along the direction of the triangle's normal. A plane moves along the Z-axis to intersect with the mesh to create bitmaps of the CAD model, and intersect with the rays to draw pixels for the hair. In this way, we created bitmaps that contain both CAD model and hair array information (Figure 8). This method allows us to apply the control of hair geometry while slicing as well. However, the generated hair array is highly dependent on the distribution and amount of the triangles. For the examples in this paper, we try to use meshes that have dense and evenly distributed triangles. One can use publicly available online tools (e.g. Meshlab) to create more uniform models. We should also notice that the 3D printer allows only 60 degree of overhang, so rays that are beyond that range are ignored. There might be also parts of the hair that penetrate the nearby surface if the surface is curved inwards. We can eliminate that by reducing the hair length correspondently.

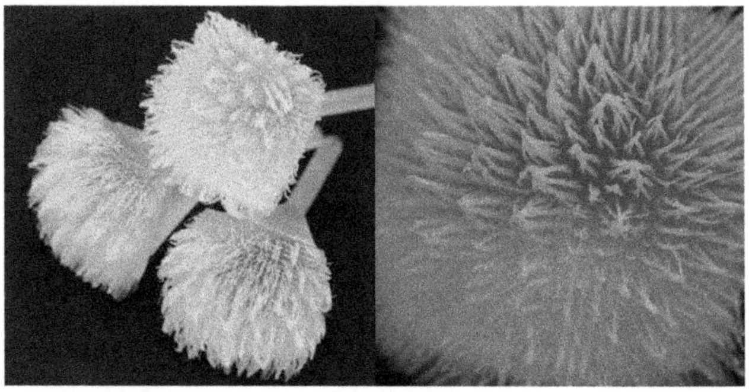

Figure 9. Successful printed hair arrays on curved surfaces.

There are three advantages when directly generating bitmaps of hair structures: 1. By manipulating single pixel, we can control single hair's geometry such as height, thickness, and angle, with the precision of 50 um. 2. Without a CAD model of the hair and slicing process, it becomes possible to print a high-density hair array. In our test, we successfully printed 20000 strands of hair on a 30 by 60 mm flat surface. 3. Hair array can "grow" on any arbitrary CAD model while the model is being sliced.

Printing with Laser Beam Based SLA

We also experimented the layer-by-layer method on a laser beam based SLA printer (Form1+. Available on formlabs.com.) In the experiment, we directly manipulate the exposure time and the moving path of the laser beam to create an array of laser "dots" for polymerizing the liquid resin. We move the laser beam to the spot where we would like to have hair structure, and turn on the laser for 2 milliseconds, then move to the next spot and turn on for another 2 millisecond. Based on our experiment, 2 milliseconds is the minimum exposure time one needs to fully polymerize the resin. It produces a dot with a 100-micron diameter. To increase the size, one can increase the exposure time (figure 11). However, we discovered that as one increases the exposure time, the polymerized dot formed into a long oval instead of circle shape. This is due the shape distortion of laser beam. Although the Form1+ has a larger build platform and potentially can be useful for more applications, we decided to use the Ember printer as it produces more uniform result.

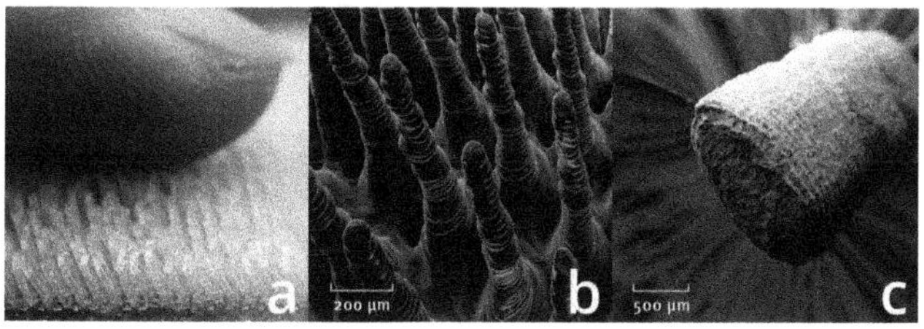

Figure 10. (a) Printed hair structure with laser beam based SLA. (b) SEM photo of (a). (c) Oval shape of the laser beam.

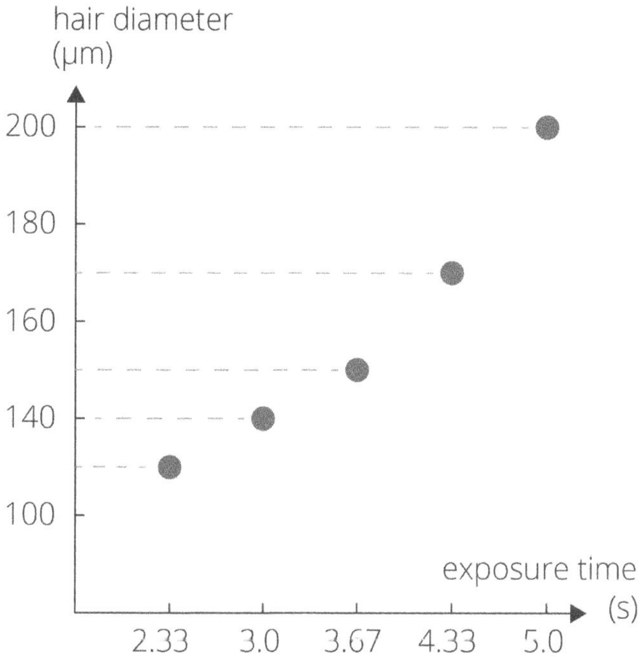

Figure 11. Laser exposure time determines diameter of the printed hair on Form1+.

Applications

To show the capability of our printing method, we create three types of possible application for designers.

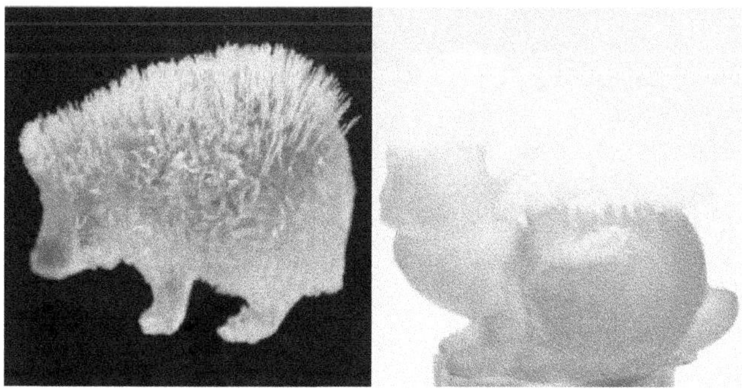

Figure 12. Printed figures with controllable hair stiffness.

Objects with fine surface texture

As we can generate hair on curved surfaces, we can now 3D print animal figures with such features. We can also vary the thickness of the hair to control its stiffness. Figure 11 shows a hedgehog that has thicker hair (6 by 6 pixels on the base), and a bunny that has a thinner patch (3 by 3 pixels on the base). In our examples, both figures' hair length is 10mm. The angle limitation is 30 degrees (figure 12).

Customized Brushes

We can also directly 3D print brushes with customized texture. Figure 13 & 14 show four brushes with different density. With the color mapping method, one could create more complex shape of a brush for artistic expression. In our example, all brushes are 30 mm in diameter. The length and density vary based on the input bitmap.

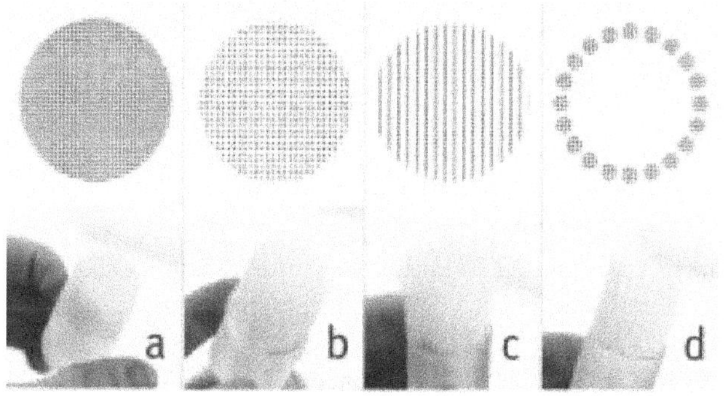

Figure 13. Printed brushes with different density and style.

Figure 14. Printed brushed can be directly use for painting.

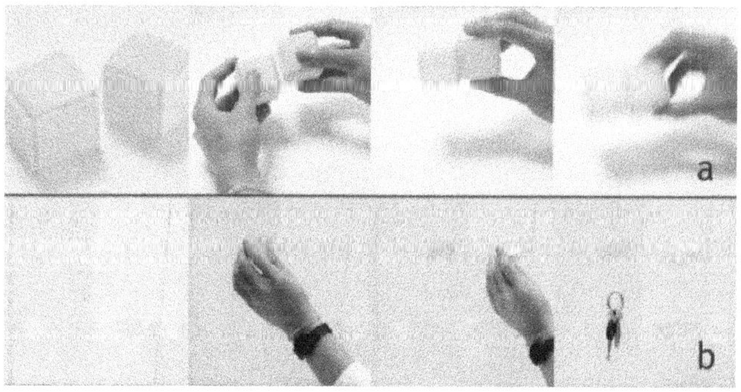

Figure 15. Printed flat surface with Cillia with mechanical adhesion property.

Mechanical Adhesion

One interesting phenomenon we found during our exploration is that two panels with dense hair can tightly stick to each other when their hair is pressed together (figure 15). This is because of the large amount of contact surface on the hair that creates friction. To demonstrate that, we printed several hair panels (40mm by 40mm) and glued them into boxes. Those boxes can be easily attached to each other. In order to keep the hairs on two panels fully in touch with each other, the gaps between the hairs must have the same size as the diameter of the hair base. In our example, the hair base and the gap are both 4 pixels (200 micron). Figure 16 shows the details of the print.

Figure 16. Large amount of contact surface on the hair creates high friction.

We tested the strength of the adhesion in relation to the tilting angle of the printed hair. In our experiment, a pair of hair panels (30mm by 30mm) were glued on a solid truncated pyramid (30mm by 30 mm by 30 mm). We push the hair surface against each other, and measured the force that was needed to pull them apart. Our test shows that as the tilting angle of the hair increases, the adhesion force raises as well (figure 17).

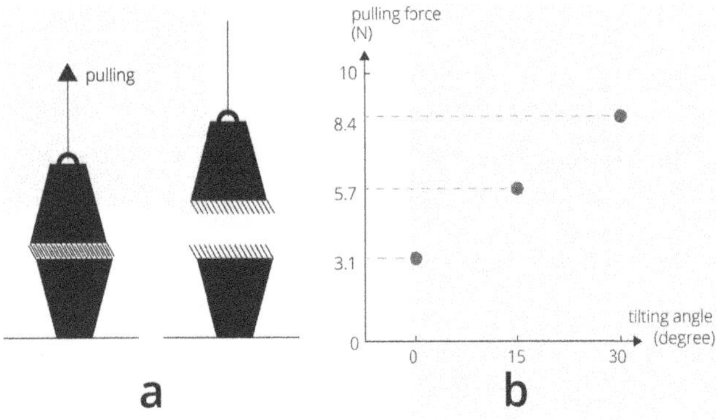

Figure 17. Adhesion force test setup and the relation between tilting angle and hairy surface adhesion force.

CILLLIA FOR PASSIVE ACTUATION

There are numerous examples of natural systems that take advantage of natural vibrations and employ anisotropic mechanical structure as a means of generating differential friction used for locomotion or particle transport. Many insects, for example, use rigid hair-like setae on their legs as a mechanism for removing debris and particles [2]. Similarly, the ciliary arrays lining the inside of our lungs produce surface standing waves that propel a mucus layer of contaminants over the surface [25]. Inspired by those phenomena, we aim to 3D print a surface that can move passive object in contact with it.

Actuated surfaces in HCI have been widely studied [9][24]. Researchers have looked into how to design a universal system that can translate an object in any direction in real time. To do so usually requires multiple actuators, and manual adding of extra components such as magnets on the actuated tangible object. Recent research on actuated tangible interfaces, especially soft shape-change interfaces [14][18] has shown that by carefully designing material structures, one can achieve compelling shape-change with one single actuator. The applications of this approach are usually designed for a situated context. Inspired by these previous works, *Cilllia* encodes the motion on the surface into the structural design of the hair array.

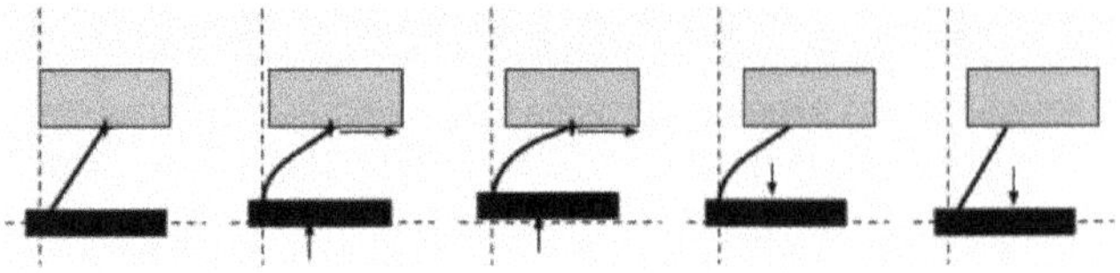

Figure 18. One cycle of the stick-slip mechanism.

Actuation Principle

A directional hair array on a surface creates anisotropic friction. When subjected to a vibration force, this property allows us to move the object in the hair's direction. One example of this actuation mechanism is the bristle-bot. A bristle-bot, which is composed of a rigid body with an array of compliant legs, moves by exciting a vibration with an onboard oscillating mass. The vibration causes the legs to stick and slip on the horizontal surface, propelling the robot forward. This simple technique is effective and has been shown to propel robots at many times their own body-length per second [1]. *Cilllia* effectively inverts this bristle mechanism and leverages it to move objects on a surface without the need for precise control of an array of actuators (figure 18). As we can fabricate hair with customized geometry and angles on both flat and curved surfaces, we demonstrate how to control the motion direction and velocity by manipulating the design of the hair.

Actuation Primitives

We studied basic translating paths enabled by *Cilllia*. Based on the surfaces where *Cilllia* is arranged, we divide the moving paths into: 1. Hair on flat surface; and 2. Hair on curved surface.

Hair on flat surface

We printed a series of 40 by 40 by 15 mm blocks. Each block contains a hair array with predefined orientation on the surface. We placed the blocks on an exciter, which vibrates the block vertically at 180Hz. By controlling the orientation of the hair array on the flat surface, we can fabricate 2D surfaces that move passive objects in: 1. Straight line; 2. Curve line; and 3. Centered rotation. Figure 19 & 20 show how the direction of the hair array changes the trajectory of the object.

We also implemented a larger actuation surface by tiling small printed panel together. (Figure 21) The surface is designed to slide the objects on top to the middle and then move them to the right side. To fabricate this, we generate a bitmap in Photoshop that contains the hair geometry information of the whole panel. Then we divided the image into 16 parts. Each part of the images was used to generate one tile for the large panel. We glued the 16 printed parts on an aluminum plate after printing.

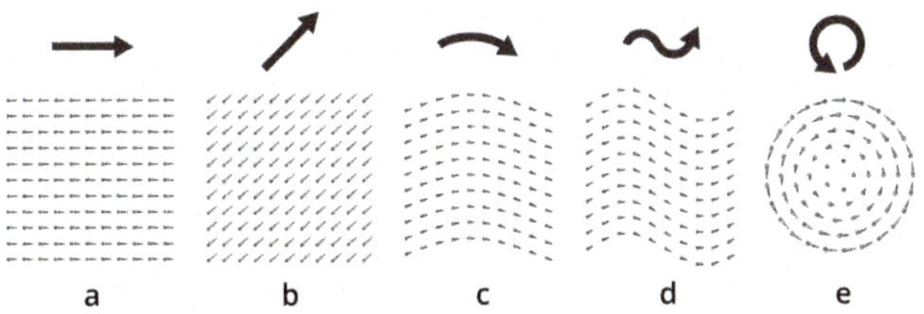

Figure 19. hair direction corresponding to figure 20. (a)(b) Straight line; (c)(d) Curved line; (e) Centered rotation.

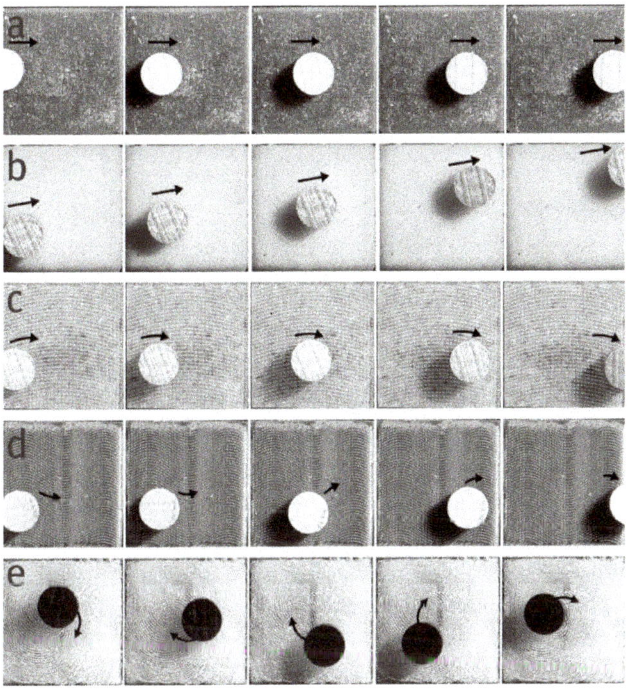

Figure 20. Actuation primitives. (a)(b) Straight line; (c)(d) Curved line; (e) Centered rotation.

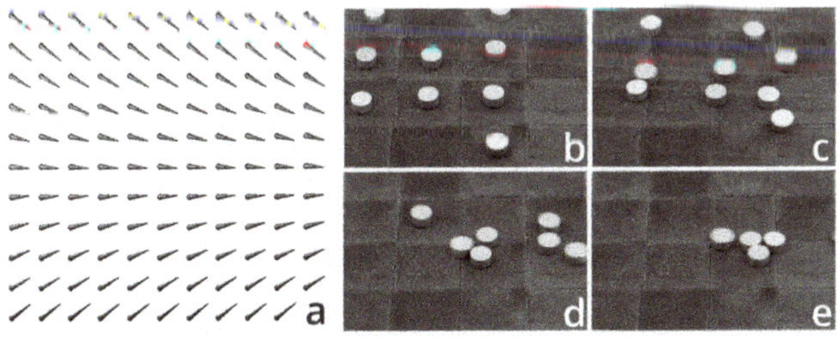

Figure 21. (a) hair direction. (b-e) a conveyor platform converges parts to the middle and the push to the right.

Hair on curved surface.

Similar to the previous example, directional hair on curved surfaces can move object along its vector. In order to fully explore this capability, we designed a block (25 by 25 by 40 mm) with a round hole in the center (Diameter 20mm). The goal was to print the hair array on the inner wall of this block. We cut the block along the long side into four identical pieces. We then placed them in the correct direction and generated identical hair arrays with directionality. After printing, we manually glued them back into the original shape. We then attached a vibrator on one side of the block. By doing this, we were able to direct the vibration force into different kinds of motion: 1. Rotary; 2. Slide; and 3. A combination of the previous two. The block can actuate a cylinder shaped material when the vibration is applied (Figure 22).

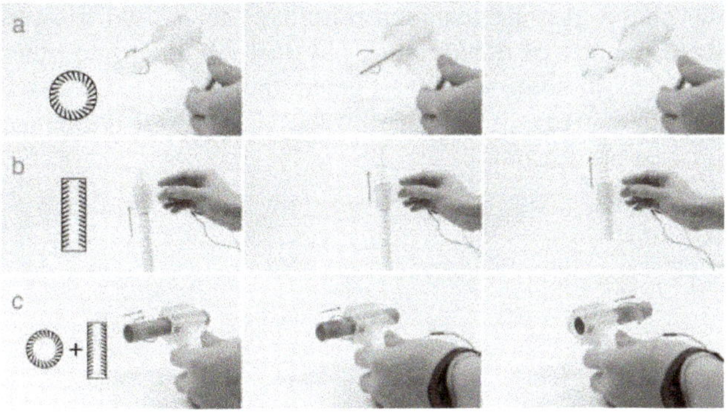

Figure 22. Actuation primitives. (a) Rotatory motion; (b) sliding motion; (c) A combination of rotation and sliding.

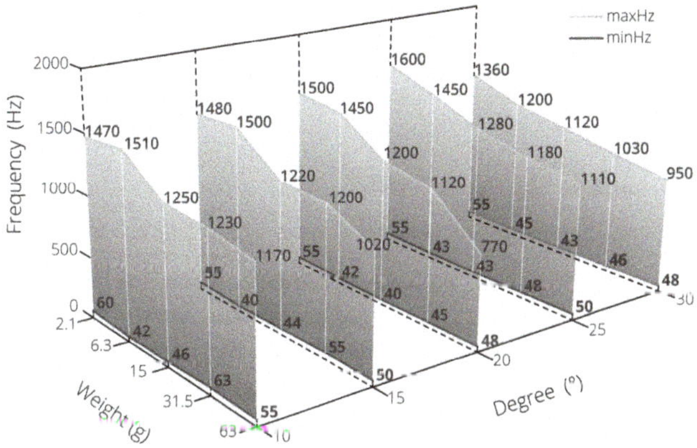

Figure 23. The relationship among the hair tilting degree, the weight of the passive objects and the frequency of the vibration source.

Velocity Dependency

The velocity of the moving object on *Cilllia* depends on the geometry of the hair, the stiffness of the material, and the weight of the passive moving object, as well as the vibration frequency and amplitude. Our preliminary test shows that velocities increase as the vibration amplitude rises. However, the relation between the vibration frequency and the velocity of the passive moving object is not linear. Therefore, instead of testing the velocity change across the vibration frequency, we measured the frequency range in which the passive object can be actuated. This is interesting for us, because our hypothesis is that when two objects with different weights are placed on the hair surface, we can selectively actuate one of them at a certain frequency. We tested five objects with different weight. Their moving velocity was all measured on five hair panels. Each panel's hair has different tilting angle to the X-axis. The result proves our hypothesis (figure 23).

Applications

We designed three applications to show how *Cilllia* surface actuation mechanism can be use in the context of HCI.

Ambient Actuated Tangibles. Recent research in HCI looks into physically moving a phone on the table to remind user of incoming phone call or text messages [24]. They require either a special table or external actuators to be attached on the phone. As our actuation primitives for *Cilllia* showed the capability of transforming physical vibration into other types of motion, we investigated the design of passive objects that can be actuated by the vibration of the phone for user notification.

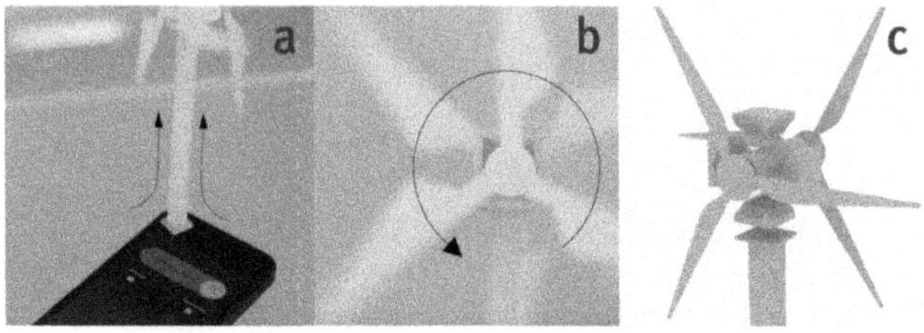

Figure 24. (a) The vibration of a phone can be conducted vertically. (b) Printed hair on the core's surface convert vertical vibration to rotation. (c) Construction of the windmill.

Figure 25. A windmill that are rotates by the phone vibration.

We designed and printed a figure of a windmill, which continuously rotates when subjected to vibration (figure 24). The rotation mechanism is same as the one shown in the last section. The stand of the windmill is hollow so it can effectively conduct the vibration of the phone. The wind turbine is symmetrically fabricated to balance the momentum when it is rotating. Figure 25 shows the user scenario.

Another possible use case could be a tangible outdoor wind speed indication. Our phone has already apps that tell us the wind speed. By modulating the vibration frequency, we can change the rotation velocity of the windmill to ambient display the outside wind speed.

Printed dancing figures. Inspired by the works of Cymatics, we also use the surface of a speaker as a platform for actuating objects. We aim to design and 3D print figures that contain embedded instruction of moving path when the music is playing.

Based on the rotation primitives mentioned above, we printed a series of ballerinas with *Cilllia* on their feet. We separated them into three groups. One had the rotation center on the edge, and the other two were in the middle. We then gave different hair tilting angles (15 and 30 degree) to the remaining two groups to vary their rotation velocity.

We constructed our own speaker/dancing table. A Dayton Audio BCT-2 Bone Conducting Transducer Exciter (Available on https://www.parts-express.com) is mounted in the middle of a round transparent acrylic plate (1" thick). The shaking component of the transducer is attached to another thinner acrylic plate (1/16"). We firmly attached the two plates on their edges by gluing them on a 1" think acrylic spacer, to ensure that only vertical vibration would conduct to the surface, as well as the vibration being propagated evenly through the surface.

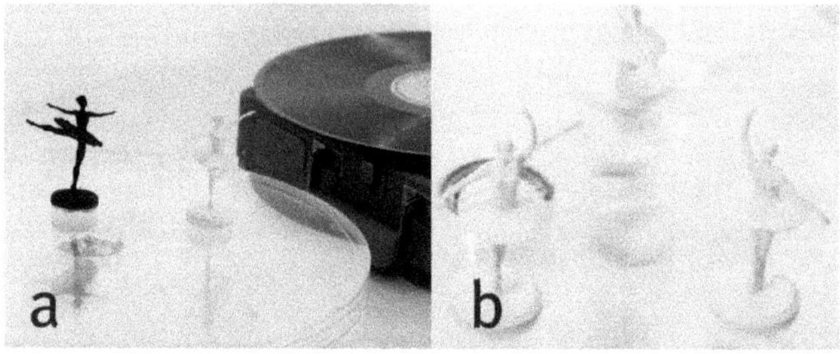

Figure 26. (a) Printed dancing figures on our customized speaker/dancing table. (b) Ballet dancers rotate in different velocity due to the difference in the tilting angle of the hair structure.

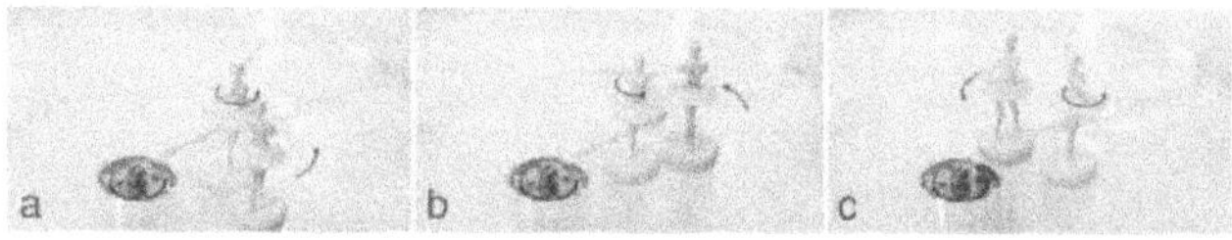

Figure 27. Ballet dancers move following different path due to the difference in hair orientation.

When music plays, we can clearly see each group of ballerinas dance differently based on their hair structure (figure 26 & 27). Sometimes the moving path of the ballerinas would drift slightly due to the uneven distribution of the vibration. In the future, we could improve both the dancing table and hair construction to improve the moving performance.

CILLLIA FOR ACOUSTIC SENSING

One of the most important features of hair in nature is the extent to which it aids in sensing changes in environmental conditions. Many animals, such as caterpillars, use hair on their skin to detect airborne disturbances [15]. In the engineering world, researchers have been learning from hair structure to build artificial flow sensors [11]. Building those sensors usually requires expensive machines and micro-fabrication processes. We utilize the ability to control the hair geometry of *Cilllia* combined with an acoustic sensing method to rapidly fabricate sensors that detect the direction and velocity of human swiping.

A number of researchers have used acoustic methods to detect human gestures [5]. Chris Harrison, et. al. [4] demonstrate the encoding of physical 2.5D barcodes on materials. Sensing on the hair is interesting for us because the sensing mechanism and the surface texture can be seamlessly combined. We can now print a furry animal that senses petting without adding any electronics or obtrusive geometry on the surface of the figure.

When being swiped, a hair array generates an almost inaudible sound by its vibration. If the hair is tilted, swiping along or against the orientation of the hair generates sound comprising different frequencies. One can therefore capture and analyze the sound to reveal the direction and velocity of swiping. In this paper, we use machine learning to classify swiping gestures on the hair.

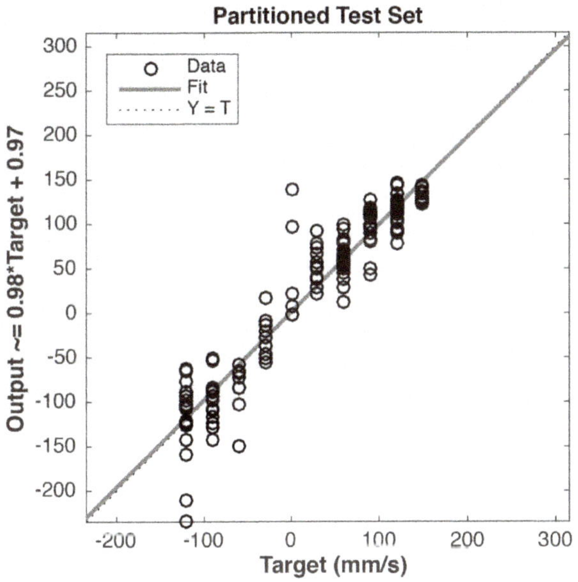

Figure 28. Regression plot compares the ANN output with ground truth target for different speeds and directions.

Swipe Classification

Using a piezo element to capture vibration, we are able to classify direction and speed of swiping along the hair structures on several different printed models. To do so, we condition the signal from the piezo sensor using a simple high impedance JFET buffer. We then digitize it using the line level audio input of a laptop computer. Next, we compute the fast Fourier Transform(FFT) of the signal and bin the resultant amplitude spectrum using a normalized 8-bin histogram. We also compute the spectral flatness (known as the Wiener entropy) of the signal. The histogram bins and the entropy are then used as features in a machine learning process. The signal is characterized by a peak in the spectrum for swipes in the direction of the hair (labeled as forwards); faster forward swipes result in higher harmonics. Swipes against the grain (labeled as backwards) produce a flatter spectrum—closer to noise in the time domain—whose profile is shaped by the speed of the swipe; the result is a noise signal which has a low-cut frequency that increases with swipe speed. In our preliminary exploration, we trained classifiers for each object, though we expect the classifiers to generalize for objects with similar geometries and plan to more thoroughly characterize this in the future.

We conducted three sets of experiments using this technique. In the preliminary experiment, we recorded 4 classes of swipes---forwards slow, forwards fast, backwards slow and backwards fast---along a flat *cilllia* surface with the piezo element attached to the bottom of the printed object with epoxy. The training and testing set consisted of 500 examples divided amongst the 4 classes. We partitioned the data randomly (70% training, 15% validation, 15% test) and used Matlab to train an artificial neural network (ANN) with a single hidden layer of 10 neurons. We ran the partitioning and training 50 times, testing the resultant ANNs each time, and achieved 96% correct classification on average. Encouraged by these results, we collected data for 6 more gradations of swipe speed (for a total of 5 backwards and 5 forwards speeds) and implemented a real-time pipeline in Python to classify swipes with a 10Hz update rate (dictated by the window size). Figure 28 shows that the results were more mixed (with a much higher degree of confusion between neighboring classes), as one might expect, though the fit is apparent. We preliminarily tested the real-time pipeline with a simple demo application that estimates and displays the speed in real time, using the audio input of the computer to capture the signal (figure 29).

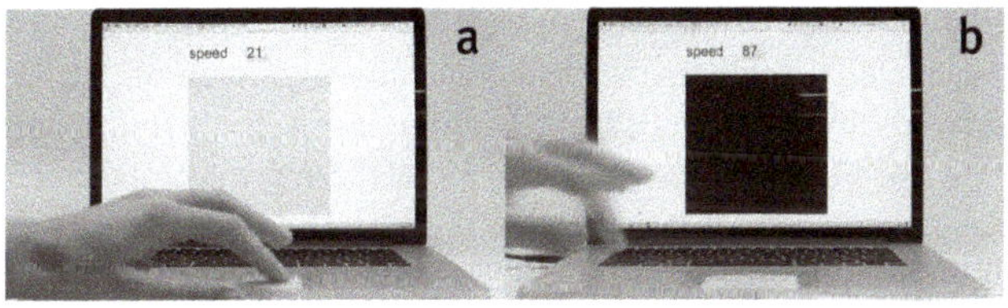

Figure 29. Swiping speed is mapped to the grey scale of the block. (a) Lower speed, (b) higher speed.

In the third experiment, we recorded forwards and backwards swipes along a curved surface. In this case, it is along the back of a model of a rabbit. As in the first experiment, the signal was captured with the piezo element glued to the bottom of the object. In this experiment, the classes were well separated using only the lowest 2 bins (figure 30) of the 8-bin histogram of the amplitude spectrum. We used a support vector machine (SVM) with a linear kernel to classify the swipe direction, with the feature vectors standardized (scaled to zero-mean and unit variance). Because the model was small, we did not attempt to classify swipe speed. To demonstrate feasibility of real-time classification, we ran the classifier online on 500-ms sliding windows over the input signal, overlapping by half the window. We chose this window size to balance the update rate with classification performance, finding a 2-Hz update rate both sufficient for the application and quite high performing. We used a naïve time-domain signal energy metric for onset and outset detection, summing the rectified signal over the window, dividing by the window length, and thresholding. Training on only 10 examples per class, just under 5% of 350 sample windows (corresponding to 200 distinct swipes) were misclassified. As shown in figure 26, only forwards swipes on the bunny were misclassified.

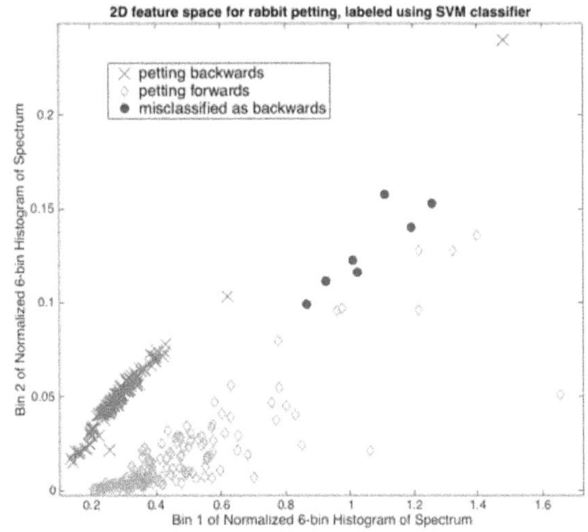

Figure 30. 2D feature space for rabbit petting, labeled using SVM classifier.

Applications

The ability to sense finger swiping on the hair allows us to design interactive toys that combine the sensing mechanism and surface texture seamlessly. To demonstrate that, we fabricated a furry bunny that shows the right way of petting animals by changing the LED color inside its body. When one swipes along the hair direction, the bunny turns green to indicate it's OK; when one swipes against the hair direction, it turns red to show it's unhappy (figure 31).

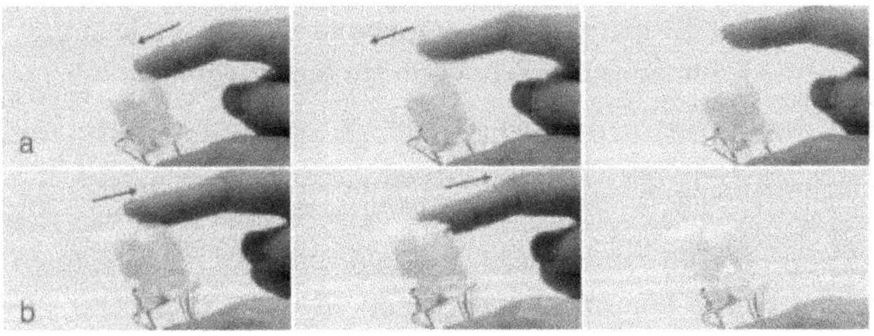

Figure 31. The direction of the swiping on the hairy surface can be differentiated.

We modified the bunny that was used in the second sensing experiment so that we can insert a full color LED inside. A Piezo microphone is firmly glued on the bottom of the bunny. We then attached another acrylic rod to the other side of the piezo so that user can easily grab it.

DISCUSSION AND FUTURE WORKS

While we demonstrated methods and a possible design space for 3D printed micro-pillar structures, we are aware that the technique is very much limited by the physical constraints of current SLA 3D printers. For example, if we had to create an arbitrarily shaped object that is fully covered by hair, we would have to split the object so that the curvature of the surface can still be printed without a supporting structure. The printable materials are also limited in terms of color and stiffness.

Our current algorithm for generating hair on curved surfaces is also highly dependent on the amount and distribution of the triangles of the CAD model. This means that to print high quality hair requires either a nice and clean mesh model or a pre-processing step for the model. In the future, we plan to further develop this technique by focusing on the following aspects:

Hair Generation

As mentioned above, our current approach for hair generation on arbitrary meshes is based on the triangles of the CAD model. In the future, we will add re-mesh functions in our software platform to control hair distribution. It would be also very interesting to test if tilted hair is mechanically weaker than the straight one, as the contact area for each layer of the voxel is less.

Actuation

We plan to embed hair arrays with two opposite orientations at the same area. They also have two different geometries (thickness or angle). Since the two oriented hair arrays can have different resonant frequencies, the platform might be able to actuate objects towards different orientations under different frequencies.

From our material performance characterization, we conclude that objects with a certain weight can only be actuated within a specific range of frequencies (Figure 19). In the future, we hope to design a sorting table that can sort objects with different weight by carefully choosing the vibration frequency. Through our preliminary test, we also observed that hair stiffness may affect the actuation or sorting capability. The ultimate goal is to mathematically model the relation among the hair's geometry (angle, density, thickness), object's weight, vibration frequency and actuation velocity.

Sensing

As the next step, we would like to conduct tests and classifications on more gestures beyond single swiping. Some potential gestures include multi-finger gestures, location of touch and intensity of touch.

Furthermore, we would like to explore the design of analog circuits that would perform real time frequency filtering to recognize gestures without a machine learning process.

CONCLUSION

We present a method of 3D printing hair-like structures on both flat and curved surfaces. It allows a user to design and fabricate hair geometry at the resolution of 50 um. We built a software platform to let one quickly define a hair's angle, thickness, density, and height. The ability to fabricate customized hair-like structures not only expands the library of 3D-printable shapes, but also enables us to design alternative actuator and sensors. We also present several applications to show how the 3D-printed hair can be used for designing everyday interactive objects.

REFERENCES

1. A DeSimone and A Tatone, "Crawling motility through the analysis of model locomotors: two case studies.," Eur. Phys. J. E. Soft Matter, vol. 35, no. 9, p. 85, Sep. 2012.
2. A. Filippov and S. N. Gorb, "Frictional-anisotropy-based systems in biology: structural diversity and numerical model.," Sci. Rep., vol. 3, p. 1240, Jan. 2013.
3. A. Selle, M. Lentine, and R. Fedkiw. 2008. A mass spring model for hair simulation. ACM Trans. Graph. 27, 3, Article 64 (August 2008),
4. C. Harrison, R. Xiao, and S. Hudson. 2012. Acoustic barcodes: passive, durable and inexpensive notched identification tags. In Proceedings of the 25th annual ACM symposium on User interface software and technology (UIST '12). ACM, New York, NY, USA, 563-568.
5. C. Harrison and S. Hudson. 2008. Scratch input: creating large, inexpensive, unpowered and mobile finger input surfaces. In Proceedings of the 21st annual ACM symposium on User interface software and technology (UIST '08). ACM, New York, NY, USA, 205-208.
6. D. K. Rosner and K. Ryokai. 2009. Reflections on craft: probing the creative process of everyday knitters. In Proceedings of the seventh ACM conference on Creativity and cognition (C&C '09). ACM, New York, NY, USA.
7. D. Nowacka, K. Ladha, N. Y. Hammerla, D. Jackson, C. Ladha, E. Rukzio, and P. Olivier. 2013. Touchbugs: actuated tangibles on multi-touch tables. In Proceedings of the SIGCHI Conference on Human Factors in Computing Systems (CHI '13). ACM, New York, NY, USA, 759-762.
8. G. Laput, X. Chen, and C. Harrison. 2015. 3D Printed Hair: Fused Deposition Modeling of Soft Strands, Fibers, and Bristles. In Proceedings of the 28th Annual ACM Symposium on User Interface Software & Technology (UIST '15). ACM, New York, NY, USA, 593-597.
9. G. Pangaro, D. Maynes-Aminzade, and H. Ishii. 2002. The actuated workbench: computer-controlled actuation in tabletop tangible interfaces. In Proceedings of the 15th annual ACM symposium on User interface software and technology (UIST '02). ACM, New York, NY, USA, 181-190.
10. H. Perner-Wilson and L. Buechley. 2010. Making textile sensors from scratch. In Proceedings of the fourth international conference on Tangible, embedded, and embodied interaction (TEI '10). ACM, New York, NY, USA, 349-352.
11. H. Devaraj, J. Travas-Sejdic, R. Sharma, N. Aydemir, D. Williams, E. Haemmerle, Bio-inspired flow sensor from printed PEDOT:PSS micro-hairs 2015 Bioinspir. Biomim. 10 016017
12. H. Ishii, D. Lakatos, L. Bonanni, and JB. Labrune. 2012. Radical atoms: beyond tangible bits, toward transformable materials. *interactions* 19, 1 (January 2012), 38-51.
13. I. Poupyrev, C. Harrison, and M. Sato. 2012. Touché: touch and gesture sensing for the real world. In Proceedings of the 2012 ACM Conference on Ubiquitous Computing (UbiComp '12). ACM, New York, NY, USA, 536-536.
14. J. Ou, L. Yao, D. Tauber, J. Steimle, R. Niiyama, and H. Ishii. 2014. jamSheets: thin interfaces with tunable stiffness enabled by layer jamming. In Proceedings of the 8th International Conference on Tangible, Embedded and Embodied Interaction (TEI '14). ACM, New York, NY, USA, 65-72.
15. J. Tautz and H. Markl, Caterpillars Detect Flying Wasps by Hairs Sensitive to Airborne Vibration, Behavioral Ecology and Sociobiology. Vol. 4, No. 1 (1978), pp. 101-110, Springer
16. K. Willis, E. Brockmeyer, S. Hudson, and I. Poupyrev. 2012. Printed optics: 3D printing of embedded optical elements for interactive devices. In Proceedings of the 25th annual ACM symposium on User interface software and technology (UIST '12). ACM, New York, NY, USA, 589-598.
17. L. Amato, S. S. Keller, A. Heiskanen, M. Dimaki, J. Emnéus, A. Boisen, M. Tenje, Fabrication of high-aspect ratio SU-8 micropillar arrays, Microelectronic Engineering, Volume 98, October 2012, Pages 483-487, ISSN 0167-9317,
18. L. Yao, R. Niiyama, J. Ou, S. Follmer, C. D. Silva, and H. Ishii. 2013. PneUI: pneumatically actuated soft composite materials for shape changing interfaces. In Proceedings of the 26th annual ACM symposium on User interface software and technology (UIST '13). ACM, New York, NY, USA, 13-22.
19. M. Weiss, F. Schwarz, S. Jakubowski, and J. Borchers. 2010. Madgets: actuating widgets on interactive tabletops. In Proceedings of the 23nd annual ACM symposium on User interface software and technology (UIST '10). ACM, New York, NY, USA, 293-302.
20. N. Hopkinson, R.J.M. Hague, P.M. Dickens. Rapid Manufacturing, An Industrial Revolution For The Digital Age. Chichester, Wiley Publication, 2006, pp. 43 – 45.
21. J. Paek, and J. Kim Microsphere-assisted fabrication of high aspect-ratio elastomeric micropillars and waveguides. Nature Communication, 5. 2014.

22. R. Slyper, I. Poupyrev, and J. Hodgins. 2010. Sensing through structure: designing soft silicone sensors. In Proceedings of the fifth international conference on Tangible, embedded, and embodied interaction (TEI '11). ACM, New York, NY, USA, 213-220.
23. S. Hudson. 2014. Printing teddy bears: a technique for 3D printing of soft interactive objects. In Proceedings of the SIGCHI Conference on Human Factors in Computing Systems (CHI '14). ACM, New York, NY, USA, 459-468.
24. S. Follmer, D. Leithinger, A. Olwal, A. Hogge, and H. Ishii. 2013. inFORM: dynamic physical affordances and constraints through shape and object actuation. In Proceedings of the 26th annual ACM symposium on User interface software and technology (UIST '13). ACM, New York, NY, USA, 417-426.
25. S. Gueron, K. Levit-Gurevich, N. Liron, and J. J. Blum, "Cilia internal mechanism and metachronal coordination as the result of hydrodynamical coupling," Appl. Math., vol. 94, no. June, pp. 6001–6006, 1997.

Foldem: Heterogeneous Object Fabrication via Selective Ablation of Multi-Material Sheets

Varun Perumal C, Daniel Wigdor
Department of Computer Science
University of Toronto, Toronto, ON, Canada
{varun | daniel}@dgp.toronto.edu

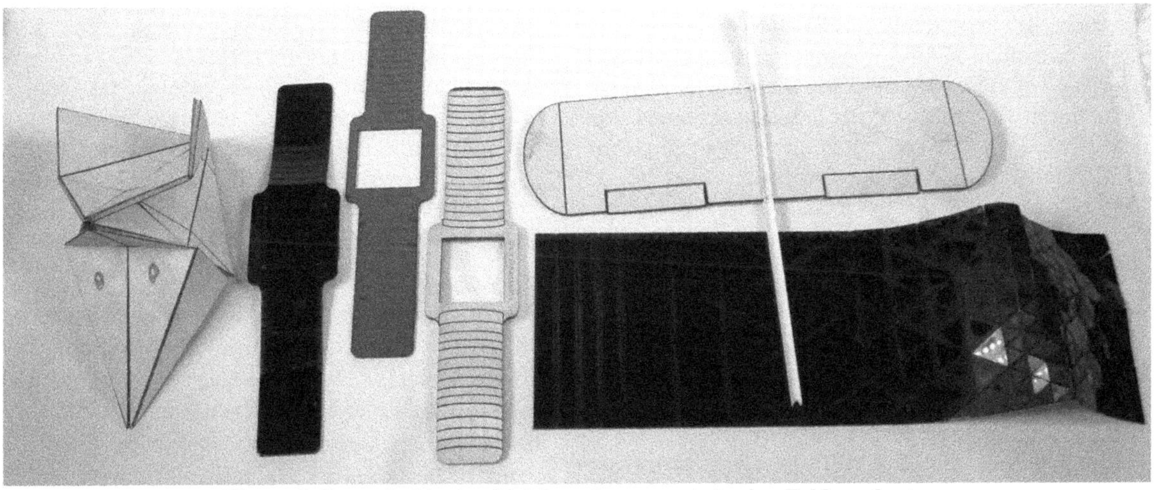

Figure 1. Several objects which have been created using Foldem sheets.

ABSTRACT
Foldem, a novel method of rapid fabrication of objects with multi-material properties is presented. Our specially formulated Foldem sheet allows users to fabricate and easily assemble objects with rigid, bendable, and flexible properties using a standard laser-cutter. The user begins by creating his designs in a vector graphics software package. A laser cutter is then used to fabricate the design by selectively ablating/vaporizing one or more layers of the Foldem sheet to achieve the desired physical properties for each joint. Herein the composition of the Foldem sheet, as well as various design considerations taken into account while building and designing the method, are described. Sample objects made with Foldem are demonstrated, each showcasing the unique attributes of Foldem. Additionally, a novel method for carefully calibrating a laser cutter for precise ablation is presented.

CHI'16, May 07 - 12, 2016, San Jose, CA, USA

ACM 978-1-4503-3362-7/16/05···$15.00
DOI: http://dx.doi.org/10.1145/2858036.2858135

INTRODUCTION
The unprecedented popularity and adoption of rapid prototyping and manufacturing methods such as desktop 3D printing and laser cutting has allowed designers, engineers, and creators to not only rapidly iterate and manufacture their designs but also to fabricate new designs that were previously very difficult or impossible to make [6,9]. Such rapid prototyping tools, owing to their accessibility and ease of use, have democratized physical fabrication and have become important conduits for creative expression [11].

The majority of these rapid prototyping and fabrication methods can be broadly classified as either additive or subtractive methods. Additive fabrication methods create physical objects by sequentially depositing material in a controlled fashion to generate the final objects. The most common type of desktop 3D printers–the fused deposition modelling (FDM) 3D printers–are great examples of additive fabrication technologies. Conversely, subtractive fabrication involves the controlled removal of raw material from a stock to generate the final object. Laser cutting and computer numeric control (CNC) machines are good examples.

Most additive and subtractive fabrication methods are primarily designed to work with only one type of material. Discrete materials are typically handled and processed in separate ways, and each finished piece must be assembled to form the final object [30]. While this paradigm of fabrication enables a systematic approach, it can have a profound impact on the way in which designers and engineers approach their work, which we believe, at times, limits the gamut of possible creations as well as lengthens the time to arrive at the final product by including additional assembly steps.

To address these shortcomings, significant work has been done in developing additive and subtractive fabrication methods that enable the creation of multi-material objects in a single process [31,32]. However, these methods all face the drawbacks of being either extremely costly, slow, or unreliable. Advances in multi-material 3D printing have enabled the creation of objects with varying physical, optical, and electrical properties [18,29]. Subtractive fabrication methods such as laser cutting and CNC routing are significantly faster than additive manufacturing methods; and several varieties of affordable aesthetic multi-material stock [33]for subtractive fabrication are available, but these compound materials do not offer the wide range of mechanical, electrical and optical properties enabled by multi-material additive fabrication methods.

We propose Foldem, a novel approach that expands the space of multi-material subtractive fabrication techniques through the creation of a new compound material: The Foldem sheet, that integrates rigid, bendable, and flexible properties into a single sheet that can be laser-cut or CNC milled. Foldem aims to maintain a balanced approach to fabrication by retaining some of the advantages of additive multi-material methods, namely the control over certain physical properties particularly rigidity and flexibility, while leveraging the speed and broader options of materials enabled by subtractive techniques in order to allow the quick and easy construction of 3D objects with reduced assembly effort and multi-material properties.

To create objects with Foldem, any of the numerous 2D and 3D CAD programs may be utilized. However, to leverage the unique properties of Foldem we have designed a custom set of color coded "brushes" for Adobe Illustrator, which allow them to specify the multi-material properties in their design

We believe that the ease of assembly of the objects generated by Foldem as well as the extended choice of physical properties that the user can incorporate into their designs will be a valuable addition to the rapidly expanding set of accessible tools available to users. Our method enables the easy fabrication and assembly of objects that might normally require multiple processes, materials, and assembly steps to achieve. The philosophy behind Foldem is to enable new methods of fabrication by focusing on the material and not the machine, Similar to the instant PCB fabrication method Printem [27], Foldem attempts to achieve good results without the need for modified or new machinery.

In the next section we conduct a review of existing methods of multi-material and rapid fabrication, exploring additive and subtractive methods including the unique software design tools around them. We also describe work in fabrication using sheet technologies. We then propose Foldem, thoroughly describing the usage of the method and all the material and physical considerations taken into account while designing it. Subsequently, we walk through the process of using Adobe Illustrator and our custom brush set to create the designs. Following this we demonstrate the various sample objects created with Foldem, with an emphasis on the new affordances enabled by this technique. We follow through with a report on our experience of making objects with the Foldem method, describing the advantages and limitations of the method along with guidelines/best-practices for potential users. Finally, we conclude the paper with the various opportunities and possibilities for improving and expanding on Foldem for future work.

RELATED WORK

Significant prior work has been done not only towards the development of new methods of rapid fabrication but also around the enhancement of existing methods that allow for the fabrication of a wider gamut of designs. We discuss the spectrum of relevant prior work under four broad categories: multi-material fabrication, subtractive sheet fabrication techniques, and finally interactive software tools.

Multi-Material Additive Fabrication

Several commercial solutions for multi-material additive fabrication exist such as the Objet Connex [31] and the Polyjet systems [32]. These machines use inkjet technology to deposit multiple materials in a layered fashion to create the final object; these technologies have been deployed in a broad range of uses. They have been utilized for the creation of interactive objects in Printed Optics [29] by Willis et al, enhancing mobile interactions [7], creating curved displays [3], manufacturing high performance footwear [34], and creative clothing [35], and for digitally fabricating bendable origami shapes [4]. MultiFab [21] and Ober et al.'s work [14] have further improved the capabilities of multi-material fabrication technologies through machine vision and a wider array of usable materials. However, these machines are prohibitively expensive with prices ranging from several thousand dollars to tens of thousands of dollars, putting them out of reach of the average user.

Considerable work has been done in extending traditional Fused Deposition Modeling (FDM) [46] with enhancements such as multiple extruders and novel materials, allowing for the creation of multi-colored objects [36], embedding conductive pathways [8] and simulating the look and feel of other materials [37]. These advancements; however, have been shown to be considerably unreliable and inconsistent in real world use and require significant tweaking by the user to get satisfactory results.

Our Foldem sheet offers multi-material capabilities while working on existing laser cutting machines that are more accessible and reliable when compared to multi-material additive fabrication machines. Additionally, a Foldem sheet can be made using low cost materials making it accessible to a comparatively larger set of users.

Sheet Fabrication Methods

Using laser-cutting and other sheet fabrication methods to manufacture prototypes is a fast method of rapid prototyping. But the 2D nature of the fabrication process implies that post fabrication assembly is required to create the final object. Several innovative solutions have been proposed to address this problem. Traditionally, heat bending of plastic sheets [38] has been a standard manufacturing process to create 3D objects out of 2D sheets. Mueller et al. [12] introduced a novel method for using laser-cutting machines to both cut and bend flat plastic sheets into 3D forms. Peng et al.[15] demonstrated the use of fabric sheets in creating soft, interactive 3D objects. ElectronicPoppables [16] showcased the integration of electronics in 3D popup books. Olberding et al. [20] and Oxman et al. [23] further explored the integration of electronics into flat sheets that fold to form 3D objects. These methods all offer fast turnaround time for prototyping, but they limit the gamut of possible designs.

The ability to fabricate 3D forms form 2D sheets is also of great interest to the mechanical engineering and robotics research communities. Several of these approaches use self folding mechanisms fabricated form 2D sheets to form the final structures [1,24]. These methods predominantly involve the individual cutting various materials first followed by the assembly of these sheets into a laminate and finally a self-assembly process. Foldem on the other hand starts with a preformed compound laminate followed by a cutting and manual folding process.

The assembly of discrete 2D sheets into 3D forms is viable for a small number of pieces but very difficult to do for objects with a large number of pieces. Additionally, it is difficult to create movable joints between these pieces. To solve this, researchers have been exploring self-assembly techniques to automatically form the final object. Several approaches to this paradigm of fabrication have been explored [22], including the use of shape memory materials [17,25] and heat reactive polymers [10]. These techniques reduce assembly time on the user's part but place significant constraints on the design of the object, where only certain geometries are possible.

Hybrid fabrication techniques that merge additive and subtractive fabrication methods have been proposed and implemented in various ways. Mueller et al. demonstrate highly rapid fabrication of objects through the use of Lego bricks and 3D printing [13], the substitution of laser-cut parts [2], and the stacking and laser welding of plastic sheets [26]. Commercially available solutions such as the DMG Mori Lasertec [39] combine additive material deposition with CNC milling to achieve good surface finishes.

Foldem is comparable in speed to traditional laser cutting processes, and it uses multi-material properties of the Foldem sheet to allow for the creation of 3D objects through bending and folding operations. By providing joints which the user can quickly bend to create a shape, its use for assembly of 3D objects is significantly faster than fastening separately-cut components. Additionally, Foldem, much like [4], allows the user to control the angle's degree of bend at design time to create more precise folds in 3D objects.

Design Software

Substantial work has been done to address the unique challenges of creating manufacture-able designs for multi-material processes. OpenFab [28] creates a generic pipeline for dealing with multi-material design processes. Fogarty et al. [5] have explored methods of specifying semantic meaning in drawing packages, such methods can be used to extend existing drawing packages to specify special material properties as in the case of Foldem. Foldio [20] demonstrates a software tool that allows users to easily create interactive, foldable objects from a flat material. Software such as Pepakura [40] also allows the user to turn 3D models into foldable paper objects. Additionally, several widely available CAD design tools allow users to easily remix [19], create, and modify [41] designs for digital fabrication.

To create objects with Foldem, users are free to choose from any of the available CAD software, provided that an output in the form of a PDF file can be generated. Alternatively, the user can choose to use our custom set of brushes in Adobe Illustrator to specify the desired multi-material properties.

FOLDEM SHEET

Our proposed method - the Foldem sheet is a compound stack of materials, each with different properties. This sheet can be laser-cut or milled with a CNC. In addition to enabling the creation of objects with multi-material properties, Foldem sheets allow for the quick creation of 3D objects by allowing the 2D sheet to be selectively folded along cut lines and bent to form 3D structures. In summary, the Foldem sheet offers the following key advantages:

1. *Allows for the fabrication of objects with multi-material properties*
2. *Works with traditional laser cutting and 2D CNC milling, both of which are methods that are significantly faster than additive fabrication technologies.*
3. *Allows for the creation of 3D objects with individual joints that hold their shape (are 'bent') or remain fully flexible.*
4. *Enables design-time control of the angle of folds between rigid portions, enabling rapid and controlled folding.*
5. *Is low cost: each sheet can be comprised of commodity materials.*

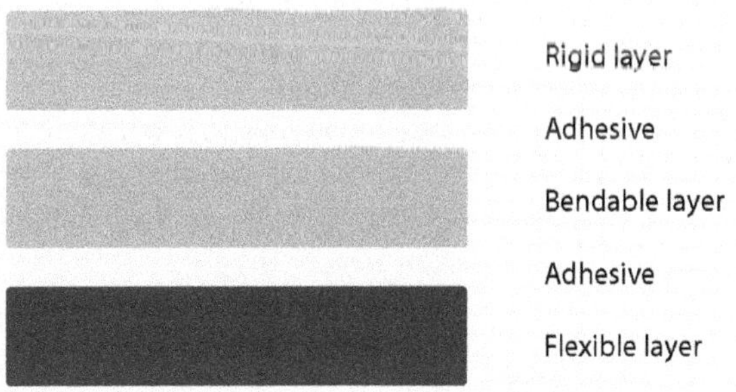

Figure 2. The layers of a Foldem sheet.

The key to enabling design-time control over fold angle, as well as a selection between permanent folds and flexible joints, is Foldem's multi-material stack. Each Foldem sheet is made up of a stack of three different layers bonded using a suitable adhesive compound, as illustrated in Figure 2. In the following section we describe the principle of operation of the Foldem sheet followed by a description of their construction and the choice of materials for each layer.

Principle of Operation and Design Implications

The Foldem sheet is a simple stack of multiple materials that have been bonded together using a suitable adhesive to form a compound sheet, very much like plywood. Unlike plywood, each of the materials in the stack has a different physical property: a different level of rigidity. The layers are stacked in an increasing order of their flexibility with the most rigid layer on top and the most flexible layer at the bottom, as illustrated in Figure 2.

This arrangement allows the laser-cutting machine or CNC milling machine to remove the layers as needed in a sequential fashion to achieve the desired material properties at a joint. The more layers that are removed, the more flexible the resulting joint becomes. Laser cutting a three layer Foldem sheet to achieve multi material properties works as follows:

1. If the layers are cut all the way through the Foldem sheet (a “full cut”), this results in a part that is similar to any of the rigid plastic sheets as illustrated in Figure 3(d).

2. When the laser ablates the rigid layer (the first layer), we are left with the bendable and the flexible layers (a “bendable cut). The bendable layer dominates the physical strength of this arrangement and the remainder of the sheet is now bendable as illustrated in Figure 3(b). The width of cut is what determines angle to which the joint may be bent: the wider the cut, the greater the bend.

3. Similarly, when the bendable layer (the second layer) of the Foldem sheet is cut through as well (a “flexible cut”, the flexible layer remains as the only connected structural component of the sheet, thus generating a joint/interface that is completely flexible as illustrated in Figure 3(c). Here too, a wider cut enables a greater of freedom of movement in the resulting joint.

This method of arranging and stacking layers can be applied to a wide variety of material. In this paper we consider Foldem sheets made with a stack of two or three materials but the same principle of operation and construction method can be applied to sheets with a larger number of layers, each increasingly flexible, in order to provide finer-grained control over the rigidity of each join.

Composition of the Foldem Sheet

The user can mix and match materials to fabricate their own Foldem sheets with their desired number of layers to suit the aesthetic and functional requirements of their application. Our current implementation of the Foldem sheet has been primarily designed for use with the most common types of laser-cutting equipment. Although Foldem sheets are, in concept, compatible with both CNC and laser cutters, we focused our present investigation on the latter due to their relatively greater availability. In particular, the materials we chose were carefully tested for use with the cutter. For our entire process we have used a VersaLaser [42] machine. This machine is rated at 70W power for the laser at a peak wavelength of 1064nm and a cutting area of 24”x12”. The machine also has an adjustable focus to adjust the laser focus for working with materials of different thicknesses.

Several considerations must be taken into account while choosing the materials for each layer, as well as the adhesive used to bind the layers together into the finished Foldem sheet. Each has a unique set of needs, but several characteristics apply to all:

1. *Must be suitable for laser cutting*
2. *Must not smoke or release harmful gas while being cut*
3. *Must possess the rigidity required for the given layer*

In addition to these common properties, each layer has its own unique considerations as well.

1. Rigid Layer

As the name indicates, this layer forms the rigid structural element of the Foldem sheet. Any rigid laser cuttable material can be used for this purpose, the most common choices being acrylic, high-density polyethylene (HDPE), soft woods, and medium density fiber boards (MDF). Owing to their common availability, acrylic and bass wood are the materials of choice in our experiments and samples. The thickness of this layer is crucial to the performance of the Foldem sheet: if this layer is too thick, it will impede the amount of bending enabled by the layer below. If the layer is too thin, it can cause the final object to be structurally weak and cause it to break. In our experiments we have found that a layer that has a thickness in the range of 1mm-3mm is most suited for this purpose. Greater thickness can be used as required, but suitable precautions must be taken while designing objects to be fabricated from such sheets.

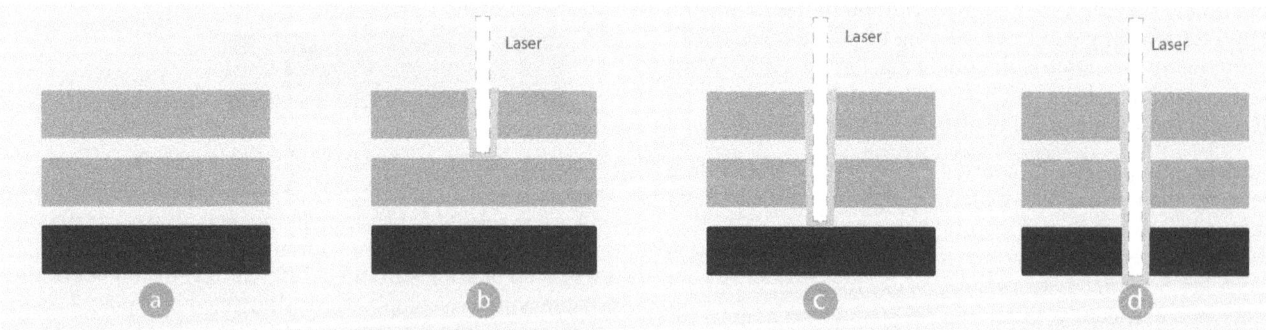

Figure 3. Generating desired multi-material properties using Foldem: (a) Foldem sheet intact; (b) Rigid layer cut through, leaving a bendable joint; (c) Rigid and bendable layers cut through, leaving a flexible joint; (d) All layers cut through for a full cut.

2. Bendable Layer

Below the rigid layer is the bendable layer, this layer is to be made up of a material that is not only malleable enough to be bent by hand but also strong enough to maintain the bend, much like a metal wire that can be bent and formed into various shapes. Metals, such as copper or tin are the natural choice for such a layer; however, the most common types of laser cutters cannot cut metallic substrates. Hence, we have chosen a special plastic that possesses similar properties for bending, while also being compatible with a laser cutter [43]. This layer should be as thin as possible while maintaining malleability. We have found a thickness of 0.8 mm is ideal for the material chosen. If compatibility with commonly available laser cutters was not a requirement, metallic materials could be used and would enable a still thinner bendable layer.

2. Flexible Layer

Finally, the bottom-most layer of the Foldem sheet provides the flexible property of the sheet and forms flexible joints and hinges that freely move. It thus must be comprised of a material that will maintain the mechanical connection between the parts cut from the acrylic, but a material that will not stretch laterally after repeated flexing. We have chosen to use cotton and satin fabrics due to favourability with respect to these factors, and its ease of laser cutting.

4. Adhesive

All the above-mentioned layers need to be bonded together to form the complete Foldem sheet. The adhesive chosen should be laser cuttable, non-reactive to the materials that are being bonded and be strong enough to hold the various materials together. Most generic adhesives such as craft glues, epoxies, and water-based glues are suitable for this purpose. In our experiments and samples we have chosen to use the 3M Super 77 [44] spray adhesive due to its ease of application and compatibility with a broad range of substrates. Additionally, the 3M DP420 Epoxy [45] can also be used for stronger bonds, however the application process for liquid adhesives is more cumbersome.

Care must be taken in process of fabricating the Foldem sheet in order to ensure good final results. We have observed that the uniform application of the adhesive between the layers and the uniform bonding of the layers are critical factors in achieving good quality output. To ensure this, we recommend that the user take great care in using the spray adhesive and spray evenly from a fixed distance. While using liquid adhesive, its recommend to use squeegees and rollers to ensure a uniform coating. Finally, the Foldem sheet must be assembled one layer at a time, ensuring enough time for each layer to bond and cure fully before moving on the next layers. While bonding each layer to the next it is also recommended that the user sandwich the work piece in between heavy flat pieces of wood to ensure uniform pressure during the curing process for the adhesive.

Degree of Bend and Fold

Another key feature of the Foldem method is that it allows the user to control, at design-time, the angle to which two adjacent features can bend with respect to each other. This is achieved by controlling the width of the laser cut into the Foldem sheet. The bend angle is a function of the width of the cutting line and the thickness of the rigid sheet. A simple derivation shows this expression to be:

$$w = 2 * t * \sin\left(\frac{\theta}{2}\right) - \mathbf{k}$$

Where t is the thickness of the rigid layer and $\boldsymbol{\theta}$ is the desired bend angle in radians, w is the width of cut that the laser needs to make. Due to a small but finite beam size, all laser-cutting machines burn off a set width of material called "kerf" when they cut, this is taken into account by the **k** term. Figure 4 illustrates how the width of the cut affects the bend angle.

A key point to note is that the process of generating a change in this cutting width must be carefully controlled. A naïve way of achieving this is to simply cut multiple parallel lines to achieve the desired cut width, but this poses a significant issue. When the laser is cutting lines very close to each other, part of the beam does not fall on the substrate, instead it reaches through the gap created by the previously ablated material and starts ablating the layers below. We use raster etching to mitigate this issue. All laser-cutting machines support the use of raster etching to generate raster graphics on the substrates. To achieve this the laser-cutting machine reduces the power of the laser as well as increases the speed of cutting, ensuring the ablation of the desired thickness of surface material.

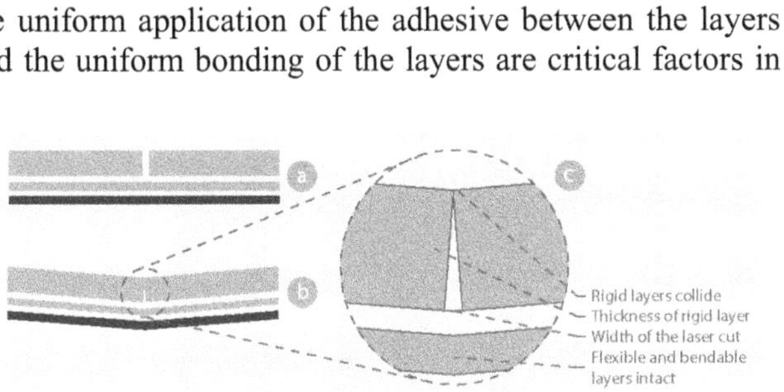

Figure 4. Process of controlling the bend angle in Foldem: (a) Foldem sheet with a laser cut line; (b) bending of the Foldem sheet; (c) Close up of the bend.

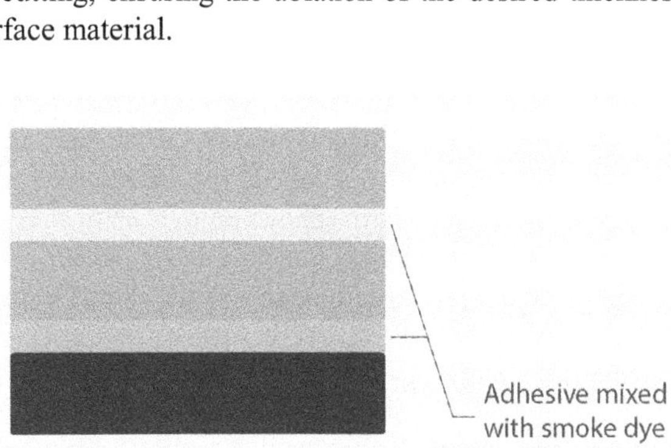

Figure 5. The layers of the Foldem calibration sheet.

In addition to the three layered Foldem sheets described, Foldem sheets with larger or fewer number of layers can be built to suit the designers purpose. For example, a five layer Foldem sheet that consists of a central flexible layer surrounded by a bendable and rigid layers on either side can be used to have controlled bending in both directions.

Choice of Materials

Several materials were tested for their compatibility for use as part of the Foldem sheet. For the rigid layers, we have tested, soft wood sheets such as balsa and bass, hardwoods such as maple and oak, plastics such as acrylic, High Density Polyethylene (HDPE) and Poly-lactic Acid (PLA). For the flexible layers we have experimented with a wide variety of natural and synthetic fabrics including, cotton, cotton canvas, polyester, nylon fabric, cotton-polyester mix, denim and faux leather.

After extensively testing various permutations and combinations of the above materials in making the Foldem sheet we recommend two combinations that have worked really well in terms of assembling the Foldem sheet as well as enabling the creation of precise clean cuts with the laser cutting machine. For smaller objects that require a lot of flexible and bendable joints and where mechanical strength of the object is not of the highest priority, we recommend a combination of acrylic (rigid), polyester and nylon blend fabric (flexible layer) and finally bendable plastic for the bendable layer. Additionally, for larger objects that require a lot of mechanical strength but do not require as much flexibility we recommend a combination of bass wood (rigid layer), cotton canvas (flexible layer) and bendable plastic for the bendable layer.

Cutter Calibration

As we have discussed, materials were carefully chosen for their compatibility with a laser cutter. Even so, individual differences between laser cutters, as well as differences in the movement of the cutting head in each cardinal direction, have meant that careful calibration has been required to use Foldem sheets. Calibration consists of adjusting instructions based on speed and power of the laser. This process can be potentially time consuming and error prone due to the lack of direct user control over the depth of the cut using the laser cutter, and the harmful nature of looking directly at the work piece during cutting.

To ease this process of calibration, we have developed the Foldem Calibration sheet, which is identical to the normal Foldem sheet, with one major exception: where a regular Foldem sheet uses standard adhesives to join the layers together to form the final compound sheet, the layers of our calibration sheet uses those same adhesives, doped with an organic dye. When heated, the dye burns, and produces non-toxic, brightly colored smoke much like a firecracker. A different color is used at the interface of each different layer of the compound sheet. When the laser breaches each layer of material, the colored smoke indicates that the layer has been cut-through. The current setting of intensity can then be saved and adjusted for use with the regular Foldem sheets. In our samples we have used a blue dye at the interface of the rigid and bendable layers and an orange dye at the interface of the bendable and flexible layers. Because all laser cutting systems are equipped with air venting and exhaust systems which sequester the colored smoke, no harm is posed.

PROCESS OF USING FOLDEM

Once the laser cutter is calibrated, the user is ready to utilize Foldem to create 3D objects. Using the Foldem is a three-step process. First, our Adobe Illustrator brush set is used to design the file. The output file is then accepted by the laser-cutting machine to cut the appropriate patterns and layers. Finally, the cut and ablated Foldem sheet is manually folded, bent, or glued in place to achieve the final form.

Creating Designs

Key to enabling users to make-use of a Foldem sheet's unique capabilities is providing a tool to enable them to specify the degree to which a given joint should be allowed to bend or fold. As we have described, significant work has been invested in creating software tools for people to create functional foldable objects with 2D fabrication technologies [20]. This software tool would be an ideal design environment for Foldem, once enhanced for our multi-material sheets and connecting of degree of fold to cut width. To demonstrate how this enhancement might be made, we built a plugin for Adobe Illustator, which includes a custom set of "brushes". Each brush encodes a different type of manufacturing operation described above: *Bendable Cut*, *Flexible Cut*, *Full Cut,* and traditional *Engraving* (see Figure 3). Additionally, the plugin allows the user to specify the angle for *Bendable* and *Flexible* cuts.

The process of using our custom brushes is nearly identical to how laser cutting is normally done: the user specifies cuts as paths in a vector drawing, where colors of the lines indicate

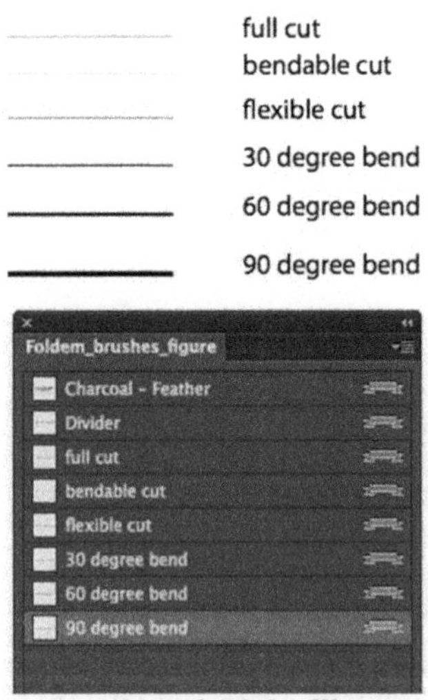

Figure 6. A screenshot of Adobe Illustrator, showing our custom tool palette (bottom) and sample cut lines.

power and speed of the laser. Our plug-in generates the appropriate color, and adds passes for width, given the user's selected brush. Finally, after achieving a satisfactory design the user simply exports his design into the PDF file format. This PDF file should then be imported into the laser cutter CAM software, which then translates the various colored lines and strokes into commands that the laser cutter implements, thus fabricating the object, which the user can bend, fold, and assemble into the final form.

PROPERTIES OF OBJECTS CREATED WITH FOLDEM

The unique construction of the Foldem sheet as well as the novel way in which the laser cutter works with it allow for unique affordances that the user can exploit in his design process, fabricating objects that are not only functional but also possessing a unique aesthetic. We believe that a confluence of theses discrete properties when combined and used, form a powerful feature set for the user to deploy.

Rigidity

The rigidity of the Foldem sheet is similar to typical materials used for fabrication using a laser cutter; in fact, the top layer of the Foldem sheet can be composed of whatever material is desired for a given application. This implies that the majority of designs that are made for use on normal laser cutting substrates such as acrylic and HDPE can be simply be used alongside the Foldem sheet with little to no modifications, allowing for co-existence of traditional laser cut designs and the new ones made possible through Foldem. Additionally, the bonding of the rigid layers with the flexible and bendable layers provides additional strength to the entire sheet.

Bendability

The Foldem sheet is also bendable; much like a sheet of metal, it can be bent to a specific position that is retained until sufficient force is applied to move it to a new position. This allows the user to generate features that require a bendable joint that maintains its position, much like the appendages of a pose able action figure. This allows the user to adjust the model after fabrication for any number of reasons ranging from changing the orientation of certain features to using it as a deformable surface.

Flexibility

Cloth-like flexibility is a key feature of the Foldem sheet. This property allows for the generation of features that require free flowing motion. This property also serves as the basic connective tissue that keeps the assembly of the rigid and bendable pieces together, allowing the parts made with Foldem to be easily assembled by folding.

Ease of Assembly

Owing to the presence of the flexible layer in the Foldem sheet, the final laser cut sheet can be easily folded into the right shape. The flexible layer does the job of providing a foldable "hinge" as well as keeping the various pieces of the object fixed in their lateral positions with the sheet. This is advantageous in several ways over traditional assembly of laser cut objects. It reduces the cognitive load on the user to align and place the various pieces in the right orientation; a crucial benefit when the object has dozens of individual parts that need to be assembled together.

SAMPLE OBJECTS

To showcase the unique affordances and the breadth of designs made possible through Foldem, we have produced five samples of objects made with the Foldem sheets. Each of these examples showcase a group of specific attributes of our method and demonstrate how they can be used in tandem to create practical and unique designs.

Wearable Bracelet

Wearable devices and electronics naturally require multi-material properties in their construction; several traditional wearable objects such as watches and bracelets employ rigid sections that are linked with flexible joints to ensure a comfortable wearing experience and good fit. We believe that Foldem is ideally placed to fabricate parts for such devices, and we present a bracelet made for a smart watch using a three layer Foldem sheet. The simple bracelet is constructed with alternating bendable and flexible joints to allow for adjustment to various wrist sizes and a comfortable fit. The unique bracelet incorporates both a traditional watch on the front and a smart watch on the underside, giving the user a wide choice in self-expression without compromising on connectivity.

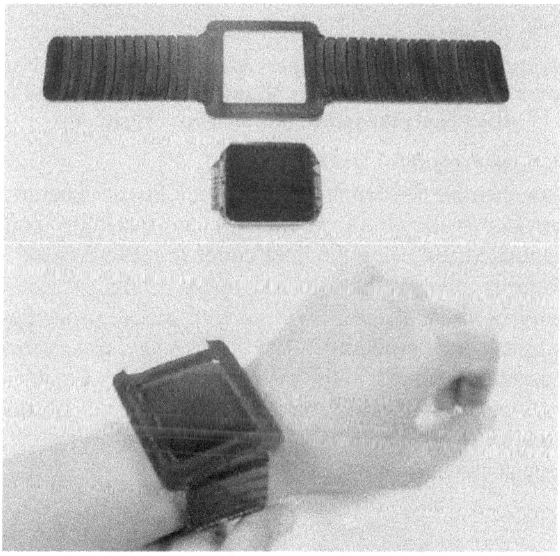

Figure 8. The Foldem-based watchband, custom cut to fit an Android smart watch (a), on the user's wrist (b)

User-Adjustable Glider Ailerons

Foldem can be used to produce objects whose physical shape can be modified continuously by end-users. In this example, we demonstrate how a simple yet functional glider can be laser-cut using a Foldem sheet. The glider's flight is directed by the positioning of ailerons, shown in Figure 9. Each time the glider is thrown, its path is altered by the user's positioning. Each aileron may be individually positioned. The interface between the sides of the aileron and the wings has been cut through, while the joint between them has been ablated to the bendable layer.

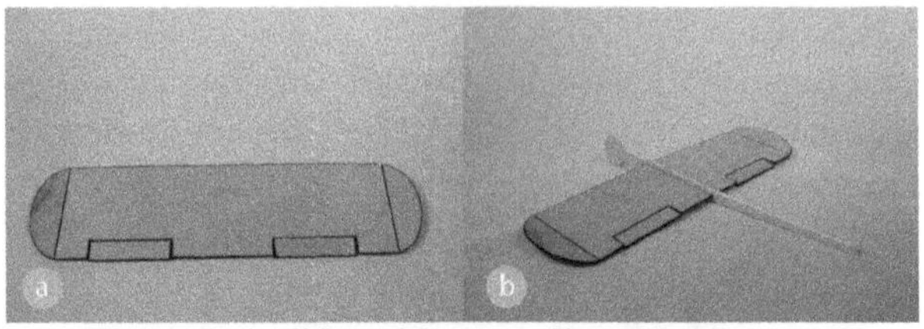

Figure 9. A glider with user-adjustable ailerons. The bendable layer provides sufficient rigidity to maintain the ailerons' position after each user adjustment.

Origami Fox

Foldem can be used to trivially create origami that is made easy to fold by the pre-cutting of joints, and made rigid by the solid materials used. As Figure 10 illustrates, the folds in the origami are ablated from the Foldem sheet. The user must then perform the folds in the correct order to create the finished model This Foldem sheet also demonstrates the use of wood as the rigid layer.

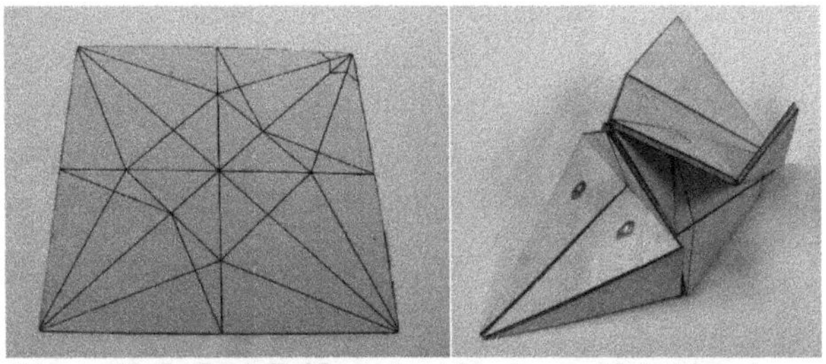

Figure 10. Left: A Foldem sheet has been ablated in a laser cutter to create several joints. Right: the user has folded the sheet, using the joints, into a classic origami fox.

Cloth-Like Material

In this example we demonstrate the viability of generating a fabric like material whose stiffness and flexibility can be manipulated. By using the laser cutter to make flexible cuts of various repeating shapes and by adjusting the size and density of these shapes, surfaces with different degrees of flexibility are produced. The user can also generate directional flexibility in the material by making flexible and bendable cuts in only one direction. Such fabric-like materials can be used to "drape" objects and projects to create unique aesthetics.

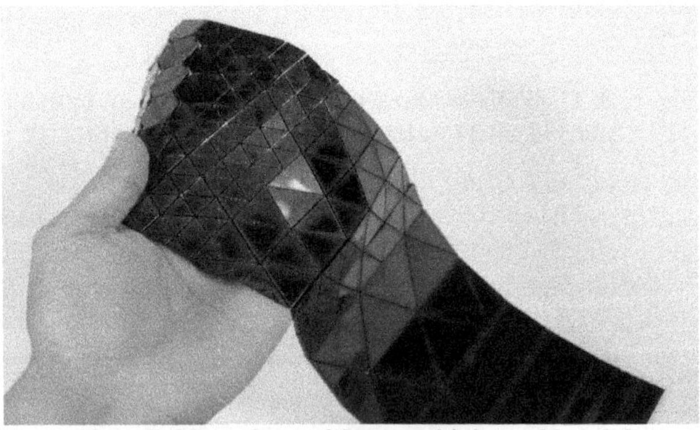

Figure 11. A Foldem sheet with several joints, ablated down to the flexible layer, creates a rigid material that moves like cloth.

DISCUSSION

Foldem is a unique method of subtractive digital fabrication that relies on a special substrate to achieve multi-material properties. As demonstrated in the samples above, it can be used to generate a wide variety of objects and designs, with unique characteristics.

The primary advantage of Foldem is its ability to fabricate objects with multi-material properties using laser-cutting machines. It is recommended that the objects made through Foldem leverage the multi-material properties in two ways. First, to use the flexible and bendable hinges to generate 3D shapes from the 2D sheet. Secondly, to generate unique features in the final objects such as flexible sub-sections. As with any fabrication method, Foldem has its limitations that must be carefully considered: by its very nature it is highly suitable for the fabrication of certain kinds of objects and not suitable for some other kinds of designs. Foldem is not suitable for constructing objects that are intended to be rigid or uniformly flexible: these objects are best manufactured through traditional rapid prototyping techniques such as desktop 3D printing or laser-cutting.

Foldem also reduces the time for required for assembly of laser-cut parts. However, it must be noted that this reduction in time only applies to parts that require manual assembly such as parts made with traditional materials on a laser-cutter. For standard objects made with 3D printers however, objects are generally printed as a whole and assembly is usually not required. Of course, the use of a 3D printer can add significantly to fabrication time. Foldem can produce a wider gamut of objects and shapes when compared to other 2D fabrication methods; however, unlike LaserOrigami [12], where a laser is used to cut and bend plastic sheets into 3D shapes Foldem cannot produce 3D structures without manual assembly.

Although Foldem can be used to fabricate simple 2D shapes, it does not offer a significant advantage over normal laser-cuttable materials in this regard. But leveraging the multi-material properties of Foldem to fabricate 2D shapes can result in the creation of objects such as the cloth-like material sample presented in this paper. Such objects can be very difficult or expensive to manufacture using traditional materials and processes.

The price of the Foldem sheet depends on the materials chosen for each of its layers. The Foldem sheet in some of our examples is more expensive than traditional laser cutting materials of similar thickness and dimension. The majority of the increase in cost comes from the addition of the bendable plastic layer, which is expensive to procure in prototype quantities. The assembly of the various materials into a single sheet also adds to the cost of the Foldem sheet. However, we see that with the use of metal for the bendable layer and mass manufacturing this cost can be significantly cut down.

Foldem combines the speeds of traditional laser cutting processes with the ability to fabricate multi-material 3D objects. As a fabrication method, Foldem trades complexity and fidelity for speed and flexibility. Hence, when time is not an important constraint, Foldem does not offer a significant advantage over traditional 3D printing techniques. Similarly, Foldem is not suitable for making complex objects with intricate shapes; these types of objects are best suited to be manufactured using traditional 3D printing and CNC milling technologies.

To summarize, we see Foldem as a method that bridges the gap between 3D printing methods and 2D fabrication methods, as an additional tool for increasing the gamut of creations possible with existing machinery by creating and using novel materials.

FUTURE WORK AND CONCLUSION

To extend and improve on Foldem we foresee future work in multiple areas. Primarily, we intend to improve the Foldem sheet by adding additional layers, and experimenting with alternative layers, in order to generate even more interesting physical properties. The variation of material properties across the sheet in addition through the variation through the sheet could be explored. Additionally, the concept of self-assembling objects can be explored further using Foldem as the foundation. We also intend to work on building custom software tailored for use with multi-material sheet fabrication, which can allow for the automatic generation of the necessary geometric patterns when the user specifies a set of desired physical properties.

We believe that the unique properties of objects constructed using Foldem make it a worthy addition to the field of multi-material manufacturing, as well as to the more nascent field of rapid prototyping and digital fabrication. We have found Foldem to be a valuable addition to our digital fabrication facility, and hope others will benefit as well.

ACKNOWLEDGEMENTS

We thank Katie Barker, Khai Truong, and Peter Hamilton for their assistance with this work and members of DGP for their valuable inputs and discussions.

REFERENCES

1. Daniel M Aukes, Benjamin Goldberg, Mark R Cutkosky, and Robert J Wood. 2014. An analytic framework for developing inherently-manufacturable pop-up laminate devices. *Smart Materials and Structures* 23, 9: 094013. http://doi.org/10.1088/0964-1726/23/9/094013
2. Dustin Beyer, Serafima Gurevich, Stefanie Mueller, Hsiang-ting Chen, and Patrick Baudisch. Platener : Low-Fidelity Fabrication of 3D Objects by Substituting 3D Print with Laser-Cut Plates. 3–10.
3. Eric Brockmeyer, Ivan Poupyrev, and Scott Hudson. 2013. PAPILLON. *Proceedings of the 26th annual ACM symposium on User interface software and technology - UIST '13*, ACM Press, 457–462. http://doi.org/10.1145/2501988.2502027
4. Dongping Deng and Yong Chen. 2012. Design of Origami Sheets for Foldable Object Fabrication. *Volume 3: 38th Design Automation Conference, Parts A and B*, ASME, 223. http://doi.org/10.1115/DETC2012-71530
5. James Fogarty, Jodi Forlizzi, and Scott E. Hudson. 2002. Specifying behavior and semantic meaning in an unmodified layered drawing package. *Proceedings of the 15th annual ACM symposium on User interface software and technology - UIST '02*, ACM Press, 61. http://doi.org/10.1145/571985.571995
6. Neil Gershenfeld. 2007. Fab: The Coming Revolution on Your Desktop--from Personal Computers to Personal Fabrication. Retrieved September 20, 2015 from http://dl.acm.org/citation.cfm?id=1211574
7. Gierad Laput, Eric Brockmeyer, Scott E. Hudson, and Chris Harrison. 2015. Acoustruments. *Proceedings of the 33rd Annual ACM Conference on Human Factors in Computing Systems - CHI '15*, ACM Press, 2161–2170. http://doi.org/10.1145/2702123.2702414
8. Simon J Leigh, Robert J Bradley, Christopher P Purssell, Duncan R Billson, and David A Hutchins. 2012. A simple, low-cost conductive composite material for 3D printing of electronic sensors. *PloS one* 7, 11: e49365. http://doi.org/10.1371/journal.pone.0049365
9. Hod Lipson and Melba Kurman. 2013. *Fabricated: The New World of 3D Printing*. John Wiley & Sons. Retrieved September 24, 2015 from https://books.google.com/books?hl=en&lr=&id=MpLXWIIp orIC&pgis=1
10. Shuhei Miyashita and Daniela Rus. 2013. Multi-Crease Self-Folding by Uniform Heating Self-Folding Method. *Ecal 2013*, 1: 955–956.
11. Catarina Mota. 2011. The rise of personal fabrication. *Proceedings of the 8th ACM conference on Creativity and cognition - C&C '11*, ACM Press, 279. http://doi.org/10.1145/2069618.2069665
12. Stefanie Mueller, Bastian Kruck, and Patrick Baudisch. 2013. LaserOrigami. *Proceedings of the SIGCHI Conference on Human Factors in Computing Systems - CHI '13*, ACM Press, 2585. http://doi.org/10.1145/2470654.2481358
13. Stefanie Mueller, Tobias Mohr, Kerstin Guenther, Johannes Frohnhofen, and Patrick Baudisch. 2014. faBrickation. *Proceedings of the 32nd annual ACM conference on Human factors in computing systems*

- *CHI '14*, ACM Press, 3827–3834. http://doi.org/10.1145/2556288.2557005

14. Thomas J. Ober, Daniele Foresti, and Jennifer a. Lewis. 2015. Active mixing of complex fluids at the microscale. *Proceedings of the National Academy of Sciences* 2015, 2: 201509224. http://doi.org/10.1073/pnas.1509224112
15. Huaishu Peng, Jennifer Mankoff, Scott E. Hudson, and James McCann. 2015. A Layered Fabric 3D Printer for Soft Interactive Objects. *Proceedings of the 33rd Annual ACM Conference on Human Factors in Computing Systems - CHI '15*, ACM Press, 1789–1798. http://doi.org/10.1145/2702123.2702327
16. Jie Qi and Leah Buechley. 2010. Electronic popables. *Proceedings of the fourth international conference on Tangible, embedded, and embodied interaction - TEI '10*, ACM Press, 121. http://doi.org/10.1145/1709886.1709909
17. Jie Qi and Leah Buechley. 2012. Animating paper using shape memory alloys. *Proceedings of the 2012 ACM annual conference on Human Factors in Computing Systems - CHI '12*, ACM Press, 749. http://doi.org/10.1145/2207676.2207783
18. Valkyrie Savage, Ryan Schmidt, Tovi Grossman, George Fitzmaurice, and Björn Hartmann. 2014. A series of tubes. *Proceedings of the 27th annual ACM symposium on User interface software and technology - UIST '14*, ACM Press, 3–12. http://doi.org/10.1145/2642918.2647374
19. Ryan Schmidt and Karan Singh. 2010. meshmixer. *ACM SIGGRAPH 2010 Talks on - SIGGRAPH '10*, ACM Press, 1. http://doi.org/10.1145/1837026.1837034
20. Jürgen Steimle Simon Olberding, Sergio Soto Ortega, Klaus Hildebrandt. 2015. Foldio: Digital Fabrication of Interactive and Shape--Changing Objects With Foldable Printed Electronics. *Proceedings of the 28th annual ACM symposium on User interface software and technology.*
21. Pitchaya Sitthi-Amorn, Javier E. Ramos, Yuwang Wangy, et al. 2015. MultiFab. *ACM Transactions on Graphics* 34, 4: 129:1–129:11. http://doi.org/10.1145/2766962
22. J Am Chem Soc, George M Whitesides, and Bartosz Grzybowski. 2002. Self-Assembly at All Scales. 295, March: 2418–2422.
23. Yoav Sterman, Erik D. Demaine, and Neri Oxman. 2013. PCB Origami: A Material-Based Design Approach to Computer-Aided Foldable Electronic Devices. *Journal of Mechanical Design* 135, 11: 114502. http://doi.org/10.1115/1.4025370
24. Michael T Tolley, Samuel M Felton, Shuhei Miyashita, Daniel Aukes, Daniela Rus, and Robert J Wood. 2014. Self-folding origami: shape memory composites activated by uniform heating. *Smart Materials and Structures* 23, 9: 094006. http://doi.org/10.1088/0964-1726/23/9/094006
25. Michael T. Tolley, Samuel M. Felton, Shuhei Miyashita, et al. 2013. Self-folding shape memory laminates for automated fabrication. *IEEE International Conference on Intelligent Robots and Systems*: 4931–4936. http://doi.org/10.1109/IROS.2013.6697068
26. Patrick Baudisch Udayan Umapathi, Hsiang-Ting Chen, Stefanie Mueller, Ludwig Wall, Anna Seufert. 2015. LaserStacker: Fabricating 3D Objects by Laser Cutting and Welding. *Proceedings of the 28th annual ACM symposium on User interface software and technologyth annual ACM symposium on User interface software and technology.*
27. Daniel Wigdor Varun Perumal C. 2015. Printem: Instant Printed Circuit Boards with Standard Office Printers & Inks. *Proceedings of the 28th annual ACM symposium on User interface software and technology.*
28. Kiril Vidimče, Szu-Po Wang, Jonathan Ragan-Kelley, and Wojciech Matusik. 2013. OpenFab. *ACM Transactions on Graphics* 32, 4: 1. http://doi.org/10.1145/2461912.2461993
29. Karl Willis, Eric Brockmeyer, Scott Hudson, and Ivan Poupyrev. 2012. Printed optics. *Proceedings of the 25th annual ACM symposium on User interface software and technology - UIST '12*, ACM Press, 589. http://doi.org/10.1145/2380116.2380190
30. 3D Printing 2015-2025: Technologies, Markets, Players: IDTechEx. Retrieved September 23, 2015 from http://www.idtechex.com/research/reports/3d-printing-2015-2025-technologies-markets-players-000423.asp
31. Objet Connex Multi-Material 3D Printers | Stratasys. Retrieved September 23, 2015 from http://www.stratasys.com/3d-printers/design-series/connex-systems
32. Polyjet Matrix 3D Printing | Simultaneous Multi-material 3D Printing. Retrieved September 23, 2015 from http://proto3000.com/polyjet-matrix-3D-printing-technology-services.php
33. Purple on White Laserable Acrylic Sheet. Retrieved September 23, 2015 from https://www.inventables.com/technologies/purple-on-white-laserable-acrylic-sheet
34. Nike News - Nike Football Accelerates Innovation with 3D printed "Concept Cleat" for Shuttle.

Retrieved September 23, 2015 from http://news.nike.com/news/nike-football-accelerates-innovation-with-3d-printed-concept-cleat-for-shuttle

35. Zuhal, Saturn's Wonderer | by Neri Oxman. Retrieved September 23, 2015 from http://www.materialecology.com/projects/details/zuhal

36. Multicolor-extruder - RepRapWiki. Retrieved September 23, 2015 from http://reprap.org/wiki/Multicolor-extruder

37. ColorFabb - woodFill Fine 3D Printing WOOD Filament. Retrieved September 23, 2015 from http://colorfabb.com/woodfill-fine

38. Workshop Wednesday: How To Heat-Bend Acrylic Enclosures | Make: DIY Projects, How-Tos, Electronics, Crafts and Ideas for Makers. Retrieved September 24, 2015 from http://makezine.com/2013/02/06/workshop-wednesday-heat-bending-acrylic-enclosures/

39. Product overview by DMG MORI. Retrieved September 24, 2015 from http://ca-en.dmgmori.com/products/lasertec/lasertec-additivemanufacturing/lasertec-65-3d

40. Pepakura Designer. Retrieved September 24, 2015 from http://www.tamasoft.co.jp/pepakura-en/

41. Autodesk 123D Design. Retrieved September 24, 2015 from http://www.123dapp.com/design

42. VersaLaser | Specification. Retrieved September 24, 2015 from http://www.versalaser.com.au/specification.html

43. PAGE6. Retrieved September 24, 2015 from http://www.bendableplastic.com/PAGE6.html

44. Super 77 Anniversary Promotion. Retrieved September 24, 2015 from http://solutions.3m.com/wps/portal/3M/en_US/Adhesives/Tapes/Promotions/Super77-Anniversary-Promotion/

45. 3M™ Scotch-Weld™ Epoxy Adhesive DP420 Black, 37 mL, 12 per case. Retrieved January 8, 2016 from http://solutions.3m.com/wps/portal/3M/en_US/Adhesives/Tapes/Products/~/3M-Scotch-Weld-Epoxy-Adhesive-DP420-Black-37-mL-12-per-case?N=6081606+4294871756&rt=rud

46. 1992. Apparatus and method for creating three-dimensional objects. Retrieved September 23, 2015 from https://www.google.com/patents/US5121329

A Model Relating Pupil Diameter to Mental Workload and Lighting Conditions

Bastian Pfleging[1,3], Drea K. Fekety[2], Albrecht Schmidt[3], Andrew L. Kun[4]
[1]University of Munich (LMU), Munich, Germany
[2]Clemson University, Clemson, SC, USA
[3]University of Stuttgart, Stuttgart, Germany
[4]University of New Hampshire, Durham, NH, USA
bastian.pfleging@ifi.lmu.de, dfekety@g.clemson.edu,
albrecht.schmidt@vis.uni-stuttgart.de, andrew.kun@unh.edu

ABSTRACT
In this paper, we present a proof-of-concept approach to estimating mental workload by measuring the user's pupil diameter under various controlled lighting conditions. Knowing the user's mental workload is desirable for many application scenarios, ranging from driving a car, to adaptive workplace setups. Typically, physiological sensors allow inferring mental workload, but these sensors might be rather uncomfortable to wear.

Measuring pupil diameter through remote eye-tracking instead is an unobtrusive method. However, a practical eye-tracking-based system must also account for pupil changes due to variable lighting conditions. Based on the results of a study with tasks of varying mental demand and six different lighting conditions, we built a simple model that is able to infer the workload independently of the lighting condition in 75 % of the tested conditions.

Author Keywords
Estimation of mental workload; eye-tracking; task-evoked pupillary response; cognitive workload; compensation of pupillary light reflex; adaptive user interfaces; psychophysiology; lighting.

ACM Classification Keywords
H.5.2. Information interfaces and presentation (e.g., HCI): User Interfaces;

INTRODUCTION
A large body of literature exists on the topic of estimating a person's mental workload while engaged in cognitively-demanding tasks. Although mental workload is not something that can be measured directly, in recent years many different

CHI'16, May 07 - 12, 2016, San Jose, CA, USA

ACM 978-1-4503-3362-7/16/05...$15.00
DOI: http://dx.doi.org/10.1145/2858036.2858117

	Light (large impact)		Task (small impact)	
	low	high	difficult	easy
Pupil diameter	↗	↘	↗	↘

Model: $PD = PD_{light} + PD_{task}$

$PD_{task} = PD - PD_{light}$

Estimate: $mental\ workload \approx f(PD_{task})$

Figure 1: For many applications (e.g., online learning), knowing the user's workload is beneficial for instance to adapt the interface. With a model extracted from our study, we are able to estimate mental workload based on pupil diameter retrieved through remote eye-tracking under different controlled lighting.

technologies have been used to gather data that can accurately infer a person's mental workload. Measurements in this area can be in the form of pupil diameter (collected from remote as well as head-worn eye-trackers), electroencephalography (EEG), heart rate (HR), heart rate variability (HRV), skin conductance (GSR), skin temperature, and respiration rate, to name a few. These methods have their strengths and weaknesses, but all have been used in some capacity to estimate how a person uses mental resources to process information and where a person's upper limits of cognitive capabilities lie. One important advantage of remote eye-trackers in comparison to other established physiological measurements of mental workload is that they are rather unobtrusive and do not require the user to be tethered to measurement equipment.

The study outlined in this paper uses pupil diameter data to estimate mental workload (Figure 1). A large number of studies have confirmed that, in an effect called the task-evoked pupillary response (TEPR), pupil diameter increases when the cognitive difficulty of a task increases [3]. This change in pupil diameter occurs rapidly, both when the pupil dilates and when it contracts, making eye trackers attractive in efforts to estimate mental workload. However, pupil diameter also depends strongly on lighting conditions: the pupillary light reflex constricts the pupil in response to increased light levels and vice versa. Pupil size can change by several millimeters due to the pupillary light reflex. In contrast, changes related to mental workload are an order of magnitude smaller–usually between 0.1 mm and 0.5 mm [3]. These small changes can be overwhelmed by the large changes due to the pupillary light reflex. This work addresses this issue by modeling the effects of TEPR and the pupillary light reflex on pupil size, and by using this model to separate the two effects.

We propose a simple model as a proof of concept that we extracted from our experiment data on pupil size changes under different known levels of light reaching the eye, and under different levels of task difficulty. We then use this model to estimate pupil diameter changes occurring as a result of cognitive load, and ultimately to estimate the task difficulty that resulted in the measured pupil diameter. In this work we constrain the model to cases when both the light reaching the eye and the mental task difficulty are constant during a certain condition.

The pupillary light reflex will respond to both ambient light (such as room illumination) and visual target luminance (such as the light emitted from a computer screen). We demonstrate these effects in the different lighting conditions of the experiment.

CONTRIBUTION STATEMENT

The contribution of this paper is an investigation of the combined influence of light and mental workload on the user's pupil size. Previous studies investigating eye-tracking and mental workload often fixed lighting conditions to one level in order to eliminate the effects of the pupillary light reflex. Instead, we conducted a study in which users performed different tasks and were exposed to six different (and controlled) lighting conditions. We used the results of this study to create a simple model of pupil diameter change that incorporates both the pupillary light reflex (for our controlled conditions), and the pupil diameter change that is due to changes in mental workload. We see this model as a first step towards pupil-based illumination-independent workload estimation.

Estimating the user's workload is helpful for many situations where people interact with computing devices or machines. One example is the automotive domain where it is important not to overload the driver as they interact with in-vehicle devices [28] or communicate with remote conversants [21, 38], since performance degrades with increasing workload [6]. With automated driving modes and non-driving-related activities [37], workload estimation can be useful to track and support the driver's reengagement in the driving task [20]. In a desktop setup, one application domain would be online learning where the estimation of mental workload is used to adapt the content and/or interface to improve the learner's performance.

RELATED WORK

Measuring the user's mental workload has been the subject of various studies.

Eye-Tracking Data Used as Indices of Mental Workload

Eye gaze data has been established as an effective method for measuring mental workload in response to a cognitively demanding task, by focusing on certain parameters of autonomically-driven eye behavior. Pupils tend to dilate in response to greater mental workload (often called the task-evoked pupillary response). A number of early studies supported this relationship between pupillary changes and workload, and in a way established the foundation for this approach to psychophysiology [15, 16]. A dated but thorough review of the literature surrounding task-evoked pupillary responses outlined the relationship between changes in pupil size and mental workload [3].

Other early research with eye-tracking indicated a greater time interval between blinks for a visual identification task compared to a visual detection task [8]. Blink duration and frequency were also found to decrease in response to increased difficulty of a visual identification game [46]. Nunes & Recarte [32] found increased pupil diameter and higher blink rates when participants were engaged in more difficult secondary tasks while driving an automobile. Ahlstrom & Friedman-Berg [1] found that air traffic controllers exhibited greater pupil diameter and shorter blink duration in response to increased task difficulty. In response to performing an auditory workload task while driving, Tsai et al. [45] found that participants' blink frequencies and pupil diameters significantly increased, though measures of blink duration did not reflect these results. Benedetto and colleagues [4] also recently found that increased dual-task difficulty was accompanied by shorter blink duration and longer duration between blinks in a simulated driving environment, though the former provided more reliable data. The contextual qualities of these selected studies suggest that inferences about mental workload indicated by eye-tracking data are robust and not necessarily domain-specific.

A key issue with using eye-tracking data to infer mental workload is that physiological changes in the eye are influenced both by lighting conditions and the difficulty of the task a person is engaged in. In creating algorithms to predict eye gaze changes based on mental workload, researchers have to parse out the effects of changes in lighting and mostly do so by choosing constant lighting conditions for experiments. A series of recent preliminary studies have addressed this issue in further detail, in the context of a simulated driving environment [23, 34, 35]. Methods have also been developed to gather eye gaze data in sub-optimal lighting conditions [49, 50]. Furthermore, Marshall proposed the Index of Cognitive Activity, which attempts to estimate cognitive load [24] independent of lighting, based on rapid fluctuations of pupil size. However, Marshall's proprietary algorithm by default outputs a sequence of estimates once a second, which can obscure interesting changes in cognitive activity that occur at a quicker pace, such as those observed in spoken interactions [14, 22, 36]. Using TEPR and compensating for lighting conditions should allow us to detect such changes.

Presentation Modalities of Workload Tasks

In many studies where eye-tracking data were used as indices of mental workload, the task used to induce workload was often a visually-based stimulus [7]. This highlights the need to identify and isolate the separate influences of lighting and workload on gaze data. One potential solution to this issue could be to introduce an auditory-based workload task and have participants focus on a single point in a visually neutral or uninteresting stimulus [18]. Ideally, this would allow for the measurement of gaze data in response to a cognitively-demanding task without the interference of changing lighting conditions.

Tasks used to induce mental workload, such as the N-back test, delayed digit recall test, or the PASAT [12, 17, 27] can be presented as either a visual stimulus or as an auditory stimulus. The auditory N-back task has been successfully used to induce workload, with different physiological measures (e.g., [25, 39]). This protocol has been used in a number of studies in the realm of automobile driving. Mehler and colleagues found that heart rate and skin conductance were reliably indicative of driver workload estimates in simulated driving tasks [25, 26]. In an on-road driving study they also found similar changes in heart rate and eye gaze measurements with respect to task difficulty [48]. The same research group showed that pupil diameter can be used to estimate workload for drivers engaged in the N-back task [47]. More recently Gable et al. found evidence that in driving simulator studies pupil diameter might be a more sensitive measure of cognitive load changes than heart rate [9].

Klingner et al. [19] found that the difficulty of a task may change between different perceptual modalities. However, the peer-reviewed literature has yet to fully explore the differences between these modalities. For our study, we chose to use an auditory presentation, working memory mental workload task to minimize the effects of extraneous visual stimuli which may influence eye-tracking measurements.

Other Physiological Measures of Mental Workload

Physiological measures such as functional near-infrared spectroscopy (fNIRS) [11, 44], electroencephalography EEG [5, 10, 33, 42], heart rate [31, 40] and heart rate variability [31, 41], and skin conductance [13, 43], have also been used to track mental workload while engaged in a cognitively demanding task. One advantage of using these physiological measures instead of eye-trackers is that they are not dependent upon the lighting conditions of the environmental configuration used for data collection. However, these methods can be rather obtrusive since they require the user to wear or connect sensor technology and also reveal health-relevant personal data. Furthermore, these types of solutions can invoke unnatural participant behaviors which confound the data (e.g., jaw clenching with EEG). Remote eye-tracking is advantageous in this domain as it can maintain reliable recordings while alleviating participant discomfort, which could otherwise negatively influence experimenters' data yield.

Summary: Measuring Mental Workload

As outlined in this section, various methods have already been used to measure and estimate mental workload. With regard to unobtrusiveness, measuring the pupil diameter through a (remote) eye-tracker seems to be one of the most promising approaches. In contrast, many of the approaches that employ physiological sensors require the user to wear specific sensor hardware.

For eye-tracking, one drawback is the concurrent influence of the pupillary light reflex and the task-evoked pupillary reflex on pupil diameter. That is why previous work often required strongly controlled lighting setups. With the experiment presented in this paper, we want to broaden the flexibility of this approach by investigating different lighting conditions and generating a model that allows for workload estimation in different cases.

EXPERIMENT: ANALYIZING THE INFLUENCE OF LIGHT AND WORKLOAD ON PUPIL DIAMETER

Our study explores how we can separate the effects of light and mental workload on pupil diameter. We therefore conducted an experiment where we explored the combined effect of lighting (variable ambient light or visual target luminance) and cognitive load on pupil diameter.

Variable Light Conditions

We used six different lighting conditions in order to demonstrate pupil changes in typical situations of varying ambient light (such as differences from office lighting); and target illumination (such as screen content). The six lighting conditions consisted of three conditions (part 1) where the environmental illumination was varied using different lamps (1 lamp, 2 lamps, 3 lamps) while keeping the target constant, and three conditions (part 2) where the target illumination (screen content) was varied (25%, 50%, 75 % grey) while keeping the environmental illumination constant (3 lamps).

Auditory Delayed Digit Recall Task

In the experiment we utilized an auditory delayed digit recall task [27] as the primary task to induce workload. For each trial of the delayed digit recall task, participants heard a randomized set of 20 digits ranging between 0 and 9 spoken by a computerized voice, with a 1.5-second interval between each spoken number. In total, each trial was 30 seconds long.

You hear:	6	5	2	7	4	4
You say (0-back):	6	5	2	7	4	4
You say (1-back):		6	5	2	7	4
You say (2-back):			6	5	2	7

Table 1: Example numbers spoken by a computer voice, followed by correct participant responses for the three task difficulties of the auditory delayed digit recall task. Blank cells indicate that the correct response for the participant is to say nothing.

Our pilot testing revealed this rate of presentation to be optimal for participants engaged in our workload test (i.e., no secondary tasks) after sufficient practice. For each trial, participants were instructed to verbally repeat the number that they heard N numbers ago. The number N corresponded to the difficulty level of the task they were currently performing, i.e. 0-, 1-, or 2-back. Table 1 shows examples of the tasks performed. The same delayed digit recall tasks were employed throughout the whole experiment, and numbers were randomly generated for each trial.

Participants were allowed one minute of resting time between the end of one trial and the start of the next trial. This was done to allow for a recovery to a baseline state of workload before the next trial. In situations where lighting conditions changed between the end of one trial and the start of the next trial, the experimenters allowed a 2.5-minute recovery period in order to allow the participants' eyes to appropriately adjust to the new lighting conditions.

Design

The experiment was designed as a within-subject experiment. Participants completed three trials with different levels of difficulty (0-back, 1-back, 2-back) for each of the six lighting conditions. This results in a total of 3 x 6 = 18 trials with level of difficulty (3 levels) and lighting (6 levels) as independent variables. Given that the pauses between tasks of different difficulty were between one minute and 2.5 minutes, we did not expect any need to counterbalance the order of task presentation. After all, prior research shows that after the end of a cognitively-demanding task, pupil diameter returns to its pre-task level within a few seconds (see for instance [3, 22]). Nevertheless, we introduced two task orders, such that in each lighting condition participants started with the 0-back task, while the order of the next two tasks (1-back and 2-back) was counterbalanced between participants.

As dependent variables, we recorded workload task performance (percentage of correct responses), pupil diameter (as well as other eye-tracking measurements), and eye behavior (blinks, saccades, and fixations). Due to time restrictions, subjective workload ratings (NASA TLX) were collected only at the end of the experiments to get a summative rating for each level of difficulty.

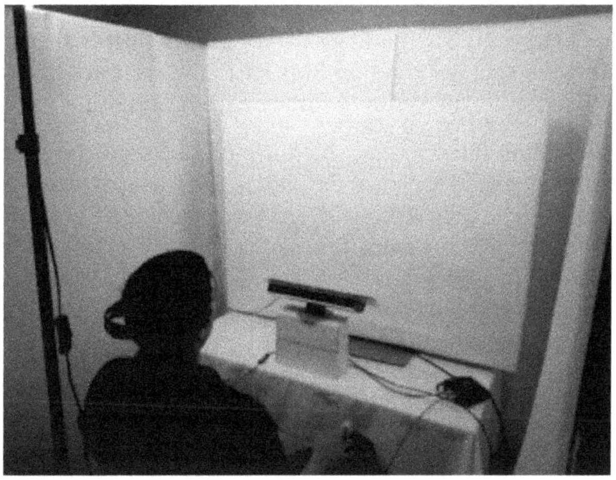

Figure 2: Experiment setup. The eye-tracker was placed between participant and wall/ TV; the computers to log all measurements were located out of the participant's sight next to the cubicle. Lamps as illumination sources were placed on tripods behind the participants about 40 cm above the participants' heads. This figure shows the configuration as it was used for part 1 of the experiment.

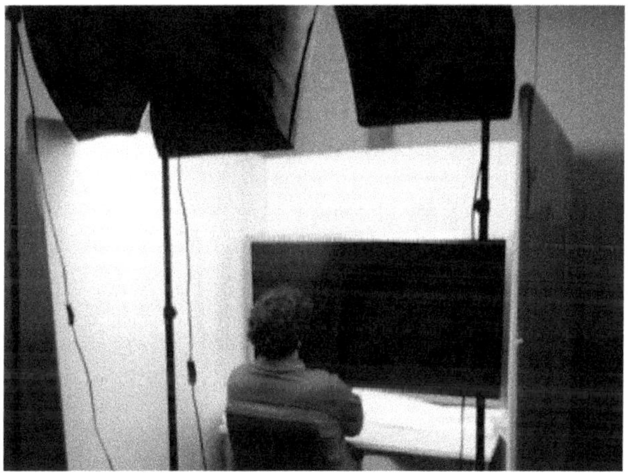

Figure 3: In part 2 of the study participants sat in the 3-walled white 'cubicle' with the LCD TV in front of them.

Participants

In total, 24 participants (19 male, 5 female) aged between 19 and 42 (M=25.00 years, SD=6.16 years) took part in this study. Participants were recruited from students and faculty members of the University of Stuttgart. All participants were compensated for their time by receiving a small give-away. Student recruits also received course credit for their participation in the study. Eye tracking data from 3 participants were excluded from our analysis due to technical difficulties. We also excluded data from one other participant because he did not follow instructions in completing the delayed digit recall task. Thus, our sample size is N=20.

Apparatus and Data Collection

The study took place in a windowless room. The participant's seat was placed in a white-walled "cubicle" in which three (temporary) poster walls surrounded the participant.

These walls were covered with large white sheets of paper (see Figure 2). The participants' eye movement and pupil data were sourced from an SMI RED250 eye-tracker[1] and recorded using the iView X software from SMI.

The lighting intensity variable for part 1 of the experiment was manipulated such that the participant's cubicle was illuminated by 1, 2, or 3 professional-grade studio lamps (Product number 400894 from TecTake.de) as only sources of illumination with 55-watt white fluorescent bulbs. The TV as gaze target was covered with white paper in this part 1 of the study to have a homogeneous, constant target.

For part 2 of the experiment, we used a 55-inch FullHD (1920x1080 pixels) Philips 55PFL7606/K02 television (see Figure 3 for equipment setup) displaying a full-screen view of one of three gray images with different brightness. The major device settings were: Contrast: 90, Brightness 76, Color 67, Sharpness 5, Color Temperature Cold, Dynamic Contrast: Minimum, Light Sensor: Off, Ambilight: Off. In this part, the environmental illumination was kept constant (all three lamps on).

The lamps and the TV screen were the only light sources in the windowless room. At the beginning of each trial, we measured the amount of light reaching the participant's eyes with a lux meter (iClever digital lux meter LX1330B[2]) placed at the participant's forehead. The amount of illumination reaching the participant's eye (in lux) for the three different levels of environmental illumination (part 1) were M=133.50, SD=5.45 (1 lamp); M=247.55, SD=23.55 (2 lamps); M=387.14, SD=22.81 (3 lamps). The amount of illumination reaching the participant's eye (in lux) for the three levels of different target brightness (part 2) were M=255.19, SD=31.51 (25%); M=308.10, SD=28.69 (50%); M=364.76, SD=35.07 (75%).

Procedure

When the participants arrived at our lab, we first introduced them to the topic and procedure of our experiment. Next, the participants read and signed the consent forms and filled out an initial demographic questionnaire. The participants were then seated in the experiment room. Participants remained seated for the duration of the experimental session, and were asked to visually focus on a small crosshair at a centrally located position in front of them.

Before the start of the experiment, we introduced the participants to the cognitive workload task (the auditory delayed digit recall test). Participants were given up to 12 practice sessions of non-scored trials at each level of task difficulty in order to fully familiarize themselves with the different difficulty levels of the task. Also, we presented them an empty copy of the NASA TLX questionnaire as a preparation for those sheets that should be filled out at the end of the experiment. Afterwards, the eye-tracker was calibrated using a nine-point calibration method that was provided with the eye-tracking software.

As explained before, the experiment itself was then conducted in two parts. The difference between the two parts was the way in which the participant experienced lighting conditions. We chose to split the experiment into these parts, since technical reasons prevented us from switching easily between these setups. The order between the two experiment parts was counter-balanced such that half of the participants started with part one and the other half with part two.

For each scored delayed digit recall trial in both parts, we asked participants to focus on a small "+"-shaped target located on the white board / TV set seen in front of the participant. This was done to minimize the possibility of eye movements interfering with eye-tracking data while the participant performed the task.

Part 1: Controlling Environmental Illumination

In this part, we controlled the amount of environmental illumination that reaches the participant's viewing perspective. We manipulated ambient room illumination such that the influence of illumination and workload on pupil diameter could be examined in different lighting conditions.

Part 2: Controlling Large Field-of-View Stimulus Brightness

In this part, we controlled the intensity of target luminance the participant was viewing. Participants were seated in the same location (with illumination provided by all three lamps at the same time) and viewed a homogeneous single-color gray image on the TV screen while engaged in the same delayed digit recall test. These gray images were created such that they represented 25%, 50%, and 75% brightness relative to a full-white color image. The TV screen covered much of the participants' field of view (see Figure 3). All other factors between the two experiments were kept constant.

Both independent variables were manipulated in the same order as in experiment part 1. Because all data were collected from participants in the same session, participants experienced the conditions of experiment part 2 either immediately before or immediately after experiment part 1 (depending on the condition they were assigned).

At the end of the experiment, the participants were asked to fill out three NASA TLX questionnaires, one for each level of the cognitive workload task.

DATA SET

We compiled the recordings made during the experiment into a data set that is publicly available under an open data license. Details about the full dataset are available at http://www.hcilab.org/research/workload-pupil-diameter/.

Apart from the analysis in this paper, we believe that this data set will be helpful for the research community in various purposes. Especially, it will be helpful towards the development

[1] http://www.smivision.com, last access 2016-01-07

[2] http://goo.gl/qNCdNB, last access 2016-01-07

		Part 1: Environmental Illumination								
		1 lamp ("low")			2 lamps ("medium")			3 lamps ("high")		
Metric	**Units**	**0-back**	**1-back**	**2-back**	**0-back**	**1-back**	**2-back**	**0-back**	**1-back**	**2-back**
Left pupil diameter	**mm**	3.889 (0.492)	4.044 (0.483)	4.210 (0.578)	3.406 (0.382)	3.610 (0.416)	3.742 (0.478)	3.139 (0.317)	3.206 (0.313)	3.328 (0.367)

Table 2: Means and standard deviations of pupil diameter measurements of workload under each condition in Part 1

		Part 2: Stimulus Brightness								
		25% ("low")			50% ("medium")			75% ("high")		
Metric	**Units**	**0-back**	**1-back**	**2-back**	**0-back**	**1-back**	**2-back**	**0-back**	**1-back**	**2-back**
Left pupil diameter	**mm**	3.719 (0.434)	3.947 (0.482)	4.100 (0.467)	3.086 (0.298)	3.203 (0.342)	3.318 (0.321)	2.903 (0.283)	3.010 (0.316)	3.099 (0.313)

Table 3: Means and standard deviations of pupil diameter measurements of workload under each condition in Part 2

of generalizable models that allow for workload detection based on eye-tracking data independent from the current illumination situation.

Participants performed a total of 18 delayed digit recall tasks across the two experiment parts, and a counter-balanced design controlled the order in which participants experienced the conditions of each trial (i.e., some combination of lighting conditions, and task difficulty). While we excluded data for four of the 24 participants from the dataset, and subsequently used data from 20 participants, the loss of data did not skew our counter-balanced design; approximately equal sample sizes were maintained between groups. Additionally, main effects of trial order on task performance were not present. Means and standard deviations for pupil diameters for all participants can be found in Table 2 and Table 3.

Eye-Tracking Data
The eye-tracking data was recorded using the SMI RED 250 remote eye-tracker. This time-stamped data was recorded at 120 Hz. The measurements include all available information the SMI software provided. This includes pupil diameter for both eyes, and gaze position (on the screen). Also, details about the current eye behavior, i.e., blinks, saccades, and fixations were recorded and added using the SMI-internal software using default parameters for the event detection.

Hand-Coded Data
We collected NASA-TLX scores, the participants' error rates on the delayed digit recall task, and measurements of the amount of light reaching the participants' head in each lighting condition.

NASA TLX
After both experiments, the participants were asked to also complete NASA TLX questionnaires. Due to time restrictions of the experiment, we could not ask for subjective ratings after each condition. In order to get at least some subjective feedback, we did an overall assessment for each of the levels of the digit recall task (rating across all conditions with the corresponding level).

Participant Performance / Error Rates
We hand coded the participants' responses to the delayed digit recall task on paper. We later transcribed these scores and stored them in electronic form.

Illumination Measurements
Whenever the lighting conditions were changed we measured and recorded the illumination (in lux) reaching the participant's eye.

Pupil Diameter Data Preprocessing
For each of the 20 participants we found the average pupil diameter for each of the experimental condition. Given that the participants experienced 3 task difficulty levels at each of the 6 lighting levels, we calculated 20 x 3 x 6 = 360 pupil diameter averages.

To calculate the pupil diameter averages we started with the raw measurements from the SMI software. Since some of the data from the SMI software was provided with non-uniform sampling rates, we first used the "interp1" Matlab function to resample the raw measurements to attain a uniform sampling rate of 120 Hz. Next, we excluded samples for which the raw measurement values remained constant for at least 100 ms, as these samples were generated when the eye tracker failed to accurately track pupil diameter. Finally, we plotted pupil diameter changes over the 30 second periods delayed of the digit recall tasks for each of the 360 measurements. By visual inspection we identified three cases where the pupil diameter data was noisy for the majority of the experimental condition, and we rejected this data. We then calculated averages for 360 – 3 = 357 cases. Finally, we used a single imputation method [2] to fill in the remaining 3 averages: in our method the missing average is set equal to an average calculated for the same participant, and same lighting conditions, but a different task difficulty. Note that this method is conservative in that it does not artificially improve our chances of confirming our expectation that pupil diameter will increase with increased task difficulty.

DATA ANALYSIS AND DISCUSSION

Lighting Conditions

We analyzed whether the settings chosen for our lights created measurable differences in the stimulus and room lighting. At the same time, we analyzed potential order effects related to the counter-balanced lighting conditions. A one-way ANOVA comparing the lighting conditions of each trial to the lighting condition order showed no significant differences in lighting conditions based on order effects (p>.05).

For the purposes of this analysis, we treated all 6 lighting conditions as levels in one variable. Consequently, we compared the average illumination reaching the participants' eyes between all 6 lighting conditions using a one-way repeated measures ANOVA.

Mauchly's test failed to detect a violation of the sphericity assumption in our illumination data, $\chi^2(14)=14.672$, $p>.05$, therefore no corrections to degrees of freedom are needed. The results indicate a significant main effect of lighting manipulations on illumination reaching the eye, $F(5,100)=461.987$, $p<.001$, $\eta^2=.959$. Least Significant Difference (LSD) post-hoc analyses within lighting conditions revealed significant differences ($p<.001$) in average illumination reaching the eye between all levels, except for the "2 lamps" vs. "50%" conditions ($p>.05$).

Task Performance

Participants' performance on each delayed digit recall task was measured in terms of percentage of correct responses. Percentage correct was used instead of a measure of frequency of correct responses, because the 3 different difficulty levels of the task are designed in such a way that yields a different number of responses from the participant. In other words, the 2-back task (if performed correctly) yields fewer responses from the participant compared to the 1-back and 0-back tasks, because the participant has no response for the first two numbers they hear. This effectively means that 0-back tasks produce 20 responses from participants, where 1-back tasks produce 19 and 2-back tasks produce 18 responses.

A one-way ANOVA revealed statistically significant differences in average task performance among difficulty levels, $F(2,63)=27.300$, $p<.001$, $\eta^2=.464$. A Least Significant Difference (LSD) post-hoc analysis showed statistically significant differences between all pairwise comparisons of difficulty level except for the 0-back-to-1-back comparison ($p=.247$). This suggests our participants were able to perform equally well on the easiest and middle-difficulty tasks featured here. However, it is important to remember that the focus of this paper is estimating users' workload and not their ability to perform tasks. Thus our measurements of TEPR inferring workload should have more value to our model than task performance in this situation.

Subjective Workload

Subjective workload was measured after the end of the experiment, where participants were asked to fill out a NASA-TLX form for each task difficulty level. Each subjective workload rating (one per difficulty level) represents the participants' average workload from 6 trials of that difficulty level. Unweighted subjective workload scores for each participant were calculated by averaging participants' ratings on a scale of 1-20 over the six dimensions of the NASA-TLX questionnaire [29].

A one-way ANOVA revealed statistically significant differences in average subjective workload among task difficulty levels, $F(2,63)=94.660$, $p<.05$, $\eta^2=.750$. A Least Significant Difference (LSD) post-hoc analysis showed statistically significant differences between all pairwise comparisons of difficulty level such that 0-back<1-back<2-back, $p<.001$.

There are moderate, negative correlations between participants' task performance (percentage of correct responses) and their subjective ratings of workload (NASA-TLX) for the 1-back task ($r=-0.445$, $p<.05$) and the 2-back task ($r=-0.466$, $p<.05$). In other words, as participants performed better on the workload task, they felt that the task was less workload-inducing. However, a weak positive correlation exists between task performance and subjective workload for the 0-back task, although this relationship is not significant ($r=0.154$, $p>.05$).

Eye-Tracking: Pupil Diameter

We conducted a 6 (lighting level) x 3 (task difficulty) repeated measures ANOVA to examine the separate and combined influences of these factors on pupil diameter. For the remainder of this section, we only consider the left eye's pupil diameter because we observed fewer inaccurate/missing data points in this eye throughout our data set. Mauchly's tests detected a violation of the sphericity assumption in our pupil data for the main effect of lighting ($\chi^2(14)=63.728$, $p<.001$, $\varepsilon=.478$), the main effect of task difficulty ($\chi^2(2)=11.162$, $p<.05$, $\varepsilon=.684$), and the interaction between lighting and task difficulty ($\chi^2(54)=107.262$, $p<.001$, $\varepsilon=.436$). Therefore, Greenhouse-Geisser corrections are reported here. We observed a significant main effect of lighting level on pupil diameter, $F(2.391,45.424)=167.143$, $p<.001$, $\eta^2=.898$. Post-hoc LSD comparisons revealed significant differences in pupil diameter among all lighting levels ($p<.001$), except for the comparisons between "1 lamp" vs. "25%" and "3 lamps" vs. "50%" ($p>.05$). This omnibus test also revealed a significant main effect of task difficulty on pupil diameter, $F(1.368,25.990)=71.903$, $p<.001$, $\eta^2=.791$. Further, post-hoc LSD comparisons showed significant differences in pupil diameter among all task difficulty levels, $p<.001$.

Another result observed within this omnibus test was the significant interaction between lighting level and task difficulty on pupil diameter, $F(4.356,82.767)=3.633$, $p<.05$, $\eta^2=.161$. Post-hoc LSD comparisons of pupil diameter also revealed significant differences among all task difficulty levels within each of the 6 lighting conditions ($p<.05$).

TOWARDS A MODEL FOR WORKLOAD ESTIMATION

The eye-tracking results indicate that average pupil diameter increases with increased task difficulty, and that we can detect this under all lighting conditions. These results are also in agreement with the performance results and the subjective workload ratings.

But how well can individual measurements of pupil diameter be used to assess workload? To answer this question we first plotted all of the pupil diameter measurements (18 data points for 20 participants) as shown in Figure 4. On the x-axis of Figure 4 we vary the task difficulty – this results in 3 groups of data points, one for each delayed digit recall task. Within each group we also vary the lighting condition – this results in the six columns of measurements, one for each lighting condition.

Two trends are visible in the data in Figure 4. First, the average pupil diameter clearly changes with light. Second, the average pupil diameter also increases with task difficulty. However, the data shows that, if we want to use individual pupil diameter measurements to assess the user's current workload we have to address two problems. First, we must account for lighting conditions. As the data in Figure 4 demonstrates, the same pupil diameter can be the result of different workloads under different lighting conditions. Second, pupil diameter measurements are noisy. Thus, even if we know the lighting conditions we might not be able to always correctly identify workload.

To address these issues we introduce a model that serves as a proof-of-concept for the idea that if we know the lighting conditions then we can use pupil diameter values to identify the task difficulty. Thus, for each participant *p*, we model pupil diameter PD_p as a sum of two contributing factors:

$$PD_p = PD_{p,light} + PD_{p,task}$$

Equation 1 Modelling pupil diameter.

In Equation 1, $PD_{p,light}$ is the pupil diameter for participant *p* given lighting condition *light*, while $PD_{p,task}$ is the normalized pupil diameter for that participant's pupil diameter given task difficulty *task*.

For a given level of *light* we calculate $PD_{p,light}$ as the average pupil diameter for all three levels of *task*. Expressing $PD_{p,task}$ as the difference between PD_p and $PD_{p,light}$, we get the normalized pupil diameter data presented in Figure 5.

Next, we classify the normalized pupil diameter readings as indicating one of the three task difficulties. We perform the classification by comparing the normalized pupil diameter to the lower and upper limit of the 1-back region (shown as blue lines in Figure 5): pupil diameters below the lower limit are classified as indicating a 0-back task, diameters between the limits as indicating a 1-back task, and those above the upper limit as indicating a 2-back task. In this paper we identify the upper and lower limits using a simple heuristic approach: we first find the mean of the normalized pupil diameter values

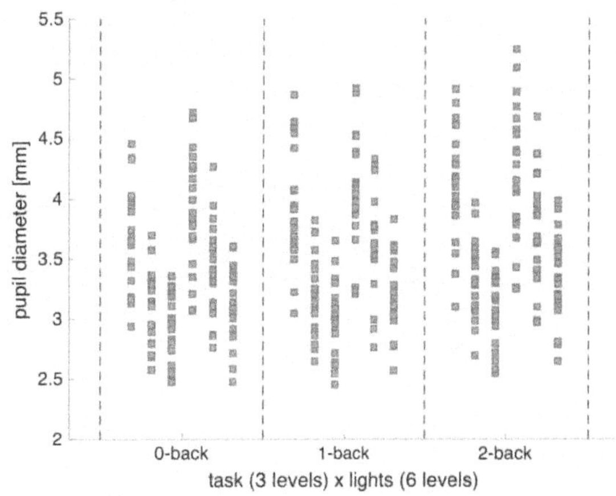

Figure 4: Pupil diameter measurements. Each data point shows the average pupil diameter (y-axis, in mm) of one participant during one 30 second-long trial. The trials on the x-axis are grouped by task (0-, 1-, and 2-back) and lighting (1, 2, and 3 lamps, and 25%, 50%, and 75% brightness).

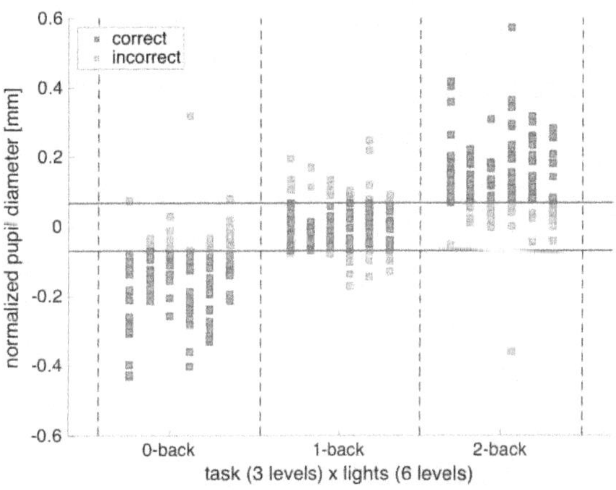

Figure 5: Using Equation 1, we can calculate the normalized pupil diameter by subtracting the participant's average pupil diameter for a given level of light ($PD_{p,light}$) from the pupil diameter of the trial. This diagram shows the normalized pupil diameter (y-axis) using the pupil diameters shown in Figure 4, for all participants during the different trials (x-axis) separated by task and illumination. Blue lines indicate the thresholds we used to classify the underlying workload: data above the top line was classified as workload due to 2-back task, between the two lines as due to 1-back, and below bottom line as due to 0-back. For correctly classified workloads we marked the data points in green, and for incorrectly classified workloads we marked them in red.

for the 1-back task, and set the upper and lower limits one standard deviation away from this mean. We visually demonstrate the results of this approach in Figure 5. Here we use all of the 360 data points to calculate the limits, and then apply the limits to the same 360 data points, and the correctly classified data points are shown in green. We evaluated this approach using k-fold cross-validation. With k = 4, we get result of 75% correct classification. In our k-fold cross validation we found the threshold values based on data from ¾ of the participants (15 of 20), and tested them with data from ¼ of the participants (5 of 20).

GENERAL DISCUSSION

In this study we explored the combined effects of light and cognitive load on pupil diameter and we proposed a model that allows us to estimate task difficulty based on pupil diameter measurements. Having such an estimate of task difficulty would be useful in a number of situations. In software environments it might allow us to identify when users are confused or overwhelmed, which in turn could trigger a change in the interaction approach for the user interface. In learning environments, the estimate of task difficulty might help us find the optimal way to present the material based on the user's current state.

Our results are encouraging. We explored the combined effect of lighting and task difficulty on pupil diameter for indoor lighting conditions commonly found in offices and homes, and for plausible task difficulty levels. We found that we must account for the effects of light if we intend to use pupil diameter as a measure of task difficulty. This is demonstrated in Figure 6, which shows pupil diameter measurements for one participant at two different lighting levels: 25% gray scale brightness, and 2 lamps. Note that the participant's average pupil diameter is 3.484 mm when engaged the 0-back task and viewing the screen at 25% gray scale brightness, and it is 3.496 mm when engaged in the 1-back task with 2 lamps as the light source. In practice the two pupil diameters are indistinguishable from each other. This situation demonstrates that in general we cannot estimate task difficulty from pupil diameter without separating the effects of task difficulty and light.

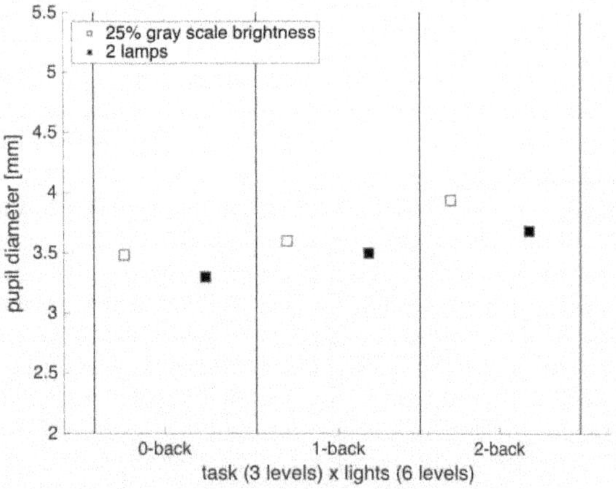

Figure 6: Pupil diameter data for one participant for two different lighting conditions. Note that raw pupil diameter measurements result in indistinguishable results for the 0-back task performed while looking at the LCD screen set to 25% gray scale brightness, and for the 1-back task performed with 2 lamps.

To be able to separate these effects we introduce a simple model, which treats the effects of light and cognitive load as additive parts of the overall pupil diameter. We show that we can use the model to classify pupil diameter readings according to the underlying task difficulty if we have two pieces of information available: the current lighting level and the average size of the user's pupil for that lighting level. Our results demonstrate that it is possible to use the model to estimate the difficulty of the underlying task with about 75% accuracy. As an example, if we apply our model to the data in Figure 6 the resulting normalized pupil diameters are -0.188 mm and 0.005 mm, respectively. Our model correctly classifies these values as resulting from 0-back and 1-back task difficulty, respectively.

Our simple model builds on the work of Palinko and Kun [34], in which they proposed a model of pupil diameter that incorporated both the effects of visual target luminance and task difficulty. However, the parameters of their model [34] were manually derived to demonstrate the idea of separating the effects of light and task difficulty for a small portion of the data collected in that experiment. There was no attempt to systematically evaluate their model's performance using all of the data from the experiment. In contrast, the model presented in this paper was created and evaluated using the entire dataset collected in this experiment, allowing us to quantify what we might expect to achieve in estimating task difficulty based on pupil diameter measurements.

The results also provide indication that the system might be able to use training data from existing users in order to accommodate new users. Specifically, in our k-fold validation we found thresholds for our model based on data from 15 of the 20 participants, and tested the model on data from the remaining 5 participants. With this approach we were able to correctly classify the workload based on pupil diameter measurement in 75% of the cases.

Using the current model as input for adaptive UIs could be challenging since this accuracy could (negatively) impact the user in case of misclassifications. Thus, further work is required to increase accuracy and investigate the required level of accuracy. However, our approach cannot only be used for UI adaptation, but also as a tool to highlight challenges of the interaction during UI design, and provide ideas how/what to modify. For UI adaptation as one of the long-term goals we see our approach as one of the steps towards this goal but agree that further aspects need to be considered (e.g., [30]).

Finally, our data also demonstrates that using pupil diameter measurements to estimate task difficulty is complicated by measurement noise. Noise can result from eye blinks, head motion, and other natural user actions and environmental conditions. We can expect such noisy measurements to occur with remote eye trackers, although the situation might improve if we use head-worn eye trackers. Head-worn eye trackers might become widespread with the advent of devices similar to Google Glass, or the upcoming Microsoft

HoloLens (although neither of these two devices has eye tracking capabilities at this time).

PRACTICALLY ESTIMATING WORKLOAD

Looking ahead, based on the findings presented in this paper it becomes possible to continuously estimate workload for new users and new tasks. To apply our model in an office or home environment, for example to track a user's task difficulty while coding, or playing a game, we would need three types of information: the user's pupil diameter, the current lighting conditions, and the average pupil diameter for those lighting conditions.

Pupil diameter measurement will likely become inexpensive soon. Even today we can purchase eye trackers at about $200, and we can imagine that in the near future eye tracking applications will be able to utilize a high-resolution webcam (and infrared illumination) integrated into a computing device. And, at least for applications where the user's visual attention is focused on a screen, we should be able to easily assess lighting conditions: e.g., for a user writing code on a computer we can track the user's gaze, and assess the luminance of the screen around the user's visual focus as well as the environmental illumination. We can also assess ambient light – mobile devices can already measure the intensity of ambient light to control their display luminance. Finally, assessing the average pupil diameter for a given lighting level would require a calibration process: this might be as simple as instructing the user to look at different areas of the screen and it collecting pupil diameter data as a function of screen luminance. In this process the pupil size would be measured at expected lighting levels (e.g. lighter and darker application windows), and at extremes (e.g., a white and a black screen), while there is no workload present. One could calculate, based on these data, an illumination-dependent average pupil diameter for the user. Using these values for the pupil size and knowing the current lighting level (e.g., based on what is shown on the screen) the proposed model can be used to estimate the workload while engaged in arbitrary tasks.

LIMITATIONS

One limitation of our work is that our model was implemented and tested using discrete levels of lighting and task difficulty. Furthermore, we avoided transitions between these discrete levels by introducing long rest periods between experimental conditions. Finally, the time resolution of our estimate is low, as we estimate workload for 30-second segments. We averaged measurements from the eye-tracker to reduce the effect of measurement noise. For future work, we plan to separate the two effects for each measurement point (at the frequency of the eye-tracker). However, we see this model as a first step towards high time-resolution workload estimation through pupil diameter, independent of lighting.

In a natural setting, a number of variables will change continuously in time and value, including the luminance and color of visual targets, ambient lighting, as well as task modality and difficulty. Thus, future work will have to address modeling pupil diameter changes in these realistic environments. If we can model pupil diameter changes due to factors other than cognitive workload, then we expect that we can use this model to estimate the changes that are due to cognitive workload. Our plan is to first explore this question in the context of interactions with user interfaces presented on screens, both small and large.

Another limitation is that our calculations are completed after all of the data has been collected, and not in real-time. While this approach would be useful in the design phase of a user interface, more work is needed to create a model that can be used to provide real-time feedback to UI algorithms.

Furthermore, in this work we use a simple heuristic classifier. It is possible that we could attain better classification with a more sophisticated classifier. However, the classifier we implemented serves the intended purpose of providing a proof of concept that separating the effects of light and task difficulty is possible. One of the next steps is to investigate continuously changing levels of light and task difficulty and present a system that can do this in real-time. With this step we will also introduce a sophisticated new classifier.

CONCLUSION

With the increasing proliferation of eye-tracking devices, it becomes more and more feasible to rely on this technology when interacting with computers and intelligent devices. One desire is to use eye-tracking to estimate the user's mental workload. This work seeks to tackle potential limitations of using eye-tracking methods in estimating mental workload such as the influence of illumination. By conducting a fully controlled experiment under different lighting and workload conditions, we are able to provide a dataset and preliminary model that can be used to estimate mental workload based on eye-tracking employing the user's pupil diameter.

ACKNOWLEDGMENTS

This work was funded in part by the NSF under grant IIA-1358096. We thank Micah Lucas, Michael Nguyen, and Rudra Timsina for their help in conducting the study and processing the data. We also thank the German Research Foundation (DFG) for financial support of the project within the Cluster of Excellence in Simulation Technology (EXC 310/2) and within the projects C02 of SFB / Transregio 161 "Quantitative Methods for Visual Computing" at the University of Stuttgart.

REFERENCES

1. Ulf Ahlstrom and Ferne J. Friedman-Berg. 2006. Using eye movement activity as a correlate of cognitive workload. *International Journal of Industrial Ergonomics* 36, 7 (Jul. 2006), 623-636. DOI: http://dx.doi.org/10.1016/j.ergon.2006.04.002
2. Amanda N. Baraldi and Craig K. Enders. 2010. An introduction to modern missing data analyses. *Journal of School Psychology* 48, 1 (Feb. 2010), 5-37. DOI: http://dx.doi.org/10.1016/j.jsp.2009.10.001
3. Jackson Beatty. 1982. Task-evoked pupillary responses, processing load, and the structure of processing resources. *Psychological Bulletin* 91, 2 (Mar. 1982), 276-292. DOI: http://dx.doi.org/10.1037/0033-2909.91.2.276
4. Simone Benedetto, Marco Pedrotti, Luca Minin, Thierry Baccino, Alessandra Re, and Roberto Montanari. 2011. Driver workload and eye blink duration. *Transportation Research Part F: Traffic Psychology and Behavior* 14, 3 (May 2011), 199-208. DOI: http://dx.doi.org/10.1016/j.trf.2010.12.001
5. Anne-Marie Brouwer, Maarten A. Hogervorst1, Jan B. F. van Erp, Tobias Heffelaar, Patrick H. Zimmerman, and Robert Oostenveld. 2012. Estimating workload using EEG spectral power and ERPs in the n-back task. *Journal of Neural Engineering* 9, 4, Article 045008 (Jul. 2012), 045008, 14 pages. DOI: http://dx.doi.org/10.1088/1741-2560/9/4/045008
6. Joseph F. Coughlin, Bryan Reimer, and Bruce Mehler. 2009. *Driver Wellness, Safety & the Development of an AwareCar*. MIT AgeLab White Paper. Massachusetts Institute of Technology, Cambridge, MA. http://web.mit.edu/reimer/www/pdfs/coughlin_wellness_2009.pdf
7. Andrew T. Duchowski. 2002. A breadth-first survey of eye-tracking applications. *Behavior Research Methods, Instruments, & Computers* 34, 4 (Nov. 2002), 455-470. DOI: http://dx.doi.org/10.3758/BF03195475
8. Christine Fogarty, and John A. Stern, 1989. Eye movements and blinks: Their relationship to higher cognitive processes. *International Journal of Psychophysiology* 8, 1 (Sep. 1983), 35-42. http://dx.doi.org/10.1016/0167-8760(89)90017-2
9. Thomas M. Gable, Andrew L. Kun, Bruce N. Walker, and Riley J. Winton. 2015. Comparing heart rate and pupil size as objective measures of workload in the driving context: initial look. In *Adjunct Proceedings of the 7th International Conference on Automotive User Interfaces and Interactive Vehicular Applications (AutomotiveUI '15)*. ACM, New York, NY, USA, 20-25. DOI: http://doi.acm.org/10.1145/2809730.2809745
10. Alan Gevins, and Michael E. Smith. 2003. Neurophysiological measures of cognitive workload during human-computer interaction. *Theoretical Issues in Ergonomics Science 4*, 1-2 (2003), 113-131. DOI: http://dx.doi.org/10.1080/14639220210159717
11. Audrey Girouard and Erin Treacy Solovey and Robert J.K. Jacob. 2013. Designing a passive brain computer interface using real time classification of functional near-infrared spectroscopy. *International Journal of Autonomous and Adaptive Communication Systems* 6,1 (2013), 26-44. DOI: http://dx.doi.org/10.1504/IJAACS.2013.050689
12. D. M. A. Gronwall. 1977. Paced Auditory Serial-Addition Task: A Measure of Recovery From Concussion. *Perceptual and Motor Skills* 44 (1977), 367-373. DOI: http://dx.doi.org/10.2466/pms.1977.44.2.367
13. Jennifer A. Healey, and Rosalind W. Picard. 2005. Detecting stress during real-world driving tasks using physiological sensors. *IEEE Trans. Intelligent Transportation Systems* 6, 2 (June 2005), 156-166. DOI: http://dx.doi.org/10.1109/TITS.2005.848368
14. Peter A. Heeman, Tomer Meshorer, Andrew L. Kun, Oskar Palinko, and Zeljko Medenica. 2013. Estimating cognitive load using pupil diameter during a spoken dialogue task. In *Proceedings of the 5th International Conference on Automotive User Interfaces and Interactive Vehicular Applications* (AutomotiveUI '13). ACM, New York, NY, USA, 242-245. DOI: http://dx.doi.org/10.1145/2516540.2516570
15. Daniel Kahneman, D., and Jackson Beatty. 1966. Pupil Diameter and Load on Memory. *Science* 154, 3756 (Dec. 1966), 1583-1585. DOI: http://dx.doi.org/10.1126/science.154.3756.1583
16. Daniel Kahneman, Linda Onuska, L., and Ruth E. Wolman. 1968. Effects of pupillary response in a short-term memory task. *The Quarterly Journal of Experimental Psychology* 20, 3 (1968), 309-311. DOI: http://dx.doi.org/10.1080/14640746808400168
17. W. K. Kirchner. Age differences in short-term retention of rapidly changing information. *Journal of experimental psychology* 55, 4 (Apr. 1958), 352-358.
18. Jeff Klingner, Rakshit Kumar, and Pat Hanrahan. 2008. Measuring the task-evoked pupillary response with a remote eye tracker. In *Proceedings of the 2008 symposium on Eye tracking research & applications* (ETRA '08). ACM, New York, NY, USA, 69-72. DOI: http://dx.doi.org/10.1145/1344471.1344489
19. Jeff Klingner, Barbara Tversky, and Pat Hanrahan. 2011. Effects of visual and verbal presentation on cognitive load in vigilance, memory, and arithmetic tasks. *Psychophysiology* 48, 3 (Mar. 2011), 323-332. DOI: http://dx.doi.org/10.1111/j.1469-8986.2010.01069.x
20. Andrew L. Kun, Susanne Boll, and Albrecht Schmidt. 2016. Shirting gears: User interfaces in the age of autonomous driving. *IEEE Pervasive Computing* 15, 1

(January-March 2016), 32-37. DOI: http://dx.doi.org/10.1109/MPRV.2016.14

21. Andrew L. Kun, and Zeljko Medenica. 2012. Video call or not, that is the question. In *CHI '12 Extended Abstracts on Human Factors in Computing Systems*. ACM, New York, NY, USA, 1631-1636. DOI: http://dx.doi.org/10.1145/2212776.2223684
22. Andrew L. Kun, Oskar Palinko, Zeljko Medenica, and Peter A. Heeman. 2013. On the Feasibility of Using Pupil Diameter to Estimate Cognitive Load Changes for In-Vehicle Spoken Dialogues. In INTERSPEECH, (2013), 3766-3770.
23. Andrew L. Kun, Oskar Palinko, and Razumenić, I. Exploring the effects of size and luminance of visual targets on the pupillary light reflex. In *Proceedings of the 4th International Conference on Automotive User Interfaces and Interactive Vehicular Applications* (AutomotiveUI '12). ACM, New York, NY, USA, 183-186. DOI: http://doi.acm.org/10.1145/2390256.2390287
24. Sandra P. Marshall, 2002. The Index of Cognitive Activity: measuring cognitive workload. In *Proceedings of the 2002 IEEE 7th Conference on Human Factors and Power Plants*. IEEE, 7-5 – 7-9. DOI: http://dx.doi.org/10.1109/HFPP.2002.1042860
25. Bruce Mehler, Bryan Reimer, Joseph F. Coughlin, and Jeffery A. Dusek. 2009. Impact of incremental increases in cognitive workload on physiological arousal and performance in young adult drivers. *Transportation Research Record: Journal of the Transportation Research Board* 2138, 1 (2009), 6-12. DOI: http://dx.doi.org/10.3141/2138-02
26. Bruce Mehler, Bryan Reimer, and Joseph F. Coughlin. 2012. Sensitivity of physiological measures for detecting systematic variations in cognitive demand from a working memory task an on-road study across three age groups. *Human Factors* 54, 3 (2010), 396-412. DOI: http://dx.doi.org/10.1177/0018720812442086
27. Bruce Mehler, Bryan Reimer and Jeffery A. Dusek. 2011. *MIT AgeLab Delayed Digit Recall Task (n-back)* Working Paper 2011-3B. Massachusetts Institute of Technology, Cambridge, MA. http://agelab.mit.edu/system/files/Mehler_et_al_n-back-white-paper_2011_B.pdf
28. W. Thomas Miller, and Andrew L. Kun. 2013. Using speech, GUIs and buttons in police vehicles: field data on user preferences for the Project54 system. In *Proceedings of the 5th International Conference on Automotive User Interfaces and Interactive Vehicular Applications* (AutomotiveUI '13). ACM, New York, NY, USA, 108-113. DOI: http://dx.doi.org/10.1145/2516540.2516564
29. William F. Moroney, David W. Biers, Thomas Eggemeier, and Jennifer A. Mitchell. 1992. A comparison of two scoring procedures with the NASA Task Load Index in a simulated flight task. In *Proceedings of the IEEE 1992 National Aerospace and Electronics Conference, NAECON 1992*. IEEE, 734-740. DOI: http://dx.doi.org/10.1109/NAECON.1992.220513
30. Nesrine Mezhoudi, Iyad Khaddam, and Jean Vanderdonckt. 2015. Toward Usable Intelligent User Interface. In: *Proceedings of the 17th International Conference on Human-Computer Interaction (HCII '15), Part II*, LNCS 9170, Springer International Publishing, 459-471. DOI: http://dx.doi.org/10.1007/978-3-319-20916-6_43
31. Michael Myrtek, Doris Weber, Georg Brügner, and Wolfgang Müller. 1996. Occupational stress and strain of female students: results of physiological, behavioral, and psychological monitoring. *Biological Psychology* 42, 3 (Feb. 1996), 379-391. DOI: http://dx.doi.org/10.1016/0301-0511(95)05168-6
32. Luis Nunes and Miguel A. Rescarte 2002. Cognitive demands of hands-free-phone conversation while driving. *Transportation Research Part F* 5, 2 (Jun. 2002), 133-144. DOI: http://dx.doi.org/10.1016/S1369-8478(02)00012-8
33. Julie Onton, Arnaud Delorme, and Scott Makeig. 2005. Frontal midline EEG dynamics during working memory. *NeuroImage* 27, 2 (Aug. 2005), 341-356. DOI: http://dx.doi.org/10.1016/j.neuroimage.2005.04.014
34. Oskar Palinko and Andrew Kun. 2011. Exploring the influence of light and cognitive load on pupil diameter in driving simulator studies. In *Proceedings of the Sixth International Driving Symposium on Human Factors in Driver Assessment, Training and Vehicle Design (Driving Assessment 2011)*, University of Iowa, Iowa City, IA, 329-336. http://drivingassessment.uiowa.edu/sites/default/files/DA2011/Papers/048_PalinkoKun.pdf
35. Oskar Palinko and Andrew Kun. 2012. Exploring the effects of visual cognitive load and illumination on pupil diameter in driving simulators. In *Proceedings of the Symposium on Eye Tracking Research and Applications (ETRA '12)*, ACM, New York, NY, 413-416. DOI: http://dx.doi.org/10.1145/2168556.2168650
36. Oskar Palinko, Andrew L. Kun, Alexander Shyrokov, and Peter A. Heeman. 2010. Estimating cognitive load using remote eye tracking in a driving simulator. In *Proceedings of the Symposium on Eye Tracking Research and Applications (ETRA '10)*, ACM, New York, NY, 141-144. DOI: http://dx.doi.org/10.1145/1743666.1743701
37. Bastian Pfleging and Albrecht Schmidt. 2015. (Non-) Driving-Related Activities in the Car: Defining Driver Activitgies for Manual and Automated Driving. In Workshop on Experiencing Autonomous Vehicles: Crossing the Boundaries between a Drive and a Ride at

CHI '15. http://www.hcilab.org/wp-content/uploads/pfleging-2015-drivingrelatedactivities.pdf

38. Bastian Pfleging, Stefan Schneegass, and Albrecht Schmidt. 2013. Exploring user expectations for context and road video sharing while calling and driving. In *Proceedings of the 5th International Conference on Automotive User Interfaces and Interactive Vehicular Applications (AutomotiveUI '13)*. ACM, New York, NY, USA, 132-139. DOI: http://dx.doi.org/10.1145/2516540.2516547

39. Bryan Reimer, Bruce Mehler, Joseph F. Coughlin, Kathryn M. Godfrey, and Chauanzhong Tan. 2009. An on-road assessment of the impact of cognitive workload on physiological arousal in young adult drivers. In *Proceedings of the 1st International Conference on Automotive User Interfaces and Interactive Vehicular Application (AutomotiveUI '09)*, ACM, New York, NY, 115-118. DOI: http://dx.doi.org/10.1145/1620509.1620531

40. A. H. Roscoe. 1992. Assessing pilot workload. Why measure heart rate, HRV and respiration? *Biological Psychology* 34, 2 (Nov. 1992), 259-287. DOI: http://dx.doi.org/10.1016/0301-0511(92)90018-P

41. Dennis W. Rowe, John Sibert, and Don Irwin. 1998. Heart rate variability: Indicator of user state as an aid to human-computer interaction. In *Proceedings of the SIGCHI Conference on Human Factors in Computing Systems (CHI '98)*, ACM, New York, NY, 480-487. DOI: http://dx.doi.org/10.1145/274644.274709

42. Kilseop Ryu and Rohae Myung. 2005. Evaluation of mental workload with a combined measure based on physiological indices during a dual task of tracking and mental arithmetic. *International Journal of Industrial Ergonomics* 35, 11 (Nov. 2005), 991-1009. DOI: http://dx.doi.org/10.1016/j.ergon.2005.04.005

43. Stefan Schneegass, Bastian Pfleging, Nora Broy, Frederik Heinrich, and Albrecht Schmidt. A data set of real world driving to assess driver workload. In *Proceedings of the 5th International Conference on Automotive User Interfaces and Interactive Vehicular Applications (AutomotiveUI 2013)*. ACM, New York, NY, 150-157. DOI: http://dx.doi.org/10.1145/2516540.2516561

44. Erin T. Solovey, Paul Schermerhorn, Matthias Scheutz, Angelo Sassaroli, Sergio Fantini, and Robert J.K. Jacob. 2012. Brainput: Enhancing Interactive Systems with Streaming fNIRS Brain Input. In *Proceedings of the SIGCHI Conference on Human Factors in Computing Systems (CHI '12)*. ACM, New York, NY, USA, 2193-2202. DOI: http://dx.doi.org/10.1145/2207676.2208372

45. Yi-Fang Tsai, Erik Viirre, Christopher Strychacz, Bradley Chase, and Tzyy-Ping Jung. 2007. Task performance and eye activity: Predicting behavior relating to cognitive workload. *Aviation, Space, and Environmental Medicine* 78, 5 (May 2007), B176-B185.

46. Karl F. Van Orden, Wendy Limbert, Scott Makeig, and Tzyy-Ping Jung. 2001. Eye activity correlates of workload during visuospatial memory task. *Human Factors: The Journal of the Human Factors and Ergonomics Society* 43, 1 (Spring 2001), 111-121. DOI: http://dx.doi.org/10.1518/001872001775992570

47. Ying Wang, Bryan Reimer, Bruce Mehler, Jun Zhang, Alea Mehler, and Joseph F. Coughlin. 2010. The Impact of Repeated Cognitive Tasks on Driving Performance and Visual Attention. In *Proceedings of the 3rd International Conference on Applied Human Factors and Ergonomics (AHFE' 10)*, Miami, FL, USA.

48. Yan Yang, Bryan Reimer, Bruce Mehler,and Jonathan Dobres. 2013. A field study assessing driving performance, visual attention, heart rate and subjective ratings in response to two types of cognitive workload. In *Proceedings of the 7th International Driving Symposium on Human Factors in Driver Assessment, Training, and Vehicle Design (Driving Assessment 2013)*. University of Iowa, Iowa City, IA, 397-403.

49. Yabo Yang, Keith Thompson, and Stephen A. Burns. 2002. Pupil location under mesopic, photopic, and pharmacologically dilated conditions. *Investigative Ophthalmology & Visual Science* 43, 7 (Jul. 2002), 2508-2512.

50. Zhiwei Zhu, Kikuo Fujimura, and Qiang Ji. 2002. Real-time eye detection and tracking under various light conditions. In *Proceedings of the 2002 Symposium on Eye Tracking Research & Applications (ETRA 2002)*. ACM, New York, NY, 139-144. DOI: http://dx.doi.org/10.1145/507072.507100

Pointing while Looking Elsewhere: Designing for Varying Degrees of Visual Guidance during Manual Input

Barış Serim[1,3], Giulio Jacucci[1,2]
[1] Helsinki Institute for Information Technology HIIT, Dept. of Computer Science, University of Helsinki
[2] Helsinki Institute for Information Technology HIIT, Aalto University
[3] Department of Design, Aalto University
firstname.lastname@hiit.fi

ABSTRACT
We propose using eye tracking to support interface use with decreased reliance on visual guidance. While the design of most graphical user interfaces take visual guidance during manual input for granted, eye tracking allows distinguishing between the cases when the manual input is conducted with or without guidance. We conceptualize the latter cases as input with uncertainty that require separate handling. We describe the design space of input handling by utilizing input resources available to the system, possible actions the system can realize and various feedback techniques for informing the user. We demonstrate the particular action mechanisms and feedback techniques through three applications we developed for touch interaction on a large screen. We conducted a two stage study of positional accuracy during target acquisition with varying visual guidance, to determine the selection range around a touch point due to positional uncertainty. We also conducted a qualitative evaluation of example applications with participants to identify perceived utility and hand eye coordination challenges while using interfaces with decreased visual guidance.

Author Keywords
Gaze input; eye tracking; multimodal interaction; uncertain input; interaction techniques; interactive surface

ACM Classification Keywords
H.5.2. Information interfaces and presentation: Input devices and strategies

INTRODUCTION
In HCI, terms such as eyes-on or eyes-free input are used to describe the degree of visual guidance an input action is performed with, in other words, the extent sight is used to guide action. Input actions vary regarding their degree of visual guidance. While typing on a physical keyboard can be conducted with little visual guidance, selecting items from a graphical interface often demands users to look where they are pointing to. Visual guidance of input actions gains particular importance with the use of eye tracking as a real time input for interaction. Examples of gaze input often feature gaze as a pointer for selection [30, 33, 41], assuming user's visual focus at the region of interest [3, 21]. Human visual attention, however, is a limited resource and there are a number of reasons to support input without extensive reliance on visual guidance:

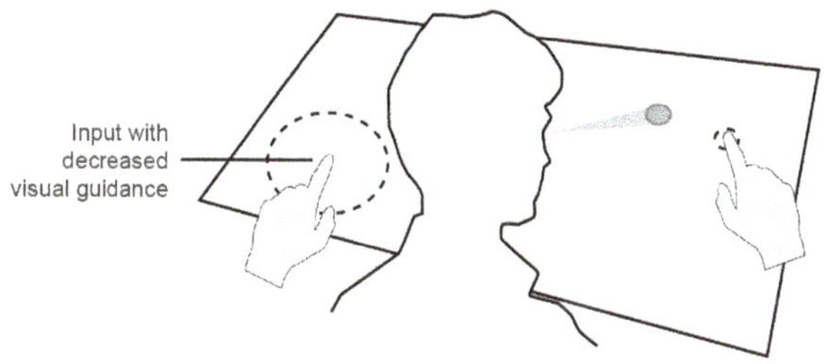

Figure 1. The user's manual input can be handled based on the degree of visual guidance it is conducted with. The input position is interpreted as exact when the action is realized eyes-on, while the system increases the potential selection range around touch and utilizes contextual resources and feedback techniques for input handling in the case of decreased visual guidance.

- It can be desirable or necessary to remain visually focused at a certain region of interest without having to redirect gaze to another region in the interface.
- Input accuracy can be uncritical for certain cases, when the user is casual or wishes to delegate a certain level of control to the system.
- The task can require concurrent pointing at multiple regions of interest within the interface.

In this paper, we propose *using eye tracking to support manual input in the absence of or with little visual guidance*. The design of most graphical interfaces takes user's full visual guidance during manual input for granted. System interpretation of input is accordingly definitive; pointing actions on the interface are processed as exact coordinates. As an alternative to the current adoption, eye tracking can be used to understand the degree of visual guidance that a manual action is accomplished with and adapt the system interpretation and handling of the user input. Our main design strategy is to use manual input as a direct input and utilize gaze to increase

CHI'16, May 07 - 12, 2016, San Jose, CA, USA

ACM 978-1-4503-3362-7/16/05$15.00
DOI: http://dx.doi.org/10.1145/2858036.2858480

its expressiveness. This approach is fundamentally different than many current examples of gaze interaction that complement gaze with indirect manual input [21, 30, 33].

We make a number of contributions to support manual input with varying visual guidance. We conceptualize user input performed with decreased visual guidance as input with uncertainty and adopt an uncertain input handling framework for adapting system behavior. We describe action mechanisms and novel feedback techniques for handling such input and demonstrate their use through three example applications. We conducted a two part study to guide future design. In the first part, we determine the selection range of manual input on a large touch screen by measuring the positional offset with different degrees of visual guidance. In the second part, we report the perceived utility and the hand-eye coordination challenges that emerge during the interaction through a qualitative evaluation of the applications.

BACKGROUND

We motivate our design approach by discussing earlier work on gaze input, hand-eye coordination and input with uncertainty.

Gaze as Input Modality

Our work falls under the design approach that utilizes gaze as an additional modality rather than replacing manual input. Research in this direction aims to compensate the lack of a confirmation mechanism in gaze input (known as "Midas Touch" [16]) by using physical keyboard [19], mouse [41], touch [30] or gesture.

Previous studies conducted in controlled, isolated settings show that gaze can be faster than other pointing devices for target selection [28, 34]. Thus, a strong motivation for most previous work that combine gaze and manual input has been motor performance gains in target acquisition [4, 18, 21, 30, 31, 33, 41]. A pioneering application is Zhai et al.'s MAGIC pointing [41], a manual and gaze hybrid pointing method, that eliminates part of the mouse movement by warping the mouse cursor to the eye fixation coordinates and then accomplishes the selection action through the mouse, thus cascading the two input modalities. Recently, interaction with large and distant displays, where direct input is impractical, has been an application area for utilizing gaze. In these applications gaze is complemented by touch input on a hand-held device [30, 31, 33] or free air gestures [18].

In general, previous work capitalizes on the rapid switching of spatial context afforded by gaze to decrease the amplitude of movement by hand. Thus, a common feature among them is the separation of the hand from the target, namely the indirect and relative use of manual input to complement the absolute coordinates provided by gaze. Two hybrid exceptions are GazeTouch [21] and Gaze-Shifting [22] that utilize manual input both as a direct and indirect input, based on the distance of gaze point to the input position.

Some of the examples cited above are similar to our approach in that they facilitate manual input without visual guidance. This is achieved through different means, such as using touch as a relative, indirect input [21] or in small handheld devices that enable eyes-free interaction [31]. Our approach departs from them by *always using manual input directly*, even in the case of input without visual guidance. We use manual input for selection and use gaze input to qualify manual input. While earlier work advocates the separation of the hand from the target, summarized as *"gaze suggests and touch confirms"* [30] or *"gaze selects, touch manipulates"* [21], we propose an alternative use in which *"gaze qualifies hand input."*

Hand-Eye Coordination

Our approach is partly motivated by the simultaneous use of gaze and manual input on multiple points of interest. Previous work in eye cursor coordination in web search shows that mouse use is not purely *incidental*, (i.e. performed for the purpose of clicking) [24]. Instead, the cursor can be used for other purposes such as keeping track of what is read and as a placeholder on interesting items, while eyes switch to other regions [15, 24]. Additionally, as Bieg et al. [3] argue, one assumption in techniques that aim to decrease the amplitude in target acquisition using gaze is that eye movement precedes pointing actions. Contrary to this, their study reports that pointing behavior is initiated without visual guidance for items whose approximate locations are known.

In the above described situations gaze and pointing accomplish parallel tasks in different regions within interface. However, such parallel use of eye and cursor movements might not be well supported by design approaches that cascade (i.e., sequence) manual and gaze input such as MAGIC pointing [41].

While approaches like MAGIC pointing focus on increasing the performance in a sequential set of actions using gaze, we target supporting concurrent access to multiple regions on the interface, without necessarily redirecting gaze. A usable distinction has been made by Fitzmaurice et al. [9, 10] between spatial and time multiplexing for user input. While time multiplexing refers to sequential and mutually exclusive techniques, spatial multiplexing refers to the concurrent access to dedicated input fields. Their observation of manual interaction with domino bricks is illustrative of spatial multiplexing: *"...Tactile feedback was often used to grab dominos while visually attending to other tasks. The non-dominant hand was often used to reposition and align the dominos into their final resting place while, in parallel, the dominant hand was used to retrieve new dominos..."* [10]. Fitzmaurice et al., accordingly, design for spatial multiplexing through graspable input devices by citing the benefits of tactile confirmation and possible use without visual guidance.

On the other hand, the advent of multi-touch devices enabled spatial multiplexing in graphical interfaces. Even though interaction with tactile interfaces has shown to be more robust and efficient [32, 37], multi-touch input surfaces allow similar benefits like bimanualism. Previous work on touch screens aims to support eyes-free interaction in various ways such as using touch as a gestural input or directing finger to predefined locations using magnetic attraction [36]. In contrast, we support eyes-free interaction through appropriate interpretation and handling of the user input. We interpret lack of visual guidance as situations of inputs with uncertainty.

Input with Uncertainty

Proliferation of inherently uncertain inputs, such as speech recognition, gestures and touch, motivated a number of techniques and frameworks for the flexible handling of user input and communicating system interpretation of input back to the user [20, 23, 25, 26, 38, 39].

A large body of research on input positional uncertainty deals with the "fat finger problem", namely the large touch contact area and visual occlusion caused by the finger [2, 26, 35, 38]. In the context of this paper, the source of uncertainty is the user's lack of exact information about how his/her manual input coordinates map to the visual content on the user interface *due to decreased visual guidance*. The most closely related work in this direction is by Hagiya and Kato [14], who use gaze point information to model touch distribution on a hand-size mobile display. Although particularly focused on text entry, their distinction between accurate and ambiguous touch is parallel to our approach. Different from their work, we consider the overall design space of input handling and demonstrate their use in diverse applications with multi-touch interaction on a large screen. Previous work on the accuracy of target acquisition using arm movements without visual guidance suggests that errors increase in relation to the amplitude of movement [5, 29] and cumulatively [6].

Users' lack of information about their exact input region allows system to interpret the input as positionally ambiguous and less decisive. Conversely, high visual guidance reinforces user's manual input. In HCI various design frameworks aim to adapt system behaviour depending on user's varying degrees of control. In vehicle design, "horse metaphor" [12] refers to a level of delegation of decision making to the system, based on how tight or loose the user's control is. Pohl and Murray-Smith propose design approaches for mobile systems that allow users to vary their level of engagement along a focused-casual continuum [23]. When user input is casual (i.e., lacking in precision and deliberation) the system partly takes control using available personal and contextual information. In the same spirit, we use the degree of visual guidance for a partial delegation of decision making to the system. However, while user attention is inhibited or reserved for another activity in mobile use [23], we are primarily interested in the cases in which user attention is divided between two actions related to the same task and two regions within the same interface. This enables using gaze position on the interface as a resource for interpreting the user's input and providing feedback to the user through various channels.

DESIGN SPACE

Previous work [20, 25] on handling input with uncertainty separates handling process into successive stages of modeling input, event dispatch, interpretation and action, in which the system component "mediator" is responsible for deciding on the action. We used a similar structure and provide an inexhaustive list of considerations and techniques that are particularly relevant for handling input with varying degrees of visual guidance.

User input involves both user manual input position and other contextual information. The system handles user input through various *action mechanisms* (i.e. select, defer or inaction). *Feedback techniques* aim to remedy users' lack of visual guidance by making manual input information and system interpretation of input available to the user.

User input

Manual input position. The primary resource for interpreting user's manual input is the position (such as x,y values) of the input. Potential selection range around a manual input position increases with decreasing visual guidance (Figure 2), due to positional uncertainty. We operationalized visual guidance as the distance between the gaze and manual input position and use it to compute the potential selection range around touch input. The interpretation of manual input is exact up to a certain distance threshold between gaze and input position. Beyond this threshold, the selection range increases in linear relation to the distance between gaze and manual input position. For touch input the selection range is greater than a single pixel, even when it is conducted with visual guidance, due to the inherent uncertainty of touch. During the design process we heuristically defined the threshold and linear relation values. A two stage target acquisition study described further in the paper shows how the threshold and linear relation can be empirically determined.

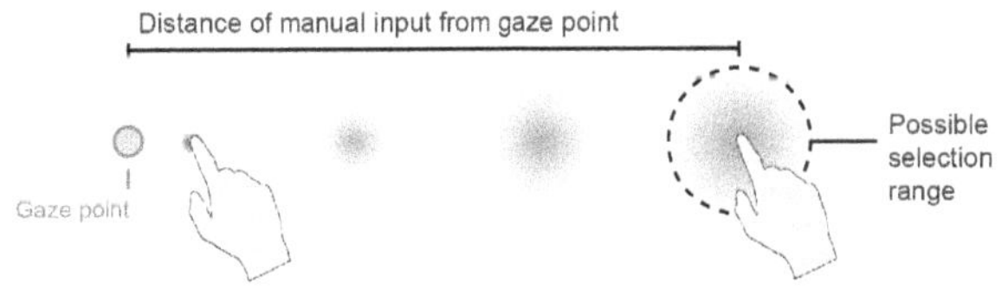

Figure 2. Input selection range increases the further gaze point is located from the manual input position (where the touch or cursor is located).

Additionally, the determination of visual guidance is dependent on a number of design decisions:

- **Continuous, discrete.** For a manual input event, visual guidance can be determined along a discrete (such as only covering the two opposite ends eyes-on and eyes-free) or continuous scale.
- **Conservative, liberal approaches.** The determination of visual guidance and thus the selection range around an input position can change upon eye movements (liberal approach) or only upon the movement of the hand (conservative approach). We borrow the terms from Zhai et al. [41], who used them to distinguish the cases in which a mouse cursor is continuously warped to the gaze point coordinates (liberal) or only upon a cursor movement event (conservative). For many cases, conservative approach can be more suitable, since elements pointed with visual guidance will persist in the user's short term memory even after the gaze shifts to another location.

When scaling the range of uncertainty upon movement, our general principle is to a) decrease the uncertainty *instantly* when the user increases visual guidance and b) increase the uncertainty *gradually* when the user decreases the visual guidance. The difference is due to the gradual deviation in position with increasing amplitude of movement [5]. It should be noted that for cursor input (e.g., mouse), the uncertainty can always be determined upon movement as the cursor is always present at the interface. On the other hand, touch input involves finger enter and exit events.

Gaze context. Interpersonal interaction can involve "referential gaze" in combination with speech and manual pointing to ground and disambiguate meaning. The use of "dual pointing" to two different regions of interest in the environment, one with gaze the other with the hand, to semantically associate them, has been documented [13]. Similarly, eye tracking information can be used beyond determining the positional uncertainty of manual input. The information of where the user is gazing at the interface can be used to resolve uncertainty in manual input by prioritizing actions that are related to the gaze context.

There are multiple possibilities regarding how the gaze context can be determined in relation to manual input. First, the gaze context position can be determined at the beginning of manual interaction and remain fixed until the user ends the manual input (such as by releasing a mouse or in a touch up event). Second, the gaze context position can be constantly updated upon eye movements. However, during the design process we noticed that continuous synchronization of gaze context with eye movements can be intrusive and unstable. A more viable option is to update gaze context only upon touch or cursor movements.

Interaction history. Another resource for resolving positional uncertainty is the interaction history of the user. A possible reason for the lack of visual guidance and loose hand-eye coordination could be that the location of the item is remembered [11]. Thus, decreased visual guidance can be attributed to the user expectation of repeating a previous action. The system can also resolve uncertainty by keeping track of how user changes the application state. Application functionality makes certain action sequences more probable over others in an interface configuration. As an example, if the user previously opened a dropdown menu, it is more probable that a selection action on one of the menu items will follow.

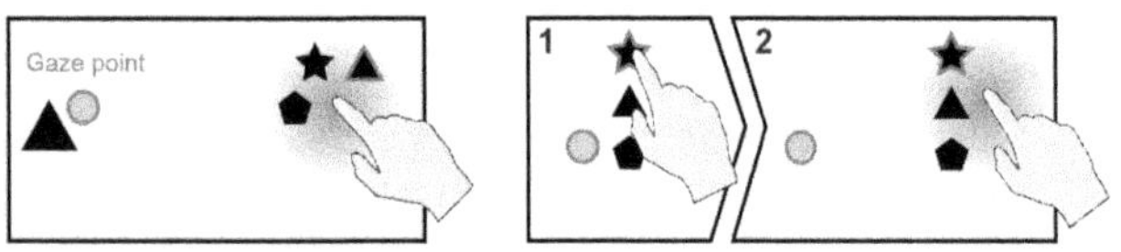

Figure 3. Two possible ways of resolving positional uncertainty are using gaze context (left) and interaction history (right).

Action Mechanisms

Select action. The system can respond to positional uncertainty in a number of ways for selecting action (Figure 4). One is positional selection between different actions, such as selecting between different discrete input fields like buttons. The selection can also occur between different actions that positionally overlap. For example, a touch action on a text field can be intended for scrolling or text selection [26]. These different actions require different degrees of visual guidance: scrolling has an area effect and does not require exact pointing, while selection requires accurate pointing. Decreased visual guidance in such cases can aid the system decision making between various actions types. Finally, if the input field allows range selection, positional uncertainty can be handled by expanding the selection range.

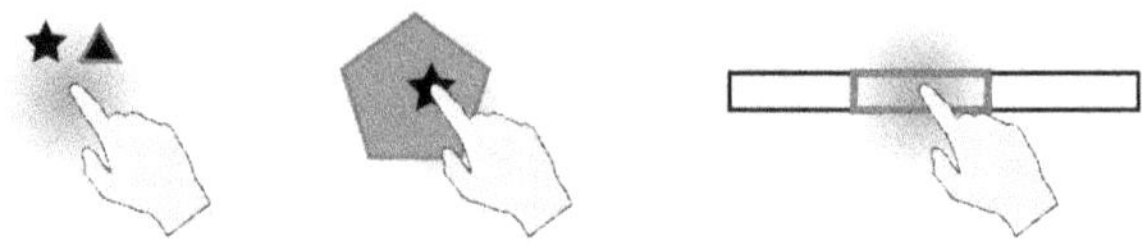

Figure 4. Action selection can involve positional selection (left), selecting between actions that positionally overlap (middle) or range selection (right).

Defer action. Another potential response is to defer action until enough information is gathered for disambiguation. A common example is the press-release sequence for inherently uncertain inputs such as touch [25] or gaze [19]. System interpretation of user command is communicated as a feedback after key or touch press event and the final action is deferred to a key or touch release event.

Inaction. Input without visual guidance can be interpreted as unintentional or unfocused, resulting in the system not taking action.

Feedback Techniques

In addition to possible non-visual notifications such as sound or tactile feedback, eye tracking allows various visual strategies to provide feedback about user actions and the system interpretation of them:

Support peripheral awareness. In the case of manual input without visual guidance the system can remedy the lack of information by supporting peripheral awareness. The system can increase the visual footprint of the cursor a) to support the peripheral awareness of where the cursor or finger is located within interface and b) to indicate the degree of positional uncertainty as determined by the system (Figure 5). The visual footprint of potential targets can also be increased, informing users about the system interpretation of their action.

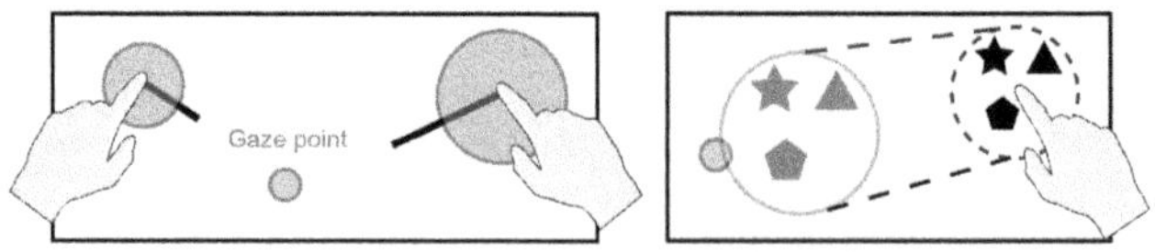

Figure 5. Providing peripheral awareness (left) and warping information content around manual input position to gaze point (right) are two possible visual feedback techniques to communicate system interpretation of user input back to user.

Warp information to gaze point. Warping information to the gaze point is the counterpart of warping cursor to the gaze point location (e.g. [41]). The information content around the user's manual input position or the system interpretation of user action is overlaid to where the user's gaze is directed (Figure 5).

Figure 6 provides a summary of the design space. It should be noted that providing feedback and uncertain input handling are two competing approaches, since feedback techniques decrease the uncertainty by providing information to the user. However, they are not mutually exclusive and can be integrated in various stages of interaction as can be seen in the applications described further in the paper.

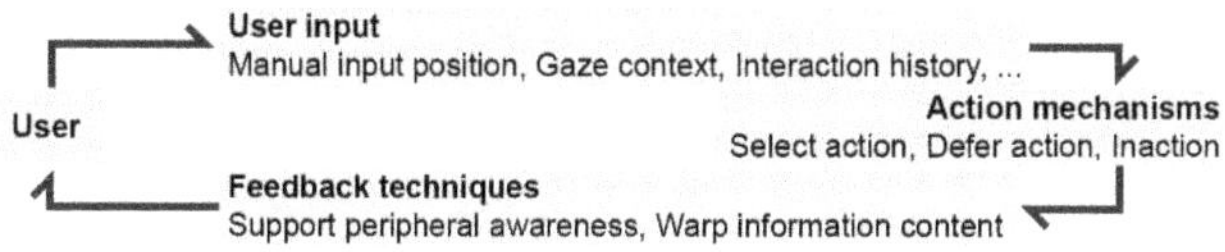

Figure 6. Summary of the design space.

DETERMINING SELECTION RANGE

An important design question related to positional uncertainty is determining selection range for input with varying levels of visual guidance.

We conducted a two stage study of target acquisition to determine the potential selection range around a touch point. 12 participants (4 female) aged between 20 to 34 (m=28, sd=3.95) took part in our evaluation. Each session started with 9 point eye tracking calibration and proceeded if the calibration was successful (below 2° deviation in accuracy). The height of the table on which the screen and eye tracker were mounted was adjusted for each participant and the participants remained standing during the evaluation.

Apparatus

The study has been conducted using a 10 finger multi-touch screen (27", 2,560x1,440 pixels) combined with an SMI RED eye tracker that is positioned below the touch screen running at 60Hz. The screen was tilted 30° to enable easier hand reach for touch input. The screen and eye tracker were positioned respectively 50cm and 70cm in front of the eyes (approximate values).

Study Design

Each participant performed two set of tasks. The first set of tasks aimed to determine positional inaccuracy (variable) for varying distances between gaze and target (invariable). The second task set aimed to determine the distance between gaze and the target (variable) for accurate pointing tasks (invariable).

We logged gaze, touch and target positions for each task. During the study there were brief moments when eye tracking signal was not available due to hand occlusion or head movement. Thus, a task was completed only when the gaze point was available to the system.

Position Inaccuracy for Gaze Distance

Earlier work suggests a decreased positional accuracy for motor target acquisition without visual guidance [5, 29]. At the first stage, we aimed to determine the positional uncertainty for target acquisition in varying degrees of visual guidance, which we operationalized as *the distance between the target and where the gaze is directed.*

To complete a target acquisition task, the participants had to keep their gaze (controlled by eye tracking) inside a circle while tapping on one of the 15 targets (on a 5×3 matrix) on the touch screen (Figure 7). The participants were instructed to tap as correctly and as fast as possible to determine the positional offset for acquisition. We used the 6 lower middle points within the matrix, where the eye tracking is most accurate, as gaze fixation points. While keeping their gaze within the defined area, the participants tapped on all the defined targets on the matrix at a randomized order. The target acquisition tasks were accepted only if the participants kept their gaze within the circle (indicated to the participants by changing the circle area to green).

To prevent giving any visual cues, the entire target matrix was visible during the tasks. However, information of which target to tap on was shown within the circle. The pairing of 6 eye fixation regions with 15 target positions resulted in 90 tasks, that show varying distances between the target and the gaze point. To prevent the misidentification of the target, each column was assigned a different shape (from left to right: circle, cross, triangle, square and pentagon).

The degree of visual guidance as we operationalized in the study is not easily comparable to index of difficulty in Fitts' law. First, the amplitude of motion is not dependent on the distance of the target from the gaze, since the participants initiated the movement from the previous target location in the matrix. Second, the visual boundary of the targets does not accurately represent target width as the system did not require the participants to touch on the exact position.

At the same time Fitts' law has implications for acquisition with restricted visual guidance. It has been shown that Fitts' law is valid for restricted visual guidance on the target or hand [40]. By increasing the selection range for manual input, we increase the target width and thus decrease the index of difficulty. How the increased target width compensates the lack of visual guidance for acquisition performance is a highly relevant question for future research. However, we limit the scope of this study to determining the selection range around touch point.

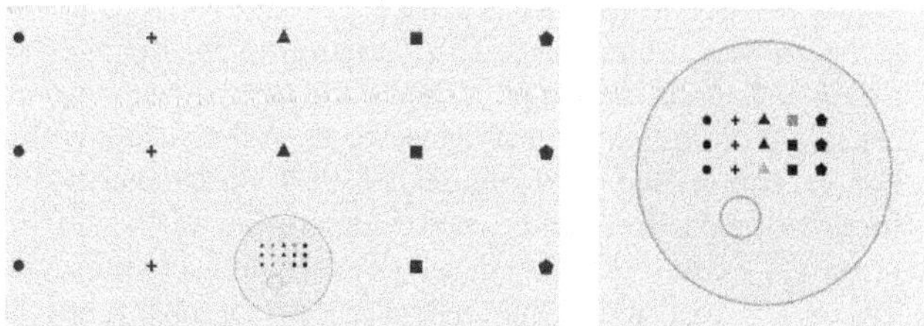

Figure 7. The experimental screen (left) and the close up of the circle (rad = 52.5mm) in which the participants need to keep their gaze inside (right). The target is shown in red inside the circle, while the position of the circle is shown in green.

Gaze Distance for Accurate Acquisition

While the first stage aimed to understand the positional inaccuracy with varying visual guidance, second stage aimed to understand the distance of gaze from the target for accurate pointing. Participants were instructed to touch circular targets, without any constraints on where they look. This stage forced participants to be accurate since a task was considered complete only when the touch point fell within the circular target (rad = 5.8mm). Each participant completed 3 repetitions of 6 target acquisition tasks (randomized order).

Results

The first stage yielded 1080 trials from 12 participants (× 90 tasks). The scatter plot in Figure 8 shows the relationship between the distance of the gaze point to the target position (invariable) to the positional offset (distance between the touch and target positions). The outliers in the scatter plot refer to the trials in which there was a large positional offset (M=120.8 mm, sd = 13.4), but the touch point was close to an adjacent target on the matrix (M=19 mm, sd = 8.8). We categorize these 31 outliers as cases in which participants misidentified the target, and exclude them from the analysis.

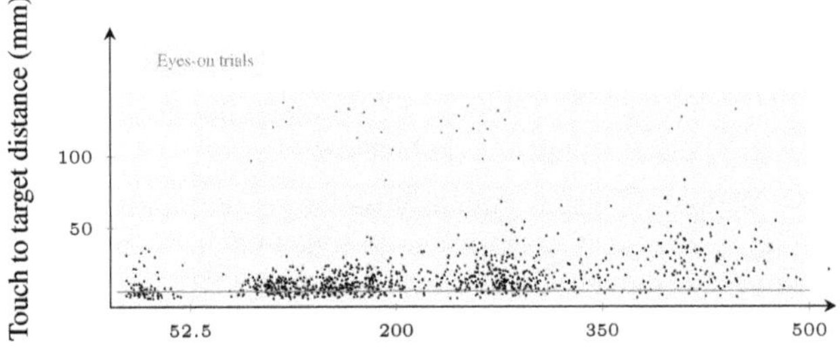

Figure 8. Scatter plot of peripheral target acquisition tasks across all participants. Outliers are shown in blue. Horizontal red line indicates the visual boundary of the circle target (rad=5.8mm). Green background indicates the eyes-on in which the target was within the boundary of the circle the participants had to keep their gaze inside(rad=52.5mm).

We divide the data in four continuous bins that correspond to varying levels of visual guidance. The intervals of the first bin (0-52.5) were determined by eyes-on tasks, in which the distance between the gaze point and the target are smaller than the radius of the circle in which the participants had to keep their gaze inside. We divided the rest of the data in three bins of even intervals. Figure 9 shows the distribution of touch points relative to the target across all users for four chosen levels of visual guidance. The deviation in the distance between gaze point and target is due to the large diameter of circle in which the participants need to keep their gaze within. For varying visual guidance levels, 95% confidence values for positional offset can be used to determine touch selection range. The results (Table 1) suggest an increasing positional inaccuracy with increasing distance between gaze point and target.

An unusual result from the first stage is the very large deviation for eyes-on tasks (0-52.5mm) when compared to a previous study [2] that reports an accuracy rate higher than 95% for 5mm radius target acquisition. We relate the unusual result to the experimental design of the first stage, in which participants did not have to touch within the target to complete the task. This is in contrast to the second stage, in which participants had to touch within the target visual border. In 216 total trials gathered from the second stage, 95% of gaze

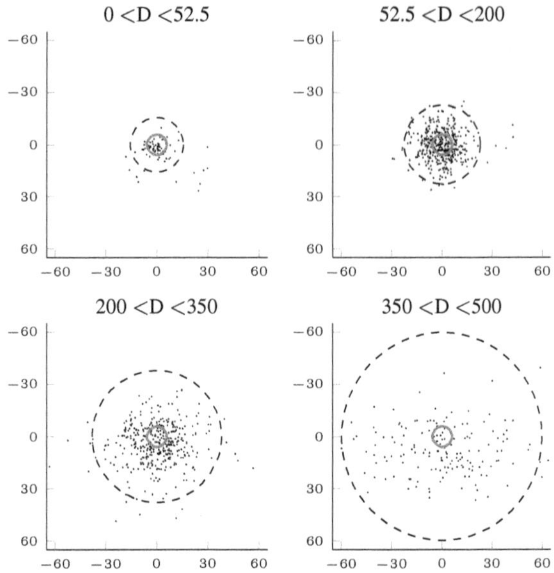

Figure 9. The distribution of touch points relative to the target across all users for chosen ranges of distance between gaze point and target. The dashed circles are the 95 % confidence circles. The red circles show the target visual boundary. All units in mm.

Distance range (Gaze to Target)	Mean distance (Gaze to Target)	95% confidence (Touch offset)
0-52.5mm	20.7mm (sd=9.3)	15.6mm
52.5-200mm	146.0mm (sd=29.6)	22.6mm
200-350mm	272.8mm (sd=33.1)	37.9mm
350-500mm	414.8mm (sd=32.1)	56.7mm

Table 1. 95% confidence values of positional offset for distance between touch and target for different visual guidance ranges. The range 0-52.5mm represent eyes-on tasks.

points were within a 61.0mm radius range around the target (M=26.3mm, sd=20.0).

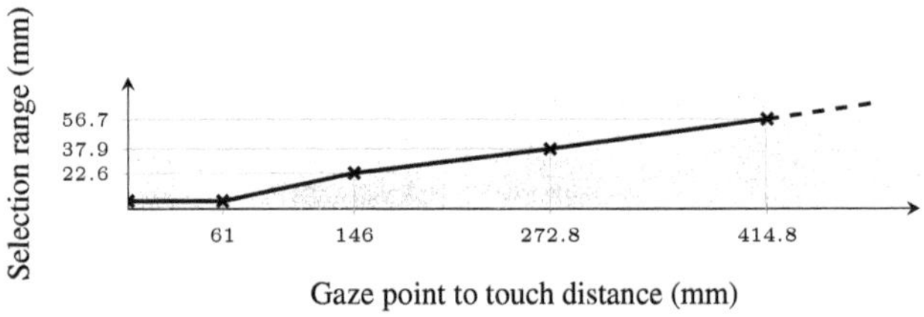

Figure 10. Selection range profile showing 95% confidence ranges from the first and second stages. Note that the minimum selection range on y axis does not need to start from a single pixel width for inputs that are inherently uncertain, such as touch.

We use the 95% confidence value (61.0mm) for the distance between gaze and target in accurate pointing tasks as a threshold for increasing positional uncertainty due to decreased visual guidance. Together with the values from the peripheral target acquisition tasks at the first stage (Table 1), we plot a tentative profile of selection range with varying degrees of guidance (Figure 10). We should stress that the profile is intended as a provisional design guide. More importantly, not every potential action within the input selection range should be given the same weight for input handling. We consider a discrete confidence threshold to be most useful for cases that require making the selection range visually explicit to the user.

APPLICATIONS

We developed a number of applications to demonstrate the applicability of our design approach for a variety of use cases. The applications feature different combinations of input handling components. Below, we provide a conceptual breakdown of each application in terms of user input, action mechanisms and feedback techniques described above.

Application 1: Multifocus Image Exploration

A potential application case is multifocus interfaces (e.g., [7, 8]) that involve spatial juxtaposition of multiple points of interest. As opposed to time multiplexed methods such as zooming, multifocus interaction utilizes spatial multiplexing to display information [7]. A common aim in juxtaposition is to compare and correlate between multiple foci [8] and avoid redirecting gaze over long distances. The process of declaring multiple foci can be sequential or concurrent (e.g. using multi-touch). Gaze input can be a useful addition to multifocus interaction tasks, both as a focus point and for supporting input with decreased visual guidance.

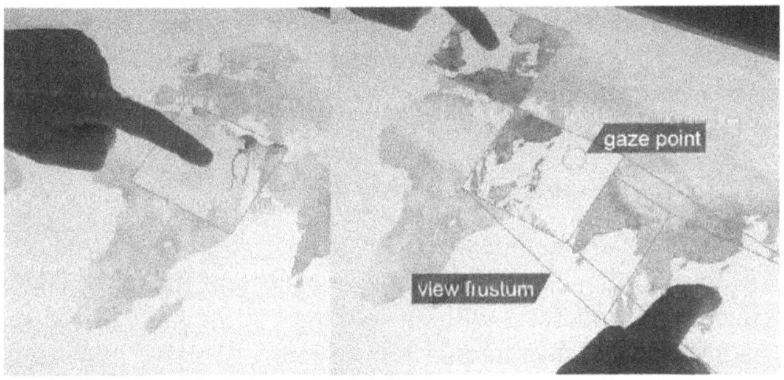

User input: Manual input position (discrete, conservative), Interaction history (previously zoomed in regions are used to resolve positional ambiguity)
Action mechanisms: Select action (resolve positional uncertainty, increase selection range by zooming out)
Feedback techniques: Peripheral awareness (show view frustum from finger to the gaze context), warp information content (warp lens near the primary touch point)

Figure 11. The degree of visual guidance is used to determine the position of lenses in image exploration. In the case of a touch event with visual guidance, the lens is shown at the touch position (left). In the case of a touch event with decreased visual guidance, the lens is warped near an existing lens (right).

Here, we demonstrate the use of input without visual guidance for exploring a map image that shows world population density (Figure 11). The application allows creating multiple lenses that are aligned edge to edge and controlled by individual touch points. The degree of visual guidance on different touch events is used to determine the primary touch point near the other lenses are aligned by its edge. The primary touch point is reevaluated with each touch down event. In the case of a touch event with visual guidance, the other lenses are warped to the new touch location. In the case of a touch event with decreased visual guidance, the lens is warped near the primary lens that the user's gaze is directed. In the latter case, positional uncertainty is handled in two ways. First, the lens covers an increased areal range. Second, positional uncertainty can be resolved by using interaction history by zooming into a previously viewed location.

Application 2: Exploring Relational Data

Another multifocus application case is interaction with relational data. We created a geospatial visualization of flight connections in the US (Figure 12). Interaction with the graph allows filtering flight connections based on the airports near the manual input. The degree of visual guidance is used to determine the positional uncertainty of touch points. For touch actions with high visual guidance, the application visualizes the connections from a single node that the user is pointing to. Positional uncertainty is increased and the cursor is expanded for pointing actions with decreased visual guidance. In this case, the gaze context of the user is used to resolve positional uncertainty; only the connections between manual selection range and airports near gaze point are visualized. In contrast to multifocus image application, the gaze context is not associated with an existing touch point and updates continuously with the movement of the touch.

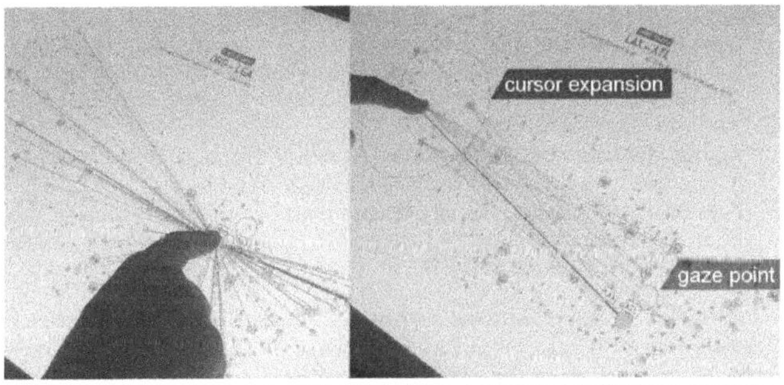

User input: Manual input position (continuous, conservative), Gaze context (updates based on manual movement on touch surface, resolve positional uncertainty using relational data)
Action mechanisms: Select action (resolve positional uncertainty)
Feedback techniques: Peripheral awareness (expand the cursor to show positional uncertainty), Warp information content (show airport code on the gaze context)

Figure 12. If the manual positions are interpreted as exact, the application visualizes all the connections from a single node (left). If the user gaze is directed elsewhere at the graph, the cursor is expanded to show increased positional uncertainty (right).

Application 3: Color Switching in Paint

Many interfaces involve sequences of tool switching and manipulation actions. Tool switching can be realized using toolbars, keyboard shortcuts or in-place selection techniques such as pie menus. Direct input devices such as touch screens allow bimanual action, where one hand performs tool selection while the other manipulates the target. In these cases, visual guidance can be used to qualify tool selection and manipulation actions. In this application we take color selection and painting on a canvas as an example of pair actions. Our application features two input fields: a continuous color selection bar and a virtual painting canvas.

Input field: Color palette

The color palette is configured as a vertical bar with varying hues along the y axis (Figure 13). The degree of visual guidance is determined continuously, corresponding to increased positional uncertainty for selection. In the case of selection with visual guidance, the system only considers the touch position for selecting a hue. In case of decreased visual guidance, the positional uncertainty is increased and the system uses additional user input resources for selection, namely the previous color selections (interaction history) and the colors in the gaze context of the user. The actual color selection is deferred to a touch release event. In the meantime, feedback of selection is displayed to the user through a radial color palette that appears on the gaze point. The gaze context is fixed at the start of a touch event and remains constant until the touch is released.

User input: Manual input position(continuous, conservative), Gaze context (the colors on the canvas region that the user looks at are used to resolve uncertainty for selection), Interaction history (previously used colors are used to resolve uncertainty)

Action mechanisms: Select action (resolve positional uncertainty), Defer action (defer the actual color selection to touch up event)

Feedback techniques: Peripheral awareness (increase the cursor size to show positional uncertainty), warp information content (create a color palette around gaze the context)

Figure 13. When conducted with a high degree of visual guidance the manual input is interpreted as exact (left). If the user gaze is directed elsewhere, such as on the canvas, the positional uncertainty is increased. In this case system provides feedback by visualizing a radial color palette at the gaze point (right).

Input field: Canvas

For input on canvas (Figure 14), the degree of visual guidance is determined discretely and is used to select action type. The degree of visual guidance at the moment of touch is used to determine if the action type is intended for painting (requiring fine degree of control) or moving the canvas (has area visual effect, thus requiring less visual guidance). The input type associated with a touch point remains stable until the touch is released.

EVALUATION OF APPLICATIONS

The various applications we developed combined different input handling techniques. We evaluated different applications to investigate 1) possible hand-eye coordination challenges that are general for input with decreased visual guidance and 2) the particular interaction challenges related to the action mechanisms and feedback techniques that vary among applications.

After finishing the target acquisition tasks, the participants proceeded into using the three applications. They were asked to perform open ended tasks with the example applications

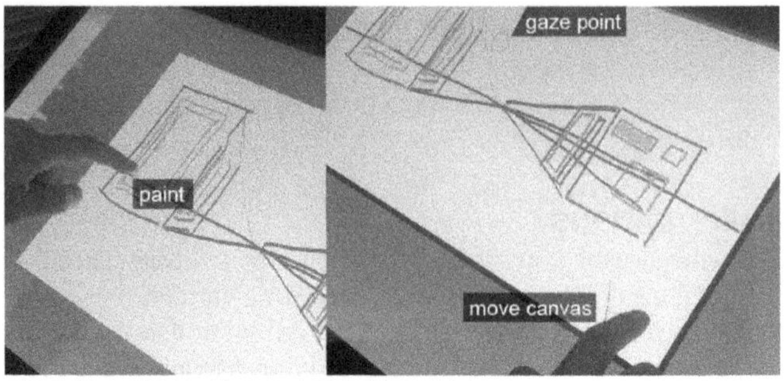

User input: Manual input position (discreet)

Action mechanisms: Select action (between types "paint" or "move")

Figure 14. Touch event on a canvas can be interpreted either as a paint (left) or move the canvas function (right) depending on the degree of visual guidance.

until they felt comfortable using the system (approximately 5 minutes). While our design approach does not require gaze point to be made explicit to the user, we still visualized the gaze as a translucent gray ring to inform participants in case the system loses track of their gaze. In this case, the translucent ring turned opaque, warning participants to correct their posture.

We video recorded participant interactions and collected their feedback after using each application. We also interviewed the participants at the end of the study to gather their overall feedback. In this section we report the participant feedback and observational data.

Participant Feedback & Video Analysis

Adjustment through Use

A common reaction among participants was the reported difficulty of "touching without looking" at the start of the session followed by gradual adjustment. Words "unnatural", "unintuitive", "strange" were often used to describe the initial experience, while the participants described their later experience as "natural" and "easier". Deliberately "avoiding drifting" of gaze to the touch location was observed during interaction and was also reported by participants as one reason for initial difficulty. *"At first it was of course quiet strange, pointing to a place where you can't see and your gaze tries to go there and you try to use your peripheral vision, but that also gets easier as you use it, you get used to the feeling of touching somewhere that you don't see."* (P4). The experience has also been compared to typing on a keyboard: *"... you start to write in the keyboard without looking, initially you look but you can try to do without looking..."* (P1)

Some participants described input handling mechanisms as "forgiving" and assistive of eyes-free input. *"I don't trust at all what I am seeing in my peripheral vision... knowing that it (eye tracking) being taken into account I trusted it even more and could predict and had some expectation of what will happen"* (P12). while others highlighted the need to know *"exactly where everything is"* before being able to point without looking. Although participant reaction differed regarding the degree of proficiency needed, individual confidence during eyes-free or peripheral pointing was a common dimension of use experience.

Being able to concentrate on the task such as drawing and *"using peripheral vision to do other specific tasks that are very obvious"* were highlighted as benefits. One participant also reported that gradual adjustment was useful for *"using two hands"*.

Gaze as Additional Pointer

The three applications are different regarding how explicitly they use the gaze context and how gaze updates in relation to touch events. The participant feedback helped identify potential benefits and drawbacks of different ways of using the gaze context. Explicit use of the gaze context has been welcomed as an additional "third hand" in flight visualization application and enabled concurrent access to three different locations (Figure 15). *"So the same feature can be done with two hands... but then I realized we only have two hands so maybe some possibility could be use your gaze as a third hand."* (P1)

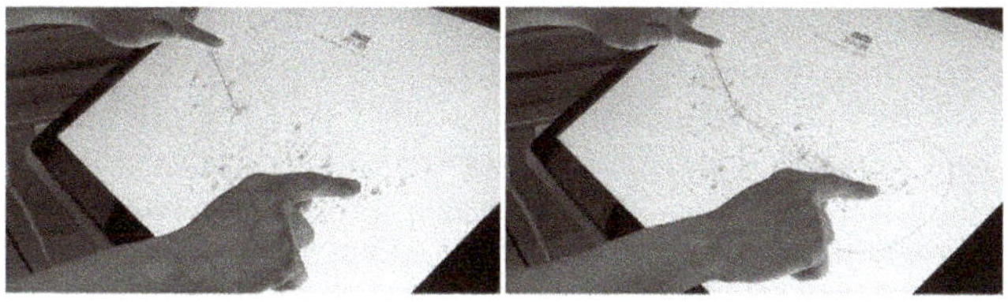

Figure 15. Gaze being used as a third pointer in addition to two hands.

On the other hand, the use of gaze as an additional pointer, especially with dynamic update, caused hand eye coordination challenges. An additional challenge is the difference between the system and user interpretation of gaze context. Participants compared between the use of gaze in the multifocus image and flight visualization applications. *"I think it is easier to use it updating in a static way, because there is nothing that constantly change, I can compare more easily, there is nothing unexpected, but in dynamic I had more options, was good that it updates fast where I look, but then it was loosing..."* (P9).

Misinterpretation of Positional Uncertainty

We observed a number of instances in which a manual input action was wrongly interpreted as positionally uncertain due to the system's lack of awareness of the movement before the actual touch event. The instances usually involved the participant keeping his finger just above a specific point on the interface and performing the touch action while looking elsewhere (Figure 16). In these cases, although the participants knew exactly where they were pointing to, the application interpreted it as positionally uncertain and handled accordingly. The participant occasionally identified this as a "problem".

Screen Edge as Ambiguous Border and Tactile Guide

Although a touch screen is an input field with definite boundaries, decreased visual guidance can cause ambiguity for users regarding whether they are *addressing* the system during touch. In some instances, while aiming for the color palette near the edge of the screen, participants touched the insensitive bezel area of the screen (Figure 17). The lack

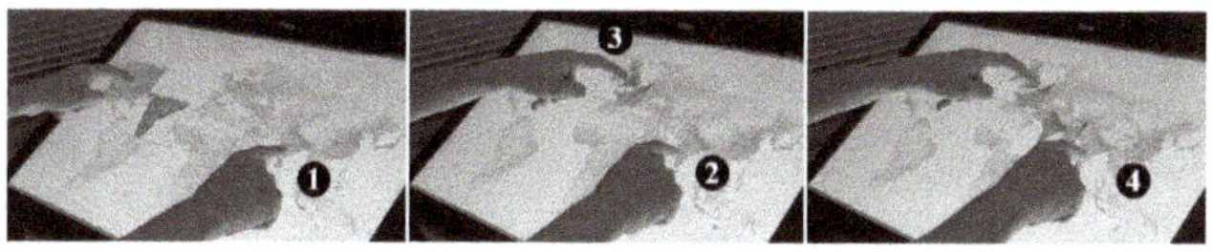

Figure 16. Interaction sequence leading to misinterpretation of positional uncertainty. The participant placed his right index finger on a region on the image (1). After a brief look, he lifted his right index finger from the touch screen but held it just above the surface (2), while pointing to another location with his left index finger (3). This was followed by a touch on the same point with the right index finger (4).

of visual feedback (color palette warped to the gaze point) in this case communicated that the system is not addressed, which led the users to a repeated touch action. On the other hand, device borders provide potential tactile cues for eyes-free use. This was observed again for selecting colors, when participants *anchored* their left hand on the screen edge for sliding along the color palette with their thumb or index finger while keeping their gaze on the canvas (Figure 17).

Figure 17. Instances of tapping on the bezel rather than the display area (left) and using the screen edge as a tactile guide (right).

DISCUSSION

We presented a design approach that targets supporting manual input with decreased visual guidance. Informed by previous literature [5, 14, 29], our main assumption was an increased positional uncertainty for input with decreased visual guidance. The first part of evaluation confirmed our assumption and provided a tentative profile for scaling selection range for different levels of visual guidance. The conceptualization of input with decreased visual guidance as input with uncertainty led to the design of various input handling and feedback techniques. The feedback we gathered from the participants during evaluation provides evidence for the viability of input with decreased visual guidance, although cognitive challenges related to hand-eye coordination and confidence during input were reported. Moreover, some such as addressing challenges and misinterpretation problems are mainly communicative challenges that might emerge in sensing or adaptive interfaces [1, 17, 27].

While we formulated manual input with decreased visual guidance as a design motivation, the specific benefits like increased functionality or satisfaction depends on a number of contextual factors such as physical setup and task. Manual input with decreased visual guidance can be forced by application context or preferred by the user. Similarly, various feedback techniques can be necessary when decreased visual guidance is forced by application context while they are not as essential when the users are able to direct their gaze to the input location.

At this point, we would like to discuss what we learned along the design process and evaluation through the analytical lens of spatial multiplexis [9]. Tuddenham et al. [32] limit the use of *bimanualism* to "two-handed one-object interaction", while using the terms *concurrent unimanualism* and *lateral sequential unimanualism* for "two-handed two-object interaction". The distinction is highly relevant regarding the degree of visual guidance during input. We argue that the benefit of supporting manual input with decreased guidance is most valid for multiple object interactions, since these cases involve direct and concurrent access to multiple interface regions. In painting application, this was observed when participants switched between colors with left hand and painted with their right hand (lateral sequential unimanualism) without redirecting their gaze. For multifocus image exploration and flight visualization the main pattern of interaction was concurrent unimanualism.

At the same time, gaze input requires revisiting the scope of space multiplexed user input. In their seminal paper, Fitzmaurice and Buxton investigate space-multiplexis through parallel use of hands [9]. However, the parallel use of manual input and eyes on different regions of interest [3, 15, 24] suggests that the scope of spatial multiplexis can be extended to the concurrent use of visual perception and input actions at different regions. In addition, spatial multiplexis can be extended to the interactions in which gaze is used not only for perception but also as a pointer. Many recent examples that combine gaze with indirect touch can be described as "one-hand+gaze one-object" or "two-hand+gaze one-object" interactions [21, 30, 33]. In contrast, during evaluation sessions, participants interpreted the explicit use of the gaze context as an additional "third hand", and performed "one-hand+gaze two-object", or "two-hand+gaze three-object" interactions.

Finally, gaze input requires revisiting the rationale of multiple object, space multiplexed input. Unlike multi-touch, gaze is a single channel but a very rapid input. Thus, using gaze coordinates for selection might favor sequential interaction over simultaneous selection of multiple targets, as in the case of sequential multiple target acquisition by gaze [21]. In this paper, we presented a design approach that targets multiple object interaction by supporting the use of touch with varying visual guidance as a direct input. However, further research is needed to evaluate the drawbacks and benefits of both approaches for different applications.

Limitations

Determining Visual Guidance

In the experimental design and applications we operationalized visual guidance as the distance of gaze point from the touch position at the moment of touch. This does not account for the complex hand-eye coordination over time that leads to a touch event: the motor movements can be accompanied by different levels of visual guidance between the initiation of the movement and touch. Planar input on the screen alone is not always sufficient for sensing this coordination, occasionally resulting in misinterpretation of positional uncertainty as reported above. A potential solution is over-the-screen sensing of the hand and finger movement to increase resources available to the system. The problem is not as significant for mouse or other cursor based movement, since the cursor position information is always available to the system.

Stability of Input Field

Our design approach assumes the stability of the input field. Keyboard, fixed toolbars and geospatial data are relatively stable input fields, which users either have prior knowledge of or get accustomed to. However, more information is needed to determine the viable scope of performing manual input with decreased visual guidance.

Non-planar Surfaces

It should also be noted that we limited our scope of investigation to a single planar interactive surface. However, our design approach can be applied to a range of settings that are spatially more diverse, such as distributed, on-body or virtual interfaces. These settings raise a number of questions such as determining positional uncertainty and solving the addressing problems described earlier.

CONCLUSION

Potential ubiquity of eye tracking in the near future calls for reevaluating the division of labor between different input modalities and the role of gaze within. In this paper, we contributed to the ongoing discussion on how gaze can be integrated with other modalities. Our proposed design approach utilizes gaze to qualify direct manual input by taking into account the level of visual guidance the input is performed with. In the case of input with visual guidance the system allows familiar interaction, while the input with decreased visual guidance is supported through various action mechanisms and feedback techniques for handling input with uncertainty. Adaptive handling of input, in return, supports concurrent access to multiple locations in an interface. We consider the design space we developed as a starting point for a systematic exploration of interfaces that adapt manual input handling in relation to visual guidance.

ACKNOWLEDGMENTS

This work has been partly supported by MindSee (FP7 ICT; Grant Agreement #611570). We would like to thank the anonymous reviewers for their insightful comments and to the participants of the study.

REFERENCES

1. Bellotti, V., Back, M., Edwards, W. K., Grinter, R. E., Henderson, A., and Lopes, C. Making sense of sensing systems: five questions for designers and researchers. In *Proc. CHI'02*, ACM (2002), 415–422.
2. Bi, X., and Zhai, S. Bayesian touch: a statistical criterion of target selection with finger touch. In *Proc. UIST'13*, ACM (2013), 51–60.
3. Bieg, H.-J., Chuang, L. L., Fleming, R. W., Reiterer, H., and Bülthoff, H. H. Eye and pointer coordination in search and selection tasks. In *Proc. ETRA'10*, ACM (2010), 89–92.
4. Blanch, R., and Ortega, M. Rake cursor: improving pointing performance with concurrent input channels. In *Proc. CHI'09*, ACM (2009), 1415–1418.

5. Bock, O., and Eckmiller, R. Goal-directed arm movements in absence of visual guidance: evidence for amplitude rather than position control. *Experimental Brain Research 62*, 3 (1986), 451–458.
6. Brown, L. E., Rosenbaum, D. A., and Sainburg, R. L. Limb position drift: implications for control of posture and movement. *Journal of Neurophysiology 90*, 5 (2003), 3105–3118.
7. Butscher, S., Hornbæk, K., and Reiterer, H. Spacefold and physiclenses: simultaneous multifocus navigation on touch surfaces. In *Proc. AVI'14*, ACM (2014), 209–216.
8. Elmqvist, N., Riche, Y., Henry-Riche, N., and Fekete, J.-D. Mélange: Space folding for visual exploration. *IEEE TVCG 16*, 3 (2010), 468–483.
9. Fitzmaurice, G. W., and Buxton, W. An empirical evaluation of graspable user interfaces: towards specialized, space-multiplexed input. In *Proc. UIST'97*, ACM (1997), 43–50.
10. Fitzmaurice, G. W., Ishii, H., and Buxton, W. A. Bricks: laying the foundations for graspable user interfaces. In *Proc. CHI'95*, ACM (1995), 442–449.
11. Flanagan, J. R., Terao, Y., and Johansson, R. S. Gaze behavior when reaching to remembered targets. *Journal of neurophysiology 100*, 3 (2008), 1533–1543.
12. Flemisch, F. O., Adams, C. A., Conway, S. R., Goodrich, K. H., Palmer, M. T., and Schutte, P. C. The h-metaphor as a guideline for vehicle automation and interaction.
13. Goodwin, C. *Pointing: Where language, culture and cognition meet.* Lawrence Erlbaum Associates, 2003, ch. Pointing as situated practice, 217–241.
14. Hagiya, T., and Kato, T. Probabilistic touchscreen text entry method incorporating gaze point information. *Journal of Information Processing 23*, 5 (2015), 708–715.
15. Huang, J., White, R., and Buscher, G. User see, user point: gaze and cursor alignment in web search. In *Proc. CHI'12*, ACM (2012), 1341–1350.
16. Jacob, R. J. What you look at is what you get: eye movement-based interaction techniques. In *Proc. CHI'90*, ACM (1990), 11–18.
17. Jacucci, G., Spagnolli, A., Freeman, J., and Gamberini, L. Symbiotic interaction: a critical definition and comparison to other human-computer paradigms. In *Symbiotic Interaction'14*. Springer, 2014, 3–20.
18. Kosunen, I., Jylha, A., Ahmed, I., An, C., Chech, L., Gamberini, L., Cavazza, M., and Jacucci, G. Comparing eye and gesture pointing to drag items on large screens. In *Proc. ITS'13*, ACM (2013), 425–428.
19. Kumar, M., Paepcke, A., and Winograd, T. Eyepoint: practical pointing and selection using gaze and keyboard. In *Proc. CHI'07*, ACM (2007), 421–430.
20. Mankoff, J., Hudson, S. E., and Abowd, G. D. Providing integrated toolkit-level support for ambiguity in recognition-based interfaces. In *Proc. CHI'00*, ACM (2000), 368–375.
21. Pfeuffer, K., Alexander, J., Chong, M. K., and Gellersen, H. Gaze-touch: Combining gaze with multi-touch for interaction on the same surface. In *Proc. UIST'14*, ACM (2014), 509–518.
22. Pfeuffer, K., Alexander, J., Chong, M. K., Zhang, Y., and Gellersen, H. Gaze-shifting: Direct-indirect input with pen and touch modulated by gaze. In *Proc. UIST'15*, ACM (2015), 373–383.
23. Pohl, H., and Murray-Smith, R. Focused and casual interactions: Allowing users to vary their level of engagement. In *Proc. CHI'13*, ACM (2013), 2223–2232.
24. Rodden, K., Fu, X., Aula, A., and Spiro, I. Eye-mouse coordination patterns on web search results pages. In *Proc. CHI EA'08*, ACM (2008), 2997–3002.
25. Schwarz, J., Hudson, S., Mankoff, J., and Wilson, A. D. A framework for robust and flexible handling of inputs with uncertainty. In *Proc. UIST'10*, ACM (2010), 47–56.
26. Schwarz, J., Mankoff, J., and Hudson, S. E. An architecture for generating interactive feedback in probabilistic user interfaces. In *Proc. CHI'15*, ACM (2015), 2545–2554.
27. Serim, B. Querying and display of information: symbiosis in exploratory search interaction scenarios. In *Symbiotic Interaction'14*. Springer, 2014, 115–120.
28. Sibert, L. E., and Jacob, R. J. Evaluation of eye gaze interaction. In *Proc. CHI'00*, ACM (2000), 281–288.
29. Spijkers, W., and Spellerberg, S. On-line visual control of aiming movements? *Acta psychologica 90*, 1 (1995), 333–348.
30. Stellmach, S., and Dachselt, R. Look & touch: gaze-supported target acquisition. In *Proc. CHI'12*, ACM (2012), 2981–2990.
31. Stellmach, S., and Dachselt, R. Still looking: investigating seamless gaze-supported selection, positioning, and manipulation of distant targets. In *Proc. CHI'13*, ACM (2013), 285–294.
32. Tuddenham, P., Kirk, D., and Izadi, S. Graspables revisited: multi-touch vs. tangible input for tabletop displays in acquisition and manipulation tasks. In *Proc. CHI'10*, ACM (2010), 2223–2232.
33. Turner, J., Alexander, J., Bulling, A., Schmidt, D., and Gellersen, H. Eye pull, eye push: Moving objects between large screens and personal devices with gaze and touch. In *INTERACT'2013*. Springer, 2013, 170–186.
34. Ware, C., and Mikaelian, H. H. An evaluation of an eye tracker as a device for computer input. In *Proc. CHI'87*, ACM (1987), 183–188.
35. Weir, D., Pohl, H., Rogers, S., Vertanen, K., and Kristensson, P. O. Uncertain text entry on mobile devices. In *Proc. CHI'14*, ACM (2014), 2307–2316.
36. Weiss, M., Wacharamanotham, C., Voelker, S., and Borchers, J. Fingerflux: near-surface haptic feedback on tabletops. In *Proc. UIST'11*, ACM (2011), 615–620.

37. Weiss, M., Wagner, J., Jansen, Y., Jennings, R., Khoshabeh, R., Hollan, J. D., and Borchers, J. Slap widgets: bridging the gap between virtual and physical controls on tabletops. In *Proc. CHI'09*, ACM (2009), 481–490.

38. Wigdor, D., Williams, S., Cronin, M., Levy, R., White, K., Mazeev, M., and Benko, H. Ripples: utilizing per-contact visualizations to improve user interaction with touch displays. In *Proc. UIST'09*, ACM (2009), 3–12.

39. Williamson, J. *Continuous uncertain interaction*. PhD thesis, University of Glasgow, 2006.

40. Wu, J., Yang, J., and Honda, T. Fitts law holds for pointing movements under conditions of restricted visual feedback. *Human movement science 29*, 6 (2010), 882–892.

41. Zhai, S., Morimoto, C., and Ihde, S. Manual and gaze input cascaded (magic) pointing. In *Proc. CHI'99*, ACM (1999), 246–253.

EyeGrip: Detecting Targets in a Series of Uni-directional Moving Objects Using Optokinetic Nystagmus Eye Movements

Shahram Jalaliniya
IT University of Copenhagen
Copenhagen, Denmark
jsha@itu.dk

Diako Mardanbegi
IT University of Copenhagen
Copenhagen, Denmark
dima@itu.dk

ABSTRACT

EyeGrip proposes a novel and yet simple technique of analysing eye movements for automatically detecting the users objects of interest in a sequence of visual stimuli moving horizontally or vertically in front of the user's view. We assess the viability of this technique in a scenario where the user looks at a sequence of images moving horizontally on the display while the user's eye movements are tracked by an eye tracker. We conducted an experiment that shows the performance of the proposed approach. We also investigated the influence of the speed and maximum number of visible images in the screen, on the accuracy of EyeGrip. Based on the experiment results, we propose guidelines for designing EyeGrip-based interfaces. EyeGrip can be considered as an implicit gaze interaction technique with potential use in broad range of applications such as large screens, mobile devices and eyewear computers. In this paper, we demonstrate the rich capabilities of EyeGrip with two example applications: 1) a mind reading game, and 2) a picture selection system. Our study shows that by selecting an appropriate speed and maximum number of visible images in the screen the proposed method can be used in a fast scrolling task where the system accurately (87%) detects the moving images that are visually appealing to the user, stops the scrolling and brings the item(s) of interest back to the screen.

Author Keywords

Gaze tracking, Optokinetic Nystagmus (OKN) eye movements, Implicit interaction, Scrolling

ACM Classification Keywords

H.5.m. Information Interfaces and Presentation (e.g. HCI): Miscellaneous

INTRODUCTION

We are living in the digital information age where companies, organizations, and even end users are producing an enormous and rapidly growing flow of digital information. Users

CHI'16, May 07-12, 2016, San Jose, CA, USA.
© 2016 ACM. ISBN 978-1-4503-3362-7/16/05...$15.00
DOI: http://dx.doi.org/10.1145/2858036.2858584

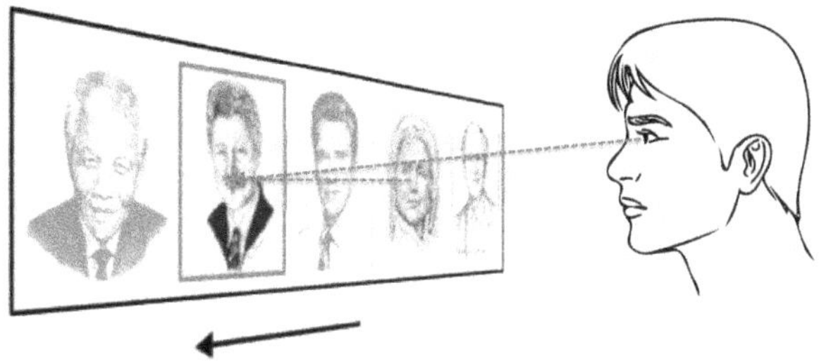

Figure 1. EyGrip technique to detect an object of interest among horizontally moving images

of Internet applications such as social networks have already been overloaded by tremendous amount of digital information ranged from textual to graphical contents. This has resulted in us to make our browsing more efficient by quickly moving our eyes across the contents and picking the contents that seem more interesting to us. The fact that our brain processes images significantly faster than text [4] might be one of the reasons of why we are often more engaged with images than textual information and why viewing pictures is among the most popular functions in social networks such as Facebook [19].

When people are browsing their Facebook [1] page on their mobile device, it's often that they quickly scan the Newsfeed by scrolling down or up the Facebook page until they find some interesting information. However, scrolling for navigation on small-screen devices has its own usability and inefficiency problems [9]. The three steps of a) scrolling, b) stopping the page, and c) bringing the desired content back to the display by scrolling back up are the main parts of browsing the contents. We go through the same steps when we search for a particular image in our photo gallery. Our ability to rapidly scan and process the visual cues that are quickly moving across our eyes, enables us to speed up the scrolling task. However, the third step (bringing the desired content back) can be a cumbersome task for users in a fast scrolling task since it requires a very high coordination between eyes, brain and our motor control system (e.g. touching the display with our fingers). Finding the target image that has gone out of the screen during a fast scrolling is not always easy and it sets a limitation to how fast the scrolling can be done.

[1] www.facebook.com

This paper proposes the EyeGrip method that enables computer systems to automatically detect the moving content that seems to be interesting for a user by monitoring and analysing the user's eye movements. Depending on the application, such systems can for example tag the content of interest in a series of scrolling contents or they can immediately react by stopping the content of interest in front of the user's view. EyeGrip provides an attentive scrolling mechanism which analyses the user's natural eye movements (Optokinetic Nystagmus) subtly in the background and it does not require any explicit command from the user or any change in their gaze behavior. Optokinetic Nystagmus (OKN) is a type of eye movement that occurs when a person tracks a moving field. OKN stabilizes images on the retina while viewing a sequence of moving objects. OKN has a sawtooth-like pattern that consists of alternating pursuit movements made in the direction of stimulus (slow phase) followed by saccacdes (fast phases). Generally, two forms of OKN have been described in the literature [26]. One is called Stare OKN which is a reflexive response that occurs when a viewer passively follows a moving visual field [16] and the other one is called Look OKN when a viewer voluntarily tracks moving stimulus in the visual field.

The principle behind the EyeGrip method is to analyze the combination of the saccades and smooth pursuits in the OKN eye movements to detect deviations in the OKN signal which is related to the long smooth pursuits or slow phase in the OKN eye movements (peaks in Figure 2). We used a machine learning approach to detect these peaks by feeding a window of the horizontal eye movement signal as a feature into the WEKA classifier. As we discuss this further in the paper, implementing EyeGrip does not necessarily require gaze estimation or any gaze calibration between the eye tracker and the display. However, depending on what approach is used for detecting a peak in the signal, we might need some algorithm calibration (not gaze calibration) or a learning phase to build a classifier as we did in our implementation.

In this paper, we show the feasibility of the EyeGrip method by detecting the images of interest in an image scrolling application. We further investigate the effect of two independent variables on the accuracy of the classification through a lab experiment. The first independent variable is *speed of scrolling*, and the second one is *maximum number of visible images in a single frame*. We manipulated the latter variable by changing image width. Based on our findings from the experiment, we propose some design guidelines for implementing EyeGrip. Finally, to demonstrate the utility of the EyeGrip technique in interactive systems, two follow up usability studies have been presented: 1) a picture selection application and 2) a mind reading game.

RELATED WORK

Gaze-based interaction

Using gaze as an input modality for computing devices has long been a topic of interest in HCI community, and it is due to the fact that humans naturally tend to direct eyes toward the target of interest. Gaze can be used both as an explicit and implicit input modality. Implicit input are actions and behaviors of humans, which are done to achieve a goal and are not primarily regarded as interaction with a computer, but captured, recognized, and interpreted by a computer system as input [23]. While explicit input are our intended commands to the system through mouse, keyboard, voice commands, body gestures, and etc.

Gaze for explicit input

One of the most explored explicit ways of using gaze to interact with computers is to use gaze as a direct pointing modality instead of mouse in a target acquisition task [12]. The target can be selected either by fixating the gaze for a while on a particular area (dwell-time) [25] or using a mouse click [14]. However, controlling cursor with eye movements is limited to pointing towards big targets due to the inaccuracy of gaze tracking methods and subconscious jittery motions of the eyes [29]. Eye-gesture is another explicit approach for gaze-based interaction where user performs predefined eye-strokes [8]. Previous studies [3, 14] have shown that using gaze as an explicit input modality is not always a convenient method for users. In fact, overloading eyes as humans' perceptual channel with a motor control task is not convenient [29].

Gaze for implicit input

In implicit method of using gaze in user interface design, natural movements of the eyes can be used to detect context, for example looking at certain objects in an environment can reveal interest of humans to those objects [17]. Gaze can also be used to infer about user's behaviour, for instance which objects attracts user attention during an everyday activity like cooking [20]. Another example of using gaze as an implicit input is to detect user's attention point and react to the users eye contact [24], or adapt user interface behavior [11] accordingly. The gaze data can also be used indirectly for interaction purposes [29, 13, 18, 28]. For instance, in the MAGIC pointing technique [29, 13], gaze data is used to move the cursor as close as possible to the target. Mardanbegi et al. [18] proposed a gaze-based interaction technique where the gaze data is used indirectly for head-gesture recognition. The other relevant work to our study is Pursuits interaction technique [28] which enables users to select an object on the screen by correlating eye pursuit movements with objects moving on the screen. The accuracy of their proposed technique depends on the difference of trajectories which means it fails to detect uni-directional moving objects due to the similarity of the trajectories in a uni-directional movement. On the contrary, our proposed EyeGrip method enables computer devices to detect the object of interest among uni-directional moving objects. EyeGrip is an implicit way of using gaze since we do not ask users to perform any kind of predefined eye-strokes or fixating on a particular target. The EyeGrip technique is based on analyzing natural eye movements for automatically detecting object of interest in a user interface.

Smooth pursuit recognition

The main part of our proposed approach is to automatically detect a deviation in the OKN eye movements when a particular object grabs user's attention. This deviation is related

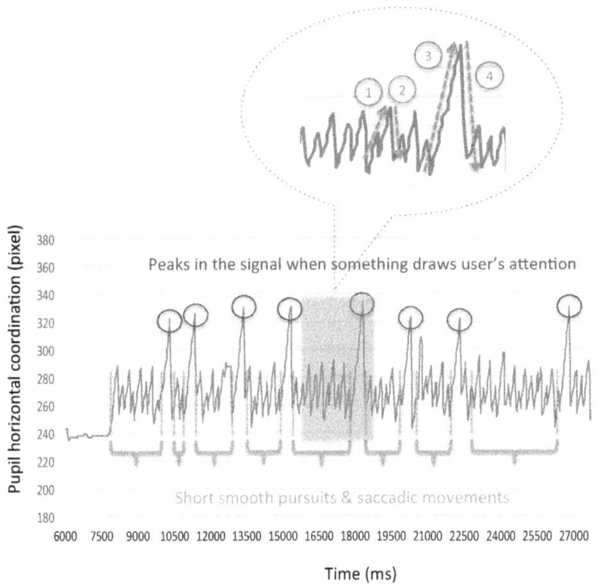

Figure 2. OKN signal generated from horizontal eye movements in a visual search task among uni-directional moving objects that move from the right side of the screen to the left. 1- Short smooth pursuit movements when eyes are scanning pictures, 2- Short saccade after a short pursuit when eyes are about to scan the next picture, 3- Long smooth pursuit (which may be supplemented by saccadic movements for fast moving objects) when an object draws user's attention, 4- Long saccade that takes the gaze back to the right area of the screen

to the slow phase of the OKN which is basically a combination of long smooth pursuits and saccadic movements. To the best of our knowledge this is the first study on using OKN in HCI. In the earlier studies, Kalman filters was used to process smooth pursuits [5, 1] while more recent works have analyzed both dispersion and velocity of the signal to classify smooth pursuits [21, 15]. Vidal and et al. [27] used a machine learning-based approach to detect pursuits by analyzing a combination of different features. In this study, we also use a machine learning algorithm to recognize patterns in the eye movement data. However, in contrast to the Pursuits [21, 15] method, we just use a single feature for classification. Our approach is explained in the next section.

THE EYEGRIP METHOD

When an object catches our visual attention, the eyes try to follow that moving object closely. This type of eye movements is called smooth pursuit. In contrast to other types of eye movements such as saccades and micro-saccades and also fixations that occur between saccades, pursuit parameters are generally more difficult to measure and are not as stereotyped as saccades [15]. Smooth pursuit consists of two phases: initiation and maintenance. Measures of initiation parameters can reveal information about the visual motion processing that is necessary for pursuit. Maintenance involves the construction of an internal, mental, representation of target motion which is used to update and enhance pursuit performance.

When we look at a series of linearly moving images, and we search for a particular image, our eyes perform a combination of saccadic and smooth pursuit movements (OKN). The smooth pursuit movements are relatively short when our eyes do not see an interesting image. As soon as an image draws user's attention, the maintenance phase of the smooth pursuit movement gets longer. In the EyeGrip technique, we exploit the difference between smooth pursuit lengths when the eyes are looking for an interesting object and when an object catches user's attention. In a visual search task among a series of uni-directional moving images, the viewer's eyes mainly move in the same direction as the moving contents. If we record the amplitude of the user's horizontal eye movements while looking at a series of moving images in the horizontal direction on the display, the generated signal looks like Figure 2 that illustrates a sawtooth like OKN signal. This figure shows the short saccadic and smooth pursuit eye movements that happen in a visual search task. The longer smooth pursuit movements occur when an object draws users' attention. In this phase of the visual search task (slow phase in OKN), eyes follow the object of interest for a longer time which generates a peak (deviation) in the signal. By detecting the moment and location of this peak (deviation), we are able to detect the object of interest among other moving objects.

We used a machine learning approach (Multilayer perceptron classifier) to detect these peaks by feeding a window of the horizontal eye movement signal as a feature into the WEKA classifier. To generate the OKN signal, we only need to detect eye movements which means there is no need for any gaze estimation or gaze calibration. In our experiment, we used a camera-based eye tracker to detect eye movements; however, to generate the OKN signal it is also possible to use other eye tracking methods such as Electrooculography (EOG) [6]. In our implementation, the classifier needs to be trained first. We collected training data from 15 participants in the experiment, and we used the same trained classifier for new participants in the follow up usability studies without adding any new training data. Since the accuracy of EyeGrip in the both usability studies for unseen data remained in the same range as the accuracy of EyeGrip in the experiment, we can conclude that the EyeGrip does not necessarily need any training phase for new users.

EXPERIMENTAL DESIGN

To characterise the eye movements in different conditions and investigate the accuracy of different algorithms, we conducted an experiment with two independent variables: 1) the speed of scrolling, and 2) the maximum number of images visible in the view-port (visible part of the sequence on the screen). To manipulate the maximum number of visible images, we can change either the size of the view-port, offset between images, or image width. Assuming that the offset between images and the width of the view-port are fixed, we changed the image width to manipulate the maximum number of images visible in the view-port. This means in some conditions the images are squeezed (Figure 4 (a) and (b)) however, since humans are extremely good in detecting faces even when they are deformed, we believe slightly squeezing images by only changing the image width has not a considerable effect on the recognition rate.

Con	Speed	Image width
1	Slow (1400 pixel/s ≃ 26.5°/s)	Small (480 pixels)
2	Slow (1400 pixel/s ≃ 26.5°/s)	Big (960 pixels)
3	Med (2000 pixel/s ≃ 37.5°/s)	Small (480 pixels)
4	Med (2000 pixel/s ≃ 37.5°/s)	Big (960 pixels)
5	Fast (2600 pixel/s ≃ 49°/s)	Small (480 pixels)
6	Fast (2600 pixel/s ≃ 49°/s)	Big (960 pixels)

Table 1. 6 different conditions used in the experiment

The dependent variables in our experiment are: 1) accuracy of the classification for detecting the moment when an image draws users' visual attention and 2) the error rate which is defined as number of target images missed by the participants divided by total number of target images.

Method

Participants

20 participants (mean age = 28, ranged from 20 to 56 years old, and 2 females) were recruited among local university staff and students to participate in the experiment. After preprocessing the data we removed the data of 5 participants which was not usable due to the inaccuracy of the eye detection for them. All of the participants had perfect visual acuity or wearing contact lens.

Apparatus

We used a home-made wearable monocular gaze tracker and the open-source Haytham gaze tracking software [2] to record the eye movement data (see Figure 4 (c)). The eye tracker was set to track the left eye for all the participants without considering the eye dominance. We assume that any possible difference between the movements of the left and right eyes will not be significant for our study. However, investigation of whether left and right eyes move differently in OKN due to the eye-dominance could be an interesting subject for the future research. The accuracy of our eye tracker is about 1 degree, and the frequency of the sampling eye data is 20 Hz. Although, in our experiment, we have not used the gaze data provided by the software. In fact, we did not calibrate the gaze tracker to calculate the gaze coordinate on the screen. We developed an application to display a series of horizontally moving images at a certain speed. The speed, direction, and the size of the images in the screen can be adjusted in the application. Both our gaze tracker software and the picture display application run on a HP laptop with a 8G RAM, Corei7 processor with the speed of 2.6 GHz, and a display with 1600 × 900 pixels resolution and 34.5 × 19.5 cm dimensions. The viewing distance form the display is about 60cm.

Procedure

The experiment started with a short introduction to the purpose of the experiment and the use of the apparatus. Then participants were asked to wear the gaze tracker, and we controlled if the gaze tracker is positioned appropriately in front of the participant's eye. Then each participant was asked to complete the task in six different conditions. The task was to look at a series of horizontally moving images of famous people's face (e.g. politicians, athletes, actors/actresses) on

[2]http://eyeinfo.itu.dk

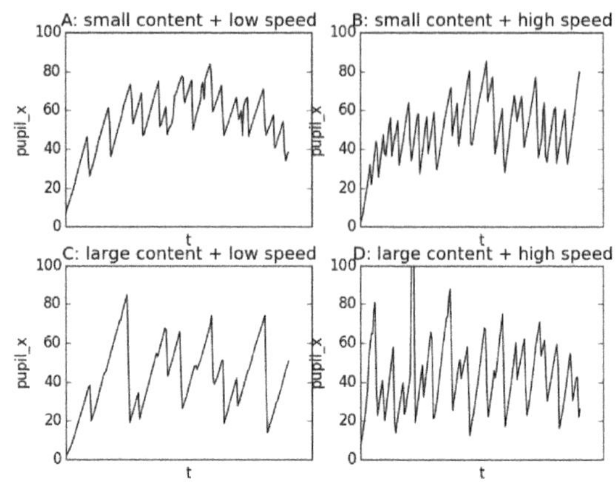

Figure 3. Optokinetik Nystagmus pattern sampled for 4 extreme conditions while viewing a set of scrolling images. W is defined as the size of the image divided by the size of the display and S is defined as the scrolling speed measured in degrees of visual field per second. The four images show the OKN pattern for conditions A) $\{W = 0.2, S = 19°/s\}$ **B)** $\{W = 0.2, S = 50°/s\}$ **C)** $\{W = 0.8, S = 19°/s\}$ **D)** $\{W = 0.8, S = 50°/s\}$

the screen and find the Bill Clinton's picture as target image. As soon as the participant recognizes Bill Clinton's face among other faces he/she should press space bar on the keyboard. Before starting the task, the participants were asked if they are familiar with Bill Clintons face or not. All of the participants mentioned that they know Bill Clinton, and they are able to recognize his face.

During each condition 40 pictures were displayed where 7 of them were target images. We recorded the eye movement data in the horizontal direction and the moment participants pressed the space key. In our study, the eye movement data is defined as pupil horizontal position in the eye image. The conditions were counterbalanced to avoid any learning effect. Also the position of the target images were counterbalanced in each condition.

Design

The experiment was an 3 × 2 within-subjects design with 15 participants, and each participant completed all conditions in one experimental session that lasted for approximately 10 minutes. In each condition, participants completed the task with three different speeds (1400, 2000, 2600 pixel/s which are respectively equal to 26.5, 37.5, and 49 degrees/s) and two different image widths (480, 960 pixels equal to 9.1 and 18.2 degrees). To change the image width we kept the height of the image fixed and just rescaled the image width. All combinations of speed and image width parameters generated 6 different conditions (see Table 1.)

Event detection algorithm

In order to recognize the moment and the location of the peak in the eye movement signal when a user performs a visual search task, we used machine learning algorithms in WEKA software [3]. A comparative analysis between different classifiers in WEKA showed that Multilayer perceptron algorithm

[3]http://www.cs.waikato.ac.nz/ml/weka/

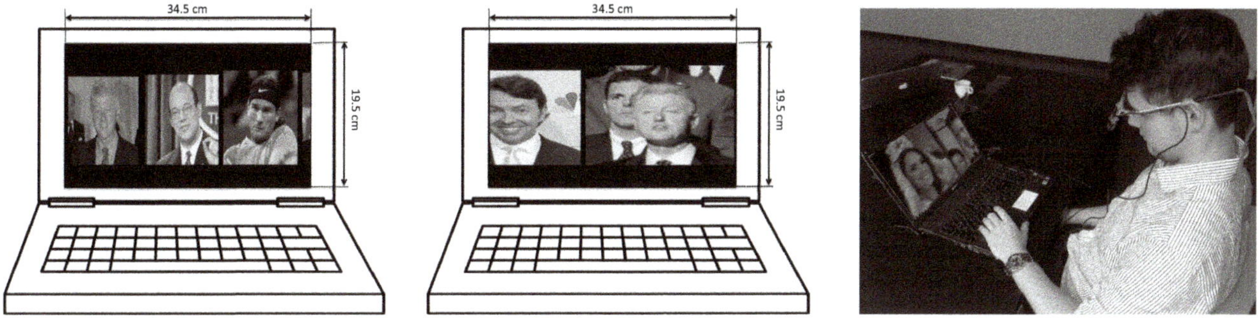

Small width conditions: 1, 3,and 5 (a) Big width condition: 2, 4, and 6 (b) (c)

Figure 4. a) a screen-shot of the system in small width conditions: 1, 3, and 5, b) a screen-shot of the system in big width conditions: 2, 4, and 6, c) a participant wearing the home-made mobile eye tracker performing the task

is the most accurate and reliable classifier among other available classifiers in WEKA. We used the default setting for the Multilayer perceptron algorithm in the WEKA with a single hidden layer. The eye movement data is used as the only feature in our classification. We used a sliding window to detect the moment when something draws users' visual attention. Since the experiment included three different speeds and two different widths of moving images, the best window size needed to be found for each condition. In the following sections, we briefly explain the data preparation and classification steps.

Pre-processing data

Removing outliers: as mentioned in the participant section, 20 participants were recruited for the experiment. First of all, the eye movement data of each participant is reviewed to investigate whether the eye tracker detected the pupil of the user appropriately or not. If pupil of the participant is not detected more than 25% of times, we removed the data of the participant from the experiment. After analyzing data from 20 participants, 5 participants were removed from the experiment. For the remaining participants, the missing values of pupil coordination are calculated based on the linear regression method.

Data cleaning & normalization: Before starting the experiment and after performing the task, participants were asked to look at the center of two red circles on the left and right sides of the screen. Each circle was displayed for 3 seconds. These two targets were later used for determining the lower and upper bounds of the eye movement signal. In order to prepare the data for aggregated data sets for each condition, the lower and upper values were used to normalize the eye movement data for all participants using the min-max method. The process of removing noise and outliers from the eye signal was easier after data normalization. We also used these two target points and the corresponding pupil positions while looking at each target, for roughly estimating the gaze area in the screen and locating the image of interest in small size image conditions.

Data aggregation: To calculate the performance of the classifier for each condition, we aggregated the normalized data from all participants in 6 data sets.

Sliding window & classification

To detect the event when an image draws user's attention, we used a sliding window with 50% overlap between two neighbor windows. To find the best window size for each condition, we used 4 different window sizes (10, 16, 20, 30). These window sizes have been chosen to cover the minimum and maximum duration that takes for an image to appear on the screen and disappear from the screen. This time period depends on the speed of the moving images (ranged from 1400 to 2600 pixels/s), the image widths (ranged from 480 to 960 pixels), the screen width (1600 pixels), and the sampling rate (20 Hz). The time needed for appearing an image on the screen and disappearing from the screen can be calculated using this equation: $time = (screenwidth + imagewidth)/speed$. Using the above values for screen width, image width, and speed the maximum time duration can be calculated as $time_{max} = (1600 + 960)/1400 = 1.8 seconds$, and the minimum time is equal to $time_{min} = (1600 + 480)/2600 = 0.8 seconds$. Since the sampling rate is 20 Hz, the minimum window size is equal to $0.8 \times 20 = 16$ and the maximum window size is equal to $1.8 \times 20 = 36$.

The performance of the classification is calculated for each condition using the aggregated data sets. The data sets are labeled based on the moment of pressing space key by participants as the center of each window with "Event" label. The accuracy and precision of the classification is measured using 10 folds cross-validation method. Figure 5-a illustrates the performance of classification for each condition with 4 different window sizes. We tried to find the highest classification performance where precision of classification is high for both classes: 1) "Event" and 2) "No event". We finally selected window size 30 for the first, second, and fourth conditions, window size 20 for the third and sixth conditions, and window size 16 for the fifth condition.

Results

To analyze the effect of speed and maximum number of visible images in the view-port on the classifier, the performance of classification is calculated for each participant in different conditions using 10 folds cross-validation method. Figure 6 (a) shows the mean and standard deviation of the performance of the classifier in each condition. A repeated measure

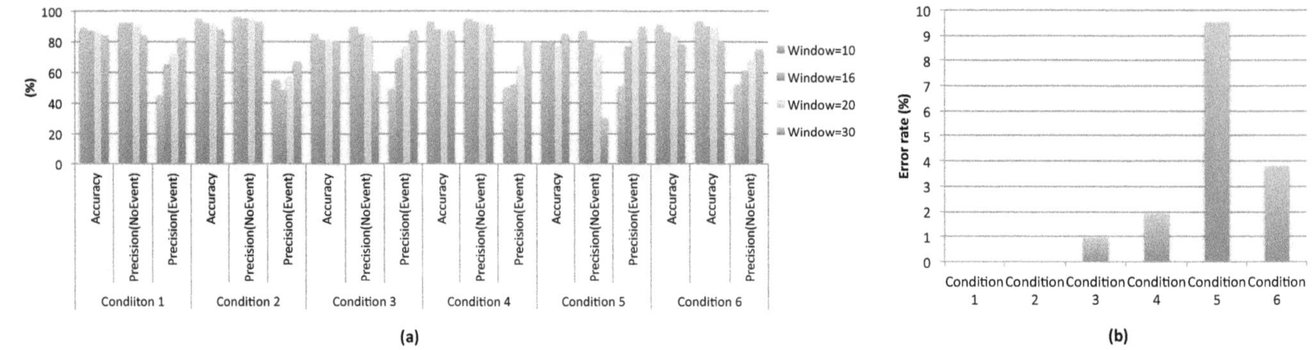

Figure 5. a) Accuracy and precision of the classification for each condition with 4 different window sizes, b) Error rate (percentage of missing targets)

ANOVA is used to investigate the differences in performance of the classifier. Post-hoc paired samples analysis with a Bonferroni correction is used for pairwise comparisons ($\alpha = .05$).

In order to measure the robustness of the classifier against unseen data, the performance of the classifier is also evaluated for the condition 4 taking a leave-one-out approach where the data of each participant was removed from the training data and used as test data. The leave-one-out evaluation for condition 4 reported an average accuracy of 87.2% (σ = 11.5) for the classification. The results of leave-one-out evaluations is illustrated in a box plot diagram (Figure 7).

The error rate (total missing target images by participants divided by total number of targets) is represented in Figure 5-b.

Effect of image width

The result of statistical analysis showed that the classification performance significantly varied with the image width: $F(1, 14) = 34.9$, $p < .0001$. The post-hoc pairwise comparisons revealed that the accuracy of the classifier is significantly higher when the image width is bigger. Figure 6 (c) illustrates changing the average accuracy of the classification when the image width changes.

Effect of speed

The statistical analysis indicated no significant effect of speed on the classification performance (see Figure 6 (b)). However, the medium speed shows a higher performance specially for small images. Moreover, participants missed more target images in the high speed conditions. Moreover, some of the participants mentioned after the experiment that it was difficult for them to complete them the task in high speed conditions specially in condition 5 where the speed was maximum and the image width was minimum.

Discussion

The results of the experiment indicates that our EyeGrip technique is more accurate for the lower number of visible images in the view-port where the image width is 960 pixels (equal to 60% of the screen width) moving with the medium speed (2000 pixel/s). As it is visible in Figure 3, increasing number of visible images in the view-port makes the sawtooth shapes in the OKN signal more homogeneous which decreases the accuracy of the classifier. Increasing the speed of moving images has a similar effect on the OKN signal (Figure 3). When images move faster on the screen, even the smooth pursuit component of the OKN eye movements have a sacadic characteristics. This makes harder for the classifier to detect slow phase of the OKN. Apart from the classification challenges, the high number of missing images in the fast conditions (see Figure 5-b) shows that following and processing fast-moving objects is harder for humans particularly when they need to see more complex images. On the other hand, there is also a lower limitation for the speed. Very low speeds let users follow all images one by one which means the shape of the smooth pursuit component of the OKN becomes more homogeneous and harder to detect for the classifier.

DESIGN GUIDELINES

We believe that the EyeGrip method is applicable to different application areas. To increase the usability of the EyeGrip technique and minimize the limitations of using the EyeGrip method, we propose the following guidelines for user interface designers.

Uni-directional moving objects

In the EyeGrip method, there is no limitation for the number of detectable objects. The important assumption is that objects need to move next to each other in the same direction at a certain speed. The objects might be placed dynamically in the queue but the system needs to know the position of each object within the sequence. In some applications, we may not be interested in detecting which content has grabbed the user's attention, and we only want to know which part of the sequence was visible in the display at the time the system has detected a long slow phase. In this case, the system can bring that part of the sequence back to the display even though there might be multiple contents visible in that moment.

Balance between moving speed & number of images

As we mentioned in the discussion section before, there are upper and lower limits for the speed of moving objects. If the objects move at lower speed the accuracy of the event detection classifier decreases. Also higher speeds increases the human error rate and risk of missing objects by user. Since the effect of increasing number of image in the view-port is similar to the increasing the speed, to maximize the accuracy of EyeGrip we need to find a balance between speed of the objects and the number of images in the view-port. Actually

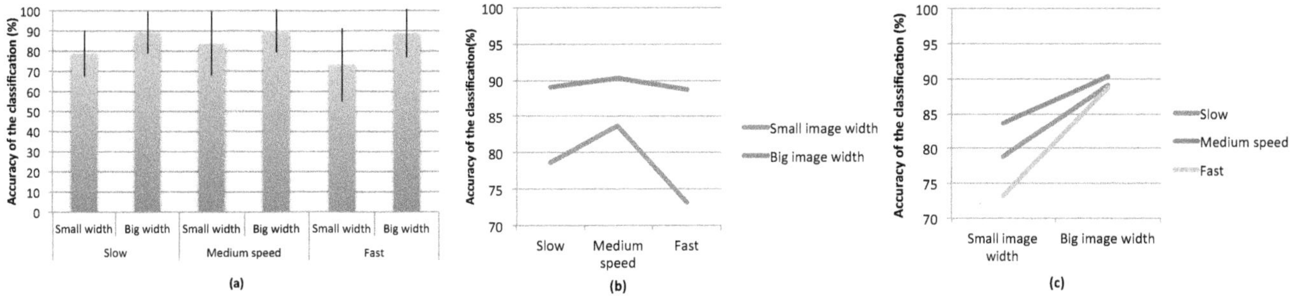

Figure 6. a) Performance of classification for each participants in different conditions, b) no significant effect of speed is observed, c) the effect of image width on the accuracy of the classifier is significant.

the EyeGrip technique works when there is a temporal tension in the visual search task. We need to be sure that we generate enough temporal tension by adjusting an appropriate speed and number of images in the view-port. At the same time, the speed should not exceed the upper limit to let users easily follow images on the screen.

Complexity of the visual search task

One of the limitations of using EyeGrip in user interface design is the fact that when a lot of images draw users' visual attention, the number of false positives increases. In other words, if users spend equal visual attention on each image in the line, the classifier cannot differentiate between target images and other objects. This limitation might be important for some applications where there is a need for high accurate recognition such as a visual inspection task. In such occasions, we can implement a two-stage algorithm where the system filters out some irrelevant objects at the first stage, and in the next step the user reviews the remaining objects to control the false positive detections.

POTENTIAL APPLICATIONS

Most of the existing gaze-based interfaces use gaze location as input. Which means for a graceful interaction, they need a very accurate gaze tracker with a cumbersome calibration procedure. In contrast, EyeGrip uses just one dimension eye movement which is much easier to achieve specially in mobile and wearable settings. This opens up a wide range of application areas that can use EyeGrip. In the following sections, we explain some of the applications that can use the EyeGrip technique for interaction.

Mind reading game

The EyeGrip technique helps the system know what attracts users' attention. This can be used in a mind reading game where the user is asked to select a person among some faces displayed on the screen. Then the user is asked to count the number of repetitions in displaying the face of that particular person among other faces while all images move horizontally in one direction with a fixed speed. The main purpose of asking users to count the number of repetitions is to draw their visual attention to a particular object. At the end the system predicts the identity of the selected person. Since EyeGrip does not need calibration and an accurate gaze tracker, the mind reading game can be installed on public displays to entertain passers-by in public places such as train stations, airports, or waiting halls.

Picture explorer on head-mounted display

One of the main challenges of interaction with eyewear computers such as Google Glass is providing input to the device. There are many situations where the hands of the user are busy with real-world task and providing a hands-free input channel can be a big advantage. The EyeGrip technique helps users with a fast and hands-free method for browsing graphical contents in eyewear computers. If we assume that in mobile scenarios, interaction with an eyewear computer should not take so much time [2], the EyeGrip method seems to be a promising technique for fast scanning visual contents on the HMD. For instance, users of the social network applications such as Facebook will be able to scan many graphical contents in a short time without any explicit input to the eyewear computer. In this case, to start scrolling the user can perform a head gesture to the left or right side or use voice commands. The graphical or textual content will start scrolling in one direction at a fixed speed. As soon as something draws the user's visual attention, the system stops scrolling and lets the user to look at that particular image or Facebook post. The user can continue scanning other contents by performing head gestures or voice commands. The beauty of using EyeGrip technique for implicitly finding users' interests is the fact that it does not need to work 100% accurate since users will always have an explicit way such as voice commands, hitting the touch-pad in Google Glass, or performing head gestures to stop scrolling. In this application, if the EyeGrip method detects object of interest in 80% of cases, it means EyeGrip has reduced the need for providing an explicit command in 80% of the times which can be a big success.

Public displays

Public displays have long been used for advertisement purposes. However, they have always been in a one-direction communication with passers-by. The EyeGrip method can help the public displays get feedback from users. One example could be to show a series of mono-directional moving images of different products on a public display where the scrolling stops whenever an image attracts attention of a user who is standing in front of the display and his/her eye is being tracked by a stationary eye tracker. EyeGrip method can

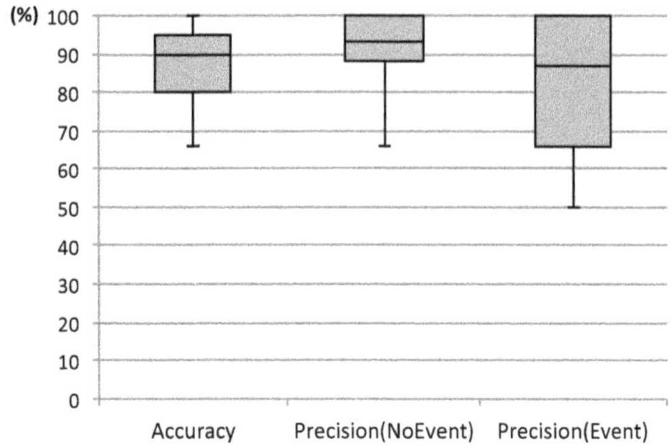

Figure 7. The performance of the classifier for condition 4 taking a leave-one-out approach.

for example be implemented using the Pupil-canthi-ratio approach [30] which is an interesting calibration-free approach for interaction with public displays. Because the relative movement between the user and the display may change the range of the horizontal movements of the eye, such a system requires the users to only move their eyes and to keep their head direction towards the center of the display. This challenge can be solved by placing a stationary infrared light source and using pupil-corneal reflection method. It is also possible that within a few seconds of recording the eye movement data while the user is looking at the moving (scrolling) contents on the display, the system figures out the lower and upper range of the eye movement signal. This can be an implicit way of calibrating the gaze direction and makes it possible to detect the images attracted users' visual attention after the scrolling has stopped.

Text reading assistant for small displays

Reading large amount of texts on small displays such as mobile devices, smart glasses, or smart watches is still challenging. One of the common approaches to facilitate reading in small displays is to enlarge the text and move it based on reader's eye movement [22]. The EyeGrip technique can be applied to such applications in order to give feedback to the system about the words which are harder to read or understand for the reader. When a user follows a word for a longer time the system can slow down the speed of moving text on the screen and provide some help, e.g. synonyms, to the user to better understand the challenging part of the text.

Assistant for visual inspection in production lines

Visual inspection is still part of quality control process in many production lines. In many cases, one or more workers control the appearance properties of the products while product move on a conveyor belt with a fixed speed. In a visual inspection task, quality controllers detect the potentially unqualified products and manually separate them from the others. If we use a gaze tracker to capture the eye movements of the quality controllers, the EyGrip technique can automatize the detection of unqualified products. If the system detects the target objects, a robot or other machines can separate them automatically. EyeGrip can potentially increases the speed of inspection by removing the manual part of the task.

Figure 8. A screen-shot of the picture selection system (study1).

USABILITY STUDIES

To evaluate the usability of the EyeGrip method from users' point of view, we conducted two user studies: 1) a picture selection system and 2) a mind reading game. The picture selection system utilizes EyeGrip in a live interaction scenario, while the mind reading game uses EyeGrip as a context recognition method to detect what draws users' visual attention. In the following sections, we report the results of the usability evaluation in each study.

Study1: A picture selection system

We designed a desktop application to select a predefined set of images among scrolling pictures on the screen. A screen-shot of the system user interface is illustrated in Figure 8. The system starts scrolling by pressing the space bar on the keyboard. To use the picture selection system in a mobile scenario, the start mechanism can change to head gestures, voice commands, etc.

Participants

8 participants (mean age = 25, ranged from 20 to 37 years old, and 1 female) were recruited among local university students to try the system. All of the participants had perfect visual acuity.

Procedure

The session started with a short introduction to the purpose of the experiment and the instruction of using the system. After preparing participants for the experiment, they were asked to wear the eye tracker apparatus and perform the task. To maximize the accuracy of the EyeGrip, we adjusted the scrolling speed equal to 2000 pixel/s and the number of visible images in the view-port (image width = 960 pixels) based on the results of our experiment. The task was similar to our experiment. The participants were asked to look at a series of moving images in the upper rectangle (see Figure 8) and count the number of Bill Clinton's pictures. Whenever the participant pays extra attention to an image, the image is selected and moved to the thumbnail panel at the bottom of the page. To give users a visual feedback about the selection mechanism, the moving procedure is animated in the user interface.

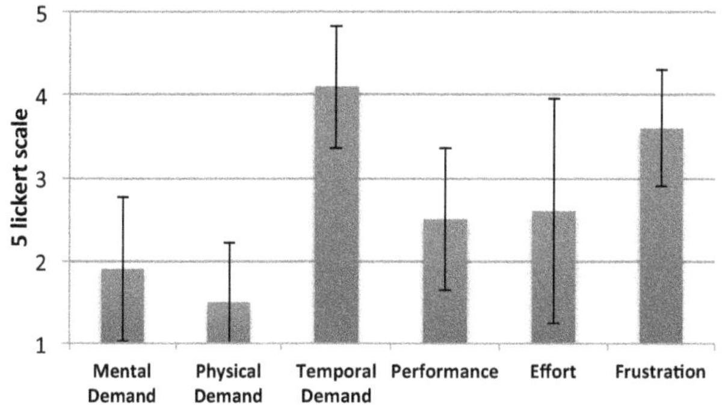

Figure 9. The result of usability questionnaire (NASA-TLX) for the picture selection system (study 1).

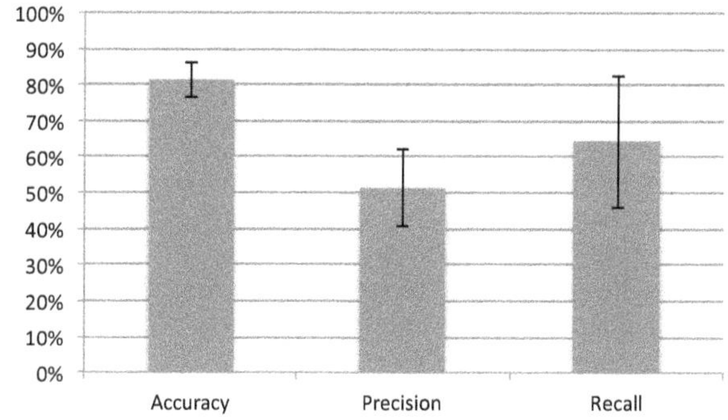

Figure 10. Performance of the EyeGrip classifier in picture selection application (study 1).

Evaluation results

To calculate the accuracy of the system, we recorded the number of correct selections, missed pictures, and wrong selections. The average accuracy, precision, and recall of the classification for all 8 participant is illustrated in Figure 10. After performing the task, the participants were asked to complete a usability questionnaire designed based on NASA-TLX [10] to reflect their experience. The result of the questionnaire is illustrated in Figure 9. The participants' general impression was also asked in an open question. They found the EyeGrip interaction technique *different* and *fun*. However, some of the participants found the EyeGrip method a bit confusing since they do not exactly know how the system selects images. Moreover, animating the image selection procedure was distracting for some users.

As it is illustrated in Figure 10, the performance of EyeGrip in the picture selection task (mean = 81%, σ = 5) is relatively close to the performance of EyeGrip in our controlled experiment (87% in Condition 4). This shows the robustness of the classifier to detect the object of interest even for the unseen data which means EyeGrip can be trained only once.

The result of the NASA-TLX questionnaire, indicates that using EyeGrip for picture selection puts time pressure on the users. This might be the reason why they felt a relatively high amount of frustration while performing the task and the accuracy of EyeGrip was slightly lower than what we observed in the experiment. Nevertheless, the task has not been physically and mentally demanding for users because the picture selection happens automatically based on their natural OKN eye movements without providing any explicit input.

Study2: A mind reading game

We also developed a mind reading game based on the software and hardware platform that we used as apparatus in the experiment. We adjusted the speed and the maximum visible number of images in the view-port similar to the condition 4 in the experiment and the picture selection application in the first usability study.

Participants

10 participants (mean age = 29, ranged from 21 to 44 years old, no female) among local university students and staff participated in the study. All of the participants had perfect visual acuity or wearing contact lens.

Procedure

We asked the participants to select a person among 4 faces printed on an A4 paper without telling us who has been chosen. Next we asked participants to wear the eye tracker hardware and sit in front of the laptop screen. They were asked to count the number of images of the selected person among other moving images on the screen. After finishing the task, the name of the selected person is displayed to the participants. All of the target images are repeated 4 times in the queue among 50 images of other people.

Evaluation results

The mind reading game was 100% accurate, and users got exited when they saw the result. Some of the participants even asked to repeat the game. Since the mind reading game has the chance to guess the selected person in 4 different occasions the probability of guessing the right person increases significantly.

Top-down & bottom up attention mechanisms

The two above-mentioned applications for EyeGrip utilize a top-down attention mechanisms in the brain. In both applications, the user knows what s/he is looking for; therefore, the visual attention is directed based on the user's longer-term cognitive strategies which is more like a top-down mechanism [7]. The EyeGrip technique can also be useful in applications where the user does not have any predefined plan for the visual search such as the Facebook Newsfeed reader explained earlier in the paper. In such applications the user's attention can be directed based on raw sensory input such as an attractive colour or fast movements (bottom-up mechanism).

DISCUSSION & CONCLUSIONS

In this paper, we introduced EyeGrip which is a novel interaction technique to support users in a visual search task in desktop, mobile, and wearable settings. EyeGrip analyzes Optokinetic Nystagmus eye movements to detect the object or area of interest among a sequence of uni-directional moving objects. This information enables users to potentially select an object without providing any explicit input to the computer.

Since OKN is a natural reaction of the eyes to the moving visual field, EyeGrip opens room for designing more intuitive methods of eye-based interaction.

We also tried to characterise the EyeGrip technique by empirically investigating the effect of scrolling speed and maximum number of visible images in the view-port (manipulated by changing image width) on the accuracy of the system and users' performance. The results of our experiment indicated a significant effect from number of image in the view-port on the performance of the classification while the effect of speed on the classification accuracy was not statistically significant. However, increasing the speed of moving images indicated a significant effect on the users' performance. But there is also a lower limit for the speed of moving objects. If the objects move very slow the user has enough time to pay equal visual attention to all of the objects. This makes the sawtooth shapes of the OKN signal more homogeneous which means it will be difficult to detect a deviation in the OKN signal when something draws user's attention.

EyeGrip utilizes the limitation of humans visual perception system in temporally intensive visual tasks where the user's visual perception mechanism needs to prioritize the time spent on following visual cues. To use the EyeGrip technique in user interface design we need to find an optimum speed and number of images in view-port to create a temporal intention, but we need to keep the speed low enough in order to minimize users' error. The temporal intention might seem to be a limitation for EyeGrip, but considering the increasing pace of producing visual contents in the Internet, we will need such mechanisms in the future to support users in quickly scanning a lot of visual contents.

In this paper, we used a home-made eye tracker, a very simple eye movement feature and classification algorithm to demonstrate the concept of EyeGrip. Using this setting we reached the accuracy of 87% where the scrolling speed is equal to 2000 pixels/s and the maximum number of visible images in the view-port is 3 (image width = 960 pixels). We believe by using more advanced features and classification models the accuracy of EyeGrip can be improved even more than what we reached in this study.

The results of the usability studies and the leave-one-out evaluation indicated an acceptable level of classification performance for the unseen data. The leave-one-out evaluation for condition 4 reported an average accuracy of 87.2% ($\sigma = 11.5$) for the classification. Furthermore, in the picture selection study, as a real-time interactive application, the average accuracy was 81% ($\sigma = 5$) and in the mind reading game the EyeGrip technique was 100% accurate. This shows that the EyeGrip technique can be used pretty accurate without any additional training for new users.

In the future work, we will implement the EyeGrip method by capturing the eye movement data from stationary eye trackers and other sensing technologies such as EOG for wearable systems. In that case, the OKN signal will be generated based on only eye movement data, and other peak detection algorithms can be used for finding local peaks in the OKN signal.

ACKNOWLEDGEMENTS

We would like to thank our fellow PIT Lab members for their valuable input at various stages of the work.

REFERENCES

1. W. Abd-Almageed, M.S. Fadali, and G. Bebis. 2002. A non-intrusive Kalman filter-based tracker for pursuit eye movement. In *American Control Conference, 2002. Proceedings of the 2002*, Vol. 2. 1443–1447 vol.2. DOI: http://dx.doi.org/10.1109/ACC.2002.1023224
2. Daniel L. Ashbrook. 2010. *Enabling Mobile Microinteractions*. Ph.D. Dissertation. Atlanta, GA, USA. Advisor(s) Starner, Thad E. AAI3414437.
3. Richard Bates and Howell O Istance. 2003. Why are eye mice unpopular? A detailed comparison of head and eye controlled assistive technology pointing devices. *UAIS* 2, 3 (2003), 280–290.
4. L Burmark. 2004. Visual Presentations That Prompt, Flash & Transform Here are some great ways to have more visually interesting class sessions. *Media and methods* 40 (2004), 4–5.
5. T. Cecchin, D. Sauter, D. Brie, and B. Martin. 1990. On-line Separation Of Smooth Pursuit And Saccadic Eye Movements. In *Engineering in Medicine and Biology Society, 1990., Proceedings of the Twelfth Annual International Conference of the IEEE*. 777–778. DOI: http://dx.doi.org/10.1109/IEMBS.1990.691327
6. M. Cheng and J.S. Outerbridge. 1975. Optokinetic nystagmus during selective retinal stimulation. *Experimental Brain Research* 23, 2 (1975), 129–139. DOI: http://dx.doi.org/10.1007/BF00235455
7. Charles E Connor, Howard E Egeth, and Steven Yantis. 2004. Visual attention: bottom-up versus top-down. *Current Biology* 14, 19 (2004), R850–R852. DOI: http://dx.doi.org/doi:10.1016/j.cub.2004.09.041
8. Heiko Drewes and Albrecht Schmidt. 2007. Interacting with the Computer Using Gaze Gestures. In *Human-Computer Interaction INTERACT 2007*. Lecture Notes in Computer Science, Vol. 4663. Springer Berlin Heidelberg, 475–488. DOI: http://dx.doi.org/10.1007/978-3-540-74800-7_43
9. Johannes Harms, Martina Kratky, Christoph Wimmer, Karin Kappel, and Thomas Grechenig. 2015. Navigation in Long Forms on Smartphones: Scrolling Worse than Tabs, Menus, and Collapsible Fieldsets. In *INTERACT 2015*. Lecture Notes in Computer Science, Vol. 9298. Springer, 333–340. DOI: http://dx.doi.org/10.1007/978-3-319-22698-9_21
10. Sandra G Hart and Lowell E Staveland. 1988. Development of NASA-TLX (Task Load Index): Results of empirical and theoretical research. *Advances in psychology* 52 (1988), 139–183. DOI: http://dx.doi.org/doi:10.1016/S0166-4115(08)62386-9

11. Aulikki Hyrskykari, Päivi Majaranta, and Kari-Jouko Räihä. 2005. From gaze control to attentive interfaces. In *Proceedings of HCII*, Vol. 2.

12. Robert J. K. Jacob. 1990. What You Look at is What You Get: Eye Movement-based Interaction Techniques. In *Proceedings of the SIGCHI Conference on Human Factors in Computing Systems (CHI '90)*. ACM, New York, NY, USA, 11–18. DOI: http://dx.doi.org/10.1145/97243.97246

13. Shahram Jalaliniya, Diako Mardanbegi, and Thomas Pederson. 2015. MAGIC Pointing for Eyewear Computers. In *Proceedings of the 2015 ACM International Symposium on Wearable Computers (ISWC '15)*. ACM, New York, NY, USA, 155–158. DOI: http://dx.doi.org/10.1145/2802083.2802094

14. Shahram Jalaliniya, Diako Mardanbegi, Thomas Pederson, and Dan Witzner. 2014. Head and Eye Movement as Pointing Modalities for Eyewear Computers. In *Wearable and Implantable Body Sensor Networks Workshops (BSN Workshops), 2014 11th International Conference on*. 50–53. DOI: http://dx.doi.org/10.1109/BSN.Workshops.2014.14

15. Do Hyong Koh, Sandeep Munikrishne Gowda, and Oleg V. Komogortsev. 2010. Real Time Eye Movement Identification Protocol. In *CHI '10 Extended Abstracts on Human Factors in Computing Systems (CHI EA '10)*. ACM, New York, NY, USA, 3499–3504. DOI: http://dx.doi.org/10.1145/1753846.1754008

16. Lori A Lott and Robert B Post. 1993. Up-down asymmetry in vertical induced motion. *PERCEPTION-LONDON-* 22 (1993), 527–527.

17. PaulP. Maglio, Teenie Matlock, ChristopherS. Campbell, Shumin Zhai, and BartonA. Smith. 2000. Gaze and Speech in Attentive User Interfaces. In *Advances in Multimodal Interfaces ICMI 2000*. Lecture Notes in Computer Science, Vol. 1948. Springer Berlin Heidelberg, 1–7. DOI: http://dx.doi.org/10.1007/3-540-40063-X_1

18. Diako Mardanbegi, Dan Witzner Hansen, and Thomas Pederson. 2012. Eye-based Head Gestures. In *Proceedings of the Symposium on Eye Tracking Research and Applications (ETRA '12)*. ACM, New York, NY, USA, 139–146. DOI: http://dx.doi.org/10.1145/2168556.2168578

19. Thomas Paul, Daniel Puscher, and Thorsten Strufe. 2015. The User Behavior in Facebook and its Development from 2009 until 2014. *arXiv preprint arXiv:1505.04943* (2015).

20. Ravikrishna Ruddarraju, Antonio Haro, Kris Nagel, Quan T. Tran, Irfan A. Essa, Gregory Abowd, and Elizabeth D. Mynatt. 2003. Perceptual User Interfaces Using Vision-based Eye Tracking. In *Proceedings of ICMI '03*. ACM, New York, NY, USA, 227–233. DOI: http://dx.doi.org/10.1145/958432.958475

21. Javier San Agustin. 2009. *Off-the-shelf gaze interaction*. Ph.D. Dissertation. IT-Universitetet i KøbenhavnIT University of Copenhagen, DirektionenManagement, InstituttetThe Department, Innovative CommunicationInnovative Communication.

22. Christopher A Sanchez and James Z Goolsbee. 2010. Character size and reading to remember from small displays. *Computers & Education* 55, 3 (2010), 1056–1062. DOI: http://dx.doi.org/doi:10.1016/j.compedu.2010.05.001

23. Albrecht Schmidt. 2005. Interactive context-aware systems interacting with ambient intelligence. *Ambient intelligence* 159 (2005).

24. Jeffrey S Shell, Roel Vertegaal, and Alexander W Skaburskis. 2003. EyePliances: attention-seeking devices that respond to visual attention. In *CHI'03 extended abstracts on Human factors in computing systems*. ACM, 770–771.

25. Linda E. Sibert and Robert J. K. Jacob. 2000. Evaluation of Eye Gaze Interaction. In *Proceedings of the SIGCHI Conference on Human Factors in Computing Systems (CHI '00)*. ACM, New York, NY, USA, 281–288. DOI: http://dx.doi.org/10.1145/332040.332445

26. JWG Ter Braak. 1936. Untersuchungen über optokinetischen Nystagmus. *Arch Neerl Physiol* 21 (1936), 309–376.

27. Mélodie Vidal, Andreas Bulling, and Hans Gellersen. 2012. Detection of Smooth Pursuits Using Eye Movement Shape Features. In *Proceedings of the Symposium on Eye Tracking Research and Applications (ETRA '12)*. ACM, New York, NY, USA, 177–180. DOI: http://dx.doi.org/10.1145/2168556.2168586

28. Mélodie Vidal, Andreas Bulling, and Hans Gellersen. 2013. Pursuits: Spontaneous Interaction with Displays Based on Smooth Pursuit Eye Movement and Moving Targets. In *Proceedings of UbiComp '13*. ACM, New York, NY, USA, 439–448. DOI: http://dx.doi.org/10.1145/2493432.2493477

29. Shumin Zhai, Carlos Morimoto, and Steven Ihde. 1999. Manual and Gaze Input Cascaded (MAGIC) Pointing. In *Proc. of the CHI '99*. ACM, 246–253. DOI: http://dx.doi.org/10.1145/302979.303053

30. Yanxia Zhang, Andreas Bulling, and Hans Gellersen. 2014. Pupil-canthi-ratio: A Calibration-free Method for Tracking Horizontal Gaze Direction. In *Proceedings of the 2014 International Working Conference on Advanced Visual Interfaces (AVI '14)*. ACM, New York, NY, USA, 129–132. DOI: http://dx.doi.org/10.1145/2598153.2598186

Eye-Trace: Segmentation of Volumetric Microscopy Images with Eyegaze

Thomas Templier, Kenan Bektas, Richard H.R. Hahnloser
Institute of Neuroinformatics
University of Zurich and ETH Zurich
Neuroscience Center Zurich, Zurich, Switzerland
{templier,rich}@ini.ethz.ch

ABSTRACT
We introduce an image annotation approach for the analysis of volumetric electron microscopic imagery of brain tissue. The core task is to identify and link tubular objects (neuronal fibers) in images taken from consecutive ultrathin sections of brain tissue. In our approach an individual 'flies' through the 3D data at a high speed and maintains eye gaze focus on a single neuronal fiber, aided by navigation with a handheld gamepad controller. The continuous foveation on a fiber of interest constitutes an intuitive means to define a trace that is seamlessly recorded with a desktop eyetracker and transformed into precise 3D coordinates of the annotated fiber (skeleton tracing). In a participant experiment we validate the approach by demonstrating a tracing accuracy of about the respective radiuses of the traced fibers with browsing speeds of up to 40 brain sections per second.

Author Keywords
Connectomics; brain mapping; array tomography; neural circuit reconstruction; segmentation; annotation; user interface design; eye tracking.

ACM Classification Keywords
H.5.2. User Interfaces: Input devices and strategies interfaces and presentation.

INTRODUCTION

Connectomics
Cellular connectomics (watch a video introduction from pioneer Jeff Lichtman [29]), a field of neuroscience that aims to decipher the organization of brain neural networks, is facing a data analysis challenge. Dozens of terabytes of high resolution volumetric electron microscopy (EM) images of brain tissue need to be analyzed in order to detect neuronal fibers and their contacts with other fibers across thousands of consecutive images (neuron tracing). Successful tracing of these fibers provides the neuron morphologies and is a prerequisite for revealing the wiring diagram of the neural network (illustrated in a short animation from the online game Eyewire [12]). Such neural circuit reconstruction is an impressively challenging and yet unsolved computer vision problem which has resisted a decade of sustained efforts in developing automated algorithms [17, 23–25, 33, 44]. All recent discoveries in the field [5, 6, 8, 22, 26, 27, 43] have extensively relied on large numbers of trained humans who annotated manually or semi-automatically these large data sets. For instance the study by Takemura et al. [43] necessitated about 15,000 person-hours of manual annotation and proofreading. In this project we explored a multimodal interaction (eyetracker and gamepad controller) approach for cellular connectomics with the aim to increase the tracing throughput of single individuals. We do so by letting users navigate through the data at high speed while continuously recording their decisions at the first easily measurable source: the eye gaze.

CHI'16, May 07-12, 2016, San Jose, CA, USA.
© 2016 ACM. ISBN 978-1-4503-3362-7/16/05…$15.00.
DOI: http://dx.doi.org/10.1145/2858036.2858578

RELATED WORK

Current Annotation Methods
Neuronal fibers are tubular objects that appear as roundish structures in high-resolution EM images taken from consecutive ultrathin sections (of 5 to 50 nm thickness) cut from a small piece of animal brain tissue (Figure 1).

Typically, skeletonization of neuronal fibers is used in purely manual methods [21, 36] and in semi-automated methods [4]. It consists of identifying fiber cross-sections with mouse clicks near their center of mass in every or in every few consecutive sections (Figure 1b). Each click can be decomposed into a) locating the fiber, b) locating the mouse cursor, c) positioning the cursor and d) clicking on the fiber. According to Fitts's Law [14], the time required to finish the mouse based annotation operation (steps b and c) is proportional to the logarithm of the ratio of target distance to target size. Put simply, more time is required for small targets which are further away.

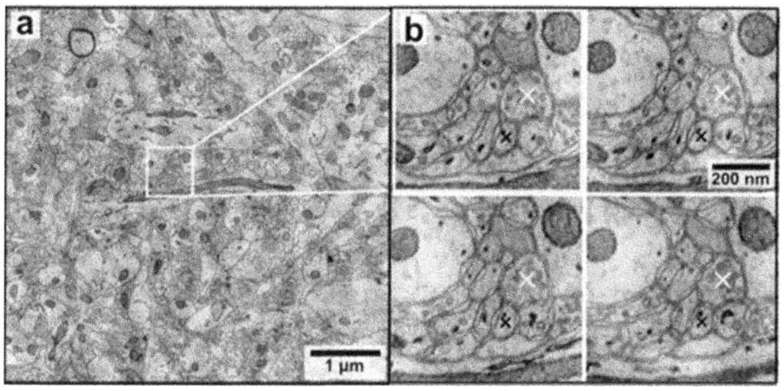

Figure 1. Electron micrographs of brain tissue. a: micrograph of a part of a section cut from a piece of mouse brain tissue. b: zoomed inset across 4 consecutive sections. Two labeled fibers are shown in red and green. The yellow and black crosses represent centers of mass of two separate fibers (skeletonization).

Also, in semi-automated methods aided by machine learning [19, 26, 27, 42], a candidate annotation that fills the inner part of each putative fiber is produced by means of computer vision algorithms (such as the green and red labels in Figure 1b). These annotations are then overlaid on the data and finally are proofread by humans.

To be able to deal with increasingly large volumes, such annotation pipelines need to be scaled up accordingly, which can be achieved by a) a better automated assessment of the locations that require manual intervention to efficiently guide proofreading, b) increasing the tracing throughput of single individuals and c) making the manual tasks easy to learn to minimize overhead from training new annotators. Both proofreading and skeletonization tasks suffer from the lack of intrinsic incentives, implying that human annotators typically must get paid or the task must be gamified [27].

Eyegaze as Input

Eye tracking consists of measuring the geometrical orientation of the eyegaze. When an individual is looking at a screen, the gaze orientation can be converted into the coordinates of the point on screen where the user is looking at.

Recently, various applications using the eye gaze as input have emerged, such as: selection of large menu items in desktop and mobile applications [28], scrolling, typing, emotion monitoring, gaze contingent visualization [3] and immersive interaction in online virtual reality environments and games. Most of these applications require a certain level of concentration known as overt attention, which occurs when an individual has the sensation of mentally focusing on a point and the measured eyegaze orientation points precisely at that same point [18].

Considering the fundamental limitations of using gaze as an input channel, Zhai et al. [45] combined gaze with mouse input by warping the pointer position to the gaze position. Their experimental study demonstrated that this system, taking advantage of Fitt´s law [14], can reduce manual effort. In an experimental study among different age groups, Murata [31] has compared the target pointing performance of participants as they use either mouse or gaze as the input modality. The results showed that with gaze input the pointing times of participants were up to 50% shorter than with mouse only. Especially for older participants with declined motor skills the target pointing with gaze was easier and simpler. Other studies with comparable setups showed that pointing with gaze is as accurate as conventional mouse pointing, and exhibits significantly shorter dwell times [13, 30, 39]. A user-centered design approach and a formative user study [41] integrated gaze as an input modality to a multi-modal environment. The findings indicate that gaze input is an intuitive modality for tasks that are in pointing nature.

To our knowledge, there is only one report of the use of eyegaze input for image analysis tasks [37]: there, a user interactively segments an object in a static (typically radiologic) image. This segmentation is achieved by feeding the eyegaze inputs to a segmentation algorithm that updates the predicted segmentation of the object of interest.

EYEGAZE FOR NEURON TRACING

In our approach, microscopy images from consecutive sections of brain tissue are displayed on a screen one after the other at a high frame rate (10 to 40 sections per second). As the sections are only a few nanometers thick, flying through them produces a pleasant impression of smooth navigation because the visible cellular structures (membranes, mitochondria, microtubuli, vesicles, myelin) evolve slowly. An observer can then perform a smooth eye pursuit and follow seamlessly these well delineated objects that they keep in their attentional spotlight. As skeletonization of neuronal tubular fibers requires a single localized label every section or every few sections, we realized that an eyegaze readout would be well suited as input to a neuron tracing system. We therefore let humans browse through the consecutive images at a constant speed and record their eyegaze with an eye tracker, infer the location on screen at which the user is foveating, and use that location as the answer to the question "Where is the cross section of the fiber currently located?". To our knowledge, this is the first attempt of performing frame-based image annotation using eyegaze input.

EXPERIMENT

After extensive tests, a short pilot experiment with 6 participants confirmed our impression that the eyegaze tracing approach was feasible and accurate enough even by novices who are unfamiliar with the data. We therefore refined the design of the pilot experiment and conducted a within subject design experiment with the goal of answering the following main question:

Q1. What is the accuracy of tracing neuronal fibers as a function of browsing speed and fiber size?

Additionally we sought answers to the following annex questions:

q2. Can neuron tracing tasks be performed by novice untrained individuals?

q3. Does the performance improve when a user repetitively traces the same fiber?

q4. Can users maintain high accuracy while tracing long segments of fibers (1200 sections)?

Finally and more generally we also sought to know whether eyegaze based neuron tracing would potentially be accurate and reliable enough to feed data into semi-automated machine vision pipelines.

Setup

The experimental setup is shown in Figure 2. Eyegaze is measured with a desktop eyetracker (Eyetribe, 30Hz sampling rate, 0.5-1° accuracy). The navigation is controlled with a gamepad (Logitech F310) with the following functionalities: Left joystick: panning in the x-y plane; Button 1: start of browsing; Button 2: task termination. A primary display (17 inch LCD, 1280x1024, 75 Hz), presents images to the user while a secondary one, invisible to the participant, is used by the experimenter to monitor the procedure (Figure 2). The head of the user is kept with a chinrest at about 60 cm distance from the display, leading to an accuracy of the eyetracker of 40 screen-pixels. An orchestrator script (Matlab, MIJI) loads tasks consecutively by calling a custom Fiji [38] plugin for display and navigation of the image stacks. Custom scripts (python) monitored the communication with the eye tracker and the gamepad. The browsing speed reported in frames per second (fps) indicates the number of consecutive sections displayed per second.

Neuroanatomical Data

The data was generated from consecutive scanning electron micrographs of a piece of mouse neocortex brain tissue with a voxel size of 3 nm x 3 nm x 29 nm [26] downloaded from the openconnectome.org website [9] (Figure 1). Images were displayed in a Fiji canvas with a fixed magnification factor appropriately set for each task, depending on the initial size of the fiber to be traced. The magnification varied between 200% for large fibers up to 500% for small fibers. At 500% magnification, 8 image pixels correspond to 1 screen pixel. Six image stacks were extracted from the large online dataset: five stacks were of dimensions 2000 x 2000 x 300 voxels (6 µm x 6µm x 8.8 µm) and one stack, containing long fibers, was of dimensions 2000 x 2000 x 1200 voxels (6 µm x 6 µm x 35.3µm).

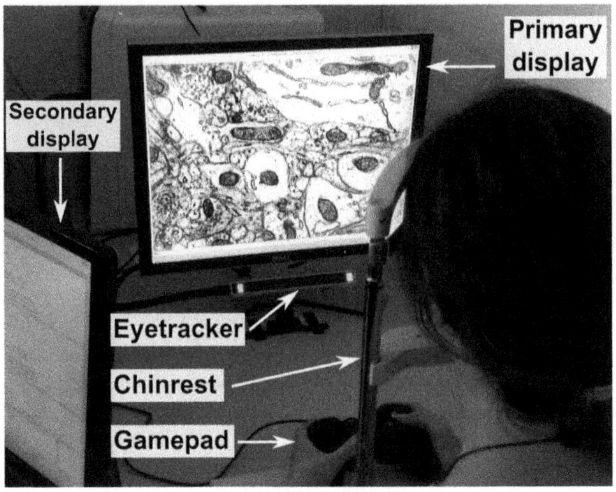

Figure 2. Experimental setup.

From these image stacks we chose 18 unique fibers to be used within the study tasks, described below. The chosen fibers did not terminate before reaching the boundary of the stack volumes. To avoid a possible bias towards more easily traceable fibers that run along the browsing axis (i.e., perpendicular to the tissue sectioning plane), we took care of selecting fibers that exhibited sharp turns.

In order to reveal the relationship between tracing speed and tracing accuracy, we classified fibers based on their diameter size. Small fibers have an average diameter of about 45 pixels (135 nm), medium fibers of 45 to 65 pixels, and large fibers of more than 65 pixels.

Participants

20 students (10 female, MSc. and PhD levels, and ages 23 to 33 years, normal or corrected-to-normal vision) participated in the experiment, provided their written consent and received a small compensation.

Procedure

Guided by the experimenter (2nd author), each participant underwent the following procedure: 1) welcoming and giving consent; 2) initial training (eye tracker calibration and 4 training tasks); 3) experiment: consecutive tracing tasks interleaved with calibrations, breaks and difficulty ratings; 4) system usability scale (SUS) rating; and 5) short debriefing.

Tasks

The experiment was divided into 129 tasks. We analyzed only the first 62 tasks, the remaining ones were designed to test further functionalities that are not reported here (branching points, complex terminations). When a task started, the initial image of a stack of sections was displayed on screen with a red cross placed in the center of the fiber that the participant had to trace. When the participant was ready, she pressed a button on the gamepad triggering the start of the browsing through the stack at a given frame rate that depends on the task. During the browsing, the participant followed the fiber of interest with her eyes and adjusted the field of view in the x-y plane with the joystick if necessary.

The task could terminate in two ways: 1) the participant followed the fiber until the end of the stack was reached (typically after 300 sections, that is, after 15 seconds if browsing was done at 20 fps); or 2) the participant pressed the termination button before the end of the stack was reached to signify that she was not able to follow the fiber any more for whatever reason.

After the termination of a task, the participant had to briefly rate its difficulty on a Likert scale. Thereafter either the next task started five seconds later or a short thirty seconds break was given.

Experimental Design

The participants were exposed to a succession of tasks that were interleaved systematically by breaks, calibrations, or instructions.

Warmup

The first four tasks provided a short initial training and exhibited four different fibers at increasing browsing speeds of 10, 20, 30 and 40 fps. These fibers were not reused in other tasks.

Speed/Size Experiment

Tasks 5-52 constituted the **speed/size experiment** and showed small, medium and large fibers at 10, 20, 30 and 40 fps. Each of the 12 tracing conditions (4 speeds x 3 sizes) was tested 4 times, for a total of 48 tasks.

For these 48 tasks, we used a total of 12 unique fibers: 4 small, 4 medium and 4 large. All 12 fibers were 300 sections long. To prevent a task from displaying the exact same fiber as a previous task, we created four different tasks from each unique fiber by displaying the stack 1) from the first to the last section (forwards); 2) from the last to the first section (backwards); 3) forwards with a 180° rotation around the browsing axis (forward rotated); 4) backwards rotated. The 4 tasks created from a unique fiber were used across the 4 different speeds. For example, fiber number 7 has been traced in the following conditions: (10fps, backwards), (20 fps, forwards rotated), (30 fps, forwards) and (40 fps, backwards rotated).

The 48 tasks were first randomized, then we reordered two tasks to number 5 and 10 for the task repetition experiment described below. This order was the same for all participants.

Repetition Experiments

The two groups of tasks {53,54,55,56} and {58,59,60,61} constituted the **fiber repetition experiment** and displayed 4 times consecutively at 20 fps the same medium and small fiber, respectively.

Task 53 (small fiber, 20 fps) was equivalent to task 5, and task 58 (medium fiber, 20 fps) was equivalent to task 10. The two pairs of identical tasks {5,53} and {10,58} constituted the **task repetition experiment** to assess improvement of the participants between the start and the end of the approximately 1 hour long experiment.

Long Fiber Experiment

Task 57 and 62, that we named **long fiber experiment,** displayed at 20 fps a medium and a small fiber, respectively, that were 1200 sections long.

Calibration

A nine-point eye tracking calibration was performed before the initial training tasks, and before tasks 1, 25 and 49. Calibrations were repeated until an accuracy measure given by the Eyetribe server (v.0.9.49) smaller than 0.4 was achieved. This calibration criterion is slightly more conservative than the "Excellent calibration" criterion implemented in the Eyetribe user interface.

Measures

Completeness

We assessed **completeness** of a tracing task by dividing the number of correctly foveated sections by the total number of sections spanned by the fiber. A section is considered correctly annotated if the participant has not pressed the termination button beforehand. For example if the participant presses the button during section 200 in a task displaying a 300 sections long fiber, then the task completeness is 0.66 (200/300).

Tracing accuracy

Each fiber was skeleton traced by an experienced neuroscientist (1st author) by clicking in each section k ($k = 1, \dots, K$) on the apparent center f_k of the fiber (in image pixel coordinates). The trace $(f_1, \dots, f_K)$ was defined as the ground truth trace of the fiber. The tracing **accuracy** of a task, expressed in pixels, is defined as the root-mean-square-error (RMSE) $\frac{1}{n}\sqrt{\sum_{k=1}^{n}(f_k - e_k)^2}$ of the gaze positions e_k across all sections, where e_k is the raw unfiltered gaze coordinate fetched from the eye tracker while section k is displayed, and n is the number of validly traced sections (validly traced sections are sections during which the participant was reportedly tracing, that is, he had not pressed the termination button). We computed a **collaborative trace** of a given fiber by averaging gaze coordinates over validly traced portions of fibers across participants. Intuitively, the collaborative trace is the mean trace, which represents the consensus from the crowd. The **collaborative accuracy** is the accuracy of the collaborative trace. We computed a **smoothed bias-corrected trace** by first subtracting from e_k the bias $b = \frac{1}{n}\sum_{k=1}^{n}(e_k - f_k)$ followed by applying two median filters separately on the x and y coordinates, where the respective medians are computed over 10 consecutive sections. The resulting accuracy of the smoothed bias-corrected trace was $\frac{1}{n}\sqrt{\sum_{k=1}^{n}(f_k - M(e_k - b))^2}$, where M represents the two median filters. In our hands, our desktop eye tracker was sufficiently precise but sometimes introduced some offset. To compensate for such accuracy offsets, we made the bias correction. The median smoothing was computed to improve the precision.

For 40 fps tracing, given that eyegaze sampling is only done at 30 Hz, there was no foveation point measurement for one fourth of the sections. We chose to not interpolate and to discard these sections for RMSE calculation.

Subjective Difficulty Rating

The fiber difficulty was measured with a Single Ease Question (SEQ). After each task, participants were asked to immediately rate the difficulty they encountered in tracing that particular fiber on a Likert scale from 1 (very easy) to 5 (very difficult).

System Usability

The system usability was assessed with a standard system usability scale (SUS) [7] immediately after the end of the experiment.

RESULTS

Speed/Size Experiment

The heat maps in Figures 3 and 4 depict in detail the accuracy and completeness of all participants for the 48 tasks of the speed/size experiment. As can be seen in these heatmaps, the accuracy values roughly oscillate between 20 and 50 pixels and the task completeness is most often 100%. These data illustrate the validation of the eyegaze tracing approach by showing that the error is about the same as the extent of the fibers while the participants rarely lost track during tracing, except for small fibers at speeds 20 fps and higher.

The accuracy tended to decrease with higher flying speeds, as intuitively expected. Somewhat counter-intuitively at low speeds (10 and 20 fps, first two meta-columns on the left, Figure 3) the accuracy decreases with increasing fiber sizes. We attribute this decrease to our definition of accuracy rather than to an inherent difficulty of tracing larger fibers (see discussion).

For a convenient representation, we depict in Figure 5 some accuracy values on representative fibers of our size classes.

Main effects of speed and size

We run a 2-way factorial repeated measures ANOVA (f-rmAN) for 3 size levels and 4 speed levels. The assumption of sphericity was violated (Mauchly´s test) for the main effects of the size, ($\chi 2(2) = 6.5$, $p = .04$), for the speed, ($\chi 2(5) = 15.1$, $p = .01$), and for the interaction speed/size, ($\chi 2(20) = 66.3$, $p = .000$). The Greenhouse-Geisser estimates of corrected degrees of freedom became .76, .66 and .53 respectively.

There was a significant main effect of the size on the accuracy, ($F(1.5, 27.3) = 85.1$, $p = .000$, $\eta 2 = .825$). Contrasts with small fibers revealed that the average accuracy for large fibers ($F(1,18) = 112.8$, $r = .37$, $\eta 2 = .862$) and medium fibers ($F(1,18) = 21.6$, $r = .67$, $\eta 2 = .545$) were larger than that of small fibers.

There was a significant main effect of the speed on the average accuracy, ($F(1.98, 35.6) = 3.49$, $p = .042$, $\eta 2 =.162$). There was a significant interaction effect between the size and speed of tracing, ($F(3.2, 57.2) = 4.98$, $p = .003$, $\eta 2 =.217$). The size of the fiber to be traced had therefore a different effect on tracing accuracy depending on the speed.

Interplay of speed and size

In order to characterize the effect of the speed for each different size level we run three separate 1-way repeated measures ANOVA (rmAN) with Bonferroni corrections. Figure 6 shows the accuracy values for the 12 speed/size conditions tested.

The tracing accuracy for **large fibers** (yellow bars, Figure 6) was independent of the speed and its mean was 50 ± 5 pixels ($F(3, 54) = 3358$, $P = 0.25$, $\eta 2 = 0.157$), no significant difference between pairs (post hoc comparisons, $p > 0.05$). Because large fibers have a diameter larger than 65 pixels, the gaze input therefore sometimes was located outside of the fiber boundary.

The accuracy for **medium fibers** (red bars, Figure 6) depended on tracing speeds ($F(3, 54) = 53.55$, $p < 0.0005$, $\eta 2 = 0.933$) and the average accuracy decreased linearly with speed from 34 ± 8 pixels for 10 fps to 48 ± 7 pixels for 40 fps, as intuitively expected. Post hoc tests (with Bonferroni correction) showed a statistically significant accuracy decrease ($p = .000$) for the speed pairs (10, 30) and (10, 40).

The accuracy for **small fibers** (blue bars, Figure 6) also decreased with increasing speeds ($F(3, 54) = 17.207$, $p < 0.0005$, $\eta 2 = 0.489$) from 27 ± 15 pixels for 10 fps to 62 ± 28 pixels for 40 fps. Post hoc tests (with Bonferroni correction) showed a statistically significant accuracy decrease ($p = .000$) between the pairs (10, 30), (10, 40) and (20, 40) fps.

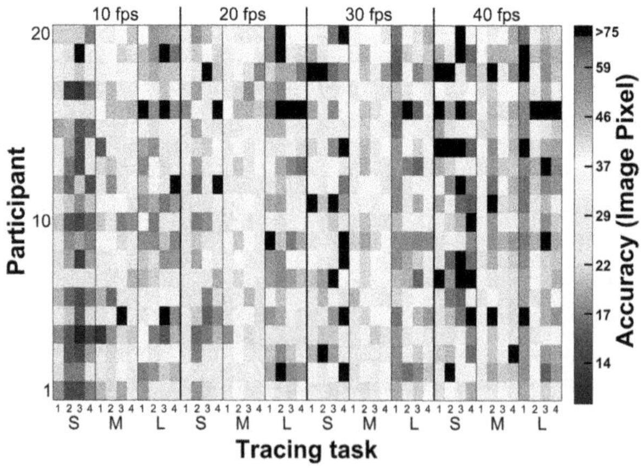

Figure 3. Heat map of the accuracy for each task from the speed/size experiment for all participants. S: small, M: medium, L: large

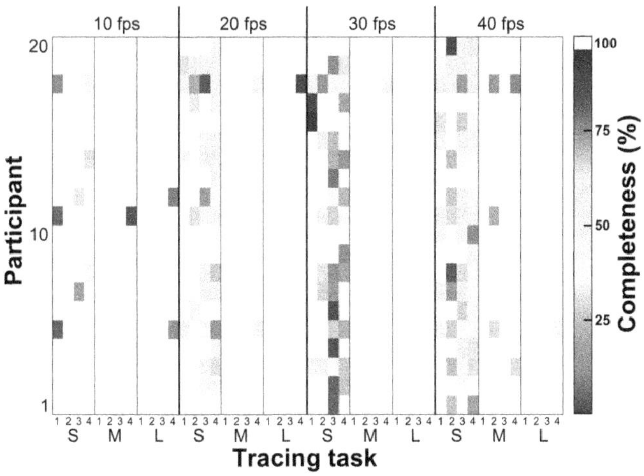

Figure 4. Heat map of the completeness for each task from the speed/size experiment for all participants. S: small, M: medium, L: large

In summary rmAN results are supplementing the general findings we obtained from f-rmAN: rmAN reveals the effect of tracing speed for each fiber size individually and f-rmAN shows that the effect of speed differs depending on size.

Collaborative traces

The accuracies of the collaborative traces for all tasks of the speed/size experiment are shown in Figure 7. In all tasks of the speed/size experiment, the collaborative trace (Figure 7) has higher accuracy than the averaged accuracies of the traces taken individually (Figure 6). This improvement in tracing accuracy is shown in detail in Figure 8 for each of the 48 tasks of the speed/size experiment.

Smoothed bias-corrected traces

The accuracies of the smoothed bias-corrected traces are shown in Figure 9. The bias and smoothing corrections show the greatest effect at low speeds.

Fiber Repetition Experiment

In the repetition experiment, a medium and a small fiber were repetitively traced consecutively 4 times at 20 fps. Some participants noticed the repetition. The average accuracy for the medium fiber was not affected by the repetition (Figure 10 left, red bars, 1-way rmAN, $F(3, 54) = 1.233$, $p = 0.307$). The same was true for the small fiber, (Figure 10 left, blue bars, 1-way rmAN, $F(3, 54) = 1.415$, $p = 0.25$).

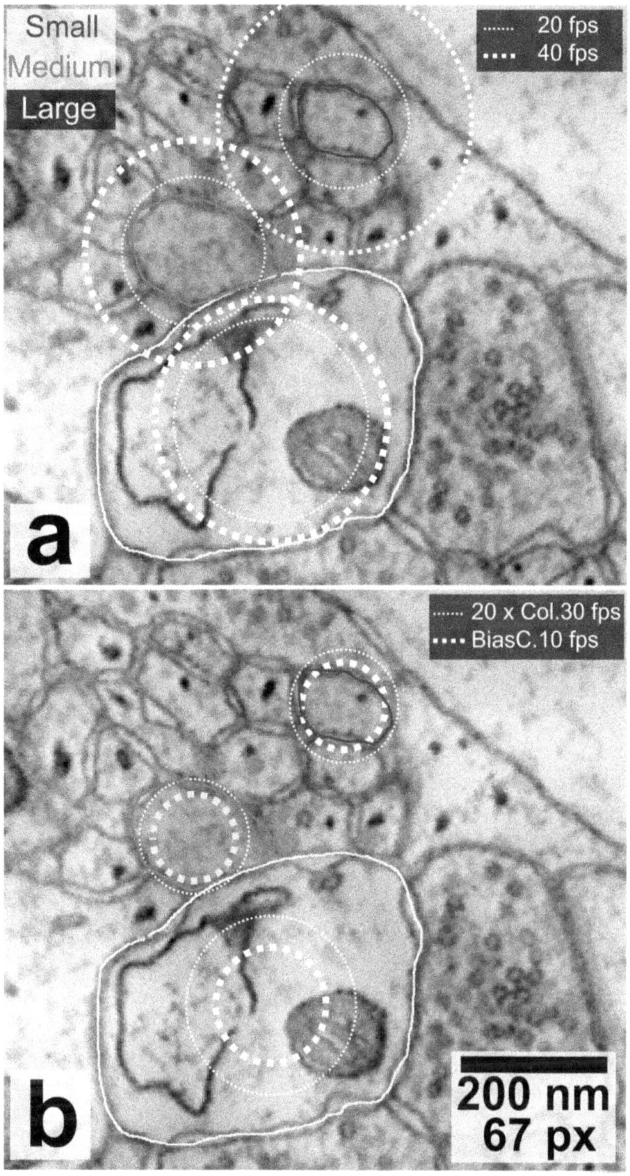

Figure 5. Accuracy of eyegaze tracing as a function of fiber size and browsing speed. Discs with a radius equal to the accuracy are centered on an example small (blue), medium (red), and large fiber (blue). Fiber boundaries are highlighted in corresponding colors. Px:image pixels (3 nm/pixel). a: fine and coarse dotted circles depict the average accuracy of all participants at 20 and 40 fps, respectively; b: fine dotted circles depict the collaborative RMSE at 30 fps. Coarse dotted circles depict the average accuracy of the smoothed bias corrected traces at 10 fps.

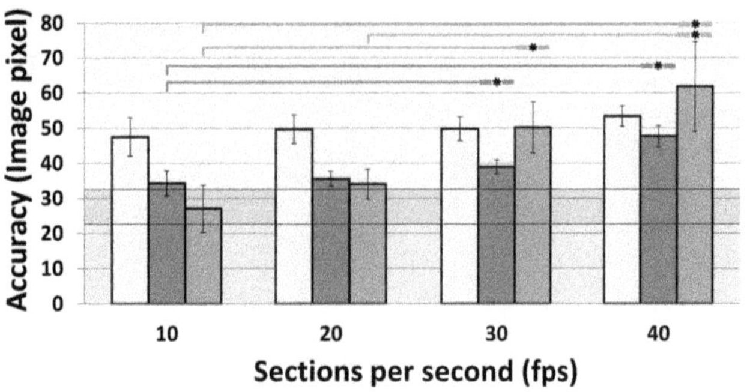

Figure 6. Accuracies for all browsing speeds (x-axis) and fiber sizes (color code as in Figure 3: Yellow: large, red: medium, blue: small.). Error bars show two standard errors of the mean. The colored background indicates the three size classes with the same color code. Stars indicate significance (* = p<0.05, post-hoc Bonferroni).

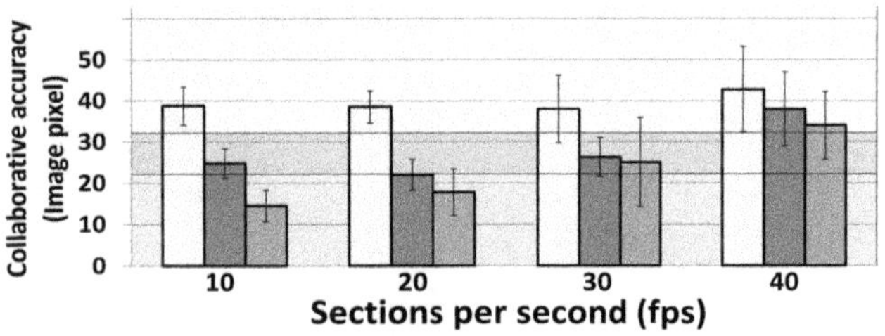

Figure 7. Accuracies of the collaborative trace for all browsing speeds (x-axis) and fiber sizes. Error bars and color codes as in Figure 6.

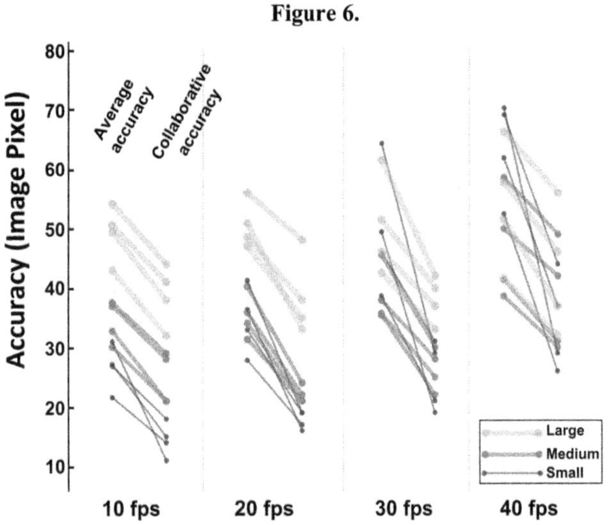

Figure 8. Collaborative tracing. Comparison of the average across all participants of the accuracies of a task with the accuracy of the corresponding collaborative trace.

Task Repetition Experiment

To assess learning of the eyegaze tracing task, participants repeated two tasks (one small, one medium fiber), with the first instance appearing within the first 10 tasks and the second instance appearing more than 40 tasks later. Figure 10 right shows the accuracy for the two repeated pairs of tasks. A pairwise t-test showed a significant increase in accuracy only for the medium fiber (t(18) = 4.77, p < 0.0005) from 40 ± 6 to 33 ± 6 pixels, and no significant difference for the small fiber (t(18) = 1.52, p = 0.146). The relatively small differences observed (though statistically significant for the medium fiber) combined with the high accuracies values show that users reach their good performance almost immediately. No participant reportedly noticed that the same fiber was being presented again after 40 tasks.

The task completeness for the repetitively traced medium fiber did not change with repetition and was on average 0.98. (1-way rmAN with Greenhouse-Geisser correction (violated sphericity), F (1.006, 19.123) = 0.991, P = 0.33). Hence fibers were already completely traced at the first repetition. For the group of small fibers, there was a slight increase in the task completeness after repetition (1st trial: 0.89 ± 0.22 and 4th trial: 0.98 ±0.04) but it was not a significant effect (F (1.802, 34.244) = 1.264, P = 0.293).

Long Fiber Experiment

The RMSE of the long medium (task 57) and long small (task 62) fibers were 23 ± 3 and 24 ± 3 pixels, respectively (2 traces were excluded as the communication with the eye tracker broke during task 62). These tracing accuracies are comparable with the ones for the short fibers (no tests performed).

Difficulty and Usability Ratings

Figure 11 shows a summary of the difficulty ratings. The subjective difficulty depended on tracing speed (non-parametric Friedman test, $\chi^2(3) = 8.647$, $p = .034$, Figure 11 left) and there was an increase in difficulty as a function of speed, as intuitively expected (though not significant).

The subjective difficulty also significantly depended on fiber size (non-parametric Friedman test , $\chi^2(2) = 24.5$, $p < 0.005$, Figure 11 middle). Small fibers were clearly perceived as the most difficult ones to trace with a statistically significant increase in perceived difficulty between large and small fibers, (Z =-3.52, $p < 0.005$) as well as between medium and small fibers, (Z =-3.52, $p < 0.005$).

Did the perceived difficulty change when a same tracing task was repeated multiple times? Figure 11, right, shows a slight decrease in difficulty after repetition, however a statistically significant reduction was only found from the first to the fourth presentations for the small fiber (Z=-3.27, $p = 0.001$) and no statistically significant changes were found for the repeated medium fiber.

Usability Assessment

The average SUS score of our setup was 68.1, *SD*: 13.2. Based on the literature [2] our score is in the marginal-high part (62.5 to 70 on a scale from 0 to 100) of the *Acceptability Range* and is classified as "good" (between *"ok"* and *"excellent"*) in terms of *Adjective Ratings*.

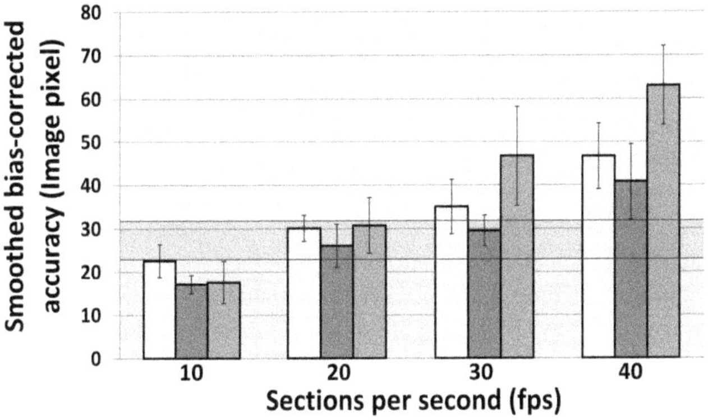

Figure 9. Accuracies of all smoothed bias-corrected traces. Error bars and color codes as in Figure 6.

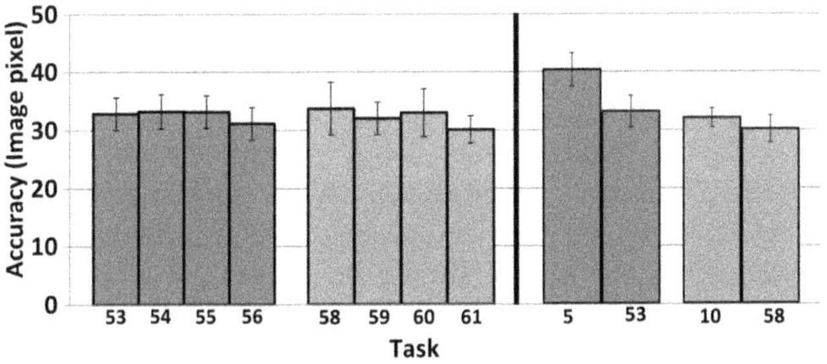

Figure 10. Learning effects with eyegaze tracing. Left: A medium (red) and a small (blue) fibers have been traced four times in a row by each participant; there are no accuracy benefits due to repetition; Right: A same task with a medium (red) and a small (blue) fiber is performed at the beginning of the experiment and more than 40 tasks later.

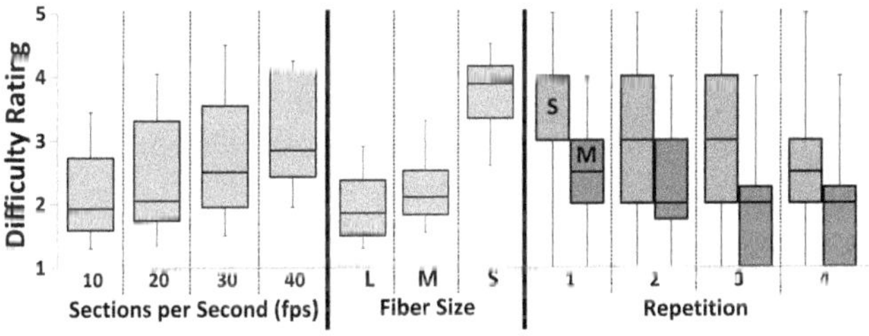

Figure 11. Subjective difficulty ratings (1: very easy, 5: very difficult) as a function of speed, of fiber size, and of repetitions in the fiber repetition experiment.

DISCUSSION

Validity of the Approach

The general impression given by the results of the participant experiment is that our eyegaze tracing approach provides acceptable skeleton traces of neuronal fibers. We found that users can follow fibers (high completeness) at high speed (10 to 40 fps) with reasonable accuracy (accuracy ~ fiber size) and that we see no severe bottleneck in performance that could arise from the technology platform chosen.

Q1. Accuracy

From Figures 3 and 6 we see that for all fiber sizes the gaze remains within the vicinity of the targeted fiber at speeds 10 and 20 fps. The study from Berning et al. [4] reports a state of the art tracing speed of 7.2h/mm, i.e., 1.3 sections/second, using accurate mouse inputs. By comparison, our system is less accurate, but allows for 10 to 40 fps browsing, which is about 15 times faster. To what extent can these numbers be compared? Clearly, the classic mouse-based approach is more accurate because users always click inside the boundary of the fiber of interest. Also, the speed comparison should be interpreted with caution because branching and termination points were not addressed here whereas these are taken into account in the speed reported for the mouse approach. In this sense it might not make sense to compare these tracing speeds.

In our approach we focus on the fact that humans are still unsurpassed in their ability to track intermingled objects and we increase the speed at the expense of the pointer accuracy. A non-automated segmentation system relying exclusively on eye gaze input would probably suffer from the lack of accuracy observed. Therefore, we believe that in future work gaze input can help automated methods to select fiber paths among diverse candidates. For example, if a fiber is erroneously traced as turning to the left by an automated method and that a user is following the fiber to the right, then the rough skeleton of the fiber would be very valuable input to correct the automated segmentation. In this sense, we hope that the achieved accuracy will be acceptable. We therefore do not see this study as a solution ready to be deployed but instead as a proof-of-principle for a scalable system that could eventually be fed into automated machine vision pipelines.

At 10 fps, smoothing and bias-correcting a trace leads to improved tracing accuracy, successfully compensating for jitter and offset produced by the eye tracker. As the ground truth and hence the bias are not known in a real application setting, querying the annotator about the exact location of his eyegaze could be a solution. For example, a salient point such as a bright item could be presented in a way to trigger the foveation of the user for a short moment on that known location, thus inferring the bias. Such a procedure could be seamlessly integrated into the workflow of a game. We note also that the quality of eye trackers is likely to improve quickly in the next few years.

As shown in Figures 3 and 5, at first glance it might be counter-intuitive that the accuracy decreases when the fiber size increases, that is, when the difficulty decreases. Our interpretation is that the gaze actually remains close to the boundaries of the fiber rather than close to the center. Instead of quantifying tracing accuracy as the simple RMSE to the approximate centers of mass, we could have added a penalty cost accounting for when the gaze is located outside of the boundary of the fiber of interest. We believe that this unexpected effect would then have vanished. However we chose to not perform the time-consuming manual contour tracing of all fibers necessary to compute such a refined accuracy.

Finally, rather specific to our neuronal reconstruction goal, it was recently demonstrated by Pallotto et al. [32] that a non-conventional brain sample preparation preserving the extracellular space between fibers aided automated machine vision algorithms. Neighboring fibers come indeed into contact much more rarely and are separated by large white gaps. We imagine that this sample preparation could compensate for the relatively lower accuracy of the eyegaze compared to a precise mouse approach.

q2. Crowd Accessibility

Scaling up the annotation task can not only be achieved by increasing the throughput of single individuals, but also by making the task accessible to a large number of individuals. Is our approach accessible to reach a large crowd? As shown in Figure 10, participants reached a high level of accuracy within a few minutes and they did not significantly improve after performing 40 tasks. Also, the heat maps in Figures 3 and 4 show qualitatively that all participants except one performed roughly equally well. From the questionnaires we learned that 14 out of the 20 participants had never manipulated such microscopy data. This therefore lets us encouragingly conclude that our approach is broadly feasible.

q3. Learning a fiber

At 20 fps, there was no significant improvement in the accuracy of participants annotating repetitively four times the same fiber, showing that the accuracy is already close to its maximum at the first attempt. This confirms also that the eyegaze approach relies on a robust mechanism of human vision to identify moving targets. A minor positive effect was observed for the completeness of these repetitively traced fibers showing that users were less likely to lose track of the fiber as they were tracing the fiber again.

q4. Long fiber segments

Our results show that users can continuously maintain attention with an appropriate foveation for at least one minute without problem (1200 sections at 20 fps). The accuracy of the long medium fiber (Task 57) was even slightly higher than the average of the short medium fibers tested in the speed/size experiment (although this long fiber might have inherently been easier to trace compared to the set of medium fibers from the speed/size experiment). We believe that this can be valuable information for the implementation of our approach for large datasets, namely to calibrate the size of the tasks presented to users. Nevertheless, such long fibers are not likely to be presented in a proofreading context as most computer errors are local and therefore users are more likely to be asked to trace short segments for local disambiguation.

Choice of the fibers

Finding a large number of fibers that were contained in a small stack from the first to the last section revealed to be a difficult task, therefore we chose to select a few (12 unique fibers for the size/speed experiment) and to apply the backward and/or the 180° rotation transformations. We were concerned that fibers could be learned, which would have biased our speed/size analysis. However we observed that the fibers displayed at such a high speed in such different settings cannot be learned. The repetition experiments tend to show that there is no learning effect even when the same fiber is repeated 4 times in a row. Also the four tasks based on a same fiber were conducted at four different speeds and therefore helped to reduce bias between different speed conditions that could have arisen from diverse difficulty levels (we assume that a fiber exhibits the same difficulty when displayed in the 4 different settings).

Another limitation maybe arose from the choice of fibers that were present from the first to the last section of the 2000x2000x300 voxels stacks which represent volumes of 6 µm x 6 µm x 9 µm. The fibers might therefore have exhibited a bias towards evolving in the direction perpendicular to the imaging plane, thus appearing more like roundish structures and maybe easing the tracing. Nevertheless, though a subjective precaution, among the candidate fibers we found, we chose on purpose some that looked tortuous to us to compensate for this possible bias. Nonetheless, our results should be considered with some degree of caution, given the limited number of fibers which have been tested.

Navigation

Magnification

In a preliminary pilot experiment, we observed that accuracy tends to increase at high magnification factors. Therefore in a different user interface version we implemented an interactive zoom to let the user adapt the display to the size of the traced fiber. However we thought that this interactive zoom would have made the task too difficult to learn as the participants were present for only about an hour.

Browsing speed

For convenience we decided to simply let the participants browse at a predefined frame rate to focus on the speed and the size of the fibers for the first characterization of our eyegaze approach. In a real setting, these speed parameters could be made easily adjustable, namely accelerating and breaking as in a racing game could also be used to navigate through the data conveniently.

Eyegaze panning

Panning laterally in the x-y plane was performed with a joystick actuated with the left thumb. It could also be done with gaze input only with appropriate treatment of the gaze signal, so that whenever the fiber deviates from the center of the display, the field of view is translated to bring the fiber back to the center of the display. Such an implementation would be desirable in mobile devices to free the hands of the user.

Complex controllers
Improving navigation probably calls for more complex control mechanisms to manipulate the data in a more efficient way, see the virtual reality system from Cali et al. [10] for example. Special handheld controllers, wearable controllers or gesture sensing devices might provide seamless navigation through such complex datasets. However a tradeoff arises between the efficiency and complexity of the human machine interaction and the accessibility of the setup to large crowds.

Collaborative Annotation
Figure 8 convincingly shows a significant increase in accuracy when averaging the trace of a fiber across the 20 participants of the study, even without removing outliers. This improvement means that if a certain level of accuracy is desired, for example as requirement from an automated pipeline, more annotators can be recruited to trace independently the same fibers. As eye tracking is about to reach mass markets, crowdsourcing our proposed eyegaze approach with the aid of online tools appears feasible.

Semi-Automated Eyegaze Tracing
Some semi-automated pipelines require that a proofreader focuses on a given fiber, follows it while the data are browsed for a couple of sections, and finally indicates the new location of the fiber. Using eyegaze information during this procedure might add some noise to the final location of the fiber provided by the annotator, however the complete approximate path would also be recorded, which could also be a valuable input to the algorithms. In a similar fashion, [4] has developed a semi-automated method that currently takes as inputs manually generated skeletons of fibers. The SOPNET framework for neuron circuit reconstruction [15–17] also interestingly makes use of candidate 2-dimensional segmentations of the fibers and could integrate our eyegaze data as input. It will be interesting in the future to assess the minimal accuracy required by these pipelines and whether our eyegaze traced fibers can be fed to them.

From the point of view of the management of the tasks given to annotators, short segments that need to be traced could be distributed among different users or players, as currently implemented in the Eyewire game and other applications [4, 20, 27]. A possible very large scale implementation of that approach could be a login procedure for new generation wearable glasses [35] during which the user has to foveate on a fiber across a few sections while his gaze is recorded. Such login procedure could constitute a new generation of recaptchas [1] with a currently unsolved complex computer vision problem that would immediately receive a great attention from the machine vision community, maybe leading to a resolution faster than without this publicity.

General Applications
The eyegaze tracing approach might be suitable for any visual data in which spatial or temporal trajectories have to be drawn: tracing of tubular objects (neurons, vasculature) in various microscopy modalities, tracking of objects over time (dividing cells, growing neurons, interacting animals, evolving particles in a gas, vehicles and humans in surveillance imagery). Automated tracking or guidance of fast moving or occluded military targets such as soldiers, vehicles or missiles could also be enhanced with gaze input.

We think that our application in itself could also be seen as a novel contribution to the field of human machine interaction as to our knowledge, it uniquely (apart from games) challenges individuals with complex tasks at an unprecedentedly high temporal rate, in some way similar to a trained pianist hitting more than 10 keys per second. Complex high throughput human computer interaction systems may not have appeared yet because the applications were missing.

Future Work
In other tasks of the experiment not analyzed in this article, participants were instructed to press a button whenever the currently traced fiber was splitting into two fibers or was merging with another one. In future work the collaborative detection of branches or objects of interest such as synaptic contacts between fibers might be achieved to create wiring diagrams of the neuroanatomical networks.

The current most promising way to scale up this approach to the analysis of large volumes of electron microscopy imagery of brain tissue would be to feed semi-automated pipelines [4, 17] with eyegaze-traced skeletons.

CONCLUSION
The analysis of increasingly large and complex data requires not only the improvement of automated methods such as machine learning but also new ways for individuals to visualize and manipulate them, making the link between the data and the automated algorithms.

In this paper we designed and implemented a novel image annotation method for the analysis of large volumetric imagery of brain tissue. By displaying dynamically the data, we enabled the readout of the decisions of the individuals directly at the earliest possible sense: the eyegaze. We performed a participant experiment to validate the approach and showed acceptable accuracy during fast visualization of the data. We also showed that our approach is scalable to be used by crowds of novice users, making our approach a good candidate for analyzing increasingly large datasets.

ACKNOWLEDGMENTS
We thank the openconnectome project, the Lichtman laboratory for making the data available and the participants. We thank Andrew Duchowski and Bart Knijnenburg for comments.

REFERENCES
1. Luis von Ahn, Benjamin Maurer, Colin McMillen, David Abraham, and Manuel Blum. 2008. reCAPTCHA: human-based character recognition via Web security measures. *Science (New York, N.Y.)* 321: 1465–1468. http://doi.org/10.1126/science.1160379

2. Aaron Bangor, Philip Kortum, and James Miller. 2009. Determining what individual SUS scores mean: Adding an adjective rating scale. *Journal of usability studies* 4, 3: 114–123.

3. Kenan Bektas, Arzu Cöltekin, Jens Krüger, and Andrew T Duchowski. 2015. A Testbed Combining Visual Perception Models for Geographic Gaze Contingent Displays. *https://diglib.eg.org/handle/10.2312/eurovisshort.20151127.067-071.*

4. Manuel Berning, Kevin M. Boergens, and Moritz Helmstaedter. 2015. SegEM: Efficient Image Analysis for High-Resolution Connectomics. *Neuron* 87, 6: 1193–1206. http://doi.org/10.1016/j.neuron.2015.09.003

5. Davi D Bock, Wei-Chung Allen Lee, Aaron M Kerlin, et al. 2011. Network anatomy and in vivo physiology of visual cortical neurons. *Nature* 471, 7337: 177–182. http://doi.org/10.1038/nature09802

6. Kevin L Briggman, Moritz Helmstaedter, and Winfried Denk. 2011. Wiring specificity in the direction-selectivity circuit of the retina. *Nature* 471, 7337: 183–188. Retrieved from http://dx.doi.org/10.1038/nature09818

7. John Brooke. 1996. SUS-A quick and dirty usability scale. *Usability evaluation in industry* 189: 194.

8. Daniel J Bumbarger, Metta Riebesell, Christian Rödelsperger, and Ralf J Sommer. 2013. System-wide rewiring underlies behavioral differences in predatory and bacterial-feeding nematodes. *Cell* 152, 1-2: 109–19. http://doi.org/10.1016/j.cell.2012.12.013

9. Randal Burns, William Gray Roncal, Dean Kleissas, et al. 2013. The Open Connectome Project Data Cluster: Scalable Analysis and Vision for High-Throughput Neuroscience. *International Conference on Scientific and Statistical Database Management*: 1–11. http://doi.org/10.1145/2484838.2484870

10. Corrado Calì, Jumana Baghabra, Daniya J Boges, et al. 2015. Three-dimensional immersive virtual reality for studying cellular compartments in 3D models from EM preparations of neural tissues. *Journal of Comparative Neurology*: n/a–n/a. http://doi.org/10.1002/cne.23852

11. K R Cave and N P Bichot. 1999. Visuospatial attention: beyond a spotlight model. *Psychonomic bulletin & review* 6, 2: 204–223.

12. Eyewire. 2014. *Reconstructing a Neuron in 3D.* Retrieved from https://www.youtube.com/watch?v=noDx7TmMr8Q

13. Ribel Fares, Shaomin Fang, and Oleg Komogortsev. 2013. Can we beat the mouse with MAGIC? *Proceedings of the SIGCHI Conference on Human Factors in Computing Systems - CHI '13*: 1387. http://doi.org/10.1145/2470654.2466183

14. P M Fitts. 1992. The information capacity of the human motor system in controlling the amplitude of movement. 1954. *Journal of experimental psychology. General* 121, 3: 262–269.

15. Jan Funke, Bjoern Andres, Fred a. Hamprecht, Albert Cardona, and Matthew Cook. 2012. Efficient automatic 3D-reconstruction of branching neurons from em data. *Proceedings of the IEEE Computer Society Conference on Computer Vision and Pattern Recognition*: 1004–1011. http://doi.org/10.1109/CVPR.2012.6247777

16. Jan Funke, Björn Andres, Fred Hamprecht, Albert Cardona, and Matthew Cook. 2011. Multi-Hypothesis CRF-Segmentation of Neural Tissue in Anisotropic EM Volumes. i: 1–8. Retrieved from http://arxiv.org/abs/1109.2449

17. Jan Funke, Julien N P Martel, Stephan Gerhard, and Bjoern Andres. 2014. Candidate Sampling for Neuron Reconstruction from Anisotropic Electron Microscopy Volumes. *MICCAI Supplement*, 1: 0–5. http://doi.org/10.1007/978-3-319-10404-1_3

18. Wilson S Geisler and Lawrence K Cormack. 2011. Models of overt attention. In *The Oxford handbook of eye movements*. 439–454. http://doi.org/10.1093/oxfordhb/9780199539789.013.0024

19. Daniel Haehn, Seymour Knowles-barley, Mike Roberts, et al. 2014. Design and Evaluation of Interactive Proofreading Tools for Connectomics. http://doi.org/10.1109/TVCG.2014.2346371

20. Moritz Helmstaedter, Kevin L Briggman, and Winfried Denk. 2011. High-accuracy neurite reconstruction for high-throughput neuroanatomy. *Nature neuroscience* 14, 8: 1081–1088. http://doi.org/10.1038/nn.2868

21. Moritz Helmstaedter, Kevin L Briggman, and Winfried Denk. 2011. High-accuracy neurite reconstruction for high-throughput neuroanatomy. *Nat Neurosci* 14, 8: 1081–1088. http://doi.org/10.1038/nn.2868

22. Moritz Helmstaedter, Kevin L Briggman, Srinivas C Turaga, Viren Jain, H Sebastian Seung, and Winfried Denk. 2013. Connectomic reconstruction of the inner plexiform layer in the mouse retina. *Nature* 500, 7461: 168–74. http://doi.org/10.1038/nature12346

23. Moritz Helmstaedter and Partha P Mitra. 2012. Computational methods and challenges for large-scale circuit mapping. *Curr Opin Neurobiol* 22, 1: 162–169. http://doi.org/10.1016/j.conb.2011.11.010

24. V Jain, J F Murray, F Roth, et al. 2007. Supervised Learning of Image Restoration with Convolutional Networks. *Computer Vision, 2007. ICCV 2007. IEEE 11th International Conference on*, 1–8. http://doi.org/10.1109/ICCV.2007.4408909

25. Viren Jain, H Sebastian Seung, and Srinivas C Turaga. 2010. Machines that learn to segment images: a crucial technology for connectomics. *Curr Opin Neurobiol* 20, 5: 653–666. http://doi.org/10.1016/j.conb.2010.07.004

26. Narayanan Kasthuri, Kenneth Jeffrey Hayworth, Daniel Raimund Berger, et al. 2015. Saturated Reconstruction of a Volume of Neocortex. *Cell* 162: 648–661. http://doi.org/10.1016/j.cell.2015.06.054

27. Jinseop S. Kim, Matthew J. Greene, Aleksandar Zlateski, et al. 2014. Space–time wiring specificity supports direction selectivity in the retina. *Nature*, 4. http://doi.org/10.1038/nature13240

28. Manu Kumar, Andreas Paepcke, and Terry Winograd. 2007. EyePoint: practical pointing and selection using gaze and keyboard. *Proceedings of the SIGCHI conference on Human factors in computing systems*, 430. http://doi.org/10.1145/1240624.1240692

29. Jeff William Lichtman. 2014. *Brain Connectomics?* Retrieved from https://www.youtube.com/watch?v=2QVy0n_rdBI

30. Julio C Mateo. 2008. Gaze Beats Mouse : Hands-free Selection by Combining Gaze and EMG. *Chi Ea*: 3039–3044. http://doi.org/10.1145/1358628.1358804

31. Atsuo Murata. 2006. Eye-Gaze Input Versus Mouse: Cursor Control as a Function of Age. *International Journal of Human-Computer Interaction* 21, 1: 1–14. http://doi.org/10.1207/s15327590ijhc2101_1

32. Marta Pallotto, Paul V Watkins, Boma Fubara, Joshua H Singer, and Kevin L Briggman. 2015. Extracellular space preservation aids the connectomic analysis of neural circuits. *eLife*. http://doi.org/10.7554/eLife.08206

33. Stephen M Plaza, Louis K Scheffer, and Dmitri B Chklovskii. 2014. Toward large-scale connectome reconstructions. *Current opinion in neurobiology* 25C: 201–210. http://doi.org/10.1016/j.conb.2014.01.019

34. M I Posner, C R Snyder, and B J Davidson. 1980. Attention and the detection of signals. *Journal of experimental psychology* 109, 2: 160–174.

35. H S Raffle, A Wong, and R Geiss. 2012. Unlocking a screen using eye tracking information.

36. Stephan Saalfeld, Albert Cardona, Volker Hartenstein, and Pavel Tomančák. 2009. CATMAID: Collaborative annotation toolkit for massive amounts of image data. *Bioinformatics* 25, 15: 1984–1986. http://doi.org/10.1093/bioinformatics/btp266

37. M. Sadeghi, G. Tien, G. Hamarneh, and Ms Atkins. 2009. Hands-free interactive image segmentation using eyegaze. *Proc. of SPIE Vol* 7260: 72601H–1. http://doi.org/10.1117/12.813452

38. Johannes Schindelin, Ignacio Arganda-Carreras, Erwin Frise, et al. 2012. Fiji: an open-source platform for biological-image analysis. *Nature Methods* 9, 7: 676–682. http://doi.org/10.1038/nmeth.2019

39. Linda E. Sibert and Robert J. K. Jacob. 2000. Evaluation of eye gaze interaction. *Proc. CHI* 2, 1: 281–288. http://doi.org/10.1145/332040.332445

40. Sophie Stellmach and Raimund Dachselt. 2012. Look & Touch : Gaze-supported Target Acquisition. 2981–2990. http://doi.org/10.1145/2207676.2208709

41. Sophie Stellmach, Sebastian Stober, Andreas Nürnberger, and Raimund Dachselt. 2011. Designing gaze-supported multimodal interactions for the exploration of large image collections. *Proceedings of the 1st Conference on Novel Gaze-Controlled Applications - NGCA '11*: 1–8. http://doi.org/10.1145/1983302.1983303

42. Shin-ya Takemura, Arjun Bharioke, Zhiyuan Lu, et al. 2013. A visual motion detection circuit suggested by Drosophila connectomics. *Nature* 500, 7461: 175–181. Retrieved from http://dx.doi.org/10.1038/nature12450

43. Shin-ya Takemura, Arjun Bharioke, Zhiyuan Lu, et al. 2013. A visual motion detection circuit suggested by Drosophila connectomics. *Nature* 500, 7461: 175–81. http://doi.org/10.1038/nature12450

44. Srinivas C Turaga, Joseph F Murray, Viren Jain, et al. 2010. Convolutional networks can learn to generate affinity graphs for image segmentation. *Neural Comput.* 22, 2: 511–538. http://doi.org/http://dx.doi.org/10.1162/neco.2009.10-08-881

45. Shumin Zhai, Carlos Morimoto, and Steven Ihde. 1999. Manual and gaze input cascaded (MAGIC) pointing. *Proceedings of the SIGCHI conference on Human factors in computing systems the CHI is the limit CHI 99*: 246–253. http://doi.org/10.1145/302979.303053

46. Eyewire A Game To Map The Brain. Retrieved from https://eyewire.org

The Bicycle Barometer: Design and Evaluation of Cyclist-Specific Interaction for a Public Display

Sandy Claes
Research[x]Design
KU Leuven
sandy.claes@kuleuven.be

Karin Slegers
CUO
KU Leuven/ iMinds
karin.slegers@kuleuven.be

Andrew Vande Moere
Research[x]Design
KU Leuven
andrew.vandemoere@kuleuven.be

Figure 1. Cyclist confirms personal opinion with a button press, located on a handrail (left); two cyclists, both at location SUB (middle); and the polling question shown on the LED display at location URB (right).

ABSTRACT
As cycling is increasingly promoted as an environment-friendly, cheap and even fast alternative, there exists an increasing need to civically involve the potentially engaged and opinionated user group of cyclists. Therefore, we designed and evaluated *Bicycle Barometer*, an interactive bicycle count display that gathers the opinions from cyclists and conveys real-time, multi-dimensional data to them regarding cycling behavior. Our user-centered design process focused on optimizing the user experience by comparing several alternative cyclist-specific interaction designs, which resulted in the combination of a pressure sensitive floor mat, push button and low-resolution LED display. An in-the-wild evaluation study resulted in a set of design recommendations for cyclist-specific interaction, providing concrete insights into how a specifically targeted interaction method for public display is able to afford engagement and enthusiasm from a particular target audience.

Author Keywords
Urban visualization; public polling; citizen participation; cyclist-specific interaction; in the wild, bicycle HCI

CHI'16, May 07 - 12, 2016, San Jose, CA, USA

ACM 978-1-4503-3362-7/16/05···$15.00
DOI: http://dx.doi.org/10.1145/2858036.2858429

ACM Classification Keywords
H.5.m. Information interfaces and presentation (e.g., HCI): Miscellaneous

INTRODUCTION
Our cities are increasingly permeated by different forms of sensing and monitoring technology, offering new opportunities for overlaying the physical space with a digital world of data. Within the context of smart cities, it has been hypothesized that this digital, real-time lens will allow us to tackle various contemporary urban challenges, such as traffic congestion, scarcity of energy or cultural diversity [10]. These emerging data sources also provide novel opportunities to inform citizens more effectively, such as how their collective activities cause (or may help solve) these urban challenges, with the ultimate goal to nudge their behavior to more sustainable alternatives. Within this context, research efforts on urban visualization aim to make such urban data more accessible and actionable by communicating this data situated within the urban environment itself [37], in order to encourage citizens to reflect upon their own environment [16] or actively participate in civic discussions [16, 35]. A bicycle count display (e.g. [7]) forms a particularly intriguing example of urban visualization, as it captures and conveys simple, quantitative information within the situated setting of the city. Moreover, the presence of a bicycle count display acknowledges and reinforces a sense of belonging for a particular (cyclist) community [9]. Most interactive, public display installations (e.g. [34, 36]) specifically target pedestrians, which however form only a particular subset of a typical urban population. We thus believe that cyclists to date are often overlooked as engaged citizens, as well as potential HCI users. Moreover, as cycling has been

increasingly promoted as being instrumental to help solve modern urban mobility issues [22], this target group is increasing and quickly gaining civic importance.

We therefore investigated a novel interaction design for a bicycle count display that is able to to convey richer forms of information and gather qualitative data from cyclists. Within this challenge, we investigated aspects of usefulness and usability, including the ergonomic efficient and playful facilitation of the input, as well as the insight generating capacities of the output media. As one of the first HCI studies to explore interactive public displays specifically targeting cyclists, our research questions are exploratory in nature:

- RQ1 (input): How can cyclists efficiently participate in public polling? With sub-RQ1a: What is impact of several types of interaction design? And sub-RQ1b: What is the impact of context, such as location?
- RQ2 (output): How can cyclists be informed by an urban visualization? With sub-RQ2a: How to communicate information with public displays to fast-moving users? And sub-RQ2b: How to generate insights on the displayed information?

By describing our rationale during the user-centered design process, and evaluating how people engaged with the hi-fidelity prototype in a real world setting, this paper provides insight in how well-specified and limited forms of interaction encourages according community members to civically participate. Specific attention was given to guide cyclists through successive phases of engagement. The design was constrained by realistic demands, such as low-resolution, yet affordable and robust input and output devices.

RELATED WORK

Interaction in public environments

Interaction with public displays typically occurs by pedestrians, facilitated via touch screens [17], gestures [36] or by the use of personal devices such as smartphones [27]. However, public displays are often faced by 'interaction blindness', i.e. passers-by often do not recognize their interactive capacities [24], while smartphone applications rely on less opportunistic and more dedicated ways of considering or commencing engagement. More contextual ways of public interaction have been explored, such as blending elements of the built environment with public polling (e.g. [16]), deploying a large screen for full-body interaction [13], adding tangible elements (e.g. [4]), or placing other curiosity-triggering elements [14]. For instance, interacting with one's feet by means of an interactive floor [29] or floor-based buttons [34] have a low-threshold to engagement, and makes civic participation by pedestrians more effortless, both mentally as physically.

Cyclist-specific interaction

Most interactive applications targeting cyclists focus on aiding way-finding or creating personal experiences via smartphone applications (e.g. [25, 26]). Efforts to integrate the physical environment in the interaction experience include a bike-mounted projection that displays navigational information on the ground [6] or - when cycling in group - a display that is mounted on the back of a bicycle helmet conveying health information to following cyclists [39]. Integrated displays, such as t-shirts with wearable flexible displays [19] and projectors integrated in bicycle seats that display unto clothing [32] are potentially useful for public information sharing on bicycles.

Another range of cyclist-specific interaction modalities exemplify how the environment can act as the information carrier, such as a bicycle tunnel with an app-based adjustable LED lightning schema [1], or a display that asks passers-by questions like *"which bird do you hear?"* above the entrance, and displaying the correct answer at the exit [33]. Both tunnel installations aim for cyclists to feel safer and at ease. In turn, *Bicycle Counts* creates a public experience via a public projection that represents each passing cyclist in terms of individual and collective financial savings [2]. Dedicated polling systems exist that specifically target cyclists, such as by allowing passers-by to answer a survey question through riding on the appropriate 'yes' or 'no' cycle path [38].

DESIGN

For this study, we collaborated with the civic government of Leuven, a mid-sized city in Belgium, who expressed the goal to invest in a mobile bicycle count display.

Design Requirements

In spite of not yet having an appropriate way of displaying any form of public feedback, the local government already utilizes numerous bicycle counter devices underneath several local cycle paths. These devices continuously capture data such as the number of passing cyclists, the speed of passing cyclists, the time and date they passed, the type of their bicycles (e.g. child bicycle, adult bicycle or motorized bicycle), precipitation, and outdoor temperature. Due to the richness of the available data, we specifically aimed to design for ways to display more than simple statistical facts to cyclists (e.g. number of cyclists passing by), allowing for deeper forms of insight generation. In addition, we wished to contextualize the available quantitative data by exploring how qualitative opinions could be collected from the cyclists themselves. As the combination of both user input and output/feedback requires several physical and perceptual activities, we chose to target cyclists when they stand still, such as at a traffic light or an intersection. As a final design goal, we aimed to design a system that was playful and fun to use, yet still realistic, safe, affordable and easily deployable at diverse locations, hereby noting the required robust nature of urban infrastructure. Accordingly, we quickly disregarded the notion of higher resolution LCD or LED displays, as well as touch-enabled displays.

Figure 2. Footrest: physical buttons (left) versus non-physical buttons (right).

The local government proposed additional requirements, i.e. being inexpensive while also being mobile (so that it could be placed at various frequented locations), yet be weather- and vandalism-proof (so that it could be left unsupervised for longer periods of time). Furthermore, the bicycle counter display should be legible for multiple cyclists (and other passers-by) at once, both close-by as from a distance, in order to warrant an accessible and public character.

INPUT: EVALUATING INTERACTION ALTERNATIVES

We introduce *Bicycle Barometer*, which is based on a novel interaction method to vote and operate a public, informative display. The construction and design of the input interaction method followed a three-phased user-centered, iterative design approach consisting of: 1) field observations that inspired two low-fidelity input device mockups; 2) the design and evaluation of low-tech prototypes of three interaction alternatives; and 3) the comparative evaluation of the ideal interaction methods to select the most effective.

1. Exploratory interaction design study

In order to assure our system would be perceived as unobtrusive, we conducted an ethnographic pre-study to reveal how cyclists typically behave during waiting situations. During two consecutive hours (i.e. noon, 11am-1pm on a Wednesday), one researcher observed a busy, 4-armed intersection at the edge of the city. Of the 152 observed cyclists, we noticed how 62 (41%) cyclists used the raised curb to rest their feet. Few individuals (5) grabbed a traffic sign attached to the traffic light to lean on while their feet stayed on the pedals, and a single individual balanced his bike during the entire waiting time. This behavior was different for those not positioned at prime, frontal positions, as less or no physical supports like curbs were available further away from the crossing. To allow cyclists to likewise exploit a physical structure to lean on, we inspired our physical design on existing cyclist-specific urban furniture, such as a footrest (e.g. [5]) or a traffic light handle (e.g. [11]).

Accordingly, we evaluated a low-fidelity mockup of an interactive footrest and an interactive handrail, constructed out of materials such as wood and foam. Small evaluation studies with 24 volunteering participants captured the influence of the shape, size and height on the balance, comfort and support while people interacted. We noticed how many cyclists liked to keep going back and forth with their bicycle while finding support via the handrail or footrest. As a result, we were inspired to design a third interaction method, which tracks the relative front wheel position of a bicycle on a pressure-sensitive floor mat.

2. Low-tech prototypes

For each of the three chosen interaction methods, we integrated an identical feedback method that revealed a clear and immediate confirmation of one's interaction. We built two low-tech prototype alternatives for each of the three interaction methods, and evaluated them individually in a real world setup, i.e. a cycle path on a university campus. 30 volunteering cyclists were recruited per interaction method, and invited on the spot. The feedback was simulated through a Wizard-of-Oz setup: participants selected and confirmed their personal response (i.e. a 5-point agreement scale) for a particular question that was displayed on a common LCD screen, e.g. *"Are there sufficient parking lots for bicycles?"* Afterwards, participants answered a short semi-structured interview, based on four questions of the NASA task load index [12] in order to measure the physical load and comfort, for both the polling as the feedback features.

Footrest. We compared the user experience of a physical button versus a touch sensitive footrest, both operated with a single foot (Fig. 2). The use of a footrest for interaction implies that a cyclist needs to support both body and bicycle with a foot at all times. While pressing a physical button with a foot might be less comfortable than touching a platform, a physical button provides some form of direct feedback (e.g. the shifting movement of the button) that does not require any other external feedback for confirmation, like sound, vibration or a visual alert. Most participants did not rate the footrest button as comfortable because they needed to lift their foot to press, causing some instances of instability. The non-physical footrest buttons were also rated as uncomfortable because participants had to switch their gaze from their feet up to the display to notice the visual feedback.

Handrail. We preferred to evaluate a horizontally positioned bar support as it is more flexible to temporally place in the environment than a vertical one. The bar was equipped with physical buttons in order to facilitate easily perceivable tangible feedback. The two prototypes compared large, hand-sized buttons versus

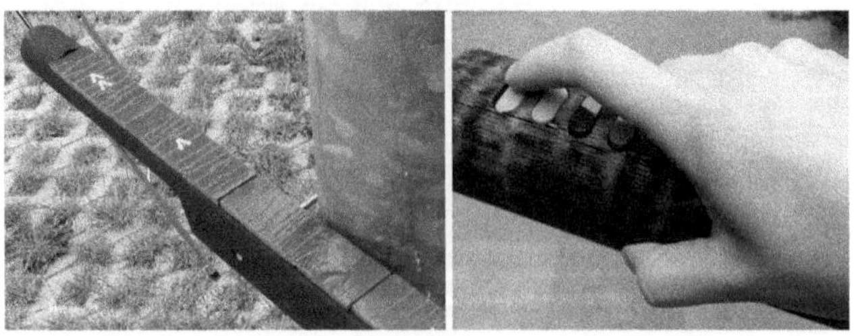

Figure 3. Handrail: large buttons (left) versus small buttons (right).

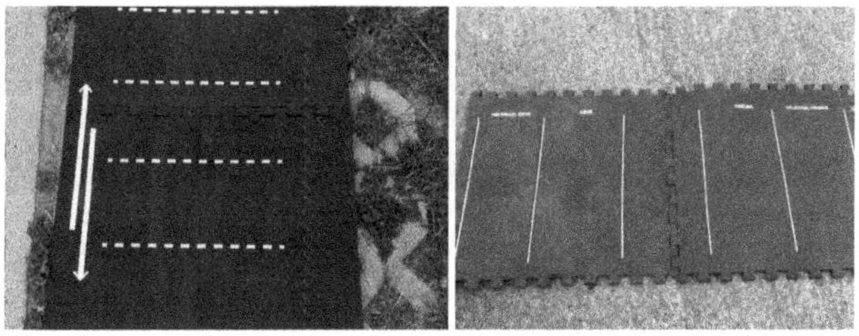

Figure 4. Floor mat: horizontal layout (left) versus vertical layout (right).

small, finger-scaled physical buttons (Fig. 3). Most participants pressed the large buttons with one finger, denying support with the rest of the hand at that time. All the small buttons were in reach of the pointing finger while supporting the rest of the hand at all times, which was also rated as most comfortable.

Floor Mat. We designed two floor mat layouts. One floor mat featured a vertical layout, allowing a form of up-and-down 'scrolling' like a window scrollbar (Fig. 4, left). In turn, a horizontal layout framed each answer in a separate compartment (Fig. 4, right) that forced cyclists to determine the desired wheel position before entering the mat, or reposition the wheel by first putting both feet on the ground.

Like the footrest, gazing up and down from the mat to the display for feedback was not rated comfortable for both layout alternatives. The horizontal layout provided more certainty about the selection of their response, while selecting and interacting with the vertical layout was considered playful and fun. The maximal, interactive vertical zone of the floor mat is 60cm, as it is not comfortable when a bicycle wheel needs to bridge more space.

3. Combined interaction methods

The three most promising interaction alternatives (handrail with small buttons, footrest with non-physical buttons and floor mat with vertical layout) were also evaluated in parallel, all integrated in a single system (see Figure 6). Again, 30 coincidental passing cyclists were stopped and asked to participate. After testing one alternative, they were asked to fill in a survey based on 4 questions of the NASA task load index to measure physical load and ergonomics [12]. After testing all remaining interaction methods, they were invited to give a preference rating in terms of user experience, fun and attractiveness, and were administered a semi-structured interview to further explain their replies.

Overall, the footrest scored lowest in all preference ratings. The handrail was considered most comfortable and provided most reliable feedback. The floor mat was rated as most fun and most attractive in appearance. Furthermore, the floor was considered to specifically accommodate the use of a bicycle, which was mentioned as a potential motivation for use.

OUTPUT: CO-DESIGNING THE INFORMATION DISPLAY

To include the cyclists' informational needs in the design of the output, we organized a 2-hour co-design workshop with 9 participants (3 female, mean age: 35, SD: 5), consisting of eight cyclists and one local government representative. The workshop structure was based on a mapping method [15], which was divided into three successive phases: 1) the kind of information cyclists want to be informed about in the urban environment; 2) types of data that cyclists consider relevant; and 3) types of visualization that are can be used to present the statistical data in comprehensible ways.

Figure 5. Participant is adding a card sticker with a type of data in the workshop.

The discussions revealed that cyclists did not want to become aware of distinct facts and statistics, but were rather interested in receiving contextual information and stories, specifically targeting their personal situation and potentially connecting this to other meaningful trends. The subsequent co-design of data-driven stories then focused on using common frustrations as starting points for engaging cyclists to answer specific questions in public. We deployed the card sorting technique to relate existing frustrations to what is typically captured in existing data sources. Lastly, we used card sorting again to discuss possible visualization techniques that combine the accessible style of infographics (i.e. pictograms, emoticons), with more '*trustworthy*' bar and line graph diagrams (see Figure 6).

IMPLEMENTATION

Based on the insights from our exploratory design studies described above, we developed a working, hi-fidelity prototype. We selected the floor mat (vertical layout) as the main interaction method to browse between possible poll answers. As the floor method did not provide intuitive or efficient ways of confirming one's vote, we decided to keep one button on the handrail as the interaction method for confirming the interaction (e.g. submitting the vote) while also facilitating physical support (see Figure 9 for an overview of the prototype set up). Based on the input from the workshop, we selected the provocative frustration *"Cyclist-terrorists are a burden"*. Inspired by actual quantitative data from the existing bicycle counters which we thus could visualize, we rephrased it into an open-ended question, i.e. *"What do you think of fast cyclists?"*. The system allows passing cyclists to vote by selecting one out of five possible smiley faces, ranging from very unhappy to

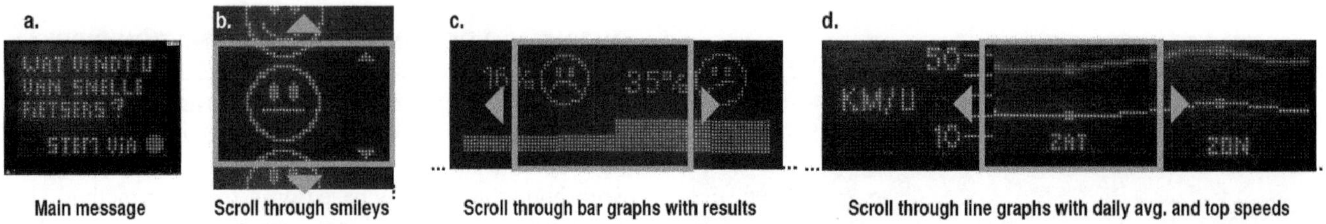

Figure 6. Screen shots of the narrative flow on the LED display: main message "*What do you think of fast cyclists? Vote with [red dot]*" (a), selection of smiley faces (b), results as a rolling bar graph (d) and average versus top speed in km/h ("*Km/u*") on Saturday ("*ZAT*") and Sunday ("*ZON*"), presented as a rolling line graph (d).

very happy. After the poll, the system then continues with a data-driven story, which encourages cyclists to browse through past polling results. Finally, the system offers to explore a specific yet relevant data set captured by the bicycle count system, i.e. the top and average speed per day.

Constrained by the already mentioned technical and practical requirements, we chose to integrate a small, low-resolution LED display as output device (resolution of 32x46px, 6mm pixel pitch, and sized 24x38cm). Such small and light display can be easily transported and installed, is reasonably affordable, robust and weather resistant, and can potentially run on solar energy. Next to its excellent contrast even in very bright, outdoor circumstances, a LED display resembles typical urban furniture like common digital traffic signs and does not appear as desirable as a common hi-res LCD display to be potentially stolen or vandalized. However, its extreme low-resolution limited the potential output to minimalistic graphics or four lines of (readable) text. We therefore custom-designed the textual characters, allowing approximately 13 characters per line. Furthermore, as communicating information-dense stories on a low-resolution output is a challenge [23], we custom designed each visualization as one large horizontally stretched graph of which the display only shows a specific, cropped fragment (see Figure 6). The cyclist can then horizontally scroll through the graph to understand the full overview.

The narrative flow

The display guided the cyclist through a narrative flow, as illustrated in Figure 9. It was structured as an interactive slideshow structure, one of the three possible narrative structures of narrative visualization [31]. Accordingly, the sequence of low-resolution visualization fragments could be explored both backwards or forwards by moving one's bicycle wheel respectively towards the back, or the front, of the interactive floor mat. To avoid obvious usability issues, the slides sequence continued in an endless loop. Moving the bicycle wheel to the middle of the mat halted this sequence, and a specific slide could be 'confirmed' or 'selected' by pressing the button on the handrail. More detailed instructions were provided in pictograms right below the display.

To avoid that fast-riding cyclists would not notice the installation in time, we extended the display-driven narrative flow with a physical '*teaser*' in the form of a wooden trestle that announced the installation by the engaging message: "*Cyclist, give your opinion!*". This teaser, located approx. 5 meters in front of the floor mat, thus functioned as a curiosity object [14], triggering cyclists to pay attention to the immediate environment. The second stage of the narrative flow consisted of the main displayed question and instructions, i.e. "*vote with [a red circle]*" referring to the red button (Fig. 6, a). Then, users could scroll through the five possible smiley faces (Fig. 6, b). After the polling, the overall polling results for each option were represented as one continuous bar chart (i.e. 5 vertical bars arranged horizontally) with percentile values, of which only a fragment is displayed (Fig. 6, c). Through the scrolling mechanism, visual comparisons between bars were made possible. The top and average speed data were represented as two rolling line graphs (Fig. 6, d) showing data from over a period of a week, and as such allowed comparisons between two data dimensions and time.

Technical and Physical Setup

The higher-fidelity prototype was built with off-the-shelf hardware parts. A *Raspberry Pi* was connected with the LED display via a standard HDMI to DVI input. An industry-grade push button was integrated in the wooden handrail (Fig. 1, left). The foam floor mat concealed two tracks, i.e. forward (fwd) and backward (bwd), with each track consisting of a series of three pressure sensitive zones in order to evenly distribute the sensors over the width of the floor (i.e. 60cm). On the software side, a set of custom programs was developed in Python to implement the appropriate interaction functionalities.

The physical setup was designed to be mobile yet sturdy, but sufficient for shorter-term evaluation study purposes. Obviously, longer-term deployments would require more robust renditions of similar components. A wooden trestle (120cm high) supported the LED display. The wooden construction of the handrail was 80cm long by 110cm high, and the floor mat was 60cm wide by 120cm long.

IN THE WILD STUDY

Bicycle Barometer was deployed during six days, and set up at two different types of locations: an intersection at 1) an urban area (URB); and 2) a suburban area (SUB) (see Figure 8 and Figure 11). Permission to use the public domain for the in-the-wild study was obtained by the local council beforehand in order to ensure the system would not

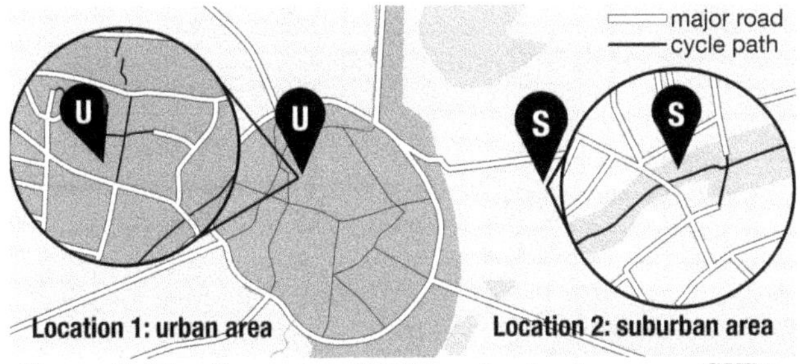

Figure 7. Situating urban (URB) and suburban area (SUB).

obstruct traffic or be removed by city cleaning services. At SUB, the *Bicycle Barometer* was deployed from Tuesday to Friday (8am – 6pm). We were not able to record any results on Thursday due to stormy weather conditions, making a total of three days. At URB, the installation was set up during two days, on a Wednesday and Friday (8am – 6pm), in order to capture data during comparable weekdays.

All evaluation data was collected via a mixed method approach, such as by: i) electronically logging every interaction (i.e. movements with wheel and button presses); ii) a hidden video camera; and iii) observations from one researcher who was present in the vicinity (hidden from sight) at all times. Cyclists were registered as male or female, and their age category was estimated. The behaviors of each passing cyclist were categorized according to the Passive, Active Engagement and Discovery (PACD) model [20]. Passive engagement comprised of glimpsing at the teaser or the display (e.g. turning head towards), or more *immersive forms of interaction* [20] such as reading while cycling (i.e. keeping one's head turned towards), or riding over the floor mat. Active engagement occurred when cyclists read in a more active way, such as when braking to facilitate reading, or *read 'n interact* (i.e. pressing the button but not confirming). As indicated on Figure 8, cyclists in the discovery phase were actively voting, browsed the polling results or explored the statistical data. Furthermore, we also noted at which moment of the narrative flow of the setup (see Figure 9), cyclists executed these behaviors.

In total, we interviewed 63 people. 53 semi-structured interviews were held with cyclists who engaged with the installation in some way or form (N=53, 27 Female, Mean age: 45, SD: 17), and 10 with cyclists who did not stop to interact (N=10, 3 Female, Mean age: 53).

After they turned their attention away from the *Bicycle Barometer* installation, we asked participants for demographic information (i.e. age, place of residence); the reasons that triggered them to stop and interact; how they experienced the interaction; and what they remembered of the content they had just explored. The latter question was explicitly formulated in a very broad way in order to encourage participants to report any kind of insight. The reported insights were categorized according to type of data used in the narrative. The insight depth was then scaled according to the insight reporting methodology [28]. This scale was divided in 3 subcategories of *insight depth*: 1) *factual*, a mere description of data values; 2) *interpretive*, the synthesis of data values with objective knowledge or an existing experience; and 3) *reflective*, which is similar to interpretative, yet contains some subjective, personal or emotional connotations. The electronic logs were analyzed according to the time between events, the number of button presses and when in the narrative flow they occurred.

RESULTS & DISCUSSION

Based upon the PACD model [20] we grouped the behaviors caused by *Bicycle Barometer* in different forms of engagement (see Figure 8) and according phases (see Figure 9). As our results show some overlap with previous research on pedestrian-centric public displays, our recommendations will focus on particular aspects that are relevant for cyclist-specific interaction.

1. Passive engagement

Only 13% of the passing cyclists ignored the *Bicycle Barometer* completely (see Figure 8). Interviews revealed how several cyclists (16 of 53) were particularly intrigued by the handrail and/or floor, which directed their attention to the display (e.g. *"I wanted to find out what this* [referring to the floor] *was doing here, so I looked at the display").*

The display seemed to be considered as a natural part of the built environment, as cyclists connected its physical manifestation to typical warning signs around schools or hospitals (e.g. *"At first, I thought the display was meant to make us aware of the dangerous situation here, and then I saw the other parts [referring to the handrail and floor]"*). Also the floor was considered unobtrusive, as 19 cyclists (10% of all passers-by) fluently rode over the floor as if it was intrinsic part of the cycle route. Fifteen cyclists of all passers-by riding over the floor glanced to the immediate response shown on the display, and almost half (47%, N=7) returned to the installation (e.g. *"I was surprised it responded when I rode over it, then I saw 'Cyclists' and I wanted to find out what it was about exactly").*

Design Recommendation: Past research has shown how interactivity cues like silhouettes [21] or tangible objects [14] can effectively lure pedestrians into interacting with a public display. However, as cyclists approach at various yet often faster speeds, more appropriate strategies to attract their attention should be designed. Therefore, a) both the display content and the interactive features offered should become evident in a quick glance. For instance, the use of 'interactive teasers' that react even upon a brief form of interaction (e.g. riding over the floor) seems to be able to sufficiently attract cyclists' attention. b) To alert cyclists who ride too fast or are otherwise distracted to be able to notice the purpose of the installation while riding, the purpose can be gradually announced, such as pictorial or short but readable messages on both teasers as display. Cyclists who become curious yet are still cautious can be potentially convinced by c) allowing low-thresholds to the

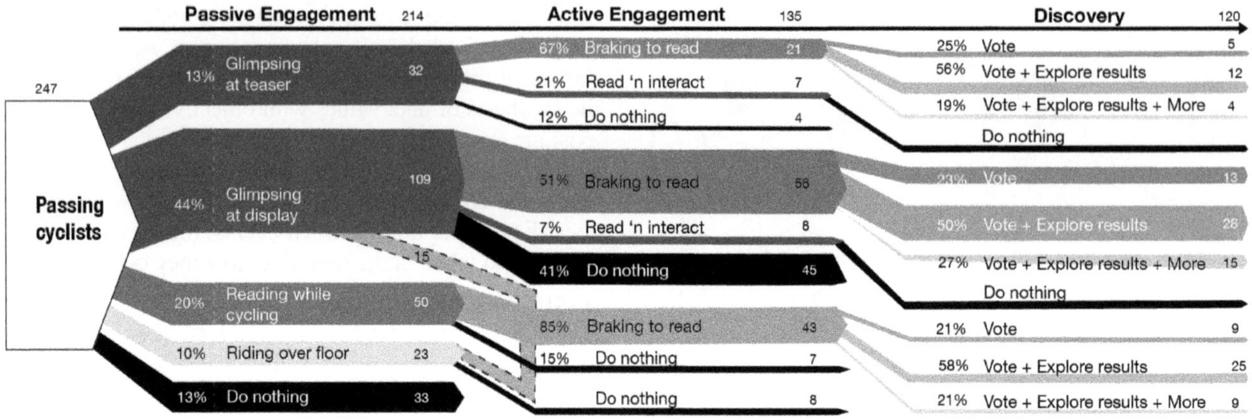

Figure 8. Distribution of the number of passing cyclists from passive over active engagement to discovery.

interaction that do not disturb their cycling activity. Cyclists can also be attracted because of the efficacy of interacting, such by d) optimizing the ergonomic usability so that they are not required to stop or dismount; and by e) designing the physical appearance so that it unmistakably and specifically targets cyclists. As cyclist-specific interfaces are very rare, some of these results might strongly correlate with the novelty effect. However, we believe that specific interfaces targeting clearly distinguishable user groups in the public domain brings powerful advantages, from solving obvious usability issues to calling upon the personal responsibility of belonging to a specific community.

2. Active engagement

21 of 33 cyclists who initially glanced at the teaser braked, slowed down to read the display and eventually stopped. We grouped these active engagement events in a *situational braking zone* (see Figure 9), in analogy with the landing zone for pedestrians [21]. Subsequently, these cyclists scanned the environment (e.g. "*In a blink I noticed a wooden trestle that said 'Cyclist,…', and then I noticed this bigger wooden 'thing'* [referring to the handrail] *and a screen with again 'cyclists' on it, which made me believe it was meant for me*"). Half of these cyclists (10) then approached the installation by getting off their bike and walking towards it, or by riding at a very slow speed towards the interactive floor. As all of these cyclists then decided to interact with the installation, we consider this behavior that disturbs the normal cycling flow not as unwanted, as it seems to accommodate those people who are more cautious in nature (e.g. "*I wanted to take a closer look at the installation but then I understood it"*). The other half continued riding directly towards the handrail and stopped on the floor. Accordingly, we define an *engagement braking zone* around the physical setup of the handrail, floor and display. Of those cyclists not noticing the teaser but only the display, 51% glanced at the display and slowed down and stopped in the *engagement braking zone* to read the question and vote. Interviews during the first two hours of the study at URB revealed how cyclists who noticed the teaser did not link its message to the display as they were distracted by the traffic situation. We thus relocated the teaser closer to the display.

Design Recommendation: Designers aim to balance teasing potential users and effectively guiding them to the ideal interaction entry point in the pedestrian landing zone [21]. For cyclists, this zone needs to be extended as seemingly unwanted effects like halting or dismounting prematurely can actually accommodate personal exploration strategies. Some persons initially require a *situational overview* whereas others have no issue with instantly *engaging* with an interface. In addition, the optimal placement of teasers depends on many contextual factors in the built environment, as teaser and setup should be interpreted as a single, consistent installation. Obstacles that break consistency (e.g. a passage, a garbage can) distract users from commencing or following the narrative flow. These teasers should therefore also be designed to complement the design language of the setup (i.e. use of same materials, color scheme, font, etc.).

3. Discovery

Although most cyclists in the active engagement phase (N=97) landed their bike next to the handrail to read, we observed cyclists (N=42, or 31%) who stopped closer to the display, with their rear wheel on the floor, and looking around to find the red button. Yet as all cyclists eventually grabbed the red button after reading the question, its purpose seemed to be clear. 15 cyclists pressed the red button purposefully to go to the second stage but did not select and confirm an opinion. Generally, we noticed most of these cyclists (N=13) to be elderly (age category: 65 y.). We interviewed 2 of them; they mentioned that they did not understand how to navigate further, even after they read instructions (e.g. "*I just did not get it! Aargh, probably I am too old to understand. I just gave up.*"). Although the digital divide might be an obvious reason for such interaction difficulties, many other elderly cyclists (N=34 > 65 y.) did succeed to select and confirm their vote. The other two cyclists that did not vote were teenagers (both 15 y.o.) who were not interested in the question (e.g. "*I wanted to see how it worked but I don't care about that question").*

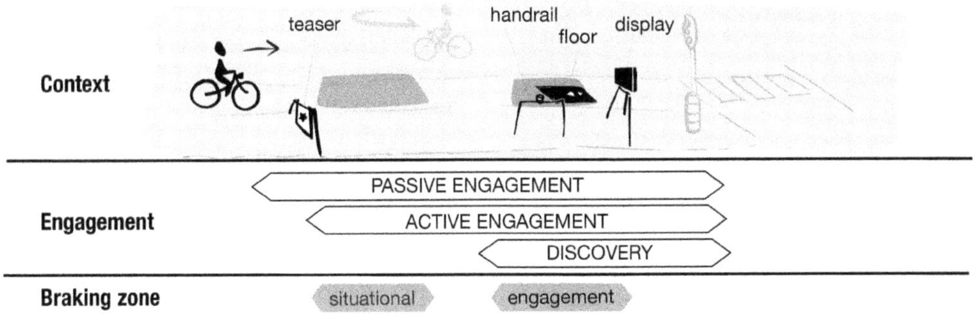

Figure 10. Setup of Bicycle Barometer in the context, and the physical distribution of the engagement phases and braking zones.

Design recommendation: As cyclists are seated on, or at least holding onto a bicycle when interacting, they make their participation noticeable, potentially causing social embarrassment [3]. We revealed that gradually introducing users to less-familiar interaction methods through the combined use of more familiar methods can be an strategy to overcome this issue. Although *Bicycle Barometer* had a specific bicycle-wheel interaction design by way of an interactive floor, the first affordance was often discovered via the more familiar physical button. As button presses were immediately followed by an on-screen response, users were confident the system worked, which empowered them to more challenging, less familiar interaction via the floor.

4. Cyclist-specific interaction

While the cyclists were engaged in reading the question and voting, the majority (58%) had both feet on the ground with one foot on each side of the bicycle (see also Figure 1, left and middle). Others (37%) stayed seated on their saddle and utilized the handrail support, while the rest (5%) stood next to their bike. The floor mat interaction seemed sufficiently intuitive to select the appropriate opinion. Although most cyclists (112 of 120) used both forward and backward floor motions to navigate around, a few participants (8 of 120) seemed unaware of the backward possibility and only used the forward motion (e.g. *"I missed the one I wanted to vote, so I had to go through all of them again [...], Oh, I didn't see you could go backward as well*").

Interacting via the bicycle wheel was considered exclusive for cyclists (*"I like that you had to do it with a wheel, specific for us - cyclists"),* which made some interviewed participants feel honored (e.g. "*It makes me feel privileged*"). Interaction with the wheel was considered fun (e.g. *"It made it feel like a computer game or something"),* and even when combined with the handrail, the interaction was found to be comfortable (e.g. "*comfortable that you can stay on your bike").* Some interviewed cyclists (N= 6) mentioned the specific design as a reason to participate (e.g. *"When I saw it was meant for us – cyclists - I had to try it*"). Despite the cyclist-oriented design, some pedestrians participated, of which we interviewed 5 persons (e.g. *"I am annoyed by fast cyclists too").* Although the pedestrians interacted in rather strange looking ways (i.e. dancing on the floor), they did not seem to mind the possible social embarrassment.

Design Recommendation: The use of interaction methods that target specific user groups allows for provoking curiosity, lowers the engagement barrier [30] and calls upon the sense of belonging to a community (see also design recommendation on passive engagement). Yet, it also seems to encourage subsequent, deeper engagement, such that some people might engage longer because they wish to explore the interaction method for itself. Even if such specific interaction methods might be less intuitive than more established alternatives, its specificity, exclusivity and playfulness helps to overcome apparent usability issues.

5. Encouraging participation

193 votes were registered in total, of which 73 were discarded for this research, e.g. because of too many consecutive button presses. More people voted 'unhappy' (N=35), with a close tie for 'neutral' (N=33). Overall, cyclists appear to be a more engaged audience than pedestrians, at least when the voting rate (i.e. amount of people that voted of all passers-by) of *Bicycle Barometer* (49% or 120 out of 247) is compared to a previous study on public polling displays (24,5%) [36]. Of those who voted, the majority (74%) also explored the data, at least the stage with the results (see 'Discovery' in Figure 8).

Most interviewed cyclists (29 of 53) voted because they cared about the subject matter (e.g. *"I believe fast cyclists are a problem, yes").* As such, they related their opinion to personal experiences (e.g. "*Once I did not see them coming and they scared me so much"),* or the location (e.g. "*Many cyclists just cross the street without stopping. That's so dangerous!").* Others (N=9) indicated to have voted because they were curious what would follow after the question was answered. Some (N=4) mentioned that they expected more explanation (e.g. *"I expected more context to the question"),* clarification on the definitions (N=3, e.g. *"What is meant with fast cyclists exactly? Do I count with my electric bicycle?"*), or the possibility to leave a more detailed reaction (N=1). Six cyclists indicated that a poll with smiley faces was not as nuanced as they desired.

19 cyclists only voted out of idealistic reasons, i.e. they wanted to support the polling initiative to signal the government that they appreciated the perceived interest in cyclists. As such, some of those cyclists (N=15) wanted to support the polling initiative to signal the government that

Figure 10. ***Bicycle Barometer*** **in urban area URB (left) and in the suburban area SUB (right).**

they appreciated the interest in cyclists (e.g. "*It's good that they* [local government] *ask our opinion, so I wanted to take part although I do not have really an opinion*"). Another example of idealistic participation was exemplified by an elderly pedestrian (Male, 74 y.o.), who stopped individual cyclists to convince them to vote: *"it is an important topic as the situation is often dangerous"*. Remarkably, he did not vote himself, as he felt *Bicycle Barometer* was only meant for cyclists.

Design Recommendation: Similarly to the appeal of urban visualization [37], public engagement seems not only to depend on the physical qualities of the interaction design but also on the relevancy of the content within a specific, situated context. Therefore, the main displayed message should be carefully formulated as a motivational point for interaction and reflection. One strategy is to include controversial topics [16] that are relevant yet provocative to the target user group. We also propose to use an open formulation, as this entices people to interact in order to unravel the true purpose or context of the question. This way, participants appropriate the question to their own experience, or feel sufficiently motivated to send a signal to those asking the question. However, including ambiguity might also turn polling results less representative, as voters might interpret the meaning differently.

6. Location depending contextual differences

More passing cyclists voted in the suburban area (SUB, 54%) than in the urban area (URB, 37%), although a similar amount of passing cyclists did nothing (13% SUB versus 15% URB). There may be several explanations for this behavior. For instance, the question might be perceived as more relevant or pertinent in SUB as it was located at a known dangerous intersection (e.g. *"I was not interested in the question displayed, so I did not respond. I wanted to give my opinion on the quality of the cycling paths, though")*. There might also exist a difference in the time that a cyclist has available: SUB cyclists generally plan longer trajectories and thus have less strict time constraints. Lastly, urban environments might be more distracting, and its occupants might be more inclined to ignore unknown visual stimuli.

Design Recommendation: The participation rate is impacted by objective parameters such as the built environment (i.e. suburb or urban), and more subjective parameters such as the contextual meaning of a location [29] (e.g. a dangerous intersection), or the relative time availability of the passers-by (e.g. SUB participants have more time). We therefore propose choosing locations in relation to longer trajectories, such as for commuting or recreation. Designers could also become familiar with the situated context through informal conversations with local inhabitants or authorities, and potentially exploit the discovered subjective meanings.

7. Exploring the urban visualization

Most cyclists who voted (93 of 120) also explored the subsequent visualization of the results. They seemed especially interested in discovering where 'their vote' was situated, as almost half (N=23) of the 53 interviewed participants were able to remember the percentile number of the most popular vote, and the percentile number of their choice. Participants reported making comparisons between the polling results, during which they made broad generalizations instead of recalling exact numerical values (e.g. "*more people voted unhappy than neutral*").

The subsequent option to explore the general data in the form of rolling line graphs seemed less popular. Although this feature was announced on the display (i.e. when the results were displayed) and on the instructions, people seemed eager to continue their trip and did not seem to notice the graphical option to commence exploring – (e.g. *"Oh, after I found out how other people voted I just left, I did not know there was more [...] But I wanted to move along anyway")*. Some cyclists (N=3) also explained that they disliked the way the data was represented because it was too difficult (e.g. "*It was something with a graph, but I do not understand that")*.

Cyclists who explored the line graph visualization (28 in total, but interviewed N=13) were able to extract insights, and interpreted them according to their personal opinion (e.g. *"On Sunday, we cycle much faster in general, I would expect the opposite.")* or situation (e.g. "*Wow! Top speed on Sunday was 50 km per hour? I can only get that when I cycle down from a hill")*. These insights also encouraged cyclists to nuance their opinions (e.g. an amateur road bike cyclist said *"When I see it in numbers, we cycle much, much faster than the average cyclist, more than double! However, I think there is space for both of us"*).

Design Recommendation: In public space, physically situating a display at a specific, context-rich location, e.g. positioning it on or nearby a bicycle path, forms a particular approach to nudge passers-by into personal sense-making [37]. Moreover, we also demonstrated how the specificity of the interaction design itself, e.g. accommodating people to manipulate their bicycles without needing to get off or stand down, further contributes to this sense-making process. In addition, our results show that most people were encouraged to interact further after leaving their vote. As some people were interested in knowing the overall polling results, while others wanted to discover more detailed information, it is advisable to design a particular interaction flow that 1) provides some gratification in terms of informing participants; and 2) allows for different information consumption behaviors; from browsing bite-sized facts to allowing more sophisticated analysis.

8. Social cyclist-specific interaction

Honeypot effects occurred in 18 occasions, although it was not obvious in terms of waiting behavior. We noticed two types of grouping attitudes: 1) in 12 occasions, one or more cyclists waited next to the floor mat (as illustrated in Figure 1, middle) on which the interacting cycling was standing; 2) in six occasions, cyclists formed a neat queue behind the interacting cyclist. During one of those occasions, a recreational cycling group of 13 people arrived, to whom the purpose of the installation was passed down verbally, This prompted five cyclists to wait in line in order to participate, while the other eight were grouped around them to wait and gaze at the display. We also observed that when cyclists stand next or behind each other, they needed to talk loudly to bridge the distance between them, which might be influenced by the physical dimensions of the bicycles. However, the physical dispersion of cyclists probably influenced their willingness to start a conversation. Groups discussed their opinion with each other (e.g. "*The problem is the speed of the cars" – "I don't agree with you on that"*) or were imagining solutions (e.g. *"They should install a bridge for us, than there is no problem")*. Furthermore, multi-user bicycle use afforded collaborative efforts. For instance, we observed cyclists with young children (e.g. on a child seat, in a cargo bike) who interacted together, i.e. an adult navigated via the floor while the child pressed the button (Figure 11).

Design Recommendation: When designing for a social interaction space around a public display [8], bicycles occupy more space than pedestrians. As a result, both the physical dimensions of the interaction space and the potential waiting line occupy a larger space than with more traditional public displays, potentially causing traffic obstructions. These physical constraints also limited spontaneous social interaction. Future work could explore collaborative possibilities of cyclist-specific interaction.

LIMITATIONS

Overall, identifying appropriate locations and receiving the permissions to undertake in the wild research in traffic-sensitive situations is a cumbersome undertaking, as it involves the joint agreement of many different authorities. Upholding security is of utmost importance, as any intervention in traffic potentially interferes with the personal wellbeing of participants. Therefore, as the performance of a public installation like *Bicycle Barometer* is influenced by the contextual situation existing in its immediate vicinity, benchmarking different interventions, comparing otherwise controlled conditions, or even reproducing results is potentially challenging. Moreover, even environmental factors like the physical availability of space, the type of neighborhood or the time of day need to be taken into account. Therefore, the reported percentages provide only general indications, in spite of the considerable large number of in-the-wild study participants.

Figure 11. Multi-user interaction at location SUB.

The choice of display technology may influence the results in terms of output qualities. For instance, our low-resolution LED display output was limited to basic visual mappings, which required additional interaction modalities (i.e. scrolling). Similarly, a high-resolution display may present more data in a glance.

FUTURE WORK: CIVICALLY INVOLVED CYCLISTS

Our results open up new opportunities to facilitate cyclists to become publically involved citizens who are better informed and able to participate in relevant civic debates. Involving the cyclist community in the generation of statements and questions causes more accessible and relevant debates [16], and cyclist-specific questions could be generated by bottom-up public participation projects as [18]. Alternatively, questions that are generated from a top-down perspective allow local governments to retrieve qualitative opinions in relation to the quantitative data they already capture, facilitating more informed forms of policy making. For instance, installations like the Bicycle Barometer could gather hyperlocal sentiments about potential planning alternatives, or clarify patterns within bicycle count data.

CONCLUSION

This study demonstrated the potential qualities of a cyclist-specific polling interface. More importantly, the participation rate in addition to the participant comments demonstrates the apparent societal demand for these kinds of public, interactive interfaces. We have shown how designing an interaction modality targeting a specific user group is able to overcome usability issues and instead generate sufficient engagement to participate. In addition, our public polling approach has demonstrated that when people are encouraged to vote, they also are sufficiently motivated to explore the relevant results and dive into insight-generating processes. As such, our research forms the evidence towards how new forms of interaction can target specific user groups to become involved citizens.

ACKNOWLEDGMENTS

We thank codewerken.be and Daan Wampers for the technical support.

REFERENCES

1. Ateliereen Architecten. 2015. Light-Artwork in Bicycle Tunnet at Rijnwijlpad. Artwork. Retrieved September 12, 2015 from http://www.ateliereen.nl/projecten/rijnwaalpad.html.
2. Arlene Birt. 2012. Bicycling Counts. Artwork. Retrieved September 12, 2015 from http://backgroundstories.com/portfolio-item/bicycling-counts/.
3. Harry Brignull and Yvonne Rogers. 2003. Enticing People to Interact with Large Public Displays in Public Spaces. In *Proceedings of INTERACT*. 17-24. http://dx.doi.org/10.1.1.129.603
4. Sandy Claes and Andrew Vande Moere. 2015. The Role of Tangible Interaction in Exploring Information on Public Visualization Displays. In *International Symposium on Pervasive Displays*. 201-207 http://dx.doi.org/10.1145/2757710.2757733
5. Copenhagenize.eu. 2014. Holding on to Cyclists in Copenhagen. Urban Intervention. Retrieved September 11, 2015 http://www.copenhagenize.com/2010/01/holding-on-to-cyclists-in-copenhagen.html.
6. Alexandru Dancu, Zlatko Franjcic and Morten Fjeld. 2014. Smart Flashlight: Map Navigation Using a Bike-Mounted Projector. In *Proceedings of the SIGCHI Conference on Human Factors in Computing Systems*. ACM, 2557289, 3627-3630. http://dx.doi.org/10.1145/2556288.2557289
7. Eco-compteur. 2015. Eco Totem Displays Bicycle Count Data. Retrieved September 11, 2015 From http://www.eco-compteur.com/en/products/eco-totem.
8. Patrick Tobias Fischer and Eva Hornecker. 2012. Urban Hci: Spatial Aspects in the Design of Shared Encounters for Media Facades. In *Proceedings of the SIGCHI Conference on Human Factors in Computing Systems*. ACM, 307-316. http://dx.doi.org/10.1145/2207676.2207719
9. Ray Forrest and Ade Kearns. Social Cohesion, Social Capital and the Neighbourhood. *Urban studies* 38, 12 (2001), 2125-2143. http://dx.doi.org/10.1080/00420980120087081
10. Anne Galloway. Intimations of Everyday Life: Ubiquitous Computing and the City. *Cultural studies* 18, 2-3 (2004), 384-408. http://dx.doi.org/ 10.1080/0950238042000201572
11. Gaby Grix-Saar. 2015. Traffic Light Grip - Ampelgriff. Urban Intervention. Retrieved September 11, 2015 From http://www.ampelgriff.de/.
12. Sandra G Hart and Lowell E Staveland. Development of Nasa-Tlx (Task Load Index): Results of Empirical and Theoretical Research. *Advances in psychology* 52 (1988), 139-183. http://dx.doi.org/10.1016/S0166-4115(08)62386-9
13. Luke Hespanhol, Martin Tomitsch, Ian McArthur, Joel Fredericks, Ronald Schroeter and Marcus Foth. 2015. Vote as You Go: Blending Interfaces for Community Engagement into the Urban Space. In *Proceedings of the 7th International Conference on Communities and Technologies (C&T)*. ACM. http://dx.doi.org/10.1145/2768545.2768553
14. Steven Houben and Christian Weichel. 2013. Overcoming Interaction Blindness through Curiosity Objects. In *Extended Abstracts on Human Factors in Computing Systems (CHI '13)*. ACM, 2468631, 1539-1544. http://dx.doi.org/10.1145/2468356.2468631
15. Liesbeth Huybrechts, Katrien Dreessen and Selina Schepers. 2012. Mapping Design Practices: On Risk, Hybridity and Participation. In *Proceedings of the 12th Participatory Design Conference: Exploratory Papers, Workshop Descriptions, Industry Cases - Volume 2*. ACM, 2348155, 29-32. http://dx.doi.org/10.1145/2348144.2348155
16. Lisa Koeman, Vaiva Kalnikait and Yvonne Rogers. 2015. "Everyone Is Talking About It!": A Distributed Approach to Urban Voting Technology and Visualisations. In *Proceedings of the 33rd Annual ACM Conference on Human Factors in Computing Systems*. ACM, 2702263, 3127-3136. http://dx.doi.org/10.1145/2702123.2702263
17. Hannu Kukka, Vassilis Kostakos, Timo Ojala, Johanna Ylipulli, Tiina Suopajärvi, Marko Jurmu and Simo Hosio. This Is Not Classified: Everyday Information Seeking and Encountering in Smart Urban Spaces. *Personal and Ubiquitous Computing* 17, 1 (2013), 15-27. http://dx.doi.org/10.1007/s00779-011-0474-1
18. Christopher A Le Dantec, Kari E Watkins, Russ Clark and Elizabeth Mynatt. 2015. Cycle Atlanta and Onebusaway: Driving Innovation through the Data Ecosystems of Civic Computing. *Human-Computer Interaction Users and Contexts: Proceedings 17th International Conference, HCI International*, 327–338. Springer.
19. Matthew Mauriello, Michael Gubbels and Jon E. Froehlich. 2014. Social Fabric Fitness: The Design and Evaluation of Wearable E-Textile Displays to Support Group Running. In *Proceedings of the SIGCHI Conference on Human Factors in Computing Systems*. ACM, 2557299, 2833-2842. http://dx.doi.org/10.1145/2556288.2557299
20. Nemanja Memarovic, Marc Langheinrich, Florian Alt, Ivan Elhart, Simo Hosio and Elisa Rubegni. 2012. Using Public Displays to Stimulate Passive Engagement, Active Engagement, and Discovery in Public Spaces. In *Procedings of Media Architecture Biennale 2012*. ACM, 55-64.

21. Jörg Müller, Robert Walter, Gilles Bailly, Michael Nischt and Florian Alt. 2012. Looking Glass: A Field Study on Noticing Interactivity of a Shop Window. In *Proceedings of the SIGCHI Conference on Human Factors in Computing Systems*. ACM, 297-306. http://dx.doi.org/10.1145/2207676.2207718
22. P. Newman and J. Kenworthy. *The End of Automobile Dependence: How Cities Are Moving Beyond Car-Based Planning*. Island Press, 2015.
23. Dietmar Offenhuber and Susanne Seitinger. 2014. Over the Rainbow: Information Design for Low-Resolution Urban Displays. In *Proceedings of the 2nd Media Architecture Biennale Conference: World Cities*. ACM, 2682886, 40-47. http://dx.doi.org/10.1145/2682884.2682886
24. Timo Ojala, Vassilis Kostakos, Hannu Kukka, Tommi Heikkinen, Tomas Linden, Marko Jurmu, Simo Hosio, Fabio Kruger and Daniele Zanni. Multipurpose Interactive Public Displays in the Wild: Three Years Later. *Computer* 45, 5 (2012), 42-49. http://dx.doi.org/10.1109/mc.2012.115
25. Martin Pielot, Benjamin Poppinga, Wilko Heuten and Susanne Boll. 2012. Tacticycle: Supporting Exploratory Bicycle Trips. In *Proceedings of the 14th international conference on Human-computer interaction with mobile devices and services*. ACM, 369-378. http://dx.doi.org/10.1145/2371574.2371631
26. Duncan Rowland, Martin Flintham, Leif Oppermann, Joe Marshall, Alan Chamberlain, Boriana Koleva, Steve Benford and Citlali Perez. 2009. Ubikequitous Computing: Designing Interactive Experiences for Cyclists. In *Proceedings of the 11th International Conference on Human-Computer Interaction with Mobile Devices and Services*. ACM, 21. http://dx.doi.org/10.1145/1613858.1613886
27. Enrico Rukzio, Michael Müller and Robert Hardy. 2009. Design, Implementation and Evaluation of a Novel Public Display for Pedestrian Navigation: The Rotating Compass. In *Proceedings of the SIGCHI Conference on Human Factors in Computing Systems*. ACM, 113-122. http://dx.doi.org/10.1145/1518701.1518722
28. Purvi Saraiya, Chris North and Karen Duca. An Insight-Based Methodology for Evaluating Bioinformatics Visualizations. *Visualization and Computer Graphics, IEEE Transactions on* 11, 4 (2005), 443-456. http://dx.doi.org/10.1109/TVCG.2005.53
29. Ava Fatah gen. Schieck, Carolina Briones and Chiron Mottram. The Urban Screen as a Socialising Platform: Exploring the Role of Place within the Urban Space. *F. Eckardt et al., eds., MEDIACITY: Situations, Practices and Encounters Frank & Timme GmbH, Berlin, Germany,* (2008), 285-305.
30. Ronald Schroeter. 2012. Engaging New Digital Locals with Interactive Urban Screens to Collaboratively Improve the City. In *Proceedings of the ACM 2012 conference on Computer Supported Cooperative Work*. ACM, 227-236. http://dx.doi.org/10.1145/2145204.2145239
31. Edward Segel and Jeffrey Heer. Narrative Visualization: Telling Stories with Data. *Visualization and Computer Graphics, IEEE Transactions on* 16, 6 (2010), 1139-1148. http://dx.doi.org/10.1109/TVCG.2010.179
32. Sarang Sheth. 2015. Indicator Innovation. Online Article. Retrieved September 12, 2015 From http://www.yankodesign.com/2015/06/30/indicator-innovation/.
33. Pieter Jan Stallen. 2012. Public Passes. Artwork. Retrieved September 12, 2015 From http://www.publicpasses.com/.
34. Fabius Steinberger, Marcus Foth and Florian Alt. 2014. Vote with Your Feet: Local Community Polling on Urban Screens. In *Proceedings of The International Symposium on Pervasive Displays*. ACM, 44. http://dx.doi.org/10.1145/2611009.2611015
35. Alex S. Taylor, Sian Lindley, Tim Regan, David Sweeney, Vasillis Vlachokyriakos, Lillie Grainger and Jessica Lingel. 2015. Data-in-Place: Thinking through the Relations between Data and Community. In *Proceedings of the 33rd Annual ACM Conference on Human Factors in Computing Systems*. ACM, 2702558, 2863-2872. http://dx.doi.org/10.1145/2702123.2702558
36. Nina Valkanova, Robert Walter, Andrew Vande Moere and Jörg Müller. 2014. Myposition: A Public Polling Projection Display Designed to Spark Civic Participation. In *Proceedings of the 17th ACM conference on Computer supported cooperative work & social computing (CSCW'14)*. 1323-1332. http://dx.doi.org/10.1145/2531602.2531639
37. Andrew Vande Moere and Dan Hill. Designing for the Situated and Public Visualization of Urban Data. *Journal of Urban Technology* 19, 2 (2012), 25-46. http://dx.doi.org/10.1080/10630732.2012.698065
38. Verkeersnet. 2015. Surveying Cyclists without Stopping. Retrieved September 12, 2015 from http://www.verkeersnet.nl/15593/fietsers-enqueteren-zonder-stoppen/.
39. Wouter Walmink, Danielle Wilde and Florian 'Floyd' Mueller. 2014. Displaying Heart Rate Data on a Bicycle Helmet to Support Social Exertion Experiences. In *Proceedings of the 8th International Conference on Tangible, Embedded and Embodied Interaction*. ACM, 97-104. http://dx.doi.org/10.1145/2540930.2540970

HandMark Menus: Rapid Command Selection and Large Command Sets on Multi-Touch Displays

Md. Sami Uddin[1], Carl Gutwin[1], and Benjamin Lafreniere[2]
[1]Computer Science, University of Saskatchewan, Saskatoon, Canada
[2]Autodesk Research, Toronto, Canada
sami.uddin@usask.ca, gutwin@cs.usask.ca, ben.lafreniere@autodesk.com

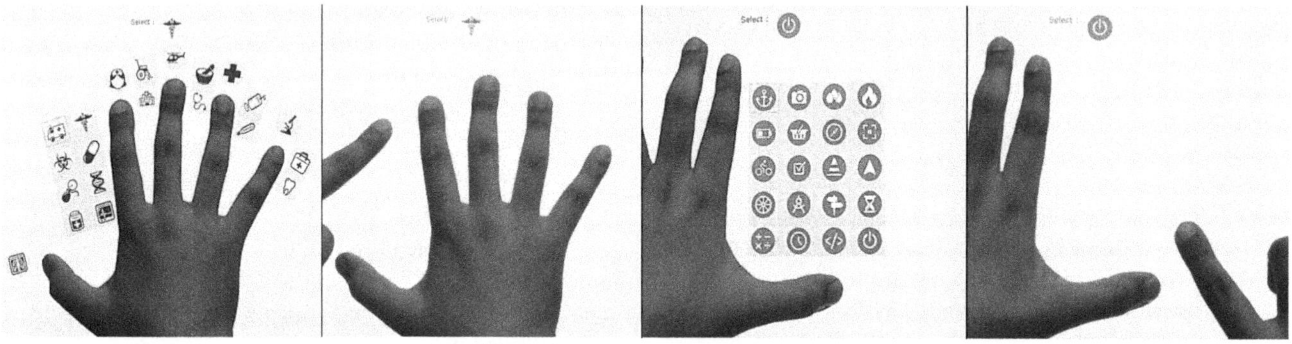

Figure 1. HandMark Menus. From left, 1: HandMark-Finger (novice mode). 2: HandMark-Finger chorded selection (expert mode), 3: HandMark-Multi (novice mode), 4: HandMark-Multi chorded selection (expert mode).

ABSTRACT
Command selection on large multi-touch surfaces can be difficult, because the large surface means that there are few landmarks to help users build up familiarity with controls. However, people's hands and fingers are landmarks that are always present when interacting with a touch display. To explore the use of hands as landmarks, we designed two hand-centric techniques for multi-touch displays – one allowing 42 commands, and one allowing 160 – and tested them in an empirical comparison against standard tab widgets. We found that the small version (HandMark-Fingers) was significantly faster at all stages of use, and that the large version (HandMark-Multi) was slower at the start but equivalent to tabs after people gained experience with the technique. There was no difference in error rates, and participants strongly preferred both of the HandMark menus over tabs. We demonstrate that people's intimate knowledge of their hands can be the basis for fast and feasible interaction techniques that can improve the performance and usability of interactive tables and other multi-touch systems.

Author Keywords
Command selection; landmarks; multi-touch; tabletops.

ACM Classification Keywords
H.5.2. Information interfaces (e.g., HCI): User Interfaces.

ACM 978-1-4503-3362-7/16/05…$15.00
DOI: http://dx.doi.org/10.1145/2858036.2858211

INTRODUCTION
Command selection on large multi-touch surfaces, such as tabletops, can be a difficult task. Selection techniques and widgets from desktop interfaces are often a poor match for the physical characteristics of a table – for example, menus or ribbons are typically placed at the edges of the screen, making them hard to reach on large displays, and hard to see on horizontal displays (due to the oblique angle to the user). As a result, researchers have proposed several techniques that bring tools closer to the user's work area, such as moveable palettes and toolsheets controlled by the non-dominant hand [8, 26], gestural commands [31], finger-count menus [5], or multi-touch marking menus [33]. These techniques can work well, but are limited in the number of commands that they can show (e.g., finger-count menus are limited to 25 commands, marking menus to about 64 [29]).

Part of the difficulty in developing new high-capacity selection techniques for large surfaces is that there are few landmarks that can help people learn the tool locations. Once a widget such as a tool palette is displayed on the screen, people can learn the locations of items by using visual landmarks in the palette (e.g., corners or colored items), but if the selection widget is hidden by default, the user must first invoke the menu before they can make use of this familiarity.

There is, however, a well-known landmark that is always present and visible to the user of a touch surface – their hands. People are intimately familiar with the size and shape of their hands, and proprioception allows people to easily locate features (e.g., touching your right index finger to the tip of your left thumb can be done without looking). This intimate knowledge of hands, however, is not exploited for command selection. For example, widgets such as tool palettes [26] are held by the non-dominant hand, but the palette does not use the details of the hand as a reference frame. Although people can use proprioception to bring a palette close to the selecting finger, the palette can be held in many different ways relative to the hand, and so any detailed familiarity with the tool locations is based mainly on the visual display of the palette. One technique that does use detailed knowledge of the hands is finger-count menus [5], which select commands based on the pattern of fingers touching the surface. This allows the development of proprioceptive memory for command invocation, but is limited to 25 commands, and does not make extensive use of people's familiarity with the size and shape of their hands.

To explore the use of people's hands as a landmarking technique for command selection, we developed and tested two hand-centric menu techniques for multi-touch displays. The first, HandMark-Finger, places command icons in the spaces between a user's spread-out fingers (Figure 1.1). This technique uses the hand as a clear external reference frame – once the locations of different items are learned, people can use their hand as a frame for setting up the selection action even before the fingers are placed on the touchscreen. The technique can be used with both hands to increase the number of available items.

The second technique, HandMark-Multi, provides multiple sets of commands, where the set is chosen by the number of fingers touching the surface (Figure 1.3). The technique is therefore similar to finger-count menus in the way that a category is selected, but allows many more items per category because a larger menu is displayed between the thumb and index finger (20 items in a 4x5 grid). HandMark-Multi also allows people to prepare for their selection before the hands are placed on the screen, once they have learned what menu an item is in and its location in the grid.

We carried out a study that compared HandMark menus to equivalent tab widgets presented at the top of the display. The study showed that HandMark-Finger was significantly faster than standard tabs (0.6 seconds per selection) with a similar error rate. The study also showed that although HandMark-Multi was slower than a tab UI in the early stages of use, there was no difference between the techniques as people gained experience. For both menus, it was clear that people did use their hands as a reference frame that aided memory of tool locations (e.g., people increasingly prepared their two hands for a correct selection as they gained experience). Participants also strongly preferred HandMark menus over the tab interfaces. Our work shows that the hands, and people's intimate knowledge of them, are an under-used resource that can improve the performance and usability of interfaces for tables and multi-touch systems.

HANDMARK DESIGN GOALS AND RELATED WORK

HandMark menus display command sets in specific places on the touch surface based on the sensed position of the left or right hand and the specific combination of fingers (see Figures 1.1 and 1.3). They are a design descendant of early bimanual techniques such as Palettes and Toolglasses [26], which allowed users to control a menu of tools with the non-dominant hand, and make selections with a pointing device in the dominant hand. This division allows one hand to act in a supporting role to the other (e.g., following Guiard's Kinematic Chain model [19]).

However, although techniques such as Toolglasses can improve performance compared to traditional selection widgets [8], they only allow users to build up a coarse understanding of the locations of specific commands in relation to the hand, and only when used with an absolute input space. The intent of HandMark menus is to go beyond the design of other multi-hand selection techniques, and use the hands as a more detailed absolute reference frame for developing memory of specific item locations. This allows people to remember commands using features on their hands, and allows them to position their hands and fingers for a selection even before the hands have touched the surface.

Design Goal 1: Rapid multi-touch command selection

A well-established method for improving selection speed is to enable memory-based command invocation rather than visually-guided navigation [10, 21, 22]. Researchers have used several mechanisms to enable memory-based interaction, such as spatial locations [23], gestures [32], multitouch chords [18] or hotkeys [37]. HandMark menus associate command icons with locations around the user's hands, so they use a spatial-memory mechanism – as users learn command locations, they can make selections using recall rather than visual search. Spatial memory is built up through interactions with a stable visual representation [13], and as people gain experience with a particular location, they can remember it easily. Studies have shown that people can quickly learn and retrieve command locations [15, 23, 39].

Multi-touch surfaces provide new opportunities for rich interaction and proprioceptive memory. For example, Wu and Balakrishnan [48] describe multi-finger and whole-hand interaction techniques for tables, including a selection mechanism that posts a toolglass with the thumb, allowing selection with another finger. Multi-touch marking menus [33] and finger-count menus [5] both allow users to specify a menu category by changing the number of fingers used to touch the screen. However, since a more-complex control action may take more time to retrieve and execute, these techniques do not always improve performance [27].

The efficiency of a command selection interface depends on the number of separate actions needed to find and execute a command. Using a full-screen overlay to display all commands at once, Scarr et al.'s CommandMap [41] successfully reduced the number of actions for desktop systems, an approach also used by the Hotbox technique [30]. Similarly, FastTap [23] uses chorded thumb and finger touches on a spatially stable grid interface to accelerate command selection for tablets. However, some of these techniques are difficult to use on large touch tables because the user can be at any location and any orientation, making it difficult to accurately position a visual representation.

Design Goal 2: Use hands as landmarks

Landmarks play a vital role in retrieval by providing a reference frame for other objects' locations. For example, the FastTap technique uses the corners and sides of a tablet's screen as the reference frame for organizing a grid menu [23]. However, on a large surface, these natural landmarks are not readily available (because people may be working in the middle of the screen and not near an edge or corner). In these situations, artificial visual landmarks can be useful to support spatial memory (e.g., Alexander et al.'s Footprints Scrollbar [1]); in addition, the visual layout of a toolbar can also show implicit landmarks, such as the corners and sides of the palette. Artificial visual landmarks can only be used once the toolbar is displayed, however.

In touch-based systems, there is another set of natural visual landmarks that are readily available and well known to the user – their hands. Therefore, we may be able to use hands and fingers as landmarks to support the development of spatial memory for item locations. There is considerable space around each hand and its fingers; if we use that space to represent command items, people can use their knowledge of their hands' shapes and sizes to remember those locations. In addition, the hands are a natural reference frame that is always visible, meaning that users can prepare for a selection even before they touch the surface. For example, if a command is stored near the user's left thumb, they can move their selection finger near to the thumb as they touch down on the surface, potentially reducing selection time.

Numerous other selection techniques have also used the hands in some fashion. As described above, bimanual techniques like Toolglasses [8] and Palettes [26] use one hand to control a palette's position and other hand to select. However, these techniques differ from HandMarks in that they do not use the details of the hand as a reference frame. In the original version, the palette was controlled by an indirect pointing device [26], so the hand was not visible at all; and when used with touch surfaces, the way in which the user holds the palette can change (thus changing the frame). Users can use proprioception at a coarse level (e.g., to quickly bring the tools to the work area and orient them appropriately, but there is no detailed mapping between commands and specific hand locations.

Other techniques also use proprioceptive memory of the hands as a non-visual reference frame. For example, Finger Count menus [5] rely on people's memory of finger patterns, and other systems use multi-finger chords to represent commands [18, 46]. Finally, although not intended for table-based interactions, techniques such as Imaginary Interfaces [21], Body Mnemonics [2], and Virtual Shelves [35] also rely on proprioceptive memory for command selection.

Design Goal 3: Hand detection

In order to use hands as the landmarks for a menu, we need to know the shape and orientation of the hand once it has touched the surface. Earlier work has explored hand detection using several methods: computer vision approaches, specialized hardware, and glove-based tracking. Several systems use computer vision to track the position of hands and to identify fingers [3, 16, 34]. Another uses distance, orientation, and movement information of touch blobs to identify fingers and people [12, 47]. Schmidt et al's HandsDown [42] system allows hand detection on tabletops, and provides lenses for interaction [43]. The reliability and accuracy of vision-based recognition, however, remains a challenge for all of these systems.

Other methods use specialized hardware to distinguish between hand parts and between users. For example, the DiamondTouch system [14] uses capacitive coupling to identify different users. Other hardware approaches distinguish hand parts: for example, an EMG muscle-sensing armband identifies a person's fingers touching a surface [7], while fingerprint recognition could provide similarly precise touch information and user identification [25]. Other techniques distinguish a user's hands and their posture in space by using colored patches or markers on gloves [9, 48].

As described below, we developed a new hand identification technique for HandMark menus that does not use either vision or specialized hardware, and relies only on the touch points that are reported by a multi-touch surface.

Design Goal 4: Support a large number of commands

Many memory-based command selection interfaces provide a limited number of commands. For example, FastTap supports only 19 commands [23], and Finger Count menus [5] provide only 25. Several approaches have been used to increase the number of commands in selection techniques. Marking Menus uses multiple levels to provide more commands (allowing about eight items per level [32]); other techniques such as Polygon menus [49], Flower menus [4], Augmented letters [40], Gesture avatar [36], Arpège [18], FlowMenu [20] and OctoPocus [6] increase the command vocabulary by expanding the range of gestures.

For HandMark menus, rapid execution is our priority, but we also want to support a large command vocabulary. Our prototypes place as many items as possible around the hands, while still ensuring that hands and fingers can be used as landmarks to facilitate rapid development of spatial memory.

HANDMARK DESIGN AND IMPLEMENTATION

We developed two variants of the HandMark technique to explore different kinds of hand-based landmarks and different menu sizes.

Design 1: HandMark-Finger

This technique provides modal access to two different sets of commands, each belonging to one hand (Figures 1.1 and 2). To access commands, the five fingers of the left or right hand are touched down in any order, spreading the hand to provide space between the fingers.

Commands are displayed in the space around the hand and between the fingers (Figure 2), and selections are made by touching an item with the other hand. We place pairs of icons between fingers, and one command at the top of each finger. As the space between the thumb and index finger is larger, we place eight commands there in a 4x2 grid. The size of the grid was determined using the average width of an adult index finger (16-20mm [11]) as a guideline and considering Parhi et al.'s recommendation that touch targets be no smaller than 9.6mm [38]. In total, HandMark-Finger supports 42 items (21 in each hand).

The user can rotate and move the menu in any direction. Following a hand touch, the menu appears after a short 300ms delay, but selections can be made immediately. This enables two types of selections. Novice users can wait until the menu appears and use visual search to select a target. Expert users, who have built up spatial memory of the location of a desired item, can tap the location without waiting for the menu to be displayed (Figure 1.2). This follows Kurtenbach's principle of rehearsal, which states that novice actions should be a rehearsal of the expert mode [28].

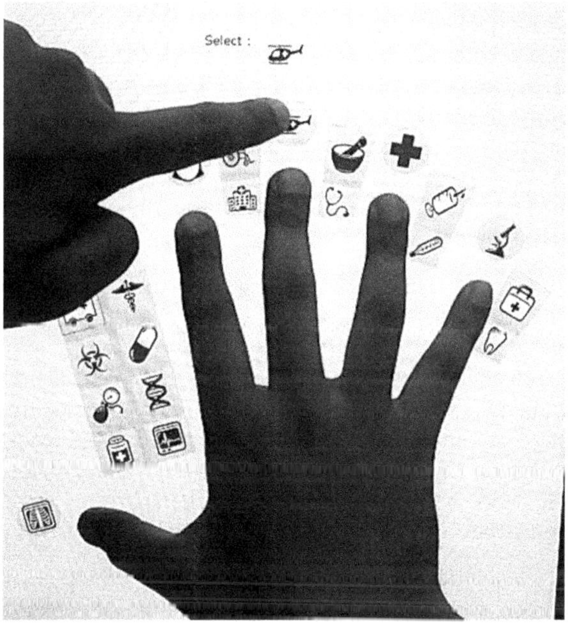

Figure 2. Making a selection with HandMark-Finger.

Design 2: HandMark-Multi

This interface also provides modal access to different sets of commands (Figures 1.3 and 3) and has a similar selection method to that described above. In HM-Multi, however, there are eight command sets (four in each hand) and each set can be accessed by touching on the screen with a specific number of fingers and thumb in an L-shaped posture (see Figure 3). The index finger and thumb are always used, and adding other fingers accesses other sets – e.g., to access the second set on the left hand, the index and middle fingers of the left hand are touched down along with the thumb.

A spatially-stable grid of items is then shown in the space between the thumb and index finger (Figure 3). We placed 20 commands (a 5x4 grid) in the space between thumb and index finger [11, 38]. Since these two fingers are always used to frame the grid, we can provide four sets in total (the first uses only thumb and index finger, and the others add the middle, ring, and pinky fingers). HandMark-Multi supports 160 items (20 in each tab, and 4 tabs in each hand). The menu follows the user's hand as it moves or rotates on the screen. Handmark-Multi also supports the novice and expert selection methods described for HandMark-Finger above.

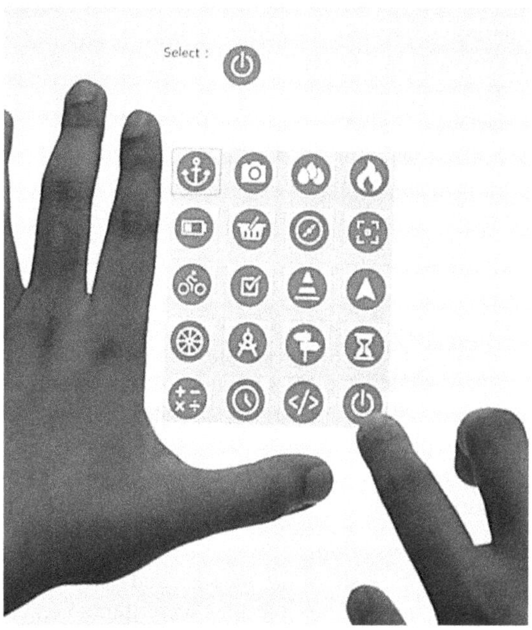

Figure 3. Making a selection with HandMark-Multi.

Hand identification

HandMark requires accurate identification of the left and right hand using only the fingers' touch points. We make use of the distinctive geometrics of people's hands in terms of the position of the thumb compared to other fingers and the individual positions of the fingers compared to the thumb. For example, the position of thumb is always below the other fingers if the hand points upwards, and the rightmost touch is always the thumb for the left hand (and reversed for the right). Using these features, we are reliably able to differentiate the left and right hand. Other fingers (index, middle, ring, and pinky) can be found from the touch points once the hand and thumb are identified.

The algorithm we use is as follows. For each set of points touched down simultaneously, determine whether the rightmost or leftmost point is lower than the others in the set. Identify this as the thumb (which also determines the left or right hand). The remaining points can then be identified using left-to-right ordering for the right hand, and right-to-left for the left hand. This algorithm requires that users place the fingers of one hand (all five fingers for HM-Finger, and at least two for HM-Multi) on the surface in an approximately upright posture, and at approximately the same time (but in any order). Other finger-identification techniques exist that are more robust (see Vogel [45]), but our simplistic approach works well for the prototypes described here.

In-place tools and occlusion of content

All in-place interfaces occlude parts of the work surface [44] (e.g., pop-up menus) or the whole screen (e.g., FastTap). For HandMark menus we chose a hybrid overlay presentation – when used in novice mode, the menu covers part of the screen, but in expert mode, no visual presentation is needed. In addition, it is easy for the user to control the presence of the overlay (by lifting the fingers from the touch surface), allowing rapid switching between menu and content. It is also easy to move the menu hand after activating the menu, which allows the user to further manage occlusion.

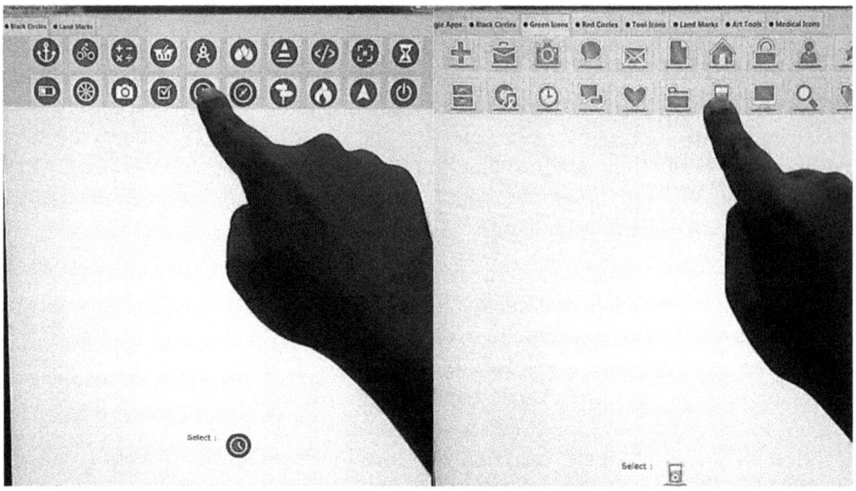

Figure 5. Left: Tabs-2, Right: Tabs-8.

EXPERIMENT

To assess the performance of command selection using hands as landmarks, we conducted a study comparing HandMark menus to standard tab-based menus. We compared the interfaces in a controlled experiment where participants selected a series of commands over several blocks, allowing us to examine selection behaviors and learning in each interface.

Experimental Conditions

Two versions of HandMark menus, and two equivalent versions of a standard tab interface were implemented in a tabletop environment (see Figures 2, 3 and 5).

HandMark-Finger was implemented as described above. The interface used in the experiment contained 21 commands in each hand's set, for a total of 42 items. Eight items were used as study targets – four from each hand (Figure 4).

HandMark-Multi was also implemented as described above. There were 20 command buttons in a 5x4 grid for each set. There were eight sets (grouped by color) for a total of 160 command buttons. Eight targets were used in the study, one from each set (Figure 4 shows command locations within the grid; note that each command was from a different set).

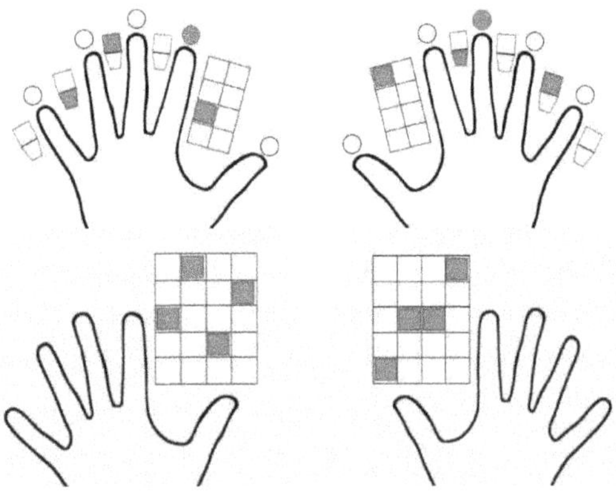

Figure 4. Target locations for HM-Finger and HM-Multi (collapsed across different command sets).

Standard tab interfaces. We implemented two versions of standard tabbed ribbon interface (Tabs-2 and Tabs-8) to compare with the two HandMark menus. Tabs-2 (Figure 5 left) had only two tabs (each consisting of 20 command buttons) to match HandMark-Finger. For Tabs-8 (Figure 5 right), there were eight tabs each with 20 items in a 2x10 grid (total of 160). Items were grouped by type and color, and the named tabs were placed side by side as a ribbon interface at the top left edge of the screen.

We compared HandMarks to Tabs rather than other research systems for several reasons: Tabs offer equitable command range to our prototypes (which is not provided by several research techniques), and they are the de facto standard UI; in addition, a main goal of the evaluation was to compare the strong landmarking and proprioceptive approach of HandMarks to a traditional visually-guided approach. In future work we will also extend the comparisons to other systems such as Marking Menus and other recent designs

For all interfaces (and both expert and novice mode), feedback was shown for 300ms after a command was selected by displaying the icon in its home location.

Procedure

The study was divided into two parts. Part 1 tested HandMark-Finger and Tabs-2, and part 2 tested HandMark-Multi and Tabs-8. Participants completed a demographics questionnaire, and then performed a sequence of selections in the custom study system with both interfaces. For each version, a command stimulus (one of eight icons, Figure 4) was displayed in the middle of the screen; the participants had to tap one large (easily accessible) button placed at bottom to view the command stimulus and start the trial. Trials were timed from the appearance of the stimulus until that icon was correctly selected. Participants were instructed to complete tasks as quickly and accurately as possible, and were told that errors could be corrected simply by selecting the correct item. In our analysis, we include error correction in completion times.

The study was carried out using a 24-inch multitouch monitor placed flat on a table in front of the participant in portrait mode. Although this is not a large-scale surface, it adequately simulated the combination of a local work area and a far edge that participants needed to reach in order to use. Participants were stationed at a fixed seat and allowed to lean forward for selecting items using both hands.

For both interfaces, only eight commands were used as stimuli, in order to allow faster development of spatial memory. For each interface, selections were organized into blocks of eight trials. Participants first performed one practice session which was consisted of two commands and ten blocks (data discarded) to ensure that they could use the interfaces successfully. They then carried out 17 blocks of eight selections each. Targets were presented in random order (sampling without replacement) for each block. After each interface, participants were allowed to rest, and filled out a questionnaire based on the NASA-TLX survey [24]. At the end of each pair of techniques, participants gave their preferences between two the systems. Order of the interfaces in each part, along with the order of study parts was counterbalanced using a Latin square design.

Participants and Apparatus

Fourteen participants were recruited from a local university; one person's data could not be used due to technical difficulties, leaving 13 participants (6 female; mean age 24 years). The study was conducted on a Dell multitouch monitor (24-inch screen, 1920x1080 resolution) and a Windows 7 PC. The interfaces were written in JavaFx, and the study software recorded all experimental data including selection times, errors, and incorrect set selections.

Design and Hypotheses

The study used 2×17 within-participants RM-ANOVAs; with factors *Interface* (HandMark-Finger vs. Tabs-2; and HandMark-Multi vs. Tabs-8), and *Block* (1-17). Dependent measures were selection time per command, errors per block, and incorrect tabs per block. Interfaces and sets were counterbalanced. Hypotheses were:

H1. Selection will be faster for *HandMark* than for *Tabs*.

H2. *HandMark* will be faster both for novices and experts.

H3. There will be no evidence of a difference in error rates between *HandMark* and *Tabs*.

H4. There will be no evidence of a difference in selecting the wrong set between *HandMark* and *Tabs*.

H5. There will be no evidence of a difference in perception of effort for *HandMark* and *Tabs*.

H6. Users will prefer *HandMark* over *Tabs*.

Results: HandMark-Finger vs. Tabs-2

Selection Time per Command

We calculated mean selection time for each command by dividing the total trial time by the number of commands in that block. Mean selection times were 0.62 seconds faster per command with *HandMark-Finger* (2.32, s.d. 0.79s) than with *Tabs-2* (2.94s, s.d. 0.95s), see Figure 6.

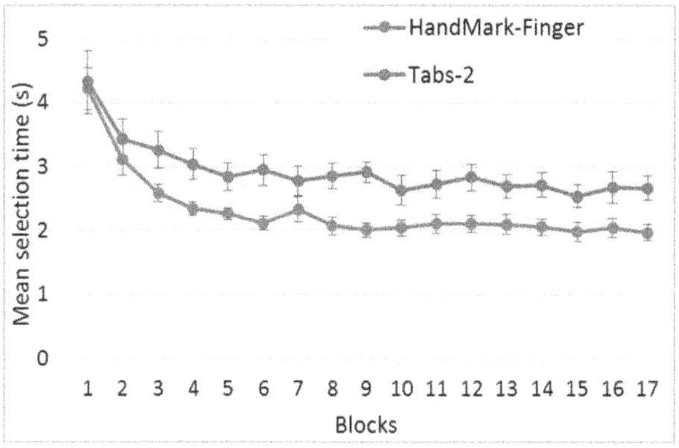

Figure 6. Mean selection time by Interface and Block.

RM-ANOVA showed a significant main effect of *Interface* ($F_{1,12}$=37.59, p<.0001). For the small menus, we therefore accept **H1** – HandMark-Finger was 21% faster than Tabs-2. As shown in Figure 6, selection times decreased across trial blocks for both interfaces; RM-ANOVA showed a significant effect of *Block* ($F_{16,192}$=18.04, p<.0001). There was no interaction between *Interface* and *Block* ($F_{16,192}$=1.00, p=.456) as HandMark-Finger was faster than Tabs-2 throughout. For HandMark-Finger, we therefore accept **H2**.

Errors

We also analyzed errors per command (counted as any incorrect selection). RM-ANOVA showed no effect of *Interface* on errors, with HandMark-Finger at 0.04 errors/command, s.d. 0.09, and *Tabs-2* at 0.04 errors/command, s.d. 0.08 ($F_{1,12}$=0.01, p=.924). We therefore accept **H3** (errors are considered further below). There were no effects of *Block* ($F_{16,192}$=1.07, p=.388) on errors, and no *Interface* x *Block* interaction ($F_{16,192}$=1.42, p=.138).

Incorrect Set Selection

We also recorded the number of times participants selected the wrong command set (e.g., the wrong tab or the wrong hand/finger combination). RM-ANOVA showed no effect of *Interface* ($F_{1,12}$=0.26, p=.623) on errors, with 0.05 incorrect sets/command, s.d. 0.09 for both *HandMark-Finger* and *Tabs-2*. There was also no effect of *Block* ($F_{16,192}$=0.6, p=.88). Therefore we accept **H4** for HandMark-Finger.

Subjective Responses: Effort and Preferences

Participants' responses were positive for both interfaces, but there were no strong differences in NASA-TLX scores (Friedman test, Table 1) for HandMark-Finger and Tabs-2. There were no significant differences on any question, and the mean scores were similar. Therefore, we accept **H5**.

	HandMark-Finger	Tabs-2	χ^2_r	p
Mental	5.54(2.73)	5.46(2.37)	0.08	0.78
Physical	5.38(2.79)	6.62(2.47)	1.23	0.27
Temporal	5.00(2.89)	4.77(1.74)	0.08	0.78
Performance	8.69(0.95)	6.92(1.93)	7.69	0.01
Effort	5.31(2.75)	6.77(2.35)	0.31	0.58
Frustration	2.00(1.78)	4.69(3.01)	4.92	0.03

Table 1. Mean (s.d.) effort scores (0-10 scale, low to high).

We also asked participants about their preferred interface in terms of several qualities (Table 2). Counts were easily distinguishable, and overall, 92% of participants preferred HandMark-Finger. We therefore accept **H6.**

	HandMark-Finger	Neither	Tabs-2
Speed	12	0	1
Accuracy	9	2	2
Memorization	11	2	0
Comfort	12	0	1
Overall	12	0	1

Table 2. Counts of participant preferences.

Results: HandMark-Multi vs. Tabs-8

Selection Time per Command

Mean selection times were 0.62 sec/command slower with *HandMark-Multi* (3.84s, s.d. 2.1s) than with *Tabs-8* (3.22s, s.d. 1.43s), giving a main effect of *Interface* ($F_{1,12}$=4.86, p=.048). However, this result must be interpreted in light of the significant interaction between *Interface* and *Block* ($F_{16,192}$=4.96, p<.0001). In early blocks, Tabs-8 was faster than HM-Multi, but by the final four blocks, the two techniques were similar (RM-ANOVA for blocks 14-17 showed no significant effect of *Interface*, $F_{1,12}$=.008, p=.932). Hypotheses **H1** and **H2** therefore cannot be clearly rejected – HM-Multi was slower overall, but there was no difference in performance once users learned item locations.

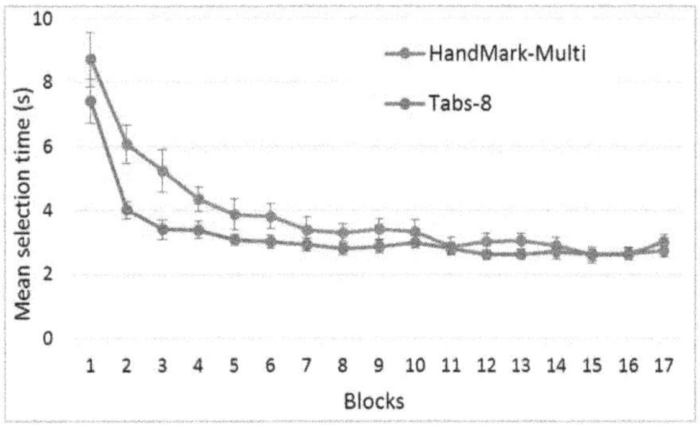

Figure 7. Mean selection time by Interface and Block.

Errors

RM-ANOVA showed similar trends to the smaller menus: *HandMark-Multi* had 0.06 errors/command, s.d. 0.1, and *Tabs-8* had 0.04 errors/command, s.d. 0.09, with no main effect ($F_{1,12}$=2.47, p=.142). We therefore accept **H3** (errors are considered further below). There was no effect of *Block* ($F_{16,192}$=1.6, p=.07), and no interaction ($F_{16,192}$=.75, p=.74).

Incorrect Set Selection

RM-ANOVA showed a different trend to the smaller menus: *HandMark-Multi* had more incorrect set selections (0.64 per command, s.d. 0.86) than *Tabs-8* (0.18 per command, s.d. 0.38) ($F_{1,12}$=9.78, p<.01). There was also a significant interaction between *Interface* and *Block* ($F_{16,192}$=6.51, p<.0001). We therefore reject **H4** for HandMark-Multi.

Subjective Responses: Effort and Preferences

Again, participants gave positive responses for both interfaces, with no significant differences (Friedman test, Table 3) between HandMark-Multi and Tabs-8. Mean scores were close in all cases; therefore, we accept **H5**.

Participant preference counts (Table 4) were again easily distinguishable, with a strong preference for HandMark-Multi (73% overall). We therefore accept **H6**.

	HandMark-Multi	Tabs-8	χ^2_r	p
Mental	7.62(2.36)	6.23(1.83)	2.77	0.10
Physical	6.00(2.71)	7.23(2.13)	1.23	0.27
Temporal	6.46(2.76)	6.31(2.06)	0.08	0.78
Performance	7.62(1.5)	7.54(2.26)	0.69	0.41
Effort	7.00(2.45)	7.54(1.61)	0.08	0.78
Frustration	3.69(2.02)	4.08(2.5)	1.23	0.27

Table 3. Mean (s.d.) effort scores (0-10 scale, low to high).

	HandMark-Multi	Neither	Tabs-8
Speed	10	0	3
Accuracy	6	2	5
Memorization	12	1	0
Comfort	10	1	2
Overall	10	1	2

Table 4. Counts of participant preferences.

Use of Hands as Landmarks

To consider whether participants made use of their hands as landmarks, we analyzed the number of selections made without any visual feedback (meaning that people used only their hands as a reference for selection) and the performance of different locations around the hand.

Selection with no visual feedback

We recorded the number of selections made without waiting the 300ms for visual feedback (i.e., "expert mode"). For both types of HandMark menu, selection without feedback started near zero in the early blocks, but increased to approximately 8% of selections in the final block.

In addition, experimenter's informal visual observations showed that all users moved their selection finger towards the correct region on the menu hand even before the menu hand was placed. That is, even when people did wait for system feedback, they were preparing for a correct selection by correctly positioning their finger before the menu was displayed. These preparatory actions suggest that people were developing proprioceptive memory and were remembering the mapping of commands to hand locations.

Performance of Selection by Target Location

We also analyzed selection time and expert mode use by target location. For HandMark-Finger, three areas were defined: finger-top, between-fingers and near-thumb. RM-ANOVA showed finger-top locations were better than others with 0.03 expert-selections/command, s.d. 0.12 ($F_{2,24}$=1.41, p=.26) and faster command selection (mean 2.3s, s.d. 0.1) ($F_{2,24}$=0.74, p=.5). For HandMark-Multi, two areas were defined: close and far from index and thumb. Here, the targets located close to index and thumb performed best – for these better-landmarked locations, selections were faster and expert mode was used more (0.08 selections/command, s.d. 0.16) with a significant main effect ($F_{1,12}$=6.67, p<.05).

Participant Comments

Participant comments followed the pattern of preference results. Participants made several comments on how spatial stability and quick activation using both hands helped the speed of HandMark menus: one participant said *"Really neat technique that allows you to browse through different tabs based on the number of fingers."* One person, however, remarked on the difficulty of remembering the different hands' sets: *"It was difficult to remember which hand has the right kind of tool."*

Other comments suggested that the HandMark interfaces helped participants to learn command locations: one said *"It was easier to remember where icons were relative to spaces on fingers instead of just on the tabs."* Another said "*[HandMark was] easier to use and faster to remember,*" and another stated "*[Tabs were] more difficult to memorize.*"

Some participants stated that they were initially concerned with slow memorization in HandMark-Multi, but eventually preferred it. One person stated *"Remembering was slightly slower at early stage but in a short amount of time it became quite strong and it became easier to answer."* This participant also stated that the Tab interface *"was fast at the beginning but it could not build up strong memory and hence it became tough to apply them later."*

DISCUSSION

Our study of HandMark menus provides six main results:

- HandMark-Finger was significantly faster than Tabs-2 (0.62s/selection), and was faster in all blocks.
- HandMark-Multi was slower overall than Tabs-8 (0.62s per selection), but only in the early blocks.
- The only difference in errors between the two approaches was that HM-Multi had a slightly higher rate than Tabs-8.
- There were no significant differences for perceived effort between interfaces in either pair, but most participants preferred both HandMark menu types.

Explanation and Interpretation of Results

Performance analysis of HandMark menus

The study showed that HandMark-Finger was faster than a visually-guided tab menu (at all stages) and HandMark-Multi was slower (although only during early use). There are a few reasons for these results, based on the command selection steps for both novice and expert. For novices, there are three steps needed: invoking the correct command set, searching for the target command, and executing a selection action. Invoking the menu was different for both interfaces. For HandMark-Finger, invocation involves pressing with all five fingers anywhere on the touch surface, which was easy and fast. In contrast, the Tabs-2 required touching at a specific position (the tab buttons at the top of the screen). Participants had to reach further for the tab interface, and had to be more precise in their selections because of the lower angle of the display. These factors likely led to additional time to invoke the tab interface.

For HandMark-Multi, displaying a command set involves different combinations of fingers. With eight sets, there were eight different combinations of fingers. Novices spent a large amount of time determining which finger combination belonged to which set; in contrast, Tabs-8 showed names and specific positions for each tab. Even though novices also had to spend time searching through the different tabs, the visual presentation allowed people to better organize their task.

Searching for a specific command within a set required a similar strategy for all interfaces. The visual search needed for HandMark-Finger could take longer initially, since the commands are shown at different places around the hand compared to the grid presentation of Tabs-2. In particular, in some cases people's hands could partially occlude the menu items. However, as people became more experienced, the additional landmarks in HandMark-Finger appeared to help people with retrieval [23]. HandMark-Multi also supports development of spatial memory, although the grid of items does not contain as many landmarks as HandMark-Finger, and so there was not as large an advantage in spatial memory as was seen in the smaller menu.

The final step – executing the selection action – was similar for all interfaces, although accurate touches appeared to be more difficult with Tabs due to the screen's oblique angle.

For experts, selection in HandMark menus requires only two steps: retrieval of the command's set and location from memory, and execution of the selection action at any position on the touch surface. The lack of a spatial reference frame for Tabs, however, means that users must still perform some degree of visual search, even when they are familiar with the location. The performance advantage for expert use of HandMark menus arises in the speed of execution, which can be achieved by chording the menu choice with the selection.

In addition, the amount of time taken for reaching to the tabs (at the top edge of the display) was a substantial component of the overall performance of the Tabs technique. This is not the case for HandMark menus, since these are always invoked close to the user. Therefore, the performance difference between a tab interface and HandMarks will to some degree depend on where the tabs are located – as tabs become further away, the performance advantage for HandMarks will increase. In future work we will also compare against palette-based techniques like Toolglasses [8]: these methods bring tools close to the work area, but often require that the user execute additional actions (e.g., to grab the palette and drag it near to the selection hand).

Error rates with HandMark

Error rates per command were high in all the techniques: 4% for both HandMark-Finger and Tabs-2; 6% and 4% for HandMark-Multi and Tabs-8. This high error rate might be an artifact of our experimental protocol, which instructed participants to select commands quickly, and noted that errors could be corrected afterwards. There are other possible explanations for the error rates, however. First, the quick execution of a selection in all the interfaces may have encouraged participants to view errors as amenable to rapid correction, thereby encouraging users towards a 'guess and correct' mode of operation [23].

Second, it is possible that people's memory of a command's spatial location was imperfect, and so participants may have experienced 'near misses' more often with larger sets (HandMark-Multi and Tabs-8). Third, it is very easy to touch down with fingers on touch surface but, it is somewhat more difficult to change the combination of fingers very quickly, which sometimes caused unintentional touches for HandMark-Multi. Last, for both Tabs-2 and Tabs-8, the oblique viewing angle may also have increased errors. Further work is needed to explore these sources of error, and to determine whether the high error rates for both techniques occur in real-world use.

Command-set browsing with HandMark

Incorrect command-set selections were also relatively high for all the interfaces: 0.05 sets/command for both HandMark-Finger and Tabs-2; 0.64 and 0.18 tabs/command for HandMark-Multi and Tabs-8. As the number of tabs was smaller for the first pair, participants made fewer errors; in the larger menus, the rate was considerably higher. This can be explained by the larger number of items, and the increased need for visual search overall. As described above, the visual representation of the tabs in the standard interface may have allowed participants to better organize their visual search, whereas people's search in HandMark-Multi was often poorly organized. This indicates one disadvantage of hand-centric interfaces – information such as the name of the set cannot be shown on the reference frame (i.e., the hand).

An additional reason for differences in set-selection errors is the physical position of fingers in HandMark-Multi. As fingers are very close to one another, people sometimes touched the wrong finger onto the surface. More work is needed to evaluate the ergonomic and effort characteristics of different hand and finger combinations – it may be that a smaller number of menus (using only the easy-to-produce finger combinations) will improve browsing performance.

Real-world use of HandMarks

The two HandMark prototypes represent a tradeoff between landmarks and command capacity – HM-Finger makes more extensive use of the hands and is faster overall, but is limited in size; HM-Multi can accommodate more commands, but overloads one region (between thumb and index finger).

Although further studies with the techniques are needed, we speculate that people will be more successful at learning locations with HM-Finger, due to its richer landmarking, and therefore more likely to use the expert selection mode in real-world use. We are also interested in how continued use will change the ways that people carry out preparatory actions – for example, once the locations around the hand are learned, it is possible to use tactile feedback alone to prepare for a selection (e.g., register the pointing finger between two fingers of the menu hand, and then touch the surface).

Although HandMark-Multi does not have the same rich landmarks, the consistent presentation of command sets between thumb and index finger is still likely to be valuable in real-world use. HM-Multi can be considered as a version of earlier Palette techniques, but with the tool items always presented using a consistent spatial reference frame.

In future work we will also compare HandMark menus to other recent designs, such as Marking Menus [32], Flower Menus [4], and Arpège [18]. One area of particular interest is how the different approaches support transitions from novice to expert use – both HandMarks and Marking Menus, for example, are based on the principle of rehearsing expert actions in the novice mode; in other gesture-based and chord-based systems such as Arpège, learning the commands requires explicit training.

Limitations and design possibilities

Our investigation of HandMark menus considers only a portion of the likely issues present in real-world use, and there are several ways in which the HandMark techniques can be extended in future.

Hand postures and ergonomics. A few participants reported difficulties with the finger combinations required to choose different command sets with HandMark-Multi. Participants noted that changing quickly between sets was initially difficult as it required good finger dexterity (even though all of our hand postures are "relaxed" [18]). These initial problems were quickly overcome, and it was seen as helpful that the menus move and adapt as the hands are moved, allowing users to choose comfortable hand positions. Finally, two participants had longer fingernails in our study, but they did not have difficulty using HandMark menus.

Mapping of commands to menus and locations. In our study, we arbitrarily assigned commands to locations, and command sets to different hands – in real use, performance and learning could likely be substantially improved with a more thoughtful mapping. For example, with HandMark-Multi, both the left and right hands "held" four different command sets, and some participants initially had difficulty remembering which hand contained their desired set. The study suggested that choosing the wrong hand was a costly error, as participants tended to check each of the sets on that hand before trying the other hand. Therefore, further work is needed to determine how menu contents are best mapped to different hands. In addition, since some locations around the hand appeared to be faster and easier to learn, frequent or important commands could be assigned to these locations.

Occlusion of the menu. HM-Finger shows items between fingers, so it is possible for the hand itself to occlude the menu, particularly if the hand is not directly in front of the user. In the study, some participants with smaller fingers occasionally experienced this problem. In future work we will explore solutions to this problem, such as better determination of the actual shape of the hand, automatically scaling the icons for different hand sizes, or moving the icons upwards (while still maintaining relative spatial positioning) if there is not enough space between fingers. Previous work by Vogel and colleagues [44] has shown that unrestricted models of hand occlusion can be inferred from touch points, so we are confident that our technique can be extended to the general usage case. The problem of occlusion primarily affects the learning stages, however, when users are still using the visual guidance of the displayed menu; once item locations are known, users can position their selection finger using the hand rather than the display.

Multiple users and different orientations. The prototype system supported only one person at a fixed location, and further work is needed to determine how the hand detection technique will perform with multiple hands and with hands at any orientation. We believe that our hand-posture algorithms can handle these additional demands with additional sensing of the environment, such as finger-contact areas and shapes, or a depth camera that can track each person's approximate location around the table [17].

Increasing the number of commands. Our prototypes explored two command-set sizes (42 for HandMark-Finger, and 160 for HandMark-Multi). It is possible to increase these numbers (e.g., by having a larger grid between thumb and index finger [11, 38], by stacking additional layers above the fingers in HM-Finger, or by using the different positions in HM-Finger as triggers for second-level sets). However, further work is needed to determine whether larger command sets are beneficial – for example, our study showed that initial learning was more difficult for the multiple sets in HM-Multi, and it may be advantageous to restrict the number of commands to improve learnability.

Indicating hand menu contents. One problem identified in the study was that HandMark-Multi does not provide any visual indication of the mapping between finger combinations and command sets in order to assist users who are in the novice stages of learning. A visual "map legend" could be shown on the display as a reminder, but it would also be possible to use augmented-reality techniques to show menu contents (e.g., project symbols on the display near the hands above the table, or on the hands themselves).

Device orientation and size. In our experiment we used a relatively small tabletop touch surface (24-inch diagonal). We believe that this setup reasonably approximates the actions that will be needed on a larger table, but we will confirm this in future studies with larger surfaces. In addition, we are interested in how HandMarks will work on smaller surfaces such as tablets. Many devices are now large enough to accommodate a whole hand, and a technique such as HandMark-Finger could be successful on smaller devices (although comparisons will be needed to other techniques such as FastTap and bezel-based interaction).

Advanced interactions. Most interfaces include widgets that are more advanced than buttons – for example, sliders or color pickers can be used to provide a finer degree of control over application parameters. We will explore how these kinds of widgets can be converted to work with HandMark menus – for example, HandMark could be adapted to use a Toolglass-style interaction in which users click through the command and start their manipulation at the same time. It may also be possible to combine HandMarks with other gesture-based techniques such as marking menus [29]. For example, people could activate different command modes with one hand and perform gestures with the other.

Single-handed use. It is not currently possible to use HandMark menus with one hand – both hands are required for novice and expert mode. The two-handed nature of the technique increases interaction bandwidth, and is one of the reasons why it performed well. However, it would be possible to modify the technique to be usable with one hand. Although chorded operation would not be possible, it would be relatively easy to have the menu stay present for a short time after being invoked – this would allow people to invoke the menu and then select with the same hand (still being able to take advantage of spatial memory).

CONCLUSIONS

Command selection on large multi-touch surfaces can be difficult, because techniques are not well suited to the display setting, and because the lack of landmarks makes it harder for users to build up familiarity with spatial locations. People's hands are always present in the workspace, however, and can be used as a reference frame for designing touch-based selection techniques. A few techniques take advantage of hands, but often these methods are limited in the number of items they can accommodate.

We designed two hand-centric techniques for multitouch displays – one allowing 42 commands, and one allowing 160 – and tested them in an empirical comparison against standard tab widgets. We found that the small version (HandMark-Finger) was significantly faster at all stages of use, and that the large version (HandMark-Multi) was slower at the start but equivalent to tabs after people gained experience with the technique. Participants strongly preferred both of the HandMark menus over tabs.

Our work shows that the hands, and people's intimate knowledge of them, are an under-used resource for interaction. We demonstrate that hand-centric interfaces are feasible, can be faster than standard techniques, and are preferred by users. Techniques using hands as landmarks can improve the performance and usability of interfaces for tables and other multi-touch systems.

ACKNOWLEDGMENTS

This work was supported by NSERC and the Surfnet research network. Our thanks to Andy Cockburn and to the anonymous referees for valuable comments and suggestions.

REFERENCES

1. Jason Alexander, Andy Cockburn, Stephen Fitchett, Carl Gutwin, and Saul Greenberg. 2009. Revisiting read wear. In *Proceedings of the 27th international conference on Human factors in computing systems* (CHI '09), 1665–1674. http://dx.doi.org/10.1145/1518701.1518957
2. Jussi Ängeslevä, Ian Oakley, Stephen Hughes and Sile O'Modhrain. 2003. Body Mnemonics - Portable device interaction design concept. In *Proceedings of the 16th annual ACM symposium on User interface software and technology* (UIST '03).
3. Oscar Kin-Chung Au and Chiew-Lan Tai. 2010. Multitouch finger registration and its applications. In *Proceedings of the 22nd Conference of the Computer-Human Interaction Special Interest Group of Australia on Computer-Human Interaction* (OZCHI '10), 41-48. http://dx.doi.org/10.1145/1952222.1952233
4. Gilles Bailly, Eric Lecolinet, and Laurence Nigay. 2008. Flower menus. In *Proceedings of the working conference on Advanced visual interfaces* (AVI '08), 15-22. http://dx.doi.org/10.1145/1385569.1385575
5. Gilles Bailly, Jörg Müller, and Eric Lecolinet. 2012. Design and evaluation of finger-count interaction: Combining multitouch gestures and menus. *Int. J. Hum.-Comput. Stud.* 70, 10 (October 2012), 673-689. http://dx.doi.org/10.1016/j.ijhcs.2012.05.006
6. Olivier Bau and Wendy E. Mackay. 2008. OctoPocus. In *Proceedings of the 21st annual ACM symposium on User interface software and technology* (UIST '08), 37-46. http://dx.doi.org/10.1145/1449715.1449724
7. Hrvoje Benko, T. Scott Saponas, Dan Morris, and Desney Tan. 2009. Enhancing input on and above the interactive surface with muscle sensing. In *Proceedings of the ACM International Conference on Interactive Tabletops and Surfaces* (ITS '09), 93-100. http://dx.doi.org/10.1145/1731903.1731924
8. Eric A. Bier, Maureen C. Stone, Ken Pier, William Buxton, Tony D. DeRose. 1993. Toolglass and magic lenses: the see-through interface. In *Proceedings of the 20th annual conference on Computer graphics and interactive techniques* (SIGGRAPH '93), 73-80.
9. Volkert Buchmann, Stephen Violich, Mark Billinghurst, and Andy Cockburn. 2004. FingARtips. In *Proceedings of the 2nd international conference on Computer graphics and interactive techniques in Austalasia and Southe East Asia* (GRAPHITE '04), 212-221. http://dx.doi.org/10.1145/988834.988871
10. Andy Cockburn, Philip Quinn, Carl Gutwin, Gonzalo Ramos, and Julian Looser. 2011. Air pointing: Design and evaluation of spatial target acquisition with and without visual feedback. *Int. J. Hum.-Comput. Stud.* 69, 6 (June 2011), 401-414. http://dx.doi.org/10.1016/j.ijhcs.2011.02.005
11. Kiran Dandekar, Balasundar I. Raju, and Mandayam A. Srinivasan. 2003. 3-D Finite-Element Models of Human and Monkey Fingertips to Investigate the Mechanics of Tactile Sense. *Journal of Biomechanical Engineering* 125, 5 (2003), 682-691. http://dx.doi.org/10.1115/1.1613673
12. Chi Tai Dang, Martin Straub, and Elisabeth André. 2009. Hand distinction for multi-touch tabletop interaction. In *Proceedings of the ACM International Conference on Interactive Tabletops and Surfaces* (ITS '09), 101-108. http://doi.acm.org/10.1145/1731903.1731925
13. Rudolph P. Darken and John L. Sibert. 1996. Wayfinding strategies and behaviors in large virtual worlds. In *Proceedings of the SIGCHI conference on Human factors in computing systems common ground* (CHI '96), 142-150. http://dx.doi.org/10.1145/238386.238459
14. Paul Dietz and Darren Leigh. 2001. DiamondTouch. In *Proceedings of the 14th annual ACM symposium on User interface software and technology* (UIST '01), 219-226. http://dx.doi.org/10.1145/502348.502389
15. Brian D. Ehret. 2002. Learning where to look. In *Proceedings of the SIGCHI conference on Human factors in computing systems Changing our world, changing ourselves* (CHI '02), 211-218. http://dx.doi.org/10.1145/503376.503414
16. Philipp Ewerling, Alexander Kulik, and Bernd Froehlich. 2012. Finger and hand detection for multi-touch interfaces based on maximally stable extremal regions. In *Proceedings of the 2012 ACM international conference on Interactive tabletops and surfaces* (ITS '12, 173-182. http://dx.doi.org/10.1145/2396636.2396663
17. Aaron M. Genest, Carl Gutwin, Anthony Tang, Michael Kalyn, and Zenja Ivkovic. 2013. KinectArms: a toolkit for capturing and displaying arm embodiments in distributed tabletop groupware. In *Proceedings of the 2013 conference on Computer supported cooperative work* (CSCW '13, 157-166. http://dx.doi.org/10.1145/2441776.2441796
18. Emilien Ghomi, Stéphane Huot, Olivier Bau, Michel Beaudouin-Lafon, and Wendy E. Mackay. 2013. Arpège: learning multitouch chord gestures vocabularies. In *Proceedings of the 2013 ACM international conference on Interactive tabletops and surfaces* (ITS '13), 209-218. http://dx.doi.org/10.1145/2512349.2512795
19. Yves Guiard. 1987. Asymmetric Division of Labor in Human Skilled Bimanual Action: The Kinematic Chain as a Model. *Journal of Motor Behaviour* 1987, Vol. 19, No. 4, 486-517.
20. François Guimbretiére and Terry Winograd. 2000. FlowMenu: combining command, text, and data entry.

In *Proceedings of the 13th annual ACM symposium on User interface software and technology* (UIST '00), 213-216. http://dx.doi.org/10.1145/354401.354778

21. Sean Gustafson, Daniel Bierwirth, and Patrick Baudisch. 2010. Imaginary interfaces: spatial interaction with empty hands and without visual feedback. In *Proceedings of the 23nd annual ACM symposium on User interface software and technology* (UIST '10), 3-12. http://dx.doi.org/10.1145/1866029.1866033
22. Sean Gustafson, Christian Holz, and Patrick Baudisch. 2011. Imaginary phone: learning imaginary interfaces by transferring spatial memory from a familiar device. In *Proceedings of the 24th annual ACM symposium on User interface software and technology* (UIST '11), 283-292. http://dx.doi.org/10.1145/2047196.2047233
23. Carl Gutwin, Andy Cockburn, Joey Scarr, Sylvain Malacria, and Scott C. Olson. 2014. Faster command selection on tablets with FastTap. In *Proceedings of the 32nd annual ACM conference on Human factors in computing systems* (CHI '14), 2617-2626. http://dx.doi.org/10.1145/2556288.2557136
24. Sandra G. Hart and Lowell E. Staveland. 1988. Development of NASA-TLX (Task Load Index): Results of empirical and theoretical research. In *P. A. Hancock and N. Meshkati (Eds.)* Human Mental Workload. Amsterdam: North Holland Press.
25. Christian Holz and Patrick Baudisch. 2010. The generalized perceived input point model and how to double touch accuracy by extracting fingerprints. In *Proceedings of the 28th international conference on Human factors in computing systems* (CHI '10), 581 590. http://dx.doi.org/10.1145/1753326.1753413
26. Paul Kabbash, William Buxton, and Abigail Sellen. 1994. Two-handed input in a compound task. In *Proceedings of the SIGCHI Conference on Human Factors in Computing Systems* (CHI '94), 417-423. http://dx.doi.org/10.1145/191666.191808
27. Kenrick Kin, Björn Hartmann, and Maneesh Agrawala. 2011. Two-handed marking menus for multitouch devices. *ACM Transactions on Computer-Human Interaction* 18, 3, Article 16 (August 2011), 23 pages. http://dx.doi.org/10.1145/1993060.1993066
28. Gordon Paul Kurtenbach. 1993. *The design and evaluation of marking menus*. PhD Thesis, University of Toronto.
29. Gordon Kurtenbach and William Buxton. 1994. User learning and performance with marking menus. In *Conference companion on Human factors in computing systems* (CHI '94), 258-264. http://dx.doi.org/10.1145/259963.260376
30. Gordon Kurtenbach, George W. Fitzmaurice, Russell N. Owen, and Thomas Baudel. 1999. The Hotbox: efficient access to a large number of menu-items. In *Proceedings of the SIGCHI conference on Human Factors in Computing Systems* (CHI '99), 231-237. http://dx.doi.org/10.1145/302979.303047
31. Gordon Kurtenbach, Thomas P. Moran, and William Buxton. 1994. Contextual animation of gestural commands. *Computer Graphics Forum*. Vol. 13. No. 5. Blackwell Science Ltd.
32. Gordon Kurtenbach, Abigail Sellen, and William Buxton. 1993. An Empirical Evaluation of Some Articulatory and Cognitive Aspects of Marking Menus. *Human-Comp. Interaction* 8, 1 (mar 1993), 1-23. http://dx.doi.org/10.1207/s15327051hci0801_1
33. G. Julian Lepinski, Tovi Grossman, and George Fitzmaurice. 2010. The design and evaluation of multitouch marking menus. In *Proceedings of the 28th international conference on Human factors in computing systems* (CHI '10), 2233-2242. http://dx.doi.org/10.1145/1753326.1753663
34. Julien Letessier and François Bérard. 2004. Visual tracking of bare fingers for interactive surfaces. In *Proceedings of the 17th annual ACM symposium on User interface software and technology* (UIST '04), 119-122. http://doi.acm.org/10.1145/1029632.1029652
35. Frank Chun Yat Li, David Dearman, and Khai N. Truong. 2009. Virtual shelves: interactions with orientation aware devices. In *Proceedings of the 22nd annual ACM symposium on User interface software and technology* (UIST '09), 125-128. http://dx.doi.org/10.1145/1622176.1622200
36. Hao Lü and Yang Li. 2011. Gesture avatar: a technique for operating mobile user interfaces using gestures. In *Proceedings of the SIGCHI Conference on Human Factors in Computing Systems* (CHI '11, 207-216. http://dx.doi.org/10.1145/1978942.1978972
37. Sylvain Malacria, Gilles Bailly, Joel Harrison, Andy Cockburn, and Carl Gutwin. 2013. Promoting Hotkey use through rehearsal with ExposeHK. In *Proceedings of the SIGCHI Conference on Human Factors in Computing Systems* (CHI '13, 573-582. http://dx.doi.org/10.1145/2470654.2470735
38. Pekka Parhi, Amy K. Karlson, and Benjamin B. Bederson. 2006. Target size study for one-handed thumb use on small touchscreen devices. In *Proceedings of the 8th conference on Human-computer interaction with mobile devices and services* (MobileHCI '06), 203-210. http://dx.doi.org/10.1145/1152215.1152260
39. George Robertson, Mary Czerwinski, Kevin Larson, Daniel C. Robbins, David Thiel, and Maarten van Dantzich. 1998. Data mountain. In *Proceedings of the 11th annual ACM symposium on User interface software and technology* (UIST '98), 153-162. http://dx.doi.org/10.1145/288392.288596

40. Quentin Roy, Sylvain Malacria, Yves Guiard, Eric Lecolinet, and James Eagan. 2013. Augmented letters: mnemonic gesture-based shortcuts. In *Proceedings of the SIGCHI Conference on Human Factors in Computing Systems* (CHI '13, 2325-2328. http://dx.doi.org/10.1145/2470654.2481321

41. Joey Scarr, Andy Cockburn, Carl Gutwin, and Andrea Bunt. 2012. Improving command selection with CommandMaps. In *Proceedings of the 2012 ACM annual conference on Human Factors in Computing Systems* (CHI '12), 257-266. http://dx.doi.org/10.1145/2207676.2207713

42. Dominik Schmidt, Ming Ki Chong, and Hans Gellersen. 2010. HandsDown. In *Proceedings of the 6th Nordic Conference on Human-Computer Interaction Extending Boundaries* (NordiCHI '10), 432–441. http://dx.doi.org/10.1145/1868914.1868964

43. Dominik Schmidt, Ming Ki Chong, and Hans Gellersen. 2010. IdLenses. In *ACM International Conference on Interactive Tabletops and Surfaces* (ITS '10), 131–134. http://dx.doi.org/10.1145/1936652.1936678

44. Daniel Vogel. 2010. *Direct Pen Input and Hand Occlusion.* Ph.D Dissertation. University of Toronto. Retrieved from http://tspace.library.utoronto.ca/handle/1807/24905

45. Daniel Vogel and Géry Casiez. 2012. Hand occlusion on a multi-touch tabletop. In *Proceedings of the SIGCHI Conference on Human Factors in Computing Systems* (CHI '12). 2307-2316. http://dx.doi.org/10.1145/2207676.2208390

46. Julie Wagner, Eric Lecolinet, and Ted Selker. 2014. Multi-finger chords for hand-held tablets: recognizable and memorable. In *Proceedings of the SIGCHI Conference on Human Factors in Computing Systems* (CHI '14), 2883-2892. http://dx.doi.org/10.1145/2556288.2556958

47. Robert Y. Wang and Jovan Popović. 2009. Real-time hand-tracking with a color glove. *ACM Trans. Graph*. 28, 3, Article 63 (July 2009), 8 pages. http://doi.acm.org/10.1145/1531326.1531369

48. Mike Wu and Ravin Balakrishnan. 2003. Multi-finger and whole hand gestural interaction techniques for multi-user tabletop displays. In *Proceedings of the 16th annual ACM symposium on User interface software and technology* (UIST '03), 193-202. http://dx.doi.org/10.1145/964696.964718

49. Shengdong Zhao, Maneesh Agrawala, and Ken Hinckley. 2006. Zone and polygon menus. In *Proceedings of the SIGCHI conference on Human Factors in computing systems* (CHI '06), 1077-1086. http://dx.doi.org/10.1145/1124772.1124933

Glowworms and Fireflies: Ambient Light on Large Interactive Surfaces

Florian Perteneder[1], Eva-Maria Grossauer[1], Joanne Leong[1], Wolfgang Stuerzlinger[2], Michael Haller[1]

[1]Media Interaction Lab, University of Applied Sciences Upper Austria, Austria

[2]School of Interactive Arts + Technology, Simon Fraser University, Canada

ABSTRACT

Ambient light is starting to be commercially used to enhance the viewing experience for watching TV. We believe that ambient light can add value in meeting and control rooms that use large vertical interactive surfaces. Therefore, we equipped a large interactive whiteboard with a peripheral ambient light display and explored its utility for different scenarios by conducting two controlled experiments. In the first experiment, we investigated how ambient light can be used for peripheral notifications, and how perception is influenced by the user's position and the type of work they are engaged in. The second experiment investigated the utility of ambient light for off-screen visualization. We condense our findings into several design recommendations that we then applied to application scenarios to show the versatility and usefulness of ambient light for large surfaces.

Author Keywords

Ambient light display; peripheral display; large interactive surfaces; interactive whiteboard; evaluations;

ACM Classification Keywords

H5.2 Information interfaces and presentation: User Interfaces

INTRODUCTION

Introduced by Philips, Ambilight (*ambient light*) is known as a lighting effect for TVs to illuminate the environment around the TV based on the predominant colors in the video image. This leads to enhanced visual comfort, less fatigue [10], and a subjective enlargement of the perceived screen size [7]. Early models provided only a static illumination to reduce eye-strain that occurs while watching TV in a dark room. Later versions aimed to adapt the illumination dynamically for providing a better and more immersive viewing experience [12]. Although Philips is offering the only commercial solution, several DIY-projects and open source projects (e.g. LiveLight Project[1], Atmolight[2]) aim to provide a similar experience by equipping screens with LED strips.

CHI'16, May 07 - 12, 2016, San Jose, CA, USA

ACM978-1-4503-3362-7/16/05...$15.00

DOI: http://dx.doi.org/10.1145/2858036.2858524

All these efforts focus on enhancing the viewing experience while watching videos or playing games on TVs, where the ambient light depends on the content currently shown on screen. We believe that ambient light can enhance how people work with *large interactive surfaces.* It can extend the screen-space and provide a peripheral information space (see Figure 1) across multiple applications and scenarios. Ambient light can ameliorate the resolution limitations of current large interactive surfaces, such as wall projections, by preserving valuable display space, as notifications can be displayed in the periphery.

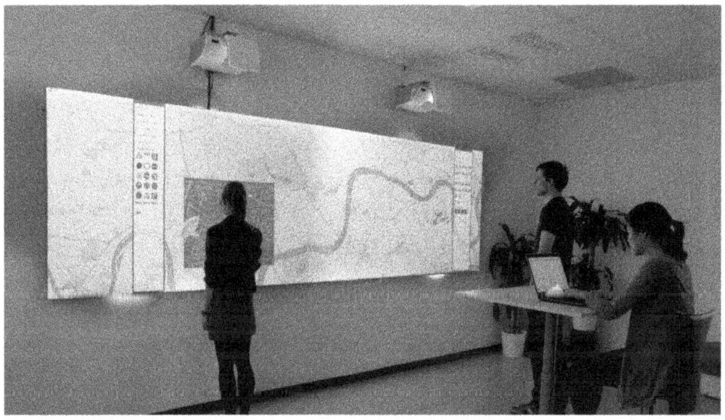

Figure 1: Using ambient light to support work on large interactive surfaces via peripheral information display.

In this paper, we are mainly interested in establishing an understanding of how best to use ambient light to display information and support work on large interactive surfaces within a productive environment, such as in discussion or control rooms. For this, we firstly equipped a digital whiteboard with an ambient lighting system. Drawing upon related work and our own insights, we formulate a number of hypotheses and conduct a series of two user studies using our setup to explore the design space provided by peripheral LEDs. The first experiment deals with the issue of different tasks, different user positions, and the limits of peripheral perception. The second experiment examines the utility of ambient light visualizations for off-screen object visualization by comparing it to the well-established techniques Halo [6] and Wedge [14]. Based on the results of the studies, we present a number of design recommendations for how best to use ambient light to display information and enhance how people work with large interactive surfaces. Finally, we present a number of different usage scenarios to highlight the design principles.

[1] http://www.livelightproject.com/

[2] http://www.vdr-wiki.de/wiki/index.php/Atmo-plugin

RELATED WORK

According to the definitions of Pousman and Stasko [35] our setup, which extends a large interactive surface with ambient light, is a peripheral display. Therefore, after discussing various related projects that use *ambient light*, we present insights on *peripheral vision*, and provide examples of systems that apply these principles. Finally, we also provide a brief overview on *territoriality* in the context of large surfaces as well as *off-screen visualizations,* as these topics are relevant for our experiments.

The taxonomy for ambient information systems by Pousman and Stasko [35] includes the following four design dimensions: *information capacity*, *notification level*, *representation fidelity,* and *aesthetical emphasis*. In this paper, we focus on exploring the information capacity and notification level of ambient light. A peripheral display can also oftentimes be understood as a notification system. Matthews et al. [30] distinguish between five types of notifications: *ignore*, *change blind*, *make aware*, *interrupt*, and *demand action*. In the context of this paper, we are especially interested in the third type, classified as *make aware*.

Ambient Light

While there are many ambient light displays that use only light as a source of output [1,18,26,34], there are only a few examples where ambient light is used in combination with high-resolution displays [32,33]. AmbiX [31] provides valuable insights on how to use ambient light displays to provide visual cues in an unobtrusive manner. Löcken et al. [27] explored the design space of ambient light displays by simulating various ambient light properties, such as the optimal LED arrangement in software, before actually building an entire hardware setup. Their tool was used to create Sparkle [33] an ambient light display for dynamic off-screen points of interest. From a technical perspective our setup has many similarities with Ambilight by Philips, with the previously mentioned DIY projects, and with the Ambient Timer [32].

Peripheral Vision

While the perception of color is lacking in the periphery [45], the human vision system is exceptionally capable of perceiving movement and brightness in the peripheral area [43]. Therefore, Bartram et al. [4] suggest using movement to increase perception in the periphery, which we also investigate in one of our studies by observing blinking notifications. Ball and North [3] investigated why visualization tasks benefit from large-scale displays. They conclude that the major factor is physical navigation, but also found that the effect is amplified by peripheral vision. Bezerianos et al. [8] studied the perception of visualizations on wall-sized displays. Their findings suggest that perception accuracy is negatively impacted when users are close to the wall. Therefore, they suggest that users stand further away when examining data.

Peripheral Displays

There are various examples for ambient displays that demand the use of peripheral vision. ambientRoom [22] is an early project of utilizing an entire room for providing information in an ambient way. IllumiRoom [23] also follows the idea of focus and context [5]. It casts a projection on the wall around the TV to extend the screen and provide a more immersive gaming experience. Perifoveal Display [20], a large visualization display for a desktop workstation, was designed for observing large amounts of data. Kimura [28] and the Peripheral-Vision Display presented by Birnholtz [9] are examples of using a peripheral display to support background activities within an office context. We observe peripheral perception of ambient light and on-screen notifications in our first study.

Territoriality in the Context of Large Vertical Displays

Various work deals with territoriality in the context of public ambient displays [41] and large vertical displays [2]. Range [24] and Hello.wall [36] use proximity sensing to provide a smooth transition between different modes of interaction. Based on this, we study three scenarios that utilize different interaction zones in front of large interactive displays.

Off-screen Visualizations

Two well-known examples of off-screen visualization methods are Halo [6] and Wedge [14]. Although both were initially designed for small devices, they are also used as reference strategies on larger surfaces [21], since there are few alternatives. Another popular way to help users to find off-screen visualizations are minimaps [37]. Folding metaphors like in Melange [12] or Canyon [21] require high-res screen space to be available outside of the main working area.

DESIGN SPACE OF AMBIENT LIGHT

At first glance, it may seem that ambient light has a very limited set of properties that can be used to convey information. However, light offers quite a large number of different parameters to encode information [31]. The most obvious parameter is *color*, which contains three subcomponents: *hue*, *brightness*, *saturation*. These single parameters can also be found in the enumeration of Visual Variables by Mackinlay, who referred to them as *Color Hue*, *Color Saturation* and *Density* (*Brightness*) [29]. While hue is a very good parameter to encode nominal data, brightness and saturation are more suitable to encode ordinal or quantitative data. We assume this kind of encoding transfers to ambient light. Besides color, *duration* and *frequency of changes* (=*animation*) [25,31] can also be used. In addition, the specific physical setting along the rim of a large surface also provides the *position* and the *size* of the luminous area as useful properties.

Besides these properties, another important factor that has to be considered is the *user's position* [31]. When watching TV, the position and the view of the user are well defined. In contrast, the situation in front of a large interactive wall is fundamentally different. Dependent on the task, users may be standing directly in front of the board, moving around, discussing the content with others, standing a couple of meters away, or sitting at the back of the room. This variety of possible user positions and visual perspectives requires a closer look at the dependencies of position, focus and perception of peripheral visual stimuli.

DECODING WORKING STYLES AND DISTANCE

Interactive surfaces are designed to support a wide variety of tasks and working styles [15,38,44]. A very common use case for these systems is to support people in gaining an overview of large amounts of data [44]. They can also be used for focused work, where users either work directly on the surface [15], or use it in an ambient manner while performing primary tasks on other devices [28,39]. Based on these insights, we classified the work on interactive whiteboards into two dimensions: *distance* and the *type of work*, which yields four scenarios:

The ***Close-Focused*** scenario for an interactive wall setup comprises a large degree of user involvement. Users are typically very close to the wall and have a limited field of view.

In the ***Close-Overview*** scenario specific UI elements, such as mini-maps are used to provide overview on a small area.

The ***Distant-Overview*** scenario involves discussion or taking in a lot of content. People try to gain an overview, rearrange, and structure content. To gain such an overview, users often step back from the wall to widen their field of view.

The ***Distant-Focused*** scenario involves focused tasks performed on a different, personal or stationary device. The interactive wall is then used as a peripheral or ambient display where public information is updated and visible to others.

We acknowledge techniques such as mini-maps or similar approaches that provide an overview through additional UI elements. However, on very large display surfaces these can easily be too far away to be useful. Moreover, people naturally take a step back from the board to get an overview. Thus, *Close-Overview* does not present a typical working style to us and we focus on the other three scenarios here: *Close-Focused, Distant-Overview, and Distant-Focused* (see Figure 2).

Related work suggests that the perception of ambient information is closely related to the user position [31]. We also expect that the type of *Distant-Focused* work has a considerable effect on the perception. Therefore, in our first experiment we explored these notions regarding perception of ambient light notifications within these three scenarios.

EVALUATION

Two empirical studies were conducted to explore the benefits and limitations of the ambient light equipped whiteboard. All experiments were carried out with the same apparatus.

Apparatus

The studies were conducted in a quiet white room with a large interactive whiteboard, equipped with an ambient light display system. For the ambient light we used multiple Adafruit NeoPixel LED strips with 680 LEDs in total, driven by an Arduino Leonardo and external power supplies. The whiteboard had a resolution of 3840 × 1080 pixels and was operated by two Vivitek D795WT short-throw projectors, with input through Anoto digital pens (ADP 601). The bottom edge of the whiteboard was mounted at 90cm. During

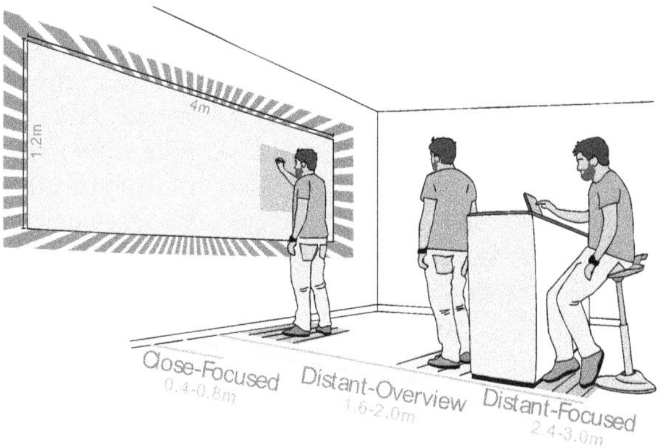

Figure 2: The three scenarios evaluated in experiment 1: *Close-Focused* on the whiteboard (orange), *Distant-Overview* (yellow), and *Distant-Focused* on an external device (green). The red striped area highlights the notification area.

the study we aimed to create realistic and reproducible lighting conditions. We used artificial light sources to provide an average brightness of 600 lx in the back where the participants worked in the *Distant-Focused* scenario and 300 lx next to the interactive wall. These values fulfill the lighting and energy standard defined in ISO 8995-1 – CIE S008/E.

EXPERIMENT 1: PERCEPTION OF NOTIFICATIONS

In the first experiment, *Ambient Light* was compared to *On-Screen* notifications in the three scenarios, *Close-Focused, Distant-Overview*, and *Distant-Focused* as described earlier. A blinking animation effect was also explored as a means of improving peripheral perception.

Hypothesis

The experiment was designed and conducted with the following hypotheses in mind.

Hypothesis 1.1: *Ambient Light vs. On-screen Notifications.* Due to their brighter appearance on the non-cluttered wall, Ambient Light notifications will be spotted more frequently than *On-Screen* notifications in the *Distant-Overview* and the Distant Focused scenario. There will be no big difference in the Close-Focused scenario, due to steep visual angles.

Hypothesis 1.2: *Impact of Scenarios on Visual Perception.* The perception of stimuli for the *Close-Focused* scenario will be low compared to the *Distant-Overview* and *Distant-Focused* scenarios, as both types of notifications are outside of the peripheral view.

Hypothesis 1.3: *Blinking vs. Static Notifications.* People's perceptional system is trained to notice changes. Therefore, blinking notifications will increase people's ability to perceive the notifications regardless of the scenarios and whether *On-Screen* or *Ambient Light* visualizations are used.

Design

We conducted a controlled experiment, where we assigned three different primary tasks to the participants that were designed to engage them in focused work on the board (*Close-Focused*), a task that required them to get an instant overview (*Distant-Overview*), and focused work on an external device within the room (*Distant-Focused*). We asked participants to work on the right side of the board (see Figure 2), as users usually do not work at the border between two projections. While the participants were executing the primary task, we triggered Ambient Light and On-Screen notifications and asked participants to identify the position of the notification when it was perceived. This way we calculated the percentage of perceived notification, which we used as the main metric in this experiment. In addition, we also added the *blinking* and *static* conditions; we assumed that blinking would increase the perception of notifications dramatically.

A within-subject design was used. The 3 scenarios × 2 (ambient light vs. on-screen) × 2 (blink vs. no blink) conditions were counterbalanced using a Latin square design. For each *position* (*left, right, top, bottom, top left, bottom left, top right, bottom right*) a total of two *trials* had to be completed. Summarizing, each participant completed a total of 192 trials (3 scenarios × 4 conditions × 8 positions × 2 trials). After each condition, participants were asked to rate the different techniques. The whole test, including instruction, training sessions, questionnaires, and a final interview lasted for approximately 80 minutes for each participant.

Tasks

Primary Tasks

For both the *Close-Focused* and *Distant-Focused* scenarios, we initially implemented a square click task [40], where participants have to click on a black square that randomly changes position every second. As our pilots revealed, participants still had enough time to actively search for notifications during performing this task. Thus, we decided to increase the task difficulty. Inspired by Hausen et al. [19], we provided four squares of different color. A colored border indicated the color of the square that had to be selected.

In the *Distant-Focused* scenario the colored square click task was performed full-screen on a 10.6" screen (MS Surface Pro) using touch for input (see Figure 3, *right).*

In the *Close-Focused* scenario, an adapted version of the colored square task was executed directly on the whiteboard using a digital pen (see Figure 3, *left*). To simulate focused work, the interaction area was limited to an area of 50 cm × 50 cm; moreover, the height was adjusted to suit the height of each participant.

As the *Distant-Overview* scenario does not involve continuous interaction, we had to search for a scenario that required gaining an overview of a large amount of data displayed on the board, but which also was mentally demanding so that participants would focus on it. Therefore, we used a word-search task (see Figure 3, *middle*) and asked participants to find as many words as possible and to strike them out once found on the board, and to step back for the next search.

Secondary Task

All participants were told to focus on the primary tasks while notifications appeared on the edges of the board. We asked

Figure 3: The primary tasks for the Close-Focused scenario (left), the Distant-Overview scenario (middle), and the Distant-Focused scenario (right).

the participants to name the position of the notification once they have been recognized. As shown in Figure 4, both *Ambient Light* as well as *On-screen Notifications* were colored red as we considered it as being an attention-demanding color. Both notification designs had the same length, 200px (~24cm). *On-Screen Notifications* were 25px high, as this size can fit text labels, which are comfortable to read up to a 4m distance, as humans mainly react to change. Additionally, the *On-screen Notifications* were given a white border and a drop shadow to stand out. Presented next to each other in Figure 4, Ambient Light undoubtedly stands out more. Due to the use of different technology, its visual footprint is larger. However, we decided not to mimic the visual footprint of the ambient light in the *On-Screen Notifications* as notifications of this size would be hardly used in a real world application where it is important and common practice to conserve limited display space. Moreover, our pilots revealed that sudden change is much more important than notification size. Therefore, *Static Notifications*, while they stayed for 3s, were faded in and out for 0.5s to minimize the 'one-time' blinking effect. In contrast, in the *Blinking Notifications*, alternated between on and off every 0.5s without any fading effect.

Figure 4: Notifications were shown as Ambient Light (*left*) as well as in an On-Screen condition (*right*).

Participants

We recruited 12 participants (4 female) from various computer science research labs at our university. Their ages ranged from 22 to 38 and their height ranged from 160 to 185 cm. Two of the participants were left-handed and four of them wore glasses. None of them were color-blind.

Results

In all analyses reported here, the assumption of sphericity was not violated, so no corrections were necessary. We used repeated measures ANOVA ($\alpha = .05$) and pairwise tests with Bonferroni corrections for post-hoc analysis.

Hypothesis 1.1: Ambient Light vs. On-Screen Notifications

A three-way ANOVA showed a significant interaction between the factors ($F_{2,11} = 9.02$, $p < .001$) with power = .972.The post-hoc tests showed that in the *Distant-Overview* scenario as well in the *Distant-Focused* scenario, the percentage of perceived notifications with *Ambient Light* was higher than for *On-Screen Notifications*. A repeated

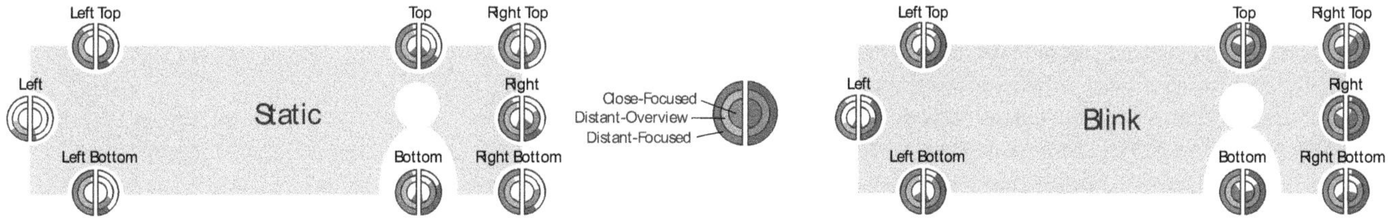

Figure 5: Perception of notifications in different spots. The green part of the circles shows the recognition rates for Ambient Light, the blue part the rates for on-screen notifications.

measures ANOVA unveiled an overall highly significant difference between *Ambient Light* and *On-Screen* Notifications ($F_{1,11}$ = 298.82, $p < .001$) with power = 1. Post-hoc tests showed that there was no significant difference in the *Close-Focused* scenario. However, there was a highly significant difference in the *Distant-Overview Static* scenario ($F_{1,11}$ = 75.94, $p < .001$) with power = 1 as well as in the *Distant-Focused Static* scenario ($F_{1,11}$ = 166.26, $p < .001$) with power = 1. Thus, *Hypothesis 1.1* is confirmed. For the *Static* condition (*Distant-Overview* and *Distant-Focused* scenarios), there was a vast difference between *Ambient Light* and *On-Screen Notifications* (see Figure 5). For the *Blinking* condition, the difference was significant for the *Distant-Overview* scenario ($F_{1,11}$ = 9.0, $p < .05$) with power .78, and for the *Distant-Focused* scenario ($F_{1,11}$ = 11.0, $p < .01$) with power .86.

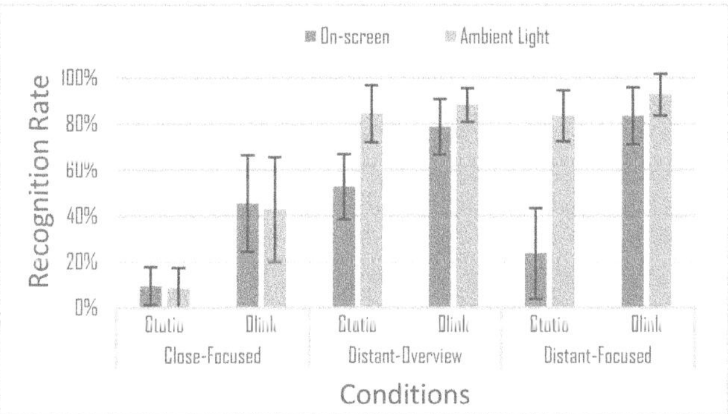

Figure 6: Results *Ambient Light* vs. *On-Screen* Notifications. The error bars indicate the range of two standard errors of the mean (above and below the mean).

Hypothesis 1.2: Impact of Scenarios on Visual Perception

Generally, notifications were difficult to perceive in the *Close-Focused* scenario. However, the percentage of perceived notifications was much higher with 75.9% (*Distant-Overview*) and 70.7% (*Distant-Focused*) respectively. Thus, the collected data confirms *Hypothesis 1.2*. Examining Figure 6 more closely, we see that the percentages given above differ, particularly because the proportion of *Static On-Screen* Notifications that was noticed in the *Distant-Focused* scenario was low. Another interesting observation was that more *Blinking Ambient Lights* were perceived in the *Distant-Focused* scenario than in the *Distant-Overview* scenario, which had lower temporal demand and gave participants more time to look around.

Hypothesis 1.3: Blinking vs. Static Notifications

As humans are good in perceiving changes within their peripheral vision [4], it is not surprising that blinking improves the visual perception of notifications in all conditions and scenarios. The analysis showed a highly significant difference between *Static* and *Blinking* overall ($F_{1,11}$ = 78.28, $p < .001$) with power = 1. A highly significant difference between *Static* and *Blinking* was found in the *Close-Focused Ambient Light* scenario ($F_{1,11}$ = 25.76, $p < .001$) with power = .99, where the percentage of identified notifications increased from 8.3% (*Static*) to 42.7% (*Blinking*), as shown in Figure 6. There was also a significant difference for the *Distant-Focused* scenario, ($F_{1,11}$ = 6.6, $p < .05$) with power = .65. This demonstrates that blinking has the highest impact when users are engaged in focused work and rely on their peripheral vision for monitoring notifications.

Further Insights

Perceived Positions

Figure 5 shows how well notifications were perceived in each location. Note that the participants worked at the right side of the board. Unsurprisingly, notifications were perceived less likely the further they were away from the participant. Although the perception rates were quite low in the *Close-Focused* scenario overall, blinking notifications close to the user could be perceived relatively well. Also in the *Distant-Overview* and the *Distant-Focused* scenario, the distance and consequently the viewing angle of the notifications had a considerable effect.

Task Performance Comparison

We used two different primary tasks, which was a potential source of bias when comparing results. However, there was no statistically significant difference in the performance of the primary task for participants, regardless of which secondary task conditions were applied. Results from a NASA TLX questionnaire confirm this observation.

Qualitative Results

Semi-structured interviews and a post-study questionnaire revealed additional insights. Existing literature suggests blinking could be irritating [31]. The responses we collected did not reflect that, but, such feedback might be different with other blinking patterns or frequencies. Some participants reported that they actively searched for notifications at some times, but ultimately felt that this did not help their performance for the secondary task. Furthermore, participants' subjective perception of their performance using *Ambient Light* in each scenario did not match their actual performance; they rated their performance in the *Distant-Overview* scenario highest, but performed best in *Distant-Focused*.

Discussion

In general, focused tasks as investigated in the *Close-Focused* and *Distant-Focused* scenarios relied more on peripheral perception than in the *Distant-Overview* scenario. As a blinking animation effect supports visual perception in the periphery, it is highly recommended for capturing the attention of users who are engaged in focused work. However, this effect might not work as well if other parts of the UI also blink. The results show that Ambient Light notifications could be very useful in multi-user scenarios (e.g. in control rooms), where users working directly at the board should not be disturbed, while people in the background need to be alarmed if a status change happens. In such a scenario it is beneficial to use a technology that prevents clutter on the screen by moving notifications off-screen.

THE RIGHT 'GAMMA' – CORRECTING THE BRIGHTNESS

When altering the intensity value of the Ambient Light display it becomes apparent that the value sent to the LED strips and the perceived brightness do not match well. The task of transforming a linearly growing value that is not perceived in a linear way by humans is traditionally solved using Gamma correction [13,42].

The Adafruit NeoPixel strips and other addressable LEDs use *pulse-width modulation.* This means in order to display different intensity levels the LEDs quickly toggle on and off [11]. The ratio between the on and off state defines the intensity level. However, to our perceptional system the perceived brightness is close to 100%, even if the LEDs are only on for 50% of the time. To compensate for humans' non-linear perception, it is thus necessary to perform gamma correction. The gamma values suggested for the LED strips we used are around 2.8 [11]. We ended up using a gamma-factor of 3.0, as we achieved the best results with this value.

The blue line in Figure 7 maps the perceived brightness levels to the displayed ambient light levels. As our LED strips cannot represent the small differences in brightness that could be perceived at lower levels, we compromised by taking the smallest available steps for these low levels (see Figure 7, dashed red line).

EXPERIMENT 2: COMPARISON TO OTHER OFF-SCREEN VISUALIZATIONS (HALOS AND WEDGES)

As an array of controllable lights around the periphery of the whiteboard, ambient light can show off-screen information. In this experiment we aim to examine this use-case and explore the advantages and disadvantages of different types of visualizations to gain insights on how to use some of the different properties of ambient light discussed earlier. Specifically, we use *color* to distinguish between different sets of notes, *brightness* and *size* to encode distance of off-screen objects, and *position* to indicate direction.

We developed two different variations of ambient light visualizations and compared them to the well-established off-screen visualization methods Halo [6] and Wedge [14]. This is because unlike other techniques, they work in the periphery of the screen. In comparison to these on-screen visualizations, ambient light has a much smaller design-space. It provides only a single line of LEDs and therefore cannot use geometric shapes to provide a hint of the off-screens objects position. Thus, we used the size of notifications in one and the brightness in another condition. As Halo and Wedge were mainly designed for small screens, we carefully adapted them for use on large surfaces without changing their main principles. Moreover, they were initially not designed to supply color information and required adaption.

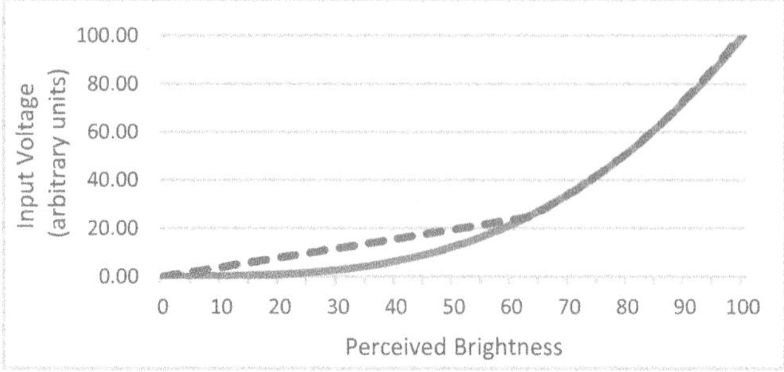

Figure 7: The blue line shows the ideal brightness mapping when using gamma correction (γ=3.0). The red dashed line shows the actual brightness mapping due to the limitations of our LEDs.

Halo

We re-implemented Halo (see Figure 8, *left*) as described in the paper [6]. As we felt that in contrast to ambient light the small ring segments were quite difficult to spot, we filled the circles. In a pilot study we compared the filled with the non-filled version. We kept the filled version as it performed better. As in the original paper, close circles are stacked, and the visible part of the circle is divided, with displaying the color of a smaller circle (closer object) in the middle.

Wedge

Similar to Halo, we re-implemented Wedge (see Figure 8, *middle-left*) as described in the paper [14]. We also tested a filled version against an outline version in a pilot study, with a similar result. Therefore, we used filled Wedges in our final experiment. Corners are challenging, as a large amount of off-screen space needs to be represented in a small area [5,9]. Due to the large number of off-screen notes in our study and the limited space in corners, overlaps could not always be resolved. For these cases we ensured that at least all wedges are visible by moving smaller indicators to the front so that none is fully hidden.

Ambient Light – Glowworm

Glowworm (see Figure 8, *middle-right*) is an ambient light implementation that uses *brightness*. Starting with the closest objects, it displays all off-screen objects. Distant objects do not overwrite closer ones but are shifted to a nearby free spot. The accuracy of the displayed position decreases in this situation. The brightness indicates the 'rank' of the represented note in contrast to other notes of the same color. This means that the closest yellow note is the brightest, while the furthest is the dimmest.

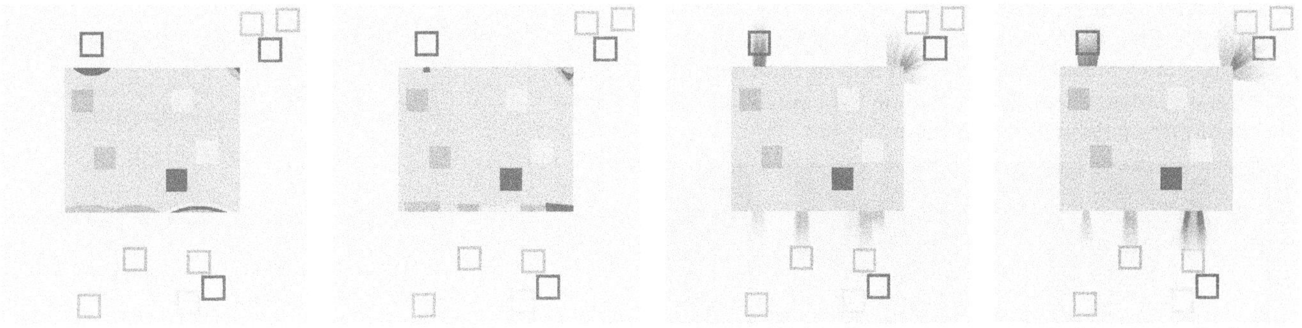

Figure 8: The four conditions that were compared in experiment 2. Please note that figures are not to scale.

Ambient Light – Firefly
Firefly (see Figure 8, *right*) maps the distance of the off-screen object to the *size* of the spot. Starting with a size of 200px the notification gets smaller as the object moves away. There is no change in brightness. If two indications are overlapping they get stacked. In this case the closer note is placed inside and the furthest outside. The size of the stack is calculated by using the size of the closest element as a basis. For each added note to the stack, the size of the combined notification is increased by 20%.

Hypothesis

Hypothesis 2.1: Performance: Ambient light will not be significantly slower than Halos or Wedges from a performance perspective. On-screen solutions can show more complex information about the note location than ambient light. Nevertheless, the ambient light techniques can compete with the on-screen solutions, due their bigger visual footprint which does not require valuable screen space.

Hypothesis 2.2: Preference: Ambient Light will be preferred. Ambient light benefits from a clear visual separation to the screen, resulting in less clutter on the screen. Users will prefer ambient light over on-screen solutions.

Design

In this controlled experiment we compared the four mentioned notification conditions. In addition, we also ran a baseline condition without any visualization of off-screen objects, which resulted in a total number of five conditions. The conditions were tested in a repeated-measures, Latin Square study design, balanced for first-order carry-over effects. In our first experiment we learned that the ambient light works best at a certain distance from the board. We applied this knowledge in this comparison in a setting similar to the Distant-Focused condition from experiment 1 (see Figure 9). The participants sat facing the whiteboard on a height adjustable chair, in front of a small height adjustable table. A wireless computer mouse was used as the input device.

We provided participants with a virtual canvas of 6 × 6 screens (11.520 × 6480 pixels). As the whiteboard is a two projector setup, they could see a section of two of these 36 screens side by side at once (3860 × 1080 pixels). On the whole canvas 30 sticky notes of different color (10 yellow, 8 pink, 6 blue, 4 green, 2 orange) and with different content were placed pseudo-randomly. Participants were presented with an image of a sticky note on a small screen on their desk. Their task was then to find this particular note on the virtual canvas, using the off-screen visualizations to make their search more efficient. Each condition consisted of three blocks of 10 notes with the option to pause in between. Each block was carried out on a different data set (different placement of notes) to avoid location memory effects.

Figure 9: Setup in experiment two: On the tablet the target note is shown. Glowworm refers to the chains of colored lights.

The study started with a demographic questionnaire. No training was done. Between the different conditions we asked the participants to rate the task load using a NASA TLX [17] test. The study was concluded with another short questionnaire and a semi-structured interview, lasting approximately 50 minutes overall for each participant.

Apparatus Adaption

When performing the first pilots for this experiment we soon noticed that the lower resolution of ambient light was a considerable disadvantage for this condition in comparison to the on-screen solutions. Especially the natural additive mixing of colors was a problem, as close off-screen objects of different color blended into a white spot and could not be distinguished (see Figure 10, *left*). Therefore, we decided to alter our hardware setup. We installed small separators (35×40 mm white cardboard) between the individual LEDs around the whiteboard, which keep the lights separated and enhance visibility (see Figure 10, *right*). This installation decreases the general possible brightness of the ambient light installation. Overall this effect is only minor and can be diminished further by using a reflective material for the separators (e.g. mirror cardboard), as initial tests have shown. In all other regards the installation and the light conditions in the room was similar to first experiment.

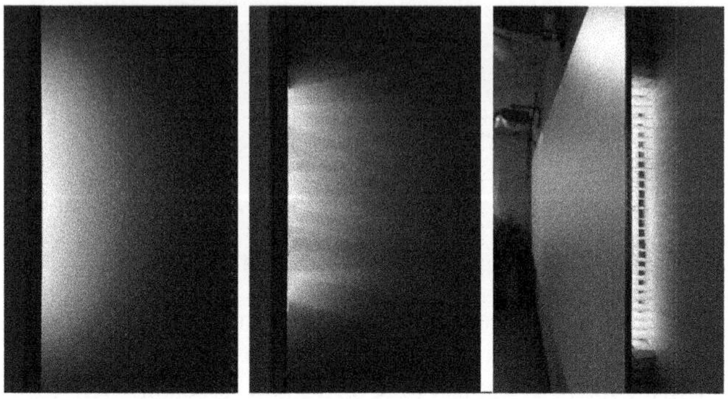

Figure 10: Comparison between ambient light with and without separators. *Left*: The light blends and different colors can hardly be distinguished. Middle: The separators prevent the blending of colors to make identification easier. *Right*: The separators in the whiteboard context.

Participants

We recruited 10 participants (3 female) with an age range between 22 and 53 from various computer science research labs and administration staff at our university. Six wore glasses and nobody was color-blind. All were regular computer users, but only five had experience with interactive whiteboards.

Results

The quantitative results show only small deviations between the different conditions.

Hypothesis 2.1: Performance

For the performance analysis we measured the task execution time of the individual trials. Trials with times greater than average + three time SD were considered as outliers and eliminated for further analysis (1.3% of the data). Execution time was analyzed by a repeated-measures ANOVA (α = .05). The assumption of sphericity was violated, so the Greenhouse Geisser corrected values are reported. It showed that the Baseline (M = 17.35s, SD = 4.75) was significantly slower than all the other conditions ($F_{2.28,9}$ = 10.339, p < .005) with power = .982. Our test confirmed the measures in [14]. Post-hoc tests showed that although Wedge was the fastest technique (M = 12.61s, SD = 4.42) tightly followed by Firefly (M = 12.68s, SD = 2.86), it was not significantly faster than both of the ambient light conditions. Thus *Hypothesis 2.1* is confirmed.

Hypothesis 2.2: Preference

All of the participants preferred using ambient light visualizations (6 participants Firefly, 4 participants Glowworm) over On-Screen solutions. From an aesthetic point of view, seven participants preferred Firefly, and two Glowworm. One person liked Halo best from an aesthetic point of view.

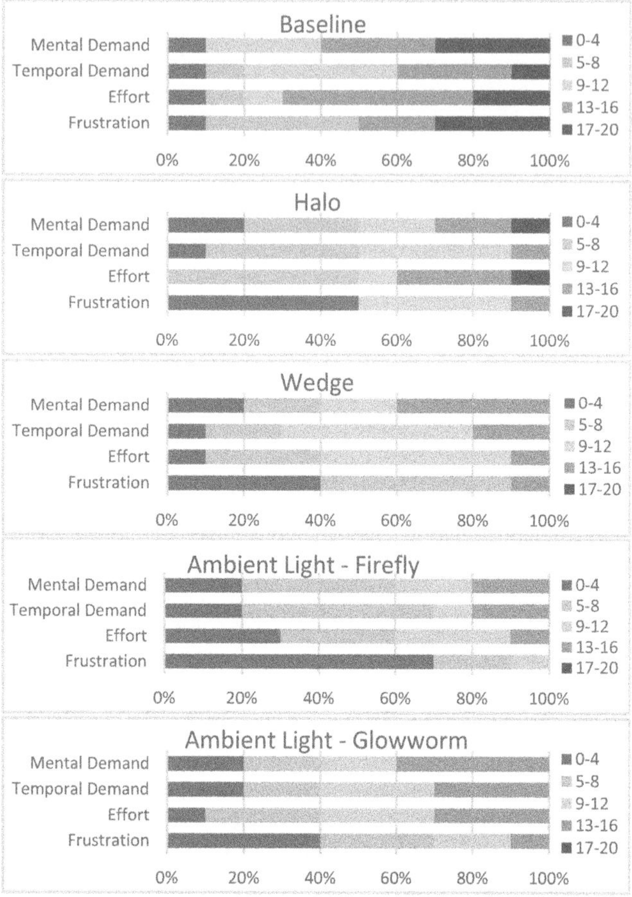

Figure 11: NASA-TLX results of the second experiment.

The NASA-TLX ratings (see Figure 11) show the lowest task load for the Firefly condition. A Friedman test indicated significant results for the overall task load ($\chi^2(4)$ = 15.82, p = .003) and Frustration ($\chi^2(4)$=15.94, p = .003). In depth analysis by performing a Wilcoxon Signed Rank test showed that the overall task load for Firefly was significantly lower than for Wedge (Z = -2.193, p < .05) and Halo (Z = -2.654, p < .01). Further investigations unveiled that this was mainly due to a significantly lower *frustration* level compared to Wedge (Z = -2.059, p < .05) and Halo (Z = -2.657, p < .01). Firefly also has a low load of *Effort* and *Mental Demand* (see Figure 11). In contrast, we measured a higher task load for Glowworm, which indicates that the better performance caused also higher overall task load, effort, and frustration. All participants stated a preference for one of the ambient light solutions. Due to this and the significantly lower task-load and frustration level for Firefly, we can confirm *Hypotheses 2.2*.

Additional Insights

The way how distance is mapped in the different conditions is quite diverse. We were interested in how intuitive the different mappings were to the participants. In the post-experiment interviews six participants stated that they had problems interpreting Wedge in the right way. P2 stated: *"I understand it from a logical point of view but it is unintuitive that they (the visualizations) are bigger when they are fur-*

Figure 12: Example applications. *Left*: Off-Screen content visualization in a virtual 2D workspace; *Middle*: Visualizing notifications; *Right*: Indicating the position of a remote user – the colored silhouettes are not part of the actual visualization.

ther away". Seven participants considered the mapping of close objects to a bigger visualization as used in Firefly as "*intuitive*" and "*right*", confirming insights in [33]. Obviously the different mapping are a source of potential bias. However, we implemented Wedge and Halo close to the original techniques to provide maximum comparability to existing state-of-the-art-work. We still implemented the best possible ambient light technique.

Regarding Glowworm the opinions were divided. While some of the more technologically-literate participants could use the different cues well and also performed quite well, novice users had a hard time with this condition. We are hesitant to draw strong conclusions, due to our small sample size. However, we assume this difference is due to the fact that brightness is not used to indicate the absolute distance, but a ranking between the different off-screen notes of similar color. We observed that this worked particularly well for participants whose strategy was to identify the closest note and move there. Others, who tried to gain an overview of the note positioning had a harder time. As P8 put it: *"Firefly gives a better understanding of the whole picture"*.

Discussion
The experiment showed that ambient light is not significantly inferior to state-of-the-art off-screen visualizations, despite its smaller design space, and was even preferred by users. While ambient light requires some additional hardware, it does not require any screen-space. The natural separation between on-screen objects and off-screen visualization helps to reduce clutter and reduces users' workload. This is reflected in the analyses of the overall task load and frustration, which were significantly reduced when using Firefly.

DESIGN RECOMMENDATIONS
Based on our two experiments that created new insights and confirmed existing knowledge, we present the following design implications that designers should consider when using ambient light to enhance large interactive surfaces. Drawing on the existing literature, we suggest to apply the concept of Visual Variables [29] for encoding parameters.

D1: Accommodating User Positions: Standing close to the whiteboard decreases one's ability to perceive ambient light notifications. Hence, they are best suited to support scenarios that involve distant interaction or observation. For scenarios where the user is standing close to the board visibility can be increased by using animation.

D2: Using Animation for Notifications: The animation of ambient light notifications increases its perceptibility in all scenarios, confirming insights of related work [4,43]. Use blinking or animated ambient light for high priority notification to ensure that it is perceived.

D3: Enhance Brightness Perception: We recommend to apply gamma correction to make better use of the available and perceivable brightness levels (c.f. [13,42]). If the user position is static, one can accommodate for different viewing angles, increasing intensity when the viewing angle is flatter.

D4: Size is Interpreted Faster than Brightness: Most users are quicker to detect size than brightness. While it is not too difficult to distinguish different brightness levels, most users seem faster in interpreting the meaning of different sizes.

D5: If Resolution is Important, Add Light Separators: Separators are a great way to prevent light blending. This enables the system designer to show notifications of different colors close to each other. Moreover, the separators aid in the perception of changes in notification size.

APPLICATION SCENARIOS
Based on the design recommendations we showcase a variety of applications, which highlight the benefits of using ambient light to enhance work on large interactive surfaces. While the Virtual 2D Workspace and Emergency Response scenario build directly on the performed studies, the others suggest different domains where ambient light could be beneficial.

Virtual 2D Workspace (see Figure 12, *left*): Having spatial awareness of off-screen objects in a virtual 2D workspace is often crucial, yet challenging to sustain. As shown in experiment 2 using ambient light is very suitable for visualizing off-screen content. It also showed that using the property of size to encode for distance, such as in Firefly, is easier for users to interpret than brightness in the Glowworm visualization (*D4*). However, if brightness is used for encoding, gamma correction is of great benefit to account for human perception (*D3*). For spatially close notifications, separators are a great help to enhance light visibility (*D5*). Finally, considering the user position is also important in this scenario. Ambient light has the advantage of not disturbing users who work close to the board. However, when stepping back to gain overview it can help to enhance understanding of the relation to off-screen content. In this case the use of ambient light for off-screen visualizations is beneficial (*D1*).

Emergency Response (see Figure 12, *middle*): Ambient light is very well suited for emergency response applications where operators work in collaboration with each other. Firstly, the flexibility to determine the position of ambient light notifications means that spatial data can be conveyed to operators working independently at the back of the room, while users close to the board are hardly affected (*D1*). Secondly, using animation can trigger attention more aggressively in an emergency situation (*D2*). Off-screen notifications are not any more disruptive than on-screen notifications for operators working close to the board, yet they help operators to understand the overall situation quicker. Thirdly, the ability to vary size or brightness levels allows for events to be portrayed in order of importance or priority (*D4*). Finally, the ability to increase the resolution might be helpful in this scenario to provide more sophisticated notifications that contain more information (*D5*).

Remote Activity (see Figure 12, *right*): Ambient lights can be used to facilitate remote collaboration. By showing the position of a remote person, ambient light enables users to perceive and avoid entering occupied working space. The approach is more abstract than, e.g., [46], but has the advantage of not occluding on-screen content. Notification size and brightness levels can be used to provide an estimate of the remote user's distance from the whiteboard (*D4*), while the position of the ambient light can indicate the viewing angle. As seen in Figure 12 (*right*), the light bars are shown at the bottom and top of the whiteboard to improve visual perception for users close to the board (*D1*).

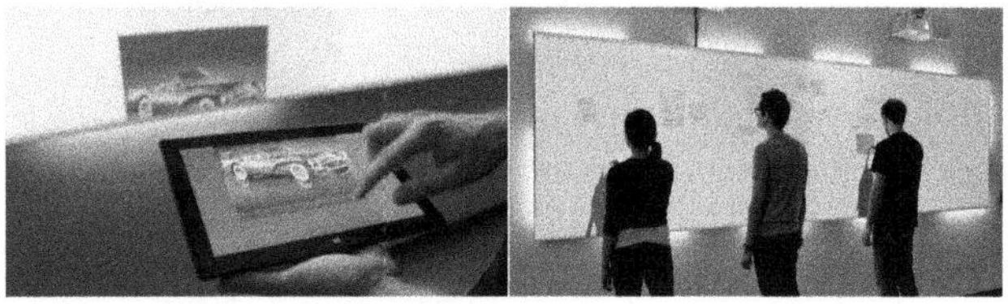

Figure 13: Additional applications: *Left*: A virtual border to an external device; *Right*: Visualization of a timed process.

Linking to Remote Devices (see Figure 13, *left*): Ambient light can be used to bridge real and virtual space. Using it in the context of remote device tracking, the position of the lights along the perimeter of the whiteboard can map directly to the real space occupied by a remote device. The light creates a border of virtual space that serves as a portal through which content can be transferred. Different colors identify different devices and while people working on external devices can easily detect the ambient light from the distance, users, standing close to the board, are hardly disturbed (*D1*).

Progress Indicators (see Figure 13, *right*): Peripheral ambient light can be used to convey information, such as the progression of time [32,34], without occluding valuable workspace, and without requiring users to explicitly switch their gaze and attention away from their primary tasks. To accommodate for various possible user locations close to the board (*D1*), we would suggest a design that provides progress indication at multiple spots, so that users can perceive changes close to them. Finally, blinking (*D2*) assures that every user is informed when the process ends.

LIMITATIONS

In this paper we summarize our insights in using ambient light on a large interactive surface, and more specifically, to augment an interactive whiteboard. We aimed to keep our insights transferable to similar and related setups and therefore reported variables such as the size of the board, distance of the users and lighting conditions. Nevertheless, when conducting the studies and pilots we learned that small changes can have considerable impact and that perception is ultimately a very personal issue that may differ between users. Nevertheless, we believe that ambient light has notable potential in the context of large interactive surfaces and that our experiments provide some valuable insights for others.

CONCLUSIONS & FUTURE WORK

In this paper, we considered how ambient light can be used for more than enhancing the TV viewing experience. We explored the applicability of ambient light for extending screen space and depicting peripheral information on large interactive surfaces. Based on the findings from two experiments, we developed design recommendations regarding how best to leverage ambient light for use in this context. These cover differences in the perception of notifications in three possible work scenarios, and insights on how to depict various types of information. Finally, we applied these design recommendations to five application scenarios to highlight the strengths of using ambient light in various situations.

We explored the influence of location and different working scenarios, concluding that ambient light is particularly suitable for giving notifications to people distant from the board. While we included a blinking animation effect in our first experiment, animations could potentially provide a much larger design space to communicate information [16], especially for peripheral use [4]. This would be an interesting topic for future work. We also examined the utility of ambient light as a tool for off-screen visualization. Our findings suggest that when making use of the property of size, ambient light lowers the task load and the frustration level. In the future, it would be interesting to see how ambient light performs in combination with interactive surfaces when used for longer periods of time in real-life scenarios.

Although there are topics to explore further, we believe that our studies and design recommendations provide helpful insights for designing applications that use ambient light. Moreover, the versatile scenarios we depict in this paper show that there is a general benefit in using ambient light to extend large interactive surfaces.

ACKNOWLEDGEMENTS

The presented research was funded by the European Unions Seventh Framework Programme FP7/2007 - 2001 under grant agreement n°318552. We would like to thank our colleagues for their help and insights.

REFERENCES

1. Mark Altosaar, Roel Vertegaal, Changuk Sohn, and Daniel Cheng. 2006. AuraOrb. *Proceedings of the 20th conference of the computer-human interaction special interest group (CHISIG) of Australia on Computer-human interaction: design: activities, artefacts and environments (OZCHI '06)*, 159–166. http://doi.org/10.1145/1228175.1228204

2. Alec Azad, Jaime Ruiz, Daniel Vogel, Mark Hancock, and Edward Lank. 2012. Territoriality and behaviour on and around large vertical publicly-shared displays. *Proceedings of the Designing Interactive Systems Conference (DIS '12)*, 468–477. http://doi.org/10.1145/2317956.2318025

3. Robert Ball and Chris North. 2008. The effects of peripheral vision and physical navigation on large scale visualization. *Proceedings of Graphics Interface 2008*: 9–16. Retrieved August 22, 2014 from http://portal.acm.org/citation.cfm?id=1375714.1375717

4. Lyn Bartram, Colin Ware, and Tom Calvert. 2001. Moving Icons : Detection And Distraction. 157–166. Retrieved September 22, 2015 from http://www.ccom.unh.edu/vislab/PDFs/Interact2001.pdf

5. Patrick Baudisch, Nathaniel Good, and Paul Stewart. 2001. Focus plus context screens. *Proceedings of the 14th annual ACM symposium on User interface software and technology (UIST '01)*, 31–40. http://doi.org/10.1145/502348.502354

6. Patrick Baudisch and Ruth Rosenholtz. 2003. Halo. *Proceedings of the SIGCHI Conference on Human factors in Computing Systems (CHI '03)*, 481–488. http://doi.org/10.1145/642611.642695

7. Simon H.A. Begemann. 2005. A scientific study on the effects of Ambilight in flat-panel displays. 2005. Retrieved September 25, 2015 from http://www.embedded.com/design/real-time-and-performance/4012996/A-scientific-study-on-the-effects-of-Ambilight-in-flat-panel-displays

8. A Bezerianos and P Isenberg. 2012. Perception of Visual Variables on Tiled Wall-Sized Displays for Information Visualization Applications. *IEEE transactions on visualization and computer graphics (GI '08)* 18, 12: 2516–25. http://doi.org/10.1109/TVCG.2012.251

9. Jeremy Birnholtz, Lindsay Reynolds, Eli Luxenberg, Carl Gutwin, and Maryam Mustafa. 2010. Awareness Beyond the Desktop : Exploring Attention and Distraction with a Projected Peripheral-Vision Display. *Proceedings of Graphics Interface 2010 (GI '10)*, 55–62. http://doi.org/10.1306/74D71041-2B21-11D7-8648000102C1865D

10. John D. Bullough, Yukio Akashi, Charles R. Fay, and Mariana G. Figueiro. 2006. Impact of surrounding illumination on visual fatigue and eyestrain while viewing television. *Journal of Applied Sciences* 6, 8: 1664–1670. http://doi.org/10.3923/jas.2006.1664.1670

11. Phillip Burgess. LED Tricks: Gamma Correction. Retrieved September 23, 2015 from https://learn.adafruit.com/led-tricks-gamma-correction/the-issue

12. Niklas Elmqvist, Nathalie Henry, Yann Ri he, and Jean-Daniel Fekete. 2008. Mélange: Space Folding for Multi-Focus Interaction. *Proceedings of the SIGCHI Conference on Human Factors in Computing Systems (CHI '08)*, 1333–1342. http://doi.org/10.1145/1357054.1357263

13. Mark D. Fairchild. 2013. *Color Appearance Models*. Wiley, Chinester.

14. Sean Gustafson, Patrick Baudisch, Carl Gutwin, and Pourang Irani. 2008. Wedge: Clutter-Free Visualization of Off-Screen Locations. *Proceedings of the SIGCHI Conference on Human Factors in Computing Systems (CHI '08)*, 787–796. http://doi.org/10.1145/1357054.1357179

15. Michael Haller, Jakob Leitner, Thomas Seifried, et al. 2010. The NICE discussion room. *Proceedings of the SIGCHI Conference on Human Factors in Computing Systems (CHI '10)*, 609–618. http://doi.org/10.1145/1753326.1753418

16. Chris Harrison, John Horstman, Gary Hsieh, and Scott Hudson. 2012. Unlocking the expressivity of point lights. *Proceedings of the SIGCHI Conference on Human Factors in Computing Systems (CHI '12)*, 1683–1692. http://doi.org/10.1145/2207676.2208296

17. Sandra G. Hart and Lowell E. Staveland. 1988. *Development of NASA-TLX (Task Load Index): Results of Empirical and Theoretical Research.* http://doi.org/10.1016/S0166-4115(08)62386-9

18. Doris Hausen, Sebastian Boring, Clara Lueling, Simone Rodestock, and Andreas Butz. 2012. StaTube: facilitating state management in instant messaging systems. *Proceedings of the Sixth International Conference on Tangible, Embedded and Embodied Interaction (TEI '12)*, 283–290. http://doi.org/10.1145/2148131.2148191

19. Doris Hausen, Christine Wagner, Sebastian Boring, and Andreas Butz. 2013. Comparing modalities and feedback for peripheral interaction. *CHI '13*

Extended Abstracts on Human Factors in Computing Systems on (CHI EA '13), 1263–1268. http://doi.org/10.1145/2468356.2468582

20. Valentin Heun, Anette von Kapri, and Pattie Maes. 2012. Perifoveal display. *Proceedings of the 2012 ACM Conference on Ubiquitous Computing (UbiComp '12)*, 1150–155. http://doi.org/10.1145/2370216.2370460

21. Alexandra Ion, Y.-L. Betty Chang, Michael Haller, Mark Hancock, and Stacey D. Scott. 2013. Canyon: Providing Location Awareness of Multiple Moving Objects in a Detail View on Large Displays. *Proceedings of the SIGCHI Conference on Human Factors in Computing Systems (CHI '13)*, 3149–3158. http://doi.org/10.1145/2470654.2466431

22. Hiroshi Ishii, Craig Wisneski, Scott Brave, et al. 1998. ambientROOM: Integrating Ambient Media with Architectural Space. *Proceedings of the SIGCHI Conference on Human Factors in Computing Systems (CHI '98)*, 173–174. http://doi.org/10.1145/286498.286652

23. Brett R. Jones, Hrvoje Benko, Eyal Ofek, and Andrew D. Wilson. 2013. IllumiRoom: peripheral projected illusions for interactive experiences. *Proceedings of the SIGCHI Conference on Human Factors in Computing Systems (CHI '13)*, 869–878. http://doi.org/10.1145/2470654.2466112

24. Wendy Ju, Brian a. Lee, and Scott R. Klemmer. 2008. Range: Exploring Implicit Interaction through Electronic Whiteboard Design. *Proceedings of the ACM 2008 Conference on Computer Supported Cooperative Work (CSCW '08)*, 17–26. http://doi.org/10.1145/1460563.1460569

25. Min H. Kim, Tim Weyrich, and Jan Kautz. 2009. Modeling human color perception under extended luminance levels. *ACM Transactions on Graphics* 28, 3: 1. http://doi.org/10.1145/1531326.1531333

26. Brian Y. Lim, Aubrey Shick, Chris Harrison, and Scott E. Hudson. 2011. Pediluma: motivating physical activity through contextual information and social influence. *Proceedings of the fifth international conference on Tangible, embedded, and embodied interaction (TEI '11)*, 173–180. http://doi.org/10.1145/1935701.1935736

27. Andreas Löcken, Heiko Müller, Wilko Heuten, and Susanne Cj Boll. 2014. Exploring the design space of ambient light displays. *Proceedings of the extended abstracts of the 32nd annual ACM conference on Human factors in computing systems (CHI EA '14)*, 387–390. http://doi.org/10.1145/2559206.2574793

28. Blair MacIntyre, Elizabeth D. Mynatt, Stephen Voida, Klaus M. Hansen, Joe Tullio, and Gregory M. Corso. 2001. Support for multitasking and background awareness using interactive peripheral displays. *Proceedings of the 14th annual ACM symposium on User interface software and technology (UIST '01)*, 41–50. http://doi.org/10.1145/502348.502355

29. Jock Mackinlay. 1986. Automating the design of graphical presentations of relational information. *ACM Transactions on Graphics* 5, 2: 110–141. http://doi.org/10.1145/22949.22950

30. Tara Matthews, Anind K Dey, Jennifer Mankoff, Scott Carter, and Tye Rattenbury. 2004. A toolkit for managing user attention in peripheral displays. *Proceedings of the 17th annual ACM symposium on User interface software and technology (UIST '04)*, 247–256. http://doi.org/10.1145/1029632.1029676

31. Heiko Müller, Jutta Fortmann, Martin Pielot, et al. 2012. Ambix: Designing Ambient Light Information Displays. *Designing Interactive Lighting Workshop at DIS 2012*. Retrieved June 20, 2014 from http://www.researchgate.net/publication/257186115_AmbiX_Designing_Ambient_Light_Information_Displays/file/60b7d526240c2a9e2b.pdf

32. Heiko Müller, Anastasia Kazakova, Martin Pielot, Wilko Heuten, and Susanne Boll. 2013. Ambient Timer – Unobtrusively Reminding Users of Upcoming Tasks with Ambient Light. In *Lecture Notes in Computer Science (including subseries Lecture Notes in Artificial Intelligence and Lecture Notes in Bioinformatics)*. 211–228. http://doi.org/10.1007/978-3-642-40483-2_15

33. Heiko Müller, Andreas Löcken, Wilko Heuten, and Susanne Boll. 2014. Sparkle : An Ambient Light Display for Dynamic Off-Screen Points of Interest. *Proceedings of the 8th Nordic Conference on Human-Computer Interaction: Fun, Fast, Foundational (NordCHI '14)*, 51–60.

34. Valentina Occhialini, Harm van Essen, and Berry Eggen. 2011. Design and Evaluation of an Ambient Display to Support Time Management during Meetings. In *Lecture Notes in Computer Science (including subseries Lecture Notes in Artificial Intelligence and Lecture Notes in Bioinformatics)*. 263–280. http://doi.org/10.1007/978-3-642-23771-3_20

35. Z. Pousman and J. Stasko. 2006. A taxonomy of ambient information systems: four patterns of design. *Proceedings of the working conference on Advanced visual interfaces (AVI '06)*, 67–74. http://doi.org/10.1145/1133265.1133277

36. Thorsten Prante, Carsten Röcker, Norbert Streitz, et al. 2003. Hello . Wall – Beyond Ambient Displays AMBIENTE – Workspaces of the Future. *5th International Conference on Ubiquitous Computing (UBICOMP '03)*, 277 – 278.

37. Hanan Samet. 2014. Using minimaps to enable toponym resolution with an effective 100% rate of recall. *Proceedings of the 8th Workshop on Geographic Information Retrieval - GIR '14*, ACM Press, 1–8. http://doi.org/10.1145/2675354.2675698

38. Izadi Shahram, Harry Brignull, Tom Rodden, Yvonne Rogers, and Mia Underwood. 2003. Dynamo: A public interactive surface supporting the cooperative sharing and exchange of media. *Proceedings of the 16th annual ACM symposium on User interface software and technology (UIST '03)*, 159–168. http://doi.org/10.1145/964696.964714

39. Izadi Sharam, Geraldine Fitzpatrick, Tom Rodden, Harry Brignull, Yvonne Rogers, and Siân Lindley. 2005. The iterative design and study of a large display for shared and sociable spaces. *Proceedings of the 2005 conference on Designing for User eXperience (DUX '05)*: 59. Retrieved September 8, 2014 from http://discovery.ucl.ac.uk/1324312/

40. Xiaobin Shen. 2007. An Evaluation Methodology for Ambient Displays. *Journal of Engineering, Computing and Architecture* 1, 2. Retrieved from http://www.scientificjournals.org/journals2007/articles/1129.pdf

41. Daniel Vogel and Ravin Balakrishnan. 2004. Interactive public ambient displays. *Proceedings of the 2004 ACM Symposium on User Interface Software and Technology (UIST '04)*, 137–146. http://doi.org/10.1145/1029632.1029656

42. Colin Ware. 2004. *Information Visualization.* Morgan Kaufmann, San Francisco.

43. Harald Wasser. 2007. *Im Auge des Betrachters.* Stäubli-Verlag, Zürich.

44. Daniel Wigdor, Hao Jiang, Clifton Forlines, Michelle Borkin, and Chia Shen. 2009. WeSpace: The Design, Development, and Deployment of a Walk-Up and Share Multi-Surface Collaboration System. *Proceedings of the SIGCHI Conference on Human Factors in Computing Systems (CHI 09)*, 1237–1246. http://doi.org/10.1145/1518701.1518886

45. Günther Wyszecki and W. S. Stiles. 1982. *Color Science: Concepts and Methods.* Wiley, New York.

46. Jakob Zillner, Christoph Rhemann, Shahram Izadi, and Michael Haller. 2014. 3D-board. *Proceedings of the 27th annual ACM symposium on User interface software and technology (UIST '14)*, 471–479. http://doi.org/10.1145/2642918.2647393

Off-Limits: Interacting Beyond the Boundaries of Large Displays

Anders Markussen, Sebastian Boring, Mikkel R. Jakobsen and Kasper Hornbæk
Department of Computer Science, University of Copenhagen, Copenhagen, Denmark
{amark, sebastian.boring, mikkelrj, kash}@di.ku.dk

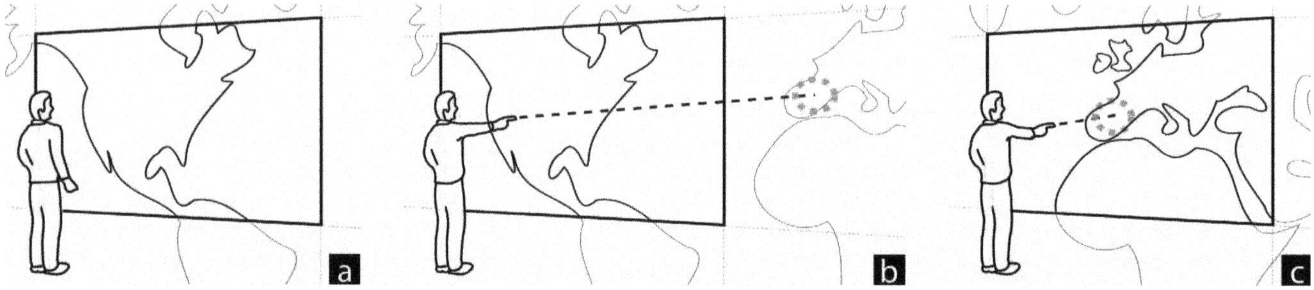

Figure 1. An illustration of the *Off-Limits* concept: (a) a user looks at a view of North America on a display; (b) the user points at the location of Europe in off-screen space; (c) the user drags Europe onto the screen from its off-screen location.

ABSTRACT
The size of information spaces often exceeds the limits of even the largest displays. This makes navigating such spaces through on-screen interactions demanding. However, if users imagine the information space extending in a plane beyond the display's boundaries, they might be able to use the space beyond the display for input. This paper investigates *Off-Limits*, an interaction concept extending the input space of a large display into the space beyond the screen through the use of mid-air pointing. We develop and evaluate the concept through three empirical studies in one-dimensional space: First, we explore benefits and limitations of off-screen pointing compared to touch interaction and mid-air on-screen pointing; next, we assess users' accuracy in off-screen pointing to model the distance-to-screen vs. accuracy trade-off; and finally, we show how *Off-Limits* is further improved by applying that model to the naïve approach. Overall, we found that the final *Off-Limits* concept provides significant performance benefits over on-screen and touch pointing conditions.

Author Keywords
Mid-air pointing; Off-screen pointing; In-air pointing; Spatial user interfaces; Freehand pointing.

ACM Classification Keywords
I.3.6 Methodology and Techniques: Interaction techniques

CHI'16, May 07-12, 2016, San Jose, CA, USA
© 2016 ACM. ISBN 978-1-4503-3362-7/16/05…$15.00
DOI: http://dx.doi.org/10.1145/2858036.2858083

INTRODUCTION
Many information spaces (e.g., detailed maps) exceed the limits of even wall-sized displays. The display is thus a viewport into these spaces and information residing *off-screen* can be brought *on-screen* (i.e., inside the viewport) through navigation. Users commonly do this by moving the information space (and its digital representation respectively) through either mouse and keyboard [17], personal devices (e.g., tablets or phones [25]), touch input, or mid-air interaction to interact from afar on larger displays [29].

Although users may be able to imagine the information extending into *off-screen* space, the physical dimensions of a display often determine the available input space: touch is performed directly *on-screen*; and mid-air pointing commonly uses ray casting onto the display's surface. More traditional input methods (e.g., a mouse pointer) are also bound to the screen, as users have to keep track of cursors. As a consequence, the input space is usually tied to the display containing the visual output and is thus much smaller than the actual information space that users interact with.

Display size constraints on mobile devices have forced researchers to think *outside the box*, allowing for interactions to occur *around* the device rather than on its display (e.g., [14,15]). In this paper, we adapt the general idea of using off-screen space to large displays. Unlike previous approaches for mobile devices, however, we *extend* the input space beyond a large display's boundaries – thus allowing people to seamlessly use both *on-screen* and *off-screen* space throughout an interaction.

OFF-LIMITS
As illustrated by Figure 1, *Off-Limits* allows the use of mid-air interaction within an input space that extends beyond display boundaries, thereby enabling a much larger input space than previous techniques (e.g., [22,34]). In doing so, we match the input space to a much larger part of the in-

formation space instead of tying it to the space within the display's boundaries. With *Off-Limits*, people can use their knowledge of spatial relations in the presented information. For example, locations on a map have certain distances and orientations relative to each other. Despite being out of view, points of interest can be addressed in off-screen space directly, using the parts of the information space that are visible on the display as reference.

Figure 1 illustrates this idea using a map shown on a large display: (a) in the beginning the display shows North America, but the user wants to display the map of Europe; (b) the well-defined relation between the two continents allows the user to point at Europe's location in off-screen space; (c) Europe can now be dragged into the viewport in a single dragging operation, where that drag started in off-screen space and ends in on-screen space (in case the user underestimated the distance to Europe, the drag may even continue into off-screen space on the opposite side of the display).

The main benefit of *Off-Limits* is that it frees the input space from the physical limitations of a display. It extends two common operations: (1) it allows for addressing a point of interest (of which users know the spatial location) directly in *off-screen* space, without using repeated on-screen dragging operations (i.e., clutching); and (2) it allows for starting and/or continuing dragging operations in *off-screen* space (i.e., beyond the display's border), without interrupting interaction when the display's borders are reached. Further, *Off-Limits* can be implemented to allow for bi-manual operation (similar to bi-manual *Multipoint* [2], yet in off-screen space), where users may address two off-screen areas simultaneously (e.g., to perform on-screen comparison).

In this paper, we contribute three experiments that help develop and evaluate this concept on large displays: the first experiment demonstrates that off-screen space is suitable (and complementary) for interacting with large displays. In the second study, we assess users' accuracy in pointing to locations in off-screen space, leading to a model for estimating the perceived location of a point in off-screen space based on the points' distance from the display's center. With this model we refine the naïve adaptation of *Off-Limits*. In the third experiment, we demonstrate *Off-Limit*'s superior performance compared to the naïve implementation regarding interaction time, number of interactions and user satisfaction. Our improvements make *Off-Limits* a compelling candidate for future large display interactions.

RELATED WORK

The work presented in this paper builds on research in interaction techniques for large displays, techniques that allow for distant interaction, and off-screen interaction.

Interaction Techniques for Large Displays

Large, high-resolution displays have introduced new challenges for designers of touch- or pen-based interaction techniques: (1) due to the display's size, content may be out of the users' reach; and (2) content is not always readable to users even though it is shown on the display, due to its distance to the user. Previous work, discussed below, has focused on these challenges and presented a number of techniques to improve the interaction with distant content, when being close to the display.

Approaches either virtually increase the user's reach or bring distant objects or areas closer to the user for selection. With *HybridPointing* [10], users can switch back-and-forth between absolute and relative pointing (using a direct input device) to increase their reach. *Drag-and-throw* and *Push-and-throw* [8] allow users to bridge large distances while dragging an object. The user only has to move a short distance, which is then amplified. *Press-and-flick* [26] works similarly for moving objects across large distances, but it does not allow for controlling the object's movement once it is released (i.e., open-loop). *Drag-and-pop* [31] brings remote objects of interest closer (e.g., dragging a document brings potential targets closer to the user). *Frisbee* [21], on the other hand, creates a portal to a distant area of the display, allowing for fast interchange of objects between both the local and remote area.

Each of these techniques enables access to distant (and potentially off-screen) locations on large displays. At the same time, however, they discourage using the inherent benefits of large displays – namely the users' ability to move freely (e.g., to get an overview of the information space [1]).

Interaction at a Distance

To free users from having to interact up close to the display, researchers have explored how to support interacting while further away from the display. One such way is to use dedicated devices, such as keyboards or gyroscopic mice. A user's personal device (e.g., a phone or a tablet) can also be used. *Touch Projector* [4] is one such system that allows interacting with distant displays using a phone's camera. Jansen et al. [18] present tangible remote controllers that can be used in concert with a tablet to allow for rich input to a large display from afar. *ARC-Pad* [25] uses a world-in-miniature view on a handheld device in combination with absolute and relative pointing. Nancel et al. [27] increase pointing accuracy, despite the mismatch in size between a mobile device and a large display.

To avoid having secondary and dedicated interaction devices, research turned to mid-air pointing techniques, where people point using their arms and fingers (e.g., [7,20,28]). In addition to pointing at targets, previous work also focused on target selection using mid-air techniques. Vogel & Balakrishnan [34] created two techniques for triggering a selection: *AirTap* and *ThumbTrigger*. They further evaluated techniques for distant freehand pointing, and found absolute pointing to be beneficial when tasks required bridging larger *on-screen* distances. Banerjee et al. [2] presented techniques for bi-manual on-screen manipulation of objects and found them superior to laser pointer based techniques. Nancel et al. [29] extended such interactions to also allow for zooming (besides panning) using mid-air gestures. Unlike *Off-Limits*, these interactions operate on-screen: they improve on-screen selection performance or bring off-screen content into the display through a series of on-screen pan and zoom interactions.

Kopper et al. [22] explored distal pointing tasks on large displays. They intended to model such techniques using Fitts' Law, and found that it is possible as a function of angular amplitude (i.e., the distance of the target in degrees) and angular target size. In contrast to Fitts' Law, however, the task difficulty grew as a quadratic function, indicating that pointing difficulty grows rapidly with increasing angular amplitudes. Further, a target's angular size had an even larger impact than angular amplitude. This is highly relevant for *Off-Limits*, as angular amplitudes further increase when going beyond the display.

Off-Screen Interaction

When the display acts as a viewport onto a larger information space, parts of the information space will reside *off-screen*. Users can access off-screen content through pan-and-zoom interfaces, where they must integrate overview and detail over time [6] or by using world-in-miniature representations of the entire information space [32]. Proxy-based interfaces further allow for accessing off-screen content: *Halo* [3], *Wedge* [12], and *City Lights* [36] are examples of such interfaces, which provide on-screen visual cues of an object's distance and orientation. Irani et al.'s work on off-screen content validates that proxies are useful for quickly accessing off-screen objects [15,16]. However, proxy-based systems require that the system knows the objects of interest before the interaction takes place.

Each of these techniques still uses the display as input space. Instead of changing the information space's representation through on-screen operations, a device can (if possible) also be moved to change its viewport into that space. *Peephole Displays* [35] is one such approach, where the information space remains fixed and a mobile device instead is moved within that space. *Virtual Shelves* [23] similarly makes use of a larger information space (here: applications sorted in a grid), which users can select by pointing at their invisible location in space. Like *Off-Limits*, these systems enable users to move to an off-screen location, rather than moving digital information on-screen.

Finally, and most related to our work, is research on free-hand off-screen pointing and interaction. Ens et al.'s work [9] and *AD-Binning* [13] allows placing and retrieving objects or locations in the proximity of small handheld devices. Hasan et al. [14] found that using off-screen pointing does outperform on-screen navigation at the expense of accuracy. Jones et al. [19] further used the off-screen space of a mobile device to allow for a greater interaction volume, as well as removing the apparent screen occlusion. Takashima et al. [33] explored how users can start dragging operations on-screen and continue them outside the device after crossing its boundary. Despite being designed for small-screen devices, these techniques were inspiring for our work on *Off-Limits*. Due to the different display sizes (and thus motor spaces), we do not expect that off-screen interaction performance on mobile devices can be generalized directly to large displays. Hence, directly porting techniques from small devices to large displays is not straightforward, as the different devices afford substantially different motions when interacting with them.

USER STUDIES

We contribute three user studies, each of which investigates the users' perception and use of off-screen space. Our goal is to successfully bring off-screen interaction to large displays. To do so, we first evaluate the performance of naïvely applying the concept of off-screen pointing. Then, we investigate how the information space extends beyond the display. Given the display as the frame of reference, we explore whether users can extrapolate locations in the information space in a linear fashion beyond the display's boundaries, or whether the information is scaled based on how far users point into off-screen space. Finally, we create a model based on the findings, improve the concept, and evaluate it against the naïve approach. We chose to not give on-screen visual guidance regarding the current pointing location, although such guidance may increase users' pointing accuracy. Instead, our focus is to assess users' perception of off-screen space with the display being the only frame of reference. We leave an exploration of the effects of visual guidance for future work.

In all experiments, we used an OptiTrack motion capturing system with eight Flex 13 cameras (with 56° field of view). Each camera runs at 120 fps with a resolution of 1280 × 1024 pixels. Thus, we are able to track a volume of 3 × 3 meters at sub-millimeter accuracy. To track pointing interactions, participants wore a glove on their right hand with reflective markers attached to it as follows: one rigid body to find the hand, one marker on the dorsal side of the distal phalanx and one marker on the dorsal side of the proximal phalanx (see inlay in Figure 2). We used the ray emanating through those markers onto the planar extension of the display for interaction. As display, we used an 84" SMART Board 8084i with an active display area of 1.86 × 1.04 meters (3840 × 2160 pixels). Figure 2 shows our setup.

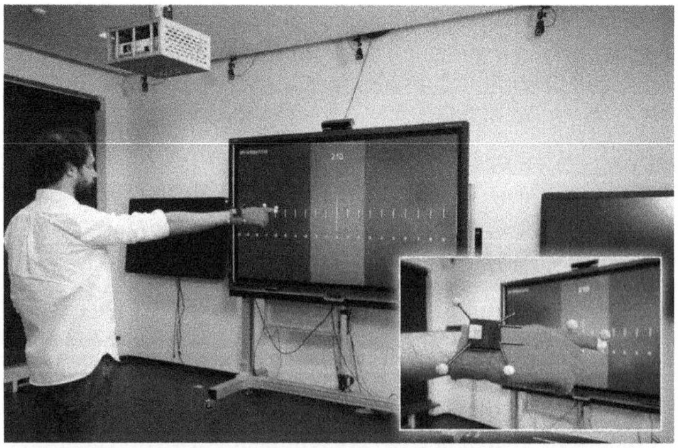

Figure 2. The experimental setup used in all three studies.

STUDY 1: OFF-SCREEN INTERACTION PERFORMANCE

The first experiment compares the naïve implementation of off-screen interaction to an on-screen mid-air condition and a touch condition. Participants performed 1D-docking operations by panning a horizontal line of numbers.

Task

Participants performed a 1D-docking task, where they had to drag a horizontal line of numbers until a given number is within the target area in the center of the display (which covered a quarter of the display's width). At the beginning of each trial, the display showed the initial range of -10 to 10 (both inclusive), with 0 in the center. At the top of the display, the number participants had to dock was shown (see Figure 2). Task values ranged from ±10 to ±210 (i.e., most numbers were initially off-screen). Participants had to drag the horizontal line, so that the desired number appeared on-screen. The correct number was indicated with a thick red line. Once the number entered the target area, the area changed its color to green. A trial ended when the target was stationary within the target area for 500ms. We recorded time from the first interaction until the docking was completed (with the 500ms stationary dwell time excluded), as well as the number of dragging operations.

Interfaces

Participants used three interfaces: two baseline conditions, Touch and On-screen mid-air pointing, and the experimental condition, Off-screen mid-air pointing. We included touch as a condition, because it is widespread even on large displays. In detail, the interfaces were:

Touch. This baseline interface is implemented to allow for dragging operations using single-touch. We added inertia (which is common in touch interfaces), and implemented it as follows: while dragging, we compute the velocity of the drag. Once a finger is lifted (end of a drag), we multiply that velocity with a factor 0.985 for every 10ms passed since the release (i.e., the start of an inertia scroll). Velocity was capped to a maximum value determined through a pilot study with four participants.

On-screen Mid-air Pointing (*On-Screen*)**.** Like *Touch*, this technique is bound to the display (i.e., an interaction can only occur while a user is pointing at the display). To determine the on-screen location users point at, we used an approach similar to Vogel and Balakrishnan [34], where an imagined ray was emanating from the tip of the extended index finger. As our task was a 1D-docking task, however, we only used the x-coordinate of the intersection to give feedback to participants regarding the pointing location.

Unlike other mid-air techniques (e.g., [5,34]), we chose to have participants click a mouse in their non-dominant hand. Note that this suggests bi-manual operation where one hand points at an off-screen location while the other hand is used for selecting that location. We did so to ensure robust operation, and to minimize the effects of clicking on pointing performance. The mouse's left button acted as selection trigger (dragging was enabled while the button was pressed). Once participants pointed off-screen, an automatic *release* event was triggered to tie the interaction to the display. If the button remained pressed and the cursor reentered the display, we trigged a *press* event. This technique used the same inertia implementation as *Touch*.

Off-screen Mid-air Pointing (*Off-Screen*)**.** The off-screen pointing technique was implemented in the same way as its on-screen counterpart. The important difference, however, was that there were no automatic *press* and *release* events when the cursor left the display. Thus, participants could freely make use of off-screen space. That is, they could point at locations not residing on-screen, and perform dragging operations beyond the display's boundaries (i.e., either start or end in off-screen space). This technique allowed for the same inertia behavior as the other two.

Study Design & Procedure

The experiment used a within-subjects design with *Interface* (*Touch*, *On-Screen*, and *Off-Screen*) and *Value* (*±10*, *±50*, *±90*, *±130*, *±170*, and *±210*) as independent variables. The values represent equally distributed numbers up to ten times the display width to either side of the display. The order of *Interfaces* was systematically varied between participants using a balanced Latin Square. The order of *Value* was randomized. In total, we collected *12 Participants* × *3 Interfaces* × *12 Values* × *5 Repetitions* = *2160 Trials* (180 data points per participant).

First, participants were asked to complete a demographic questionnaire, and were introduced to the experiment. Before performing tasks with an *Interface*, participants received a short introduction and then practiced until they felt comfortable using the interface. All participants used less than 10 practice trials for each *Interface*. For *Touch*, participants were standing in front of the center of the display; for the two mid-air conditions, participants stood 2 meters away from the display. Once they completed all trials with an *Interface*, they were administered a device assessment questionnaire (ISO-9241-9). At the end of the study, participants ranked the three *Interfaces* (1 was best). Participants completed the study on average in 60 minutes.

Participants

We recruited 12 paid participants (7 female, 5 male) ranging in age from 18 to 36 (M=25.3, SD=5.0). All were right-handed or ambidextrous. Furthermore, participants reported normal mobility in both arms as well as hands.

Hypotheses

We hypothesized that *Off-Screen* would outperform the other two techniques. In particular, we (H1) expected *Off-Screen* to have shorter interaction times for targets further in off-screen space, due to (H2) fewer dragging operations.

Results

We performed separate Repeated Measures Analysis Of Variance (RM-ANOVA) tests on task completion time and number of operations. Outliers calculated for each interac-

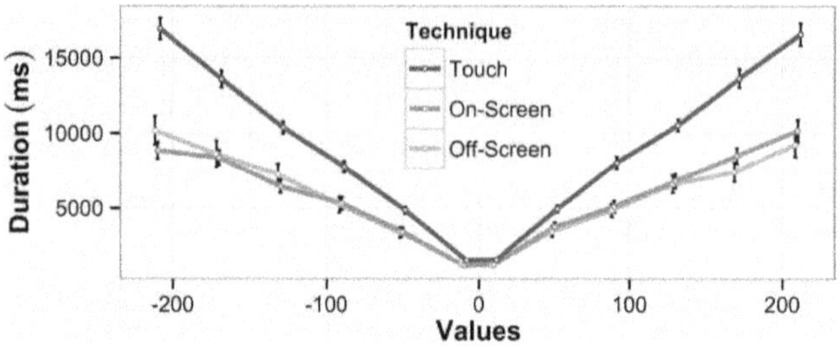

Figure 3. Task durations across values. Error bars denote 95% confidence intervals.

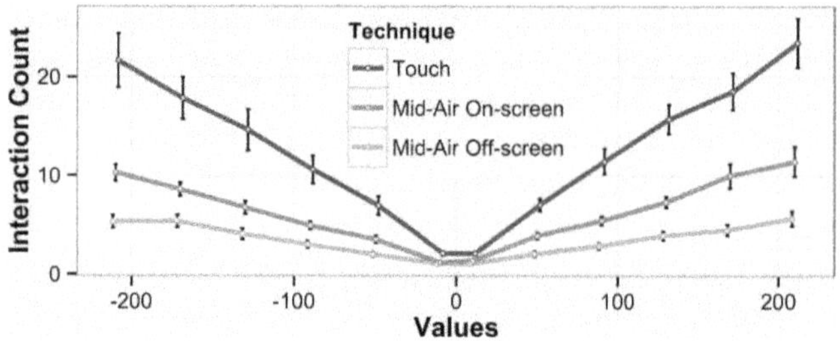

Figure 4. Interaction count (drags) across values. Error bars denote 95% confidence intervals.

tion technique and value combination were removed. A trial was regarded as an outlier if task duration was more than three interquartile ranges above the upper quartile (Q3) or below the lower quartile (Q1). In total, we removed 32 trials (*Touch*: 4, *On-Screen*: 3, and *Off-Screen*: 25). In cases where sphericity was violated, we corrected the degrees of freedom using Greenhouse-Geisser correction. For pairwise post-hoc comparisons, we used Bonferroni correction. Unstated *p*-values were non-significant ($p > 0.05$).

Completion time. We found significant main effects for *Interface* ($F_{2,22} = 60.663$, $p < .001$) and *Value* ($F_{3.352,36.869} = 501.713$, $p < .001$). Pairwise comparisons revealed that *Touch* was slower than both *On-Screen* and *Off-Screen*. The effect of *Value* was unsurprising, as larger values naturally require longer time to reach them. Pairs of *values* of the same absolute value (e.g., +10 versus -10) did not differ significantly, but all others did (all $p < .05$).

We also found an *Interface* × *Value* interaction ($F_{22,242} = 28.111$, $p < .001$). As shown in Figure 3, *Touch* was consistently slower than the other two *Techniques* for all *Values* but *-10* (all $p < .023$). For *-10*, *Touch* was only slower than *On-Screen* ($p < .007$), but no difference was found between *Touch* and *Off-Screen*. Across all *Values*, there was no significant difference between the two mid-air conditions. Overall, *Touch* (*M*=9211ms, *SD*=5391) was slower than both *On-Screen* (*M*=5774ms, *SD*=3286), and *Off-Screen* (*M*=5687ms, *SD*=3631).

Number of operations. Since no difference in performance was found between *On-Screen* and *Off-Screen*, we investigated the number of dragging operations used to see if participants used *Off-Screen* similar to *On-Screen* (i.e., not making use of off-screen space). Note that a lower number indicates larger dragging distances, and thus the use of off-screen space. We again found significant main effects for both *Interface* ($F_{1.337,14.709} = 476.461$, $p < .001$) and *Value* ($F_{3.212,35.332} = 515.353$, $p < .001$). The main effect of *Values* was unsurprising, as larger ranges require more dragging operations. Again, *Values* of the same absolute value (e.g., +10 versus -10) did not differ significantly, but all others except for the two largest *Values* did (all $p < .05$).

An *Interface* × *Value* interaction ($F_{22,242} = 160.583$, $p < .001$) was also observed. Figure 4 reveals the source of the detected interaction, where – as the absolute *Values* increase – *Off-Screen* had fewer and fewer operations than both *On-Screen* and *Touch* (all $p < .001$). Even for the smallest *Value* (±10), *Off-Screen* had the lowest number of operations (all $p < .001$). Overall, *Touch* (*M*=12.69, *SD*=9.36) required most operations, followed by *On-Screen* (*M*=6.21, *SD*=4.31) and *Off-Screen* (*M*=3.37, *SD*=2.32). Figure 4 summarizes these results.

To further support the differences in interaction strategies, we observed large differences in the percentage of viewport movement being caused by inertia per participant and *Interface*. A higher percentage indicates that participants more strongly relied on inertia. In total, *Touch* had 59.8% (*SD*=2.72), *On-Screen* 36.3% (*SD*=4.55), and *Off-Screen* 10.6% (*SD*=9.19) of movement caused by inertia. Fewer interactions paired with less inertia-based movement supports that off-screen interaction was used actively.

Subjective feedback. One participant did not answer all the questions of the ISO-9241-9 questionnaire, and we removed that participant's answers before further analysis. A MANOVA analysis using Wilks' lambda revealed significant differences between the *Interfaces* (Λ=.165, $F_{26,36} = 2.022$, $p < .05$). Post-hoc comparisons showed no significant differences between the two mid-air conditions. *Touch*, however, was regarded as requiring more physical effort, being slower, being less comfortable, and to cause higher fatigue in the finger, the arm and shoulder (all $p < .05$) than *On-Screen*. In addition, *Touch* was regarded as being slower, but as being more accurate than *Off-Screen* (all $p < .05$).

We further asked participants to rank the three *Interfaces*. We found a significant difference in ranks ($\chi^2(2) = 12.667$, $p < .002$). A post-hoc analysis using Wilcoxon Signed-Rank Tests then revealed that *On-Screen* was the preferred *Interface* (all $p < .005$), whilst *Touch* and *Off-Screen* showed no significant difference. Overall, *On-Screen* was ranked first ten times, the other two only once each.

Discussion

We hypothesized that *Off-Screen* would outperform both *Touch* and *Off-Screen* in terms of completion time by reducing the number of operations required. However, we found that both mid-air *Interfaces* exhibited similar performance regarding completion time, which means that we reject H1. We further found that *Interfaces* were used differently, which is outlined by the number of operations using during a trial. Here, *Off-Screen* required significantly fewer dragging operations than the other two techniques, which we believe stems from the larger range available for interaction. This supports H2. During the experiment, we made important observations (which were supported by participants' comments during and after the study):

First, for all *Interfaces*, participants often adjusted their speed of panning to a level that allowed reading the numbers on the display. One participant specifically commented that this was the case and that he had to go slower in *Touch* than with the mid-air interfaces to see the numbers (because he was very close to the display).

Second, for *Touch* and *On-Screen*, all participants heavily relied on inertia. For *Off-Screen*, participants fell into two groups: either they relied on a similar inertia strategy as for *Touch* and *On-Screen*, or they attempted to accurately point in off-screen space to directly drag the target on-screen. We observed that the latter group often undershot the target and continued the dragging operation across the display to end in the off-screen space opposite to where they had started. This resulted in increased effects of hand-tremor.

Third, when using *Off-Screen*, participants attempted to correct for the undershooting they experienced. This often resulted in severe overshooting when trying to point at large values due to the planar and linear extension of the plane. After experiencing this a few times, participants adopted a similar usage pattern as observed for *On-Screen*, i.e., mostly using the display instead of off-screen space.

In summary, *Off-Screen* did not outperform the two baseline conditions *Touch* and *On-Screen*, as we had anticipated, but performed on par. We also identified issues with the off-screen pointing *Interface*, namely severe undershooting and overshooting effects that encouraged further work.

STUDY 2: UNDERSTANDING OFF-SCREEN SPACE

The aforementioned challenges may stem from the users' perception of off-screen space and their ability to point accurately within that space. In the first experiment, it became clear that users' perception of off-screen space is not necessarily a linear extension of the display. Instead, there may be a different function that relies on a target's distance to the display. In this experiment, we explore the users' perception of locations in off-screen space.

To assess participants' perception of off-screen pointing, we adopted a method from *Psychophysics* and applied the so-called *Magnitude Production* using a predefined scale [11]. Despite its design for physical stimuli (e.g., force, or sound pressure), we found the experimental setup to be a good fit for this experiment. We chose a predefined scale, because we foresee off-screen use cases that are based on scales defined by on-screen content, rather than scales defined by a user's mental model.

Interface

As we were interested in assessing off-screen pointing accuracy, we only used one interface – namely *Off-Screen*. Compared to the first experiment, the visual representation was simplified: a horizontal line was the basis of the scale. The number 0 was in the center, and ±10 were located at the edges of the display. No additional numbers were on the scale. Note, that ±10 here was not exactly at the edge (as in experiment 1), but slightly moved inward, so that the numbers were better readable.

Task

At the beginning of each trial, participants were presented with a number (visually on-screen through a textbox at the bottom of the display), which they had to acquire using *Off-Screen* pointing. That is, they had to point at the location where they thought the number should be. While pointing at the number's location, they clicked the mouse button. No visual feedback was given to indicate their accuracy.

We instructed participants as follows: "(1) Imagine that the straight line shown on the display extends horizontally to both sides (into off-screen space) without any defined limits. (2) A linear scale ranging from -10 to 10 is defined on the display. 0 is at the center of the display. (3) You will be given a set of numbers. For each number, we ask you to point to the number on the extended line. (4) Please be aware that both negative and positive number will occur". For each trial, we measured where participants actually pointed at in off-screen space.

Experimental Design & Setup

The first experiment revealed that pointing accuracy in off-screen space seemingly degrades with an increased angular distance (where an angle of 0° is equal to pointing directly at the display's center). Unlike in experiment 1, we chose to distribute *Values* based on an equal spread across *pointing angles* to the display. As the largest numbers in the first experiment (i.e., ±210) correspond to pointing angles of ±84.9°, we chose to use ±84° as largest values. In between, we chose six degree intervals (rounded to the closest integer), leading to the following 29 *Values*: 0, ±2, ±5, ±7, ±10, ±12, ±16, ±20, ±24, ±30, ±38, ±49, ±67, ±102, and ±207. *Values* were presented in random order. Note that nine *Values* reside on-screen (with only 0, and ±10 being indicated on the horizontal line as ticks). In total, we recorded *29 Values × 12 Repetitions = 384 trials* per participant. *Values* were presented in random order.

Environmental features (e.g., room size, display size, and objects) might affect users' ability to point accurately. We attempted to minimize such effects by suspending black fabric from the ceiling, covering the walls and any objects that could be used as landmarks.

Procedure

Participants were first asked to complete a demographic questionnaire, and they were introduced to the experiment. Before beginning the pointing tasks, participants completed a VZ-2 paper-folding test for spatial visualization [30]. The test provides an assessment of the participants' ability to imagine/visualize spatial relationships. Results range between 0 and 20 (higher is better) based on 20 imagined paper-folding/whole-punching tasks. During the pointing task,

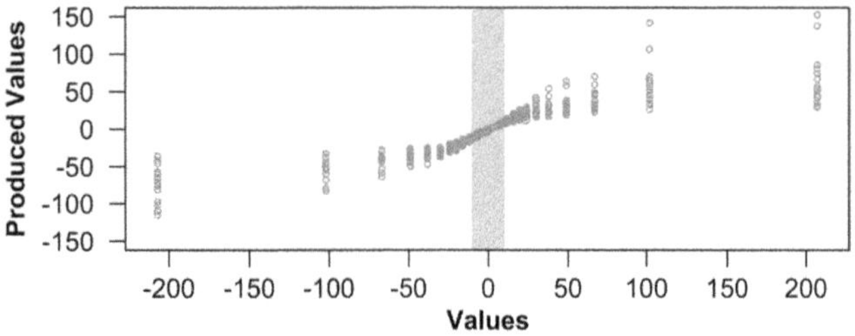

Figure 5. Scatter plot of participants' mean pointing performance. The grey area indicates the display area.

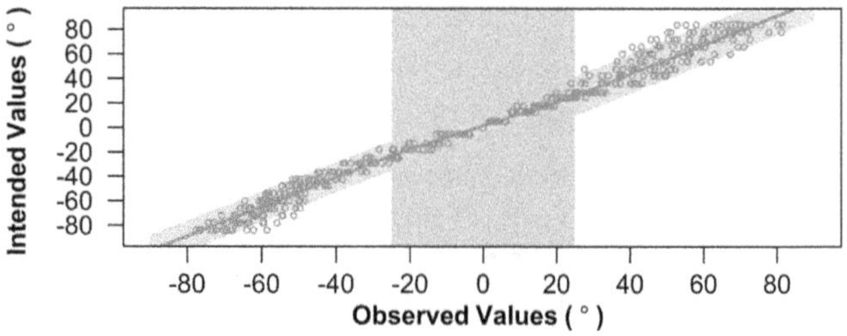

Figure 6. Scatter plot and regressions of our model. Grey indicates the display; green areas show 95% prediction intervals.

participants stood 2 meters away from the center of the display (as in experiment 1). When needed, users were allowed to take short breaks. Participants completed the experiment on average in 30 minutes.

Participants
We recruited 15 paid participants (6 female, 9 male) ranging in age from 21 to 64 (*M*=36.1, *SD*=11.2). All were right handed and all reported normal mobility in both arms and hands. Participants scored between 8 and 20 (*M*=13.1) on the VZ-2 paper-folding test.

Results
Before beginning the analysis, we removed 149 trials, where participants misread the number's sign and hence pointed in the wrong direction; and 107 outliers (i.e., more than three interquartile ranges above the upper quartile or below the lower quartile). In total, 265 trials were removed.

Next, we computed the *Value* error, which is the absolute difference between *Value* (the cued value) and the *Produced Value* (the value participants actually pointed at). For each participant, we compared this error to the VZ-2 test scores using linear regression. The associated analysis of variance did not show any significant predictive power of a participant's test score on their pointing accuracy ($F_{1,13}$ = .087, $p = .38$), which suggests that individual spatial visualization abilities cannot predict errors in *Value*.

To minimize the effects of within user variance, we calculated each participant's average per *Value*. As expected, participants' accuracy degraded rapidly as *Values* (and thus angles) increased (see Figure 5). A closer examination of outliers supports this: the four largest *Values* (i.e., ±102 and ±207) accounted for 71% of all outliers. As we suspected, Figure 5 further reveals a non-linear correlation between a trial's *Value* and the *Produced Value*. Participants consistently tended to undershoot the *Value*, which supports our observation from study 1.

Modeling Off-Screen Space
The presented data can be used to improve the performance of off-screen pointing in experiment 1. To do so, we created a model that predicts a user's *intended value* (*iv*) based on an *observed value* (*ov*). The intended value is the location the user *intends* to point at, whereas the observed value is the location the user *actually* points at (in the system's coordinate system, based on the display's pixel grid).

We experimented with different regression models (i.e., *linear*, *logarithmic*, and *exponential*) on values in pixel space, but were unable to find a model that explained all data well enough. For that reason, we transformed the values from pixel-space into the corresponding angular values, and found that linear regression worked more promising with angles. However, because accuracy seems to differ between on- and off-screen pointing, we decided to divide the data into on- and off-screen values: *Negative Off-Screen* (i.e., left of the display), *On-Screen* (i.e., within the display), and *Positive Off-Screen* (i.e., right of the display). *On-Screen* data was modeled well using linear regression ($iv = 0.974 \times ov + 1.656, R^2 = .971$).

We then fitted similar models to both off-screen areas. We decided to include on-screen points (i.e., the *Positive On-Screen* model would include on-screen points on the right/positive part of the display). *Negative Off-Screen* led to $iv = 1.159 \times ov + 4.262$ with $R^2 = .947$, and *Positive Off-Screen* led to $iv = 1.121 \times ov + 1.317$ with $R^2 = .909$. However, this led to unwanted, non-seamless transitions when crossing the display's edges (i.e., discontinuous predictions). To achieve a continuous connection between the models, we adjusted the model slightly to allow for seamless transitions (by forcing the off-screen linear regressions to go through the endpoints of the on-screen regression): *Negative Off-Screen* was then $iv = 1.202 \times ov + 7.356$ with $R^2 = .934$, and *Positive Off-Screen* changed to $iv = 1.188 \times ov - 3.694$ with $R^2 = .896$. Equation 1 shows the final combination of the three models (note that predictions larger that or equal to ±90 degrees is not applicable).

$$iv = \begin{cases} 1.202 \times ov + 7.356 & \text{if } -80.995 < ov < -25 \\ 0.974 \times ov + 1.656 & \text{if } -25 \leq ov \leq 25 \\ 1.188 \times ov - 3.694 & \text{if } 25 < ov < 78.867 \\ N/A & \text{if } ov \leq -80.995 \vee ov \geq 78.867 \end{cases} \quad (1)$$

Figure 6 shows a scatter plot of the pointing data together with the final model (the shaded area represents the 95% prediction intervals). Our model gives an estimate of the user's intended pointing position based on an observation, allowing for correcting previously observed undershooting effects. The prediction interval reveals in which interval a user intended to point in case of a new observation, with 95% confidence. Predicting a user's intended position and identifying the limits of off-screen pointing may be useful for future techniques, such as zooming automatically based on the uncertainty of an observation.

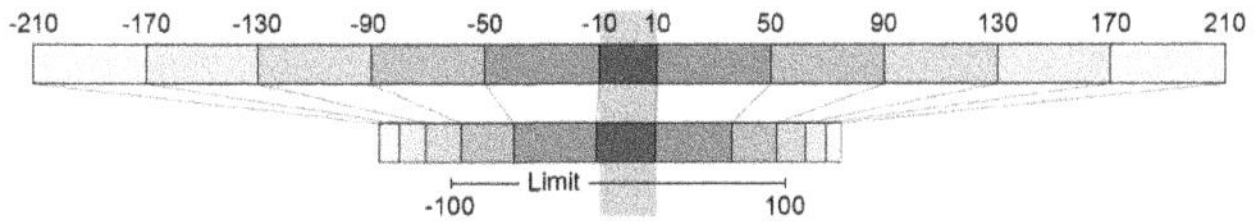

Figure 7. Relationship between *values* in original input space (top) and corrected input space (bottom).

OFF-LIMITS: MAKING OFF-SCREEN POINTING WORK

Based on the results and observations of the two experiments, we refined the naïve implementation and created the *Off-Limits* technique, which improves off-screen pointing in two important aspects: (1) we correct for the intended value using our defined model; and (2) we limit the interaction when users point too far away from the display. Figure 7 outlines the model and the limits used.

Model-based Correction. We found that participants systematically undershot their intended target. The model defined in the second experiment corrects for this – particularly in off-screen space. To ensure seamless transitions across the display's edges, we make use of the adjusted model explained in the previous section (see Equation 1).

Constrained Interaction Space. Despite the original intention of allowing for limitless off-screen interaction, results from the first two experiments suggest that the uncertainty associated with off-screen pointing quickly reaches levels where this becomes a hindering factor. More precisely, for locations far away from the display's center, slight angular changes result in large positional changes. The results of the second experiment suggested a maximum meaningful limit of 5 times the display width from the display's center. The limit is enforced on the *model-corrected* input.

STUDY 3: OFF-LIMITS' PERFORMANCE

In the first experiment, off-screen pointing showed competitive, yet not superior, performance to touch and mid-air on-screen pointing. In this experiment, we evaluate *Off-Limits* and compare it to off-screen pointing.

Interfaces

We compared two interfaces: (1) *Off-Screen* was implemented as in the first experiment; and (2) *Off-Limits* was implemented using the model and constraints as described in the previous section. We did not include the *Touch* interface, which was shown inferior in experiment 1, and neither included *On-Screen*, as it was comparable to *Off-Screen*.

Task, Study Design & Procedure

The task was modeled in the same way as in the first experiment. That is, participants performed a 1D-docking task using each of the two interfaces. We recorded the same data, namely time (from the first interaction until the docking was completed) and the number of dragging operations.

Like the first experiment, this study used a within-subjects design with the two independent variables *Interface* and *Value*. To allow for informal comparisons to the original experiment, we kept the *Values* identical (i.e., ranging from -210 to +210). Note, that the enforced limit for *Off-Limits* therefore is ±100. In contrast to the first study, we did increase the number of repetitions from 5 to 10 per *Interface* and *Value* combination. In total, each participant completed *2 Techniques × 12 Values × 10 Repetitions = 3120 trials.*

The procedure was also adapted from the first experiment. On average, participants spent approximately 60 minutes.

Participants

We recruited 13 paid participants (9 female, 4 male) ranging in age from 20 to 33 years (*M*=23.8, *SD*=3.4). Two participants had previously participated in experiment 1. All of our participants were right-handed and reported normal mobility in both arms as well as hands.

Hypotheses

We hypothesized, that (H1) *Off-Limits* is faster than *Off-Screen* with increasing *Values* (i.e., larger distances to the display's center), and (H2) requires fewer operations.

Results

We performed RM-ANOVA tests on task completion time and number of operations. We removed outliers before beginning our analysis (as described for experiment 1). We removed 87 outliers (*Off-Screen*: 59; *Off-Limits*: 28). We corrected degrees of freedom using Greenhouse-Geisser when sphericity was violated. For pair-wise post-hoc comparisons, we used Bonferroni correction.

Completion time. We found significant main effects for *Interface* ($F_{1,12}$ = 7.093, $p < .021$) and *Value* ($F_{2.666,31.997}$ = 104.643, $p < .001$) and an *Interface* × *Value* interaction ($F_{3.621,43.448}$ = 6.973, $p < .001$). As for the first experiment, the *Value* effect is explained by requiring more time to reach targets further away. The results are in line with the previous studies, in that neither values of the same absolute value nor values with an absolute value of 170 or larger differed significantly.

Figure 8 reveals the source of the interesting interaction. While *Off-Screen* seems to perform equally well compared to *Off-Limits* when *Values* are on-screen or only slightly beyond the display, *Off-Limits* outperforms *Off-Screen* for *Values* further away from the display. In particular, we found that *Off-Limits* was faster than *Off-Screen* for the following *Values*: +130, +210, -170, and -210 (all $p < .015$). Although there are no significant differences between the two *Interfaces* for -130 and +170, Figure 8 indicates a trend in that *Off-Limits* may work better in the off-screen space further away. On the other hand, for *Values* -10 ($p < .007$)

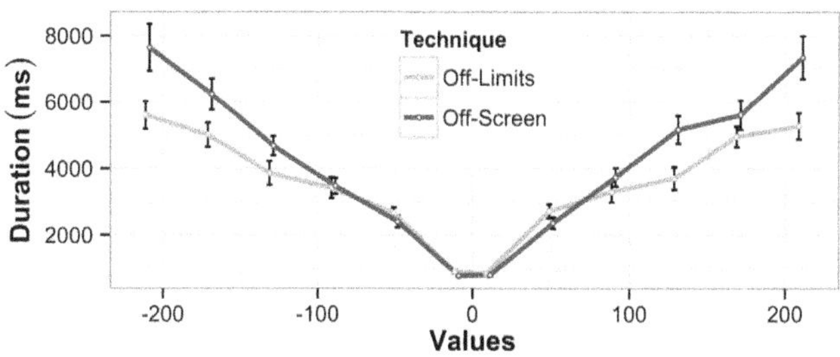

Figure 8. Task durations across values. Error bars denote 95% confidence intervals.

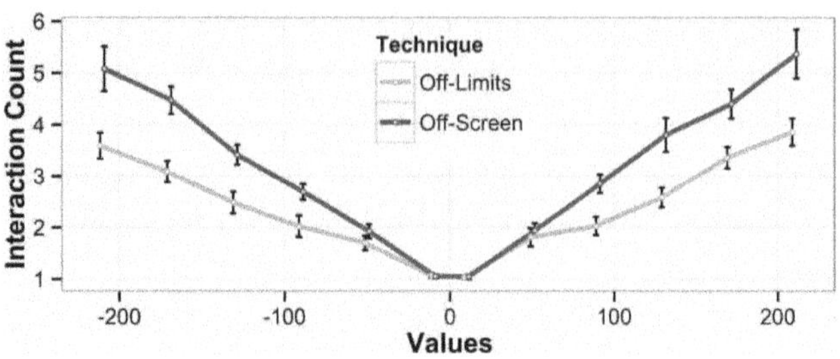

Figure 9. Interaction count (drags) across values. Error bars denote 95% confidence intervals.

and +50 ($p < .049$), *Off-Screen* was slightly faster, suggesting that the off-screen correction may have had a slight influence. Overall, however, *Off-Limits* (M=3526.81, SD=216.94) was faster than the original *Off-Screen* interface (M=4209.7, SD=285.42). These results support H1.

Number of operations. We found significant main effects for *Interface* ($F_{1,12}$ = 23.238, $p < .001$) and *Value* ($F_{3.925,47.095}$ = 142.108, $p < .001$) and an *Interface* × *Value* interaction ($F_{3.769,45.234}$ = 8.277, $p < .001$). As for completion time, *Values* further away require more operations. Like in the other experiments, post-hoc pair-wise multiple means comparisons revealed that positive/negative *Values* of the same absolute value did not differ, and neither did *Values* from ±170 onward (all $p < .05$).

The source of the *Interface* × *Value* interaction is shown in Figure 9. Both *Interfaces* did not differ significantly for the lowest two *Values* (i.e., ±10 and ±50). For all other *Values*, *Off-Limits* required fewer operations than pure *Off-Screen* pointing (all $p < .013$). This is in line with completion times and further supports that *Off-Limits* works well for *Values* further away from the display's center. This supports our hypothesis H2. Overall, *Off-Limits* (M=2.384, SD=0.095) required fewer operations than *Off-Screen* (M=3.165, SD=0.145). Figure 9 summarizes the results.

Subjective feedback. As in study 1, we ran a MANOVA using Wilks' lambda on the ISO-9241-9 questionnaire answers. Overall, the MANOVA did not find the *Interfaces* to be different (Λ=.354, $F_{12,13}$ = 1.688, $p > .05$). Post-hoc comparisons of the individual questions, however, showed significant differences on the accuracy of pointing and the overall ease of use (both $p < .05$). *Off-Limits* was perceived more accurate and easier to use. All 13 participants preferred the use of *Off-Limits*. One stated that "*I feel that I hit what I'm aiming at more accurately, using this technique*", another that "*I don't need to slow down to see the numbers because I know what I'm holding onto*". Others had similar comments. Only one stated that she "*had to slow down to see the numbers in both techniques*".

All participants preferred *Off-Limits*. Interestingly, one participant who was part of the first experiment commented that *Off-Limits* was "***by far** the best technique I have tried*". These results and statements indicate that our improvements to the naïve off-screen pointing implementation had the desired effect.

DISCUSSION

We set out to explore off-screen pointing as an interaction technique for navigating large information spaces on large displays. Our main hypothesis was that off-screen pointing provides significant advantages over state-of-the-art interaction techniques (e.g., touch and mid-air), whose input is bound to the display.

The first experiment found *Touch* to perform slower than the mid-air techniques. The study did not show a performance increase when using off-screen space, as participants consistently undershot the target when they tried to directly point at it. Undershooting greatly decreased performance, and brought it overall closer to the mid-air on-screen technique. One reason for this is that users do not perceive off-screen space as linearly extending the on-screen space.

The second study, which collected data to understand and model users' behavior, showed that users' pointing accuracy degraded rapidly when pointing further away from the display. We also observed that participants systematically undershot the target. We derived a model that predicts the value a user intends to point at, which can be used to correct for undershooting. The model limits output to only the range in off-screen space where users can accurately point (i.e., to avoid angles close to 90 degrees that are problematic). The results led to the final design of *Off-Limits*.

The third experiment compared *Off-Limits* to the naïve *Off-Screen* implementation of the first experiment. The results show significant improvements: *Off-Limits* is significantly faster, requires fewer (clutching) operations, and is preferred by participants. Figure 10 highlights that participants used off-screen space (and particularly the limit of ±100) more extensively with *Off-Limits* compared to the naïve approach (where participants pointed closer to the display).

Angular vs. Orthogonal Pointing

Our results show that naïvely extending the plane linearly did not lower task completion time significantly, when working on large displays. However, earlier work on mobile devices successfully used this style of off-screen pointing [13,14]. We believe that this stems from the way people point: on mobile devices, people would point orthogonally into the extended space with off-screen locations reasonably close to the display. On large displays, pointing orthogonally in off-screen space would require people to move parallel to the display. Instead, people point in an angular fashion by turning their forearm. During the process of deriving our model, we found that angular pointing was used.

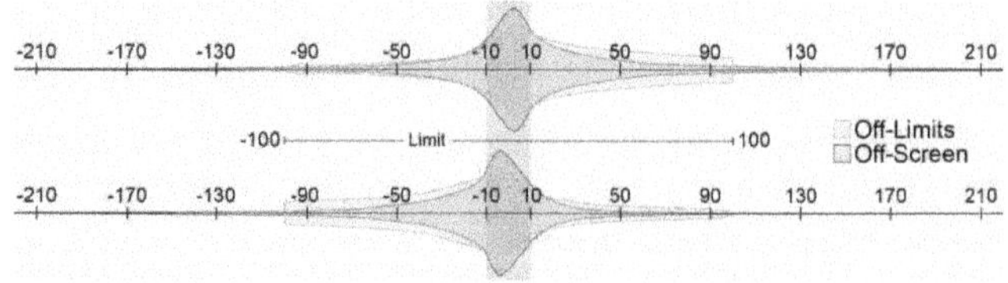

Figure 10. Aggregation of drag movement across positive (top) and negative (bottom) values. The shaded areas show the proportion of interactions in different parts of the motor space.

Figure 11. A user interacting with the Kinect prototype: (a) a user looks at a view of North America on a display; (b) the user points the location of Europe in off-screen space; (c) the user drags Europe onto the screen from its off-screen location.

A second, yet unconfirmed, reason might be that users have a different perception of off-screen space. Although we had instructed them to imagine a *planar* extension of the display, it is not clear that they actually did. Also, imagining positions further off-screen may be linked to the motor space. That is, when we point using our forearm (or potentially the entire arm), the extension may become *spherical* instead of *planar*. While our angular model reflects this, there is potential for future work.

Limitations of the Results

We acknowledge that there are limitations to the generalizability of our results. First, most information spaces are two-dimensional, and not one-dimensional as we used in our experiments. It is not yet clear, whether the model would hold for 2D off-screen interaction. However, our approach to defining a model may inform future work on deriving similar models for 2D spaces.

Second, participants were standing at a fixed distance (2m) from the fixed-size (84"). However, distance and size may influence off-screen pointing: there is a possibility that our model might need to be adapted to other distances and displays sizes. We believe, however, that this affects the cutoff of *Off-Limits*, whereas the angular model itself should translate well to other distances and displays. Tracking the user's position continuously can update the model dynamically. However, we leave the exploration for future work.

Finally, our results are affected by the chosen ray-casting and selection mechanism (as previously found by Mayer et al. [24]). Yet, we believe that the dominant factor is the uncertainty in users' perception of off-screen space. Thus, we expect similar results with other ray-casting and selection mechanisms. Nonetheless, this is left for future work.

Possible Applications using Off-Limits

To further illustrate potential use cases for *Off-Limits*, we developed an example application that allowed for visualizing high-resolution tiled images (we chose: maps, satellite images, high resolution deep space image, and electronic microscope samples). Our application makes use of three interaction techniques, each of which takes advantage of off-screen pointing: (1) *Off-Screen Panning*, which is similar to our experiments; (2) *Off-Screen Jumping* allows for jumping to a selected off-screen location using a zooming transition; and (3) *Uncertainty Feedback*, which shows an on-screen popup when a user interacts off-screen. The popup provides a real-time view into off-screen space, with automatic zooming based on pointing uncertainty.

Moreover, we implemented *Off-Limits* using an off-the-shelf Kinect v2 depth sensor mounted on top of the display to control the application, to demonstrate that *Off-Limits* is useful with less sophisticated tracking systems than the one used in the studies (see Figure 11). The Kinect was calibrated to the OptiTrack's coordinate system by capturing a person's wrist with both tracking systems while that person moved around. Naturally, the tracking accuracy is lower than using OptiTrack, yet the Kinect did provide sufficient accuracy to allow for effective off-screen pointing. The accompanying video figure illustrates the interaction techniques using OptiTrack and Kinect in operation.

CONCLUSIONS & FUTURE WORK

In this paper, we presented our findings from an exploration of off-screen pointing as an interaction technique for large displays. In three studies, we found that off-screen pointing provides significant benefits over state-of-the-art interaction techniques (*Touch* and *Mid-Air On-Screen* pointing). We systematically explored users' ability to point to off-screen locations in a horizontal extension of the on-screen information space. The results help better understand off-screen pointing, and have informed the design of *Off-Limits*, a novel off-screen interaction technique for large displays.

Our focus has been on quantitatively assessing users' abilities and to quantify performance gains of *Off-Limits*. We also gathered some positive subjective feedback on the use of *Off-Limits*, but future work could further investigate user's experience with *Off-Limit*. An obvious next step is to apply our work to two-dimensional information spaces; the applications we presented here that use *Off-Limits* already hint at the potential of off-screen pointing in 2D. A third direction for future work is to explore the effect of a person's distance to the display, as well as varying display sizes. Overall, we conclude that off-screen pointing (on large displays) has shown potential and will receive future improvements to create even better opportunities for interacting with large information spaces.

ACKNOWLEDGMENTS

This work was supported by the European Research Council under Grant Agreement n. 648785.

REFERENCES

1. Robert Ball, Chris North, and Doug A. Bowman. 2007. Move to Improve: Promoting Physical Navigation to Increase User Performance with Large Displays. *Proceedings of the SIGCHI Conference on Human Factors in Computing Systems*, ACM, 191–200. http://doi.org/10.1145/1240624.1240656

2. Amartya Banerjee, Jesse Burstyn, Audrey Girouard, and Roel Vertegaal. 2012. MultiPoint: Comparing laser and manual pointing as remote input in large display interactions. *International Journal of Human-Computer Studies* 70, 10: 690–702. http://doi.org/10.1016/j.ijhcs.2012.05.009

3. Patrick Baudisch and Ruth Rosenholtz. 2003. Halo: A Technique for Visualizing Off-screen Objects. *Proceedings of the SIGCHI Conference on Human Factors in Computing Systems*, ACM, 481–488. http://doi.org/10.1145/642611.642695

4. Sebastian Boring, Dominikus Baur, Andreas Butz, Sean Gustafson, and Patrick Baudisch. 2010. Touch Projector: Mobile Interaction Through Video. *Proceedings of the SIGCHI Conference on Human Factors in Computing Systems*, ACM, 2287–2296. http://doi.org/10.1145/1753326.1753671

5. Florian van de Camp, Alexander Schick, and Rainer Stiefelhagen. 2013. How to Click in Mid-Air. In *Distributed, Ambient, and Pervasive Interactions*, Norbert Streitz and Constantine Stephanidis (eds.). Springer Berlin Heidelberg, 78–86. http://link.springer.com/chapter/10.1007/978-3-642-39351-8_9

6. Andy Cockburn, Amy Karlson, and Benjamin B. Bederson. 2009. A Review of Overview+Detail, Zooming, and Focus+Context Interfaces. *ACM Comput. Surv.* 41, 1: 2:1–2:31. http://doi.org/10.1145/1456650.1456652

7. Andy Cockburn, Philip Quinn, Carl Gutwin, Gonzalo Ramos, and Julian Looser. 2011. Air pointing: Design and evaluation of spatial target acquisition with and without visual feedback. *Int. J. Hum.-Comput. Stud.* 69, 6: 401–414. http://doi.org/10.1016/j.ijhcs.2011.02.005

8. Maxime Collomb, Mountaz Hascoët, Patrick Baudisch, and Brian Lee. 2005. Improving Drag-and-drop on Wall-size Displays. *Proceedings of Graphics Interface 2005*, Canadian Human-Computer Communications Society, 25–32. http://dl.acm.org/citation.cfm?id=1089508.1089514

9. Barrett Ens, David Ahlström, Andy Cockburn, and Pourang Irani. 2011. Characterizing User Performance with Assisted Direct Off-screen Pointing. *Proceedings of the 13th International Conference on Human Computer Interaction with Mobile Devices and Services*, ACM, 485–494. http://doi.org/10.1145/2037373.2037445

10. Clifton Forlines, Daniel Vogel, and Ravin Balakrishnan. 2006. HybridPointing: Fluid Switching Between Absolute and Relative Pointing with a Direct Input Device. *Proceedings of the 19th Annual ACM Symposium on User Interface Software and Technology*, ACM, 211–220. http://doi.org/10.1145/1166253.1166286

11. George A. Gescheider. *Psychophysics: The Fundamentals.* Lawrence Erlbaum Associates, Publishers.

12. Sean Gustafson, Patrick Baudisch, Carl Gutwin, and Pourang Irani. 2008. Wedge: Clutter-free Visualization of Off-screen Locations. *Proceedings of the SIGCHI Conference on Human Factors in Computing Systems*, ACM, 787–796. http://doi.org/10.1145/1357054.1357179

13. Khalad Hasan, David Ahlström, and Pourang Irani. 2013. Ad-binning: Leveraging Around Device Space for Storing, Browsing and Retrieving Mobile Device Content. *Proceedings of the SIGCHI Conference on Human Factors in Computing Systems*, ACM, 899–908. http://doi.org/10.1145/2470654.2466115

14. Khalad Hasan, David Ahlström, and Pourang P. Irani. 2015. Comparing Direct Off-Screen Pointing, Peephole, and Flick & Pinch Interaction for Map Navigation. *Proceedings of the 3rd ACM Symposium on Spatial User Interaction*, ACM, 99–102. http://doi.org/10.1145/2788940.2788957

15. Pourang Irani, Carl Gutwin, Grant Partridge, and Mahtab Nezhadasl. 2007. Techniques for Interacting with Off-Screen Content. In *Human-Computer Interaction – INTERACT 2007*, Cécilia Baranauskas, Philippe Palanque, Julio Abascal and Simone Diniz Junqueira Barbosa (eds.). Springer Berlin Heidelberg, 234–249. http://link.springer.com/chapter/10.1007/978-3-540-74800-7_19

16. Pourang Irani, Carl Gutwin, and Xing Dong Yang. 2006. Improving Selection of Off-screen Targets with Hopping. *Proceedings of the SIGCHI Conference on Human Factors in Computing Systems*, ACM, 299–308. http://doi.org/10.1145/1124772.1124818

17. Mikkel R. Jakobsen and Kasper Hornb\a ek. 2015. Is Moving Improving?: Some Effects of Locomotion in Wall-Display Interaction. *Proceedings of the 33rd Annual ACM Conference on Human Factors in Computing Systems*, ACM, 4169–4178. http://doi.org/10.1145/2702123.2702312

18. Yvonne Jansen, Pierre Dragicevic, and Jean-Daniel Fekete. 2012. Tangible Remote Controllers for Wall-size Displays. *Proceedings of the SIGCHI Conference*

on Human Factors in Computing Systems, ACM, 2865–2874. http://doi.org/10.1145/2207676.2208691

19. Brett Jones, Rajinder Sodhi, David Forsyth, Brian Bailey, and Giuliano Maciocci. 2012. Around Device Interaction for Multiscale Navigation. *Proceedings of the 14th International Conference on Human-computer Interaction with Mobile Devices and Services*, ACM, 83–92. http://doi.org/10.1145/2371574.2371589

20. Ricardo Jota, Miguel A. Nacenta, Joaquim A. Jorge, Sheelagh Carpendale, and Saul Greenberg. 2010. A comparison of ray pointing techniques for very large displays. *Proceedings of Graphics Interface 2010*, Canadian Information Processing Society, 269–276. http://dl.acm.org/citation.cfm?id=1839214.1839261

21. Azam Khan, George Fitzmaurice, Don Almeida, Nicolas Burtnyk, and Gordon Kurtenbach. 2004. A Remote Control Interface for Large Displays. *Proceedings of the 17th Annual ACM Symposium on User Interface Software and Technology*, ACM, 127–136. http://doi.org/10.1145/1029632.1029655

22. Regis Kopper, Doug A. Bowman, Mara G. Silva, and Ryan P. McMahan. 2010. A Human Motor Behavior Model for Distal Pointing Tasks. *Int. J. Hum.-Comput. Stud.* 68, 10: 603–615. http://doi.org/10.1016/j.ijhcs.2010.05.001

23. Frank Chun Yat Li, David Dearman, and Khai N. Truong. 2009. Virtual Shelves: Interactions with Orientation Aware Devices. *Proceedings of the 22Nd Annual ACM Symposium on User Interface Software and Technology*, ACM, 125–128. http://doi.org/10.1145/1622176.1622200

24. Sven Mayer, Katrin Wolf, Stefan Schneegass, and Niels Henze. 2015. Modeling Distant Pointing for Compensating Systematic Displacements. *Proceedings of the 33rd Annual ACM Conference on Human Factors in Computing Systems*, ACM, 4165–4168. http://doi.org/10.1145/2702123.2702332

25. David C. McCallum and Pourang Irani. 2009. ARC-Pad: Absolute+Relative Cursor Positioning for Large Displays with a Mobile Touchscreen. *Proceedings of the 22Nd Annual ACM Symposium on User Interface Software and Technology*, ACM, 153–156. http://doi.org/10.1145/1622176.1622205

26. Miguel A. Nacenta, Dzmitry Aliakseyeu, Sriram Subramanian, and Carl Gutwin. 2005. A Comparison of Techniques for Multi-display Reaching. *Proceedings of the SIGCHI Conference on Human Factors in Computing Systems*, ACM, 371–380. http://doi.org/10.1145/1054972.1055024

27. Mathieu Nancel, Olivier Chapuis, Emmanuel Pietriga, Xing-Dong Yang, Pourang P. Irani, and Michel Beaudouin-Lafon. 2013. High-precision Pointing on Large Wall Displays Using Small Handheld Devices. *Proceedings of the SIGCHI Conference on Human Factors in Computing Systems*, ACM, 831–840. http://doi.org/10.1145/2470654.2470773

28. Mathieu Nancel, Emmanuel Pietriga, Olivier Chapuis, and Michel Beaudouin-Lafon. 2015. Mid-Air Pointing on Ultra-Walls. *ACM Trans. Comput.-Hum. Interact.* 22, 5: 21:1–21:62. http://doi.org/10.1145/2766448

29. Mathieu Nancel, Julie Wagner, Emmanuel Pietriga, Olivier Chapuis, and Wendy Mackay. 2011. Mid-air Pan-and-zoom on Wall-sized Displays. *Proceedings of the SIGCHI Conference on Human Factors in Computing Systems*, ACM, 177–186. http://doi.org/10.1145/1978942.1978969

30. J. W. French R. B. Ekstrom. 1976. Kit of Factor-Referenced Cognitive Tests.

31. George Robertson, Mary Czerwinski, Patrick Baudisch, et al. 2005. The Large-Display User Experience. *IEEE Comput. Graph. Appl.* 25, 4: 44–51. http://doi.org/10.1109/MCG.2005.88

32. Richard Stoakley, Matthew J. Conway, and Randy Pausch. 1995. Virtual Reality on a WIM: Interactive Worlds in Miniature. *Proceedings of the SIGCHI Conference on Human Factors in Computing Systems*, ACM Press/Addison-Wesley Publishing Co., 265–272. http://doi.org/10.1145/223904.223938

33. Kazuki Takashima, Nana Shinshi, and Yoshifumi Kitamura. 2015. Exploring Boundless Scroll by Extending Motor Space. *Proceedings of the 17th International Conference on Human-Computer Interaction with Mobile Devices and Services*, ACM, 557–566. http://doi.org/10.1145/2785830.2785884

34. Daniel Vogel and Ravin Balakrishnan. 2005. Distant freehand pointing and clicking on very large, high resolution displays. *Proceedings of the 18th annual ACM symposium on User interface software and technology*, ACM, 33–42. http://doi.org/10.1145/1095034.1095041

35. Ka-Ping Yee. 2003. Peephole Displays: Pen Interaction on Spatially Aware Handheld Computers. *Proceedings of the SIGCHI Conference on Human Factors in Computing Systems*, ACM, 1–8. http://doi.org/10.1145/642611.642613

36. Polle T. Zellweger, Jock D. Mackinlay, Lance Good, Mark Stefik, and Patrick Baudisch. 2003. City Lights: Contextual Views in Minimal Space. *CHI '03 Extended Abstracts on Human Factors in Computing Systems*, ACM, 838–839. http://doi.org/10.1145/765891.766022

Pressing Not Tapping: Comparing a Physical Button with a Smartphone App for Tagging Music in Radio Programmes

Lianne Kerlin
BBC R&D, Salford, UK
lianne.kerlin@bbc.co.uk

Jasmine Cox
BBC R&D, Salford, UK
jasmine.cox@bbc.co.uk

Stephen Jolly
BBC R&D, Salford, UK
stephen.jolly@bbc.co.uk

Michael Evans
BBC R&D, Salford, UK
michael.evans@bbc.co.uk

George Green
Amberlight Partners
London, UK
gcgreen@gmail.com

David Regan
Amberlight Partners
London, UK
dave.e.regan@gmail.com

ABSTRACT

A physical hardware prototype—*The Button*—was developed as a research probe to understand how radio audiences could discover, organise and consume music radio content at the touch of a physical button, the only control on a tiny handheld device. The Button allows listeners to tag tracks they like via a simple one-touch interaction, and save them to a non-commercial online playlist service: BBC Playlister[1]. Users can then export these tags to other music streaming platforms, such as Spotify, Deezer, etc. Following a user-centric design process, a large in-the-wild study was conducted over several weeks to investigate the value of the Button in aiding listeners' discovery of music. One group of participants was given a mobile phone app designed to facilitate tagging music heard on BBC radio stations; two other groups were given both the app and a Button (in one of two hardware versions). The findings revealed that Button users made significantly more tags on average than app users, indicating that a physical device could add significant value for radio listeners who want to tag music. Participants valued the simple one-touch interaction method, especially in situations where their smartphones were out of reach or contextual constraints meant that interaction with a complex device was undesirable or difficult.

ACM Classification Keywords

H.5.1 Information interfaces and presentation (e.g., HCI): Multimedia Information Systems; H.5.2 Information interfaces and presentation (e.g., HCI): User Interfaces

Author Keywords

Radio; Connected Devices; Internet of Things; Interactive Product Design; Research in the Wild; Music; User-Centred Design

[1]http://www.bbc.co.uk/music/playlister

CHI'16, May 07 - 12, 2016, San Jose, CA, USA

ACM 978-1-4503-3362-7/16/05...$15.00
DOI: http://dx.doi.org/10.1145/2858036.2858325

INTRODUCTION

Radio remains one of the most important means by which people discover new music. It was the top source for new music discoveries in 2014 in both the UK and the USA [16, 3]. However, the user experience of radio provides little assistance to the listener when it comes to remembering and retrieving music of interest: the most common platforms for radio provide no help at all, and it is left to the listener to find ways to record or remember whatever information may be given regarding a track in the radio programme itself.

This is a particular issue in the common environments in which a radio listener is contextually constrained from recording information (e.g. in places of work, while washing dishes, while carrying things or while driving a vehicle). Even when these constraints do not apply, the process that leads from a serendipitous discovery while listening to a radio programme to a point where the listener can achieve goals such as listening to the music again, exploring other music by the same artist or buying recordings of the music is complex and unreliable.

Commercial music fingerprinting services such as Shazam [26] have been launched to address this need, and make the task of identifying music simpler. They use a smartphone or other device running a dedicated application to recognise the music that is being played in its vicinity by recording a short snippet using the device's microphone and analysing it to determine its identity. The app then presents that identity to the user, and may also offer *'onward journeys'* to help the listener fulfil their goals, via links to music stores, for example.

A service of this kind requires the listener to undertake a sequence of actions from the point where music of interest has been identified, such as obtaining a smartphone with the app installed, launching the app and recording the snippet. Additional steps may be required, such as unlocking the phone, entering a password and identifying and launching the app via the device's user interface. Use of devices and apps in this way will, in some contexts, be impossible for the listener. They also will not generally work when headphones are being used, and they work less reliably in environments with significant levels of background noise.

To address these issues, we set out to design and test a system for "tagging" music in radio programmes that minimises the steps between hearing an interesting piece of music and fulfilling a consequential goal, that works for live radio broadcasts on all platforms, and that can be used in as many contextually constrained environments as possible.

Our system is a prototype smart device—*The Button*—that allows users to tag music with a single button press. The Button transfers tag data to a paired smartphone app, which gives the user information about the most recently tagged music, and uploads tagged track information to the *BBC Playlister* service. The system enables the tagging of music playing on live radio in a wide range of contexts, including those in which the user is unable to perform more complex tasks. In addition, the cognitive load of remembering information about the song and the inefficiency of using general-purpose tools such as Internet searches to fulfil user goals at a later date are eliminated. The system works with any live radio platform, including analogue and digital broadcasts and online streaming.

Our empirical study, conducted over a three-week period with 125 users, shows that listeners tag significantly more music when given a physical Button than when using just a smartphone app. This is largely explained by the tangibility of the Button and its speed and simplicity.

RELATED WORK

Single-Function Connected Button Devices

A number of recent products and prototypes seek to fulfil particular user goals in response to presses on a self-contained physical button, communicating wirelessly. For example, the *Amazon Dash Button*[2] allows consumers to purchase household items for delivery from Amazon automatically. Different patterns of press on the *Flic* button[3] trigger behaviour in a paired smartphone app such as controlling automated features of a smart home, or making phone calls to predetermined numbers. The *bt.tn*[4] makes a call to a user-defined web service when it is pressed. The *Droplet*[5] is a button that the user attaches to objects associated with specific tasks, such as medicines that must be taken regularly: if a user has not presssed the button to indicate completion of the task in a timely fashion, an app can remind them to carry it out.

The use of Internet-connected buttons to help people remember to carry out tasks has also been explored by Tang *et al.* [21], who developed such a device for tracking the number of times a healthcare activity has been performed. Their device features LED lights and a loudspeaker for user feedback, a seven-segment display that can display locally the number of times that the activity has been accomplished, and has two buttons: one to increase the count and one to decrease it in the event of accidental presses. The goal to be tracked is defined by a user in a separate graphical user interface, with which the button communicates via a cloud service. The button can be placed in a location of significance to the user (e.g. on the fridge in the case of a food-related daily goal).

The *Radio Bookmark* [10] is a key-fob device with buttons that can be used to tag programmes on National Public Radio affiliate stations in the USA. The device does not possess a wireless communication capability: users plug the device into a computer's USB port to upload the tagging data to a website.

Physical Objects

Attention theory signifies that mental resources can be divided between a number of activities [11]. Tasks at the periphery of attention (e.g. tagging radio content) require less cognitive resource and can be performed alongside other activities [1]. They can be defined as tasks carried out in short bursts of secondary activity lasting less than 4 seconds [17, 13]. There has been an increase in interactions designed to support peripheral attention tasks that fit seamlessly into everyday behaviour [1, 22]. Since interfaces are designed primarily to use vision and hearing it is difficult to use these channels for peripheral tasks without distracting from a main activity. Therefore, this work continues efforts seeking to leverage the physical world for tasks that require little attention [1, 17].

The physical world is an interesting design space for short peripheral, digital tasks, drawing on simple and intuitive interaction methods [17]. Physical objects can take advantage of users' pre-existing skills and knowledge [20] and can be familiar and intuitive when the link between action and system feedback is effective (e.g. perceived coupling [7]). Physical objects can also increase engagement [14, 7], especially when making the initial interaction that is required for continued engagement. Ma *et al* [14] compared the use of a physical object (a physical ring) and a digital equivalent (virtual ring) to explore the population of plankton in the ocean in a tabletop tangible user interface. They found that the physical ring attracted more visitors, allowing people to touch and interact with the display, as well as encouraging the initial interaction that resulted in an increase in prolonged engagement. Bakker *et al* [1] designed three case studies in a school classroom to explore the use of interactive systems for supporting periphery actions. They found that periphery tasks frequently but briefly shift to be main focus tasks, and when designing for such shifts in attention it is important to account for context and routine, with the interactions themselves needing to be easy to initiate and discard. This paper extends the scale of these studies, including over time.

Our Button puts into practice elements of the frameworks of *Embodied Interaction* (e.g. [6, 24]), whereby physical objects are augmented with digital capabilities to fit in with the social world around us. Specifically, the Button is designed to have affordance in its ecology and supports *situated action*. Its singular function is a fundamental physical/digital *binding*.

Recent Tangible Interaction Research

This Button study adds to the body of research that explores interaction with screenless objects. Comparisons can be drawn to other simple interaction techniques, such as tapping, or *whacking* (e.g. striking a device with a hand or palm) [18, 8], and gesture based interactions on screenless devices (e.g. [13]). These techniques have in common appropriate procedures for carrying out short interactions to record signals that can be retrieved at a later date. Loclair *et al*'s *PinchWatch*[13], a wearable watch device that allows users to carry out gesture based interactions such as touching the palm, was designed for

[2] http://www.amazon.com/oc/dash-button
[3] https://flic.io/
[4] http://bt.tn
[5] http://www.dropletlife.com

situations when users would wish to carry out short (<4s) interactions with a device to record a piece of information, but not interrupt focus on their activity. In the context of rock climbing, PinchWatch allows users to made a brief microinteraction on a screenless device, completing a task while minimising distraction from the physical world. Our Button affords the ability to record interesting moments in time while users are engaged in everyday activities, facilitating or even enabling the task of *taking a note* in situations where hands are not free to use a phone—such as washing the dishes or driving. These interactions all feature simple and accurate affordances.

Wolf *et al* [27] developed a taxonomy of 21 microgestures for completing a secondary task in a mobile application that minimally interrupts a primary task, thus enabling concurrency of both tasks and allowing for secondary goals to be completed on the go. They interviewed experts (sports and physiotherapists) about appropriate secondary micro-gestures that could be completed as a secondary task alongside the primary task of driving a car. The palm grasp was favoured as a microgesture that is best suited to secondary tasks whilst driving, because this requires minimal attention.

Single-Purpose Functionality

Single-purpose functionality helps users make associations between the device and its action when the link between action and device feedback is strong [7]. The device can act as a physical prompt for the single function that it offers. Multipurpose devices may not offer the same physical prompts to carry out actions, and the intention for desired outcomes may also become confused. This occured in Ronakinen *et al*'s findings [18] of single tap recordings on a phone, where a number of false positives occurred due to the phone's accelerometer. The current study investigates the use of a single-purpose portable connected button, focussing on the use case of tagging interesting music from the radio. The findings contribute to the wider body of work investigating the use of physical objects with single purpose interactions.

RESEARCH QUESTIONS

We wanted to understand the role of a physical device in supporting music tagging, compared to a smartphone app with the same purpose. Specifically:

- When given such an app or Button for a period of several weeks, how, when and where do people use it?
- Does possession of a physical Button result in different tagging behaviour than just having access to a smartphone app with the same essential functionality?
- Does the form and size of the physical Button significantly affect the experiences that people have when using it? Does it affect the number of tags that people make with it?

SYSTEM DESIGN

Humans have a natural appreciation for the material affordances of texture, weight, delicacy and temperature: we use them to interact unthinkingly with the objects we encounter in everyday life. Designers of new objects and devices thus face a challenge to design their products to take full advantage of this intuition. For example, one of the challenges of touchscreen user interfaces is that sliding fingers across a glass surface is only a natural interaction in limited circumstances [25].

In designing the Button, we aimed to eliminate this lack of naturalness for the act of tagging music in radio programmes. We wanted to create a screenless interface to simplify otherwise complex user journeys—an object of the kind described by Rose [19]: 'dedicated to a single task... quietly waiting to do [its] job', that can be glanceable (tangibly as well as visually), designed for minimally-disruptive information exchange between user and device (and *vice-versa*). We therefore looked to adopt recognisable forms and affordances to suggest functionality to the user rather than use text to instruct them in the device's use. For example, an object that fits comfortably in the hand and has a keychain attached to it invites being carried on the person or in a bag or pocket. A single button on a single-purpose device suggests to the user that the device's purpose can be realised by pushing that button. A simple form also helps the user accomplish that purpose even when they are only interacting with the device using their sense of touch.

A key opportunity arises when designing a dedicated physical device that aims to offer functionality that would otherwise be implemented as software on a general purpose computing device: a chance to enable that functionality in contexts where the user is prevented from using general purpose devices such as PCs or smartphones. Such constrained situations include those where the user has one or more primary foci of attention from which lengthy distractions are undesirable, or those that require technology that can be used discreetly, such as:

- A user in a restricted space or with limited zones of reach.
- A user with occupied hands or split attention (e.g. driving).
- A user in a socially constrained situation.
- A user lacking the dexterity to use general purpose devices.

From a design perspective, exploring these contexts not only identifies use cases for which the product may be uniquely suited, but it helps identify the interactions that are strictly essential. Both of these insights are critical, since additional physical objects in our lives must be justified in terms of the value they offer: they must not only be attractive both in terms of styling and personal resonance, but essential (as well as uncomplicated) in function.

Design Process

The design process for the Button consisted of six explorative, generative, and evaluative phases: *Observe*, *Play*, *Reflect*, *Make*, *Talk* and *Implement*, as shown in Figure 1 and described

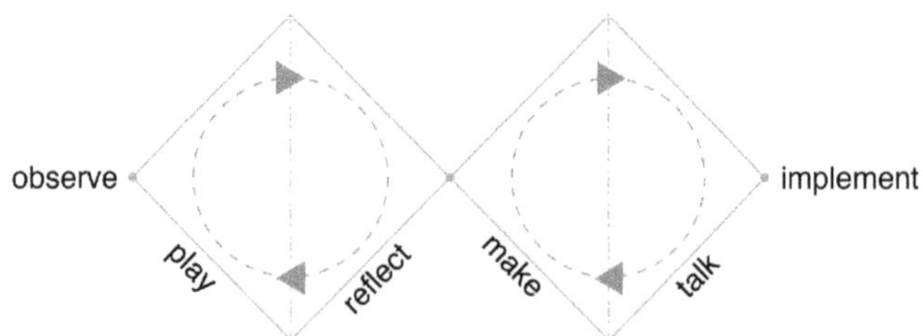

Figure 1. The relationship between phases in our design process, including the reflective cycles.

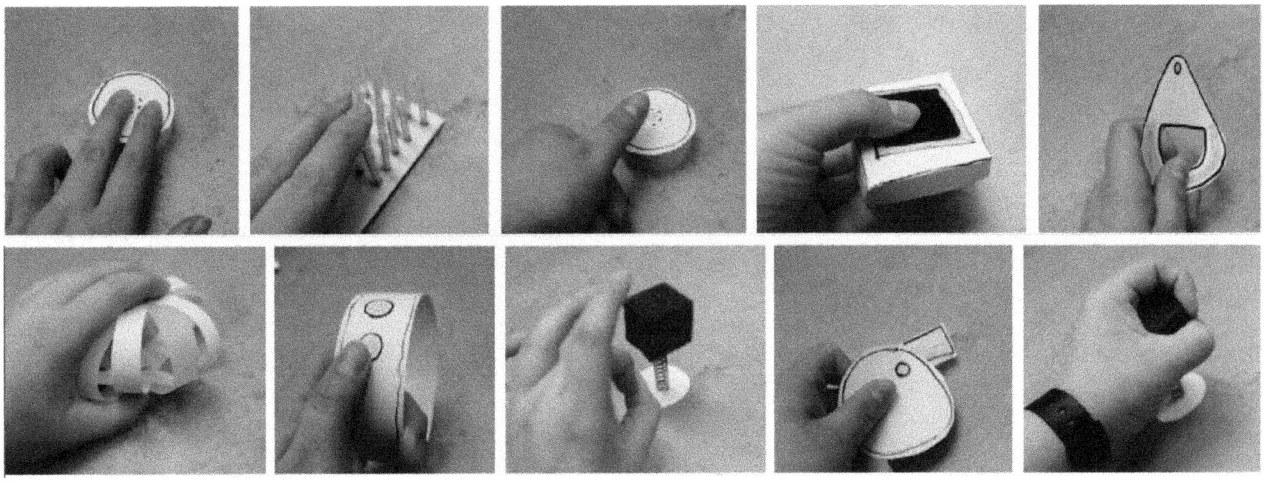

Figure 2. Photographs of paper prototypes constructed at an early stage of the design process. Rough models made from card and other materials allow form and texture to be explored

below. This was not a rigid process: the *Play-Reflect* and *Make-Talk* stages were iterated, creating reflective cycles that improved the product. We took the Design Council's *'double diamond'* structure [5] as the basis of our process, modifying their *Discover*, *Define*, *Develop* and *Deliver* phases. The process required insights both from potential users—including behaviour, needs, expectation, aspiration—and technical expertise (embodied in the design team itself and from the literature) in specific design features and usability, including UI design, material properties and ergonomics.

Our journey through the process was as follows. In the *Observe* phase, starting with our concept of a pocketable device for recording interesting things in radio programmes while driving, we set out to investigate and observe music listening habits in cars.

In the *Play* phase, the team used a variety of design approaches to broaden the scope of the concept. A team member gained insight into the implications of introducing such a device into everyday life by carrying a small foam block around with them (and attaching it to their keys). Rapid sketching [2] and paper prototyping were used to explore design concepts and the implications of different forms and textures rapidly (see Figure 2). Candidate technologies for implementing the device's functionality were investigated, and simple electronic Button prototypes constructed to understand the extent to which engineering concerns would affect the size and form of a working device. Initial development of user personas also took place.

Reflecting on the outcomes of these activities, the team refined the concept by seeking rapid feedback from people outside the team and by running a heuristic evaluation workshop [15] (described below) with external participants. The *Play-Reflect* cycle was iterated until the team achieved a design fulfilling its aims.

In the *Make* phase, the team moved beyond simple prototypes of the Button device and developed a working end-to-end system. This phase included the development of mass-produceable electronic hardware prototypes using custom PCBs and the creation of user interaction wireframes and a system architecture, leading to the development of a smartphone app that could communicate with the prototype.

The *Talk* phase took place once an end-to-end system existed. People both in and out of the team were asked to test the system and its components. In later iterations, draft user guides were also tested. The *Make-Talk* cycle was also iterated, refining the specifics of a range of design features, including fascia shape, button choices, press actuation frameworks, material affordances, visual feedback signalling, and the app's UI.

Once the whole product met the aims of the team, the process entered the *Implement* phase, in which the electronics and enclosure were produced in volume, the user study was designed and analytics incorporated into the software, and packaging was designed for safe transit and to make the act of receiving and unpacking a Button as delightful as possible.

User-Centred Design

During a *Reflect* phase, fundamental questions about the device's purpose were explored at a heuristic evaluation workshop with twenty radio listeners. The workshop introduced the concept of a physical device as an alternative to a smartphone app, and attendees were asked to consider the negative and positive aspects of the approach. Our evaluation method was one of inspection of the product's usability based on a predefined set of criteria, which was followed by the evaluator during the analysis to identify the key benefits and disadvantages of addressing the music tagging use case with a dedicated physical device in defined contexts. Attendees were presented with example situations such as driving in a car, preparing a meal, jogging in the park, and relaxing at home—all with a particular user desire to capture a piece of radio content. Example personas were also shared; these were devised based on the listenership of the six main BBC radio stations.

Following an individual heuristic evaluation, workshop members then shared their evaluations with the group. After this the

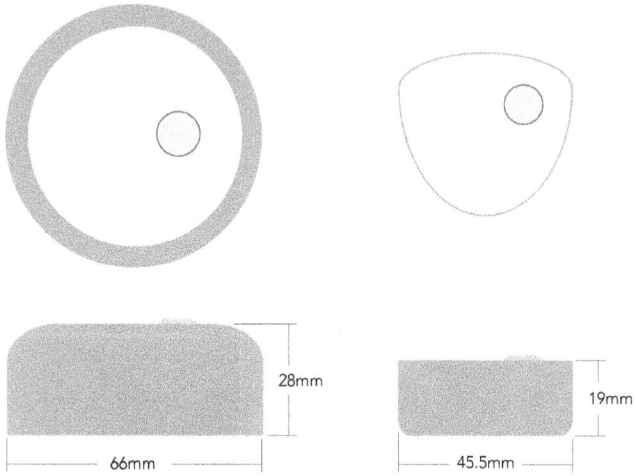

Figure 3. Top-down and profile views showing the dimensions of both Button variants trialled

group discussed their thoughts as a *Group Interview* mediated by a facilitator (a member of the design team) with a structure as outlined in the methods section of IDEO's Field Guide to HCD [9]. Finally, attendees were shown a model Button and asked to suggest improvements to its form.

The key advantages of a physical device identified by the attendees were that it can help you in situations when the primary focus of your attention is elsewhere; it can help you discover new music; it could help you identify things that you only half heard; it could generate data to help the broadcaster understand their audiences better; it could be safer and more convenient than a smartphone app in constrained contexts and it could have strong aesthetic value. Balancing these, attendees identified that incorporating another electronic device into the user's life is inconvenient, and that physical devices cost money—someone needs a reason to pay for them.

We also carried out experiments using Arduino[6] microcontroller prototyping boards with added sensing and actuating components, to prototype functioning circuits embedded into paper or 3D-printed prototype housings.

As we iterated the design process, we asked people to try out the prototypes and collected feedback on their experiences. We knew that a major challenge of the project was to communicate the capability of the Buttons and provide feedback when they were pressed without relying on a screen-based interaction: reflections on the iterations of our design were invaluable to the success of deploying these devices to remote study participants. Colleagues, visitors and members of the public were asked questions like, *'Do people feel distracted by it?'*, *'How easy is the device to use?'*, *'How can it be simpler?'*, *'Do people like the concept?'*, and *'How would people use a simple one-touch device in other contexts with BBC services?'*. Their responses regarding ergonomics and ease of use informed onward design of the Button and of the system as a whole.

Figure 4. The large Button, shown being used as a fridge magnet

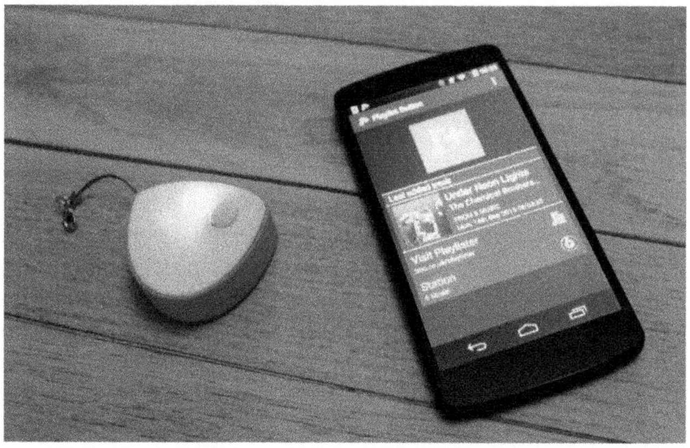

Figure 5. The small Button (with its LED illuminated) and the smartphone app, showing the result of a tagging operation

The Button: Physical Design

The Button has a small rigid plastic two-part shell with a multi-function tactile button on the top that constitutes the sole affordance for user input (see Figure 3). A multi-colour LED that shines through the translucent top panel of the shell provides the user with direct feedback about the Button's actions in response to user input.

Two variants of the Button were designed and manufactured:

- A large cylindrical Button with a magnetic back to allow it to adhere to a metal surface such as a fridge door. This Button is powered by two standard AAA batteries, and was designed to be left by the user in a location selected by them for convenience. (See Figure 4.)
- A small three-cornered Button: a smaller and lighter object that is comfortable to hold in the palm of a hand. This version has a slimline rechargeable battery and a keychain clip; it was designed to be portable enough to carry on the person at all times. (See Figure 5.)

The Button: Interaction Design

When the Button is pressed briefly, it makes a record of the current time and starts connecting to the smartphone app,

[6] `https://www.arduino.cc/`

informing the user that the process of tagging is taking place by means of visual feedback via a flashing LED. The same button can be used to place the device into a pairing mode (by pressing and holding the Button for at least one second), or a synchronisation mode (two short presses in quick succession) in which stored tags are sent to the phone app without a new tag being created. Quick tests with a number of people outside the project team suggested that 'traffic light' colours should be used to communicate the success or failure of operations. When the Button has successfully completed tagging, syncing, or pairing it again conveys this visually to the user with a long green pulse and fade to black. If any of these tasks were not immediately successful the user would see an amber pulse and fade. Trial participants who had Buttons were supplied with simple written material explaining this user interface.

The App: Interaction Design

Regardless of whether or not they were supplied with a Button, trialists could tag music directly within a smartphone app via a large square *'Add to Playlister'* button on its landing page.

In addition to tagging music, app users can select and change radio stations, view information about the most recently-tagged track, and navigate to their Playlister account on the Web, where they can browse a list of the tracks they have tagged, listen to 30s clips or transfer the playlist to commercial music services such as YouTube and Spotify. The app displays information about the artist, title and album art for the last track tagged via either the app or a paired Button (thus offering a particularly convenient solution when the user goal is to identify that information), along with information about the date and time when it was tagged and the radio station it was on at the time. Information about tagged tracks is also presented to the user via system-wide notifications.

On its first launch, the app takes users through an *onboarding* flow during which they pair their Button device (if they have one) with the smartphone, enter an identifying number provided to trialists to allow their usage to be tracked, and log in to the Playlister service, optionally creating an account.

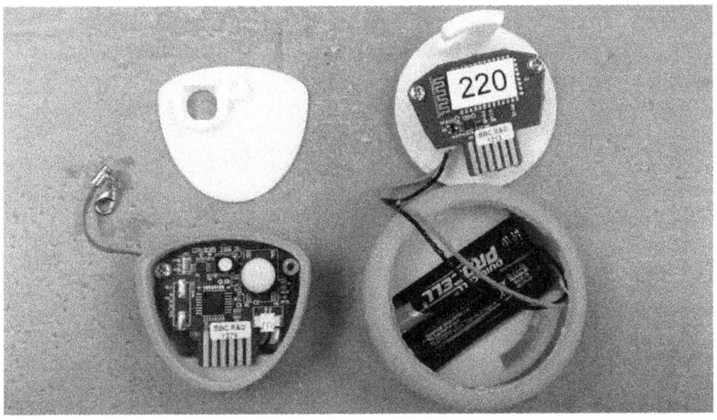

Figure 6. Internal views of large and small Buttons showing custom electronics in 3D-printed casings

Engineering Aspects

The Button was initially prototyped using the Arduino microcontroller development environment, with components for creating timestamps and communicating via Bluetooth connected via simple breadboarding. A custom printed circuit board was subsequently designed and produced. The casing designs were commercially 3D printed (see Figure 6).

The smartphone app was developed as a native Android app, using the Android Bluetooth stack for communication with the Button hardware. The RadioTAG protocol[7] was used to identify the music playing on specific stations at particular times and to add the tracks to the user's Playlister account.

STUDY METHOD

A study was conducted in order to understand the ways in which people use the Button as part of everyday, unprompted behaviour. This was a large, *in-the-wild* trial, taking place over the course of several weeks. It was designed to compare groups of people using the two variations of the physical hardware against those just using the app. We chose this approach to obtain adequate statistical power to distinguish quantitatively between different groups of users, and to test the Button in users' everyday lives over a time period of several weeks and weekends: long enough for the Button and app to have the opportunity to become natural parts of people's lives.

Participants

A panel process was undertaken to recruit suitable participants for the trial. Participants were required to be older than 18 years and to be an existing listener to one of the stations served by the BBC Playlister service (Radio 1, Radio 1Xtra, Radio 2, Radio 3, 6 Music, and Asian Network), but not an existing user of that service. 209 trialists were recruited, with 125 choosing to go through the onboarding process (signing a consent form, installing the app, pairing their Button (if relevant) and creating a Playlister account) and making tags (60% retention rate). 62 were recruited into both the large and small Button groups, with 48 and 45 participating respectively (77% and 73% retention). 85 were recruited into the app group with 32 participating (38% retention).

The participants were recruited with the intention of selecting a cross-section of the audiences of the radio stations covered by the trial. We aimed for good representation in each of four age groups (16-24; 25-34; 35-54 and over 55 years). The final trial included 52, 31, 46 and 18 in each group respectively. Compared to the audience demographics for the stations in question [23] this under-represents the 25-34 and 55+ groups. The decision was taken not to reduce the size of the participant panel further by excluding people in order to get a more even demographic balance, as this would reduce the size and power of the trial. A statistical test during the analysis (see "Quantitative Findings" below) found no significant evidence that age affected tagging behaviour ($p>0.05$), supporting the decision to proceed with an unbalanced age profile. Participants came from a mixture of socio-economic backgrounds, and were recruited from all areas of the UK.

[7] http://www.bbc.co.uk/rd/projects/radiotag

18 participants who were invited to attend a post-trial interview were recruited separately by a specialist agency so that a human screener could select people with a high probability of engagement. They were otherwise selected according to the standard criteria, and divided equally between trial groups.

Participants were given a £20 incentive for completing the onboarding process and an initial survey at the end of the first week of the trial. An additional £10 was given to participants who completed a second survey at the end of the third week of the trial, and the 18 participants that attended a 90 minute post-trial interview were paid £100 more. Participants in all trial groups who had not completed the onboarding process within a few days of receiving their Button and/or app were contacted to ask if help was needed in completing the necessary steps.

User Trial Design

The 125 participants who completed the onboarding process had the use of the Button and/or app with which they were provided for a period of several weeks (inclusive of weekends) during which their use of these tools was recorded. They completed a survey about their experience after their first and third weeks, with 105 and 111 responses respectively. Data was collected for most users over a three week period, but to limit the impact of any last-minute software or hardware issues, ten people in each group were designated as pilot users and started the trial a week earlier than the cohort; an additional week's quantitative data was collected for these users.

Data Collection

We used Google Analytics[8] to capture information about each tag made by a user, along with information about how users interacted with the app. We captured the type of tag (whether it originated from a Button or an app); the tag offset (whether a Button tag was made and sent to the paired smartphone app immediately, or synchronised at a later time); the time and date of each tag; the radio station selected by the user before the tag in question was made or synchronised, and the song title and artist, retrieved from the BBC's RadioTag service. Where this information was not available (for example when no song was playing), the radio programme information was stored instead. We also recorded every occasion when user interaction with the app triggered the display of a different screen to the user (eg progress through the onboarding process; in-app viewing of playlists on the Playlister website).

The data was anonymised at the point of collection: individual activity was indexed using a unique number that participants were allocated at the start of the trial. Only those individuals who were responsible for supporting the trial users and managing the distribution and return of Buttons had access to personally identifying information about participants.

Qualitative data was collected in the form of surveys and semi-structured interviews. A first survey collected initial impressions and ratings after week one of the trial, and a second survey gathered more in-depth thoughts and further ratings after week three. The surveys consisted of open-ended questions and ratings based on a four-point Likert scale (i.e. with no neutral option, to force a choice), allowing participants to rate aspects of the experience such as the utility and ease of use of the Button from *"very easy to use"* to *"very difficult to use"*. The data was analysed by two researchers independently through thematic analysis [4]; each coding the data into themes and sub-themes that naturally emerged using a grounded theory approach, which were then harmonised.

[8] http://www.google.com/analytics/

RESULTS

Quantitative Findings

To answer our primary research question about the impact of tag ownership on tagging behaviour, we analysed the distributions of the total number of tracks tagged across the three trial groups. Visual inspection of the distributions and of quartile-quartile plots indicated that the distributions were skewed, and did not satisfy assumptions of normality. A number of transformations were applied to attempt to normalise the data (square root, $1/x$ and natural log), however, these did not correct the skew and indeed resulted in negative skew. There were significant outliers in the data, but an inspection of the qualitative data did not reveal any reasons to exclude the participants in question from the analyses. Consequently, these outliers were retained in the data set and the analysis was carried out using nonparametric techniques.

Total Tags

A total of 4016 tags were made by participants within the three week trial period. The large-Button group made the most tags (2063), followed by the small-Button (1501 tags) and app-only (452) groups.

Average Tags

Taking the median as the non-parametric average, participants with Buttons (both large and small-Button groups combined) made an average of 29 tags (see Figure 7), with large Button users averaging 30 tags and small Button users 27 tags (Figure 8). The app-only group made an average of 14.5 tags.

Comparing Average Tags

Using a nonparametric alternative to ANOVA to compare averages across the groups, Kruskal-Wallis tests were performed on the data. First, the two Button groups were combined to examine differences between people with a Button and people

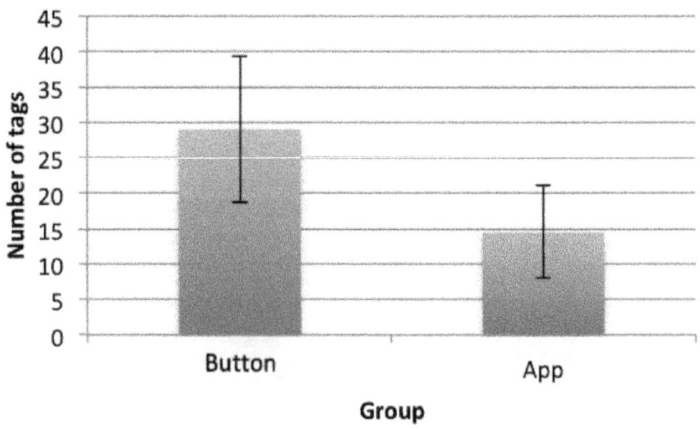

Figure 7. Median number of tags by all Button users and by app users

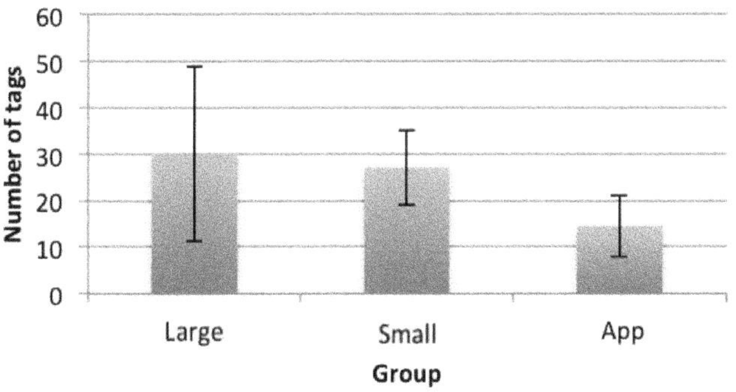

Figure 8. Median number of tags made by Button users (large and small) and app users

with an app, and then the Button groups were separated (large Button and small Button) to examine whether there was any difference between the three groups.

Examining the differences between Button and app users, significant differences were found between the two groups (K=9.711, df=1, $p<0.05$ Kruskal-Wallis, Bonferroni corrected). Button users made significantly more tags (mean rank=63.73) than app users (mean rank=40.40).

Further significant differences were found when considering the three trial groups separately (K=9.587, df=2, $p<0.05$, Kruskal-Wallis, Bonferroni corrected). Post hoc Dunnet C analysis indicated that both the Button groups made significantly more tags (large Button mean rank=64.99; small Button mean rank=62.47) than the app group (mean rank=40.40) $p<0.05$. However, there was no significant difference found between the large and small Button groups. Both tests indicate that people with a Button made more tags than those without.

Age

The over 55 year old age group tagged a median of 30 times, with the 24-34 year olds making an average of 27, and the 16-24 year olds and 35-54 year olds making 24 tags and 23 tags respectively. To examine the significance between these average tags and to determine whether age was a factor, a Kruskal-Wallis test was applied between the four groups (16-24; 25-34; 35-54 and over 55 years). This test demonstrated no significant differences between the different age groups (K=0.194, df=3, $p>0.05$).

Qualitative Findings

The general message in post-trial feedback from participants was enthusiasm for the Button, both in terms of concept and ease of use. Thematic analysis revealed six themes: positive impressions of the concept; simplicity; discovery and onward journeys; frustrations and ideas for future iterations.

Positive Impressions of the Concept

The qualitative data revealed 55 positive comments made in relation to the concept of the Button. Participants praised it for being *"handy for keeping a track of songs that I like on the radio" (Participant P1)*, as well as for onward journeys such as creating playlists and discovering music.

"It's been so useful not only for discovering who and what song was on, but for creating my own playlists that I can use over and over again... There are so many times I listen to a song and want to save it, and this has made it so easy for me to do that." (P2)

The concept was also highly praised in terms of convenience, with 78% of participants rating it as either *Convenient* or *Very Convenient*. Participants highlighted situations that were not only valuable to them, but envisaged the benefits for others.

"I think it is a great idea to have around the house especially somewhere like the kitchen where most people will listen to the radio." (P3)

Simplicity

Ease of use featured strongly within participant feedback. A consistently positive rating was seen across both first and second surveys, with 89% of participants making an initial rating of the Button as *Easy* or *Very Easy* to use in the first survey, rising to 77% after participants had used the Button for three weeks. This finding was supported in answers to the open-ended question about their impression of the Button after living with it for three weeks, with 44 participants stating that its strongest asset was the simplicity of interacting with it. A majority described the Button easy to use and synchronise.

"You don't have to fiddle about to find [the app] on your phone. Pressing the Button on the device was so much easier." (P3)

The main advantage of the Button emerged as being this simplicity of *"One click of a button" (P3)*. A simple, dedicated button press to save songs for later was clearly valued by participants. By carrying out this single press they were able to handover the conscious need to think about or remember an artist or track name.

"You can take it with you whilst washing up [...] and if there is a song you like, click the Button. You don't have to do anything else straight away" (P4)

This was praised for saving time and reducing the need to identify a song via alternate methods.

"I am extremely busy most of the time but with the Button I am able to get hold of good quality material and enjoy it while doing everything I have to do." (P5)

"It works very well, easier than writing songs down which is what I usually do!" (P6)

It was also reported to be simpler than using the app.

"Having to pick up your phone, open the app and then press it is more time consuming, and not as suitable for on the move in the car or whilst you are doing other jobs." (P7)

It was also clear that the simplicity of this interaction design only became problematic when additional features were added, such as use of the LED to signify different functions.

"Pink light, blue light, maybe green. One was for saving, I can't remember now" (P8)

Discovery and Onward Journeys

It was clear in both the feedback surveys and the interviews that participants preferred to use their Buttons by putting them in defined locations, such as in the car to use whilst driving, on a bedside table at home or in a desk drawer at work. 67 participants indicated that they used or would use the Button in the home, placing the device within reach of the location of a particular task, or one associated with music listening.

"The Button now lives next to the radio in my kitchen—which is where I normally listen—and has essentially become a part of it." (P9)

This was also strongly communicated during the interviews, with participants using their Buttons in the home by placing them somewhere they would remember. The visibility of the Button prompted people to use it: the very fact that people could see a dedicated physical device was a reminder that its functionality was immediately available to them.

"If I heard a song I liked, I'd just hit the Button on my way past the fridge" (P10)

"It's convenient for when I'm at home, as I can put next to my computer." (P11)

Only ten participants said they would use their Button in situations where it would be carried on the person such as whilst commuting, travelling on public transport or walking. There were opposing opinions on the subject of the Buttons' portability in both the small and large-Button groups:

"easy to use, ideal way to store great music. easy to transport and carry around" (P12 - large Button)

"I think it is maybe a little too inconvenient for everyday use and awkward to carry around all the time. I found myself forgetting it and being uninterested in using it daily." (P13 - small Button)

For some participants, an extra item to carry around did not work for them. However, it is notable that despite the constraints on the size, weight and form of the Button, participants remained positive about the prototype and app.

"The idea is brilliant but the Button is too big. It would be better keyfob size." (P14)

For most participants, radio offers daytime background noise with the opportunity for spontaneous discovery, in contrast to directed music listening in the evening—listening to specific tracks or albums, generally on a computer. The Button enabled participants to save tracks for later use. 21 comments were made in relation to being able to save tracks for later.

"The device is handy for keeping a track of songs that I like on the radio." (P15)

The Button made it easier for participants to save a track heard on the radio without having to use their memory or employ alternate methods to find the song at a later point.

"There are so many times I listen to a song and want to save it, and this has made it so easy for me to do that." (P16)

"It works very well, easier than writing songs down which is what I usually do!" (P17)

The Button was regarded as great for *"creating my own playlists that I can use over and over again" (P18)*, whilst using means that the playlist *"builds up with all your favourite songs from the radio that you would otherwise forget about" (P17)*. The collated playlist was used as a collection of jump-off points for directed listening later on in the day or week.

"[The Button] lets me record a list of the songs I've heard that I like on the radio." (P18)

Twelve participants expressed that they would like to use the Button to build playlists with a specific purpose in mind (e.g. a wedding playlist), and a few spontaneously requested the ability to add music to multiple playlists. Participants valued this idea because tracks they added had various uses (e.g. gym, relaxation, and by genre).

Frustrations

Participants were frustrated by errors made by the system during the user trial. Seven indicated that songs appeared in their playlist that they had not intentionally tagged. This generally occurred when the Button was carried in a bag.

"Having transported it in my bag to work I found that it saved a song without me know." (P19)

Two participants reported frustrating delays between pressing the Button and seeing the tagged track appear in the Playlister service, and three participants reported that having *"to remember to change the station on the app was getting annoying!" (P20)*. There was also a desire for the Button to support use with non-BBC stations (three participants).

Recommendations for Further Iterations

Participants in both Button groups expressed concerns about the current forms of the devices as being *"...at times bulky" (P21)*. Even the small Button is still comparable in volume to a small smartphone – lending itself to the same locations for storage, such as the pocket or the handbag, and offering little additional convenience. In total, 25 participants requested the Buttons to be made smaller or more portable (12 large Button users and 13 small Button users). For example, one individual suggested simply that the Button *"could do with being smaller so it fits better on your keys" (P22)*. Other individuals requested a Button the size of *"a USB drive" (P23)* or *"a car key fob" (P24)*, with the possibility of attaching it to a lanyard, keys or a waistband.

Other suggestions included station selection direct from the Button, or design changes to reduce accidental presses.

DISCUSSION

Our surveys and interviews suggest two key reasons why Button users tagged more frequently than app users: Firstly, as a single-purpose physical device, the Button acts as a visible and tangible reminder of its own functionality. Secondly, the process of tagging music with the Button is faster, and requires the user to undertake fewer consecutive tasks.

There is some evidence to suggest that the two form factors were too physically similar to drive different user behaviour: people from both trial groups suggested that the Button should be made smaller and more portable, and reported a general preference for placing their Button in a defined location rather than carrying it.

It is interesting to note that the Button trial groups not only had significantly higher levels of tagging behaviour, but also retained a much higher fraction of their recruits after the on-boarding phase: 73% and 77% compared to 38% for the app-only group. This latter difference in behaviour between groups selected to be similar suggests that there is something significant about the act of being given (or otherwise acquiring) a novel physical object that drives interest and engagement.

Considering the Button alongside other commercially available connected buttons—including Flic and Amazon's Dash—as well as other prototypes, such as Tang *et al*'s [21], there is clear interest in the potential of developing single-purpose buttons that offer users a simple way to perform a single, well-defined task each time that button is pressed. A number of business models for funding these buttons are being considered.

The Button and the Radio Bookmark can be used to fulfil their purpose anywhere that radio stations can be listened to, without requiring Internet connectivity or proximity to a smartphone at the point of use. Music evokes strong emotions in people [12], so as a device intimately connected with a user's experience of music, the Button has the opportunity to become an emotionally significant object to them.

Our participants recommended improving the Button by allowing radio stations to be selected on the hardware itself. This could be incorporated into the current hardware in a way that minimally increases complexity by adding a dial or switch to 'tune' infrequently between a few favourite stations. This would increase the unit cost of the device, however. The Button could also be branded and marketed as a device dedicated to one specific radio station, helping reinforce the relationship between station and listener, and targeting users that identify themselves as fans of particular stations or presenters.

It is significant that the trial participants were not given prompts or guidance about how or where to use the Button other than basic instruction in how to set it up and use it to tag music. This resulted in participants discovering its value over the course of the trial. Participants were strong advocates for the Button, praising its concept and describing situations where it was used or where they could envisage it being used in the future. Despite the constraints of the size and weight of the Button, participants were positive about the concept of using it to tag radio content, with some even requesting to keep their Buttons, or suggesting improvements.

FURTHER WORK

Wider Implications

The Button is an exemplar of a single function device that makes modest demands on user attention, and has physical affordance. The use case of tagging music during radio listening illustrates the potential these devices have for providing a simple way to record *ad hoc* events during daily life.

There is clear wider appplicability and other use cases where encouraging people to *diarise* has benefits, such as recording the occurrence of breathlessness or other health symptoms. Devices could also be deployed selectively in space, time and population: for example, to monitor real-time sentiment (i.e. as a *Like Button*) amongst the audience of a live event.

Research in the Wild and the Internet of Things

Answering our research questions, in an ecologically valid manner and at sufficient scale to provide valuable and reliable insights, required us to conduct a large in-the-wild study. Specifically, we worked with 125 participants over a study period of several weeks. There are practical and methodological challenges in studies of this scale when the research probe is just a website or a mobile application. In this case, we created not just an app, but two different instances of a physical device. These had to be designed, manufactured, distributed and supported for the duration of the trial.

One of our main findings therefore is methodological: as UX research increasingly takes place in a world of connected devices and the *Internet of Things*, deployments like this, together with their challenges and excitements, are likely to become more and more a part of useful UX research practice. Developing scalable and rigorous approaches to this kind of research will be very important.

CONCLUSION

This study has explored supporting radio listeners in tagging the music they hear throughout their day. Our design process identified user goals of identifying, remembering and building playlists from interesting tracks, and study participants used our system to fulfil these. Integration into users' lives varied; some choosing to carry a Button with them and others leaving it wherever they commonly listen to the radio.

Secondly, the study shows that giving people a physical Button changes their behaviour, and they tag more music than users of an equivalent smartphone app. In addition, trial participants were predominantly positive about the Button's value, rating it positively for both convenience and ease of use. This suggests that providing this kind of device to listeners could be an effective way for broadcasters to reinforce the value of radio as a means of discovering new music.

Thirdly, deploying different form factors for the device had no significanct impact on tagging behaviour, and similar numbers of users from both trial groups called for smaller Buttons, suggesting that even the smaller of the two was too large to be considered portable. Additional follow-up work should include smaller physical devices, and also explore comparison to alternative non-physical interaction, such as tagging by voice command.

REFERENCES

1. Saskia Bakker, Elise van den Hoven, and Berry Eggen. 2015. Peripheral interaction: characteristics and

considerations. *Personal and Ubiquitous Computing* 19, 1 (2015), 239–254.

2. Bill Buxton. 2007. *Sketching User Experiences: Getting the Design Right and the Right Design (Interactive Technologies)*. Morgan Kaufmann, San Francisco, USA.
3. The Nielsen Company. 2014. 2014 Nielsen Music U.S. Report. (7 January 2014). Retrieved January 12, 2016 from http://www.nielsen.com/content/dam/corporate/us/en/public%20factsheets/Soundscan/nielsen-2014-year-end-music-report-us.pdf.
4. Juliet M. Corbin and Anselm Strauss. 1990. Grounded theory research: Procedures, canons, and evaluative criteria. *Qualitative Sociology* 13, 1 (1990), 3–21. DOI: http://dx.doi.org/10.1007/BF00988593
5. Design Council. 2007. A Study of the Design Process, Eleven lessons: managing design in eleven global brands. (2007). Retrieved January 12, 2016 from http://www.designcouncil.org.uk/resources/report/11-lessons-managing-design-global-brands.
6. Paul Dourish. 2001. *Where the action is: the foundations of embodied interaction*. MIT Press.
7. Eva Hornecker and Jacob Buur. 2006. Getting a grip on tangible interaction: a framework on physical space and social interaction. In *Proceedings of the SIGCHI conference on Human Factors in computing systems*. ACM, 437–446.
8. Scott E Hudson, Chris Harrison, Beverly L Harrison, and Anthony LaMarca. 2010. Whack gestures: inexact and inattentive interaction with mobile devices. In *Proceedings of the fourth international conference on Tangible, embedded, and embodied interaction*. ACM, 109–112.
9. IDEO.org. 2015. *The Field Guide to Human-Centred Design*. IDEO. Retrieved January 12, 2016 from http://www.designkit.org/resources/1.
10. SkyBlue Technologies Inc. 2008. Learn about the small portable device that saves NPR and public radio stories. (2008). Retrieved January 12, 2016 from http://www.radiobookmark.com/static/learn_more.
11. D Kahneman. 1973. *Attention and Effort*. Prentice-Hall.
12. Ai Kawakami, Kiyoshi Furukawa, and Kazuo Okanoya. 2014. Music evokes vicarious emotions in listeners. *Frontiers in Psychology* 5, Article 431 (2014), 7 pages.
13. Christian Loclair, Sean Gustafson, and Patrick Baudisch. 2010. PinchWatch: a wearable device for one-handed microinteractions. In *Proceedings of the Workshop on Ensembles of On-Body Devices at the Conference on Human-Computer Interaction with Mobile Devices and Services*, Vol. 10. ACM, 4.
14. Joyce Ma, Lisa Sindorf, Isaac Liao, and Jennifer Frazier. 2015. Using a Tangible Versus a Multi-touch Graphical User Interface to Support Data Exploration at a Museum Exhibit. In *Proceedings of the Ninth International Conference on Tangible, Embedded, and Embodied Interaction*. ACM, 33–40.
15. Jakob Nielsen. 1994. *Usability engineering*. Elsevier.
16. Ofcom. 2015. The Communications Market 2015: Radio and Audio. (August 2015). Retrieved January 12, 2016 from http://stakeholders.ofcom.org.uk/binaries/research/cmr/cmr15/UK_3.pdf.
17. Fernando Olivera, Manuel García-Herranz, Pablo A Haya, and Pablo Llinás. 2011. Do not disturb: physical interfaces for parallel peripheral interactions. In *Human-Computer Interaction–INTERACT 2011*. Springer, 479–486.
18. Sami Ronkainen, Jonna Häkkilä, Saana Kaleva, Ashley Colley, and Jukka Linjama. 2007. Tap input as an embedded interaction method for mobile devices. In *Proceedings of the 1st international conference on Tangible and embedded interaction*. ACM, 263–270.
19. David Rose. 2014. *Enchanted Objects: Design, Human Desire, and the Internet of Things*. Scribner.
20. Orit Shaer and Robert JK Jacob. 2009. A specification paradigm for the design and implementation of tangible user interfaces. *ACM Transactions on Computer-Human Interaction (TOCHI)* 16, 4 (2009), 20.
21. Lie Ming Tang, Judy Kay, and Bob Kummerfeld. 2015. Gamification of tangible internet connected buttons towards long term goals. *The University of Sydney, School of Information Technologies Technical Reports* 701 (June 2015), 4.
22. Peter Tolmie, James Pycock, Tim Diggins, Allan MacLean, and Alain Karsenty. 2002. Unremarkable computing. In *Proceedings of the SIGCHI conference on Human factors in computing systems*. ACM, 399–406.
23. BBC Trust. 2015. BBC Trust Service Review: Radio 1, 1Xtra, Radio 2, Radio 3, 6 Music and Asian Network. (19 March 2015). Retrieved January 12, 2016 from http://downloads.bbc.co.uk/bbctrust/assets/files/pdf/our_work/music_radio/music_radio.pdf.
24. B. Ullmer and H. Ishii. 2000. Emerging Frameworks for Tangible User Interfaces. *IBM Syst. J.* 39, 3-4 (July 2000), 915–931. DOI:http://dx.doi.org/10.1147/sj.393.0915
25. Bret Victor. 2011. A brief rant on the future of interaction design. (8 November 2011). Retrieved January 12, 2016 from http://worrydream.com/ABriefRantOnTheFutureOfInteractionDesign/.
26. Avery Wang. 2006. The Shazam Music Recognition Service. *Commun. ACM* 49, Article 8 (Aug. 2006), 5 pages. DOI:http://dx.doi.org/10.1145/1145287.1145312
27. Katrin Wolf, Anja Naumann, Michael Rohs, and Jörg Müller. 2011. Taxonomy of Microinteractions: Defining Microgestures Based on Ergonomic and Scenario-dependent Requirements. In *Proceedings of the 13th IFIP TC 13 International Conference on Human-computer Interaction - Volume Part I (INTERACT'11)*. Springer-Verlag, Berlin, Heidelberg, 559–575. http://dl.acm.org/citation.cfm?id=2042053.2042111

PaperID: A Technique for Drawing Functional Battery-Free Wireless Interfaces on Paper

Hanchuan Li[1,2], Eric Brockmeyer[1], Elizabeth J. Carter[1], Josh Fromm[2], Scott E. Hudson[1,3], Shwetak N. Patel[2], Alanson Sample[1]

Disney Research[1]
Pittsburgh, USA
{eric.brockmeyer, liz.carter, alanson.sample}
@disneyresearch.com

Computer Science & Engineering[2]
University of Washington
Seattle, USA
{hanchuan, jwfromm, shwetak}
@cs.washington.edu

School of Computer Science[3]
Carnegie Mellon University
Pittsburgh, USA
scott.hudson@cs.cmu.edu

Figure 1. Left to right: A wireless polling device, a pinwheel animation that adapts with spin speed, a conducting baton, a dollhouse controlled with custom RFID tags on paper interfaces, and a pop-up book with embedded tags which trigger audio content.

ABSTRACT

We describe techniques that allow inexpensive, ultra-thin, battery-free Radio Frequency Identification (*RFID*) tags to be turned into simple paper input devices. We use sensing and signal processing techniques that determine how a tag is being manipulated by the user via an RFID reader and show how tags may be enhanced with a simple set of conductive traces that can be printed on paper, stencil-traced, or even hand-drawn. These traces modify the behavior of contiguous tags to serve as input devices. Our techniques provide the capability to use off-the-shelf RFID tags to sense touch, cover, overlap of tags by conductive or dielectric (insulating) materials, and tag movement trajectories. Paper prototypes can be made functional in seconds. Due to the rapid deployability and low cost of the tags used, we can create a new class of interactive paper devices that are drawn on demand for simple tasks. These capabilities allow new interactive possibilities for pop-up books and other papercraft objects.

Author Keywords

RFID; paper interfaces; tangible; battery free

ACM Classification Keywords

H.5.2. Information Interfaces and Presentation (e.g. HCI): User Interfaces

CHI'16, May 07 - 12, 2016, San Jose, CA, USA

ACM 978-1-4503-3362-7/16/05...$15.00
DOI: http://dx.doi.org/10.1145/2858036.2858249

INTRODUCTION

Modern tools and techniques now make it quite easy to construct a graphical interface with only minimal training and effort. Advances in low-cost, micro-controller-based electronics (e.g., [1]) and accompanying tools such as hardware toolkits (e.g., [13, 8, 10]) have sought to bring that same ease of creation to physical interactive devices as well. However, because of physical constraints, such as the size of electronic circuits, required wiring, and the need to supply and/or replenish power to those circuits, creation of physical interfaces has remained difficult. Thus, construction of such devices still cannot really be considered easy, lightweight, or simple. As a result, we might normally start any design effort aimed at creating such an artifact with an exercise in paper prototyping [21]. We do this in part because the paper is *lightweight* – both in a physical and economic sense, but also with respect to the ease with which we can work with it and modify it on demand. For prototyping, this lightweight nature is useful to keep our investment in early concepts to a minimum and, as a result, it allows more alternatives to be quickly explored.

However, these (and other) good properties of using paper as an interface medium could be taken further. We ask the question: What if we could (nearly) as easily make interfaces that *actually function* using paper as a central medium? This could be of substantial interest for our well-established prototyping practices. In addition, the lightweight nature of the medium may also offer the possibility of a new class of simple but highly customized interface devices that are created quickly on demand for small tasks [17] and possibly discarded (or recycled) when the task was completed or changed.

In this work, we develop technology that provides a new set of capabilities in this direction for the creation of functioning interfaces affixed to, or even partially drawn on, paper. In particular, we describe techniques for processing signals from inexpensive off-the-shelf UHF Radio Frequency Identification (*RFID*) tags, which can be easily affixed to sheets of paper in the form of small adhesive-backed *stickers*. These techniques use details about the low-level radio frequency signals normally used to retrieve identification information to also infer properties of how each tag is being manipulated by a user. For example, when the user touches the antenna of the tag, even without making direct electrical contact, the touch changes how the antenna functions. Similarly, when a tag moves in space, a shifting in the phase of the signal occurs. These subtle changes can be detected in properties of the low-level signals from the tag that are detected by a remote reader (that can be positioned up to several meters away). With sufficient processing, several types of basic user manipulations – touch, covering of the tag by a conductive or dielectric (insulating) materials, and tag movement – can be detected and differentiated. This allows the tags to provide the basic functions necessary to act as sensors for user inputs, despite the fact that they are ultra-thin (coming in a paper sticker form factor), inexpensive (as little as USD$0.10 [15] per tag and therefore usable in applications where they are considered disposable), and have no power source of their own (as they are powered entirely by the reader).

Our contributions in this paper are multifold. We first introduced a new approach for augmenting tags that increases their usefulness as input sensors. In particular, we describe how specifically designed conductive traces can be placed underneath the commercially available UHF loop tag containing an integrated circuit (IC) (henceforth called a "loop IC"). These traces capacitively couple to the existing tag antenna and change how it functions, essentially providing a new antenna for the loop tag without requiring removal of, or even electrical contact with, the existing antenna. As described in detail later, one form of these conductive traces creates an unbalanced monopole antenna that detunes the resulting tag sufficiently that it can no longer be read. However, the traces are constructed in such a way that if a particular spot is touched by the user (and capacitively couples to them), their body serves as the ground plane, boosting the reflected signal, and the tag begins to operate again, creating what amounts to a touch-sensitive antenna. These augmenting traces can be very easily constructed using conductive inks. We demonstrate that they can be inkjet-printed either directly onto the paper that will form part of the interface or onto adhesive stickers that can be placed onto the final interface as needed. Furthermore, we show that they can be constructed using simple stencils and even drawn by hand using a commercially available pen filled with conductive ink. Small RFID loop IC tag stickers can then be placed over the augmenting conductive traces to provide fully functional input sensors.

Furthermore, we introduce our Trace Recovery techniques to enable the continuous tracking of the tag's velocity, motion magnitude, and relative direction of motion towards and away from the reader. Finally, we introduce new RF features that (when combined with a SVM classifier) can support real-time multi-class gesture classification including hand-waving over the tag, light finger touch, whole-hand cover, swipe touch, and no touch. Even though these two techniques share similarity with the motion and touch sensing in previous work [14], this work introduces new signal processing techniques that allow the continuous trajectory of a tag's motion to be monitored as well as support a rich set of interactions that significantly expands upon previous work.

RELATED WORK

Paper is one of the most ubiquitous forms of media in everyday life. In this work, we demonstrate the lightweight, passive, and recyclable nature of our sensing approach by augmenting paper with sensing capabilities for gesture and object state. Previous research has leveraged paper-based input interfaces for interactive applications that include cross-media hyperlinking, documentation tagging, and other interactions [2, 16, 9, 11, 25]. The challenge is how to enable paper-based, unobtrusive input sensing while still preserving the lightweight, passive, and disposable nature of the paper.

Paper-based interfaces have been explored previously as a method for rapid prototyping. Qi and colleagues [20] introduced a paper circuitry approach where a user could build control interfaces on a sheet of paper, attaching electronic components with conductive ink and copper tape. Kawahara and colleagues [12] extended this work by creating inkjet-printed circuits on photo paper for rapid prototyping. They demonstrated easy and effective ways for printing connection circuits or even sensors to enable interactive scenarios. However, the utility of the paper-based control interfaces is limited to on-paper devices, which in turn are constrained by the difficulty of augmenting paper with wireless communication capacities. Attaching wireless communication components, such as Bluetooth and Wi-Fi modules, or a power source makes it very difficult to retain the flexibility and lightweight nature of paper. Additionally, using active components counteracts the benefit of using inexpensive paper as a medium due to the high price of components.

Enabling sensing capabilities on RFID tags could make the technology an ideal alternative for use in paper-based wireless control interfaces. Early work on the use of RFID tags for input constructed power-free buttons from modified RFID tags [4]. In more advanced work, the Wireless Identification and Sensing Platform (WISP) [24] provided custom-built RFID tags with an embedded micro-controller. Although expensive due to their special-purpose nature (about USD $100 per unit), these tags were capable of a number of sensing tasks. For example, prior work [5] describes its use for tracking the movement of tags within a large room and was able to distinguish between 12 common household activities. Other sensing approaches that use RFID technology have required a large number of tags or reader antennas. For example, Asadzadeh and colleagues [3] implemented an 80cm by 80cm matrix with 64 tags and 3 antennas to detect hand gestures. Their system was able to classify 12 predefined hand gestures with 93% accuracy. Later, Wang and colleagues [27] proposed a system for tracking tag movement that used 8 anten-

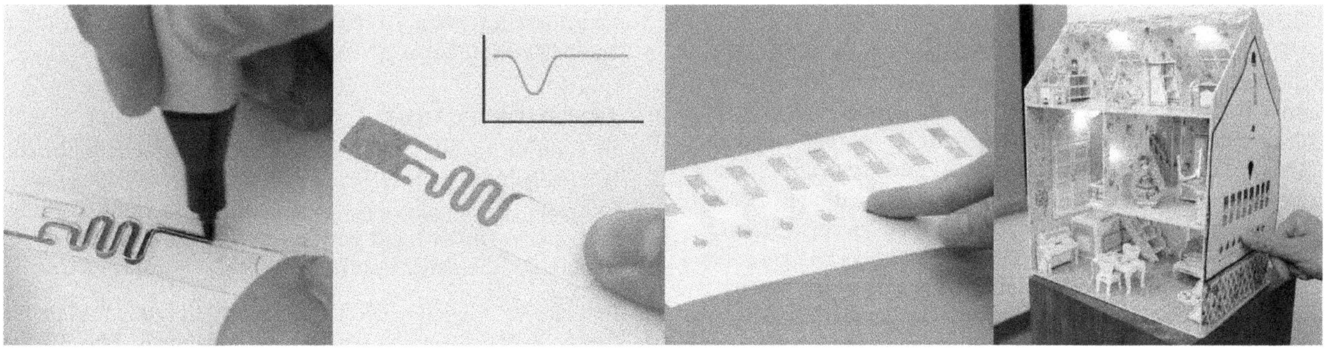

Figure 2. Left to right: A user creates an antenna with a stencil, affixes a loop IC, builds a slider, and uses the slider to control light brightness in a dollhouse.

nas in 4 pairs; they enabled trace tracking of a tag with a median error of 3.7cm. Marquardt and colleagues [18] explored the implementation of input buttons and sliders by modifying RFID circuits and adding electrical components around RFID chips. Together, these projects demonstrated the feasibility of basic RFID-based input sensing. However, constraints in size, installment cost, or user burden make them undesirable for augmenting paper in realistic scenarios.

In work that is more similar to the type of sensing used in the approach described here, Fishkin *et al.* [7] was able to demonstrate the use of inexpensive, passive UHF RFID tags as a sensor for detecting motion. However, only rotational motion was detected robustly and required both multiple tags per object and multiple readers. Parlak and colleagues [19] presented a passive UHF RFID motion detection system designed for a trauma resuscitation scenario. The authors focused on detecting constant tag movement and rotations which showed 90% accuracy in four lab-controlled experiments. However, the motion detection classifier described in their system is solely based on received signal strength (the *RSSI* measure described later) and therefore requires multiple antennas to distinguish between the binary states of still and moving. Li and colleagues [14] used a single antenna to enable motion detection in their object interaction detection system, detecting motion faster than 10cm/s with 93% accuracy.

These previous research projects demonstrate the feasibility of using UHF RFID systems to monitor the state of an object. However, their state detection is limited to binary classification using fixed function off-the-shelf RFID tags. In this paper, we extend prior work by creating new tag types that can be quickly prototyped using conductive inks. Specifically, we introduce the "half antenna tag" which is a passive RFID tag that can use the human body as part of the antenna structure for operation when touched. Additionally, we enable a number of new input modalities that include several types of on-tag and free-air interaction types, such as hand waving around the tag, as well as sensing the real-time motion velocity and trajectory of the tag relative to the reader.

TECHNICAL OVERVIEW

The process for creating an RFID-enhanced paper interface employs a familiar set of supplies and techniques consisting of paper, RFID tags in the form of stickers, and pens with conductive ink, along with extras such as glue, scissors, tape, and markers. Here, we provide a brief overview of the necessary steps and techniques as an outline for the in-depth discussion in the following sections where we focus on the fabrication, signal processing, and machine learning techniques related to prototyping interactive interfaces using off-the-shelf tags as well as customized tags.

As shown in Figure 2, fabrication using tags with customized antennas typically begins with placement of an RFID tag on the paper or by drawing the antenna itself and adding a loop IC sticker to form a fully functional RFID tag. The ability to hand draw, ink-jet print, or use commercial RFID tags provides a great deal of flexibility in visual design, RF performance, and the types of interactions. We discuss the fabrication of these antennas in the Custom Tag Fabrication section.

In order to harness the wireless sensing capabilities of commonplace RFID tags (Figure 3 panel d), we monitor changes in the low level channel parameters of the reader / tag communication to infer human / tag interaction events. In the Signal Detection section, we discuss in detail the signal processing and machine learning techniques applied to low-channel parameters of this commonplace tag to enable a wide variety of on-tag and free-air interaction sensing capabilities.

Once the mechanics of building and sensing interactions are established, a number of primitives can be built in the form of paper knobs, sliders, pop-ups, etc. These building blocks are then combined with on-tag and free-air RFID tag gestures to create a variety of interaction types that can be used to build and prototype new interfaces and applications.

Background

In this work, we utilized a commercially available EPC Gen 2 UHF RFID system [6] that operates with a carrier signal at a frequency from 902 MHz to 928 MHz and is capable of powering and reading hundreds of RFID tags simultaneously within a range of 6-10 meters. RFID readers vary in shape, size and performance with prices from $200 to $1,500. Generally, any full-featured reader that reports RSSI and RF phase can be used. We utilized commodity UHF Squiggle RFID tags and UHF loop tags that are inexpensive (10 cents), disposable, and completely passive in conjunction with user-customized tag antennas created with conductive ink.

CUSTOM TAG FABRICATION

UHF RFID tags are readily available in a wide variety of shapes and sizes that typically take the form of two-dimensional stickers or labels. While commercial tags offer the greatest possible performance in terms of read range, they are not suitable for dense deployment due to near-field interference. In this paper, we overcome this limitation by presenting a half-antenna design together with a sticker RFID IC as depicted in Figure 2(a,b,c). The design acts as an ungrounded monopole antenna, which performs poorly at harvesting RF energy thus making the tag invisible to the reader. When the antenna pad is touched, the human body (which is reasonably conductive at these frequencies) acts as a ground plane, which improves received signal power allowing the tag to harvest enough power for operation. The design of these "silent" touch buttons will dramatically reduce interference between near-field tags. For rapid touch interface prototyping, we outline a few antenna construction methods that can be used to fabricate this type of customized RFID tag.

One standard approach to designing custom antennas is to use an inkjet printer with conductive ink [22, 28], which was used to print the half-antenna in figure 3(e). This provides the greatest amount of control and repeatability. One challenge to this approach is bonding the RFID IC (which is approximately 0.5mm x 0.5mm) to the printed antenna, which cannot be hand-soldered. This can be overcome by re-purposing an ultra small form-factor, near-field UHF RFID tag [26] into what we refer to as a loop IC, as shown in Figure 3(d). Instead of having to mechanically and electrically bond an IC to the antenna, we use the loop IC to inductively couple to the spine of the printed antenna, thereby forming a fully functional custom RFID tag (i.e., antenna plus IC).

An alternative approach is to use conductive ink pens to draw the antenna freehand (Figure 3(a)). While it is quite simple to draw a straight line design, other more compact antenna shapes can also be drawn, as shown in Figure 3. While hand drawn antennas do not have the 10-meter read range of their commercially available counterparts, with a little trial and error, it is quite easy to make hand drawn RFID antennas with a functional range of 5-6 meters. In order to help users become comfortable with drawing UHF antennas, a plastic antenna stencil can be used as a guide (Figure 3(b)). This also insures consistent performance from one tag to the next while still allowing people to prototype their interface quickly. In practice, we noticed that the conductive ink should have a resistance less than 10 ohms per inch in order to ensure an antenna with reliable performance.

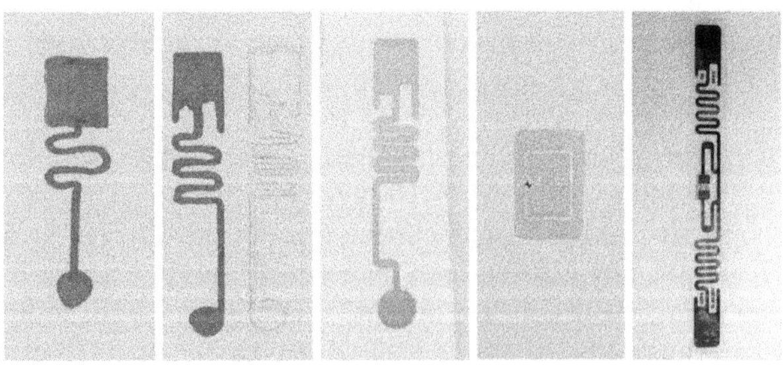

(a) Drawn (b) Stencil (c) Printed (d) Loop IC (e) Sticker

Figure 3. Tag antenna types.

SIGNAL DETECTION

In addition to fabricating conductive ink antennas for loop ICs to enable responsive hand touching detection, we also utilize other commodity tags to support interactions, including on-paper or in-air hand gesture detection as well as motion tracking of the paper interface.

In order to integrate rich hand interaction types that include touch, wave, swipe, cover and tag movement into a single tag (Figure 6(a)-(e)), we employ the channel parameters reported by the RFID reader, such as Received Signal Strength Indicator (RSSI), RF Phase, and Read Rate, which represent a unique signature of the RF environment of each individual tag. Each tag's RF environment is comprised of the far-field signal path from the reader to the tag (including all multipath elements), as well as the near-field region of the tag, which has an effective radius around the tag of half of a wavelength (~16cm). Thus, any changes in either the far-field or near-field regions of the tag, such as hand touch, wave, cover gestures, or tag movements, will result in altering the signal paths and be reported as changes in RF channel parameters. By putting tags onto the paper interface and observing and extracting the patterns of each tag's channel parameters, we can establish a quantitative understanding of people's interactions with the interface. In the following subsections, we explain how we make use of low-level channel parameters including RSSI, RF Phase and read rate to enable tag motion tracking, as well as on-tag and free air gesture detection.

Understanding Channel Parameters

RSSI

When an RFID tag receives power from a reader, part of the received power is reflected back to the RFID reader. This reflection is called backscatter and RSSI is a power measurement of the backscattered signal from each tag received by the reader. RSSI is predominantly determined by the distance to the tag as well as the power level of the reader, as shown in equation 1.

$$RSSI = 10log(P_r) = 10log(\frac{G_t\lambda^2\sigma}{(4\pi)^3d^4}) + 10log(P_t) \qquad (1)$$

where P_r = backscatter signal power, P_t = reader transmit power, G_t = reader antenna gain, λ = carrier wavelength, σ = tag radar cross section, and d = distance between the reader and tag.

Phase

The difference in phase between the signal transmitted by the reader and the backscattered signal from the tag as seen by the reader provides additional insight into the state of the tag. RF phase is dominated by the antenna-tag distance d as well as signal carrier frequency $f = 1/\lambda$, and repeats every wavelength. The constant shown in Equation 2 is introduced by the transmit circuits, receiver circuits, and the tag's reflection

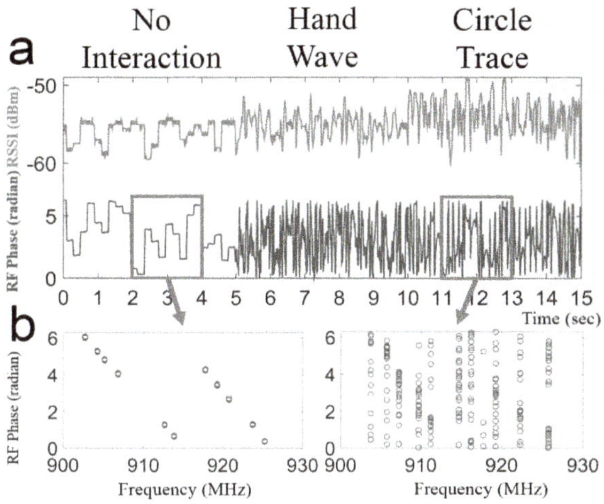

Figure 4. (a) Raw RSSI and Phase data for a single RFID tag remaining still or experiencing near-field hand waving and circular movement. (b) Due to pseudo-random frequency hopping, a 2-second window of RF phase is sorted by channel to reveal characteristics of these events.

characteristic.

$$\theta = 2\pi \frac{2d}{\lambda} mod(2\pi) + constant \quad (2)$$

Read Rate

The RFID read rate is defined as the number of packets received from each tag per second. Read rate can be influenced by dramatic changes in signal strength as a result of blocking or capacitive coupling of the human body. To get a better understanding of these RF parameters, we attached a tag to a sheet of paper and show 15 seconds of the raw RSSI and phase signal streams of the tag in Figure 4. There was no interaction during the first 5 seconds, and for the next 5 seconds, the tag is undergoing constant hand waving in the near-field region. For the last 5 seconds, the tag is moving in a circular trace. The still state with no interaction can be distinguished from other states by observing the RSSI and phase raw signal variations shown in Figure 4(a), noting larger variations in RSSI as well as Phase signal.

We noticed discontinuity in RSSI and phase samples in the first 5 seconds of Figure 4(a). When there is no interaction involving the tag, this is a result of the RFID reader constantly changing its transmit signal frequency. FCC regulations require RFID readers in the 915 MHz ISM band to pseudo-randomly change their transmit frequency in order to minimize interference with other devices. To satisfy this requirement, RFID readers frequency hop across 50 channels from 902 MHz to 928 MHz (in the USA) at a time interval of approximately 0.2 seconds.

To better reveal the underlying characteristics of phase hidden by frequency hopping, we take a 1-second slice of phase from the still state and one from interaction state and re-plot against channel frequency in Figure 4(b). For the first 5 seconds, phase is linearly correlated with the carrier signal and wrapped into segments within $[0, 2\pi]$. Hand waving around the tag as well as circular movement of the tag resulted in

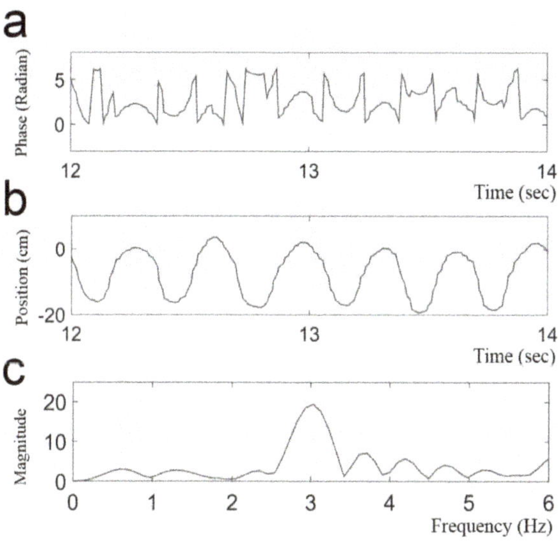

Figure 5. (a) Two segments of raw phase data; (b) application of the trace recovering technique to reveal the moving trace relative to the RFID reader; (c) applying a Fast Fourier transform to reveal the frequency of the movement.

dramatic phase variations within each channel, as depicted in the right panel of Figure 4(b).

Trace Recovering

Here, we demonstrate a technique for tracking the movement traces of tags using the phase signal. This technique enables the "continuous tracking" of the tag's velocity, motion magnitude, and relative direction of motion towards and away from the reader. Figure 5(a) is a 2-second slice of seconds 12 to 14 shown in Figure 4. According to the phase definition in Equation 2, after unwrapping the phase signals, we can calculate the distance change d_1 and d_2 with the following equation:

$$d_1 - d_2 = \frac{1}{2} \frac{\lambda}{2\pi} (\theta_1 - \theta_2). \quad (3)$$

We apply this equation to the phase signal in panel (a) and then apply signal smoothing between timestamps where frequency hopping occurs. We recover the trace of the circular movement of the paper, as represented in Figure 5(b). Note that according to Equation 2, distance d is the relative distance between the tag and the reader. In this case, the movement represented in the recovered trace is a 1-dimensional component of the circular trace, which is close to a sine wave.

We apply a Fast Fourier transform to this trace signal to get the frequency component of the trace in panel (c). This trace-tracking technique is later applied to paper-based toy applications. Consider the "conductors wand" application where the frequency at which the wand is waved side-to-side is mapped to the tempo of the music while the magnitude of motion is mapped to volume. Our technique provides a rich user interface, in contrast to the binary motion detection in IDSense [14], which would only be able to turn the music on or off.

Multi-Gesture Classifier

Here, we discuss the technical details of a multi-gesture classifier that is later utilized to enable controlling applications. Here we support interactions including finger touch, cover, swipe and in-air directional hand waving on a single tag.

In order to enable a variety of gesture input methods on paper interfaces, we apply machine learning to these lower RF channel parameters to describe the unique RF environment of each tag on paper interfaces. For each segment, we calculate the following features.

Read Rate

- Read Rate: This feature is defined as the number of packets received from each RFID tag per second. This feature is effective for characterizing interactions that dramatically change the ambient RF environment, such as a cover gesture, or detuning events happening on the tag, such as a touch gesture.

Phase Features

- Tag position change: The relative position change within each segment characterized by our trace recovering technique. This feature is effective for describing motions related to a paper interface.
- Standard deviation of phase within each channel: This feature is effective for describing periodic hand gestures in the near-field region of the tag, such as swiping or touching the tag surface.
- Standard error of the linear regression of phase versus channel frequencies: As demonstrated in the left panel of Figure 4(b), when no interaction is happening on the paper interface, the phase is linearly correlated with the channel. Here, we unwrap the phase samples and calculate the error of the linear fit, which is useful for separating non-interaction states from other interactions on the paper interface.

RSSI Features

- Average Standard Deviation of RSSI per channel: As demonstrated in Figure 4, RSSI variation will increase when there are interaction events happening with the paper interface. The magnitude of the variation is dependent on the interaction type, so we include this feature here to describe the variation in signal strength related to different interaction types.
- Sum of RSSI difference per channel: This feature describes the directional changes of the RSSI magnitude, which is useful for monitoring immediate change in reflected signal as a result of near-field interference, such as hand touching.
- RSSI Average Value: The RSSI value can vary according to the relative distance, antenna orientation, and power level of the reader, so uncontrolled RSSI values cannot provide effective information about the interaction states of the paper interface to which it is attached; however, we actively calibrate the initial RSSI value to approximately -25dBm. In this case, we can utilize the RSSI Average Value (within each segment) to indicate the interaction types that will change the RSSI, including on-tag and free-air interactions.

Machine Learning

Here, we introduce the machine learning pipeline for the purpose of distinguishing multiple simultaneous gestures on RFID tags. More details on how we apply this pipeline to gesture classification applications will be discussed in later sections. First, we segment the RF channel parameters reported by the reader. Through experimentation, we decided to utilize a window size of 1 second that advances every half second with 50% overlap. This achieves a good balance between classification accuracy and delay in real-time. A longer window may help to further boost classification accuracy, but it would also increase the latency of the real-time system.

Phase, RSSI and read rate features are utilized to implement a Support Vector Machine (SVM) with the Radial Basis Function (RBF) kernel. Training data is collected offline. We record and label training data for each of the interaction classes at multiple locations to improve the robustness of our classifier. Then, we optimize parameters of the RBF kernel by maximizing 10-fold cross-validation results. Our classifier makes real-time predictions based on the most recent 1-second RF parameters and refreshes prediction results every 0.5 seconds.

INTERACTION METHODS AND PRIMITIVES

Thus far, we have presented several methods for quickly building custom RFID antennas using construction techniques consistent with prototyping on paper. By applying the signal processing techniques described above, we are able to turn our custom tags and commercial tags (that normally only report their ID number) into battery-free, ultra-thin, wireless user input devices.

In this section, we describe several user interaction primitives that can easily be made with RFID tags. The first set of primitives consists of a single RFID tag that can be implemented in several ways. Next, we combine multiple RFID tags together to make complex interactive structures, such as rotary dials and sliders. Finally, free air gestures and actions are presented wherein the user is either interacting with a static paper object or is manipulating the paper object dynamically.

Single Tag Primitives

This is the simplest interface we present as it only requires the use of a single RFID tag. We describe gestures including cover, two types of finger touch, swipe touch, and hand waving (represented in Figure 6(a)-(d)). By applying the SVM classifier onto the RF features discussed earlier, all of these primitives can be integrated onto a single tag for real-time interaction detection and classification.

Waving

This technique is for detection of the free air hand waving gesture proximate to a paper interface. It can be applied to a single tag or multiple tags on one paper interface.

With a single tag, we can detect the binary wave / no wave as represented in Figure 6(a). This is achieved by applying the SVM classifier to RF features. With the support of multiple tags on the paper interface, we can also detect the direction

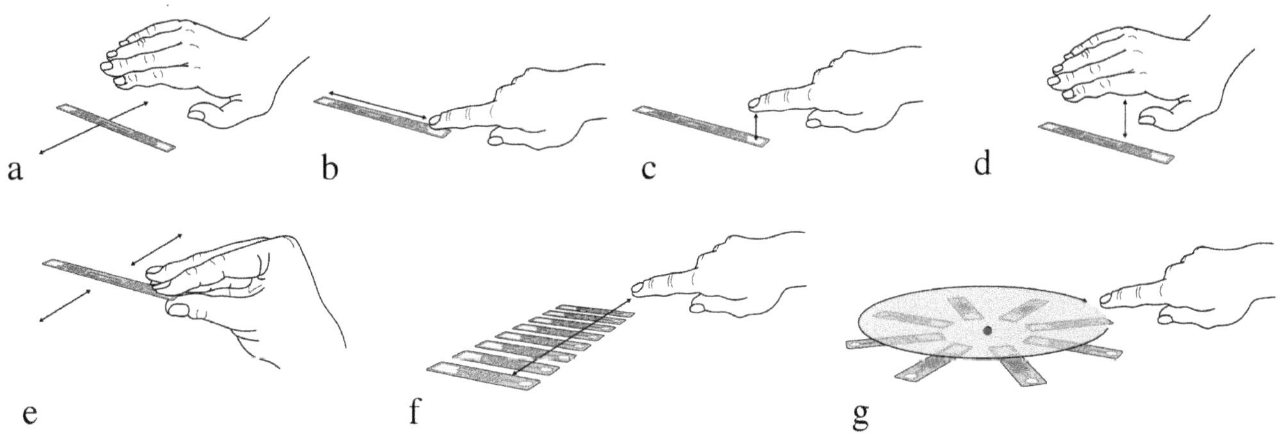

Figure 6. (a) Wave (b) Swipe (c) Finger Touch (d) Cover Touch (e) Free air tag motion (f) Slider (g) Knob

of waving by monitoring the sequence of variation in RF features of the two corresponding tags.

Button Touch

Button touch interactions can be accomplished in two different ways. First, a commonplace RFID tag will be affected when a finger touches either end of its antenna. This type of touch will cause a change in the RSSI and RF phase as reported by the reader, but will not block the signal such that the tag can no longer be read as is the case with cover touch. Using SVM, it is easy to reliably classify touch events when the tag is still. However, if this type of button is used to prototype a remote control for a TV, it would be challenging to detect button pushes while the remote control is in motion.

To overcome this limitation, a second type of touch button based on a "half antenna" has been developed, as described in the Antenna Fabrication section. In this configuration, the tag operates as a button or key press. Multiple tags can be set up on a single sheet of paper and multiple buttons can be touched simultaneously. Because the actual operation of the tag is binary, it is very robust to the motion of the prototyped device the tag is on. However, since the button is *normally off / momentarily on*, the RFID reader will not know that the device is present until the button is pushed. If desired, the designer can add a second normal tag to the prototype to indicate if the button is within view of the reader.

Cover Touch

One of the most basic RFID interaction methods is covering the RFID tag such that the signal from the reader is completely blocked or such that the tag's antenna becomes detuned to the point where it cannot receive enough power for operation (Figure 6 (d)). This can be done by covering the tag with a person's hand or body or with a conductor like copper tape. The most effective way to detect these cover events is to measure the read rate of the tag and set a threshold for activation. One drawback is that when the tag leaves the interrogation zone of the RFID reader, its read rate will also appear to drop (i.e., go to zero) and will be registered as user input. To overcome this edge condition, a time-dependent interaction can be employed, such as covering the tag for a window of 1-2 seconds and then uncovering it.

Swipe Touch

We also include a swipe touch interaction, which is the interaction of swiping a fingertip across the tag surface (Figure 6(b)). This gesture brings dramatic variation to both RSSI and phase signals, which can be characterized using our RF features.

Multi-Tag Primitives

The "silent" nature of the customized touch button tag type makes them ideal for dense deployment. Below, we introduce more complicated primitives using multiple customized touch button tags.

Slider

For the slider interface, the user slides his or her finger across a row of customized button tags as depicted in figure 6(f)). Multiple tags with half antennas are placed on one static layer of paper; the finger is placed near the edge of the tab. As the finger is moved across the static half antennas, it can couple with each one to provide enough power to backscatter signals to the reader. Thus, the reader can detect the position of the finger as a discrete touch state sensor. For example, each static tag can be paired with a different light bulb/LED, sound effect, or onscreen event that is activated when the moving hand and static half antennas align.

Rotary

This interface relies upon a group of static tags with half antennas and a single moving half antenna that triggers a unique response when moved to pair with each static tag. In our sample implementation, the static tags are placed on the front of a single sheet of paper in a spoke-like design. On top of this, a single circle is attached that has a single half antenna placed on one radius. The circle can spin freely, rotating the half antenna on the circle relative to the static tags (Figure 6 (g)). When the rotating antenna contacts a static tag, it provides enough power to backscatter signals to the reader for detection and triggers a set response.

Note that in addition to using the hand as a ground plane to enable touch interaction, we can also overlay a second antenna to complete the circuits as a dipole antenna, which can also trigger the same effect as hand touching. In this case, the state of the slider and rotary will stay in place even if the hand moves away.

Free Air Motion Primitives

We also create tag-based interfaces that track motion signals over single and multiple tags. Below, we describe a free air system with a single tag moving in space. This primitive can be applied to a paper interface of a stand-alone RFID tag where we provide functionality for fine-grain trace tracking of the interface relative to the RFID reader as well as frequency tracking for periodic movements. This primitive is supported by our trace tracking technique introduced in the Signal Processing section.

LED User Feedback

Most of the RFID tags described thus far are geared to user input. However, it is possible to construct an LED-enhanced RFID tag that harvests enough power for the RFID reader to flash an LED. Although not as complex and full-featured as prior work [23], this tag does not need a "loop IC" to communicate with the reader. Instead, the RFID reader can programmatically modulate its output power from high to low to turn the LED on or off. The LED tag can also be made into a half tag such that the user completes the antenna and lights the LED when touched.

APPLICATIONS

In this section, we present several applications that use combinations of the primitives described above to build new interactive paper interfaces that come to life when read by an RFID reader.

Polling Device

One of the most widely used test-taking and grading methods involves the Scantron test form. In this classic paper interface, users fill in bubbles with a number two pencil to denote answers to multiple choice test questions. By using the RFID half tag concept, we are able to re-imagine test taking as a real-time, interactive experience. In Figure 7, we demonstrate two methods to use RFID tags to create polling/multiple choice devices. First, users can indicate a choice among multiple tags by either covering a complete RFID tag (touch interaction) or by completing a half antenna with a finger (button interaction). Second, users can complete one of multiple half antennas by coloring in the end of the antenna with a conductive pen. In both cases, data can be collected and assessed in near real time. This method allows nearly instantaneous processing of users' opinions or knowledge without requiring that each user has access to an individual wired or otherwise powered system, resulting in lower cost.

Magic Wand/Conducting Baton

Besides augmenting a static 2D piece of paper with touch controls, the "free air" gestures described above can be used to transform a piece of paper into a tangible gesture interface.

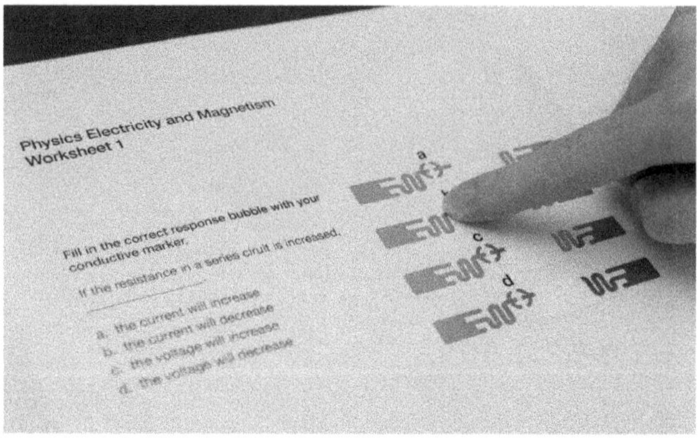

Figure 7. In this polling application, a student can pick a response on a worksheet and receive live feedback.

Figure 8. The wand frequency is mapped to music tempo and the velocity is mapped to gain.

In this example, a commercially available RFID tag sticker is placed on a single sheet of paper that is then rolled up into a cylinder to form a magic wand, as shown in Figure 8. As a user waves the wand back and forth through the air, the RFID reader streams the RF channel parameters to the signal processing pipeline (on a host PC) to extract wand motion in terms of frequency content and velocity. These two metrics are then used to control the tempo and the volume of music played through the host PC. The effect is that the user can control the tempo of the music by the rate at which they swing the wand back and forth. To increase the volume of the music, the user increases the size of the gesture (i.e., the velocity it takes to complete one repetitive swinging motion). Thus, large, repetitive gestures make the music play louder and small, repetitive gestures make the music play softer.

Pinwheel

A corollary to the wand application is the pinwheel made of construction paper shown in Figure 9. For this application, we attach a single RFID tag sticker to a pinwheel. A user can blow on the pinwheel and use the velocity of the tag to control the animation flow of blowing particles with varying number and force, as shown in the supplementary video.

Figure 9. The speed of the spinning tag on the pinwheel is mapped to onscreen graphics.

Figure 10. This pop-up book contains a knob interactor which selects audio tracks and a shielded tag in the pop-up barn.

Figure 11. Paper interfaces can be used to create new sensors to control the lighting and doorbell of this foam doll house.

Pop-Up Books

Pop-up books offer a wide array of mechanical motions where pieces of paper are sliding across each other, bending, folding, and lifting. Using the RFID interaction primitives described above, these motions can inexpensively be instrumented to stream interaction events back to a computing device via the RFID reader.

For this application (Figure 10), we create an interactive, pop-up book page with a barn. First, we create an LED light circuit that turns on when the page is opened and the barn pops out. Next, a single tag is placed on an exterior wall of the barn that is blocked by a piece of copper tape when the page is closed. Opening the page stops the copper from blocking the RF signals so that the tag can be read, which in turn triggers the host PC to play the song "Old McDonald Had a Farm". Second, we present a rotary dial that allows the user to trigger various sounds. By aligning the customized button tag on the dial with the half antenna on the paper underneath, the RFID reader can determine the state of the rotary and prompt the sound that corresponds with that particular state. In the pop-up book example, the rotatory dial is covered with images of barnyard animals. Thus, when the child rotates the wheel to an image of a sheep, a "baa" sound is played.

Dollhouse

In the dollhouse example shown in Figure 11, we use both the button and the slider. When a user presses the button, the house emits a doorbell sound. For the slider, there a set of stationary half tags connected to LEDs in each room in the house. As a finger is dragged across the stationary tags, it completes each tag antenna to adjust the brightness of the lights.

Interactive Light Control

We combine our cover, swipe, and wave interactors into a single RFID tag to create a control system for a desk lamp with a Phillips Hue light bulb that can be controlled remotely by Bluetooth® and offers a full-color spectrum at varying levels of brightness (Figure 12). We use the cover action to turn the light on and off. The touch interaction changes the color of the light bulb across the light spectrum, and the swipe and wave gestures control the brightness.

RFID Powered LED

Although RFID is primarily designed for communication, it also transmits RF power that is harvested by the RFID tag for operation. This mechanism of wireless power transfer can be hijacked and used to wirelessly power LEDs. In the example application shown in Figure 13, an image of a cartoon skull is augmented with two LED enabled RFID tags in the eyes, and one hand-drawn stub antenna for a button tag in the mouth. When the user touches the button tag. the RFID reader is commanded to increase its output power level and cause enough power to be harvested by the two LEDs for them to turn on, creating the effect of shining eyes in the paper skull.

EVALUATION

In this section, we evaluate our interaction methods and primitives used in our applications. One factor influencing performance is the reflected signal strength. To control this factor, we automatically calibrate the antenna power so that RSSI is at approximately -25dBm.

Figure 12. The intensity and color of light can be altered using wave and touch gestures.

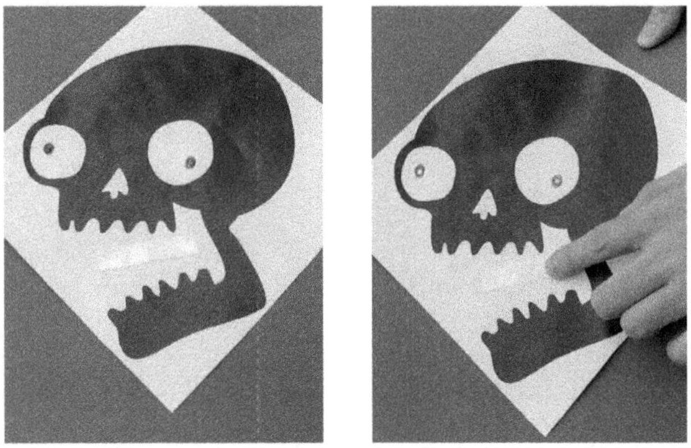

Figure 13. Using the same antenna with which we sense our input tags, we can wirelessly power LEDs. We are using a single touch tag as our input to increase or decrease the reader's power output.

Gesture Sensing Evaluation

We integrate our wave (Figure 6(a)), swipe (Figure 6(b)), touch (Figure 6(c)) and cover (Figure 6(d)) interaction primitives into a tag gesture-sensing application using features and classification methods described in the Signal Detection Section. Our training data was recorded at 3 locations (2m, 4m, and 6m away from the reader). Our classifier has 5 classes, including the 4 gestures and the still state when no interaction is performed. We recorded 30 instances from each class, 10 at each of the 3 locations. Training is done offline by optimizing parameters in the RBF kernel maximizing the 10-fold cross validation results of gesture classification. We recruited 5 participants (4 male, 1 female) with a mean age of 24.4 years. Each participant was asked to follow visual instructions on a monitor to perform 20 instances of each of the 5 gesture classes. Each participant repeated the task 3 times at each of the 3 locations (2m, 4m, and 6m away from the antenna). Visual gesture instructions were given once every 4 seconds, and pauses between gestures were utilized to generate still instances. The instruction script was used as ground truth and user mistakes were manually annotated. We achieved an average of 94.1% accuracy classifying gestures into 5 categories with a 2.4% STD across participants and 1.4% STD across locations. This study result demonstrates the high performance of our system across all locations with low variations, showcasing the promising potential for deploying our technique for real-world user interfaces.

Customized Touch Button Evaluation

We evaluated the effectiveness of our customized touch button design in this study for when we detect touch vs no-touch states using a read rate threshold of 5 reads/per second. We arrayed 10 hand-drawn touch buttons in a row on a sheet of paper. Note that there are 3 ways to fabricate the button antenna: hand-drawn, stencil-traced, and inject printing. We evaluated the most challenging hand-drawn ones to establish a performance baseline. We recruited 5 participants (3 male, 2 female) with a mean age of 26.0 years. Each participant was asked to follow visual instructions on a monitor to perform 10 touches on each of the 10 tags, one tag at a time. The study was repeated 3 times at 3 different locations (2m, 4m, and 6m away from the reader). Instructions were given once every 2 seconds. The instruction script was used as ground truth and user mistakes were manually annotated. Pauses between touches were utilized to generate no-touch instances. Our design achieved an average of 96.2% accuracy on detecting touch events, with a 1.1% STD across participants and a 0.4% STD across locations. Because the Knob and Slider primitives were designed based on customized touch button elements, their performance will be similar to what we see in this evaluation.

Velocity Metric Evaluation

We utilized the magic wand described in the Applications section to evaluate our Trace Recovering technique. We moved a tagged wand between 2 points with a separation of 20 centimeters back and forth at 1, 2, 4, 6 Hz per second from 2, 4, and 6 meters away from the antenna, each for 20 seconds. Velocity is calculated by accumulated displacement divided by time difference and frequency is estimated by the most significant frequency component after the Fast Fourier Transform is performed. These two metrics are calculated in real time using window length of 2 seconds and updated every 1 second. Study results demonstrated that velocity sensing had an average standard error of 6.4% and frequency sensing had an average standard error of 8.2%.

CONCLUSION

We demonstrate techniques to create simple, lightweight, recyclable paper interfaces that rely on RFID technology. Using a single RFID reader antenna and inexpensive passive tags, we can create applications with numerous controllable features, including lights, sounds, software control, and animations. Subtle changes in the low-level radio frequency signals that typically retrieve tag identification information are leveraged to determine how each tag is manipulated by the user. Additionally, we introduce multiple techniques for creating RFID tag antennas in order to customize tags for different contexts. Our methodology expands the functionality of RFID tags to quickly and easily create user interfaces on paper, a ubiquitous, lightweight medium.

REFERENCES

1. 2015. Arduino & Genuino Product Page. (sep 2015). https://www.arduino.cc/en/Main/Products
2. Toshifumi Arai, Dietmar Aust, and Scott E. Hudson. 1997. PaperLink: A Technique for Hyperlinking from Real Paper to Electronic Content. In *Proceedings of the ACM SIGCHI Conference on Human Factors in Computing Systems (CHI '97)*. ACM, New York, NY, USA, 327–334. DOI: http://dx.doi.org/10.1145/258549.258782
3. Parvin Asadzadeh, Lars Kulik, and Egemen Tanin. 2012. Gesture recognition using RFID technology. *Personal and Ubiquitous Computing* 16, 3 (2012), 225–234. DOI: http://dx.doi.org/10.1007/s00779-011-0395-z
4. Daniel Avrahami and Scott E. Hudson. 2002. Forming Interactivity: A Tool for Rapid Prototyping of Physical Interactive Products. In *Proceedings of the 4th Conference on Designing Interactive Systems: Processes, Practices, Methods, and Techniques (DIS '02)*. ACM, New York, NY, USA, 141–146. DOI: http://dx.doi.org/10.1145/778712.778735
5. Michael Buettner, Richa Prasad, Matthai Philipose, and David Wetherall. 2009. Recognizing Daily Activities with RFID-based Sensors. In *Proceedings of the 11th International Conference on Ubiquitous Computing (UbiComp '09)*. ACM, New York, NY, USA, 51–60. DOI: http://dx.doi.org/10.1145/1620545.1620553
6. EPCglobal. *EPC^TM Radio-frequency identity protocols generation-2 UHF RFID specification for RFID air interface, Version 2.0*.
7. K. Fishkin, B. Jiang, M. Philipose, S. Roy, Kenneth P. Fishkin, Bing Jiang, Matthai Philipose, and Sumit Roy. 2004. I Sense a Disturbance in the Force: Unobtrusive Detection of Interactions with RFID-tagged Objects. Springer-Verlag, 268–282. DOI: http://dx.doi.org/10.1007/978-3-540-30119-6_16
8. Saul Greenberg and Chester Fitchett. 2001. Phidgets: Easy Development of Physical Interfaces Through Physical Widgets. In *Proceedings of the 14th Annual ACM Symposium on User Interface Software and Technology (UIST '01)*. ACM, New York, NY, USA, 209–218. DOI: http://dx.doi.org/10.1145/502348.502388
9. François Guimbretière. 2003. Paper Augmented Digital Documents. In *Proceedings of the 16th Annual ACM Symposium on User Interface Software and Technology (UIST '03)*. ACM, New York, NY, USA, 51–60. DOI: http://dx.doi.org/10.1145/964696.964702
10. Björn Hartmann, Scott R. Klemmer, Michael Bernstein, Leith Abdulla, Brandon Burr, Avi Robinson-Mosher, and Jennifer Gee. 2006. Reflective Physical Prototyping Through Integrated Design, Test, and Analysis. In *Proceedings of the 19th Annual ACM Symposium on User Interface Software and Technology (UIST '06)*. ACM, New York, NY, USA, 299–308. DOI: http://dx.doi.org/10.1145/1166253.1166300
11. David Holman, Roel Vertegaal, Mark Altosaar, Nikolaus Troje, and Derek Johns. 2005. Paper Windows: Interaction Techniques for Digital Paper. In *Proceedings of the SIGCHI Conference on Human Factors in Computing Systems (CHI '05)*. ACM, New York, NY, USA, 591–599. DOI: http://dx.doi.org/10.1145/1054972.1055054
12. Yoshihiro Kawahara, Steve Hodges, Benjamin S Cook, Cheng Zhang, and Gregory D Abowd. 2013. Instant inkjet circuits: lab-based inkjet printing to support rapid prototyping of UbiComp devices. In *Proceedings of the 2013 ACM international joint conference on Pervasive and ubiquitous computing*. ACM, 363–372. DOI: http://dx.doi.org/10.1145/2493432.2493486
13. Johnny C. Lee, Daniel Avrahami, Scott E. Hudson, Jodi Forlizzi, Paul H. Dietz, and Darren Leigh. 2004. The Calder Toolkit: Wired and Wireless Components for Rapidly Prototyping Interactive Devices. In *Proceedings of the 5th Conference on Designing Interactive Systems: Processes, Practices, Methods, and Techniques (DIS '04)*. ACM, New York, NY, USA, 167–175. DOI: http://dx.doi.org/10.1145/1013115.1013139
14. Hanchuan Li, Can Ye, and Alanson P Sample. 2015. IDSense: A Human Object Interaction Detection System Based on Passive UHF RFID. In *Proceedings of the SIGCHI Conference on Human Factors in Computing Systems (CHI '15)*. ACM, New York, NY, USA, 2555–2564. DOI: http://dx.doi.org/10.1145/2702123.2702178
15. RFID Journal LLC. 2015. How much does an RFID tag cost today? (sep 2015). http://www.rfidjournal.com/faq/show?85
16. Wendy E. Mackay, Guillaume Pothier, Catherine Letondal, Kaare Bøegh, and Hans Erik Sørensen. 2002. The Missing Link: Augmenting Biology Laboratory Notebooks. In *Proceedings of the 15th Annual ACM Symposium on User Interface Software and Technology (UIST '02)*. ACM, New York, NY, USA, 41–50. DOI: http://dx.doi.org/10.1145/571985.571992
17. Allan MacLean, Kathleen Carter, Lennart Lövstrand, and Thomas Moran. 1990. User-tailorable Systems: Pressing the Issues with Buttons. In *Proceedings of the SIGCHI Conference on Human Factors in Computing Systems (CHI '90)*. ACM, New York, NY, USA, 175–182. DOI: http://dx.doi.org/10.1145/97243.97271
18. Nicolai Marquardt, Alex S Taylor, Nicolas Villar, and Saul Greenberg. 2010. Rethinking RFID: awareness and control for interaction with RFID systems. In *Proceedings of the SIGCHI Conference on Human Factors in Computing Systems*. ACM, 2307–2316. DOI: http://dx.doi.org/10.1145/1753326.1753674

19. Siddika Parlak and Ivan Marsic. 2013. Detecting object motion using passive RFID: A trauma resuscitation case study. *Instrumentation and Measurement, IEEE Transactions on* 62, 9 (2013), 2430–2437. DOI: http://dx.doi.org/10.1109/TIM.2013.2258772

20. Jie Qi and Leah Buechley. 2014. Sketching in circuits: designing and building electronics on paper. In *Proceedings of the SIGCHI Conference on Human Factors in Computing Systems*. ACM, 1713–1722. DOI:http://dx.doi.org/10.1145/2556288.2557391

21. Marc Rettig. 1994. Prototyping for Tiny Fingers. *Commun. ACM* 37, 4 (April 1994), 21–27. DOI: http://dx.doi.org/10.1145/175276.175288

22. A. Rida, Li Yang, R. Vyas, and M.M. Tentzeris. 2009. Conductive Inkjet-Printed Antennas on Flexible Low-Cost Paper-Based Substrates for RFID and WSN Applications. *Antennas and Propagation Magazine, IEEE* 51, 3 (June 2009), 13–23. DOI: http://dx.doi.org/10.1109/MAP.2009.5251188

23. Alanson Sample, Craig Macomber, Liang-Ting Jiang, and Joshua R Smith. 2012. Optical localization of passive UHF RFID tags with integrated LEDs. In *RFID (RFID), 2012 IEEE International Conference on*. 116–123. DOI: http://dx.doi.org/10.1109/RFID.2012.6193038

24. A.P. Sample, D.J. Yeager, P.S. Powledge, and J.R. Smith. 2007. Design of a Passively-Powered, Programmable Sensing Platform for UHF RFID Systems. In *RFID, 2007. IEEE International Conference on*. 149–156. DOI: http://dx.doi.org/10.1109/RFID.2007.346163

25. Jürgen Steimle. 2009. Designing pen-and-paper user interfaces for interaction with documents. In *Proceedings of the 3rd International Conference on Tangible and Embedded Interaction*. ACM, 197–204. DOI:http://dx.doi.org/10.1145/1517664.1517707

26. Alien Technology. 2014. ALN-9713 SIT Inlay. (March 2014). http://www.alientechnology.com/wp-content/uploads/Alien-Technology-Higgs-4-ALN-9713-SIT.pdf

27. Jue Wang, Deepak Vasisht, and Dina Katabi. RF-IDraw: virtual touch screen in the air using RF signals. In *Proceedings of the 2014 ACM conference on SIGCOMM*. DOI: http://dx.doi.org/10.1145/2740070.2626330

28. Li Yang, A. Rida, R. Vyas, and M.M. Tentzeris. 2007. RFID Tag and RF Structures on a Paper Substrate Using Inkjet-Printing Technology. *Microwave Theory and Techniques, IEEE Transactions on* 55, 12 (Dec 2007), 2894–2901. DOI: http://dx.doi.org/10.1109/TMTT.2007.909886

RapID: A Framework for Fabricating Low-Latency Interactive Objects with RFID Tags

Andrew Spielberg[*†] aespielberg@csail.mit.edu
Alanson Sample[*] alanson.sample@disneyresearch.com
Scott E. Hudson[*‡] scott.hudson@cs.cmu.edu
Jennifer Mankoff[*‡] jmankoff@cs.cmu.edu
James McCann[*] jmccann@disneyresearch.com

[*]Disney Research Pittsburgh, Pittsburgh, PA
[†]Massachusetts Institute of Technology, Cambridge, MA
[‡]Carnegie Mellon University, Pittsburgh, PA

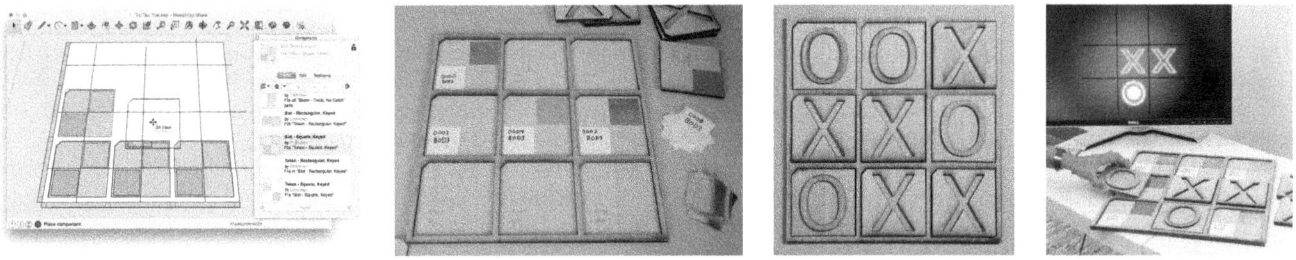

Figure 1. A wireless, batteryless game of Tic-tac-toe is designed using components in the RapID standard library, fabricated using laser cutting along with stick-on RFID tags and foil, and tracked with low latency using the RapID runtime library.

ABSTRACT
RFID tags can be used to add inexpensive, wireless, batteryless sensing to objects. However, quickly and accurately estimating the state of an RFID tag is difficult. In this work, we show how to achieve low-latency manipulation and movement sensing with off-the-shelf RFID tags and readers. Our approach couples a probabilistic filtering layer with a monte-carlo-sampling-based interaction layer, preserving uncertainty in tag reads until they can be resolved in the context of interactions. This allows designers' code to reason about inputs at a high level. We demonstrate the effectiveness of our approach with a number of interactive objects, along with a library of components that can be combined to make new designs.

Author Keywords
RFID; probabilistic modeling; computational fabrication

INTRODUCTION
Currently, graphical user interfaces can be constructed very quickly by composing them from a component library and writing a small amount of "glue" code to carry out user actions. Unfortunately, the same cannot yet be said for interfaces constructed with physical objects although there have been significant advances in this direction (*e.g.*, [6, 9, 15]). One challenge in the design of interactive physical objects is integrating sensing, processing, and communications components and their associated circuitry. For example, physical objects must usually be specially designed to make room for circuit boards, wiring, and power sources. Passive Radio Frequency Identification (*RFID*) tags offer a number of potential advantages which might overcome many of these difficulties. Passive RFID tags use very tiny electronic circuits which can be easily affixed to, or embedded in, many objects. Each RFID tag can be programmed with a 12-byte identifier known as an Electronic Product Code (*EPC*), which can be wirelessly queried by devices known as readers. Importantly, they also operate without a local power source, as they draw power from the remote reading antenna.

Recent advances in the analysis of the underlying RFID signals used for identifying tags have demonstrated that manipulations of tags, such as human touch, cover by conductive or dielectric materials, and tag motion, can be reliably detected using standard RFID tags and conventional readers positioned up to several meters away [16]. This opens up the possibility of using these tags as input devices. To produce high accuracy inputs from these low level signals takes time, waiting for multiple tag reads or other evidence that the system is correctly understanding what manipulations have caused the signal changes before reporting inputs. This can produce delays on the order of two seconds for most types of manipulations, limitinga the kinds of interactions they can be used for.

In this work, we introduce a new probabilistic framework for processing RFID tag signals which allows the application to

CHI'16, May 07 - 12, 2016, San Jose, CA, USA

ACM 978-1-4503-3362-7/16/05...$15.00
DOI: http://dx.doi.org/10.1145/2858036.2858243

respond to input much more quickly. By accurately modeling the probabilities of partially understood input (using methods related to [31]), it is possible to make less conservative, but more informed decisions, and to deliver them faster – with typical delays under 200 msec. This means that input can generally be reported with a latency at, or under, typical minimum human perception-action cycle times [3] – more in line with most interactive systems than the two second delay that characterized previous work [16]. Further, the probabilistic formulation used to process the RFID tag signals can smoothly incorporate state information from an application, and probabilistic estimates can optionally be exposed to the application so that it can reason about them in an informed fashion.

To facilitate use of the techniques described here, we have also built an extension to the SketchUp 3D drawing package [18] which allows a library of interactive components built using our techniques to be easily integrated with physical objects The library we currently provide is implemented entirely with small, inexpensive UHF RFID tags (which in quantity can cost as little as USD$0.10 per tag [17]). Fabrication also requires cut to size copper foil to provide covers that can hide the RFID tag signal, which is important for several of the tag manipulations we support. Our system includes the code necessary to use each library component in our probabilistic framework at runtime.

After reviewing background on RFID sensing and key concepts needed to interact with them under uncertainty, we provide a system overview of RapID, our framework for RFID-based interaction. Following that, we describe the main contribution of this paper, our solution for speeding up interaction by interpreting interaction with RFID tags as probabilistic inputs and managing probabilistic states. We then present a developer API for creating more advanced applications using these probabilistic inputs, along with a CAD extension for quickly designing and fabricating interactive objects. Finally, we validate our method through a series of example applications implemented with our framework including a tic-tac-toe game, a pong game and an audio controller, and conclude by analyzing the strengths and limitations of our approach.

Background and Related Work

There is a rich history of developing systems which enable users to rapidly prototype interactive objects (*e.g.*, [6, 21, 34, 29]). Since the beginning, such work has emphasized simplicity of programming, often in a fashion mimetic to traditional UI programming environments (*e.g.*,[6]). More recently, work has added a facility to embed electronics in ordinary objects (*e.g.*, [21, 34, 26]). However these interactive circuits are limited in scope by the size of their setting, requiring users to make a tradeoff between small circuit footprints and larger component devices. An onboard power source must also be supplied. Further, while these frameworks automate much of the low-level design work, fabricating circuits is still a manual process which does not exploit digital manufacturing tools or the quick peel-and-stick advantages of RFID tags.

Other competing technologies for fabricating custom interactive components within physcial objects include acoustic sensing of gestures and other physical manipulation (*e.g.*, [14, 28] and capacitive touch sensing (*e.g.*,[10, 29, 7]). However, each of these technologies needs to create or use intricate and somewhat bulky components and/or wiring inside objects, all of which must typically be designed around when creating the object. It is also possible to use computer vision with depth or conventional cameras [36]. However, this approach suffers from occlusion problems and recognition of fine manipulations is difficult. One approach to overcoming this limitation is to place the camera inside the object [27]. This overcomes occlusion and resolution issues, but requires hollow objects with mostly unoccluded interiors, and still requires bulky and possibly costly electronics and power for each object.

RFID technologies fill an important gap in this body of work by enabling real-time interaction with objects that are easily fabricatable, require no on-board power, and require nothing more than stick-on tags and copper covers to add functionality. RFID systems consist of small, robust and inexpensive *tags* and more complex *readers* which can interrogate tags within range. RFID readers are designed to be part of the infrastructure of a space and to communicate with a host computer. Current RFID readers can cost around $130 for embedded modules [32], and around $1,000 for enterprise grade readers [13]. The readers used in this work make use of *far-field* RF effects at distances as far as 9 meters from the reader antenna to the tag(s). This can be contrasted with the *near-field* effects of readers now being built into some cell phones, which are limited to a few centimeters in range.

Our work uses passive UHF tags, which are ultra-thin tags powered solely by the radio frequency energy emitted by the reader, making them battery-free. Tags operate with low power because instead of generating a signal, they communicate with a reader by modulated backscatter, which reflects the reader's carrier signal back to the reader along with an encoded tag id. Manipulations of tags can influence the details of this signal and past work has demonstrated that it is feasible to detect these signal changes and interpret them in terms of user input.

Prior work has used RFID tags for input in a number of ways. Philipose *et al.* instrumented people with near-field detectors, and objects with RFID tags to detect activities [25]. Buettner *et al.* use a custom platform for detecting movement of tagged objects in large rooms instrumented with RFID readers to disambiguate between twelve daily household activities [2]. Recent work has demonstrated the feasibility of using passive UHF RFID tags for detecting motion [5, 24, 16], tag coverage [16], and touch and swipe gestures [16]. However, robust detection has required multiple readers and antennas [5], multiple tags per object [5], or accumulated signal data for up to 2 seconds [16], limiting the viability of the approach for interaction. In this paper we demonstrate how to overcome many of these limitations.

SYSTEM OVERVIEW AND MOTIVATING EXAMPLE

RapID allows for RFID-based interaction at low latencies by exploiting a probabilistic model of tag state. These probabilities are then managed in an intelligent way by a downstream application. This process is diagrammed in Figure 2.

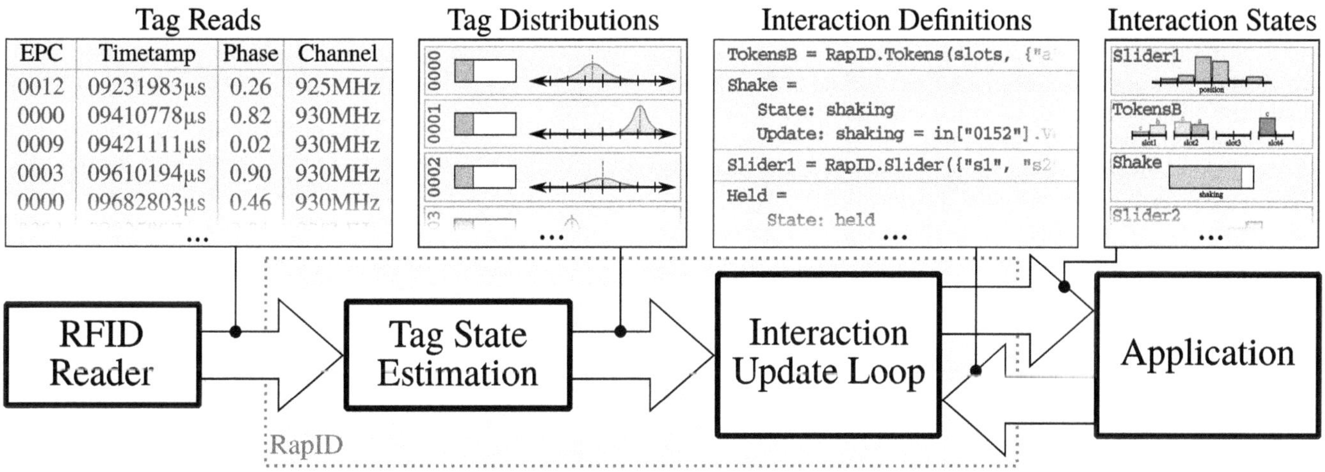

Figure 2. RapID propagates uncertainty about RFID tag states to applications by maintaining probability distributions over tag velocity and cover state, and sampling from these to update the state distributions of application-defined interactions.

Our solution is comprised of:

1. A *Tag State Estimation* method, which allows a system to incrementally update probability distributions over the state of each RFID tag, given a stream of reads from an RFID reader.

2. An *Interaction Update* method, which translates these low-level probabilistic inputs into a probability distribution over the states of states of higher-level interactions. These interactions can reason about multiple tags at once, and only need to be written using straightforward, non-probabilistic code.

3. A runtime API, which makes it easy for a developer to launch and monitor interactions (both pre-defined and developer-created).

4. An extension for SketchUp [18], including a standard library of pre-defined starter interactors and associated code, for designing physical objects for interaction, including code to export descriptions of designed objects for use by the API.

Together, these components allow a user to design physical objects, and with little to no additional code, enable user input to an application based on how the physical objects are manipulated.

As a motivating example, consider a scenario in which a developer desires to create an interactive game of Tic-Tac-Toe. The application must have the ability to track the game state, which includes detecting moves and when the game has ended. The application must also be able to provide feedback to players by both visually displaying the game state and providing audio feedback at key moments during the game, such as the game start, the start of each player's move, and the game's end.

Creating Tic-Tac-Toe with our framework is straightforward (see Figure 1 and video figure). The developer designs the board in SketchUp. Using our extensions, she creates a 3x3 array of game pieces and slots. The developer then assigns groups (X, O, board) and IDs (board positions) to the pieces, and uses our extension to export a table associating these names with the EPC numbers she will program into the RFID tags during construction. She exports a .dxf file for laser-cutting, and fabricates the board and game pieces – attaching foil and RFID tags where indicated.

In her game code, the developer writes code to initialize our API (passing it the exported name/EPC table), instantiate a token/slot interaction from our standard library, associate it with the appropriate tags, and translate the events it produces into game actions such as visual and auditory feedback, all of which can be written compactly.

PROBABILISTIC FORMULATION

One of the challenges in interpreting RFID interaction data at high speeds is the high level of uncertainty caused by the noisy signal. Uncertain input is an issue in other domains that involve recognition such as touch [1] and speech [23].

Several approaches exist for dealing with uncertainty. The most common but least pliable approach is to remove uncertainty before generating any application input. This approach is what led to the two second delay in Li *et al.*'s work, as they waited to inform the application until input presence and type was known with high confidence [16]. A second approach is to model the interface as a type of signal feedback system, engaging the user in a tight loop that visualizes uncertainty across the user interface [35]. However, this method requires a radically different approach to interface construction. A final approach is to maintain distribution over possible inputs that could have happened [11, 19, 20, 30, 31]. By modeling this as a monte-carlo sampling of a distribution over possible application states [31], it is possible for the developer to reason deterministically about the application, while the underlying infrastructure keeps track of any uncertainty.

This final approach is well suited to handling the type of uncertainty that arises when interpreting RFID signals as input. Schwarz *et al.* [30, 31] assume that each event is a complete distribution of possible inputs. RFID reads, however, only provide data on a single tag at a time, providing an incomplete view of the true interaction state of the population. Attempting to change the state of the interface from each read event can cause the *order* of tag reads to have a serious impact on behavior. Thus, some way of accumulating information over time is needed. Therefore, we have taken a two-level approach, where we probabilistically model the state of each tag based on signal-level information, and use these models to generate higher level inputs that describe how we believe the tag is being manipulated. These in turn are used to (probabilistically) update interactor state.

In the remainder of this section, we first describe the low-level tag state distribution estimators in more detail, and then discuss how RapID translates probabilistic input state into probabilistic interaction state.

Tag State Estimation

For each tag in the environment, RapID maintains a probabilistic estimate of *a)* whether it is covered/visible and *b)* its velocity.

As tag reads arrive, RapID updates these distributions using Bayes filters. Chapter 2 of [33] provides an introductory background to Bayes filters. A Bayes filter is a procedure that, given a system evolving over time and a sequence of i observations $\mathbf{z}_{1:i}$, estimates the current distribution of possible states $\mathbf{x}_i$. The variable $\mathbf{x}_i$ can be a discrete or continuous. In our setting, $\mathbf{x}_i$ will either correspond to whether the tag is in a discrete covered or visible state, or it will correspond to a continuous value representing the tag's velocity. The conditional distribution of the current tag state, given the sequence of observations, $bel(\mathbf{x_i}) \equiv p(\mathbf{x}_i|\mathbf{z}_{1:i})$, is known as the current *belief*. The belief at step $i-1$, is used to estimate the belief at step i recursively:

$$\overline{bel}(\mathbf{x_i}) = \int_{\mathbf{x}_{i-1}} p(\mathbf{x}_i|\mathbf{x}_{i-1})bel(\mathbf{x_{i-1}}) \quad (1)$$

$$bel(\mathbf{x_i}) \propto p(\mathbf{z}_i|\mathbf{x}_i)\overline{bel}(\mathbf{x_i}) \quad (2)$$

These equations first account for the evolution of the system's state between observations using a *transition model* prior, $p(\mathbf{x}_i|\mathbf{x}_{i-1})$; the updated state estimate $\overline{bel}(\mathbf{x}_i)$ is then re-weighted using an *observation model* $p(\mathbf{z}|\mathbf{x})$. We use $\propto$ in Equation (2) to indicate that the calculated belief is proportional to the true belief and thus normalization may be required after this step. The Bayes filter is thus a recursive application of Bayes' rule, *modulo* normalization. For readers who are familiar with particle filtering, we note that a particle filter is a special class of Bayes filter where the belief distributions are approximated through a collection of samples; in our Bayes filter, the belief distributions are calculated and maintained explicitly. Since we maintain a visibility filter and a velocity estimation filter for each tag, for a collection of m tags, we maintain $2m$ filters.

In the following sections, we describe the transition and update models for our filters for visibility and velocity estimation. First, however, we take a moment to describe the RFID protocol, which provides our system with its observations.

RFID Protocol

The Gen2 UHF RFID protocol [8] allows a single reader to inventory a collection of tags. These tags have no local power source, and communicate by harvesting energy from the reader's transmissions and using it to selectively change the RF reflectivity of their antennae. The reader measures these reflected emissions to receive information from the tags.

However, if multiple tags modulate their reflectivity at the same time, the reader cannot properly decode their transmissions. Thus, tag inventory proceeds in a series of rounds, where, in each round, the reader repeatedly allocates a number of response slots, and asks all tags that have not yet replied to reply in one of these slots. When a tag replies in a slot, the reader queries it for its EPC, and sends this number, along with ancillary data – in our case, a timestamp, the phase of the reflected carrier wave, and the channel frequency – to the host computer. Once no more tags reply, the reader starts a new round.

In practice, this means that the time between reads of RFID tags is randomly distributed, and depends on the total number of uncovered tags.

In turn, we now describe the how we formulate our tag cover and velocity filters as applications of the general Bayes filter as described above.

Tag Cover State

When a user action causes a tag to be covered (*e.g.,* by a foil-covered X or O in Tic-Tac-Toe), it is effectively invisible to the reader. Conductive (*e.g.* foil) or dielectric (*e.g.* hand) material very close to the tag will have this effect. Thus, the *lack* of a read can indicate a user action. The longer the reader fails to receive reads from a tag over time, the more probable it is that that tag is covered.

The state space for tag cover state is binary: $\mathbf{x}_i \in \{\text{visible}, \text{covered}\}$ – so the corresponding Bayes filter operates on a distribution represented by a single value $v_i \equiv \mathbb{P}(\mathbf{x_i} = \text{visible}|\mathbf{z_{1:i}})$. The observation space is continuous: $\mathbf{z}_i \in \mathbb{R}^+$, and is equal to the time that has elapsed since the previous read.

The transition function is straightforward – given the amount of time t since the last observation, the unobserved visibility distribution $\overline{v}_i = \overline{bel}(\mathbf{x_i})$ is computed from the previous visibility v_{i-1} by decaying toward a uniform distribution:

$$\overline{v}_i \leftarrow \frac{1}{2} + \frac{1}{2^{t/h}}\left(v_{i-1} - \frac{1}{2}\right) \quad (3)$$

where h sets the half-life of the decay. RapID's default value of h is 1 second. Developers may override this value if they know a better model for their application.

Unfortunately, the RFID protocol does not provide information about a "missed read." While the start-of-round signal might provide some evidence, it isn't exposed by common reader interfaces. Instead, we build our observation model on the elapsed time between subsequent reads. To estimate

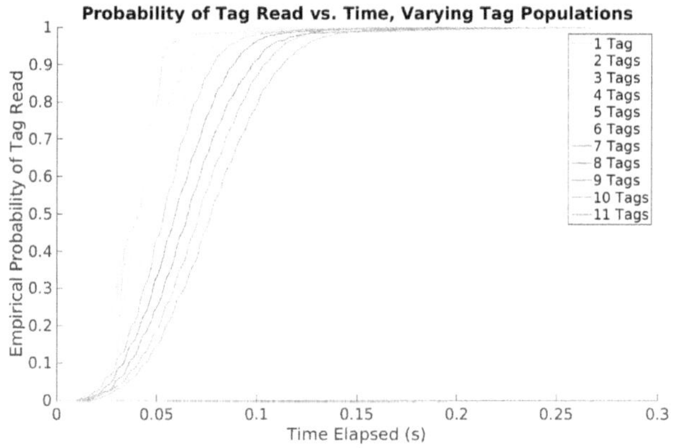

Figure 3. The probability a tag will have been read after a given amount of time, over various tag population sizes. On average, adding another tag adds approximately 5.13 **ms of latency, with a tag in a population of** 10 **being seen after** 140 **ms with 95% probability.**

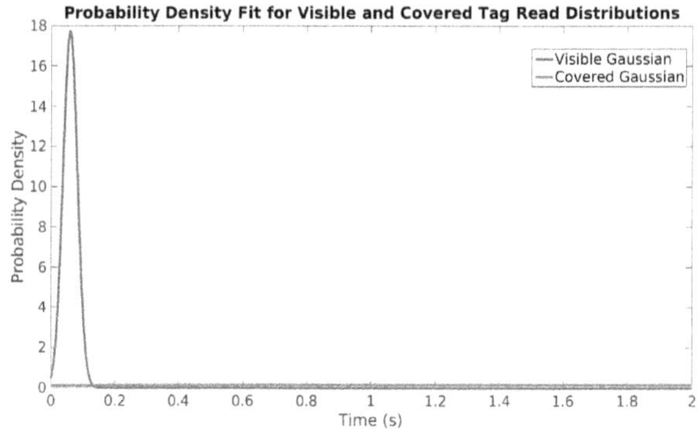

Figure 4. An example of the fit Gaussians to the covered and uncovered distributions for populations of 8 **tags. The variance on the covered distribution is so large that it appears nearly flat. The covered state becomes more probable after** 133 **ms without a read.**

the probability densities $p(\mathbf{z_i}|\text{visible})$ and $p(\mathbf{z_i}|\text{covered})$ from data, we conducted two sets of observations.

In the first, we recorded the time between reads for an uncovered tag with a varying total numbers of tags. The cumulative densities of these read times are shown in Figure 3. As expected, tag reads are randomly distributed, with larger population size correlated with more time between reads.

For the second set of observations we measured responses of covered tags. We used the same setup but covered one of the tags partially with aluminum foil. The read latency distributions of this covered tag – as one might expect – had large variance and mean (on the order of 2 s).

Our final observation model approximates these distributions as Gaussians, where the visible observation model depends on tag population size:

$$z_{\text{visible}} \sim \mathcal{N}^+(\mu_v(m), \sigma_v^2(m)) \quad (4)$$

$$z_{\text{covered}} \sim \mathcal{N}^+(\mu_c, \sigma_c^2) \quad (5)$$

$\mu_v(m)$ and $\sigma_v^2(m)$ correspond to the mean and variance respectively for the observed uncovered populations of size m; μ_c and σ_c^2 correspond to the mean and variance respectively for the covered observations. We found that in the uncovered case, both the mean and variance of the Gaussian had a strong linear correlation with the tag population size (R^2 with mean: 0.92, R^2 with standard deviation: 0.9072). Thus, our distribution for visible tags is parameteric in the tag population size, m. In the covered case, the mean and variance were mostly constant with respect to population size. We write $\mathcal{N}^+$ to indicate that RapID discards the negative portion of each Gaussian (negative read latencies don't make sense) and normalizes the remainder.

These Gaussians are well separated (Figure 4), making the observation very informative.

These transition and observation models serve to update the visibility belief for each tag whenever a new read is received.

However, the visibility distribution is also required between (potentially sporadic) reads in order to update interaction state. Between reads, RapID constantly maintains the state belief by applying the transtion model and then integrating over the observation model, in order to estimate the probability of having not read the tag for t seconds:

$$\mathbb{P}(\text{no read for } t = T \mid \text{visible}) \propto 1 - \int_0^T \mathcal{N}^+(\mu_v(m), \sigma_v^2(m))dt \quad (6)$$

$$\mathbb{P}(\text{no read for } t = T \mid \text{covered}) \propto 1 - \int_0^T \mathcal{N}^+(\mu_c, \sigma_c^2)dt \quad (7)$$

Finally, we note that the filters are initialized with a default $v_0 = 0.5$ for each tag.

Velocity

User interactions that involve motion of a tag can also easily be sensed in terms of velocity relative to the tag reader. In this case, the state space is continuous – $\mathbf{x}_i \in \mathbb{R}$ – so the corresponding Bayes filter operates on a continuous distribution (modeled as a Gaussian) $\mathbf{x_i}|\mathbf{z_{1:i}} \sim \mathcal{N}(\mu_{\mathcal{V}i}, \sigma_{\mathcal{V}i}^2)$. The observation space is continuous: $\mathbf{z}_i \in \mathbb{R}$, and in this case is dependent on the difference in RF phase angles between subsequent tag reads. RapID represents the tag velocity as a normal distribution, and updates the distribution's mean, $\mu_{\mathcal{V}i}$, and standard deviation, $\sigma_{\mathcal{V}i}$, at observation i as follows.

RapID models velocity as being influenced by a normally-distributed acceleration over time t. We let $\overline{\mu}_{\mathcal{V}i}, \overline{\sigma}_{\mathcal{V}i}^2$ represent the updated mean and variance of the velocity estimate after the transition update. The transition update at observation i is thus:

$$\overline{\mu}_{\mathcal{V}i} \leftarrow \mu_{\mathcal{V}i-1} \quad (8)$$

$$\overline{\sigma}_{\mathcal{V}i}^2 \leftarrow \sigma_{\mathcal{V}i-1}^2 + at \quad (9)$$

We set a to 1m/s, which works well in practice, though developers using RapID may override this selection if they have a better model for their application.

In UHF RFID, the phase of the carrier wave returning to the reader is proportional to the path length between the antenna and tag (modulo the wavelength of the signal) [22]. Thus, given two subsequent reads separated by t seconds and a tag velocity of $\mathscr{V}$, one would expect to observe a phase difference of

$$\Delta\phi = \frac{2t\mathscr{V}}{\lambda} + N \quad (10)$$

where wavelength $\lambda = \frac{c}{f}$ can be computed from the frequency of the carrier wave and the speed of light, with noise $N \sim \mathscr{N}(0, 0.01\pi^{-2})$ according to the manufacturer of our reader [12]. From this equation, one can immediately compute the observation model $p(\Delta\phi|\mathscr{V})$. This model works well as long as t is small; this is typically the case when the tag is uncovered, and it is not an unnatural constraint to require uncovered tags for motion-based interactions. Note that both the observation and transition models are Gaussian, and thus the velocity belief can be computed as a closed form Gaussian at each step.

The velocity distribution is updated whenever two consecutive reads of the same tag are performed on the same channel (that is, with a carrier wave of the same frequency). However, RFID readers are required by the FCC to change their carrier frequency every 400ms [4]. In practice, about 80% of reads are same-channel, which still provides plenty of data to keep the model updated.

UHF RFID employs carrier frequencies in the 900-930MHz range, giving it a wavelength of approximately 32 cm. However, the reader we are using can only determine phase ϕ up to a half-wavelength, so any object that moves more than 8cm between reads ($\approx$ 2m/s) runs the risk of having its velocity underestimated; of course, an object moving 2m/s will also quickly leave the working volume of the reader.

Finally, we note that the filters are initialized with a default $\mu_{\mathscr{V}0} = 0, \sigma_{\mathscr{V}0} = 1$ for each tag.

Interaction State Distributions

Since interactions in RapID have uncertain inputs, they may be in uncertain states. Given a developer-supplied deterministic state update rule, RapID uses sampling to approximate the distribution of possible interaction states, similar to [30].

Developers specify an interaction by providing a sampling budget q, a starting state r_0, and an update function $u(r,i,t) \to r'$ which, given a current interaction state r and a sample i drawn from the current *joint* tag state distribution distribution, along with an elapsed time t, produces an updated state sample. Note that this function does not need to reason about probability distributions or weights, as it takes as input only concrete samples, rather than distributions. A typical update function might do things like implement a finite-state controller for an interactor.

For every current interaction, RapID maintains a population of states R, which it updates every timestep in Monte Carlo fashion by applying u to q sampled inputs and states (Algorithm 1).

Algorithm 1 The update loop run for every interaction.

```
function UPDATELOOP(q, r_0, u)
    R_0 ← {r_0}
    k ← 0
    while InteractionIsRunning do
        t ← ElapsedTime()
        for i = 1 to q do
            r'_i ← u(SampleStates(R_k), SampleInput(I_k), t)
        end for
        R_{k+1} ← {r'_i}
        k ← k + 1
    end while
end function
```

A nice property of this method is that the solution is scalable: updates among samples can occur in embarrassingly parallel fashion. This means that although R_k is an approximation of the true distribution, q can be increased and the approximation thus improved simply by adding more CPU or GPU cores.

By default, interactions run indefinitely. However, developers may choose to specify a post-update function which is called after every update step. This function examines the current interaction state distribution and can, *e.g.*, dispatch events, update summary statistics, terminate the interaction, or even modify the sample population. One such post-update function that we have found convenient terminates the interaction and dispatches an event whenever an interaction state accounts for more than a (user-specified) proportion p of the total pool of states.

DEVELOPER API

Our Development API, which is implemented in C#, includes three developer-facing classes, **Application**, **Interaction**, and **InteractionState**. Though these classes may be extended for custom behavior, RapID already includes subclasses to support the interactors in its standard library. For example, with the game piece interactor, developers can use an off-the-shelf Interaction to track piece placement, and must only specify what happens when specific game pieces are placed. Figure 5 provides a visualization of how these classes are related in our API.

Application is a singleton class which handles interaction with the RFID reader hardware, including setting a tag mask to avoid reading tags that are currently irrelevant to the Interactions. It also runs tag state estimation and the Interaction update loop.

We have produced a version of RapID whose Application class includes additional functionality, including a general-purpose main loop and functions to visualize the superposition of interaction states; however, the demos shown in the video were all produced using a version of RapID whose Application class sits alongside user code, rather than subsuming it.

The **Interaction** class represents interaction processes which run in an Application. Each Interaction is responsible for

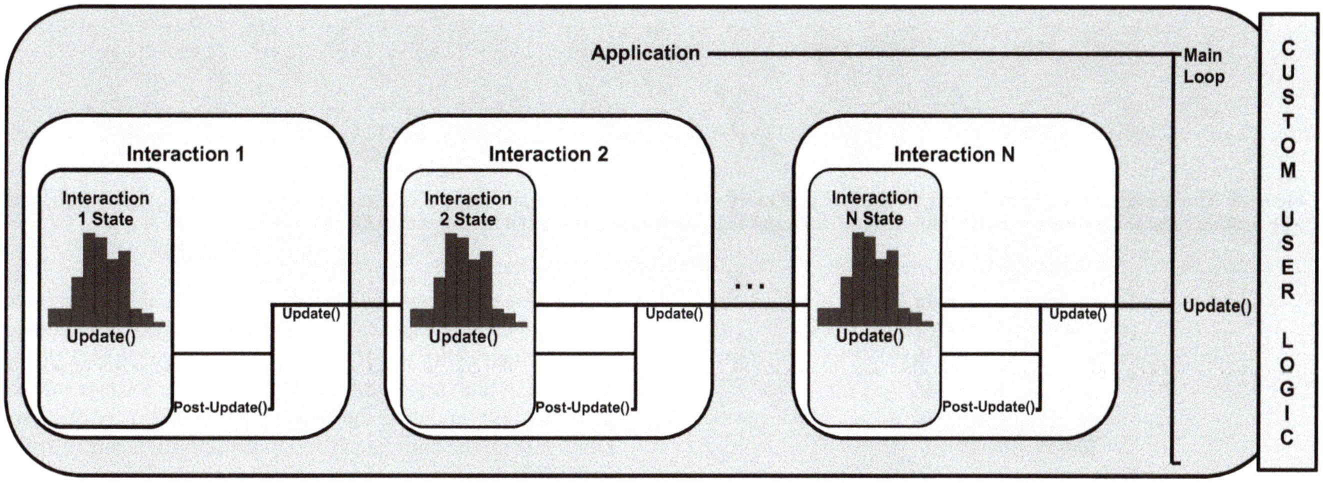

Figure 5. A visualization of our API. A main application contains a collection of Interactions, each with its own internal probabilistic InteractionState representation. The application iteratively updates each Interaction, which in turn update their InteractionStates. Additional user code discrete from inputs can live inside the Application but distinct from our RapID API.

maintaining and updating a distribution over possible InteractionStates and contains an overridable post-update function, as discussed in the previous section.

Finally, **InteractionState** wraps the state and update function for each interaction. Developers creating a new interaction will generally create a subclass of InteractionState and override its Update method.

STANDARD COMPONENT LIBRARY

While RFID tags can be embedded on any object, we provide an interface for designing new objects from scratch. Our interface is designed as a component library and extension for SketchUp [18], a commonly used CAD package aimed at novice designers, which can export designs to .obj and .dxf files for digital manufacturing.

The component library (Figure 6) contains several basic interactive elements, already marked up with special materials to indicate where to place foil and tags. The extension script assigns a unique EPC to every RFID tag placed in the model; creates a text label so that the developer will know what EPC to set on their RFID tags during construction; and saves a table mapping these EPCs to SketchUp object names, for use when referencing tags in the API.

RapID's standard library contains the following objects:

Bare Tags and Covers Tags and foil covers are the building blocks of any interaction, and tags can also be used on their own to sense motion or touch.

Game Pieces and Slots. Game pieces and slots have tags and covers placed so that when a piece is inserted into a slot, both the piece's tag and the slot's tag will be covered. Corresponding Interaction code identifies correlated (dis)appearances of tags to keep track of which pieces have been placed into which slots. Such objects are a useful building-block for defining most board games (our Tic-Tac-Toe application uses pieces for both the "x"'s and the "o"'s; they can also represent pawns in checkers or various chess pieces), or registration of figurines for applications such as Skylanders or Amiibo[1]. Pieces are keyed by trimming a corner to ensure that they are always placed in an orientation in which the respective tags and covers to touch.

Sliders. A slider is a row of tags with a sliding cover, allowing it to take on a range of states depending on which tags are covered. Sliders are especially useful for range-based inputs, and the slider can be fabricated at arbitrary lengths. The number of slider states is linear in its length. The standard Interaction for sliders estimates the slider state by looking for either a single covered tag or two adjacent covered tags. Our standard library provides sliders with and without rails to hold the cover in place (since "cover not present" can be a useful interaction signal).

Rotary Encoder. Our rotary encoder places n tags radially from its center, and uses a foil spinnable cover cut into an n-bit circular gray-code pattern. An encoder with n tags will have 2^n states. The state is estimated by sampling the cover state of each of the tags - each subset of covered tag states corresponds to a unique encoder state.

EXAMPLE APPLICATIONS

In order to test the RapID framework and component library, we created several applications which use tracked RFID tags. We encourage readers to view the accompanying video to see these applications in action.

Our testing environment (Figure 7) was a general-purpose office space. We placed an Alien ALR-9611-CR antenna under small wooden table (chosen because it is RF-transparent). Atop the table we placed a monitor for visual feedback, along with our custom RFID-tracked input devices. We connected the antenna to an Impinj Speedway Revolution R420 UHF RFID reader, which, in turn, was connected to the computer

[1] See `http://www.skylanderscharacters.com/figures.asp` and `http://www.nintendo.com/amiibo` respectively.

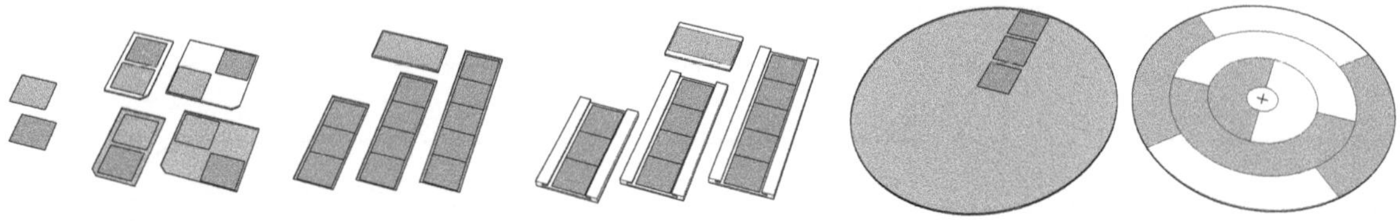

Figure 6. Our standard component library for SketchUp includes – from left to right – bare tags and covers, game pieces and slots, sliders without and with locking rails, and a rotary encoder. Blue material indicates tags, while orange material indicates metallic foil covers.

Figure 7. Our testing area consisted of an RFID antenna placed on the floor, a non-metallic table, and a monitor for visual feedback. The RFID reader and the computer running the application (both not shown) are placed to the side, and connected *via* ethernet.

running the application *via* ethernet. Latency of the ethernet connection, as reported by the 'ping' command, was less than 1 ms.

Our applications use our RapID C# API for input, and the Unity game engine for graphics and sound. All reported numbers are from application tests run on a Late 2013 MacBook Pro Retina, 15-inch, with a 2.6 GHz Intel Core i7 processor and 16 GB of RAM. In all cases RapID-related processing was a negligible part (< 10%) of the overall runtime of the application.

Each example application required fewer than 200 lines of code to be explicitly written by the developer, with the most complex (Pong) taking 188 lines (mostly concerned with complex ball physics), and the least complex (Spaceship) only requiring 73. Sampling budgets were never an isuse.

Figure 8. Our Tic-Tac-Toe application's X and O markers. From left to right: as designed in SketchUp; pending RFID and foil attachment; completed.

Tic-Tac-Toe

Our Tic-tac-toe application, Figure 1 and 8, provides visual and audio feedback about a game of Tic-tac-toe, prompting players to place game pieces into slots on a physical fabricated board, and congratulating them if they win.

Tic-tac-toe was designed by using our SketchUp components for the physical design, fabricated from laser-cut plywood, and programmed using RapID's default "game piece and slot" interaction, which maintains a list of piece/slot correspondences, incrementally updating the state when the majority of its samples agree on the correlated (dis)appearance of a pair of "piece" and "slot" tags.

The finished example has the most tags (18) of any example, but at 530 reads per second, each tag state is still updated at approximately 29Hz.

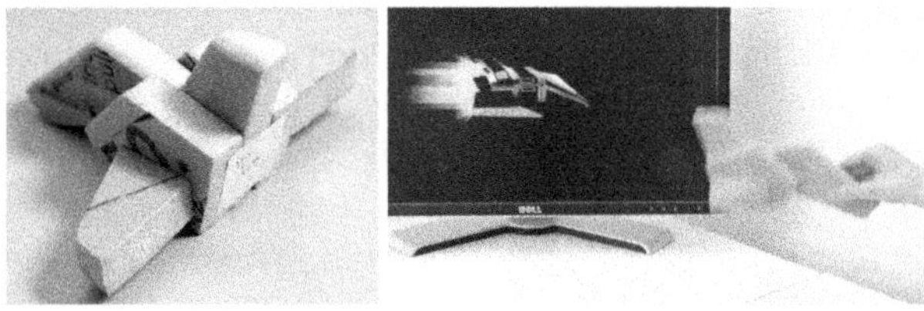

Figure 9. In our spaceship application, a single tag is used to track the motion of a spaceship model. This motion is used to animate an on-screen ship.

Spaceship

Our spaceship application (Figure 9) demonstrates how single-tag motion tracking can add interactivity to an otherwise inert object. When the user shakes the spaceship prop on the table, the spaceship on the screen accelerates.

This application animates the on-screen ship using the value reported by our our default "speed" interaction, which computes the average magnitude of its state's samples of a tag's velocity. This application also serves to test the upper bound on single-tag update speed – 146 reads per second, of which approximately 140 were same-channel reads suitable for velocity updates.

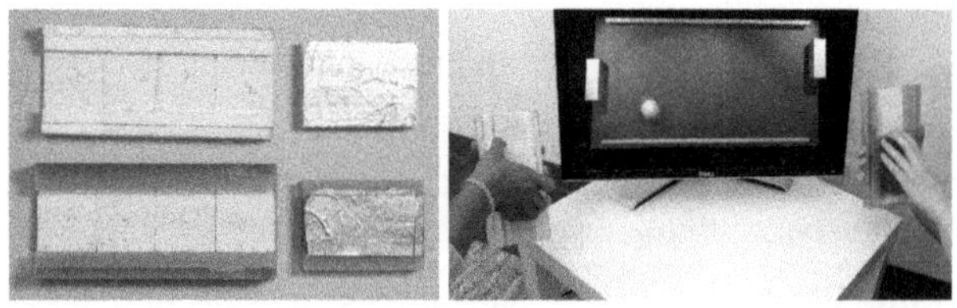

Figure 10. In our pong-like application, two slider components fabricated using different technologies are used to control the paddles in the game.

Pong

Our pong application (Figure 10) uses two slider components from the component library to control a pong-like game.

Such a game requires responsive (low-latency) controls to be playable.

The sliders are basic parts, included in our SketchUp component library. We chose to use a different fabrication process for each slider to show that RapID is material-agnostic. One slider was printed on an Object Connex 260 3D printer using Vero Clear material, while the other was made from laser-cut acrylic, stacked and glued. Both perform well, providing no noticable advantage in play to one side or the other.

Each slider is read using RapID's default "slider" interaction. This interaction's states each estimate the slider position based on which tags they see as covered in their sample of the tag distributions, and a post-update function combines these estimates with a weighted average.

During our tests, RapID processed about 415 reads per second – that is, it was able to update each of the eight tags at approximately 50Hz.

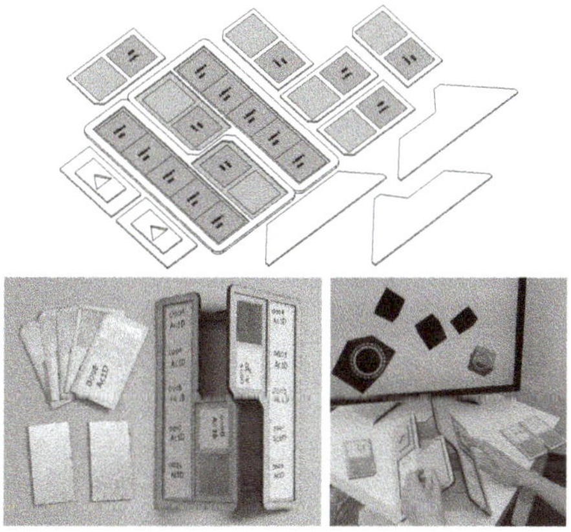

Figure 11. Our audio controller application uses several RapID components and associated interactions to enable an interactive music-mixing experience.

Audio Controller

Another application example is an audio controller (Figure 11). Users of the controller place pieces associated with music loops into two slots to activate them, and move sliders to change the volume of the respective currently active loops. This audio controller shows how a device can be quickly composed using different components and interactions from RapID's library, and shows how multiple interactions (two slider interactions and a piece/slot interaction) can be combined to build a more sophisticated experience.

The completed device contains 17 tags, and – in our tests – produces about 490 reads per second, resulting in an approximately 28 Hz per-tag update rate.

Quiz Game

In our quiz game application (Figure 12), players are asked a multiple choice trivia question; players then select their answer by launching a puff of air from a vortex cannon at one of three flags. The quiz game example demonstrates how RFID tracking can be used to build large interactive experiences (the read range of the tags we are using is several meters), and shows how custom interactions can be useful.

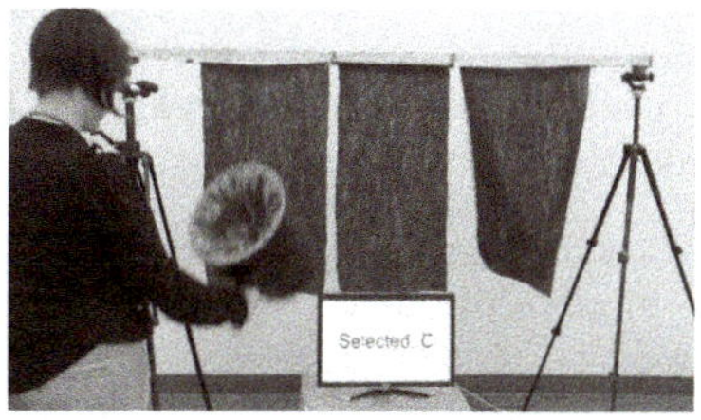

Figure 12. In this quiz game, the player answers each question by shooting a puff of air at one of three curtains using a vortex cannon toy. A custom RapID interaction reads the velocities of tags attached to the bottom of each curtain to decide which (if any) has been hit.

For this example, an interaction was written that compares the average speeds of tags attached to the three flags, terminating with a confirmed selection whenever one tag's speed is significantly higher than the others with high probability.

Discussion

As we have demonstrated, off-the-shelf RFID tags and readers can support reasonably low-latency wireless interactivity. However, our system is not without limitations. Velocity can only be detected for motion toward or away from the antenna, so extra antennas would be needed to extract full 3D motion. Another limitation is that tags cannot be placed directly on dielectric surfaces, meaning that intermediate surfaces must be put in between the tags and any dielectric surfaces.

Since the average time between tag reads scales linearly with the number of tags in view, there is a limit on the number of tags that can be added before the responsiveness for touch events begins to suffer. Similarly, because only a limited number number of tag reads happens within a single channel, and two reads of the same tag must happen within the same channel in order to extract motion features, with enough tags tracking quick motion accurately becomes infeasible. This wasn't an issue in any of our demonstrations (up to 20 tags), but with enough tags we expect it to become one.

The UHF RFID Gen2 protocol includes support for the selection of subsets of tags using tag masking. This should allow for responsive interactions with large populations of tags, as long as only a small subset needed to be read at once, such as only the X's and board tags or only the O's and board tags in Tic-Tac-Toe. While we did test dynamically changing the tag mask, we did not include it in any of our examples because we found changing the mask to be an expensive operation for our reader (with delays up to 150 ms), and this added overhead was not worth the increased tag responsiveness in any of our applications.

While classification with RapID is roughly ten times faster than the prior state of the art, IDSense [16], the methods cannot be compared directly. IDSense relies on a discriminative model for activity recognition whereas RapID employs a generative model. Thus, IDSense waits and collects sufficient information about a tag before giving a definitive answer about its state; while RapID immediately responds but only converges over time to the correct label. In practice, RapID converges to the correct cover/uncover labels with high probability and high accuracy within 200ms, ten times faster than the flat 2s required for IDSense's method. A more rigorous probabilistic evaluation and benchmarking of RapID's methods may be desired in the future.

Hardware or reader firmware modifications could further lower latency and improve the range of possible interactions. For example, modified reader firmware that was more careful about frequency hopping would allow more tags to be simultaneously tracked for speed; while firmware that could poll different tags at different frequencies would allow for more flexible interface designs. In addition, it might be possible to create custom RFID tags specifically for interaction, e.g., by having them perform some sort of low-power sensing locally, rather than just reporting an ID. It might also be possible to create tags which can be placed on more kinds of material surfaces. Finally, the RFID protocol itself wasn't designed for interactive applications; it could be revised to better support the sorts of sensing we have described. In the future, it would also be valuable to explore processes that can embed the tags into objects during digital fabrication.

CONCLUSION

We demonstrated how a designer can use RFID tags to add inexpensive, wireless, low-footprint, batteryless, low-latency input sensing to objects. The key to our approach was a probabilistic formulation which enabled low-level uncertainty to be handled in a high-level fashion. This, coupled with an API for managing probabilistic interactions and a simple design interface embedded in SketchUp makes RapID both an easy to use and flexible design and development platform. By making it easy to add RFID-based sensing to objects, RapID enables the design of new, custom interactive objects with a very fast development cycle.

Acknowledgments

We thank Moshe Mahler, Sahana Vijai, and Kyna McIntosh for our demos' digital assets. We thank Hanchuan Li for providing starter code for interfacing with the RFID Reader. We thank Lea Albaugh, Eric Brockmeyer, and Alex Alspach for their advice and assistance in the fabrication of widgets.

REFERENCES

1. Xiaojun Bi and Shumin Zhai. 2013. Bayesian touch: a statistical criterion of target selection with finger touch. In *The 26th Annual ACM Symposium on User Interface Software and Technology, UIST'13, St. Andrews, United Kingdom, October 8-11, 2013*. 51–60. DOI: http://dx.doi.org/10.1145/2501988.2502058

2. Michael Buettner, Richa Prasad, Matthai Philipose, and David Wetherall. 2009. Recognizing daily activities with RFID-based sensors. In *UbiComp 2009: Ubiquitous Computing, 11th International Conference, UbiComp 2009, Orlando, Florida, USA, September 30 - October 3, 2009, Proceedings*. 51–60. DOI: http://dx.doi.org/10.1145/1620545.1620553

3. Stuart K Card, Allen Newell, and Thomas P Moran. 1983. *The psychology of human-computer interaction*. L. Erlbaum Associates Inc.

4. Federal Communication Commission (FCC). 2011. Title 47: Telecommunication, Part 15 Radio Frequency Devices. www.fcc.gov. (January, 31 2011). http://www.fcc.gov/

5. Kenneth P. Fishkin, Bing Jiang, Matthai Philipose, and Sumit Roy. 2004. I Sense a Disturbance in the Force: Unobtrusive Detection of Interactions with RFID-tagged Objects. In *UbiComp 2004: Ubiquitous Computing: 6th International Conference, Nottingham, UK, September 7-10, 2004. Proceedings*. 268–282. DOI: http://dx.doi.org/10.1007/978-3-540-30119-6_16

6. Saul Greenberg and Chester Fitchett. 2001. Phidgets: easy development of physical interfaces through physical widgets. In *Proceedings of the 14th Annual ACM Symposium on User Interface Software and Technology, UIST 2001, Disney's BoardWalk Inn Resort, Walt Disney World, Orlando, Florida, USA, November 11-14, 2001*. 209–218. DOI: http://dx.doi.org/10.1145/502348.502388

7. Tobias Alexander Große-Puppendahl, Yannick Berghoefer, Andreas Braun, Raphael Wimmer, and Arjan Kuijper. 2013. OpenCapSense: A rapid prototyping toolkit for pervasive interaction using capacitive sensing. In *2013 IEEE International Conference on Pervasive Computing and Communications, PerCom 2013, San Diego, CA, USA, March 18-22, 2013*. 152–159. DOI: http://dx.doi.org/10.1109/PerCom.2013.6526726

8. GS1. 2004. EPC Radio-Frequency Identity Protocols Generation-2 UHF RFID. (2004). http://www.gs1.org/sites/default/files/docs/epc/Gen2_Protocol_Standard.pdf.

9. Björn Hartmann, Scott R. Klemmer, Michael S. Bernstein, Leith Abdulla, Brandon Burr, Avi Robinson-Mosher, and Jennifer Gee. 2006. Reflective physical prototyping through integrated design, test, and analysis. In *Proceedings of the 19th Annual ACM Symposium on User Interface Software and Technology, Montreux, Switzerland, October 15-18, 2006*. 299–308. DOI: http://dx.doi.org/10.1145/1166253.1166300

10. Scott E. Hudson and Jennifer Mankoff. 2006. Rapid construction of functioning physical interfaces from cardboard, thumbtacks, tin foil and masking tape. In *Proceedings of the 19th Annual ACM Symposium on User Interface Software and Technology, Montreux, Switzerland, October 15-18, 2006*. 289–298. DOI: http://dx.doi.org/10.1145/1166253.1166299

11. Scott E. Hudson and Gary L. Newell. 1992. Probabilistic State Machines: Dialog Management for Inputs with Uncertainty. In *Proceedings of the Fifth ACM Symposium on User Interface Software and Technology, UIST 1992, Monteray, CA, USA, November 15-18, 1992*. 199–208. DOI: http://dx.doi.org/10.1145/142621.142650

12. Impinj. 2013. Low Level User Data Support. Application Note. (2013). https://support.impinj.com/hc/en-us/articles/202755318-Application-Note-Low-Level-User-Data-Support.

13. Impinj, Inc. 2011. *Impinj Speedway Revolution R220* (www.impinj.com ed.). Impinj, Inc., 701 N. 34th Street, Suite 300 Seattle, WA 98103.

14. Gierad Laput, Eric Brockmeyer, Scott E. Hudson, and Chris Harrison. 2015. Acoustruments: Passive, Acoustically-Driven, Interactive Controls for Handheld Devices. In *Proceedings of the 33rd Annual ACM Conference on Human Factors in Computing Systems, CHI 2015, Seoul, Republic of Korea, April 18-23, 2015.* 2161–2170. DOI: http://dx.doi.org/10.1145/2702123.2702414

15. Johnny C. Lee, Daniel Avrahami, Scott E. Hudson, Jodi Forlizzi, Paul H. Dietz, and Darren Leigh. 2004. The calder toolkit: wired and wireless components for rapidly prototyping interactive devices. In *Proceedings of the Conference on Designing Interactive Systems: Processes, Practices, Methods, and Techniques, Cambridge, MA, USA, August 1-4, 2004.* 167–175. DOI: http://dx.doi.org/10.1145/1013115.1013139

16. Hanchuan Li, Can Ye, and Alanson P. Sample. 2015. IDSense: A Human Object Interaction Detection System Based on Passive UHF RFID. In *Proceedings of the 33rd Annual ACM Conference on Human Factors in Computing Systems, CHI 2015, Seoul, Republic of Korea, April 18-23, 2015.* 2555–2564. DOI: http://dx.doi.org/10.1145/2702123.2702178

17. RFID Journal LLC. 2015. How much does an RFID tag cost today? (sep 2015). http://www.rfidjournal.com/faq/show?85

18. Trimble Navigation Ltd. 2000–2015. Sketchup. http://www.sketchup.com/. (2000–2015).

19. Jennifer Mankoff, Scott E. Hudson, and Gregory D. Abowd. 2000a. Interaction techniques for ambiguity resolution in recognition-based interfaces. In *Proceedings of the 13th Annual ACM Symposium on User Interface Software and Technology, UIST 2000, San Diego, California, USA, November 6-8, 2000.* 11–20. DOI: http://dx.doi.org/10.1145/354401.354407

20. Jennifer Mankoff, Scott E. Hudson, and Gregory D. Abowd. 2000b. Providing integrated toolkit-level support for ambiguity in recognition-based interfaces. In *Proceedings of the CHI 2000 Conference on Human factors in computing systems, The Hague, The Netherlands, April 1-6, 2000.* 368–375. DOI: http://dx.doi.org/10.1145/332040.332459

21. David Mellis, Sam Jacoby, Leah Buechley, Hannah Perner-Wilson, and Jie Qi. 2013. Microcontrollers as material: crafting circuits with paper, conductive ink, electronic components, and an "untoolkit". In *Seventh International Conference on Tangible, Embedded, and Embodied Interaction, TEI'13, Barcelona, Spain, February 10-13, 2013.* 83–90. DOI: http://dx.doi.org/10.1145/2460625.2460638

22. P.V. Nikitin, R. Martinez, S. Ramamurthy, H. Leland, G. Spiess, and K.V.S. Rao. 2010. Phase based spatial identification of UHF RFID tags. In *2010 IEEE International Conference on RFID.* 102–109. DOI: http://dx.doi.org/10.1109/RFID.2010.5467253

23. Sharon L. Oviatt. 1999. Mutual Disambiguation of Recognition Errors in a Multimodel Architecture. In *Proceeding of the CHI '99 Conference on Human Factors in Computing Systems: The CHI is the Limit, Pittsburgh, PA, USA, May 15-20, 1999.* 576–583. DOI: http://dx.doi.org/10.1145/302979.303163

24. Siddika Parlak and Ivan Marsic. 2013. Detecting object motion using passive RFID: A trauma resuscitation case study. *Instrumentation and Measurement, IEEE Transactions on* 62, 9 (2013), 2430–2437.

25. Matthai Philipose. 2005. Large-Scale human activity recognition using ultra-dense sensing. *The Bridge, National Academy of Engineering* 35, 4 (2005).

26. Raf Ramakers, Kashyap Todi, and Kris Luyten. 2015. PaperPulse: An Integrated Approach for Embedding Electronics in Paper Designs. In *Proceedings of the 33rd Annual ACM Conference on Human Factors in Computing Systems, CHI 2015, Seoul, Republic of Korea, April 18-23, 2015.* 2457–2466. DOI: http://dx.doi.org/10.1145/2702123.2702487

27. Valkyrie Savage, Colin Chang, and Björn Hartmann. 2013. Sauron: embedded single-camera sensing of printed physical user interfaces. In *The 26th Annual ACM Symposium on User Interface Software and Technology, UIST'13, St. Andrews, United Kingdom, October 8-11, 2013.* 447–456. DOI: http://dx.doi.org/10.1145/2501988.2501992

28. Valkyrie Savage, Andrew Head, Björn Hartmann, Dan B. Goldman, Gautham J. Mysore, and Wilmot Li. 2015. Lamello: Passive Acoustic Sensing for Tangible Input Components. In *Proceedings of the 33rd Annual ACM Conference on Human Factors in Computing Systems, CHI 2015, Seoul, Republic of Korea, April 18-23, 2015.* 1277–1280. DOI: http://dx.doi.org/10.1145/2702123.2702207

29. Valkyrie Savage, Xiaohan Zhang, and Björn Hartmann. 2012. Midas: fabricating custom capacitive touch sensors to prototype interactive objects. In *The 25th Annual ACM Symposium on User Interface Software and Technology, UIST '12, Cambridge, MA, USA, October 7-10, 2012.* 579–588. DOI: http://dx.doi.org/10.1145/2380116.2380189

30. Julia Schwarz, Jennifer Mankoff, and Scott E. Hudson. 2011. Monte carlo methods for managing interactive state, action and feedback under uncertainty. In *Proceedings of the 24th Annual ACM Symposium on User Interface Software and Technology, Santa Barbara, CA, USA, October 16-19, 2011.* 235–244. DOI: http://dx.doi.org/10.1145/2047196.2047227

31. Julia Schwarz, Jennifer Mankoff, and Scott E. Hudson. 2015. An Architecture for Generating Interactive Feedback in Probabilistic User Interfaces. In *Proceedings of the 33rd Annual ACM Conference on Human Factors in Computing Systems, CHI 2015, Seoul, Republic of Korea, April 18-23, 2015*. 2545–2554. DOI: http://dx.doi.org/10.1145/2702123.2702228

32. ThingMagic, A Division of Trimble 2015. *M6E-NANO: Embedded UHF RFID Module* (www.thingmagic.com ed.). ThingMagic, A Division of Trimble, One Merrill Street Woburn, MA 01801.

33. Sebastian Thrun, Wolfram Burgard, and Dieter Fox. 2005. *Probabilistic Robotics (Intelligent Robotics and Autonomous Agents)*. The MIT Press.

34. Alexander Wiethoff, Hanna Schneider, Julia Küfner, Michael Rohs, Andreas Butz, and Saul Greenberg. 2013. Paperbox: a toolkit for exploring tangible interaction on interactive surfaces. In *Creativity and Cognition 2013, C&C '13, Sydney, NSW, Australia, June 17-20, 2013*. 64–73. DOI: http://dx.doi.org/10.1145/2466627.2466635

35. John Williamson. 2006. *Continuous uncertain interaction*. Ph.D. Dissertation. University of Glasgow.

36. Robert Xiao, Chris Harrison, and Scott E. Hudson. 2013. WorldKit: rapid and easy creation of ad-hoc interactive applications on everyday surfaces. In *2013 ACM SIGCHI Conference on Human Factors in Computing Systems, CHI '13, Paris, France, April 27 - May 2, 2013*. 879–888. DOI: http://dx.doi.org/10.1145/2470654.2466113

Snap-To-It: A User-Inspired Platform for Opportunistic Device Interactions

Adrian A. de Freitas[1], Michael Nebeling[1], Xiang 'Anthony' Chen[1], Junrui Yang[2], Akshaye Shreenithi Kirupa Karthikeyan Ranithangam[3], Anind K. Dey[1]
[1] Human-Computer Interaction Institute, Carnegie Mellon University, Pittsburgh, PA, USA
[2] Peking University, Beijing, China [3] Coimbatore Institute of Technology, Tamil Nadu, India
(adefreit, mnebelin, xiangche, anind)@cs.cmu.edu, (jackieyang51, akshaya.kar)@gmail.com

ABSTRACT
The ability to quickly interact with any nearby appliance from a mobile device would allow people to perform a wide range of one-time tasks (*e.g.,* printing a document in an unfamiliar office location). However, users currently lack this capability, and must instead manually configure their devices for each appliance they want to use. To address this problem, we created Snap-To-It, a system that allows users to opportunistically interact with any appliance simply by taking a picture of it. Snap-To-It shares the image of the appliance a user wants to interact with over a local area network. Appliances then analyze this image (along with the user's location and device orientation) to see if they are being "selected," and deliver the corresponding control interface to the user's mobile device. Snap-To-It's design was informed by two technology probes that explored how users would like to select and interact with appliances using their mobile phone. These studies highlighted the need to be able to select hardware *and* software *via* a camera, and identified several novel use cases not supported by existing systems (*e.g.,* interacting with disconnected objects, transferring settings between appliances). In this paper, we show how Snap-To-It's design is informed by our probes and how developers can utilize our system. We then show that Snap-To-It can identify appliances with over 95.3% accuracy, and demonstrate through a two-month deployment that our approach is robust to gradual changes to the environment.

ACM Classification Keywords
H.5.2 Information Interfaces and Presentation (e.g. HCI): User Interfaces: Input Devices and Strategies, Interaction Styles

Author Keywords
Internet of things, mobile interaction

INTRODUCTION
The rapid proliferation of "smart" appliances (*e.g.,* printers, speakers) has created new opportunities for users to interact and engage with technology in meaningful ways. Taking advantage of this connectivity, however, is a well-known problem [7, 19, 23, 25, 31]. For example, if users want to use a networked printer, they have to know its IP address and install the correct drivers. Similarly, if a user wants to play music on a Bluetooth speaker, they must set the appliance to be discoverable, and then find and pair with it. While this level of effort is acceptable for appliances used frequently, it makes one-time or spontaneous use impractical. This discourages users from interacting with new or unfamiliar appliances, and can even force them to seek alternative solutions (*e.g.,* asking a friend or stranger to print a document on their behalf).

CHI'16, May 07–12, 2016, San Jose, CA, USA
©2016 ACM. ISBN 978-1-4503-3362-7/16/05...$15.00
DOI: http://dx.doi.org/10.1145/2858036.2858177

Figure 1. A user takes a photo of the appliance they want to control (left). Our system shares this image (along with the user's location and device orientation) with nearby appliances. The user's device connects to the appliance that best matches the image, and receives a custom UI (right).

Our goal is to empower users with the ability to quickly and easily connect and interact with ubiquitously distributed appliances in *any* environment. To achieve this, we have developed Snap-To-It, a software system that transforms a mobile phone into a universal interaction tool. Inspired by how people already use their smartphones, Snap-To-It lets users select a nearby appliance by "snapping" a photo of it. The Snap-To-It app then transmits this image (along with the user's location and device orientation) across a local area network so that appliances and/or software proxies can analyze it. If a photo matches an appliance, the app connects to it and renders a custom interface (Figure 1). Otherwise, the user receives a list of the most likely candidates and is asked to select from them.

Prior research has explored several solutions for users to control appliances from their mobile device [8, 27, 34, 30, 35]; Snap-to-It expands on this work in three important ways.

First, our work broadens our understanding of the types of opportunistic interactions users would like to perform using a mobile device. Prior to developing Snap-To-It, we conducted two probes to learn 1) how users would like to select an appliance in an unfamiliar environment, and 2) how they would like to interact with that appliance using their mobile phone. These probes revealed that participants preferred selecting appliances by taking a photograph (as opposed to scanning QR codes or selecting them from a list), and identified six categories of general use cases, respectively. Snap-To-It's design is directly informed by these findings, providing a research platform that not only shows what types of interactions are *possible* using a mobile device, but that are actually *desired* by end users.

Secondly, Snap-To-It provides a truly opportunistic way of interacting with a wide range of appliances. Rather than require the user to download a list of nearby appliances [19] or connect to a well-known server [10], our system uses multicasting to identify an appliance based on its photo. This makes it particularly useful when users are visiting a location for the first time, and need to use an appliance once or spontaneously. Additionally, while prior work has shown that mobile devices can be used to select and interact with hardware [29, 33] and software [11], they have focused on one *or* the other. In contrast, Snap-To-It compares user-taken photographs against stock images and real-time screenshots. This lets it support both types of appliances using a single interaction technique. Finally, since Snap-To-It works with any photograph, our system can even be used to make non-computational objects (*e.g.,* signs, maps) selectable. This increases the range of appliances, applications, and information that users can interact with without requiring each one to have an embedded computer.

Third, Snap-To-It provides a developer-friendly way to allow appliances to be selectable *via* camera. Our system's middleware automatically processes incoming photos, establishes connections with user devices, and delivers arbitrary HTML/JavaScript-based user interfaces. This allows developers to incorporate Snap-To-It's functionality into appliances without having to implement their own photo recognition. Additionally, our middleware can act as a software wrapper for existing appliances and applications. This greatly expands the range of appliances that can utilize our system without forcing users or site administrators to purchase additional hardware.

In the following section, we describe our probes, and show how user responses have influenced Snap-To-It's design. Afterwards, we describe Snap-To-It's architecture, and present four prototypes that highlight its capabilities. Through three studies, we show that Snap-To-It is sufficiently accurate to be deployed in real-world environments. Finally, we address issues such as usability, responsiveness, and hardware requirements, and close with a discussion of related and future work.

TECHNOLOGY PROBES AND DERIVED REQUIREMENTS

With Snap-To-It, we aim to let users quickly select and interact with any object in their physical environment. Yet while prior work has shown that this two-step interaction model supports many use cases, they focus on the challenges associated with connecting to devices and receiving and/or rendering custom interfaces [19, 27]. Consequently, we lack general knowledge of 1) how users would *like* to select appliances using their mobile devices, and 2) the specific types of interactions they would like to perform, both of which are crucial for building a usable and effective system.

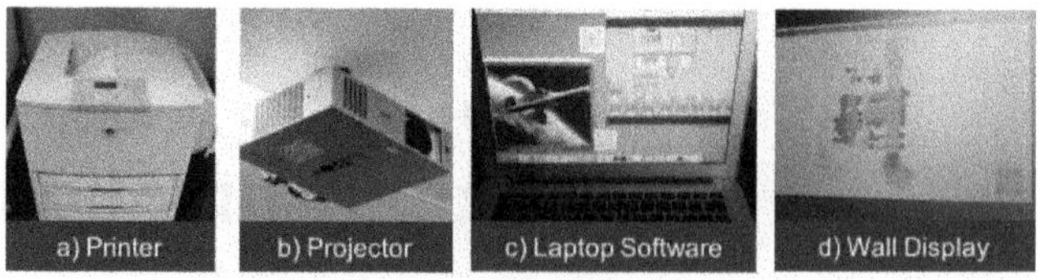

Figure 2. Appliances used in our first probe.

To fill these gaps, we conducted two technology probes that examine the process of selecting and using appliances in detail. In this section, we describe both probes and show how their findings have informed Snap-To-It's design.

Probe 1: Selecting an Appliance from the Environment

Our first probe was targeted towards learning how users would like to select an appliance using their mobile device. To investigate this, we asked 10 participants (6 male, 4 female; 22-42 years old; mix of novices and experts with mobile phones and QR codes) to try out a variety of techniques and provide feedback. Prior to the study, we gave participants a list of 7 techniques that could be implemented on existing smartphones: taking a photograph, scanning a QR code (on and off the device), near-field communication, "bumping" the phone against the appliance, text search, and selecting the appliance from a list. We then had participants rank order each technique for a variety of appliances (Figure 2), and evaluated the three techniques that were both rated the highest and compatible with the widest range of appliances: taking a picture, scanning a QR code, and selecting from a list.

The probe was conducted in our institution's common area. We selected a mix of hardware/software (Figure 2) that visitors might want to interact with using their phones. Prior to the study, we placed QR codes on each appliance and/or application using best practices for the size and positioning established in [5], and created a list of every appliance within 30 feet of the room (*i.e.,* Bluetooth range). We then gave participants an app that lets them take a photo, scan a QR code (using a common QR code reader app [4]), and select an appliance from an alphabetized list. Participants spent 30 minutes trying each technique in random order from both touching distance and 5-10 feet away, and were compensated with $15 USD.

Feedback on the list-based technique was overwhelmingly negative. Despite being conceptually simple, participants had difficulty identifying a specific appliance from a list of names. While this problem might be overcome by choosing names other than the ones assigned by our network administrators (*e.g.,* "Zircon", "Pewter"), prior research suggests that no naming convention works well with every user [12]. Even though the list only had 11 items, participants reported that they were "scrolling and scrolling and scrolling" (P1). This led them to unanimously rate the list technique as the worst.

Feedback on the QR code technique was also negative. While participants could see the codes on each appliance, eight of them had trouble getting the phone to successfully scan one or more of them. The digital projector (Figure 2b) was especially problematic since it was located above a conference table; this forced users to scan its code from an angle. While placing multiple codes on each appliance (*e.g.,* one on each side) might help, participants also noted that they disliked having QR codes appear on a screen, especially when multiple codes are needed to differentiate between different applications (Figure 2c). Consequently, while participants felt that QR codes were better than lists, only one rated it as the best technique.

In contrast to the list and QR code methods, feedback on the camera technique was almost universally positive. Participants called the technique "fun" (P3, P4, P7), and noted that it was easy to understand: "I can hand it to my 4-year old, and he'll understand" (P1). Others noted that the time to take a photograph felt shorter than the time needed to scan the QR code, as they did not have to continually hold their phones up to the code for it to be recognized. In fairness, several participants did state that the difference between QR codes and the camera was negligible when the appliance being selected is physically close. However, for software applications and objects farther away, participants agreed that the photo-based selection method offered a better overall experience.

Collectively, these findings illustrate the value of photo-based selection. While our participants were eventually able to interact with every appliance using all three techniques, 9 out of 10 stated that they *preferred* selecting appliances by taking a photo. This motivated us to develop a system that could make camera-based selection a reality.

Probe 2: Types of Interactions

For our second probe, we wanted to know how users would like to interact with appliances once they have been selected. To investigate this, we asked 28 participants (14 male, 14 female; 19-60 years old; mix of novice and experts) to create a "wish list" of interactions that they would like to perform. For this probe, we developed an Android app that let users take photos of appliances and annotate how they would use them. We then asked them to use the app for a week as they went about their normal routine, and compensated them with $20.

Through this process, we collected a total of 195 photographs. Each photo was categorized according to 1) the interaction being performed, and 2) the technologies needed to support them. This information was then directly used to identify general use cases and derive critical technical requirements. Although the number of photos submitted by participants varied, our analysis found that each identified roughly the same number of general use cases (avg=2.1, SD=1.1), making sure that the findings were not overly influenced by any one participant.

Use Case Categories

Participants had a wide range of ideas as to how they wanted to interact with appliances using their mobile phone. In all, we identified six general use case categories (Figure 3).

Nineteen participants (68%) wanted to use their mobile phones to quickly interact with new or unfamiliar appliances (Figure 3, Column 1). The majority took photographs of office appliances such as printers, projectors, and multimedia controls. Others took photos of specialized equipment such as laser cutters and 3D printers. In each case, users wanted to use the appliance without installing software/drivers.

Another popular use case was to control appliances from afar (Column 2). Twenty participants (71%) took pictures of household/office appliances, vehicles and industrial equipment, and stated that they wanted to be able to control these devices from anywhere. In some cases, it was purely for added convenience (*e.g.,* "[I want to] turn off the lights when I'm in bed"). Others viewed their phone as a more hygienic way to interact with public objects (*e.g.,* lights, toilet handles) without having to physically touch them. Finally, several participants noted that being able to activate controls from a distance would be particularly helpful to disabled individuals. We found this to be an unexpected, but interesting use case that we wanted to support.

While we anticipated that participants would want to use their smartphones as a remote control, participants also identified several other ways to interact with appliances. Eight participants (29%) wanted to use their mobile device as a way to upload and download content (Column 3). Several users took pictures of public displays and televisions, and stated that they wanted to be able to send or receive content (*e.g., push* a PowerPoint presentation, *pull* a closed-caption feed). Interestingly, the idea of pushing/pulling content was not limited to computer devices. Several participants took photos of *disconnected objects* such as campus maps and public museum displays, and stated that they wanted to extract the information represented by the object using their phone (*e.g.,* converting a picture of a map into a digital version). In these cases, participants viewed these objects as "physical hyperlinks", and were interested in being able to use their mobile phone as a way to access an object's digital representation.

Seven participants (25%) wanted to use their phone to perform secure transactions (Column 4). Several of them took pictures of locked doors and computers, and noted how it would save them time and effort if they could authenticate to these devices while approaching them. Others took photographs of payment systems (*e.g.,* vending machines), and noted that it would be convenient if they could make purchases electronically.

A fifth use case identified by four participants (14%) was to learn more about a particular appliance (Column 5). One participant photographed a light switch, and wrote: "I am not so sure what these buttons control." Others took pictures of fire alarms, defibrillators, and household appliances, and asked for 1) what the appliance does, and 2) how to use it.

Finally, two participants (7%) wanted to use camera-based selection to easily transfer settings and preferences between appliances (Column 6). One participant took a photo of a treadmill, and said that he wanted to easily carry over his exercise preferences (*e.g.,* speed, incline) to another machine during his next workout session. The other took a photograph of a public television, and stated that he wanted to quickly find and tune to his favorite channels without having to search for them. In both cases, users wanted their phone to remember their past interactions. This would allow them to seamlessly transfer these preferences to new appliances.

Collectively, these responses highlight the need for a system like Snap-To-It. While only 18% of our participants stated that they use more than three devices daily, our probe reveals that

Use Case Category	Quick Control	Long Distance Operation	Transfer Content	Secure Transactions	Increase Intelligibility	Share Preferences
Motivation	*Connect and use a nearby device.*	*Operate a device from a remote location.*	*Allows users to post and receive data.*	*Be able to securely send information to a device.*	*Improves users' knowledge of how a device operates.*	*Allow settings/preferences to be shared across devices.*
Sample Participant Responses and Appliances	 "I want to print"	 "I would like to . . . heat my food before I reach home."	 "Extend my phone screen to a bigger display."	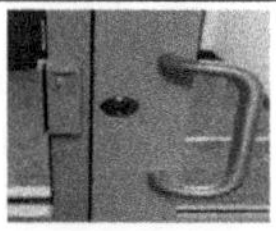 "Access doors to let me in"	 "I am not so sure what these button controls"	 "Preset my treadmill"
	 "Changing slides in a powerpoint presentation"	 "Hold elevator when I'm in my apartment"	 "If I took a photo of a map, then a 3D map appears, it would be useful."	 "Enter choice thru my phone N pay through my phone"	 "How does this work?"	 "Set my favorite TV channel."

Figure 3. General use cases for Snap-To-It, as derived from user responses in our second technology probe.

1) all of them *wanted* to interact with more devices than they currently do, and 2) that this desire extends beyond simple remote controls. This emphasizes the relevance of our work, and the need for a more versatile way of interacting with appliances than is currently available.

Functional Requirements
Our probes show that users seek a simple but versatile way of interacting with a wide range of objects/appliances. From their responses, we have identified five functional requirements:

R1: Support Photo-Based Selection. Our first probe shows that users prefer selecting appliances *via* photos. Consequently, while other methods (*e.g.,* QR codes) may be necessary at times, camera-based selection should be used when possible.

R2: Interact with Software and Hardware. Current systems typically focus on interacting with hardware [19, 2] *or* software [11]. Our second probe, however, shows that users frequently interact with both types of appliances (Figure 3). For this reason, tools like Snap-To-It need to support both hardware and software interactions through a single interface.

R3: Interact with Appliances from Afar. Our second probe shows that users want to interact with appliances that are out of sight (Figure 3, Column 2). This points to the need to remember previously used appliances (*i.e.,* a "favorites list") so that remote operation is possible.

R4: Render Complex Interfaces. Many of the use cases identified in Figure 3 call for complex user interfaces (*e.g.,* interactive maps, real-time closed-captioning feeds). These interfaces are more dynamic than the button/slider interfaces supported by existing remote control systems, and illustrate the need to be able to render any arbitrary UI "on the fly."

R5: Support Expandability. The final insight gained from our probes is that users use new technologies in unexpected ways. While we know that there are several obvious use cases that our system *needs* to support (*e.g.,* sending commands to remote appliances), our participants have also identified a number of use cases that are important to them, such as the ability to perform remote transactions and save/transfer settings. These findings highlight the real world challenges of creating a universal interaction tool, and that systems such as Snap-To-It need to be flexible enough to accommodate these use cases as they are discovered.

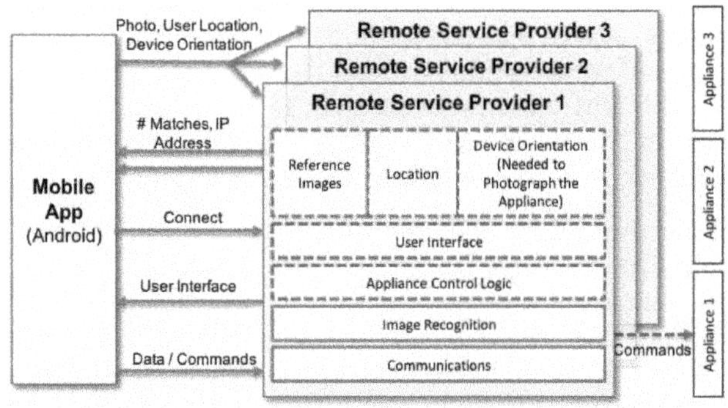

Figure 4. High level system architecture. Solid boxed components are provided by Snap-To-It, dotted boxes by developers/administrators.

In the following section, we show how Snap-To-It's design is directly influenced by our probes. Our system satisfies all five requirements described above, and provides a middleware that makes it easy to add our system's functionality to new or existing appliances. This allows it to support all six use case categories while still leaving room for future expansion.

SYSTEM DESIGN
Snap-To-It consists of two components (Figure 4): 1) a mobile app, and 2) a series of remote service providers (RSP), each of which controls one or more appliances and resides either on the appliance itself or a designated proxy (*i.e.,* a server). When users take a photo, the app sends a multicast datagram containing a URL to the photo, as well as the phone's location and device orientation. RSPs on the same subnet can then use this information to determine if the user is looking at them, and respond with their IP address and port. In our system, RSPs analyze photos, deliver interfaces, and transmit remote commands to the appliance(s) they control. The app, in turn, acts as a thin client, and can interact with any appliance without having to know about it or its capabilities in advance.

This section describes Snap-To-It's important technical details. First, we show how our system recognizes appliances. Afterwards, we show how it renders interfaces, shares preferences, authenticates users, and supports extensibility.

Selecting an Appliance via the Mobile App
Snap-To-It offers two ways to select an appliance. The primary way is by using the mobile device's camera (**R1**). Each time

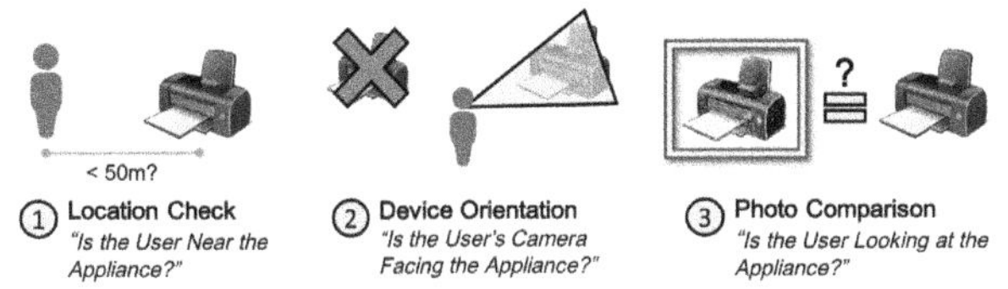

Figure 5. Snap-To-It's appliance recognition process.

a user takes a photo of an appliance, our app automatically uploads a 640 × 480 JPEG version of it to a cloud server (which simply hosts the photo for RSPs to access), and records the phone's location and orientation (azimuth, pitch, roll). It then transmits a *request message* containing the photo URL, location, and device orientation, and waits for a response. If an RSP reports that it matches a photo with a high degree of confidence, our app automatically connects to it. If no high confidence match is found (or the appliance is obstructed), the app provides users with the five highest matching appliances based on their reported context, and lets them choose which one they want to use. Our app always lets users return to the list of top matches for the most recently taken photo. This lets them gracefully recover in the event they (or the system) select the wrong appliance.

In support of **R3**, our mobile app also allows users to select appliances over long distances. Our system maintains a history of previously connected appliances, and lets users explicitly add appliances to a favorites list. The user can then use either list to reconnect to an appliance without having to be nearby.

Recognizing an Appliance

Snap-To-It matches user requests to specific appliances in three stages (Figure 5). In the first stage, each RSP extracts the latitude/longitude from the request message and calculates the distance between itself and the user. The RSP only then proceeds to the next stage if the user is within a predefined distance (*e.g.,* 50 meters). Since indoor location tracking is imprecise, our system only checks to see if the user is in the general vicinity of the appliance (*i.e.,* the same building). This lets RSPs disregard requests from users that are clearly out of visual range, and lets our system work in networks where a subnet covers a large area (*e.g.,* a college campus).

In the second stage, RSPs check to see if the user's camera is pointing towards the appliance they represent. Each RSP knows what direction a user needs to be facing in order to take a picture of it (specified *a priori* or obtained by using its onboard compass). RSPs can then check to see if the user's device is pointing towards it. Similar to before, this test cannot definitively tell if a user is looking at it. Instead, it only prevents appliances from comparing photos that are obviously taken from the wrong direction. This improves accuracy when appliances look similar, but face different directions.

The third stage examines the user's photograph. Here, each of the remaining RSPs under consideration downloads the user photo and extracts its salient features using the Scale-Invariant Feature Transform (SIFT) algorithm [22]. These features are then compared to reference photos (*i.e.,* photos of the appliance that are either provided in advance, or taken programmatically), and the results (*i.e.,* the maximum number of matches) are sent back to the mobile app. We use SIFT because the features it identifies are resilient against changes in the orientation of the camera and distance from appliances. This lets it effectively compare two images, even when they are taken from slightly different angles and distances.

For the above process to work, each RSP needs to know 1) what it looks like, 2) where its appliance is located, and 3) what direction the user needs to face to photograph it. For appliances with a GPS, compass, and display, this information can be automatically obtained by directing the RSP to periodically poll its sensors and take screenshots of its display, respectively. Many appliances (*e.g.,* printers), however, lack this capability. To support them, developers and/or administrators can collect this information *via* our mobile app, and provide the photos (and their associated metadata) to the RSP. While cumbersome, we have empirically found that this approach yields good results with as few as 3 reference photos (one taken from the front, and two from opposite 45 degree angles). This makes it easy for developers to create RSPs for a wide range of hardware, software, and non-computational objects (satisfying **R2**).

Additionally, our process requires that every reference photo contain *some* information about an appliance's surroundings. To achieve this, our app provides users with a targeting reticule (*i.e.,* a box), and instructs them to keep the appliance in the center of the image (Figure 1, left). The resulting photos contain enough background scenery to give the RSP a sense of where it is located in relation to the environment, as well as what appliances are near it. This lets our system differentiate between similar looking appliances, even when they are physically near each other (an examination of Snap-To-It's accuracy is provided in our validation).

Updating/Maintaining Reference Photos

Snap-To-It's accuracy largely depends on the quality of its reference photos. When these photos closely match the appliance's actual appearance, our system is able to identify appliances with a high degree of confidence. However, reference photos become stale over time as the environment changes. Consequently, there needs to be a way for RSPs to update their reference images with minimal assistance.

Snap-To-It overcomes this problem by utilizing user photographs. When users connect to an RSP, the photo they took is compared to the RSP's reference images. If the photo was taken at a similar angle to an existing photo (*e.g.,* within 10 degrees azimuth/pitch/roll) and has a low number of SIFT matches, the RSP replaces the older reference image. Otherwise, the system adds the photo to its current library (up to a specified limit). By letting RSPs update their reference images when the SIFT accuracy drops below a threshold, our system is able to learn how an environment is changing over time. This keeps them up to date, while simultaneously allowing them to recognize appliances from a wider range of angles.

Although this provides RSPs with new photos, it also opens the possibility of RSPs receiving blurry or inaccurate images by mistake (*e.g.,* an image of another appliance). To overcome this, RSPs ask users to judge another user's photo before

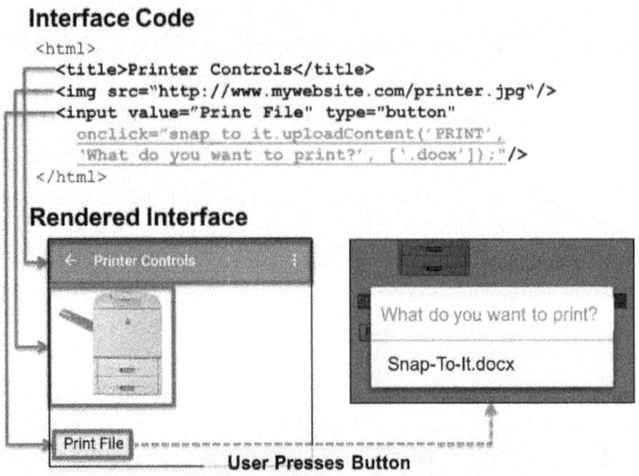

Figure 6. Sample controls for a printer. When users press the "Print File" button, it invokes our JavaScript API (red/underlined) to select and upload a file (bottom right).

adding it to its library. By leveraging user responses, RSPs can "weed out" low quality photos from its library. Moreover, since judging is only needed when a new photo is added, the impact on the end user experience is kept to a minimum.

Defining User Interfaces

From our second technology probe, we know that there are a handful of common operations that users need to perform in order to effectively control an appliance, such as the ability to transmit remote commands. As a result, Snap-To-It provides a JavaScript API that supports these core functions. When developers specify their interface, they can insert calls to our API at key events (*e.g.,* when a button is pressed). These calls then direct the app to perform a desired action (Figure 6).

This approach lets Snap-To-It perform operations that are normally inaccessible (or difficult to perform) from a mobile web browser. Our system allows developers to customize these operations (*e.g.,* specify what command is transmitted), and "push" new UIs without requiring the user to refresh their display. This allows them to create responsive, arbitrarily complex UIs (supporting **R4**), and makes our system extensible to a wide range of appliances and use cases.

Sharing Preferences

RSPs can also store preferences (*e.g.,* favorite TV channels, exercise settings) on the user's device, similar to the way that websites store cookies on a client device. When an RSP needs to save a preference, it calls our API's *setPreference* method, and specifies the name of the preference and its value. These values are then stored in the mobile app, and are provided to the RSP in future sessions.

Moreover, preferences can be shared *across appliances* (supporting **R5**). Each time an RSP replies to a request, it specifies the preference(s) it needs. The mobile app then delivers these preferences (if authorized by the user) to the RSP when it connects. Since RSPs can ask for any preference, our system lets appliances configure themselves (*e.g.,* transfer exercise settings) based on the user's interactions with similar and/or complementary appliances. In doing so, we reduce the need for manual configuration in many situations.

```
public class Printer_RSP extends RemoteServiceProvider {
 public Printer_RSP () {
  addPhoto("Photo1.jpeg",
    LOCATION, AZIMUTH, PITCH, YAW);
 }

 public String getInterface(User u) {
  return "<html> . . . </html>";
 }

 public void onRemoteCommand(User u, Command c) {
  if (c.getCommand().equals("PRINT")){
   // Print File Using URL Stored in c
  }
 }
}
```

STEP 1: Add Reference Photo(s)
STEP 2: Specify the UI
STEP 3: Process Commands

Figure 7. Pseudocode for a remote service provider.

Identifying Users

There are many situations where an RSP needs to customize the services it offers on a per-user basis. For example, an RSP for a printer on a college campus might want to provide students and faculty members with an interface to print in color, while limiting visitors to black and white.

To support these situations, Snap-To-It allows appliances to distinguish between individual users. Each time a mobile app connects to the RSP, it transmits a set of identifying credentials to the RSP. The RSP can then use these values to determine what level of service to provide. For now, our credentials contain the device's Android ID and a hash of the user's email address, as this information is sufficient to identify a particular user (provided the email address or ID is known beforehand). In the future, however, a more robust authentication method (*i.e.,* digital signatures) could be used in its place. This would provide greater security, while still allowing our system to offer relevant and *appropriate* services (supporting **R5** as well).

Creating a New RSP

Snap-To-It's middleware makes it easy for both first and third party developers to create and deploy their own RSPs. To demonstrate this, Figure 7 provides a sample implementation of a printer RSP. This code is simplified for brevity, but highlights the three steps needed to create an RSP from scratch:

1. Add Reference Photos. In the first step, we tell the RSP what its appliance looks like. For this example, we only provide a single image (along with its location, azimuth, pitch, and roll). However, more photos will obviously improve its ability to recognize itself in a user-submitted image (at the cost of increased computation time).

2. Specify the UI. The second step is to specify the user interface that the mobile app will display. Here, we return the HTML code that is described in Figure 6. Alternatively, we can provide the user with an HTTP/S link.

3. Process Commands. The final step is to process incoming commands from the mobile app. From Figure 6, we see that the app will automatically transmit a command (*e.g.,* "PRINT") to the RSP each time the user uploads a file. To detect this command, we check for this string in the `onRemoteCommand` method. We then use the URL contained within the command to download and print the file.

We implemented Snap-To-It in Java. It uses the OpenImaj library [17] to perform image comparisons, and UDP multicast and TCP sockets to transmit requests and send commands, respectively. Our system currently works in any environment with a local area network, but is targeted towards work areas such as offices. In the future, however, we hope to use *ad hoc* networking in order to support a wider range of locations.

VALIDATION

We validate Snap-To-It in two parts. First, we present four examples that were created using our system. We then evaluate Snap-To-It's accuracy, both under controlled conditions and after a two-month deployment.

Example Applications

In this section, we describe four applications (Figure 8a-d) that were developed using Snap-To-It. Each application is inspired by our general use cases, and demonstrates the range of interactions (hardware and software) our middleware supports.

Application #1: Game Controller

Our first application uses Snap-To-It to quickly control an appliance. For this application, we deployed a laptop running both a commercial game and an RSP. When a user takes a photo of the screen, Snap-To-It sends a multicast datagram containing a link to the image, as well as the user's location and device orientation. Our RSP then verifies that the user's phone was pointed towards the laptop and looking at the screen, and sends back a response containing the number of visual feature matches and its IP address. When the user connects to the RSP, the mobile app receives an HTML interface for a gamepad and renders it on the screen. As the user presses buttons on the UI, the interface directs the mobile app to send commands to the RSP (*e.g.*, "LEFT"). These commands are then translated into keyboard presses that control the game.

This application demonstrates our system's ability to select appliances, render interfaces, and transmit commands without requiring either the mobile app or the RSP to know of each other *a priori*. Additionally, this application also shows how preferences can be shared through our system. In addition to the default controller shown in Figure 8a, the application also lets users choose between multiple controller layouts. This preference is then stored on the user's device, and can recreate their control settings when playing on a different computer.

Note that we did not use a special API to control the game. Instead, our RSP merely translates the user's controller commands into keyboard presses to give the user the impression that they are controlling the game directly. The ability to wrap Snap-To-It around existing applications is inspired by prior work in software overloading [14], and we believe that this is a general technique that can be used to instrument a wide range of existing hardware and software appliances.

Application #2: Digital Projector

Our second application shows how Snap-To-It can be used to upload/download content. We created an RSP that is linked to a conference room's multimedia control system. When users take a photo of the room's digital projector, the RSP provides them with an interface that lets them upload a presentation. The RSP then downloads and projects the presentation, and provides the user with slide deck controls (Figure 8b).

This application also shows how Snap-To-It can support multiple users at once. Our RSP differentiates between the user that uploaded the presentation and users that connect afterwards (*i.e.,* audience members). The RSP can then provide audience members with a separate interface to 1) see the currently visible slide, and 2) download a copy of the presentation. Although simple in concept, this application shows how Snap-To-It can support multiple user types through a single RSP. This allows our system to support a wide range of collaborative and cooperative activities—a capability not explicitly supported in existing remote control systems.

Application #3: Paint App

Our third application uses Snap-To-It to enhance a traditional software UI. By taking a photo of a paint application, users are provided with a series of drawing tools on their mobile display. The user can spread these controls across multiple devices (Figure 8c) so that they can access these controls without taking up room on the main display.

This application is heavily inspired by prior research in cross-device interactions [16]. However, our system builds on this work by allowing devices to share interfaces without having to install the same software or pair in advance. This lets users utilize any nearby device as an extended control surface, while simultaneously making these types of interactions easy to develop and deploy.

Application #4: Campus Map

Our last application uses Snap-To-It to interact with a non-computational object (*i.e.,* a campus map). When users photograph the map (Figure 8d), the RSP provides them with a digital version. They can then search for points of interest without having to remain near the physical object.

Note that the sign was not instrumented in any way. Instead, we simply gave the RSP a photo of the sign, and linked it to our institution's online map. In doing so, we show how Snap-To-It could one day be used to help users extract deep knowledge directly from their environment.

Experimental Evaluation

To evaluate Snap-To-It, we performed three small studies. The first compares Snap-To-It to SIFT, and shows how our system's use of multiple contexts helps it identify appliances with higher accuracy. The second compares Snap-To-It to QR codes, and shows how our system supports a wider range of angles and ranges. The third was conducted after a two-month live deployment, and shows how our system can continue to accurately identify appliances after an extended period of time.

Snap-To-It vs. SIFT Photo Recognition Accuracy

For the first study, we took eleven pictures of every printer (13), copy machine (3), and fax machine (2) in our institution's building (18 appliances total). The first five photos served as reference images, and were taken from the front and sides. The following six images served as our test set, and were taken by two experimenters on different days. The test images were taken from multiple angles from separate phones, and were

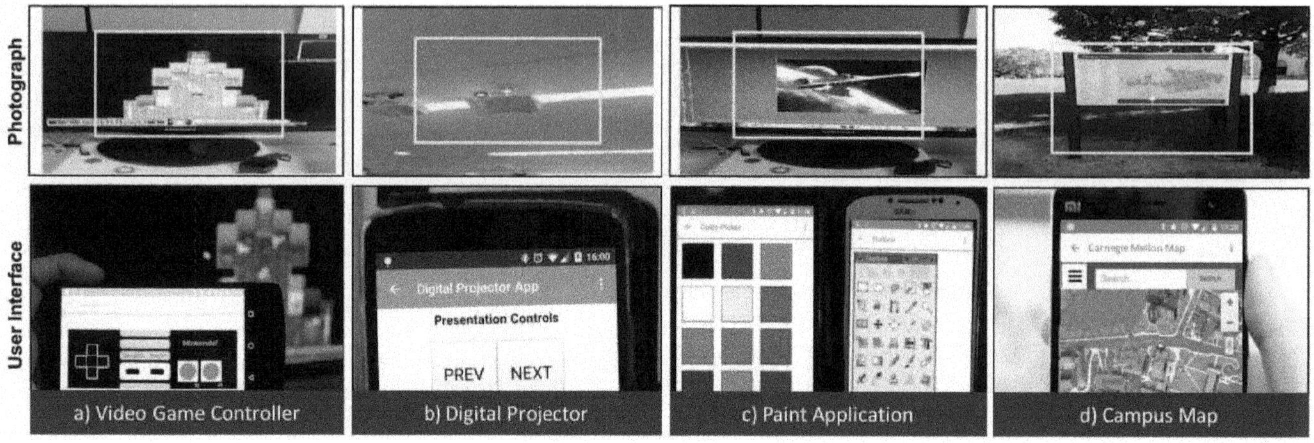

Figure 8. Example Snap-To-It applications. By taking a picture (top), our system can support a wide range of interactions (bottom).

List Position	SNAP TO IT 1 Ref Photo	SNAP TO IT 3 Ref Photos	SNAP TO IT 5 Ref Photos	SIFT ONLY 1 Ref Photo	SIFT ONLY 3 Ref Photo	SIFT ONLY 5 Ref Photo
Top 1	81.5%	87.0%	89.0%	67.6%	79.6%	85.2%
Top 3	87.0%	92.5%	94.6%	75.9%	92.6%	90.7%
Top 5	88.8%	95.3%	95.5%	83.3%	93.5%	92.5%

Table 1. Comparison of Snap-To-It and SIFT's photo recognition accuracy. Percentages show the number of times the correct appliance (out of 18) appeared in a list of the top 1, 3 and 5 matches.

not filtered to remove blurry images. For our evaluation, we created 18 RSPs (1 for each appliance), and provided each with 1, 3, or 5 reference photographs. We then had the RSPs evaluate each photo using both our system and pure SIFT.

As expected, Snap-To-It's ability to recognize an appliance depends on the quality and variety of its reference photos (Table 1). When we only provided a single reference image (taken from the front), there was an 82% chance that the correct appliance appeared at the top of the list and an 89% chance it was in the top five. With three and five reference photos, however, the chance of the correct appliance appearing at the top increased to 87% and 89%, respectively. The chance of the device appearing in the top five then exceeded 95%.

There are two important takeaways from this study. First, it shows that our system does not need a large number of reference images. Table 1 shows that our system's accuracy starts to level off with three reference images. This means that on-site administrators and/or developers only have to provide RSPs with a handful of images to obtain good performance.

Second, these results show how our system outperforms standard image recognition in a real-world setting. Of the 18 printers, six were the same make/model and ten were either located next to each other (and hence appear in each others' photographs) or placed in similar looking office rooms. While these similarities confused SIFT (especially in situations when the photo contains only a small amount of background scenery), Snap-To-It was able to more accurately differentiate between appliances that looked the same but faced different directions. Moreover, while SIFT came closer to Snap-To-It's accuracy with more reference photos, the results also reveal that our system is more likely to have the correct appliance at the *top* of the list. This makes our system more user-friendly in an opportunistic setting, and lets users be more confident that the appliance at the top of the list is the correct one.

Snap-To-It vs. QR-Code-Based Device Selection

Our second study compared device selection using Snap-To-It and QR codes. We placed 3 and 8-inch tall QR codes on the front and sides of a printer used in the previous study. We then tried to scan the code with a popular mobile app [4] from a variety of angles, starting from the front of the appliance and moving around at 20 degree increments from distances of three and six feet. At each location, we tried three times to see if the app could recognize any of the codes visible on the appliance within five seconds (the amount of time it typically takes Snap-To-It to identify the appliance). We then used Snap-To-It three times from the same location to see how it would perform (using three reference photos).

The results (Figure 9) show that QR codes are sensitive to both angle and distance. When the user was directly in front of the QR code, the app had no trouble scanning it. However, when the user looked at the code from an angle (40-60 degrees), the app was often unable to scan it reliably. Even after placing the code on multiple sides, there were some angles where none of the codes could be successfully scanned. Additionally, while a 3-inch code was sufficient when the user was one meter away, an 8-inch code was required for the app to recognize it from two meters. This may be acceptable for larger appliances such as the printer we used, but it is likely too big for smaller or narrower devices (*e.g.,* projectors). Snap-To-It was able to identify the printer from *all* of the locations at both distances. While the system's confidence varied depending on the angle (with the best results when angle and distance were closest to the three supplied reference images), the printer was always the top match from the 18 possible appliances. Our system's ability to collect and process reference photos from additional angles lets it become even more accurate, and suggests that Snap-To-It can be more reliable than using multiple QR codes.

Long Term Feasibility

While our first two studies show that Snap-To-It is accurate, we were also interested in seeing how well our system performs over time. To evaluate this, we deployed 24 RSPs in our environment for common appliances such as printers (18),

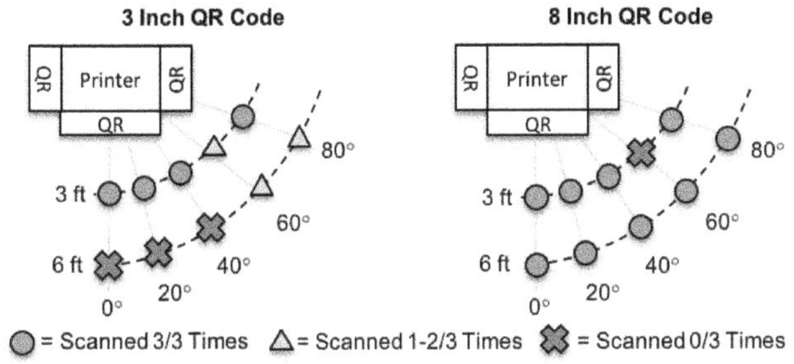

Figure 9. QR code scanning accuracy for a single appliance from multiple angles (codes placed on the front and sides).

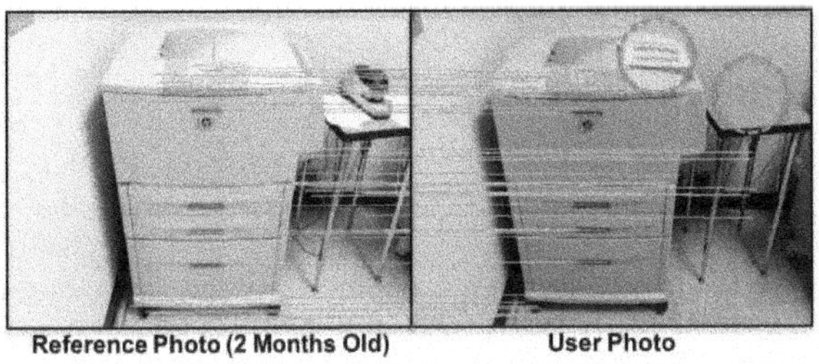

Figure 10. Sample from our long term feasibility study. Despite noticeable differences (circled), our system still identified the correct appliance using two month old reference photos (SIFT matches shown as lines).

computer displays (2), and digital projectors (4). We then published the Snap-To-It app in the Google Play store, and placed advertisements throughout our building letting users know that the app was available. During that time, a total of nine different users interacted with one or more appliances, and provided our RSPs with 25 new photographs (using the updating logic described earlier).

After running Snap-To-It for 59 days, we asked 16 new participants to interact with an appliance using our system. Our participants consisted of first year Ph.D. students and visitors, as both groups were new to our environment and not affiliated with our work. For this study, we emailed them a document or a PowerPoint presentation, and asked them to use Snap-To-It to either print or project them on an appliance that they have never used before, respectively. We then observed them as they performed the task on their phones.

Even though nine participants interacted with appliances with two-month old reference photographs, our system was still able to identify the correct appliance in all 16 cases (Figure 10). Additionally, in all but one case, the correct appliance was at the top of the list; in the other case, the correct appliance was second. While additional studies are needed to verify that Snap-To-It works over longer stretches of time, these results show that it works despite small but frequent changes to an environment (*e.g.,* papers placed on a printer). This suggests that our system is robust enough to be used outside of the lab.

DISCUSSION

In this section, we highlight three important aspects of our system: usability, responsiveness, and hardware requirements.

Usability

There are two factors that affect Snap-To-It's usability:

Which Appliances are Compatible? One challenge with deploying a system like Snap-To-It is letting users know which appliances are selectable. This is a well-known problem for Ubicomp systems [9]. Although icons/markers can help, tagging every hardware/software appliance goes against the simplicity our system offers. At the same time, however, we know that users will stop using a system if it does not work consistently [13]. Consequently, it is important to provide *some* guidance so that users never feel like they are guessing.

We expect that users' uncertainty with Snap-To-It will decrease as more appliances become compatible. To expedite this process, however, we used multiple strategies. First, we posted a series of advertisements throughout our institution to let users know when they are entering/leaving a Snap-To-It enabled area. In addition, we are also experimenting with letting the user know when they are in Bluetooth range of a Snap-To-It compatible appliance, either by displaying a notification on the user's mobile device, or by allowing appliances to display an icon and/or beep. No approach works for all appliances. Collectively, however, they reduce the chances of users taking a photo when no services are available.

Security. Although Snap-To-It provides basic mechanisms for user authentication, it assumes that the appliances in an environment are trustworthy. This creates two security concerns. If a malicious RSP states that it strongly matches every user photograph, it can prevent users from connecting to other appliances. Additionally, since Snap-To-It uses JavaScript for its interfaces, rogue developers can potentially use it to execute malicious code on a user's device.

While concerning, it is important to remember that establishing trust is an issue in every networked system. One way to overcome this is to use blacklists to block rogue RSPs. A more robust solution, however is to mandate the use of digital certificates. The infrastructure to support this already exists, and would allow our mobile app to ignore advertisements from an RSP that has not been vetted by a trusted authority.

Responsiveness

On average, Snap-To-It takes 4 seconds to find an appliance from a photograph. This includes the time needed for our app to upload an image (1360ms) and for the RSP (running on a Macbook) to download it (1043ms), calculate its features (780ms), and compare it against one or more reference images (267ms each). Once the app has connected, an additional delay is required to download the interface. This delay varies depending on internet connectivity and complexity of the UI, but ranged between 1-3 seconds in our tests.

Although 5-7 seconds may seem long, the participants in our final study found it to be fast compared to the time it takes for a user to pair with an appliance or install a driver/app. This time could be reduced even further by including the photograph in the *request message*, as opposed to using URLs. Furthermore, we have also improved the responsiveness of our mobile app so that it displays results as they arrive, rather than forcing users to wait for all RSPs to respond. This, combined with our system's sub-100ms latency for sending/receiving commands, makes Snap-To-It fast enough for many interactive use cases.

Hardware Requirements

Snap-To-It's architecture assumes that each appliance runs its own RSP. However, many appliances currently lack the computational power to analyze photos on their own. This is especially the case when it comes to *calculating* SIFT features, as the process can take upwards of 28 seconds *per image* on low-powered hardware (*e.g.,* a Raspberry Pi).

Fortunately, Snap-To-It can take advantage of existing infrastructure to give users the impression that they are directly interacting with an appliance. All of the RSPs described in this paper were hosted on laptop/desktop computers; servers can provide similar functionality. Additionally, our approach does not require appliances to process images on their own. In our ongoing work, we have modified the mobile app so that it calculates the SIFT features of its photos *via* a web service prior to sending a request. This approach increases the time needed for the app to upload a photo (from 1360ms to 3564ms), making it slightly slower for RSPs that can already calculate SIFT features quickly. However, this strategy only requires low-powered RSPs to *compare* SIFT features (which takes 2.4s per image on a Raspberry Pi), thereby making our goal of running RSPs on appliances technically feasible.

RELATED WORK

The idea of using mobile devices to control appliances has been explored often in previous work. In [19], Hodes *et al.* developed an architecture that rendered arbitrary controls on a handheld device. Their system let users control appliances from a PDA, but required them to connect to a well known server and select devices from a list/map. This made the system cumbersome when the user was new to the environment, or when the list contained dozens of appliances.

Since then, researchers have developed numerous techniques to let users specify which appliance(s) they want to use (or "address" [9]). Prior work has experimented with laser pointers [8, 29, 31], handheld projectors [33], RFID tags [32], and head mounted wearables [12] to allow users to physically point, tap, or stare at the devices they want to select. While accurate, these techniques rely heavily on non-standard hardware (*e.g.,* transmitters/receivers), making them difficult to deploy outside of the lab. Other systems use mounted cameras [10, 15] and magnetometers [36, 35] in order to determine where a user is and what appliance(s) he/she is pointing at. These systems prevent *every* appliance from having to be instrumented, but only work in preinstrumented areas. Finally, researchers have explored using smartphone cameras to select objects, either by affixing fiducial markers to each appliance [26, 18, 20], or by utilizing image recognition [11, 21] or machine learning [24].

While Snap-To-It also relies on visual recognition, our approach differs in three ways. First, our system does not require the user's device to have *a priori* knowledge of an image processing server, as is required by systems such as [26, 18, 20]. Instead, it uses multicasting to share images, which lets it discover and connect to appliances in any network-connected environment. Secondly, our approach does not limit users to appliances that they already own (as was done in [11]), require the user's device to know which devices are selectable beforehand [24], or require the user to keep the appliance in view in order to use it (as is the case with augmented reality systems). This lets us support a wider range of opportunistic interactions through a single system. Finally, while other systems rely entirely on images to identify appliances, Snap-To-It also takes the user's location and device orientation into consideration. This allows our system to more accurately differentiate between similar looking appliances, thereby improving our system's ability to be used in real-world environments.

In addition to selection techniques, researchers have also looked into the *types* of interactions that are possible using a mobile device. While much work still focuses on remote control functionality (*e.g.,* rendering control interfaces [27], supporting multiple interaction modalities [28], sending remote commands [34]), there is now increasing interest in other types of interactions. Pick and Drag and Drop, for example, supports cross-device interactions by allowing users to "grab" a file from one machine and move it to another. The Digifieds system, on the other hand, uses smartphones to modify public displays, allowing users to easily post a quick note or reposition content [6]. Deep Shot lets devices easily transfer program tasks between one another, thus allowing users to start a task on one device and finish it on another [11]. In the Open Project, researchers allowed users to project their phone's screen on unused public displays, thereby allowing them to share content with friends or strangers. Finally, products such as AllJoyn [2], Bonjour/ZeroConf [1], and Universal Plug and Play [3] are not designed for a single interaction, but instead provide a general solution to allow appliances to communicate with each other without prior coordination. However, these systems still require users to know a device's name or capabilities before they can (manually) select them.

Snap-To-It contributes to this body of work by helping us better understand the types of interactions users *want* to have, and how we can support them through a single system. We do not claim that our system is feature complete. It does, however, support a wide range of use cases, and its ability to be deployed in real-world environments provides a solid foundation for future research.

CONCLUSION

This paper has presented Snap-To-It, a system that allows users to select and control nearby appliances using their mobile device's camera. Our work takes an important step towards increasing a user's ability to interact with new and unfamiliar appliances. Yet while Snap-To-It's interaction technique already works with many appliances, it can be improved further. One idea is to use Snap-To-It to interact with multiple appliances at the same time. For example, it would be interesting to allow users to connect to multiple appliances (*e.g.,* all of the lamps in a room) by photographing them all at once. Additionally, while our system already uses background scenery and compass orientation to differentiate between objects that look the same, it would be interesting to incorporate additional types of context (*e.g.,* barometric pressure to estimate elevation) into the recognition pipeline to further increase accuracy.

ACKNOWLEDGMENTS

This work is supported by the Software Engineering Institute, Carnegie Mellon University.

REFERENCES

1. 2014. Bonjour. (2014). https://www.apple.com/support/bonjour/.
2. 2014. A Common Language for the Internet of Everything - AllJoyn. (2014). https://www.alljoyn.org/.
3. 2014. UPnP Forum. (2014). http://www.upnp.org/.
4. 2015. Barcode Scanner. (2015). https://play.google.com/store/apps/details?id=com.google.zxing.client.android&hl=en.
5. 2015. QRcode.com. (2015). http://www.qrcode.com/en/index.html.
6. Florian Alt, Alireza Sahami Shirazi, Thomas Kubitza, and Albrecht Schmidt. 2013. Interaction techniques for creating and exchanging content with public displays. In *Proceedings of the SIGCHI Conference on Human Factors in Computing Systems - CHI '13*. ACM Press, New York, New York, USA, 1709. DOI: http://dx.doi.org/10.1145/2470654.2466226
7. Debasis Bandyopadhyay and Jaydip Sen. 2011. Internet of Things: Applications and Challenges in Technology and Standardization. *Wireless Personal Communications* 58, 1 (April 2011), 49–69. DOI: http://dx.doi.org/10.1007/s11277-011-0288-5
8. Michael Beigl. 1999. Point & click-interaction in smart environments. In *Handheld and Ubiquitous Computing*. Springer, 311–313. DOI: http://dx.doi.org/10.1007/3-540-48157-5_31
9. Victoria Bellotti, Maribeth Back, W Keith Edwards, Rebecca E Grinter, Austin Henderson, and Cristina Lopes. 2002. Making Sense of Sensing Systems: Five Questions for Designers and Researchers. 1 (2002), 415–422. DOI: http://dx.doi.org/10.1145/503376.503450
10. Matthias Budde, Matthias Berning, Christopher Baumgärtner, Florian Kinn, Timo Kopf, Sven Ochs, Frederik Reiche, Till Riedel, and Michael Beigl. 2013. Point & control–interaction in smart environments: you only click twice. In *Proceedings of the 2013 ACM conference on Pervasive and ubiquitous computing adjunct publication*. ACM, 303–306. DOI: http://dx.doi.org/10.1145/2494091.2494184
11. Tsung-Hsiang Chang and Yang Li. Deep shot: a framework for migrating tasks across devices using mobile phone cameras. In *CHI '11*. New York, New York, USA, 2163–2172. DOI: http://dx.doi.org/10.1145/1978942.1979257
12. Yu-Hsiang Chen, Ben Zhang, Claire Tuna, Yang Li, Edward A Lee, and Bjï£¡rn Hartmann. 2013. *A Context Menu for the Real World: Controlling Physical Appliances Through Head-Worn Infrared Targeting*. Technical Report UCB/EECS-2013-200. EECS Department, University of California, Berkeley. DOI: http://dx.doi.org/No.UCB/EECS-2013-182
13. Fred D Davis. 1985. *A technology acceptance model for empirically testing new end-user information systems : theory and results*. Ph.D. Dissertation. http://dspace.mit.edu/handle/1721.1/15192
14. James R. Eagan, Michel Beaudouin-Lafon, and Wendy E. Mackay. 2011. Cracking the Cocoa Nut: User Interface Programming at Runtime. In *Proceedings of the 24th Annual ACM Symposium on User Interface Software and Technology (UIST '11)*. ACM, New York, NY, USA, 225–234. DOI: http://dx.doi.org/10.1145/2047196.2047226
15. David Fleer and Christian Leichsenring. 2012. MISO: a context-sensitive multimodal interface for smart objects based on hand gestures and finger snaps. In *UIST Adjunct Proceedings '12*. New York, New York, USA, 93–94. DOI: http://dx.doi.org/10.1145/2380296.2380338
16. Peter Hamilton and Daniel J. Wigdor. 2014. Conductor. In *CHI '14*. New York, New York, USA, 2773–2782. DOI: http://dx.doi.org/10.1145/2556288.2557170
17. Jonathon S Hare, Sina Samangooei, and David P Dupplaw. 2011. OpenIMAJ and ImageTerrier: Java libraries and tools for scalable multimedia analysis and indexing of images. In *MM '11*. New York, NY, USA, 691–694. DOI: http://dx.doi.org/10.1145/2072298.2072421
18. Valentin Heun, Shunichi Kasahara, and Pattie Maes. 2013. Smarter Objects: Using AR Technology to Program Physical Objects and Their Interactions. In *CHI '13 Extended Abstracts on Human Factors in Computing Systems (CHI EA '13)*. ACM, New York, NY, USA, 961–966. DOI: http://dx.doi.org/10.1145/2468356.2468528
19. Todd D. Hodes, Randy H. Katz, Edouard Servan-Schreiber, and Lawrence Rowe. 1997. Composable ad-hoc mobile services for universal interaction. In *MobiCom '97*. New York, New York, USA, 1–12. DOI: http://dx.doi.org/10.1145/262116.262121
20. Can Liu, Stephane Huot, Jonathan Diehl, Wendy Mackay, and Michel Beaudouin-Lafon. 2012. Evaluating the Benefits of Real-time Feedback in Mobile Augmented Reality with Hand-held Devices. In *Proceedings of the SIGCHI Conference on Human Factors in Computing Systems (CHI '12)*. ACM, New York, NY, USA, 2973–2976. DOI: http://dx.doi.org/10.1145/2207676.2208706
21. Qiong Liu, Paul McEvoy, Don Kimber, Patrick Chiu, and Hanning Zhou. 2006. On Redirecting Documents with a Mobile Camera. In *Workshop on Multimedia Signal Processing*. 467–470. DOI: http://dx.doi.org/10.1109/MMSP.2006.285352
22. D.G. Lowe. 1999. Object recognition from local scale-invariant features. In *International Conference on Computer Vision*, Vol. 2. 1150–1157. DOI: http://dx.doi.org/10.1109/ICCV.1999.790410

23. Friedemann Mattern and Christian Floerkemeier. 2010. From the Internet of Computers to the Internet of Things. *From Active Data Management to Event-Based Systems and More* (Jan. 2010), 242–259. http://dl.acm.org/citation.cfm?id=1985625.1985645

24. Simon Mayer, Markus Schalch, Marian George, and Gábor Sörös. 2013. Device recognition for intuitive interaction with the web of things. In *UbiComp '13 Adjunct Proceedings*. New York, New York, USA, 239–242. DOI: http://dx.doi.org/10.1145/2494091.2494168

25. Daniele Miorandi, Sabrina Sicari, Francesco De Pellegrini, and Imrich Chlamtac. 2012. Internet of things: Vision, applications and research challenges. *Ad Hoc Networks* 10, 7 (Sept. 2012), 1497–1516. DOI: http://dx.doi.org/10.1016/j.adhoc.2012.02.016

26. Matei Negulescu and Yang Li. 2013. Open project: a lightweight framework for remote sharing of mobile applications. In *UIST '13*. New York, New York, USA, 281–290. DOI: http://dx.doi.org/10.1145/2501988.2502030

27. Jeffrey Nichols, Brad A. Myers, Michael Higgins, Joseph Hughes, Thomas K. Harris, Roni Rosenfeld, and Mathilde Pignol. 2002. Generating remote control interfaces for complex appliances. In *UIST '02*. New York, New York, USA, 161–170. DOI: http://dx.doi.org/10.1145/571985.572008

28. Jeffrey Nichols, Brad A. Myers, and Brandon Rothrock. 2006. UNIFORM: automatically generating consistent remote control user interfaces. In *CHI '06*. New York, New York, USA, 611–620. DOI: http://dx.doi.org/10.1145/1124772.1124865

29. Shwetak N Patel and Gregory D Abowd. 2003. A 2-way laser-assisted selection scheme for handhelds in a physical environment. In *UbiComp '03*. Springer, 200–207. DOI: http://dx.doi.org/10.1007/978-3-540-39653-6_16

30. Jukka Riekki, Ivan Sanchez, and Mikko Pyykkönen. 2008. Universal Remote Control for the Smart World. In *Ubiquitous Intelligence and Computing (Lecture Notes in Computer Science)*, Frode Eika Sandnes, Yan Zhang, Chunming Rong, Laurence T. Yang, and Jianhua Ma (Eds.), Vol. 5061. Berlin, Heidelberg, 563–577. DOI: http://dx.doi.org/10.1007/978-3-540-69293-5

31. Matthias Ringwald. 2002. UbiControl: Providing New and Easy Ways to Interact with Various Consumer Devices. In *UbiComp '02*. 81,82.

32. Ichiro Satoh. 2011. A Management Framework for Context-Aware Multimedia Services.. In *DMS*. 165–170.

33. Dominik Schmidt, David Molyneaux, and Xiang Cao. 2012. PICOntrol: using a handheld projector for direct control of physical devices through visible light. In *UIST '12*. ACM Press, New York, New York, USA, 379–388. DOI: http://dx.doi.org/10.1145/2380116.2380166

34. Chuong Cong Vo. 2013. *A Framework for a Task-Oriented User Interaction with Smart Environments Using Mobile Devices*. Ph.D. Dissertation. La Trobe University.

35. Hanno Wirtz, Jan Rüth, Martin Serror, Jó Ágila Bitsch Link, and Klaus Wehrle. 2014. Opportunistic interaction in the challenged internet of things. *Proceedings of the 9th ACM MobiCom workshop on Challenged networks - CHANTS '14* (2014), 7–12. DOI: http://dx.doi.org/10.1145/2645672.2645679

36. Jiahui Wu, Gang Pan, Daqing Zhang, Shijian Li, and Zhaohui Wu. 2010. MagicPhone: pointing & interacting. In *UbiComp '10*. New York, New York, USA, 451–452. DOI: http://dx.doi.org/10.1145/1864431.1864483

"She'll just grab any device that's closer": A Study of Everyday Device & Account Sharing in Households

Tara Matthews, Kerwell Liao, Anna Turner,
Marianne Berkovich, Rob Reeder, Sunny Consolvo
Google
Mountain View, CA, USA
{taramatthews, kerwell, annaturn, mberkovich, rreeder, sconsolvo}@google.com

ABSTRACT
Many technologies assume a single user will use an account or device. But account and device sharing situations (when 2+ people use a single device or account) may arise during everyday life. We present results from a multiple-methods study of device and account sharing practices among household members and their relations. Among our findings are that device and account sharing was common, and mobile phones were often shared despite being considered "personal" devices. Based on our study results, we organize sharing practices into a taxonomy of six sharing types—distinct patterns of what, why, and how people shared. We also present two themes that cut across sharing types: that (1) trust in sharees and (2) convenience highly influenced sharing practices. Based on these findings, we discuss implications for study and technology design.

Author Keywords
Device sharing; account sharing; household; CSCW; usable privacy and security; user study.

ACM Classification Keywords
H.5.m. Information interfaces and presentation (e.g., HCI): Miscellaneous.

INTRODUCTION
Many technologies rely on the assumption that they will be used by a single person. For example, personalization systems create a user model based on actions in a single signed-in account or device [33]. Also relying on this assumption are authentication solutions that keep users signed in across sessions, systems that offer to save passwords, OS-level authentication that grants access to an entire device, and systems that auto-backup to cloud accounts.

However, the 'single user' assumption may not consider the many account and device sharing situations that arise during everyday life. For this paper, we define *sharing* as any situation in which two or more people use a single device or account, either at the same time or taking turns. A common sharing scenario revealed in the study presented in this paper involved household members borrowing each others' mobile phones. They would do a quick web search or play a game with whoever's phone was closest, available (e.g., not out of batteries or in use), and had the desired content or capability (e.g., the right game). Other examples abound: kids watch videos on a parent's account, friends navigate maps using each others' phones in the car, one spouse sets up a device on behalf of the other, a family uses a single desktop computer at home, and so on.

In sharing situations like these, systems designed for a single user can break down. For example, personalization systems may surface inconsistencies or private activities if they incorporate the actions of others into their models [1,33]. Password management systems may save the credentials of a sharee on the sharer's account or grant a sharee access to a sharer's accounts. Authentication systems that keep users logged in across sessions may enable a sharee unexpected access to a sharer's accounts.

Prior work has shown that people share devices [8,9,14,18,19,24,25,31] and accounts [3,11,15,30], but we lack a systematic understanding of the nature of device and account sharing, across multiple device and account types, in households today. This understanding is critical to our ability to design systems that consider everyday device and account sharing practices. Further, this understanding could inspire novel systems that better support the realities of how people share technology.

We present results from a multiple-methods study of device and account sharing practices among household members and their relations, and discuss implications for design. Our study involved (1) a survey of 99 households about their devices; (2) a 21-day diary study with 25 participants to collect in situ device sharing instances about phones, tablets, and computers; and (3) interviews with 24 participants about why and how device and account sharing occurred. We address the following research questions:

- What devices and accounts are shared? With whom? Why? With what frequency? To do what activities? Using what security measures?

CHI'16, May 07-12, 2016, San Jose, CA, USA
ACM 978-1-4503-3362-7/16/05.
http://dx.doi.org/10.1145/2858036.2858051

- What are implications of device and account sharing for study and technology design?

Among our key findings are that device and account sharing is common, and that mobile phones were shared as much as computers and more often than tablets—even though participants typically perceived phones as *personal* devices and did not realize how often they were shared until participating in our diary study. Technology sharing was messy, varied, and frequent. Thus, *the major contribution of this work is a taxonomy of six sharing types*—distinct patterns of what, why, and how people shared their devices and accounts—developed from our study results. We found that sharing was often intentional, but sometimes accidental or unsupervised sharing occurred. We also present two themes that cut across sharing types: that (1) trust in sharees and (2) convenience highly influenced sharing practices. Based on these empirical findings, we discuss implications for designing studies and technologies.

RELATED WORK

We focus on everyday sharing of *common devices and accounts* among household members and their relations. This excludes prior research on sharing *content* in which each user authenticates to their own account (e.g., sharing photos [22], files [29] across accounts), as well as *specialized multi-user devices or accounts* designed for specific use cases (e.g., tabletop [23] or whiteboard [26] displays, or specialized calendars [7]). Given this focus, we scope this section to prior research on sharing of common devices (phones, tablets, computers) and accounts (email, social, financial, etc.). We discuss prior studies of device and account sharing, what influences sharing, and security and privacy practices when sharing.

Studies Documenting Device and Account Sharing

The fact that *people share common devices* has been documented [6,8,9,14,18,19,24,25,31], though most studies have focused on practices around a single device (e.g., mobile phones *or* tablets). Some studies have shown that mobile phone sharing is common [6,9,19], especially in developing countries [18,25,31]. Based on an ethnographic study in Bangalore, Steenson and Donner [31] described two categories of sharing: *proximate* (multiple close relations use a single phone) and *distributed* (person A will call person B to reach person C, who may not have a phone). Karlson et al. [19] documented how often 12 U.S. participants shared their phones, based on their recall during interviews. Research on tablet use has found that for some activities—playing games, reading books, educational work—multiple family members will use a device together [24]. Bødker and Christiansen [6] interviewed 12 early mobile phone users and noted ad hoc sharing with family and friends. Frohlich and Kraut [14] conducted an early study on in-home technology use and found participants using the computer together for entertainment and parents logging into their children's accounts to monitor activity.

Fewer studies have explored *sharing behaviors across multiple common devices*. Based on visits to 15 households in the U.S., Brush and Inkpen [8] found that family members shared a range of technologies, though computers were shared more often than mobile phones. They also found that sharing occurred more frequently with devices located in public spaces within the home.

Some work has explored *account sharing* [3,11,15,30]—that is, when two or more people use the same credentials for a single account. Egelman et al. [11] studied computer OS-level profile use in families and found that family members frequently used each others' profiles. In a study of home network use, Grinter et al. [15] found that when Tivo viewer profiles were not used as intended, personalization was affected. Alghamdi et al. [3] and Singh et al. [30] studied bank account sharing, finding that it was motivated in part by the sharers needing help from the sharees.

Sharing Influencers

Prior studies have identified factors that influence sharing, including *trust* [3,8,10,16,21,27,30,31,34], *culture* [3,4,31], and *utility* [10,12,16–18,25,31].

People often share based on the trust they have in the sharee or the dictates of their culture. Brush and Inkpen [8] found that trust between family members was evident in the extent of open sharing that occurred, though this did not always extend to parent-child relationships. In a survey of people in Vancouver, Cherapau et al. [10] found that respondents often shared their phone passcodes with people they trusted. Steenson and Donner [31] found that phone sharing practices in Bangalore often involved family members, friends, and nearby neighbors, to the extent that it was common to call one person's phone to reach somebody else. Alghamdi et al. [3] studied couples in Saudi Arabia, finding that bank credentials were not only shared or withheld as a sign of trust, but also because sharing fit within the cultural expectations of spousal access. In a study of Australian participants, Singh et al. [30] found that couples shared internet banking passwords as a sign of trust.

Utility and convenience are other strong influencers: people share because it is useful or easy. In some socio-economic situations, technology sharing is essential due to limited resources [18,25,31]. Prior work in the U.S. and Europe describes sharing as 'spontaneous' [16,19] and motivated by quick access to digital content [16]. This work suggests that people weigh the potential cost of sharing a device (loss of privacy/security or a temporary inability to access one's technology) with the usefulness of sharing [10,12,16,17]. Frohlich and Kraut [14] found that within a household, convenience was a frequent motivator for sharing when performing quick information-seeking tasks.

Security and Privacy When Sharing

Sharing common devices and accounts may make the sharer's data or online activities accessible to the sharee, and vice versa. Prior research has explored how people regulate access to sensitive data when sharing their devices [16,17,19,21] and technology solutions that aim to make sharing more secure or easier [5,8,11,17,20,28].

Sharers sometimes attempt to regulate sharees' access to data. Karlson et al. [19] interviewed 12 U.S. mobile phone users about what data they were comfortable sharing and why, suggesting an all-or-nothing sharing model is not sufficient to meet user needs. Mazurek et al. [21] interviewed 33 Pittsburgh-based participants about how they controlled access to digital content within their households. Sharers described deleting or hiding sensitive data, using device-level PINs or passwords, mandatory supervision during sharing, or refusal to share with certain individuals. In a study of smartphone sharing, Hang et al. [16] similarly found that participants reported staying in proximity to the sharee or refusing to share with those they did not trust.

Profile switching is a commonly proposed solution to handle many issues that arise when sharing, including mitigating privacy and security risks. However, prior work has shown that the cost (in time and mental effort) of switching profiles is often too high [5,8,11]. Brush and Inkpen [8] and Egelman et al. [11] found that even families who set up and intended to use profiles often did not.

Authentication solutions have been proposed to provide more control in ad hoc sharing situations, something studies of technology sharing have found participants want [16,17,19]. Hayashi et al. [17] introduced authentication mechanisms that would provide limited access in situ, including allowing sharers to lock access to all but the current active application. Liu et al. [20] proposed xShare, which allows users to set custom access controls right before sharing. Seifert et al. [28] proposed TreasurePhone, which uses context to automatically add access controls.

Our work adds new knowledge to this literature. We use a multiple methods to study device and account sharing within a variety of household types, including those with room mates, childless couples, and adult children living with their parents. We describe the six *types of sharing* we observed (e.g., *borrowing*, *mutual use*, etc.), and for each type, discuss what is shared, why it is shared, how it is shared, how often this type of sharing happens, and what activities are usually performed. This novel taxonomy gives designers a range of concrete sharing types to inform their technology. While prior studies cover themes about sharing, none have systematically organized and described the range of sharing behavior types for designers. We also expand on the roles of trust and convenience in device and account sharing.

METHOD

Our study, conducted between June and September 2014, involved (1) an inventory survey of 99 households about their devices; (2) a 21-day diary study with 25 participants to collect in situ device sharing instances; and (3) interviews with 24 participants about why and how device and account sharing occurred. We provide details below.

Participants

Our participants were English speakers in the U.S. Each participant responded on behalf of their household, which we categorized into one of 6 arrangements:

1. Lives only w/significant other (N=25 for the survey, N=3 for the diary and interviews)
2. Lives w/kids <13 years old (22 survey, 6 diary, 5 int.)
3. Lives w/kids 13-18 (16 survey, 4 diary/int.)
4. Lives w/kids under *and* over 13 (6 survey, 1 diary/int.)
5. Lives only w/nonrelated others (16 survey, 6 diary/int.)
6. Miscellaneous (e.g., adult living with parents, lives with children + roommates) (14 survey, 5 diary/int.)

Participants were recruited via our institution's external participant database and sent a screening survey via email. An incentive was provided for participating.

The *99 survey participants* included 44 females, 54 males, 1 unspecified; 11 age 18-22, 25 age 23-39, 22 age 30-39, 27 age 40-49, 11 age 50-59, 3 age 60+; and 59 were employed, 8 unemployed, 19 students, 13 other. The *25 diary study participants* included 13 females, 12 males; 2 age 18-22, 8 age 23-39, 8 age 30-39, 3 age 40-49, 4 age 50-59+; and 16 were employed, 3 unemployed, 2 were students, 3 other. The *24 interview participants* were the same as the diary study with one fewer female age 23-39. Occupations of participants varied, including law clerk, broker, teacher, administrate assistant, pastor, and small business owner.

Device Inventory Survey

Based on responses from the screening survey, we invited 120 English-speaking people who used a mobile phone *and* desktop or laptop computer at least once per month to participate. We sent invitees a paper-based device inventory survey packet that included a welcome note, instructions, household member survey (who lives in the household), device inventory survey (what devices are in the household, for what they are used, and who uses them), and a return envelope with pre-paid postage. We received completed packets from 99 respondents in 34 states.

Diary Study on Device Sharing

We selected 25 of our 99 survey respondents, from 17 U.S. states, to participate in the follow-up diary study. Since we were interested in learning about device sharing, we selected respondents from the inventory survey who reported that they and at least one other household member used the same mobile phone, tablet/e-reader, or laptop/desktop computer at least once per month. All participant households had at least one of each device type, except one household that had no tablet/e-reader. The diary was conducted via the PACO smartphone app [13], which required that participants use a smartphone running iOS 7+ or Android 2.2+.

Participants were notified 3 times a day for 21 days to report instances of device sharing they observed, defined as 2+ people using the same mobile phone, tablet/e-reader, or laptop/desktop computer, either one after another or together. Notifications asked if participants had seen any sharing recently. If they indicated that there was a recent example of sharing, we asked them what device was shared (select one type), whether the individuals used the device at the *same time* or *one after another*, who the individuals were (select one or more relationship types). Participants could also submit responses if they observed a sharing instance but did not have an active notification. In total, 25 participants reported 591 in situ instances of sharing over 21 days, 445 of which were in response to a notification. (These numbers exclude 14 reported sharing instances we deemed outside the study's scope of sharing among household members and their relations, e.g., observing two strangers share a library computer or a computer in the Apple Store.)

Interviews on Device & Account Sharing

Finally, we conducted 1-hour long, semi-structured one-on-one phone interviews with 24 of the diary study participants to further explore device and account sharing. Interview questions focused on mobile phones, tablets/e-readers, and laptop/desktop computers. In cases where participants spontaneously discussed account sharing—which happened for all participants—we explored how and why *accounts* were shared, and included those findings in our results. Interviews were audio recorded and transcribed for analysis.

Piloting

We conducted multiple rounds of pilot testing to ensure the high quality of our data. Participants for all pilot studies were colleagues at our institution. Based on feedback from piloting, we converted the inventory survey from digital to paper form and improved the structure and clarity of questions in the survey, diary, and interviews.

Analysis

From the inventory survey, we calculated descriptive statistics such as the average number of devices per household. From the diary study, we calculated descriptive statistics such as the average percentage of sharing instances reported per participant, broken down by device type and with whom devices were shared. Where we report significant differences below, we include details on the statistics used.

To analyze the interview data, we used a general inductive approach [32]. All transcripts were read by three of the authors who collaboratively developed a coding scheme that focused on characterizing device and account sharing practices, as guided by the research questions. The three researchers each coded one-third of the transcripts, meeting after each new transcript was completed to discuss and refine the coding scheme. Early in our analysis, we realized the importance of coding attributes of *sharing stories* participants described. A sharing story was any time a participant described sharing a single device or account, for example a phone or a bank account. From this analysis emerged 228 *sharing stories*. In this paper, we focus on the following attributes of sharing stories:

- **What**: phone, tablet, computer, or account type (e.g., entertainment, email, bank, etc.)
- **Why**: reasons for sharing, such as convenience, helping someone, and so on.
- **How**: any security measures or social norms involved in the sharing, such as staying nearby to monitor use, using together, and so on.
- **Frequency**: once, rarely, sometimes, often.
- **Activities**: entertainment (watching videos, listening to music, playing games), messaging, browsing the Internet, installing an app, and so on.

We observed common patterns of the *why*, *how*, and *frequency* attributes that distinguished the sharing stories. A final analysis pass organized the 228 sharing stories into the *types* in Table 1 based on patterns of the *why*, *how*, and *frequency* attributes. Sub-sections in Results describe each *sharing type* in turn, their attributes, and how they are distinguished from other types.

Limitations

Our study is subject to some limitations. We relied on self-report data, which is subject to biases such as social desirability and recall. Regarding sampling, our participants are not necessarily representative of the U.S. population. Furthermore, they were willing to speak with us about their households and technology use; those unwilling to do so may have characteristics or issues we did not discover. Also, the numbers we present should be interpreted carefully. We include them to indicate broad trends from our study, not to represent sharing practices within a broader population. This is particularly true for the numbers associated with interview data, as the interviews depended on what participants remembered and chose to discuss. To minimize recall bias in interviews, we asked about devices and sharing instances reported during the inventory survey and diary study. However, participants discussed *accounts* in a more ad hoc manner. Also, we had not developed our full set of attributes and codes until the analysis phase, so follow up questions were not asked to fully explore all attributes of each sharing story. Thus the numbers associated with account sharing and to characterize the frequency of different sharing story attributes should be interpreted with caution.

RESULTS

We begin with results from the diary study and inventory survey; key findings are that (1) device and account sharing are common, and (2) mobile phones were frequently reported as shared. Next, we present a taxonomy of sharing types—patterns of what, why, and how people shared—developed from our interview results. Finally, we present two themes that cut across sharing types: that (1) trust in sharees and (2) convenience highly influenced sharing.

Diary & Inventory: Overview of Devices and Sharing

Diary study participants reported sharing instances that they participated in and that they observed others participating in without being involved themselves. Averaging all of these sharing instances per participant, the main findings from our diary study were that device sharing was common (with a median 14 sharing instances per participant over the 21-

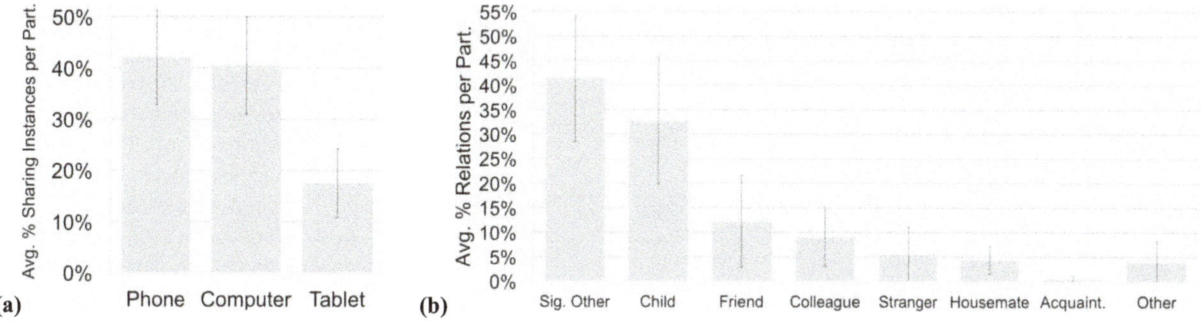

Figure 1. Diary study results. (a) Sharing by device, shown as the average percent of sharing instances per participant (591 total instances reported by 25 participants). (b) Who participants shared with, shown as the average percent of relations reported per participant (533 total relations reported by 25 participants during 468 sharing instances; 1 relation listed in 413 instances, >1 relation listed in 55 instances). Sig. others and children were most common relations shared with. Error bars represent 95% CIs.

day study period), and mobile phones were shared as often as computers and more often than tablets (phones were shared significantly more than tablets, $t(43.91)=4.22$, $p<.001$, as were computers, $t(43.26)=3.88$, $p=.001$, according to pairwise t-tests, corrected for multiple tests using the Bonferroni method). Of the 591 sharing instances reported in the diary study, an average of 42.0% per participant involved phones, 40.5% involved computers and 17.5% involved tablets (Figure 1a). Our *inventory survey*, for just the 25 participants who also completed the diary study, revealed that participants' households contained fewer mobile phones (3.0 average per household) than computers (4.0 average per household), so the extensive sharing of phones is notable. The *inventory survey* indicates that more partici pants (100% of 25 diary study participants) reported someone in their household *using* at least one household phone and computer on a weekly basis, and fewer (88%) reported weekly usage of at least one household tablet. Thus sharing and usage patterns may roughly align.

To examine the *relations* participants shared with, we analyzed the subset of diary study sharing instances in which the participant was involved (468 out of 591 total sharing instances). Restricting the data in this way was important to ensuring a consistent point of reference (the participant) for defining the relationship type (e.g., the participant's children, friends, etc.). Overall, participants shared most often with their significant others and children (see Figure 1b; significant according to one sample, two-sided t-tests of the null hypothesis that all relation types are equally likely, corrected for multiple tests using the Bonferroni method; significant others $t(23)=4.37$, $p=.0018$ and children $t(23)=3.06$, $p=.045$).

An interesting finding from triangulating our diary study, inventory survey, and interviews was that sharing was often invisible to participants. In the inventory survey (prior to the diary study), we asked participants to self-report which of their devices were shared with one or more others at least once per month. Then in the diary study, we asked them to report each sharing instance that they participated in or observed in situ. A priori, they reported that more tablets were shared (34.5%) and computers were shared (31.8%) than were phones (27.6%). However, the average amount of sharing they reported in situ was higher for phones and computers than for tablets (Figure 1a). While these two metrics do not contradict (since they are not directly comparable), it was not until the in situ exercise that participants *realized* the prevalence of phone sharing. Multiple participants expressed their surprise in interviews at learning from the diary study how often they shared devices they had previously thought of as personal:

> *"We weren't really paying attention how much of [my wife's and my phones] [our kids] were using... Every time the app called for making the survey, my kids were always involved." (P20)*

Taxonomy of Sharing Types

From our survey and diary study, we learned that device sharing occurred frequently. From our subsequent interviews, we learned that technology sharing was messy and highly varied. It was messy in that participants did not share their devices and accounts the same way with every person or in every situation. It was varied, in that our initial definition of sharing as 'more than one person using a device or account' was too simple to characterize the many ways and reasons participants shared. Through our analysis of interview data, we discovered that there were distinct patterns of what, why, how, and how often participants shared devices and accounts, which we call *sharing types*. What follows is a taxonomy of six sharing types that occurred in the households studied: *borrowing*, *mutual use*, *setup*, *helping*, *broadcasting*, and *accidental* (see Table 1 for an overview).

Borrowing

The most common sharing type described was *borrowing*, an ad hoc, temporary lending of a device or account to benefit the sharee (all 24 participants reported *borrowing*, which accounted for 47% of sharing stories). Example sharing stories of the *borrowing* type include:

> *Friends Sharing PINs: Lisa[1] sometimes uses her friends' phones when out. She usually uses their phone browser to check her accounts, but occasionally uses apps, if they are easy to set up. Some friends have told her their phone passcodes. (P6)*

[1] Pseudonyms are used throughout the paper.

Sharing Type	Description *Applies to devices and accounts*	# (%) Sharing Stories (N=228)	% Ps
Borrowing	Temporary lending that benefits the sharee	107 (47%)	100%
Mutual Use	2+ people regularly use device/account as one of their primary of that type	48 (21%)	75%
Setup	Sharee sets up device/account on behalf of sharer	26 (11%)	58%
Helping	Sharee helps sharer do a task other than setup	16 (7%)	46%
Broadcasting	2+ people view a device/account at same time	10 (4%)	29%
Accidental	Unintentional access of data while sharing device/account	21 (9%)	42%

Table 1. Taxonomy of 6 sharing types—distinct patterns of what, why, how, and how frequently participants shared their devices and accounts—identified from interview data.

Out of Batteries: Everyone in the Chang family has their own tablet, but sometimes one of the kids will forget to charge theirs, so they borrow someone else's. (P22)

Attributes

What: Phones were a commonly borrowed device (47% of sharing stories), followed by computers (30%), then tablets (16%). Accounts were rarely borrowed—it did not tend to make sense to temporarily borrow someone's email account, whereas it did sometimes make sense to borrow another's phone to sign in to one's own email account.

Why: There were three main motivations for *borrowing*: *convenience*, *content*, and *capabilities*. The "out of batteries" story above is an example of *convenience*—rather than wait for one's own tablet battery to charge, it is more convenient to use someone else's tablet. Participants commonly borrowed someone else's device if it was more conveniently located than their own, as described by P20:

"We're watching TV and my phone is more handy than [my wife's] phone, and she'll grab my phone and start Facebooking or playing [a game]... She'll just grab any device that's closer to her. Same with me. If I need to make a call and her phone is next to me, I'll grab her phone."

The *capabilities* of or *content* available on a device were also important rationales for *borrowing*, such as a child playing a particular game on her parent's tablet or a spouse *borrowing* a phone for its better camera:

"[My wife] likes the camera on my phone better, so sometimes she'll use it for those purposes." (P24)

How: A mixture of security approaches were used for *borrowing*, reacting to a range of trusted to untrusted sharees. In 60% of sharing stories, participants described trusting the sharee and allowing them full, unsupervised access. For the remaining 40%, participants described limited trust in the sharee, allowing supervised use after entering credentials themselves. P16 described sharing with a trusted daughter:

"[My kids] usually take my phone and I don't really pay too much attention to what they're doing on it. Last night my daughter took my phone to video chat with a friend."

Frequency: *Borrowing* was characterized by happening at ad hoc occasions. *Borrowing* frequency was idiosyncratic by participant, ranging from rare to often. However, borrowers usually had their own device of the same type they were *borrowing*, so there was an expectation that they would limit the amount of time they borrowed.

Activities: The top activities done on borrowed devices were entertainment, social/messaging, and web browsing.

Mutual Use

The next most common sharing type was *mutual use*, when 2 or more people regularly used a device or account as one of their primary of that type (75% of participants, 21% of sharing stories). Unlike the other sharing types, *mutual use* often did not involve a sharer and sharee, but rather two (or more) people who had fairly equal ownership of a device or account. Example *sharing stories* of *mutual use* include:

Shared Netflix Account: The Martinez family mutually use one Netflix account. It has one profile for the parents and one kid-specific profile for the two kids. The family's devices have PINs to prevent the kids from using them without permission, but once the device is unlocked, they can freely access Netflix. (P19)

Family Computers: The Smith's (Mom, Dad, 13 y/o Daughter) have 2 shared desktop computers: upstairs and downstairs. Mom only uses the downstairs computer. Dad and Daughter use whichever is most convenient. The downstairs computer has 3 Chrome browser profiles (one per person), and the upstairs computer has 2 Chrome browser profiles (for Dad and Daughter). They mostly use their own profiles, but sometimes forget to log out and will use each others'. (P17)

Attributes

What: 37% of *mutual use* sharing stories were about computers or tablets and 63% were about accounts. No phones were mutually used—a result that might be different in other countries [18,25,31]. The lack of mutually used phones may have contributed to perceptions of phones as "personal" devices (we return to this in the Discussion). The most common *mutually used* accounts were entertainment focused (TV, video, music, and games), representing half of the account sharing stories for this type. The other half were often critical household accounts, like a couple's bank account or family calendar.

Why: The three main drivers of *mutual use* were *mutual need*, *limited resources*, and *convenience*. For example, spouses often mix finances and thus *mutually need* a shared bank account. *Limited resources*, such as the money to purchase an extra device or subscription-based account, also led to sharing. Finally, *convenience* motivated the Smith family (in the story above) to keep two mutually used computers—upstairs and downstairs—so they would not have to walk far to get to one. Sometimes these motivations combined: for example, participants demonstrated a strong desire for household-wide entertainment accounts, both for convenience (e.g., it was easier to maintain one music library) and to avoid multiple subscription fees.

How: For most of the *mutual use* stories (81%), participants shared with trusted others and all knew the authentication credentials for the device or account. Participants of six households described "common passwords" known by all household members so anyone could easily access household-wide mutually used devices and accounts:

> *"I think all families kind of have a couple of passwords that they use... So it's just kind of like a guess-which-one-it-is and you're probably going to be right." (P7)*

In 23% of stories, participants described setting up profiles (e.g., OS-level profiles on a desktop or browser profiles on any device); each user usually knew only their own credentials, but sometimes they knew each others'. As illustrated in the "family computers" story above, several participants described using the profile of whoever was logged in. As we discuss in the *accidental* sharing type below, unintentional access to data was often caused by not logging out of accounts or profiles on mutually used devices.

Frequency: For mutual users, sharing occurred often, and typically no one user got consistent priority over others.

Activities: A wide variety of computing activities were performed on/with mutually used devices and accounts.

Setup

The *setup* sharing type involved a sharee performing device or account initialization or major maintenance / configuration activities on behalf of the sharer (58% of participants, 11% of sharing stories).

> *The Family Sysadmin: Maya set up both of her parents' phones because they aren't very tech literate. She made the decision to not put a passcode on their devices, because she says they mainly use their phones for calling. She also set up their email accounts, so she knows how to get into those accounts. (P11)*

> *Phone Favor: Jake sets up cool new apps he discovers on his girlfriend's phone, because they are both early adopters. (P23)*

<u>Attributes</u>

What: More of the *setup* sharing stories were about devices rather than accounts (69% of stories for devices, with a fairly even mix of phones, tablets, and computers, compared to 31% of stories for accounts). Most accounts set up by a sharee included critical or sensitive information, such as bank, password manager, and email accounts.

Why: Almost all *setup* stories occurred because the sharer did not know how to initialize or maintain their device or account. We may have seen so many sensitive accounts set up by others because these are critical accounts most people need, even if they do not know how to set them up. The remaining *setup* stories occurred as a favor to the sharee.

How: In 81% of *setup* stories, the sharee retained full access to the device or account. They usually set up credentials, which sharers with low tech know-how often didn't change.

Frequency: The *setup* type was nearly always rare or one-time. However, the potential consequences of a sharee configuring and having continued access to a sharer's device or account was long-term.

Activities: Device or account initialization accounted for most of the *setup* stories (88%), followed by app installation without an account initialization, and factory resets to enable an ownership change.

Five of the 24 participants reported transferring a device to another person (usually their child) *without* removing their own accounts. Participants did not always factory reset these "hand-me-down" devices for the next owner, in part due to trusted relationships. Thus, participants described a variety of problems, from botched personalization (for themselves as well as for the new device owner) to accidental access to others' files or communication:

> *Reusing a Tablet: Dan gave his iPad to his son. Dan had originally set it up with his Google work account which is synced across all his devices. As a result, his son's Google-related activity on the iPad—which is often watching YouTube videos—shows up on all of Dan's devices. (P21)*

> *Hand-me-down Phone: Jen's daughter, Rose, uses Jen's old iPhone. Jen keeps her Apple account on the phone. When Rose takes photos, they show up in Jen's photostream, which Jen finds annoying. (P3)*

Helping

In the *helping* sharing type, the sharee uses the sharer's device or account to help the sharer with a task other than setup (46% of participants, 7% of sharing stories).

> *Busy Driving: Lisa and her boyfriend, Rick, use each others' phones in the car, getting directions, or texting. For example, if she gets a text message in the car, she'll ask Rick to read it. (P6)*

> *Setup then Help: Maya's dad doesn't use the computer. He asks Maya to do banking tasks on his behalf in his online banking account (which Maya also set up and has full access to). (P11)*

<u>Attributes</u>

What: For *helping* stories, 63% involved devices (mostly phones) and 37% involved accounts (a variety, including password managers, bank, and email).

Why: There were two main reasons for sharing by *helping*: (1) the sharer was indisposed or would be inconvenienced by using technology at that moment (as in the "busy driving" story above), or (2) the sharer did not know how to do the task (as in the "setup then help" example above).

How: In 75% of stories about *helping*, the sharee had full access to the device or account, and in nearly all stories, the sharee was described as a trusted individual.

Frequency: *Helping* occurred from often to rare, depending on the activity. For example, taking an ad hoc photo for a friend may be a fairly infrequent activity, but backing up the photos on a spouse's various devices may occur often.

Activities: Sharees helped with a range of activities for the sharer including: in-car navigation, answering calls or texts, taking photos, backing up devices, creating calendar entries or emails, doing online banking, and managing passwords.

Broadcasting

For *broadcasting*, two or more people viewed the same device or account at the same time, usually to enjoy content together (29% of participants, 4% of sharing stories).

> *Viewing Content: Sometimes Mike's daughter will show him a music video that she's watching on her phone. Or, his wife will ask for his opinion on a chat message or email by showing it to him on the phone or tablet screen. He says, "I mean if we're sharing things we'll share it using our own device. My daughter will say, 'Can I show you this music video?' She'll bring the phone over rather than sending a link." (P17)*

> *Enjoying Media Together: When Jake has friends over, they like to watch movies or play music together. Someone will stream content from their phone or computer for all to enjoy. (P23)*

Attributes

What: Despite their small screens, phones were commonly used for *broadcasting* (40% of *broadcasting* stories). Participants explained that their phones were always with them, and they enjoyed a great deal of content on their phones—some of which they wanted to share. The remaining 60% of *broadcasting* stories were fairly evenly split between tablets and computers.

Why: The predominant motivation for *broadcasting* was to enjoy content with others.

How: Participants usually *broadcasted* with sharees they trusted, so they seldom voiced concerns about security. Further, in 60% of *broadcasting* stories, participants described the sharee(s) as viewing the content only, and in 20% of stories, the sharee interacted only briefly with the device or account. A methodological note is important here: the wording of our interview question ("Tell us about when someone else used your device/account, or you used their device/account") may have caused participants to underestimate *broadcasting*, since the sharer often retained control.

Frequency: Despite relatively few *broadcasting* stories (compared to the other types), participants described these events as occurring frequently.

Activities: Common activities included watching videos, viewing photos, playing games, listening to music, and reading messages or articles.

Accidental

The *accidental* sharing type is substantially different from the others. It involved the sharee gaining access to the sharer's device or account (and hence the associated data), when the sharer *did not intend* for that access to happen (42% of participants, 9% of sharing stories).

> *Shared Work Computer: Dan and Matt are coworkers who share a computer at work and log in with different accounts. Dan has accidentally seen Matt's email and files when Matt has forgotten to log out. Dan usually just logs Matt out. Dan has heard of other coworkers who share a computer accidentally emailing from the wrong account before, saying: "Not that I think anyone's doing anything maliciously, but you don't want somebody else to be sending email even accidentally from my email account to their customer saying, 'Send me your financial data.' That's not a good idea." (P21)*

> *Spying: A Chromebook is mutually used by Mom and teenage Daughter because Daughter's laptop died part way through the school year. Each has their own Google account, and they usually log in/out between sessions, but not always. Sometimes they browse the web in each others' accounts. When her daughter forgets to log out, Mom looks through Daughter's browsing history to see what Daughter has been doing online. Mom is not sure if Daughter knows Mom looks. Mom uses LastPass on the Chromebook, so Daughter could get into Mom's accounts (including bank), but Mom doesn't worry about it. (P2)*

Attributes

What: All *accidental* sharing stories were about *accounts* being unintentionally accessed during an otherwise intended device sharing situation. Most stories (62%) involved communication accounts (social, email, and texting). Several (19%) were work accounts accidentally being shared—some participants described mutually using computers at work, which sometimes led to *accidental* account accesses.

Why: As noted, this sharing type usually involved an intended device sharing situation that led to *accidental* account sharing. In 57% of *accidental* stories, the sharee was *borrowing* the device, and in 29% the sharee was *mutually using* the device—for both types, the first user had not logged out of the accounts that were accidentally shared.

How: Problematically, in 57% of *accidental* stories, participants described the sharee who gained access to their account as someone they did not fully trust.

Frequency: The frequency of *accidental* sharing is unclear. Participants sometimes became aware of these accidents or admitted to accessing others' accounts (e.g., see the "Spying" story above). However, a limitation of our method is that participants were unable to report what they did not know, or they may have avoided admitting they looked at others' accounts.

Influences on Sharing Behaviors & Security Decisions

The sharing types taxonomy adds structure and detail to our understanding of how participants shared devices and accounts. Across sharing types, two major themes emerged from the interviews: that motivation to share and security-related decisions were highly influenced by (1) trust in sharees and (2) convenience. These themes were so prevalent that they are an essential part of understanding everyday sharing. While prior work has identified trust [3,8,10,16,21,27,30,31,34] and convenience [10,12,16–18,25,31] as factors that influence technology sharing, our results add detail on how they influence the different sharing types differently, and the effects of trust- and convenience-based sharing decisions (e.g., leaving participants open to security threats from trusted relations, or *accidental* sharing due to not logging out of accounts before sharing a device).

Trust in Sharees

Trust in sharees, which is often invisible to technology designers, highly influenced *whether* and *how* people shared devices and accounts. In more than half of sharing stories, participants described behaviors that implicitly communicated their trust in sharees (e.g., not supervising the sharee's use of a device) and in many of these, they explicitly described trust as impacting whether and how they shared.

A sharer's level of trust in a sharee strongly influenced the *level of security* the sharer enforced. Sharers used fewer security precautions to share with trusted sharees: the sharer would often give their password to the sharee and would not supervise use of the device or account. Significant others were nearly always described as a trusted sharee in interviews, corroborated by diary study data, which shows them as one of the most shared with relationship types (Figure 1b). P6 described open sharing with her spouse:

> *"I think the trust is a big factor, in any relationship so if you're comfortable with someone seeing your messages and you don't have anything to hide, like, there's no reason to have to keep logging in and out." (P6)*

Conversely, sharers used more security precautions with less trusted sharees: they either kept the device in their possession or supervised the sharee; applied rules (such as requiring the sharee to ask permission to use a device or account); and rather than giving their password to the sharee, the sharer would enter it themselves. For example, P23 gave his password to his girlfriend, but did not give it to visitors to his home who he let use his computer:

> *"[Visitors] definitely use my profile to do stuff... I have no problem letting people use it, like, if I'm around and it's already open... I do wanna keep my password to myself." (P23)*

Because sharing practices implicitly communicated a sharer's trust in a sharee, participants sometimes felt obligated to share more openly than they may have felt comfortable with, in order to avoid communicating a lack of trust that could harm a relationship. For example, P14 described how building a relationship with his new wife took precedence:

> *"We've only been married two years... and we're just trying to figure out how to share things at this point, let alone worrying about sharing too much."*

Trust was based on past experiences with and expectations of the sharee's behavior. For example, P6 trusted her spouse with her phone or laptop, but did not trust her mom:

> *"[My parents are] just, like, very curious people. They want to know everything that's going on in my life, so I just know that they will, if given the opportunity, typically my mother, like, want to check my messages and stuff."*

Because it was experience-based, security decisions based on trust were dynamic and reactive. If a trusted person broke expectations (e.g., by snooping or pranking), they would become less trusted and sharers would change how they shared with that individual. Thus, social role (e.g., spouse, child, friend) was not necessarily a predictor of trust—it was possible that one participant would trust their significant other and another would not, or that a parent would trust one of their children but not their other child. Also, making security decisions based on trust left people open to harm from their social relations. In other words, trusted people could become potential threats. For example, P24 described why he put a password on his laptop:

> *"[My roommates] kept putting weird files and images onto my laptop when I wasn't there, so I was like, 'All right, we need to draw some boundaries here.'" (P24)*

Convenience

For over a third of sharing stories in interviews, participants described that *convenience* motivated *why* or *how* they shared. It motivated many of the *helping* and *borrowing* stories. For example, it is inconvenient to pull over while driving to answer the phone, so a passenger may answer it (*helping*). Likewise, it is more convenient to borrow your sibling's tablet if yours is out of batteries (*borrowing*).

For devices, their proximity to the sharee or location in the home was a major sub-theme that affected sharing. Devices that were located *nearby*, were simply more convenient to use. In a *borrowing* example from above, P20 noted that his wife will, "*just grab any device that's closer to her.*"

Not surprisingly, phones tended to be located nearby, which helps explain the diary study finding that phones were more frequently shared than tablets—they were often closer than tablets. P18 describes sharing his phone more than his tablet with his son, because "*I have my phone with me when I'm with [my son], when we're out... more often.*"

The desire for convenience also affected the adoption of security features, which led to many *accidental* sharing stories. Most often, sharers did not want to log out/in of accounts when someone temporarily used their device because it was inconvenient, which enabled *accidental* account sharing. This affected all sharing types except *mutual use*, which was not characterized by temporary use (though even in cases of *mutual use*, sharers sometimes forgot to log out; see the "spying" story above). Also related to adoption of security features, sharers commonly described not using lock screen PINs/patterns (in about one-quarter of sharing stories), in part to enable more convenient sharing. P11 lends her phone to her boyfriend and has no security lock because, *"It's easier for us to check something really quick."* For those who did have PINs or passwords on their devices or accounts, they usually told them to frequent sharees, in part because this enabled easier sharing (see the "friends sharing PINs" example in *borrowing*). As noted above, six households had common passwords known by all family members to make it easier to access *mutually used* accounts. For over a third of sharing stories, participants described providing their credentials to sharees.

The pervasiveness of convenience as a motivator for *how* and *why* people shared their devices and accounts is critical to how designers approach the creation of technology. We discuss implications of this and our other findings next.

DISCUSSION

Overall, our study contributes to understanding everyday device and account sharing practices. Here, we discuss implications for (1) research methods, and (2) designing technologies that are likely impacted by sharing.

Implications for Research Methods

Importantly, our study shows that what participants thought of as "personal" devices or accounts are not exclusively personal in practice. After the diary study, participants expressed surprise at how often they shared their "personal" mobile phones. The *invisibility* of certain types of sharing is important to call out. *Borrowing* and *helping* sharing types tended to be *unplanned*, which may have contributed to their invisibility. People may forget the situations when their spouse quickly looks up something on their phone or answers a call on their behalf; they may not see all the times their kids borrow their tablet to watch a video. Our results highlight that the language used to describe devices and accounts can be deceiving: "personal" devices are often shared; and sharing occurs in multiple ways and for a variety of reasons beyond the most obvious or visible.

This invisibility of sharing and potential ambiguity around the language has implications for research methods. Questions about sharing must be carefully worded. The terms "sharing" and "personal" are fraught with issues, potentially being overloaded or interpreted differently by different people. Even with clearly worded questions that we piloted and which specified sharing as "use of a device by more than one person," participants did not understand or recall the extent of their sharing until they completed the diary study. Our results show that certain types of sharing may be more or less top-of-mind. Thus in future research, it will be important to mitigate these risks, for example by including in situ or complementary methods, or providing examples of different types of sharing to help participants consider the range of relevant behaviors.

Implications for Technology Design

The major contribution of this paper for designers is the taxonomy of sharing types, which provides a framework for thinking about a variety of common sharing practices. Designers can use the taxonomy to evaluate how different sharing types would impact the use of new technologies being designed. To illustrate this, we present an example of how our taxonomy can be used by designers of *entertainment* accounts (e.g., music, video, or game accounts).

Designers of entertainment accounts can expect *mutual use* to be a very common sharing type among household members, according to our results. *Mutual use* was motivated by convenient access to shared content (e.g., a music or video library) and avoidance of extra subscription or content purchases. Thus, designers should consider group accounts that enable multiple users to sign up together and organize a shared library of content. Because all mutual users may frequently use the account, any personalization system employed (e.g., to make video recommendations) must consider sharing to avoid developing incorrect models that could result in poor personalization, consistent with prior work on Tivo viewer profiles [15]. To account for sharing, such personalization systems might try to detect who is currently using the account. *Mutual use* was common with one's significant other and children in our study. Systems may be able to leverage this knowledge by, for example, modeling differences between adult and child behavior to separate user activities. Finally, since creating and switching profiles was an issue with mutual users, improving profile interfaces is an important area for future design, though prior work has noted the challenges in doing so [5,8,11].

Borrowing and *broadcasting* were also common on entertainment accounts. Designers would help users avoid *accidental* sharing in these cases by creating easy-to-use guest modes. Within those guest modes, designers could consider suppressing notifications or auto-completes in text entry boxes. Many notifications pop-up previews of incoming messages, emails, calendar entries, and so on, which can reveal personal information to a sharee. Likewise, autocompletes in text entry boxes, which can improve usability, may unintentionally reveal previous web browsing, personal information entered into forms, and so on.

Setup is also an issue for shared entertainment accounts: one person likely initializes the account, meaning that all the other sharers may never see notice and consent material or know how privacy-related settings were configured. Designers of entertainment accounts should consider using approaches like "privacy check-ups" [2,35] to ensure all account users understand and agree to the privacy settings.

CONCLUSION

We have presented results from a multiple-methods study of common device and account sharing practices among household members and their relations. Among our key findings were that device and account sharing is common, and that mobile phones were often shared. The major contribution of this work is the organization of technology sharing practices into a taxonomy of six sharing types—distinct patterns of what, why, and how people shared. We also presented two themes that cut across sharing types: that (1) trust in sharees and (2) convenience highly influenced sharing behaviors and security-related decisions. Future work could explore device and account sharing among a different type of social group than household members (e.g., teens, friend groups, coworkers, and so on), in special situations (e.g., when traveling or during disaster response), or deeply within a single sharing type (e.g., *accidental*) using observation or other qualitative methods.

REFERENCES

1. Lalit Agarwal, Nisheeth Shrivastava, Sharad Jaiswal, and Saurabh Panjwani. 2013. Do Not Embarrass: Re-examining User Concerns for Online Tracking and Advertising. *Proceedings of the Ninth Symposium on Usable Privacy and Security*, 8:1–8:13. http://doi.org/10.1145/2501604.2501612
2. Mario Aguilar. Go Check Up On Your Google Privacy Settings in the New Accounts Page. *Gizmodo*. Retrieved August 21, 2015 from http://gizmodo.com/go-check-up-on-your-google-privacy-settings-in-the-new-1708171674
3. Deena Alghamdi, Ivan Flechais, and Marina Jirotka. 2015. Security Practices for Households Bank Customers in the Kingdom of Saudi Arabia. *Eleventh Symposium On Usable Privacy and Security (SOUPS 2015)*, 297–308.
4. Antonella De Angeli, Uday Athavankar, Anirudha Joshi, Lynne Coventry, and Graham I. Johnson. 2004. Introducing ATMs in India: a contextual inquiry. *Interacting with Computers* 16, 1: 29–44.
5. Jakob E. Bardram. 2005. The trouble with login: on usability and computer security in ubiquitous computing. *Personal Ubiquitous Computing* 9: 357–367. http://doi.org/10.1007/s00779-005-0347-6
6. Susanne Bødker and Ellen Christiansen. 2012. Poetry in motion – Appropriation of the world of Apps. ACM.
7. Susanne Bødker and Erik Grönvall. 2013. Calendars: Time Coordination and Overview in Families and Beyond. *Proceedings of the 13th European Conference on Computer Supported Cooperative Work*, Springer-Verlag.
8. A. J. Bernheim Brush and Kori M. Inkpen. 2007. Yours, Mine and Ours? Sharing and Use of Technology in Domestic Environments. *Proceedings of the 9th International Conference on Ubiquitous Computing (UbiComp '07)*, 109–126.
9. Britta Busse and Marek Fuchs. 2013. Prevalence of Cell Phone Sharing. *Survey Methods: Insights from the Field*. http://doi.org/10.13094/SMIF-2013-00004
10. Ivan Cherapau, Ildar Muslukhov, Nalin Asanka, and Konstantin Beznosov. 2015. On the Impact of Touch ID on iPhone Passcodes. *Eleventh Symposium On Usable Privacy and Security (SOUPS 2015)*, 257–276.
11. Serge Egelman, A.J. Bernheim Brush, and Kori M. Inkpen. 2008. Family Accounts: A New Paradigm for User Accounts Within the Home Environment. *Proceedings of the 2008 ACM conference on Computer supported cooperative work (CSCW '08)*, 669–678. http://doi.org/10.1145/1460563.1460666
12. Serge Egelman, Sakshi Jain, Rebecca S. Portnoff, Kerwell Liao, Sunny Consolvo, and David Wagner. 2014. Are You Ready to Lock? Understanding User Motivations for Smartphone Locking Behaviors. *Proceedings of the 2014 ACM SIGSAC Conference on Computer and Communications Security (CCS '14)*, 750–761. http://doi.org/10.1145/2660267.2660273
13. Bob Evans. 2014. *PACO*. Retrieved from https://www.pacoapp.com/
14. David Frohlich and Robert Kraut. 2003. The Social Context of Home Computing. In *Inside the Smart Home*, R. Harper (ed.). Springer-Verlag, London, 127–162.
15. Rebecca E. Grinter, W. Keith Edwards, Mark W. Newman, and Nicolas Ducheneaut. 2005. The Work to Make a Home Network Work. *Proceedings of the Ninth Conference on European Conference on Computer Supported Cooperative Work (ECSCW '05)*, 469–488.
16. Alina Hang, Emanuel Von Zezschwitz, Er De Luca, and Heinrich Hussmann. 2012. Too much Information! User Attitudes towards Smartphone Sharing. *Proceedings of the 7th Nordic Conference on Human-Computer Interaction (NordiCHI '12)*, 284–287. http://doi.org/10.1145/2399016.2399061
17. Eiji Hayashi, Oriana Riva, Karin Strauss, A.J. Bernheim Brush, and Schechter Stuart. 2012. Goldilocks and the Two Mobile Devices: Going Beyond All-Or-Nothing Access to a Device's Applications. *Symposium On Usable Privacy and Security (SOUPS)*. http://doi.org/10.1145/2335356.2335359
18. Jeffrey James and Mila Versteeg. 2007. Mobile phones in Africa: How much do we really know? *Social Indicators Research* 84, 1: 117–126. http://doi.org/10.1007/s11205-006-9079-x
19. Amy K. Karlson, A.J. Bernheim Brush, and Stuart Schechter. 2009. Can I Borrow Your Phone?: Understanding Concerns when Sharing Mobile Phones. *Proceedings of the SIGCHI Conference on Human Factors in Computing Systems (CHI '09)*, 1647–1650. http://doi.org/10.1145/1518701.1518953
20. Yunxin Liu, Ahmad Rahmati, Yuanhe Huang, et al. 2009. xShare: Supporting Impromptu Sharing of Mobile Phones. *Proceedings of the 7th international conference on Mobile systems, applications, and services (MobiSys '09)*, 15–28. http://doi.org/10.1145/1555816.1555819
21. Michelle L. Mazurek, J.P. Arsenault, Joanna Bresee, et al. 2010. Access Control for Home Data Sharing: Attitudes, Needs and Practices. *Proceedings of the SIGCHI Conference on Human Factors in Computing Systems (CHI '10)*. http://doi.org/10.1145/1753326.1753421
22. Andrew D. Miller and W. Keith Edwards. 2007. Give and Take: A Study of Consumer Photo-sharing Culture and Practice. *Proceedings of the SIGCHI Conference*

on Human Factors in Computing Systems (CHI '07), 347–356. http://doi.org/10.1145/1240624.1240682

23. M.R. Morris, A. Cassanego, A. Paepcke, T. Winograd, A.M. Piper, and A. Huang. 2006. Mediating Group Dynamics through Tabletop Interface Design. *IEEE Computer Graphics and Applications* 26, 5: 65–73. http://doi.org/10.1109/MCG.2006.114
24. Hendrik Muller, Jennifer L. Gove, and John S. Webb. 2012. Understanding Tablet Use: A Multi-Method Exploration. *Proceedings of the 14th international conference on Human-computer interaction with mobile devices and services (MobileHCI '12)*, 1–10. http://doi.org/10.1145/2371574.2371576
25. Laura L. Murphy and Alexandra E. Priebe. 2011. "My co-wife can borrow my mobile phone!" Gendered Geographies of Cell Phone Usage and Significance for Rural Kenyans. *Gender Technology and Development* 15, 1: 1–23. http://doi.org/10.1177/097185241101500101
26. Elizabeth D. Mynatt, Takeo Igarashi, W. Keith Edwards, and Anthony LaMarca. 1999. Flatland: New Dimensions in Office Whiteboards. *Proceedings of the SIGCHI Conference on Human Factors in Computing Systems (CHI '99)*, 346–353. http://doi.org/10.1145/302979.303108
27. Stuart Schechter. 2013. The User IS the Enemy, and (S)he Keeps Reaching for that Bright Shiny Power Button! The Security and Privacy Impacts of Children and Childhood on Technology for the Home. *Symposium On Usable Privacy and Security (SOUPS), Workshop on Home Usable Privacy and Security (HUPS).*
28. Julian Seifert, Alexander De Luca, Bettina Conradi, and Heinrich Hussmann. 2010. TreasurePhone: Context-sensitive User Data Protection on Mobile Phones. *Proceedings of the 8th International Conference on Pervasive Computing (Pervasive '10)*, 130–137. http://doi.org/10.1007/978-3-642-12654-3_8
29. N. Sadat Shami, Michael Muller, and David Millen. 2011. Browse and discover: Social file sharing in the enterprise. *Proceedings of the ACM 2011 conference on Computer supported cooperative work (CSCW '11)*, 295–304. http://doi.org/10.1145/1958824.1958868
30. Supriya Singh, Anuja Cabraal, Catherine Demosthenous, Gunela Astbrink, and Michele Furlong. 2007. Password Sharing: Implications for Security Design Based on Social Practice. *Proceedings of the SIGCHI Conference on Human Factors in Computing Systems (CHI '07)*, 895–904. http://doi.org/10.1145/1240624.1240759
31. Molly Wright Steenson and Jonathan Donner. 2008. Beyond the Personal and Private: Modes of Mobile Phone Sharing in Urban India. In *The Reconstruction of Space and Time: Mobile Communication Practices*, S.W. Campbell and R. Ling (eds.). Transaction Publishers, 231–250.
32. David R. Thomas. 2006. A General Inductive Approach for Analyzing Qualitative Evaluation Data. *American Journal of Evaluation* 27, 2: 237–246. http://doi.org/10.1177/1098214005283748
33. Eran Toch, Yang Wang, and Lorrie Faith Cranor. 2012. Personalization and privacy: a survey of privacy risks and remedies in personalization-based systems. *User Modeling and User-Adapted Interaction* 22, 1-2: 203–220. http://doi.org/10.1007/s11257-011-9110-z
34. Charlotte D. W. Vinkers, Catrin Finkenauer, and Skyler T. Hawk. 2011. Why do close partners snoop? Predictors of intrusive behavior in newlywed couples. *Personal Relationships* 18: 110–124. http://doi.org/10.1111/j.1475-6811.2010.01314.x
35. Blue dinosaur to help Facebook privacy push. *BBC News*. Retrieved August 21, 2015 from http://www.bbc.com/news/technology-29111393

"Just whack it on until it gets hot": Working with IoT Data in the Home

Joel E. Fischer, Andy Crabtree, Tom Rodden, James A. Colley
Mixed Reality Laboratory
School of Computer Science
University of Nottingham
{jef, axc, tar, jzc}@cs.nott.ac.uk

Enrico Costanza, Michael O. Jewell, Sarvapali D. Ramchurn
Agents, Interaction and Complexity Group
Electronics and Computer Science
University of Southampton
{ec, moj, sdr}@ecs.soton.ac.uk

ABSTRACT

This paper presents findings from a co-design project that aims to augment the practices of professional energy advisors with environmental data from sensors deployed in clients' homes. Premised on prior ethnographic observations we prototyped a sensor platform to support the work of tailoring advice-giving to particular homes. We report on the deployment process and the findings to emerge, particularly the work involved in making sense of or accounting for the data in the course of advice-giving. Our ethnomethodological analysis focuses on the ways in which data is drawn upon as a resource in the home visit, and how understanding and advice-giving turns upon unpacking the indexical relationship of the data to the situated goings-on in the home. This insight, coupled with further design workshops with the advisors, shaped requirements for an interactive system that makes the sensor data available for visual inspection and annotation to support the situated sense-making that is key to giving energy advice.

Author Keywords

Internet of Things, sensor data; energy advice; non-profit; ethnomethodology; data work.

ACM Classification Keywords

H.5.3 Information interfaces and presentation (e.g., HCI). Group and Organization Interfaces.

INTRODUCTION

The Internet of Things (IoT) promises to provide 'the right service at the right time' and in doing so to increase well-being, productivity and convenience [24]. The widespread availability of relatively cheap sensors coupled to networks and computing platforms brings this vision a step closer to reality. It is a vision that assumes people can afford such novel consumer devices (whereas the expense may preclude a great many from the IoT vision in practice) and, more tractably, that the data produced by IoT applications can be readily 'read off' and acted upon. This latter assumption is turning out to be problematic (just as the former might do), with recent research revealing the difficulties encountered in the use of 'smart' domestic applications [39] and the sophisticated reasoning implicated in making sense of sensor-based data [35]. The work presented in this paper chimes with these emerging findings.

The paper builds on prior ethnographic research [13] to support the work of energy advisors through design. Energy advisors typically provide in-home advice to low-income households in a bid to help them manage energy consumption, reduce bills, and deal with problems such as damp and mould. Previous ethnographic observations (ibid.) suggested that it might be possible to augment the advisors' work practices with sensor data, providing useful insights into the domestic environment (temperature, humidity, etc.) to enable advisors to better tailor advice around their clients' everyday lives. We prototyped a sensor kit to explore the possibility and deployed it concurrently in twelve UK homes.

We adopted an ethnomethodological perspective [16] to analyse the collaborative nature of the 'data work' the advisors and their clients had to engage in to understand the data coming out of the sensor kit and to tailor bespoke advice around it. Our analysis reveals that this kind of data work turns upon unpacking the 'indexicality' of the data. This suggests that the sense of the data is not found in the data itself, but in collaborative *talk* about the data (e.g., between advisors and clients). Indexicality thus refers to,

> " ... expressions whose sense cannot be decided by an auditor without his necessarily knowing or assuming something about the biography and the purpose of the user of the expression, the circumstances of the utterance, the previous course of the conversation, or the particular relationship of actual or potential interaction that exists between the expressor and the auditor." (ibid.: 4).

One consequence of indexicality is that the meaning of the data cannot simply be 'read off' representations of it (e.g., graphs and charts). Rather, what the data means, what it refers to, what it reveals is, without remedy, wrapped up in the *situated* interaction between parties to its use. Thus,

CHI'16, May 07-12, 2016, San Jose, CA, USA
© 2016 ACM. ISBN 978-1-4503-3362-7/16/05…$15.00
DOI: http://dx.doi.org/10.1145/2858036.2858518

sensor data requires 'articulation' to make sense of it [35] and arrive at an account of what it means 'here and now', in this case, *in* the giving of energy advice.

Our study unpacks the articulated character of data work in the giving of energy advice. We describe and document the broad lifecycle involved, where sensor data is *anticipated* during installation, the presentation of data is *rehearsed* prior to home visits, and data presentation is *performed* during in-home visits. Anticipating, rehearsing and performing data are collaborative matters through and through. They reflect the articulated character of the data work occasioned by the deployments and have informed our thinking about future systems to support the work of advice-giving, human and automated.

RELATED WORK

Our work is located at the intersection of a number topics in HCI, UbiComp and CSCW, including energy and sustainability, sensing, workplace studies, and the home as a 'wild' setting, which we briefly review here.

Energy, sustainability and environmental sensing

A significant body of work has been aimed at raising awareness of energy consumption and encouraging behaviour change [10,28]. Electricity consumption feedback [14]; advanced sensing techniques for monitoring use [20], and interactive systems to visualise and annotate this information and promote understanding have all been studied [3]. Advances in sensor technology further allow novel applications based on sensing of air quality [22,23], occupancy [31], and CO_2 data [21]. While our work is not specifically aimed at behaviour change, we apply techniques from sensing and visualisation to augment and support energy advice practice with sensor data. Technical work has been complemented by studies of energy use in low-income homes highlighting relevant social issues, such as that lack of control and ownership can act as barriers to energy saving [8], and that designing for rented properties should engage with conflicts between landlords and tenants [9]. Our work is related to research concerned with how people with few means at their disposal can be supported, and what the implications might be for technology design [6,11]. It also speaks to research concerned with the relationship between sensor data and its intelligibility in a domestic context [e.g., 2,12,30].

Designing for non-profit workplaces

Our research has a focus on *work practice* [1] and draws on fieldwork with a view to inform a co-design process. We note that studies of work practice are not confined to the workplace [4], but this approach has been widely used to study organisations, occupations and professions in CSCW [29], emphasising a social perspective on the development of technological infrastructure [32]. Applied to non-profit workplace settings, related work has for example looked at information management [27], coordination and awareness [7,33], participatory design with community groups [26], fundraising [18], and volunteer coordination [38]. In this paper, we focus on novel work practices implicated in the conduct of not-for-profit energy advice work that makes use of sensor data in order to feed the results back into an ongoing co-design process.

Deploying technology in homes

A notable difference to the workplace studies literature is that the workplace setting of energy advisors is more often than not the home of their clients. This overlap warrants consideration of some of the concerns that have emerged about the home as a setting for the deployment of technology. Tolmie and Crabtree highlight that deployments are often oriented to by household members as something done *to* them rather than done *for* them, which impacts our understanding of how new technologies might actually be adopted in the real world [36]. Further research has highlighted the extensive work required to make the technology work in the home [19], social and technical, including the work of 'digital plumbing' [34]. Our work touches upon all of these concerns. It seeks to exploit technology to deliver beneficial outcomes *for* clients; it touches upon the work of digital plumbing in accounting for salient aspects of the work of deployment; and it unpacks the inherently collaborative or social character of the data work that advice-giving turns upon.

THE PROJECT

This work is part of the CharIoT project aimed at using the IoT to support the work of energy advisors through the co-design of sensor kits for collecting environmental data in homes and interactive systems that support sense-making and the provisioning of tailored advice. The project follows a participatory co-design philosophy, including ethnographic studies of advice-giving work practice, participatory design workshops, cooperative prototyping, real world deployments, and studies in the wild.

Energy advice

This project aims to support the work of energy advisors working for the Centre for Sustainable Energy (CSE), a non-profit charity based in Bristol, UK. CSE's energy advisors provide advice through in-home visits, particularly to vulnerable households affected by fuel poverty. Fuel poverty is a key societal problem not just in the UK, with millions of people struggling to pay fuel bills in order to maintain adequate heating in winter months, affecting financial, physical, and emotional wellbeing [25]. CSE's energy advice work involves diagnosing the causes of high bills and health risks (e.g., damp and mould), recommending material and behavioural improvements, and reporting to third parties to make the case for improvements on their client's behalf (e.g. landlords, councils, and energy suppliers); a detailed account of the advisors' work practices has been reported elsewhere [13]. The project team consists of three full time advisors and CSE's senior development manager, who collaborate with a number of interdisciplinary academic researchers. The team collaborates by means of meetings, workshops, shared workspaces, and remote communication.

Supporting Advisors

CSE's advisors currently suffer from a paucity of information about the causes of problems in households, which limits their ability to tailor advice to clients and to provide evidence when acting on their behalf. Our work explores whether and how data from environmental sensors may mitigate this paucity in information and support advisory practice. The key goal is to augment and thereby improve existing advisory practices in homes by enabling personalised, data-driven advice-giving. Prior work [13] suggested multiple opportunities for technological support including:

- ***Enhancing advice visits with data***, by providing and discussing data visualisations that show the impact of the client's activity;
- ***Supporting remote advice work,*** by providing access to the client's household's data prior to the home visit to enable better preparation and comparison;
- ***Supporting upward accountability,*** by enabling data representations as evidence of practices and property conditions in third party negotiations.

We prototyped a sensor kit for deployment in CSE's clients' homes to explore these opportunities in the wild.

The sensor kit

The sensor kit was assembled using off the shelf components including:

- A wireless temperature, (relative) humidity and light sensor (Figure 1), including WiFi connectivity to send the data to our server via the portable 3G router.

Figure 1. The prototype temperature, humidity and light sensor.

- An off the shelf electricity sensor (CT clamp) which sends data wirelessly over the zigbee to a hub. The hub is connected to the internet via an Ethernet connection to the portable 3G router or broadband modem if available.
- A small form factor 3G mobile broadband router which is preconfigured to allow access from the wireless environmental sensor and off the shelf CT clamp.
- A rudimentary web interface was also developed to enable checking during installation that data from the home was received in our database, and to plot the raw data in simple line charts (Figure 2).

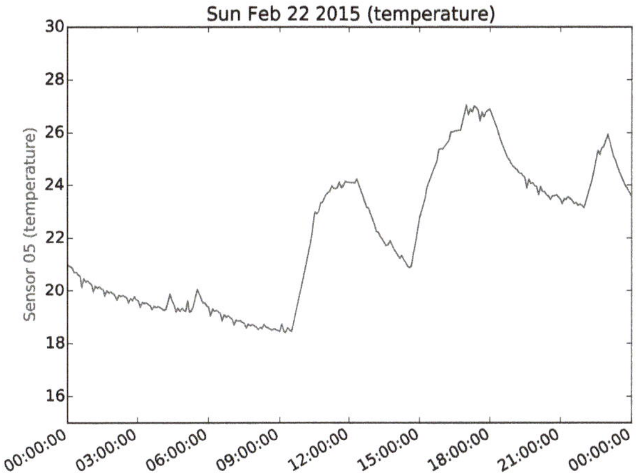

Figure 2. Sample temperature data.

Participants

After approval by the University's ethics committee, we recruited 12 homes as participants. Six homes were recruited via an energy supplier, which was recruiting new pre-paid smart meter customers. Pre-paid meters are prevalent among low-income communities in Britain; the majority of CSE's clients are on a pre-paid tariff. We hoped that there would be participants among the energy supplier's new customer base who would benefit from advice by CSE. Eligibility was ensured on a case-by-case basis, as described below. In addition, our relationship with the supplier provided access to otherwise unavailable gas consumption data.

We took steps to ensure that participants understood the research was not being conducted on the part of their energy company. For example, the company's representatives were instructed to advertise the research project only after new customers had agreed to smart meter installation, and to stress that participation was voluntary and independent of their contractual relationship with the company. CSE advisors then phoned the potential participants after a 'cooling-off' period of two weeks to establish whether they would benefit from a home visit. This interview followed CSE's procedures to establish client eligibility, and included probing whether the client has a cold home in winter, or problems with damp and mould, or sometimes struggled to pay their bills.

An additional six households were recruited from CSE's existing client base. These clients are tenants of council properties in the city of Bristol and were referred to CSE by the city council, which for various and specific reasons identified these households as 'vulnerable', e.g., members include children, elderly or disabled people, or those with long term illnesses. Out of our 12 participating households, two households had people over 70 years of age, four had children below the age of five, seven had a low household income (less than £16,000/year), eight reported their homes were colder than they preferred in winter, five reported problems with damp and mould, and eight reported they sometimes struggle to pay their fuel bills.

Project phases

The sensor kit was deployed in each of the participant's homes for between 4 and 6 weeks. Deployment, use and study of the sensor kit was accomplished over a number of discrete phases. The first of these involved an *installation visit* to situate the sensor kit in participants' homes. The second consisted of a *seed workshop*, where collected data samples were reviewed by the academic researchers and CSE staff. Third, the advisors conducted *in-home visits* using the data to work through perceived problems. Forth, a *final visit* was conducted by the advisors to collect the sensor kit and offer further advice. Fifth, a *reflective workshop* was held between the advisors and academic staff to review the experience.

Data collection and analysis

In addition to the data that was captured by the sensor kit, we treated each of the phases outlined above as opportunities and subject matter for fieldwork. CSE's operating procedures require two people to conduct a home visit, so a field worker accompanied the advisor and documented the work s/he engaged the client in. Data captured included audio and video, along with fieldnotes, which was transcribed and then initially analysed to identify the sequential organisation of advice-giving work (cf. [5], chapter 6). This reflects an ethnomethodological orientation, which seeks to identify the methodical ways in which the members of a setting naturally and accountably order their activities in interaction [17]. Identifying the sequential organisation of interaction orients us to the naturally accountable order of interactional work and subsequently enables its unpacking.

Thus we focus below on the ways in which sensor data is *anticipated* during installation, gets *rehearsed* before the visit, is *performed* during visits, and how these methodical features of data work impacted reflection on sensor-based advisory practice. While a host of research lenses could be interesting to adopt, we are especially concerned here to understand *the work to make the sensor data work* in support of the advisors' advice-giving practice, both in collaboration with one another (in workshops) and with their clients (during in-home visits). We elaborate key findings by offering conversational vignettes or extracts from the field studies to unpack the work involved in making sensor data accountable in and to interaction.

DATA WORK

Data work occurs across the 3 main stages of deployment, during installation of the kit, the pre-visit workshops were sample data is reviewed, and during the in-home visits where they are drawn upon as a resource in the work of advice-giving. We explicate key features of data work in each of these stages below.[1]

[1] It is worth noting that our aim here is not to provide an exhaustive account of data work in each stage; more could be said. What we want to do here is tease out what we take to be the most salient features of the work to design.

Installation: anticipating data work

As a preface to installation advisors first assemble the sensor kit at the offices to check that it is complete and working. At the client's home the advisor explains the project and runs through an initial interview to get a "general sense" of the property and its occupants. The purpose of this interview is to *profile the property* (e.g., fuel type, heating system, appliances) and *the occupants* (e.g., number, type and age of people living in the home), and their *everyday routines* (e.g., how do they use the heating system, how do they dry their clothes, how do they ventilate the home, whether or not they keep doors open or closed), and to *establish the client's main concerns* (e.g., damp and mould, high bills or a cold home).

Deploying the sensor kit is not simply a matter of physically installing it and making sure it works. It also, and crucially, relies upon a process of negotiation that involves introducing the kit to the client, explaining what it does, getting their permission to install it, which frequently involves articulating potential benefits for the client, and figuring out where to place the kit. Placement can be challenging as the advisor needs to balance the desire to equip a room that is frequently used or that has problems (such as damp) with technical constraints, including access to plug sockets, distance between sensor and hub (which affects connectivity), and avoiding direct sunlight or extreme heat (which produces misleading data). Installation also involves accounting for follow up actions (e.g., potential repair visits if the kit breaks down and the planned advice visit).

The following vignette shows something of the work involved in installing the sensor kit:

Vignette 1

After introducing the project, the advisor retrieves the sensor kit from her bag:
Advisor: (Picks up sensor) So this - basically what we'll be doing - this is a sensor - and it records the temperature in a room, and the light, and the humidity.
Client: Yes.
Advisor: And it (picks up hub) sends a signal to this router, and this (picks up 3G dongle) is like a 3G connection.
Client: Yes, it's a dongle. Yes. Yes.
Advisor: And then we can receive the information and we can get charts on those readings.
Client: Yes, not a problem.
Advisor: And then we come back in a couple of weeks.
Client: Yes.
Advisor: And share that information with you, and offer advice about what you might be able to do to reduce your fuel bills.

The vignette makes it visible that the advisor introduces the sensor kit piece-by-piece, explaining the kinds of data that will be collected and how it will be transmitted. It is of note that in doing this the advisor brings up the *anticipated use* of the data - "we can get charts on those readings", and can "share that information with you"; its *purpose* – to "reduce your fuel bills"; and the *projected actions* through which this will be achieved – "we come back in a couple of weeks ... and offer advice". The client's utterances indicate both his understanding of the kit and the procedure, as well as his permission – "yes, not a problem".

Communicating the anticipated use (what will be done with the data) and its purpose (why) is essential to gaining the participant's acceptance and permission to install the kit. If omitted, the client may in turn *prompt an account*. Consider the following vignette:

Vignette 2

The advisor has just clipped the CT-clamp around the meter's main cable.
Client: So what does that do now, the part you've just put on there?
Advisor: That's on the live electric cable.
Client: Right.
Advisor: And so what that does, that'll send to the little white box we're going to plug in now, and that is recording the electricity that you use.
Client: Right.

Here we can see that clients do not simply accept the installation of the kit: reasons have to be given to account for what is being done, and good ones at that. Thus, the client's requests for an account of what the installed sensor does is provided by the advisor in saying that it records "the electricity that you use". We can see too that the advisor accounts for the next action she is going to perform in saying that the sensor sends data "to the little white box we're going to plug in now". Accounting for installation is critical but it is not sufficient simply to say what something is or does, for what is absent from this kind of exchange is an account of the anticipated use and purpose of the sensor data, and particularly the *relevance* of these matters to the household, which clients are not blind to:

Vignette 3

Client: So when you've got all this data and everything, how does this benefit us then? How would this benefit us?
Advisor: So, what we'll be able to - what it'll give us is the humidity in the room, the light, and the temperature.
Client: Yes.
Advisor: So say, for example, we could see that there was a sudden drop in temperature. We could ask why that might be, and what that might mean in terms of helping you with your heating? That kind of thing.
Client: OK.

A further important characteristic of note in the installation visits is an attempt to sensitise clients to *the relationship between their activities and the data*. This is most strikingly evident in how the advisors ask for a "diary of unusual activities" to be kept by clients:

Advisor: So if you just record down unusual, out-of-the-ordinary activity - so if you have more people around than normal, just write it there (gestures towards diary) to say tonight there are people coming around. If you dry clothes in there (points to living room), just write that down as well, because when we get the graphs back that will help us to be able to read things. If your humidity levels or the heat suddenly shoots up and you've got more bodies in there that will explain that.

Here we can see that the advisor not only provides examples of the kinds of activities or events that might constitute "out-of-the ordinary" – e.g., having "more people around than normal" or "drying clothes" in the living room – but also accounts for the purpose of providing this kind of information – it "will help us to be able to read things" or the data to be more precise. The advisor also accounts for what being "able to read things" means – "if your humidity levels or heat shoots up and you've got more bodies in there that will explain that." *Explaining the data* is key to data work and, while trading in the "out-of-the-ordinary" here, it is clear that advisors are aware of and anticipate its indexical character – i.e., that what the data means, what it reveals, is irremediably tied to what Garfinkel [16] refers to as the biography, the purposes, the circumstances of data production and the relationship of parties who generate the data to it. Thus, the advisors *presume in advance* of data collection that the data will not account for itself: more will be required to make sense of the data, with the more of the matter consisting of perceptibly salient aspects of the day-to-day business of domestic life.

It is notable too that that none of the participants recorded any information in the diary. This underscores the orientation of participants to the ordinarily *unremarkable* nature of domestic life: that having more people round than normal is not, in itself, particularly noteworthy, anymore than drying the clothes in the living room, bedroom or bathroom is. If you doubt it, try saying such things to your friends and colleagues and see what they make of them. Many aspects of domestic life are deliberately "opaque" [36] and for good reason in that surfacing them opens members up to potential moral account [35]. We might say then that members have a vested interest in making domestic life into a largely unremarkable matter, and that everyday life in general turns upon this mundane matter of fact [37]. A key challenge to data work involves opening the unremarkable up [35].

In summary, the work of installation is not merely about installing the sensor kit. It turns upon a range of practical concerns *with the data*. These include accounting for what data will be gathered and how, the purpose of data gathering and its anticipated use, and the projected actions through which this will be achieved, all of which turns upon accounting for the relevance (or benefits) of the data to the participants. Furthermore, these anticipatory concerns with the data are accompanied by a concern with the indexicality of the data, particularly its relationship to the activities and events that generate it and the need to make the data accountable to these. Much of this work may be seen as incidental to the work of advising, but it is key both to installation and to building a cooperative relationship between advisor and client in the use of sensor-based applications.

Pre-home visit: rehearsing data work

Once sufficient sensor data had been collected, a workshop was organised by the researchers to prepare the advisors for the in-home visits. The researchers plotted and overlaid the raw sensor data from the various sensors (gas, electricity, temperature, humidity and light) in simple line charts (as in Figure 2). One household was discussed at a time, to explore the richness and completeness of the available data.

The advisor who led the installation visit gave an overview of the household (issues, occupancy, routines, etc.) and the property (fuel, heating system, thermostat settings, major appliances, etc.), and the data was then reviewed and discussed. Recalling where the sensor kit was placed was important to understanding what the data might be saying about each home.

The advisors first set about trying to spot *expected patterns* in the data by correlating data streams. As one advisor put it,

Straight away you can see temperature falls, boiler fires up and there's a spike in gas consumption, and then the temperature increases immediately after this.

The advisor here correlates temperature, electricity, and gas data; knowing that the client has thermostat controlled central heating with a combination boiler, the expected pattern of cause (temperature falls) and effect (boiler fires up) is 'straightforward' to read from the data. This, however, is not always the case and the advisors spent a great deal of the time discussing *remarkable* data segments – i.e., data segments that were difficult to interpret or counter-intuitive.

For example, the participants spent quite a while discussing a case in which the temperature one day goes up hours before the gas comes on. The advisors *speculated* about what may have caused the temperature to go up, for example, "bodies in the space might do that" or electrical devices such as the "TV, Xbox, or computer." *Cross-referencing* between days was frequently engaged in by the advisors in a bid to verify unusual patterns, for example, examining the previous days' heating profile.

Temperature data was read for its maximum and minimum values, and temporal range. Time of day also served as a reference for the effect of outdoor temperature. The steepness of the slopes of the line chart gave an indication how quickly the home heats up and cools down, and insulation measures were often evoked in relation to this. Temperature was frequently correlated with humidity (laws of physics prescribe that relative humidity increases as the temperature drops) and gas (indicating the use of central heating). The advisors reasoned that repeating patterns in temperature were indicative of heating *rhythms and routines*.[2]

The humidity data was inspected for signs of increased humidity. Values over 70% for prolonged periods of time are particularly worrisome, and may be indicative of issues with damp and condensation. Humidity can also be affected by the presence of humans and pets, (lack of) ventilation, or drying of clothes. Peaks and troughs in the electricity data were accounted for in terms of what was known about appliances in a home, time of day, occupancy patterns, and the *domestic activities* that could have caused them (e.g., cooking, washing, using electric heaters). Both gas and electricity data were frequently related to cost.

The advisors frequently *labelled* patterns to reflect their understanding of the data, e.g., one segment was referred to as 'having the heating on all night'. Based on the workshop, the advisors compiled a "checklist for the advice visit", a sort of crib sheet detailing their inspection of the data and the issues they wanted to explore during the in-home visit. For some visits where the data was particularly opaque, printouts of the data were annotated as well.

To summarise the workshop, data work revolved around identifying patterns in the data, both expected and unusual, and speculating for what caused them and their potential detrimental effects. This work was oriented to understanding the local indexicality of the data and opening up the unremarkable nature of domestic life for inspection and *analysis*. The work of analysis might be usefully characterised as attempting to reverse engineer the data, tracking back from the data through the use of common-sense, local and technical reasoning to the situated activities and events that produced it. While some patterns may be 'straightforward' to detect, this work is not unproblematic and is inhabited by uncertainty. Speculation, no matter how informed it may be, is still speculation. The best it can do is suggesting possible causes and effects, and this is what data work seeks to arrive at here. The next step is to verify these working assumptions with clients during in-home visits.

In-home visit: performing data work

The in-home visit begins with a further interview focusing on the physical condition of the house, whether or not energy efficiency measures are in place (e.g., insulation), if the clients have health problems that might be related or exacerbated by the condition of the property, and how much they spend on energy bills. The advisor then moves on to discuss the data, using a tablet to look at (non-interactive) line charts or printouts of the data. Annotations of the printouts or the crib sheet detailing issues arising from the pre-visit workshop are drawn on as prompts to discuss particular data streams and to establish whether or not there is link between them and the client's potential issues on energy bills, energy efficiency, housing condition, health or well-being. The following extended and edited vignette illustrates data work here:

Vignette 4.1

The client reports in the interview that himself and his children suffer from "coughs and colds all the time". There are also issues with mould and damp in bedrooms, and high gas bills.

Advisor: So this is like a week of your temperature changes, with the time along here (pointing at chart – shown in Figure 2). So that's when you're getting up for work.

Client: Yes.

Advisor: You can see there's a number of peaks - one in the morning, normally, and then one kind of around about three o'clock, and then also continuing a bit into the evening.

Client: It all depends on how cold it is, doesn't it?

[2] Although the researchers had initially hoped that light data might be indicative of external temperature (brightness), this proved too unreliable in practice; light data was barely brought up in the workshop, nor in the home visits.

Advisor: Yes. But also looking at your charts - for example on the Sunday, yes (pointing at chart)? So the temperature went up quite high, then dropped over a few hours, and then went back up to nearly 28 degrees.
Client: Yes, just before bed.
Advisor: Yes. So 28 degrees is like really, really, really high - like Mediterranean temperature really.
Client: Well we always have - it's just set at that. That box in the hall, I think that's what keeps it at that, whatever it does.
Advisor: OK
Client: When I put it on, I don't change it. I haven't changed it since the day I walked in this house - what we just tend to do is just whack it on until it gets hot, then turn it off.

In the first part of this exchange we can see the advisor verifying his pre-visit understanding of the data with client: e.g., "that's when you're getting up for work" – "yes." We can also see that the advisor suggests there are stable characteristics to the data - "a number of peaks" at distinct times of the day (morning, afternoon, evening). These are not contested by the client, though they are seen as contingent – "it all depends on how cold it is." The advisor draws on the data to make it visible to the client that, contingent or not, there is something problematic about the temperature cycle, that it is "quite high", unusually so, i.e., "Mediterranean". Importantly an account is offered by the client as to why the data looks like it does: we "just whack it on until it gets hot, then turn it off". This account, in turn, becomes a resource not only for understanding the data but also proposing remedial actions:

Vignette 4.2
Advisor: So there's a sort of pattern in your heating - morning time, kind of roughly three o'clock time, before the kids get home from school …
Client: Yes.
Advisor: … and then maybe a bit more in the evening as well; people relaxing, whatever.
Client: Yes, it all depends what the weather's like to be honest you know.
Advisor: So that might be one thing to try, to bring your temperature down a little bit, looking at your room thermostat in the hall, seeing if you can take that down a bit.
Client: I just put it - I didn't have a clue how to do it to be honest. So I just thought oh, I'll just put it up to full and see what happens.
Advisor: OK. The timer - you can program it to come on at certain times a day.
Client: I'm not really into that programming thing. I'd rather just put it on when I want it on.
Advisor: OK. It's just a suggestion, so it's set …
Client: If I want it on, I'll put it on, and if I don't - it's the same with my partner, she's the same. I'm never going to use a timer on it, never. I'll just put it on when we need it.
Advisor: Let's just have a quick look at the other …
Client: Yes, but it's just easier for us to just put it on when we need it. The way I see it, if my house is cold, and my kids are cold, I don't care if we have to pay, I'll put it on. Because I'm not going to make my kids cold. If I have to put more money on, I will.
Advisor: OK.

Here we can see that the client's account of what causes the unusually high temperature enables the advisor to assert that there *is* a pattern to the heating. This is verified by the client, though still seen as contingent. However, establishing that there is a pattern and its cause enables the advisor to propose a potential solution that would reduce the client's bills: turning the thermostat "down a bit". The client initially responds to this proposal by saying he doesn't know how to do this. The advisor informs him that the thermostat can be programmed. The client rejects the proposal again: "I'm not really into programming". The advisor recognises that potential for conflict here and tries to mollify the client and then move on to another topic. However, the client provides further accounts for his actions that not only justify them, but do so ostensibly on moral grounds (his duty of care for his children) and with respect to a primordial imperative or priority in family life (ensuring the children aren't cold). This is not to say that the data cannot be acted upon:

Vignette 4.3
Advisor: You might want to have a look at the boiler because …
Client: The boiler is rubbish.
Advisor: … that will reduce the temperature of the water that's going into your radiators and will help to improve the temperature.
Client: Yes, OK.
Advisor: You know the thermostat valves on the radiators?
Client: Yes.
Advisor: Do you use those much, or do you just leave them?
Client: No, I leave them on full.
Advisor: So you could turn …
Client: There's one room where we don't have the radiator on in. That's the room which has got the damp in. There's no point in burning gas having that one on when no one's ever in there.
Advisor: Well yes, actually, what might help is if you put the one in the mouldy room on a little bit, on like a one.
Client: Just to keep some warmth in it you mean?
Advisor: Yes. And then in the other rooms, turn them off completely during the day. So when the girls get up in the morning, tell them to turn their radiators off. Then at night, just before they go to bed …
Client: Turn them back on again. Yes, I see what you mean there.
Advisor: Because that's going to save you …
Client: So we put the heating on in the day down here …
Advisor: Yes, and because also what's going to happen, the heat's going to rise.
Client: Because it's heating upstairs and downstairs for no reason isn't it.
Advisor: Yes, the heat's going to rise anyway, and you could try that, try it for a week.
Client: I will do that, actually.

Here we can see that the heating problem has various aspects to it: it is not just about the thermostat but the boiler and the radiator valves, the settings on each being directly implicated in the problematic heating pattern. The advisor proposes further potential solutions, which might address both the heating and the damp problem. It is notable here that data is *not* appealed to. Its use is confined to establishing patterns and elaborating causes, but with these in hand the business of working out solutions turns upon the further elaboration of current practice and proposing novel future practices that will mitigate or resolve the problems to hand. Importantly the work here turns upon accounting for the consequences of current and prospective actions. So again, just as with installation, it is not enough to account for what is (or in this case could be done), but why or to what end.

In summary, performing data work involves verifying pre-visit understandings, which provides a basis for unpacking the indexicality of the data, particularly the rhythms and routines that provide for it. This, in turn enables the identif-

Anticipating data work → **Rehearsing data work** → **Performing data work**

Anticipating data work

Capturing context
- Profile property (e.g., fuel type, heating system, appliances
- Profile practices (e.g., how heating system is used)
- Identify client's concerns (e.g., high bills)

Accounting for data capture
- What sensors are and how they work
- Data transmission

Accounting for data use and purpose
- What happens with the data (incl. future actions)
- Benefits to the client

Rehearsing data work

Reading the data
- Identifying peaks and troughs (min-max range)
- Identifying patterns (recurrence, co-occurrence and anomalies)
- Identifying slopes (e.g., heat up/cool down times)

Speculating cause
- Reverse engineering the data
- Drawing common-sense, local and technical knowledge

Annotating data
- To support reading and speculation
- And to identify issues for verification with client

Performing data work

Verifying pre-visit speculations
- Articulating stable characteristics of the data (e.g. peaks and troughs)
- Drawing on data characteristics to articulate problems
- Tying problems to rhythms and routines

Identifying definitive patterns and causes
- Verifying with client
- Drawing on verified patterns and causes to propose solutions

Working up solutions
- Elaborating current practice
- Shaping solutions around domestic priorities
- Articulating future practice and its benefits

Figure 3. Key stages of sensor data work.

cation of definitive patterns and their causes,[3] which in turn provides a basis for elaborating potential solutions. Where the client is in a position to remedy problems, these matters are worked up and out in the course of interaction between advisor and client. Importantly, they turn not only on the data and working out its indexical relationship to human practice, but on the morally accountable grounds on which practice stands. Not anything will do as a solution then, no matter how reasonable it may appear from the outside. Solutions are, evidently, contestable and must chime with the priorities of domestic life.

The naturally accountable order of sensor data work

The vignettes presented above elaborate what Sacks [24] called the "machinery of interaction". What Sacks is driving at here is that interaction is possessed of generalisable features that order it *in situ*. So while each data set is unique, just as each home is in its problems and practices, the ways in which data work gets done *in* interaction is possessed of stable properties or "procedures" that organise its conduct. These are reflected in Figure 3. They not only consist of anticipating, rehearsing performing the data. Each of these key stages is possessed of its own unique methodical procedures [15].

Thus data work begins with the installation of the sensor kit, which is methodically occupied with the work of *anticipating the data*. This involves capturing context, which is an important resource in subsequently making sense of the data, accounting for data capture, use and purpose, and the benefits the data will bring to the client. *Rehearsing the data* follows on from this and is methodically occupied with reading the data to identify patterns, their causes and consequences. This involves speculation and draws on various orders of reasoning to "reverse engineer" the data and explain how it could have been brought about, and annotating the data in preparation for in-home visits. *Performing the data* is methodically occupied with verifying pre-visit assumptions and identifying definitive patterns and causes, which turns upon unpacking the indexicality of the data to domestic rhythms and routines. This in turn enables solutions to be proposed and shaped around domestic priorities.

SENSING FOR ADVICE GIVING

The stages of sensor data work bring to the fore its *retrospective-prospective* character. Anticipating the data is oriented to what it will be used for, rehearsal to what produced it, performance to what action can be taken on its basis, all of which turns upon articulating the data and making it accountable to the orderliness of domestic life and the rhythms and routines at work in 'this' home. Key to this achievement is the householder or client. Should his or her input on what the data means be absent, what can be done on its basis cannot be definitively established.

It is worth stressing here that our sensor kit seeks to enhance the delivery of advice from an expert; rather than

[3] Often this is sufficient for the advisor to provide *evidence* to third parties (e.g., landlords) that problems exist and need to be addressed.

to deliver information to the householder for them to understand and act upon, or provide information to a remote entity charged with undertaking some form of 'big data' analysis. Thus, we deliver information *in support of a relationship* between client and advisor and the tailoring of bespoke advice. We undertook a workshop with the advisors following collection of the sensor kit from the clients' homes to explore in more detail the impact of this approach and the ways in which the sensor data impacts advice giving. In this section we wish to highlight specific issues that arose for advisors in the use of sensor data and the implications this might have for the design of an improved sensor kit and interactive system for data work.

Data helps build trust

The consensus among advisors was that the data was useful in establishing and supporting their relationship with clients. One of the key problems they have to deal with as advisors is getting the client to listen to them, or "getting close to the client." They found that the data helped build a better relationship with clients, both in terms of understanding the problems that confronted them and being able to evidence their claims, which in turned helped build trust. This was seen as key to being able to get client's to act on advice. As one advisor put it,

"The woman had problems with humidity in her kitchen, and I think that being able to see that on the graphs showed her that I believed her ... gave her a bit more faith in me actually understanding the problem ... and that then helped me to give her further advice."

It was felt that "being able to see" problems in the data increased the advisors' ability to engage effectively with the client and the client's confidence in their advice. The provision of the data allowed the advisor and client to work together to address identified issues, rather than the advisor having to debate the issues with the client and convince them that the phenomena was occurring.

The challenges in elaborating data to clients

The deployment of sensors and the collection of data also impacted the advisors' work practices, changing how they oriented to the task of providing advice. Although recognising the value in enhancing the relationship with clients, advisors also stressed that this was not without issue. They outlined three particular challenges that arose from the use of data as an integral part of advice giving.

Enriching the Data

The advisors drew particular attention to the work required prior to a consultation with clients. Working through and annotating the data in preparation for the in-home visit was time-consuming. Advisors argued that this preparatory work requires explicit support.

"So if there's a way to annotate electronically, that would be good."

In addition to supporting the enrichment of data through annotation prior to visits, advisors also though that it would be useful to have more sensors including outdoor temperature (to disambiguate indoor temperature fluctuations) and CO2 (to disambiguate occupancy).

Client involvement

The advisors stressed the critical role of the client in making sense of the data. The data was often made legible by the client in conversation with the advisor as part of the visit. Consequently, the advisors thought more could be done to improve clients' input and aid their recall of events.

"The data we looked at was actually quite old. Often it was a month old. So it's really important to be quite temporally close to the date that you're looking at, because then they will actually remember and say, Tuesday, I did this and that. So you have people that remember and have more certainty as to what actually caused the data that you're seeing."

The advisors argued that the work of "rehearsing data" prior to advice-giving fell too much to the advisor and that some balance, where the client also prepared the data prior to an in-home visit, might be beneficial. They wondered if a deployed system could be enhanced to allow clients to provide self-annotation and develop a range of services and functionality to allow the client to make notes to support their preparation for the advice sessions.

Conveying Savings

The advisors emphasised that giving advice was the principle purpose of their visits and that saving their clients money was the driving focus of their work, rather than data interpretation. Consequently, they thought that it would add value to their dialogue with clients and other parties to convert raw electricity and gas measurements for selected periods of time into monetary values, which in turn could be converted into 'value for money' savings. In addition to being directly useful to advice work with clients, this would speak to the city council's concerns with the affordability of their properties. As one of the advisors put it,

"If it's clear that the house is not enabling the tenants to live comfortably and affordably, and we have evidence, then I would have thought it would go into their decision making in some way."

BROADER IMPLICATIONS FOR IOT SENSING

Deployment of the sensor kit to support energy advice-giving and reflection on its use has raised requirements for future work, including the extension of the sensor kit and development of interactive systems to support data elaboration and articulation. However, our experiences also speak to a number of broader issues concerning the IoT and its use, particularly in domestic settings. Our study demonstrates the way in which data work turns upon *unpacking the indexicality* of sensor data and making it accountable to the temporally-ordered practices that organise domestic life. These practices are manifest as domestic domestic rhythms and routines, motivated by the priorities of domestic life. Their articulation is key to advisory work, both to understanding problems, their causes, and consequences, and to working up acceptable solutions. Advisory work turns upon reasoning through the data in relation to these matters to identify problems and formulate alternative practices that resolve them.

Our findings support emerging ethnographic work that reveals the legibility of sensor data relies upon various orders of situated reasoning, including reasoning about time, activities, routines, exceptions, people and the moral order of the home [35]. These findings underscore the *essentially* indexical character of sensor data – i.e., that its sense is *irremediably* bound up with situated action and the temporally-ordered practices that organise it. This is not to say that what sensor data means or reveals cannot be inferred – common-sense reasoning along with other kinds of reasoning (e.g., mathematical) can always be applied. It is to say that such readings have the character of speculations, informed guesses at best, and these of course may be erroneous. The inability of a learning thermostat to understand 'context, situations, and intent' [39] provides a point in case, and this is but a single sensor.

The essential indexicality of sensor data occasions the need to build people whose behaviour is sensed into the loop, at least insofar as systems are designed to respond to their conduct. System-supported dialogues might enable this, but they will need to be two-way (not just machine to human) insofar as a) inference about practices in the home is necessarily limited by the indexicality of sensed data, and b) the formulation of alternatives is contingent upon the client's domestic priorities, which are not captured by the data. There is a need then to actively involve data producers in a dialogue a) to understand the action that generates data and the reasoning implicated in it, and b) where remedial actions are required, to formulate viable alternatives.

If sensor data is to be appropriated to augment human action, whether it be in human-human interaction or automated machine-based interaction, it is crucial that sensor-based systems provide ways for collected data to be mapped to local goings-on in much the same way as is apparent in the negotiations between advisor and client in our fieldwork. Here the sensor data is a *resource* drawn upon to support the situated reasoning involved in attempting to answer whichever question is at stake and figure out appropriate responses.

The workshop with the advisors has provided important insight into how this resource may be improved by providing an interactive system that supports the various orders of reasoning implicated in reading the data, and annotating it with speculations about the local indexicality of the data. The purpose of the interactive sensor data system is not to automate sense-making, but to provide people with the tools they need to make sense of the data and formulate appropriate responses. The broader challenge will involve working out how to build such tools into automated sensor-based advice-giving systems of the kinds that large utility providers are beginning to adopt and other help-giving IoT systems in the home. In short, if you want to help the householder, you ought to provide the means to understand what he or she does. Data alone is not sufficient.

CONCLUSIONS

This paper has focused on exploiting sensor data to support the work of energy advisors. It is premised on prior ethnographic studies of advice-giving practice [13], which shaped the design of a sensor kit capturing energy and environmental data in clients' homes. The sensor kit was deployed in 12 homes for between 4 and 6 weeks and the data made available to the energy advisors and their clients. The deployment was studied through fieldwork, including studying installation of the sensor kit, pre-visit reviews of the data by advisors, in-home visits between advisors and clients, and post-deployment reflection on the experience.

The study focused on the collaborative nature of sensor data work, and revealed 3 key stages to its accomplishment: anticipating the data during installation, rehearsing the data during pre-visit review, and performing the data during in-home visits. Unpacking each of these achievements through ethnomethodological analysis has made it perspicuous that data work turns upon articulating the *indexical* character of sensor data, particularly the domestic rhythms, routines and priorities that order domestic life and make the data look like it does. These matters drive data production but are not contained within the data itself. Their articulation enables advisor and client to build a collaborative understanding of the problems 'at work' in a particular home, their causes and consequences, which in turn provides the grounds for formulating remedial actions.

The advisors have found that the use of sensor data has added value to advice-giving practice, enabling them to get closer to their clients, build trust, and better evidence problems to clients and third parties (e.g., landlords). Their experiences have also raised further requirements for extending the sensor kit and developing interactive systems to better support sensor data work. However, the indexical character of sensor data has broader implications for the design of IoT applications that seek to offer in-home advice. The need to articulate sensor data makes it perspicuous that its factual status *cannot* be established independently of the circumstances of its production; a finding that echoes Garfinkel's comment on 'organizational data' [20:138]. This means that it will be necessary to build support for articulation work into advice-giving IoT systems and enable a dialogue between householders and service providers to establish what the data is really all about and what should really be done in response.

While much may be read off sensor data, either through common-sense reasoning or big data analytics, the veracity of the data in this context inevitably turns upon the clients' input: the data is indexical to his or her everyday life and the parties they live with. Whether building systems to augment advice-giving or to automate it, there is a need on both counts to *build the user into the loop* and enable articulation of its essentially indexical character if the IoT is to gain traction and deliver the envisioned benefit to users.

ACKNOWLEDGEMENTS

This research was funded by EPSRC grants EP/L02392X/1, EP/N014243/1, and EP/M001636/1. EPSRC data access: the data that this paper is based on is provided in this paper.

REFERENCES

1. Graham Button and Richard Harper. 1995. The Relevance of "Work-practice" for Design. *Comput. Supported Coop. Work* 4, 4: 263–280. http://doi.org/10.1007/BF00749172
2. Marshini Chetty, Richard Banks, Richard Harper, et al. 2010. Who's hogging the bandwidth: the consequences of revealing the invisible in the home. *Proceedings of the 28th international conference on Human factors in computing systems - CHI '10*, ACM Press, 659–668. http://doi.org/10.1145/1753326.1753423
3. Enrico Costanza, Sarvapali D. Ramchurn, and Nicholas R. Jennings. 2012. Understanding domestic energy consumption through interactive visualisation. *Proceedings of the 2012 ACM Conference on Ubiquitous Computing - UbiComp '12*, ACM Press, 216–225. http://dl.acm.org/citation.cfm?id=2370216.2370251
4. Andrew Crabtree, Tom Rodden, Peter Tolmie, and Graham Button. 2009. Ethnography Considered Harmful. *Proceedings of the SIGCHI Conference on Human Factors in Computing Systems*, ACM, 879–888. http://doi.org/10.1145/1518701.1518835
5. Andrew Crabtree, Mark Rouncefield, and Peter Tolmie. 2012. *Doing Design Ethnography*. Springer, London, UK.
6. Christopher A. Le Dantec and W. Keith Edwards. 2008. The view from the trenches: organization, power, and technology at two nonprofit homeless outreach centers. *Proceedings of the ACM 2008 conference on Computer supported cooperative work - CSCW '08*, ACM Press, 589–598. http://dl.acm.org/citation.cfm?id=1460563.1460656
7. Christopher A. Le Dantec and W. Keith Edwards. 2010. Across boundaries of influence and accountability: the multiple scales of public sector information systems. *Proceedings of the 28th international conference on Human factors in computing systems - CHI '10*, ACM Press, 113–122. http://dl.acm.org/citation.cfm?id=1753326.1753345
8. Tawanna Dillahunt, Jennifer Mankoff, Eric Paulos, and Susan Fussell. 2009. It's not all about "Green": energy use in low-income communities. *Proceedings of the 11th international conference on Ubiquitous computing - Ubicomp '09*, ACM Press, 255–264. http://dl.acm.org/citation.cfm?id=1620545.1620583
9. Tawanna Dillahunt, Jennifer Mankoff, and Eric Paulos. 2010. Understanding conflict between landlords and tenants. *Proceedings of the 12th ACM international conference on Ubiquitous computing - Ubicomp '10*, ACM Press, 149–158. http://dl.acm.org/citation.cfm?id=1864349.1864376
10. C DiSalvo and P Sengers. 2010. Mapping the landscape of sustainable HCI. *CHI '10 Proceedings of the 28th international conference on Human factors in computing systems*. http://dl.acm.org/citation.cfm?id=1753625
11. Lynn Dombrowski, Jed R. Brubaker, Sen H. Hirano, Melissa Mazmanian, and Gillian R. Hayes. 2013. It takes a network to get dinner. *Proceedings of the 2013 ACM international joint conference on Pervasive and ubiquitous computing - UbiComp '13*, ACM Press, 519–528. http://dl.acm.org/citation.cfm?id=2493432.2493493
12. Tao Dong, Mark W. Newman, Mark S. Ackerman, and Sarita Schoenebeck. 2015. Supporting reflection through play: field testing the home trivia system. *Proceedings of the 2015 ACM International Joint Conference on Pervasive and Ubiquitous Computing - UbiComp '15*, ACM Press, 251–262. http://doi.org/10.1145/2750858.2804294
13. Joel E. Fischer, Enrico Costanza, Sarvapali D. Ramchurn, James Colley, and Tom Rodden. 2014. Energy advisors at work: charity work practices to support people in fuel poverty. *Proceedings of the 2014 ACM International Joint Conference on Pervasive and Ubiquitous Computing - UbiComp '14*, ACM Press, 447–458. http://dl.acm.org/citation.cfm?id=2632048.2636081
14. Jon Froehlich, Leah Findlater, and James Landay. 2010. The design of eco-feedback technology. *CHI '10 Proceedings of the 28th international conference on Human factors in computing systems*, 1999–2008. http://dl.acm.org/citation.cfm?id=1753629
15. Harold Garfinkel, Michael Lynch, and Eric Livingston. 1981. I. 1 The Work of a Discovering Science Construed with Materials from the Optically Discovered Pulsar. *Philosophy of the social sciences* 11, 2: 131–158.
16. Harold Garfinkel. 1967. *Studies in Ethnomethodology*. Polity.
17. Harold Garfinkel. 1991. Respecification: Evidence for locally produced, naturally accountable phenomena of order, logic, reason, meaning, method, etc. in and as of the essential haecceity of immortal ordinary society (I)—an announcement of studies. In *Ethnomethodology and the Human Sciences*, Graham Button (ed.). Cambridge University Press, 10–19.
18. Jeremy Goecks, Amy Voida, Stephen Voida, and Elizabeth D. Mynatt. 2008. Charitable technologies: Opportunities for Collaborative Computing in Nonprofit Fundraising. *Proceedings of the ACM 2008 conference on Computer supported cooperative work - CSCW '08*, ACM Press, 689–698. http://doi.org/10.1145/1460563.1460669
19. Rebecca E. Grinter, W. Keith Edwards, Mark W. Newman, and Nicolas Ducheneaut. 2005. The work to make a home network work. 469–488. http://dl.acm.org/citation.cfm?id=1242029.1242053
20. Sidhant Gupta, Matthew S. Reynolds, and Shwetak N. Patel. 2010. ElectriSense: single-point sensing using EMI for electrical event detection and classification in the home. *Proceedings of the 12th ACM international conference on Ubiquitous computing - Ubicomp '10*,

ACM Press, 139–148. http://dl.acm.org/citation.cfm?id=1864349.1864375

21. Rachel Jacobs, Steve Benford, Mark Selby, Michael Golembewski, Dominic Price, and Gabriella Giannachi. 2013. A conversation between trees: what data feels like in the forest. *Proceedings of the SIGCHI Conference on Human Factors in Computing Systems - CHI '13*, ACM Press, 129-138. http://dl.acm.org/citation.cfm?id=2470654.2470673
22. Yifei Jiang, Li Shang, Kun Li, et al. 2011. MAQS: a personalized mobile sensing system for indoor air quality monitoring. *Proceedings of the 13th international conference on Ubiquitous computing - UbiComp '11*, ACM Press, 271–280. http://dl.acm.org/citation.cfm?id=2030112.2030150
23. Sunyoung Kim and Eric Paulos. 2010. InAir: sharing indoor air quality measurements and visualizations. *Proceedings of the 28th international conference on Human factors in computing systems - CHI '10*, ACM Press, 1861–1870. http://dl.acm.org/citation.cfm?id=1753326.1753605
24. Gierad Laput, Walter S. Lasecki, Jason Wiese, Robert Xiao, Jeffrey P. Bigham, and Chris Harrison. 2015. Zensors: Adaptive, Rapidly Deployable, Human-Intelligent Sensor Feeds. *Proceedings of the 33rd Annual ACM Conference on Human Factors in Computing Systems - CHI '15*, ACM Press, 1935–1944. http://doi.org/10.1145/2702123.2702416
25. Marmot Review Team. 2011. *The health impacts of cold homes and fuel poverty*. London, England.
26. Cecelia B. Merkel, Lu Xiao, Umer Farooq, et al. 2004. Participatory design in community computing contexts. *Proceedings of the eighth conference on Participatory design Artful integration: interweaving media, materials and practices - PDC 04*, ACM Press, 1–10. http://doi.org/10.1145/1011870.1011872
27. Cecelia Merkel, Umer Farooq, Lu Xiao, Craig Ganoe, Mary Beth Rosson, and John M. Carroll. 2007. Managing technology use and learning in nonprofit community organizations. *Proceedings of the 2007 symposium on Computer human interaction for the management of information technology - CHIMIT '07*, ACM Press. http://doi.org/10.1145/1234772.1234783
28. James Pierce and Eric Paulos. 2012. Beyond energy monitors: interaction, energy, and emerging energy systems. *Proceedings of the 2012 ACM annual conference on Human Factors in Computing Systems - CHI '12*, ACM Press, 665. http://dl.acm.org/citation.cfm?id=2207676.2207771
29. Lydia Plowman, Yvonne Rogers, and Magnus Ramage. 1995. What are workplace studies for? *ECSCW*, 309–324. http://dl.acm.org/citation.cfm?id=1241958.1241978
30. Zachary Pousman, Mario Romero, Adam Smith, and Michael Mateas. 2008. Living with tableau machine: a longitudinal investigation of a curious domestic intelligence. *Proceedings of the 10th international conference on Ubiquitous computing - UbiComp '08*, ACM Press, 370–379. http://doi.org/10.1145/1409635.1409685
31. James Scott, A.J. Bernheim Brush, John Krumm, et al. 2011. PreHeat: controlling home heating using occupancy prediction. *Proceedings of the 13th international conference on Ubiquitous computing - UbiComp '11*, ACM Press, 281–290. http://dl.acm.org/citation.cfm?id=2030112.2030151
32. Susan Leigh Star and Geoffrey C Bowker. 2002. How to infrastructure. In *The Handbook of New Media*, L.A. Lievrouw and S.M. Livingstone (eds.). Sage, London, UK, 151–162.
33. Jennifer Stoll, W. Keith Edwards, and Elizabeth D. Mynatt. 2010. Interorganizational coordination and awareness in a nonprofit ecosystem. *Proceedings of the 2010 ACM conference on Computer supported cooperative work - CSCW '10*, ACM Press, 51–60. http://doi.org/10.1145/1718918.1718930
34. Peter Tolmie, Andy Crabtree, Stefan Egglestone, Jan Humble, Chris Greenhalgh, and Tom Rodden. 2009. Digital plumbing: the mundane work of deploying UbiComp in the home. *Personal and Ubiquitous Computing* 14, 3: 181–196. http://doi.org/10.1007/s00779-009-0260-5
35. Peter Tolmie, Andy Crabtree, Tom Rodden, James Colley, and Ewa Luger. 2016. "This has to be the cats" - personal data legibility in networked sensing systems. *Proceedings of the 2016 ACM Conference on Computer Supported Cooperative Work.*
36. Peter Tolmie and Andy Crabtree. 2008. Deploying research technology in the home. *Proceedings of the ACM 2008 conference on Computer supported cooperative work - CSCW '08*, ACM Press, 639–648. http://doi.org/10.1145/1460563.1460662
37. Peter Tolmie. 2011. Uncovering the Unremarkable. In *Making Work Visible: Ethnographically Grounded Case Studies of Work Practice*, Margaret H. Szymanski and Jack Whalen (eds.). Cambridge University Press, 53–73.
38. Amy Voida, Ellie Harmon, and Ban Al-Ani. 2012. Bridging between organizations and the public: volunteer coordinators' uneasy relationship with social computing. *Proceedings of the 2012 ACM annual conference on Human Factors in Computing Systems - CHI '12*, ACM Press, 1967–1976. http://doi.org/10.1145/2207676.2208341
39. Rayoung Yang and Mark W. Newman. 2013. Learning from a learning thermostat: lessons for intelligent systems for the home. *Proceedings of the 2013 ACM international joint conference on Pervasive and ubiquitous computing - UbiComp '13*, ACM Press, 93–102. http://dl.acm.org/citation.cfm?id=2493432.2493489

Designing for Domestic Memorialization and Remembrance: A Field Study of Fenestra in Japan

Daisuke Uriu
Keio University
Graduate School of Media Design
Yokohama, Kanagawa, Japan
uriu@kmd.keio.ac.jp

William Odom
Simon Fraser University
School of Interactive Arts + Technology
Surrey, British Columbia, Canada
wodom@sfu.ca

ABSTRACT
We describe the design, implementation, and deployment of Fenestra, a domestic technology embodied in the form of a wirelessly connected round mirror, photo frame, and candle that displays photos of departed loved ones. Fenestra's interaction design, form, and materials are inspired by Japanese domestic practices of memorializing departed loved ones with a home altar called *butsudan*. We deployed Fenestra in three Japanese households to explore how this design artifact might support everyday domestic practices of memorialization, and where complications might potentially emerge. Findings reveal that a range of outcomes emerged across our participants' experiences of living with Fenestra—from profound remembrance to unexpected uses to unsettling encounters. These findings are interpreted to present opportunities for future research and practice initiatives in the HCI community.

Author Keywords
Domestic Memorialization; Thanatosensitive Design; Techno-Spirituality; Research through Design.

ACM Classification Keywords
H.5.m. Information interfaces and presentation (e.g., HCI): Miscellaneous.

INTRODUCTION
While it can be a delicate and complex research area, technological trends are compelling the HCI community to engage with issues related to bereavement and memorialization. Recent work has begun to explore issues such as the appropriate transfer of the departed's digital data [e.g., 4,39] to how technology could better support grieving processes among various stakeholders [e.g., 33,34,35,41] to the ways in which digital content might be used in practices of memorialization [e.g., 23,28,37,38]. In this paper, we focus on expanding design-oriented research in this latter theme: how digital materials can be embodied in interactive systems to open up new ways of supporting everyday practices of memorialization in the home.

Figure 1. Emi-H1 integrated a quilt made by her grandmother and other objects in this Fenestra installation displayed in her living room. Emi's reflection in the round mirror is subtly present in the backdrop of her grandmother's cropped image.

While people worldwide are amassing diverse kinds of digital possessions [44], this paper focuses specifically on digital photos—one of the most enduring and expansive contemporary forms of personal content. We wanted to investigate how new forms of interaction might enable meaningful experiences with photos in the context of everyday domestic experiences of memorialization. We also wanted to explore any unintended yet possible tensions that might result from creating new technologies in this nascent and sensitive design space.

Importantly, we situate our design work and field study in the greater Tokyo, Japan area. There is growing interest in the HCI community in understanding how interactive systems are intersecting with social, cultural, and spiritual practices concerning remembrance of one's ancestors [e.g., 2]. However, the majority of HCI research on bereavement and memorialization has emphasized on Western contexts. More generally, few examples exist of HCI research that has progressed beyond investigations of current practice to explore how people's everyday practices of memorializing the lives of departed loved ones could be supported through the design of new interactive systems.

With this in mind, we designed *Fenestra*—an interactive system embodied in the form of a wirelessly connected round mirror display, photo frame display, and candle (see figure 1). Fenestra's design draws inspiration from

DOI: http://dx.doi.org/10.1145/2858036.2858069

butsudan—the Japanese Buddhist home altar that is a highly significant site for practices of memorializing departed loved ones. Lighting a candle in the candleholder activates the main interactive feature of Fenestra; indeterminate changes in the brightness and movement of its flame control how photos of the departed are surfaced, cycled through, and remain present on the photo frame and mirror displays. A secondary feature is triggered when the user gazes directly at the round mirror, which causes cropped digital portraits of the deceased to be displayed. We deployed Fenestra in the homes of three participants that each represented different life stages, but had experienced the loss of a family member in recent years. Findings revealed that participants drew on Fenestra as a resource for their everyday memorialization practices in valued and, at times, unexpected ways. They also reveal the need for new strategies to better support people's evolving self-determined practices of living with digital materials evoking the lives of departed loved ones. Our study also led to unanticipated encounters for household members, which revealed several critical issues bound to conducting research in this nascent and growing design space.

This paper makes two contributions. First, it offers a rare example of a research-through-design study situated within the non-western context of contemporary Japanese memorialization practices in the home. Second, it offers several considerations aimed at sensitizing the design space toward better supporting the work of living and engaging with digital materials evoking people's departed loved ones.

BACKGROUND AND RELATED WORK

There exists extensive literature from many perspectives within the social sciences that explore how people deal with death. While these works are expansive, *memorialization*—the intentional act of preserving the memory of a person or event—has gained significant attention. A central thread in this work explores how social and cultural values shape memorialization practices on individual and societal levels [e.g., 10,26]. Scholars have also turned their attention towards the materiality of memorials and the various roles they play in the lives of the bereaved over time [20]. Researchers have described how memorials can be leveraged as resources for the bereaved to move on from the death of a loved one [3], while others have documented how they can help maintain connections to departed ancestors [32,60]. Practices for memorializing the lives of departed loved ones have existed for hundreds of years in Japan [e.g., 29,50,57]. The widespread adoption of these practices is tied to traditional Buddhist rituals, where the Japanese Buddhist altar, the butsudan, plays a central role. Traditionally, each Japanese family would possess one altar. This family altar was handed down across generations through a patriarchal structure, from the eldest son to next oldest male within the family [1].

However, perspectives on traditional Buddhist home altar practices have been changing due to several reasons [51,58]. First, it is more common for family members to live long distances away from each other, often to pursue professional careers. Second, contemporary home life in urban settings, such as Tokyo, unfolds within small apartments, which are difficult to accommodate large traditional altars. Third, the patriarchal structure of traditional altar practices largely restricted women from living with their family's altar [1]. Hence, now smaller altars with modern aesthetics are beginning to emerge in the Japanese marketplace. Recent research has also indicated a trend toward memorializing departed loved ones with framed deceased's photos instead of traditional butsudans in Japanese households [51]. The proliferation of digital content presents an opportunity for rich new materials to support home memorialization practices in ways that could be more extensible and easier to mobilize than physical materials. Yet, little is known about how people would react to a digital materials and interactive technology augmenting home altar practices, and what the potential benefits and tensions might be.

Within the HCI community, there has been growing interest in how interactive technology is intersecting with experiences of bereavement. Massimi and others argue *thanatosensitive design*—design that engages with the many issues bound to mortality, dying, and death through the creation of interactive systems—is a critical emerging area for HCI research and practice [34]. A range of recent works has since explored issues, such as the transfer of digital possessions belonging to the departed [4,18,19,35,39] support for emotional grief [5,33], and even potential issues for researchers operating in the space themselves [40].

A handful of works in HCI have begun to consider how digital technology is intersecting with memorialization efforts. Foong and Kera [11] adopt a reflective design lens to interpreting experiences of digital memorials. Uriu et al. [54] propose a digital family shrine concept for people to remember deceased relatives. Following this work, Uriu & Okude [53] describe a speculative interactive altar for supporting ritual prayer with one's ancestors. Drawing on these examples and many others, Moncur and Kirk [38] offer a framework for designing digital memorials. They articulate the need for future research to explore how interactive systems shape practices related to the *post-self*—how the identity of the departed is socially constructed.

In parallel to these works, there has been an ongoing interest in the HCI community on how interactive technology and spiritual practices are becoming entangled. Bell [2] and Wyche et al. [62] describe emerging *techno-spiritual* practices and the implications they suggest for critically reframing the design of domestic technologies to better support extraordinary experiences in everyday life. With the exception of the Prayer Companion [13] and Sun Dial [61], few other research-through-design projects have emerged in the HCI community since Bell and Wyche et al.'s seminal work [see 6]. More generally, the increasing prevalence of personal digital content, such as digital photos [e.g., 28,43,45], video [e.g., 47], audio [e.g., 46], and social media [7], has led to a stream of work in HCI exploring how experiences of reflection and reminiscence might be better supported.

Collectively, these strands of research have made important contributions to understanding how interactive technology is intersecting with experiences of memorialization. They also call attention to how complex and culturally situated this design space is and the need to better understand possible opportunities and tensions existing in it. Our work attempts to bring these strands together. We want to explore how interactive technologies could be designed to leverage pre-existing cultural rituals tied to contemporary domestic memorialization practices in Japan. We also want to understand how technology mediates people's experiences of living with digital representations of their departed loved ones. Beyond work that has gone before, we do this by grounding discussion around the design and deployment of the Fenestra system in three Japanese households.

METHODOLOGY

We designed Fenestra with the goal of exploring how embodying digital photos within a domestic technology could support everyday memorialization practices in Japan. The design of Fenestra's interaction and aesthetics draws inspiration from Japanese Buddhist home altars, and symbolic forms commonly found in Japanese Buddhist temples. We intended to craft an interaction design artifact that could provoke reflection on the system itself and encourage a dialogue about (and beyond) the potential future it embodies. Our methodology drew on several related approaches including reflective design [48], technology probes [24], and research through design [63].

Design Process and Rationale

In an earlier speculative design project, Uriu and Okude [53] developed an interactive installation called ThanatoFenestra (see Figure 2) that explored a potential future where bereaved family members could remember their ancestors by experiencing photographs projected onto a circular canvas. The installation used stock images and was far too fragile and cumbersome to viably deploy in a person's home. Yet the form and experience appeared compelling. In the Fenestra project, we wanted to develop a robust system that could more easily fit within people's everyday domestic settings.

The process leading to the development of Fenestra consisted of the following. We reviewed theoretical literature and empirical studies (a sample of which are noted in the prior section). We also conducted in-person observations of in-home practices for memorialization as well as several different traditional Japanese *Zen* Buddhist temples to help orient our design sensibility toward the forms, materials, and practices characterizing these sites. During our in-home visits, we interviewed and video-recorded three different households, asking them to walk us through their practices of memorializing departed loved ones with and without utilizing traditional butsudans. When visiting public temples, we took photographs and field notes to document emerging insights.

We intended the design of Fenestra to reference some key elements emerging in our observations. Circle and square shaped windows were common across Buddhist temples we visited (see Right of Figure 2). Indeed, the name *Fenestra* is a reference to the Latin word for window. In Zen Buddhism, the circle symbolizes the afterlife paradise, whereas the square represents the lower (i.e. living) world. Candles also populated altars and temples, and are used in many different kinds of Buddhist ceremonies including funerals and memorial services. Here, candlelight symbolizes the journey of the departed's spirit to the afterlife.

Figure 2. Left: Prototype of ThanatoFenestra [53], Right: *Genko-an* temple (Kyoto-city, Japan) we visited during our design process; the circular window is symbolic of the afterlife; the square-shape entrance is a gate to the living world.

Fenestra consists of three artifacts a mirror, photo frame, and candleholder. These artifacts are designed as a visual family, each handcrafted from teakwood. All technical components are embedded within the wooden cases. These design choices were motivated in part by our desire to craft artifacts whose materials could inspire a sense of *perceived durability* [42] often associated with domestic altars.

Fenestra artifacts, implementation, and interaction design

The *Round Mirror* is comprised of a custom cut circular piece of one-way mirror glass, which has an LCD display embedded behind it. An Arduino Fio paired with an Xbee module and an IR distance sensor are embedded in the front of the mirror stand; the IR sensor will detect obstruction within 300 mm from the mirror (e.g., if a person is directly in front of the mirror and not moving). We gave the mirror a circular form as a subtle cultural reference to the afterlife in Zen Buddhism. We used mirror glass to potentially evoke contemplation on the connection between the owner's life and their ancestors (e.g., through seeing the subtle reflection of one's own face while gazing at images of departed loved ones).

The *Photo Frame* consists of a tablet computer embedded in a wooden case; a Xbee Explorer module is housed in the base of the photo frame and connected to the tablet via USB. The module wirelessly receives signals from the candleholder and mirror. Swiping the photo frame touchscreen enables people to cycle through photos if desired. We gave the Photo Frame a quadrilateral, square-

Figure 3. From left to right: **(A)** current photos can be viewed on the photo frame through simple swipe interactions (no image appears on the round mirror); **(B)** changes in the candle flame's brightness and movement unpredictably triggers how old photos (on the photo frame) and face photos (on the round mirror) surface and are cycled through; **(C)** if the IR sensor is obstructed by a person or object (in this case the candleholder) a face photo will appear on the round mirror, even if current photos are being display (such as in this case).

like form as a subtle symbolic reference to the type of digital content it presents—mostly images of people still existing in the 'lower', living world.

The *Candleholder* components include an Arduino Pro Mini paired with a Xbee module, two light (CdS) sensors, an infrared temperature sensor, a thermistor temperature sensor, and a lithium-ion battery; all are embedded within a handcrafted spherical candleholder. The candleholder is intended to hold a lit candle. The light sensors detect variations in the candle flame movement and brightness. The infrared sensor detects the temperature of candle flame, and the thermistor detects the temperature inside of the candleholder. The candleholder sits on top of a custom designed teak cradle with a micro USB connection for charging the lithium battery. While a candle is lit, all sensors continuously send data to the Photo Frame. This choice enabled the candle to be moved elsewhere in the home; this aimed to offer more flexibility for people to adapt Fenestra artifacts to their own practices and domestic spaces. We decided on using a candle as the primary 'input' sensed by the system for two main reasons: (i) it provided an opportunity to leverage a pre-existing cultural ritual tied to Japanese Buddhist memorialization practices and (ii) the ephemeral, wavering quality of the candlelight offered a poetic way to unpredictably surface digital content, while not requiring direct further interaction by the user(s).

Before installing Fenestra, we asked participants to assemble an archive of photos to include in the system. We also created high-resolution scanned images of any physical photographs they wanted to include in the system. While participants knew that Fenestra was related to home altar practices, no specific criteria were given to about the kinds of photos they should select. We did make participants aware that they could include photos that they may more generally want to display in the home if desired. We wanted to explore how a mix of digital content related to departed ancestors and one's own everyday life might shape perceptions of Fenestra as a domestic technology.

Based on the images participants provided, three main types of photos were displayed through Fenestra: *Current*, *Old*, and *Face*. Current is the most general category and often consisted of images of living family or friends. They could only be viewed on the Photo Frame when the candle was not lit (see Figure 3A).

Old photos consisted of (often scanned) images taken when the departed was still alive. We developed a script to generate cropped, circular portrait-like images of the departed in all instances in which she or he appeared. These Face photos would simultaneously appear on the Round Mirror when the corresponding Old photo was displayed on the Photo Frame. The cropped Face photos reference to the *iei*—a photo typically created by a third party Japanese funeral company. The *iei* photo is always edited to depict a portrait of the departed against a neutral background; a large print of it is then made, framed, and shown at the departed's Japanese memorial ceremony. Since the *iei* photo is closely tied to formal ceremonies, we chose to not edit out the backgrounds of the Face photos to emphasize the everyday nature of Fenestra as a domestic technology. The mirror image in Figure 3B and C is an example of this cropped *iei* inspired Face photo.

When a candle is lit in the candleholder, the system transitions to showing Old Photos on the Photo Frame and Face photos of the Round Mirror (see Figure 3B). Additional parings of Old/Face photos are surfaced depending changes in the candlelight's brightness and movement. If the candlelight shimmered from a slight breeze, a similar shimmering visual effect manifests in the Old/Face Photo pairing. If the flame wavers more strongly, Fenestra cycles through Old/Face images in a motion closely tied to the flame's movement. As the candle dims over time, the photos do too. When the candle goes out, all screens are dimmed and remain off to signify the end of the ritual (however, at any point after this, the owner could touch the Photo Frame to begin viewing Current Photos).

Face photos can also appear on the Round Mirror when the IR sensor is obstructed (see Figure 3C). This triggers a Face photo to randomly surface through the mirror, although the owner's reflection in the mirror is still slightly visible. When the sensor is no longer obstructed the Face photo will disappear. In addition to gazing into the mirror, a person can trigger a Face photo by placing an object (or offering) directly in front of the mirror.

Participants, Data Collection, and Analysis

We recruited three primary participants from three different households from the Tokyo area to participate in our study. This approach clearly has limitations; for example, it makes the results hard to generalize to a wide population of users. Similar to the seminal technology probes paper [24], and several field studies since then [e.g., 14,22,43,52], we wanted to initially focus on a small selection of participants to gain a richer descriptive understanding of the space as a whole to inform what might be salient issues for future research and practice. Considering the sensitive nature of our study, flyers and advertisements did not prove effective for recruitment. By spreading information via word-of-mouth through a snowball sampling approach—beginning by asking many people we knew that exhibited various ages and occupations, and then asking them to pass along information about our study to their social contacts—we were recruited three participants; each represented very different life stages and domestic settings. We recruited this participant pool as it could offer a diverse range of experiences with home memorialization practices. We use pseudonyms to describe household members in this paper.

Our primary participant in household 1 (H1) is Emi, a woman in her mid-20s whom had lost her grandmother Yoshiko six months prior to the study. Emi lives alone in her apartment, often working at home as director of her design company. Her grandfather Joji lives a short walk away from her apartment and owns a Buddhist altar in his home. Emi uploaded 15 current, 29 old, 22 face photos.

Satoko was the primary participant in household 2 (H2); she was in her late-80s and lost her husband Kenta eight years ago. She had recently transitioned to living in an eldercare home, where she shared a room with three other elder women. Her daughter Masako and her granddaughter Chisa visited her frequently, as did care workers. She had a Buddhist altar with many material possessions owning to her departed husband at her home, but could no longer see them. Satoko uploaded 17 current, 14 old, and 14 face photos. Satoko passed away approximately one year after the conclusion of our field study.

Rikako, a woman in her late-50s, was the primary participant in household 3 (H3). She had lost her mother Toshiko six years ago and her father Shun two years prior. She lives with her husband Gen and second son Tsuyoshi; her first son Taku lives in an apartment nearby and visits frequently. Rikako purchased a Buddhist altar when Toshiko died; she has it featured centrally in her living room with two small framed photos of departed her parents. She uploaded 9 current, 22 old, and 34 face photos.

We deployed Fenestra in each household for one week. It is important to note that considerable discussion among our design research team shaped this field study deployment period. Recent research has indicated that even under 'normal' circumstances of the death of a loved one, individuals can experience complicated grief disorder (CGD), which can prolong experiences of grief, causing imbalances in autobiographical and biographical memory [17]. CGD and related disorders (e.g., prolonged grief and depression) have been shown to be prevalent within the Japanese population [8,25]. While American Psychological Association (APA) metrics for questionnaires [e.g., 49] do exist to help screen participants for CGD, nearly all findings from prior studies that inform this approach are derived from Western cultures; their effectiveness within non-western cultures is not fully established [25]. Considering how little is known about the design space we are investigating—especially within a non-western context like Japan—we had to proceed cautiously. Fenestra could trigger unpredictable emotional reactions and we went to great lengths to make participants aware of the possible effects that could come from participating in our study. We decided on the one-week period as it presented enough time to understand participants' everyday experiences, while not putting them at potential long-term risk of unanticipated effects. This duration does suggest limitations in terms of a possible novelty effect shaping participants' perceptions of Fenestra. We were careful to be mindful of this throughout the development of our interview protocol, data analysis, and interpretation of the study findings.

We aimed to collect rich, descriptive accounts from participants through semi-structured interviews. This included an introductory interview when installing Fenestra and a final interview at the end of the deployment. During our initial home visit (which lasted 3-4 hours) we aimed to understand members' everyday lives, personal memorialization practices, perceptions of digital or physical materials belonging to the departed, and general technology-usage. Our primary participants gave us a tour of their living spaces and decided where Fenestra should be installed. We also provided participants with candles, matches, a trash bin, and an iPad. Participants could use the iPad if they wanted to take pictures, videos, or voice recordings capturing their experiences with Fenestra (but this was not a requirement). We gave an introduction to how Fenestra works and provided a instructional pamphlet. We did not explicitly encourage participants to interact with the Fenestra and all were aware they could drop out of the study at any time. At the conclusion of each study, we conducted a final interview to understand participants' experiences with Fenestra. Questions were designed to explore topics such as: initial impressions and shifting perceptions; potential unanticipated experiences; how others reacted to Fenestra. We also reviewed the experiences participants may have captured on the iPad.

All interview sessions were audio recorded. All recordings were transcribed first in Japanese; then, relevant segments (as opposed to idle chitchat) were translated into English. Researchers took field notes and documentary photographs during each interview session. Field notes were reviewed following each interview, and tentative insights were noted in reflective field memos [16]. We held ongoing meetings to discuss emergent findings. Analysis of the data was an ongoing process. After each home visit, we conducted preliminary analysis, searching for emergent patterns across recordings, field notes, and photos to draw out underlying themes [36]. We coded raw data documents with these themes. We also created affinity diagrams to model connections and differences among households.

FINDINGS

Interviews, observations, and participants' diary reflections revealed that Fenestra was frequently used across all three primary participants. The references to Buddhist home altars and the ease with which other cherished objects could be integrated with Fenestra helped evoke a sense of familiarity around its place in everyday life. However, several differences surfaced in how household members adopted Fenestra. Extraordinary and unnerving encounters emerged in some cases as participants struggled to interpret unexpected behaviors exhibited by the system. In the following sections, we present examples taken from across our field study that help to capture these themes.

Pre-existing rituals and emergent practices

Interviews with participants revealed a range of ways that Fenestra was drawn on as a resource for supporting the memorialization and remembrance of departed loved ones. Yet each household represented different life stages, domestic configurations, and orientations toward Buddhist home altar practices. Next, we detail how Fenestra became uniquely situated within our primary participants' lives and practices, and perceptions that emerged.

While Emi-H1 had a few possessions that she used to remember her departed grandmother Yoshiko's life, she did not have a butsudan in her small apartment. She noted that her grandfather Joji-H1 had purchased a traditional butsudan following the death of his wife, but felt inclined to follow traditional Japanese Buddhist practices and not integrate any materials belonging to her life into the altar. Emi-H1 described growing dissatisfaction over this choice: "*It's all about praying for butsudan itself and not much about grandmother* [Yoshiko]." This issue produced an ongoing unresolved tension for her. She expressed disinterest in traditional Japanese Buddhist practice and a reluctance to visit her grandfather's home altar.

Emi-H1 situated Fenestra on a table in her living room near where she spends most her time working from home. Soon after the initial installation, she integrated a quilt her grandmother had made under the photo frame, along with a small plant that symbolized Yoshiko's love of nature (see Figure 1). Emi-H1 later noted that these decisions were highly meaningful in enabling Fenestra to find its place within her home by bringing the few material possessions belonging to her grandmother into an ensemble with the more expansive digital materials embodied in Fenestra. In this way, the openness of Fenestra's design enabled Emi-H1 to create a unique assembly of material traces and digital artifacts associated with her grandmother's life in a way that was intimately situated to her home.

Emi-H1 also reported that she was able to easily engage in practices with Fenestra and highlighted the significance of the candle as a control mechanism for the system. She lit the candle every night and sometimes in the morning. During these times, her attention oscillated between the photo frame, mirror, and the candle flame itself when a subtle visual flickering effect manifested on the photos. She described an emergent practice of exhaling a deep breathe onto the candle to trigger it to cycle to a different juxtaposition of photos on the mirror and frame. When reflecting on her experience, Emi-H1 emphasized how this subtle kind interaction paired with not having direct control over the specific photos manifested through Fenestra enabled her to better concentrate on contemplating her grandmother's life.

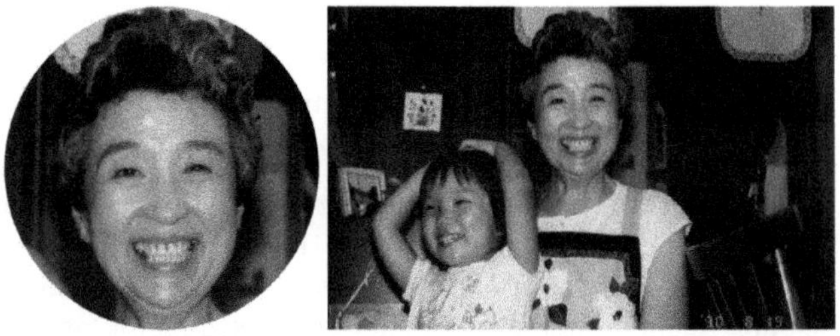

Figure 4. Emi-H1 favored contemplating juxtapostitions of images on the mirror and photoframe that depicted intimate, one-to-one social relationships that shaped the life of her grandmother.

As Emi-H1's experiences accumulated, she described becoming particularly drawn to instances in which images highlighting one-to-one social bonds appeared: "*I love photos showing only me and grandma* (e.g. Figure 4)*, which is the best combination for me. ... I* [also] *love the photo of my grandparents Yoshiko and Joji that my father took during his childhood.*" Emi noted that the combination of the photo frame image depicting a deeply meaningful one-to-one social bond, paired with viewing the photo of her grandmother's faced slightly imposed over the reflection of her own face produced a meaningful space for remembrance and reflection. Interestingly, Emi-H1 stated that other *old* images depicting her grandmother in larger groups of people often did not produce the same result. For her, they drew emphasis away from honoring the intimacy bound to social relationships between her grandmother, other specific people, and her desire to contemplate how these bonds shaped her own life. She desired to have a curated set of photos that reflected these kinds of instances.

Similar to Emi-H1, Satoko-H2 did not currently inhabit a dwelling with a butsudan. She had purchased one after her husband Kenta's death six years ago and frequently drew on it as a resource for memorializing his life, but had been separated from it since moving to the care facility. Masako-H2 and Chisa-H2 helped Satoko-H2 set up Fenestra on a shelf next to her bed (see Figure 5). Fenestra's simple tangible interaction design enabled Satoko-H2 to fluidly adopt it into an everyday practice. She contrasted Fenestra's use of familiar input mechanisms (i.e. a candle) and her comfortable relation to it with other contemporary digital technologies, which she perceived as designed for younger generations and had largely avoided. Satoko described engaging with Fenestra several times each day from morning until evening. She habitually cared for the system by covering the photo frame with a special cover each night. Satoko also ritualistically closed the curtain to the outside facing window each night as a way of symbolically bidding her departed husband farewell before going to bed: *"I could meet Kenta everyday, but have to say 'Good bye' when I sleep at night. Please close this curtain now. He* [Kenta] *does not appear when it is too bright!"*

Figure 5. Fenestra near Satoko-H2's bed where it was habitually cared for and sometimes triggered extraordinary experiences.

When we probed further on this statement, it became clear that the subtle changes in light produced when Satoko closed the curtain could sometimes trigger the IR sensor in the round mirror to momentarily display an image of her deceased husband. Interestingly, when this accidental sensing occurred Satoko reported always perceiving it as an extraordinary serendipitous encounter. She interpreted these instances as good omens—*"like he's watching over me"*—making her feel calm before going to bed. Further, Satoko enthusiastically noted *"Kenta sometimes appeared even at midnight"* and described seeing a momentary image of him a handful of times when she had briefly awoken during the night. This kind of unexpected accidental sensing resulted in positive serendipitous experiences for Satoko and catalyzed a meaningful nightly ritual. However, as we describe later, other instances of accidental sensing did not always produce such positively perceived effects.

Rikako-H3 possessed a very large, immobile butsudan in her home, which she purchased six years ago after the death of her mother (her father had since passed away). Among our participants, Rikako-H3 most strictly adhered to norms surrounding Buddhist altar practices. She displayed formal, framed *iei* pictures of each of her deceased parents in the butsudan, where she frequently lit candles and incense sticks, and placed food offerings for the departed loved ones (a ceremonial Buddhist practice).

Throughout the field study, several instances emerged that illustrated how Rikako-H3 developed a different, yet significant relation to Fenestra compared to her traditional butsudan. Rikako-H3 situated Fenestra as a fixture in her living room, making it available for casual encounters and direct, purposed engagements. She contrasted this decision with the location of her butsudan in a small nearby room that was only used for altar rituals. Rikako-H3 also viewed Fenestra as an opportunity to integrate cherished material possessions within a domestic display honoring her parents, which she perceived were not appropriate for her traditional butsudan. She recognized the references to Buddhist forms embodied in the Fenestra, which prompted her to artfully situate preserved flowers from her mother's memorial service between the photo frame and the mirror as a symbol of her journey from the lower-world to the afterlife. She also placed dolls alongside Fenestra that she had acquired when living in Spain with her parents and brought back many memories from this time in her life (see Figure 6).

In Rikako-H3's initial Fenestra deployment, we had generated two different cropped images (one for each departed parent) to appear on her round mirror. After using Fenestra during the initial interview, she asked us to depart from the reference to customary *iei* portrait photos (where only one person can be featured). Since she perceived Fenestra as existing outside of butsudan norms and believed her parents would have wanted to be together, we were asked to generate a new set of mirror images in which they were collocated (one such image is visible in Figure 6).

Figure 6. Rikako's practice of placing the candleholder in front of the mirror to trigger a collocated image of her parents to 'show' them a more recent photo frame image of her nephew's wedding.

This subtle decision led to an emergent valued ritual. Rikako-H3 described that when the photo frame displayed her current photos, she would subtly orient the mirror toward the frame and place the candleholder in front of it, triggering a collocated cropped image of her parents to appear. She perceived this action as enabling her parents, together, to view experiences in her life that she wished they could have attended. Rikako-H3 reflects on enacting this practice when a photo of her nephew Sayaka's recent wedding reception appeared on the photo frame: *"It's a way for them to celebrate the wedding. ...I love the combination. The faces* [of my parents] *on the mirror and the recent photos on the photo frame. ...It felt like it* [Fenestra] *provided an experience of living with the deceased in a way that very different from* [traditional] *Buddhist altars."*

When reflecting further on this distinction, Rikako-H3 characterized Fenestra as having a lightweight quality that could exist in her everyday life and easily shift between being directly experienced and simply being lived with. She contrasted this with the more involved process of dedicated contemplation and honoring of ancestors at her butsudan. For Rikako-H3, Fenestra emerged as a resource for seeing her departed parents, momentarily "*greeting them*", perhaps showing them a part of her life that they had missed, and then letting them fade away into the background as the mirror eclipsed their image. She reflected further: "*gradually I began to feel the calm presence of my parents. ...When I woke up in the morning or came back home, the photos are changing, which made me happy to take a few moments to see them.*"

Collectively, these reflections illustrate how on a general level Fenestra functioned as a valued resource for supporting everyday memorialization practices in our participants' lives. They also reveal that the specific ways it was drawn on varied considerably and, at times, in unexpected ways as participants sought to adapt it to their domestic practices and values in unique self-determined ways. In the next section we describe how Fenestra intersected with our participants' broader everyday domestic environments as others also encountered it.

Broader intersections and effects in everyday life

While Fenestra was arranged for our three main participants, unexpected experiences were triggered by its situation in domestic spaces. Next, we present examples that illustrate how the everyday orientation of Fenestra produced both positive outcomes and unsettling encounters.

Emergent social interactions triggered by Fenestra

All participants reported that the tangible nature of Fenestra opened it up to being noticed and manipulated by other people occupying their domestic environment. For example, Rikako-H3's son Taku initiated a practice of lighting a candle and bringing the candleholder to the dining table when household 3 had dinner. The simple presence of the candleholder itself during meals could stimulate recollection and discussion of fond memories associated with Rikako's departed parents. In some cases, family members reported enjoying the anticipation that grew around which photos might be displayed when they returned to Fenestra with the candle. Yet, household 3 described equally appreciating that if their discussion continued on and the candle faded out, so too would the images on Fenestra. The photos flickered and disappeared against the backdrop of domestic life just as the candlelight had, instead of lingering on and demanding the attention of family members.

In Satoko-H2's case, the presence of Fenestra triggered a resurgence of social activity in her everyday life. Visiting family members and care facility workers described a remarkable change in Satoko-H2's desire to engage others in conversations about her own life. Both Masako-H2 and Chisa-H2 conveyed unresolved reservations about Satoko-H2's living for years separated from nearly all material possessions reminiscent of her husband. They described how the range of images embodied through Fenestra prompted Satoko-H2 to tell rarely heard stories about the life she shared with her husband. One example centered on when an image of Satoko-H2's husband against the backdrop of many tents surfaced (see Figure 7), Masako-H2 and Chisa-H2 learned about the meaning and significance of the photograph they had never known, but were soon going to inherit. Yet, it is unclear if this kind of behavior would have continued in a longer study. This example does illustrate how the extensibility of digital materials embodied in Fenestra provided a resource for Sataoko-H2 to memorialize and remember her husband's life in ways that largely would have been impossible with material possessions due to her living conditions.

Figure 7. Fenestra emerged as a 'ticket to talk' about the personal and historical significance of old photos depicting Satoko-H2's life with Kenta that her family members had never heard.

Fenestra also provided a platform for family members from different generations to express their opinions on shifting perspectives in Japan around the butsudan and memorialization rituals. For example, Emi-H1's grandfather Joji-H1 visited her home while she was living with Fenestra. To her surprise, after lighting a candle and interacting with Fenestra during his visit, he was highly receptive to its presence within her home. While it was a topic they seldom discussed, Joji-H1 opened up about his thoughts on the needs of the younger generation in Tokyo today: "*I don't know what we should pray with* [in my] *butsudan to memorialize them. There is nothing there that really reminds us them. ...Traditional rituals should be updated for the contemporary needs that people have to remember their lost loved ones. ...Japanese people don't have to use butsudan anymore. ...*[Fenestra] *could be an alternative. It could even be produced in Buddhist temples. ...We can all actually remember the deceased with it.*"

Unexpected re-animations of the departed through Fenestra

Despite the optimism voiced in Joji's statement above, several unsettling experiences also emerged when participants struggled to interpret unexpected behaviors exhibited by Fenestra. Nearly all of these cases centered on instances in which the IR sensor was accidentally triggered, causing an image of a departed loved one to momentarily manifest on the round mirror and then disappear. Emi-H1 reflects on how this effect could have a disruptive effect on her everyday routine of working from home: "*I had a kind of dark mood when seeing photos that sometimes appeared on the mirror when I was busy working in daytime. I thought photos of the deceased should have been shown only when I lit the candle. I love grandma and want to remember her, but not all of the time."* This example illustrates how accidental sensing introduced digital content into Emi's domestic life at a time that was socially inappropriate. She also speculated that if her grandmother had not passed away in such a peaceful way, this kind of unrequested momentary manifestation could have serious emotional consequences.

Family members in household 3 also reported occasionally encountering temporary manifestations of a departed loved one. As these experiences accumulated, household members decided to unplug Fenestra at night when they go to bed: "*We decided to switch it off every night when we go to sleep. It started when my son came back home late one night and saw it* [accidentally trigger]. *He felt scared and turned it off*" (Rikako-H3). Gen-H3 then noted: "*And, when I went to the rest room late at night I was scared. The deceased's face appeared!*" These experiences prompted household 3 to reflect on their own everyday domestic practices and consider activities that, as Rikako-H3 noted, "*wouldn't want the deceased to see.*" As a preemptive practice, household 3 began unplugging Fenestra when they watched television together in the living room. Similar to Emi-H1, they wanted to avoid a momentary re-animation of the departed disrupting the social order of the home (e.g., during family leisure time). Comparable to both Emi-H1 and Rikako-H3's accounts, a night manager at Satoko-H2's care facility described the uneasy effects generated from occasionally encountering an unexpected flicker of her elderly client's deceased husband in the middle of the night.

Collectively, these examples highlight unintended consequences that emerged when images of the departed unexpectedly manifested through Fenestra. While some participants developed workarounds, these undesired intrusions complicated the social and moral expectations that our participants had for a technology like Fenestra.

DISCUSSION AND IMPLICATIONS

Our findings reveal various ways households desired to draw on Fenestra. In several instances participants desired to further situate Fenestra to their own unique, self-determined memorialization practices. Other cases suggested how technology could better support a wider range of experiences bound to domestic memorialization beyond direct interaction. Our study also raises several consequences that could emerge if critical consideration is not given to new technological interventions. Next, we present several research and design considerations for the HCI community that emerged from our work.

Designing for momentary and lived-with experiences— A core goal of our study was to explore how the design of Fenestra could leverage people's pre-existing material practices. We decided on using candlelight as a primary material for interaction because it drew on a familiar cultural practice with Japanese memorialization ceremonies. We also felt that the candle flame could offer a poetic quality to the experience of Fenestra. Similar to how it can be challenging for people to connect with and imagine death, candle flames too are complex. It can be difficult to anticipate how they will move and, like life, a candle flame can quickly be blown out unexpectedly. Participants reflected on how the input method of candlelight offered a simple, appropriate way to open up contemplative rituals with Fenestra (e.g., Emi-H1's practice of navigating photos through slow, deep exhalations). Surprisingly, participants did not report tensions in abdicating control over photo selection to changes to the unpredictable, indeterminate nature of the candlelight. Rather, this design choice was often cited as helping participants to momentarily concentrate on the lives of departed loved ones, growing anticipation around the digital photos, and enabling experiences with Fenestra fade to a close as the candlelight dimmed and went out.

While prior work has explored how qualities of randomness and machine autonomy can productively open up experiences of pause, reflection, and anticipation [e.g., 14, 22,30,31,43,59], nearly all research to date has manifested these qualities of experience through hidden computational processes. Our study contributes to this growing area of HCI research by demonstrating the value and potential in leveraging easy to manipulate, ephemeral input [9,23, 53,55], which, in our case manifested a quality of unpredictability that supported rich experiences and rituals for memorializing the departed. There is an opportunity to explore how additional kinds of highly sensorial, momentary input (e.g., incense smoke, light from multiple candles, etc.) could be combined with other forms of digital content (e.g., audio, video, music) to artfully support experiences of memorialization. Developing more meaningful strategies for supporting the remembrance of lost loved ones through carefully crafted ways of re-experiencing digital content in everyday life marks a clear space for future research in the HCI community.

We also found that participants created and re-configured assemblies of material possessions with Fenestra. While subtle, these actions enabled Fenestra to bring into relation digital materials, physical things, domestic space, and household members in ways that were unique, nuanced, and evolving. As these kinds of actions accumulated, Fenestra emerged as a *background technology*—one that could dynamically shift from the forefront of domestic experience, to being passively encountered, to fading out of sight entirely. In this way, Fenestra offers an example of how digital materials can be embodied with material qualities that enable them to be situated in the familiar context of artifact-mediated memorialization practices. These findings build on and expand prior work articulating the need for new design strategies that move beyond designing explicitly for 'use' and emphasize the aesthetics of integrating cherished digital materials into environments in more holistic ways over time [e.g., 15,21,43,48].

Supporting evolving personalization of digital materials for domestic memorialization—Another goal of our study was to explore how digital photos could provide a meaningful resource for domestic memorialization. The spaceless quality of digital photos—that an archive could be manifested through Fenestra in ways that could not have been easily achieved with physical photos—created opportunities to support memorialization activities. For Emi-H1 and Satoko-H2 it provided a resource to support practices that their material conditions had largely prevented. For Rikako-H3, Fenestra enabled her to draw on new materials that opened up a wider range of experiences than would have not been permitted in her formal butsudan. Yet participants also desired to augment Fenestra in diverse and unexpected ways. Emi-H1 wanted to only include images that highlighted one-to-one social bonds to honor these relationships and her grandmother's life. While Rikako-H3 requested that both of her parents be present in the cropped mirror image, which prompted her ritual of 'showing' her parents photos of experiences she wished they could have been present at.

These examples help illustrate the complex, idiosyncratic, and evolving processes of socially constructing the identity of a departed loved one. As conceptualizations of the departed's identity change, so too might rituals and practices of memorializing their life. However, tools to support these shifts as they unfold over time remain underdeveloped. These findings are in parallel to recent efforts in the HCI community articulating the need to critically consider how interactive systems might shape people's practices over long periods of time [e.g., 12,39]. There is a need for future research to explore more flexible ways new technologies might be designed to represent digital content associated with a departed loved one's life as perspectives change, practices evolve, and these technologies themselves may change hands across generations in the future.

Unintended consequences and broader implications—Undesirable encounters also emerged with Fenestra. These instances were triggered when the IR sensor embedded in the round mirror was inadvertently triggered by lighting changes in the local environment. Although Satoko-H2 interpreted such instances as extraordinary encounters, they produced uncomfortable emotions for other participants. These findings illustrate the sensitive threshold memorialization technologies operate on and how serious consequences can emerge if the system manifests behaviors that are unexpected and difficult interpret.

One possibility is that future research could engineer a higher degree of contextual awareness into memorialization systems to avoid such disruptions. Yet, it is possible that other disturbing encounters could emerge from errors in computational inferences about who is socially present and what digital content ought to be manifested. Our goal was not to engineer a perfect 'solution' to digital domestic memorialization. Rather, we aimed to sensitize this nascent design space for future exploration within the HCI community. These findings make clear that sensing processes within memorialization technologies need to be treated with critical caution and come with significant potential pitfalls.

On a broader level, this study produced an unexpected dilemma for our own research team. Fenestra is a bespoke design artifact that participants knew they would not live with after the study concluded. However, participants did develop visible emotional connections to Fenestra and removing it from their lives left us, the research team, feeling uneasy. Yet, it is likely unrealistic (or impossible) for researchers to provide robust bespoke systems for participants to have and use indefinitely into the future. New initiatives are emerging to support the appropriate transfer of the departed's online accounts to the bereaved [4,39]. However, it remains unclear how these issues should be handled with bespoke design artifacts—they could open up radically new way of conceptualizing memorialization technologies, but also come with potentially serious consequences. Recent work is starting to articulate potential dangers for researchers operating in this nascent research space [40]. There is a need to expand this discourse to develop more effective strategies for sensitively handling potential issues for all stakeholders surrounding the deployment (and possible extraction) of research products and prototypes in the future.

CONCLUSION

We designed Fenestra to critically explore how interactive technology could open up new opportunities for leveraging digital materials to support practices of domestic memorialization in Japan. Findings revealed opportunities to support such practices in unique and meaningful ways, and unintended consequences that new systems could raise. Our study provided a rare example of a research-through-design project situated in the context of Tokyo, Japan. There is a clear need for future work to expand to sites and practices elsewhere in the world. Ultimately, we hope this research will inspire the HCI community to explore designing technology aimed at supporting people's self-determined, evolving practices of memorializing and remembrance, now and well into the future.

ACKNOWLEDGMENTS

We thank Naohito Okude, Masa Inakage, Hideki Sunahara, Masahiko Inami, and Susumu Shimazono for their supervision on the Fenestra project. We also thank our study participants, the reviewers for their insightful suggestions, and Carman Neustaedter and Rebecca Gulotta for feedback on earlier drafts of this paper. This work is supported in part by Keio University Graduate School of Media Design and a Banting Postdoctoral Fellowship through the Social Science and Humanities Research Council of Canada.

REFERENCES

1. Toshimaro Ama. 2005. *Why are the Japanese non-religious?: Japanese spirituality: being non-religious in a religious culture*. University Press of America.
2. Genevieve Bell. 2006. No more SMS from Jesus: ubicomp, religion and techno-spiritual practices. In *UbiComp 2006: Ubiquitous Computing*. Springer, 141–158.
3. George A. Bonanno and Stacey Kaltman. 1999. Toward an integrative perspective on bereavement. *Psychological bulletin 125*, 6: 760.
4. Jed R. Brubaker, Lynn S. Dombrowski, Anita M. Gilbert, Nafiri Kusumakaulika, and Gillian R. Hayes. 2014. Stewarding a Legacy: Responsibilities and Relationships in the Management of Post-mortem Data. *Proceedings of the 32Nd Annual ACM Conference on Human Factors in Computing Systems*, ACM, 4157–4166. http://doi.org/10.1145/2556288.2557059
5. Jed R. Brubaker and Gillian R. Hayes. 2011. We will never forget you [online]: an empirical investigation of post-mortem myspace comments. *Proceedings of the ACM 2011 conference on Computer supported cooperative work*, ACM, 123–132.
6. Elizabeth Buie and Mark Blythe. 2013. Spirituality: there's an app for that!(but not a lot of research). *CHI'13 Extended Abstracts on Human Factors in Computing Systems*, ACM, 2315–2324.
7. Dan Cosley, Victoria Schwanda Sosik, Johnathon Schultz, S. Tejaswi Peesapati, and Soyoung Lee. 2012. Experiences with designing tools for everyday reminiscing. *Human–Computer Interaction 27*, 1-2: 175–198.
8. Minako Deno, Mitsunori Miyashita, Daisuke Fujisawa, Satomi Nakajima, and Masaya Ito. 2011. The relationships between complicated grief, depression, and alexithymia according to the seriousness of complicated grief in the Japanese general population. *Journal of affective disorders 135*, 1: 122–127.
9. Tanja Döring, Axel Sylvester, and Albrecht Schmidt. 2013. Ephemeral user interfaces: valuing the aesthetics of interface components that do not last. *interactions* 20, 4: 32–37.
10. Ruth M. Van Dyke and Susan E. Alcock. 2003. *Archaeologies of memory: An introduction*. Archaeologies of memory: 1–13. Cambridge University Press.
11. Pin Sym Foong and Denisa Kera. 2008. Applying reflective design to digital memorials. In *Proceedings of International Workshop on Social and Mundane Technologies.*
12. Batya Friedman and Lisa P. Nathan. 2010. Multi-lifespan information system design: a research initiative for the hci community. *Proceedings of the SIGCHI Conference on Human Factors in Computing Systems*, ACM, 2243–2246.
13. William Gaver, Mark Blythe, Andy Boucher, Nadine Jarvis, John Bowers, and Peter Wright. 2010. The prayer companion: openness and specificity, materiality and spirituality. *Proceedings of the SIGCHI conference on Human factors in computing systems*, ACM, 2055–2064.
14. William Gaver, Phoebe Sengers, Tobie Kerridge, Joseph Kaye, and John Bowers. 2007. Enhancing Ubiquitous Computing with User Interpretation: Field Testing the Home Health Horoscope. *Proceedings of the SIGCHI Conference on Human Factors in Computing Systems*, ACM, 537–546. http://doi.org/10.1145/1240624.1240711
15. William W. Gaver, John Bowers, Kirsten Boehner, et al. 2013. Indoor Weather Stations: Investigating a Ludic Approach to Environmental HCI Through Batch Prototyping. *Proceedings of the SIGCHI Conference on Human Factors in Computing Systems*, ACM, 3451–3460. http://doi.org/10.1145/2470654.2466474
16. Barney Glaser and Anselm L. Strauss. 2009. *The discovery of grounded theory: Strategies for qualitative research.* Transaction Publishers.
17. Ann-Marie Golden, Tim Dalgleish, and Bundy Mackintosh. 2007. Levels of specificity of autobiographical memories and of biographical memories of the deceased in bereaved individuals with and without complicated grief. *Journal of abnormal psychology 116*, no. 4: 786.
18. Rebecca Gulotta, William Odom, Haakon Faste, and Jodi Forlizzi. 2014. Legacy in the Age of the Internet: Reflections on How Interactive Systems Shape How We Are Remembered. *Proceedings of the 2014 Conference on Designing Interactive Systems*, ACM, 975–984. http://doi.org/10.1145/2598510.2598579
19. Rebecca Gulotta, William Odom, Jodi Forlizzi, and Haakon Faste. 2013. Digital Artifacts As Legacy: Exploring the Lifespan and Value of Digital Data. *Proceedings of the SIGCHI Conference on Human Factors in Computing Systems*, ACM, 1813–1822. http://doi.org/10.1145/2470654.2466240
20. Elizabeth Hallam and Jenny Hockey. 2001. *Death, memory and material culture*. Bloomsbury Academic.
21. Lars Hallnäs and Johan Redström. 2001. Slow technology–designing for reflection. *Personal and ubiquitous computing 5*, 3: 201–212.
22. John Helmes, Alex S. Taylor, Xiang Cao, Kristina Höök, Peter Schmitt, and Nicolas Villar. 2010. Rudiments 1, 2 & 3: design speculations on autonomy. In *Proceedings of the fifth international conference on Tangible, embedded, and embodied interaction* (TEI '11). ACM, New York, NY, USA, 145-152.

23. Michelle Hlubinka, Jennifer Beaudin, Emmanuel Munguia Tapia, and John S. An. 2002. AltarNation: interface design for meditative communities. *CHI'02 Extended Abstracts on Human Factors in Computing Systems*, ACM, 612–613.

24. Hilary Hutchinson, Wendy Mackay, Bo Westerlund, et al. 2003. Technology probes: inspiring design for and with families. *Proceedings of the SIGCHI conference on Human factors in computing systems*, ACM, 17–24.

25. Masaya Ito, Satomi Nakajima, Daisuke Fujisawa, et al. 2012. Brief measure for screening complicated grief: reliability and discriminant validity. *PloS one* 7, 2: e31209.

26. Jack B. Kamerman. 1988. *Death in the midst of life: Social and cultural influences on death, grief, and mourning.* Prentice Hall.

27. Dave Kirk, Rolf Wiesemes, Adam Moore, and Jim Kosem. 2010. Towards Pervasive Monuments. *Proceedings of Digital Futures 10.*

28. David S. Kirk and Abigail Sellen. 2010. On human remains: Values and practice in the home archiving of cherished objects. *ACM Transactions on Computer-Human Interaction* (TOCHI) 17, 3: 10.

29. Dennis Klass, Phyllis R. Silverman, and Steven Nickman. 2014. *Continuing bonds: New understandings of grief.* Taylor & Francis.

30. Tuck Leong, Frank Vetere, and Steve Howard. 2008. Abdicating choice: the rewards of letting go. *Digital Creativity 19*, 4: 233–243.

31. Tuck Wah Leong, Frank Vetere, and Steve Howard. 2006. Randomness as a resource for design. *Proceedings of the 6th conference on Designing Interactive Systems*, ACM, 132–139.

32. Avril Maddrell and James D. Sidaway. 2010. *Deathscapes: Spaces for death, dying, mourning and remembrance.* Ashgate Publishing.

33. Michael Massimi and Ronald M. Baecker. 2011. Dealing with death in design: Developing systems for the bereaved. *Proceedings of the 2011 annual conference on Human factors in computing systems*, ACM, 1001–1010.

34. Michael Massimi and Andrea Charise. 2009. Dying, death, and mortality: towards thanatosensitivity in HCI. *CHI'09 Extended Abstracts on Human Factors in Computing Systems*, ACM, 2459–2468.

35. Michael Massimi, William Odom, Richard Banks, and David Kirk. 2011. Matters of Life and Death: Locating the End of Life in Lifespan-oriented Hci Research. *Proceedings of the SIGCHI Conference on Human Factors in Computing Systems*, ACM, 987–996. http://doi.org/10.1145/1978942.1979090

36. Matthew Miles and A. Michael Huberman. *Qualitative data analysis: An expanded sourcebook.* Sage, 1994.

37. Wendy Moncur, Miriam Julius, Elise van Denhoven, and David Kirk. 2015. Story Shell: The Participatory Design of a Bespoke Digital Memorial. *In Proceedings of 4th Participatory Innovation Conference*, 470-477.

38. Wendy Moncur and David Kirk. 2014. An emergent framework for digital memorials. *Proceedings of the 2014 conference on Designing interactive systems*, ACM, 965–974.

39. Wendy Moncur, Jan Bikker, Elaine Kasket, and John Troyer. 2012. From death to final disposition: roles of technology in the post-mortem interval. In *Proceedings of the SIGCHI Conference on Human Factors in Computing Systems* (CHI '12). ACM, New York, NY, USA, 531-540. DOI=10.1145/2207676.2207750

40. Wendy Moncur. 2013. The emotional wellbeing of researchers: considerations for practice. In *Proceedings of the SIGCHI Conference on Human Factors in Computing Systems* (CHI '13). ACM, New York, NY, USA, 1883-1890. DOI=10.1145/2470654.2466248

41. William Odom, Richard Harper, Abigail Sellen, David Kirk, and Richard Banks. 2010. Passing on & putting to rest: understanding bereavement in the context of interactive technologies. *Proceedings of the SIGCHI conference on Human Factors in computing systems*, ACM, 1831–1840.

42. William Odom, James Pierce, Erik Stolterman, and Eli Blevis. 2009. Understanding why we preserve some things and discard others in the context of interaction design. *Proceedings of the SIGCHI Conference on Human Factors in Computing Systems*, ACM, 1053–1062. http://doi.org/10.1145/1518701.1518862

43. William T. Odom, Abigail J. Sellen, Richard Banks, et al. 2014. Designing for Slowness, Anticipation and Re-visitation: A Long Term Field Study of the Photobox. *Proceedings of the 32nd Annual ACM Conference on Human Factors in Computing Systems*, ACM, 1961–1970. http://doi.org/10.1145/2556288.2557178

44. William Odom, John Zimmerman, and Jodi Forlizzi. 2014. Placelessness, Spacelessness, and Formlessness: Experiential Qualities of Virtual Possessions. *Proceedings of the 2014 Conference on Designing Interactive Systems*, ACM, 985–994. http://doi.org/10.1145/2598510.2598577

45. Daniela Petrelli, Simon Bowen, and Steve Whittaker. 2014. Photo Mementos: Designing Digital Media to Represent Ourselves at Home. *Int. J. Hum.-Comput.* Stud. 72, 3: 320–336. http://doi.org/10.1016/j.ijhcs.2013.09.009

46. Daniela Petrelli, Nicolas Villar, Vaiva Kalnikaite, Lina Dib, and Steve Whittaker. 2010. FM radio: family interplay with sonic mementos. *Proceedings of the*

SIGCHI Conference on Human Factors in Computing Systems, ACM, 2371–2380.

47. Jason Procyk and Carman Neustaedter. 2014. GEMS: The Design and Evaluation of a Location-based Storytelling Game. *Proceedings of the 17th ACM Conference on Computer Supported Cooperative Work & Social Computing*, ACM, 1156–1166. http://doi.org/10.1145/2531602.2531701

48. Phoebe Sengers, Kirsten Boehner, Shay David, and Joseph "Jofish" Kaye. 2005. Reflective Design. *Proceedings of the 4th Decennial Conference on Critical Computing: Between Sense and Sensibility*, ACM, 49–58. http://doi.org/10.1145/1094562.1094569

49. M. Katherine Shear, Naomi Simon, Melanie Wall, et al. 2011. Complicated grief and related bereavement issues for DSM-5. *Depression and anxiety 28*, 2: 103–117.

50. Robert John Smith. 1974. *Ancestor worship in contemporary Japan*. Stanford University Press.

51. Hikaru Suzuki. 2013. "Beyond Ancestor Worship: Continued Relationship With Significant Others." In *Death and Dying in Contemporary Japan*, 141-141.

52. Wenn-Chieh Tsai, Po-Hao Wang, Hung-Chi Lee, Rung-Huei Liang, and Jane Hsu. 2014. The reflexive printer: toward making sense of perceived drawbacks in technology-mediated reminiscence. In *Proceedings of the 2014 conference on Designing interactive systems* (DIS '14). ACM, New York, NY, USA, 995-1004. DOI=10.1145/2598510.2598589

53. Daisuke Uriu and Naohito Okude. 2010. ThanatoFenestra: photographic family altar supporting a ritual to pray for the deceased. In *Adjunct Proceedings of the 8th ACM Conference on Designing Interactive Systems* (DIS '10). ACM, New York, NY, USA, 422-425. DOI=10.1145/1858171.1858253

54. Daisuke Uriu, Takahiro Ogasawara, Naohito Shimizu, and Naohito Okude. 2006. MASTABA: the household shrine in the future archived digital pictures. *ACM SIGGRAPH 2006 Sketches*, ACM, 151.

55. Jay Vidyarthi, Bernhard E. Riecke, and Diane Gromala. 2012. Sonic Cradle: Designing for an Immersive Experience of Meditation by Connecting Respiration to Music. *Proceedings of the Designing Interactive Systems Conference*, ACM, 408–417. http://doi.org/10.1145/2317956.2318017

56. Tony Walter, Rachid Hourizi, Wendy Moncur, and Stacey Pitsillides. 2012. Does the internet change how we die and mourn? Overview and analysis. *Omega-Journal of Death and Dying 64*, 4: 275–302.

57. Jonathan Watts. 2012. The vihara of compassion: an introduction to Buddhist care for the dying and bereaved in the modern world. *Contemporary Buddhism 13*, 1: 139–155.

58. Franz Winter. 2014. Handbook of Contemporary Japanese Religions. *Religious Studies Review 40*, 4: 191–194.

59. Allison Woodruff, Sally Augustin, and Brooke Foucault. 2007. Sabbath day home automation: it's like mixing technology and religion. *Proceedings of the SIGCHI conference on Human factors in computing systems*, ACM, 527–536.

60. Kate Woodthorpe. 2011. Using bereavement theory to understand memorialising behaviour. *Bereavement Care 30*, 2: 29–32.

61. Susan P. Wyche, Kelly E. Caine, Benjamin K. Davison, Shwetak N. Patel, Michael Arteaga, and Rebecca E. Grinter. 2009. Sacred imagery in techno-spiritual design. *Proceedings of the SIGCHI Conference on Human Factors in Computing Systems*, ACM, 55–58.

62. Susan P. Wyche and Rebecca E. Grinter. 2009. Extraordinary computing: religion as a lens for reconsidering the home. *Proceedings of the SIGCHI Conference on Human Factors in Computing Systems*, ACM, 749–758.

63. John Zimmerman, Jodi Forlizzi, and Shelley Evenson. 2007. Research Through Design As a Method for Interaction Design Research in HCI. *Proceedings of the SIGCHI Conference on Human Factors in Computing Systems*, ACM, 493–502. http://doi.org/10.1145/1240624.1240704

Integrating the Smart Home into the Digital Calendar

Sarah Mennicken
University of Zurich
Zurich, Switzerland
mennicken@ifi.uzh.ch

David Kim
Microsoft Research
Redmond, WA, USA
davidkim@microsoft.com

Elaine May Huang
University of Zurich
Zurich, Switzerland
huang@ifi.uzh.ch

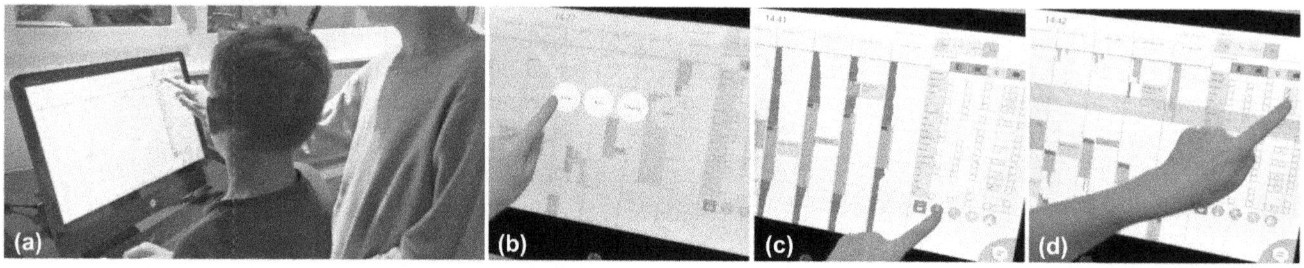

Figure 1: (a) The smart home digital calendar touch interface allows easy access for all household members at a central location at home; (b) each user can retrieve a tailored view of the smart home data via one-touch login; (c) the 7-day week view allows users to see behavior patterns of the home at a glance; (d) smart home and personal calendar events are shown side-by-side on each timeline and users can filter entries based on the device category and location.

ABSTRACT
With the growing adoption of smart home technologies, inhabitants are faced with the challenge of making sense of the data that their homes can collect to configure automated behaviors that benefit their routines. Current commercial smart home interfaces usually provide information on individual devices instead of a more comprehensive overview of a home's behavior. To reduce the complexity of smart home data and integrate it better into inhabitants' lives, we turned to the familiar metaphor of a calendar and developed our smart home interface *Casalendar*. In order to investigate the concept and evaluate our goals to facilitate the understanding of smart home data, we created a prototype that we installed in two commercial smart homes for a month. The results we present in this paper are based on our analysis of user data from questionnaires, semi-structured interviews, participant-driven audio and screenshot feedback as well as logged interactions with our system. Our findings exposed advantages and disadvantages of this metaphor, emerging usage patterns, privacy concerns and challenges for information visualization. We further report on implications for design and open challenges we revealed through this work.

CHI'16, May 07 - 12, 2016, San Jose, CA, USA

ACM 978-1-4503-3362-7/16/05...$15.00
DOI: http://dx.doi.org/10.1145/2858036.2858168

Author Keywords
Smart home; calendar; domestic routines; in-the-wild study; interface design; home automation

ACM Classification Keywords
H.5.m

INTRODUCTION AND BACKGROUND
A variety of data on behavior in homes is collected as a result of the increasing adoption of connected sensors and actuators in domestic environments. Most currently available smart home interfaces allow inhabitants to view the state of individual devices or functions and access log files about past events or sensor values. Much of this data, such as numerical values for temperature and brightness or binary values for motion triggers, is presented in raw form as numbers and text in log entries that are not helpful for most inhabitants for forming a useful mental model of one's automated home [28]. However, having a proper understanding is crucial for being able to control such a system and develop trust in it [1], which ultimately affects how satisfied people can be with their most personal space – their home [12].

The way data is represented can also impede accessibility to the technology for household members without the required background or training. We previously found that people sharing a home not only differ in technical background, but also in motivation to actively engage with the smart home, and responsibility for such tasks [37]. There are particular groups of users with little interest in engaging with the home, who have more issues with current UIs, as well as users who actively take charge in maintaining the technical infrastructure of the home [25] and who often even consider smart homes their hobby [38]. The tools used to configure an automated home or to visualize collected sensor data are not tailored to the various user groups, which often results in low accessibility. This negatively impacts the overall user experience and leaves opportunities for automation untapped [39]. Especially for users without strong technical skills, this can lead to frustration over the lack of transparency and control of things happening in the home. Given the data that is already captured in the home, there is an opportunity to alleviate this issue with a better presentation that reveals behavior patterns of the home and the household. This could facilitate the understanding of the home's behavior and provide a more accessible interface that lowers the barrier to access to the technology and data within smart homes.

Once a smart home is set up and programmed, its installation is rather inflexible [29] and acts according to a set of preconfigured automation rules and its own schedule. In some ways, it could be seen as an entity of its own in the household, which could be incorporated in the planning and coordination of all household members' routines. A tool that has already proven successful for managing routines, communicating and coordinating with others in typical households is the calendar; often, a family calendar that all members have access to (e.g. many households use a paper calendar in the kitchen or another common area [22]).

In this paper, we investigate the suitability and value of calendars as a familiar interface metaphor to visualize a smart home's behavior and its collected sensor data, to facilitate understanding of its actions. We designed a prototype called *Casalendar* (Figure 1) to investigate potential benefits and drawbacks of calendars and deployed it in two real-world smart homes to gauge its value over a period of a month. The findings are intended to inform our future work, with the long-term goal to support a better inclusion of all different user groups and their routines and exceptions in the home. Our contributions in this paper are: (i) to provide an evaluation of the shortfalls of current smart home interfaces and uncover new opportunities for calendars in this context; (ii) to consider the key factors for designing a tool for communication and coordination between the home and its inhabitants and control of the automation technology; (iii) the design and development of the *Casalendar* interface and prototype; and (iv) our findings about the emerged usage patterns, the appropriateness of the calendar metaphor and how it supported lowering barriers to access within smart homes, resulting in several design implications.

RELATED WORK

Facilitating the understanding and control of environments equipped with sensors and capabilities to actuate devices has been a longstanding interest in research [19]. One big aspect of this is to inform inhabitants about the collected data, the carried out actions, and underlying reasons for this automated behavior [1]. In the following, we describe related work on the visualization of such data and how it inspired us to explore the metaphor of calendars further.

Feedback and Control in Smart Homes

In research, related work on visualizations of logged sensor data in the home often has a specific application focus, such as increasing awareness of energy consumption [21], network usage [4], or water consumption [9]. Related work for smart home interfaces often focuses on improving end-user programming of context-aware environments [8,30] or exploring different means of input [3,14]. Commercial interfaces usually simply offer users an interface (e.g. on a tablet PC, mobile phone, or in a web browser [13]) they can use to access the controls for the various devices and functionalities in the home, however, without support for specific higher-level activities, such as preparing the house for a party or a longer vacation. Our *Casalendar* interface is similar in this respect and does not afford a specific use case or promote a specific functionality. Its primary aim is to elicit data on inhabitants' interests and the way they intend to apply the knowledge they may gain in order to learn about advantages and disadvantages of the metaphor we chose to investigate.

Visualization of Data in Calendars

The calendar has been used as a canvas for visualizations in many areas of application. Costanza et al. [5] made use of calendars to allow people to better understand varying costs of energy in the context of smart grid applications, while Laschke et al. [15] provided an in-situ visualization in the shower using the calendar metaphor to increase awareness for water consumption. Informative data were also integrated in Huang et al.'s [11] work that visualized step counts from activity trackers next to people's calendar entries in order to increase awareness of such data and lower the threshold for engaging with them. Our prototype aims to incorporate the multiplicity of different devices comprised in a home and offer an overview of the provided functions. The goal is to learn whether aspects of the calendar metaphor have a different meaning when representing smart home data opposed to personal events and how suitable it is for allowing people to improve their understanding of their home's behavior.

Calendar Usage

Besides providing a strong metaphor for time-related data, calendars are a well-established tool for coordination, communication, and collaboration between people [24]. In the context of families, this has been looked at in depth by Neustaedter et al. [22]. Calendars have proven to be helpful for families in managing routines and manage conflicts [7]. Motivated by this, we explore whether similar benefits can be transferred to interactions between the home and its inhabitants.

Tullio et al. [31] created a shared calendar augmented with additional information and explored its use in the work context. This calendar interface contained predictive information for users, aiming to facilitate interpersonal communication. In our interface and case study, we explore the usefulness of the calendar metaphor mostly by looking at the participants' interaction with past smart home data, but we included potential predictions of smart home behavior in order to allow us to preliminarily probe on potential uses of such information. However, the contribution of our studies and the insights derived aim to add to the understanding of how to facilitate interactions with a smart home and are less about advancing the research on calendar interaction itself.

DESIGNING SMART HOME INTERFACES

Previous studies [25,26] provide us with motivations to improve the visualization of smart home behavior to support the inclusion of inhabitants with less technical background, both in terms of understanding and controlling the home. Common commercial smart home interfaces are usually designed with a focus on a few specific use cases, such as (1) **viewing the current state**, (2) **configuring settings** of a specific device at a specific known location, and (3) **getting a spatial overview** of the current state of a subset of functions.

Categorical Menu. Interfaces for the first use case are usually organized in categorical, often hierarchical, menus based on the device category or location. They usually contain specific control elements for each device type, which allows one to see the current state of each device and change its configuration. The main advantage of such menus is quick access to the settings, assuming one already knows what one is looking for. Moreover, the interface of each device type typically takes up the entire screen and can display detailed state information and options for control.

Spatial Map. Interfaces that are based on spatial maps provide a hierarchy-less overview of the entire home or selected floors. They allow users to locate the control element for a specific device based on their knowledge of the home's spatial layout, and thus provide direct access to a specific set of functions or devices. Such floor plan-like interfaces provide glanceability, allowing users to spot any irregularities of device states at a glance, for example by indicating any open windows with a red circle.

Log list. Log list interfaces are often included alongside the two other interface types described above and all three are based on the same underlying data. These lists are most practical when one is interested in viewing the event history and filtering for past events that happened within a specific timeframe.

The interface types described above suffice when a user is interested in changing simple settings or when she can specify what data she wants to access. However, they are not suited for developing a causal understanding of the complex interactions between multiple devices and programs running within a smart home. This is mainly due to the lack of an appropriate way to meaningfully present interactions and interdependencies between devices, rules, and users that occur over time.

There are further usage scenarios that are often overlooked but could contribute to a better inclusion of the different user groups through a more appropriate presentation of temporal data across the entire home. For example, (4) **finding the reason** for an unexpected actuation of a device that has multiple potential sources, (5) **discovering new opportunities** for automation and potential conflicts by detecting behavior patterns, and (6) **adapting the home's behavior** to the user's own personal schedule (i.e. routines and exceptions, as opposed to manually overriding the program every time or putting up with a sub-optimal configuration).

The above-mentioned interface types are most commonly used in current interfaces for smart homes. Yet, they are not ideal for addressing these scenarios, as they either require users to already know which devices, category of device, or location they want to look for, or they isolate the various devices without the option to view multiple devices and their behavior in the same view.

Timelines. In contrast to spatial maps, a timeline view consists of past events and allows users to see emerging temporal behavior patterns at a glance. This enables the user to retrace the actions executed by the home (e.g. light turned on) for multiple devices or functions on the same timeline, even for automation that does not have a specific location (e.g. time-based triggers or sending alerts). The view can also include information on the sensors that triggered them (e.g. brightness sensor) and reveal potential chains of causality.

Calendar as a Smart Home Interface

A calendar represents a specific type of timeline interface that allows routines, repetitive behavior and exceptions to be easily visible. In the context of smart homes, such events could reflect state changes of devices. Events that recur daily or weekly are often effects of pre-programmed rules of a home that are in turn based on the household's routines (e.g. heating that is based on sleeping and waking up times). We found the calendar to be a suitable metaphor for our purposes as it is an accessible and already widely used tool that would allow users to view and match both the household's and the home's routines within the same interface.

Existing calendar views are currently not used as the main smart home interface, but just for visualizing the data of a single device or function, such as heating or air conditioning [35]. Thus, we seek to learn about the suitability of interfaces that focus on the use of the calendar metaphor and aim to explore it in the context of smart home interaction with the longer-term goal to support a better inclusion of all user groups and their routines in the home.

DESIGN AND IMPLEMENTATION OF CASALENDAR

Based on the goals and the usage scenarios we set out earlier, we designed an interaction concept and developed a working prototype that would allow us to collect insights about the everyday use of our concept in real homes.

Interface Design

The general design of our prototype is primarily based on the week view of a digital calendar containing seven vertical timelines, one for each weekday. The content consists of calendar entries added by the smart home and the inhabitants, each with an icon or text headline indicating the entry type, and color-coded to indicate who or which function it pertains to.

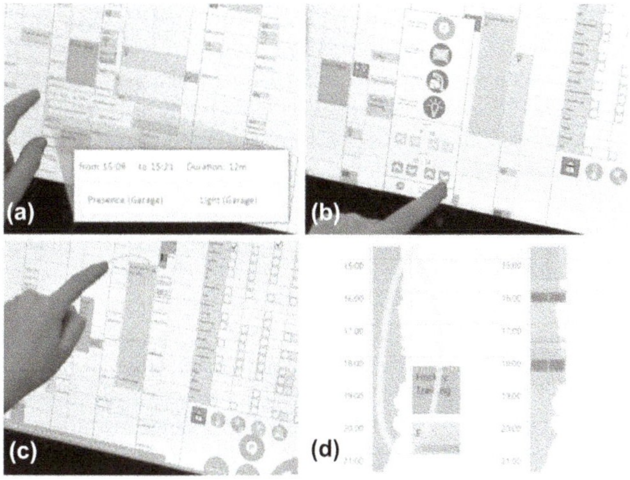

Figure 2: (a) Detail view of a *light* calendar entry. Shows the time, type and location of the light trigger (*presence* sensor); (b) user programs a smart home function in the calendar; (c) smart home and personal events are shown side-by-side and can be annotated; (d-left) H1H's annotation of an unusual peak in the brightness sensor data; (d-right) between 5 and 7 pm: unwanted behavior of shades observed by H1W

Timeline Layout. Our prototype emphasizes personal events, as it aims to recreate a calendar, which has the additional benefit of providing integrated access to additional information on and control of the smart home. To provide a clear visual distinction: smart home's events are displayed in left third of the timeline while household members' personal events use the remaining two thirds of the timeline (Figure 2c and 2d).

Dealing with Visual Clutter. A potential danger of providing a one-week overview of events across multiple devices of the same and different types, in addition to calendar events of household members, is visual clutter and information overload which would defeat our purpose. Therefore, we allowed users to view calendar entries of only certain household members and specific types of devices in specific locations which can be selected through a filter panel on the side of our interface (Figure 1d). We anticipated different viewing preferences for each participant and added a one-touch login mechanism (Figure 1b) that allowed household members to identify themselves and to retrieve and store their individual view settings. A future version could incorporate an automatic face-recognition-based login mechanism to simplify the identification process further.

Representation of Smart Home Entries. We preselected a set of sensor and actuation devices to be displayed on the calendar based on their importance and potential impact on the inhabitants of the smart home. Our selection included: window shades (see turquoise calendar entries in Figure 1c and 2 d-right), lights, sensors detecting the door/window state (as open or closed), heating, temperature, brightness, music player and a vacuum-cleaning robot. Discrete events and data are visualized as rectangular blocks (e.g. shades down or door open) whose vertical height depends on their duration. Continuous sensor data, such as temperature and brightness, is displayed as graphs that span the entire timeline (see blue graphs in Figure 1c or yellow graphs in Figure 2d).

Additional Details and Control on Demand. Our interface allows inhabitants to retrieve additional details for an event, such as a list of possible causes that might have triggered it, exact duration of the event (Figure 2a) and other contextual sensor data (e.g. brightness and temperature). To elicit usage data beyond only consumption of information, we enabled inhabitants to perform simple control actions, e.g. locking specific motion triggered lights or controlling their vacuum-cleaning robot directly through calendar entries (Figure 2b).

Technical Implementation

We deployed our prototypes on 23″ all-in-one multi-touch PCs that allowed users to access the calendar interface comfortably via touch. The smart home infrastructure of our participants used *KNX*[1], a standardized network protocol for smart home devices. To easily communicate with KNX, we used a software controller called *nomos System*[2] which can be installed on a Raspberry Pi mini-computer and facilitates retrieving messages as well as sending commands from or to the connected KNX devices. The prototype was implemented in C# and WPF and is able to import iCal streams of our participants' personal digital calendars.

Limitations of the Deployable Prototype

Our interaction concept for *Casalendar* included several features that we were not able to implement in our prototype, such as determining the root cause of certain events with absolute certainty. For instance, the actuation of shades in the participating homes was determined by a complex decision structure involving a weather station whose internal logic unit we could not access. Direct control of devices through our interface was somewhat limited, as it would not have been feasible to break apart the existing smart home configuration and reprogram all involved sensors and actors. Due to the complexity of this task and potential liability issues that could result from a breakdown of our research prototype, we decided to do this for only a limited subset of the home's functionalities. To make up for this restriction and to elicit further data on active usage, we allowed users to create "fake events" and record short audio clips that let them express their interest in particular smart home features missing in *Casalendar*. We would have liked to implement several features known to be important for the adoption of calendar interfaces, such as mobile access from multiple locations [20]. However, we were not able to address them in this first case study due to technical constraints.

FIELD-RESEARCHED CASE STUDY

Living in a smart home and using its functionalities in everyday life differs considerably from staged usage

[1] knx.org/in/knx/association/what-is-knx/index.php

[2] nomos-system.com/

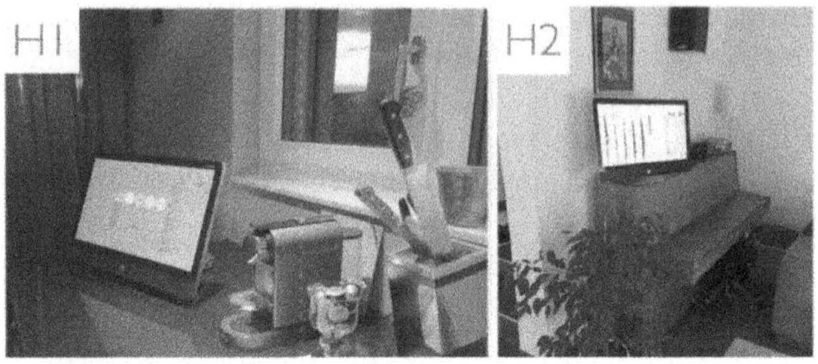

Figure 3: Locations in which our participants set up our prototype. Kitchen in H1 (left), living area in H2 (right).

scenarios in lab settings. We conducted an in-the-wild deployment of our prototype design for an entire month (June 2015) to assess its applicability to real homes.

Procedure

Recruiting of Participants. Two smart home households, which originally had been recruited via a smart home forum for previous studies [18], were recruited again for this study for two reasons: firstly, we had to ask them for full access to all of their smart home as well as their personal calendar data, thus, we wanted participants with whom we had already established a trust relationship. Secondly, we were familiar with their installations and several specifics about their configurations that would allow us to smoothly integrate our prototype into their existing systems. Both households were willing to participate without any compensation but were given an equivalent of USD 320 as an incentive to maintain their participation over the course of the month.

Preparation for Deployment. As the integration of our prototype involved major individual customizations, we had two meetings with one member of each household beforehand. In these meetings, we retrieved their configuration files that were required to prepare our prototype for each home. We also discussed specifics of their respective installations and gave our participants the opportunity to express any concerns or questions they had regarding our deployment and evaluation. Even with careful preparation prior to the on-site installation, it took several hours to fully deploy our prototype in the actual setting.

The prototypes were placed in locations chosen by the households. These locations were highly frequented spots that allowed family members easy access and promoted shared awareness [22]: in the kitchen (Figure 3 left) and in the open space for living and dining (Figure 3 right). After the prototypes were running, we introduced all family members to the interface, and explained the features of our system to them, including the feature for recording feedback. We also provided a manual that repeats these explanations visually.

Participating Households

For our case studies, we intentionally recruited two households with different characteristics, apart from similar age and family composition, to gain broader insights about our concepts. The first household (H1) consisted of two parents in their early 40s and their three children between 8 and 14 years old. The second household (H2) also consisted of two parents in their early 40s and two teenagers, ages 14 and 15. In both cases, the husbands were working full-time and the wives part-time. The wives had less interest in engaging with the smart home and less technical skills compared to the husbands, who considered smart homes a hobby.

H1 built their house with integrated smart home technology and moved in approximately two years ago, while H2 installed their smart home functionalities during a major renovation almost eight years ago. While in H1 both parents used digital calendars extensively and maintained digital calendars for their kids, in H2 only the father used a personal digital calendar and maintained a minimal shared calendar to which other family members were subscribed. The mother maintained a traditional paper calendar for the entire family which was placed at a central location that could be easily accessed by everyone in the family.

Data collection

We gave participants questionnaires that inquired about their opinions and attitudes towards smart home technologies before and after the study. The questions intentionally left out any items related to our prototype in order to isolate and learn about changes in the participants' general perception of their own smart home and interactions with it. In addition, we also asked them to complete a questionnaire which contained items specifically targeting our interface. The questionnaire was an adapted UTAUT [33] survey, which is a standardized set of questions that assesses the technology acceptance by probing users' expectations and intentions for use. While our intention was to learn about potential usability or user experience issues that could affect other collected data from our case study participants, we did not use this data to make general claims about the ease of use of our interface. All questionnaire items were statements and participants rated their agreement with each on a Likert scale between 1 for 'I fully disagree' to 5 for 'I fully agree'. All participants, except two children, answered the surveys.

During the study, we logged interactions with the interface and participants captured additional qualitative feedback through the 'feedback mode' of the interface (Figure 4). Once invoked, this mode captures a screenshot of the interface and allows users to add freehand annotation on the screen by using their finger to draw on the touchscreen (see yellow annotation in Figure 4) and/or record an audio file. Feedback and snapshots of the calendar entries are instantly stored on a password-protected cloud data storage, which can be directly accessed by the researchers. This way, we were able to review participants' screenshots and audio feedback and prepare follow-up questions for the final interview while the study was still running. These interviews, which were conducted at the participants' homes, also contained more general questions such as whether there were any unusual events during the duration of the study that might have affected the use of the calendar, whether *Casalendar* was a topic of family conversations and if their experiences with the interface inspired ideas about what they would have liked

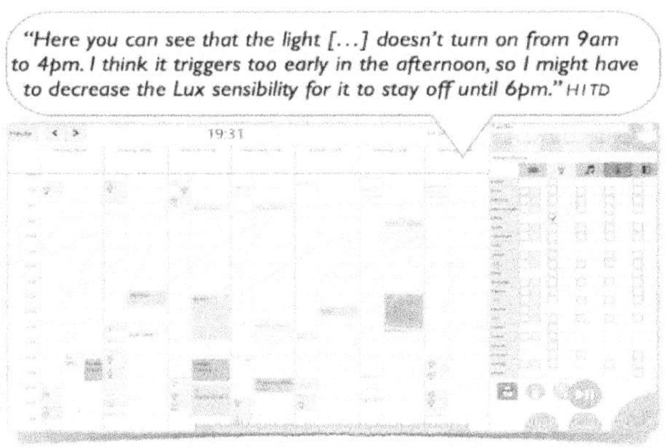

Figure 4: Freehand annotation (yellow) on a screenshot of the current calendar view and transcribed audio feedback.

to change about it. We further sent three reminder emails to participants over the course of the study to maintain their participation and prompt feedback.

FINDINGS

First, we evaluated the UTAUT survey to learn whether issues with the usability or acceptance of the system could have severely influenced the use of the system. Then we looked at differences between the pre- and post-deployment surveys about participants' opinions and attitudes regarding smart home technologies. As the data sample was too small for statistically significant results, we instead focused on looking at noticeable differences among individuals, between households, or user types. We classified changes as noticeable if the answer before the study differed by at least two points from the answer given after the study, or if multiple participants' answers changed in the same way. As those changes might have occurred by chance, we checked for consistency with the qualitative feedback from interviews and feedback given through *Casalendar*, which was partially transcribed and analyzed using open coding. We only considered insights from our quantitative analysis that were consistent with the qualitative feedback.

In the following sections, we present what we learned about the appropriateness of the calendar metaphor in the smart home context, emerging usage patterns with our interface, and social implications we observed. We refer to the participants by using the household number and H for husband, W for wife, and C# for their children (e.g. H1C1 describing the oldest child of H1W and H1H).

Appropriateness of the Calendar Metaphor

The use of our interface we observed and feedback we collected revealed several benefits and limitations regarding the suitability of a calendar metaphor for smart home user interfaces.

Beneficial for Providing an Overview of Behavioral Patterns

Participants reported that the weekly overview that incorporated multiple functions and sensors was good for giving an overview of behavioral patterns of the home and the family. H1W described this as *"You quickly have an overview [of] what my family is up to"* and *"[I can] see the whole week, how the home has behaved."* As mentioned earlier, many commercially available smart home interfaces displayed the various functions in individual, isolated visualizations. While this allows one to choose the best-fitting representation of the data, it makes it more difficult to draw insights about the overall behavior of the home.

We found that visualizing the data on a timeline provided an easy way to spot issues in the configuration, as when one event causes another, they are often close together in time. In some cases, it also facilitated the definition of actionable changes to the existing configuration. For example, H1W noticed that the shades were not acting as she wanted them to in the afternoon and early evening. By visual inspection of the calendar, her husband was able to identify unexpected brightness changes and the effects to the currently set threshold values as one potential cause (Figure 2d), which he could use to update the configuration. Additionally, this is an example of the calendar offering a means to facilitate communication between family members to solve suboptimal configurations of a smart home.

Establish Trust in the Home Through Temporal Anchors

Participants' responses to several questionnaire items about trust and understanding were slightly increased after they had used *Casalendar* for a month. For example, their average agreement on *"If something happens automatically in the home, I know why it happened"* increased consistently by 0.5 points for all participants. H2H, who was previously wondering about a specific function in his home further reported: *"It's visually obvious to me now that there are no malfunctions. Till now, I've assumed that the light in the basement is periodically turned on without any reason."* One potential explanation could be that the familiarity of the calendar metaphor, with calendar entries being associated with events taking place, increased feelings of trust. However, even in a personal calendar it can be uncertain whether personal entries actually took place [31]. We assume that participants may think of the home's events as a defined schedule rather than a dynamically adapting calendar. This understanding may be challenged by a future version of *Casalendar*, which could include future event predictions that are automatically inserted by the home and continually adjusted over time.

Usage Patterns Around Smart Home Events

Two primary use cases emerged in our deployment: *checking on the home's behavior retrospectively* and *verifying the configuration.*

Retrospective Check

Our participants reported enjoying having a familiar tool to turn to when they wanted to check on what was happening at home while they were absent. This included information on the family and the home's functions. For example, H1W wanted to know what her kids had been up to, while H2W wanted to learn about the Roomba's activities. The information they retrieved from *Casalendar* also became a conversation topic and a tool for reflecting on the patterns, not only for the adults but also for the kids, as expressed by H1C2: *"We just saw for how long the light was on, or whether we forgot to turn it off, or whether we forgot and left the music playing."*

Configuration Verification

Participants appreciated having visual feedback that allowed them to confirm that the home had worked as expected. For example, H2H wondered whether the motion-triggered lights in the basement were working properly, and H1W wanted to verify whether the configuration changes that her husband had carried out actually worked.

While these usage patterns seem similar, their intentions are slightly different: In case of the *retrospective check*, the inhabitants' focus was on learning about details of the automation technology's behavior or other household members' behaviors without a specific expectation. In case of the *configuration verification*, they focused on whether or not something worked as expected, and compared their expectation with what was visualized.

Although our sample size is limited, participants' feedback indicated that the duration of habitation in a home may have affected the benefits an interface can provide. We hypothesized before the study that H1, who had been living in their home for less than two years and was still frequently changing the home's configuration, would consider *Casalendar* more useful than H2 who had been living in their home for more than eight years and who reached a phase of stability in which they had already fixed many issues of its behavior through many iterations. This was confirmed by their responses in our questionnaire: H1's perception of whether *Casalendar* increased the chance to set the home in the way they wanted it to be was higher than H2's. Similarly, H1 agreed that *Casalendar* could help identify and understand problems quickly, while H2 disagreed. H2 reflected on the usefulness of our interface in the early stages of the smart home adoption. H2H: *"I had to change so many things over and over again, and then it still wasn't like the way you had thought. The temporal sequence [of actions] took a lot of adjustments [to get it right]."* H2W: *"You could have simply looked at the whole week [in Casalendar] to see how the home has behaved."* They considered the calendar-based interface to be useful to see patterns and exceptions in the weekly overview at a glance. H2W was generally happy with the interface she was using after several adjustments had been made and she reported having gotten used to interacting with these tools. However, she noted that she would have adopted *Casalendar*, if she had been given this option earlier, since *"[with Casalendar] you simply have it all, [the different devices and calendar] in one [interface]."*

Usage Patterns Around the Integrated Calendar

When designing the interface, we considered scenarios in which the context of the personal calendar could potentially be connected to the smart home's behavior (e.g., by having the robot vacuum clean the house before a visit that is entered as a personal event, or deactivating the shades to the garden when guests come over for dinner in order to not disturb them). Yet, neither in the annotated screenshots collected nor in the follow-up interviews did examples like this, or any other specific interest in connecting personal calendar entries with smart home behavior, come up. However, participants mentioned the usefulness of seeing their calendar entries collocated with the behavior of the home. E.g., H1W expressed the wish to define exceptions for the shades when seeing that a school holiday was coming up. Despite having the potential to be a promising approach, stronger evidence for the usefulness of such functionality has yet to arise. This idea might be worthwhile reevaluating when our prototype a) offers control over various devices and b) when calendar entries have more automatically generated contextual information, such as locations of events or commute times.

In general, our participants felt that they had lost interest in the smart home's actions after living there for a while. They believed that the true purpose of a smart home should simply be to *"function optimally in any situation, so the user wouldn't need to worry about questions like 'will the shades go up and when will they go down?'"* (H1W). H2 had substantially less interaction with the interface than H1. We attribute that to the fact that there is generally little need and interest in the smart home data most of the time. This makes sense: smart home inhabitants want to enjoy peace of mind [2] and worry about fewer things, not more. H1W expressed interest in using one single interface for both smart homes functions and the family's calendar and said: *"I would like to also be able to edit the [personal] calendar entries [in Casalendar], so that I could get rid of the iPad entirely."* The same household also reported how they were using *Casalendar* exclusively to look at their own calendars when they had a very busy week during our study. Therefore, we propose integrating informative data about the smart home's behavior into an interface that is frequently used in the user's everyday life. The integration should be carried out in such a way that it only draws the user's attention when it is needed and otherwise stays in the background or can easily be ignored.

H1 used their digital calendars extensively and we observed a more natural integration of their interaction with *Casalendar* into the daily habits of the family compared to H2. We argue that the acceptance of such an interface will be highest if a) users already habitually use digital calendars and b) are still in a phase with frequent adjustments to their home's configuration.

Tradeoff Between Completeness and Visual Clutter

The challenge of designing usable interfaces which incorporate dense information is certainly not new. One of the many guidelines for good design states that "the display should be designed to convey 'just enough' information" [17]. Although we tried to address this issue with user-specific information and view filters beforehand, we observed a frequent tension between having access to more information and viewing less data in our participants' feedback. Our participants reported sometimes being overwhelmed by the amount of information presented. H1H reported: *"[...] I simply selected all shades [...] and now there's a bunch of individual bars and that's all very confusing."* At the same time, they also expressed the wish to include more data in the interface. H1H and H2H would have liked to see numerical values next to the temperature and brightness graphs on the timeline. Ideally, the interface would manage high information density and create a view that is useful and actionable for the user.

More Reflection and Context Needed Over Time

We observed that our interface was only interesting for a short period for the participants who have been living in their smart home for a longer time and who were already familiar with their home's behavior. H2H commented: *"In the beginning [Casalendar] was very interesting, however, over time it wasn't [...] interesting to look at it over and over again because in the end it doesn't really change a lot."* He felt that his trust in the home's behavior was confirmed after a while and he *"doesn't check all the time whether it still runs correctly as [when he checked it] last time."* He stated that he would instead be interested in learning about certain trends in the home's behavior and recent changes to the configuration. Strengers [28] made a similar observation of saturation on inhabitants who have been provided with eco-feedback for some time.

Presenting information that is relevant to the user at a specific moment is essential. Related work looked at various techniques on how to prepare information for people in context-aware environments to make it useful [34]. This concerns events that actually took place, but also events that did not, because people will also still wonder why expected events did not take place [16]. For example, H2W stated a strong interest in these questions and other unusual behavior. She wanted answers to questions such as *"did the iRobot really run, or was there a black out?"*

Other participants stated that they would not only want to see entries that would allow them to understand the home better, but also support them in spotting exceptions in the sensor data or home's behavior. H2H described it as: *"[It would be helpful] if you could see [...] 'was that only an exception?' or is that the typical course of action. At the moment, I always have to figure out, was it an exception or my mistake [in the configuration]?"*

Lower Barrier to Access for Smart Home Interactions

Mennicken and Huang [41] revealed that many common smart home technologies require people to have technical skills to gain access to all information and control functionalities. We were therefore interested in how our approach would be perceived by user of different technical abilities.

Access for the Entire Household

Our interface was well received also by inhabitants with strong technical skills that already used existing interfaces as it was simpler to access and the calendar visualization was easier to parse, as reported by H2H: *"Well, I could go into the logs and see that there, but here in Casalendar it's visualized very comfortably."* A shared visualization that is usable by all family members, regardless of their technical skills, could help to support communication of problems and ideas for the configuration, and thus improve the initial configuration phase.

Our interface design was based on the metaphor of shared, physical calendars that can be accessed by everyone at any time, as opposed to tools on personal devices that are often access-restricted. In the participating households, some family members had limited access to the devices on which the control interfaces resided. For example, in case of H1 the data on sensor data (temperature, brightness) was only accessible through interfaces that were never introduced (or of any real interest) to most household members, and only installed on devices that had restricted access, as described by H1C2: *"On mama's [iPad] we can't do that because [the iPad] is locked."* Our prototype *Casalendar* was not access-restricted, which was well received, as described by H1W: *"The kids enjoy using the calendar view, but they also play around with the smart home functions in there because the iPad is locked."*

Emerging Questions of Privacy

Contrary to our expectations, our participants had no privacy concerns about *Casalendar* revealing information to other household members and only those with a strong technical background (H1H, H2H) agreed or strongly agreed they would not want information to be shared outside of their household. Those with less technical skills (H1W, H2W) disagreed or strongly disagreed and thus, did not share this concern. Privacy concerns did not come up in the interviews either, although we specifically probed for them. Only H1W commented that her children could potentially have concerns in the future: *"We could associate the fingerprints to the kids sometime in the future. We could check which kid got home at what time after they have been going out at night. Hm, they will probably not be overly happy about that."*

While data collected from individual devices (for motion-triggered lights in the basement or electricity measurements of the kitchen stove) might not instantly raise privacy concerns for the inhabitants, it could easily be turned into a sophisticated surveillance system just by being put in the context of the entire home [32]. This is not unique to calendar representations; however, the increased accessibility and the potential resulting awareness make careful design to maintain privacy especially important. From the patterns in the timeline, H1W was able to infer when the kids came home and whether they actually heated up their lunch or whether they went straight to the basement to play computer games. We found that our visual representation of data helped users to easily capture exceptions or outliers in certain patterns or events at unusual times. For example, H1W noticed an unusual entry located in the basement one night, which she recorded via an annotated screenshot in our feedback mode. After casually talking to her husband about it, he admitted having fallen asleep after watching TV for too long and then checking up on the cats before going to bed. In this case, both household members felt comfortable sharing; in other cases, a simple smart home calendar entry might violate a person's privacy or cause arguments.

DISCUSSION AND IMPLICATIONS

In this section, we discuss our findings and provide several implications that aim to support the design of future systems. Moreover, our discussion aims to raise emerging questions that take into account the limitations of our interface prototype and our case study.

Calendar or Smart Home Interface

We designed our interface primarily to look like a regular calendar interface, as reflected in our decision to give personal calendar events more space than smart home events. However, we noticed that the perception of whether our hybrid interface was primarily a calendar or a calendar-style smart home interface varied based on the usage and configuration, and the extent to which digital calendars were already in use in a household. As a consequence, the question arises whether and when it makes sense to present *Casalendar* primarily as a smart home interface in the form of a calendar and when to present it as a subtle integration into something that is primarily a calendar interface. Both would share similar properties, such as presenting smart home events on a timeline and providing an overview across devices and days that makes it easy to spot patterns, exceptions, and causalities. From our study, we learned that the smart home data and logs themselves are not interesting enough to justify a stand-alone interface most of the time. Additionally, work by Palen [24] revealed that simply replacing the calendar artifacts that people use can create major challenges with regard to their routines. Thus, we believe that integrating smart home data into frequently used tools will be the more promising approach compared to only focusing on visualizing the data – as long as it does not compromise existing practices with these tools or require extra effort from the user.

A calendar interface is without a doubt more familiar and accessible to the wider population than technical smart home interfaces or log files. In our study, we found that no one had trouble understanding our interface concept. However, we also reached the understanding that one interface cannot serve all purposes equally well. Although we only offered limited options to control features of the home (as this was not the primary focus of our study), it gave us some early insights about participants' opinions of the metaphor of a central calendar for control purposes. H1W raised concerns regarding the limited practicality for simple controls, such as letting the shades down. She expressed that she does not want *"to have to walk up to the calendar for this simple action."* This would be a problem for any interface that is not mobile and has to be accessed from a specific location. While this might be addressed by making *Casalendar* accessible from mobile devices, it also hints that immediate control of devices may not be well supported by this metaphor. Still, participants expressed that they want to be able to access specific control functions when they see events of this function in the interface. Hence, such a visualization interface should include the means to control the devices presented or their configuration, even if it will probably remain only a complementary tool to other means of control. When integrating means for control of multiple devices into a single interface, the design challenges that are known from previous approaches to "universal remotes" [23], such as preventing mode errors, will have to be taken into account.

Our interface helped our participants get a better idea of the temporal behavior of their home, and they could create focused views of it using the different filter functionalities. Yet, for use cases in which only the current state is of interest, a spatial metaphor might serve better. For example, when leaving the home and trying to find out which windows are still open, a spatial interface such as a map would only require one view. In our interface, users would first have to orient themselves within the timeline and then see whether there were events related to all the devices of interest. As mentioned earlier, we believe that the visualization of smart home data we propose here will probably not suffice as a stand-alone application. Integration with another interface might offer other advantages as well. For example, by integrating temporal and spatial interfaces the use of a selected location could customize the calendar view and reduce visual clutter. Offering multiple metaphors could also allow for a more versatile use of the system.

Calendar as a Sensor and Tool to Facilitate Future Controls

Despite the small sample size, our deployment of *Casalendar* in real households indicated that a familiar representation of information that is usually captured but hidden in log files can be useful for inhabitants. But capturing this information could also serve another purpose: in addition to offering automated behavior that remains rather static and inflexible after the initial setup [29], the house could use it to play a more active role in the household. By aggregating information about the context of everyone's whereabouts through the calendar, the home could better understand the dynamics of the household and adjust to them. Prior work by Davidoff [6] demonstrated how such information on people's routines can be used to create more valuable ubiquitous computing systems. Other work used calendars as sensors to collect information, in order to automatically annotate images with context information [10]. People already use calendars for tracking past actions [24], and annotations on the calendar have been used to support awareness within the family [20]. A smart home could potentially do the same thing: it could use the information about interactions with the building infrastructure to allow a better adaptation to the family or to create a means for the inhabitants to more easily set their home to a specific state. For example, the home could look back at personal events (such as "Spring break", "Dinner party", etc.) and try to correlate them with the changes to its configuration to learn about how it could interpret them. Then, it could offer "autocomplete"-style suggestions when adding or changing a device or configuration or when adding a new personal calendar event. This could permit a more optimized use of the technologies and reduction of manual overrides, assuming that the reconfiguration was previously too demanding for the user.

The only potential future events we showed was manually generated information about the behavior of the shades. Therefore, we could not gain much insight about how people would interact with predictive events from our study. Yet, participants expressed interest in having the various scheduled events of different devices or functions included in the calendar interface. For example, H1W believed it would be helpful if she could see the starting time of her stove in *Casalendar* when she programmed it in the morning. That way she could react to potential conflicts during the course of the day by adjusting the preprogrammed time or canceling it. H2W wanted to include the weekly cleaning schedule of the robot vacuum in the calendar for the same reasons. She also wished to include contextual information that was potentially relevant to the home, like the weather forecast, so that she could easily change the home's settings accordingly. Merging all this data into one interface could help create a mutual understanding of what the home bases its actions on. Yet, when introducing uncertain and potentially changing data, a challenge that is already known for shared calendars will have to be considered: how does the inhabitant stay ahead of changes that occur throughout the day [20]?

Transparency vs. Privacy

Our interface has the potential to provide more transparency, to act as a base for communication and to allow the less technical household members to understand and refer more easily to certain behaviors of the automation technology. In the case of H1, we also observed how the home can act as an extended monitoring system that provides a more tangible way for parents to address some behavior patterns of their children.

Our interface raised an additional question regarding privacy, besides the general questions of collecting such data: what does it imply if smart home data is offered in an accessible tool that makes it very visual, and thus easily consumable for all household members? Should the entirety of the data collected be available to all household members? Even regular calendar entries can make users vulnerable to external judgment [24]. What will happen when a teenager misses curfew by a couple of minutes, leaving a distinct visual pattern on the calendar? Will a tolerated "white lie" become intolerable because of the calendar entry it creates? This scenario has been studied by Ur et al. [32], revealing attitudes of parents and teenagers. One of their recommendations is to make the logs less granular, such as showing "around 11pm" instead of the exact timestamp. A calendar interface that visualizes logs would therefore need to be able to offer a suitable representation for such fuzzy entries.

Privacy issues in smart homes are not new; the data in such homes has always been available but accessible only by one or few members of the household and buried in a list of log entries. In some ways, this has created an imbalance in access to information about other family members. If interfaces like *Casalendar* suddenly make previously obscure data usable and lower barriers to access, new privacy issues and questions regarding the rights to access smart home data will be exposed. Who should know about what in a household? Who should be able to filter this information? Behavioral patterns can be spotted easily in the calendar interface as they have a specific visual appearance. There are several approaches in privacy research, such as adapting information to context in ambient calendar displays [27] that could be considered, even for interfaces situated in a more private context. Most importantly, these questions need to be recognized as major challenges that will require sensible design choices, in order to avoid negative social implications on family dynamics.

CONCLUSION

Casalendar is a first attempt to provide a combined, holistic view of a home's and inhabitants' events and routines through a temporal interface containing actual smart home logs and participants' calendars. Based on a one-month deployment in two households, we presented several observations and insights, such as how the metaphor of a calendar supported building trust in the home's behavior and how such an interface can lower barriers to accessing smart home information. We reflected on the usefulness of the calendar metaphor for giving an overview of the home's and family's behavioral patterns. However, we also learned that with the current state of our interface such information is mostly of interest if changes to the home's configuration were still being made. We further found that the proposed visualization of smart home data would most likely be useful if integrated into existing tools rather than considered as a stand-alone application. By discussing the limitations of our work, we identified remaining challenges that need to be addressed.

ACKNOWLEDGEMENTS

We would like to express our gratitude to the families that participated in our study for their time, patience, and understanding. We also thank *nomos* for providing us with their hardware, particularly Mike Eudenbach, who supported us in technical questions. Thanks to Peter Sperlich for showing us how to deal with "real-life" KNX installations and providing us with training hardware. Thanks to Gunnar Harboe, Helen He, Nemanja Memarovic, and Christian Remy for their support in the various phases of this research project.

REFERENCES

1. Victoria Bellotti and Keith Edwards. 2001. Intelligibility and accountability: human considerations in context-aware systems. Hum.-Comput. Interact. 16, 2 (December 2001), 193-212. http://dx.doi.org/10.1207/S15327051HCI16234_05
2. A.J. Bernheim Brush, Bongshin Lee, Ratul Mahajan, Sharad Agarwal, Stefan Saroiu, and Colin Dixon. 2011. Home automation in the wild: challenges and opportunities. In *Proceedings of the SIGCHI Conference on Human Factors in Computing Systems* (CHI '11). ACM, New York, NY, USA, 2115-2124. http://dx.doi.org/10.1145/1978942.1979249
3. Dario Bonino, Emiliano Castellina, Fulvio Corno, and Luigi De Russis. 2011. DOGeye: Controlling your home with eye interaction. *Interact. Comput.* 23, 5 (September 2011), 484-498. http://dx.doi.org/10.1016/j.intcom.2011.06.002
4. Marshini Chetty, Richard Banks, Richard Harper, Tim Regan, Abigail Sellen, Christos Gkantsidis, Thomas Karagiannis, and Peter Key. 2010. Who's hogging the bandwidth: the consequences of revealing the invisible in the home. In Proceedings of the SIGCHI Conference on Human Factors in Computing Systems (CHI '10). ACM, New York, NY, USA, 659-668. http://dx.doi.org/10.1145/1753326.1753423
5. Enrico Costanza, Joel E. Fischer, James A. Colley, Tom Rodden, Sarvapali D. Ramchurn, and Nicholas R. Jennings. 2014. Doing the laundry with agents: a field trial of a future smart energy system in the home. In Proceedings of the SIGCHI Conference on Human Factors in Computing Systems (CHI '14). ACM, New York, NY, USA, 813-822. http://dx.doi.org/10.1145/2556288.2557167
6. Scott Davidoff, Min Kyung Lee, Anind K. Dey, and John Zimmerman. 2007. Rapidly exploring application design through speed dating. In Proceedings of the 9th international conference on Ubiquitous computing (UbiComp '07), John Krumm, Gregory D. Abowd, Aruna Seneviratne, and Thomas Strang (Eds.). Springer-Verlag, Berlin, Heidelberg, 429-446. http://dx.doi.org/10.1007/978-3-540-74853-3_25
7. Scott Davidoff. 2011. Routine as resource for the design of learning systems. (Doctoral Dissertation) (CMU-HCII-11-103). 344 p. Available from the Carnegie Mellon SCS Technical Report Collection.
8. Anind K. Dey, Raffay Hamid, Chris Beckmann, Ian Li, and Daniel Hsu. 2004. a CAPpella: programming by demonstration of context-aware applications. In Proceedings of the SIGCHI Conference on Human Factors in Computing Systems (CHI '04). ACM, New York, NY, USA, 33-40. http://dx.doi.org/10.1145/985692.985697
9. Jon Froehlich, Leah Findlater, Marilyn Ostergren, Solai Ramanathan, Josh Peterson, Inness Wragg, Eric Larson, Fabia Fu, Mazhengmin Bai, Shwetak Patel, and James A. Landay. 2012. The design and evaluation of prototype eco-feedback displays for fixture-level water usage data. In Proceedings of the SIGCHI Conference on Human Factors in Computing Systems (CHI '12). ACM, New York, NY, USA, 2367-2376. http://dx.doi.org/10.1145/2207676.2208397
10. Andrew C. Gallagher, Carman G. Neustaedter, Liangliang Cao, Jiebo Luo, and Tsuhan Chen. 2008. Image annotation using personal calendars as context. In Proceedings of the 16th ACM international conference on Multimedia (MM '08). ACM, New York, NY, USA, 681-684. http://dx.doi.org/10.1145/1459359.1459458
11. Dandan Huang, Melanie Tory, and Lyn Bartram. 2014. Data in everyday life: Visualizing time-varying data on a calendar. In *Proc. Poster Compendium IEEE VIS.*
12. Antonio Isalgue, Massimo Palme, Helena Coch, and Rafael Serra. 2006. The importance of users' actions for the sensation of comfort in buildings. In *Proceedings PLEA*, 6-8.
13. Tiiu Koskela and Kaisa Väänänen-Vainio-Mattila. 2004. Evolution towards smart home environments: empirical evaluation of three user interfaces. Personal Ubiquitous Comput. 8, 3-4 (July 2004), 234-240. http://dx.doi.org/10.1007/s00779-004-0283-x
14. Christine Kühnel, Tilo Westermann, Fabian Hemmert, Sven Kratz, Alexander Müller, and Sebastian Möller. 2011. I'm home: Defining and evaluating a gesture set for smart-home control. *International Journal of Human-Computer Studies* 69, 11: 693–704. http://doi.org/10.1016/j.ijhcs.2011.04.005
15. Matthias Laschke, Marc Hassenzahl, Sarah Diefenbach, and Marius Tippkämper. 2011. With a little help from a friend: a shower calendar to save water. In CHI '11 Extended Abstracts on Human Factors in Computing Systems (CHI EA '11). ACM, New York, NY, USA, 633-646. http://dx.doi.org/10.1145/1979742.1979659
16. Brian Y. Lim and Anind K. Dey. 2011. Investigating intelligibility for uncertain context-aware applications. In Proceedings of the 13th international conference on Ubiquitous computing (UbiComp '11). ACM, New York, NY, USA, 415-424. http://dx.doi.org/10.1145/2030112.2030168
17. Jennifer Mankoff, Anind K. Dey, Gary Hsieh, Julie Kientz, Scott Lederer, and Morgan Ames. 2003. Heuristic evaluation of ambient displays. In Proceedings of the SIGCHI Conference on Human Factors in Computing Systems (CHI '03). ACM, New York, NY, USA, 169-176. http://dx.doi.org/10.1145/642611.642642
18. Sarah Mennicken and Elaine M. Huang. 2012. Hacking the natural habitat: an in-the-wild study of smart homes, their development, and the people who live in them. In Proceedings of the 10th international conference on Pervasive Computing (Pervasive'12), Judy Kay, Paul Lukowicz, Hideyuki Tokuda, Patrick Olivier, and Antonio Krüger (Eds.). Springer-Verlag, Berlin, Heidelberg, 143-160. http://dx.doi.org/10.1007/978-3-642-31205-2_10

19. Sarah Mennicken, Jo Vermeulen, and Elaine M. Huang. 2014. From today's augmented houses to tomorrow's smart homes: new directions for home automation research. In Proceedings of the 2014 ACM International Joint Conference on Pervasive and Ubiquitous Computing (UbiComp '14). ACM, New York, NY, USA, 105-115. http://dx.doi.org/10.1145/2632048.2636076
20. Carman Neustaedter and A. J. Bernheim Brush. 2006. "LINC-ing" the family: the participatory design of an inkable family calendar. In Proceedings of the SIGCHI Conference on Human Factors in Computing Systems (CHI '06), Rebecca Grinter, Thomas Rodden, Paul Aoki, Ed Cutrell, Robin Jeffries, and Gary Olson (Eds.). ACM, New York, NY, USA, 141-150. http://dx.doi.org/10.1145/1124772.1124796
21. Carman Neustaedter, Lyn Bartram, and Aaron Mah. 2013. Everyday activities and energy consumption: how families understand the relationship. In Proceedings of the SIGCHI Conference on Human Factors in Computing Systems (CHI '13). ACM, New York, NY, USA, 1183-1192. http://dx.doi.org/10.1145/2470654.2466153
22. Carman Neustaedter, A. J. Bernheim Brush, and Saul Greenberg. 2009. The calendar is crucial: Coordination and awareness through the family calendar. ACM Trans. Comput.-Hum. Interact. 16, 1, Article 6 (April 2009), 48 pages. http://dx.doi.org/10.1145/1502800.1502806
23. Jeffrey Nichols, Brad A. Myers, Michael Higgins, Joseph Hughes, Thomas K. Harris, Roni Rosenfeld, and Mathilde Pignol. 2002. Generating remote control interfaces for complex appliances. In Proceedings of the 15th annual ACM symposium on User interface software and technology (UIST '02). ACM, New York, NY, USA, 161-170. http://dx.doi.org/10.1145/571985.572008
24. Leysia Palen. 1999. Social, individual and technological issues for groupware calendar systems. In Proceedings of the SIGCHI conference on Human Factors in Computing Systems (CHI '99). ACM, New York, NY, USA, 17-24. http://dx.doi.org/10.1145/302979.302982
25. Erika Shehan Poole, Marshini Chetty, Rebecca E. Grinter, and W. Keith Edwards. 2008. More than meets the eye: transforming the user experience of home network management. In Proceedings of the 7th ACM conference on Designing interactive systems (DIS '08). ACM, New York, NY, USA, 455-464. http://dx.doi.org/10.1145/1394445.1394494
26. Jennifer A. Rode, Eleanor F. Toye, and Alan F. Blackwell. 2004. The fuzzy felt ethnography—understanding the programming patterns of domestic appliances. Personal Ubiquitous Comput. 8, 3-4 (July 2004), 161-176. http://dx.doi.org/10.1007/s00779-004-0272-0
27. Florian Schaub, Peter Lang, Bastian Könings, and Michael Weber. 2013. PriCal: dynamic privacy adaptation of collaborative calendar displays. In Proceedings of the 2013 ACM conference on Pervasive and ubiquitous computing adjunct publication (UbiComp '13 Adjunct). ACM, New York, NY, USA, 223-226. http://dx.doi.org/10.1145/2494091.2494163
28. Yolande A.A. Strengers. 2011. Designing eco-feedback systems for everyday life. In Proceedings of the SIGCHI Conference on Human Factors in Computing Systems (CHI '11). ACM, New York, NY, USA, 2135-2144. http://dx.doi.org/10.1145/1978942.1979252
29. Mark Stringer, Geraldine Fitzpatrick, and Eric Harris. 2006. Lessons for the Future: Experiences with the Installation and Use of Today's Domestic Sensors & Technologies. In Proceedings of the 4th international conference on Pervasive Computing (Pervasive '06), Kenneth P. Fishkin, Bernt Schiele, Paddy Nixon, and Aaron Quigley (Eds.). Springer-Verlag, Berlin Heidelberg, 383–399. http://dx.doi.org/10.1007/11748625_24
30. Truong, Khai N., Elaine M. Huang, and Gregory D. Abowd. "CAMP: A magnetic poetry interface for end-user programming of capture applications for the home." In Proceedings of the 6th International Conference on Ubiquitous Computing (UbiComp '04), Nigel Davies, Elizabeth Mynatt, and Itiro Siio (Eds.). Springer-Verlag, Berlin Heidelberg, 143-160. http://dx.doi.org/10.1007/b99948
31. Joe Tullio and Elizabeth D. Mynatt. 2007. Use and implications of a shared, forecasting calendar. In Proceedings of the 11th IFIP TC 13 international conference on Human-computer interaction (INTERACT'07), Cécilia Baranauskas, Philippe Palanque, Julio Abascal, and Simone Diniz Junqueira Barbosa (Eds.). Springer-Verlag, Berlin Heidelberg, 269-282. http://dx.doi.org/ 10.1007/978-3-540-74796-3_26
32. Blase Ur, Jaeyeon Jung, and Stuart Schechter. 2014. Intruders versus intrusiveness: teens' and parents' perspectives on home-entryway surveillance. In Proceedings of the 2014 ACM International Joint Conference on Pervasive and Ubiquitous Computing (UbiComp '14). ACM, New York, NY, USA, 129-139. http://dx.doi.org/10.1145/2632048.2632107
33. Viswanath Venkatesh, Michael G. Morris, Gordon B. Davis, and Fred D. Davis. 2003. User acceptance of information technology: toward a unified view. MIS Q. 27, 3 (September 2003), 425-478.
34. Jo Vermeulen, Geert Vanderhulst, Kris Luyten, and Karin Coninx. 2010. PervasiveCrystal: Asking and answering why and why not questions about pervasive computing applications. In Proceedings of the 6th International Conference on Intelligent Environments (IE'10), IEEE, 271-276. http://dx.doi.org/10.1109/IE.2010.56
35. Rayoung Yang, Mark W. Newman, and Jodi Forlizzi. 2014. Making sustainability sustainable: challenges in the design of eco-interaction technologies. In Proceedings of the SIGCHI Conference on Human Factors in Computing Systems (CHI '14). ACM, New York, NY, USA, 823-832. http://dx.doi.org/10.1145/2556288.2557380

Expanding on Wabi-Sabi as a Design Resource in HCI

Vasiliki Tsaknaki & Ylva Fernaeus
Mobile Life @ KTH, Royal Institute of Technology
Stockholm, Sweden
{tsaknaki, fernaeus}@kth.se

ABSTRACT
The material foundations of computer systems and interactive technology is a topic that gained an increased interest within the HCI community during the last years. In this paper we discuss this topic through the Japanese concept of Wabi-Sabi, a philosophy that embraces three basic realities of the material world: 'nothing lasts', 'nothing is finished', and 'nothing is perfect'. We use these concepts to reflect on four unique interactive artefacts, which all in different ways embrace aspects of Wabi-Sabi, in terms of their design gestalt, materiality, but also in terms of use practices. Further, we use our analysis to articulate three high-level principles that may help addressing the long-term realities faced in physical interaction design, and for the design of interactive systems in general.

Author Keywords
Interaction design; impermanence; incompleteness; imperfection; Wabi-Sabi; materiality; design practice

ACM Classification Keywords
H.5.m. Information interfaces and presentation (e.g., HCI): Miscellaneous.

INTRODUCTION
A practical challenge for designers as well as users of interactive products today lies in how the engineering discourse of technology tends to promote values of designs to be finished, lasting, and perfect, while at the same time contradicting the same notions by technology that easily breaks or quickly becomes out of fashion. Several scholars have discussed this in relation to topics such as sustainability and obsolescence (e.g. [8,20,29]) but also by further emphasising the concrete circumstances for *crafting* with interactive technology (e.g. [9,35,62]). Studying interaction design from a perspective of crafting has highlighted not only notions related to the skilled practice of working with specific tools and materials, but also the material foundations of design work in this domain [3,22]. An important aspect of this discussion concerns how the design of interactive systems is physically tied to the material foundations that define possible interactions, computations and media expressions [5,11,15,67]. Developments in hardware for representing, storing and displaying electronic media have fundamentally affected not only the types of software that can be produced, but also how that software may be practically used and interacted with. Software and hardware is thereby *"intimately connected to a cycle of mutual obsolescence"*, as phrased by Blevis ([8], p503). In this context it is increasingly relevant to reflect on how we, as a community concerned with design and user experiences, may provide advice and guidelines for new solutions to be not just attractive and easy to use, but also of relevance over time.

In this paper we use the philosophy of *Wabi-Sabi* [33,50] to ground a discussion around how the above situation could be embraced in the design of interactive technology. Wabi-Sabi is a traditional Japanese philosophy that *"nurtures all that is authentic by acknowledging three simple realities: nothing lasts, nothing is finished, and nothing is perfect."* ([50], p23). We explore the realities of Wabi-Sabi in interactive artefacts by first providing an extended overview of how its three themes have previously been addressed in HCI, followed by an articulation of our own understanding of the concept through analysing four distinct design cases.

Our analysis result in the formulation of three principles, which we suggest might help guiding designers who aim to approach Wabi-Sabi more concretely in their design work. The three principles each involves an element of contradiction, and are framed as: 1) Design for long-term interaction through conscious use of impermanent materials and media, 2) Approach perfection through explicitly unfinished designs, and 3) Engage with the richness of interactive expressions by embracing limitations in current technology.

Thus, we contribute by elaborating on Wabi-Sabi as a conceptual framework to reflect on crucial aspects that seem predominant in contemporary computing, but also as a practical resource to guide the design of new interactive solutions. Compared to previous work that has brought up Wabi-Sabi to the context of HCI [24,27] our aim is to provide a higher-level account of how this concept can be approached on a more conceptual level, beyond merely the surface appearance of designed systems and artefacts.

 ACM 978-1-4503-3362-7/16/05···$15.00
DOI: http://dx.doi.org/10.1145/2858036.2858459

BACKGROUND

As an aesthetic concept within the field of physical product design [30,44], Wabi-Sabi is sometimes used to describe objects with a family resemblance to traditional Japanese folklore, characterized through terms such as simplicity, patina, raw materials, and uneven and naturally shaped surfaces. In the area of computing, this notion of Wabi-Sabi has been introduced as a way of reflecting on design features primarily in the domain of physical interfaces and interaction. In their description of what they call *organic interfaces*, Holman & Vertegaal for instance, use it to pose questions: *"what might computers look like if they were designed with a little more wabi-sabi? More curved, like a piece of earthenware, more flexible, like a sheet of Japanese Washi rice paper and more delicate, like handmade knitwear?"* ([24], p51). Wabi-Sabi has also been approached by Ikemya and Rosner in their articulation of *worn media* as a manifestation of wear among digital things [27].

In this paper we further elaborate the concept of Wabi-Sabi in HCI, but from a more philosophically oriented and holistic direction. The term Wabi-Sabi consists of two parts: *Wabi* refers to the essence of simplification, of cutting down the things to the important, whereas *Sabi* refers to the passage of time, and more specifically to the fact that the core of something remains the same, even though the facade or surface may change over time [50]. While *Wabi* resonates directly with standard principles of product- and interface design, such as the Bauhaus ideals of minimalism, *Sabi* has a less straightforward counterpart in (post) modern ideals of (predominantly Western) design thinking. However, the notion of *Sabi* is still very much present in traditional crafting practices observed also in non-Japanese contexts. Some examples include the resourceful use of material by a leather craftsman in Basel [64] and the central role of patina in repair work at a bookbinding workshop in Cambridge [55] – both observed for elaborating notions of craft in the context of HCI.

Thus, apart from being used to describe a physical form that has organic and delicate attributes, the concept of Wabi-Sabi also embodies aspects of long-term deployment and use over time, which is an important concern for research in human-computer interaction. To emphasize this aspect, we will, in this paper, focus our analysis and discussion based on the three main themes of Wabi-Sabi, mentioned already in introduction: '*nothing lasts, nothing is finished, and nothing is perfect*' [50]. We see this as forming a particularly well-articulated design philosophy, providing us with a lens through which to approach and guide a broader discussion around materiality in the context of interaction design, HCI, and computing at large.

Wabi-Sabi is a complex and rich philosophical concept, and we would like to acknowledge that we will be using it in a rather pragmatic way, based on simplified definitions as interpreted and summarized by predominantly western scholars and from a perspective of design theory [30,33,50]. Apart from being a guiding principle for design work, the concept of Wabi-Sabi is strongly associated with customs such as the Japanese tea ceremony, as well as with nature itself [33]. We would also like to emphasise that Wabi-Sabi is just one of many design philosophies that co-exist, and if studying Japanese high-tech product designs for example, this would not be the most prominent. Instead Wabi-Sabi to us, is better described as a globally occurring theme, or genre in contemporary product design, in which attention is directed towards traditional crafting and resourceful use of authentic and organic materials [44].

THE THREE THEMES OF WABI-SABI IN HCI

We will now delve briefly into how the three poetic themes of Wabi-Sabi – 'nothing lasts', 'nothing is finished', and 'nothing is perfect' – have been addressed in prior work within the field of HCI. Each of these three topics has a long existing discourse within the field, although most often using another vocabulary and without Wabi-Sabi as its guiding framework. Here we will give an overview of what we see as main topics within these works, separated into sections for each of the three themes.

Impermanence – 'Nothing Lasts'

Several scholars have stressed the importance of increasing the longevity and endurance of interactive products, most notably from a perspective of environmental sustainability (e.g. [6,29,46]). Others have highlighted the value of more long-term historical perspectives on interaction over all, such as Fernaeus *et al.* in their analysis of a 150 year old Jacquard loom still in use [13]. Even more broadly, Irwin, Kossoff and Tonkinwise [70], proposed the term *transition design,* as a way of framing design as dealing with societal transition towards more sustainable futures. The interaction design community within HCI has also highlighted several aspects around transience and temporality in accordance to the topics of materiality (e.g. [21,53]) and recent research on time-related issues in HCI [20,38]. In these, and other related works, concepts such as material traces [53], promoting quality and equality [7], or the ephemerality of social networks [23,36] have been discussed as emergent throughout the lifetime of an interactive product or software system. Another direction from which impermanence has been discussed is through the lens of ephemeral user interfaces [10], designed from explicitly temporal materials such as ice or fog, taking the idea of impermanence to the extreme.

That the technology built, tested and reported on in the areas of electronics and computing is in constant development has also been discussed in terms of knowledge production. Hornbæk *et al.* [25] suggest that replacing old technologies with new in replication studies can help researchers reflect upon acquired knowledge on a specific research topic. In similar terms, the concept of an interaction design remake has been explored [4], pointing to the reality of technologies and experiences as shaped by changes in socio-technical contexts over time.

Incompleteness – 'Nothing is Finished'

The impermanent nature of technology is also related to the question of what is considered a *finished* interactive product [62]. In a research context, a finished or complete system or product may refer to a state of being ready to be adopted or deployed by users for user studies, in contrast to e.g. product design, where a finished product is ready to be mass-produced and released on the market [43]. In HCI, terms such as prototypes, probes or experiments are used to describe products that are part of a design exploration. Pierce and Paulos, for instance, use the term *experiments* to refer to a series of counterfunctional cameras they designed, since their aim was to explore this topic *"without overly focusing on specific applications or finished, usable artifacts"* ([48], p377).

However, all material entities are characterized by constant changes being either slow and subtle, or abrupt and drastic. This is also the case with interactive products, as they get filled with media content, get updated, or personalised. This was however not always the standard perspective taken in computational designs. An example is personal webpages, which in the 1990's often were accompanied with visual signage to indicate that they were 'under construction'. In reflecting on this, Rettberg concludes how this highlighted a tension between *"the desire for completion that we had inherited from print and the constant flux of the web"* ([51],p7*).* The early homepages could be seen as predecessors of today's blogs, were being 'unfinished', or having more updates to come, is rather a positive aspect of being 'live'. Computer systems being understood as in a constant state of development is now also evident e.g. in agile software development methodologies, and can also be illustrated by software companies, such as Adobe, who recently shifted their business model to sell subscriptions of a service, rather than licenses of products. An example from the other end of the spectrum is hardware hacking practices, practices of replacing or modding the physical casings or surfaces of interactive devices [61], or repair as an everyday design practice [38]. Thus, incompleteness from a perspective of being in progress is not to be read as bearing only negative connotations in the field of HCI, but rather as a reality that designers, companies and end users make use of actively as a resource. Embracing the idea of incompleteness in more positive terms, Seok *et al.* recently introduced a new design space of intentionally unfinished designs that help end-users solve their own problems, which they named *Non-Finito Products* [57].

Imperfection – 'Nothing is Perfect'

Perfection, within a traditional design discourse, has been associated with the properties of mass-produced objects in terms of form, shape, geometry or texture [34]. In that context, perfection is associated with ideals of symmetry, uniformity and lack of features acquired by use. Moving from mass production to personal fabrication, some designers and makers have now started to put the ideals of perfection as uniformity into question. In interaction design, there now seems to be an increasing number of makers and crafters inspired by the unique and thus 'imperfect' outcomes of making things by hand, or by using personal, local and small-scale fabrication tools (e.g. [17,43,69]). According to Ingold, the designer, as a creator or inventor of things, is the 'manager of imperfection' [28].

The notion of perfection gains relevance with increased emphasis on interaction design as a process of *crafting*, which can be described as "*thinking through making things by hand*" ([45], p2) or "*the skilled manipulation of physical materials*" ([52], p195). A major characteristic of a crafting process is the uniqueness of the produced outcomes, depended on the skilled work of the crafts specialist, but also on decisions taken on the spot. In a similar way, computer programming, and making in software in general, has been conceptualized as a crafting practice [41]. Similar to any crafting process, unintentional mistakes or decisions taken on the spot, based on circumstances in the digital tools, can lead to unique and unexpected outcomes, which greatly might impact the final design [15]. Along with the development of a rich variety of post-desktop computing devices, many alternative types of physical materials such as glass [56], leather and wood [64] or paper [42] become more common in the design of interactive artefacts. By integrating such types of materials in interaction design contexts, not only new types of crafting practices, but also different interactive qualities emerge, putting ideals of 'perfection' associated with mass-produced products into question. As mentioned by Vallgårda and Fernaeus, tangible and material computing thereby stresses the incomplete and imperfect reality of interaction design [66].

The notion of perfection also relates on a deep philosophical level to how user experience can be understood and approached by designers, e.g. as in McCarthy and Wright's pragmatically based account: *"In a world of change, the same action can have different meaning and significance, as the context is always different. In an open world, all action is creative, a fresh use of intelligence producing something surprising and new every time."* ([40], p71). In terms of experience, perfection thereby seems as nothing but a floating target – changing with practice, fashions and with technical development.

FOUR DESIGN EXAMPLES

We will here articulate our understanding of Wabi-Sabi in interaction design by presenting four distinctly different interactive objects, focusing on their respective design gestalt, materiality, but also their intended use. The presentation can be understood as a form of interaction critique [2], with explicit focus on how each of the objects can be interpreted in terms of impermanence, incompleteness and imperfection. These artefacts were chosen firstly because they all resonated with our

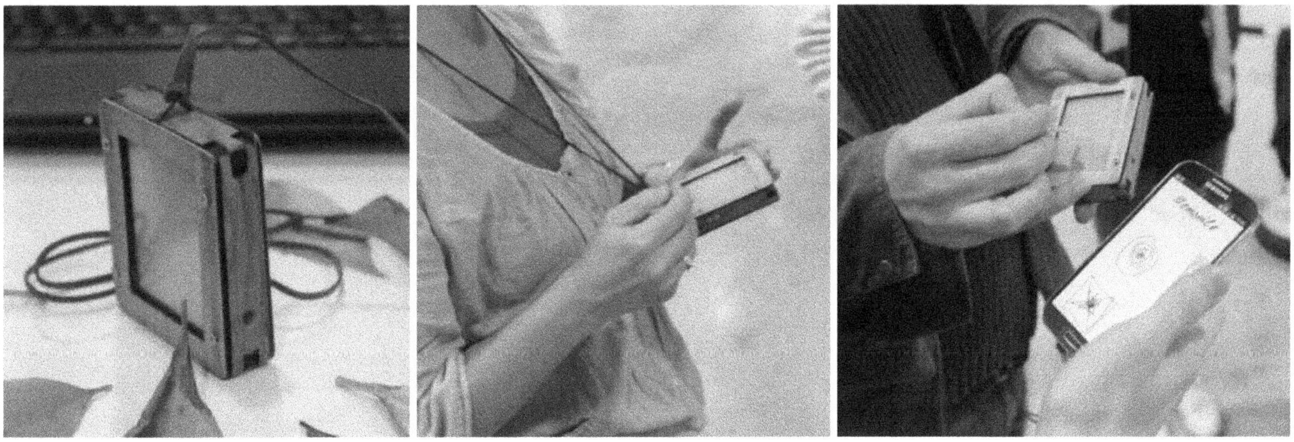

Figure 1. Memonile Necklace; a) overview picture of the device, b) device in use, c) device next to a smartphone, showing feed tracking the screenless doodles and gestures performed on the Memonile.

understanding of Wabi-Sabi, by presenting physical as well as interactive gestalts that emphasise aspects of repair, tweaking, and customisation. We also found them intriguing since their overall appearances depart in different ways from common norms in the design of interactive gadgets. Further, these artefacts were physically accessible to us, as we were able to experience their interactive qualities hands on, and discuss them with their makers. Finally, they cover a range of interactive arenas (design, performance, haptics, art), which allowed a discussion across different types of use settings.

The artefacts we will discuss here are:

- The Memonile, a note-taking device based on DIY aesthetics.
- Ajna, a complex musical cabinet, created in a bricolage fashion.
- Woody, an open-source haptic manipulation device.
- The Seaweed speaker, an exploration of physical form factors and interaction.

The analysis was conducted by articulating our subjective experience of interacting with each artefact, as well as from the descriptions given by their makers. This we used as a base for 'reading' the artefacts through the lens of the three themes presented above. The three realities highlighted by Wabi-Sabi were thereby used as a guide to foreground certain aspects of these designs, and to help us articulate different ways that these notions could be practically understood in relation to interactive products.

Memonile

The Memonile is a wireless interactive device worn as a necklace that can be used for sightlessly taking quick notes or doodles, which are stored as a feed on a mobile phone or other device (Figure 1). It was developed by a group of interaction design students during a three-week workshop, organized by our research group in the context of physical interaction design education [65]. Conceptualised by its designers as a kind of jewellery, it speaks to its explicit context of the maker culture, where the idea of personally manufactured technology, using tools such as laser cutters and latest microcontroller boards, are idealized, and possibly even worn on display. Its physical form factors and interactive gestalt are reminiscent of the since long obsolete Palm Pilot and similar devices of the late 1990's, which adds a quirky historical perspective to the design.

The physical object is made out of 3mm plywood, cut using a laser cutter and assembled in a compact box that hangs around the neck by a leather cord. At the front of the box is a touch-sensitive input surface made of glass, interacted with a stylus pen, also made of wood. Inside the box is an Arduino compatible circuit board, the rFlea [60], which has a built-in Bluetooth Low Energy module in order to communicate wirelessly to the mobile phone of the person wearing the Memonile. When writing or doodling something on the screen, the word or the sketch is sent and saved as a feed on the user's mobile phone. This 'blindfolded' interaction with the input surface, without direct visual feedback on the device itself, adds a dimension of surprise, 'secrecy' and ambiguity to the performance of interaction.

The simple and rough 'quick and dirty' design of the Memonile points to a rather imperfect prototype. It is basically a wooden box assembled without any redundant elements or decorative details. At the same time, in terms of the physical form factors, the wooden parts assembled with screws in combination with the darker wooden surfaces, burnt from the laser beam, are traces inscribed from the fabrication process, which manifest deliberate and non-deliberate signs that become an important part of the design itself. The way it has been fabricated, also communicates the possibility to be disassembled in order to replace the electronics hosted inside the box, or change the glass input screen in case it breaks. In a similar way, the software was designed in an open-source fashion so that it can be programmed for different purposes, thus leaving the interaction open for personal appropriation and re-design.

Figure 2. Ajna interactive musical cabinet; a) Ajna performing with orchestra, b) the main drum with projection, c) physical interface for controlling Ajna.

Ajna

Our second design case illustrates a more complex interactive construction (Figure 2). Ajna [16] is a human-sized interactive musical object created by the art- and music collective *I Skogen Ibland.* Ajna is designed to perform along with a live orchestra in concert settings, but it has also been displayed in various music festivals and art gallery settings as an interactive music sculpture for audiences to interact with, using a variety of setups. Fernaeus and Vallgårda describe the design as *"an obscure, musical bricolage, made from a heterogeneous collection of parts including electromechanical devices, old musical instruments, microcontrollers, wood, feathers, skin, motors, potentiometers – all hosted within the frame of a vintage rococo cabinet"* ([16], p915). The different parts are put together as mechanical systems, which are controlled via midi signals, thus creating a complex physical form in combination with a rich musical soundscape.

In this design, we see Wabi-Sabi as represented through the on-going state of being 'in construction'. The artists are improving and adjusting the design before every show, this partly due to the fragile materials used for the separate parts, but also since they want to improve and test new ideas. This is the case not only for the physical structure, for instance that mechanical parts need to be re-adjusted or screws need to be tightened, but also in terms of software and audio used. Working as a composer, one of its designers constantly provides new media expressions for Ajna to perform. That the design is constantly changing increases the sense of *liveness* of Ajna, where each performance is unique and highly authentic.

The design is essentially a material assemblage, consisting of found and available objects which have been tailored to fit with a rather loose original idea shared and negotiated by two artists. Constructing Ajna from such a rich variety of materials and objects that each has its own unique history is also an important quality that makes the artefact seem like an organic being, with its own material history, unique visual appearance, and functionality.

Importantly, the reuse of artefacts was by the artists not expressed as for the purpose of eco design or environmental sustainability, instead this was rather of aesthetic and practical reasons, to make something that would work musically and also to fit with the cultural context of a live orchestra. The designers have thereby directed their efforts towards a rather narrow niche of cultural expression, in which e.g. clean white surfaces and blinking LED displays would make a less natural fit. This opened the design space for new solutions also in terms of interaction. The feathers of the marimba-like instrument at the top (see Figure 2a), were for instance not placed there merely for decorative purposes, but in order for the musicians to be able to read

Figure 3. Woody, a haptic feedback device that can be physically adapted to fit the needs of specific haptic manipulation scenarios; a) overview of testing the device with on-screen model, b) the device with another design of arm, c) box with electrical interface.

and follow the movements of Ajna while performing. Thus, the use of fragile organic physical matter is here shown to have functional as well as aesthetic uses in this specific interactive setting.

Woody

Woody (Figure 3) is an *"open-source, open-hardware module-based kit"* for spatial haptics [18]. Like other spatial haptic devices, it is based on a mechanical arm that a person can hold and manipulate, and through force feedback get a haptic experience of the shape and materials in 3D computer models. Such technology is used for instancc in surgcry simulations, for communication between blind, and other cases where physical feedback is central to the experience of interactive manipulation of media content.

One aspect that is unique about Woody is that the choice of wood as a material for the robotic arm means that designers, but also users, more easily can adapt the length and shape of the arm, and thereby more readily tune important parameters to fit a particular task or application (Figure 3b). With the classic 'set' design of similar devices, which are all based on an industrial design that cannot be modified, the interaction scenarios are limited to desktop settings with a very defined space for allowed gestures and manipulations.

The wood itself, and especially the production process of making use of laser cutting, also points to the quickness and ease that the device could be modified, and that the design itself is open for change. Wood may not seem the most durable material for this type of applications, but it does speak to common knowledge of sustainable practices of repair and use. Or, as expressed by one of its designers: *'they may paint it pink if they like to'*. The need for a personalized device may be more important for a specific application, rather than a stable solution that may not be modified. Moreover, the makers of Woody chose not to encapsulate parts of the construction, specifically, the mechanical structure and wire rope power transmission, but leave them exposed. According to the authors, *"this was intended to help designers focus more on designing for their application rather than problem solving through mechanical and electrical nuances and details"* ([18], p134). Designers, in this case, refer to other people who like to use Woody as part of their own interactive setup.

The specific design embraces the fact that one solution may not fit all, and thus that the 'perfect' shape of a spatial haptic device is contextually dependent and shifts with specific applications.

Seaweed Speaker

Our last example is a simplistic case of a modded loudspeaker, made to emphasize the offline aspect of interacting with physical forms, as described by Esteves *et al.* [12]. This design was created by the first author in collaboration with a professional silversmith artist, as part of a six-month project exploring the intersection of jewellery and interaction design [63].

It functions as a mobile speaker, crafted in a sculptural form out of leather, which resembles a seaweed plant. On a surface level, the main function of this artefact could be read to provide another way of using and experiencing a mobile speaker as an electronic and mobile device. The Seaweed speaker connects to a device such as a mobile phone or a laptop, and can be either worn as a necklace (Figure 4a), placed on a surface (Figure 4b), or probably hung on the wall, leaving an increased openness or ambiguity in terms of where it can be placed, and accordingly, how it can be used or experienced as a device. But the user can also decide whether to fully expand it as a sculptural object, or entangle it in order to occupy less space. In the case of wearing the Seaweed speaker as a necklace, the user can bring the copper seashell, where the speaker is hosted, close to the ear to listen to the music, as shown in Figure 4c. Leather was chosen as a material to host the cables of the device because it can be easily deformed and shaped in different directions. The floppy leather parts can be placed in different ways, while no way is ever to be expected as better than any other. The organic shape reduces any expectations for symmetrical perfection

Figure 4. The Seaweed speaker; a) wearing the Seaweed speaker as a necklace, b) the Seaweed speaker with laptop, c) listening to the music from the copper shell-speaker.

and points to the property of living things as growing and ever changing, pointing to the Wabi-Sabi notion of imperfection.

We also read this design as a commentary on the short-lived reality of most technical gadgets, where the mobile speaker/headphones may be one of the most common. Most of the cheap mobile speakers sold in the market will function only for a limited time, whereas the way they have been manufactured does not allow for repair. The carefully handcrafted copper, silver and leather parts, in a way intend to hide the electronic components, cables and battery, similar to most portable gadgets. But in contrast to most such devices, the entire electronic parts, which will likely be damaged at some point, have been made accessible in order to be replaced. The handcrafted case containing the circuit board is shaped as a mussel shell and has a small hinge and can open and close, providing access to the main electronics. In a similar way, the speaker with the cables attached to it is placed inside the copper spiral and can be removed by following around the spiral form. Thus, the way the Seaweed speaker has been crafted stresses, and probably takes to the extreme, the impermanent attributes of common electronic devices and gadgets.

Insights from Analysing the Four Artefacts

The most striking common feature of the designs above is probably how they all emphasise aspects of Wabi-Sabi through their physical properties. In our first interpretation, their surface appearances, made from organic materials, gave them a sense of *liveness*, for instance that they will age with time, which mapped well with our own preconception of Wabi-Sabi. This was also partly why these particular artefacts were selected for this study, and became an important part of our analysis. However, through our broadened insights from the analysis we would like to bring forth a more holistic perspective, including aspects of software, electronic behaviour, and user interaction.

The four design examples presented here all make explicit that the impermanent nature of software and hardware could be considered a design opportunity rather than only an obstacle. The Memonile with its lightweight prototype construction, Ajna through recycling of found objects, Woody through explicit instructions for modding and re-design, and the design for repairability in the Seaweed speaker. That said, it would probably be too drastic to say that these handcrafted interactive devices would be able to compete fully with mass-manufactured devices in terms of robustness, which often have had large groups of professional designers behind them, with much resources for testing and debugging. However, their explicit use of fragile materials and technologies, and that they thereby have been consciously designed to upgrade, repair, extend, and tweak, point to a shift in attitude compared to most other designs in this field.

Importantly, the physical materials chosen for each artefact, were not just interesting materials tried out together with electronics, but were actively chosen for practical reasons as for example the leather drums in the Ajna, or wood in the Woody. From a perspective of product design, these materials seem to have a greater potential for adaptation and repair, and also address a more varied view on culture and ever-changing contexts of use. The standard materials of plastic and metals used in most processes of mass-production are indeed often more robust and easier to mass-produce, but also less straightforward to modify, repair, or to use in practices of making and crafting. A contradiction that the four design examples in different ways make explicit is thereby the mutual dependency of physical devices and interactive behaviour, in which, negative connotations of fragility and the positive discourse around constant progress can be seen as two sides of the same coin.

Further, all of the designs presented above point to a rather pluralistic view of interaction design, in which many parallel cultural values, aesthetic genres, and tastes are allowed to coexist. Taking Woody as an example, the 'openness' it allows for, embraces incompleteness in both hardware and software, through the possibility of making new variations. The possibility to replace or modify parts of the Woody in terms of hardware or software is assumed as a necessity in order to get closer to anything near 'perfection'. Similarly, this can be observed with the way the Memonile, Ajna and the Seaweed speaker have been designed. The Memonile that can be re-programmed, Ajna adapted to fit in the context of an orchestra, and the unusual gestalt of the Seaweed speaker.

There is no coincidence that all of the artefacts presented in this study are explicitly grounded in culture, but also in known limitations of current technology. In each of the examples, imperfections of current technology are used actively as a design resource, rather than a barrier for design. Looking at the Seaweed speaker for example, making accessible the electronic parts as things to be replaced, is core to its conceptual design and what it expresses, as a sculptural object. In Woody, the limitation of 'one size does not fit all' was the main motivation for its design, whereas the sightless interaction with the Memonile is what makes the interaction interesting as an interactive performance. Finally, the design case of Ajna represents a fine balance at the very limits of the technologically possible, which is also what made it into an impressively rich media art installation. Finally, it could be noted that all examples that we presented here illustrate an attitude of *tinkering*, reflected both in the making process but also as something that is welcomed and expected in use. Of course, such an attitude puts high demands on users as active co-creators and caretakers, which for sure would not be accepted by everyone. Yet, we see that these designs address an important desire, at least among certain user groups, where these use qualities are highly valued and expected.

Summarizing the insights from the critiques presented

above, we see three emerging themes, each highlighting a paradoxical circumstance. *Firstly*, each of the four designs was intended as long-lasting object through customisation, repair and tweaking, while using rather fragile materials. *Secondly*, they all exhibit a design ideal that embraces repair and customisation, rather than the status of the brand new. *Thirdly*, they each manage to display rather visionary interactions, while engaging actively with limitations of current technology.

DESIGNING INTERACTIONS WITH WABI-SABI

Here we will further elaborate our understanding of Wabi-Sabi in terms of how it could support reflection within the field of interaction design. We will structure this discussion around the three themes introduced in the analysis above. These themes, or paradoxes, could be seen as forming high-level design principles for the domain of interactive systems:

1) Design for long-term interaction through conscious use of impermanent materials and media.
2) Approach perfection through explicitly unfinished designs.
3) Engage with the richness of interactive expressions by embracing limitations in current technology.

Design for Long-term Interaction through Conscious Use of Impermanent Materials and Media

The first topic we want to discuss is how conscious use of impermanent materials and media can be used actively as a way of guiding the design of long-term interaction. By impermanence we refer to the actual fragile properties of physical materials such as wood, glass screens and electronic parts, as well as of software built on unreliable foundations in terms of operating systems, service providers, or socio-technical infrastructure.

All physical artefacts change over time and with use, and eventually they will break. For the case of interactive systems, we are all familiar with this reality through disk spaces that get full, battery life getting shorter, buttons falling apart, screens that break and hard drives that simply stop working. It is also not uncommon that software files get corrupted or deleted, software running slower over time, and certain file formats or operating systems no longer get supported. Moreover, systems and functionality may get lost in the transition to new hardware platforms. When, for instance, the curators of MoMA recently decided to put together an archive exhibition of classic video games, one of their greatest challenges was that the physical controls needed to be remade, and also that software had to be reprogrammed, in order for the games to be playable using contemporary hardware [1]. With more active emphasis on the impermanent nature of interactive systems, we believe that more designs could be prepared for more lasting use.

As an extreme example, the Jacquard loom studied by Fernaeus *et al.* [13] had been persistently used for more than 150 years, although its construction was based entirely on 'fragile' materials such as wood, cardboards and cotton string. Even though this might seem like a paradox, that design was in the end probably more robust than even the sturdiest of smartphones of today. In a similar way as the Jaquard loom, designs based on this concept could allow for use practices that treat designed objects as *live*, accepting the need for some caretaking over time. An insight is that robust materials, such as plastic or metal, or software locked for modification or upgrades by end users, are commonly also difficult to repair.

In many ways the market embraces this reality, which is reflected in 'planned obsolescence', new technological gadgets, and constant needs for software updates. An everyday example is the repair of mobile phones, which has made specialized repair shops a thriving business. As a counter-reaction, DIY community blogs show instructions for how to repair a broken screen of an iPhone, for instance. This is just one of many examples of how the fragile nature of interactive products, both in hardware and software, is a reality that affects, apart from design practitioners, many other stakeholders.

Importantly, this principle will not necessarily solve, but rather highlight the problematic aspects of existing strategies such as planned obsolescence. This can also open new directions for more varied designs that embrace this reality. In HCI, this has been reflected in how materials such as paper [58], clay [54], glass [56] or even more fragile matter such as seeds or dried leaves [14] have been used to highlight this aspect of technology. For instance, Ikemiya and Rosner [27] describe prompted actions of breakage of ceramic objects can be used for reflecting on what they call *worn media*. Similarly, Pierce and Paulos constructed a series of cameras, which they describe as being '*designed around the idea of requiring the user to physically break apart the camera in order to gain physical access to the digitally stored images*' [49]

Thus, if accepting impermanence as a reality, then longevity and endurance might not even necessarily be a design target per se. The fragility and impermanence that are inherent properties of media might instead inspire new design directions and practices that treasure the ephemeral. One well-known example here is the online communication service Snapchat [71], in which a main feature is that content will be permanently deleted, after a time limit set by the user sending the content to recipients. This takes into consideration that impermanent videos or photos can engage users in a different way and be valued as short-lasting content. The value of this media lies exactly in its temporality, grounded in existing use practices and human values, rather than the assumed preference among users towards stored files that will be retrieved again and again. A more general example is the perceived promise of free, unlimited and permanent space as provided by the so-called 'cloud'. Storing our entire digital life stories permanently in digital form does not yet seem as a viable option, so other modes of looking at information and technology might be needed. The failed promise of eternal storage has also inspired other designs, e.g. Delete by Haiku [59] , in which old text messages may be creatively repurposed into a shortened poetic format, as a form of data compression.

As interaction designers, we might make a serious mistake when taking for example hardware platforms, interaction solutions, storage space or connectivity for granted. Even such widespread concepts as the 'mouse and keyboard', or 'double-clicking' are now quickly starting to get replaced by other interaction paradigms considered as mainstream. If the impermanent nature of interaction techniques on specific platforms, for example, were embraced more fully in design, then more care might be taken to find ways for systems to be kept alive. This could be considered important also on a broader scale, given the central role of interactive technology in our society and its potential value as part of our cultural heritage. Paradoxical as it may seem, making resourceful use of the impermanent properties of materials and media is a direction that we believe could possibly increase the potential of long-lived interactive systems.

Approach Perfection through Explicitly Unfinished Designs

Our second theme concerns how explicitly unfinished or incomplete designs could be a way of working towards pleasing the specific needs of different users. The 'timeless perfection' as proposed in early modernism and industrial design through planar surfaces and strict minimalist geometric forms, and which has been inherited also to graphical interfaces, could be argued to neglect some of the multi-faceted nature of culture as changing over time, between contexts and societies. Our reading of Wabi-Sabi proposes that it is through the particular intentions and skills of the designer, crafts person, or programmer, but also the tools available a given moment, and finally the cultural and historical grounding, through which a negotiation of perfection could potentially be achieved. Given the global context of our field of studies, one may ask if 'timeless perfection' is even a sensible target for interaction design. And if so, what would such a design be like?

In the design examples presented above, this question is approached through designs that provide the possibility to be improved, altered and repaired over time and for different contexts of interaction and use. This direction links the notion of imperfection to *uniqueness*, previously discussed in product design in relation to injection moulding as a method of production [47] or from a material perspective, linking imperfection with graceful aging [32]. What we mean here is the imperfections inherent in organic materials and in handcrafted objects, rather than to a negative connotation of something that is 'not right'. This also points to the nature of making as a process of compromises and decisions taken on the spot, in contrast to a process of mass-production, which can be considered as resulting in 'perfect' products.

However, there is a danger to read this paradox as potentially welcoming attitudes such as 'anything goes', 'ad-hocism', or sloppiness in design, which is rather contradictory to the traditional crafting practices that Wabi-Sabi is fundamentally drawing on. Rather than taking responsibilities away from the judgments of designers, the aim here is to shift these to further acknowledge the potential re-designs and evolvement that may occur within use and after deployment.

The incompleteness that is inherent in a design process, but also in the way interactive products are designed and experienced by users, is mirrored by this quote from the Wabi-Sabi philosophy: *"All things are incomplete. [...] All things [...] are in constant, never-ending state of becoming or dissolving"* ([33], p49). Thus, the fact that things are constantly becoming, changing and transforming is an important aspect of reality, which successful long-lived systems will have to be designed for.

The idea of incompleteness, as interpreted through the philosophical concept of Wabi-Sabi speaks to current needs for tailorability and modifications, also in software. In that way, an interactive artefact can always be transformed and 'evolve' over time and through usage, or adapt to fit with new needs or interests. Still, the look of the 'new' is obviously to be idealised by an industry who aims to sell more products, and thus may be a challenge to address concretely in terms of industrial design practice. However, we believe that the notion of the new is now complemented by allowing practices of adapting, appropriating or updating, and for users to relate to interactive products in terms of long-term service.

Engage with the Richness of Interactive Expressions by Embracing Limitations in Current Technology

Our third proposal for how to approach Wabi-Sabi in interaction design is to embrace the limitations in current technology, as a way to engage with the full potential of interactive expressions. According to the tradition of Wabi-Sabi *'good design is design based on the materials at hand'* [31]. This view relates the concept of Wabi-Sabi to that of bricolage, which has been discussed as a making process that rather than being primarily concept-driven, is guided by a dialogue with the available materials, tools and resources, and thereby more explicitly allows for unique and unpredictable results [37]. Interaction design relies fundamentally on current technological advances and computational materials, ranging from circuit boards to software systems and other peripherals. Working knowledge of such technology, based on active experimentation with the media expressions they may produce, is often necessary in order to achieve desired user experiences.

Looking at technological artefacts from such a perspective

is grounded on the idea that *"technologies must be understood phenomenologically, as belonging in different ways to our experience and use of technologies as a human-technology relation, rather than abstractly conceiving of them as mere objects"* [26]. We believe that we have to use the possibilities and limitations of current technology in order to design rich interactions, rather than relying on visions of what technologies we might have as a resource in the future. Considering the limitations and imperfections of current technology in tandem with materials and software, there could be new framings and understandings concerning design methods, which complement approaches that start from a perspective of concepts and visions.

To us, this principle points towards a direction of 'honesty', in terms of the material properties of electronics, but also in terms of digital media being inherently limited. However, rather than referring to authenticity of materials as opposed to e.g. skeuomorphs [68], this links directly to the three paradoxes presented in this paper, i.e. that artefacts will break, they will not last and the design may never be 'finished'. Such a perspective might potentially reflect a pessimistic outlook that would not strive for new solutions, visions, and readiness for what comes next. However, looking at the second paradox presented above, leaving a design 'unfinished' can be a way to allow for integrating new technological solutions, to ideally make them both backward- and forward compatible.

CONCLUSION

In this paper we used the Japanese philosophy of Wabi-Sabi to reflect on the material circumstances for contemporary computing, and more specifically for interaction design. We did this by first presenting an overview on how the three themes of Wabi-Sabi – *'nothing lasts', 'nothing is finished', and 'nothing is perfect'* – have been previously addressed in HCI. Additionally, we presented a reflective account of four examples of uniquely designed interactive artefacts, which all in different ways embrace the three themes.

From an engineering perspective, the three themes of Wabi-Sabi could probably read as pessimistic, as problems to solve or realities that should be strived to overcome. However, through our deepened engagement with these concepts we found each of the themes as not bound to negative connotations, but rather to be highlighting cultural values that are relevant to all practices, ranging from design, to crafting, and practices of use. This led us to formulate three high-level design principles, which can be used as a way to practically engage with Wabi-Sabi in design work, or as an analytical lens to reflect on any other interactive product or system. We proposed that a way to design for long-term interaction could be through conscious use of impermanent materials and media, but also that 'perfection' could be approached through explicitly unfinished designs that allow for modifications and repair. Additionally, by embracing the limitations in current technology, it is possible to engage fully with the richness of interactive expressions.

The above directions are pointing to alternative ways of discussing the long-term impact of digital media on the one hand, but they also speak to a more general desire for more authentic interactive products on the other, which is essentially what the philosophy of Wabi-Sabi is about. The first has to do with the equilibrium between designing for long-term interaction, while at the same time embracing the reality that the software and hardware of each artefact will evidently become obsolete. The second paradox proposed to embrace artefacts as 'unfinished' entities, as a way to eventually come closer to a 'perfect' design. Finally, the third theme was about accepting and making creative use of given technological limitations.

We would also like to note that although we found the examples presented here as highly intriguing, these should not be read as direct proposals to turn into mass production, but rather as reflections on how interaction designs could be allowed to exist also outside of the limited frames of capitalist structures. This topic opens up broader discussions in relation to socio-economic and political agendas, from considering various modes of open source as an attitude and political stance. With the democratization of knowledge that the Internet, social networks and globalization brought, people learn to fix things themselves, but also to exchange services and knowledge on topics that cover a vast spectrum. Such a direction supports alternative modes of making and sharing, in contrast to supporting ideals of the 'ready-made', which are more related to traditional exchange systems. Even though we find this topic very important to be further addressed, it goes beyond the scope of the study presented here.

Finally, we believe that looking at interactive products from a Wabi-Sabi perspective, or using Wabi-Sabi as a resource in design practice, is an important direction that can raise more discussions around the material aspects of computing and interactive technologies, placing them in their cultural and time-specific contexts.

ACKNOWLEDGMENTS

The research has been funded by the Arts and Crafts project at Mobile Life Vinn Excellence Centre, with a grant from Vinnova. We would like to thank all the designers and artists of the four artefacts discussed in this paper for their insightful comments.

REFERENCES

1. Paola Antonelli. 2013. The New Frontiers of Design. *Opening plenary keynote, CHI'13.*

2. Jeffrey Bardzell. 2009. Interaction criticism and aesthetics. *Proceedings of the 27th international conference on Human factors in computing systems - CHI 09*: 2357. http://doi.org/10.1145/1518701.1519063

3. Shaowen Bardzell, Daniela K. Rosner, and Jeffrey Bardzell. 2012. Crafting quality in design. *Proceedings of the Designing Interactive Systems Conference on - DIS '12*, ACM Press, 11. Retrieved September 25, 2015 from http://dl.acm.org/citation.cfm?id=2317956.2317959

4. Moa Bergsmark and Ylva Fernaeus. 2016. From Patchwork to Appliqué: Reflections from an Interaction Design Remake. *Proceedings of the International Conference on Tangible, Embedded and Embodied Interaction (TEI '16)*, ACM.

5. Jean-françois Blanchette. 2011. A Material History of Bits. *Journal of the American Society for Information Science and Technology* 62, 6: 1042–1057.

6. Eli Blevis, Kevin Makice, William Odom, et al. 2007. Luxury & new luxury, quality & equality. *Proceedings of the 2007 conference on Designing pleasurable products and interfaces - DPPI '07*, ACM Press, 296. Retrieved September 25, 2015 from http://dl.acm.org/citation.cfm?id=1314161.1314188

7. Eli Blevis and Erik Stolterman. 2007. Ensoulment and Sustainable Interaction Design. *IASDR07, Hong Kong Polytechnic University*, 1–23.

8. Eli Blevis. 2007. Sustainable interaction design: invention & disposal, renewal & reuse. In *Proceedings of the SIGCHI Conference on Human Factors in Computing Systems* (CHI '07). ACM, New York, NY, USA, 503-512. DOI=http://dx.doi.org/10.1145/1240624.1240705.

9. Leah Buechley and Hannah Perner-Wilson. 2012. Crafting technology. *ACM Transactions on Computer-Human Interaction* 19, 3: 1–21. http://doi.org/10.1145/2362364.2362369

10. Tanja Döring, Axel Sylvester, and Albrecht Schmidt. 2013. A design space for ephemeral user interfaces. *Proceedings of the 7th International Conference on Tangible, Embedded and Embodied Interaction - TEI '13*: 75. http://doi.org/10.1145/2460625.2460637

11. Paul Dourish and Melissa Mazmanian. 2011. Media as Material : Information Representations as Material Foundations for Organizational Practice. *International Symposium on Process Organization Studie*, 1–24.

12. Augusto Esteves, Michelle Scott, and Ian Oakley. 2013. Supporting offline activities on interactive surfaces. *TEI '13*, ACM Press, 147. http://doi.org/10.1145/2460625.2460648

13. Ylva Fernaeus, Martin Jonsson, and Jakob Tholander. 2012. Revisiting the jacquard loom: threads of history and current patterns in HCI. In *Proceedings of the SIGCHI Conference on Human Factors in Computing Systems* (CHI '12). ACM, New York, NY, USA, 1593-1602. DOI=http://dx.doi.org/10.1145/2207676.2208280

14. Ylva Fernaeus, Martin Murer, Vasiliki Tsaknaki, and Jordi Solsona Belenguer. 2013. Handcrafting electronic accessories using “raw” materials. *TEI '14*, ACM Press, 369–372. http://doi.org/10.1145/2540930.2567906

15. Ylva Fernaeus and Petra Sundström. 2012. The material move how materials matter in interaction design research. In *Proceedings of the Designing Interactive Systems Conference* (DIS '12). ACM, New York, NY, USA, 486-495. DOI=10.1145/2317956.2318029 http://doi.acm.org/10.1145/2317956.2318029

16. Ylva Fernaeus and Anna Vallgårda. 2014. Ajna: negotiating forms in the making of a musical cabinet. In *Proceedings of the 2014 conference on Designing interactive systems* (DIS '14). ACM, New York, NY, USA, 915-924. DOI=http://dx.doi.org/10.1145/2598510.2600883

17. Patrick Tobias Fischer, Eva Hornecker, and Christian Zoellner. 2013. SMSlingshot: an expert amateur DIY case study. *Proceedings of the International Conference on Tangible, Embedded and Embodied Interaction TEI '13*, ACM Press, 9–16. http://doi.org/10.1145/2460625.2460627

18. Jonas Forsslund, Michael Yip, and Eva-Lotta Sallnäs. 2015. WoodenHaptics: A Starting Kit for Crafting Force-Reflecting Spatial Haptic Devices. *Proceedings of the Ninth International Conference on Tangible, Embedded, and Embodied Interaction - TEI '15*, ACM Press, 133–140. http://doi.org/10.1145/2677199.2680595

19. Verena Fuchsberger, Martin Murer, and Manfred Tscheligi. 2015. Time and Design. *TEI '14*, ACM Press, 581–586. http://doi.org/10.1145/2677199.2687911

20. Silke Gegenbauer and Elaine M. Huang. 2012. Inspiring the design of longer-lived electronics through an understanding of personal attachment. *DIS '12*, ACM Press, 635. http://doi.org/10.1145/2317956.2318052

21. Elisa Giaccardi, Elvin Karana, Holly Robbins, and Patrizia D'Olivo. 2014. Growing traces on objects of daily use: a product design perspective for HCI. In *Proceedings of the 2014 conference on Designing interactive systems* (DIS '14). ACM, New York, NY, USA, 473-482. DOI=http://dx.doi.org/10.1145/2598510.2602964

22. Shad Gross, Jeffrey Bardzell, and Shaowen Bardzell. 2013. Structures, forms, and stuff: the materiality and medium of interaction. *Personal and Ubiquitous Computing* 18, 3: 637–649. http://doi.org/10.1007/s00779-013-0689-4

23. Richard Harper, Eryn Whitworth, and Ruth Page. 2012. | Harper | Selected Papers of Internet Research. *Selected Papers of Internet Research 2*. Retrieved September 25, 2015 from http://spir.aoir.org/index.php/spir/article/view/8

24. David Holman and Roel Vertegaal. 2008. Organic user interfaces. *Communications of the ACM* 51, 6: 48. http://doi.org/10.1145/1349026.1349037

25. Kasper Hornbæk, Søren S. Sander, Javier Andrés Bargas-Avila, and Jakob Grue Simonsen. 2014. Is once enough?: on the extent and content of replications in human-computer interaction. *CHI '14*, ACM Press, 3523–3532. http://doi.org/10.1145/2556288.2557004

26. Don Ihde. 1995. *Postphenomenology: Essays in the Postmodern Context*. Retrieved May 15, 2015 from https://books.google.com/books?hl=el&lr=&id=l49PYEDFSbgC&pgis=1

27. Miwa Ikemiya and Daniela K. Rosner. 2013. Broken probes: toward the design of worn media. *Personal and Ubiquitous Computing* 18, 3: 671–683. http://doi.org/10.1007/s00779-013-0690-y

28. Tim Ingold and Social Anthropology. 2013. *Making: Anthropology, Archaeology, Art and Architecture*. Routledge.

29. Heekyoung Jung, Shaowen Bardzell, Eli Blevis, James Pierce, and Erik Stolterman. 2011. How Deep Is Your Love: Deep Narratives of Ensoulment and Heirloom Status. 5, 1: 59–71.

30. Andrew Juniper. 2011. *Wabi Sabi: The Japanese Art of Impermanence*. Tuttle Publishing. Retrieved September 22, 2015 from https://books.google.com/books?id=objWAgAAQBAJ&pgis=1

31. Anne Marie Kanstrup and Ellen Christiansen. 2006. Selecting and evoking innovators. *NordiCHI '06*, ACM Press, 321–330. http://doi.org/10.1145/1182475.1182509

32. Elvin Karana, Owain Pedgley, and Valentina Rognoli. 2013. *Materials Experience: fundamentals of materials and design*. Butterworth-Heinemann.

33. Leonard Koren. 1994. *Wabi-Sabi: For Artists, Designers, Poets and Philosophers*. Stone Bridge Press, Berkeley, California.

34. William Lidwell, Kritina Holden, and Jill Butler. 2003. *Universal Principles of Design: 100 Ways to Enhance Usability, Influence Perception, Increase Appeal, Make Better Design Decisions, and Teach Through Design*. Rockport Publishers. Retrieved September 25, 2015 from https://books.google.com/books?id=juX1nCMWkPkC&pgis=1

35. Rikard Lindell. 2013. Crafting interaction: The epistemology of modern programming. *Personal and Ubiquitous Computing* 18, 3: 613–624. Retrieved March 18, 2015 from http://link.springer.com/10.1007/s00779-013-0687-6

36. Siân Lindley, Robert Corish, Elsa Kosmack Vaara, Pedro Ferreira, and Vygandas Simbelis. 2013. Changing perspectives of time in HCI. *CHI EA '13*, ACM Press, 3211. http://doi.org/10.1145/2468356.2479649

37. Panagiotis Louridas. 1999. Design as bricolage: anthropology meets design thinking. *Design Studies* 20, 6: 517–535. http://doi.org/10.1016/S0142-694X(98)00044-1

38. Leah Maestri and Ron Wakkary. 2011. Understanding repair as a creative process of everyday design. *Proceedings of the 8th ACM conference on Creativity and cognition - C&C '11*, ACM Press, 81. http://doi.org/10.1145/2069618.2069633

39. Ramia Mazé. 2007. *Occupying Time: Design, technology and the form of interaction*. Axl Books.

40. John McCarthy and Peter Wright. 2004. *Technology as Experience*. MIT Press.

41. Malcolm McCullough. 1998. *Abstracting Craft: The Practiced Digital Hand*. Retrieved September 24, 2015 from https://books.google.com/books?hl=el&lr=&id=PcwH1WricJEC&pgis=1

42. David A. Mellis, Sam Jacoby, Leah Buechley, Hannah Perner-Wilson, and Jie Qi. 2013. Microcontrollers as material. *TEI '13*, ACM Press, 83. http://doi.org/10.1145/2460625.2460638

43. David A. Mellis. 2013. Do-it-yourself electronic products and the people who make them. *International Conference on Tangible, Embedded and Embodied Interaction (TEI '13)*, ACM Press, 357. http://doi.org/10.1145/2460625.2460692

44. Boye De Mente. 2006. *Elements of Japanese Design*. Retrieved September 24, 2015 from https://books.google.com/books?hl=el&lr=&id=jy7Y2wTBXUwC&pgis=1

45. Nithikul Nimkulrat. 2012. Hands-on Intellect : Integrating Craft Practice into Design Research Introduction : *IJDesign* 6, 3: 1–14.

46. William Odom and James Pierce. 2009. Improving with age. *Proceedings of the 27th international conference extended abstracts on Human factors in computing systems - CHI EA '09*, ACM Press, 3793. Retrieved September 25, 2015 from http://dl.acm.org/citation.cfm?id=1520340.1520573

47. Giuseppe Salvia, Francesca Ostuzzi, Valentina Rognoli and Marinella Levi. 2012. The value of imperfection in sustainable design: The emotional tie with perfectible artefacts for longer lifespan. Retrieved from Academia.edu

48. James Pierce and Eric Paulos. 2014. Counterfunctional things. *DIS '14*, ACM Press, 375–384. http://doi.org/10.1145/2598510.2598522

49. James Pierce and Eric Paulos. 2015. Making Multiple Uses of the Obscura 1C Digital Camera. *CHI '15*, ACM Press, 2103–2112. http://doi.org/10.1145/2702123.2702405

50. Richard R. Powell. 2004. *Wabi Sabi Simple*. Adams Media.

51. Jill Walker Rettberg. 2013. *Blogging*. Polity.

52. Daniela K. Rosner and Kimiko Ryokai. 2009. Reflections on craft: probing the creative process of everyday knitters. In *Proceedings of the seventh ACM conference on Creativity and cognition* (C&C '09). ACM, New York, NY, USA, 195-204. DOI=http://dx.doi.org/10.1145/1640233.1640264

53. Daniela K. Rosner, Miwa Ikemiya, Diana Kim, and Kristin Koch. 2013. Designing with traces. *Proceedings of the SIGCHI Conference on Human Factors in Computing Systems - CHI '13*, ACM Press, 1649. Retrieved January 7, 2016 from http://dl.acm.org/citation.cfm?id=2470654.2466218

54. Daniela K. Rosner, Miwa Ikemiya, and Tim Regan. 2015. Resisting Alignment: Code and Clay. In *Proceedings of the Ninth International Conference on Tangible, Embedded, and Embodied Interaction* (TEI '15). ACM, New York, NY, USA, 181-188. DOI=http://dx.doi.org/10.1145/2677199.2680587

55. Daniela K. Rosner. 2012. The material practices of collaboration. *Proceedings of the ACM 2012 conference on Computer Supported Cooperative Work - CSCW '12*: 1155. http://doi.org/10.1145/2145204.2145375

56. Magdalena Schmid, Sonja Rümelin, and Hendrik Richter. Empowering Materiality : Inspiring the Design of Tangible Interactions. 91–98.

57. Jin-min Seok, Jong-bum Woo, and Youn-kyung Lim. 2014. Non-finito products. *Proceedings of the 32nd annual ACM conference on Human factors in computing systems - CHI '14*, ACM Press, 693–702. http://doi.org/10.1145/2556288.2557222

58. Michael Shorter, Jon Rogers, and John McGhee. 2014. Enhancing everyday paper interactions with paper circuits. *Proceedings of the 2014 conference on Designing interactive systems - DIS '14*: 39–42. http://doi.org/10.1145/2598510.2598584

59. Vygandas "Vegas" Šimbelis, Pedro Ferreira, Elsa Vaara, Kristina Höök, and Jarmo Laaksolahti. 2016. Repurposing Bits and Pieces of the Digital. *ACM CHI'16*.

60. Jordi Solsona Belenguer. 2015. Engineering through Designerly Conversations with the Digital Material : The Approach, the Tools and the Design Space. Retrieved January 8, 2016 from http://kth.diva-portal.org/smash/record.jsf?pid=diva2%3A875831&dswid=2205

61. Joshua Tanenbaum, Karen Tanenbaum, and Ron Wakkary. 2012. Steampunk as design fiction. *Proceedings of the 2012 ACM annual conference on Human Factors in Computing Systems - CHI '12*: 1583. http://doi.org/10.1145/2207676.2208279

62. Robyn Taylor, Guy Schofield, Jonathan Hook, Karim Ladha, John Bowers, and Peter Wright. 2013. Crafting interactive systems. *CHI EA '13*, ACM Press, 3223. http://doi.org/10.1145/2468356.2479652

63. Vasiliki Tsaknaki, Ylva Fernaeus, and Martin Jonsson. 2015. Precious Materials of Interaction - Exploring Interactive Accessories as Jewellery Items. *Nordes'15* 1, 6.

64. Vasiliki Tsaknaki, Ylva Fernaeus, and Mischa Schaub. 2014. Leather as a material for crafting interactive and physical artifacts. In *Proceedings of the 2014 conference on Designing interactive systems* (DIS '14). ACM, New York, NY, USA, 5-14. DOI=http://dx.doi.org/10.1145/2598510.2598574

65. John Turesson, Anxiao Chen, Erik Dahlström, Dan Carino, and Niclas Ericsson. 2015.The Memonile. *Proceedings of SIDER'15*, 162–164.

66. Anna Vallgårda and Ylva Fernaeus. 2015. Interaction Design as a Bricolage Practice. *Proceedings of the Ninth International Conference on Tangible, Embedded, and Embodied Interaction - TEI '15*: 173–180. http://doi.org/10.1145/2677199.2680594

67. Anna Vallgårda and Tomas Sokoler. 2010. A Material Strategy: Exploring Material Properties of Computers. *IJDesign* 4, 3.

68. Mikael Wiberg. 2013. Methodology for materiality: interaction design research through a material lens. *Personal and Ubiquitous Computing* 18, 3: 625–636. http://doi.org/10.1007/s00779-013-0686-7

69. Zoran, Amit and Leah Buechley. Hybrid Reassemblage: An Exploration of Craft, Digital Fabrication and Artifact Uniqueness. Retrieved August 24, 2015 from http://web.media.mit.edu/~amitz/Publications_files/Leonardo_HybridreAssemblage.pdf

70. Terry Irwin, Gideon Kossoff, and Cameron Tonkinwise. 2015. Transition Design: The Importance of Everyday Life and Lifestyles as a Leverage Point for Sustainability Transitions |Academia.edu. Retrieved September 25, 2015 from http://www.academia.edu.

71. Snapchat. Retrieved from https://www.snapchat.com

The Hybrid Bricolage - Bridging Parametric Design with Craft through Algorithmic Modularity

Tamara Anna Efrat[1*] **Moran Mizrahi**[2*] **Amit Zoran**[12]
tamara.anna.efrat@gmail.com moran.mizrahi@mail.huji.ac.il zoran@cs.huji.ac.il
Bezalel Academy of Arts and Design[1] & The Hebrew University of Jerusalem[2], Jerusalem, Israel

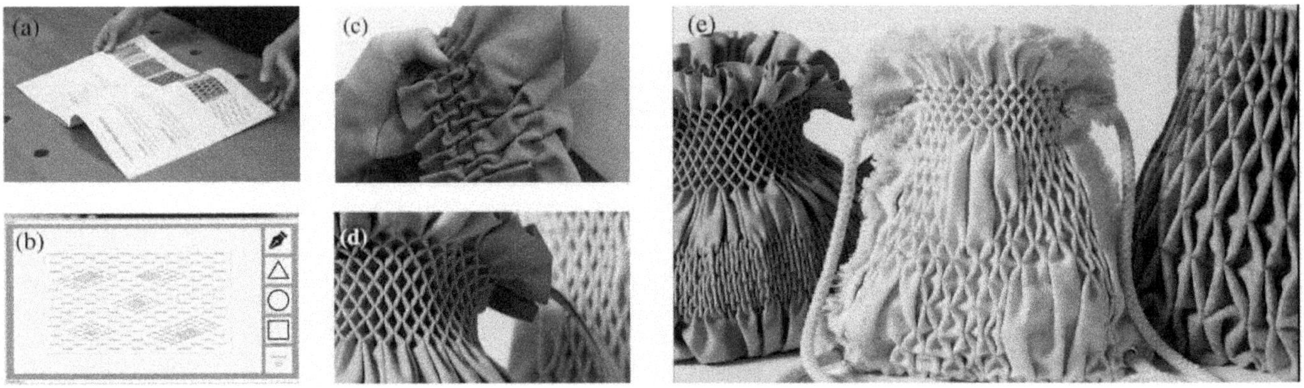

Figure 1 Hybrid Bricolage process: (a) The designer selects generated patterns using the Honeycomb Smocking Pattern Catalog, (b) applies the patterns using Computer-Aided Smocking (CAS) design software, and (c-d) manually completes the work. (e) A portfolio of honeycomb smocking embroidery bags designed by the first author. Photograph (d & e) by Daniel Shechter.

ABSTRACT
The digital design space, unlimited by its virtual freedom, differs from traditional craft, which is bounded by a fixed set of given materials. We study how to introduce parametric design tools to craftspersons. Our hypothesis is that the arrangement of parametric design in modular representation, in the form of a catalog, can assist makers unfamiliar with this practice. We evaluate this assumption in the realm of bag design, through a Honeycomb Smocking Pattern Catalog and custom Computer-Aided Smocking (CAS) design software. We describe the technical work and designs made with our tools, present a user study that validates our assumptions, and conclude with ideas for future work developing additional tools to bridge computational design and craft.

* These authors contributed equally to this work.

CHI'16, May 07-12, 2016, San Jose, CA, USA

DOI: http://dx.doi.org/10.1145/2858036.2858441

Author Keywords
Smocking; Parametric design; Craft; Computer-Aided Design (CAD); Tinkering; Bricolage; Fabrication.

ACM Classification Keywords
H.5.2. User Interfaces: User-centered design.

INTRODUCTION
Parametric design has gained a central place in today's making trends, from architecture to jewelry making, ceramics, and fashion design. Automatic and semi-automatic generated patterns controlled by a small set of designer inputs can achieve complex aesthetics [27]. However, as these parametric design tools rely on formal knowledge in mathematics, they are not accessible to all designers. Designers from non-digital practices may be uncomfortable with the sterile realm of numbers and code [15, 28], thus avoiding opportunities to explore the new design possibilities the computational domain holds.

Motivated to introduce parametric design to craftspersons, we hypothesize that *the arrangement of parametric design space in modular representation can assist makers unfamiliar with this practice.* Similar to work with a *fixed* set of physical materials, such as beads or fabrics, *Hybrid Bricolage* allows craftspersons to tinker with a limited set of computer-generated *meta-patterns*. Using a catalog of generated patterns, we draw an analogy between computational practices and the workset of traditional craft. Nevertheless, with Hybrid Bricolage, the user can digitally tweak and modify the patterns to fine-tune the design.

To evaluate Hybrid Bricolage, we apply parametric pattern design to the manual craft of *honeycomb smocking embroidery* (see Fig. 1). Because the complexity of this embroidery makes it difficult to automate, it requires manual labor. At the same time, it benefits from computational representation, as it includes extensive use of repetitive patterns.

Hybrid Bricolage consists of two tools: a *Honeycomb Smocking Pattern Catalog* (see Table 1 at the end of the paper), and *Computer-Aided Smocking* (CAS) design software. The catalog assists in the design process by visualizing eight different patterns, allowing the designers to choose between alternatives. Our CAS software allows the designer to choose and fine-tune settings in each pattern and combine different patterns from the catalog. When the design is ready, the stitching instructions are marked on a selected sheet of fabric using a laser-cutting machine, before the maker manually stitches the piece together and completes the design.

This paper is structured around the conceptual background of Hybrid Bricolage, the technical discussion of the catalog and the accompanying software, and the user study. In the next section we present the motivation of the work, before discussing related work in textile technologies, design and HCI research. In *Discretization of the Parametric Design Space*, we introduce the Honeycomb Smocking Pattern catalog, the CAS software, and our experimentations with these tools. The *User Study* presents a workshop in which eight fashion designers evaluated our tools, including a review of its outcomes, and suggests implications for HCI, before we conclude the work in the last section.

BACKGROUND: DESIGN TINKERING

In *The Savage Mind*, Lévi-Strauss discusses bricolage, defining a bricoleur as "someone who works with his hands… he does not subordinate each of [his means] to the availability of raw materials and tools conceived and procured for the purpose of the project… the rules of his game are always to make do with 'whatever is at hand'" [19]. While Lévi-Strauss did not emphasize the relative strengths of the bricoleur, Papert described the advantages of the improvised and intuitive making engagement of the bricoleur, especially when applied to education [10].

Since then, many scholars have discussed bricolage as an epistemological contrast to modern engineering. A relevant discourse has arisen within the design terrain, pointing to the limitations of digital design practice in comparison to traditional craft [20]. The emphasis on the process rather than the final product [12], the unstructural practice, the manual engagement, and the intimacy between maker and raw material are fundamental to craft, but almost neglected in engineering and industrial design. These qualities have encouraged researchers to investigate and study hybrid territories, where craft values and practices are reintroduced to digital mediums [3, 6, 30, 37].

Prior art suggests several ways merging digital and craft practices: constructing physical artifacts made by both practices separately [36, 38]; developing physical tools to allow for limited digital assistance [39]; or developing CAD tools dedicated to parametric design, allowing for continuous and expressive modification of the virtual design [13, 14, 34]. However, none of these options acknowledge that the high degree of digital freedom of most parametric design may discourage traditional makers.

Jacobs and Zoran, in their work with a group of former foragers, suggested that "in seeking ways to make digital tools that better facilitate exploratory modular practices, one approach is to design domain-specific CAD tools that enable designers to reconfigure virtual and physical modular parts through a small number of operations that are derived from the topology of the parts themselves" [15]. Hence, we propose modifying the digital planning stage to virtually resemble bricolage procedure, while still retaining the CAD hierarchy of planning before (physically) building.

Our work follows these lines and suggests a paradigm to make tools that facilitate exploratory modular practices. Complementing the line of STEM projects that encourage a bricolage practice within the digital realm [28], we seek a hybrid procedure that manipulates parametric design in the same *tinkering* manner. Thus, we contribute a paradigm of discretizing parametric design space in the form of a catalog containing a finite set of patterns that function as a toolset for the designer (the bricoleur).

RELATED WORK: DIGITAL FABRICATION AND TEXTILE

As fabrication technologies and textiles have been intertwined for millennia, it is not surprising to see the development of new digital projects involving textiles. Johnson and Hawley studied the influence of the Internet on quilters in 2004 [16]. More recent projects allow users to customize sweaters [18], apply mathematical patterns to scarves [1, 32] and design garments interactively [5, 7, 23]. The endless options of textile design encourage researchers to seek ways of integrating textile products with electronics [2] or develop new materials to allow textile-based sensing [26]. Considering the fabrication process, Hudson [11] and Peng et al. [25] suggest 3D printing with traditional textile materials, while Melnikova et al. [21] developed a system for 3D printing textile-like structures using polymers. Nervous Systems created parametric design tools for 3D printing foldable forms composed of articulated modules [17], and Sosanya has presented a 2.5D weaving machine [33]. Though it is not a textile project, Mueller et al. have used a laser-cutting machine to explore new design possibilities [22] in a manner similar to our work.

HONEYCOMB SMOCKING PATTERN

Here we focus on the honeycomb smocking pattern. Smocking is an embroidery technique whose basic form, the honeycomb pattern, was invented to provide an elastic quality to non-elastic fabrics in laborers' clothes in the 18th and early 19th centuries [4, 8, 9]. By the late 19th century, smocking embroidery had become popular for aristocrats' clothing, due to its decorative look, and several non-elastic smocking stitches had been invented.

Today, smocking is not a common design practice. It is an old, difficult and time-consuming handicraft technique. Yet, a few specialized designers utilize smocking patterns in some of their works. Moroso, for example, took the traditional smocking technique and integrated it into the company's industrial process, resulting in a small collection of special furniture [35].

While there are pleating machines that can speed some parts of the creation of a honeycomb smocking pattern, their contribution to the process is minor; most of the work will still be handmade. Like origami, the maker is constantly changing the fabric position and form while sewing a honeycomb smocking pattern. Although robots with high degrees of freedom might enable automation of this process, most industrial manufacturers are looking for easy and inexpensive ways to produce products. Because smocking does not meet these criteria, it does not hold a central place in today's design.

Yet, while the production of smocking is hard to automate, the grid of points that creates it is easy to represent numerically, making it a good platform for our research. As our aim is to create parametric tools that engage craftspeople, smocking embroidery is a medium that benefits from computational representation, but still requires manual labor.

DISCRETIZATION OF THE PARAMETRIC DESIGN SPACE

The implementation of Hybrid Bricolage combines computational honeycomb smocking patterns with manual craft, using a catalog and special software. While researchers have already investigated the use of a style-based design exploration tool [29], our intent is to search for a possible revision to common computer-aided design (CAD) processes, focusing only on the part we wish to study: *designing patterns for craft using a computer*. We rely on *pre-fabrication design* process, a common approach in CAD practices. While many craftspersons choose to work differently, the art of honeycomb smocking is based on careful pattern planning *prior to execution*.

This section presents our investigation and development of Hybrid Bricolage. After designing the patterns using the computer, we transfer computerized sewing instructions composed of lines or points to the fabric. The designer then finishes the work manually. We use two methods to transfer the instructions to the fabric:

Transfer paper Printing the instructions onto transfer paper, then pressing it against the fabric. This enables us to transfer the design onto large expanses of fabric.

Laser cutting and marking Cutting or marking thin fabrics such as canvas, or thick ones like felt or leather, with a laser-cutting machine. This method is advantageous for synthetic fabrics, as the laser sears the edges to produce a high-quality finish. Although this method limits the size of material we can mark at one time, we rely on it for most of the work.

Hands-on investigations preceded the development of the catalog and the software. Therefore, we start by discussing the lessons learned in this early stage, then present the catalog, the software, and a portfolio of bags that demonstrates the quality of the results.

Smocking Investigations and Design Constraints

To embroider honeycomb smocking, the user draws a two-dimensional grid of points with equal distances between them on the fabric, and then sews neighboring points in a consistent order (see Fig. 3(c-e)). During the sewing process the fabric twists into a manifold in 3D space and reveals an interconnected diamond pattern in which the diamond edges are ridges, and the diamond diagonals vertical to the sewing direction are valleys (see Fig. 2(a)). We define these stitches as triples $(\vec{r}, \vec{v}, \Delta)$, where r is a vector that starts on the origin and ends at the beginning of the stitch, v is a vector from the beginning of the stitch to its end, and Δ is the length of the stitch (Fig. 2(h)). Then, a pattern p is simply a set of n stitches $p = \{s_1, s_2, \dots, s_n\}$ where $s_i = (\vec{r_i}, \vec{v_i}, \Delta_i)$.

To achieve new results, we physically explored about a hundred different test patterns based on transformations of the original embroidery. Some of these experiments led to new patterns, while others were less appealing but revealed important constraints (see Fig. 2(b-g)). These experiments allowed us to define the following design constraints for a set of four neighboring stitches $\{s_0, s_1, s_2, s_3, s_4\}$, where $s_0 = s_4$ (see Fig. 2(i)), to result in a single elastic diamond after sewing it:

1. There exists a vector $\vec{v}$ such for every $0 \leq i \leq 3$:

$$\vec{v_i} = \Delta_i \cdot \vec{v}$$

2. For every $0 \leq i \leq 3$:

$$\frac{\pi}{2} \leq \theta_i \leq \frac{\pi}{2} + c$$

When θ_i is defined as (see figure 2(i)):

$$\theta_i = \max\left\{\cos^{-1}\left(\frac{(\vec{r_i} + \vec{v_i} - \vec{r_{i+1}}) \cdot \vec{v_i}}{\|\vec{r_i} + \vec{v_i} - \vec{r_{i+1}}\| \cdot \|\vec{v_i}\|}\right), \cos^{-1}\left(\frac{(\vec{r_{i+1}} + \vec{v_{i+1}} - \vec{r_i}) \cdot \vec{v_i}}{\|\vec{r_{i+1}} + \vec{v_{i+1}} - \vec{r_i}\| \cdot \|\vec{v_i}\|}\right)\right\}$$

And c is a small constant depends on the elasticity and thickness of the fabric.

3. For every $0 \leq i \leq 3$:

$$\min\left\{\frac{\Delta_i}{d_i}, \frac{\Delta_{i+1}}{d_i}\right\} \geq 1$$

When d_i is defined as (see figure 2(i)):

$$d_i = \min\{\|\vec{r_i} + \vec{v_i} - \vec{r_{i+1}}\|, \|\vec{r_{i+1}} + \vec{v_{i+1}} - \vec{r_i}\|\}$$

While incompliance with these constraints will damage the pattern or its elasticity, it may also produce interesting results. For example, choosing $\theta_i > \frac{\pi}{2} + c$ may produce an elastic pattern with diamond-like shapes that appear only when the fabric is stretched; sewing non-parallel stitches in circles produces an attractive, inelastic 3D cylinder. Other designs may impact the intrinsic forces that (as a function of the fabric type) mold the fabric into a 3D form or make the pattern looser at rest.

All the above make the creation of advanced honeycomb smocking patterns by hand very difficult. They demand a lot of experience, or mathematical skills and technical engagement. Yet, because these criteria are easy to translate into code, software can assist smocking novices and facilitate their work.

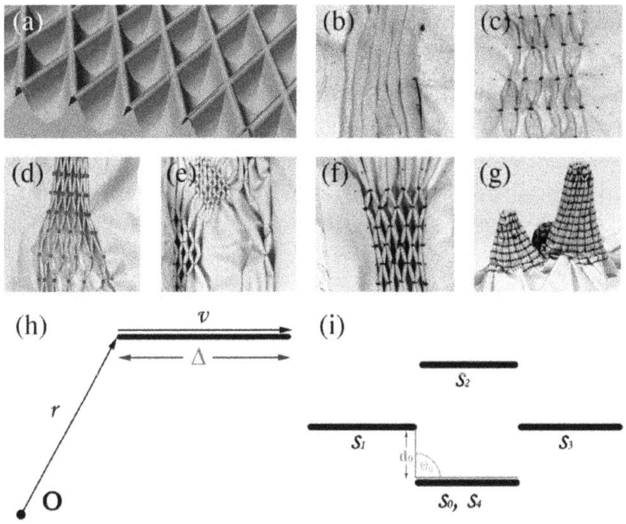

Figure 2 Analyzing the honeycomb smocking pattern: (a) 3D Grasshopper simulation of the basic honeycomb pattern, (b-g) examples of our early investigations with smocking, (h) basic smocking stitch triple, and (i) a representation of four neighboring stitches.

Digital Smocking Design Catalog

Our work focuses on traditional craftspersons unskilled with smocking embroidery. We wish to evaluate to what extent the computer can assist them in parametric design. Such designers (1) may be not familiar with the technical constraints, and/or (2) may not be comfortable working with computers. To close this gap in knowledge and skills, we pack computational outcomes into a traditional frame: a physical design catalog. The catalog presents available design possibilities in an accessible visual format, while limiting the possibilities to a small (and therefore mentally digestible) set of options. In a sense, this allows for design tinkering, as the parametric space being presented acts as raw material for a modular making process.

Based on our early investigation, we reduced the portfolio to a set of eight *meta-patterns* that constitute our catalog (see Table 1 on the last page). The patterns in the catalog allow a limited degree of parametric tweaking, varying from basic options—elastic/non-elastic—to more complicated ones, like a pattern of varying diamonds that allows the designer to create a good approximation of any new diamond-like pattern, even something non-symmetrical and curved.

The purpose of this combination of basic and complicated patterns was to give the designers maximum freedom in choosing their building blocks. This way the users can rely on basic/low-level building blocks (patterns a-e, h), or customize high-level building blocks (patterns f-g). For every pattern in the catalog, we included a short explanation, sewing instructions, photos to illustrate the sewing results (front, back, front in stretch, and back in stretch), and the pseudocode we used to implement it (dropped from Table 1 due to limited space). For example, here is a pseudocode of the varying diamond pattern:

```
Input: diamonds_grid (any diamonds grid)
Let V be the set of all vertices in diamonds_grid
for every point p in V do
  min_dist = ∞
  for each neighbor np of p in diamonds_grid do
    dist_x = np.x – p.x
    if dist_x < min_dist then
      min_dist = dist_x
      Draw a line of length 2*min_dist starts at point (p.x – min_dist, p.y)
Scale obtained image according to fabric params
```

The learning curve for manual smocking may be long, but we believe the catalog can significantly shorten the time needed for a successful outcome, inviting manual practitioners to use our software without engaging with the design constraints and/or the parametric procedural code.

Computer-Aided Smocking Software (CAS)

While the catalog communicates and visualizes our discrete set of pattern design possibilities, a dedicated CAS allows the users to implement their designs on a virtual sheet after browsing the catalog and selecting patterns from it. Based on the initial exploration stage, together with the prior theoretical discussion on tinkering and design, we defined the following software requirements:

1. A simple, direct-manipulation GUI.
2. A small and limited (yet not limiting) number of smocking patterns, based on the catalog.
3. A high degree of freedom in placing, tweaking and combining these patterns.
4. Smooth and easy implementation of the transition from digital design to physical sewing.

While early investigation relied on *Grasshopper* (a plugin to Rhino), we implemented the final version of our software in *Processing*. It includes a simple GUI that lays out a virtual canvas, corresponding to a 100x70 cm sheet of fabric (Fig. 3(a-b)) The software allows the designer to choose different design primitives (polygon, ellipse, free pen tool), manipulate them (drag, rotate, resize, delete), apply a pattern to them, and tweak its inner design if possible (patterns (f), (g)). After applying a pattern, the user can easily change its parameters, and combine it with another pattern if possible. For example, pattern (a) (non-elastic) cannot be combined with pattern (b) (elastic), while pattern (e) (separating axes) can be merged with patterns (a), (b) or (d). Using these tools, the designer defines the general outline of the work and composes his or her own patterns.

The transition from digital design to physical sewing relies on two exported files from the CAS (Fig. 3). One, in SVG format, contains instructions for the laser-cutting machine indicating which points need to be cut or printed on the fabric; a second PDF file contains instructions for the designers on sewing the digital fabricated points. We chose to mark only points on the fabric, instead of including full instructions in the form of lines, to minimize unnecessary marks.

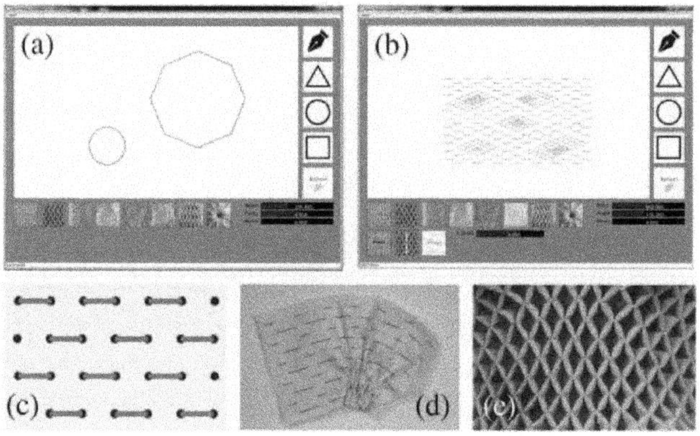

Figure 3 (a-b) Computer-Aided Smocking Software (CAS) GUI, (c) virtual stitching instructions (d) transferred to a fabric using a transfer paper, (e) and the final pattern after sewing.

Honeycomb Smocking Embroidery Bags Example

To self-validate our Hybrid Bricolage prior to conducting the user study, the first author designed and hand-sewed a collection of eighteen honeycomb smocking embroidery bags based on our catalog and using the CAS (see Fig. 1 and 4). This selection of bags, in particular, demonstrates the elasticity of the sewn fabric, an important quality in honeycomb smocking patterns: an elastic bag is a very useful container that grows and shrinks according to its content and use.

With each of these bags, the process included an early manual sketching step based on the catalog; another step preparing the files prior to cutting and marking the instructions on the fabric; and finally, a manual sewing step to complete the work. This collection spans the variety of designs enabled by our tools. For example, an urn-form bag, which is narrow at the top

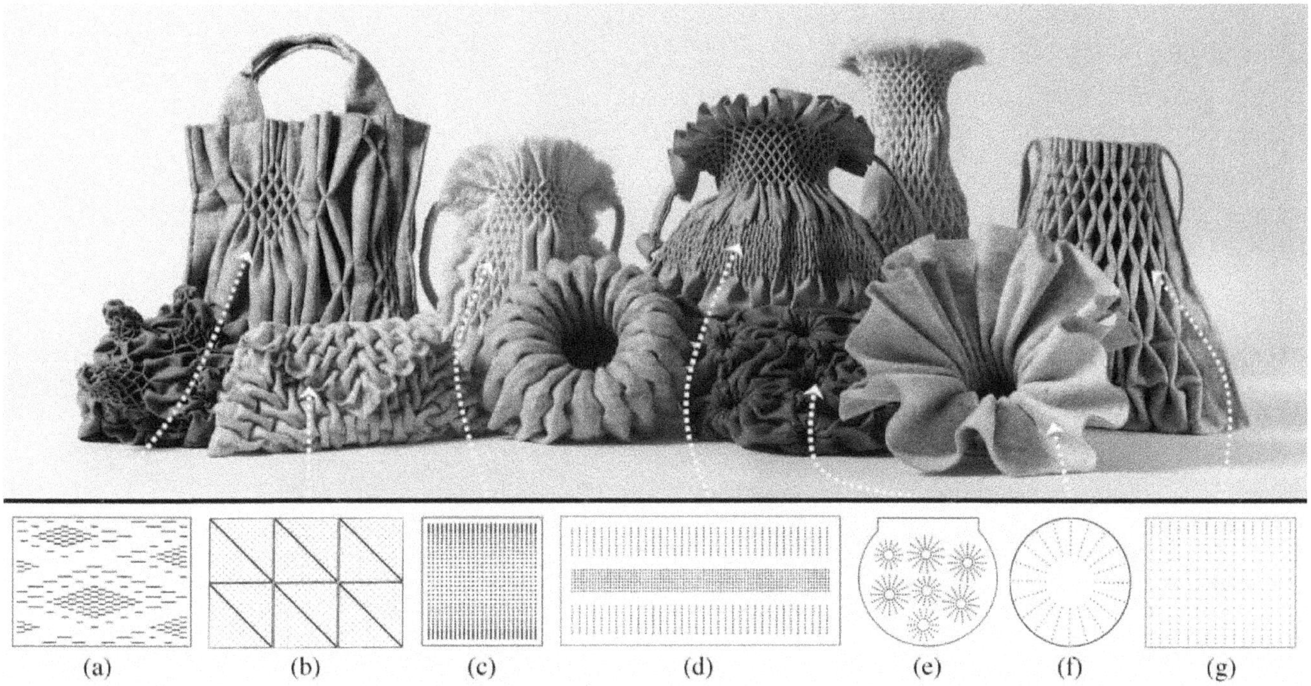

Figure 4 (a-g) A portfolio of honeycomb smocking embroidery bags designed by the first author, based on the Digital Smocking Design Catalog and the Computer-Aided Smocking Software (CAS). Below are CAS generated instructions sent to the laser cutting machine for marking. Photograph by Daniel Shechter.

and wide across the body, uses two patterns: the elastic diamond pattern on the top and bottom, and a non-elastic diamond pattern in the middle. Another bag has two faces; one side contains topological holes, while a second, exaggerated side, contains spikes. The spikes/holes diamond pattern is used here several times. Finally, an entirely different example is a tree trunk bag; while the other two bags were composed of several basic patterns, this one comprises a single varying diamonds pattern.

USER STUDY

Our initial hypothesis was that *the arrangement of parametric design space in modular representation can assist makers unfamiliar with the parametric design practice*. To validate this, after constructing the catalog and the CAS software, we conducted a study with a group of skilled fashion designers who were familiar with computers, but not with honeycomb smocking embroidery or parametric design. We evaluate the ease of use of our tools, the integration of the Hybrid Bricolage paradigm in a traditional craft workset, and the quality of the outcomes. In addition, we use this opportunity to study general qualities of the Hybrid Bricolage paradigm and our new tools.

Methodology

We led a two-day workshop in which the participants designed and hand-sewed their bags. The workshop contained eight fashion design students (seven female and one male), varying in age from 21 to 27. All of the participants had experience in fashion design, and six of them had prior experience in designing bags. They all had experience in designing with a computer, but none had ever worked with parametric design tools nor with honeycomb smocking embroidery (one designer, M., had a modicum of experience in a different smocking technique). Selecting a group of textile- and computer-literate craftspersons helped us evaluate the contribution of Hybrid Bricolage to skilled makers.

To get a broad understanding of the participants' experience, we administered formal surveys before and after the workshop; interviewed the participants before, during, and after the workshop; and documented the process and its final outcomes. In the surveys we asked participants about their backgrounds and design preferences, their experience with the workshop, general reflection on technology and craft, and so on. Where relevant, the participants ranked their answers on a quantitative scale between 1 to 5 (where 1 was the lowest mark and 5 was the highest).

On the first day of the workshop we provided the participants with a general explanation of smocking embroidery, and a one-hour tutorial in which they practiced some basic honeycomb smocking examples.

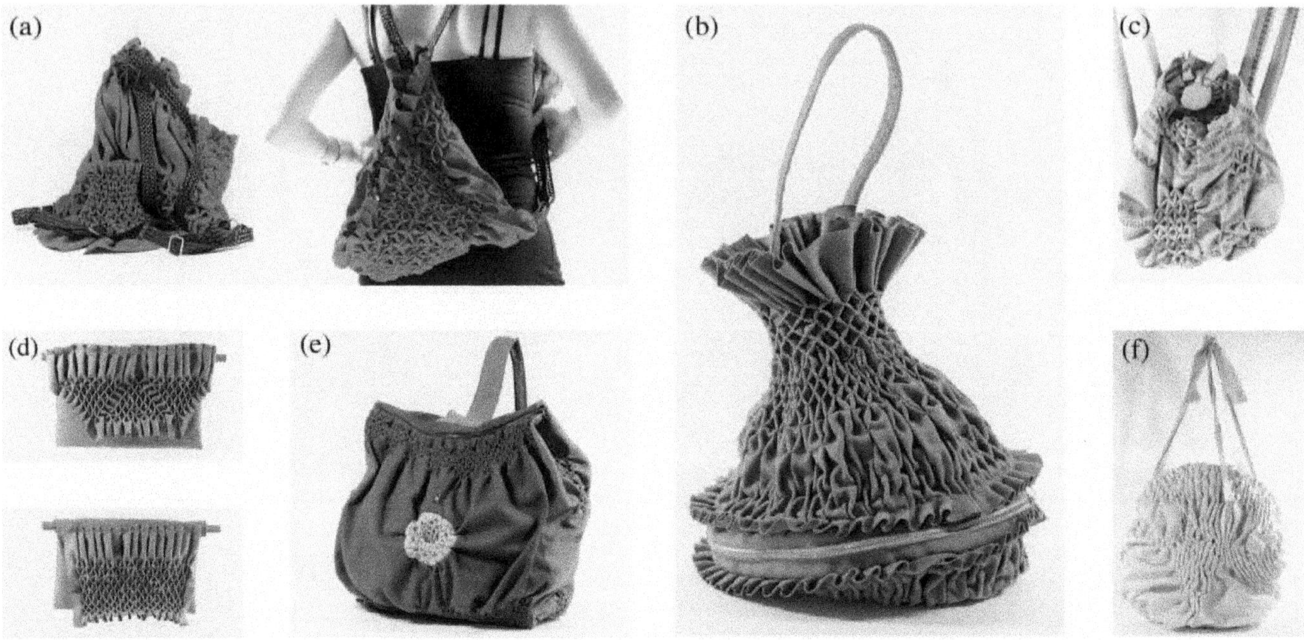

Figure 5 (a-f) Outcomes of the Hybrid Bricolage workshop made by 6 designers.

Afterwards we practiced more basic smocking, introduced the catalog and CAS, and asked the participants to design their own bags with CAS. As the same patterns appear in both the catalog and CAS, the participants could search for patterns before starting to design, or ignore the catalog and approach the CAS directly. Two participants immediately started using our CAS, while others sketched their initial ideas manually. All of the participants browsed the physical catalog *while* investigating their designs, each of which corresponded to the presented patterns. During this stage participants also choose their preferred fabric type and color from a given collection we supplied.

After the participants completed their designs, we applied the instructions to the fabric with a laser-cutting machine, marking and cutting the outline of the bags. On the second day of the workshop, the participants sewed their chosen fabric according to instructions generated by the software. All of the participants needed more time to complete their designs and continued to work at home.

Workshop Experience, Outcomes and Reflections

A diverse portfolio of final bags is presented in Fig. 5, demonstrating the variety of design possibilities and styles that came out of the workshop. These outcomes diverge from the original collection we created: one participant made a bag with replaceable covers with different smocking patterns (Fig 5(d)); several participants explored the application of smocking patterns to 3D shapes, such as a vase-like form that could be opened from the bottom (Fig. 5(b)), or a pyramid-shaped bag (Fig. 5(a)). One participant made a hole in the center of the bag, which functioned as a small pocket (Fig. 5(e)). Another participant (who did not complete her bag) tried to draw the New York City skyline using the smocking embroidery. Two participants picked a pattern and applied it to the fabric prior to designing the general form of the bag: they simply used the pattern as a raw material, and only after preparing this new "material" did they move forward designing *for* it manually (Fig. 5(c,f)).

Six of the eight participants invested between ten and thirty *extra hours at home*, and arrived at an additional closing session with their finished products, and/or visited our lab in between the official meetings. Moreover, we witnessed a good atmosphere throughout the workshop, with lush social interactions. When we asked the participants if they would like to continue working at home, they all preferred to stay together at the lab. All of the participants indicated they would like to participate in a similar workshop in the future, and six of the eight rated their enjoyment of the workshop as a 5. Furthermore, many of the participants said they were excited to continue working this way in the future and use what they learned in their regular work process. They *all* wished to have future access to the software.

"I really like my bag and I am going to produce several more, it's definitely going to be part of my portfolio..." (S, a week after the workshop ended)

Mastering traditional honeycomb smocking embroidery requires a lot of experience. Considering the lack of previous experience for our participants in parametric design or smocking, the complexity and diversity of the designs support our initial hypothesis: our tools improve the accessibility of computationally enhanced parametric smocking craft for novices in parametric design. Yet, the joy of our creative participants and their beautifully designed projects may positively bias our observations. Thus, we now investigate to what extent Hybrid Bricolage empowers makers, what needs to be improved, and what other lessons can be learned from the experience.

The Hybrid Bricolage Paradigm

Discretizing the design space into a catalog with a limited number of meta-patterns maintained the practicality of the concept, but may have harmed the designers' sense of freedom. An early work by Oehlberg et al. discussed creative freedom with respect to generative and non-generative design [24], pointing to the power of hybrid practices. With Hybrid Bricolage, users can combine several generative and non-generative design options: (1) the outline of the design is unlimited and the designer can sew any desired shape; (2) the user selects from a fixed set of raw materials and generated meta-patterns; (3) each meta pattern allows for a limited degree of parametric tweaking; (4) the designer is not bound to complete the pattern instructions and can improvise in real-time.

To gain a better understanding of this quality of the Hybrid Bricolage, we asked the participants to rate their *sense of freedom* in the design process. Seven of the participants rated the two relevant questions at least 4. However, when asked to rate their sense of freedom to insert changes while sewing, the answers were not as absolute—two rated it 5, three rated it 4, one rated it 3, one rated it 2, and one rated it 1.

"At the beginning... I didn't know exactly what I wanted [...] I chose a pattern to work with and wanted to replicate it several times on the fabric... I tried to sew only part of the points, while leaving other points free. I felt a total freedom while sewing and designing the bag and I really liked it." (N.)

Hybrid Bricolage seeks to provide a balanced experience using CAD and manual practice: the maker determines the pattern to be designed in the software, while the sewing is all done by hand. The importance of manual craft practice has been widely discussed elsewhere, but the application of Hybrid Bricolage to honeycomb smocking embroidery presents a unique case. Here, craftspersons apply manual techniques to implement a repetitive generated mass of elements, instead of a digitally automating their production. Moreover, the outcome cannot be reproduced nor easily predicted, since it depends on real-time decisions and the precision of the maker:

"In the beginning [...] I thought I would sew all the points... Then I understood I was too optimistic... so I [...] sewed just some of the points and the outcome was kind of a surprise for me." (N.)

Looking more closely, we noticed two different creative approaches. Some people arrived with a concept design and continued with their ideas even though they did not fit the smocking embroidery constraints, while others developed their designs while using the catalog. We theorize that the participants from the first group were fixed on prior assumptions about the elasticity of the computer-aided design process. Hence, they did not properly adapt to virtual tinkering, and were less satisfied with the results. When asked "How much do you feel the physical catalog was a tool in designing your sketch?", most of the participants in the first group marked 3, while all of the participants in the second group marked 4 or 5. Moreover, none of the participants in the second group followed the instructions in their entirety. In stark contrast, the students in the first group did, and when asked to rate their sense of freedom to insert changes during sewing, they rated it significantly lower than the participants in the first group. Moreover, when asked to rate the originality of their bags and the reasons for it, the answers of the participants in the second group were based on the uniqueness of the embroidery, while the answers in the first group didn't mention the embroidery at all.

"The form, the details, the color combinations and the gatherings that are getting deeper and making the bag narrower are all special." (M., second group)

Creative investment and ownership maintain a complex affiliation. Although the computer optimizes part of the process, the smocking embroidery still requires a significant manual investment, which none of the participants predicted properly beforehand. The average amount of time invested in sewing a bag was twenty hours, varying from nine to forty hours. We noticed a curious, yet likely, link between the time invested in the bag and the sense of ownership. As Hybrid Bricolage assists makers in implementing parametric design into their craft, but does not alter the manual making practice, these observations are in agreement with prior knowledge on traditional craft practice, where investment, intimacy and engagement impact the quality of the practice and the sense of joy and ownership [31].

Interaction with CAS Software and Its Outcomes

All of the participants stated that the manual instructions were easy and straightforward, and rated the clearness at least 4. Our CAS was ranked as intuitive (two rated it 5, four rated it 4, two rated it 3) and unintimidating (four of the participants rated their fear 1, one rated it 2, and three rated it 3). The Hybrid Bricolage procedure is simple, accessible, and does not require prior knowledge.

While most of the participants showed no interest in knowing more about the underlying constraints and the mathematics, their use of CAS allowed them to create a varied set of new patterns that would have been difficult to achieve without a computer, and spared them the tedious work of marking the points on the fabric by hand. Most of the participants said they could not reach the same results without a computer. When asked to rate the usefulness of the marked points, however, they were slightly more restrained: four participants rated it 5, one rated it 4 and three rated it 3.

" If I had to mark them [the points] by myself, it would send me into despair..." (M.)

Yet, we noticed that almost all of the participants would have liked a visual simulation of the predicted outcomes. This specific requirement may have derived from their prior technological experience and knowledge in CAD, which raised their expectations:

"I would add an option [...] that enables to sew or unpick stitches and see the result simulated on the screen." (N.)

Prediction and Expectations

Our CAS currently produces instructions to assist in the manual labor of smocking embroidery rather than final design renderings. Yet there is early evidence that the participants tend to expect computational assistance in the design process, rather than the manual fabrication. The participants' lack of experience with smocking embroidery probably influenced them to seek information minimizing the unpredictability of the final artifacts in a form of 3D simulation rather than our 2D planning. While our participants were all familiar with virtual design simulations and computer renderings, Jacobs and Zoran did not observe similar expectations in their workshop with former hunter-gatherers [15], demonstrating that users' expectations of technological agency depend on cultural context. Along the same lines, participants fixated on a preliminary design were less satisfied with the outcome of the workshop. To summarize, there is evidence of a link between preliminary expectations and satisfaction from the process and its outcomes.

Hybrid Bricolage contributes a new arrangement of the parametric design space, and does not supply a prediction of the process and its outcomes. As with traditional bricolage, creative freedom is constricted by a fixed set of raw patterns and materials, and a successful practice requires mastering these existing sets of design primitives. Moreover, the intuitive practice of traditional bricolage consists of *trial and error* rather than *planning and prediction.* Nevertheless, we see future potential in extending our paradigm to designers who wish to stretch this domain, allowing them to predict the aesthetics and required labor of the planned work, and enabling alternatives modes of working.

CONCLUSIONS

Within this work, we present Hybrid Bricolage, a new parametric design paradigm using a fixed set of computer-generated, tweakable meta-patterns. After experimenting with parametric design and honeycomb smocking embroidery, we developed a physical Honeycomb Smocking Pattern Catalog and Computer-Aided Smocking design software, and evaluated them in a user study, while presenting a diverse portfolio of bags. This work draws on other studies in the realm of hybrid design, aiming to link traditional creative practices with contemporary technology. While the concept of tinkering or bricolage already influences HCI and STEM projects, we build upon prior work and contribute a new perspective, replacing the presentation of mathematical (or code-based) formality with a discrete set of given patterns.

Our user study validated our assumption that such modular presentation can be easily integrated by craftspersons who are novice parametric designers, although the results pointed to important future work in improving the flexibility and predictability of our digital bricolage paradigm. Additionally, we envision a design process where makers could import external patterns into CAS. While our emphasis on computationally enhanced labor seems fruitful, the participants also showed interest in articulated visualization to predict the completed designs. We hope this work will encourage others to continue investigating the development of tools incorporating wide creative audiences, and provide accessibility to hybrid approaches to craft.

Name	Technique	Characteristics	Sewing instructions	Front	Back	Stretched front	Stretched back	Object
(a) **Elastic diamonds**	To create a pattern of elastic diamonds: $\frac{stitch\ width}{rows\ distance} \geq 1.5$ (= 2.5 for maximum elasticity)	Very elastic pattern that returns to its original state after stretching. Requires approximately 250 percent more fabric than a non-elastic pattern.	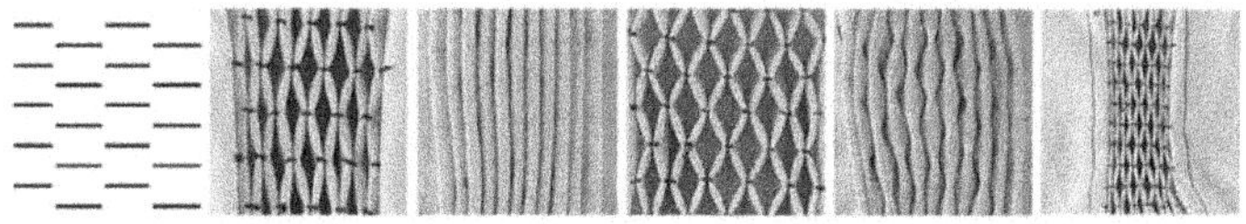					
(b) **Non-elastic diamonds**	To create a pattern of non-elastic diamonds: $\frac{stitch\ width}{rows\ distance} = 1$	The pattern remains opened after stretching. Of all of the patterns in the catalog, the non-elastic diamonds consume the smallest quantity of fabric.	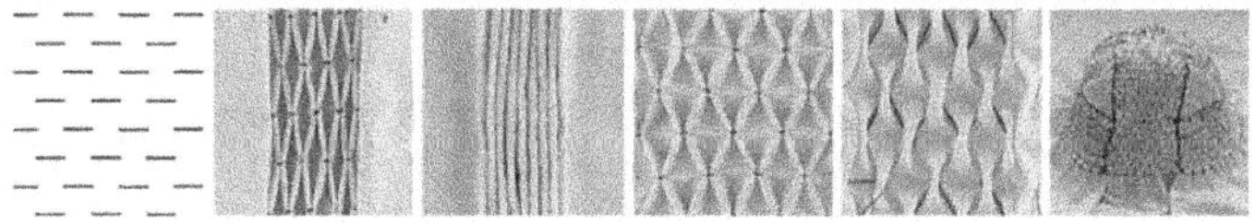					
(c) **Diamonds only when stretched**	To create a pattern of visible only when the fabric is stretched, there should be a limited non-overlapping area between every two neighboring diagonal stitches.	There is an element of "surprise" when stretching this pattern. The pattern returns to its original state (with no visible diamonds) after stretching.	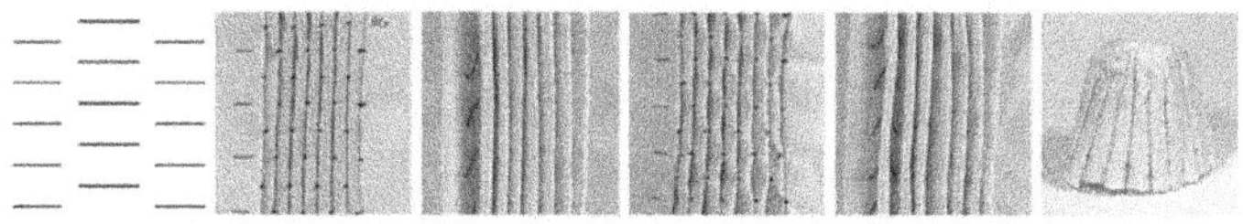					
(d) **From narrow diamonds to wide**	To create this kind of pattern, the ratio between the width of the stitches and the distance between the rows should grow slowly from 1 to 2.5.	The pattern is tight and elastic on one side and loose and non-elastic on the other.	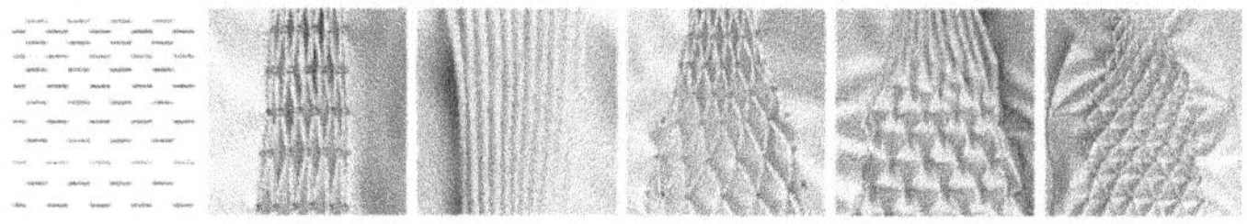					
(e) **Diamonds with separating axes**	To create a pattern with diamonds separated by axes, the different parts need to be completed separately, with a relatively small gap between them.	The elasticity depends on the different patterns in each part. The axes allow a wider range of motion.	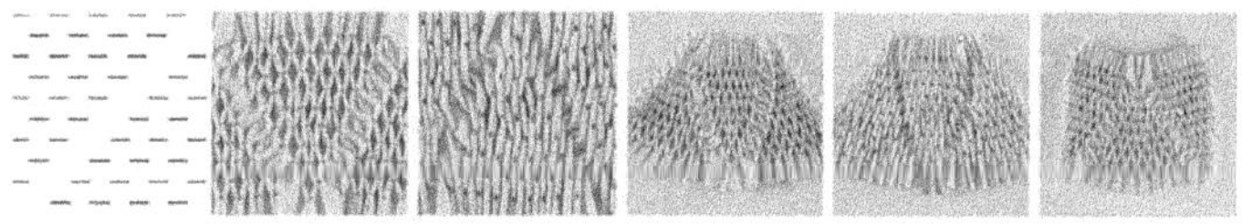					
(f) **Varying diamonds**	To create a pattern of varying diamonds, the sewing instructions should be produced according to a given algorithm that enables the creation of any non-homogenous diamonds pattern.	The elasticity of the sewn fabric varies along the pattern.	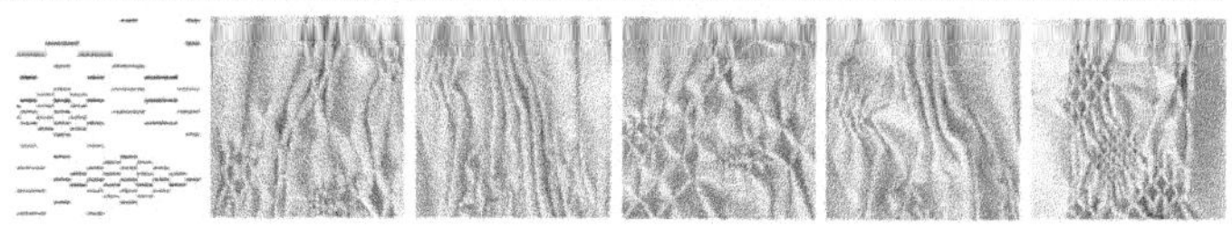					
(h) **Diamonds of varying depths**	To create a diamond pattern that varies by depth, the length of the stitches should change along the sewn rows. Long stitches will result in deep diamonds, while short stitches will result in shallow ones.	The elasticity of the sewn fabric varies along the pattern.	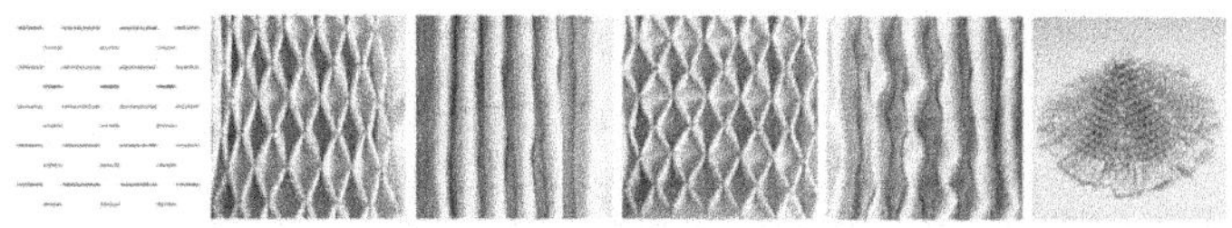					
(g) **Diamonds with spikes or holes**	to create a spike or hole, the pattern should be sewn in circles, from the center to the outside.	The sewn pattern has four interesting states: (1) spike, (2) hole, (3) inverse spike, (4) inverse hole. The elasticity of the sewn pattern depends on the distance between the circles and the number of stitches in each circle.	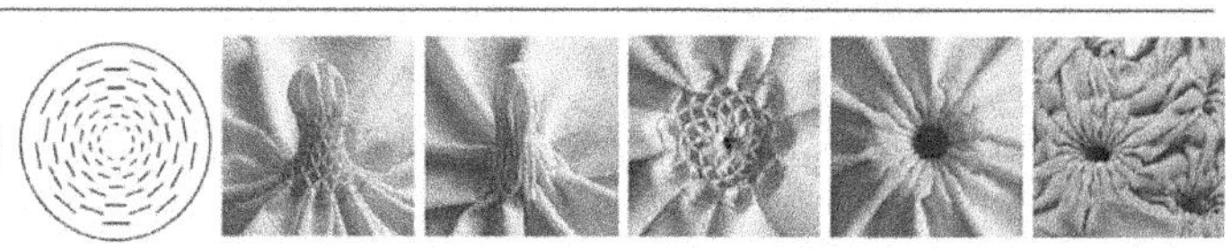					

Table 1. Honeycomb Smocking Pattern Catalog

ACKNOWLEDGMENT

We would like to thank J. Jacobs, D. A. Mellis, R. Fattal, L. Dubinsky, A. Aharon, C. Zorea, T. Vasilevitsky, G. Medan, T. Nussbaum, A. Rotem, C. L. Evers and all the participants in our user study.

REFERENCES

1. Abboudeh, M. 2014. Palestinian Parametric Patterns {P}^{3}. Retrieved December 21, 2015, from http://www.mu-abboudeh.com/palestinian-parametric-patterns/
2. Buechley, L., Eisenberg, M., Catchen, J. and Crockett, A. 2008. "The LilyPad Arduino: Using Computational Textiles to Investigate Engagement, Aesthetics, and Diversity in Computer Science Education", In Proc. of the SIGCHI on Human factors in Computing Systems (CHI '08), pp. 423-432.
3. Buechley. L., and Perner-Wilson, H. 2012. Crafting technology: Reimagining the processes, materials, and cultures of electronics. ACM Trans. Comput.-Hum. Interact. 19, 3, Article 21, October, 21 pages.
4. Cane, O., and Hodges, J. 1985. Smocking, Traditional and Modern Approach. B T Batsford Ltd; First edition (August 1985).
5. D.dress. (n.d.). Continuum. Retrieved December 21, 2015, from http://www.continuumfashion.com/D.php
6. Devendorf, L., and Ryokai, K. 2015. Being the Machine: Reconfiguring Agency and Control in Hybrid Fabrication. In Proceedings of the 33rd Annual ACM Conference on Human Factors in Computing Systems (CHI '15). ACM, New York, NY, USA, 2477-2486.
7. Floraine Berthouzoz, Akash Garg, Danny M. Kaufman, Eitan Grinspun, and Maneesh Agrawala. 2013. Parsing sewing patterns into 3D garments. ACM Trans. Graph.
8. Gostelow, M. 2003. The Complete Guide to Needlework, Technique and Materials. QUANTUM PUBLISHING (January 1, 2003)
9. Hall, M. 2008. Smocks (Shire Library). Shire (March 4, 2008)
10. Harel, I., and Papert, S. 1991. Situating Constructionism [first chapter]. In Constructionism: Research Reports and Essays, 1985-1990. Ablex Publishing (January 1, 1991).
11. Hudson, S. E. 2014. Printing teddy bears: a technique for 3D printing of soft interactive objects. In Proceedings of the SIGCHI Conference on Human Factors in Computing Systems (CHI '14). ACM, New York, NY, USA, 459-468.
12. Ingold, T. 2010. The textility of making. Cambridge Journal of Economics 34, 1 (2010), 91--102.
13. Jacobs, J., and Buechley, L. 2013. Codeable objects: computational design and digital fabrication for novice programmers. In Proceedings of the SIGCHI Conference on Human Factors in Computing Systems (CHI '13). ACM, New York, NY, USA, 1589-1598.
14. Jacobs, J., Resnick, M., and Buechley, L. 2014. Dresscode: supporting youth in computational design and making. In Proceedings of Constructionism 2014 Conference. Vienna, Austria.
15. Jacobs, J., and Zoran, A. 2015. Hybrid Practice in the Kalahari: Design Collaboration through Digital Tools and Hunter-Gatherer Craft. In Proceedings of the 33rd Annual ACM Conference on Human Factors in Computing Systems (CHI '15). ACM, New York, NY, USA, 619-628.
16. Johnson, J. S., Hawley, J. (2004) Technology's impact on creative traditions: Pieceful coexistence in quilting. In Clothing and Textiles Research Journal, 22(1/2), pp. 69-78.
17. KINEMATICS. 2013. Nervous System. Retrieved September 5, 2015, from http://n-e-r-v-o-u-s.com/
18. Knyttan. (n.d.). Retrieved September 5, 2015, from http://knyttan.com/
19. Lévi-Strauss, C. (1966). The savage mind. Chicago, IL: University of Chicago Pres
20. McCullough, M. 1998. Abstracting Craft: The Practiced Digital Hand. The MIT Press.
21. Melnikova,R., Ehrmann, A., and Finsterbusch, K. 2014. 3D printing of textile-based structures by Fused Deposition Modelling (FDM) with different polymer materials. IOP Conference

Series: Materials Science and Engineering, Volume 62, conference 1.

22. Mueller, S., Kruck, B., and Baudisch, P. (2013) "LaserOrigami: laser-cutting 3D objects", In Proc. of the SIGCHI Conf. on Human Factors in Computing Systems (CHI '13), pp. 2585-2592.
23. Nobuyuki Umetani, Danny M. Kaufman, Takeo Igarashi, and Eitan Grinspun. 2011. Sensitive couture for interactive garment modeling and editing. ACM Trans. Graph. 30, 4, Article 90 (July 2011)
24. Oehlberg, L., Willett, W., and Mackay, W. E. 2015. Patterns of Physical Design Remixing in Online Maker Communities. In Proceedings of the 33rd Annual ACM Conference on Human Factors in Computing Systems (CHI '15). ACM, New York, NY, USA, 639-648.
25. Peng, H., Mankoff, J., Hudson, S. E. and McCann, J. 2015. A Layered Fabric 3D Printer for Soft Interactive Objects. In Proceedings of the 33rd Annual ACM Conference on Human Factors in Computing Systems (CHI '15). ACM, New York, NY, USA, 1789-1798.
26. Project Jacquard. 2015. Google. Retrieved September 5, 2015, from http://www.google.com/atap/project-jacquard/.
27. Reas, C., McWilliams, C., and LUST. 2010. Form and Code: In Design, Art and Architecture, A Guide to Computational Aesthetics. Princeton Architectural Press.
28. Resnick, M., and Rosenbaum, E. 2013. DESIGNING FOR TINKERABILITY [Chapter 10]. In Honey, M., and Kanter, D. E. (Eds.) Design, Make, Play: Growing the Next Generation of STEM Innovators (pp. 163-181), Routledge; 1st edition (March 15, 2013).
29. Ritchie, D., Kejriwal, A. A., and Klemmer, S. R. d.tour: Style-based exploration of design example galleries. In Proc. UIST'11, ACM (2011), 165–174.
30. Rosner, D., and Ryokai, K., (2009) "Reflections on craft: probing the creative process of everyday knitters", In Proc. of the ACM Conf. on Creativity and Cognition, pp. 195-204.
31. Sennet, R. 2008. The Craftsman. New Haven: Yale University Press.
32. Serriere, F. 2015, June 23. KnitYak: Custom mathematical knit scarves. Retrieved September 5, 2015, from https://www.kickstarter.com/projects/fbz/knityak-custom-mathematical-knit-scarves
33. Sosanya, O. 2014. 3D Weaver. Retrieved September 5, 2015, from http://www.sosafresh.com/3d-weave
34. Torres, C., and Paulos, E. 2015. MetaMorphe: Designing Expressive 3D Models for Digital Fabrication. In Proceedings of the 2015 ACM SIGCHI Conference on Creativity and Cognition (C&C '15). ACM, New York, NY, USA, 73-82.
35. Urquiola, Patricia. 2005. Smock, Sofa. Moroso. Retrieved September 5, 2015, from http://www.moroso.it/catalogo/smock-divani/?lang=en.
36. Zoran, A. 2013. Hybrid basketry: interweaving digital practice within contemporary craft. In ACM SIGGRAPH 2013 Art Gallery (SIGGRAPH '13). ACM, New York, NY, USA, 324-331.
37. Zoran, A. 2015. Hybrid craft: showcase of physical and digital integration of design and craft skills. In ACM SIGGRAPH Art Gallery (SIGGRAPH '15). ACM, New York, NY, USA, 384-398.
38. Zoran, A. and Buechley, L. 2013. Hybrid reAssemblage: An Exploration of Craft, Digital Fabrication and Artifact Uniqueness. Leonardo, Journal of Arts, Sciences and Technology, volume 46, issue 1, February 2013.
39. Zoran, A., Shilkrot, R., Nanyakkara, S., and Paradiso, J.A. 2014. The Hybrid Artisans: A Case Study in Smart Tools. ACM Trans. Comput.-Hum. Interact. 21, 3, Article 15 (June 2014), 29 pages.

ExoSkin: On-Body Fabrication

Madeline Gannon[1,2], Tovi Grossman[1], George Fitzmaurice[1]

[1]Autodesk Research
{firstname.lastname}@autodesk.com

[2]Carnegie Mellon University
mgannon@andrew.cmu.edu

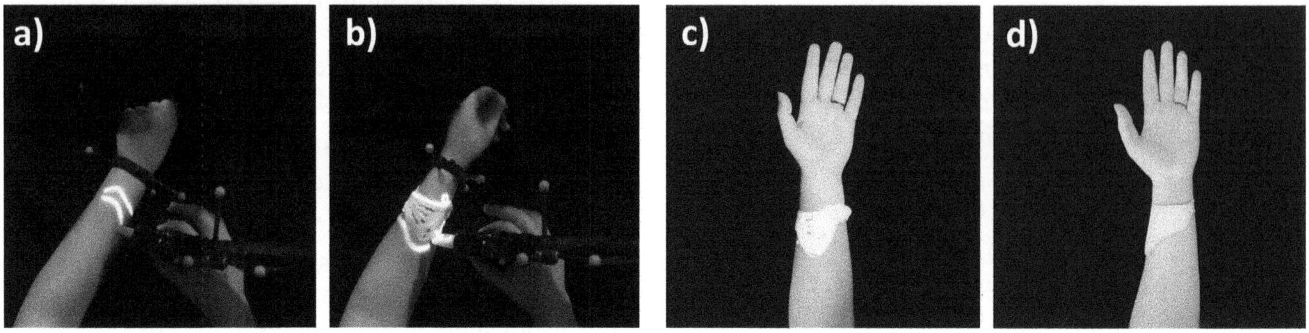

Figure 1. *ExoSkin* is a hybrid fabrication system for designing and printing digital artifacts directly on the body. a) A user sketches directly on the body using the tip of the extruder as a stylus. b) The user can then use a custom built handheld extruder to print directly on the body, tracing over the projected toolpaths. c) The printed material is adhesive and can be worn. d) The final geometry can also be exported and 3D printed using traditional 3D printers and materials.

ABSTRACT

There is a long tradition for crafting wearable objects directly on the body, such as garments, casts, and orthotics. However, these high-skill, analog practices have yet to be augmented by digital fabrication techniques. In this paper, we explore the use of hybrid fabrication workflows for on-body printing. We outline design considerations for creating on-body fabrication systems, and identify several human, machine, and material challenges unique to this endeavor. Based on our explorations, we present *ExoSkin*, a hybrid fabrication system for designing and printing digital artifacts directly on the body. ExoSkin utilizes a custom built fabrication machine designed specifically for on-body printing. We demonstrate the potential of on-body fabrication with a set of sample workflows, and share feedback from initial observation sessions.

INTRODUCTION

In art and design communities, there is a strong tradition for crafting directly on the body, or on proxies for the body. Fashion designers and tailors create bespoke garments on models or mannequins; special effects artists craft prosthetics and props on actors or lifecasts; tattoo artists inscribe their graphic designs onto their client's skin. In many of these domains, the techniques for on-body design and fabrication are purely *analog*. In each of these scenarios, the artifact is customized and hand-crafted on an individual's body by highly trained fabricators.

More recently, engineering communities have been developing *digital* fabrication workflows, such as 3D modeling and 3D printing. Such processes make iterating between design and physical objects a more facile, flexible, and scalable operation [12]. Moreover, pragmatic functionalities like archiving, sharing, and reproducing a body-fabricated design are enabled. However, with such processes, the user, who may be an artist or designer, typically loses agency within the process, when creativity and control may be desired [8].

While today it may seem as a topic of science fiction[1,2], we foresee a future where these art and engineering spaces come together, and wearable artifacts, such as clothing, jewelry, and medical braces are fabricated in real-time directly on the body through a human-machine collaboration.

However, there are several human, machine, and material challenges unique to on-body fabrication that would make it difficult to realize this vision. With traditional Computer-Numeric Control (CNC) processes, material is added or removed on a flat, stabilized build platform. By contrast, when fabricating on the body, the build platform — the body — is a highly deformable, highly curved surface in constant motion. Moreover, materials for on-body fabrication, such as silicones, plasters, clays, or textiles, are dynamic, and are actively transformed by gravity, temperature, and the environment. Last, for safety reasons, traditional CNC processes are not designed for close-quarter human

CHI'16, May 07-12, 2016, San Jose, CA, USA

DOI: http://dx.doi.org/10.1145/2858036.2858576

[1] Iron Man [Suit Up]. https://youtu.be/Fcm7OjoOz4A
[2] Spray on Shoes. https://youtu.be/JpVtVUSYMRw

interaction. This requirement cannot be satisfied in on-body fabrication, where the human can be both the operator and the canvas for fabrication.

These challenges have impeded the development of digital workflows specific to on-body fabrication. For example, 3D printers *can* produce wearable objects, however this fabrication process is fairly inefficient: the form of objects that wrap the arms, legs, or shoulders tend to have high volumes of space, but low material densities [11]. This high volume-to-density ratio is particularly inefficient in material and time for 3D printing, where a form is sequentially built up layer by layer. By contrast, a printing process specifically designed for on-body fabrication could integrate the body as a three-dimensional support structure, which could reduce time and material wasted in fabrication. Moreover, printing on the body can provide a more direct and engaging user experience, which to date, has not been explored.

In this paper, we make several contributions towards enabling digital models to be fabricated directly on the body, synthesizing a diverse range of knowledge from Computer-Aided Design, computer vision, material science, and hardware design. Most notably, we outline a set of design considerations for digital on-body printing, including material choice, machine configurations, appropriate content, and hybrid workflows. We then present *ExoSkin*, a proof-of-concept system which demonstrates the feasibility of digitally designing and fabricating directly on the body (Figure 1). While ExoSkin does not yet produce product ready artifacts, it shows how some of the challenges of on-body fabrication can be addressed. The core technology of ExoSkin is a custom hand-held extruder for digitally fabricating a single layer of material directly on the body. We discuss the range of workflows enabled by our system, and share feedback from an initial observation session.

Our work is positioned at the intersection of engineering and artistic practice. We build upon existing extrusion devices developed in the engineering communities, but make the necessary modifications to support on-body fabrication. Furthermore, we adapt the existing crafts of on-body design from the art and design communities to leverage the advantages of digital fabrication workflows while still supporting user agency throughout the process.

RELATED WORK

Our research builds upon existing *on-body design* and *hybrid fabrication* processes developed for artistic practices as well the engineering process of *free form 3D printing*. Furthermore, we leverage skin-based interfaces, as developed within the HCI community.

Crafting on the On Body

There are many existing fabrication methods for creating things on and around the body: including molding, extruding, weaving, wrapping, spraying, and draping.

These analog methods are often used to create wearable artifacts on proxies, and are then transferred onto the body of the wearer. For example, dressmakers and seamstresses will often use mannequins or dress forms as a canvas for patternmaking [35]. Fabric can be draped on the mannequin to better visualize the final shape and produce a better fit. On-body fabrication could adapt this practice to allow a better personalization of the final form.

Some crafts, such as lifecasting [1], involve working directly on the human body. Human models take on a desired stationary pose, and then the artist applies a mold material to the surface of the body. A casting material can then be used to create a duplicate of the molded body part. Prosthetic makeup artists may similarly use lifecasting techniques to create advanced cosmetic effects [2]. ExoSkin adapts these types of crafts to provide digital guidance and manipulation tools while designing and fabricating on the human body.

Hybrid Fabrication

Hybrid fabrication, or hybrid craft, is a method of integrating digital and analog fabrication techniques to augment traditional craft with digital workflows [38, 40]. Craft practices hybridized with digital techniques include drawing [25], carving [38], weaving [39], painting [32], sculpting [29], and fashion design [36]. Tools developed for hybrid fabrication are often hand-held devices that use mechanical or computational interventions to increase precision and accuracy [29, 31, 32, 38]. These tools have an awareness of the material they are manipulating and their location in space, and provide visual [24, 30, 32] or tangible [29] feedback. However, hybrid fabrication systems typically rely on static build volumes and canvases. Fabrication on the body — a constantly moving canvas with a high degree of freedom — is an added technical challenge.

The role of a hybrid fabrication machine during the production process can vary: from passive to neutral to active. With a *passive* approach, digital techniques may be used to print a static formwork that artisans can build upon [39]. A *neutral* approach could involve using digital techniques to guide the user, but not intervene if they deviate [32]. With an *active* approach, actuated tool-heads can be used to correct or constrain user actions to match a desired digital model [29, 31, 32, 38].

Recent research offers a more critical view of the role of the human in the hybrid fabrication processes. *The Hybrid Artisans* examines the value added and value lost to traditional craft practices [40]. *Being the Machine* reflects on the tradeoffs in agency and control between a user and hybrid fabrication machine [8].

While we take inspiration from these existing hybrid fabrication systems, we are unaware of existing hybrid fabrication systems that are designed to fabricate on complex, moving surfaces, such as the body.

Free Form 3D Printing

Free form 3D printing is a digital fabrication process in which Computer Numeric Control (CNC) machines three-dimensionally extrude material in free space. It differs from traditional 3D printing processes in that it does not build up geometry by printing horizontal layers and it does not fabricate its own support structure. As a result, artifacts fabricated through freeform printing can see a reduction in build time and material waste [28].

Freeform printers are often built using industrial robots, and use a variety of materials, such as thermoplastics [28], clays [4], metals [20], waxes [14], or photopolymers [19] to extrude geometry in free space. Many examples use external formworks such as machined foam [4], water [14], or inflatable shells [23] to receive the printing medium.

Closely related to freeform printing is the concept of printing directly onto existing objects, or *patching* [34]. This can be accomplished by placing the existing object on a 5 axis rotating platform [34] or on a custom 3D printed support [7]. These techniques still require traditional 3D printer devices, and thus do not directly adapt to fabrication on the body.

Finally, many hand-held devices for manually extruding materials exist (e.g., glue guns, UV curing pens, plastic extruding pens, motorized caulk guns). However none of these commercially available options provide a way to fabricate on the body without extensive modification.

To our knowledge the only such machines capable of operating on the body are experimental robotic tattoo printers [3]. Otherwise, these systems have yet to develop materials that are safe to print on the skin, nor have they used the body as a support structure for freeform printing.

Skin-based Interfaces

Skin-based interfaces appropriate the body as an always-available, spatio-tangible surface for sensing and displaying information. A number of techniques have been developed for sensing input on one's skin. This includes sensors worn on the body [5, 6, 15, 21, 27, 37], implanted under the skin [17], and embedded in the environment [13, 16].

To display information, projection-based systems can overlay traditional mobile interfaces, including buttons, menus, or games, directly onto the body [15, 16]. Projection-based skin interfaces have also been explored as a method to spatially guide the movement of a user [33], as well as a way of overlaying medical information directly on patients [26].

Most related to our work is our recent Tactum system, which explores the use of skin as an input platform for 3D modeling directly on the body [11]. While Tactum's design system is fabrication-aware, the resulting wearable models still must be printed on an external 3D printer and then subsequently attached to the body. This provides a disconnect in the overall workflow that could be remedied if the fabrication process also occurred directly on the body.

In summary, our review reveals that on-body fabrication has yet to be explored in the context of hybrid fabrication or freeform printing. Thus, combining skin interfaces with techniques in hybrid craft and freeform printing present a new thread of exploration in on-body fabrication.

DESIGN CONSIDERATIONS

In this section we present a number of considerations required for designing on-body fabrication systems.

Fabrication Methods

As described earlier, many crafts exist for manually creating on-body artifacts. With ExoSkin, we wish to adapt these practices by leveraging to benefits of digital tools, such as providing guidance and feedback, and supporting importing and exporting operations. Currently, we know of no CNC machines that are specifically designed to use these processes for fabricating directly on the body.

Each of the abovementioned fabrication methods insinuate the body to be in a specific location in relation to the fabrication machine. For example, a CNC loom that weaves directly onto a body would need that area to be positioned inside of it. Similarly, a CNC draping machine would need the body to be placed under, and a CNC spraying machine would need the body to be placed in front of it.

To use extrusion, the nozzle of the extrusion machine should remain perpendicular to its surface during printing. This spatial limitation prevents traditional 3-axis 3D printers to be used for on-body fabrication. The complex curvature of the body requires a minimum of 4 axes for the extruder to be normal to the printing surface. Machines with 5 or more degrees-of-freedom, such as hand-held extruders or robotic arms, have the ideal flexibility for printing on the body.

If hand-held devices are used, it may be hard to reach certain body regions, and there may be challenges in orienting the device to perform the fabrication. These constraints could be remedied if a third-party is performing the fabrication on a subject's body.

Safety

In every case where a fabrication machine comes in close contact with the human body, safety should be a primary concern. The risk of entanglement should be minimized by keeping moving machine parts fully enclosed and away from the body. Pinch points must be avoided by positioning the body in free space and not on a rigid platform. Most importantly, irritations and burns need to be prevented by using skin-safe materials.

Materials

Finding appropriate materials for on-body printing was one of the steeper challenges for this research. There are a number of constraints and limitations that impact the choice of materials for on-body fabrication. As described above, the material must be skin-safe, including its temperature at the time of extrusion. Second, it must be easy to remove and clean, unless the print is meant to be permanent. Third, the material must be resilient to movements and deformation on the body. Lastly, it must be a workable medium for a given fabrication process (*e.g.* extrudable).

The safety requirements immediately rule out materials that change states using heat. For example, polymers that liquefy with heat, such as the thermosoftening plastics used in Fused

Deposition Modeling (FDM) 3D printers, or materials that cure with heat, such as the thermosetting plastics, concrete, resins, clays, and plaster often used in freeform printing, are not appropriate for on-body printing. Photopolymers may be applicable, however they were avoided in this research due to concerns of prolonged UV exposure to the skin.

The second consideration for skin-safe material is that it can be removed from the body. Latex and silicones are commonly used to make prosthetics, masks, and molds for the body, however they often require adhesives to remain stuck to the skin and must be peeled off the body when done. Water-soluble clays and pastes, by contrast, will stick to skin during fabrication, and can be simply washed off after use. Excessive body sweat or humidity, however, may impede drying and can deteriorate the printed material over time.

Other considerations are the specific material properties in relation to a chosen fabrication process. In extrusion, for example, the viscosity of a material plays a critical role. If the material is not viscous enough, it will take a long time to set, and consequently slide off the body during printing. But if the material is too viscous, it will be extremely difficult and slow to extrude. Moreover, attributes like drying rate, drying time, and layer adhesion all influence the performance of the material during extrusion, as well as the finish quality of the fully cured material.

Hybrid Fabrication Workflows

Integrating analog and digital craft into a hybrid fabrication workflow can be strategically challenging. As discussed in our related work section, there is a spectrum of possible influence in which the digital tools can control the process, from *active* to *neutral* to *passive*. If the workflow becomes too digitally oriented (*active*), the benefit of the human agency is minimized. Likewise, if the advantages of digital fabrication processes are not leveraged (*passive)*, the existing analog methods may be limited. In designing hybrid workflows for on-body fabrication it is important to consider where in this spectrum the system should fall.

Design

One important aspect of any fabrication workflow is the design phase. Existing research has developed techniques for designing digital models on and around the body [11, 36]. Developing additional digital input modes based on tools currently used in on-body fabrication may be a more contextual approach to hybridizing these analog crafts. For example, a tailor could digitally design a garment directly on a customer's body, rather than manually measuring the body dimensions and subsequently producing the design.

Adapting body-based input as a digital process also enables us to augment several existing analog design methods. For example, positioning, scaling, copying, or reorienting a 2D pattern on the body can be a time consuming analog process. However, these geometric transformations are trivial in digital design. Moreover, in many analog on-body processes, such as creating garments or prosthetics, the design and fabrication stages happen simultaneously. The ability to visualize a digital design on the body prior to fabricating can enhance the design-to-production workflow, and enable more rapid design iteration before committing to fabrication.

A final benefit of utilizing digital design is that it could enable a design fabricated on the body to be more easily replicated, shared with others, archived, fabricated remotely, or adapted to different bodies. This increases the potential impact of a design beyond a single individual's body.

Fabrication

In terms of the actual fabrication process, a fully digital fabrication process could be preferred to ensure the highest level of precision in the final fabricated model. However, there are certain practices that may be best suited as an analog technique within hybrid workflows.

For example, the person who will wear the artifact may desire more agency and control over the final outcome. In this case, keeping human input integrated into the design process may increase overall satisfaction, since people have complex sensitivities and preferences to what gets put on their bodies.

Additionally, in certain scenarios, a fully digitized fabrication process may not be appropriate for hybrid workflows. For example, fabricating near sensitive or injured areas of the body require a level of delicate and dexterous control that goes far beyond the sensing and actuation capabilities of current fabrication machines. In these scenarios, integrating a hand-held or assistive fabrication device into the hybrid workflow may be most effective.

EXOSKIN

To initiate the exploration and investigation of these design considerations, we developed ExoSkin, a proof-of-concept system for printing digital designs directly on the body. Similar to existing on-body crafts which we reviewed, a user can design and fabricate directly on a human body. However, we adapt these analog arts with digital tools, to provide guidance, feedback, and to support additional operations such as importing and exporting designs.

The general workflow of ExoSkin allows users to first use a handheld fabrication machine as a stylus, to provide design input directly on the body. The resulting geometry is projected in real time directly on the body. Once satisfied with a design the user can switch to an output mode and fabricate the design by extruding a single layer of material. This fabrication process is facilitated by a projection guidance system which visualize the required tool paths.

ExoSkin uses a *neutral* hybrid fabrication process, where digital guidance is provided to the user, but there is no actuation or force feedback to control or constrain the geometry as it is fabricated.

For our system development, we focus on a single body part: the arm. We chose the arm as a representative body part, as it is highly mobile, has a complex curved form, and tires quickly when unsupported. However, we believe the techniques and ideas explored through the arm are largely applicable to other parts of the body.

The designs which can be generated by ExoSkin are simple and abstract. Our emphasis is less on generating product-ready models, and more on demonstrating the feasibility of on-body fabrication. Domain-specific applications and potential use cases are discussed later.

Fabrication Material

Guided by the constraints identified in our design considerations section, we explored three types of clays as a possible printing medium: an oil-based polymer clay, a water-based polymer clay, and a natural stoneware clay. We controlled the viscosity of each substance by adding a thinner to the first oil-based polymer clay, and water to the second polymer clay and stoneware clay. Each material was extrudable, however the oil-based polymer clay would not harden at room temperature. The stoneware clay would harden too quickly, and was prone to cracking and chipping.

In the end, we chose the water-based polymer clay (Jumping Clay) as our printing medium (Figure 2). It has a few unique affordances that make it an ideal candidate for on-body printing. First, it is an air-dry clay, so it cures from liquid to solid at room temperature. Second, when cured it is a lightweight, semi-flexible foam (Figure 3). This flexibility is an ideal material property for printing on the body, as the surface finish is resistant to cracking as the skin deforms. Lastly, the clay is reusable. Even when fully cured, this clay can be harvested and returned to its paste-like state by submerging it in water. This last material attribute is particularly compelling, as the majority of materials currently used in 3D printing are either one-time use only, or have a complex recycling process.

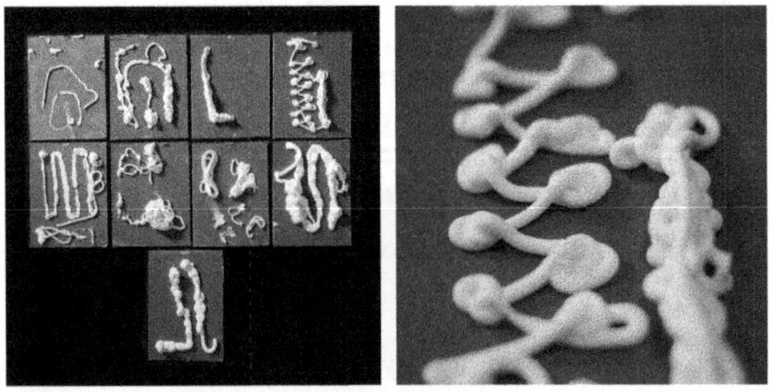

Figure 2. ExoSkin uses a water-based polymer clay as the printing medium.

Figure 3. ExoSkin prints with an air-dry polymer clay (0 minutes, 2 minutes, and 6 minutes after extrusion). The clay dries with a smooth surface finish and a foam-like flexibility.

Fabrication Hardware

The main hardware component of ExoSkin is the custom fabrication machine designed specifically for on-body printing. The system uses extrusion as its hybrid fabrication method. We choose to develop a hand-held extruder instead of adapting an industrial robot for on-body printing over concerns of safety and user engagement. Developing the additional safety measures needed for a robotic arm to safely touch a human body were beyond the scope of this research. Although a hand-held extruder will be less precise than a robotic arm, users can gain an increased sense of control and agency throughout the design and fabrication process [8].

Our on-body fabrication machine consists of three parts: a motorized clay extruder, a hose, and a hand-held extrusion nozzle (Figure 4). The clay extruder is a Potterbot linear RAM extruder, which has a 2-liter material reservoir. We add an 18" high-pressure polyester reinforced PVC tubing to transfer material from the extruder reservoir to the hand-held effector. The hand-held portion of the extruder consists of a hose adaptor, motorized ball valve, a set of interchangeable nozzle tips, two input/output buttons, and motion capture markers (Figure 5). The hose adaptor and nozzle tip screw into the motorized ball valve.

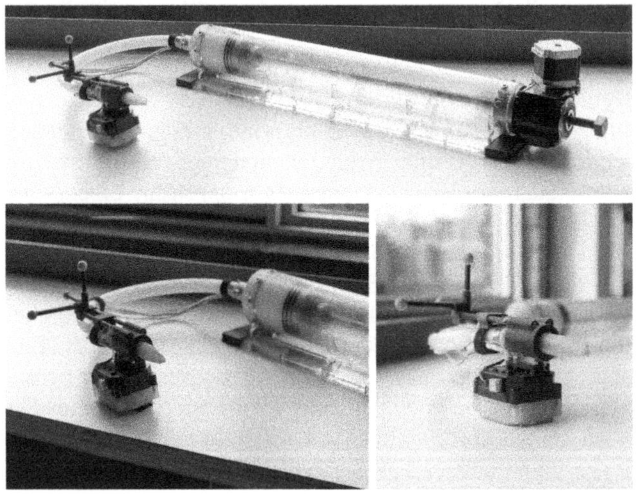

Figure 4. Our custom fabrication machine designed for on-body printing. The machine consists of a motorized clay extruder, a hose, and a hand-held extrusion nozzle.

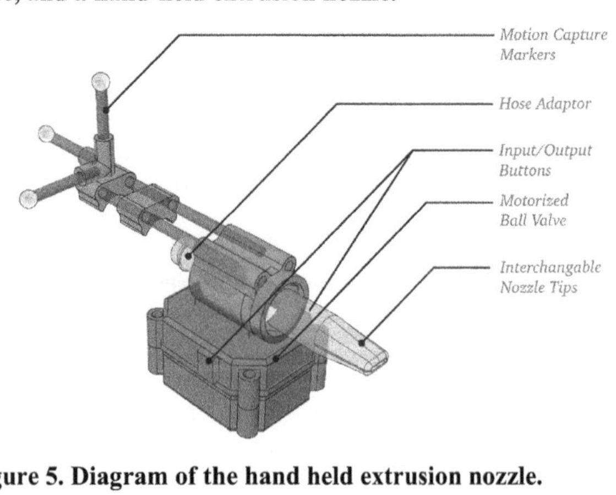

Figure 5. Diagram of the hand held extrusion nozzle.

The motorized ball valve has a slow 3-second phase cycle, which means it takes 3 seconds to fully open or close. However, it can operate with high viscosity material, unlike quicker, but weaker solenoid valves. Prior to fabricating, we pre-pressurize the extruder to push our clay paste from the material reservoir, through the hose, and to the hand-held effector. An output button under the thumb triggers the ball valve to open or close for extruding material. An input button, positioned on the ball valve under the index finger, switches to an input mode which is described later.

The profile of the extruded material can be changed throughout a fabrication session by exchanging nozzles tips on the extruder (Figure 6). Swapping a small diameter for a large diameter nozzle will help rapidly increase the volume of material extruded. Swapping a low perimeter tip for a high perimeter tip will improve drying times for our air-dry clay, since increasing the surface area-to-volume ratio exposes the extruded section to more air.

Many factors contribute to the flow rate of the material from the extruder nozzle: the viscosity of the material, the shape of the nozzle profile, the length of tube between the material reservoir and the hand-held effector. In our system, the flow rate would vary from approximately one to four inches per second, mostly depending on the viscosity of the material and the size of the nozzle being used.

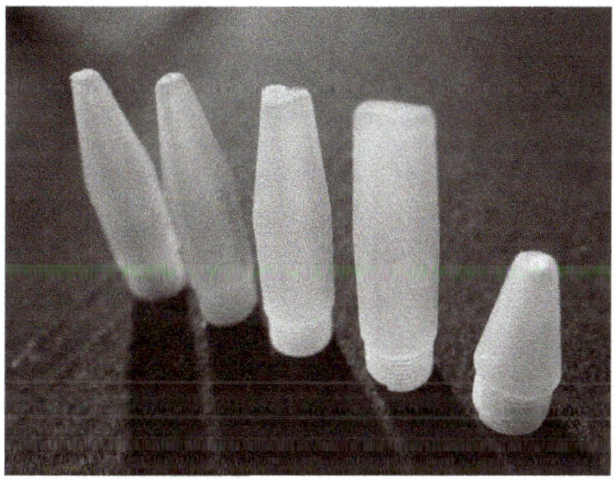

Figure 6. The nozzle tips on the extruder can be exchanged.

Fabrication Guidance System

ExoSkin uses a fabrication guidance system for tracking and visualizing toolpaths data directly on the body. The guidance system is comprised of a motion capture tracking system, projection-mapped visual feedback, and user input.

Motion Tracking

We use a six camera OptiTrack motion capture system mounted above a 3'x 4'x 3' tracking area. Motion capture cameras are mounted from above and below in order to track the full rotation of the arm. Passive markers attached to the wrist of the user track the position and orientation for the arm in world space. Markers attached to the end of the extruder track the position and orientation of the nozzle tip.

Motion capture is handled by OptiTrack's Arena (version 1.7.3). It tracks two pre-defined rigid bodies: the wrist worn marker set and the marker set on the extrusion tool. The position and orientation of these markers are streamed over Open Sound Control (OSC) to our software that controls body-based input, output, and projection mapping.

Visual Feedback

Generic toolpaths used by traditional CNC machines are sometimes visualized in software as simple lines that map how a tool head will move across a volume of space. However, the body is a more complex canvas for fabrication, and brings a number of complications for the generic toolpath. To begin, the user is printing with a hand-held extruder, which is inherently less accurate than a CNC controlled extruder. Moreover, the extruder must move relative to the arm not a volume of space. As a result, this highly curved, constantly shifting surface will have parts of toolpaths that go around the body, and can't be seen by the user. Our system projects custom toolpath visualizations directly on the body to mitigate these challenges unique to on-body fabrication.

A DLP projector is mounted above the tracking area to provide on-body visual feedback. To accurately project onto the body, we first calibrate the projector to the motion capture system using a simple one-time routine that correlates projected 2D points with tracked 3D world points.

User Input

In addition to fabricating, the hand-held extruder serves as a digital input device. The user enters an input mode by pressing the input button on the extruder. In this input mode, the user can draw digital content on their physical arm by using the tip of the extruder as an on-body stylus.

A CAD backend records the world coordinates of the extrusion nozzle's tip. These user-recorded points are down sampled and smoothed from the initial motion capture data. The motion capture system streams coordinates at 100 fps at sub-millimeter precision. The filtered coordinates are then attached to the virtual representation of the arm. This lets the user freely move and rotate their physical arm, while keeping the user input geometry fixed to its original location relative to the reoriented arm.

CAD Backend

The underlying software of our system is a backend CAD program not seen by the user. It holds the pre-scanned mesh of the body part intended for on-body fabrication, a mesh of the extrusion tool, and the 3D model of the current design. The meshes are dynamically rigged to the rigid body data streaming from the Arena software. The CAD backend aligns the arm's mesh to the incoming tracking data by translating the mesh from a known offset to the incoming marker coordinate, and then reorients the medial axis of the mesh to the normal of the wrist-marker plane. Similarly, the mesh and tip of the extrusion tool is transformed from a known offset to the position and orientation streaming from the tool-marker set. Synchronizing a virtual representation of the arm and extrusion tool with the physical arm and extrusion tool enables the CAD backend to record user input in coordinates that are relative to the moving body.

Software Implementation

ExoSkin was implemented using the Java programming language at 60 FPS. It uses the following open-source libraries: processing for graphics, OpenCV for projection mapping, toxiclibs for computational geometry, and oscP5 for streaming data over Open Sound Control (OSC). Rhinoceros 3D and Grasshopper 3D are used to illustrate how our system can send and receive geometry from external CAD software.

User Interaction and Workflow

ExoSkin strategically implements a hybrid fabrication workflow that enables digital designs to be printed directly on the body. In designing our hybrid workflow, we build upon analog techniques in on-body fabrication. The analog design process for on-body fabrication happens *in-situ* — within the local context of the body. This enables a fabricator to dynamically adapt a design in response to the surface, the person, or other conditions that would otherwise impact the final outcome. ExoSkin adapts this dynamic, in-situ design process as a digital workflow. The designs which are created are meant to demonstrate the capabilities of the system, and do not necessarily represent product-ready models.

Design

A user begins by digitally drawing on the skin by pressing and holding the input button on the extruder. As they move the extruder over the arm in world space, the sketched lines are projected as toolpaths directly onto the body (Figure 7). Together, the tracking system and projection mapping keeps a persistent rendering of the artwork relative to the moving arm. This means that when the user moves or rotates their arm, only the correct, visible portions of the design are rendered.

To smooth user input, the system down samples motion capture data to have a minimum distance of 3mm between points. Additionally, ExoSkin automatically snaps user input points to the closest points on the virtual surface. These filtered surface points are then interpolated into a smooth 3-degree spline.

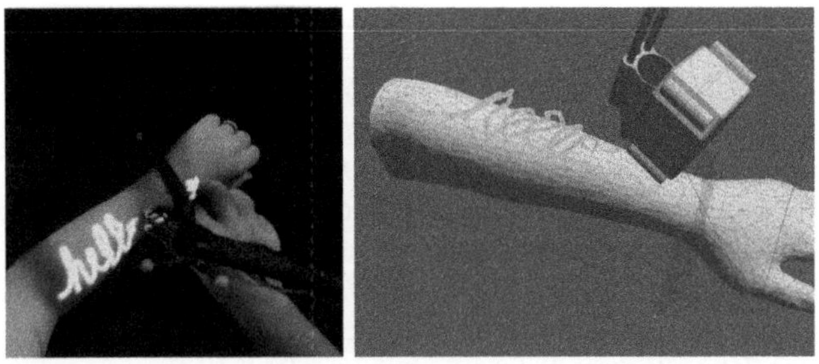

Figure 7. The user can directly sketch virtual strokes onto their body.

Fabricate

Once a sketch is complete the user can transition to the output mode of the extruder. To begin extruding, the user holds down the output button on the nozzle, which opens the ball valve to begin extruding material. The user can then slowly trace the rendered design on their body (Figure 8). During fabrication, ExoSkin displays Toolpaths that are designed to provide multiple layers of information to assist the user during the fabrication process.

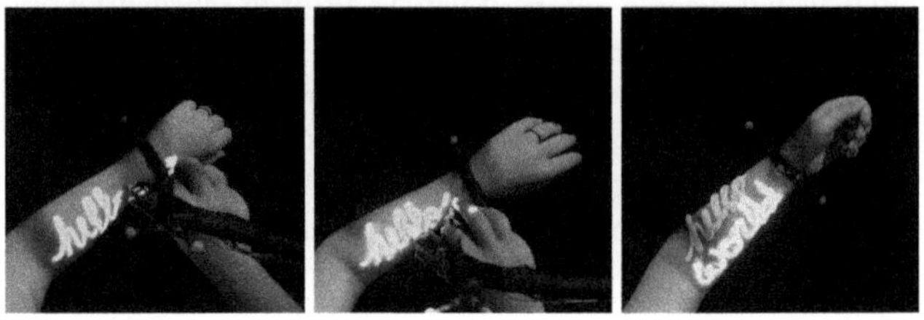

Figure 8. The user holds down the output button and extrudes over the rendered design.

To help improve accuracy for fabricating with a hand-held device, our system provides continuous visual feedback relating the nozzle location in relation to the toolpath. As the user brings the extruder near a toolpath, a halo around the tip of the extruder and the closest point on the toolpath is projected (Figure 9a). The halo illustrates the disparity between locations and visually prompts the user to adapt their tool position.

Next, to indicate the continuation of a toolpath towards a non-visible part of the body, we dynamically animate the line thickness and color gradient of the toolpath. Toolpaths grow thicker and brighter directly under the extruder. However, as the user moves the extruder tip from one side of the body to the other, the thickness and color of the toolpath thins and dims, as if it is wrapping around to the backside of the surface (Figure 9b). This serves as guidance for the extruder paths.

Users can also physically manipulate the material once it is extruded, if they do not get a desired result. A minor error can be corrected by nudging the material to better match a desired toolpath. A larger error can be corrected by removing portions of the fabricated path and re-printing it.

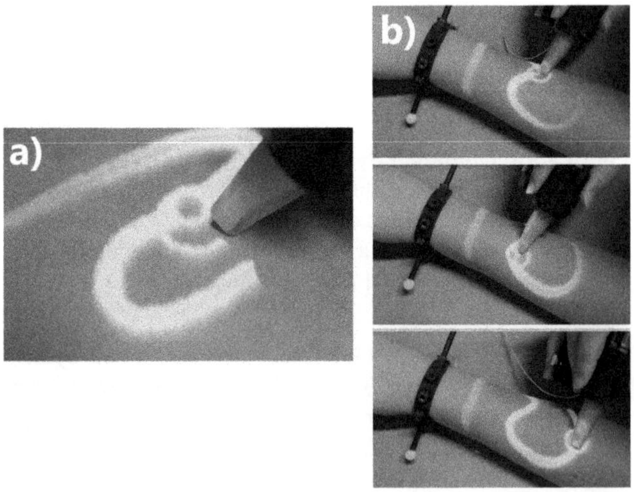

Figure 9. Visual feedback during fabrication. a) A halo around the extruder directs the user to the closest point on the toolpath. b) A dynamic toolpath indicates the path that the extruder should follow.

Sketch Beautification

Our system implements simple sketch beautification [18] to transform imprecise user input into precise geometric objects. In Figure 10, the user quickly sketches a circular shape onto their body using the input mode of the extruder. The system then recognizes the sketch as a circle, creates the idealized geometry on the virtual arm, and then projects the 3D dimensional perfect circle as a toolpath, and the user can press the output button to extrude material while tracing the toolpath. Likewise, a triangle is sketched on the body, processed into an idealized polygon, and then projected back as a precise shape. Again, the user presses the output button on the extruder and traces the toolpath to fabricate the shape.

Figure 10. Precise sketching demo.

Importing Geometry

As an alternative workflow, ExoSkin can connect to conventional 3D modeling software for importing geometry. This lets a user create precise digital designs for the body, which are then sent to our system for on-body projection and fabrication. In Figure 11, a user designs an organic 2D pattern in Rhinoceros3D, a commercially available CAD software (Figure 11a). We developed a script running in the CAD program to map the 2D pattern to the 3D mesh stored in our system, and then send the 3D geometry to ExoSkin via OSC. ExoSkin stores the geometry as toolpaths attached to the virtual arm. This keeps the CAD-generated geometry attached to the user's arm as they move and rotate around the workstation. These CAD-generated geometries are projected onto the body, and are ready for printing (Figure 11b). ExoSkin's pipeline to existing 3D modeling software enables users to quickly test out a design directly on the body. Users can easily translate, rotate, copy, or scale a design in the CAD program, which then updates the geometry projected onto the body in real-time. The floral pattern armlet in Figure 11b demonstrates ExoSkin's capability of fabricating highly intricate toolpaths.

Exporting Geometry

ExoSkin's connection to external CAD software brings an additional benefit to the hybrid fabrication process: the ability to export an artifact designed or fabricated on the body as a ready-to-print 3D model (Figure 1). In Figure 1a, the extruder is used as an input device to draw the design of a bracelet directly on the arm. ExoSkin stores the user input as a set of toolpaths, which it also sends to a connected CAD program. The user then prints the bracelet on the body by tracing the projected toolpaths, then infilling the defined region (Figure 1b). Simultaneously, a script running in the CAD program generates a thickened surface from the user's input geometry, and exports a valid mesh for conventional 3D printing (Figure 1d). This allows users to obtain a quick physical prototype printed directly on the body, and then print a more robust model on an external 3D printer with rigid 3D printing materials.

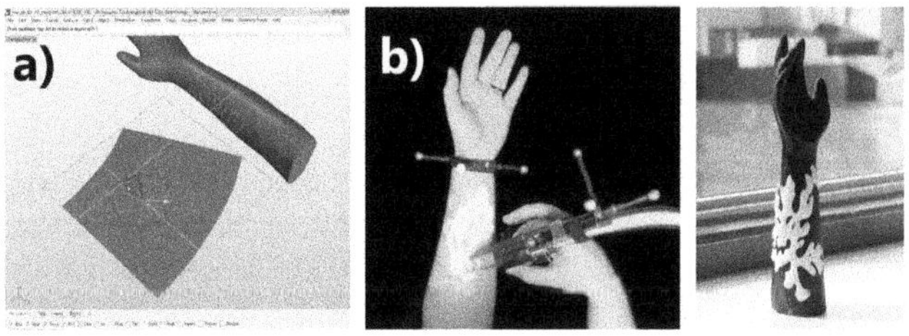

Figure 11. a) Design can be generated in commercial CAD software. b) The CAD geometries are projected onto the body.

A Framework of On-Body Fabrication

Figure 12 contrasts the input and output workflow paradigms facilitated with ExoSkin, to existing workflows for the design and fabrication of wearable objects. Our system provides several new design and fabrication workflows that sit in between fully analog and full digital methods for on-body fabrication. We believe the flexibility to mix input and output methods offer a number of opportunities for future exploration.

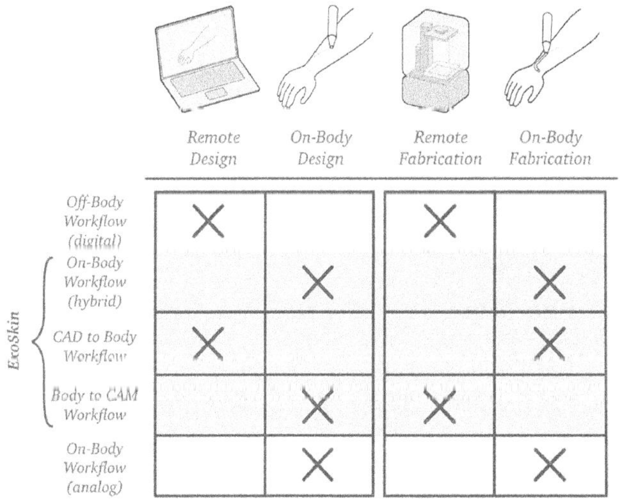

Figure 12. Input and output paradigms for the design and fabrication of wearable objects. ExoSkin provides several new design and fabrication workflows (highlighted blue) that sit in between a fully analog on-body workflow and a traditional fully digital off-body workflow.

INITIAL USER OBSERVATION SESSION

ExoSkin is an exploratory system designed to investigate the concept of on-body fabrication. As such, it was not our goal to evaluate the system or conduct formal caparisons to other fabrication techniques. However, we still felt it would be useful to get initial user feedback on the system and the concepts which it represents.

We invited four users to participate in a single workshop session — two male and two female, aged 20–30. Participants were internal to our organization but were not members of our research group and had no prior knowledge or exposure to the ExoSkin system.

All four participants had engineering or computer science backgrounds, but had very little previous experience with digital design and fabrication methods. One participant had basic knowledge of 3D modeling and only one participant had ever used a 3D printer.

Procedure

During the workshop session, we first explained the system configuration, providing an overview of the fabrication, sensing, and projection technology. The fabrication workflows were then demonstrated to participants, highlighting the main features of the system. Each of the four participants were then given an opportunity to use the system, and were prompted to design and fabricate a simple model directly on their arm. The entire session took approximately 45 minutes. Below we discuss the main observations and feedback which were collected.

Participant Feedback

In general, participants reflected positively on our system and were enthusiastic about on-body fabrication. When initially extruding onto the skin, each participant made a comment on the printing material's texture. They were surprised by its stickiness and cool temperature, with one participant exclaiming *"It tickles!" (p2)*.

Participants did see the value in printing with a washable, reusable material, however there was also a desire to preserve a print so that it can be worn multiple times:

"I would like to be able to take it off my body without destroying my beautiful design." (p1)

When prompted for their thoughts on the extrusion tool, three participants noted a potential preference for a robotic instead of hand-held tool. They felt a robotic system would increase the speed and accuracy of the fabrication process and would take less effort on their part. There was also a sense that a machine would do a better job than they themselves could:

"I don't trust myself to make it right... I'd rather trust a machine." (p3)

P4 enjoyed the hand-held device, and also noted the desire to use it on others, in addition to using it on his own body:

"I'd use it to give someone a tattoo!" (p4)

Participants were also asked if they would entrust a machine to fabricate on sensitive areas of their body, such as the face or back. Three participants gave a definitive *'No'*, however one participant said they would feel comfortable as long as there was a human overseer:

"I wouldn't mind a machine printing on my face ... as long as a person would come check up on me every once in while. You know ... to check if I'm still alive." (p2)

At the end of the workshop, participants were asked to think about the kinds of thing they would print on their bodies. Clothing and accessories were immediately mentioned, and one participant wanted to print custom electronics:

"I'd print a game controller right on my arm!" (p3)

DISCUSSION

We believe there are many analog craft processes that can be adapted for hybrid workflows in on-body fabrication. We are optimistic that further exploration into on-body fabrication will prompt additional innovative interaction techniques that circumvent the unique challenge of crafting digital designs directly on the body.

Domain Specific Applications

Our research was focused on the interaction implications and hardware configurations for printing on the body. We have provided some abstract examples of the artifacts which could be generated with such a system. Further work could investigate specific applications for fabricating functional objects on the body.

Body-centric design industries that rely on one-off, handcrafted designs are currently limited in their ability to rapidly create, iterate, and share a given design. Augmenting these high-skill analog craft practices with digital techniques brings an opportunity to streamline design-to-production workflows for on-body fabrication. In particular, we see four primary domains that would benefit from on-body digital fabrication: skin-centric industries (such as cosmetics), fashion and wearables industries, film and special effects industries, and the medical device industry. Such domains may specifically benefit from on-body design, on-body fabrication, or both.

In applications that modify the skin, such as cosmetics, digital drawing or brushing instructions that are projected onto the body can help non-experts learn expert techniques. In the movie and special effects industries, body-worn props or prosthetics can be precisely designed in a CAD environment, then digitally fabricated directly onto an actor. For fashion and wearable devices, on-body design could give both the artist and the model agency in a customized design process, while direct-to-body fabrication enables bespoke designs to be customized to many bodies, and inherently ensures the design will fit the wearer. Lastly, for medical applications, the design of prosthetic sockets or silicone dressings, for example, can be created by an expert then sent to remote locations for technicians to fabricate directly on a patient.

Body Parts

Our discussion of possible content domains indicates that many areas of the body may be appropriate for on-body fabrication. However, each specific location brings unique challenges and considerations that impact the choice of machine configuration. This can relate to *physically sensitive* areas of the body — such as the face, head, neck, and spine — *socially sensitive* areas — such as the chest and nether regions — or *highly mobile* areas — such as the arms, hands, legs, and feet.

Printing on physically sensitive areas require continuous, nuanced feedback on how the fabrication device is touching the body. In these scenarios, hand-held devices may be most reliable and appropriate as fabrication devices. Socially sensitive parts of the body, may be less desirable for direct on-body fabrication or may be preferred to be operated by the person being printed on instead of a third party. For highly mobile areas of the body, the fabrication system cannot assume that the body part will remain still for long periods of time. Therefore, the configuration of the system must be designed to adapt to continuous changes in position and orientation of the fabrication surface.

LIMITATIONS AND FUTURE WORK

We chose to develop a hand-held extruder as the fabrication device for our on-body fabrication system. Our decision was guided by the relatively quick development time for a hand-held device, as well as the low risk of injury for the end user. However, what we gained in agile deployment and increased safety, we lost in precision and accuracy when compared to existing multi-axis CNC machines. Future work could focus on developing compliant, multi-axis systems that strike a more even balance between precision, accuracy, and safety for on-body fabrication. For example, worker-friendly robotic arms, such as Universal Robots, would be particularly interesting to explore.

Our implementation uses a motion capture system as a low-latency, high accuracy, and highly flexible solution to track bodies in space. However there are other spatial tracking technologies that could be used in on-body fabrication systems. In particular, markerless tracking would be desirable for any sort of deployment. We experimented with both Kinect and Leap motion tracking, but found the accuracy was not yet reliable for the purpose of our project.

We use a single projector to visualize fabrication instructions on the body. Although the throw of the projector adequately covered the volume of our work area, shadows cast by the extrusion tool could hide portions of projected toolpaths from the user's view. Future fabrication systems could mitigate this problem by using alternative visualization configurations; for example, switching multiple projectors or using augmented reality devices, such as translucent screens or head-mounted displays would eliminate the shadows cast by physical objects in the workstation.

With regards to our implementation, we examine the implications of direct on-body printing using a single, skin-safe material. However, there are many more materials to be developed and explored. We are particular excited for composites that layer skin-safe and non-skin-safe materials together. For example, a skin-safe paste could be printed as an insulating layer against other heat-transferring materials, like thermosoftening or thermosetting plastics. Moreover, edible materials such as frostings, pastes, or foams may also be applicable for on-body fabrication.

One notable limitation of our implementation is that it supports extrusion of only a single layer of material. While ExoSkin supports complex toolpaths that are curved and three-dimensional geometry, it does not provide traditional multi-layer three-dimensional fabrication. To support this, the set time of the material would need to be accounted for. Furthermore, or toolpath generation algorithm would need to be advanced to support multi-later digitization.

Our work could also be extended to support printing on areas of the body under high amounts of deformation or stress, such as joints, hands, and feet. Moreover, fabricating electronics directly on the body could be explored by combining skin-safe materials and conductive pastes or inks.

The machine processes for on-body fabrication also warrant further investigation. In our implementation, we create a custom material to use in an extrusion device. However, existing everyday materials could prove useful if the appropriate fabrication process were developed. For example, threads and textiles could be used in fabrication machines that weave or drape directly on the body, and medical tapes or gauzes could be used in machines that wrap bandages, braces, casts, or splints around patients.

Fabricating with a custom-made material also limits quality control from batch to batch. Despite our best efforts the water content of each hand-mixed batch of polymer clay would vary slightly. As a result, the behavior of the material, its viscosity and drying time, would differ each time the material reservoir was reloaded. Future implementations could integrate an air-assist onto the extrusion tool to actively dry the clay when too wet.

Finally, we would like to conduct more thorough and formal evaluations of on-body fabrication. Our preliminary observation session provided some interesting insights. For example, the issue of reusability came up – how can models printed directly on the body be preserved and re-worn? Furthermore, the topic of human agency revealed subjectivity and trade-offs – while some identified the manual extrusion tool as potentially imprecise, others valued the ability it gave them to control the fabrication process. Follow-up studies could explore these and other related topics.

CONCLUSION

We have shown how existing crafts of on-body design can be adapted with hybrid fabrication workflows to enable digital designs to be crafted directly on the body. Our initial observation session indicates that this new paradigm for interactive 3D modeling involves curiosity and intrigue, motivating further explorations and implementations. Moreover, we have outlined design considerations for future on-body fabrication systems, and have identified the unique human, machine, and material challenges that these systems will need to solve. We acknowledge that digital on-body fabrication is a challenging domain. However, we believe the potential impact of digitizing this previous analog craft to be an important area for future explorations.

REFERENCES

1. Lifecasting. *Wikipedia.* https://en.wikipedia.org/wiki/Lifecasting. Retrieved Jan 5, 2016.
2. Prosthetic makeup. *Wikipedia.* https://en.wikipedia.org/wiki/Prosthetic_makeup. Retrieved Jan 5, 2016.
3. Appropriate Audiences. 3d Printer X Tattoo Machine. *Instructables.* http://www.instructables.com/id/3D-PRINTER-X-TATTOO-MACHINE/. Retrieved Jan 4, 2016.
4. Martin Bechthold, Jonathan King, Anthony Kane, Jeffrey Niemasz, Christoph Reinhart. Integrated Environmental Design and Robotic Fabrication Workflow for Ceramic Shading Systems. In *Proceedings of the 28th ISARC* (ISARC '11), Seoul, Korea, 70-75.
5. Liwei Chan, Rong-Hao Liang, Ming-Chang Tsai, Kai-Yin Cheng, Chao-Huai Su, Mike Y. Chen, Wen-Huang Cheng, and Bing-Yu Chen. 2013. FingerPad: private and subtle interaction using fingertips. In Proceedings of the 26th annual ACM symposium on User interface software and technology (UIST '13). ACM, New York, NY, USA, 255-260. DOI=10.1145/2501988.2502016
6. Ke-Yu Chen, Kent Lyons, Sean White, and Shwetak Patel. 2013. uTrack: 3D input using two magnetic sensors. In Proceedings of the 26th annual ACM symposium on User interface software and technology (UIST '13). ACM, New York, NY, USA, 237-244. DOI=10.1145/2501988.2502035
7. Xiang 'Anthony' Chen, Stelian Coros, Jennifer Mankoff, and Scott E. Hudson. 2015. Encore: 3D Printed Augmentation of Everyday Objects with Printed-Over, Affixed and Interlocked Attachments. In Proceedings of the 28th Annual ACM Symposium on User Interface Software & Technology (UIST '15). ACM, New York, NY, USA, 73-82. DOI=http://dx.doi.org/10.1145/2807442.2807498
8. Laura Devendorf and Kimiko Ryokai. 2015. Being the Machine: Reconfiguring Agency and Control in Hybrid Fabrication. In *Proceedings of the 33rd Annual ACM Conference on Human Factors in Computing Systems* (CHI '15). ACM, New York, NY, USA, 2477-2486. http://doi.acm.org/10.1145/2702123.2702547
9. Nicholas Foley, Ryan Luke Johns, Axel Kilian. 2014. Bouyant Extrusions. Workshop In *Robotic Fabrication in Architecture, Art and Design* (RobArch '14).
10. Jared Friedman and Heamin Kim. 2014. *Experiments in Additive Clay Depositions.* In *Robotic Fabrication in Architecture, Art and Design* (RobArch '14), 261-272.
11. Madeline Gannon, Tovi Grossman, and George Fitzmaurice. 2015. Tactum: A Skin-Centric Approach to Digital Design and Fabrication. In *Proceedings of the 33rd Annual ACM Conference on Human Factors in Computing Systems* (CHI '15). ACM, New York, NY, USA, 1779-1788. http://doi.acm.org/10.1145/2702123.2702581
12. N. Gershenfeld (2008). Fab: the coming revolution on your desktop--from personal computers to personal fabrication. Basic Books.
13. Sean Gustafson, Christian Holz, and Patrick Baudisch. 2011. Imaginary phone: learning imaginary interfaces by transferring spatial memory from a familiar device. *In Proceedings of the 24th annual ACM symposium on User interface software and technology (UIST '11).* ACM, New York, NY, USA, 283-292. DOI=10.1145/2047196.2047233
14. Brian Harms. Buoyant Depositions. Retrieved Sept 2015. https://vimeo.com/65179063
15. Chris Harrison, Desney Tan, and Dan Morris. 2010. Skinput: appropriating the body as an input surface. I*n Proceedings of the SIGCHI Conference on Human Factors in Computing Systems (CHI '10).* ACM, New York, NY, USA, 453-462. DOI=10.1145/1753326.1753394.
16. Chris Harrison, Hrvoje Benko, and Andrew D. Wilson. 2011. OmniTouch: wearable multitouch interaction everywhere. In *Proceedings of the 24th annual ACM symposium on User interface software and technology* (UIST '11). ACM, New York, NY, USA, 441-450. http://doi.acm.org/10.1145/2047196.2047255
17. Christian Holz, Tovi Grossman, George Fitzmaurice, and Anne Agur. 2012. Implanted user interfaces. In Proceedings of the SIGCHI Conference on Human Factors in Computing Systems (CHI '12). ACM, New York, NY, USA, 503-512. http://doi.acm.org/10.1145/2207676.2207745
18. Takeo Igarashi, Satoshi Matsuoka, Sachiko Kawachiya, and Hidehiko Tanaka. 1997. Interactive beautification: a technique for rapid geometric design. In Proceedings of the 10th annual ACM symposium on User interface software and technology (UIST '97). ACM, New York, NY, USA, 105-114. DOI=10.1145/263407.263525 http://doi.acm.org/10.1145/263407.263525
19. Kim, J. S., Kim, D. S., & Lee, M. C. (2007, October). 3D printing method of multi Piezo head using a photopolymer resin. In Control, Automation and Systems, 2007. ICCAS'07. International Conference on (pp. 2587-2590). IEEE.
20. Joris Laarman. MX3D Metal. Retrieved Sept, 2015. http://mx3d.com/projects/metal/
21. Gierad Laput, Robert Xiao, Xiang 'Anthony' Chen, Scott E. Hudson, and Chris Harrison. 2014. Skin buttons: cheap, small, low-powered and clickable fixed-icon laser projectors. In *Proceedings of the 27th annual ACM symposium on User interface software and technology* (UIST '14). ACM, New York, NY,

USA, 389-394. http://doi.acm.org/10.1145/2642918.2647356

22. Shu-Yang Lin, Chao-Huai Su, Kai-Yin Cheng, Rong-Hao Liang, Tzu-Hao Kuo, and Bing-Yu Chen. 2011. Pub - point upon body: exploring eyes-free interaction and methods on an arm. *In Proceedings of the 24th annual ACM symposium on User interface software and technology (UIST '11).* ACM, New York, NY, USA, 481-488. DOI=10.1145/2047196.2047259.

23. Achim Menges, Jan Knippers. ICD/ITKE Research Pavilion 2014-15. Retrieved Sept 2015. http://icd.uni-stuttgart.de/?p=12965.

24. Adiyan Mujibiya, Xiang Cao, Desney S. Tan, Dan Morris, Shwetak N. Patel, and Jun Rekimoto. 2013. The sound of touch: on-body touch and gesture sensing based on transdermal ultrasound propagation. In *Proceedings of the 2013 ACM international conference on Interactive tabletops and surfaces* (ITS '13). ACM, New York, NY, USA, 189-198. DOI=10.1145/2512349.2512821

25. Stefanie Mueller, Pedro Lopes, and Patrick Baudisch. 2012. Interactive construction: interactive fabrication of functional mechanical devices. In *Proceedings of the 25th annual ACM symposium on User interface software and technology* (UIST '12). ACM, New York, NY, USA, 599-606. DOI = 10.1145/2380116.2380191

26. Tao Ni, Amy K. Karlson, and Daniel Wigdor. 2011. AnatOnMe: facilitating doctor-patient communication using a projection-based handheld device. In *Proceedings of the SIGCHI Conference on Human Factors in Computing Systems* (CHI '11). ACM, New York, NY, USA, 3333-3342. http://doi.acm.org/10.1145/1978942.1979437

27. Masa Ogata, Yuta Sugiura, Yasutoshi Makino, Masahiko Inami, and Michita Imai. 2013. SenSkin: adapting skin as a soft interface. In *Proceedings of the 26th annual ACM symposium on User interface software and technology* (UIST '13). ACM, New York, NY, USA, 539-544. DOI=10.1145/2501988.2502039.

28. Neri Oxman, J. Laucks, M. Kayser, E. Tsai & M. Firstenberg. 2013. Freeform 3D Printing: toward a Sustainable Approach to Additive Manufacturing. In *Green Design, Materials and Manufacturing Processes*. Helena Bartolo et al. (eds.). CRC Press.

29. Huaishu Peng, Amit Zoran, and François V. Guimbretière. 2015. D-Coil: A Hands-on Approach to Digital 3D Models Design. In *Proceedings of the 33rd Annual ACM Conference on Human Factors in Computing Systems* (CHI '15). ACM, New York, NY, USA, 1807-1815. DOI=10.1145/2702123.2702381

30. Alec Rivers, Andrew Adams, and Frédo Durand. 2012. Sculpting by numbers. *ACM Trans. Graph.*31, 6, Article 157 (November 2012), 7 pages. http://doi.acm.org/10.1145/2366145.2366176

31. Alec Rivers, Ilan E. Moyer, and Frédo Durand. 2012. Position-correcting tools for 2D digital fabrication. *ACM Trans. Graph.* 31, 4, Article 88 (July 2012), 7 pages. http://doi.acm.org/10.1145/2185520.2185584

32. Roy Shilkrot, Pattie Maes, Joseph A. Paradiso and Amit Zoran. 2015. "Augmented Airbrush for Computer Aided Painting (CAP)." ACM Trans. Graph. (TOG) 34, 2, Article 19, March 2015, 11 pages.

33. Rajinder Sodhi, Hrvoje Benko, and Andrew Wilson. 2012. LightGuide: projected visualizations for hand movement guidance. In *Proceedings of the SIGCHI Conference on Human Factors in Computing Systems* (CHI '12). ACM, New York, NY, USA, 179-188. http://doi.acm.org/10.1145/2207676.2207702

34. Alexander Teibrich, Stefanie Mueller, François Guimbretière, Robert Kovacs, Stefan Neubert, and Patrick Baudisch. 2015. Patching Physical Objects. In Proceedings of the 28th Annual ACM Symposium on User Interface Software & Technology (UIST '15). ACM, New York, NY, USA, 83-91. DOI=http://dx.doi.org/10.1145/2807442.2807467

35. Natalie Walsh. How to Use a Dress Form. *Instructables.* http://www.instructables.com/id/How-to-Use-a-Dress-Form/. Retrieved Jan. 5, 2016.

36. Amy Wibowo, Daisuke Sakamoto, Jun Mitani, and Takeo Igarashi. 2012. DressUp: a 3D interface for clothing design with a physical mannequin. In *Proceedings of the Sixth International Conference on Tangible, Embedded and Embodied Interaction* (TEI '12), Stephen N. Spencer (Ed.). ACM, New York, NY, USA, 99-102. http://doi.acm.org/10.1145/2148131.2148153

37. Xing-Dong Yang, Tovi Grossman, Daniel Wigdor, and George Fitzmaurice. 2012. Magic finger: always-available input through finger instrumentation. In *Proceedings of the 25th annual ACM symposium on User interface software and technology* (UIST '12). ACM, New York, NY, USA, 147-156. DOI=10.1145/2380116.2380137.

38. Amit Zoran and Joseph A. Paradiso. 2013. FreeD: a freehand digital sculpting tool. In *Proceedings of the SIGCHI Conference on Human Factors in Computing Systems* (CHI '13). ACM, New York, NY, USA, 2613-2616. http://doi.acm.org/10.1145/2470654.2481361

39. Amit Zoran. 2013. Hybrid basketry: interweaving digital practice within contemporary craft. In *ACM SIGGRAPH 2013 Art Gallery* (SIGGRAPH '13). ACM, New York, NY, USA, 324-331. http://doi.acm.org/10.1145/2503649.2503651

40. Amit Zoran, Roy Shilkrot, Suranga Nanyakkara, and Joseph Paradiso. 2014. The Hybrid Artisans: A Case Study in Smart Tools. *ACM Trans. Comput.-Hum. Interact.* 21, 3, Article 15 (June 2014), 29 pages. http://doi.acm.org/10.1145/2617570.

Mimetic Machines: Collaborative Interventions in Digital Fabrication with Arc

Hidekazu Saegusa[1] **Thomas Tran**[2] **Daniela K. Rosner**[1]
[1]Human Centered Design and Engineering
University of Washington
{chgm, dkrosner}@uw.edu
[2]Environmental Science
University of Washington
thomas.tytran@gmail.com

ABSTRACT
This paper examines the collaborative process of developing Arc, a computer numerical controlled (CNC) engraving tool for ceramics that offers a new window onto traditional forms of craft. In reflecting on this case and scholarship from the social sciences, we make two contributions. First, we show that fabrication tools may integrate multiple and distinct roles (as copiers, translators and connectors) in their production of form, selectively limiting the agency of the maker and machine. Second, we situate small-scale manufacturing in a wider historical context of "mimetic machinery": machines for mechanical reproduction that draw their symbolic power from a material connection with the phenomena represented (in this case, sound and gesture). We end by sharing lessons learned for fabrication research based on this study.

Author Keywords
Digital craft, performance, digital fabrication, research-through-design, design inquiry, mimesis.

ACM Classification Keywords
K.4.0 Computers in Society: general.

INTRODUCTION
Over the last decade, a new project of reproduction has entered HCI. Cultures of making have given rise to systems for digital fabrication that create tactile media out of metal, plastic, wood and clay. At one end, advocates within HCI contend that such systems have created nothing short of a "revolution"—enabling new forms of small-scale manufacturing and technological empowerment [26]. Laser cutters produce modular furniture in garages and workshops [25]. Shoe-boxed-sized 3D printers create jewelry through additive manufacturing [16]. And computer numerical control (CNC) looms weave textiles patterns with shared digital files [13]. At the other end, analysts view digital fabrication as commodity fetishism: extending capitalist modes of for-profit production to accommodate small-scale manufacturing, often reinforcing privileged technical authority along the way [20,23]. For instance, Roedl et al. [23] emphasize the tendency of "maker" events to speak to college-educated, upper and middle-class white men. Others break open the category of technology to detail forms of care work [29], hacking [15], and craft [24].

CHI'16, May 07 - 12, 2016, San Jose, CA, USA

ACM 978-1-4503-3362-7/16/05...$15.00
DOI: http://dx.doi.org/10.1145/2858036.2858475

Figure 1: Miller inspecting the ceramic pot he created with the Arc machine.

This paper pulls back from these productivist and critical framings to consider fabrication as a mode of inquiry, a window into the sociotechnical imagination of craft. To do this work, we developed Arc, a computer numerical controlled (CNC) engraving tool for ceramics that carves material according to surrounding sounds and actions. We draw on eight months of fieldwork and technical development of Arc in a clay studio and scholarship from science and technology studies and cultural studies to make two arguments. First, we suggest Arc exposes multiple roles for systems of digital fabrication in the workshop: as copier, as translator and as connector, selectively limiting agency through each encounter. Second, locating these machines in the historical context of "mimetic machines" shows that tactile media may throw into question the bounds and competencies of production: how algorithms shape measurement and interpretation to become a source of "fetishlike power" [16, 27]. While we developed Arc to build new imaginative frames into practices of digital fabrication, we soon found the symbolic value of small-scale manufacturing took precedence.

RELATED WORK

This examination of digital fabrication builds on studies of making and craft [5,12,13,15,17,21] and interventionist design research [6] that have gained recent traction within HCI due to the different ideas of design and use they propose. Advocates claim makers "are reshaping how people consume and interpret the handmade" [13,p.xi]. This includes the "maker movement" typified by projects featured in the popular DIY magazine *Make* and transnational Maker Faires. Around digital fabrication in particular, design researchers consider what can be learnt through the development of new tools [8,25]. Zoran and Paradiso [28], for example, present an interactive milling tool that pushes back at the hand that holds it. From computer-controlled embroidery [10] to plush toy construction [19], this machinery explores the production of custom 3D shapes through varied textures and materials. In the domain of ceramics, we find several additional examples, from audio-recorded stories inside the ceramic vessels [10] to blurring the boundary between ceramic craftsmanship and technology more broadly [17,13,16]. Artist Geoffrey Mann's *Crossfire* comprises vessels that visualize the sound of an argument passing through them.

Most connected to our project is a recent body of work examining the material performances that become core to process of meaning making [6,7], and not just background activities. Cheatle and Jackson's [5] recent examination of digital fabrication in the context of a fine art furniture studio, finding that such tools live in historically complex systems of value that shift the very content and form of their use. As a practice that inhabits the edges of manual, mechanical and digital worlds, ceramic work extends these questions of value for digital fabrication.

ARC: MILLING TOGETHER

Arc is a digital engraving machine that mimics the sounds and actions of makers based on computational analysis of surrounding gestures and sound. The machine moves a ribbon tool for cutting clay in response to the rhythm, volume and pitch of the sound, the gestures of the maker, and how the maker configures the machine's sensitivity. The core system consists of three parts: (1) a mechanism that analyzes sound and gesture data captured by simple sensors; (2) a custom engraving instrument that sculpts material on the potter's wheel in response to this analysis; and (3) mobile phone software for changing the sensitivity of the machine and software algorithms. For example, a maker can shift the association between pitch, volume, and gesture to movement by repositioning a lever on a mobile phone interface. That interface then wirelessly communicates with the engraving mechanism.

The application runs on the iOS 8.4 platform with an iPod touch (5th generation). It wirelessly connects with output using the Open Sound Control (OSC) protocol. The microphone is embedded in the phone, which processes the sound (i.e., voice, music played from a phone, etc.). The software extracts the volume of the incoming sound in reference to the value of the volume slider, which corresponds to a multiplied value of the specified volume. In addition to the volume, the software recognizes the peak frequency if its amplitude is greater than the threshold value set by the slider interface. This allows the user control over the sensitivities of pitch and volume, individually. We then send the pitch and the volume of sound input to the hub application (built with Processing) running on a laptop (Mac Book Pro) that controls the behaviors of the output machinery. The hand gesture recognition uses a Leap Motion sensor to detect velocities of the index finger, measuring its elevation and (lateral movement). We multiply the values of the sliders for depth and height as weight coefficients on each vector of velocity. We then communicate each variable to the hub desktop application. The derived value of the vector of velocity of each axis (elevation & lateral motion) is multiplied by the set slider value as weight coefficients.

The output machinery consists of a rotating table on which a material object is placed, a machine arm that engraves the object and an elevation structure to control the height of the machine arm. The elevation system is structured as a threaded rod bolstered with four linear bearings controlling the elevation of the machine arm. The stepper motors controlled by a micro controller (Arduino Uno R3) drives the machine arm and the elevation structure. The mobile software determines the elevation based on the elevation-axis velocity of the index finger or the pitch received. The machine arm is structured as a crank, and the value for volume and velocity of the lateral-axis received from the mobile software, determines the distance an arm extrudes. As the received value increases, the extrusion of the machine arm moves closer toward the center of the rotating table. The elevation-axis velocity of the index finger or the number of frequency band received from the mobile application determines the elevation. As the hub application receives the elevation-axis velocity, the elevation of the ribbon tool is responsively determined.

BUILDING COLLABORATIVELY

The Arc system came about through a collaboration between maker-scholars at the University of Washington and Seattle-based ceramic artisans Adrien Miller and John Ellefson. Miller is a sculptor with a background in painting and photography (once telling us, "*I like to sneak art into everyday objects*.") Much of his work takes the form of portraiture that he creates based on photos of individuals. Ellefson by contrast calls himself a potter because of its less "*pretentious*" connotations. His ceramic objects focus on the urn and its narrative potential.

Our work with Miller and Ellefson began at Florentia Clayworks, a ceramics studio in Seattle, Washington home seven ceramic artists who collectively rent and care for the space. The workshop contained a range of pottery wheels, electronic hand tools (such as saws and drills) and a large kiln. No tools for digital fabrication like laser cutters or 3D printers had entered the space and the artisans had no plans to bring them in. Miller and Ellefson both find the draw of clay work in the physical interaction with clay ("*as a method of understanding your world and work you lose something*," Ellefson explains.)

During our first visit we told the artisans we wished to explore the introduction of digital fabrication processes in ceramic work. We presented them with a linear motor whose movements corresponded to a digital 3D model displayed on a mobile phone. The initial prototype worked much like a subtractive 3D printer wherein digital renderings drive tangible design. In the scene that follows we describe our initial discussions that would lead to Arc.

The research team joins Ellefson and Miller at the Clay Works Studio. Ellefson begins sketching ideas for a fabrication machine. "If there's some algorithm that would alter with my gesture so that I didn't full understand how — what shape it would take," he says, staring at our prototype's jerky arm movement. "Rather than just uuuuuun," he says, imitating the recurring motor noise with regular movement. "Not that I really understand anything about how algorithms work or how to do that. But I get the sense that [...] the parameters aren't linear. And the non-linear thing is the thing that's somehow interesting." Ellefson explains how everyone has a unique way of handling clay: appreciating how people have their own habits of gesture. Miller stands back from the prototype. "One idea I'm having just looking at it," he begins, "essentially having whatever my input is with my hand be mimicked by the machine." Miller demonstrates concurrent movement wherein the machine reproduces his hand gesture at the wheel. "So you're one half of the equation and here's the other half?" Ellefson asks with excitement. Miller nods (Figure 2).

The above vignette illustrates the artisans' early responses our project, imagining an alternative engagement with machine fabrication. Miller's proposal for an interaction that blends the maker and machine — the latter mimicking the former — ultimately expands the kinds of fabrication techniques used in the studio and those used beyond it, such as within 3D ceramic fabrication labs. The idea stems from Miller's recent experience showing people how to throw clay by asking them to think of the wheel as a clock face where forces push at opposite ends. But from watching the uneven movements of a linear motor, the artisans develop other ideas for creating compelling formal interventions and imagery. Along the way, Miller embraces unexpected

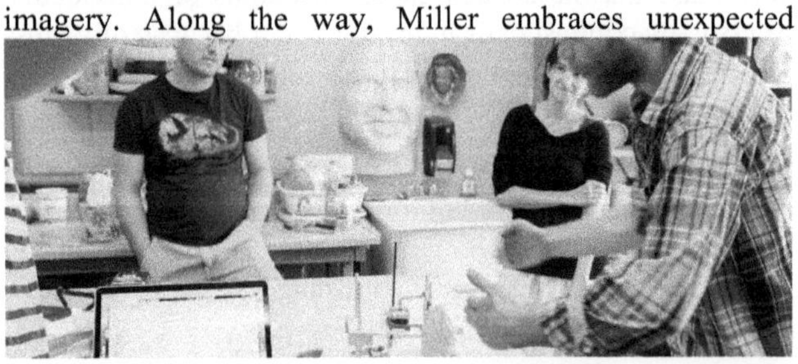

Figure 2: Miller explaining the mimicking gesture of machine.

rhythms, suggesting ideas for cultivating a soft agential presence on the ceramic stage. Soon mathematical metaphors take hold: "parameters," "algorithms," "linearity," and "equations." Ellefson focuses on non-linear parameters and mystery of computational algorithms.

In the sections that follow we see how this concern for extending the ceramicist's hand becomes indicative of the multiple roles Arc could potentially play. As Arc develops alongside other projects in the studio, it highlights unique priorities for the makers. In the process, we foreground three facets of digital production — coping, translating and connecting — each of which suggests paths for developing the symbolic life of 3D printing.

Copying

Early iterations of the machine followed on Miller's suggestion for collaborative production to begin tracking hand gestures in isolation. While experiencing this technique for the first time, Ellefson describes the instrument as a "*pantograph sort of thing*," creating patterns originated by the hand. The pantograph instrument, whose mechanism developed in the early 17th century, enables the movement of an arm (often tracing an image) to produce the movement of another arm. These movements may happen at different scales, enabling both the reproduction and magnification of an image.

However, despite developing a closer relation to the pantograph over time (increasing its accuracy), later versions of the machine could feel abrasive. At one point Ellefson refers to Arc as "a ticker tape machine," coarsely copying the finger's movements. He bends over the machine arm to inspect its precision, making several suggestions to improve this accuracy. He recommends alternate material and mechanics – from wood to metal and from a height-axis piston to a height-axis threaded screw. Miller worried that a delay in height-axis shifting inadequately constrained his movements. Much like a photocopier, Ellefson and Miller expected Arc to reproduce the forms that came before – making precision and scope core concerns.

Translating

The features of Arc that became particularly intriguing for Ellefson and Miller concerned its ability to translate a human action. Miller focused on the regularly placed incisions it made on the top of the bowl, marks he said he had trouble producing by hand. Once the machine involved mimicry of sound, Miller read new possibilities: "*You can record conversations on there*." He proceeded to ask Hidekazu to play a recording of Brian Eno, partially in jest (as a clichéd reference to performance art) and partially as a test of its boundaries (how the would machine translate these sounds). As the song played, the rhythmic sound Arc created as the Arc jutted back and forth fed back into its speakers, subtly influencing the movements of the machine.

More visibly, the song's higher pitches moved the arm's z-axis at an imperceptible pace. The volume, by contrast, moved the arm faster. Even adjusting these features proved unsettling, suggesting the delay could not be sufficiently overcome. Ellefson and Miller grew more interested in how the arm created marks along the z-axis. "*It's beautiful,*" Miller told us, reflecting on a pot he had glazed and put through kiln. As a translator, Arc selectively listened to the digital descriptions of 3D form (via gesture and sound). These invisible decisions to amplify or ignore patterns of activity, seemed to embrace ambiguity, prompting a certain desire for surprise — affective, formal, and aesthetic. Through translation, Arc presented possibilities for revision, iteration, deletion and breakdown, concepts that push at HCI's current understandings of digital craft. These roles not only suggest attending to digital fabrication beyond moments of imitation, they also recommend recovering alternative characterizations of reproduction that have long emerged through the craft practices and representations.

Connecting

What surprised the makers most visibly, however, concerned a desire for extending the sensitivity of the machine. Early on, Miller described clay work as *"a quiet and self-contained performance."* While watching the movement of the Arc arm, Miller wanted the machine to react to more than his touch, suggesting it should respond to sounds as well. He explained: "*I think of performance as being very body based: the physical gesture of moving limbs. How do we stretch out and bring awareness of the space around us into this small container of what we're focusing on?"* Through music, Miller positioned Arc to provide a window onto the wheel, a contained and focused performance.

During our final session, the height-axis refused to budge. Miller stopped using the machine in frustration. He turned to Ellefson in disappointment, noting the machine's impoverished ability to demonstrate the subtlety of the hand's gesture. By entering into a theater of digital fabrication, the makers exposed pottery production to new questions of performance and control. How should the machine interpret the hand? How should the hand interpret the machine? Through making marks in clay with Arc, the potters created a visible and durable connection to those moments of breakdown and adoption of Arc. While copying implies an imitation of form or content, connecting here highlights the maker's continual ties with the phenomena reproduced, a process that invites questions of authenticity, or ways of evidencing the presence of the maker in the act of making.

POSITIONING ARC AS A MIMETIC MACHINE

In his brief 1933 essay on mimesis, cultural critic Walter Benjamin outlined the key role of mimicry in all human endeavor. "*Perhaps there is none of [a person's] higher functions in which his mimetic faculty does not play a decisive role*" [2, p.343]. In a remote past, imitations of astrological processes took the form of dances signifying recognizable reenactments of the sky. Mimesis sustained more than similarity; it captured "magical correspondences" [2, p.334] with the phenomena represented.

Decades later, anthropologist Michel Taussig read Benjamin's commentary as a statement on sociotechnical life. He argued that contemporary "mimetic machinery" enables a resurgence of ancient "magic" (1993: 59). Film cameras create powerful analogies with the phenomena depicted by its moving imagery, and sound recorders apprehend the same from audio traces. This mimetic machinery comprises a range of apparatuses, from engraving and etching to lithography, photography, and film. It also began to explain the holding power of technology, or what Ames [1] has recently called charisma.

Like the analogue photograph and film cameras that came before them, our integrative program of ceramic work showed how tools of digital fabrication (and here Arc) hold a certain symbolic power. Despite finding themselves "*skeptical*" of 3D printing technology, Ellefson and Miller enlivened our ideas of what fabricators could become. The "*fetishlike power*" [27, p. 59] of their fabricated form did not rely solely on imitation or translation.

This form of contagion—or what anthropologist James George Frazer called the *Law of Contact*—represents a crucial aspect of Arc's integration of roles [8, p.220]. Confronting the fetish quality of fabrication requires us to create a kind of "relating to" that displaces the concept of function – framing the ceramic process as part of other relations (coping, translating, connecting). It also acknowledges an indefinable tactility of vision, how making gesture and sound durable entails stabilizing actions in tangible media (tape cassettes, CDs, vinyl, hard disks). For HCI, this contagion casts new light on "WYSIWIG" production – showing what you can see and what you get from digital fabrication is less a matter of function than a capacity for creating a symbolic hold on the thing being reproduced (and keeping that thing "*alive*" [1]).

CONCLUSION

The stories above begin to illustrate how the concepts of copying, connecting and translating extend HCI debates around human-object relations and creative practice in ways that call attention to the symbolic value of digital reproduction. This means looking beyond the human-machine interface (c.f. [28]) to the complex arrangements and histories of meaning making on which it depends. As an analytic matter, Arc's multiple roles suggest recognizing the limits of mimetic metaphors for characterizing digital craft processes (both their content and form). Approaching the connecting and translating of material expression expands the "capture and extraction" logic underpinning many HCI projects of fabrication. In doing so it also adds precision to the socio-material metaphors of "entanglement" or "intra-action" [2,30] that characterize the co-constitution of matter and meaning underway.

ACKNOWLEDGEMENTS

We would like to thank Adrien Miller and John Ellefson and the grant supported provided under NSF #1453329.

REFERENCES

1. Morgan G Ames. "Charismatic Technology." *Critical Alternatives Aarhus '15.*
2. Karen Barad. *Meeting the universe halfway: Quantum physics and the entanglement of matter and meaning.* duke university Press, 2007.
3. Walter Benjamin. "On the mimetic faculty." *Reflections* 334 (1978).
4. Walter Benjamin. 2007 [1968]. *Illuminations*, ed. H. Arendt, trans. H. Zohn. New York: Schocken Books.
5. Amy Cheatle and Steven J. Jackson. "Digital Entanglements: Craft, Computation and Collaboration in Fine Art Furniture Production." In Proceedings of the 18th ACM Conference on Computer Supported Cooperative Work & Social Computing, pp. 958-968. ACM. http://doi.org/10.1145/2675133.2675291
6. Laura Devendorf and Daniela K. Rosner. "Reimagining Digital Fabrication as Performance Art." In *Proceedings of the 33rd Annual ACM Conference Extended Abstracts on Human Factors in Computing Systems*, pp. 555-566. ACM, 2015. http://doi.org/10.1145/2702613.2732507
7. Laura Devendorf and Kimiko Ryokai. "Being the Machine: Reconfiguring Agency and Control in Hybrid Fabrication." In *CHI*, pp. 2477-2486. 2015. http://doi.org/10.1145/2702123.2702547
8. James George Frazer. *The golden bough.* NuVision Publications, LLC, 2004.
9. Follmer, Sean, and Hiroshi Ishii. "KidCAD: digitally remixing toys through tangible tools." In *Proceedings of the SIGCHI Conference on Human Factors in Computing Systems*, pp. 2401-2410. ACM, 2012. http://doi.org/10.1145/2207676.2208403
10. Green Eyl design group's *Whispering Table.* Online at: http://thegreeneyl.com/whispering-table
11. Scott E Hudson. "Printing teddy bears: a technique for 3D printing of soft interactive objects." In Proceedings of the 32nd annual ACM conference on Human factors in computing systems, pp. 459-468. ACM, 2014. http://doi.org/10.1145/2556288.2557338
12. Steven J. Jackson and Laewoo Kang. "Breakdown, obsolescence and reuse: HCI and the art of repair." In *Proceedings of the 32nd annual ACM conference on Human factors in computing systems*, pp. 449-458. ACM, 2014. http://doi.org/10.1145/2556288.2557332
13. Jonathan Keep. Online at: http://www.keep-art.co.uk
14. Faythe Levine and Cortney Heimerl. 2008. *Handmade Nation: The Rise of DIY, Art, Craft, and Design.* Princeton Architectural Press.
15. Silvia Lindtner, Garnet D. Hertz, and Paul Dourish. "Emerging sites of HCI innovation: hackerspaces, hardware startups & incubators." In *Proceedings of the SIGCHI Conference on Human Factors in Computing Systems*, pp. 439-448. ACM, 2014.
16. Geoffrey Mann. Online at: http://www.mrmann.co.uk Marvin, Carolyn. *When old technologies were new.* Oxford University Press, 1997.
17. Rupert Meese, Shakir Ali, Emily-Clare Thorne, Steve D. Benford, Anthony Quinn, Richard Mortier, Boriana N. Koleva, Tony Pridmore, and Sharon L. Baurley. "From codes to patterns: designing interactive decoration for tableware." In *Proceedings of the SIGCHI Conference on Human Factors in Computing Systems*, pp. 931-940. ACM, 2013. http://doi.org/10.1145/2470654.2466119
18. David A. Mellis and Leah Buechley. "Case studies in the personal fabrication of electronic products." In *Proceedings of the Designing Interactive Systems Conference*, pp. 268-277. ACM, 2012. http://doi.org/10.1145/2317956.2317998
19. Yuki Mori and Takeo Igarashi. "Plushie: an interactive design system for plush toys." In *ACM Transactions on Graphics (TOG)*, vol. 26, no. 3, p. 45. ACM, 2007. http://doi.org/10.1145/1276377.1276433
20. Evgeny Morozov. *The net delusion: The dark side of Internet freedom.* PublicAffairs Store, 2012.
21. The Particules Studio. Online at: http://particules-studio.com/objets-sans-âge.html
22. Matt Ratto. "Critical making: conceptual and material studies in technology and social life." *The Information Society* 27, no. 4 (2011): 252-260.
23. David Roedl, Shaowen Bardzell, and Jeffrey Bardzell. "Sustainable Making? Balancing Optimism and Criticism in HCI Discourse." *ACM Transactions on Computer-Human Interaction (TOCHI)* 22, no. 3 (2015): 15.
24. Daniela K. Rosner and Kimiko Ryokai. "Reflections on craft: probing the creative process of everyday knitters." In *Proceedings of the seventh ACM conference on Creativity and cognition*, pp. 195-204. ACM, 2009. http://doi.org/10.1145/1640233.1640264
25. Greg Saul, Manfred Lau, Jun Mitani, and Takeo Igarashi. "SketchChair: an all-in-one chair design system for end users." In *Proceedings of the fifth international conference on Tangible, embedded, and embodied interaction*, pp. 73-80. ACM, 2011. http://doi.org/10.1145/1935701.1935717
26. Joshua G. Tanenbaum, Amanda M. Williams, Audrey Desjardins, and Karen Tanenbaum. "Democratizing technology: pleasure, utility and expressiveness in DIY and maker practice." In Proceedings of the SIGCHI Conference on Human Factors in Computing Systems, pp. 2603-2612. ACM, 2013. http://doi.org/10.1145/2470654.2481360

27. Michael T. Taussig, *Mimesis and alterity: A particular history of the senses*. Psychology Press, 1993.
28. Alex Taylor. "After interaction." *interactions* 22, no. 5 (2015): 48-53.
29. Austin Toombs. "Enacting Care Through Collaboration in Communities of Makers." In *Proceedings of the 18th ACM Conference Companion on Computer Supported Cooperative Work & Social Computing*, pp. 81-84. ACM, 2015. http://doi.org/10.1145/2685553.2699326
30. Jakob Tholander, Maria Normark, and Chiara Rossitto. "Understanding agency in interaction design materials." In *Proceedings of the SIGCHI Conference on Human Factors in Computing Systems*, pp. 2499-2508. ACM, 2012. http://doi.org/10.1145/2207676.2208417
31. Amit Zoran, and Joseph A. Paradiso. "FreeD: a free-hand digital sculpting tool." In *Proceedings of the SIGCHI Conference on Human Factors in Computing Systems*, pp. 2613-2616. ACM, 2013. http://doi.org/10.1145/2470654.2481361

Embodied Sketching

Elena Márquez Segura*, Laia Turmo Vidal*, Asreen Rostami, Annika Waern***

*Uppsala University
Uppsala, Sweden
{elena.marquez; laia.turmo;
annika.waern}@im.uu.se

**Mobile Life Centre,
Stockholm University, Sweden
asreen@dsv.su.se

ABSTRACT

Designing bodily experiences is challenging. In this paper, we propose *embodied sketching* as a way of practicing design that involves understanding and designing for bodily experiences early in the design process. Embodied sketching encompasses ideation methods that are grounded in, and inspired by, the lived experience and includes the social and spatial settings as design resources in the sketching. Embodied sketching is also based on harnessing play and playfulness as the principal way to elicit creative physical engagement. We present three different ways to implement and use embodied sketching in the application domain of co-located social play. These include *bodystorming* of ideas, *co-designing with users*, and *sensitizing designers*. The latter helps to uncover and articulate significant, as well as novel embodied experiences, whilst the first two are useful for developing a better understanding of possible design resources.

Author Keywords

Ideation; Bodystorming; Embodied Sketching; Embodied Interaction; Design Methods; Sensitizing; Somaesthetics.

ACM Classification Keywords

H.5.m. Information interfaces and presentation (e.g., HCI): Miscellaneous.

INTRODUCTION

More than fifteen years ago, Djajadiningrat, Gaver, and Frens discussed the difficulty of designing when considering the aesthetic experience and interaction together [13]. As time has passed there has been plenty of research into how to fill this gap by establishing methods, guiding principles, and supporting techniques [1,14,20,28,58]. Recently, the call for methods that can tap into the aesthetic experience has been renewed with the development of technology that can recognize bodily gestures, movements, and physiological reactions, [30,38,41,42,70]. Nonetheless, as in many other domains, technology has advanced faster than research [16], and we have found ourselves surrounded by a plethora of research prototypes and commercial examples that use gestures and movement as input, using diverse controllers and input mechanisms. These have focused on recognizing and harnessing our everyday gestures [55], so that we can operate in a virtual world in a way that bears resemblance with how we act in our everyday life, in a "natural way". This presented a powerful narrative, from which followed a variety of movement-based interfaces [55]. In the application domain of interactive games in particular these interfaces were embraced by industry, researchers, and the gaming public [36,69]. However, this phenomenon soon lost momentum, as reflected in a significant decrease in sales [15,50].

CHI'16, May 07 - 12, 2016, San Jose, CA, USA

ACM 978-1-4503-3362-7/16/05...$15.00
DOI: http://dx.doi.org/10.1145/2858036.2858486

The approach of instrumentalizing the body [30], and the technical limitations of the technology to capture and map body movements [2,40], have been highlighted as issues due to the constraints they imposed on the moving body [14, 20]. While we have long passed the period of technical limitations, we have not yet witnessed the foreseen paradigm shift. Body-controlled game experiences do not come off as exciting and engaging to players in the long run, and gesture-based interaction fails to offer an interesting experience once the novelty effect passes [73]. Sony acknowledges with this comment about the PlayStation Move controller: "[...] great tech, probably not so great applications so far [...]"[71].

A positivistic understanding of action that has dominated the field underlies many of these issues [55]; movements have been seen as something that can be specified, represented, and modeled without considering the context where they take place. This makes the design problem an "engineering" one, and gestures have been considered as "an afterthought", once the technology in "in place" [73].

In this paper, we present a design practice that we call *embodied sketching*, which is intended to: i) support *ideation* rather than evaluation, ii) support the *inclusion of bodily experiences* early in the design process, before the construction of fully-functional prototypes, and iii) *spur creativity* by harnessing play and playfulness, in a way that is grounded in and inspired by the lived experience. By using the word *embodied* we foreground the embodied perspective from which we draw [16]. By using the word *sketching*, we wish to highlight that the methods are directed towards ideation as well as the exploratory, suggestive, and tentative character of the resulting sketches [6].

We illustrate the concept of embodied sketching through three case examples, which represent three design situations where embodied sketching can be useful: in *bodystorming* with designers, in *co-creating with users*, and in *sensitizing designers*. While the former two are useful for ideation related to the available design resources (including, but not restricted to, technology), the latter helps in uncovering and articulating qualities of a novel embodied experience that share traits with that for which designers design.

With this paper, we contribute to HCI by adding to the body of work that aims to translate the abstract theory of embodied interaction into design practice, in this case in the domain of design for movement and play.

BACKGROUND

Spurring creativity

There exist a plethora of methods for spurring creativity and ideation that are used with enthusiasm by practitioners [27] in Interaction Design (IxD) processes. This includes well-known practices such as classical brainstorming [56], personas, affinity maps, and various sketching methods. However, these are not always rigorously studied or validated [18]. Recent research efforts in IxD have been devoted to develop, study, and validate such methods [18].

Among these methods we find bodystorming [27,57,66], which has been characterized as a situated ideation method in which designers prototype in context, using enactment [66]. Schleicher et al. [66] named *user-case theater* a variation of bodystorming that involves actors, and props, to simulate the activity for which to design. Related but with a more evaluative focus are methods of *strong prototyping,* which replicate the end environment so that design prototypes can be tested [66]. Particularly interesting for this article, is the concept of *embodied storming*, a pre-brainstorming activity in which participants engage in simulations of an envisioned scenario, which they collaborate to sustain by enactment. Through enactment, the participants can gain personal insight into the situation for which they are to design.

Understanding the embodied experience

While all of the above are inspirational, they are not specifically purposed for the design of bodily activities.

Design scholars have emphasized that bodily experience and awareness are key when designing technologically supported aesthetic experiences [29,39,41,48,63,65,81]. Much of this work is theoretically grounded in somaesthetics [38], an interdisciplinary field that foregrounds the role of the body not only as an object of aesthetic representation, but as subjectivity for aesthetic appreciation [67]. The field embraces "bodily perception, performance and presentation" theories and practices [68]. Analytic somaesthetics in particular has provided a theoretical foundation to researchers and designers dealing with the lived, and felt experience. Its theories about "the nature of our bodily perceptions and practices and their function in our knowledge and construction of the world" [68] have been useful for explaining the importance of bodily perception and awareness. For example, in [29] Höök presents a detailed analysis of the experience of horseback riding, which yields interesting themes that are then translated into design considerations.

Other work in this area has relied on the pragmatic branch of somaesthetics, which concerns the postulation of disciplines and techniques for improving our somatic sensibilities, typically accompanied by a particular way of understanding and shaping of the body (e.g. Feldenkrais, Tai Chi). Recognized work in this domain includes Klooster's explorations on the usage of artefacts and the creation of cycles of attention to (and through) the body, and the artefact [32,81], and Schiphorst's suggestion of introducing a "connoisseur", in which the design process is supported by a facilitator with heightened somatic and empathic skills, who is able to resonate with the experience of the participants, connect, and guide them to access subtle qualities of bodily knowledge that would otherwise not be accessible to them [65]. Schiphorst works with a shift from a third-person "everyday-type" perspective on movement towards a first-person, inwards-type of awareness [63–65]. that runs through the work of Shusterman. Also Lee et al. emphasise somatic introspection methods as a way to heighten attention and interest [38].

HCI has to a lesser extent explored the use of practical somaesthetics, which is the third branch of somaesthetics. This is perhaps the most straightforward of them all, as it involves the actual "doing", the practice of a certain discipline such as what practitioners do when they go to a Feldenkrais class. In this article, we take the opportunity to include practical somaesthetics in one of our embodied sketching techniques.

Drawing from other fields

A crucial issue for enactment-based ideation processes is how to facilitate enactment. Performance anxiety and body perception issues may affect the participants' ability to engage in physical performance in a co-located social setting [9]. Methods from other creative fields have been used to mitigate these issues. The use of scenario-based and character creation techniques [4,54] for understanding of prospective scenarios [3] and users is well understood, as it is the use of performative techniques in design [33]. Such methods have been used also in participatory design [43] to allow designers to explore, communicate and test the prototypes in a fictional space. Improvisational methods adopted from theatre can bridge the gap between users and designers [53], and have shown potential as a way to investigate the human behaviour in space, with or around objects [5]. Situated performance activities, including role playing and embodied fiction have been used as ways to co-design and generate creative ideas [34]. Experience Design Theatre (EDT) as introduced by Vines et al [77] is a method that investigates participants interaction in a shared lived experience through the use of role playing. Finally Gerber [24,25], uses improvisation techniques to support designers and improve brainstorming, by building up skills and a mindset that is productive during ideation phases. These techniques will often work to reinforce the imperatives of brainstorming (withholding judgment, building on one another's ideas, focus on quantity, etcetera), and contribute to foster innovation, spontaneity, and the ability to embrace failure. In this article, we rely on play activities in a similar way.

OUR APPROACH

In this section, we discuss the design values that underlie embodied sketching.

Design resources for co-located physical & social play

In the introduction we elaborated on how the design space of movement-based interfaces remains narrow. This is in part due to a lack of acknowledgement of how such interfaces shape the space around the technology, including the social and emotional experience of the players [35], but also in how shaping the space around an activity can influence the play experience. We see a missed opportunity in not considering that space as a design resource [46,47,73], in particular, the socio-spatial arrangement of players and artefacts in the space [46,47].

The technology has not yet caught up with this [69], and we find plenty of "playing, seating, and viewing arrangements that hinder mechanisms such as mutual eye contact, natural reciprocation of approach or avoidance cues and mirroring, or emotionally relevant communication signals" [47]. The "social factor", which is one of the main motivations why players like playing multiplayer games [9,17,22,78], remains often set aside as a backdrop, without having direct involvement, participation, and interaction in the gameplay. This has been known by the moniker of "playing alone together" [17,72,76] .

The potential of the socio-spatial configurations for shaping the situated experience is well documented [22,37,44,45]. Hence, although the mere presence of others can add to the game experience even in cases of solo play [7], play schemes along the lines of "alone together" miss the benefits associated with taking the social aspect into account when designing for co-located social play – among others, higher engagement, arousal, affect, and positive emotions [9,22,61].

In line with the concepts reported in [47], we take a technology-supported approach [79] and consider the technology to be just one of the resources to design. The others include socio-spatial elements, such as arrangements of players, or the placement of displays used for monitoring actions and effects. Our approach typically involves designing an activity by selecting an amalgam of design resources (e.g. digital and physical artefacts, participants, audience), each to whom/which an important role to support the activity is assigned. Their spatial arrangement is also designed, so that the whole configuration promotes mutual orientation, awareness, and communication and coordination of joint action [32,47].

A practice to access the experience

As discussed in the background section, techniques from other disciplines like play and theatre have been imported to spark a mindset that is conducive of creativity

We propose that practical somaesthetics can function as a way to access to, and articulate bodily experiences in a manner that informs design. . We suggest that designers prepare for ideation by engaging in an activity very similar to that for which they design, containing similar elements, and physical core mechanics[1]. This allows designers to develop a heightened embodied sensibility attentive to both the designers' somatic experience (intero-, proprio-, and exteroceptive sensations), as well as important contextual elements (e.g. social, physical, and spatial). We argue that this in turn inspires and influences the emergence of design ideas that take the embodied experience at their core.

Play as a medium and a goal

Play and playfulness have proven themselves useful in instilling a mindset that is conducive of creative thinking [12,27]. Play can also help to lower performance anxiety due to its power to re-signify [11,26,31,59] anything that happens within the "magic circle of play"[31]. As Gaver puts it: *play is not just mindless entertainment, but an essential way of engaging with and learning about our world and ourselves—for adults as well as children. As we toy with things and ideas, as we chat and daydream, we find new perspectives and new ways to create, new ambitions, relationships, and ideals.*[23].

Before, we mentioned how methods from improvisational theatre could positively impact ideation activities. We argue that play and playfulness can spark off creativity in very similar ways [23].

EMBODIED SKETCHING

We define *Embodied sketching* as a characterization of design practices in the domain of embodied interaction that

[1] In game studies, core mechanics are recurring or continuous actions and procedures required to advance in a game [62:316]. As we are designing for physical play, we introduce 'physical', to highlight those core mechanics that rely on substantial physical engagement by players. They can be simple actions (e.g. jumping when you are playing on a jump rope) or combination of these (e.g. shooting while hiding and dodging when playing laser tag).

foregrounds the somaesthetic experience for the exploration of, and design for particularly interesting physical activities. This is done by: 1) physically engaging with simple actions and activities that are constituent of, or essential to, the bodily activity you design for, and 2) by looking into (and trying) how different design resources integrate and blend together to support and give rise to play activities.

Embodied sketching can be implemented in different ways, depending on the current status of a design project and the particular challenges that it faces. Below, we present examples of embodied sketching in design projects, and show some of the considcrations that comc into play. Wc introduce our example cases with a short description of the design situation at hand, then describe implementation details, and finish with our main takeaways.

The first usage scenario, *bodystorming*, is used to help designers sketch ideas for movement-based interactive systems by engaging physically in a co-design play-based ideation activity with peers. The exploration of the design space focuses on both digital and non-digital mediating artefacts, on the arrangement of contextual elements in physical space, and on the 'physical core mechanics' at work. This form of embodied sketching allows designers to develop ideas from scratch.

The second scenario, *participatory embodied sketching*, uses play as a mean to support a co-design activity with end users. As a participatory form of embodied sketching, it democratizes design and empowers end users [60], supporting them to explore, follow, play, modify, break, and create game or activity design structures. This form of embodied sketching allows designers to understand their users, and to refine and rethink existing ideas.

Finally, the practice-driven *sensitizing of designers,* employs an activity to cultivate the somaesthetic appreciation of designers, to sensitize and help them access and articulate particularly interesting embodied phenomena we want to design for, and hence it can be employed pre-ideation.

Example 1: Bodystorming

In a joint international research collaboration project, we worked with a research group that had developed an exertion game – an interactive game that "deliberately requires intense physical effort" from the participants [51]. The central physical activity had already been decided – centred around the experience of hanging. An interesting design, "hanging off a bar" [52] had been created, challenging previous exertion games designs by facilitating "exertion" without requiring big and energetic movements.

At the time of the embodied sketching exercise, the design team had already collected feedback from different play tests. However, we thought that the very interesting concept and core mechanics of hanging had not been fully explored; we felt that hanging could offer a *generative concept* from which new game ideas could arise. Hence, we decided to re-open the design space focusing on the concept of hanging. We arranged a bodystorming workshop using a non-technological tool: the TRX, an artefact for suspension training that leverages body weight [75].

Method

An expert design team of the Exertion Games Lab at RMIT, composed of four Ph.D. students and one master's student in Game Design, participated in the workshop. The TRX was hung from the ceiling in the middle of the workshop space. We also brought other artefacts gathered from throughout the lab, such as Styrofoam swords, a Pilates ball, a basketball ball, tennis balls, and Styrofoam mats.

We introduced the concept of embodied sketching to the designers: we were to come up with games by playing with the material we had around. We enforced social rules that were similar to those of ordinary brainstorming [56] in the sense that all ideas were welcome, that we would not criticize ideas, and that we wouldn't think too much about feasibility issues. Then, we suggested turn-taking as to regulate social interaction: First, a person would suggest something, which s/he would show/demo to the rest of us. Then, the rest of the group was free to participate in the idea construction by suggesting changes, e.g. adding rules, goals, and artefacts. When one idea was "done", we would come up with another idea together. The workshop was recorded in order to later discuss the session with a senior designer and two of the participants.

Overview of games and ideas

Ten ideas arose from the workshop, which we named 1) ninja swords, 2) projections on the floor, 3) sitting on a ball, 4) standing on a ball, 5) flying football, 6) dodge balls, 7) laser, 8) competitive path following, 9) hitting targets and 10) single legged. Six of them included variations, from a minimum of three to a maximum of seven (1, 2, 4, 8, 9, and 10). Variations were adds-on to an original idea, with differcnt physical corc mcchanics or artcfacts involvcd.

Physical core mechanics and artefacts shaping ideas

The ideas that emerged throughout the workshop were primarily shaped by either physical core mechanics, or

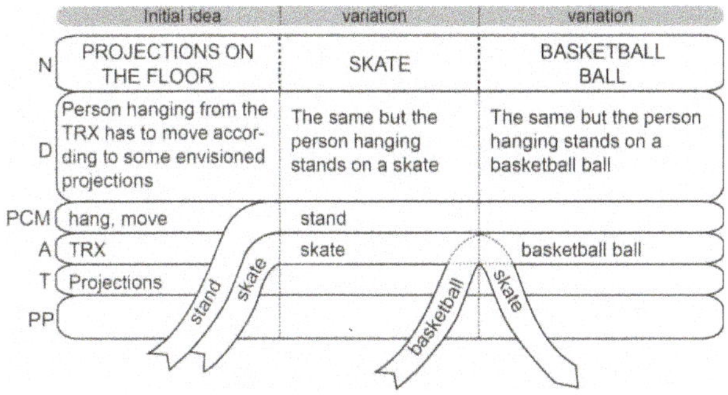

Fig. 1 © Laia Turmo Vidal & Elena Márquez Segura. Graphical representation of the evolution of one idea. N=name, D=description, PCM=physical core mechanics, A=artefacts, T=envisioned technology, PP=pretence play.

artefacts (see in Fig. 1. how different elements were added and removed, resulting into different variations of one same idea). Among the physical core mechanics that appeared, there were some that "worked", i.e. where enjoyment was visible, players showed great excitement, or an obvious wish to engage. An example of this was the idea "standing on a ball" (4), where one participant was hanging from the TRX while trying to maintain the balance on top of a Pilates ball. We engaged with the idea longer in comparison to the other ones, most of us tried it out, and the sound of laughter was present continuously.

At other times, the physical core mechanics needed some tweaking. This happened when the group identified some interesting elements in the idea but the idea itself did not "work". When this happened, the participants tended to replace an artefact to another that changed the physical core mechanic. This happened with one of the versions of the idea "projections on the floor" (2, see Fig. 1), where one participant was hanging from the TRX while standing on a skateboard, and envisioned certain projections on the floor which he should try to avoid. The skateboard turned out to constrain his movement too much. One of the participants stated: "*as long as the skateboard is there, we don't have that much of room*". In response to this it was suggested to change the skateboard for a basketball. This proved to be useful when another participant tried it out as it allowed a broader range of movements. Figure 1 depicts part of the evolution of the initial idea according to these changes[2].

Some physical core mechanics were discarded completely, i.e. when an idea emerged but was not accepted or soon abandoned. For instance, a participant suggested trying the idea "flying football" (5), where a participant would use the TRX to gather momentum, to then take her feet off the ground and hit a Pilates ball. After the first try by the proponent of the idea, the rest of the group showed no intention to try it out, change it, or build upon it. Thus it was discarded in favour of the next idea.

As with the physical core mechanics, the available artefacts also shaped the ideas. Some artefacts seemed to "work better" (in the same sense than used above) than others in particular ideas. For instance, during the exploration of the idea "standing on a ball" (4), one iteration was suggested involving tennis balls, which would be thrown to a player on the Pilates ball, who needed to dodge them. While the big ball was kept for the following ideas, the tennis balls were discarded after just one try. This is also an illustrative example of how an idea centred on an artefact (Pilates ball) allowed changes of the physical core mechanics involved (from just balance, to balance and dodging).

[2] The full evolution of all the ideas in this session can be found as auxiliary material of this paper at ACM DL.

Technology in the workshop

While this workshop was not centred on proposing technological implementations, this would still emerge as part of the game explored. One example was the idea called "projections with skateboard" (variation of 2), where the group envisioned some technology that would implement a particular feature of the game, like projecting patterns on the floor, which the participant on the skateboard holding the TRX had to follow or avoid.

In other ideas, the designers would simulate the functioning of the technology using *pretence play* [19] (PP in Fig.1). The role that the technology would take was simulated using the artefacts at hand, which promoted discussions about possible future issues. For example, in the idea called "hitting targets" (9), the group imagined the random appearance of dots in the environment, which the participants hanging from the TRX had to catch. The appearance of the dots was simulated by placing, and moving Styrofoam panels around. Playing this out allowed us to realize the need for creating some rules concerning the order of appearance of the dots, and inspired variations of the idea, such as moving the dots in the vertical plane, which was simulated by holding the panels up in the air.

Debrief

The debrief session revolved around how the TRX was a facilitator of bodily play, and the simple physical core mechanics that the TRX invited, such as hanging and swinging, from which other more complex arose. This led to a discussion about the different physical affordances of the TRX as an artefact, and the bodily impact of using it in different ways. E.g. the muscles used depending on the grip, position, and movement of the player. Moreover, we discussed unusual bodily orientations and positions with regard to the space or other participants. The TRX was seen as "an alteration mechanism to gravity", "hijacking" the usual bodily positioning, which was considered an interesting feature of the TRX as physical play mediator

Analysis

This case investigated what it means to use embodied sketching very early in the design process, as a way to explore and open up the design space. Before, we described our holistic approach to design, which considers design resources that go beyond the technology, including the socio-spatial configuration of players and other artefacts. Bodystorming is useful to physically sketch ideas that consider different arrangements of these design resources, improving our understanding of the way they intertwine with one another to form design constructs, which we called *embodied sketches*. The activity allows for a rapid arrangement and re-arrangement of resources into different embodied sketches that are tried out, keeping an eye open to how these generate interesting experiential qualities.

This activity resembles traditional brainstorming in the sense that it is done within design groups to come up with ideas on-the-fly, jointly, and includes building on one another's ideas. However, it does so while also supplying an embodied experience of each idea. Just as in brainstorming, this early form of embodied sketching is done without technology. This method relies on the evocative power of the artefacts, which the participants use to simulate the behaviour of the technology, as well as on the physical core mechanic they invite. This shifts the locus of design attention from the technology to the activity, allowing designers to think about novel ways of using different arrangements of design resources in service of the activity. The workshop does result in the creation of entire games, but on the development of more or less complex 'physical core mechanics' instead.

Example 2: Participatory embodied sketching.

This case example originates in an iteration of a design process in which we were consulting for Movinto Fun, a company that was developing a movement-based game platform, the Oriboo. The device was a ball-shaped interactive toy running on a leash that a participant would hold by its ends. It could sense the players' movements, and it produced sound and visual output (by means of its LED eyes in the front and a small display at the back). The toy was meant to encourage children to explore and expand their bodily movements' repertoire. However, the already implemented games had not met this expectation: firstly, the games encouraged an artefact-focused type of interaction [74], relying heavily on the device's small display. Secondly, the repertoire of movements that the games required was very restricted due to technological limitations [47].

At the point in the design process when this embodied sketching session was organized, we had already made a first attempt at designing a richer repertoire of games. In particular, one of the designed games focused on recognizing movement qualities and had showed potential in earlier play tests [47]. The embodied sketching workshop focused on how this game, as well as one of the original games, could be enriched by using different play patterns and socio-spatial arrangements of players. We also wanted to see how children responded to design constructs that were more or less sustained by other design resources than the technology.

Method

We organized a series of workshops, in which we first let children play freely with the mobile platform, to then play variations of the selected games. The variations made use of the implemented functions in the device, but introduced new socially agreed rules and changed the socio-spatial configuration of the players. Variations included playing one of the original games in a group sharing one Oriboo (instead of having one per child), playing a game blindfolded, or competing between groups. A detailed video analysis was done of the recorded sessions, complemented with in-between interviews where we asked for suggestions.

Fig. 2. Participatory embodied sketching. Multiplayer variation of an original Oriboo game.

Researchers modifying the games on-the-fly

Since the game variations were mostly achieved through socio-spatial and rules modifications, designers could gauge what was working for the players, and what was not, and tweak the games on-the-fly. We could add and remove obstacles in the games to level the difficulty that the game presented to the skills of the participants, or change their use of the technology and the rest of the resources by changing the rules.

For example, in a variant in which the children were blindfolded, we used the device's implemented function of emitting different sounds accordingly to the salient movement quality of the child's movement. All children were using the same function on their device, and the task we posed was to find and make groups with those children who were producing the same sound. The first time this variation was tried, the play session ended too quickly without generating the sense of surmounting a challenge. The reason was that many of the children had chosen the same sound, and since they had started the game close to one another they very quickly ended up in a joint group in the centre of the room. By changing the initial spatial placement of the children, spreading them out in the room, and by explicitly asking some children to produce a specific sound, the activity would last longer and provide a more balanced challenge. To this variation, the children reacted with signs of thrill and excitement.

However, in subsequent play sessions of this variation it turned out to be difficult to establish the right level of challenge. Sometimes, one child would happen to start out too far from others with the same sound, and therefore became clueless as to where to go. We ended up helping with clues to orient them in the "right" direction, either by physically adjusting their walking direction, or with voice cues ("I'm hearing a robot here").

Another example came from a situation where the challenge level was raised after the children had played a particular game of the mobile platform for a while. With most games, the Oriboo had implemented feedback both from its eyes and its display, although children would typically use the latter as it was easier to decode. So as soon as children seemed to have a game under control, they were instructed to turn the device around, and only use the Oriboo's eyes for feedback and guidance. This seemed to amuse the children. An unexpected effect from this change was that it inspired the children to start playing together, in front of the one another, both holding onto the device, but each one looking at one of its sides.

Children changing the rules

While these workshops were partially structured by the variations introduced by the designers, the workshop would also create social play patterns invented entirely by the children, who appropriated the implemented and suggested games to their needs and wishes. This sometimes involved a different type of holding or sharing of the technology, such as the collaborative transformation of a single-player game into a multiplayer game by finding a different way of holding the device. The children also found variations to the rules suggested by the researchers, such as when they turned a turn-taking game into a collaborative one, and suggested additional rules, like eliminating the player who had missed a move. The children also invented their own games based on basic functions of the technology, like when the children started a racing game with the technology based on the way the "Oriboo's body" moves up along the leash when it's held in a vertical position.

Movements and handling that were not accommodated by the technology

The expected way of holding of the device –from the ends of the stretched leash— was important since it had informed the movement detection algorithm of the game platform. However, during the workshops, it was clear that this would need further revisions, given the many unexpected ways of holding the device we observed. For example, children in a particular school grabbed the device from its body (the central ball), leaving the leash hanging to the sides and bringing it close to their ears. This happened during a game that primarily was based on sound output, in a school where the noise level was quite high. This way of holding the device impeded the children's use of the display as a guide, but influenced the movement recognition system.

Other common types of movements observed included children using the device as a skipping the rope, or using the leash to perform a lasso type of movement (grabbing the ends of the leash) and moving it over their head in a circular movement. All these movements, although incredibly fun for the children, did not fall within what the technology could sense, and therefore reward.

Different usage

Although it is no surprise that different target groups react in different ways to the same technology, and that different contexts in which the activity takes place also influence their reaction, it is worthwhile to understand the intricacies of such differences. In our case, we found that children at different schools found different ways of holding the device, and we were also frequently able to identify why that was the case, like in the above holding of the device close to their ear in a noisy environment. We also saw that certain implemented functions inspired different ways to hold the device in an attempt to 'trick' the device to recognize movements that were not performed. Children from different schools also varied in which core mechanics they preferred [8]. In one school in which the students characterized themselves as very competitive (during post-interviews), competitive games were seen to take most of their attention and enthusiasm. In a school where children had barely had any contact with mobile technology, they were completely engrossed by the interactivity offered by the device, paying most attention to sensorimotor types of games, in particular a game that required repetitive and highly energetic movements. Finally, in a school where children has access to loads of technology devices, and who were very much used to solitary play at home (as reported in questionnaires), they preferred single-player games.

Analysis

This case follows up on the former one in the sense that the focus is still on the interconnection between the design resources that make a particular design sketch. However, this case is less open than the previous one, as we used both implemented functionalities in a working device, and the pre-planned game variations. Still, the workshop format was kept fluent, allowing for innovative variations from both designers and the participants. In this type of embodied sketching, the designers need to act as active observers throughout the workshop, to notice emergent configurations of the social, spatial, technological and artefact resources of the setting.

The decision to leave the designs open for interventions was influenced by the ideas underlying the New Games movement [10] and Wilson's concept of "deputizing the players" [82], both in which the experience of the participants was prioritized over the consistency or stability of the design. Both recognize the entitlement of the player to "uphold, reinterpret, and negotiate the rules as provided" [82]. DeKoven [10] suggests multiple ways to incorporate such on-the-fly modifications, some of which involve the active re-configuration of the game elements by the players. While this is typically easy for players when they feel "at home", playing with their peers [21], it is less likely to happen in the context of an experiment or evaluation. We believe that the fact that the workshop organizers themselves were constantly changing the rules might have been perceived by the children as an invitation to do the same. Finally, the level of technological intervention in this form of embodied sketching is a design choice that can range from functional prototypes to mock-ups, as long as the technology is deployed as one of the many elements that sustain the play activity. This facilitates the capacity of the designer and participants to change the configurations and the rules. In cases where the technology is the only (or the major) factor responsible for sustaining the game [79], the capacity to influence the activity is lowered.

Example 3: Sensitizing designers

Our third case example was done as a follow-up on the previous workshop around the core mechanic of hanging. Where the former had been useful in creating an understanding of how artefacts of different shape and function would contribute with a range of "working" game ideas, the experience of hanging as such had been little explored. We were yet not able to fully articulate what it was in hanging that was interesting and exhilarating. So this third workshop was developed as a way to delve deeper into that particular experiential concept, and turned to a first-person perspective kind of inquiry.

Method

This workshop resonates with the goal of the embodied storming method by Schleicher et al.: *we ought to first create the experience of physical performance, not to ideate but to enact experiential awareness* [66]. The difference is that we place a higher emphasis on the context of the experience in terms of the physical space, the artefact in use, and the social interrelationships between participants, looking into how these interrelated with the first person experience.

The workshop was done in the form of an AntiGravity (AG) Fundamentals class. AntiGravity Fitness is a pragmatic somaesthetic discipline that comprises different branches or techniques. All of them share a core set of principles and a philosophy, and the use of a physical artefact, the hammock, used in all poses and movements. Many of these involved the participants hanging from the hammock, either in a vertical upright position, or in an inversion with the head towards the floor. Six design researchers were involved. Of those, four are co-authors of this paper, one of which is also a certified AG Fitness instructor who acted as a facilitator and instructed the rest. After the class, we held a brainstorming session with the goal of uncovering interesting experiential qualities and concepts that arose from the experience, which we wanted to relate with elements that sustained the activity, including spatial and social aspects, as well as the hammock itself.

Fig. 3. Sensitizing designers in an AntiGravity class.

An abridge of the experience

The AG class ran as usual AG beginners classes do. Although the class was planned in advance, the instructor changed the poses, the time spent on them, and the feedback and cueing strategy according to her perception of the skills and reactions of the participants. In the following, we illustrate this session with snippets from their impressions collected a few days after the class. *I was so surprised that I was actually able to perform the movements. I watched myself in the mirror and I felt everything was so aesthetically pleasant, my own movements just like the instructor's movements. That felt really empowering.* Another participant recollected the experience as *All excitement and joy*, and elaborated: *It's almost like experiencing flying, even though you know it is not real. It also had that feeling of uncertainty, when you are not sure if you are doing it right or not. You constantly ask and challenge yourself should I do it or should I wait to get the right instruction? It's like always to want more, and pushing forward.*

Debriefing

The analysis of the debriefing of the session resulted in several themes that were related to each other. A salient theme related to the *felt experience* of the activity: AG was empowering in the sense that allowed us to perform movements that we thought we would not be able to. Moreover, it made us reflect on the risk and the safety issues in relation to the practice and ourselves. We also reflected on our abilities and how they relate to the experience of belonging, feeling *in* the activity if we were able to perform an exercise, whereas *out* of it if we could not keep up. This was related to *social aspect* of the activity: although some were self-conscious about their bodies and abilities, we reached out for social support from the rest of the participants and the instructor while performing, wither it was for guidance or validation. When we did not perform an exercise correctly, we felt separated from the rest of the group that could.

Another theme was the *aesthetic component* of the activity. We perceived AG as a deeply aesthetic experience, which we related to the sensed flow of movements, the perception of ourselves and others in synchrony. The soft, mouldable, and yet firm material of the hammock also contributed, and how we could move in it, with it, despite of it, and because of it. It was apparent how the hammock could be shaped, but as much as how it could shape in turn the whole activity and our bodies, triggering bodily reactions, like sweat or a flush in the face, or how it trapped and compressed parts of our bodies, while leaving others free.

Analysis

This case example focuses on the use of a shared lived experience to sensitize designers to salient attributes of their in-the-moment, felt experience, which can then be used in design. In particular, we harnessed an "unusual" type of bodily activity to elicit creative thinking. In comparison with our other examples, this one is different in that it separates the act of feeling from the actual design activity. The separation was in part a necessity, due to the relative complexity of the movements as such, such as in how the feet must lock around the hammock to be able to safely hang upside down. The second motivation was our experience from the first workshop, which was successful in developing ideas but less successful in creating a good understanding of the felt experience of hanging; We saw a need to separate sensitization from ideation to allow ourselves to focus and access the quite unusual bodily experience of hanging.

The use of the hammocks as a sensitizing aid resonates with previous works in which the concept of *defamiliarization* is used as a tool to trigger creativity. Djajadiningrat et al. [13] describe the method of *interaction relabelling*, where a mechanical artefact is used to evoke possible ways of handling and interacting with a future design in an entirely unforeseen manner –in their paper, they used a toy gun to think about how to interact with an appointment management system. More closely related to our approach is Wilde's method of defamiliarization, in which she encouraged participants to move in different ways than usual [80]. But by focusing on deeply accessing the bodily experience, we take a more pre-ontological stance [49]. For this we use a practice within practical somaesthetics to allow us to sense certain qualities that have potential, and find ways to articulate these. The joint post-processing session was in this sense very important, as it allowed us to abstract from our experiences into aspects that were generalizable as well as shared between us. Finally, these were picked up upon in the design debriefing and subsequent analysis. It is important to highlight the role of the facilitator in this case example. The facilitator helped the rest to articulate, share, and structure their experiences into something that provided a useful context for design.

REFLECTIONS

The three cases illustrate three different ways to use embodied sketching in practice, for different purposes, and with different participants involved: designers/researchers in case 1, and 3, and also end users in case 2. Then, although all three instantiations are to be used early in the design process, they might fit best at different points, given their requirements. For example, while cases 1 and 3 can happen before any other design activity, case 2 require certain design ideas in place, more or less established.

During our work, we have used a bodystorming sessions (case 1) early in design projects, to invite designers to play with design resources and create novel play activity concepts. Once these start to manifest in designed rules over players, artefacts, and technological systems, an embodied sketch emerges, which in turn can inspire other modes of engagement with it. This process is clearly visible in the first case, but emerges also in the participatory setting (case 2), where participants understood and followed, but also tweaked the game structures previously designed by us, and created their own. Maintaining an open and playful approach to subsequent explorations allows us to capture, evaluate and build upon emergent ideas throughout a design project.

The embodied sketching techniques work well together; bodystorming (case 1) and participatory design (case 2) have been used in consecutive workshops in the same design project. Sensitizing workshops (case 3) work well to prepare for bodystorming (case 1), and both should ideally be used at an early stage of a design project. While the bodystorming method succeeds in eliciting design ideas, focusing on physical core mechanics and foregrounding the social aspect of play, it is less sensitive to the felt experience. This was apparent from the discussion notes gathered from the debrief after the workshop, which sometimes would mention experiential qualities but never fully explored them, nor their implications for design. This contrasts with the sensitizing designers workshop, where we were able to access and articulate them in a rich manner.

We argue that such articulation is important to inform designs so that that are in line with, and supportive of the explored felt experience. A related example can be found in [30], in which the group of designers were involved in the practice of Feldenkrais, inspired in which, and for which, they designed.

Five characterizing and distinguishing principles

Our embodied sketching design practice is similar to other embodied ideation methods presented in the background of this paper in that they all use an embodied approach to design, given that they harness the situated physical, and social context for creating and gauging design ideas. However, the goal of embodied sketching, the detailed method, and the resources used, are different.

Five principles characterize and differentiate embodied sketching from other embodied ideation methods: i) an activity-centred embodied approach to ideation, ii) the use of the complete setting as a design resource, iii) the physical and hands-on engagement of designers with a non-scripted activity, iv) the use of movement and play both as method and goal, and v) the facilitation of a sensitizing and design conducive space.

Embodied sketching is activity-centred (i), in that its goal is to design enjoyable social and physical activities that are technologically-supported. By contrast, other embodied approaches to stimulate creativity are artefact-/technology-/service- centred, so that the design activity revolves around designing, prototyping and even testing some*thing* concrete (e.g. Schleicher et al.'s example of designing a new food order system for a cafe). A second important difference is that in embodied sketching, contextual elements are used as design resources, while other embodied methods use context as a backdrop against which to evaluate design ideas (ii). In addition, although they all are to be used early in the design process, previous methods emphasize early prototype testing (bodystorming, use-case theatre, strong prototyping). In contrast, we focus on initial explorative ideation phases as a way to open up the design space (v) at the experiential level.

For this, we use physical and playful engagement (iv), which we argue to be particularly useful, as it allows designers to engage in a mind-set conducive of exploration and creativity. This is unique to our proposal; others use performative techniques (e.g. acting roles in use-case theatre), or fictional scenarios (e.g. strong prototyping relies on building a high-fi replica of the environment to test mock-ups under different controlled environmental variables, and use-case theatre requires of actors as well as less accurate environment modelling to understand people's possible accommodation and reaction to a particular problem setting and solution). We suggest to use play and playfulness as the primary mode of engagement in all versions of embodied sketching. The advantage of promoting play lies in its transformative and creative power, very similar to those of improvisational theatre but more appropriate for physical and embodied creative activities. But it is also important to realize that we used play to also *design* play and games. This made it easy for our participants to adopt a playful approach to their involvement.

FINAL COMMENTS

In this paper, we have proposed *embodied sketching* to support idea generation when designing for bodily activities in co-located settings where the spatial and physical layout of the environment plays an important role.

While a rigorous comparison between design practices would not be feasible as the goals, method, and outcomes of previous methods and ours are very different, we can reflect upon our results in the light of documented assessments of previous ideation methods. The assessment we have found is Oulasvirta et al.'s, who questioned their success since they did not find that ideas from their embodied methods were more sensitive to the "physical, social or interactional details" compared to those coming from traditional brainstorming methods, and that acting was seen as an "unnecessary factor frustrating participants" [57:7]. We argue that it is harder to motivate and engage with a physical activity during the ideation processes when it appears to be just an aftereffect of the ideation method (e.g. enacting a role), detached from the design goals/outcome. This is remarkably different in embodied sketching, where the activity that participants engage with is meaningful, as it is very close to the final design outcome: you play and move together with your peers to design for play and movement-based social activities (iv).

An important aspect for future work is how to encourage a playful mode of engagement in non-playful design contexts, since playful and physical engagement might pose a challenge for certain participants and in certain design domains. We didn't experience such difficulties in the design cases presented in this paper, but they all belong to a very particular design domain (physical play). Strategies for design projects outside this domain remain as very relevant future work, and we are currently working towards developing them.

Another point to consider for future work is to study the impact that our design practices have on both the participants and the outcome of ideation process, which we can only do by exposing our practices to multiple design contexts.

Finally, we want to conclude by highlighting a particular feature of our embodied sketches: Physical activity is the defining and critical aspect of our embodied sketching practice. It is the in-the-moment activity that shapes both the opportunities for uncovering and scrutinizing the felt experience, and the fluid and flexible space for creativity, innovation, and change. This means that the sketches obtained are not persistent but *ephemeral*, shaped in the moment and then gone. A critical issue for embodied interaction concerns how to enable participants to remember, document, and articulate these ephemeral sketches. In our case examples, this was primarily done through extensive video documentation. All our sessions were filmed, often from multiple directions with multiple cameras. Participants were also asked to talk about their experience right after the embodied sketching session, so as to capture their thoughts and experiences as rapidly and clearly as possible. It remains as future work to develop ways of packaging the observed design features of the ephemeral sketches in a way that becomes readily available to the designers.

ACKNOWLEDGMENTS

Many people have made this paper possible. First, the colleagues who participated in our workshops: Jon Back, Mareike Glöss, Floyd Mueller, Robert Cercós, Jayden Garner, William Goddard, and Harrison Smith, and the children from Ullens (Kathmandu), Rudrayanee (Kathmandu), Sophia (Stockholm), and Rico Cejudo (Seville) schools. Special thanks to those who facilitated our workshops: Medin Lamichhane (Ullens), Babu Ram Thapa (Rudrayanee), Louise Öhnfeldt (Sophia), Lola Segura (Rico Cejudo), and Yoram Chisik. Also to Jessica Söderlund, who lend us her fitness studio Yogaire for our sensitizing workshop. Thanks to our helpers Carlos Duarte, Adrián Onco, Luis Maqueda, Mathias Jonsson, and to Jin Moen, who shipped us worldwide with a bunch of Oriboos. Thanks to the CHI reviewers, who provided very helpful comments, which have helped polish our contributions, and to Donny McMillan who proofread this text. Part of the research was made possible by a grant from the Swedish Governmental Agency for Innovation Systems (VINNOVA) to the Mobile Life Vinn Excellence Center.

REFERENCES

1. Jeffrey Bardzell. 2009. Interaction Criticism and Aesthetics. In *Proceedings of the SIGCHI Conference on Human Factors in Computing Systems* (CHI '09), 2357–2366. http://doi.org/10.1145/1518701.1519063
2. Steve Benford, Holger Schnädelbach, Boriana Koleva, et al. 2005. Expected, Sensed, and Desired: A Framework for Designing Sensing-based Interaction. *ACM Trans. Comput.-Hum. Interact.* 12, 1: 3–30. http://doi.org/10.1145/1057237.1057239
3. Julian Bleecker. 2009. Design Fiction: A Short Essay on Design, Science, Fact and Fiction. *Near Future Laboratory*. Retrieved September 25, 2015 from http://blog.nearfuturelaboratory.com/2009/03/17/design-fiction-a-short-essay-on-design-science-fact-and-fiction/
4. Mark Blythe. 2014. The Hitchhiker's Guide to Ubicomp: Using Techniques from Literary and Critical Theory to Reframe Scientific Agendas. *Personal Ubiquitous Comput.* 18, 4: 795–808. http://doi.org/10.1007/s00779-013-0679-6
5. Jacob Buur and Rosa Torguet. 2013. Ethnographic findings in the organizational theatre. *Ethnographic Praxis in Industry* 1: 143–160. http://doi.org/10.1111/j.1559-8918.2013.00013.x
6. Bill Buxton. 2007. *Sketching User Experiences: Getting the Design Right and the Right Design.* Morgan Kaufmann Publishers Inc., San Francisco, CA, USA.
7. Diane Carr, Gareth Schott, Andrew Burn, and David Buckingham. 2004. Doing game studies: A multi-method approach to the study of textuality, interactivity and narrative space. *Media International Australia* 110: 19–30.
8. Yoram I. Chisik, Alissa N. Antle, Brian Birtles, Elena Márquez Segura, and Cristina Sylla. 2014. The Kathmandu Kids Entertainment Workshops. In *Entertaining the Whole World*, Adrian David Cheok, Anton Nijholt and Teresa Romão (eds.). Springer London, 5–21.
9. Yvonne A. W. De Kort and Wijnand A. Ijsselsteijn. 2008. People, Places, and Play: Player Experience in a Socio-spatial Context. *Computers in Entertainment.* 6, 2: 18:1–11. http://doi.org/10.1145/1371216.1371221
10. Bernard De Koven. Coliberation. *DeepFUN.* Retrieved September 25, 2015 from http://www.deepfun.com/coliberation/
11. Sebastian Deterding. 2009. The Game Frame: Systemizing a Goffmanian Approach to Video Game Theory. *Digital Games Research Association.*
12. Sebastian Deterding. 2011. Meaningful Play. Getting »Gamification« Right. In *Google Tech Talk.* Retrieved December 18, 2015 from http://www.slideshare.net/dings/meaningful-play-getting-gamification-right
13. J. P. Djajadiningrat, W. W. Gaver, and J. W. Frens. 2000. Interaction Relabelling and Extreme Characters: Methods for Exploring Aesthetic Interactions. In *Proceedings of the 3rd Conference on Designing Interactive Systems: Processes, Practices, Methods, and Techniques* (DIS 00), 66–71. http://doi.org/10.1145/347642.347664
14. Tom Djajadiningrat, Stephan Wensveen, Joep Frens, and Kees Overbeeke. 2004. Tangible Products: Redressing the Balance Between Appearance and Action. *Personal Ubiquitous Comput.* 8, 5: 294–309. http://doi.org/10.1007/s00779-004-0293-8.
15. Andrei Dobra. Great Games Are Needed to Make PlayStation Move Popular, Sony Admits. In *Softpedia.* Retrieved June 7, 2015 from http://news.softpedia.com/news/Great-Games-Are-Needed-to-Make-PlayStation-Move-Popular-Sony-Admits-257838.shtml
16. Paul Dourish. 2001. *Where the Action Is: The Foundations of Embodied Interaction*. The MIT Press, Cambridge, Mass.
17. Nicolas Ducheneaut, Nicholas Yee, Eric Nickell, and Robert J. Moore. 2006. "Alone Together?": Exploring the Social Dynamics of Massively Multiplayer Online Games. In *Proceedings of the SIGCHI Conference on Human Factors in Computing Systems* (CHI '06), 407–416. http://doi.org/10.1145/1124772.1124834.
18. Daniel Fallman and Erik Stolterman. 2010. Establishing Criteria of Rigor and Relevance in Interaction Design Research. In *Proceedings of the 2010 International Conference on The Interaction Design*, (Create '10), Oli Mival, John Bonner, Michael Smyth, and Shaleph O'Neill (eds.). British Computer Society, Swinton, UK, 58-63.
19. Greta G. Fein. 1981. Pretend Play in Childhood: An Integrative Review. *Child Development* 52, 4: 1095–1118. http://doi.org/10.2307/1129497
20. James Fogarty, Jodi Forlizzi, and Scott E. Hudson. 2001. Aesthetic Information Collages: Generating Decorative Displays That Contain Information. in *Proceedings of the 14th Annual ACM Symposium on User Interface Software and Technology* (UIST '01), 141–150. http://doi.org/10.1145/502348.502369
21. Tracy Fullerton. 2008. *Game Design Workshop: A Playcentric Approach to Creating Innovative Games*. Morgan Kaufmann, Amsterdam; Boston.
22. Brian Gajadhar, Yvonne de Kort, and Wijnand IJsselsteijn. 2008. Influence of Social Setting on Player Experience of Digital Games. In *CHI'08 Extended Abstracts on Human Factors in Computing Systems* (CHI EA '08), 3099–3104. http://doi.org/10.1145/1358628.1358814
23. Bill Gaver. 2002. Designing for Homo Ludens. *I3 Magazine 12*. Retrieved January 24, 2016 from https://www.gold.ac.uk/media/migrated/media/goldsmiths/departments/researchcentres/interactionresearchstudio/pdf/27gaver.ludens.02.pdf
24. Elizabeth Gerber. 2007. Improvisation Principles and Techniques for Design. In *Proceedings of the SIGCHI*

Conference on Human Factors in Computing Systems (CHI '07), 1069–1072. http://doi.org/10.1145/1240624.1240786
25. Elizabeth Gerber. 2009. Using Improvisation to Enhance the Effectiveness of Brainstorming. In *Proceedings of the SIGCHI Conference on Human Factors in Computing Systems* (CHI ' 09), 97–104. http://doi.org/10.1145/1518701.1518718
26. Erving Goffman. 1961. Fun in Games. *Encounters: Two studies in the sociology of interaction*. Bobbs-Merrill, Oxford, England, 15 – 81.
27. Dave Gray, Sunni Brown, and James Macanufo. 2010. *Gamestorming: A Playbook for Innovators, Rulebreakers, and Changemakers*. O'Reilly Media Inc., Sebastopol, CA, USA.
28. Marc Hassenzahl. 2008. The Interplay of Beauty, Goodness, and Usability in Interactive Products. *Hum.-Comput. Interact.* 19, 4: 319–349. http://doi.org/10.1207/s15327051hci1904_2
29. Kristina Höök. 2010. Transferring Qualities from Horseback Riding to Design. *Proceedings of the 6th Nordic Conference on Human-Computer Interaction: Extending Boundaries* (NordiCHI '10), ACM, 226–235. http://doi.org/10.1145/1868914.1868943
30. Kristina Höök, Anna Ståhl, Martin Jonsson, Johanna Mercurio, Anna Karlsson, and Eva-Carin Banka Johnson. 2015. Somaesthetic Design. *Interactions* 22, 4: 26–33. http://doi.org/10.1145/2770888
31. Johan Huizinga. 1971. *Homo Ludens: A Study of the Play-Element in Culture*. Beacon Press, Boston.
32. Caroline Hummels, Kees C. Overbeeke, and Sietske Klooster. 2007. Move to Get Moved: A Search for Methods, Tools and Knowledge to Design for Expressive and Rich Movement-based Interaction. *Personal Ubiquitous Comput.* 11, 8: 677–690. http://doi.org/10.1007/s00779-006-0135-y
33. Giulio Iacucci, Carlo Iacucci, and Kari Kuutti. 2002. Imagining and Experiencing in Design, the Role of Performances. *Proceedings of the Second Nordic Conference on Human-computer Interaction* (NordiCHI '02), 167–176. http://doi.org/10.1145/572020.572040
34. Giulio Iacucci and Kari Kuutti. 2002. Everyday Life as a Stage in Creating and Performing Scenarios for Wireless Devices. *Personal Ubiquitous Comput.* 6, 4: 299–306. http://doi.org/10.1007/s007790200031
35. Katherine Isbister and Kaho Abe. 2015. Costumes As Game Controllers: An Exploration of Wearables to Suit Social Play. *Proceedings of the Ninth International Conference on Tangible, Embedded, and Embodied Interaction* (TEI '15), 691–696. http://doi.org/10.1145/2677199.2688813
36. Katherine Isbister, Rahul Rao, Ulf Schwekendiek, Elizabeth Hayward, and Jessamyn Lidasan. 2011. Is More Movement Better?: A Controlled Comparison of Movement-based Games. *Proceedings of the 6th International Conference on Foundations of Digital Games* (FDG ' 11), 331–333. http://doi.org/10.1145/2159365.2159429
37. Esther Jakobs, Antony S. R. Manstead, and Agneta H. Fischer. 1996. Social context and the experience of emotion. *Journal of Nonverbal Behavior* 20, 2: 123–142. http://doi.org/10.1007/BF02253073
38. Wonjun Lee, Youn-kyung Lim, and Richard Shusterman. 2014. Practicing Somaesthetics: Exploring Its Impact on Interactive Product Design Ideation. *Proceedings of the 2014 Conference on Designing Interactive Systems* (DIS '14), 1055–1064. http://doi.org/10.1145/2598510.2598561
39. Lian Loke and George Poonkhin Khut. 2011. Surging Verticality: An Experience of Balance. *Proceedings of the Fifth International Conference on Tangible, Embedded, and Embodied Interaction* (TEI ' 11), 237–240. http://doi.org/10.1145/1935701.1935747
40. Lian Loke, Astrid T. Larssen, Toni Robertson, and Jenny Edwards. 2007. Understanding Movement for Interaction Design: Frameworks and Approaches. *Personal Ubiquitous Comput.* 11, 8: 691–701. http://doi.org/10.1007/s00779-006-0132-1
41. Lian Loke and Toni Robertson. 2011. The Lived Body in Design: Mapping the Terrain. In *Proceedings of the 23rd Australian Computer-Human Interaction Conference* (OzCHI '11), 181–184. http://doi.org/10.1145/2071536.2071565
42. Lian Loke and Toni Robertson. 2013. Moving and Making Strange: An Embodied Approach to Movement-based Interaction Design. *ACM Trans. Comput.-Hum. Interact.* 20, 1: 7:1–7:25. http://doi.org/10.1145/2442106.2442113
43. Catriona Macaulay, Giulio Jacucci, Shaleph O'Neill, Tomi Kankaineen, and Morna Simpson. 2006. Editorial: The Emerging Roles of Performance Within HCI and Interaction Design. *Interact. Comput.* 18, 5: 942–955. http://doi.org/10.1016/j.intcom.2006.07.001
44. Carsten Magerkurth, Timo Engelke, and Maral Memisoglu. 2004. Augmenting the Virtual Domain with Physical and Social Elements: Towards a Paradigm Shift in Computer Entertainment Technology. *Comput. Entertain.* 2, 4: 12–12. http://doi.org/10.1145/1037851.1037870
45. Antony Stephen Reid Manstead. 2005. The social dimension of emotion. *The Psychologist* 18, 8: 484–487.
46. Elena Márquez Segura and Katherine Isbister. 2015. Enabling Co-Located Physical Social Play: A Framework for Design and Evaluation. In *Game User Experience Evaluation*, Regina Bernhaupt (ed.). Springer International Publishing, 209–238.
47. Elena Márquez Segura, Annika Waern, Jin Moen, and Carolina Johansson. 2013. The Design Space of Body Games: Technological, Physical, and Social Design. In In *Proceedings of the SIGCHI Conference on Human Factors in Computing Systems* (CHI '13), 3365–3374. http://doi.org/10.1145/2470654.2466461

48. Helena M. Mentis, Kristina Höök, Florian Mueller, Katherine Isbister, George Poonkhin Khut, and Toni Robertson. 2014. Designing for the Experiential Body. In *CHI '14 Extended Abstracts on Human Factors in Computing Systems* (CHI EA '14), 1069–1074. http://doi.org/10.1145/2559206.2579402
49. Maurice Merleau-Ponty. 2002. *Phenomenology of Perception*. Psychology Press.
50. Angela Moscaritolo. Microsoft: Xbox One Sales Double After Dropping Kinect. *PCMAG*. Retrieved June 7, 2015 from http://www.pcmag.com/article2/0,2817,2461023,00.asp
51. Florian Mueller, Stefan Agamanolis, and Rosalind Picard. 2003. Exertion Interfaces: Sports over a Distance for Social Bonding and Fun. In *Proceedings of the SIGCHI Conference on Human Factors in Computing Systems* (CHI '03), 561–568. http://doi.org/10.1145/642611.642709
52. Florian Mueller, Cagdas Toprak, Eberhard Graether, Wouter Walmink, Bert Bongers, and Elise van den Hoven. 2012. Hanging off a Bar. In *CHI '12 Extended Abstracts on Human Factors in Computing Systems* (CHI EA '12), 1055–1058. http://doi.org/10.1145/2212776.2212384
53. A. F. Newell, M. E. Morgan, P. Gregor, and A. Carmichael. 2006. Theatre As an Intermediary Between Users and CHI Designers. In *CHI '06 Extended Abstracts on Human Factors in Computing Systems* (CHI EA ' 06), 111–116. http://doi.org/10.1145/1125451.1125479
54. Lene Nielsen. 2002. From User to Character: An Investigation into User-descriptions in Scenarios. In *Proceedings of the 4th Conference on Designing Interactive Systems: Processes, Practices, Methods, and Techniques* (DIS '02), 99–104. http://doi.org/10.1145/778712.778729
55. Kenton O'hara, Richard Harper, Helena Mentis, Abigail Sellen, and Alex Taylor. 2013. On the Naturalness of Touchless: Putting the "Interaction" Back into NUI. *ACM Trans. Comput.-Hum. Interact.* 20, 1: 5:1–5:25. http://doi.org/10.1145/2442106.2442111
56. Alex F. Osborn and Lee Hastings Bristol. 1979. *Applied Imagination: Principles and Procedures of Creative Thinking*. Charles Scribner's Sons, New York.
57. Antti Oulasvirta, Esko Kurvinen, and Tomi Kankainen. 2003. Understanding Contexts by Being There: Case Studies in Bodystorming. *Personal Ubiquitous Comput.* 7, 2: 125–134. http://doi.org/10.1007/s00779-003-0238-7
58. Marianne Graves Petersen, Ole Sejer Iversen, Peter Gall Krogh, and Martin Ludvigsen. 2004. Aesthetic Interaction: A Pragmatist's Aesthetics of Interactive Systems. In *Proceedings of the 5th Conference on Designing Interactive Systems: Processes, Practices, Methods, and Techniques* (DIS '04), 269–276. http://doi.org/10.1145/1013115.1013153
59. Cindy Poremba. 2007. Critical Potential on the Brink of the Magic Circle. Retrieved January 24, 2016 from http://www.digra.org/wp-content/uploads/digital-library/07311.42117.pdf
60. Jenny Preece, Yvonne Rogers, and Helen Sharp. 2015. *Interaction Design: Beyond Human-Computer Interaction*. John Wiley & Sons.
61. Niklas Ravaja, Timo Saari, Marko Turpeinen, Jari Laarni, Mikko Salminen, and Matias Kivikangas. 2006. Spatial Presence and Emotions During Video Game Playing: Does It Matter with Whom You Play? *Presence: Teleoper. Virtual Environ.* 15, 4: 381–392. http://doi.org/10.1162/pres.15.4.381
62. Katie Salen and Eric Zimmerman. 2003. *Rules of Play: Game Design Fundamentals*. The MIT Press, Cambridge, Mass.
63. Thecla Schiphorst. 2007. Really, Really Small: The Palpability of the Invisible. In *Proceedings of the 6th ACM SIGCHI Conference on Creativity & Cognition* (C&C '07), 7–16. http://doi.org/10.1145/1254960.1254962
64. Thecla Schiphorst. 2009. Soft(N): Toward a Somaesthetics of Touch. In *CHI '09 Extended Abstracts on Human Factors in Computing Systems* (CHI EA '09), 2427–2438. http://doi.org/10.1145/1520340.1520345
65. Thecla Schiphorst. 2011. Self-evidence: applying somatic connoisseurship to experience design. *CHI '11 Extended Abstracts on Human Factors in Computing Systems* (CHI EA '11), 145–160. http://doi.org/10.1145/1979742.1979640
66. Dennis Schleicher, Peter Jones, and Oksana Kachur. 2010. Bodystorming As Embodied Designing. *Interactions* 17, 6: 47–51. http://doi.org/10.1145/1865245.1865256
67. Richard Shusterman. 2008. *Body Consciousness: A Philosophy of Mindfulness and Somaesthetics*. Cambridge University Press, Cambridge ; New York.
68. Richard Shusterman. 2013. Somaesthetics. *The Encyclopedia of Human-Computer Interaction, 2nd Ed.* Retrieved September 25, 2015 from https://www.interaction-design.org/literature/book/the-encyclopedia-of-human-computer-interaction-2nd-ed/somaesthetics
69. Bart Simon. 2009. *Wii are Out of Control: Bodies, Game Screens and the Production of Gestural Excess*. Social Science Research Network, Rochester, NY. Retrieved June 7, 2015 from http://papers.ssrn.com/abstract=1354043
70. Dag Svanaes. 2013. Interaction Design for and with the Lived Body: Some Implications of Merleau-ponty's Phenomenology. *ACM Trans. Comput.-Hum. Interact.* 20, 1: 8:1–8:30. http://doi.org/10.1145/2442106.2442114

71. Joe Svetlik. 2012. Sony admits selection of PS Move games "not so great." *CNET*. Retrieved June 7, 2015 from http://www.cnet.com/news/sony-admits-selection-of-ps-move-games-not-so-great/
72. Christine Szentgyorgyi, Michael Terry, and Edward Lank. 2008. Renegade Gaming: Practices Surrounding Social Use of the Nintendo DS Handheld Gaming System. In *Proceedings of the SIGCHI Conference on Human Factors in Computing Systems* (CHI '08), 1463–1472. http://doi.org/10.1145/1357054.1357283
73. Joshua Tanenbaum and Karen Tanenbaum. 2015. Envisioning the Future of Wearable Play: Conceptual Models for Props and Costumes as Game Controllers. In Proceedings of the 10th International Conference on the Foundations of Digital Games (FDG '15).
74. Jakob Tholander and Carolina Johansson. 2010. Design Qualities for Whole Body Interaction: Learning from Golf, Skateboarding and BodyBugging. In *Proceedings of the 6th Nordic Conference on Human-Computer Interaction: Extending Boundaries* (NordiCHI '10), 493–502. http://doi.org/10.1145/1868914.1868970
75. TRX. 2016. Retrieved January 24, 2016 from https://www.trxtraining.com/
76. Sherry Turkle. 2012. *Alone Together: Why We Expect More from Technology and Less from Each Other*. Basic Books, New York, NY.
77. John Vines, Tess Denman-Cleaver, Paul Dunphy, Peter Wright, and Patrick Olivier. 2014. Experience Design Theatre: Exploring the Role of Live Theatre in Scaffolding Design Dialogues. In *Proceedings of the SIGCHI Conference on Human Factors in Computing Systems* (CHI '14), 683–692. http://doi.org/10.1145/2556288.2556960
78. Amy Voida and Saul Greenberg. 2009. Wii All Play: The Console Game As a Computational Meeting Place. In *Proceedings of the SIGCHI Conference on Human Factors in Computing Systems* (CHI '09), 1559–1568. http://doi.org/10.1145/1518701.1518940
79. Annika Waern. 2009. Information Technology in Pervasive Games. In *Pervasive Games*, Markus Montola, Jaakko Stenros and Annika Waern (eds.). Morgan Kaufmann, Boston, 163–174.
80. Danielle Wilde. 2008. The Hipdiskettes: Learning (Through) Wearables. *Proceedings of the 20th Australasian Conference on Computer-Human Interaction: Designing for Habitus and Habitat* (OzCHI '08), 259–262. http://doi.org/10.1145/1517744.1517771
81. Danielle Wilde, Thecla Schiphorst, and Sietske Klooster. 2011. Move to Design/Design to Move: A Conversation About Designing for the Body. *Interactions* 18, 4: 22–27. http://doi.org/10.1145/1978822.1978828
82. Douglas Wilson. 2011. Brutally Unfair Tactics Totally OK Now: On Self-Effacing Games and Unachievements. *Game Studies* 11, 1. Retrieved September 25, 2015 from http://gamestudies.org/1101/articles/wilson

"I don't want to wear a screen": Probing Perceptions of and Possibilities for Dynamic Displays on Clothing

Laura Devendorf[1], Joanne Lo[1], Noura Howell[1], Jung Lin Lee[1], Nan-Wei Gong[2], M. Emre Karagozler[2], Shiho Fukuhara[2], Ivan Poupyrev[2], Eric Paulos[1], Kimiko Ryokai[1]

[1] UC Berkeley
Berkeley, CA, USA
{ldevendorf, jlo, noura, dorislee, paulos, kimiko}@berkeley.edu

[2] Google ATAP
Mountain View, CA, USA
{ngong, karagozler, shihof, ipoupyrev}@google.com

ABSTRACT
This paper explores the role dynamic textile displays play in relation to personal style: What does it mean to wear computationally responsive clothing and why would one be motivated to do so? We developed a novel textile display technology, called *Ebb*, and created several woven and crochet fabric swatches that explored clothing-specific design possibilities. We engaged fashion designers and non-designers in imagining how Ebb would integrate into their design practice or personal style of dressing. Participants evaluated the appeal and utility of clothing-based displays according to a very different set of criteria than traditional screen-based computational displays. Specifically, the slowness, low-resolution, and volatility of Ebb tended to be seen as assets as opposed to technical limitations in the context of personal style. Additionally, participants envisioned various ways that ambiguous, ambient, and abstract displays of information could prompt new experiences in their everyday lives. Our paper details the complex relationships between display and personal style and offers a new design metaphor and extension of Gaver et al.'s original descriptions of ambiguity in order to guide the design of clothing-based displays for everyday life.

Author Keywords
Clothing-based display; dynamic textiles; style; ambiguity; weaving; crochet;

ACM Classification Keywords
H.5.m. Information interfaces and presentation (e.g., HCI): Miscellaneous.

INTRODUCTION
When people choose what to wear, they are making conscious and unconscious choices about how they want to be in the world, what they want to accomplish, and how they want to be perceived by others. These choices, which we use the term "style" to define, are driven by personal and social considerations. They are personal in the sense that people use them to craft their identities. They are social in the sense that they are crafted in relation to a broader set of cultural assumptions [13]. Cultural theorist Dick Hebdige describes style as "a visible construction, a loaded choice. It directs attention to itself; it gives itself to be read" [17]. In Hebdige's view, every detail in a garment, like the choice of a particular collar or cuff, does discursive work, speaking on behalf of the wearer. The combinations people create with their clothes signal complex identifications with particular groups, make particular experiences more or less available, and shape the way people relate to their social worlds more broadly [13,17]. As technology becomes increasingly wearable, leaving the domain of smart accessories and entering the very fabric of our clothing, it is important for HCI to consider the personal meanings and social functions technological displays foster within personal style.

In order to probe these meanings, we developed a novel textile display technology, called *Ebb*, and asked fashion designers and non-designers to describe how they might (or might not) integrate it into their practice or personal style (Figure 1). Ebb emerged from creative and technical collaboration with Google Jacquard [19,41], which was developing materials for weaving electrical conductivity into textiles at scale. The core technology of Ebb consists of conductive threads individually coated with thermochromic

Figure 1: a) Ebb consists of conductive thread coated with thermochromic paint. b, c) We created several swatches showcasing color-changing effects using weaving and crochet techniques. d) We invited fashion designers and non-designers to see and feel the swatches in order to ground a conversation about potential meanings of color-changing textiles in their design practice or personal style.

CHI'16, May 07-12, 2016, San Jose, CA, USA
ACM 978-1-4503-3362-7/16/05.
http://dx.doi.org/10.1145/2858036.2858192

paint. When electricity is supplied to the threads, they heat up and gradually change color over a few seconds. We named the system "Ebb" because the color change conjured images of the ebb and flow of the tides rather than the rapid changes of traditional screen based media. We created seven woven and crochet swatches with Ebb to explore its unique technical and aesthetic capabilities.

Participants' impressions of our fabric swatches revealed a desire for clothing-based displays to function differently than smart phones or watch-based displays. Namely, participants did not want to wear "screens" on their clothing and felt that the slowness, low-resolution, and rich texture of the swatches created with Ebb fit better with their personal sense of style. Additionally, they described scenarios in which abstract, ambient, and ambiguous representations of information on clothing could provoke intrigue, playful and serendipitous social interactions, calming experiences of personal information, or ironic commentaries on cultures of technology.

Reflecting on our findings, we contribute a new design metaphor of the textile display as an artistic canvas rather than a screen, and extend Gaver et al.'s original description of ambiguity within the context of clothing based displays. Both contributions can be engaged to guide the design of future clothing-based displays that seek to respect the complex, multi-layered, and even contradictory nature of expressing oneself through personal style.

MOTIVATION AND RELATED WORK

A growing interest in wearable technology and quantified self among researchers and everyday people has given rise to numerous explorations at the intersection of fashion and technology. Within consumer markets, the popularity of accessories like Nike's Fitbit or smart watches signals a desire to integrate technology within one's personal style of dress. Our paper joins existing work exploring *clothing* as a site for computational display. Existing work in this space explores provocative visions where garments react to the wearer's environment [39], emotional state [10,34], or physiology [16]. Others have explored how clothing-based displays can be used to enhance social interactions [22], motivate fitness behaviors [25], or give rise to increased environmental awareness [24].

Our work takes a more general approach. Rather than exploring a particular instantiation or context-dependent use of clothing-based displays, we produced several clothing-based display options in order to foster a conversation with individuals about how they envision the technology functioning within their daily life, (i.e., what data do they display, what representations do they use, how do they see other people engaging with them?). Davis et al. [8] use a similar approach to explore the emotional characteristics of physical/visual textures in fabrics. We investigate meaning through a lens of style, rather than emotion, to explore a wider range of ways for technology to function meaningfully within one's personal style.

Thermochromic Display Technologies

While a wide variety of technologies have been engaged to imbue textiles with display capabilities [3–6,30,32,34,36], our work joins others that use thermochromic pigments to create non-emissive textile displays [4,22,23,27,29,32]. We chose to work with thermochromic pigments because of the aesthetic contrast they offered to screen based technologies like smart phones and watches.

Most existing work in the technical space of thermochromic textiles uses heating elements to actuate color change [22,29], which impacts the flexibility and feel of the fabrics on the skin. Alternatively, we use conductive threads to actuate color change. Karpati [23], Nilsson [27], and Orth [28] also coat conductive threads with thermochromic paint to create dynamic textiles. In their approaches, conductive fibers are woven into fabrics and later coated with thermochromic inks through techniques like painting or silkscreen. Our approach is unique in the sense that we coat individual conductive threads with thermochromic paint *before* they are integrated into fabrics. This allows us to create subtle differences in the visual texture of the fabrics since variations in thread coating create "heathered" textures on the fabrics, similar to yarn-dyed fabrics. Additionally, it allows us to utilize a wider range of fabric production techniques, such as woven inlay, double weaving, and crochet.

Materialist Approaches to Smart Materials Research

Perhaps best typified by the term "computational composites" [35], new materials, like textile displays that blend digital and physical properties into a composite material, may benefit from materials-centric modes of development and analysis. In the words of Fernaeus and Sundström, "What [HCI] needs…when working with new forms of interactive materials, is to devise ways of bringing the materials into the explorations earlier in the design process, and also make them a shared resource for everyone involved, e.g., designers, developers, engineers, HCI-experts, dancers, psychologists and end users" [9].

We engage materials-centric modes of design and analysis [9,20,21,38] in order to *draw out* meanings that become associated with technology in the context of everyday personal style. In terms of design, our explorations of thermochromic textile displays began at the level of the material itself with open-ended explorations into the electrical properties of conductive thread, behavior of thermochromic inks, and various fabric production techniques. By "allowing material properties to guide our design" [9], we are able to probe the design space of wearable textile displays in order to identify new opportunities and challenges that might not have come into focus in context-specific or needs-driven design approaches. In terms of analysis, we engage designer and non-designer perspectives at a phase when our designs are developed enough to communicate several possibilities but not so developed as to suggest one particular usage scenario. Engaging "user" feedback at this early phase is particularly useful for exploring questions of meaning, since several different design directions can be compared and contrasted in order to reveal underlying themes and symbolic associations.

DESIGNING EBB

Our design process consisted of developing a core technology, a computationally controllable color-changing thread called Ebb, and exploring design possibilities in the form of fabric swatches made using the core technology.

Electrical Characteristics

Ebb consists of conductive threads coated with thermochromic fabric paint. The conductive thread is made from cotton thread wound with copper. The copper has a thin enamel coating for electrical insulation. These cotton-copper threads were developed in an early iteration of the Google Jacquard project and were specifically engineered for use in large scale garment manufacturing [19,41]. We coated the threads with thermochromic fabric paint to explore their potential for non-emissive display. Supplying power to the conductive thread creates heat, which changes the pigments in the fabric paint from an opaque to transparent state and results in a visual effect of the thread fading to its uncoated white color. Removing power has an inverse effect, changing pigments from transparent to opaque as they cool due to exposure to ambient air temperature. Thus, maintaining the threads in the color of the thermochromic pigment requires no power, while activating the thermochromic pigment to reveal the color beneath requires power. The most feasible display functions are those that turn threads on for limited amounts of time, creating moments of dynamism in otherwise static fabrics.

Thread Construction

The construction of Ebb is unique in that we coat individual threads with thermochromic paint *before* they are integrated into fabrics rather than applying thermochromic paints to conductive fabrics after the fabric is produced (e.g., via silkscreen). Working at the thread-level allowed us to explore intricate textile production methods, like crochet (Figures 3a and 3b), as well as detailed color combinations within woven fabrics (Figure 3c). Additionally, controlling individual threads within a weave allowed for increased computational control of the dynamic fabric patterns. We developed patterns that leveraged the physical structure of fabrics to obtain particular aesthetic effects as well as power efficiency, which we describe in more detail in the Design Explorations section.

We prepared thread in three colors: blue, magenta, and yellow (Figure 1a). Our fabric paint was created by mixing TurnThermo thermochromic pigment (which activates color change at 86°F/30°C), Utretch Acrylic Gel Medium, and Golden Acrylic Fabric Medium in a ratio of 1:2:1 respectively. This recipe offered sufficient color vibrancy while being thin enough to easily coat the threads. We coated the threads by filling small plastic palette cups with

	voltage (V)	current (mA)	rise time (s)	fall time (s)
magenta	1.0	426	4.0	7.0
yellow	1.6	515	2.5	4.0
blue	2.5	653	4.0	3.0

Table 1: Summary of voltage and current required to induce color change on a 20 inch string of thread. Rise and fall times refer to the amount of time it took for the thread to completely change color when current is applied or removed, respectively.

fabric paint, puncturing the cup with a needle, and rapidly feeding the thread through the paint using the bobbin winder on a sewing machine. This approach allowed us to make quantities of thread (~100 yards) in a relatively short amount of time. In practice, each color of thread exhibited very different heating and cooling behaviors, which are outlined in Table 1.

Ebb threads are volatile in the sense that they respond to heat generated from any source, not just electricity. For instance, a cold wind could blow a computationally generated pattern off of the fabric or body heat could induce change in particular locations. The pigments also have a limited life span and the transparent state becomes permanent after the threads has been heated a particular, but unpredictable (more than 500 short headings in our study) number of times. Longevity of the threads depends on the amount of power supplied and the duration of the heat application. While typically regarded as technical limitations, these aspects of Ebb have been strategically engaged to create aesthetic expressions. For instance, Maggie Orth leverages the limited lifespan of thermochromic pigments to reveal patterns over time [27].

Fabric Construction

We used weaving and crochet to explore the technical and aesthetic potentials of Ebb as a clothing-based display. Members of our design team produced crochet swatches in-house and we collaborated with a craft weaver to produce woven swatches. In the following subsections, we offer high-level descriptions of each technique in order to give the reader a sense of the structural properties of each fabric, which we leveraged to produce specific effects in our design explorations.

Crochet

Crochet is a technique where a single thread is continually looped around itself with a hooked needle. From combinations of relatively few basic stitches, endless patterns are possible. Crocheting with thread, rather than thicker yarn, produces lace-like fabrics with varying regions of densely and loosely packed stitches. Some crochet patterns (or "motifs") are created by combining regions made by separate threads. This is often used to produce regions of different colors within a single crochet fabric, with each color made from stitches on a single thread.

Weaving

Weaving is a common technique used in industrial fabric production. To produce a basic or "plain" woven fabric a weaver threads several individual threads along the length of a loom. These are the warp threads. A weaver then joins warp threads into a fabric by running a single thread over and under alternating warp threads (called "sheds") and working back and forth across the width of the loom to produce rows (called "shots") in a direction perpendicular to the warp. The thread used to join warp threads together is called the weft of the fabric (Figure 2a).

We used plain weaving, inlay, and double weaving techniques to create custom patterns in woven fabrics. Inlay was used to create patterns atop a base fabric (Figure 2b). To create an inlay, a weaver adds an additional thread that runs parallel to and in between each shot, which results in a pattern that is woven in and out of the warp threads but sits atop the weft. In double weaving, a weaver works multiple layers of fabric at once. We used double weaving to create patterns along the warp of the fabric (Figure 2c). While double weaving produces visible patterns on the top surface of the fabric, the bottom of the fabric reveals the inverse pattern with columns of warp threads spanning regions in between surface patterns.

Design Explorations

We created several woven and crochet fabric swatches to explore possible options for clothing-based displays. We selected seven of these swatches to explore in detail in our study. All selected weaves were woven at a density of 60 ends per inch (i.e. 60 warp threads per inch) and used silk as a non conductive base thread. We found visual quality and electrical efficiency to be optimal when there was one silk thread separating each Ebb thread along the warp and no threads separating Ebb threads along the weft. Patterns created using inlay produced better visual results than patterns woven along the weft of the fabric.

In order to actuate color change in the swatches, we soldered the copper wire from Ebb threads to thicker gauge wires and connected them to microcontrollers. Each swatch was controlled by a 5V Arduino Pro Mini and powered by a 3.7V lithium ion battery. An Adafruit Power Boost 500C module was used to supply 5V to the threads. Power to each thread was pulse width modulated. For swatches with many control threads, we used an Adafruit 16 channel, 12-bit PWM/Servo Driver to specify pulse width for up to 16 threads using I2C for communication. For demonstration purposes, we created boxes with the woven swatch placed on the lid and electronics housed inside the box. Voltage levels could be adjusted in real-time by turning knobs on the box.

Density Crochet

We observed how densely packed regions of stitches heated and changed color more quickly than loosely packed regions due to cross heating effects. In light of that observation, we designed a crochet pattern to emphasize contrasts between dense and sparse regions to explore how color change would "animate" across the fabric (Figure 3a). Applying power to the crochet created a bleeding effect, where color change slowly moved from denser to less dense regions. The resistance across the swatch was 21Ω. Dense regions changed color at a 13% duty cycle, and the entire swatch changed at a duty cycle of 100%. Full color change took roughly 30 seconds.

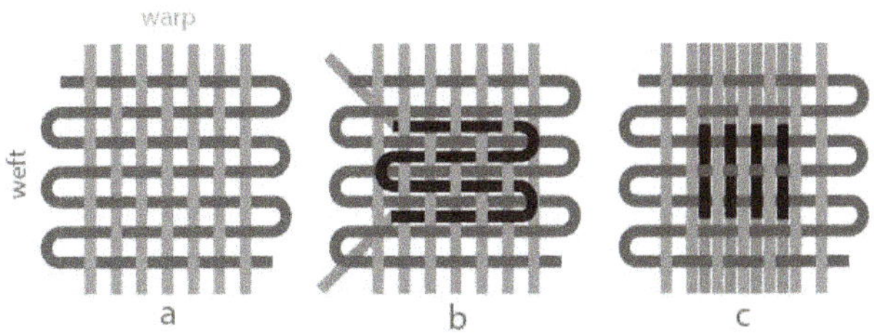

Figure 2: Weaving techniques explored with Ebb. a) plain weave b) inlay c) double weaving.

Multicolor Crochet

Our multicolor crochet swatch explores how colors could be controlled individually in order to produce different visual states on a single swatch (Figure 3b). Due to cross heating effects we could activate change on the magenta regions of the crochet without affecting blue regions but we could not change blue regions without affecting magenta regions. Thus, the swatch can take one of three states: magenta and blue both visible, magenta invisible and blue visible, and blue and magenta both invisible. We measured 14Ω and 16Ω resistance across the magenta and blue threads respectively. Magenta color change was induced at a 44% duty cycle and blue at 100%. It took roughly 20 seconds to change the color of the entire swatch.

Woven Color-Mixing Gingham

Gingham is a classic woven pattern created by running colored stripes along the warp and weft directions of a fabric (Figure 3c). We created stripes of Ebb thread along the warp with a double weave technique and stripes along the weft using inlay. The visual result is a pattern where only the overlapping sections of the stripes are visible, highlighting color combinations created by weaving different hues of Ebb thread along the warp and weft (Figure 1b). Since each row and column is controlled by a unique power source, the tint of each stripe be adjusted individually. We soldered individual warp threads together to make them function electrically as though they were one continuous thread. Each warp stripe had a resistance of 11Ω and at duty cycles ranging from 40%-75%, took roughly 5-10 seconds to fully change colors. Each weft stripe had a resistance of 5Ω and at duty cycles ranging from 15%-60%, took roughly 10-20 seconds to fully change colors.

Woven Graphic Element

We used inlay to explore activating color change on large graphic elements like logos or shapes (Figure 3d). We produced a large circle using a single continuous strand of Ebb thread. We programmed the swatch so that color would slowly appear and disappear, creating a "breathing" effect. The swatch had a resistance of 7Ω and at a 40% duty cycle, took roughly 7 seconds to fully change color.

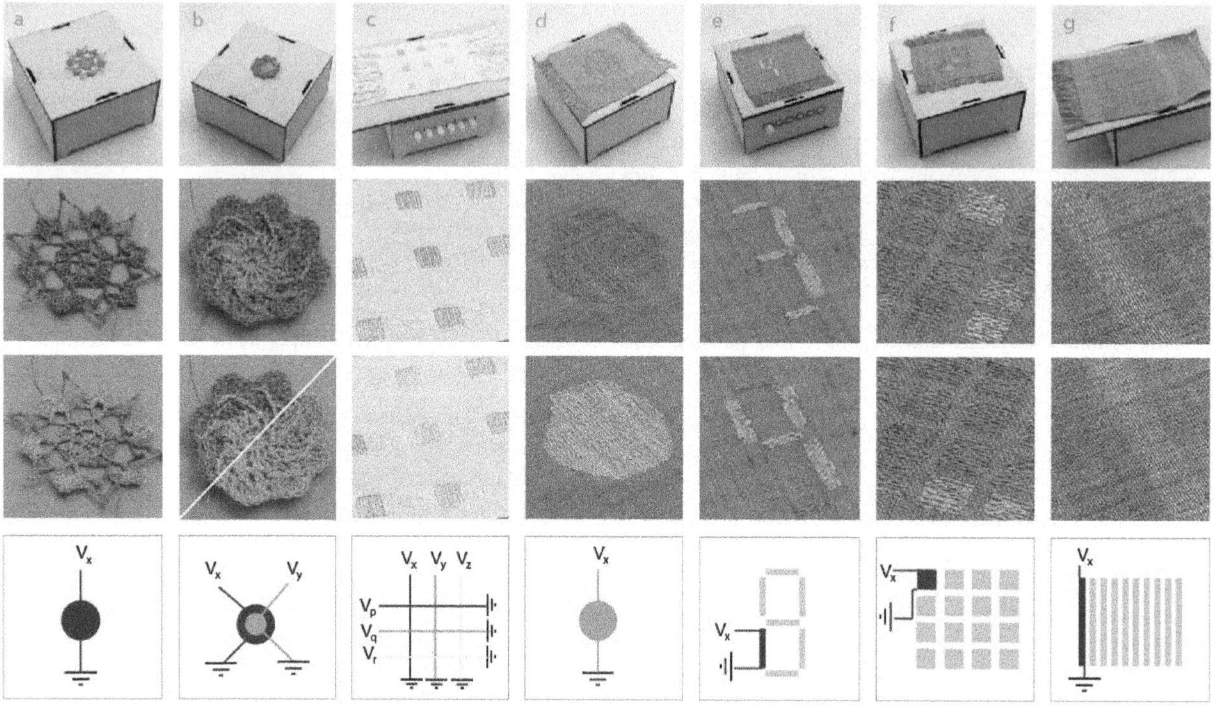

Figure 3: Swatches created from Ebb. a) density crochet, b) multicolor crochet, c) woven color-mixing gingham, d) woven graphic element, e) woven seven-segment, f) woven grid, and g) woven stripes. The bottom row shows the wiring diagrams for each swatch. On schematics e-g, grey elements each utilized identical wiring as the featured blue element.

Woven Grid

We also used inlay to create squares arranged in a four-by-four grid (Figure 3f). We controlled each square individually, which opened a space to experiment with dynamic spatial patterns and animations. When displaying the grid, we showcased a pattern that randomly turned one grid cell on at a time. The effect was a slow "shimmering" across the fabric. Each square had a resistance of 2Ω and at a 70% duty cycle, took roughly 2 seconds to fully change color.

Woven Stripes

Stripes are a common fixture in fashion as well as informational displays. We created stripes with Ebb by weaving ten separate Ebb threads into the weft of the fabric. Each stripe could be turned on an off individually (Figure 3g). Our display animation turned each stripe on and off in series, creating the effect of a single activated stripe moving down the length of the fabric. Each stripe had a resistance of 7Ω and at a 100% duty cycle, took roughly 14 seconds to fully change color.

Woven Seven-Segment

In order to explore how traditional display elements might be perceived differently with Ebb, we created a woven version of a seven-segment display (Figure 3e). Each segment was created using inlay and could be controlled independently of the other segments. For display, we showed an animation that slowly cycled through numbers from zero to nine. Each segment had a resistance of 2Ω and at a 70% duty cycle, took roughly 6 seconds to fully change color.

RESEARCH QUESTIONS

While HCI has explored domain specific and conceptual proposals for clothing-based displays, very little is known about the way such displays would be perceived and utilized within everyday life, beyond runways and outside of galleries. On a high level, we are interested in exploring why someone would choose to wear a garment with display capabilities. We approach this question through the lens of personal style, which foregrounds how self-identity shapes clothing choices [13,17]. From this perspective, a person's choice about how she might wear a clothing-based display is linked to the symbolic meaning she thinks it communicates, bringing two specific questions into focus:

What associations shape one's perceptions of a clothing-based display? According to Hebdige, the meaning of something is established among a web of associations with other meaningful things [17]. For instance, within the United States, a stovepipe may be strongly associated with former president Abraham Lincoln. When introduced into one's wardrobe, such a hat could form a bold statement: First, because the style is uncommon within the present day fashion landscape; and second, because the hat represents many of the characteristics culturally associated with Lincoln. As a new technology, Ebb lacks a distinct historical lineage of its own and must be understood in relation to things with similar function, visual appearance, or feel. Understanding what comes to mind when people see a clothing-based display can help designers understand how those perceptions could be leveraged to create spaces for particular kinds of experiences and interactions.

Second, **how do people envision clothing-based displays shaping their everyday interactions and experiences?** Drawing from Barad [2] and Balsamo [1], we argue that meaning is actively constructed and reconstructed within activities. While our first question takes a historical perspective to understand meaning, this question is future focused, exploring how people envision clothing-based displays performing within their daily lives. In addition to helping designers explore new territories of everyday clothing-based displays, investigating this question can provide insights on how specific meanings are put to work to produce particular social, personal, functional, and/or aesthetic effects.

ENGAGING DESIGNERS AND WEARERS

We presented fashion designers and wearers with our swatches in order to probe symbolic and social implications of Ebb. For clarity throughout the section we will refer to fashion designers as designers and other participants as wearers. We engaged wearers in order to unpack the factors that shaped how everyday people might bring Ebb into their wardrobes. We engaged designers as "expert" users whose understandings of the symbolism of clothing would be grounded in their practice of designing for clients.

Session Structure

We conducted 90 minute semi-structured sessions where participants were introduced to the fabric technology and asked to imagine how they would integrate it into their wardrobe or design practice. We began each session with swatch demonstrations to show how the fabrics changed color and invited participants to touch and feel the fabrics.

Next, we asked participants to select the swatches that they would be interested to integrate into their wardrobe or design practice. Focusing on their selected swatches, we asked participants to address more details about how they would design/wear it (e.g., on a scarf, shirt, inner wrist cuff, etc.), the contexts it was designed for or would be worn in, the kind of information it could display, how the participant imagined interacting with the display personally and socially, and how issues of sustainability affected their perception or ideas of use. Since the symbolism of one artifact often emerges in contrast to other artifacts, we frequently presented participants with alternatives to Ebb that could serve similar functions (i.e., woven fiber optics or flexible LED screens) and asked them to compare and contrast the technologies.

Throughout the sessions, we allowed participants to talk at length about aspects of Ebb they found personally interesting or uninteresting. To provoke discussions on topics that the participant found personally important, we based many questions on the unique responses of the participants. All sessions were video recorded and later transcribed for analysis. We analyzed video and transcripts using a grounded theory approach [7] in order to reveal common associations and themes that shaped perceptions and envisioned uses of Ebb. Audio from each interview

Figure 4: Fashion designers and wearers engaged with Ebb and discussed how they envisioned it within their style.

session was transcribed and coded in two passes by the first and third authors to identify recurring themes within the data.

FINDINGS

17 total individuals: 12 wearers (aged 23 to 56, 3 male, 9 female) and 5 designers (aged 22 to 52, all female), participated in our study. The designers had a range of experience and worked for large brands, as independent and freelance designers, or in costume design. 3 designers had knowledge of dynamic textiles and had used them within their design practice. 3 wearers had experience wearing some kind of dynamic textile or jewelry, most often with LEDs.

The range of responses, associations, and experiences from participants varied as much as their individual styles. Participants described many types of garments that could integrate the display, from dresses and shirts, to handkerchiefs and scarves, and had very different thoughts about how the garment would play into their personal styles. Designers and wearers had similar imagined uses of the technology. Yet, designers tended to address the physical texture of the fabric and used it to ground the garments they imagined.

The designer perspective also helped us contextualize our results. For one, designers did not find Ebb to be fundamentally different from other materials they engaged in their practice—design constraints based on electrical capacities were not seen to be different than constraints based on available materials or customer preferences. They saw Ebb as a new kind of material with a certain set of affordances and meanings that could be crafted in their design practices. Additionally, they were able to address the broader fashion landscapes within which color-changing clothing would be understood. Molly, for example, spoke of San Francisco having highly diverse "fashion micro-climates" and Gemma noted how "San Francisco is all about leather and feathers, where New York is very sleek and streamlined."

Among designers and wearers, themes emerged in relation to how they associated Ebb and the role they imagined it playing in their lives. We present our results in two sections in accordance with our earlier research questions: the first explores past experiences that gave rise to how designers and wearers saw Ebb and the second describes how participants thought those symbols could provoke particular kinds of experiences within the wearer's daily life.

The Symbolism of Ebb

As Hebdige notes, the symbolism of a clothing item is established among a web of symbolic historical, experiential, and material associations [17]. These associations can be multi-layered, relating to aspects like material properties as well as functionality. As we talked with participants about how they imagined integrating Ebb into their wardrobe, particular associations emerged more frequently than others.

Screen or Canvas

Participants' past experiences with dynamic displays often took place on computer or tablet screens. They tended to describe Ebb as a kind of screen and discussed how it was similar and different than other experiences with screens. Most participants had negative associations with screens: Diego, a wearer, described his phone screen as the entryway into "a world of hurt." Peter, a wearer, said "there is enough glare in my life as it is." While Ebb was seen as a kind of screen, most felt that its material qualities (lack of light emission, gradual changes, and low resolution) prevented it having the same negative effects as other screens in their life. Gemma, a designer, offered an alternative description of Ebb as a "canvas" since it offered more "painterly" uses of computation in garments.

The quality participants most disliked about typical screens was light emission. They described light emitting devices as "jarring" and distracting, like billboards or neon signs. Associations with light emission also extended beyond descriptions of screens. Participants recalled past memories of light emitting clothing: like blinking Christmas sweaters, children's sneakers that lit up when they walked, or light-up visors they might get at carnivals and amusement parks. Additionally, many referenced existing cultures of LED-enhanced clothing at clubs, large theatrical events, and Burning Man. In summary, clothing with light-emitting displays tended to be associated with parties, kids, and novelty. These associations were not strictly good or bad, but they did shape how participants imagined using textile displays in their life. For instance, Satia, a wearer, felt that LEDs in clothing were "tacky" but enjoyed wearing them to "take tacky to the extreme." For most participants, including Satia, the non-emissive quality of Ebb made it a better fit for everyday life and daytime situations.

Ebb was further differentiated from a screen because of its texture. Participants felt the patterning and the visual evidence of our swatches being made by hand gave Ebb a "warmer" appeal than traditional screens. Many participants ran their hands over the fabric and playfully draped the swatches in order to get a richer sense of its feel. The stiffness of woven fabric and its fairly coarse texture led Janet, a wearer, and Marie, a designer, to comment on its "heirloom"-like quality. In Janet's words, "[Ebb] seems a lot more tactile and something like cloth rather than plasticky…I think it's just more intimate and easier to like." The hand-crafted nature of Ebb had particular appeal for Elle and Gemma, who were concerned about the consumption and waste of textile displays. They felt that wearing clothing that was hand crafted increased its lifespan and signaled a commitment to quality and care.

The gradual color change of Ebb was also seen as an asset that made it less like a computer screen and more like a canvas. Diego, a wearer, expressed, "it's really hard to make a bad [design] decision with this kind of technology. It's really easy to make a watch, or fitness tracker, that's just the worst thing. Even the worst decision you make within the constraints of this design system would still make a really classy, nice thing." Diego attributed this observation to, "…the slowness, it has a latency that's way too high for advertising." For Diego, associations with advertising colored his impressions of our textile display. He felt that Ebb's slowness necessitated an investment of attention that sheltered it from being used for things that screens were typically used for and opened up a space for a more personally pleasurable experience of technology.

Many participants felt that Ebb could elicit different kinds of readings and interactions than other kinds of displays. They used terms such as "beautiful," "elegant," and "subtle," to describe their impressions of Ebb. Gemma, a designer with e-textiles experience, expressed how she "loved the ghostly in and out of thermochromics." Adelaine, a wearer, felt that the swatches were "more ambient than attention grabbing." Diego described Ebb as "trustworthy" because it felt more like fabric than a screen. When comparing Ebb to flexible screens he commented, "nothing is fabric but fabric." These impressions, and underlying associations, were based in past as well as imagined future experiences. While some participants felt that Ebb conjured up associations with beloved heirloom objects, others found its appeal precisely in what they felt Ebb *could not* become associated with, namely, advertising and wasteful consumption.

Envisioned Interactions & Experiences with Ebb

In this section, we focus on various ways that participants imagined leveraging the symbolic qualities of Ebb to prompt specific personal experiences and social interactions in their daily lives. Within each section, we describe how participants imagined integrating Ebb into their wardrobe.

Provoking Intrigue

Beth, Tammi, and Patrick, all wearers, liked the idea of using Ebb to mystify others, prompting interactions that began with lines such as, "Wasn't your dress blue a minute ago?" or "Wasn't that stripe on your shoulder before?" Like an inside joke, this quality of Ebb was seen to bring enjoyment, delight, or a shared sense of "being in the know" to wearers and their everyday audiences. The perceived audience for these kinds of intrigue-based interactions shifted with duration. For instance Peter imagined wearing a t-shirt with a graphic element that moved across his chest according to the time. In the morning, it would be on his left side, and as the day

Figure 5: Envisioned uses of Ebb. Participants described various ways that abstract displays of information (circles and stripes as opposed to arrows or numbers) could be strategically engaged in social scenarios.

progressed, it would move in an arc to his right side. The change would be too slow to be noticed immediately but could be discovered by people who interacted with him over the course of a day. Specifically, he imagined friends looking at his Facebook feed and discovering that his shirt had been changing in a way they had not been aware.

The gradual color change and non-emissive quality of Ebb were seen to foster a very specific kind of encounter with the public that was not explicitly attention grabbing, but a more nuanced and modest attention seeking that came from noticing and discovery. In this sense, the dynamism of Ebb was able to integrate within and represent complex personal characteristics like the ability to be cunning yet easily discovered or playful yet secretive. These statements are difficult to make with static clothing but may be too obvious when displayed through light emitting technology. The form of communication Ebb offered was not literal, but symbolic: signaling particular propensities and preferred modes of being within broader social worlds.

Data-Driven Serendipitous Encounters

Maxine, Beth, and Diego described ways Ebb could respond to their physical states or online activities. Maxine, a designer, envisioned clothing that responds to physical state in communicative, but non-literal, ways. She described how responsive garments with dynamic displays could have grammars of their own, adding a new dimension of expressivity to everyday life. Over time, she felt that users would be able to learn to control these seemingly abstract expressions and audiences may be able to read them.

Beth and Diego, wearers, imagined garments that connected their digital and physical lives. For instance, by responding to their physical proximity to someone they interacted with online. Beth imagined a shirt where a mark on her shoulder could become visible when she was near someone that she "swiped right" (a gesture to indicate potential interest) on in Tinder, a popular dating application (Figure 5a). Her choice of the shoulder as a display location signals an interest in having this information be visible to others (as opposed to wrist where only she would see). While she liked the idea of being able to connect with someone through the shirt, she also preferred the indication to be non-obvious. When asked if she would prefer an arrow pointing to the person rather than an abstract circle, she noted a preference for the circle in order to maintain a sense of not knowing, to keep her cover so to speak. Her use of Ebb was not intended to explicitly connect two people but to set up an awareness of an opportunity to potentially connect, something she felt might be more exciting, private, and comfortable. There would be a chance that the other person might notice her shirt and recognize her, or a chance that she could notice the indication and recognize the other person, or finally, a chance that both parties may not recognize the indication at all. Beth felt that chance was an asset that could infuse daily life with an element of playfulness and opportunity.

Both of the described interfaces embrace ambiguity in the display of event driven information. In the case of garments that respond to physical stimuli, Ebb was seen to support ambiguous representations that could foster multiple interpretations. Participants felt that this quality of Ebb could support playfulness and also allowed the wearer to make decisions about whether or not they would pursue particular social encounters. The slowness and subtlety off Ebb were seen to be well suited for ambiguous representations of information.

Beautiful Functional Things for Personal Enjoyment

Janet and Elle, wearers, wanted to enjoy Ebb privately instead of using it to prompt new kinds of interactions with others. They appreciated the aesthetic of Ebb but were concerned about attracting unwanted attention. Elle feared people "leering" and Janet described how she was afraid of "being at the [subway] station and waiting and sitting and wanting to just read my book and someone starring at [my] shirt and saying 'its changing colors – that's crazy!'"

Instead, Janet wanted to use Ebb as a watch located inside the wrist on her shirt because she felt it would be unexpected and beautiful, yet mundane enough to limit attention. Her interest in a fabric watch was rooted in an appreciation for the material qualities of Ebb. She was particularly fond of the unusual textured patterns created by woven inlays on the seven-segment swatch (Figure 3e). She also thought the limited lifespan of a thermochromic watch made it more interesting: "With something like clothes or functional objects, they are always so meticulously thought about that it might be nice and refreshing to add an element of chance. You'll just have to deal with how it looks [when the pigments become inoperable] and that would be part of its appeal, I think."

Ebb's physical texture, the slowness of its change, and its susceptibility to forces outside of the wearer's control combined in a way that offered Janet personal aesthetic pleasure. As a watch, it also served a functional purpose. Ebb suggested a poetic opportunity to combine new and old technology in unexpected ways.

Many Garments in One Garment

Sam, Larry, and Gemma saw Ebb as something that could increase the utility of a single garment by allowing it to change its appearance. They each imagined uses that involved waking up, setting the pattern of the garment for the day, and then having the pattern remain static throughout the day. Gemma, a designer, imagined a shirt where different kinds of collars could dynamically appear based on the wearer's preferences for the day: "A shirt completely changes its look when it's all white, including the collar, and then the collar turns into an accent color, or maybe just the tips of the collar turn bright red...like a western shirt. [Collars] all have different connotations and associations so you can say a lot with a simple, subtle change." Her personal design philosophy aimed at fostering long-term engagements between people and their clothes through the creation of garments that could be adapted and mended as the wearer's preferences changed over time. Gemma felt that Ebb increased the lifespan of a garment by offering aesthetic utility, the ability to integrate many different meaningful looks into a single garment.

Humane Information Access

Sharon and Sarah, both wearers, and Maxine, a designer, imagined Ebb offering information they typically accessed on their phones through a soft, clothing-based interface. Sharon imagined a striped scarf that could communicate real-time bus information (Figure 5b). When activated through an app on her cell phone, the stripes at the end of the scarf could change to reflect the number of minutes before her bus arrived. She preferred to represent the time information with stripes, rather than numbers, so it would not distract people she might be interacting with. She commented, "our brains are wired to recognize letters and numbers, we can't not see them." She typically accessed bus information on her phone and felt that the slowness of the information represented on the display could support a relaxing "zen-like" experience of information. Even though she imagined activating her scarf with her phone, she felt that her scarf interface would ameliorate stress by providing a slowly shifting dedicated information stream that would allow her to direct her attention to the world, interacting with others, rather than frequently checking her phone.

Most descriptions of information displays using Ebb resonated with descriptions of peripheral, calm and ambient computing [12,18,33,37] in which limited amounts of abstracted information reside in one's peripheral awareness. The information could be easily referenced or ignored on the end of a scarf or the sleeve of a shirt. The uses of Ebb as an informational display highlight how it could reduce cognitive load while also serving a social function. For instance, by allowing the wearer to maintain a sense of privacy over their data even when it is clearly on display in public spaces or allowing them to maintain conversations while staying aware of important information.

Commenting on Technology and Culture

Diego, a wearer, and Marie, a designer, felt that displaying information publicly on their clothing could be used towards critical effects. Diego described a shirt that could display his Klout score, a numeric value that is computationally derived to describe how influential a person is. For Diego, an artist who frequently explored themes of culture and technology, clearly displaying his Klout score in an outward facing position on his shirt was meant to act as an ironic commentary on our relationship with technology.

Marie, a designer, also saw clothing as a place to provoke commentary and reflection. She described a dress with accents along the bodice, which could respond to Facebook data. She saw clothing and Facebook as artificial surfaces onto which people project their ideal selves. "I think about Facebook as this curated hologram of our lives. It is very much not representative of who we are as full and complicated people...fashion is a surface too...so it feels like an appropriate comparison."

Information used towards ironic or critical affect served a much "slower" function, as Hallnäs et al. use the term [14], in the sense that it is presented for reflection and contemplation rather than efficiency or awareness. The symbolism of particular information streams represented on clothing through Ebb were seen as a way to express one's perspective about technology and culture and signal a particular orientation within those cultures.

DISCUSSION

While the variability and uniqueness of participant preferences limits the generalizability of our study to other populations and contexts, the particular body of users we studied reveals new design territories for wearable displays and new questions for designers to consider while creating such displays. The individuality of each participant and their unique perspectives of Ebb highlighted the complexity of personal style. Each aspect of the display, from the physical feel to the data represented, dramatically changed a participant's impressions and envisioned uses of Ebb. The expressions made through clothing-based displays did not have a single intended meaning, but contained many layers of sometimes contradictory meanings to produce specific effects like intrigue or irony. This poses a future design challenge for HCI, how do we go about designing clothing-based displays that can mesh well with the complex tastes and lifestyles of an individual wearer? Reflecting on the findings from our study, we suggest a new metaphor and extend Gaver et al.'s original descriptions of ambiguity in order to expand future research of clothing-based displays for everyday life.

Shifting Metaphors: From Screen To Canvas

The metaphor of a screen is an easy fit with the dynamic changes in appearance supported by textile displays. However, if designers think of these displays as "screens" they may be inclined to base their design on existing heuristics for evaluating screens (i.e., "better" screens offer higher resolution, fast switching times, and high visibility). Within the context of personal style, a very different set of heuristics was evoked. Our participants expressed value for displays that offered aesthetic pleasure and utility. In the shifting contexts of everyday life, participants described a variety of situations in which slow, specific, low-resolution displays were preferable to high fidelity display options. In many cases, the slowness, low-resolution, and volatility of

Ebb were seen as assets and opened up spaces for wearers to imagine mysterious and meditative encounters with the technology.

Drawing from the observations of our participants, we suggest that the metaphor of a *canvas* may offer designers a mental representation that expands the role of clothing-based displays within everyday life. The idea of an artistic canvas brings values for textured materials and abstraction to the foreground. Where screens might be understood in terms of their use, canvases are better understood as things that become "present" [15] within a broad spectrum of everyday life experiences. The experience of such canvases could be framed as aesthetic [31,40], enchanting [26], and slow [14].

Our study highlights how clothing-based displays can foster aesthetic and slow experiences for wearers and their publics simultaneously (e.g., Peter's slowly moving graphic t-shirt offered a personal aesthetic experience and an opportunity for surprise for others). Participants felt these kinds of shared experiences could potentially give rise to serendipitous social interactions and bring a particular kind of attention to the wearer that he or she desired. The complex and nuanced experiences provoked by the clothing reflected back on the wearer, signaling their own complexity as people.

Revisiting Ambiguity in the Context of Clothing

Ebb was seen to promote intriguing interactions through ambiguous representations of information. According to Gaver et al., ambiguity emerges from uncertainty within the "interpretative relationship linking person and artefact" [11] and can be engaged to make artifacts and situations, "evocative rather than didactic, and mysterious rather than explicit […] the artefact or situation sets the scene for meaning-making, but doesn't prescribe the result." The usage scenarios described by participants resonate with Gaver's et al.'s descriptions of ambiguity in the sense that it was seen to create potentials for various kinds of interactions and interpretations to occur without forcing those interactions. Yet, we found that ambiguity, as it was described by participants, was difficult to understand without reconfiguring the relationship between person and artifact offered in the original description.

When interactive displays enter the fabric of clothing, the artifact (i.e., the display) and the person (i.e., the wearer of the display) become tightly coupled. The person, their histories, ways of being, and other aspects of their style, contribute to the meaning of the artifact and vice versa. Thus, in the context of clothing, ambiguity might be better understood as emerging from the interpretive relationship linking the wearer and artifact *as well as* the relationship linking wearer-artifact and their publics. If we understand ambiguity in clothing through this lens, we are better able to grasp, for example, how Diego's own personality contributes to the ambiguity that emerges from his wearing of the Klout score t-shirt. As an artist whose work explores ironic uses of technology, Diego's shirt may be interpreted by his personal "audiences" along very different lines than, perhaps, a businessperson wearing the publicly displayed score at a networking event. Diego *becomes part of* the contextual discourse that shapes the interpretations others might draw from his clothing. In other cases, like Sharon's use of stripes instead of numbers on her scarf to represent transit information, ambiguity of information was pragmatically engaged to allow Sharon to maintain a level of informational awareness while remaining socially present to her friends. Ambiguity served a practical function while also reflecting Sharon's own care and value for her peers. In both cases, ambiguity between the wearer-artifact and his or her publics was strategically engaged by wearers to shape the range interpretations others might have of them, while leaving room for their publics to formulate their own meanings. Ebb uniquely allows this ambiguity to flourish in the context of clothing.

FUTURE WORK

While all envisioned uses were feasible in terms of the display capacity of Ebb, some would require significant advances in wearable power supplies in order to be comfortably worn in everyday contexts. In order to probe the everyday wearability and social implications of Ebb, we are developing sensor-driven prototypes for participants to wear throughout their daily life. Through these studies, we hope to provide richer experiential accounts of Ebb while also exploring how ambiguous displays of information affect how such signals are interpreted by the wearer and their publics.

CONCLUSION

Our study shed light on ways that clothing-based displays can function within the complex and meaning-laden landscapes of personal style. By employing a materials-centric perspective that embraces materials as meaningful communicators, we were able to draw out associations that shaped perceptions of technology in clothing. From these perceptions, we suggest that the metaphor of canvas, rather than screen, could expand the design space of clothing-based displays for everyday use. Furthermore, participants in our study envisioned scenarios in which the slowness and low resolution of Ebb could be engaged to foster serendipitous social encounters, ironic commentaries, and meditative experiences of personal data. Ambiguity played a central role in many of these scenarios. We revisit and extend Gaver et al.'s descriptions of ambiguity in the context of clothing based display in orders to highlight how ambiguity can function strategically when integrated within the complex personal and social landscapes of style.

ACKNOWLEDGMENTS

Our thanks to: all of our study participants for their time and thoughtful feedback; Rundong Tian, Chris Meyers, Mark Ohlberg for their technical guidance and assistance; and Jen Garrison Stuber for teaching us about weaving and offering her superb weaving skills; all of the reviewers.

REFERENCES

1. Anne Balsamo. 2011. *Designing Culture: The Technological Imagination at Work*. Duke University Press Books, Durham NC.
2. Karen Barad. 2007. *Meeting the Universe Halfway: Quantum Physics and the Entanglement of Matter and Meaning*. Duke University Press Books.
3. J. Berzowska and M. Coelho. 2005. Kukkia and Vilkas: kinetic electronic garments. *Ninth IEEE International Symposium on Wearable Computers, 2005. Proceedings*, 82–85. http://doi.org/10.1109/ISWC.2005.29
4. Joanna Berzowska. 2004. Very Slowly Animating Textiles: Shimmering Flower. *ACM SIGGRAPH 2004 Sketches*, ACM, 34–. http://doi.org/10.1145/1186223.1186266
5. Joanna Berzowska and Maksim Skorobogatiy. 2010. Karma Chameleon: Bragg Fiber Jacquard-woven Photonic Textiles. *Proceedings of the Fourth International Conference on Tangible, Embedded, and Embodied Interaction*, ACM, 297–298. http://doi.org/10.1145/1709886.1709950
6. Leah Buechley, Mike Eisenberg, Jaime Catchen, and Ali Crockett. 2008. The LilyPad Arduino: Using Computational Textiles to Investigate Engagement, Aesthetics, and Diversity in Computer Science Education. *Proceedings of the SIGCHI Conference on Human Factors in Computing Systems*, ACM, 423–432. http://doi.org/10.1145/1357054.1357123
7. Kathy Charmaz. 2006. *Constructing Grounded Theory: A Practical Guide Through Qualitative Analysis*. Pine Forge Press.
8. Felecia Davis. 2015. The Textility of Emotion: A Study Relating Computational Textile Textural Expression to Emotion. *Proceedings of the 2015 ACM SIGCHI Conference on Creativity and Cognition*, ACM, 23–32. http://doi.org/10.1145/2757226.2757231
9. Ylva Fernaeus and Petra Sundström. 2012. The Material Move How Materials Matter in Interaction Design Research. *Proceedings of the Designing Interactive Systems Conference*, ACM, 486–495. http://doi.org/10.1145/2317956.2318029
10. Amisha Gadani. 2010. *Porcupine Dress*. Retrieved from http://www.amishagadani.com/Work/porcupine/index.html
11. William W. Gaver, Jacob Beaver, and Steve Benford. 2003. Ambiguity As a Resource for Design. *Proceedings of the SIGCHI Conference on Human Factors in Computing Systems*, ACM, 233–240. http://doi.org/10.1145/642611.642653
12. Hans-W. Gellersen, Albrecht Schmidt, and Michael Beigl. 1999. Ambient media for peripheral information display. *Personal Technologies* 3, 4: 199–208. http://doi.org/10.1007/BF01540553
13. Erving Goffman. 1959. *The Presentation of Self in Everyday Life*. Anchor, New York.
14. Lars Hallnäs and Johan Redström. 2001. Slow Technology – Designing for Reflection. *Personal Ubiquitous Comput.* 5, 3: 201–212. http://doi.org/10.1007/PL00000019
15. Lars Hallnäs and Johan Redström. 2002. From Use to Presence: On the Expressions and Aesthetics of Everyday Computational Things. *ACM Trans. Comput.-Hum. Interact.* 9, 2: 106–124. http://doi.org/10.1145/513665.513668
16. Kate Hartman, Jackson McConnell, Boris Kourtoukov, Hillary Predko, and Izzie Colpitts-Campbell. 2015. Monarch: Self-Expression Through Wearable Kinetic Textiles. *Proceedings of the Ninth International Conference on Tangible, Embedded, and Embodied Interaction*, ACM, 413–414. http://doi.org/10.1145/2677199.2690875
17. Dick Hebdige. 1979. *Subculture: The Meaning of Style*. Routledge, London ; New York.
18. Hiroshi Ishii, Craig Wisneski, Scott Brave, et al. 1998. ambientROOM: Integrating Ambient Media with Architectural Space. *CHI 98 Cconference Summary on Human Factors in Computing Systems*, ACM, 173–174. http://doi.org/10.1145/286498.286652
19. Ivan Poupyrev, Nan-Wei Gong, Shiho Fukuhara, M. Emre Karagozler, Carsten Schwesig, and Karen Robinson. 2016. Project Jacquard: Manufacturing Digital Textiles at Scale. *Proceedings of the 34th Annual ACM Conference on Human Factors in Computing Systems*, ACM.
20. Heekyoung Jung and Erik Stolterman. 2011. Material Probe: Exploring Materiality of Digital Artifacts. *Proceedings of the Fifth International Conference on Tangible, Embedded, and Embodied Interaction*, ACM, 153–156. http://doi.org/10.1145/1935701.1935731
21. Heekyoung Jung and Erik Stolterman. 2012. Digital Form and Materiality: Propositions for a New Approach to Interaction Design Research. *Proceedings of the 7th Nordic Conference on Human-Computer Interaction: Making Sense Through Design*, ACM, 645–654. http://doi.org/10.1145/2399016.2399115
22. Viirj Kan, Katsuya Fujii, Judith Amores, Chang Long Zhu Jin, Pattie Maes, and Hiroshi Ishii. 2015. Social Textiles: Social Affordances and Icebreaking Interactions Through Wearable Social Messaging. *Proceedings of the Ninth International Conference on Tangible, Embedded, and Embodied Interaction*, ACM, 619–624. http://doi.org/10.1145/2677199.2688816
23. Judit Eszter Karpati. *Chromosonic*. Retrieved from http://chromosonic.tumblr.com/
24. Sunyoung Kim, Eric Paulos, and Mark D. Gross. 2010. WearAir: Expressive T-shirts for Air Quality Sensing. *Proceedings of the Fourth International Conference on Tangible, Embedded, and Embodied Interaction*, ACM, 295–296. http://doi.org/10.1145/1709886.1709949

25. Matthew Mauriello, Michael Gubbels, and Jon E. Froehlich. 2014. Social Fabric Fitness: The Design and Evaluation of Wearable E-textile Displays to Support Group Running. *Proceedings of the 32Nd Annual ACM Conference on Human Factors in Computing Systems*, ACM, 2833–2842. http://doi.org/10.1145/2556288.2557299
26. John McCarthy, Peter Wright, Jayne Wallace, and Andy Dearden. 2006. The Experience of Enchantment in Human–Computer Interaction. *Personal Ubiquitous Comput.* 10, 6: 369–378. http://doi.org/10.1007/s00779-005-0055-2
27. Linnéa Nilsson, Mika Satomi, Anna Vallgårda, and Linda Worbin. 2011. Understanding the complexity of designing dynamic textile patterns.
28. Maggie Orth. 2009. *100 Electronic Art Years*. Retrieved from http://www.maggieorth.com/art_100EAYears.html
29. Roshan Lalintha Peiris, Owen Noel Newton Fernando, Chua Su Bee, Adrian David Cheok, Arij Glycin Ganesan, and Prabhash Kumarasinghe. 2011. dMarkers: Ubiquitous Dynamic Makers for Augmented Reality. *Proceedings of the 10th International Conference on Virtual Reality Continuum and Its Applications in Industry*, ACM, 217–224. http://doi.org/10.1145/2087756.2087787
30. Laura Perovich, Philippa Mothersill, and Jennifer Broutin Farah. 2014. Awakened Apparel: Embedded Soft Actuators for Expressive Fashion and Functional Garments. *Proceedings of the 8th International Conference on Tangible, Embedded and Embodied Interaction*, ACM, 77–80. http://doi.org/10.1145/2540930.2540958
31. Marianne Graves Petersen, Ole Sejer Iversen, Peter Gall Krogh, and Martin Ludvigsen. 2004. Aesthetic interaction: a pragmatist's aesthetics of interactive systems. *Proceedings of the 5th conference on Designing interactive systems: processes, practices, methods, and techniques*, ACM, 269–276. http://doi.org/10.1145/1013115.1013153
32. E. R. Post, M. Orth, P. R. Russo, and N. Gershenfeld. 2000. E-broidery: Design and Fabrication of Textile-based Computing. *IBM Syst. J.* 39, 3-4: 840–860. http://doi.org/10.1147/sj.393.0840
33. Zachary Pousman and John Stasko. 2006. A Taxonomy of Ambient Information Systems: Four Patterns of Design. *Proceedings of the Working Conference on Advanced Visual Interfaces*, ACM, 67–74. http://doi.org/10.1145/1133265.1133277
34. Lisa Stead, Petar Goulev, Caroline Evans, and Ebrahim Mamdani. 2004. The Emotional Wardrobe. *Personal Ubiquitous Comput.* 8, 3-4: 282–290. http://doi.org/10.1007/s00779-004-0289-4
35. Anna Vallgårda and Johan Redström. 2007. Computational Composites. *Proceedings of the SIGCHI Conference on Human Factors in Computing Systems*, ACM, 513–522. http://doi.org/10.1145/1240624.1240706
36. Akira Wakita and Midori Shibutani. 2006. Mosaic Textile: Wearable Ambient Display with Non-emissive Color-changing Modules. *Proceedings of the 2006 ACM SIGCHI International Conference on Advances in Computer Entertainment Technology*, ACM. http://doi.org/10.1145/1178823.1178880
37. Mark Weiser and John Seely Brown. 1996. Designing Calm Technology. *POWERGRID JOURNAL* 1.
38. Mikael Wiberg, Hiroshi Ishii, Paul Dourish, et al. 2013. Materiality Matters—experience Materials. *interactions* 20, 2: 54–57. http://doi.org/10.1145/2427076.2427087
39. Anouk Wipprecht. 2013. *Spider Dress*. Retrieved from http://fashioningtech.com/profiles/blogs/robotic-couture
40. Peter Wright, Jayne Wallace, and John McCarthy. 2008. Aesthetics and experience-centered design. *ACM Trans. Comput.-Hum. Interact.* 15, 4: 18:1–18:21. http://doi.org/10.1145/1460355.1460360
41. *Google Jacquard*. Retrieved from https://www.google.com/atap/project-jacquard/

BeUpright: Posture Correction Using Relational Norm Intervention

Jaemyung Shin
KAIST
Republic of Korea
jmshin@nclab.kaist.ac.kr

Bumsoo Kang
KAIST
Republic of Korea
steve.kang@kaist.ac.kr

Taiwoo Park
Michigan State University
USA
twp@msu.edu

Jina Huh
University of California San Diego
USA
jina.huh@gmail.com

Jinhan Kim
KAIST
Republic of Korea
jinhankim@kaist.ac.kr

Junewha Song
KAIST
Republic of Korea
junesong@nclab.kaist.ac.kr

ABSTRACT
Research shows the critical role of social relationships in behavior change, and the advancement of mobile technologies brings new opportunities of using online social support for persuasive applications. In this paper, we propose Relational Norm Intervention (RNI) model for behavior change, which involves two individuals as a target user and a helper respectively. RNI model uses Negative Reinforcement and Other-Regarding Preferences as motivating factors for behavior change. The model features the passive participation of a helper who will undergo artificially generated discomforts (e.g., limited access to a mobile device) when a target user performs against a target behavior. Based on in-depth discussions from a two-phase design workshop, we designed and implemented BeUpright, a mobile application employing RNI model to correct sitting posture of a target user. Also, we conducted a two-week study to evaluate the effectiveness and user experience of BeUpright. The study showed that RNI model has a potential to increase efficacy, in terms of behavior change, compared to conventional notification approaches. The most influential factor of RNI model in the changing the behavior of target users was the intention to avoid discomforting their helpers. RNI model also showed a potential to help unmotivated individuals in behavior change. We discuss the mechanism of RNI model in relation to prior literature on behavior change and implications of exploiting discomfort in mobile behavior change services.

Author Keywords
Behavior change; relational norm intervention; posture correction; social persuasion; negative reinforcement; other-regarding preferences.

CHI'16, May 07-12, 2016, San Jose, CA, USA

DOI: http://dx.doi.org/10.1145/2858036.2858561

ACM Classification Keywords
H.5.m. Information interfaces and presentation (e.g., HCI): Miscellaneous; J.4. Social and Behavioral Sciences.

INTRODUCTION
Advances in mobile computing technologies have brought new opportunities for real-time behavior monitoring and behavior change [38]. Small-scale sensors and mobile devices have enabled a variety of measures for everyday life activities, such as step counts [42], emotions [27], sleep quality [24], and mood [34]. Based on such measures, a number of mobile services have been designed to help individuals understand their behavior patterns [22,43], as well as to deliver persuasive feedback to users in situ [19,21], thereby shaping their behavior into a better form.

Online social support has also been used for shaping an individual's behavior. A common online social support for behavior change includes forming a group to share members' behavior information such as step counts [42] and frequency of water-drinking events [28]. Researchers have also proposed direct ways to create associations between individuals' behaviors. One example is peer-rewarding [1], giving individuals an incentive, not for their own effort but for ones of other group members. With an assumption of *active* participation of users, such social supports have shown their potential in shaping individuals' behavior.

In this paper, we propose Relational Norm Intervention (RNI) model, featuring passive social support and (bad) behavior-driven discomfort. The model consists of two individuals (i.e., a target user and a pre-assigned helper) and a mobile system. Once the mobile system detects that the target user has violated a target behavior, it delivers the helper a discomfort such as locking the helper's phone for a prolonged period of time. The mechanism of the proposed model in leading the target user's behavior change is twofold: (1) the target user will stop violating the target behavior to avoid discomforting the helper, and (2) the helper will directly send the user a negative feedback.

The contributions of this paper include:

- We propose a novel intervention model for behavior change that employs discomfort to paired helpers.
- We provide design considerations for applications using the model and implement a sample application BeUpright.
- We report the effectiveness and initial user experiences of the application through a user study with 18 participants.

BACKGROUND

With the help of mobile technologies and online social networks, behavior change applications are becoming immersed in our daily lives. Smartphones and wearable devices enable real-time behavior monitoring, bringing opportunities of automated persuasion methods, such as behavior change. Also, volunteered social support from a distance has become available using online social networks.

Mobile sensing technologies for automated persuasion

Real-time sensing of human behavior using mobile devices has enabled the automated delivery of persuasive messages in situ. UbiFit [42] encourages everyday physical activities by providing summaries of activities obtained from activity motion sensors. Haug et al. and Hou et al. proposed context-aware text message reminders for smoking cessation [19] and medication adherence [21], respectively.

The major drawback of these automated intervention is user habituation, which explains a user's decreasing attention to persuasion. Anderson et al. and Kalsher et al. explained frequent exposure to intervention stimuli (e.g., messages or alarms) could lead to disregarding the stimuli [8,25]. These studies implied that there is a need to find less-structured, unanticipated stimuli that do not facilitate the habituation process. One solution is to use people to balance between machine- and peer-generated stimuli for persuasive applications. Playful bottle [28] and Houston [43] support persuasive social reminders between individuals in a group to encourage drinking-water behavior and physical activity, respectively. Several studies show social reminder was more effective. Still, such peer-generated stimuli are initiated by a few number of active participants [43].

Social networks, awareness, and norms for behavior change

Social relationships provide an effective platform for behavior change [1,5]. With the increasing number of mobile networks, the potential for using social relationships to change behavior has emerged. Social relationships in the forms of social networks, awareness, and norms influence behavior change through various mechanisms.

Shmueli et al. described two computer-mediated persuasion processes for behavior change: (1) using social networks and (2) increasing social awareness [38]. The former is to provide both a direct communication path between peers and a shared goal for peers to collaborate on; they can even compete against other groups [30,31]. The motivations behind such collaborative, mutual support in a group can stem from altruism [48] and group dynamics [4,15]. Studies showed highly context-sensitive results regarding whether competition or cooperation is more effective in behavior change [10,13].

Increasing social awareness entails providing individuals with the group's summary of a target behavior to encourage self-reflection and improvement. Example target behaviors for social awareness include participating in group activities (e.g., discussions) [14,23,44] and healthier decision-making processes [16]. Social cognitive theory [3] explains the mechanism behind this social process, by indicating that a person models her behavior based on the behaviors of others.

Performing the against behavior of surrounding others can be interpreted as a violation of social norms. A social norm violation refers to prescriptions of behaviors and attitudes that are considered unacceptable or undesirable in a given social unit [37]. Violations, also called counter-normative behaviors, are often controlled because people believe that others do not expect these behaviors from them [11]. If uncontrolled, these counter-normative behaviors are likely to result in negative reactions and feedback, including exclusion from a social group [7,35]. Social norms have been frequently employed to change socially significant behaviors, such as alcohol consumption, drug use, disordered eating, gambling, littering, and recycling [36].

Discomforting others as an aversive stimulus of negative reinforcement

In behavioral psychology, *reinforcement* is one of the core methods to increase an individual's desired behavior. Reinforcing desired behavior by avoiding an aversive stimulus is called negative reinforcement [39]. In the Skinner box, a well-known example of negative reinforcement, a rat presses a lever more frequently to avoid electric shocks. The aversive stimulus is the electric shock in this case, which is the *negative reinforcer*. We use *discomforting others* as a negative reinforcer to change one's behavior. Discomforting others can act as an effective negative reinforcer because people are reluctant to inconvenience others, due to Other-Regarding Preferences [40]. Other-Regarding Preferences describes people imagine what they expect from the others' position [12]. The dictator game [17] is a famous experiment that shows the Other-Regarding Preferences. In this experiments, the first player decides how to split an endowment to the second player. Even though they do not know each other, the first player will share the benefit. This presents people have a tendency to consider others.

Areas covered in this paper

From the aforementioned literature of mobile social networks to change behavior, we see that the following three areas need further investigation:

- *Relational norm based behavior change.* In studies examining social norms as mechanisms to change behavior, the norms have been developed mostly based on the larger social group (e.g., I learn how to maintain my trash can based on the way my neighbors maintain their trash cans). We further explore how relational norms between a small number of individuals can shape one's behavior.
- *Passive social help.* Existing social help through social networks assumes that active help comes to a peer from other peers in the same group; otherwise, the chance of such social help will decrease. Active help is triggered through motivations that are parallel to the goal of the target behavior (e.g., I want to help John lose weight to improve his health). On the other hand, passive help can be triggered by motivations that do not necessarily align with the goals of the target behavior (e.g., I want to help John lose weight because my phone will be locked otherwise).
- *Discomforting others for positive results.* One way to build passive social help is to make users want to break out of a negative event that possibly discomforts others. However, existing approaches seek to minimize the inconvenience that users might experience in voluntary tasks [32]. We argue that intentional discomfort toward the goal of behavior change is worth investigating. The primary challenge would be to find the right level of discomfort that maximizes the effectiveness of behavior change while achieving a reasonable level of helper discomfort.

RELATIONAL NORM INTERVENTION MODEL

Relational Norm Intervention (RNI) model consists of three entities: a target user, a helper, and a mobile system interacting between those of the user-helper pair. The model reinforces an individual's (i.e., target user's) desired behavior by leveraging her willingness to avoid an aversive stimulus that may discomfort a pre-assigned partner (i.e., a helper). The model requires an artificial causal relationship between the target user's violation of the desired behavior and the helper's discomfort (see Figure 1 for the overall process). As a promising medium for discomforting events, we propose mobile phones the everyday companions of many individuals with which individuals frequently interact in their daily lives [45]. For example, we can easily discomfort users by locking their phones for a while. The overall mechanism of the model is threefold:

- **Alert:** The mobile system monitors the target user and alerts her when she performs against a (desired) target behavior.
- **Discomforting Event:** If the target user continues to perform against the target behavior, the helper's phone will generate an event that will discomfort him (e.g., lock his smartphone for a while).
- **Feedback:** The helper can ask the target user to perform the target behavior in order to stop the discomforting event.

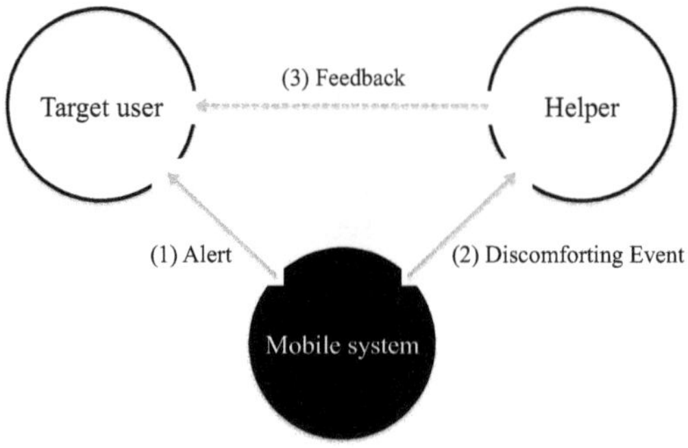

Figure 1. Overview of Relational Norm Intervention model.

APPLICATION DESIGN WORKSHOP

Method

To design prototype applications based on RNI model, we conducted a design workshop consisting of two phases. The goal of the first phase was to determine an appropriate target behavior, and the goal of the second phase was to extract design considerations for the feedback interfaces of both the target user and the helper. We recruited 16 people (6 for the first phase and 10 for the second phase) from the authors' personal contacts. The participants were students at a public research university in South Korea who are interested in mobile application development and user experiences.

In the first phase, we conducted a 2-hour focus group discussion with 6 of the participants. We began by explaining the concept of RNI model and soliciting their ideas and suggestions for potential target behaviors and discomforting events. After receiving sufficient suggestions for target behaviors and discomforting events, we further discussed the suitability of the candidates and the intervention model. At the end of the phase, we chose the most feasible target behavior and developed a conceptual prototype based on the participants' feedback.

For the second phase, we introduced a conceptual prototype developed based on the first phase workshop to the remaining 10 participants. We then solicited their feedback and suggestions using semi-structured questions followed by an open discussion. The key leading questions were: "Do you want to use the app, and why?", "Do you think this app would be helpful for behavior change?", and "Which part of the app should be improved?"

Workshop results

First phase: Good sitting posture for the target behavior

The focus group discussion resulted in the following requirements for deciding the target behavior:

- **Pervasiveness of violating the target behavior:** Violations of the target behavior should be frequently observable in daily life so as to cause helpers discomfort.
- **Change with minimal effort:** The effort required for changing the behavior should be reasonably small and should not distract from daily tasks.

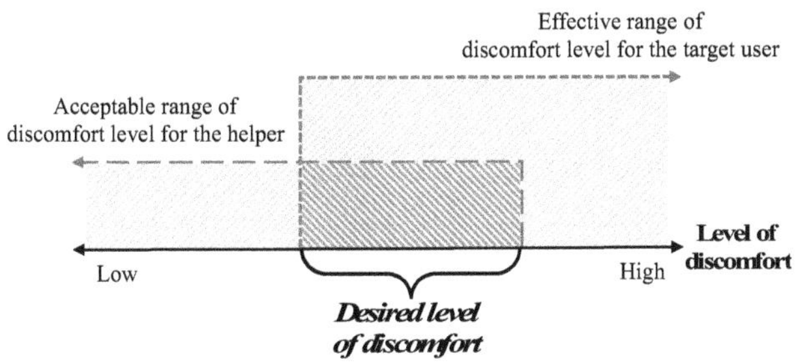

Figure 2. Conceptual diagram for discomfort level.

- **Clear benefit:** It should be generally accepted that the benefit of the behavioral change outweighs its cost.
- **Feasibility of demonstration:** In terms of complexity and ease of use, implementation should be feasible as the first demonstrative prototype of the model.

Several candidate behaviors emerged: walking 1 hour everyday, drinking 8 cups of water a day, and quitting smoking. The participants agreed to choose *good sitting posture* for the target behavior considering the above criteria. Next, the participants came to choosing *lock the phone* as a discomforting event among the several candidates, including slanting the screen and making a loud noise considering the above criteria as well.

Using the results, the conceptual prototype included the following: The mobile system will alert the target user (Figure 1, (1) *Alert*) if a poor posture is detected. If the target user continues with the poor posture, the helper's phone will be locked (Figure 1, (2) *Discomforting Event*) until the target user corrects her posture.

Second phase: Adjusting discomfort, and quick feedback

After introducing the conceptual prototype, 6 out of 10 participants responded that they were not likely to use the application. We distilled three design considerations by asking these respondents what made the model unattractive.

First, the helper needs the authority to cancel the discomforting event at any time. In our conceptual prototype, the act of locking the helper's phone may cause a severe burden to the helper, especially in situations when the helper needs to use the phone urgently. Most of the participants disliked such situations. Regardless of how close they were with the target users, the helpers refused to grant the authority to unlock their phones to an external factor over which they would not have control.

Second, setting the level of discomfort for the helpers was one of the most challenging parts of the design. The participants said they would not use the application as a helper because they could not endure the discomfort. However, the following open discussion revealed that a low discomfort level for the helper might not motivate the target users to change their behavior. Figure 2 shows the concept of this desired level of discomfort; it should be acceptable (i.e., low enough) for helpers but also effective (i.e., high enough) for target users.

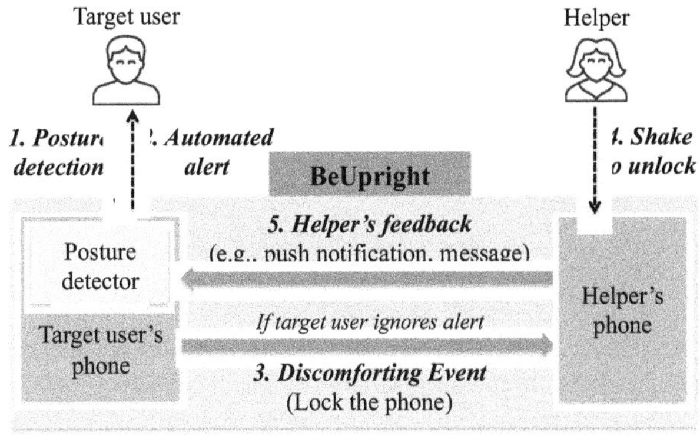

Figure 3. BeUpright overview.

Third, the participants also requested a simplified way to give feedback to their partners. Some suggested providing a shortcut for direct messages to target users. However, 2 participants argued that such messaging would be burdensome and emphasized the need for a more convenient way of communicating, such as "poking." That is, these participants only wanted to give the target user a simple signal to show that the helper has been discomforted by the target user's behavior.

After the design workshop, we revised the design of the discomforting event (i.e., the phone lock); a helper can now unlock the phone at any time. However, this reduced the level of discomfort, which has a negative effect on motivating target users. Thus, to meet a desired level of discomfort, we elicited *shaking the phone 10 times* as a way to unlock the phone. Other candidates included shaking the phone, solving a quiz, and waiting for some time period. Lastly, we decided to provide shortcuts for helpers to quickly give feedback to target users.

BEUPRIGHT: DESIGN AND IMPLEMENTATION

Following the design considerations extracted from the design workshop, we implemented BeUpright, a mobile application to help individuals maintain good sitting postures. Figure 3 shows the execution sequence of BeUpright:

1) **Posture detection:** The target user's sitting posture is monitored by the *posture detector*.
2) **Automated alert:** If a poor posture is detected, the target user's phone will give an initial alert to the target user.
3) **Discomforting Event:** If the target user ignores the alert and keeps the poor posture, the helper's phone will be locked.
4) **Shake to unlock:** The helper can unlock the phone by shaking it 10 times.
5) **Helper's feedback:** After unlocking, the helper will see a floating head on the screen which makes it easy for the helper to give feedback to the target user.

BeUpright consists of three major components: posture detector, the target user interface (target UI), and the helper

Figure 4. Sensor for sitting posture detection.

user interface (helper UI). We explain the implementation details of the three components below.

Posture detector

We implemented the sitting posture detector by referring to previous work using motion sensors, including studies on locomotion, body balance-related clinical studies, and machine learning and cybernetics studies [47,49].

The detector identifies two types of poor sitting postures: *leaning backward* and *leaning forward*—the most frequently observable cases while sitting [17]. Postures leaning more than six degrees from a "good" posture are classified as "poor" postures [46]. To detect the amount of posture leaning, we used the accelerometer to measure the target user's angle of tilt by comparing the acceleration of gravity and individual's vertically downward acceleration.

To filter out sporadic behaviors, such as body stretches, posture detector gives 20 seconds of grace period before confirming that the current posture is poor. This decision was made in consultation with an orthopedic specialist. Once a poor posture is detected, it notifies the target UI of the event. Reflecting individual differences in sitting posture, the detector allows posture calibration before use. Users can set or reset their 'good' posture before and during use (see Figure 5, right).

The detector employs the TI CC2650 SensorTag, a tiny sensor device featuring a variety of sensing modalities, including a 3-axis accelerometer as well as Bluetooth 4.0 wireless connectivity (see Figure 4). We set the position of the sensor on a user's shirt, about one inch below the collarbone[1]. For convenience of attachment, we used two small rare-earth magnets to attach the sensor to the cloth.

We implemented the detector on the Android mobile platform. It communicates with the SensorTag via the Bluetooth API provided by the Android framework. Once BeUpright runs and a wireless connection is established with the sensor, the detector is immediately initiated and begins to monitor a target user's posture.

Target and helper user interfaces

Once the target UI receives a poor posture event from the posture detector, it gives the target user a vibration alert.

[1] We borrowed the concept of placing a sensor under the collarbone from the Lumo lift, which is a commercialized product for posture detection.

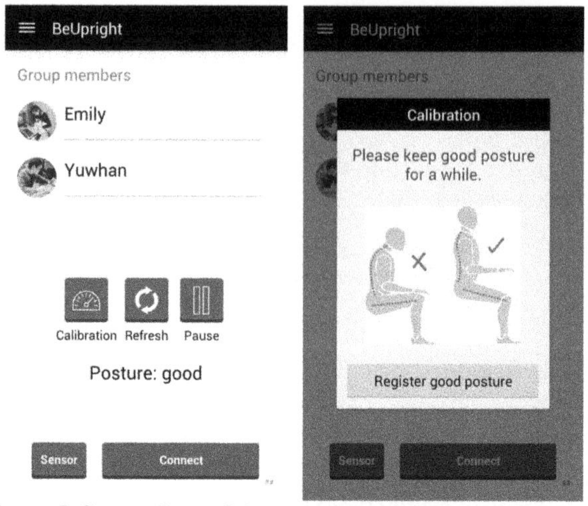

Figure 5. Screenshots of the target user interface: (left) main screen, (right) calibration dialog.

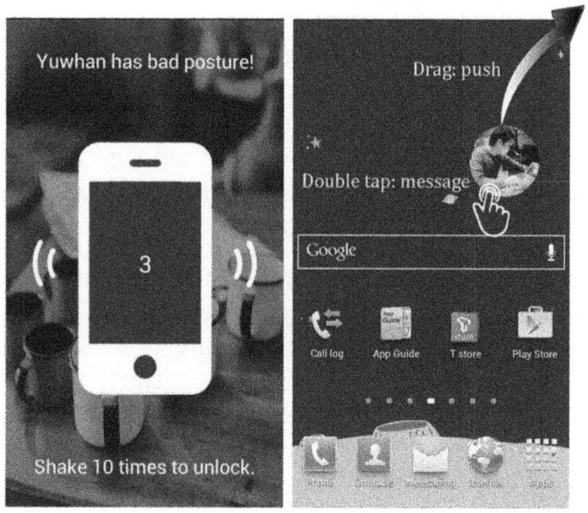

Figure 6. Screenshots of the helper user interface: (left) a screen when the phone is locked, (right) dragging out floating head sends a push feedback, and double tapping floating head helps to send a message feedback.

We set the duration of the vibration as 2 seconds, to help users distinguish it from other general phone notifications. If the user does not change her posture within 10 seconds after the first vibration alert, it requests the helper UI to give the helper the discomforting event (i.e., phone lock).

If the target users are in a situation where it is hard to keep a good posture (e.g., in a restroom), they can pause the posture detector for a while using a pause button (see Figure 5, left). Also, users can recalibrate the "good" posture whenever they want and check their posture information in real time.

Immediately after the helper UI receives a discomforting event request, it will lock the helper's phone (see Figure 6, left) and the helper is required to shake the phone 10 times to unlock it. When the helper unlocks the phone, the helper will see the target user's image as a floating head on top of the phone screen (see Figure 6, right). If the helper drags out the floating head from the screen, the helper UI will request a push notification to the target UI, informing the target user that the helper's phone had been locked recently. If the helper double taps the floating head, it will launch a messaging application for the helper to give direct feedback to the target user.

THE 2-WEEK EVALUATION STUDY

To investigate the user experience and the effectiveness of RNI model, we conducted a two-arm evaluation study (control vs. RNI) that included: (1) pre-study surveys and interviews, (2) using BeUpright for 2 weeks, and (3) a post-study survey and an interview. We measured the posture correction rate as the main outcome.

Participants

We posted a recruitment flyer to an internal online community of students and staff at a public research university in South Korea. We were interested in recruiting those who have not started to change their behavior (i.e., sitting with good posture). We recruited 12 participants and randomly assigned them into the control and test groups (i.e., RNI). We asked RNI target users to bring their helpers on their own. In total, we had 12 target users and 6 helpers. The participants were students and research staff (Ages: 21-34). All of the target users were male, and three helpers were female. All of the participants were rewarded with about $20 worth of gift certificates.

Study procedure

Procedure		AAI (control)	RNI-Target-user	RNI-Helper
Pre-study	Interviews	Motivations for posture correction		N/A
		Automated alert	Automated alert, discomforting event, helpers' feedback	
	Surveys	Q1a	Q1a, Q2a	
			$Q3a_t$	$Q3a_h$
Intervention		AAI	RNI	
Post-study	Interviews	Reflections on their experiences with BeUpright		
	Surveys	Q1b	Q1b, Q2b, Q3b	

Control group vs. test group design

As the control intervention, we used the same BeUpright interface, but without the helper and their feedback component. We will call the control group the Automated Alert Intervention (AAI) group. When the target users from AAI group maintained a poor posture for 20 seconds within the grace period, they received the same *automated alert* that RNI group received. If the target users did not change their posture within 10 seconds after that alert, the poor posture was logged to BeUpright application. As the test intervention, we used BeUpright with all components including the helpers and their feedback.

Pre-study

Introduction of BeUpright: Before the study, we first introduced the features of BeUpright system to the participants. We told AAI group about the automated alert, which is the only function their BeUpright system included; and we told RNI group how RNI works in BeUpright system.

Pre-interview: We then conducted interviews to discuss the participants' initial motivations around sitting posture correction, their relationships with their helpers (for RNI group), and their initial perceptions toward using BeUpright system.

Pre-survey: The participants also completed a survey before the study. The participants were given questions regarding their initial perceptions toward BeUpright based on the introduction. For both groups, the first survey question was: Q1a. *How much do you agree that the automated alert will be helpful in correcting [your, your target user's] posture*? The participants responded in a 5-point Likert scale—Strongly Disagree—Disagree—Neutral—Agree—Strongly Agree. RNI group was also asked the following question: Q2a. *How much do you agree that the {discomforting events, push feedback, feedback messages} will be helpful in correcting [your, your target-user's] posture.* Each item in the curly braces was asked separately. The last survey question was regarding RNI group's perception toward the discomforting event. To the target users, the survey asked: $Q3a_t$. *How much do you agree with the following statement: the helper will be bothered by the discomforting event.* To the helpers, the survey asked: $Q3a_h$. *How much do you agree with the following statement: I think I will feel bothered by the discomforting event.* The responses were again in a 5-point Likert scale—Strongly Disagree—Disagree—Neutral—Agree—Strongly Agree.

Intervention

The participants used BeUpright for 2 weeks (10 days, only on weekdays). During the intervention, the target users wore the sensor once they arrived at work, and they took off the sensor before they left the office. We logged the events of wearing and taking off the sensors with a remote server. Each day, we sent a short text message to the participants who had not worn the sensors by 10AM. We asked those who did not use the application for 10 days in 2 weeks due to business trips or personal emergencies to continue to complete 10 days.

Post-study

Post-survey: For the surveys, we asked the same set of questions: Q1b, Q2b, and Q3b, but asking about their actual experience. For instance, Q2a was modified to Q2b, which was: *How much do you agree that the {discomforting events, push feedback, feedback messages} was helpful in correcting [your, your target-user's] posture.*

Post-interview: We also conducted interviews on participants' experiences in relation to the survey results on the influential factors and the expected versus experienced discomfort levels. Also, we asked their impressions about the automated alert, the discomforting event, and the user interface. We walked through their results together to ask background information on why such results occurred.

All of the interviews were recorded and transcribed in Korean. We then conducted translation and back-translation [9] into English. We used open coding [41] to examine the emerging themes. With the open codes, we conducted axial coding using affinity diagramming [6] to understand the main themes across the interview data, narrowing the codes into a set of five themes.

EVALUATION OF THE STUDY FINDINGS

We discuss five main findings on: (1) posture correction outcomes between AAI and RNI group, (2) the target users' vs. helpers' perceptions on the discomforting event, (3) RNI and unmotivated participants, (4) the choice of push vs. message feedback, and (5) RNI and the pair's relationship.

Outcomes on target users' posture correction

Table 1 shows the average correction rates during the participating period. The correction rates indicate how many times the target users corrected the poor postures when the poor-posture alerts were given. RNI group had a higher correction rate (*M=74%, SD=10.41*) than AAI group (*M=55%, SD=15.6*). According to a t-test, the difference was significant (*t=-2.57, p=0.031*). We also conducted General Estimating Equation (GEE) analysis to take into account the autocorrelation of repeated measures, which is for analyzing longitudinal data. The results showed that the correction rates in both the controlled and treated groups (*0=AAI, 1=RNI*) were significantly different (*B=16.93, SE=3.98, p<0.001*).

Three factors that influence posture correction

Our model suggests three potential factors that influence target users' posture correction in RNI group: *the discomforting event*, the *helpers' push feedback*, and the *helpers' message feedback*. Figure 7 shows the target users' expected versus experienced impact of these three factors in RNI group. Before the study began, the participants expected that the message feedback would play the most significant role in posture correction. After the study, however, the participants reported wanting to avoid discomforting others played the biggest impact on their posture correction.

From the interviews with RNI group, the participants explained the discomforting event as the most influential factor for changing their posture. The participants did not want to bother the helpers in using their phones:

AAI group						
Participant	P7	P8	P9	P10	P11	P12
Corr. rates	41%	40%	52%	50%	82%	61%
#Correction/ #Bad posture	116/ 280	101/ 250	322/ 618	137/ 272	147/ 179	156/ 257
RNI group						
Participant	P1	P2	P3	P4	P5	P6
Corr. rates	66%	64%	86%	86%	77%	65%
#Correction/ #Bad posture	79/ 120	118/ 185	64/ 74	260/ 304	302/ 393	101/ 156

Table 1. Average correction rates in AAI and RNI groups.

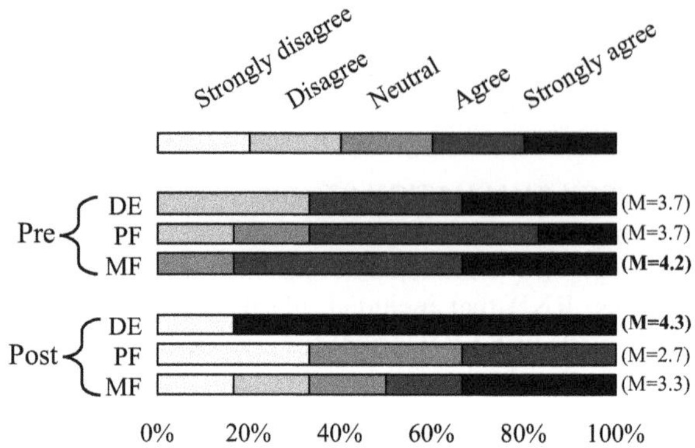

Figure 7. The survey results of how much three factors affect target user's posture correction in RNI group. (*DE: Discomforting Event, PF: Push Feedback, MF: Message Feedback*)

"The fact that my posture might annoy my partner was always on my mind... I tried as much as possible to not bother her." (RNI-T-1[2])

"If I have a poor posture, my girlfriend will become uncomfortable. So I tried not to burden her..." (RNI-T-4)

Effects of intervention over time for AAI and RNI

AAI-target users stated that they became insensitive to the alerts after being exposed to them repeatedly:

"Over time, I became insensitive to the alerts. The alerts were no longer 'alerting,' and I lost the motivation to correct my posture." (AAI-T-9)

Following the Q1 survey questions, 3 out of 6 target users in AAI group said that the effect of the stimuli diminished over time, whereas all of the target users in RNI group said the stimuli of BeUpright persistently intervened for them to correct their posture correction. Some of the target users said the stimuli bothered them more over time:

"The fact that I was causing my partner discomfort bothered me more and more over time. The feedback from my partner was a constant reminder that she was continually discomforted, and I felt sorry towards her." (RNI-T-6)

In addition, in AAI group, the correction rate was negatively associated with the days of app use (*B*=-1.139, p<0.001); however, that association was positive in RNI group (*B*=0.803, p=0.036). In other words, the intervention of AAI group had a tendency to be less affected, while the intervention of RNI group did not.

[2] We refer to each participant using the notion of the following: [AAI or RNI]-[T (Target user) or H (Helper)]-[unique participant #]

Two AAI-target users said that alerts were not enough, especially when they did not have the need to their correct posture: *I didn't change my posture each time the alert came. If my phone vibrated due to the alert, I put it away or just turned off the sensor. I'm not even interested in posture correction. Why should I correct my posture?* (AAI-T-8) They also shared that a harsher penalty might be helpful for changing their behavior, and alerts that annoy surrounding people might be effective: *When BeUpright alerted while somebody was around me, I corrected my posture because I felt bad for causing the vibration noise. I think if the alerts can annoy others, people will correct their posture a little more* (AAI-T-7).

AAI group participants were not aware of RNI group. Coincidentally, AAI group participants suggested that we should use discomforting events of others to nudge people toward behavior change, which was one of the main components of RNI model.

Perceptions on the discomforting event

In RNI group, in contrast to the initial concerns of the target users, most of the helpers did not feel bothered by the discomforting event of their phones being locked. As a result of survey Q3, 5 out of 6 target users expected that locking helpers' phones due to their poor posture would annoy the helpers (see Figure 8). An RNI target user explained his thoughts behind this expectation:

"Locking someone's phone came to me as a huge pressure because it might make the person very uncomfortable. Even if unlocking the phone required shaking the phone only once, it still would be uncomfortable for the person. Even a small discomfort—I would still feel guilty about it." (RNI-T-3)

P5 was the only target user who responded that his helper would not be agitated about his phone being locked. P5 knew that his helper did not use his phone frequently:

"I know my helper doesn't use his phone that frequently. He seemed to not mind even if I had a poor posture. So I didn't feel that guilty about bothering him that much with the feature." (RNI-T-5)

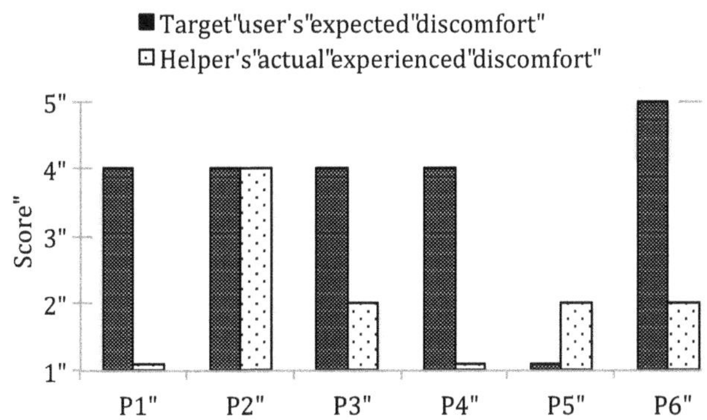

Figure 8. The level of discomfort that expected by target users and experienced by helpers.
(*1: Not at all, 2: Not really, 3: Undecided, 4: Somewhat, 5: Very much*)

In contrast with the target users, 5 out of 6 helpers said they did not feel agitated by the discomforting event (see Figure 8). Some of the helpers further said that the feature made them feel positive (e.g., glad, bonding) rather than negative (e.g., inconvenient, irritated):

"[Shaking the phone to unlock was] not that burdensome to me. It felt like an exercise. I shook my phone even harder to make it an exercise." (RNI-H-4)

"[About the floating head,] It is really funny and cute. And it didn't bother me in using the phone that much. I didn't care whether the floating head had appeared on the screen or not. " (RNI-H-1)

P2 was the only helper who responded that the discomforting event bothered him because he was very sensitive to being interrupted while using the phone:

"(Locking the phone) bothers me. I am a person who really hates any disturbance to my phone use." (RNI-H-2)

While the target users thought they might cause the helper discomfort, in reality they did not. This finding implies that the discomforting event of BeUpright has a discomfort level in the desired range, which is a crucial factor for RNI to work appropriately.

RNI and unmotivated participants

We found that RNI can be effective regardless of the target users' motivation for the target behavior. Unmotivated participants in AAI group corrected their postures less compared to motivated participants. RNI group, however, showed a more consistent and higher correction rate than AAI group in general, regardless of the participants' motivation for the target behavior.

In the post study interview of RNI group, the target user of P1, who was not motivated to correct posture, responded that he willing to continue using BeUpright, if his helper suggested him to keep using it. He just needed to find a persistent helper. Other participants also said they would keep using BeUpright if their helpers were fine with it:

"I'm not that willing to use the app because I don't have any needs for posture correction, but I will use it if my partner and I can use it together." (RNI-T-1)

"Of course I will use it. My girlfriend is saying that she will help me even thought she might face discomfort. She is totally doing this for me so I'm willing to use it." (RNI-T-4)

Here, the participants showed the importance of choosing the helpers and their willingness to help. Next, we discuss how the helpers' feedback played roles in RNI.

Choice of push vs. message feedback

Our initial assumption for potential factors playing into the helpers' choices on which feedback to use—push or message feedback—was the closeness between the helper and target user pair. We assumed that the closer the relationship, the more message feedback the helpers would send to the target users. Contrary to our belief, the closeness in the pair's relationship did not matter; the results showed that the choice on which feedback to use depended on the level of the helpers' perceived discomfort, personal preferences in communicating over the phone, and consideration for the target user.

To intervene with the target user, the helpers frequently used the push feedback over the message feedback in general. When the discomfort level increased due to repeated locking of their phones, the helpers started using the message feedback:

"I usually used the push feedback. I didn't feel the necessity to send a message since my phone was locked once or twice a day." (RNI-H-3)

"When my phone was locked many times, almost 4~5 times in a row, I sent the target user a message." (RNI-H-4)

In addition to the perceived level of discomfort, the differences in preferences of using mobile communication features, personality, and context mattered in choosing feedback. For P2, only 1% of all feedback was message feedback. P2 in general preferred not to type on the phone:

"I mostly used the push feedback because typing bothers me. I really don't like online communities or messengers... so I didn't intervene through text messages." (RNI-H-2)

Compared to P2, 49% of P5's feedback was message feedback. For P5, the choice of push feedback over message feedback was related to efficiency:

"When I want to use the phone, sending a push feedback is faster than sending a message feedback (to remove the floating head). So I used push feedback when I use the phone in purpose, and I used the message feedback when I was just checking the phone." (RNI-H-5)

Furthermore, the target users' reactions of feeling guilty for triggering the discomforting event affected the helpers' choice of feedback:

"When I received a message from my partner, it didn't feel like she was nagging me, but it reminded me that I bothered her again. This made me feel guilty." (RNI-T-4)

"I was very motivated to help my partner and intervened with him with messages in the beginning... But it seemed like he felt guilty about locking my phone, which in turn made me feel sorry for him [for sending a message]. I just wanted to let him know his posture needs to be corrected. But it seemed like I give him huge pressure. So I didn't intervene in his posture with messages later." (RNI-H-6)

The participants continued to try hard not to violate the norms, and modified their behavior (e.g., by not using messages anymore) as they observed how they reacted to one another's reactions in using BeUpright. Even with the discomforting component in the intervention, the participants expressed the positive relationship formed among the pairs.

RNI and the pairs' relationship

The participants felt that the discomforting event created an intimate communication pathway which the pair could heighten the awareness of each other. The helpers felt connected with the target users; the discomforting event constantly reminded the helpers of the target users' status, making the helpers constantly think about the target users:

"(BeUpright) feels like an interlink. It was good to know my partner's status. Also the locked screen was like an incoming message. The floating head showing his face makes me wonder what he is doing." (RNI-H-4)

3 out of 6 pairs responded that the discomforting event and the helper's message feedback in BeUpright initiated interactions between the helper and the target user and promoted continuous communication:

"Usually, during the day, we don't really communicate other than asking whether he had lunch. But now, when my phone is locked, I say something to my partner, and ask him what he is doing now. This triggers further communication not only about posture itself, but also about why he had bad posture or what situation he was in." (RNI-H-1)

"We usually didn't communicate during working hours unless there were special events... But now BeUpright locks my girlfriend's phone when I have a poor posture, and it causes her to send me messages or push feedback. It then leads to more conversations." (RNI-T-4)

The pairs replied that BeUpright has increased their interaction mostly in close relationships, including close friends or significant others. However, the participants who were not in close relationships responded that the helpers' feedback and the discomforting event initiated interaction but the interaction was hard to sustain.

Summary of the findings

We found that: (1) RNI was more effective in correcting posture compared to AAI; (2) the most influential feature of BeUpright was the discomforting event; (3) the discomforting event did not bother the helpers, unlike the target users, who were highly concerned about agitating the helpers; (4) RNI model has the potential to modify the behavior of the target users, including even unmotivated individuals; (5) the helpers' choice of feedback types depended on the discomfort level, personality, preferences, and context; and (6) BeUpright made pairs feel connected to each other and promoted increased interaction among the pairs.

DISCUSSION

In this section, we discuss how our findings translate to learning about the main components of RNI model. We first discuss the efficacy of RNI, including the effectiveness of the intervention, even with those who had low motivation to change. We then discuss at length how future researchers and designers can use RNI model to develop persuasive systems.

Efficacy of RNI

There was a disparity between the expected level of discomfort by the target users and the actual experience of the helpers (the former was higher). This result showed a unique potential for RNI model. That is, RNI model benefits from the tendency of the target users to overestimate the burden of the helpers. However, it is unclear, if the effect will diminish after the target users recognize the disparity between their perception and the actual experience. A long-term study can explain whether understanding the helpers' felt experience of the discomforting event will affect the behavior change motivation of the target users.

The finding that AAI target users' motivations to change their behavior degraded over time is consistent with previous studies showing that users are likely to be habituated to machine-generated alerts [8,25]. The target users of RNI group were receiving helpers' feedback, which was situational and not automated. Thus, RNI will help with such challenges around habituation because of the situatedness of the intervention. The helpers were in fact benefiting from the habituation process, in which they repeatedly received the same discomforting events. Our study revealed that the helpers became habituated to the discomforting events, which may decrease their level of discomfort over time.

Motivating users who are unwilling to change

Behavior change for unmotivated individuals is a critical challenge (e.g., a smoking cessation program for a person who is unwilling to stop smoking [33]). Our findings indicated that RNI motivated even unmotivated participants to change their behavior. The individuals are motivated to change their behavior due to not wanting to discomfort others, rather than the internal motivation to change their behavior. In addition, the helpers' act of good will, or an altruistic act (e.g., being a helper), can positively affect the target users to feel gratitude toward the helper, thereby motivating the target users to change [26].

Cultural factors in RNI

According to Hofstede [20], people from collectivistic societies have an increased preference for maintaining social harmony. This tendency causes people to avoid discomforting others. On the other hand, in individualist cultures, the transgression of norms leads people to feel guilty. Consequently, discomforting others may work as a light transgression, and thus, individuals will try to avoid it. This contrast shows that our approach could theoretically work in both cultural contexts, although using different underlying mechanisms.

Toward personalized relational norm intervention

RNI model uses people's general tendency to avoid violating social norm (e.g., discomforting others). We observed three factors influencing the efficacy and experience of the intervention: (1) personal and relational traits of self-pressure against discomforting others, (2) the perceived level of discomforting events, and (3) the burden for escaping from these events.

Each participant felt differently when discomforting others; some reported a significant sense of self-pressure, while others did not. Understanding such differences will help in personalizing the level of discomfort. P3 responded that he was under a high pressure when he made the system send discomforting events to his helper. However, P1 commented that he did not feel much guilt, because he believed that his wife would not get angry just for shaking the phone 10 times, if it would help him. In this case, trust between the two [29] played a role in reducing stress and tension when applying the model. Providing personalized features to fully exploit such specific traits will help RNI model to be more effective. Also, it will be worth exploring how the model works for different types of relationships. In detail, the self-pressure of a target user will be affected by the relationship with a helper (e.g., a family member, friend, acquaintance, or supervisor in a workgroup), and the pressure will affect the efficacy of behavior change.

The discomforting event should be agitating enough for the intervention to be effective, but within the boundaries of acceptable violation of relational norms. Our findings indicated that a low level of discomfort for the helpers would be appropriate when the target users frequently have a bad posture. If such bad behavior occurs only occasionally (e.g., a light smoker), a high level of discomfort would be more effective. Examples of discomforting events with various discomfort levels include (from low to high): ignorable notifications, a slanted phone screen, or a screen lock. Example activities to stop the discomforting event include (from easy to difficult): shaking a phone, answering a quiz, or jumping 5 times.

CONCLUSION

In this paper, we proposed Relational Norm Intervention model. The fundamental concept of the model is using people's tendency to avoid norm violation and translating it to motivation for behavior change. Our study proved the effectiveness of RNI model. We also gained many insights that we can apply to other areas of behavior change. Our study's sample size was relatively small, and we will have to conduct a longer intervention to see the impact on sustained behavior change. However, our first step to testing RNI model has helped us understand the feasibility of the system with rich qualitative and formative findings. This study contributes to novel ways of designing persuasive systems using intricate dynamics among social relations.

ACKNOWLEDGEMENT

This work is partly supported by the National Research Foundation of Korea (NRF, 2011-0018120) and Civil Military Technology Cooperation Centre (12-DU-EB-01). Taiwoo Park is the corresponding author.

REFERENCES

1. Aharony, Nadav, Wei Pan, Cory Ip, Inas Khayal, and Alex Pentland. Social fMRI: Investigating and shaping social mechanisms in the real world. *Pervasive and Mobile Computing* 7, no. 6 (2011): 643-659.

2. Averill, James R. Anger and Aggression in Biological Perspective. In *Anger and Aggression*, Springer New York, (1982): 33-53

3. Bandura, Albert. Social foundations of thought and action. *The health psychology reader* (2002): 94-106.

4. Beauchamp, Mark R., and Mark A. Eys. *Group dynamics in exercise and sport psychology*. Routledge, 2014.

5. Becker, Marshall H., and Lois A. Maiman. Sociobehavioral determinants of compliance with health and medical care recommendations. *Medical care* 13, no. 1 (1975): 10-24.

6. Beyer, Hugh, and Karen Holtzblatt. Contextual design: defining customer-centered systems. Elsevier, 1997.

7. Blake, J., and K. Davis. Norms, values and sanctions In Faris, REL (ed.) Handbook of Modern Sociology. *Rand McNally, Skokie* 101 (1964): 456-484.

8. Bonnie Brinton Anderson, C. Brock Kirwan, Jeffrey L. Jenkins, David Eargle, Seth Howard, and Anthony Vance. 2015. How Polymorphic Warnings Reduce Habituation in the Brain: Insights from an fMRI Study. In Proceedings of the 33rd Annual ACM Conference on Human Factors in Computing Systems (CHI '15). ACM, New York, NY, USA, 2883-2892. DOI=10.1145/2702123.2702322 http://doi.acm.org/10.1145/2702123.2702322

9. Brislin, Richard W. Back-translation for cross-cultural research. *Journal of cross-cultural psychology* 1, no. 3 (1970): 185-216.

10. Cartwright, Dorwin. Achieving Change in People: Some Applications of Group Dynamics Theory1. *Group Facilitation* 9 (2008): 59.

11. Cialdini, Robert B., Carl A. Kallgren, and Raymond R. Reno. A focus theory of normative conduct: A theoretical refinement and reevaluation of the role of norms in human behavior. *Advances in experimental social psychology* 24, no. 20 (1991): 1-243.

12. Cooper, David, and John H. Kagel. Other regarding preferences: a selective survey of experimental results. *Handbook of experimental economics* 2 (2009).

13. Deutsch, Morton. An experimental study of the effects of cooperation and competition upon group process. *Human relations* 2, no. 3 (1949): 199-231.

14. DiMicco, Joan Morris, Katherine J. Hollenbach, Anna Pandolfo, and Walter Bender. The impact of increased awareness while face-to-face. *Human–Computer Interaction* 22, no. 1-2 (2007): 47-96.

15. Dörnyei, Zoltán. Psychological processes in cooperative language learning: Group dynamics and motivation. *Modern Language Journal* (1997): 482-493.

16. Eric P.S. Baumer, Sherri Jean Katz, Jill E. Freeman, Phil Adams, Amy L. Gonzales, John Pollak, Daniela Retelny, Jeff Niederdeppe, Christine M. Olson, and Geri K. Gay. 2012. Prescriptive persuasion and open-ended social awareness: expanding the design space of mobile health. In Proceedings of the ACM 2012 conference on Computer Supported Cooperative Work (CSCW '12). ACM, New York, NY, USA, 475-484. DOI=10.1145/2145204.2145279 http://doi.acm.org/10.1145/2145204.2145279

17. Forsythe, Robert, Joel L. Horowitz, Nathan E. Savin, and Martin Sefton. Fairness in simple bargaining experiments. *Games and Economic behavior* 6, no. 3 (1994): 347-369.

18. Grandjean, Etienne, and W. Hünting. Ergonomics of posture—review of various problems of standing and sitting posture. *Applied ergonomics* 8, no. 3 (1977): 135-140.

19. Haug, Severin, Christian Meyer, Gudrun Schorr, Stephanie Bauer, and Ulrich John. Continuous individual support of smoking cessation using text messaging: a pilot experimental study. *Nicotine & Tobacco Research* (2009): ntp084.

20. Hofstede, Geert. Dimensionalizing cultures: The Hofstede model in context. *Online readings in psychology and culture* 2, no. 1 (2011): 8.

21. Hou, Melody Y., Shelley Hurwitz, Erin Kavanagh, Jennifer Fortin, and Alisa B. Goldberg. Using daily text-message reminders to improve adherence with oral contraceptives: a randomized controlled trial. *Obstetrics & Gynecology*116, no. 3 (2010): 633-640.

22. James J. Lin, Lena Mamykina, Silvia Lindtner, Gregory Delajoux, and Henry B. Strub. 2006. Fish'n'Steps: encouraging physical activity with an interactive computer game. In Proceedings of the 8th international conference on Ubiquitous Computing (UbiComp'06), Paul Dourish and Adrian Friday (Eds.). Springer-Verlag, Berlin, Heidelberg, 261-278. DOI=10.1007/11853565_16 http://dx.doi.org/10.1007/11853565_16

23. Janienke Sturm, Olga Houben-van Herwijnen, Anke Eyck, and Jacques Terken. 2007. Influencing social dynamics in meetings through a peripheral display. In Proceedings of the 9th international conference on Multimodal interfaces (ICMI '07). ACM, New York,

NY, USA, 263-270. DOI=10.1145/1322192.1322238 http://doi.acm.org/10.1145/1322192.1322238

24. Jun-Ki Min, Afsaneh Doryab, Jason Wiese, Shahriyar Amini, John Zimmerman, and Jason I. Hong. 2014. Toss 'n' turn: smartphone as sleep and sleep quality detector. In Proceedings of the SIGCHI Conference on Human Factors in Computing Systems (CHI '14). ACM, New York, NY, USA, 477-486. DOI=http://dx.doi.org/10.1145/2556288.2557220
25. Kalsher, Michael J., and Kevin J. Williams. Behavioral compliance: Theory, methodology, and results. *Handbook of warnings* (2006): 313-329.
26. Kelly, John Francis, Molly Magill, and Robert Lauren Stout. How do people recover from alcohol dependence? A systematic review of the research on mechanisms of behavior change in Alcoholics Anonymous. *Addiction Research & Theory* 17, no. 3 (2009): 236-259.
27. Kiran K. Rachuri, Mirco Musolesi, Cecilia Mascolo, Peter J. Rentfrow, Chris Longworth, and Andrius Aucinas. 2010. EmotionSense: a mobile phones based adaptive platform for experimental social psychology research. In Proceedings of the 12th ACM international conference on Ubiquitous computing (UbiComp '10). ACM, New York, NY, USA, 281-290. DOI=http://dx.doi.org/10.1145/1864349.1864393
28. Meng-Chieh Chiu, Shih-Ping Chang, Yu-Chen Chang, Hao-Hua Chu, Cheryl Chia-Hui Chen, Fei-Hsiu Hsiao, and Ju-Chun Ko. 2009. Playful bottle: a mobile social persuasion system to motivate healthy water intake. In Proceedings of the 11th international conference on Ubiquitous computing (UbiComp '09). ACM, New York, NY, USA, 185-194. DOI=10.1145/1620545.1620574 http://doi.acm.org/10.1145/1620545.1620574.
29. Manapat, Michael L., Martin A. Nowak, and David G. Rand. Information, irrationality, and the evolution of trust. *Journal of Economic Behavior & Organization* 90 (2013): S57-S75.
30. NIKE PLUS, https://secure-nikeplus.nike.com/plus/
31. Pavol Bielik, Michal Tomlein, Peter Krátky, Štefan Mitrík, Michal Barla, and Mária Bieliková. 2012. Move2Play: an innovative approach to encouraging people to be more physically active. In Proceedings of the 2nd ACM SIGHIT International Health Informatics Symposium (IHI '12). ACM, New York, NY, USA, 61-70. DOI=10.1145/2110363.2110374 http://doi.acm.org/10.1145/2110363.2110374
32. Rajan Vaish, Keith Wyngarden, Jingshu Chen, Brandon Cheung, and Michael S. Bernstein. 2014. Twitch crowdsourcing: crowd contributions in short bursts of time. In Proceedings of the SIGCHI Conference on Human Factors in Computing Systems (CHI '14). ACM, New York, NY, USA, 3645-3654. DOI=10.1145/2556288.2556996 http://doi.acm.org/10.1145/2556288.2556996
33. Riley, William, Albert Jerome, Albert Behar, and Jennifer Weil. Computer and manual self-help behavioral strategies for smoking reduction: initial feasibility and one-year follow-up. *Nicotine & tobacco research* 4, no. Suppl 2 (2002): S183-S188.
34. Robert LiKamWa, Yunxin Liu, Nicholas D. Lane, and Lin Zhong. 2013. MoodScope: building a mood sensor from smartphone usage patterns. In Proceeding of the 11th annual international conference on Mobile systems, applications, and services (MobiSys '13). ACM, New York, NY, USA, 389-402. DOI=http://dx.doi.org/10.1145/2462456.2464449
35. Schachter, Stanley. Deviation, rejection, and communication. *The Journal of Abnormal and Social Psychology* 46, no. 2 (1951): 190.
36. Schultz, P. Wesley, Jessica M. Nolan, Robert B. Cialdini, Noah J. Goldstein, and Vladas Griskevicius. The constructive, destructive, and reconstructive power of social norms. *Psychological science* 18, no. 5 (2007): 429-434.
37. Sherif, Muzafer. The psychology of social norms. (1936).
38. Shmueli, Erez, Vivek K. Singh, Bruno Lepri, and Alex Pentland. Sensing, Understanding, and Shaping Social Behavior. *Computational Social Systems, IEEE Transactions on* 1, no. 1 (2014): 22-34.
39. Skinner, Burrhus Frederic. The behavior of organisms: An experimental analysis. (1938).
40. Stout, Lynn A. Other-regarding preferences and social norms. *Georgetown Law and Economics Research Paper* 265902 (2001).
41. Strauss, Anselm, and Juliet Corbin. Grounded theory methodology. *Handbook of qualitative research* (1994): 273-285.
42. Sunny Consolvo, David W. McDonald, Tammy Toscos, Mike Y. Chen, Jon Froehlich,Beverly Harrison, Predrag Klasnja, Anthony LaMarca, Louis LeGrand, Ryan Libby, Ian Smith, and James A. Landay. 2008. Activity sensing in the wild: a field trial of ubifit garden. In Proceedings of the SIGCHI Conference on Human Factors in Computing Systems (CHI '08). ACM, New York, NY, USA, 1797-1806. DOI=10.1145/1357054.1357335 http://doi.acm.org/10.1145/1357054.1357335
43. Sunny Consolvo, Katherine Everitt, Ian Smith, and James A. Landay. 2006. Design requirements for technologies that encourage physical activity. In

Proceedings of the SIGCHI Conference on Human Factors in Computing Systems (CHI '06), Rebecca Grinter, Thomas Rodden, Paul Aoki, Ed Cutrell, Robin Jeffries, and Gary Olson (Eds.). ACM, New York, NY, USA, 457-466. DOI=10.1145/1124772.1124840 http://doi.acm.org/10.1145/1124772.1124840

44. Taemie Kim, Agnes Chang, Lindsey Holland, and Alex Sandy Pentland. 2008. Meeting mediator: enhancing group collaborationusing sociometric feedback. In Proceedings of the 2008 ACM conference on Computer supported cooperative work (CSCW '08). ACM, New York, NY, USA, 457-466. DOI=10.1145/1460563.1460636 http://doi.acm.org/10.1145/1460563.1460636.

45. Leena Ventä, Minna Isomursu, Aino Ahtinen, and Shruti Ramiah. 2008. "My Phone is a Part of My Soul" - How People Bond with Their Mobile Phones. In Proceedings of the 2008 The Second International Conference on Mobile Ubiquitous Computing, Systems, Services and Technologies (UBICOMM '08). IEEE Computer Society, Washington, DC, USA, 311-317. DOI=http://dx.doi.org/10.1109/UBICOMM.2008.48.

46. Womersley, Lauren, and Stephen May. Sitting posture of subjects with postural backache. *Journal of manipulative and physiological therapeutics* 29, no. 3 (2006): 213-218.

47. Wong, Wai Yin, and Man Sang Wong. Detecting spinal posture change in sitting positions with tri-axial accelerometers. *Gait & Posture* 27, no. 1 (2008): 168-171.

48. Yeoreum Lee, Youn-kyung Lim, and Hyeon-Jeong Suk. 2011. Altruistic interaction design: a new interaction design approach for making people care more about others. In Proceedings of the 2011 Conference on Designing Pleasurable Products and Interfaces (DPPI '11). ACM, New York, NY, USA, Article 9, 4 pages. DOI=10.1145/2347504.2347514 http://doi.acm.org/10.1145/2347504.2347514

49. Zhang, Shumei, Paul McCullagh, Chris Nugent, Huiru Zheng, and Matthias Baumgarten. Optimal model selection for posture recognition in home-based healthcare. *International Journal of Machine Learning and Cybernetics* 2, no. 1 (2011): 1-14.

Body Integrated Programmable Joints Interface

Sang-won Leigh
MIT Media Lab
75 Amherst St, Cambridge, USA
sangwon@media.mit.edu

Pattie Maes
MIT Media Lab
75 Amherst St, Cambridge, USA
pattie@media.mit.edu

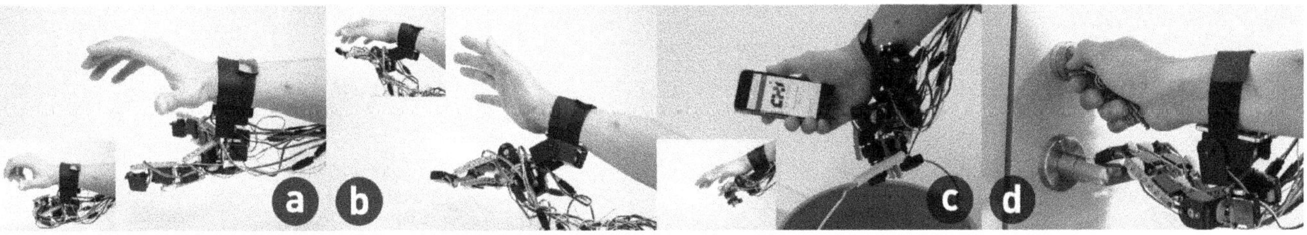

Figure 1: Different configurations for our device. a) A gripper on wrist, b) another palm to pick up big objects, c) a hook inside hand, and d) robotic joints working in tandem unlocking a door (the hand turns the key, and the joints rotate the knob).

ABSTRACT

Physical interfaces with actuation capability enable the design of wearable devices that augment human physical capabilities. Extra machine joints integrated to our biological body may allow us to achieve additional skills through programmatic reconfiguration of the joints. To that end, we present a wearable multi-joint interface that offers "synergistic interactions" by providing additional fingers, structural supports, and physical user interfaces. Motions of the machine joints can be controlled via interfacing with our muscle signals, as a direct extension of our body. On the basis of implemented applications, we demonstrate our design guidelines for creating a desirable human-machine synergy – that enhances our innate capabilities, not replacing or obstructing, and also without enforcing the augmentation. Finally we describe technical details of our muscle-based control method and implementations of the presented applications.

Author Keywords

Synergistic Interaction; Programmable Joints Interface

ACM Classification Keywords

H.5.2 User Interfaces: Input devices and strategies (e.g., mouse, touchscreen)

INTRODUCTION

Wearable computers are changing the way we access information in a real-time and ubiquitous manner. While they enable an increase in our intellectual capability, a physically engaging wearable design can lead to a functional amplification of our physiology. In order to explore this possibility, we implemented a mechanical hand augmentation device and studied potential "synergistic interactions" between our body and the device.

Human hands play a central role in creative endeavors [27] as a tool for creation and the manifestation of sophisticated skills. However, advancements in digital technology and graphical user interfaces have created an artificial blockade between our hands and the world, limiting their interaction to an increasingly infinitesimal point of contact. This not only results in a disconnect from our rich kinesthetic experience, but also a potential loss of innate skills.

A similar criticism can be applied to the trans-humanistic idea of electro-mechanical prostheses, as is depicted in science fiction often as a dystopian and dehumanized element [5]. However, we speculate that the criticism has to do with a specific "possible" future where human capability is "substituted" by lifeless machines. There have been few studies that establish design guidelines for "desirable" human-machine hybrids and corresponding applications firmly based on current human needs.

In this paper, we present a wrist-worn joints device that consists of 11 mechanical joints and is capable of rendering different physical form factors that suit to different tasks. We based our design and applications on four principles: 1) the device should not hinder or replace a user's innate capability, 2) the device should be able to disengage from the user's context without enforcing continuous use of it [16], 3) the device should remain an "interface"– that is, perceived as a tool/object rather than being a fully implanted body organ, and lastly 4) it should serve multiple purposes – as having multiple wearable devices designed for different purposes is not desirable [8, 16]. Based on these principles, we envision a synergistic electro-mechanical body extension without disregard for the natural human body and its capabilities. We also demonstrate concrete applications illustrating the use of our device in everyday contexts along with implementation details.

CHI'16, May 07-12, 2016, San Jose, CA, USA
© 2016 ACM. ISBN 978-1-4503-3362-7/16/05…$15.00
DOI: http://dx.doi.org/10.1145/2858036.2858538

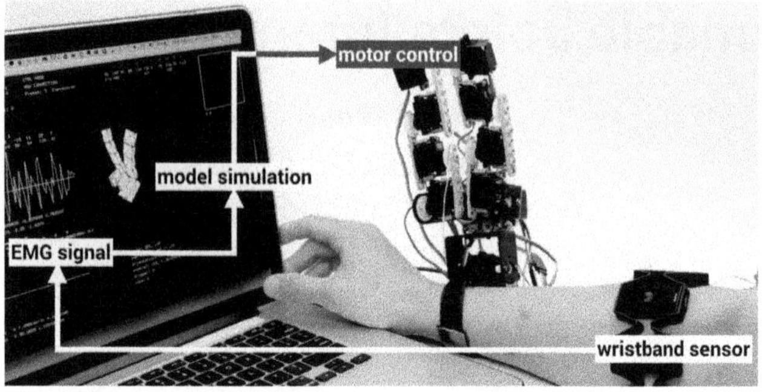

Figure 2: Sensor, control software, and the joints interface.

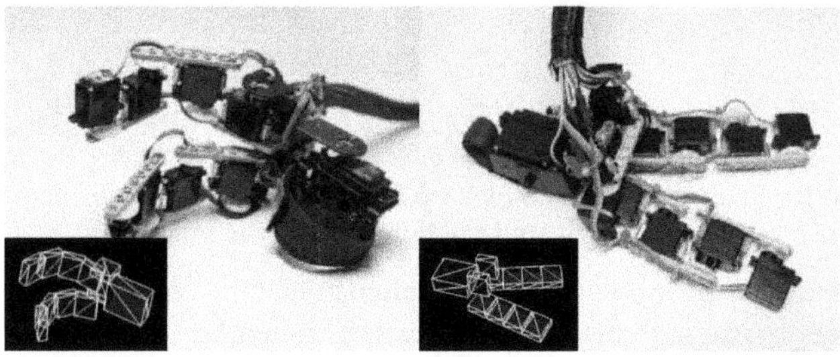

Figure 3: Our hardware. 11 motors are linked using LEGO parts, each of them with 180 degrees motion range. The wireframe diagrams illustrate the overall structure. Cables from each motor are connected to an Arduino controller.

PROGRAMMABLE JOINTS INTERFACE

The physical design of our joints device is created to maximize the rendering capability for various form factors, while maintaining a quasi-anthropomorphic setup so that a range of physical tasks can be performed [12, 15]. Therefore, our final design (Figure 3) consists of two finger-shaped segments (each with 4 pitch servos, and one yaw servo), mounted on a bigger base servo that adjusts the angular position of the entire device. The base servo can be mounted in different ways: on the forearm or the wrist, parallel or perpendicular to the arm. Each configuration provides different sets of functionalities since a segment has a wide motion range of a hemispheric coverage area (14 cm radius). For the motor control, we used Electromyography (EMG) signals from a MYO [2] sensor worn around the arm (Figure 2).

The wearable design of our device makes it easy to switch between use and non-use. Additionally, the device can disengage from the user's context by wrapping around the arm like a wristband (Figure 4). This allows the wearable design of the device less interfering, coming to the foreground only when assistance is required. The multiple use cases of the device and its compact "passive" state make it attractive as a device that is worn by the user all the time, the way one wears a watch all day long.

RELATED WORK

From Linear to Vertical Robotic Extension

Robotic exoskeletons and prosthetic limbs are closely related research fields. Exoskeletons are used for acquiring extended performance, rehabilitation, or tele-presence [18, 23]. Prostheses are designed to replace loss of body

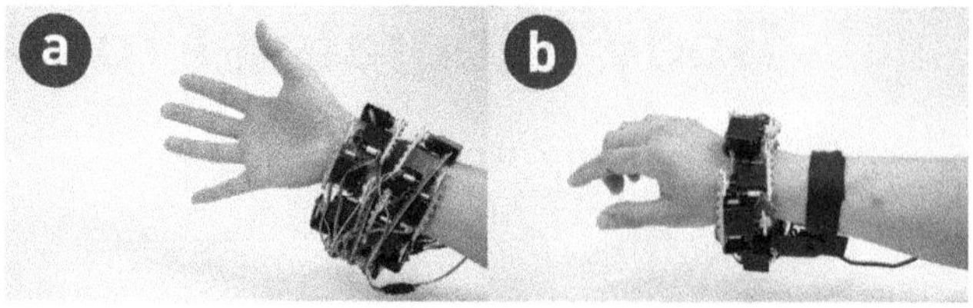

Figure 4: Disengaged wristband configurations.

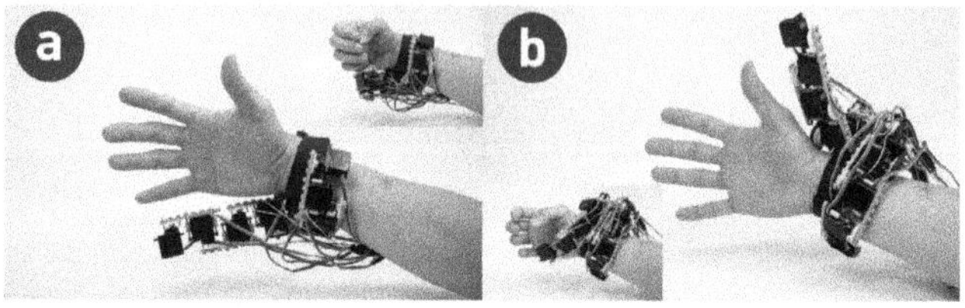

Figure 5: Additional finger configurations, a) extra little finger, b) extra thumb.

function with equivalent artificial additions, simulating sensory or functional capabilities of the human hand in the artificial limb [6, 7, 22]. In spite of their amplifying nature, the types of augmentation are limited to copying or linearly extending (e.g. stronger, longer) our innate ability.

Recently, a more radical augmentation has been explored in research on supernumerary limbs [21, 28]. This field studies additional robotic fingers or limbs that support physical tasks by reducing load or aiding in object manipulation. These works present more synergistic collaboration between human and robot, however, their control and mechanical design are heavily focused on replicating human motions, whereas more variety in form factors and motions could open up new interaction opportunities beyond increases in number.

Reconfigurable Body and Garment

In tele-presence contexts, shape displays [17] have been used to create a reconfigurable physical representation of a user's hands, although the alteration only happens in the remote space disconnected from the user's context. Electrical muscle stimulation also has been used for learning manual skills or interactions with an object [19, 25]. However, these systems only rely on existing limbs, limiting the applications to ones possible with the original body configuration. Actuated wearable garments [20, 24, 26] are also relevant, however, most of the applications are focused on information display rather than manipulation.

DESIGN OF MUSCLE-GEAR RELATION

Synergistic Action: Hand Augmentation

Our biological hands and the mechanical joints can work in synergy to provide a user with increased manipulation capability. For example, a guitarist can use extra fingers to invent a phrase formerly impossible to play, or a rubik's cube can be solved by one hand – with extra fingers holding it. These capabilities are provided in addition to the user's own hands, neither substituting nor interfering with them.

We implemented various configurations: a wrist-worn gripper (Figure 1 a), a second palm that opens against a

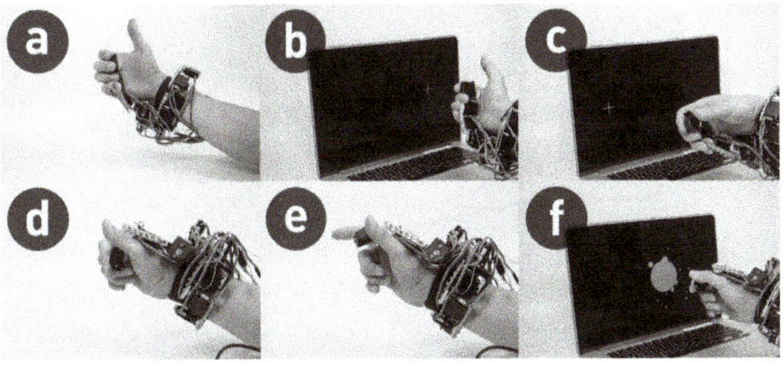

Figure 6: a) Joystick interface, b-c) two DoF pointer control with the stick, d) trigger interface, e) recoiling after the trigger action, f) aim can be adjusted by wrist motion.

user's own palm and helps with picking up large objects (Figure 1 b), a hook tool (Figure 1 c), and extra fingers with similar function and motions as the existing ones (Figure 5).

The additional joints are controlled by the EMG signal (regarded as an intuitive prosthesis control method [14]) picked up from muscles around the elbow, which can be coordinated by the user independently from normal hand movements (discussed in the implementation section). Therefore, the user can freely maneuver his/her hands separately from the joints' motion, thereby facilitating synergistic collaboration between original capabilities of hands and the extra capability acquired by the joints. Also, the control can be driven by context-awareness, e.g. the joints rotate a doorknob while the user is unlocking the key (Figure 1 d).

Additionally, we used the Gesture Recognition Toolkit [1] to utilize more sophisticated hand gestures. A fist-making gesture triggers the mechanical joints to disengage by turning into the idle wristband configuration (Figure 4), thereby switching the user's hands back to their innate capability. In the idle mode, wave-in/out gestures can be used to switch between different active modes.

Intra-Interaction: User Interface On-the-go

The device can be dynamically reconfigured to provide certain physical affordances, and utilized as a haptic User Interface (UI) on demand. In a setup similar to the extra little finger, we configured the device to be used as a *joystick controller* held by the user (Figure 6 a-c). By deactivating two of the servos, the joystick provides two degrees of freedom (DoF) control. Then we modified the two servos to read their potentiometer values (angle), and used those values for 2D pointer control.

Another implementation is a *gun-trigger* type of interface. Once the trigger is pulled, the servos get activated and provide force-feedback: "clicking" and then "recoiling" back to their original positions (Figure 6 d-f). Detailed motion parameters (recoil speed, stiffness, etc.) can be programmatically encoded to simulate different types of physical triggers. The device can also shift between states/shapes to render nested and sequential affordances [10] e.g. locking the trigger when a game player runs out of ammo and unlocking once reloaded.

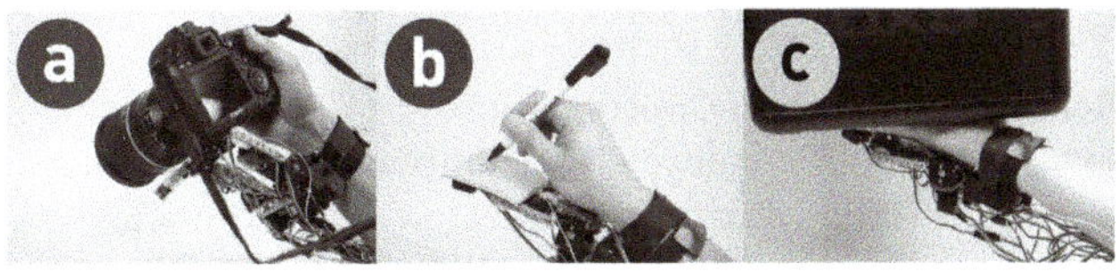

Figure 7: a) Holding support for photo shooting, b) canvas for handwriting, c) mechanical support for increased exertion capability.

These in-between interactions demonstrate the dual use for such body-mounted actuators. While hand augmentation is about ***machine-as-a-body-part***, this application is about ***machine-as-an-interface***. This duality is a key finding related to our third design principle: ***maintaining to be perceived as object/tool***.

Background Synergy: Structural Augmentation

Structural augmentation describes an inanimate form of machine engagement, where the control aspect of the joints device remains in the background. We implemented different passive support structures using the device in order to assist in bimanual tasks. The role of the non-dominant hand is offloaded to the passive joints structure (holding a camera lens or a note, Figure 7 a, b), therefore letting the user complete the tasks with one hand.

The device can also be configured to increase a user's exertion capability, e.g. help holding heavy objects like a wrist support used for bowling (Figure 7 c). An additional application is a lock mechanism that makes the user stay in a secure position e.g. locking on a bus handle.

Extended Connection

Beyond the hand-machine interactions described above, various intra-body or off-body configurations allow for connecting our hands to physically disconnected locations.

From an artistic perspective, artist Stelarc [3] deeply explored the trans-humanistic idea of having additional limbs. One interesting detail of his works was to use abdominal and leg muscles to control the third hand. Similarly, a user with an impairment of their leg muscles could drive a car by attaching our device on the ankle, so that s/he can operate a regular car's pedals by triggering the mechanical joints with their arm muscle activity (Figure 8 b). In off-body configurations such as a desk-mounted joints setup, the user can control the joints as an off-loaded body, and securely hold and maneuver a PCB board for soldering without the need of the third hand (Figure 8 a).

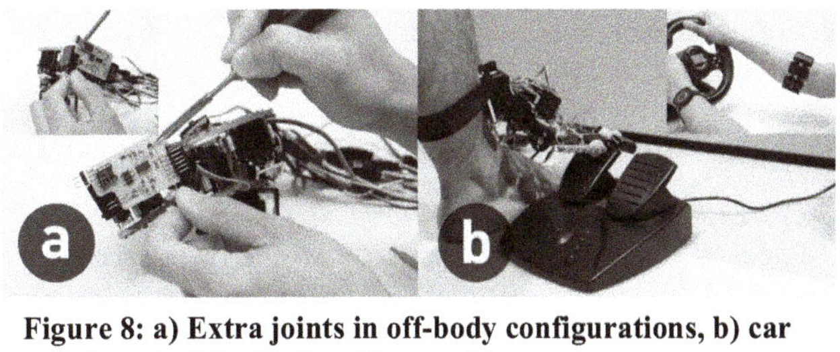

Figure 8: a) Extra joints in off-body configurations, b) car pedal control for the handicapped.

IMPLEMENTATION

Sensing and Motion Coordination

In order to achieve independent control of the robotic joints, we used EMG data from brachioradialis (muscles on forearm near the elbow, Figure 9). We collected EMG response data from 7 test participants (6 males and 1 female, age 23 – 36) during 13 different hand gestures that are commonly used (fist, thumbs up, waving in/out, palm stretched, and so on). The EMG response from the brachioradialis showed very low correlation with all of these gestures (Figure 10). Therefore, we could utilize this muscle as an additional modality alongside hand gestures. The raw EMG signal from the muscle is filtered to acquire stabilized amplitude, which is then used for control input.

The motions of the robotic joints are controlled parametrically so that a sophisticated behavior can be coordinated with low-dimension control inputs. This synergy-based control [4, 11] effectively offloads the user-side adaptation, therefore removing the learning curve for different configurations given by our device.

One limitation of the current implementation is the dynamic range of EMG signal control. A user's fine-grained linear control of the EMG signal strength may be difficult, and may require some training. To overcome that, a future implementation can generate personalized calibrations so that the signal gets adaptively linearized for a better control.

Exertion Capability and Load Capacity

The exertion capability of the joints largely differs based on their structural configurations, but to give a general idea we tested its capability in two cases. The measured maximum force exerted by the gripper is 0.49 kg, and the hook has a 0.98 kg lifting capability. The joints hold more load in a static configuration, therefore, reasonably heavy objects can be handled with passive structural support by the joints. Each of the motor has 2.3kg-cm torque.

Mode Transition

One key feature of our device is its versatility. As we have showcased, it can serve for multiple purposes by sequentially rendering different shapes and motions. This reduces the need for having multiple devices, which is especially relevant in the case of wearable systems since our body has limited space for adding extra devices and interfaces.

For a seamless switch between modes, we implemented "transition animations" for in-between behaviors. For example, when the joints move from *idle* wristband configuration to *extra little finger*, the finger segment first unrolls from the wrist, and then extends towards its final position to avoid crashing into the user's hand.

BETWEEN AUGMENTATION AND SEPARATION

Heidegger mentioned the states of a tool being ***ready-to-hand*** and being ***present-at-hand*** [13]. This describes the varying nature of the user-side perception of the tool – the tool becomes invisible when its user is engaged in an action

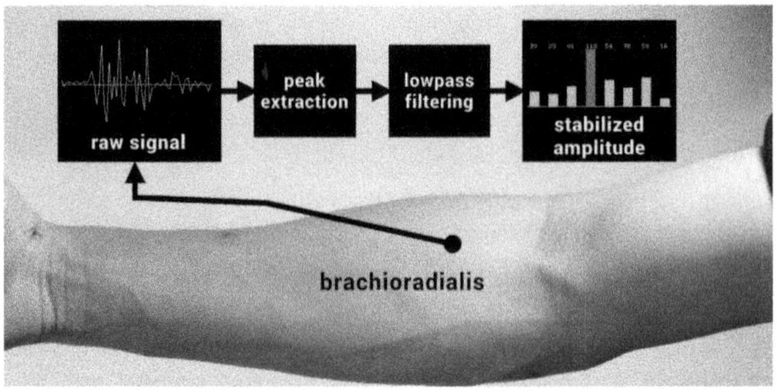

Figure 9: EMG signal from brachioradialis is processed and used for independent control of the joints.

sensor location \ gesture type	1	2	3	4	5	6	7	8	9	10	11	12	13
A	52.30	27.72	59.01	50.06	43.51	34.09	35.44	33.89	53.65	39.29	45.96	34.80	53.46
B	47.89	20.10	51.13	34.29	47.64	41.26	22.57	33.52	55.37	32.47	41.50	35.91	54.30
C	14.32	18.79	46.25	16.39	16.97	14.38	13.22	18.40	13.80	19.28	25.81	12.41	12.09
D	13.27	23.50	9.31	21.42	15.15	16.16	17.66	15.81	14.05	16.54	15.95	15.09	10.54
E	50.42	66.03	8.64	48.30	21.90	35.28	31.29	34.31	17.26	27.74	29.90	51.14	24.33
F	32.59	80.92	34.06	79.44	34.92	68.70	62.11	68.41	51.69	64.31	63.73	56.04	52.97
G	50.39	48.43	34.07	43.99	30.05	23.98	30.95	30.72	39.76	26.67	38.26	26.29	55.82
H	60.89	24.06	50.04	37.45	23.61	21.81	22.07	21.53	31.08	26.75	19.25	18.91	57.70

Figure 10: Correlation matrix between EMG signals and common hand gestures. Adjacent rows are adjacent pads of the MYO device. (D: signal from brachioradialis)

with it. Once disengaged, s/he is able to consciously inspect the tool, where Dourish explains that an effective use of tool involves continual engagement, separation, and re-engagement [9]. Through our example of a body-integrated augmentation device, we shed light on this discussion with a comparison between ***machine-as-a-body-part*** and ***machine-as-an-interface***. Continuous use of an augmentation could hinder the perceived separation between the biological and mechanical bodies, therefore, the user may fail to consciously distinguish his/her innate capabilities from the ones acquired by the augmentation. This necessitates continual transitions between "augmentation" and "separation", so as to design an augmentation technology that does not compromise human nature.

CONCLUSION

In this paper we proposed a wearable and programmable joints interface that extends our physical capabilities. Through concrete applications, ranging from mechanical hand augmentation to providing physical UI on-the-go, we demonstrated synergistic interaction between our hands and the machine joints. These are implemented on the basis of certain guidelines, so that the electro-mechanical augmentation does not replace or obstruct our innate kinesthetic skills. In order to achieve controls of the joints independent from normal hand movements, we used EMG signals from the brachioradialis muscles. This allows intuitive extension of our innate hands, and additionally, the same signal can be used for various configurations – lowering the hurdle of user adaptation. Our wearable design allows the device to easily disengage from the user's context, providing augmentations only when they are needed rather than enforcing the continuous use of them.

REFERENCES

1. Gesture Recognition Toolkit: http://www.nickgillian.com/software/grt
2. MYO Armband: http://www.myo.com
3. Third Hand: http://stelarc.org/?catID=20265
4. Brown, C., Asada, H. Inter-finger coordination and posture synergies in robot hands via mechanical implementation of Principal Component Analysis. In Proc. IROS '07. http://dx.doi.org/10.1109/IROS.2007.4399547
5. Brummett, B. Rhetoric of Machine Aesthetics. Praeger. 1999.
6. Bundhoo, V. and Park, E. J. Design of an artificial muscle actuated finger towards biomimetic prosthetic hands. In Proc. ICAR '05. http://dx.doi.org/10.1109/ICAR.2005.1507437
7. Carrozza, M. C., Massa, B., Micera, S., Lazzarini, R., Zecca, M., and Dario, P. The development of a novel prosthetic hand-ongoing research and preliminary results. IEEE/ASME Trans. Mechatronics. Aug 2002. http://dx.doi.org/10.1109/TMECH.2002.1011247
8. Clawson, J., Pater, J. A., Miller, A. D., Mynatt, E. D., Mamykina, L. No Longer Wearing: Investigating the Abandonment of Personal Health-Tracking Technologies on Craigslist. In Proc. UbiComp '15. http://dx.doi.org/10.1145/2750858.2807554
9. Dourish, P. Where the Action Is: The Foundations of Embodied Interaction. MIT Press. 2001.
10. Gaver, W. Technology affordances. In Proc. CHI 91. ACM Press: NY (1991), 79-84. http://dx.doi.org/10.1145/108844.108856
11. Gioio, G., Salvietti, G., Malvezi, M., Prattichizzo, D. Mapping synergies from human to robotic hands with dissimilar kinematics: an approach in the object domain. IEEE Trans. Robotics. Aug 2013. http://dx.doi.org/10.1109/TRO.2013.2252251
12. Hammond III, F. L., Weisz, J., de la Llera Kurth, A. A., Allen, P. K., Howe, R. D. Towards a Design Optimization Method for Reducing the Mechanical Complexity of Underactuated Robotic Hands. In Proc. ICRA '12. http://dx.doi.org/10.1109/ICRA.2012.6225010
13. Heidegger, M. Being and Time. New York: Harper & Row. 1962.
14. Ison, M., Artemiadis, P. Proportional Myoelectric Control of Robots: Muscle Synergy Development Drives Performance Enhancement, Retainment, and Generalization. IEEE Trans. Robotics '15. http://dx.doi.org/10.1109/TRO.2015.2395731
15. Jacobsen, S. C., Iversen, E. K., Knutti, D., Johnson, R., Biggers, K. Design of the Utah/MIT Dextrous Hand. In Proc. ICRA '86. http://dx.doi.org/10.1109/ROBOT.1986.1087395
16. Lazar, A., Koehler, C., Tanenbaum, J., Nguyen, D. H. Why We Use and Abandon Smart Devices. In Proc. UbiComp '15. http://dx.doi.org/10.1145/2750858.2804288
17. Leithinger, D., Follmer, S., Olwal, A., Ishii, H. Physical telepresence: shape capture and display for embodied, computer-mediated remote collaboration. In Proc. UIST '14. http://dx.doi.org/10.1145/2642918.2647377
18. Lemley, B. Really Special Forces. Discover 25–26. 2002.
19. Lopes, P., Jonell, P., Baudisch, P. Affordance++: Allowing Objects to Communicate Dynamic Use. In Proc. CHI '15. http://dx.doi.org/10.1145/2702123.2702128
20. MacLean, D., Roseway, A., Czerwinski, M. MoodWings: A Wearable Biofeedback Device for Real- Time Stress Intervention. In Proc. PETRA '13. http://dx.doi.org/10.1145/2504335.2504406
21. Parietti, F., Asada, H., Chan, K., Bracing the Human Body with Supernumerary Robotic Limbs for Physical Assistance and Load Reduction. In Proc. ICRA '14. http://dx.doi.org/10.1109/ICRA.2014.6906601
22. Popovic, M. B., Popovic, D. B., Tomovic, R. Control of Arm Movement: Reaching Synergies for Neuroprosthesis with Life-Like Control. Journal of Automatic Control. Jan 2002. http://dx.doi.org/10.2298%2fJAC0201009P
23. Pratt, J.E., Krupp, B.T., Morse, C.J., Collins, S.H. The RoboKnee: an exoskeleton for enhancing strength and endurance during walking. In Proc. ICRA '04. http://dx.doi.org/10.1109/ROBOT.2004.1307425
24. Saga, T., Munekata, N., Ono, T. Daily Support Robots that Move on Me. SIGRRAPH ASIA '14 Emerging Technologies. http://dx.doi.org/10.1145/2658861.2658882
25. Tamaki, E., Miyaki, T., Rekimoto, J. PossessedHand: techniques for controlling human hands using electrical muscles stimuli. In Proc. CHI '11. http://dx.doi.org/10.1145/1978942.1979018
26. Williams, M. A., Roseway, A., O'Dowd, C. SWARM: An Actuated Wearable for Mediating Affect. In Proc. TEI '15. http://dx.doi.org/10.1145/2677199.2680565
27. Wilson, F. The Hand: How Its Use Shapes the Brain, Language, and Human Culture. Pantheon books. 1998.
28. Wu, F. Y. and Asada, H. Bio-Artificial Synergies for Grasp Posture Control of Supernumerary Robotic Fingers. In Robotics: Science and Systems. 2014. http://hdl.handle.net/1721.1/88457

Mirror Mirror: an On-Body T-shirt Design System

Daniel Saakes [1] **Hui-Shyong Yeo** [2] **Seung-Tak Noh** [2] **Gyeol Han** [1] **Woontack Woo** [2]

[1]Department of Industrial Design [2]Department of Cultural Technologies
KAIST, Republic of Korea
{saakes, hsyeo, stnoh, hgyeols, wwoo}@kaist.ac.kr

Figure 1. ***Mirror Mirror* is a design system that combines Spatial Augmented Reality with a mirror display. Virtual garments are visible in the mirror reflection (a) as well as on the body (b). Multi user interaction is supported (c, d) and designs are readily printed (e).**

ABSTRACT

Virtual fitting rooms equipped with magic mirrors let people evaluate fashion items without actually putting them on. The mirrors superimpose virtual clothes on the user's reflection. We contribute the *Mirror Mirror* system, which not only supports mixing and matching of existing fashion items, but also lets users design new items in front of the mirror and export designs to fabric printers. While much of the related work deals with interactive cloth simulation on live user data, we focus on collaborative design activities and explore various ways of designing on the body with a mirror.

ACM Classification Keywords

H.5.2 Information Interfaces and Presentation (e.g. HCI): Graphical user interfaces.

Author Keywords

Augmented Reality; Design Interface; Magic Mirror; Fashion.

INTRODUCTION

Online shopping is popular across many product categories, but the assessment of certain products such as furniture, apparel, and eyeglasses is difficult to conduct online. These products require a situated experience, on the body or in the living environment. Retail stores offering such products apply various technologies to support the selection process [6]. Virtual fitting rooms equipped with magic mirrors superimpose virtual clothing on users' mirror images. Consumers can artificially test the "fit" without actually putting on items and can "try on" various items effortlessly.

In this note, we explore one possible future of magic mirrors. Mirrors to personalize and design custom clothes in the store or at home, to be fabricated on the spot and ready to wear. Although digital fabrication allows the creation of personalized items, the design of objects in which the "fit" of the object is established in the user's context is still an underdeveloped topic in the field of design by users [16, 31].

We present *Mirror Mirror*, a personal T-shirt design system. We combine Spatial Augmented Reality [3] with a mirror to achieve high fidelity 3D feedback. In this way, augmented graphics are visible on the body, in the reflection, and on the background, and so it is possible to employ both the foreground and background of users' attention [13]. Multiple users interact not only through the mirror but also in direct line of sight as is deemed important in shared activities [4, 11].

Our contribution is twofold: 1) A novel optical setup that combines Spatial Augmented Reality with a mirror to support multi-user interaction with a direct line of sight and third-person perspective through the reflection in the mirror. 2) We explore and evaluate several interaction scenarios for designing items with a mirror.

RELATED WORK

Several art installations [2, 20, 24] and fashion shows [27] use projectors to color persons and objects with digital video. However, this process requires a carefully calibrated setup and limits the freedom of motion. Systems that support projection mapping on free-moving 3D objects, require a sophisticated motion capture stage. For instance, dynamic shader lamps [3] and digital airbrushing with Spatial Augmented Reality [18] let users draw with virtual paint on physical surfaces using tracked

CHI'16, May 07-12, 2016, San Jose, CA, USA
 ISBN 978-1-4503-3362-7/16/05?$15.00
DOI: http://dx.doi.org/10.1145/2858036.2858282

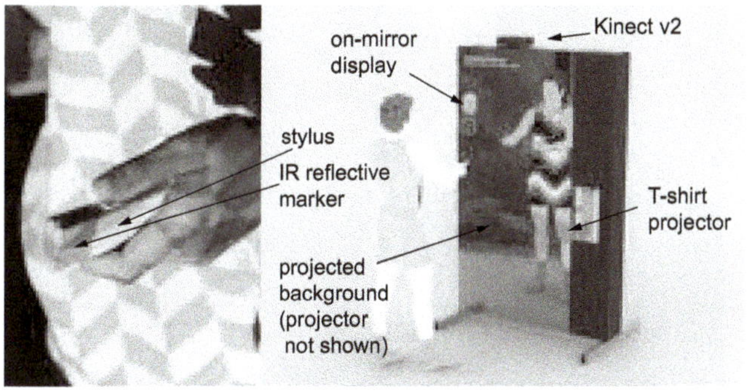

Figure 2. The *Mirror Mirror* system consists of a Kinect v2 depth sensor to capture the pose of multiple users. A projector projects virtual T-shirts on them. Gestures with tracked styli, shown on the left, support interaction directly on the body or with the on-mirror display. A second projector (not shown) projects virtual background behind the users.

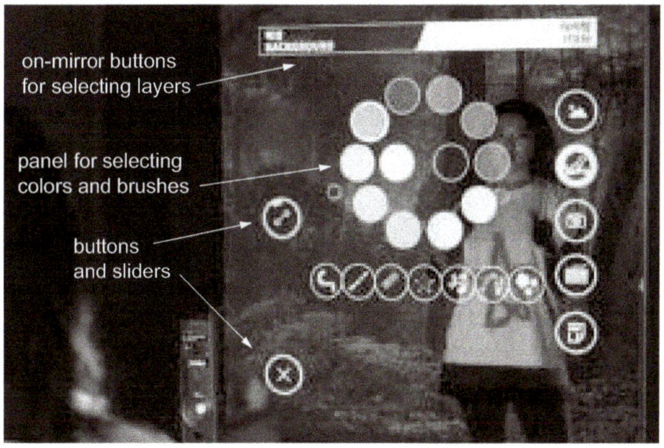

Figure 3. The display behind the Half-Silvered mirror reveals an on-mirror User Interface when a user is pointing at the mirror. Virtual buttons on the edges provide access to system functionality such as switch layer, undo, clear, take snapshot, or activate panels with additional functionality such for choosing colors and selecting brushes.

brushes. Omnitouch [9] mounts a depth camera on a user's shoulder to track hands and arms for interactive projections such as virtual watches. We build upon this work but track multiple persons in front of a mirror with a single depth sensor mounted on the mirror.

Most magic mirrors [12, 26, 28] use video based Augmented Reality that combines a camera and a display. Other systems [1, 17] optically combine real reflections with digital content using a display and a Half-Silvered Mirror (HSM). The Holoflector system [23] places the display at a distance behind the HSM equidistant to the user in front of the mirror to co-locate the digital content. By combining a regular mirror with projection mapping, *Mirror Mirror* achieves a similar 3D experience with a thin form-factor.

Related work in apparel design includes several magic mirrors [12] that have focused on real-time cloth simulation and the fit to the body [32, 33] or on accessories such as shoes [7] and handbags [30]. Whereas these systems focus on speed and accuracy *Mirror Mirror* instead target multi-user interaction and design of new items. Dressup [31] is a prototype for designing garments directly on a real tracked mannequin with tracked cutting and surfacing tools. Tactum [8] is a design system for designing wearables directly on the skin of the forearm with finger gestures. Both systems are relevant to our system, but both separate the input and visualization and thus require context switching. Nonetheless, both suggested projection mapping to situate visualization and interaction as future work.

DESIGN

With *Mirror Mirror* we explore design interfaces with a mirror and with interaction directly on the body. We aim to situate the design process; in the case of apparel, the fit on the person is an important criterion. Next, we aim to explore multi-user collaboration, because shopping is typically a social activity.

The *Mirror Mirror* system, shown in Figure 2, consists of a vertically mounted 55" display covered with HSM foil and is from top to bottom two-meter height. This mirror display provides an on-screen User Interface (UI), shown in Figure 3. Adjacent to the mirror, a short throw projector (BenQ W1080ST) projects on users in front of the mirror, and is calibrated with a Kinect v2 depth sensor using the OpenCV toolkit. We employ standard skeleton tracking to capture user pose and to dynamically generate 3D meshes for their upper body using 3D point cloud data. We render virtual T-shirts as UV textures on these meshes. Because we made graphics scale proportionally with the body size and shape, users can start right away, without calibration. This technique allows dynamic posing with interactive framerates (30fps) for up to four persons.

Users interact with the system using two wireless styli. Each stylus has a button and an absolute orientation sensor (BNO055) to determine whether users are pointing at their bodies or at the mirror and interacting with the on-screen UI. An IR reflective area on the tip of the stylus, shown in Figure 2 left, is used to estimate the position, by ray casting and blob tracking in the Kinect infrared camera feed. Kinect hand tracking, specifically near the body, has proved problematic and clicking buttons was felt to be more intuitive than hand gesture recognition. In multi-user scenarios the stylus might make the on-body interaction on the other person less uncomfortable [10] than using fingers.

Mid-air gestures with the styli are mapped to on-screen cursors to access system functionality such as activating virtual panels for selecting colors, graphics and brushes (Figure 3). Virtual buttons are located on edges of the mirror for easy access without obstructing mirror reflection and projection. Graphics and brushes can be transformed using mid-air gestures, or stamped and drawn directly on the body. Further on-body gestures place/scale/rotate graphics or strokes, similar to multi-touch applications. Dragging graphics outside the body deletes them. This seamless switching from on-screen to on-body interaction is enabled through the custom stylus and on-body, in-place, visualization.

Finally, a second projector (Benq MX842UST) projects a background in the room behind the user [14]. Immersing the users in the intended use-context helps design and evaluation.

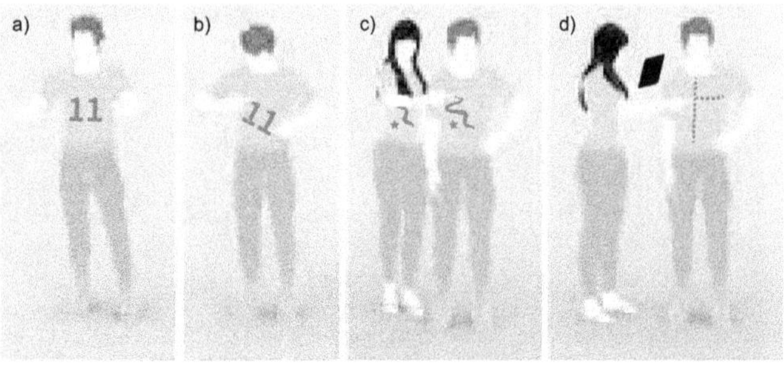

Figure 4. With *Mirror Mirror* we explored several scenarios for designing in front of a mirror. By using mid-air gestures for global transforms (a), or on-body gestures (b). Multiple users sharing a single design (c), or have a unique design. In tailor scenarios (d) a tablet replaces the on-mirror UI and lets the tailor face the client.

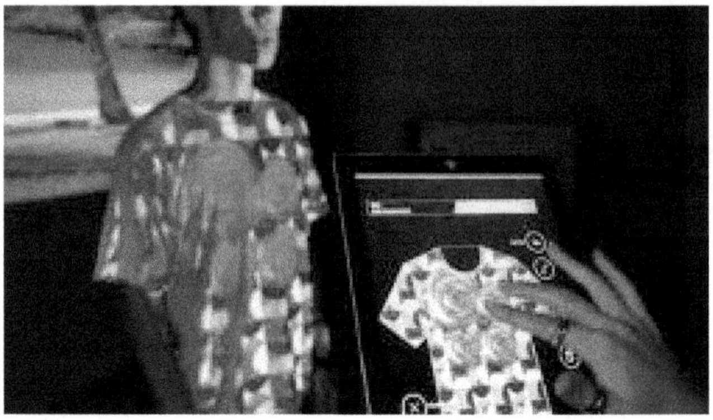

Figure 5. In a tailor scenario one user is drawing on another user. Because 'tailor' is facing the client, we provided a tablet UI in addition to the on-mirror UI. The tablet is realtime synchronized with the mirror.

When designing outdoor apparel one could select a forest and when designing suits for salarymen an office environment.

Content Creation

Mirror Mirror includes a sophisticated graphics design system with brushes for painting, and composing and patterning artwork from existing source materials, as is frequently seen in fashion design. For instance, a sports jersey can be quickly made with 1) a background color, 2) a stripe pattern scaled and rotated, 3) a club logo stamped in a new layer and 4) a hand drawn back number. Graphics are rendered as a texture for interactive projection or exported to PDF for printing. We have experience with several printing technologies including direct to garment professional T-shirt printers, shown in Figure 1e, and DIY transfer printing using irons.

Drawing on the body also supports a set of brushes with various colors, sizes and styles. Some brushes provide generative patterns, such as growing cherry blossoms or randomly sprinkled stars. Completed brush strokes are treated as objects that can be transformed and tiled. Using these features we have observed users make complicated graphics with tiling sketch strokes and masking, in similar to Vignette [15].

By using a mirror, graphics are lateral inverted. Hence, a text projected on the body appears to be mirrored in the reflection. Because the mirror provides the main feedback, we project graphics as reversed so that they look "correct" when observed in the mirror. Looking through the mirror while interacting on the body does not cause confusion in manipulation as in other mirror applications [19] because we perform on-body manipulation mostly parallel to the surface of the mirror. However, drawing text or numbers proved problematic in early user feedback. Therefore, a text input functionality was included.

Multi User Scenarios

A key feature of *Mirror Mirror* is multi-user interaction. Multiple users (Figure 4c and 1c) can design together while interacting with each other, providing feedback and recommendations. Shared design is useful for dance groups or sports teams and in couple design, for couples who want to express their affection by wearing matching outfits. Users draw on a shared T-shirt (the same design is projected on all users, but scaled to their body size), or on their own shirt. In current implementation, only one user can interact with the system and users raise hand to take control.

We explored tailor and client scenarios (Figure 4d and 5), in which one user makes a design fit another user. The tailor uses a tablet-based UI that is real time synchronized. With the tablet as a palette, brushes selected on the tablet are drawn on the body of the client, or graphics are directly manipulated on the tablet or a combination of both thanks to projection mapping. The client observes the process in the mirror.

USER STUDY

From early on we evaluated the system with pairs of design students. Several indicated that the on-body drawing was good to setup a quick sketch for a T-shirt, but it lacked the precision required for drawing a production-ready design: *"When I design with 2D programs such as Photoshop and Illustrator, I have purposes and goals for what I want to make. But this system gives me new inspiration and the chance to design something that I couldn't imagine or think of before, all using existing patterns."* Designers also wanted to continue detailing the design in Photoshop or Illustrator before having it made: *"I like this system to check the scale, position, and things like that. But I think I couldn't control things in detail with this"* and *"I think this is good for rough prototyping. I would like to move the design file to my computer after designing with this system, and edit the details."* Drawing on the body was reported to be difficult. Hence, we decided to compare the on-body and mid-air gestures with the tablet-based multi-touch interface in a within-subject user study.

We recruited 12 participants (M=23.75 years, SD=2.22) of which seven were females. Six participants were industrial designers working in industry, while the others were students without design background recruited from a local university. After a short introduction, we first demonstrated the mid-air and on-body user interface and gave the participant some time to familiarize with the system. We then asked them to reproduce two T-shirts from reference drawings with moderate complexity; the tasks involved drawing, stamping and patterning. This was followed by a free T-shirt design task. We then introduced the tablet-based interface , and let them reproduce

Figure 6. The top row T-shirts are designed during the user study using the on-body and mid-air gestures. The shirts on the center row are the corresponding designs made using the tablet. Bottom row shirts are designed by people during exhibitions.

two T-shirts from new reference drawings, also followed by a free design task. After finishing the designs, we interviewed the participants about their experiences. We videotaped the entire session which took about 40 minutes per person.

Result

All participants were much faster at completing the tasks on the tablet compared to doing so with the gesture-based interaction (in seconds: M=217.91, SD=96.64 vs. M=155.64, SD=84.99). Users felt very familiar when interacting with the multitouch surface whereas the gestures were new to them. Also, working on real scale requires more time due to the large gestures. However, fatigue due to the mid-air gestures was not reported. That being said, two-thirds of the participants experienced the gestures as more intuitive and enjoyed the novelty.

In the free task, we observed differences in the design process between the two conditions. The gestures engaged the users in an explorative process of playing with graphics and patterns while they gathered ideas for their design. In contrast, on the tablet, they were goal orientated and made their design without iteration. Although this difference can be well explained by the order of the conditions and users gaining familiarity with the system, however, as shown in Figure 6 participants made complete new designs.

When using the tablet, most users did not look in the mirror to evaluate the fit on their body as they were immersed in designing on the tablet: *"When I use the tablet, it is hard to check the mirror. I only concentrate on the tablet."* Some of the designers occasionally looked at their reflections in the mirror while scaling and positioning artwork with their fingers, using the tablet as a trackpad. Upon finishing the task, most participants realized that there was a discrepancy between what they had designed on the tablet and how it had turned out on their bodies; this caused them to make adjustments on the tablet while checking the result in the mirror.

We found differences between the novices and the professional participants. Novices preferred the tablet due to the ease of control, even though they answered that working with gestures was more intuitive. In contrast, the professionals rated the tablet as more intuitive and, two-thirds of them preferred gestures because of the situated design feedback.

DISCUSSION AND FUTURE WORK

The advantage of projection over screen based mirrors is the rich and vivid 3D on-body experience that makes the virtual clothes feel as if they are parts of the users. The situated design experience and the serendipity that occurred when designing directly on the body were highly valued. Interacting with *Mirror Mirror* engaged participants in a trial and error process of playing with graphics while generating new ideas; this is a good indication that the system supports creativity. The level of refinement and ambiguity matches qualities that are often attributed to sketching [5]. Working with gestures complements the precision and control that users said they appreciated when designing T-shirts with the tablet.

The lack of precision reported when using gestures was not an issue when we exposed the system to the public in multi-day demonstrations [25]. Novice users enjoyed designing T-shirts, did not require training, and many wanted to buy their personalized shirt. They frequently used features such as text input and making self-portraits for their designs. Introducing templates could further make the toolkit match with the user's skill [29]. Within the boundaries of such professional templates, on-body interaction is engaging and intuitive for non-professionals to customize fashion items. For professional fashion designers, on-body interactions could function as a sketching or rough prototyping stage. However, for applications that require detailing and precision, the refined control of a tablet is preferred with the occasional on-body in-place feedback. Possible a future version could explore on-mirror multi-touch interaction [21] with a hybrid on-mirror 2D representation of the T-shirt.

The current prototype has several limitations and does not implement a full body mannequin needed to support dresses and trousers. Future work should address this and explore interaction on difficult to reach places such as on the back and legs. Whereas viewing and evaluating is possible with (multiple) mirror(s), manipulation might require an on-mirror "virtual" transformable mannequin.

The "fit" and "cut" of items was frequently mentioned by consulted fashion designers and should be addressed in the future work to explore the potential for professionals. Perhaps by simulating shape through shading and with a sophisticated clothes simulation, or to use tangible fabrics, possibly encoded with invisible textures [22] to support layering of clothing, and capes and dresses [31] and apparels and accessories such as hats and bags.

With *Mirror Mirror* we have introduced and explored a novel area of mirror based design applications; the combination of multiple display and interaction surfaces provides a seamless design experience. Exported user-generated designs can be printed with fabric printers or on embroidery machines.

REFERENCES

1. Fraser Anderson, Tovi Grossman, Justin Matejka, and George Fitzmaurice. 2013. YouMove: Enhancing Movement Training with an Augmented Reality Mirror. In *Proceedings of the 26th Annual ACM Symposium on User Interface Software and Technology (UIST '13)*. ACM, New York, NY, USA, 311–320. DOI: http://dx.doi.org/10.1145/2501988.2502045
2. Nobumichi Asai. 2014. Omote Real-Time Face Tracking and Projection Mapping. (2014). Retrieved Retrieved January 1, 2016 from http://www.nobumichiasai.com/jp/omote.html.
3. Deepak Bandyopadhyay, Ramesh Raskar, and Henry Fuchs. 2001. Dynamic shader lamps : painting on movable objects. In *Augmented Reality, 2001. Proceedings. IEEE and ACM International Symposium on*. 207–216. DOI: http://dx.doi.org/10.1109/ISAR.2001.970539
4. Hrvoje Benko, Andrew D. Wilson, and Federico Zannier. 2014. Dyadic Projected Spatial Augmented Reality. In *Proceedings of the 27th Annual ACM Symposium on User Interface Software and Technology (UIST '14)*. ACM, New York, NY, USA, 645–655. DOI: http://dx.doi.org/10.1145/2642918.2647402
5. Bill Buxton. 2007. *Sketching User Experiences: Getting the Design Right and the Right Design*. Morgan Kaufmann Publishers Inc., San Francisco, CA, USA.
6. Maurice Chu, Brinda Dalal, Alan Walendowski, and Bo Begole. 2010. Countertop Responsive Mirror: Supporting Physical Retail Shopping for Sellers, Buyers and Companions. In *Proceedings of the SIGCHI Conference on Human Factors in Computing Systems (CHI '10)*. ACM, New York, NY, USA, 2533–2542. DOI: http://dx.doi.org/10.1145/1753326.1753711
7. Peter Eisert, Jürgen Rurainsky, and Philipp Fechteler. 2007. Virtual Mirror: Real-Time Tracking of Shoes in Augmented Reality Environments. In *Image Processing, 2007. ICIP 2007. IEEE International Conference on*, Vol. 2. II – 557–II – 560. DOI: http://dx.doi.org/10.1109/ICIP.2007.4379216
8. Madeline Gannon, Tovi Grossman, and George Fitzmaurice. 2015. Tactum: A Skin-Centric Approach to Digital Design and Fabrication. In *Proceedings of the 33rd Annual ACM Conference on Human Factors in Computing Systems (CHI '15)*. ACM, New York, NY, USA, 1779–1788. DOI: http://dx.doi.org/10.1145/2702123.2702581
9. Chris Harrison, Hrvoje Benko, and Andrew D. Wilson. 2011. OmniTouch: Wearable Multitouch Interaction Everywhere. In *Proceedings of the 24th Annual ACM Symposium on User Interface Software and Technology (UIST '11)*. ACM, New York, NY, USA, 441–450. DOI: http://dx.doi.org/10.1145/2047196.2047255
10. Chris Harrison and Haakon Faste. 2014. Implications of Location and Touch for On-body Projected Interfaces. In *Proceedings of the 2014 Conference on Designing Interactive Systems (DIS '14)*. ACM, New York, NY, USA, 543–552. DOI: http://dx.doi.org/10.1145/2598510.2598587
11. Heejeong Heo, Seungki Kim, Hyungkun Park, Jeeyong Chung, Geehyuk Lee, and Woohun Lee. 2013. TransWall. In *ACM SIGGRAPH 2013 Emerging Technologies (SIGGRAPH '13)*. ACM, New York, NY, USA, Article 14, 1 pages. DOI: http://dx.doi.org/10.1145/2503368.2503382
12. Anna Hilsmann and Peter Eisert. 2009. Tracking and Retexturing Cloth for Real-Time Virtual Clothing Applications. In *Computer Vision/Computer Graphics Collaboration Techniques*, André Gagalowicz and Wilfried Philips (Eds.). Lecture Notes in Computer Science, Vol. 5496. Springer Berlin Heidelberg, 94–105. DOI: http://dx.doi.org/10.1007/978-3-642-01811-4_9
13. Hiroshi Ishii and Brygg Ullmer. 1997. Tangible Bits: Towards Seamless Interfaces Between People, Bits and Atoms. In *Proceedings of the ACM SIGCHI Conference on Human Factors in Computing Systems (CHI '97)*. ACM, New York, NY, USA, 234–241. DOI: http://dx.doi.org/10.1145/258549.258715
14. Brett R. Jones, Hrvoje Benko, Eyal Ofek, and Andrew D. Wilson. 2013. IllumiRoom: Peripheral Projected Illusions for Interactive Experiences. In *Proceedings of the SIGCHI Conference on Human Factors in Computing Systems (CHI '13)*. ACM, New York, NY, USA, 869–878. DOI: http://dx.doi.org/10.1145/2470654.2466112
15. Rubaiat Habib Kazi, Takeo Igarashi, Shengdong Zhao, and Richard Davis. 2012. Vignette: Interactive Texture Design and Manipulation with Freeform Gestures for Pen-and-ink Illustration. In *Proceedings of the SIGCHI Conference on Human Factors in Computing Systems (CHI '12)*. ACM, New York, NY, USA, 1727–1736. DOI: http://dx.doi.org/10.1145/2207676.2208302
16. Manfred Lau, Masaki Hirose, Akira Ohgawara, Jun Mitani, and Takeo Igarashi. 2012. Situated Modeling: A Shape-stamping Interface with Tangible Primitives. In *Proceedings of the Sixth International Conference on Tangible, Embedded and Embodied Interaction (TEI '12)*. ACM, New York, NY, USA, 275–282. DOI: http://dx.doi.org/10.1145/2148131.2148190
17. Wing Ho Andy Li and Hongbo Fu. 2012. Augmented Reflection of Reality. In *ACM SIGGRAPH 2012 Emerging Technologies (SIGGRAPH '12)*. ACM, New York, NY, USA, Article 3, 1 pages. DOI: http://dx.doi.org/10.1145/2343456.2343459
18. Michael R. Marner, Bruce H. Thomas, and Christian Sandor. 2009. Physical-virtual tools for spatial augmented reality user interfaces. In *Mixed and Augmented Reality, 2009. ISMAR 2009. 8th IEEE International Symposium on*. 205–206. DOI: http://dx.doi.org/10.1109/ISMAR.2009.5336458

19. Diego Martinez Plasencia, Florent Berthaut, Abhijit Karnik, and Sriram Subramanian. 2014. Through the Combining Glass. In *Proceedings of the 27th Annual ACM Symposium on User Interface Software and Technology (UIST '14)*. ACM, New York, NY, USA, 341–350. DOI: http://dx.doi.org/10.1145/2642918.2647351

20. Chris Milk. 2012. The Treachery of Sanctuary. (2012). Retrieved January 1, 2016 from http://milk.co/treachery.

21. Jörg Müller, Gilles Bailly, Thor Bossuyt, and Niklas Hillgren. 2014. MirrorTouch: Combining Touch and Mid-air Gestures for Public Displays. In *Proceedings of the 16th International Conference on Human-computer Interaction with Mobile Devices and Services (MobileHCI '14)*. ACM, New York, NY, USA, 319–328. DOI:http://dx.doi.org/10.1145/2628363.2628379

22. Parinya Punpongsanon, Daisuke Iwai, and Kosuke Sato. 2013. DeforMe: Projection-based Visualization of Deformable Surfaces Using Invisible Textures. In *SIGGRAPH Asia 2013 Emerging Technologies (SA '13)*. ACM, New York, NY, USA, Article 8, 3 pages. DOI: http://dx.doi.org/10.1145/2542284.2542292

23. Microsoft Research. 2012. Holoflector. Video. (2012). Retrieved September 24, 2015 from http://research.microsoft.com/apps/video/default.aspx?id=159487.

24. Daniel Rossa, Max Goergen, Thorsten Bauer, and Till Botterweck. 2012. Sydney Opera, Lighting the sails. (2012). Retrieved Retrieved January 1, 2016 from http://www.urbanscreen.com/lightning-the-sails/.

25. Daniel Saakes, Hui-Shyong Yeo, Seung-Tak Noh, Gyeol Han, and Woontack Woo. 2015. Mirror Mirror: An On-body Clothing Design System. In *SIGGRAPH 2015: Studio (SIGGRAPH '15)*. ACM, New York, NY, USA, Article 39, 1 pages. DOI: http://dx.doi.org/10.1145/2785585.2792691

26. Hideaki Sato, Itaru Kitahara, and Yuichi Ohta. 2009. MR-Mirror: A Complex of Real and Virtual Mirrors. In *Virtual and Mixed Reality*, Randall Shumaker (Ed.). Lecture Notes in Computer Science, Vol. 5622. Springer Berlin Heidelberg, 482–491. DOI: http://dx.doi.org/10.1007/978-3-642-02771-0_54

27. Frank Sorbier. 2012. Frank Sorbier Autum/Winter 2012/13 Haute Couture show. (2012). Retrieved Retrieved January 1, 2016 from http://thecreatorsproject.vice.com/blog/designer-franck-sorbier-projects-an-haute-couture-fairy-tale.

28. Keita Ushida, Yu Tanaka, Takeshi Naemura, and Hiroshi Harashima. 2002. i-mirror: An Interaction/Information Environment Based on a Mirror Metaphor Aiming to Install into Our Life Space. In *Proceedings of the 12th International Conference on Artificial Reality and Telexistence (ICAT '02)*. 113–118.

29. Eric von Hippel. 2005. *Democratizing Innovation*. The MIT Press, Cambridge, MA, USA.

30. Lu Wang, R. Villamil, S. Samarasekera, and R. Kumar. 2012. Magic Mirror: A virtual handbag shopping system. In *Computer Vision and Pattern Recognition Workshops (CVPRW), 2012 IEEE Computer Society Conference on*. 19–24. DOI: http://dx.doi.org/10.1109/CVPRW.2012.6239181

31. Amy Wibowo, Daisuke Sakamoto, Jun Mitani, and Takeo Igarashi. 2012. DressUp: A 3D Interface for Clothing Design with a Physical Mannequin. In *Proceedings of the Sixth International Conference on Tangible, Embedded and Embodied Interaction (TEI '12)*. ACM, New York, NY, USA, 99–102. DOI: http://dx.doi.org/10.1145/2148131.2148153

32. Mao Ye, Huamin Wang, Nianchen Deng, Xubo Yang, and Ruigang Yang. 2014. Real-time Human Pose and Shape Estimation for Virtual Try-On Using a Single Commodity Depth Camera. *IEEE Transactions on Visualization and Computer Graphics* 20, 4 (April 2014), 550–559. DOI: http://dx.doi.org/10.1109/TVCG.2014.35

33. Xuaner Zhang and Lam Yuk Wong. 2014. Virtual Fitting: Real-time Garment Simulation for Online Shopping. In *ACM SIGGRAPH 2014 Posters (SIGGRAPH '14)*. ACM, New York, NY, USA, Article 41, 1 pages. DOI: http://dx.doi.org/10.1145/2614217.2633388

Author Index

www.ingramcontent.com/pod-product-compliance
Ingram Content Group UK Ltd.
Pitfield, Milton Keynes, MK11 3LW, UK
UKHW051416290926
15471UKWH00009B/1624

9 781450 346337